Introduction to Cataloging and Classification

INTRODUCTION TO CATALOGING AND CLASSIFICATION

Eleventh Edition

Daniel N. Joudrey, Arlene G. Taylor,
and David P. Miller

Library and Information Science Text Series

LIBRARIES UNLIMITED™
An Imprint of ABC-CLIO, LLC
Santa Barbara, California • Denver, Colorado

Library of Congress Cataloging-in-Publication Data

Joudrey, Daniel N., author.
  Introduction to cataloging and classification. — Eleventh edition / Daniel N. Joudrey, Arlene G. Taylor, and David P. Miller.
        pages cm — (Library and information science text series)
  Significant expansion of: Introduction to cataloging and classification. Tenth edition / Arlene G. Taylor ; with the assistance of David P. Miller.
  Includes bibliographical references and index.
    ISBN 978-1-59884-857-1 (hardback) — ISBN 978-1-59884-856-4 (pbk) — ISBN 978-1-4408-3745-6 (ebook) 1. Descriptive cataloging. 2. Subject cataloging. 3. Classification—Books. 4. Resource description & access. I. Taylor, Arlene G., 1941- author. II. Miller, David P. (David Peter), 1955- author. III. Taylor, Arlene G., 1941- Introduction to cataloging and classification. Based on (work): IV. Title.
  Z693.W94 2015
  025.3—dc23   2015012911

ISBN: 978-1-59884-857-1 (case)
        978-1-59884-856-4 (paperback)
EISBN: 978-1-4408-3745-6

19 18 17 16 15   1 2 3 4 5

This book is also available on the World Wide Web as an eBook.
Visit www.abc-clio.com for details.

Libraries Unlimited
An Imprint of ABC-CLIO, LLC

ABC-CLIO, LLC
130 Cremona Drive, P.O. Box 1911
Santa Barbara, California 93116-1911

This book is printed on acid-free paper ∞

Manufactured in the United States of America

Contents

PART V: Formatting and Presentation

PART VI: Administrative Issues

Preface to the Eleventh Edition

As Cole Porter wrote in his musical, *Anything Goes*, "Times have changed." Today, in the world of library and information science, nothing could be truer than this statement. Libraries and other information institutions continue to deal with myriad changes in all aspects of their core services; from the inclusion of Playaways, iPads, or Kindles in the collection to the 3D printers now populating a library's "makerspace," "fab lab," or "tech shop," little stays the same. Libraries and other information institutions do, however, still depend on individuals known as *catalogers* (and sometimes *indexers, archivists*, etc.) to create metadata about the resources that are available from that institution to be shared with users through the catalog. Although catalogers, on the whole, still have many of the same responsibilities that they always have had, their approaches to those activities have evolved and will continue to evolve.

Since the publication of the 10th edition of *Introduction to Cataloging and Classification* (ICC) in 2006, there have been vast changes in the processes of information organization, particularly in the area of library cataloging. In this period of time, in addition to expected technological advances that now occur between every edition of a textbook like this and the usual changes made to cataloging standards, there were critical changes to almost every aspect of cataloging and classification. In the decade since the last edition of ICC, some of the major changes have included

- fundamental shifts in the terminology used to describe cataloging,
- the adoption of new conceptual models of the bibliographic universe (i.e., *Functional Requirements for Bibliographic Records* [FRBR] and its companion documents),
- a new descriptive cataloging standard being developed (i.e., *RDA: Resource Description & Access*),

- an existing descriptive cataloging standard (i.e., *Anglo-American Cataloguing Rules*, 2nd edition [AACR2]) being replaced in many libraries,
- additional controlled vocabularies being created to address issues of genre/form in all sorts of resources and for medium of performance specifically in music resources,
- some Library of Congress (LC) subject-access resources being available freely on the web in PDF form,
- myriad new fields being created in the MAchine-Readable Cataloging (MARC) formats for bibliographic and authority records, and
- a replacement for MARC actively being pursued by LC and others.

Because of these changes and more, this edition could not be updated quickly with a few cosmetic changes and new edition numbers for cataloging standards. Instead, much of this longstanding textbook, now in its 11th edition, had to be discarded, because so much of the thinking about and the processes of cataloging have changed so radically in the intervening years. In this edition, nine chapters were written "from scratch," and the other 15 were thoroughly revised and, in many cases, greatly expanded (with some chapters doubling in size). It is not simply a revised edition, but is instead a new work.

The authors knew that this book had to "re-introduce" the topic of library cataloging and classification from a fresh, baggage-free perspective. It is intended for both students and professionals, for both novice and experienced catalogers, and for any other persons working in the information environments who want to learn more about cataloging and classification. To ensure that it is approachable to all, the text was written with no assumptions made about the readers' previous knowledge of former cataloging standards. For example, it avoids lengthy passages about how things were done in AACR2; there are other texts that cover that ground. This book is not about how cataloging has *changed* but about what cataloging *is* today.

Part I of this text provides an *introduction*. It contains two chapters that place cataloging into context: one in the context of current practices (chapter 1) and the other into historical context (chapter 2). Chapter 1 has been revised to reflect the contemporary landscape of 21st-century information organization. Basic definitions, principles, and evaluative criteria for catalogs and cataloging have been updated. For this edition, the authors aimed to cover FRBR-influenced, RDA-based, post-AACR2 library cataloging. They have also made the assumption that the online catalog is the baseline standard in most contemporary libraries in the industrialized world. Discussions of card, book, and microform catalogs have been moved to chapter 2, the history chapter, as have the discussions of the arrangement of these catalogs in classified or alphabetic form (including dictionary and divided catalogs). These additions reflect a shift in the subject matter of that chapter, now titled "Development of Catalogs and Cataloging Codes" rather than simply "Development of Cataloging Codes."

Part II addresses the concepts of *description* and *access* (i.e., *descriptive cataloging*). Part II has been rewritten completely (except for a few passages that still worked well in describing certain concepts); this was necessitated, obviously, by the replacement of AACR2 with a new content standard, RDA.

This section of the textbook begins with chapter 3, which contains a significant examination of the foundations of descriptive cataloging: the International Cataloguing Principles, FRBR, and *Functional Requirements for Authority Data* (FRAD). RDA's structure and philosophical underpinnings are based on these documents and on their interpretation of an entity-relationship model based on *groups* of entities that comprise the bibliographic universe (e.g., works, expressions, manifestations, and items). If these foundational concepts are not thoroughly understood, it is difficult to comprehend completely the activities involved in description and access. In chapter 4, readers are introduced to RDA itself. The chapter addresses the origins of RDA, data types, terminology, objectives and principles, and purpose and scope; it also provides a structural overview of the entire content standard. The chapter examines features of RDA, such as core elements, alternatives, options, exceptions, examples, and accompanying policy statements from various national libraries. Chapter 4 ends with an outline of important pre-cataloging decisions and considerations that must be addressed even before the first element is recorded. Chapters 5-8 essentially follow the outline of RDA itself, addressing the description and/ or identification of: manifestations and items (chapter 5); works and expressions (chapter 6); persons, families, corporate bodies, and places (chapter 7); and any number of relationships that may exist between those entities (chapter 8). Within each of these chapters the most common metadata elements (reflecting entities' attributes) are reviewed following some preliminary information addressing how elements are to be recorded. In addition to covering key RDA concepts in each chapter, myriad examples, illustrations, and policy statements are discussed. Besides reviewing the RDA policy statements from LC and the Program for Cooperative Cataloging, additional guidance from the authors, in the form of *ICC11 Policy Statements*, is provided for particularly tricky instructions.

After extensive discussions of RDA instructions in chapters 5-8, the authors provide a somewhat different approach in the next chapter. Chapter 9 provides step-by-step instructions for working through an original cataloging problem using RDA to describe that resource. Those instructions are followed by a step-by-step overview of the encoding process using the MARC bibliographic format. The result is an illustration of the process of creating a full bibliographic description, with access points, that has been encoded in MARC. Chapter 9 concretizes the concerns of description and access outlined in chapters 5-8.

In Part III, which contains only chapter 10, the authors discuss *authority control*. The chapter has been revised to reflect changes necessitated by the adoption of RDA. Chapter 10 addresses the relationship between authority control and the functions of the catalog, as well as outlining the fundamental concerns of authority control. It discusses authority control's relationship to system design, the dangers of a lack of authority control, the nature of authority records and authority files, and the basics of authority work, including an overview of what it takes to update an older authority record within the context of RDA.

Part IV addresses both verbal and classified approaches to *subject access*. Each chapter has been revised and updated thoroughly; many examples have been replaced to reflect current usage and some more recently added concepts. In some cases, the chapters in this section have been greatly expanded, such as in chapter 11 (Subject Access) in which the content has more than doubled. Chapter 11 now includes additional information on why one performs subject analysis, the process of determining the aboutness of a work, and challenges inherent in the process. Chapter 12, which looks at verbal approaches to subject access, also has been greatly expanded. It now includes additional and updated information on the necessity of controlled vocabularies, their structures and features, the relationships inherent in structured vocabularies, and the principles guiding the development and usage of controlled vocabularies. Chapter 13, which discusses *Library of Congress Subject Headings* (LCSH), has been restructured, updated, and expanded. It addresses the origins and characteristics of LCSH, the formats available, tools used in its application, and an overview of the types of headings and subdivisions included in the system. The chapter now discusses additional supplemental vocabularies such as the *Library of Congress Genre/Form Terms for Library and Archival Materials* and the *Library of Congress Medium of Performance Thesaurus for Music*, and the section on FAST (Faceted Application of Subject Terminology) has been updated. Chapter 14, on the *Sears List of Subject Headings*, has been revised to incorporate changes found in its 21st edition; it continues to discuss the use of terminology in the standard, the use of subject heading theory in its application, its structure, its use of subdivisions, and the formats in which it is available. Chapter 15 (Other Verbal Access Systems) has been revised to eliminate a lengthy discussion of the *Preserved Context Indexing System* (PRECIS), which is no longer used by major libraries, and to include two widely used subject heading lists: *Medical Subject Headings* (MeSH) and BISAC Subject Headings. These have been added to its longstanding sections on *Thesaurus of Psychological Index Terms*, *Thesaurus of ERIC Descriptors*, *Inspec Thesaurus*, and the *Art and Architecture Thesaurus* (AAT).

The classified approaches discussed in Part IV begin with Chapter 16 (Classification), which contains an introduction to the ideas of classification (e.g., broad versus close classification, hierarchical versus faceted classification). It has been updated and expanded in this edition to include more information about faceted classification (as illustrated in discussions of Ranganathan's Colon Classification). Chapters 17 and 18, which focus on the major classifications used in the United States, have both been revised significantly. Chapter 17 has been updated to address the 23rd edition of the Dewey Decimal Classification. In addition, the section on the Universal Decimal Classification has been expanded to include more detail about its structure and application. Chapter 18 includes recent changes to the Library of Congress Classification, including changes in the distribution of LC's classification and its accompanying *Classification and Shelflisting Manual*. Although the process of adding cutter numbers to classification notations to create call numbers has changed little, chapter 19 dealing with this topic has been revised and updated. Chapter 20, too, has been revised to include the latest information in its small overviews of other classification systems (e.g., Bliss Bibliographic Classification, Brown's Subject Classification).

Part V, a newly created section for the textbook, addresses issues of *formatting* and *presentation*. It replaces Part II: Electronic Formatting from the 10th edition. The section has been moved from the beginning of the book (before description) toward the end (after subject access). It reflects current philosophical thought on the nature of cataloging in the 21st century. Now the emphasis is on creating data without as much concern for how it will be electronically encoded or shared; the data itself is the focus. How it is encoded and formatted for presentation are concerns for later stages of the process. In Part V, a revised and greatly expanded chapter on MARC encoding has been included as have been two new chapters. Chapter 21 (MARC) now includes information on the MARC authorities format in addition to information on the bibliographic format, with many more examples added for each. Chapter 22 introduces alternatives to MARC, such as the Dublin Core, the Metadata Object Descriptive Schema (MODS), and the Bibliographic Framework Transition Initiative (BIBFRAME); it also discusses the concepts of linked data and the Semantic Web. Chapter 23 addresses the role and functions of the *International Standard Bibliographic Description* (ISBD) in the context of being a stand-alone descriptive standard, as well as in the context of its use as a display standard for RDA metadata held in MARC bibliographic records.

Part VI addresses *administrative issues*. Chapter 24, its sole occupant, includes information about integrated library systems (and their potential replacements, library services platforms), cataloging routines and tools, support services, bibliographic networks, and cooperative systems. It has been updated to reflect current practices in library technical services departments. The two appendices that follow Part VI contain (1) an outline of the chapters and sections of RDA for quick reference and (2) an RDA-based descriptive cataloging template for use with books (used in chapter 9's step-by-step cataloging instructions). A revised glossary of selected terms used in the book follows. For this edition, which spans the time of transitioning from AACR2 to RDA, many obsolete terms are marked as such rather than being deleted. Obsolete terms often refer to a replacement term whenever available. The selected bibliography also lists many new resources, as well as some significant older works, consulted in the creation of this work.

Acknowledgments

The authors wish to acknowledge the assistance and support of a number of people and organizations. Collectively we thank Janis Young, Senior Cataloging Policy Specialist at the Library of Congress's Policy and Standards Division (PSD), for her invaluable contributions and assistance on the LCSH and LCC chapters. We also wish to acknowledge the assistance of Dave Reser, Senior Cataloging Policy Specialist of PSD, and Juli Beall, Consulting Assistant Editor, *Dewey Decimal Classification*, who answered questions about RDA and DDC, respectively. We thank Christi Showman Farrar, Associate Editor, *Sears List of Subject Headings*, for her careful reading of the Sears chapter and for her suggestions for clarifications and examples, and Barbara A. Bristow, Editor of Sears, for proofreading the chapter. We also wish to express appreciation to Rebecca L. Mugridge, Associate Director, Technical Services and Library Systems, University Libraries, University at Albany, State University of New York (SUNY), for her thoughts on the status of paper shelflists, on RDA implementation issues, and on the changes occurring in cataloging and technical services in general. Because most examples of MARC records used in this edition are shown in the format that is displayed in OCLC's Connexion service, the authors are grateful to OCLC for their permission to use their format in this book. Finally, the authors would like to express our appreciation for the late Dr. Lois Mai Chan for her remarkable contributions to the study of cataloging, and for her encouragement and inspiration.

When we were writing various chapters of this work, we were dependent on a number of librarians who helped us to find, identify, select, and obtain (☺) the resources that we needed to answer various questions or explore various concepts. The authors are grateful to Dr. Carol Anne Germain, Information Literacy Librarian, University Libraries, University at Albany, SUNY; Dr. Thomas Mann, Reference Librarian, Library of Congress; and Linda Watkins, former LIS Librarian at Beatley Library, Simmons College, for exceptional reference services. These outstanding librarians provided help on some particularly thorny problems in tracking down needed materials, and, in one case, in identifying a quote from a long-forgotten resource.

We are immensely grateful to Dr. Blanche Woolls and Emma Bailey, in their respective roles in Libraries Unlimited, for running interference for us when we were confounded by unexpected changes in policy, short deadlines, and other such publishing perils. All three authors are tremendously appreciative for the assistance and support provided by all of the people listed above. Each author, however, also has some personal acknowledgments to share.

Daniel N. Joudrey: I must first thank some people associated with my home in academia—the Simmons College School of Library and Information Science (SLIS). I thank Dr. Eileen Abels, who now sits at the head of our family table as the Dean of SLIS, for her support and encouragement. I would also like to thank my former dean (and my forever friend) Dr. Michèle V. Cloonan for bringing me to Boston and Simmons College. I thank all my brilliant and dedicated colleagues at SLIS, particularly Linnea Johnson, Dr. Melanie A. Kimball, Dr. Kyong Eun Oh, Dr. Candy Schwartz, Dr. Rong Tang, Jeanne Wallace-Buckley, and Dr. Kathy Wisser, who make my time at work incredibly enjoyable and keep me sane. I would like to thank my cataloging professors for teaching me not only about cataloging and classification, but also what it means to be a dedicated and conscientious teacher. I also thank my cataloging students, particularly those who were in *LIS 416: Introduction to Cataloging and Classification* during the Fall 2014 semester, for being guinea pigs and for providing feedback on the content of this book.

I would also like to thank Dr. Mary Casserly, former Dean and Director of Libraries, and the rest of the staff and faculty of the University Libraries, University at Albany, SUNY, for providing me with office space during my sabbatical, for reference service, and for access to library materials. Their assistance made the revisions and additions to Part IV of this book much easier.

On a more personal note, I would like to thank my family for their love and support and for understanding why I could not visit over the past year or so. I've missed them terribly and hope to make up for some lost time. I would like to thank Barbara Krapohl-Birckner, my first librarian and an inspiration; she opened up the world to me and I will always be grateful. And I would especially like to thank my partner, Jesús Alonso Regalado, Subject Librarian for Romance Languages and Literatures, and Latin American, Caribbean, and U.S. Latino Studies at the University at Albany, SUNY. I have so much to thank him for, including absolutely *everything* about our life together. I thank him for his love, his unwavering support, his unrelenting faith in my abilities, his deep well of patience, and all of the selfless accommodations he made repeatedly so that for two years I could focus my attention predominantly on writing this text (I am sorry about our canceled vacation plans!). I thank him for inspiring me with his expertise, his dedication, and his complete and total love of librarianship and collection development. I also thank him for impromptu reference services (he is *still* the best librarian that I have ever known).

Arlene G. Taylor: I wish to thank all my former students for their influence on my writing. Their facial expressions were often in my mind, looking puzzled by a concept or looking very pleased with an "aha" moment they had just had. These mental images kept me always asking myself whether each sentence I wrote was going to produce the "aha" instead of the puzzlement.

I thank my husband, Dr. A. Wayne Benson, for surviving another more-than-a-year of my absorption by yet another book, for his caring, for his listening, for his wordsmithing, and for being the chief dishwasher! I also thank the rest of my family (children, grandchildren, nieces, cousins) for their understanding of my neglecting them due to my being engrossed in yet another writing project, even though I'm supposed to be retired.

David P. Miller: I am grateful to Qiang Jin, Cataloging Librarian, University of Illinois at Urbana-Champaign, for her comments on the status of paper shelflists in chapter 24, and to Jeremy Goldstein, Minuteman Library Network, for valuable input on the discussion of centralized processing centers in the same chapter. Paul Frank, Cooperative Programs Section, Library of Congress, provided essential assistance in locating hard-to-find examples of MARC linking entry fields for chapter 21. Many thanks to my wife, Jane Wiley, a life-long avid library user and non-librarian, for listening patiently, and even with interest, as I repeatedly thought out loud at breakfast and dinner about how to present concepts such as BIBFRAME and the Semantic Web. Her better-than-tolerance for matters of metadata esoterica helped make this a better book.

Part I

Introduction

Chapter 1

Cataloging in Context

INTRODUCTION

The purposes of this chapter are to set the context in which cataloging takes place and to introduce the basic concepts of cataloging. The discussion begins with an introduction to the wider sphere of information organization and addresses where catalogs and cataloging fit into that realm. Catalogs are discussed, with attention given to their functions and their component parts. Arrangements of retrieval displays in online catalogs are also presented. An overview of the entire process of cataloging is given—descriptive cataloging, subject analysis, and authority control—followed by a look at the cooperative and copy cataloging that makes original cataloging of all materials for every collection unnecessary. Finally, there is an introduction to the formats of metadata records in catalogs.

INFORMATION ORGANIZATION

Definitions

Cataloging is a subset of a larger field that is called *information organization* (sometimes referred to as *bibliographic control* or as *organization of information*), and it is helpful to view it within that context. Bibliographic control has been defined by Elaine Svenonius as "the skill or art . . . of organizing knowledge (information) for retrieval."[1] Richard P. Smiraglia defines it as "encompassing the creation, storage, manipulation, and retrieval of bibliographic data."[2] Arlene G. Taylor and Daniel N. Joudrey, in *The Organization of Information*, define information organization as a "process of describing information resources and providing name, title, and subject access to the descriptions, resulting in records that serve as surrogates for the actual items of recorded information and in resources that are logically arranged."[3] Additionally, they say that "organization of information also allows us to save for posterity copies of all kinds of works that result from human endeavors."[4]

Anyone who has attempted to maintain a list or a file of references to articles, books, and other types of materials containing information on a particular subject, or perhaps by a particular artist or author, has practiced bibliographic control over a very small part of the universe of information/knowledge. For such a project to succeed, it is necessary to decide what elements of data to record about each article, book, or other container of information/knowledge, referred to hereinafter as *resource, information resource, item,* or *object.* It may be decided to record author(s), title, keywords, abstract, and location of the information resource. These become the data to be stored, manipulated, and retrieved. As the file grows, storing, manipulating, and retrieving become more and more complex. Then art and skill become necessary for successful creation, maintenance, and use of the file.

In the universe of all knowledge, including knowledge that cannot necessarily be expressed verbally (e.g., music, art), there is a certain amount of that knowledge that has been recorded in some way—written down, printed, digitized, painted, and so on. This subset is often referred to as the *bibliographic universe.* Only the bibliographic universe can be controlled. Such control is performed by means of bibliographic tools in which each discrete item of knowledge is represented by a set of metadata statements about various aspects of a resource. A set of metadata statements may be referred to as a *bibliographic record, metadata,* a *metadata record,* or a *surrogate record.* Until recently, it was still sometimes called *an entry,* although this terminology harkens back to older forms of catalogs such as the printed book catalog or the card catalog (discussed further in chapter 2).

Bibliographic tools (also referred to as *retrieval tools*) include bibliographies, indexes, catalogs, finding aids, registers, bibliographic databases, and search engines. Futurists have predicted that when all recorded information/knowledge is digitized and available online, it will be possible to gain access to needed information directly online without the intermediate step of using bibliographic tools. However, at this time, with the technology currently available, experts are finding that there must be some kind of control and some way to have preliminary information (e.g., title, author, date, subject keywords, subject categories) before one tries to sort through thousands of information resources.[5] The creation of a number of metadata standards is a result of this need for basic information about resources. Taylor and Joudrey describe *metadata* as "structured information that describes the attributes of information resources for the purposes of identification, discovery, selection, use, access, and management."[6]

Components of Information Organization

Librarians and library users have traditionally been taught that bibliographies, indexes, catalogs, and so forth, are tools quite different from each other. In fact, they are all parts of the same realm of information organization, but they have developed separately and in somewhat different formats for various reasons. Economic factors have been pervasive in the development of catalogs in libraries. Because libraries are generally not-for-profit agencies, there have seldom been enough financial resources to allow library catalogs to provide access deeper than what might be called *macro-level indexing* (e.g., access to a whole book, but not its chapters; access to an entire serial, but not its articles). Other agencies have stepped in to create indexes with what might be called *micro-level indexing* (e.g., access to articles in serials, poetry in collections, plays collected in books). These are sold for profit—most often to libraries—whereas access to library catalogs generally has not been sold. There are also indexes that analyze the contents of a single item (e.g., *back-of-the-book indexes*), but these are usually published at the same time as the item rather than being prepared separately for the purposes of information organization.

Although this is rapidly changing, economic constraints have dictated generally that library catalogs in the past could index only materials owned and housed in that particular library, and in this sense each one has been a microcosm of the entire bibliographic universe. On the other hand, periodical indexes have covered items owned and not owned by a library; that is, an index could cover a broader portion of the bibliographic universe. Bibliographies typically cover much smaller parts of the universe than either catalogs or indexes. That is, each bibliography usually has one subject or theme—for example, works of an author, works on a particular subject, items published during a particular time or in a particular place. (Subsets of this category include discographies and art catalogs.) Because of their limited scope, bibliographies can easily include entries at both macro- and micro-levels. In the recent past, technology has enabled bibliographic databases to be developed without the earlier economic constraints that limited the level of indexing. That is, the constraints that originally applied to macro- and micro-indexing no longer apply online. Whole items can be given very in-depth metadata, with every chapter or article in a book or serial given description and access points.

Finding aids have been developed in archives as lengthy surrogates for whole collections housed by archives. In archives associated with libraries or other catalog-possessing institutions, a catalog record may be made for a finding aid or for an individual collection so that the macro-level contents of the archival collections are searchable alongside other resources in the library. *Registers* have been developed in museums and provide the means for maintaining control over the objects and artifacts housed in museums. The Internet has retrieval tools called *search engines*. Most of these do not create surrogate records ahead of time but create them on the fly, using quotations from websites that contain the word(s) sought, in response to requests made by users.

An important feature of catalogs is that they typically have some kind of authority control, whereas the other tools described above may have little or no control over names and/or titles—although indexes often have control over the subject terms they use. *Authority control* is, in part, a result of the process of maintaining consistency in the forms of standardized names, titles, and subjects used as authorized access points in a bibliographic tool. An *authorized access point* is a standardized character string chosen to represent an entity associated with information resources (e.g., a person, a family, a corporate body). In a retrieval tool that uses authority control, the access points provided in the records generally should be in the official authorized form of name (e.g., records related to Arlene Taylor should always use the authorized string **Taylor, Arlene G., 1941-** , not strings such as *Arlene Taylor* or *Taylor, A.G.*). Authority control is defined and discussed in more detail later in this chapter.

One difficulty with the fragmentation of information organization into different bibliographic tools is that users are expected to know about the existence of them all and to be able to use them all effectively. This is a somewhat unreasonable expectation, as the tools overlap in their coverage of the bibliographic universe but provide their coverage in different ways. Approaches to searching the tools differ, as do the vocabularies used for searching. Once desired descriptions are found, conventions for displaying bibliographic data differ. In tools with no authority control, one cannot know whether all possible forms of a name, title, or subject term have been found. In an ideal bibliographic control environment, a user could start with any tool and be led to other tools as needed without having to know ahead of time which tools are appropriate.

In the future, it is expected that the LIS profession's information retrieval tools and their metadata will migrate from the current closed systems to applications that are part of the linked data environment of the Semantic Web. As this occurs, bibliographic metadata will begin to inhabit the open web, living outside traditional catalogs, indexes, and other retrieval tools. It is assumed that access to this metadata will change dramatically and become just another part of typical web searches for information and resources. The profession's information organization platform and discovery platform will have both moved to the web. This is something that will not happen overnight, but it is expected in the not-so-distant future.

Functions of Bibliographic Tools

Bibliographic tools have three basic functions. The first is the *identifying function*. All tools aim at allowing a user who has a citation or has a particular bibliographic item in mind to match that known item with a resource described in the retrieval tool—limited, of course, by the scope of the tool. The scope of a library catalog, for example, is often the items owned by the institution; thus the user should be able to match or identify or find a resource that the library owns or an item that is elsewhere but to which the local institution can provide access.

The second function is the *collocating* or *gathering function*. Collocation is a means for bringing together in one place in a bibliographic tool all surrogates for like and closely related materials; for example, records for all items about dinosaurs should be grouped together. In many cases a particular work is shown in its relationship to a larger group of works—for example, the bibliographic record for a play based on *Huckleberry Finn* should be found with records for editions of the novel *Huckleberry Finn*, which are in turn found with records for other works of Mark Twain. One of the best ways of accomplishing collocation is through the process of authority control. If records for *Huckleberry Finn* are sometimes found under the letter *H* (for *Huckleberry Finn*) and sometimes under the letter *A* (for *The Adventures of Huckleberry Finn*) with no connecting references, collocation has not been accomplished.

The third function of bibliographic tools is the *evaluating function*. This function allows a user to choose from among many records the resource that best seems to represent the knowledge/information or specific physical item desired. For example, a user looking for a particular language edition of *Huckleberry Finn* should be able to select it from among several, if it is one of those resources listed in the tool; or, given a choice between a spoken sound recording on tape or one on CD, a user could choose the manifestation most appropriate for the equipment available. It can be seen that the three functions are somewhat interdependent.

Uses of Information Organization

In *Functional Requirements for Bibliographic Records* (FRBR),[7] the functions of bibliographic tools are essential for the ultimate purpose of allowing users to fulfill certain tasks. These user tasks, as listed in FRBR, are

- to find entities that correspond to the user's stated search criteria . . .
- to identify an entity . . .
- to select an entity that is appropriate to the user's needs . . .
- to acquire or obtain access to the entity described . . .[8]

Catalogers, indexers, abstractors, bibliographers, and many other information professionals establish bibliographic control over portions of the bibliographic universe. Reference librarians, readers' advisers, and information specialists create a bridge between the user and the many bibliographic tools available. The library is a major focus of these activities but is not the only one. Archives, museums, digital libraries, the Internet, individual freelance efforts, and commercial enterprises also play roles.[9]

The bibliographic tool created in the library is the catalog, although extensive use is made of all the bibliographic tools in that setting. In other words, users in libraries have access not only to the catalog, but also to indexes, finding aids, a variety of databases, web search engines, and so on. The remainder of this book concentrates on the processes involved in creating, maintaining, and providing access to catalogs and catalog-like databases.

CATALOGS

Definition and Functions

A *catalog* is an organized compilation of bibliographic metadata that represents the holdings of a particular institution and/or resources accessible in a particular location. A library's resource collection may consist of any of several types of materials—books, periodicals, maps, coins, sound recordings, paintings, and musical scores, among others. Traditionally the collection represented by a catalog has been located in one place or at least in different parts of the same institution. Increasingly, however, catalogs may represent the holdings of more than one library, as libraries form consortia and otherwise link their catalogs for the purposes of interlibrary sharing. (Such catalogs are sometimes called *union catalogs.*) In addition, catalogs may include Internet resources that are not owned but to which the library can provide access.

Why prepare catalogs? Catalogs are necessary whenever a collection grows too large for the owner/user to be able to remember and retrieve specific items. A small private library or a classroom library has little need for a formal catalog; the user can recall each book, sound recording, map, or other such item by author, title, subject, the item's shape, its color, or its position on a particular shelf. When such a collection becomes a little larger, an informal arrangement, such as grouping the items by subject categories, provides access to them. When a collection becomes too large for such simple approaches, a formal record is necessary. There are two major reasons to make such a formal record in larger collections: for retrieval and for inventory purposes. In addition to being unable to remember what is in a large collection for access purposes, it also becomes impossible for the owner to remember what has been acquired, lost, or replaced. A catalog can serve as a record of what is owned.

The functions of bibliographic tools mentioned earlier—identifying, collocating, and evaluating—are functions of every bibliographic tool, including catalogs. These functions for catalogs were described by Charles A. Cutter in his *Rules for a Printed Dictionary Catalog* in 1876, using somewhat different language. He first stated what he thought the objectives—which he called *objects*—of a catalog should be, and then he gave his view of the *means* by which the objects would be accomplished.[10] His statement serves as the basis for today's understanding of the functions of a catalog, although in modern practice the statement is somewhat incomplete:

Objects

1. To enable a person to find a book of which either
   (A) the author
   (B) the title   } is known.
   (C) the subject

2. To show what the library has
   (D) by a given author
   (E) on a given subject
   (F) in a given kind of literature.

3. To assist in the choice of a book
   (G) as to its edition (bibliographically)
   (H) as to its character (literary or topical).

Means

1. Author-entry with the necessary references (for A and D).
2. Title-entry or title-reference (for B).
3. Subject-entry, cross-references, and classed subject-table (for C and E).
4. Form-entry and language-entry (for F).
5. Giving edition and imprint, with notes when necessary (for G).
6. Notes (for H).

FIGURE 1.1 Cutter's Objects and His Means.

To conform to modern practice, the first objective needs to be rephrased as follows: "To enable a person to find any resource whether issued in a print, non-print, or electronic format." Cutter's first object is inadequate even for printed materials inasmuch as *book* does not unambiguously encompass *periodical, serial,* or *pamphlet.* Cutter's object *E* also does not go far enough for our current understanding. Rephrased, it should read "on given and related subjects." It is clearly a prime function of a catalog to guide patrons in using the system of subject headings that any particular library may have adopted. Cutter's apparent assumption that the user always has a clearly formulated given subject in mind is contrary to all observation of catalog users.

Cutter's objectives remained the primary statement of catalog principles until 1961, when the International Federation of Library Associations (IFLA) at a conference in Paris approved a statement about the purpose of an author/title catalog. It stated that the catalog should be an efficient instrument for ascertaining

1) whether the library contains a particular book specified by:
   a) its author and title, *or*
   b) if no author is named in the book, its title alone, *or*
   c) if author and title are inappropriate or insufficient for identification, a suitable substitute for the title,

and 2) a) which works by a particular author *and*
   b) which editions of a particular work are in the library.[11]

These principles, often called the *Paris Principles*, were purposely restricted to an author/title catalog, and thus no mention is made of subject access; but they, as well as Cutter's objects, bring out the three functions, already mentioned, of identifying (1.a-1.c), collocating (2.a-2.b), and evaluating (2.b). In both Cutter's statement and the Paris Principles, the evaluating function is limited to choice of edition and to Cutter's "choice of a book . . . as to its character." With time and the advent of multiple ways of presenting the same resource, both intellectually and physically, it has become more important to make certain that the catalog can assist users in making choices. This continues a long history of evolution of functions of the catalog.

New international principles were published by IFLA in 2009 after years of collaboration and discussion among cataloging experts from around the world. In these principles, the functions of the catalog are to enable a user

4.1. to **find** bibliographic resources in a collection as the result of a search using attributes or relationships of the resources . . .

4.2. to **identify** a bibliographic resource or agent . . .

4.3. to **select** a bibliographic resource that is appropriate to the user's needs . . .

4.4. to **acquire** or **obtain** access to an item described . . .

4.5. to **navigate** within a catalogue and beyond (that is, through the logical arrangement of bibliographic and authority data and presentation of clear ways to move about . . .)[12]

An additional function of a catalog brought out in the new principles is that of *locating*, a function not always served by other bibliographic tools. One can tell from a library catalog whether the library contains a certain resource and, if so, where it is physically located. This is true even of union catalogs in that the catalog identifies which libraries house particular items, although one may need more detail to know where in a particular library to find an item. With most catalogs, the circulation system is linked, making it possible for the user to learn whether an item is available at the moment. Virtual locations of Internet information resources are also provided in catalogs through uniform resource locators (URLs).

An effective catalog should possess certain qualities that will allow it to be easily consulted and maintained. If it is too difficult, too cumbersome, or too expensive, it is virtually useless. The following criteria may be considered for judging a catalog:

- **A catalog should be flexible and up to date.** A library's collection is constantly changing. Because the catalog is a record of what is available in that library, metadata should be added or removed as resources are added to or discarded from the collection. Printed catalogs—meaning all the formats of catalogs occurring before online catalogs—of the past were not flexible and up to date by today's standards; although for their times, when they were all that was available, card catalogs were considered to be very flexible compared to book or microform catalogs. Online catalogs, usually part of an integrated library system (ILS) or a library services platform (LSP), can be considered the most flexible and current of all catalog formats. Additions, deletions, and changes can be made at any time, and the results are usually instantly available to the user.

- **A catalog should support the internationally accepted functions of finding, identifying, selecting, obtaining, and navigating.**

  - **A catalog should be constructed so that all metadata can be quickly and easily found.** This is a matter of following current standards and, in the case of online catalogs, providing simple and clear screen instructions. Authority control must be practiced to the extent that, for example, a patron who wants to locate the works of Charles Dickens can find the Dickens metadata easily.

    Filing arrangement of retrieved results on a computer screen is not the same as in traditionally filed card catalogs because of the difficulty of programming computers to arrange results according to traditional library filing rules. As a result, traditional rules have been re-evaluated, and now those filing rules more closely resemble computer filing rules.[13] For example, *Henry VIII* and *Henry the Eighth* were traditionally interfiled, as if spoken and spelled out. However, in computer arrangement, *VIII* is seen as the letter *V* followed by three instances of the letter *I*; current filing rules follow the method used by computers. For more information on filing rules, see the 10th edition of Taylor's *Introduction to Cataloging and Classification*.[14]

Bibliographic records are located in online catalogs in a variety of ways. In some catalogs, the computer must be told whether an author, title, or subject search is desired. In most systems one can enter as much of the title, author, or subject as seems useful, starting at the left of the data string. Most systems also allow users to input only the words they remember in any order (called *keyword searching*), and the system searches for all records containing the words input.

Responses to searches in online catalogs also vary by system. Most systems alphabetize displays but are not consistent in the way that the arrangement is accomplished. Quite a few systems allow a user to choose display order (chronological, reverse chronological, alphabetical by author, etc.) via pull-down menus or settings.

○ **A catalog should have authority control so that users may identify what they seek and easily navigate the system.** Authority control ensures that names, subjects, and certain titles are consistent throughout the catalog. This consistency, in the form of authorized access points, allows users to unambiguously identify the entities they seek. These access points, in most online catalogs, are presented as hyperlinks, which allow users to navigate from a single record to multiple records based on the access point (e.g., navigating from a single resource about Dickens to a list of all resources about Dickens). Navigation among records in the catalog relies on the relationships identified among the entities represented in the catalog (e.g., connecting Samuel Clemens and Mark Twain in the catalog is dependent on that relationship being identified and incorporated into authority data).

○ **A catalog should contain enough metadata to allow users to select resources and to obtain those that they need.** The metadata that is used to describe a resource must be robust enough to provide users with the information they need in order to determine whether a resource is useful or not. It must also provide information on how to locate the resource either physically or through electronic means.

• **A catalog should be easy to search, with clear instructions and with explanations of the comprehensiveness of a search.** Users should be able to understand the various options available within the catalog. Today, most users, when they approach the catalog, see a simple single search box into which they are to type their inquiries for all types of resources. The default search varies among ILSs and LSPs, but it is not often a title, subject, or author search; these days, it is most often a general keyword search (i.e., a search for a term anywhere in the record). The search box may or may not indicate the default search strategy, but it should. It also may or may not provide an explanation of whether the default approach to keyword searching is using a Boolean *AND* or a Boolean *OR*, but it should.

A simple search box is often, but not always, augmented by other search options. Each ILS or LSP may allow the library to customize the interface and choose which search options are available. For example, the Voyager catalog implemented by the Library of Congress (LC) offers a *quick search* box, as well as browsing, advanced searching, and keyword searching screens for users who wish to tailor their searches more specifically. Another implementation of the Voyager catalog may offer fewer options. The more sophisticated the catalog, the more likely it is that there will be more options for searching, some of which may not be comprehensible without instructions or examples. Helpful features found in search engines, such as auto-correction, spell-checking, and auto-completion, are still rare in most online catalogs.

- **A catalog should have a search results display that is clear, understandable, and uncluttered.** Results from a search should be comprehensible and unambiguous. They should be ordered (or be able to be sorted) in a logical fashion. In most catalogs, the results may be arranged by relevance, by date, alphabetically by primary creator or title, or by some other method. Most often, the default setting is by relevance, but users usually have a choice to sort by another method by using pull-down menus or settings. A limit option should be available if there are too many results, and the search that prompted the results list should remain at the top of the display so that it can be edited and resent.

- **A catalog should be accessible to all users, regardless of whether they are sophisticated computer users and of whether they are persons who have disabilities.** Some questions about options to consider in this area are:
  - Is the use of color readable?
  - Are linking elements hyperlinked?
  - Are the words that were searched highlighted in the resulting display?
  - Are any labels that may be used stated in such a way as to be very clear?
  - When a brief display of a record is used, is it easy to get a full record?
  - Is the order of elements logical and unambiguous?
  - Is the availability of items clearly presented?

- **A catalog should be economically prepared and maintained.** The catalog that can be prepared most inexpensively and with greatest attention to currency has obvious advantages.

Arrangements of Online Catalogs

Printed catalogs required that there be multiple copies of each surrogate record—one copy for each access point associated with the resource. These could be arranged in various ways—for example, all access points might be interfiled alphabetically or there might be a divided arrangement with separate A-Z sections for name access points, title access points, and subject access points. Furthermore, subject access points might be arranged alphabetically or in a classified/categorized manner. (See further discussion in chapter 2.) Because surrogate records in online catalogs do not have to be arranged in a linear fashion, online catalogs do not have the same arrangement issues as earlier forms of catalogs. The internal arrangements of records in the computer vary greatly from system to system and make little difference to a user. What does matter to the user is how results are displayed in response to a search request. Some online catalogs are, in effect, divided catalogs because a user must choose to search through one of the indexes: author, title, subject, and sometimes classification or another category. In this kind of system, a name being used as a subject is almost always searched through the subject index, separating any records for works about a person from those representing works by that person. A number of systems allow searching of two indexes at once using the words *and, or,* and *not* or their equivalents (a form of what is called *Boolean searching*). These systems do, of course, allow a sophisticated user to find works by and about a person in a single search, but experience has shown that few library patrons are this capable of manipulating the system. Typically, such catalogs offer forms to fill in that automatically create the Boolean search *if* the user understands that a person's name must be typed in *both* the author field *and* the subject field.

Virtually all online catalogs allow for keyword searching of almost any words in any record. In such a catalog, a keyword search for a name brings together for display all records for works by and about the person, usually with the most relevant records displayed first. The definition of *relevant*, however, differs from system to system and is based on such criteria as how many times the search terms appear in the records and in which places the terms appear. In some ways, the ability to do keyword searching in the online catalog complicates the basics of searching for specific entities, in that it will search for a word as part of an author's name, a title, or a subject (as well as many other parts of the record) and will return the results no matter where the search term was found.

In online catalogs that provide for searching by classification notation, there is a semblance of the ability to search for subject entities in a categorized fashion, except that in cataloging practice in the United States, each work is limited to one place in a classification scheme. In this respect it is more like a shelflist (see discussion below). In time there may be ways to gain access to bibliographic records through the hierarchy of the classification scheme used to classify the works they represent.

Components of Catalog Systems

Basically, three components make up a whole catalog: a public access catalog, a shelflist, and an authority file or files. (In some catalogs there may also be records not available to the public, such as acquisition or *in-process* records that are part of the bibliographic file.) In printed catalogs these basic files are separate physical components. In online catalogs, the public access catalog and shelflist are really different ways to search the same file; the authority file is actually a separate file. Public access catalogs contain the records that are readily available for the use of library patrons—that is, the online catalogs just discussed in the previous section.

Shelflist was the term applied in printed catalogs to the file (or separate listing) that was a record of the holdings of a library; bibliographic descriptions were arranged in the order of items on a shelf—hence the name *shelflist*. With the cataloging of datasets, software, and web resources, for which there was often not a physical item to be placed on a shelf, or if there was a physical item not easily interfiled with books (or not interfiled by policy), the name "shelflist" became less descriptive. Records of a library's holdings for such entities were often placed in order by acquisition number, or some other device, because many librarians considered the classification number to be just part of a location device, and so a classification number was not assigned. The records making up a shelflist usually contained data about the numbers of copies owned and/or volumes held, as well as information about locations of copies, especially when a library was made up of several collections.

Shelflists in print form traditionally were kept in an area not accessible to the public. There were notable exceptions to this, however, especially in situations where the areas in which materials were shelved (called *stacks*) were not open to the public. In these situations, browsing the shelflist was a substitute for browsing in the stacks. A major change in availability of shelflists has occurred with online catalogs. When classification is an access point in the catalog, the results of classification notation searches are displayed in shelflist (i.e., classification) order, essentially making the shelflist available to everyone. In addition, in most online catalogs, when a metadata record is selected for viewing, copy and location information is provided. (See chapter 24 for further discussion.)

Authority files contain individual records of the names, titles, series, and subject headings that have been chosen as the standardized forms to use as authorized access points in a particular catalog. Authority records also contain lists of references (sometimes called *cross-references*) made in the public catalog from unauthorized forms to the standardized form, so that users do not have to know authorized forms to use the catalog. Traditionally, these files also have been kept in areas inaccessible to the public. Again, online catalogs have changed this. In most systems, authority files serve as indexes to the catalog.

Online catalogs usually contain these three components, but not always as distinctly separate as they were in printed catalogs. Authority files still are nonexistent in some online catalogs, and in some they are unlinked files; but typically they are linked to the bibliographic files so that they may serve as the index(es) to the access points used in the system, and in some cases they serve to alert catalogers automatically to inconsistencies in access points. In addition a number of other components have been added to public access catalogs. For example, as mentioned above, acquisitions and in-process records are available to the public in many systems, and circulation information—whether an item is charged out and, if so, when it is due back—is available in virtually every system.

CATALOGING

The means by which catalogs are prepared is through the process called *cataloging*. This process usually begins with descriptive cataloging and continues with subject analysis, and throughout both phases is intertwined the process of authority control.

Encoding

Encoding permeates the entire cataloging process. The results of each of the descriptive, subject, and authority processes are entered into a machine-readable form that is compatible with the online system in which the metadata will be used. Issues of encoding and presentation are addressed in Part IV of this text.

Descriptive Cataloging

Descriptive cataloging is that phase of the cataloging process that is concerned with the identification and description of an information resource, the recording of this information in the form of a cataloging record, the selection of names and titles useful for providing access to the resource, and the establishment of authorized access points for names and titles. Descriptive cataloging describes the makeup of an information resource and identifies those entities responsible for its intellectual and/or artistic contents without reference to its classification by subject or to the assignment of subject headings, both of which are the province of subject cataloging.

Description

Identification and description are interrelated processes in descriptive cataloging. Identification consists of the choice of conventional elements, guided by a set of instructions or guidelines (e.g., *RDA: Resource Description & Access*). When the cataloger has properly identified the conventional elements, they are described in a catalog record in such a fashion that the description is unique and can be applied to no other entity in the collection. In other words, each information resource should be distinguished from everything with which it could be confused. Elements considered essential for describing information resources include titles, statements of responsibility, edition information, dissemination information (e.g., publication locations, names of publishers and distributors, manufacturing information, dates), standard identifiers, and location information (e.g., URLs) as needed. Physical description—carrier type, extent, and size of resource—and series data are often necessary for this purpose as well, even though they are not applicable to all resources. In addition the cataloger gives elements of description that may be helpful to a user in evaluating potential use of the resource, such as whether it is illustrated, what equipment is needed to use it, or that its mode of access is through the web.

Access

After describing an information resource, the cataloger selects name and title access points. Names of persons, families, and corporate bodies associated with a work are chosen according to the cataloging guidelines used (e.g., RDA). Title access points also are chosen—in addition to the obvious main title (called *title proper*), there may be parallel titles, other title information, variant titles, series titles, and titles of other works related to the resource being cataloged.

In earlier cataloging practices, one of the access points was chosen as the primary one. It was usually the name of the chief creator of the work (or, if this was not clear, the first-named creator). This access point, in the past, was called the *main entry* or *primary access point*, but that terminology is no longer used in contemporary cataloging. Identification of the main entry was considered essential for identification of the intellectual or creative work embodied in an information resource. A combination of the main entry and the most widely known version of the title was the method used to refer to a work in the realm of cataloging (e.g., **Lewis, Sinclair, 1885-1951. Main Street** clearly and unambiguously identifies the 1920 novel). Although catalogers no longer identify the main entry in the same way, they still use access points associated with the work to create a standard citation for the work; these standard citations, used for naming the work, still generally comprise the primary creator's name and the most widely known title of the work. Even though catalogers approach this task somewhat differently, the resulting creator/title identifier, used to name the intellectual or artistic content of a work, is the same.

The access points chosen are formatted into the standardized forms called for by their authorized access points, which, as already mentioned, are constructed in a form that will make them readily accessible in the catalog and will enhance collocation. This is done using cataloging guidelines and through reference to the authority file.

Subject Analysis

Subject analysis involves determining what subject concept(s) are covered by the intellectual or artistic content of a work. After this has been determined, as many subject headings or indexing terms as are appropriate are chosen from a standard list. Again, an authority file must be consulted if the subject headings are to be properly collocated into the catalog with other works covering the same or related subject concepts.

The final step in the subject analysis process usually is to choose a classification notation from whatever classification scheme is used by the library. Traditionally in the United States, the classification serves both as a means for bringing an item in close proximity with other items on the same or related subjects and, in the case of tangible resources, as the first element of the *call number*, a device used to identify and locate a particular item on the shelves. The cataloger thus must choose only the one best place in the classification scheme for the item.

Authority Control

Authority control is the result of the process of maintaining consistency in the verbal form used to represent an access point and the further process of showing the relationships among names, works, and subjects. It is accomplished through use of cataloging guidelines (in the case of names and titles), use of a controlled vocabulary, and reference to an authority file to create an authorized character string (formerly called a *heading*). An authority file is a grouping of records of the forms of names, titles, or subjects chosen for use in a catalog. Each authority record in an authority file may contain, in addition to the form chosen for use as an authorized access point, a list of variant forms or terms that may be used as references. A very carefully prepared authority record also contains a list of sources consulted in the process of deciding on the standardized form and the variant forms to use as references. It is possible to practice authority control by letting the catalog itself serve as the authority file—that is, by assuming that the form of heading used in the catalog is correct. In large bibliographic files, this has proved to be difficult, and it is very difficult to keep track of references made in any size catalog without an authority file.

It is authority control that makes cataloging more than just a process of creating a series of bibliographic records to represent discrete works without apparent relationship to any other. Current cataloging practice places even more importance on relationships among the various entities represented in a catalog than was previously true. The process of cataloging can be defined as "creation of a catalog using bibliographic records," because authority control allows the cataloger to create standardized forms of names, titles, and subjects that can help with understanding relationships among the works cataloged. It means that the character string established to represent a creator is always the same in different records, so that bibliographic records for all works by and about the same person or emanating from the same corporate body can be displayed together. A standardized title can be consistently presented so that bibliographic records for all editions, translations, sound or video recordings, adaptations, abridgements, or any other kind of manifestation of a work can be displayed together. The standardized terminology used to represent the same subject concept in different works can be used always in one form (called *controlled vocabulary*) so that to the extent to which works are identified as being about the same subject concept, all such works can be displayed together. Authority control of controlled vocabulary also makes it possible to refer users from terms not used to those used and from terms used to other related terms.

As cataloging moves more and more into the international arena, connecting various national authority files with each other has become essential, resulting in the establishment of the Virtual International Authority File (VIAF).[15] Creators of catalogs in various countries using various languages need to be able to designate their own authorized forms of names while at the same time recognizing variant names for the same person or other entity in other languages. Catalogs should not be required to use the English-language authorized forms but should be able to link users to entities they seek regardless of the language used in searches.

Cooperative and Copy Cataloging

The process of cataloging described above is often referred to as *original cataloging*. Fortunately it is not necessary for every resource in every library to be cataloged originally in that library. Because libraries acquire copies of many of the same items or decide to catalog the same Internet resources, their catalogers can share metadata by adapting for their own catalogs a copy of the original cataloging data created by another library, a process commonly called *copy cataloging*.[16]

Copy cataloging has been around for quite a long time. LC began to sell its standard printed catalog cards to libraries in 1901. H. W. Wilson entered the field in the 1930s with simplified catalog cards for sale. A number of other companies created and sold catalog cards from the 1950s into the 1970s. In addition LC book catalogs were available in large libraries, and methods were devised for photocopying entries from them for adaptation and use in local catalogs.

With the development of the MARC (MAchine-Readable Cataloging) format in the late 1960s, cooperative cataloging took a new turn. At first the companies selling cards simply loaded LC's MARC tapes into their computers and printed cards from them. But the beginning of bibliographic networks based on MARC introduced a truly *cooperative* manner of using cataloging data; any member of a network could create records that could be used by any other member. The first network was OCLC—at first the Ohio College Library Center, but now OCLC Online Computer Library Center, Inc. In addition to using any records created by any other network member, any member library can use records found in the system contributed by LC or by several other national libraries.

At first the OCLC cataloging system was used only for the production of cards, and cards continue to be a product (although now only a very small part) of the system. Adaptations are easier online than changing photocopies or pre-printed cards. Now, however, most libraries download MARC records directly into their local online systems. Other major bibliographic networks in use in the United States and Canada include SkyRiver and Auto-Graphics. Smaller regional and local networks exist in large numbers.

The amount of original cataloging remaining after use of cooperative cataloging depends upon the type and size of library. The more specialized the library, the more original cataloging it has, so specialized collections can require a high percentage of original cataloging, even though they may be quite small.

In the mid-1990s there was a movement toward outsourcing both original and copy cataloging in some libraries. Outsourcing involves contracting with vendors outside the library to do some of the cataloging (or occasionally all the cataloging) for the library. The move has both advantages and disadvantages, and much has been written on the subject.[17]

FORMATS OF METADATA RECORDS IN CATALOGS

The records created in the cataloging process must be displayed in some format. Uniformity of display is very desirable so that patrons can know how to read a record and where to expect to see certain elements of data. In printed catalogs, the display of data elements has been quite standard. Most libraries and card production sources followed the LC pattern, because LC printed cards were so extensively used and because the order of elements devised by LC made a logical presentation of data. That order was codified by the various versions of the cataloging rules (e.g., until recently *The Anglo-American Cataloguing Rules, Second Edition*, 2002 Revision[18]).

Today, the vast majority of catalog records are created using one of the MARC formats. The first MARC format was developed at LC around 1965. The version used in the United States was, for many years, referred to as USMARC to distinguish it from the versions used in other countries (e.g., RUSMARC, IBERMARC, DanMARC). The latest version, published in 1999, is called MARC 21. It is a harmonization of the MARC formats used in Canada and the United States, and the name was meant to show that MARC was ready for the 21st century—although today many argue that MARC 21 is the primary reason why cataloging is perceived by some as being out of touch with contemporary information technology and communications standards. The structure of MARC 21 and its various formats is discussed in more detail in chapter 21 of this text. A general discussion of MARC and several other encoding standards can be found in Taylor and Joudrey's *Organization of Information*.[19]

Display of MARC-formatted records is far from uniform. There have been numerous calls for standards for online catalog displays so that users may once again move from catalog to catalog (now most often while looking at the same computer screen) and see displays that make sense because they are predictable. IFLA has a set of guidelines for display in online catalogs.[20] Figure 1.2 shows a record from OCLC's Connexion interface (i.e., OCLC's cataloging sub-system).

Although the catalogs of today still contain records in the MARC format, this concept is poised to change. Each catalog record is essentially a document made up of individual metadata statements about a resource. Currently, however, an entire record must be retrieved, even if the requester only wants to see, for example, the creator of a work or the subjects of that work. If the user then wishes to see further information about that creator, another entire record (document) must be retrieved. Or if the user wishes to find further resources about a topic, additional searches must be performed. This approach does not take full advantage of recent advances in data structures, communications technology, and the like. Many feel that a new, more contemporary, user-friendly approach is needed. That new approach may be found in part in the development of an extension to the World Wide Web.

METADATA AND THE SEMANTIC WEB

In today's rapidly advancing, technology-centered environment, a copious amount of the world's information (including its metadata) has migrated to the web—a place where many of the workflows performed by information professionals are now also based. In this environment, many have expressed a desire to make the currently implicit connections between entities (e.g., data, resources, creators, subjects) more obvious, more explicit, and more easily actionable. In other words, there is a desire to link related resources so that they may be more easily identifiable, better understood, and more readily retrieved.

In 1999, Sir Tim Berners-Lee expressed a dream that computers would be able to analyze all the data on the web, including all the transactions between computers and people, and when that became possible, machines talking to machines would bring about a so-called *Semantic Web* to handle our daily needs.[21] Today, the Semantic Web is an extension of the World Wide Web.

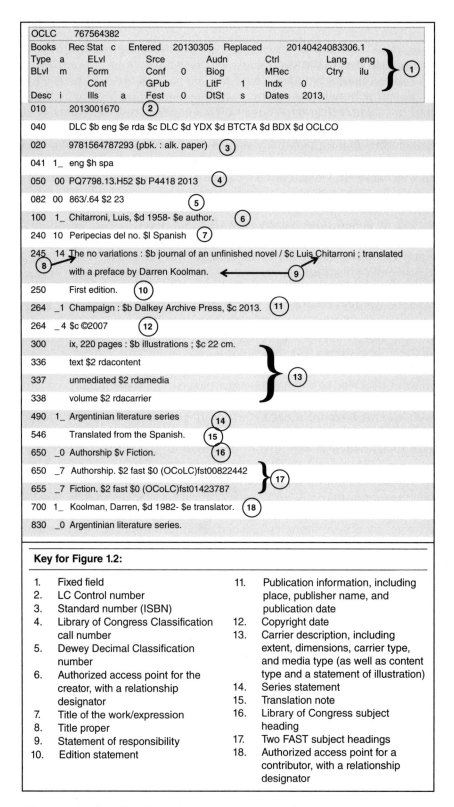

OCLC	767564382							
Books	Rec Stat c	Entered 20130305	Replaced	20140424083306.1				
Type a	ELvl	Srce	Audn	Ctrl		Lang eng		
BLvl m	Form	Conf 0	Biog	MRec		Ctry ilu		
	Cont	GPub	LitF 1	Indx 0				
Desc i	Ills a	Fest 0	DtSt s	Dates 2013,				

010   2013001670

040   DLC $b eng $e rda $c DLC $d YDX $d BTCTA $d BDX $d OCLCO

020   9781564787293 (pbk. : alk. paper)

041 1_   eng $h spa

050 00   PQ7798.13.H52 $b P4418 2013

082 00   863/.64 $2 23

100 1_   Chitarroni, Luis, $d 1958- $e author.

240 10   Peripecias del no. $l Spanish

245 14   The no variations : $b journal of an unfinished novel / $c Luis Chitarroni ; translated with a preface by Darren Koolman.

250   First edition.

264 _1   Champaign : $b Dalkey Archive Press, $c 2013.

264 _4 $c ©2007

300   ix, 220 pages : $b illustrations ; $c 22 cm.

336   text $2 rdacontent

337   unmediated $2 rdamedia

338   volume $2 rdacarrier

490 1_   Argentinian literature series

546   Translated from the Spanish.

650 _0   Authorship $v Fiction.

650 _7   Authorship. $2 fast $0 (OCoLC)fst00822442

655 _7   Fiction. $2 fast $0 (OCoLC)fst01423787

700 1_   Koolman, Darren, $d 1982- $e translator.

830 _0   Argentinian literature series.

Key for Figure 1.2:

1. Fixed field
2. LC Control number
3. Standard number (ISBN)
4. Library of Congress Classification call number
5. Dewey Decimal Classification number
6. Authorized access point for the creator, with a relationship designator
7. Title of the work/expression
8. Title proper
9. Statement of responsibility
10. Edition statement
11. Publication information, including place, publisher name, and publication date
12. Copyright date
13. Carrier description, including extent, dimensions, carrier type, and media type (as well as content type and a statement of illustration)
14. Series statement
15. Translation note
16. Library of Congress subject heading
17. Two FAST subject headings
18. Authorized access point for a contributor, with a relationship designator

Figure 1.2 Identification of Information Included in a MARC Record. (Source: OCLC Connexion, WorldCat—record number 767564382)

Whereas the traditional web provides linkages between online documents—generally at the level of the whole resource or a discrete part of it—the Semantic Web provides linkages among data statements in a format semantically meaningful to, and actionable by, computers. The basic idea is that the Semantic Web will be a *data* retriever instead of a *document* retriever. Instead of linked records, the focus is on linking individual data statements about resources being described (e.g., a person, a document, an idea). For example, computers will be able to recognize statements about a work's creator that come from different sources as being statements that are semantically equivalent (i.e., relating to the same entity).

Today, tools are being created that are bringing this dream to pass. One of these tools is *linked data*, generally considered to be the foundation for the Semantic Web. Linked data is an approach to encoding data from a wide range of different sources, and publishing it on the web, in such a way that it may be understood by computers as related to the same resource or concept. For example, if two different resources contain metadata statements that point to an authoritative representation for a subject, then both of those resources are related to that subject, and therefore, are related to each other. All resources that are related or linked are potentially of interest to a user searching for materials on that topic. This allows machines to offer a wider variety of, but also more accurately pinpointed, resources as part of their search results (i.e., not reliant solely on matching words in documents to words in search boxes). Linked data makes possible the discovery of knowledge about entities that would otherwise have been separated by disassociated means of encoding or by different data silos. The Semantic Web is currently in its infancy, but there is great excitement about its potential and the changes that will occur as the result of its maturation. There will be far-reaching effects on information organization and cataloging, but exactly how things will change is not completely evident at this time. For further discussion about the Semantic Web and linked data, refer to chapter 22 of this text.

CONCLUSION

This chapter has presented an overview of the entire cataloging process. The next chapter presents a brief historical overview. Greater detail about the content of description, including authority control of access points, is discussed in chapters 3-10. Subject analysis is given thorough treatment in part IV, with chapter 11 discussing the process of determining aboutness, chapters 12-15 devoted to subject headings, and chapters 16-20 devoted to classification. Part V addresses issues related to encoding and presentation of bibliographic data. The final chapter deals in more detail with cataloging management and discovery environments.

NOTES

1. Elaine Svenonius, "Directions for Research in Indexing, Classification, and Cataloging," *Library Resources & Technical Services* 25, no. 1 (January/March 1981): 88.

2. Richard P. Smiraglia, "Bibliographic Control Theory and Nonbook Materials," in *Policy and Practice in Bibliographic Control of Nonbook Media*, Sheila S. Intner and Richard P. Smiraglia, editors (Chicago: American Library Association, 1987), 15.

3. Arlene G. Taylor and Daniel N. Joudrey, *The Organization of Information*, 3rd ed. (Westport, Conn.: Libraries Unlimited, 2009), 459.

4. Ibid., 2.

5. For example, *see* Gregory Schymik, Robert St. Louis, and Karen Corral, "Order of Magnitude Reductions in the Size of Enterprise Search Result Sets through the Use of Subject Indexes," Americas Conference on Information Systems (AMCIS) *Proceedings*, paper 195 (2009).

6. Taylor and Joudrey, 89.

7. International Federation of Library Associations and Institutions (IFLA) Study Group on the Functional Requirements for Bibliographic Records, *Functional Requirements for Bibliographic Records, Final Report* (München, Germany: K.G. Saur, 1998), http://archive.ifla.org/VII/s13/frbr/frbr_current_toc.htm or http://www.ifla.org/files/assets/cataloguing/frbr/frbr_2008.pdf.

8. Ibid., 82.

9. These ideas are discussed in greater detail by Ronald Hagler in *The Bibliographic Record and Information Technology*, 3rd ed. (Chicago: American Library Association, 1997), 17-18; and by Taylor and Joudrey in *The Organization of Information*, 4-29.

10. Charles A. Cutter, *Rules for a Printed Dictionary Catalog* (Washington, D.C.: Government Printing Office, 1876), 10.

11. International Conference on Cataloguing Principles. Paris, 9th-18th October, 1961, *Report* (London: International Federation of Library Associations, 1963), 26.

12. IFLA Cataloguing Section and IFLA Meetings of Experts on an International Cataloguing Code, *Statement of International Cataloguing Principles*, 2009, http://www.ifla.org/files/assets/cataloguing/icp/icp_2009-en.pdf.

13. *ALA Filing Rules* (Chicago: American Library Association, 1980); *Library of Congress Filing Rules* (Washington, D.C.: Library of Congress, 1980).

14. Arlene G. Taylor, with the assistance of David P. Miller, *Introduction to Cataloging and Classification*, 10th ed. (Westport, Conn.: Libraries Unlimited, 2006), Appendix.

15. "VIAF: The Virtual International Authority File," accessed July 25, 2014, http://viaf.org/.

16. For an in-depth discussion of the decisions and adaptations that were once necessary in the process of copy cataloging, *see* Arlene G. Taylor, with the assistance of Rosanna M. O'Neil, *Cataloging with Copy: A Decision-Maker's Handbook*, 2nd ed. (Englewood, Colo.: Libraries Unlimited, 1988).

17. For example, *see* Claire-Lise Benaud and Sever Bordeianu, *Outsourcing Library Operations in Academic Libraries: An Overview of Issues and Outcomes* (Englewood, Colo.: Libraries Unlimited, 1998), and Marylou Colver and Karen Wilson, editors, *Outsourcing Library Technical Services Operations* (Chicago: American Library Association, 1997).

18. *Anglo-American Cataloguing Rules, Second Edition*, 2002 Revision, prepared under the direction of the Joint Steering Committee for Revision of AACR (Chicago: American Library Association, 2002).

19. Taylor and Joudrey, *The Organization of Information*, 129-155.

20. Martha Yee, "Guidelines for OPAC Displays," prepared for the 65th IFLA Council and General Conference, Bangkok, Thailand, 20th-28th August 1999, http://archive.ifla.org/IV/ifla65/papers/098-131e.htm.

21. Tim Berners-Lee with Mark Fischetti, *Weaving the Web: The Original Design and Ultimate Destiny of the World Wide Web by Its Inventor* (New York: HarperCollins, 1999), chap. 12.

SUGGESTED READING

Carpenter, Michael, and Elaine Svenonius, editors. *Foundations of Cataloging: A Sourcebook.* Littleton, Colo.: Libraries Unlimited, 1985.

Hagler, Ronald. *The Bibliographic Record and Information Technology*, 3rd ed. Chicago: American Library Association, 1997.

Hider, Philip. *Information Resource Description: Creating and Managing Metadata.* Chicago: ALA Editions, 2013.

Hider, Philip, with Ross Harvey. *Organising Knowledge in a Global Society: Principles and Practice in Libraries and Information Centres*, rev. ed. Wagga Wagga, NSW, Australia: Centre for Information Studies, 2008. Chapter 1: Definitions and Introductory Concepts.

Intner, Sheila S., and Jean Weihs. *Standard Cataloging for School and Public Libraries*, 5th ed. Santa Barbara, Calif.: Libraries Unlimited, 2014.

Lazarinis, Fotis. *Cataloguing and Classification: An Introduction to AACR2, RDA, DDC, LCC, LCSH and MARC 21 Standards.* Oxford: Chandos Publishing, 2014.

Sanchez, Elaine R., editor. *Conversations with Catalogers in the 21st Century.* Foreword by Michael Gorman. Santa Barbara, California: Libraries Unlimited, 2011.

Svenonius, Elaine. *The Intellectual Foundation of Information Organization.* Cambridge, Mass.: The MIT Press, 2000. Chapter 2: Bibliographic Objectives.

Taylor, Arlene G. "The Information Universe: Will We Have Chaos or Control?" *American Libraries* 25, no. 7 (July/August 1994): 629-632.

Taylor, Arlene G., and Daniel N. Joudrey. "Cataloging." In *Encyclopedia of Library and Information Science*, 3rd ed., edited by Marcia J. Bates and Mary Niles Maack. Taylor and Francis: New York, 2009.

Taylor, Arlene G., and Daniel N. Joudrey. *The Organization of Information*, 3rd ed. Westport, Conn.: Libraries Unlimited, 2009.

Taylor, Arlene G., with the assistance of Rosanna M. O'Neil. *Cataloging with Copy: A Decision-Maker's Handbook*, 2nd ed. Englewood, Colo.: Libraries Unlimited, 1988. See esp. chap. 1, "Catalogs, Procedures, and Personnel," and chap. 9, "Merits and Problems of Copy Cataloging."

Working Group on the Future of Bibliographic Control. *On the Record: Report of The Library of Congress Working Group on the Future of Bibliographic Control.* Washington, D.C.: Library of Congress, 2008, accessed August 4, 2014, http://www.loc.gov/bibliographic-future/news/lcwg-ontherecord-jan08 -final.pdf.

Chapter 2

Development of Catalogs and Cataloging Codes

INTRODUCTION

Any history must select a beginning point and an ending point. This history begins with the latter part of the 19th century and continues through the early part of the 21st century, covering, for the most part, the development of library catalogs and library cataloging codes in the United States. A more comprehensive history covering the organization of recorded information from antiquity to modern times and also presenting the perspective of organizing information with different retrieval tools in different settings may be found in *The Organization of Information*, by Arlene G. Taylor and Daniel N. Joudrey.[1]

FORMS OF CATALOGS

Library catalogs have existed since the 19th century in one of several physical formats: book, card, microform, or online, with the online version now being the common form in the most technologically developed countries. The printed book catalog is the oldest type known in the United States; it was used by many American libraries until the late 1800s. The report of the Bureau of Education in 1876 gives a list of 1,010 printed book catalogs, 382 of them published from 1870 to 1876. Because book catalogs were rather expensive to produce and quickly became outdated, they were gradually replaced by card catalogs. In a survey of 58 typical American libraries undertaken in 1893, 43 libraries had complete card catalogs and 13 had printed book catalogs with card supplements.[2] Thus, for many years, book catalogs were out of favor in American libraries.

It was only with advances in less expensive printing and with the advent of automation for quicker cumulation that book catalogs again became popular with certain types of libraries. An example of a book catalog produced by more modern production techniques was the Library of Congress's *Catalog of Books Represented by Library of Congress Printed Cards*, known after 1956 as the *National Union Catalog*. It was published only in microform from 1983 through 2002, when publication finally ceased. As its earlier title indicates, it was, for many years, produced by photographic reduction of pre-existing catalog cards; hence, it was a by-product of a card catalog. A similar technique was used by a number of commercial publishers (e.g., G. K. Hall) when they reproduced card catalogs of certain libraries in a book catalog format. Beginning in the 1950s, a new type of book catalog appeared, based on the use of computers. These catalogs, using records created by various computer-produced methods, varied widely in format, typography, extent of bibliographic detail, and pattern of updating. The Library of Congress (LC) began publishing the *National Union Catalog* via computer in the 1970s.

At the beginning of the 1990s the card catalog was still the library catalog most often found in the United States. Even in the 21st century, the card catalog is still found in some libraries that have not been able to afford the software and equipment necessary for an online catalog, and it is also found in libraries that have not been able to complete the retrospective conversion of records from card format to machine-readable format. In the card catalog, each bibliographic description was prepared on a standard 7.5 × 12.5 cm card (roughly 3 × 5 in.), although the size was not always standard. In the first card catalogs a variety of sizes was used from library to library, including 1½ × 5 in., 1½ × 10 in., and 4 × 6 in. The descriptions on cards were at first hand-written, using a standardized "library hand" type of writing developed by Melvil Dewey in the 1870s before the typewriter came into standard use. (See Figure 2.1.) Typeset cards were available for purchase from LC beginning in 1901. Later, cards were often prepared by photoreproduction of a printed or typed original. Cards produced from the last part of the 20th century to date have been most often computer-produced from machine-readable catalog records.

Microform catalogs became much more popular with the development of computer output microform (COM). COM catalogs could be produced in either microfilm or microfiche. It was feasible, with this form of catalog, to provide a

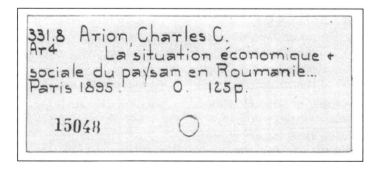

FIGURE 2.1 Example of an 1895 Catalog Card Written in "Library Hand."

completely integrated new catalog every three months or so rather than providing supplements to be used with a main catalog. However, microform catalogs were not popular with users, because microform is hard to read, may cause eye fatigue, and is difficult to take notes from. Worst of all, a film must be scrolled through or a fiche adjusted to a particular part of a grid to read what is wanted.

The online catalog, often referred to as an *online public access catalog* (OPAC), has rapidly become the catalog of choice. In first generation online catalogs, bibliographic records stored in the computer were shown on a display monitor in response to a request from a user. Displays of a metadata record were composed of either a full bibliographic record or only parts of it, depending on the system and/or the desires of the user. Until the 1990s such systems were costly, and only very large libraries were able to afford them.

Now systems have been developed for use on every size computer from network servers to personal computers and some have become quite affordable, although systems having "bells and whistles" can be costly. There are so many choices having to do with how much customization is desired, whether to opt for a discovery interface, and at what granularity the catalog should be indexed that many librarians are finding it difficult to choose among them. Our current era resembles the time before the standardization of the card catalog, when sizes of cards and order of elements of bibliographic data differed from library to library. As the profession learns what works best, online catalogs may eventually become more standardized, as did card catalogs—although with computers it will always be easier to deal with variations than it was with printed catalogs. For a discussion of the current attempts to make the best use of technology and system architecture, see the section on library services platforms in chapter 24.

CRITERIA FOR JUDGING CATALOGS

Catalogs were often judged as to whether they were effective according to criteria that developed during the 20th century. It was thought that an effective catalog in any format should possess certain qualities that would allow it to be easily consulted and maintained. The three basic criteria were (1) that it should be flexible and up to date, (2) that it should be constructed so that all access points could be quickly and easily found, and (3) that it should be economically prepared and maintained.

Because a library's collection is constantly changing, and because the catalog is a record of what is available in that library, it was thought that catalog records should be added or removed as resources were added to or discarded from the collection. The card catalog was considered to be the most flexible until the advent of the online catalog. Cards could easily be added to or removed from the files whenever necessary. However, backlogs of records to be entered often developed with card catalogs.

Book and microform catalogs were inflexible in that after they were printed, additions or deletions could not be made except in supplements or new editions of the catalog. On the other hand, because in the latter part of the 20th century they could be computer-produced, there was some flexibility in making changes in existing records for new editions of the catalog. For example, a single command could change many access points (e.g., one command could change every "Clemens, Samuel" to "Twain, Mark"), whereas with a card catalog, each card had to be changed individually. Online catalogs came to be considered the most flexible and current of all catalog formats, because additions, deletions, and changes could be made at any time, and the results were often instantly available to the user or at least available by the next day.

Constructing a catalog so that all records could be quickly and easily found was a matter of labeling, filing, and, in the case of online catalogs, simple and clear screen instructions. So far as the card catalog was concerned, the contents of each tray had to be identified well enough that, for example, a patron who wanted to locate the works of Virginia Woolf could find the Woolf catalog cards easily. The patron had to know exactly what part of the alphabet each tray contained. Within the trays themselves, arrangement of cards had to be such that items were not overlooked because the filing was not alphabetical, and guide cards had to be sufficiently plentiful to identify coverage.

Book catalogs were usually labeled on the spine, like encyclopedias. Often they had guides at the top of each page, indicating what records were covered there. Microfilm catalogs typically were stored in readers that were equipped with alphabetic index strips designed to get the user to the desired part of the alphabet. Microfiche catalogs had eye-readable labels at the top of each sheet of fiche that indicated the part of the alphabet covered. Typically, each sheet of fiche had a micro-image index in one corner that told in which cross section of the fiche particular parts of the alphabet would be found. Such systems were time-consuming to use, and reading the magnified film or fiche was often difficult. Many patrons would do almost anything to avoid using a microform catalog.

Filing arrangement in computer-produced catalogs was not the same as in traditionally filed card catalogs because of the difficulty of programming computers to arrange according to traditional library filing rules. This became a problem when users were using catalogs that were partly cards and partly microform. As a result, traditional rules were re-evaluated so that filing rules for manual filing more closely resembled computer filing rules.

Ways for locating bibliographic records in online catalogs have varied over time. At first the computer had to be told whether an author, title, or subject search was desired. In many systems one could enter as much of the title, author, or subject as seemed useful, but it was necessary to start at the left of the data string as it would have appeared in a card catalog. Some systems, after a time, also allowed users to input only the words they remembered in any order (called *keyword searching*), and the system searched for all records containing all the words input. The most recently created systems now allow sophisticated combinations of searching certain words from an author field, other words from a title field, words from a subject field, and the like—all at the same time. Accomplishing intersecting searches of this sort was very difficult, if not impossible, with all forms of printed catalogs.

Responses to searches in online catalogs have also varied by system. In some of the first systems developed, display of multiple responses (e.g., a listing of works by Frédéric Chopin) was in the order of "last in, first out"— that is, the last record cataloged or worked on in some way was the first one displayed—and there was no alphabetical collocation. (Ironically, the first web-based catalogs returned to this order of display.) In the next development, systems alphabetized displays but were not consistent among themselves in how the arrangement was accomplished. Many systems now allow a user to choose display order (chronological, reverse chronological, alphabetical by author, etc.) via pull-down menus or settings.

The third criterion was that a catalog should be economically prepared and maintained. The catalog that could be prepared most inexpensively and with greatest attention to currency had obvious advantages. The format of catalog that could be produced and maintained the most economically changed over time depending on such things as cost of paper for cards or books, costs of manual labor, costs of producing multiple copies of book and microform catalogs, availability of computer storage, availability of mechanisms to read microforms or computer data, and so on.

ARRANGEMENT OF RECORDS IN A CATALOG

A printed catalog (all the formats of catalogs occurring before online catalogs) required multiple copies of each bibliographic record so that the record could be found under any of several access points. Traditionally there was an access point for each author and any other person or corporate body associated with the creation of the intellectual or artistic work, but only if they were deemed important enough that someone might search for them. There were also access points for titles, variant titles, and subject headings assigned to the record. A copy of the entire bibliographic record usually appeared under each access point. In some book and microform catalogs, a full copy of the record appeared only at the primary creator's access point, and abbreviated versions appeared at all other access points. In all printed catalogs each access point, with its associated version of the bibliographic record, was called an *entry*, and the record that had the most information was called the *main* entry, thus giving rise to the use of *main entry* in cataloging rules to designate which access point should be chosen as the primary one.

Online catalogs do not have *entries* in the same sense. One master copy of each bibliographic record is stored by the system. Indexes are made that link each name, title, subject heading, or other entity decided upon as an access point to any associated bibliographic record. In response to a search request, selected data elements from each relevant bibliographic record are displayed on the user's screen in the format chosen for that system.

A printed catalog (unlike an online catalog) must be arranged according to some definite plan. Depending on the subject and scope of the collection, many arrangements have been possible. But no matter which one was used, it was supposed to cover the contents of the collection and guide the person who consulted it to these contents. Printed catalogs traditionally have been arranged according to one of two systems: classified or alphabetical. The differences between them lay in the arrangement of the entries.[3]

Classified Catalogs

The classified catalog has the longest history. Many American libraries used this form before they changed to the more popular alphabetical form. It was based on the system of classification used in a particular library. The *shelflist*, a record of the holdings of a library arranged by classification notation, is a classified catalog of a kind. But in a true classified catalog, a bibliographic record may be entered under as many classification notations as apply to its contents, not under just one notation as in a shelflist. In addition, the shelflist lacks an alphabetical subject index, which a true classified catalog has. In fact, classified catalogs constitute only the subject part of a divided catalog (see discussion below). They must be accompanied by a name/title catalog. Figure 2.2 shows a complete set of cards for a classified card catalog.

The major advantage of a classified catalog is that because it uses symbols, letters, and/or numbers, it is relatively unaffected by changing terminology and thus is more up to date than a subject catalog based on words. It is also useful for in-depth study of a subject. Closely related classes are brought together in sequence—often hierarchically. This is good for scanning or for moving from general to specific. In addition this arrangement permits easy compilation of subject bibliographies. Perhaps its greatest disadvantage is that it is constructed using a particular classification scheme (even though this was an advantage as noted above). Because many patrons are not familiar with classification notations, they might need special assistance when consulting a classified catalog.

Some fields—particularly the sciences—can make good use of such a catalog, as a classified catalog is flexible and can be easily updated. For example, only the index entries would have to be changed when terminology for a concept changes, rather than having to revise all records using the concept. Classified catalogs are also of value in locations where the patrons may speak two or more languages. In such a case, an alphabetical subject index may be made in each language. In Quebec, for example, where both English and French are spoken, there would be one classified catalog with French and English indexes. There are few classified catalogs in use in the United States today. They are more widely used in Europe, Canada, and a few other countries. At the end of the 20th century, predictions were made by experts in classification and bibliographic control that international cooperation would encourage the use of classification for subject exchange, because classification symbols transcend language.[4] However, currently there is no indication that this will happen.

Alphabetical Catalogs

Alphabetical catalogs came into being because of their ease of arrangement and use. An alphabetical arrangement is commonly understood by the users of that alphabet. A user is likely to find information (e.g., bibliographic records) under terms consulted first, rather than having to consult those terms to find a classification notation under which to conduct another search. Words are more easily understood than classification symbols. On the other hand, some terminology is quickly dated, and many terms have multiple meanings. In some very large catalogs in the past, alphabetic arrangement became quite complex. There have been two traditional arrangements of alphabetical catalogs: dictionary and divided.

Dictionary Catalogs

In the dictionary arrangement of card catalogs, widely used in American libraries until the 1990s, all the cards—name, title, and subject—were combined, word by word, into one alphabetical sequence. This arrangement was said to be simple; undoubtedly it was, in the sense that only one file needed to be consulted. As libraries grew, however, the dictionary arrangement became cumbersome and complex, because all the cards were inter-filed. The problem became partly one of filing (are books *by* Charles Dickens, for example, filed before those *about* him?) and partly one of dispersion (e.g., the subject *industrial relations* has many aspects; how can all these aspects be located quickly and efficiently if they are entered anywhere in the cata-log from *A* for *arbitration* to *W* for *wages*?). Two primary justifications were offered in favor of the dictionary arrangement: most patrons wanted material on one aspect of a subject rather than on the broad subject itself, and patrons were provided with ample *see* and *see also* references, which directed them to other aspects of their subjects. Ironically, as card catalogs and cataloging backlogs grew, many libraries stopped making references for subjects in the early 1980s, saying that they would be converting to online catalogs soon, and therefore, inconvenience to users would not last long. However, online catalogs began to provide subject references with regularity only in the mid- to late 1990s. Figure 2.3 shows a complete set of cards for a dictionary catalog.

Divided Catalogs

In the 1930s the realization that dictionary catalogs were becoming more and more complex led to a modification of the dictionary arrangement. The result was the divided catalog, which, in its most common form, was in reality two catalogs: one for subjects; the other for non-subject entities. The divided catalog permitted a simpler filing scheme than did the dictionary catalog, making it easier to consult; although the problem of scattered subjects still existed. There was a further complication implicit in this arrangement. The patron had to determine whether an author, a title, or a subject was wanted before knowing which part of the catalog to check. When this divided approach was used, books about Dickens and books by Dickens were not filed together in the catalog. Catalog users needed guidance and education in this matter.

Some libraries used other types of divided catalogs, such as the three-way divided catalog consisting of separate sections for authors, titles, and subjects. Although this system may have simplified the filing of cards, it was even more confusing for patrons than the two-way divided catalog. In this arrangement, entries for books by Dickens were filed under Dickens's name in the author catalog, entries for titles of his individual novels were filed in the title catalog, and entries for books about Dickens were filed in the subject catalog.

Another type of two-way divided catalog was one in which the records were separated into a name/title catalog and a topical subject catalog. In such a divided catalog, all names and titles, even those used as subject headings, were filed in the name/title section. This type of divided catalog allowed all the material by and about an author or a title to be filed together. To continue the

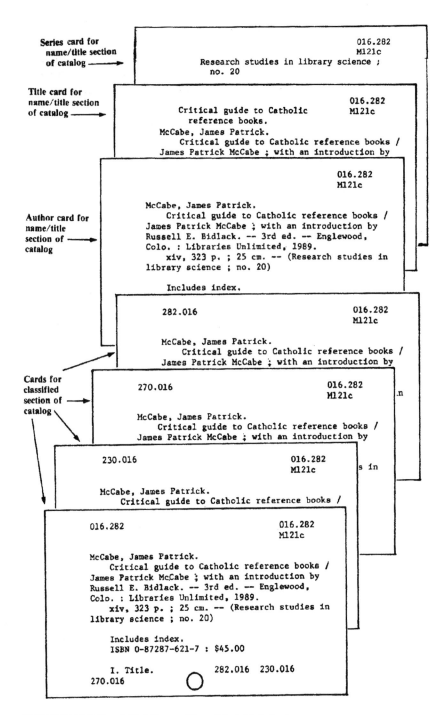

FIGURE 2.2 Card Set for a Classified Catalog.

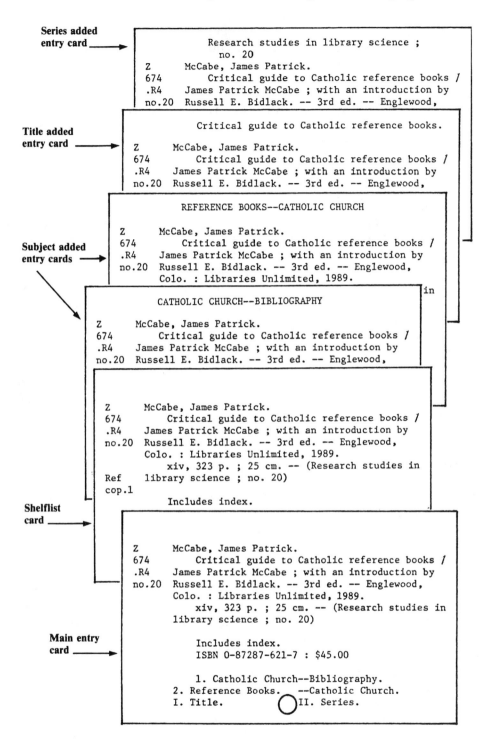

Series added
entry card

Research studies in library science ;
          no. 20
Z   McCabe, James Patrick.
674   Critical guide to Catholic reference books /
.R4   James Patrick McCabe ; with an introduction by
no.20   Russell E. Bidlack. -- 3rd ed. -- Englewood,

Title added
entry card

Critical guide to Catholic reference books.
Z   McCabe, James Patrick.
674   Critical guide to Catholic reference books /
.R4   James Patrick McCabe ; with an introduction by
no.20   Russell E. Bidlack. -- 3rd ed. -- Englewood,

REFERENCE BOOKS--CATHOLIC CHURCH
Z   McCabe, James Patrick.
674   Critical guide to Catholic reference books /
.R4   James Patrick McCabe ; with an introduction by
no.20   Russell E. Bidlack. -- 3rd ed. -- Englewood,
         Colo. : Libraries Unlimited, 1989.

Subject added
entry cards

CATHOLIC CHURCH--BIBLIOGRAPHY
Z   McCabe, James Patrick.
674   Critical guide to Catholic reference books /
.R4   James Patrick McCabe ; with an introduction by
no.20   Russell E. Bidlack. -- 3rd ed. -- Englewood,

in

Z   McCabe, James Patrick.
674   Critical guide to Catholic reference books /
.R4   James Patrick McCabe ; with an introduction by
no.20   Russell E. Bidlack. -- 3rd ed. -- Englewood,
         Colo. : Libraries Unlimited, 1989.
             xiv, 323 p. ; 25 cm. -- (Research studies in
Ref   library science ; no. 20)
cop.1
             Includes index.

Shelflist
card

Z   McCabe, James Patrick.
674   Critical guide to Catholic reference books /
.R4   James Patrick McCabe ; with an introduction by
no.20   Russell E. Bidlack. -- 3rd ed. -- Englewood,
         Colo. : Libraries Unlimited, 1989.
             xiv, 323 p. ; 25 cm. -- (Research studies in
         library science ; no. 20)

             Includes index.
             ISBN 0-87287-621-7 : $45.00

Main entry
card

             1. Catholic Church--Bibliography.
         2. Reference Books.   --Catholic Church.
         I. Title.   ◯II. Series.

FIGURE 2.3 Card Set for an Alphabetical Catalog.

previous example, books by and books about Dickens would be filed together in the same catalog. This system was potentially less confusing to the patron than any other form of divided catalog.

DEVELOPMENT OF CATALOGING RULES/GUIDELINES

In current U.S. cataloging practice no comprehensive code of rules tells a cataloger how to create bibliographic records that provide descriptive cataloging and subject access or how to create a catalog with those records. There is a widely accepted set of guidelines covering description and name and title access and addressing authority work to some extent. However, provision of subject access, authority control, and creation of catalogs depend on following both longstanding and more recent conventions—to a great extent, those established by the Library of Congress (LC) and the Program for Cooperative Cataloging (PCC). The rules for description and access, now called *RDA: Resource Description & Access*,[5] is the result of a progression of ideas about how to approach the cataloging process to prepare catalogs that provide the best possible access to library collections. RDA represents, in electronic and print forms, the current agreements that have been reached to standardize descriptive cataloging practice and thereby facilitate cooperation among libraries. It expands on the agreements presented in earlier codes and in more recently developed conceptual models (e.g., Functional Requirements for Bibliographic Records [FRBR], described below and in chapter 3 of this text) and forms the basis for further agreements that will be added to future codes.

The first cataloging rules were prepared by individuals. Anthony Panizzi, Keeper of the Printed Books at the British Museum, constructed a set of rules for that institution that was published in 1841.[6] This set of rules, often referred to as Panizzi's "91 Rules," was the first major modern statement of principles underlying cataloging rules; as such it has exerted an influence on every Western cataloging code that has been created since its publication. Panizzi believed that anyone looking for a particular work should be able to find it through the catalog, and he wrote rules with that goal in mind—e.g., he insisted on entering pseudonymous works under the pseudonym rather than under the author's real name. One characteristic of Panizzi's code was his occasional use of form headings as the primary access point (e.g., universities and learned societies were entered under the general heading **Academies**; and missals, prayer-books, and liturgies were entered under **Liturgies**). The concept of subject access as it is known today had not yet been separated from that of *main entry*, and there were no provisions for subject headings as such. Clearly, though, he thought there were some kinds of publications that ought to be *collocated* (i.e., gathered together).

Charles A. Cutter, librarian at the Boston Athenaeum, also created an important set of rules. His *Rules for a Dictionary Catalog*,[7] its fourth edition published a year after his death in 1903, asserted that catalogs not only should point the way to an individual publication, but also should assemble and organize *literary units* (groups of related works—original, editions, adaptations, etc.).[8] These rules were also the first complete set of rules for a dictionary catalog. Cutter's rules were truly comprehensive, incorporating rules for subject access and filing as well as for description and access. From the beginning of the 20th century, codes have been drawn up by committees, but the influence of these early visionary individuals has been apparent.

As mentioned earlier, the guidelines now used are for description, as well as for name and title access. After Cutter's rules for subject headings, two major American lists of subject headings were developed by LC and by Minnie Earl Sears—each containing introductions explaining conventions for use.[9] David Haykin enumerated principles for creating subject lists in 1951,[10] and LC issued its *Subject Cataloging Manual* for applying its headings in 1984 (revised as the *Subject Headings Manual* in 2008),[11] but there is no comprehensive code for subject access. Some librarians began calling for such a code in the late 1980s. History related to subject headings is discussed in more detail in Part IV of this book.

Rules for descriptive cataloging have progressed through a number of different iterations in the 20th and 21st centuries:

- LC's *Rules on Printed Cards* (1899 through the 1930s)[12]
- American Library Association (ALA) and the (British) Library Association's *Catalog Rules* (1908)[13]
- *A.L.A. Cataloging Rules* (1941)[14]
- *A.L.A. Cataloging Rules for Author and Title Entries* (1949)[15]
- LC's *Rules for Descriptive Cataloging* (1949)[16]
- *Anglo-American Cataloging Rules* (1967) (AACR)[17]
- *Anglo-American Cataloguing Rules*, 2nd ed. (1978) (AACR2)[18]
- *Anglo-American Cataloguing Rules, Second Edition*, 1988 Revision (AACR2R)[19]
- *Anglo-American Cataloguing Rules, Second Edition*, 1998 Revision (AACR2R98)[20]
- *Anglo-American Cataloguing Rules, Second Edition*, 2002 Revision (AACR2R2002)[21]
- *RDA: Resource Description & Access*[22]

The Anglo-American *Catalog Rules* of 1908 were the result of a seven-year study by a committee of ALA and a committee of the (British) Library Association.[23] In 1901 LC had begun its printed card service, with the result that libraries became interested in ways to use LC cards along with their own cards. One of the important responsibilities of the committee was to formulate rules to encourage incorporation of LC printed cards into catalogs of other libraries. The committee attempted to reconcile the cataloging practices of LC with those of other research and scholarly libraries. The use of LC cards increased dramatically between 1908 and 1941; standardization of library catalogs progressed. However, the 1908 rules were not expanded during this 33-year period, drastically curtailing attempts of cataloging practice to stay in touch with cataloging done at LC. In 1930, a subcommittee was appointed by ALA to begin work on a revision of cataloging rules, and the problems were outlined. Dissatisfaction with the 1908 code was expressed on the grounds of omissions; the basic rules were not in question. Expansion was required to meet the needs of large scholarly libraries or specialized collections:

> The preliminary edition [*A.L.A. Cataloging Rules*], published in 1941, expanded the rules of 1908 to make more provision for special classes of material: serial publications, government documents, publications of religious bodies, anonymous classics, music and maps; to amplify existing rules to cover specific cases of frequent occurrence.[24]

The *A.L.A. Cataloging Rules for Author and Title Entries* (1949) states:

> the chief changes from the preliminary [1941] edition are a rearrangement of the material to emphasize the basic rules and subordinate their amplifications, and to make the sequence of rules logical as far as possible; reduction of the number of alternate rules; omission of rules for description; rewording to avoid repetition or to make the meaning clearer; and revision, where possible, of rules inconsistent with the general principles.[25]

The 1941 and 1949 rules were sharply criticized for being too elaborate and often arbitrary; emphasis had shifted from clearly defined principles to a collection of rules developed to fit specific cases rather than the conditions that the cases illustrated. Seymour Lubetzky, then a specialist in cataloging policy at LC, commented that any logical approach to cataloging problems was blocked by the maze of arbitrary and repetitious rules and exceptions to rules.[26] The call for principles-based cataloging was echoed again more than a half-century later in the period immediately preceding the development of RDA.

Because of the omission of rules for description from the 1949 ALA rules, LC published in 1949 its *Rules for Descriptive Cataloging in the Library of Congress*.[27] This set of rules was much more simplified than had been the rules in Part II of the 1941 ALA preliminary edition. Therefore, these were not criticized, as were the rules for entry and heading (i.e., access points), and were incorporated virtually intact into the next edition of rules published by ALA in 1967.

Because the 1949 rules for entry and heading were not satisfactory, ALA invited Lubetzky in 1951 to prepare a critical study of cataloging rules. Early drafts of Lubetzky's principles came out against complete enumeration of cases in rules and pointed toward a less complex code based on well-defined principles.[28] At the International Conference on Cataloging Principles held in Paris in 1961, a draft statement of cataloging principles based on Lubetzky's *Code of Cataloging Rules* was used as the basis for consideration. The final version of the "Statement of Principles" (often called the "Paris Principles")[29] was adopted, and the participants from 53 countries agreed to work in their various countries for revised rules that would be in agreement with the accepted principles.

Anglo-American Cataloging Rules (AACR)

The Catalog Code Revision Committee that prepared the *Anglo-American Cataloging Rules* (AACR) realized that revision must be a complete reexamination of the principles and objectives of cataloging, not merely a revision of specific rules. First, the objectives of the catalog were agreed upon; it was further decided that the Paris Principles should be the basis for rules of entry and heading. This was an important step toward international bibliographic standardization. International standardization was not accepted overnight, however. The British and Americans were attempting to produce a joint code, but American conservatives were worried about the probable costs of full implementation of the Paris Principles. When the code was finally published, it was issued in two texts—one British and one North American—that were not harmonized until 1978.[30]

AACR was oriented toward large research libraries, although in a few instances of obvious conflict, alternate rules were provided for use by non-research libraries. Unlike the 1949 ALA code, which was only for entry and heading, AACR incorporated rules for entry and heading, description, and cataloging of non-book materials. An important shift occurred in the philosophy underlying the rules for entry: "The entry for a work is normally based on the statements that appear on the title page or any part of the work that is used as its substitute."[31] This meant that information appearing only in the preface, introduction, or text was not to be considered unless title page information was vague or incomplete. Another basic shift in point of view was to that of cataloging by types of authorship rather than by types of works and by classes of names rather than by classes of people.

Unlike earlier codes, AACR emphasized that choice of access points was a completely separate activity from construction of the heading used for any access point chosen. Two general principles became the basis for the rules for choice of main entry:

1. Entry should be under author or principal author when one can be determined.

2. Entry should be under title in the case of works whose authorship is diffuse, indeterminate, or unknown.

Application of rules based on these principles continued the practice of choosing a main entry, with other names and/or titles becoming added entries. However, the choice was no longer a result of first determining the type of work involved and then finding the specific rule for that type.

The construction of the headings for names that were to be main or added entries centered on two problems:

1. choice of a particular name, including both:
   a. choice among different names (e.g., Jacqueline Onassis or Jacqueline Kennedy), and
   b. choice among different forms of the same name (e.g., Morris West or Morris L. West), and

2. the form in which that name is presented (e.g., Seuss, Dr., or Dr. Seuss; Von Braun, Wernher, or Braun, Wernher von).

Rules for choice of name became based on a general principle of choosing the name used by a person or corporate body rather than the full name or official name as the 1949 ALA rules directed. This meant that a person could be entered under an assumed name, nickname, changed name, or others. A person who used both his or her real name and an assumed name, however, was still entered under the real name, and a person who used a forename initial, but also used a full form of a forename, even though rarely, was entered under the fullest form ever used. Another change was to use a firmly established English form of name rather than the vernacular form for many well-known names (e.g., Horace, not Horatius Flaccus, Quintus).

Another important area of change was in the form of access points for corporate bodies. The general rule followed the principle of using the form of name the body itself uses. Entry was usually under that form of name except when the rules provided for entry under a higher body or under the name of the government. However, the North American text gave exceptions exempting specified bodies of an institutional nature from the principle of entry under name; these were to be entered under place as in the old rules. These exceptions were contrary to the Paris Principles and to the British text of AACR, but they had been requested by the Association of Research Libraries, whose member libraries feared being overburdened with the necessity for changing thousands of entries already in catalogs.

The fear of the research libraries was also eased by LC's January 1967 announcement of the policy of *superimposition*:

> This means that the rules for choice of entry will be applied only to works that are new to the Library and that the rules for headings will be applied only to persons and corporate bodies that are being established for the first time. New editions, etc., of works previously cataloged will be entered in the same way as the earlier editions (except for revised editions in which change of authorship is indicated). New works by previously established authors will appear under the same headings.[32]

This policy continued throughout the duration of the application of AACR. As a result, thousands of access points were made between 1967 and 1981 in a form created under earlier rules and were placed on bibliographic records that were otherwise AACR records. The abandonment of the policy of superimposition with the implementation of AACR2 was a major step toward ultimate user convenience in finding entries and improved international cooperation; but for many large libraries, thousands of entries in pre-AACR form already in catalogs had to be dealt with after January 1981.

In 1974 the rule in AACR for entry of corporate bodies under place was dropped. Because of superimposition, only new corporate bodies were established and entered under their own names. Besides this change, some 40 other rules were changed, and three chapters were totally revised in the years following publication of AACR. Perhaps the most significant change was the application of international standards of description, based on the *International Standard Bibliographic Description* (ISBD), to descriptive cataloging of monographs, audiovisual media, and special instructional materials.[33] ISBD facilitated the international exchange of bibliographic information by standardizing the elements to be used in the bibliographic description, assigning an order to these elements, and specifying a system of symbols to be used in punctuating these elements.[34] (These symbols are also discussed and illustrated in Appendix D.1 of RDA.)[35] In addition, a major impact on descriptive cataloging was that "ISBD requires that a publication be totally identified by the description. It is independent of the provisions for headings, main or added, and of the provisions for the use of uniform titles; these were internationally standardized by the Paris Principles."[36]

Anglo-American Cataloguing Rules, Second Edition (AACR2)

The numerous changes to rules in AACR and the progress toward an international standard for description not only of monographs, but also of serials and all media, were two of the reasons for the meeting in 1974 of representatives of the national library associations and national libraries of Canada, the United Kingdom, and the United States to plan for the preparation of AACR2. Two other reasons were a proliferation of other rules for non-book materials that reflected dissatisfaction with AACR treatment of these materials and LC's announcement of intention to abandon the policy of superimposition.[37] The objectives established at that meeting were the following:

1. to reconcile in a single text the North American and British texts of 1967

2. to incorporate in the single text all amendments and changes already agreed upon and implemented under the previous mechanisms

3. to consider for inclusion in AACR all proposals for amendment currently under discussion

4. to provide for international interest in AACR by facilitating its use in countries other than the United States, Canada, and the United Kingdom[38]

The representatives at the 1974 meeting also agreed to establish a Joint Steering Committee for Revision of AACR (JSC) made up of one voting and one non-voting representative of each author organization. The JSC appointed an editor from each side of the Atlantic and generally oversaw the process of revision through to publication. The JSC continued from 1974 until 2007, when the committee changed its name to the Joint Steering Committee for Development of RDA. AACR2 had a process of continuous revision. Participating countries had committees that worked continually on recommendations for revisions. Approved recommendations were passed to the JSC, which then acted to accept or reject the proposals. Before recommendations were accepted, they often had to be revised, and differences of opinion had to be reconciled among the countries involved. The countries represented on the JSC continued to be Canada, Great Britain, and the United States. Australia and Germany were more recent additions to the committee.

The result of the revision process was what the preface to AACR2 calls a continuation of the first edition: "for, in spite of the changes in presentation and content which it introduces, these are still the *Anglo-American Cataloguing Rules*, having the same principles and underlying objectives as the first edition, and being firmly based on the achievement of those who created the work, first published in 1967."[39] However, AACR2, published in 1978 (but not implemented by the major national libraries until January 1981), had some differences that are worth noting here.

In the process of reconciling the North American and British texts, it was decided to use British spelling of words if the British spelling appeared as an alternative in *Webster's Third New International Dictionary of the English Language, Unabridged*. In cases of differing terminology, British usages were chosen in some cases (e.g., *full stop* instead of *period*), and American usages appeared in other cases (e.g., *parentheses* instead of the British *brackets*). Another change was in the presentation of rules for description: one general chapter presents broad provisions that can be applied in many different situations. This chapter is followed by specific chapters for different types of materials and for different conditions and patterns of publication. The rules for description were deliberately less specific in legislating ways to handle certain phenomena. The cataloger was thereby encouraged to exercise judgment in interpreting the rules in light of the needs of the user being served. (Cataloger's judgment is an idea that has again seen increased popularity in the 21st century.) One possibility for such interpretation was in AACR2's provision of three levels of description with increasing amounts of detail at each level. The cataloger chose the level that provided the amount of detail relevant to the particular library and its users and that, at the same time, met the standards called for in a set of international cataloging rules.

In the rules for choice of access points, it was significant that less emphasis was placed on *main entry*, although the concept was still present. Many people have expressed the opinion that when multiple access points are readily available, and when the bibliographic description is complete by itself, there is no need to designate one of the access points as the primary one. The original *main entry* concept, which remained basically unchanged from Panizzi's rules through AACR, was based on the idea that the purpose of the catalog is to identify works and that once the work is identified, sufficient bibliographic detail is added to facilitate finding the resource that contains the work. This was based on the assumption that there is a one-to-one correspondence between work and resource. This assumption worked fairly well until the latter part of the 20th century, when the tremendous growth of literatures and formats of all kinds rendered the assumption obsolete. Now, as noted in chapter 1, use of a main entry combined with title is the only way to identify the same work in several carriers. It is also the most common way, in a note, to identify another work that is related to the work being described in the bibliographic metadata. As long as this is true, the concept of *main entry* will not be abandoned, although it is no longer referred to in the same way. The equivalent concept in RDA is that of the authorized access point for a work, which consists of the preferred title of a work plus the authorized access point for the creator (if applicable).

A significant difference in choice of main entry in AACR2 was that a corporate body was not considered to be an *author*. Instead, there were specified categories of works that were allowed to be entered under a corporate body. This concept greatly reduced the number of corporate main entries made, although those corporate bodies that would have had main entry under earlier rules were given added entry under AACR2, resulting in the same number of corporate access points as before. These limitations on the notion of corporate body creators have continued into the latest cataloging code, RDA.

Rules for formulating headings (i.e., authorized access points) for personal names in AACR2 emphasized using the form of name most often used by a person (e.g., Benjamin Disraeli instead of Earl of Beaconsfield; Bernard Shaw instead of George Bernard Shaw). Except for pseudonyms, if a person uses more than one name, the predominant one is chosen. Rules for pseudonyms have evolved more than other rules for choice of personal name since AACR, in which only one form—the real name, if used—was chosen to represent a person who used more than one pseudonym or a real name and one or more pseudonyms. In the original 1978 version of AACR2, a predominant name was chosen; only if there were no predominant name could multiple headings be made for that author. This placed the mathematical works of Charles L. Dodgson under Lewis Carroll. In 1998, AACR2R introduced the concept of *separate bibliographic identities*, which allows separate headings in such cases as the Dodgson/Carroll example. It also called for multiple headings for all contemporary authors who use more than one pseudonym or a real name and one or more pseudonyms. These practices continue in RDA using slightly different terminology (e.g., see RDA 9.2.2.8 Individuals with More Than One Identity). Rules for corporate and geographic names similarly evolved to use names and forms of names that are more recognizable to users.

At the time of publication of AACR2, there were some general hopes for advantageous results from use of the new code. First, AACR2 laid the groundwork for much more international and national cooperative cataloging, which was expected to improve library service of a bibliographic nature and to result in considerable cost savings. Second, by providing the framework for standard description of all library materials, it made possible an integrated multimedia catalog. Third, it was expected to reduce user search time by providing headings that conform more often to the forms found in works and citations. Fourth, personal name headings were expected to be more stable than formerly, thus reducing catalog maintenance costs.[40] The first two of these expected advantages have been widely accepted as having come to pass. As to the third, Elizabeth Tate demonstrated that headings do indeed conform more often to the forms found in citations.[41] To know whether the last one has been realized, studies would have to be completed, and this has been complicated by the adoption of online catalogs, making comparisons of maintenance costs due to rule changes virtually impossible to obtain.

When AACR2 was published in 1978, a period of time was set before implementation to allow libraries to prepare for the change. The date for implementation was postponed twice, but implementation finally occurred January 2, 1981, after much angst and a flurry of local AACR2 studies to determine impact.[42] The problem was exacerbated by the fact that most libraries still had card catalogs, and changes had to be accomplished by erasing and retyping or by marking through headings and writing new forms above them. By the mid-1990s most libraries had online catalogs, in which changed access points can be modified by global search and replace methods, and new rule changes can be accommodated with more ease.

AACR2R and AACR2R98 incorporated official revisions that had been approved in the 10-year periods before each publication. For the most part, the revisions had been gradually implemented in the intervening years and the new publications were accepted easily. AACR2R2002 contained more major changes, however. Substantial changes were made to the chapters for cartographic materials, electronic resources, and serials (renamed *continuing resources*). The concept of *continuing resources* allowed the incorporation of *integrating resources* (e.g., loose-leaf updates) for the first time and went a long way toward handling the problems that web resources, which can be updated at any time, had presented for the followers of AACR2 principles.[43] After the brief interlude in which people adapted to the idea that *seriality* is not limited to print resources, RDA has returned to use of *serials* for this concept.

Rule interpretations made by LC in the process of applying AACR2 were published regularly in *Cataloging Service Bulletin*.[44] Official publications of rule changes were published annually from 2002 to 2010. The work has been translated into several languages, and its influence was widespread, but around the time of the new millennium, work toward a replacement for AACR2 began in earnest, the result being the publication of RDA.

RDA: Resource Description & Access

The preliminary work by the JSC to produce a new cataloging code, called *RDA: Resource Description & Access*, has finished. The first edition has been published, and several updates have already been incorporated into the electronic version in the web-accessible RDA Toolkit. Just as happened with AACR2, the implementation of RDA had to be postponed because of fears and concerns about how it would work. Finally, a testing period was undertaken, based on the recommendations of a panel of experts, convened by the Library of Congress, known as the Working Group on the Future of Bibliographic Control.[45] Only after achieving satisfactory testing results was RDA implemented, on March 31, 2013. Although RDA development is an ongoing process, it is on its way to becoming the new cataloging standard for the United States, Canada, Australia, Great Britain, Germany, and other locations around the world. Several international developments have led to this point, and some of the most important ones are mentioned here. First was the 1997 International Conference on the Principles and Future Development of AACR.[46] Held in Toronto, it invited experts from around the world to work on developing a plan for the future of AACR. Recommendations from that meeting are at various stages. Some have been implemented (e.g., the concerns about serials and integrating resources); some are guiding current thinking (e.g., the concern that better ways of presenting "content vs. carrier" be found); and some are waiting to be considered in the future.

A second major international set of actions involved the development of the "Functional Requirements . . . Family of Models" by study groups of the International Federation of Library Associations and Institutions (IFLA).[47] This family consists of *Functional Requirements for Bibliographic Records* (FRBR),[48] *Functional Requirements for Authority Data* (FRAD),[49] and *Functional Requirements for Subject Authority Data* (FRSAD).[50] FRBR is a conceptual model of the bibliographic universe examining the entities and relationships inherent in the creation and dissemination of information resources. The model includes three groups of entities: (1) those that are the products of creation: works, expressions, manifestations, and items; (2) those that are responsible for the existence of the Group 1 entities; and (3) those that may be the subjects of works. FRBR then explains the connections among these entities, including the high-level relationships involved in how a work gets expressed and how those expressions become manifested through individual items. More importantly, this model gives catalogers a way to show relationships among works, creators, subjects, and other entities that make up the components of the bibliographic metadata found in our catalogs, thus enabling users to find, identify, select, and obtain the information they need. FRAD defines functional requirements of authority data, continuing the work started by FRBR, and providing a framework "for the kind of authority data that is required to support authority control and for the international sharing of authority data."[51] FRBR and FRAD are two of the foundations of RDA and are discussed in more detail in the next chapter. FRSAD defines functional requirements of subject authority data and provides a framework for the "commonly shared understanding of what the subject authority data/record/file aims to provide information about, and the expectation of what such data should achieve in terms of answering user needs."[52] Chapters 33-37 of RDA are currently being held open for the future possibility of incorporating more subject entities into RDA. The reader should watch for developments on this issue.

A third international event of importance was the IFLA Meeting of Experts on an International Cataloguing Code in Frankfurt in 2003. The *Statement of International Cataloguing Principles* that came out of that meeting has replaced and broadened the Paris Principles—covering all types of materials and addressing many more aspects of bibliographic and authority records than just choice and form of entry in textual works.[53] A draft was reviewed worldwide and was finalized and published in 2009. The *Statement of International Cataloguing Principles* is another foundation of RDA; it, too, is discussed further in chapter 3.

International developments are not the only reasons why a new code for cataloging was called for. Another factor was the rapid proliferation of new types of resources along with new methods of presentation and new carriers. In addition, the relatively swift movement of the vast majority of catalogs into a networked online environment since the turn of the century has changed the way that catalogers work and the way that users search.[54] An effort was made in the development of RDA to build on the foundation of AACR2 and to maintain compatibility with the millions of bibliographic records already created according to AACR standards using the MARC format. This was accomplished while at the same time incorporating differences that are in some cases significant.[55]

RDA is meant to be a flexible framework that can accommodate a large variety of resources, not only in libraries, but also in the repositories of cultural heritage institutions, such as archives and museums, and in all kinds of digital collections. It is true that AACR2 included chapters for a number of material types other than monographic text, but incorporating new types of resources and new carriers often did not go smoothly. One issue was that a general material designation (GMD) was called for and was supposed to follow the title but precede any subtitle and/or the statement of responsibility. The GMD was usually a one- or two-word term that was supposed to incorporate the content type, media type, and carrier type. The categories for the GMD consisted of terms that could be work, expression, or manifestation attributes. RDA has introduced a framework for describing all types of resources. The RDA concepts of content type, media type, and carrier type have lists of terms acceptable to each. In addition, ISBD has accommodated the concept with a new area 0, and MARC has new tags in the 3XX range.

RDA continues moving toward creating records that will be easier for users to find and understand. For example, most abbreviations are done away with—Latin abbreviations such as *S.l.* and *et al.*, which many users may not understand, are replaced with *Place of publication not identified* and *and others*; even familiar abbreviations such as *p.* and *no.* are replaced with *pages* and *number*. Whether users understood abbreviations for illustrations such as *ill.*, *col.*, and *ports.* was debated, but they are now written out as *illustrations*, *color* or *colour*, and *portraits*. Abbreviations of dimensions and duration are maintained, and abbreviations used in the resource being described are to be transcribed as they appear.

Another change that will benefit users is that the infamous *rule of 3* is no longer in effect. This rule held that if more than three persons or corporate bodies were given as equal creators of a resource, then only the first should be named, followed by *et al.* In addition, only that first-named creator was given as an access point. In RDA, as many creators can be included as the cataloger deems useful, and all may be given as access points for the record. Additionally, families are considered to be creators, and fictitious and non-human beings are allowed the status of creators when they are presented in a resource as the creators of that resource. Also, many access points now have relationship designators telling the user the relationship of the access point to the work represented in the item described (both the expected, such as *editor* and *illustrator*, and the less well-known, including *abridger*, *narrator*, *former owner*). In authority records for names and titles, many more elements have been added for the description of the entity (e.g., place of birth and/or residence of a person, profession/occupation of a person, prominent members in families, fields of activity of a corporate body). All these user-friendly changes point to a recognition that metadata is no longer restricted to what can be typed on a 3 × 5 inch catalog card, nor are storage space and memory as expensive as they once were.

An important principle in RDA is the principle of representation, which means that information as it appears on or in a resource is more often given as found on the item than it was using AACR2. In describing publisher information, for example, the place and publisher are given as represented instead of having rules to abbreviate country names or to ignore words such as *Company* or *Inc.* Statements of responsibility may include such terms as *Jr.*, *Sr.*, *Dr.*, or *The Reverend.* Edition statements are transcribed as found (e.g., Second Edition) rather than being transformed using cataloger-supplied abbreviations and numerals. In light of this principle, RDA also allows catalogers to record what they see rather than to apply capitalization rules, to correct typos and other inaccuracies, or to change certain types of punctuation and spacing.

More information about RDA is included in Part II of this book. The reader should watch for rapid changes as this cataloging code develops.

NOTES

1. Arlene G. Taylor and Daniel N. Joudrey, *The Organization of Information* (Westport, Conn.: Libraries Unlimited, 2009), 67-87.
2. A good discussion of the historical development of cataloging practices is presented in an article written by Charles Martel, "Cataloging: 1876-1926," reprinted in *The Catalog and Cataloging*, edited by A. R. Rowland (Hamden, Conn.: Shoe String Press, 1969), 40-50.
3. *See also* discussion in: Taylor and Joudrey, *The Organization of Information*, 49-52.
4. Russell Sweeney, "The Atlantic Divide: Classification Outside the United States," in *Classification of Library Materials*, edited by Betty G. Bengtson and Janet Swan Hill (New York: Neal-Schuman, 1990), 40-51.
5. *RDA: Resource Description & Access,* developed in a collaborative process led by the Joint Steering Committee for Development of RDA (Chicago: American Library Association, 2010). Also available as *RDA Toolkit: Resource Description & Access* (Chicago: American Library Association, 2010), accessed February 15, 2014, http://www.rdatoolkit.org/. For subscription information, *see* http://www.rdatoolkit.org/subscribe.
6. Antonio Panizzi, "Rules for the Compilation of the Catalogue," in British Museum, *The Catalogue of Printed Books in the British Museum* (London, 1841), 1: v-ix.
7. Charles A. Cutter, *Rules for a Dictionary Catalog*, 4th ed., rewritten (Washington, D.C.: Government Printing Office, 1904).
8. Richard P. Smiraglia, *The Nature of "A Work": Implications for the Organization of Knowledge* (Lanham, Md.: Scarecrow Press, 2001), 19-22.
9. Library of Congress, Catalog Division, *Subject Headings Used in the Dictionary Catalogues of the Library of Congress* (Washington, D.C.: Library Branch, Government Printing Office, 1910-1914); Minnie Earl Sears, *List of Subject Headings for Small Libraries* (New York: H. W. Wilson, 1923).
10. David Judson Haykin, *Subject Headings: A Practical Guide* (Washington, D.C.: Government Printing Office, 1951).
11. Library of Congress, Cataloging Policy and Support Office, *Subject Headings Manual, 2008 ed.* (Washington, D.C.: Library of Congress Cataloging Policy and Support Office, 2008), accessed February 15, 2014, http://www.loc.gov/aba/publications/FreeSHM/freeshm.html.
12. Library of Congress, *Rules on Printed Cards* (Washington, D.C.: Library of Congress, 1899-194?).
13. *Catalog Rules, Author and Title Entries*, compiled by Committees of the American Library Association and the (British) Library Association, American ed. (Chicago: American Library Association Publishing Board, 1908).
14. *A.L.A. Cataloging Rules, Author and Title Entries*, prepared by the Catalog Code Revision Committee of the American Library Association, with the collaboration of a Committee of the (British) Library Association, Preliminary American 2nd ed. (Chicago: American Library Association, 1941).
15. *A.L.A. Cataloging Rules for Author and Title Entries*, prepared by the Division of Cataloging and Classification of the American Library Association, 2nd ed. (Chicago: American Library Association, 1949).
16. Library of Congress, Descriptive Cataloging Division, *Rules for Descriptive Cataloging in the Library of Congress* (Washington, D.C.: Library of Congress, 1949).

17. *Anglo-American Cataloging Rules, North American Text*, prepared by the American Library Association, the Library of Congress, the (British) Library Association, and the Canadian Library Association (Chicago: American Library Association, 1967).

18. *Anglo-American Cataloguing Rules*, 2nd ed., prepared by the American Library Association, the British Library, the Canadian Library Committee on Cataloguing, the (British) Library Association, and the Library of Congress, ed. by Michael Gorman and Paul W. Winkler (Chicago: American Library Association, 1978).

19. *Anglo-American Cataloguing Rules, Second Edition*, 1988 Revision, prepared by the Joint Steering Committee for Revision of AACR, ed. by Michael Gorman and Paul W. Winkler (Ottawa: Canadian Library Association; Chicago: American Library Association, 1988).

20. *Anglo-American Cataloguing Rules, Second Edition*, 1998 Revision, prepared by the Joint Steering Committee for Revision of AACR (Ottawa: Canadian Library Association; Chicago: American Library Association, 1998).

21. *Anglo-American Cataloguing Rules, Second Edition*, 2002 Revision, prepared under the direction of the Joint Steering Committee for Revision of AACR (Ottawa: Canadian Library Association; Chicago: American Library Association, 2002).

22. *RDA: Resource Description & Access,* accessed February 15, 2014, http://www.rdatoolkit.org/.

23. J.C.M. Hanson, *The Anglo-American Agreement on Cataloging Rules and Its Bearing on International Cooperation in Cataloging of Books* (Bruxelles, Belgium: Academies Royales de Belgique, 1908).

24. *A.L.A. Cataloging Rules*, 1949, viii.

25. Ibid., ix.

26. Seymour Lubetzky, *Cataloging Rules and Principles: A Critique of the A.L.A. Rules for Entry and a Proposed Design for Their Revision* (Washington, D.C.: Processing Dept., Library of Congress, 1953).

27. L.C., *Rules for Descriptive Cataloging*, 1949.

28. Seymour Lubetzky, *Code of Cataloging Rules, Author and Title: An Unfinished Draft . . . with an Explanatory Commentary by Paul Dunkin* (Chicago: American Library Association, 1960).

29. International Conference on Cataloging Principles, Paris, 9th-18th October, 1961, *Report* (London: International Federation of Library Associations, 1963).

30. *Anglo-American Cataloging Rules, North American Text* (Chicago: American Library Association, 1967); *Anglo-American Cataloguing Rules, British Text* (London: Library Association, 1967).

31. *AACR, North American Text*, 9.

32. *Cataloging Service*, bulletin 79 (January 1967): 1.

33. International Federation of Library Associations, *ISBD(G): General International Standard Bibliographic Description: Annotated Text* (London, International Office for UBC, 1977). The 1992 revised edition is available, http://archive.ifla.org/VII/s13/pubs/isbdg.htm.

34. A consolidated version of the ISBDs that had applied to different formats of resources was published in 2011: *ISBD: International Standard Bibliographic Description*, recommended by the ISBD Review Group; approved by the Standing Committee of the IFLA Cataloguing Section, Consolidated ed. (Berlin; München, Germany: De Gruyter Saur, 2011). Also available online at the IFLA website, http://www.ifla.org/files/assets/cataloguing/isbd/isbd-cons_20110321.pdf.

35. RDA, Appendix D.1: ISBD Presentation.

36. "International Standard Bibliographic Description," *Cataloging Service, bulletin* 105 (November 1972): 2.
37. "AACR 2: Background and Summary," *Library of Congress Information Bulletin* 37 (October 20, 1978): 640.
38. *AACR2*, vi-vii.
39. *AACR2*, v.
40. "AACR 2: Background and Summary," 652.
41. Elizabeth L. Tate, "Access Points and Citations: A Comparison of Four Cataloging Codes," *Library Research* 1 (Winter 1979): 347-359.
42. Arlene Taylor Dowell, *AACR 2 Headings: A Five-Year Projection of Their Impact on Catalogs* (Littleton, Colo.: Libraries Unlimited, 1982), 22-35; Arlene G. Taylor, "Implementing *AACR* and *AACR2*: A Personal Perspective and Lessons Learned," *Library Resources & Technical Services* 56, no. 3 (July 2012): 122-126.
43. Arlene G. Taylor, "Where Does AACR2 Fall Short for Internet Resources?" *Journal of Internet Cataloging* 2, no. 2 (1999): 43-50.
44. *Cataloging Service Bulletin*, no. 1-128 (Washington, D.C.: Processing Services, Library of Congress, 1978-2010).
45. *On the Record: Report of The Library of Congress Working Group on the Future of Bibliographic Control* (Washington, DC: Library of Congress, 2008), http://www.loc.gov/bibliographic-future/news/lcwg-onthe record-jan08-final.pdf.
46. Jean Weihs, ed., *The Principles and Future of AACR: Proceedings of the International Conference on the Principles and Future Development of AACR: Toronto, Ontario, Canada, October 23-25, 1997* (Ottawa: Canadian Library Association; London, UK: Library Association Publishing; Chicago: American Library Association, 1998); [web page for the Conference]: *International Conference on the Principles & Future Development of AACR,* Joint Steering Committee for Development of RDA. Web page includes the papers that were posted before the Conference and the discussion list archives, http://www .rda-jsc.org/intlconf1.html.
47. IFLA Cataloguing Section, "Functional Requirements: The FRBR Family of Models," accessed August 1, 2014, http://www.ifla.org/node/2016.
48. IFLA Study Group on the Functional Requirements for Bibliographic Records, *Functional Requirements for Bibliographic Records, Final Report* (München, Germany: K.G. Saur, 1998), http://archive.ifla.org/VII/s13/frbr/frbr_current_toc.htm or http://www.ifla.org/files/assets/cataloguing/frbr/frbr_2008.pdf.
49. IFLA Working Group on Functional Requirements and Numbering of Authority Records (FRANAR), *Functional Requirements for Authority Data: A Conceptual Model*, approved by the Standing Committees of the IFLA Cataloguing Section and IFLA Classification and Indexing Section, 2009, amended and corrected through July 2013, http://www.ifla.org/publications/functional -requirements-for-authority-data.
50. IFLA Working Group on the Functional Requirements for Subject Authority Records (FRSAR), *Functional Requirements for Subject Authority Data (FRSAD): A Conceptual Model*, approved by the Standing Committee of the IFLA Section on Classification and Indexing, 2010, accessed August 1, 2014, www.ifla.org/node/5849.
51. FRAD, 1.
52. FRSAD, section 2.2.
53. IFLA Cataloguing Section and IFLA Meetings of Experts on an International Cataloguing Code, *Statement of International Cataloguing Principles*, 2009 http://www.ifla.org/files/assets/cataloguing/icp/icp_2009-en.pdf.

54. Chris Oliver, *Introducing RDA: A Guide to the Basics* (Chicago: American Library Association, 2010), 2.

55. Adam L. Schiff, *Changes from AACR2 to RDA: A Comparison of Examples*, May 7, 2011, accessed August 2, 2014, http://faculty.washington.edu/aschiff/BCLAPresentationWithNotes-RevMay2011.pdf; Susan C. Wynne, *RDA and AACR2: What's the Difference?* (Wyoming State Library Webinar, October 11, 2011), https://www.academia.edu/1701030/RDA_and_AACR2_Whats_the_Difference.

SUGGESTED READING

Baker, Nicholson. "Discards." *New Yorker* 70, no. 7 (April 4, 1994): 64-86.

Cutter, Charles Ammi. *Rules for a Dictionary Catalog*, 4th ed., rewritten. Washington, D.C.: Government Printing Office, 1904.

Denton, William. "FRBR and the History of Cataloging." In *Understanding FRBR: What It Is and How It Will Affect Our Retrieval Tools*, edited by Arlene G. Taylor. Westport, Conn.: Libraries Unlimited, 2007, 35-57.

Dowell, Arlene Taylor. *AACR 2 Headings: A Five-Year Projection of Their Impact on Catalogs*. Littleton, Colo.: Libraries Unlimited, 1982.

Dunkin, Paul S. *Cataloging U.S.A.* Chicago: American Library Association, 1969. See esp. chap. 1, "Mr. Cutter's Catalog," and chap. 2, "The Prophet and the Law: Codes after Cutter."

International Conference on AACR2, Florida State University, 1979. *The Making of a Code: The Issues Underlying AACR2*. Chicago: American Library Association, 1980.

Joachim, Martin D., ed. *Historical Aspects of Cataloging and Classification*. Binghamton, N.Y.: Haworth Information Press, 2003.

Lubetzky, Seymour. *Cataloging Rules and Principles: A Critique of the ALA Rules for Entry and a Proposed Design for Their Revision*. Washington, D.C.: Processing Dept., Library of Congress, 1953.

Norris, Dorothy May. *A History of Cataloguing and Cataloguing Methods 1100-1850: With an Introductory Survey of Ancient Times*. Ann Arbor, Mich.: University Microfilms, 1982. (Facsimile of London: Grafton & Co., 1939).

Osborn, Andrew. "The Crisis in Cataloging." *Library Quarterly* 11 (October 1941): 393-411.

Russell, Beth M. "Hidden Wisdom and Unseen Treasure: Revisiting Cataloging in Medieval Libraries." *Cataloging & Classification Quarterly* 26, no. 3 (1998): 21-30.

Strout, Ruth French. "The Development of the Catalog and Cataloging Codes." *Library Quarterly* 26, no. 4 (October 1956): 254-275.

Taylor, Arlene G., and Daniel N. Joudrey. *The Organization of Information*, 3rd ed. Westport, Conn.: Libraries Unlimited, 2009. Chap. 3, "Development of the Organization of Recorded Information in Western Civilization."

Weihs, Jean, ed. *The Principles and Future of AACR: Proceedings of the International Conference on the Principles and Future Development of AACR, Toronto, Ontario, Canada, October 23-25, 1997*. Ottawa: Canadian Library Association; Chicago: American Library Association, 1998.

Part II

Description and Access

Chapter 3

Description and Access: Underlying Principles and Conceptual Models

INTRODUCTION

Toward the end of the 20th century, librarians had begun to discuss how traditional approaches to library cataloging were no longer sustainable. The world of information had started to change. Newer search mechanisms, for better or for worse, were often the first step on a user's road to information access.[1] Some believed that if drastic changes were not made in how description, access, and encoding were handled, the number of library patrons/ catalog users lost to search engines and the web would only increase over time. Those strongly advocating for cataloging reforms sometimes saw catalogers as being obstructionists who were anti-technology and/or resistant to change. Some catalogers assumed that library directors and other holders of purse strings were the only ones initiating these discussions and that their motives were somewhat cataloging-phobic or cataloging-illiterate. This was not true though. Although some participants may have had ulterior motives, the desire to discuss changes in bibliographic control generally was sincere and more widespread than just among administrators.

Over the following two decades, attitudes changed. Librarians and other information professionals (including many catalogers) saw technology advance rapidly. Many came to realize that standard practices that had developed in the previous century or earlier needed to be challenged. Thus began a long journey to revise cataloging standards. Over the intervening years, the attitude toward resource description has evolved from one of describing a book in hand for the purposes of retrieval and inventory to one wherein the cataloger

51

must think more about relationships and links to other similar resources in a broader landscape of information discovery on a web-based platform. No longer can catalogers and libraries afford to focus solely on siloed information in flat databases or on insular practices using standards that are completely unfamiliar to the wider world of information content providers.

To understand the contemporary approach to cataloging, a number of foundational documents and concepts must be examined. Although one could approach these chronologically, it may be more helpful to look at the general principles first and then to explore specific conceptual models. This chapter discusses the *Statement of International Cataloguing Principles* (ICP) generated by the International Federation of Library Associations and Institutions (IFLA). The basics of entity-relationship models are also introduced. Finally, two conceptual models, *Functional Requirements for Bibliographic Records* (FRBR) and *Functional Requirements for Authority Data* (FRAD), are examined in some detail.

INTERNATIONAL CATALOGUING PRINCIPLES

After a series of five meetings held around the world between 2003 and 2007, the IFLA Meeting of Experts on an International Cataloguing Code (IME ICC) disseminated a document called the *Statement of International Cataloguing Principles* (ICP) in 2009.[2] The ICP arose from concerns about the future of cataloging that had been fodder for discussions over the previous decade or longer. The purpose of the ICP was to update and expand upon the previous statement of cataloging principles produced by the International Conference on Cataloguing Principles held in Paris in 1961.[3] These "Paris Principles," based largely on Seymour Lubetzky's *Code of Cataloging Rules*,[4] have long been acknowledged as a guiding force in the development of cataloging codes around the globe concerning the choice and form of access points.

The introduction to the ICP states that the 2009 principles take into account the use of online library catalogs "and beyond" and are intended to extend the principles "from just textual works to all types of materials and from just the choice and form of entry to all aspects of bibliographic and authority data used in library catalogues."[5] From this point into the foreseeable future, the ICP is to be the basis for the international standardization of cataloging, having been built on earlier cataloging traditions and on the foundations of the FRBR and FRAD conceptual models, which were also created by IFLA working groups. The idea is that the *Statement of International Cataloguing Principles* can be used as a prefatory document that will ensure a degree of consistency among the cataloging codes created by various countries around the world. IFLA anticipates that these principles will "increase the international sharing of bibliographic and authority data and guide cataloguing rule makers in their efforts to develop an international cataloguing code."[6] IFLA also believes the ICP may be applied not only to catalogs, but also to bibliographies and other retrieval tools created by information and cultural heritage institutions (libraries, archives, museums, and so forth).

At the time of this writing, a revision of the ICP has been drafted for worldwide review. Because the document is in the early stages of development it will not be addressed thoroughly in this text. Readers should be cognizant that an updated ICP will be distributed in 2015 (or shortly thereafter) and additions to the principles are expected.

General Principles

Nine concepts make up the general principles of the ICP. These are baseline values that the makers of cataloging codes are encouraged to embrace and to reflect in their own national cataloging guidelines. Each of the principles is addressed in turn.

The first of the general principles is *Convenience of the User*. It is identified as the highest or foremost principle. The idea is that all issues, conflicts to be resolved, and decisions to be made should take into account the needs of the users. The convenience of the user, the patron, or the customer should be the primary concern (as opposed to the convenience of the cataloger). Of every decision, those writing cataloging guidelines should ask: How does this affect the user? But questions remain. How does one know what this hypothetical, generic user needs? With a world population of more than 7 billion, which users should be considered when designing a cataloging code for a diverse, multicultural, multilingual group? Although having the user as a central focus is a noble idea, it might not always be obvious just what the user wants or needs, and there may not always be a clear easy way to find out. Though one might rely on evidence obtained from practice-based or scholarly research, that research may not yet exist, or it may not be practicable to conduct that research. The point is that, at times, those in the LIS professions may just be making nothing more than an educated guess when it comes to the user. This does not mean, however, that efforts to keep users in mind are unworkable; one simply must acknowledge that there are limitations.

The second principle, *Common Usage*, is also quite reasonable in a universal sense. Its basic idea is that the terminology used when describing information resources should align itself with the vocabulary of the majority of the users. Without again getting into the question of just who those users are, one must acknowledge that terminology can be different from region to region even within a single unified country or within a population that speaks a single language. There is no common usage on an international level. Common usage, consequently, will be different from place to place. This is as it should be, particularly when thinking about the global society in which the profession operates. For example, one should not expect library users in Spain and those in Portugal to use the same character string (or form of name) to represent a creator when there are differences in how names are treated in those two countries. One also does not expect the same terminology to be used for subject matter or for bibliographic elements across different languages (e.g., edition vs. edición vs. auflage vs. útgáfa).

The third principle, *Representation*, states that names and resource descriptions should reflect how entities (resources, creators, etc.) represent themselves. For example, a name or form of name chosen for a creator should reflect the name that is most frequently used by that creator in information resources. Representation, to a certain extent, invokes another related concept: *transcription*. Transcription is the process of recording data exactly (or nearly exactly) as it is found in the resource itself. This action is often taken with certain data elements that are meant to identify a resource unambiguously. An example of transcription is when a cataloger copies a title exactly as it appears on the title page. The next principle, *Accuracy*, is fairly straightforward. One should authentically depict resources or the names associated with resources as they are. In other words, do not include incorrect information or make things up. It is expected that all catalogers will be ethical and conscientious in recording their descriptions. Typos, spelling errors, transpositions, deliberate misrepresentation, and other such mishaps, make retrieval difficult, if not impossible, so both accuracy and representation are imperative.

The fifth principle listed is *Sufficiency and Necessity*, which denotes that only data that supports the user tasks (to find, to identify, to select, to obtain, and/or to navigate) is necessary in resource descriptions or in the names used for creators, contributors, and other entities (i.e., persons, families, and corporate bodies). This means that catalogers should not add too much metadata, nor should they include too little; much like Goldilocks, catalogers are looking for the metadata that is just right. The metadata included must help fulfill the user tasks or uniquely identify the resource. For more information on the user tasks, see below.

Significance is the sixth general principle. It simply states: "Data elements should be bibliographically significant"[7]—meaning that one should not include data elements that do not matter. The ICP defines *bibliographically significant* as "a quality of an entity or attribute or relationship that has special meaning or value in the context of bibliographic resources."[8] So what does that mean? Although it no longer appears in the current cataloging rules or policy statements, for a long time the concept was discussed in the *Library of Congress Rule Interpretations* (LCRIs) for the *Anglo-American Cataloguing Rules*, 2nd edition (AACR2). In the LCRIs, it meant, "significant from the point of view of the intellectual and artistic content" of a resource.[9] For example, one would not describe in a catalog record the typeface used in a readily available and recently published trade paperback; it is not bibliographically significant. Nor would one add access points for the names of the editorial support staff; no matter how important they were in the physical production of the resource, they did not create or contribute to the artistic or intellectual content. The focus should be on the most important characteristics of the description and on those who might be sought in the catalog for their scholarly or creative contributions. In sum, the data included should be both important for identification and understanding, and should be necessary to fulfill the user tasks.

The next principle is that of *Economy*, which states that if there are alternative ways of doing something, one should select the method that involves the smallest expense in time or money. Cataloging (especially authority work) has a reputation for being expensive. When more economical options are available, the principles recommend selecting them. The eighth principle is *Consistency and Standardization*, which instructs those creating descriptions and establishing names to be consistent by following the cataloging instructions as closely as possible. The purpose of standardizing cataloging work is to ensure that there is an opportunity to share metadata widely. If all parties follow the same standards, then the metadata created should be similar enough that everyone will be able to use it (at least in theory).

Integration is the ninth and final general principle. It states that the cataloging rules established should be applicable to all types of resources and to all types of entities that may be encountered. A common set of general rules should be the basis for all cataloging codes. There is, and always will be, a need for individual rules to address the special characteristics of particular material types (serials, maps, electronic resources, etc.). These specific instructions, however, are added to the common set of rules to enhance the entire code or they may be incorporated into a supplementary manual to be used alongside the common set of guidelines. This principle instructs code-makers to start with a one-size-fits-all approach, which can be expanded to accommodate more specific requirements as needed.

In the draft revision of the ICP, additional guiding principles are proposed. These include *interoperability* (ensuring the ability to share and reuse data easily no matter the technology), *openness* (ensuring that restrictions are minimal), *accessibility* (ensuring compliance with international accessibility standards to minimize exclusion), and *rationality* (ensuring that cataloging rules are justifiable and not arbitrary). Readers should review these and other changes to the ICP after the document is finalized and distributed.

Entities, Relationships, and Attributes

In Section 3, the ICP recommends that cataloging codes consider an underlying structure based on an entity-relationship model, particularly with how it is embodied in FRBR. Before moving on to other parts of the ICP and to FRBR, it is important to take some time to understand the underlying entity-relationship structure (E-R model). In 1976, Peter Chen first proposed the idea that entities and relationships could be used as the foundation for database design.[10] In E-R models, there are three classes of concern; they obviously comprise *entities* and *relationships*, but *attributes* are included in the basic structure as well. A very simple diagram of an entity-relationship model is presented in Figure 3.1.

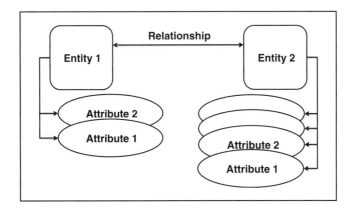

FIGURE 3.1 A Simple Entity-Relationship Model.

Entities are things. They are key objects of interest about which information is sought. Entities are capable of being distinctly identified. A person, a creative work, a corporate body, an event, and a concept are all examples of entities. An entity is often a focal point for gathering data. Determining which entities are of concern comes through the choice of a conceptual model. If the model is interested in creators and their works, then those entities will be central to the design of the code. The ICP enumerates the entities considered important in the bibliographic universe and divides them into three groups:

- **Group 1**: Work, Expression, Manifestation, and Item (WEMI)
- **Group 2**: Person, Family, and Corporate Body (PFC)
- **Group 3**: Concept, Object, Place, and Event (COPE)

These entities are taken directly from the FRBR model and will be discussed in more detail in the following section.

The second component of the E-R model is *relationships*. Relationships are reciprocal associations or connections between entities. These connections are usually expressed in a way to indicate that the relationship flows in each direction between the entities. An entity may have one or more relationships, but only relationships of bibliographic significance are usually documented in the cataloging process. Among many others, some examples of relationships include creator relationships to works, contributor relationships to expressions, whole-part relationships, derivative relationships among works, name-to-later-name relationships, and accompanying relationships.

Attributes are characteristics of entities or relationships. For the time being, current rules and practice, including the FRBR model, do not call for use of any attributes for relationships, however. Attributes for entities are identifying features that help in understanding the essence of the entities. Examples of attributes may include the title of a work, the birth date of a person, publication date, fuller form of name, a series statement, the field of activity of a corporate body, and so on. The ICP states attributes may be employed as metadata elements within a cataloging code. Attributes, however, do not provide the actual data about the entities. Attributes are fields or elements, but to describe an entity, data values must be added. It is not enough to simply know that a work has a title or that a creator has a birth date; it is the data values placed in those attributes that identify the entities. According to the ICP, an E-R model is to be the foundation for any new cataloging code. Figure 3.2 shows the same simple entity-relationship model from Figure 3.1, but with data values for the entities, attributes, and relationships specified.

To provide a loose analogy, one could equate entity-relationship models to basic grammar. One could look at entities as nouns, relationships as verbs, and attributes as adjectives and adverbs. This is not an exact correlation, however, because depending on which conceptual model is followed, some of the attributes might actually be other entities rather than simply an identifying characteristic. At times, it can be difficult to determine whether something is an entity or an attribute. For example, some cataloging students have assumed that the concept *author* was an attribute of a work, but in the FRBR model it is an entity that has a *created/created by* relationship with a particular work.

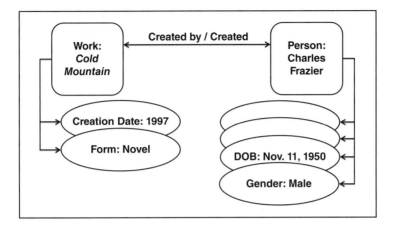

FIGURE 3.2 A Simple Entity-Relationship Model with Data Values Added.

Another example is that one might *not* treat a publisher as a separate entity but instead regard it as an attribute of a manifestation. In another model, though, one could choose to brand publishers as corporate body entities in their own right with a specific type of relationship to the manifestations they produce. How an individual concept is treated depends on choices made during the design phase of an E-R-based conceptual framework or cataloging code.

Objectives and Functions of the Catalogue

The fourth section of the ICP addresses what information professionals believe users want to do relative to the bibliographic universe. According to the ICP, catalogs should allow users to easily and effectively do the following:

1. **Find** resources corresponding to identified attributes and relationships (both single resources and sets of resources).

2. **Identify** a resource or an agent, using data values to confirm that the entity found corresponds to the entity sought or to distinguish between two similar resources.

3. **Select** an appropriate resource based on users' needs (such as having the resource available in a necessary language or operating system).

4. **Obtain** or acquire a resource.

5. **Navigate** the catalog and beyond, using relationships among resources and entities.[11]

The objectives and functions of the catalog, as outlined by the ICP, reflect the user tasks found in the FRBR conceptual model. FRBR states these objectives are "generic tasks that are performed by users when searching and making use of national bibliographies and library catalogues."[12] The user tasks will be addressed in more detail in the FRBR section that follows.

The fifth objective, *to navigate*, was not original to FRBR but was added from Elaine Svenonius's critique of the IFLA objectives.[13] The navigation task addresses the role of links, access points, and relationships to get from one resource to another. For example, a user may find a resource of interest in the catalog, see that the creator's name is a hyperlink, and on clicking be taken to all the other resources in the catalog by that same creator. It also takes into account the information-seeking behavior of some users who may not be able to articulate their information needs clearly enough to create an appropriate, effective search string. Instead, those users may take advantage of the system's internal organization structures to browse the resources described in the retrieval tool to help them find the information that they are seeking. This, of course, is only possible if the information system is able to represent adequately the relationships between entities and resources.

Svenonius is not the only one to criticize these objectives; over the years on AUTOCAT, the email discussion list for catalogers, there has been heated debate over whether the user tasks are out of date or out of touch. Some believe that catalogers do not truly know to what purposes users approach retrieval tools and that what is more important is what comes after users obtain their needed documents. Some have expressed concerns that the tasks are focused too narrowly on document retrieval rather than on information retrieval, their idea being that users want answers, not information on where to find a document that may give them the answers (e.g., Users are asking, "How big is a blue whale?" *not* "Where can I find books on blue whales?").[14]

Bibliographic Description and Access Points

Section 5 of the ICP is a relatively short one, enumerating only four points: (1) A separate description should be created for each manifestation of a resource. For example, if Charles Frazier's *Cold Mountain* were manifested in three different physical forms such as a print book, an e-book, and an audiobook, each of those forms would be described separately. Although the intellectual content is the same, the carrier is different, and that requires a separate bibliographic description. (2) When creating bibliographic descriptions, an individual copy (item) customarily will be in hand. The ICP notes that the item or copy represents the manifestation (which contains a work and its expression). In other words, when a single print copy of *Cold Mountain* is described in a bibliographic record, that metadata description can be used to represent all the single copies of it found all over the world, as long as it came from the exact same manifestation (i.e., it is the same creative work, expressed in the same language, disseminated in the same physical format by the same entities). (3) An internationally agreed-upon standard should be the basis for the bibliographic description. (4) Descriptions may have more or less metadata content depending on the catalog, the cataloging agency, the cataloging rules, or other factors; in other words, not all records will be equally comprehensive.

The sixth section, *Access Points*, reviews longstanding as well as more recent ideas on the choice and the form of access points. *Access points* are names, terms, or codes through which bibliographic data and authority data are searched and identified.[15] The ICP recognizes the need for controlled and uncontrolled access points and for authority records. Before moving forward, some explanations of these concepts might be helpful:

- *Controlled access points:* names, terms, or codes included in an authority record; they are used to represent entities in the bibliographic universe (WEMI, PFC, and COPE). For example, **Taylor, Arlene G., 1941-** and **Dowell, Arlene Taylor, 1941-** are both controlled access points for one of the authors of this book, because both names appear in her authority record.

- *Uncontrolled access points:* names, titles, and terms that do not appear in an authority record (such as a title proper, which is an access point but one that is transcribed and not standardized). For example, **Miller, D. Peter** is an uncontrolled access point for one of the authors of this book, because it does not appear in an authority record.

- *Authority record:* documentation of names, titles or subject terms associated with a particular entity; commonly contains a single established string of alphanumeric characters used to represent an entity consistently; commonly contains unauthorized forms of name, which act as references to the authorized form; authority records allow catalogers to see relationships among the names used for an entity and citations for resources where those names have appeared.

- *Authorized access points (AAP):* established strings of alphanumeric characters used to represent an entity; usually only one form of name is chosen as the basis for an authorized access point; sometimes referred to as an *authority-controlled name*. From the first example, **Taylor, Arlene G., 1941-** is the AAP, because it is the one chosen to represent that person consistently in bibliographic metadata.

- *Variant forms of names:* unauthorized strings used to represent an entity, sometimes referred to as *references*, *cross-references*, or *unauthorized forms of names*. From the first example, **Dowell, Arlene Taylor, 1941-** is a variant form of name and is generally not used in bibliographic metadata, but it does appear in Taylor's authority record.

This section of the ICP endorses the concept of *authority control*. Authority control—discussed further in the FRAD section that follows as well as in chapter 10 of this text—is the result of the process of maintaining consistency among the names, terms, or titles used to represent entities in the catalog. The foundations of authority control are *standardization* (i.e., using the same form of name consistently), *uniqueness* (i.e., ensuring that AAPs are distinctive), and *connections* (i.e., ensuring that relationships are identified so that variant forms of names or terms point to the chosen AAP). Using AAPs and authority records help to ensure that resources associated with a particular entity are collocated in catalogs. For example, all resources about Jackie Kennedy are brought together with those about Jackie Onassis because they are collocated under a single, unique, authorized access point: **Onassis, Jacqueline Kennedy, 1929-1994**.

The sixth section of the ICP goes on to discuss the choice of access points, noting that AAPs—for creators, works, expressions, and any other persons, families, corporate bodies, or subjects useful for finding and identifying a resource—are generally expected to be attached to bibliographic descriptions. The ICP states that records should also contain an access point for the title proper of the resources (generally uncontrolled), as well as access points representing any related entities. The ICP also provides general guidelines on how to create an AAP, indicating first and foremost that a cataloging standard must be followed. It then discusses issues related to languages and scripts (preference is given to the original language and script), the choice of name to be used (the most commonly known form of name is preferred), successively used names (a link to earlier and/or later names of an entity is recommended), the entry elements (follow a country's conventions for which part of a name is to be entered as the first element), handling conflicting names (use qualifiers to distinguish between entities with the same name), and references (best practice is to include them in the authority record for an entity).

Foundations for Search Capabilities

The seventh and final ICP section on search capabilities proclaims that AAPs are very important for reliable retrieval but that catalog users need a variety of methods for searching names, titles, and subjects. The ICP states that searching should be possible "by [using] full forms of names, by key words, by phrases, by truncation, by identifiers, etc."[16] It goes on to list what are considered essential access points for bibliographic records:

- The name of the creator (or the first-named creator, if more than one)
- Title of the work or expression (which may have a creator's name attached)
- Title proper of the manifestation
- Publication year
- Subject headings and classification numbers
- Standard numbers and identifiers[17]

For an authority record, the essential access points include the following:

- Controlled name or standardized title
- Standard identifiers
- Variants of the name or title[18]

The need for additional access points beyond what is deemed essential is acknowledged, citing elements such as "names of creators beyond the first, names of persons, families, or corporate bodies in roles other than creator (e.g., performers), variant titles (e.g., parallel titles, caption titles), authorized access point for the series, bibliographic record identifiers, language of the expression embodied in the manifestation, place of publication, content type, [and] carrier type."[19]

The *Statement of International Cataloguing Principles* has now fully replaced the "Paris Principles" as a foundational document in the worldwide cataloging community. The principles articulate the shared priorities for descriptive cataloging as determined by international cataloging experts. The ICP, along with the FRBR and FRAD models, provides a fresh conceptual framework for a new principles-based approach to library cataloging.

FUNCTIONAL REQUIREMENTS FOR BIBLIOGRAPHIC RECORDS (FRBR)

Modern cataloging can be somewhat incomprehensible unless one has a basic understanding of the *Functional Requirements for Bibliographic Records* conceptual model. FRBR (pronounced as *Ferber* by some and as F-R-B-R by others) is *the* theoretical model underlying the profession's contemporary perception of the bibliographic universe. The FRBR report, first published in 1998 after nearly a decade of study by IFLA working groups, is sometimes thought impenetrable by those new to the profession. Some students complain about spending time learning about FRBR before jumping into cataloging, but without its foundation, the structure of the cataloging rules in *RDA: Resource Description & Access* will not make sense; and it becomes easier to use cataloger's judgment if one understands the concepts, vocabulary, and objectives of the conceptual framework that FRBR supplies. That is why FRBR should be studied closely before examining RDA.

What Is FRBR?

Sometimes, it is easier to begin with describing what *Functional Requirements for Bibliographic Records* is not rather than what FRBR is. It is necessary to recognize that FRBR is not a data model, although it uses one—the E-R model— as its underlying structure. It is not a system design or a record structure; one cannot create a database around FRBR without a tremendous amount of additional work because that is not the purpose of FRBR. It is not a metadata schema like the Dublin Core, although it does identify some fundamental attributes that are useful as metadata elements. It is definitely not a content standard like RDA, because it does not provide detailed guidelines for constructing necessary metadata to describe a resource. And it is not an encoding format like MARC, because it is not a container or a bucket used to hold metadata.

FRBR is an abstract conceptual model. It is a basic theoretical framework for understanding the components of the bibliographic universe. "It is intended to be independent of any particular cataloguing code or implementation of the concepts it represents."[20] FRBR was developed as part of a study by cataloging experts from around the world, working under the auspices of IFLA, to address concerns related to the changing cataloging environment and to the continuous development of information technology. It was viewed as an opportunity to get a fresh perspective on what catalogers do and to review, reaffirm, and possibly reinvent the principal philosophies of cataloging, previously articulated by Cutter, Ranganathan, Lubetzky, and others.[21]

The aim of the study was to produce a framework that would provide a clear, precisely stated, and commonly shared understanding of what it is that the bibliographic record aims to provide information about, and what it is that we expect the record to achieve in terms of answering user needs. The terms of reference also gave a second charge to the study group: to recommend a basic level of functionality and basic data requirements for records created by national bibliographic agencies.[22]

To have any type of practical application of the FRBR conceptual framework, a more concrete implementation must be produced. RDA is the first cataloging code to operationalize the FRBR concepts.

The FRBR model begins by identifying why users approach information retrieval tools. These reasons, known as the *user tasks*, inform the entire model, helping information professionals remember the purposes for which the bibliographic universe is organized. It then identifies and defines the entities that may be found in the bibliographic universe, gathering them into three groups based on their functions or roles. FRBR also identifies relationships and attributes. Finally, the conceptual framework maps each entity's attributes and relationships to the user tasks, which allows catalogers to see the significance of each element in a bibliographic description or access point. This conceptual framework helps answer some important questions about what metadata might be of the most value to library users and how that metadata is used. FRBR provides the international cataloging community with baseline-level expectations about which data elements are necessary to include in resource descriptions to support the user tasks.

FRBR User Tasks

The FRBR user tasks are *find*, *identify*, *select*, and *obtain*. As stated earlier, not everyone agrees that they are comprehensive or even accurate, but they are FRBR's attempt to generalize why users approach catalogs, indexes, bibliographies, and other information retrieval tools. FRBR places all its findings about bibliographic metadata in the context of the user tasks; they are employed to justify the inclusion of data elements in bibliographic records. If a certain metadata element or an instance of data does not support at least one of the user tasks, its necessity should be questioned or at least its priority diminished. The connection between metadata and the user tasks is fundamental.

Find, the search function, is the first user task. FRBR states that users approach an information retrieval tool "*to find* entities that correspond to the user's stated search criteria."[23] Users have information needs and wants, and they are going to hunt for information, resources, or sets of resources to fulfill them. To find what they need, users may employ attributes (titles, dates, subjects, or other criteria), relationships (creator, contributor, or publisher relationships among others), or keywords that they expect might be used in connection with resources containing the information they seek. Examples of the finding task might include searching for

- the sixth edition of *Colon Classification* by S. R. Ranganathan;
- any or all music videos by Sigur Rós;

- articles on cataloging education published between 2002 and 2008;
- the limited edition Blu-ray discs for the complete series of *Battlestar Galactica*; or
- resources on blue whales.

No matter how or where users initiate a search, they are still trying to find at least one resource to help them with their information requirements.

The second user task is *identify*, which is "using the data retrieved *to identify* an entity . . . to confirm that the document described in a record corresponds to the document sought by the user, or to distinguish between two texts or recordings that have the same title."[24] This is a very important task, because neither names nor titles are unique. When a user approaches a retrieval tool, very often there are false drops among the search results. To confirm that the entities match (the one sought and the one retrieved), users must have access to enough and the right sort of metadata to distinguish between identically named or similarly described entities. The metadata held in a retrieval tool should help users with this identifying task. Examples might include distinguishing between

- the Arlene Taylor who writes about cataloging and the one who writes about brains;
- different works known as *Introduction to Psychology*;
- different editions of Ranganathan's *Colon Classification*;
- videos *by* Sigur Rós versus videos *about* Sigur Rós; or
- 21st-century articles on cataloging education versus those from the 20th century.

Select, the third task, is using the data to choose "an entity that is appropriate to the user's needs (e.g., to select a text in a language the user understands, or to choose a version of a computer program that is compatible with the hardware and operating system available to the user)."[25] This task reflects situations in which users may need to choose one resource over another based on any one of a number of characteristics, including but not limited to genre, form, language, content, edition, location, and physical format. Information retrieval tools, again, must provide enough metadata for the user to determine which resource is most appropriate for his or her need. Examples might include selecting

- a translation of *Brave New World* in Catalan rather than one in Spanish;
- a version of *Plants vs. Zombies* compatible with a Mac and not just for PC;
- the original text version of *Hamlet* and not a version rewritten for children;
- streaming music videos by Sigur Rós rather than those collected on a DVD; or
- the cataloging education articles accessible through one's local library.

The final FRBR user task is *obtain*, which "is using the data in order *to acquire or obtain* access to the entity described (e.g., to place a purchase order for a publication, to submit a request for the loan of a copy of a book in a library's collection, or to access online an electronic document stored on a remote computer)."[26] Although sometimes underappreciated, the final user task may be the most important one of all. It is undeniably essential to be able to find, to identify, and to select a resource of interest, but if one cannot obtain the resource, the endeavor is all for naught. Happily, most information institutions have mechanisms in place to provide access to information resources if they are not immediately available locally. Examples of how one may obtain a resource might include

- using a call number to locate *Brave New World* in the stacks of a library;
- approaching the interlibrary loan unit about borrowing a copy of Ranganathan's sixth edition of *Colon Classification* from another institution;
- searching an ISBN to purchase the correct *Introduction to Psychology* textbook from an online retailer;
- clicking on a URL to view Sigur Rós's "Viðrar vel til loftárása" music video; or
- finding "Graduate Education for Information Organization, Cataloging, and Metadata" in *Cataloging & Classification Quarterly* using a brief citation (volume, issue, and page numbers).

For users to successfully use an information retrieval tool of any type, those tools must have sufficient metadata to support the user tasks.

As mentioned earlier, others have augmented FRBR's four user tasks. Svenonius believed that the FRBR tasks were missing a *navigate* function, and this was added to the ICP by IFLA (see above).[27] RDA, when enumerating its version of the user tasks, added *understand* to the mix (discussed in chapter 4).[28] FRAD includes two additional tasks, *justify* and *contextualize*,[29] and *Functional Requirements for Subject Authority Data* (FRSAD), the third conceptual framework in the FRBR family of models, adds *explore*.[30]

FRBR Entities, Attributes, and Inherent Relationships

The entities used in the FRBR conceptual model are divided into three groups based on their role or function. Group 1 contains four entities—*work, expression, manifestation,* and *item* (WEMI)—that are the products or results of "intellectual or artistic endeavor that are named or described in bibliographic records."[31] Group 1 comprises the components of a bibliographic resource; it represents what is collected in libraries and other information institutions. The four entities are hierarchically connected, as can be seen in Figure 3.3, which illustrates their innate, fundamental relationships:

The FRBR User Tasks in Action!

A library user named Linda recently read a book review in the *Washington Post* about a novel titled *Inferno*. Even though she has forgotten the name of the author, she knows that the same person also wrote *The Da Vinci Code*. She goes to the library catalog to **find** the resource she wants. Linda is a skilled catalog user, so she does a title search for *Inferno* and receives 67 hits in return. They are ordered by relevance, so she sees a number of items on the first screen, including Dante's *Inferno*, Sherrilyn Kenyon's young adult novel, a book about World War II by Max Hastings, a short story collection edited by Ellen Datlow, and a 2013 novel by Dan Brown. When she sees Brown's name, she recognizes him as the author of *The Da Vinci Code,* and as the author that she is seeking today.

Linda, while going through the results, must **identify** which *Inferno* is of interest to her. Having seen that Dan Brown's *Inferno* is part of the collection, she can then use the catalog (through its facets, a hyperlink for the author, or through a more precise search combining title and author) to narrow down the results. When she does an author AND title search, she retrieves seven very precise results.

She now must **select** the resource that best fits her needs. She finds that there are Spanish, English, and Portuguese versions of the novel in her library. She reads only English, so that eliminates two of the items right off the bat. Of the five English-language resources left, two are e-books, one is large-print, one is an audiobook, and one is a hardback print version of the novel. Because Linda hates reading anything longer than a page or two on a screen, does not need larger print, and does not listen to audiobooks, she places a hold on the hardback print version, which she will **obtain** later in the month (she hopes!) when a copy becomes available. Because it may be a little while until she gets the novel she wants, Linda uses the hyperlink in the record (<u>Brown, Dan, 1964-</u>) to **navigate** the catalog to find other resources by the same author.

---

(1) a single work may be *realized through* one or more expressions—e.g., the content of a novel may be translated into many different languages; (2) one or more expressions may be *embodied in* one or more manifestations—e.g., a translated work and its original version may appear in a printed book together, and they may be distributed on microform as well; and (3) a manifestation is *exemplified by* one or more items, because widely distributed tangible resources having multiple items is the norm—e.g., thousands of copies of the latest Nicholas Sparks novel are published, because more than one institution or person will purchase a copy. Each of the Group 1 entities is explained in more detail below, as are the entities from the other two groups.

Group 2 entities are responsible for the creation, realization, production, dissemination, or ownership of the products found in Group 1. These

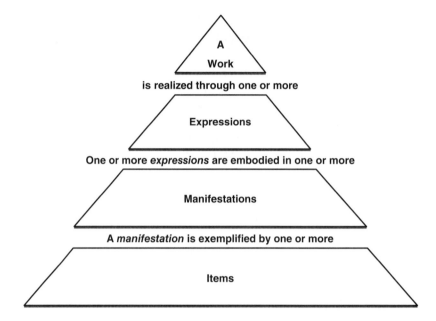

FIGURE 3.3 Group 1 Entities and Their Inherent Relationships. (Based on Figure 3.1 in FRBR, p. 14)

entities include *person, family,* and *corporate body* (PFC).[32] Actually, the previous sentence is not quite true. The entity *family* is not in the current version of the FRBR model; it was not added to Group 2 until FRAD was written.[33] Group 2 entities include creators responsible for intellectual works, such as artists, authors and coauthors, composers, and others associated with a work; contributors to an expression, such as illustrators, editors, translators, performers, musicians, and writers of added commentary; publishers, distributors, producers, and manufacturers of manifestations; and persons, families, or institutions that own or provide access to items.

The third group contains entities that represent the subjects of a work: *concept, object, place,* and *event* (COPE). Group 3 is a bit unusual in that it includes these four new entities as well as all the entities appearing in the other two groups. The full list of entities in Group 3, therefore, includes *concept, object, place, event, work, expression, manifestation, item, person, family,* and *corporate body.* In the FRBR model, subject entities are related only to the work entity from Group 1. In other words, works can have subject relationships, but expressions, manifestations, and items cannot.

Each of the entities contained in the three groups has its own set of characteristics or attributes associated with it. These attributes can be divided into two categories: inherent attributes and external attributes. "Attributes inherent in an entity can usually be determined by examining the entity itself; those that are [external] . . . often require reference to an external source."[34] Generally entities will have only one value for most attributes, although there are exceptions. Some attributes may have multiple values at

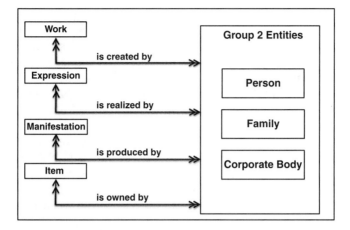

FIGURE 3.4 Group 2 Entities and Their Inherent Relationships. (Based on FRBR diagram, p. 15)

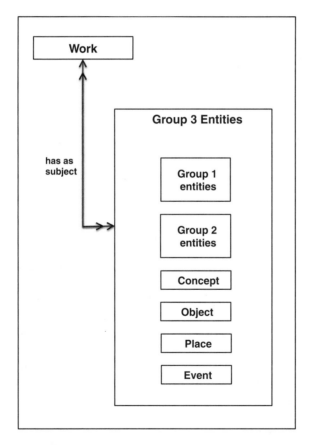

FIGURE 3.5 Group 3 Entities and Their Inherent Relationships. (Based on FRBR diagram, p. 16)

one time (multiple statements of responsibility, multiple series statements, etc.), or they may have multiple values because the value changes over time (changes in dimensions, additional creators, etc.). Not every attribute defined in the FRBR model will be used to describe every resource. Some attributes are meant to be widely applicable; others have been included only for certain resource types (e.g., attributes specifically tailored for maps or serials). If an attribute is applicable and essential, it should be included in the resource description.

Some attributes appear to duplicate information found in other parts of the bibliographic description. Those new to cataloging may perceive little difference between *title of the work* and *title of the manifestation*; they may think that the two attributes are addressing the same metadata. In some cases, the values belonging in those two different attributes will be identical, but in other cases, they will not be. For example, if a cataloger receives a Jean de Brunhoff book about the elephant Babar, then he or she must sort out the titles associated with each of the Group 1 entities. In the case of *Babar and His Children*, the following titles are applicable to this resource:

- **Title of the work**: *Babar en Famille* [the original title in its original language]
- **Title of the expression**: *Babar en Famille*. English [the original title plus language of translation]
- **Title of the manifestation**: *Babar and His Children* [the title proper transcribed directly from the title page of the resource]

Each has a different value, and each attribute has a different purpose or function.

Another example comes from the similarity between the information contained in the statement of responsibility (an attribute of manifestations) and the information describing a creator of a work. At times, the information in each attribute is the same or nearly so. For example, Arlene G. Taylor is the person responsible for the work *The Organization of Information*. For the first and second editions, her name appears as the creator as well as in the statement of responsibility, but in the third edition, another author was added. In this case, the primary creator remained the same (using the access point, **Taylor, Arlene G., 1941-**), but the statement of responsibility changed (in the third edition it is listed as "Arlene G. Taylor and Daniel N. Joudrey"). The two attributes, *creator* and *statement of responsibility*, are both necessary because they are not identical in function, even if they are sometimes identical in content. The creator attribute helps with the finding and identification of intellectual works; the statement of responsibility helps with the identification of a particular manifestation. There is another difference between the two attributes as well: how they are recorded. The creator of a work is included as an AAP to ensure collocation and consistency; the statement of responsibility is transcribed and reflects exactly what is seen on the title page, with the names recorded in direct order. Statements of responsibility might also include entities that are not involved in the creation of the work but that instead were associated with contributions to the expression (illustrators, translators, performers, editors, etc.).

The attributes in FRBR are not to be considered a finite set. FRBR states that the attributes "were derived from a logical analysis of the data that are typically reflected in bibliographic records . . . . The scope of attributes included in the model is intended to be comprehensive but not exhaustive."[35] As such, the attributes reflect the status and priorities of cataloging at the time that the model was created. There is room for expansion, clarification, and modification. Some changes have already occurred, such as when FRAD introduced *family* to the Group 2 entities. Other changes are expected in the near future, when the FR-family of models (FRBR, FRAD, and FRSAD) is harmonized.[36] Some adjustments also have been made to FRBR and FRAD attributes when they were included as metadata elements in the RDA cataloging code.

Group 1 Entities

Group 1 entities represent "products of intellectual or artistic endeavor that are named or described in bibliographic records."[37] These hierarchically ordered entities include the following:

- **Work**: an abstract intellectual or artistic creation
- **Expression**: signs, symbols, notation, sounds, images, etc., used to convey the content of a work
- **Manifestation**: a physical resource in which an expression of a work appears
- **Item**: an individual copy of the physical resource

Over the years, LIS professionals have attempted to find various analogies to help others understand the WEMI entities. Barbara Tillett uses an example, originated by Patrick Le Boeuf, to show why the use of the vocabulary found in the Group 1 entities is much more precise than just using a word such as *book* or *resource*:

> Before FRBR our cataloging rules tended to be very unclear about using the words "work," "edition," or "item." Even in everyday language, we tend to say a "book" when we may actually mean several things . . . . When we say "book" as in 'who wrote that book,' we could mean a higher level of abstraction, the conceptual content that underlies all of the linguistic versions, the story being told in the book, the ideas in a person's head for the book. FRBR calls this a "work."[38]

Tillett goes on to explain how *book* might also be used to refer to a text (*expression*), a publication (*manifestation*), or a single physical copy that can be used as a doorstop (*item*). The names of the Group 1 entities, although general in nature, are less ambiguous if they are used correctly. Using the WEMI concepts, therefore, can help librarians specify what is meant when discussing various features of the bibliographic universe.[39]

An Edible Analogy for the FRBR Group 1 Entities (WEMI)

Almost everyone has an idea of what ice cream is. We understand the overall abstract concept that it is a delicious frozen treat made from milk, sugar, and heavy cream. But we also acknowledge that not all ice cream is identical. Although the basic idea is the same, it can be rendered in a variety of ways. For example, the flavor could be raspberry-lavender, fluffer-nutter, honey-rosemary, or, for those of you who prefer more traditional flavors, vanilla, chocolate, or strawberry. There are hundreds or even thousands of flavors/recipes (*expression*) to represent the basic concept of ice cream (*work*). Once a particular expression is chosen, we must make it more concrete for it to be obtainable. For us to access this ice cream, someone must produce a batch (*manifestation*), from which we can purchase a pint (*item*) to take home and enjoy.

Works and Expressions

Work is at the top of the hierarchical chain in Group 1. A work, in FRBR, is defined as

> a distinct intellectual or artistic creation. A *work* is an abstract entity; it is the intellectual or artistic content and there is no single material object one can point to as the *work*. We recognize the *work* through individual realizations or *expressions* of the *work*, but the *work* itself exists only in the commonality of content between and among the various *expressions* of the *work*.[40]

Richard Smiraglia states that, "works are deliberate creations that stand as formal records of knowledge."[41] In this sense, the word *work* is very familiar. Surely, almost everyone has heard the phrases *a scholarly work* or *a work of art*; it is the same idea. Work includes everything from a haiku to sacred scriptures; from a nation's constitution to a computer program. It may be a single story or a compilation of individual works. An example of a work is Shakespeare's *Hamlet*. This is not referring to any particular version, translation, or edition of *Hamlet*; it is, instead, signifying the imaginative content common to every version of Shakespeare's play. It is the creator's abstract ideas that are referred to as a work. One cannot see, purchase, or touch an actual work. A work exists only in the realm of human thought; in fact, it can be helpful to think of a work as equivalent to Plato's forms or ideals.[42] To obtain a work, it must be expressed in some manner first and then manifested into some physical form or carrier.

The purpose of the work is to be able to identify unique intellectual or imaginative content and then to group expressions around it. The idea is that the work provides a name or label that may be applied to all the various expressions that orbit the same content. For example, "Shakespeare's *Hamlet*" is a label—consisting of a creator's name and a common title—that may be applied to myriad expressions of that work, including the original English-language versions from the First Quarto, Second Quarto, and First Folio, as well as various translations, such as *Hamlet, Tywysog Denmarc* (in Welsh); *Tragedien om Hamlet, prins av Danmark* (in Norwegian); more than a dozen different Mandarin translations; and, of course, *The Klingon Hamlet*. The work concept provides grouping capability so that all these expressions can be brought together under the label of "Shakespeare's *Hamlet*," and it allows relationships to be identified among sibling expressions (e.g., to connect *The Klingon Hamlet* and the Second Quarto).

In FRBR, the work entity has 12 attributes associated with it. These characteristics describe and identify individual works, *not* expressions, manifestations, or items, which have their own attributes. These characteristics also are useful in distinguishing between identically named works that contain different content (although the creator relationship is generally more important in making the distinction between them). The first seven attributes apply to all types of resources, but five additional attributes are included to address issues with two specific resource types. The general work attributes include the following:

- **Title of the work**: words or characters providing a name for a work
- **Form of work**: the category to which a work belongs, indicating form or genre (poem, play, fiction, essays, sonata, painting, sculpture, map, etc.)
- **Date of the work**: the date when a work was created, if known or discernible; may be a single date or a date range; may be date of publication if date of creation is unknown
- **Other distinguishing characteristic**: other useful features for distinguishing between works having the same name
- **Intended termination**: an indication whether a work is finite or ongoing
- **Intended audience**: an indication for whom a work is intended
- **Context for the work**: "historical, social, intellectual, artistic, or other context within which the work was originally conceived"[43]

Medium of performance, numeric designation, and *key* are attributes specifically for musical works. *Coordinates* and *equinox* are included when describing cartographic works.[44]

The next entity, *expression*, indicates how this content is communicated. An expression is the realization of a work in alphanumeric characters (for text, numeric data, etc.), musical notation (for printed music), choreographic notation (for dance documentation), movement (for performance of dance, mime, sign language),[45] sounds (for recorded music, live music, spoken word), images (for photographs, graphics, motion pictures, etc.), three-dimensional objects (man-made or naturally occurring realia, such as coins, relics, minerals, textiles, sculpture, etc.), or combinations of any of the above. "*Expression* encompasses, for example, the specific words, sentences, paragraphs, etc. that result from the realization of a *work* in the form of a text,"[46] but text that is not yet on the printed page. There can be, of course, more than one expression of a work.

An expression—like a work—is an intangible entity; it excludes physical forms. An expression is concerned with delivering the content of the work. One can neither hold nor see an expression, at least not until it has been embodied in a manifestation in some way. The concept allows catalogers to group various manifestations together as long as they share the same content and communicate it in the same way, no matter how different the physical carriers holding the content may be. The notion that an expression is an abstract entity is challenging, because some think that for an expression to be identified as being language-based and communicated through a particular series of alphanumeric character strings, one has to have those symbols appearing on a page, sheet, or screen; but this is not necessarily true in a conceptual model. As defined, an expression reflects a mode of communication (words, pictures, etc.), but it does *not* reflect a particular type of physical object (a printed book, a collage of images, etc.).

If expression seems confusing, know that you are not alone. The expression entity may become clearer with the help of some appropriate examples. Music, literary works, and drama are helpful in illustrating expressions because they contain myriad works that have been translated into other languages or that have multiple modes of communication. For example, a sonata for violin and piano by Poulenc can be conveyed in various ways. It is a particular sequence and combination of sounds and silences, but it has been expressed through musical notation, and it has been expressed aurally through numerous individual performances, each of which is a different expression. Using FRBR notation, the relationships between a work and its expressions can be communicated thus:

w_1: **Poulenc's Violin Sonata, FP 119: Intermezzo**

    e_1: composer's notated music

    e_2: performance in 1994 by Ringborg & Kilstrom

    e_3: performance in 2010 by Pryn & Olsson

    . . .

Here is another example, which comes from drama.

w_1: ***Twelfth Night* by Shakespeare**

    e_1: original English First Folio text

    e_2: Spanish translation by Jacinto Benavente

    e_3: performance by the Royal Shakespeare Company

    e_4: performance by the Folger Shakespeare Theater

    . . .

Here is a third example, this time for a non-fiction work.

w_1: ***The Organization of Information* by Arlene G. Taylor**

    e_1: 1st edition English text

    e_2: 2nd edition English text

e_3: Chinese translation of the 2nd edition

e_4: 3rd edition English text written with a coauthor

In each of these examples, there is only a single work, but there are several expressions.[47] Notice that in *The Organization of Information* example the second and third expressions (e_2 and e_3) are listed independently of each other even though there is an obvious connection between the second edition and the translation. Although that relationship does exist, the FRBR model does not allow additional hierarchical levels to accommodate it. Expressing this relationship must happen in other ways (e.g., through notes in a bibliographic description describing an expression-to-expression relationship).

The idea that a performance is an expression of a work is sometimes difficult to grasp. If one thinks about how a musical composition can sound different depending on the ensemble playing it or how the choices made by a theatre company can affect the overall experience of a play, it starts to make sense. And if one considers popular music and the prevalence of cover versions of songs, it becomes quite clear that although the work remains the same—perhaps with a few minor changes, such as gender pronouns being switched—expressions can be vastly different (e.g., compare Greg Laswell's cover of "Girls Just Want to Have Fun" to that of Cyndi Lauper's). If those examples are not convincing, the FRBR conceptual model maintains

> inasmuch as the form of *expression* is an inherent characteristic of the *expression*, any change in form (e.g., from alpha-numeric notation to spoken word) results in a new *expression*. Similarly, changes in the intellectual conventions or instruments that are employed to express a *work* (e.g., translation from one language to another) result in the production of a new *expression*. If a text is revised or modified, the resulting *expression* is considered to be a new *expression*. Minor changes, such as corrections of spelling and punctuation, etc., may be considered as variations within the same *expression*.[48]

The key idea in this passage is that changes in form (e.g., performance of alphanumeric notation as spoken word), changes in the intellectual conventions or instruments (e.g., translations), and revisions or modifications (e.g., new editions) all result in new expressions of the same work. It also states that changes such as correcting misspellings, misprints, typos, and grammatical errors are minor enough to be ignored; those changes do not result in a new expression.

The distinctions between two expressions are not always clear. For example, if a library receives two simultaneously published editions of a work (one published in the United States and the other in Great Britain), the expressions may or may not be entirely the same despite being in the same language. It may take considerable time and effort on the part of the cataloger to determine whether there are one or two expressions. In many cases, the difference, although genuine, may not be worth the effort needed to make that determination. Even in more obvious cases, the difference between expressions may be ignored. In fact, for works that have numerous translations in a single language, the different translations are generally not acknowledged as different expressions. For example, Paul Schmidt, Laurence Senelick, Peter Carson, Marian Fell, and many others have translated the plays of Anton Chekhov into English, but in the FRBR model, all these are generally lumped together as the English-language expression. Although the individual translator will likely be identified in the resource description, this is not a distinction that is currently deemed necessary at the expression level. With this in mind, the earlier example of the various expressions of Shakespeare's *Twelfth Night* could be simplified somewhat to compress all the English-language versions into a single expression as well as each foreign language translation. The live performances may or may not be combined depending on cataloger's judgment.

w_1: ***Twelfth Night* by Shakespeare**

e_1: original English text

e_2: Spanish translations

e_3: performance by the Royal Shakespeare Company

e_4: performance by the Folger Shakespeare Theater

. . .

In FRBR, there are 25 attributes associated with expression. These characteristics help describe and identify individual expressions, *not* works, manifestations, or items. There are 12 general expression attributes, some of which include the following:

- **Title of the expression**: words or phrases used to name an expression. This attribute is in FRBR, but it is not in FRAD or in RDA. Focus is placed on *title of the work* instead, adding language or some other distinguishing element as needed

- **Form of expression**: how a work is realized (text, music, sound, movement, etc.)

- **Date of the expression**: date when an expression was created, if known or discernible; may be a single date or a date range; may include date of performance, if applicable

- **Language of expression**: language used to communicate the content of a work

- **Other distinguishing characteristic**: some other useful feature for distinguishing between expressions; may include names associated with variant versions or particular editions (9th expanded edition, Today's New International Version of *The Bible*, etc.)

- **Extent of the expression**: size of an expression; may be the number of words or letters, running time of a performance, etc.; a surprisingly concrete measurement of an abstract entity

- **Summarization of content**: "abstract, summary, synopsis, etc., or a list of chapter headings, songs, parts, etc. included in the expression"[49]

Other attributes include *extensibility of expression, revisability of expression, context for the expression, critical response to the expression,* and *use restrictions on the expression,* as well as three attributes specifically designated for serials, two for music, five for cartographic images or objects, two for remote sensing images, and one for graphics or projected images. See the full FRBR report to review all 25 expression-level attributes.[50]

One of the more difficult aspects of FRBR, especially for those new to the conceptual model, is determining the boundaries of a work. Determining that some content has changed may be somewhat simple, but it takes considerable effort and judgment to determine whether those changes have resulted in a new work or simply in a new expression of the original work. The FRBR model states

> the concept of what constitutes a *work* and where the line of demarcation lies between one *work* and another may in fact be viewed differently from one culture to another. Consequently the bibliographic conventions established by various cultures or national groups may differ in terms of the criteria they use for determining the boundaries between one *work* and another.[51]

The process of determining the differences between a new work and a new expression of an existing work introduces the concept of *bibliographic relationships.* These relationships will be addressed in more detail later in this chapter, but suffice it to say that there are different types of relationships that can exist among resources, including a class called *derivative relationships.* Derivative relationships include modifications such as new editions, abridgements, translations, revisions, adaptations, changes in genre, parodies, summarizations, and so on. When describing these resources, it can be difficult to determine whether the work represented is truly new or not. Tillett has created a chart to help identify where the "magic line" lies between the two.[52] For example, under new expressions of the same work, she lists the following:

- variations or versions
- simultaneous publication
- slight modifications
- arrangements
- translations
- new editions
  - revisions or updates
  - illustrated editions
  - abridged editions
  - expurgated editions

In other words, updates, revisions, translations, subtitled or dubbed films, and modest changes in content usually result in new expressions. On the other side of the line, Tillett lists the following:

- summary, abstract, or digest
- free translation

- parody
- imitations
- adaptations
- change of genre
  - dramatization
  - novelization
  - versification
  - screenplay
  - libretto

When there are significant changes in form and/or genre, when those responsible for the content have transformed the original work into something new, or when there is significant, independent intellectual or creative endeavor, then a new work has been generated. Thus paraphrases, rewritings, and adaptations for children are just some of what are considered to be new works, even though each has a relationship to an original work. Table 3.1 contains a flowchart to assist the reader when determining the boundaries of a work.

An example of a new work being created—one that many students find frustrating—is that of film adaptations. Although many films are original works, some films are based on other forms of media, such as books, video games, television programs, comic books, graphic novels, plays, and so forth. Are films new works, or new expressions of a novel or a play? What are the relationships among the entities involved in film adaptations? In the case of film adaptations, it all begins with the original source material. Playwright Philip Barry's *Philadelphia Story* is used below as an example to explore these questions.

In the late 1930s, Philip Barry wrote the script for a play, *The Philadelphia Story*, based on a real-life couple that he knew. This original work has many expressions, including the original script in English used for the first Broadway production, a radio adaptation of that script, a French translation, and various performances of each of these scripts. They can be enumerated thus:

w_1: ***The Philadelphia Story* by Philip Barry**

e_1: original English script

e_2: performances of the play (1939-1940), starring Katherine Hepburn, Joseph Cotton, and Van Heflin

e_3: radio adaptation of the play

e_4: performances of the radio adaptation by Katherine Hepburn, Cary Grant, and Jimmy Stewart

e_5: French translation of the script known as *Vie Privée*; translated by French theater director Pierre Laville

. . .

TABLE 3.1 Flowchart for Bibliographic Families.

A Flowchart for Bibliographic Families: Relationships among Resources

1. Is the resource a copy, reproduction, facsimile, reissue, or reprint of a work?	**Yes**	Then it is an equivalent representation of the *original* work and the *original* expression.
	No	Then go to #2.
2. Does the resource contain the same basic content, but with minor changes? For example: • a new edition or revision with additional or updated content • a translation into a different language • a modified or illustrated version • a dubbed, subtitled, or colorized film • a new recording or arrangement of a musical work • an abridgement • other variations or versions	**Yes**	Then it is the *original* work, but a new derivative expression.
	No	Then go to #3.
3. Does the resource contain major changes or is it an adaptation? Such as: • a paraphrase • a free translation • a change in genre/form (e.g., dramatization, novelization, a libretto) • a parody or imitation • summary or abstract • other major adaptations	**Yes**	Then it is a *new* derivative work, with its own expression.
	No	Then go to #4.
4. Is the resource about another work, such as a review, criticism, evaluation, or commentary?	**Yes**	Then it is a *new* work with a descriptive relationship to the original work.
	No	Then one must explore other relationships that might exist. This relationship might need to be explained in detail in the metadata.

What is *not* listed is the famous film of the same name that was based on the play. The motion picture—directed by George Cukor from a screenplay by Donald Ogden Stewart and starring Katherine Hepburn, Cary Grant, and Jimmy Stewart—is an entirely separate work, as are the musical comedy film *High Society* and the Broadway musical *High Society*, both of which also have a relationship with Barry's play. All three are transformations of Barry's original work, all three have different creators involved, and all three certainly display changes in genre and form; these are all indicators that a new work has been created.

Barry's play thus is the progenitor of a *bibliographic family* (a set of resources with extensive bibliographic relationships centered around an originating work).[53] This bibliographic family is not unusually large, but it is sizable enough to help reveal some of the complexities that occur within a family of related resources. Just a small portion of the entities in this bibliographic family is itemized in the following list of works and expressions:

w_1: ***The Philadelphia Story* by Philip Barry**

e_1: original English script

e_2: performances of the play (1939-1940), starring Katherine Hepburn, Joseph Cotton, and Van Heflin

e_3: radio adaptation of the play

e_4: performances of the radio adaptation in 1942 by Katherine Hepburn, Cary Grant, and Jimmy Stewart

e_5: French translation of the script known as *Vie Privée*; translated by French theater director Pierre Laville

e_6: performances of the French translation *Vie Privée*

. . .

w_2: ***The Philadelphia Story* (film), based on Barry's play**

e_1: original director's cut of the English-language film

e_2: digitally remastered version of the film

e_3: colorized version

e_4: dubbed Spanish-language version

e_5: film with Turkish subtitles

. . .

w_3: ***The Philadelphia Story* screenplay by Donald Ogden Stewart, based on Barry's play**

e_1: temporary, incomplete version of the screenplay

e_2: final shooting script of the screenplay

. . .

w_4: ***High Society* (a musical film), based on Barry's play, with music by Cole Porter**

e_1: original director's cut of the English-language film

e_2: French-dubbed version

e_3: English-language film with Spanish subtitles

. . .

w_5: *High Society* (a musical play) based on Barry's play and the film *High Society*, with music by Cole Porter and book by Arthur Kopit

e_1: original English-language script and score

e_2: performances by the West End cast in 1987

e_3: performances by the Broadway cast in 1998

. . .

This example, which includes only five different works, is actually pretty simple. It does not acknowledge the myriad other relationships that may exist among these works (e.g., the whole-part relationship between the score of *High Society* and the musical theatre work as a whole). When a film or multiple films are included, many separate works with whole-part relationships may be identified as part of the bibliographic family (e.g., screenplays, soundtracks, musical scores, individual songs, costume designs, cinematography). An example of this is the third work in the list, the screenplay for the film *The Philadelphia Story*. It is a work in its own right, having a relationship to Barry's original play, but it is also a component of the film, which is its own work, too. Whole-part relationships add layers of complexity and are seen in almost every type of resource, but are typically found in connection to serials, collections of literary works, compilations of articles, conference proceedings, and the like.

Once the FRBR conceptual model is used to start examining resources in the bibliographic universe, complexities appear and thoughtful analysis is necessary. Tillett's chart of derivative works (new expressions versus new works) is only a loose guideline to help catalogers use their judgment to interpret specific situations. The examples provided here are only intended to illustrate some of the issues that may be encountered. What a cataloger may confront in everyday practice might be more or less convoluted and might or might not be very time-consuming to unravel. The so-called "magic line" between new works and new expressions of the same work is not a fixed one, and cataloger's judgment must be relied on in every decision. After one goes beyond a single print manifestation containing a single expression of a single work, it can get complicated quickly, but that—understanding and describing these bibliographic relationships—is part of the rewarding challenge of modern cataloging.

Manifestations and Items

Manifestation, the third entity in Group 1, is the point in the hierarchy where the focus shifts from the purely abstract to the tangible. It is

the physical embodiment of an *expression* of a *work* . . . . As an entity, *manifestation* represents all the physical objects that bear the same characteristics, in respect to both intellectual content and [mode of expression and] physical form. When a *work* is realized, the resulting *expression* of the *work* may be physically embodied on or in a medium such as paper, audio tape, video tape, canvas, plaster, etc. That physical embodiment constitutes a *manifestation* of the *work*.[54]

There can be multiple manifestations of the same expression of a work. A manifestation may comprise a single object (such as a unique work of art) or multiple copies to allow for widespread dissemination (such as a sizeable print run of a book). Changes to the physical format indicate the production of a new manifestation. For example, if the resource is produced first as a printed book but then is offered as an e-book, the e-book is a new manifestation. If that same book is later offered via microfilm, then yet another manifestation is available. If the printed book is later republished in large print or is reprinted using the Chalkboard typeface in blue-violet ink, these would be new manifestations as well. Changes in the display characteristics, the physical medium, or the container all result in new manifestations. If there are any changes in the content (for example, a new edition), that is also a new manifestation certainly, but in this case it is a manifestation of a *new expression* of the same work and will be treated somewhat differently, for the changes are higher in the Group 1 hierarchy. Any changes that occur after the manifestation has been produced happen on the item level (e.g., the spine is damaged or two leaves are ripped out).

The manifestation concept allows for gathering and describing the entirety of the items belonging to a single physical instantiation of the work/expression—i.e., it is a gathering point for all copies of a particular embodiment of the resource. If the items belong to the same manifestation, then all the items within it will be identical (or nearly so). The manifestation concept allows catalogers to use an item that is in hand to create a description that can be used over and over again to catalog the other copies that have been distributed around the world. Hence, metadata that is created based on a single exemplar (item) may be used to represent the entire set (manifestation) of those exemplars. When cataloging, it is very common to start the process by identifying the important attributes of a manifestation through an examination of the item in hand. This does not mean that work, expression, and item-level metadata are not included; they are. It is simply that the manifestation is the usual starting point for cataloging. Here are a few examples incorporating the first three entities of Group 1:

w_1: ***Twelfth Night* by Shakespeare**

   e_1: original English text

   m_1: 1892 American Book Company edition

   m_2: microform of 1892 American Book Company edition

   m_3: 2008 Arden Shakespeare edition

   m_4: electronic text via Project Gutenberg

   . . .

e₂: Spanish translations

 m₁: 1899 Revista nueva edition

 m₂: 1928 Rivadeneyra edition

 . . .

e₃: performance by the Royal Shakespeare Company

 m₁: DVD of recorded live performance

 m₁: VHS tape of recorded live performance

 . . .

In this example, one might think there should be a hierarchical relationship between **m₁** and **m₂** under the English expression. Despite the existence of that relationship, it cannot be represented in a hierarchical display of the FRBR Group 1 entities. As discussed with expressions, the model does not allow for multiple levels of hierarchy within a single entity.

w₁: Bach's ***Wedding Cantata***

 e₁: composer's notated music

 e₂: performance by Edith Mathis in 1960

  m₁: Eterna LP in 1977

  m₂: Corona compact disc in 2009

  . . .

 e₃: performance by Kathleen Battle in 1977

  m₁: RCA LP in 1977

  m₂: RCA compact disc in 2006

  . . .

 . . .

In this example, two performances and the original score are listed as expressions. Under each performance, two manifestations are listed; one is for long-playing record albums and the other for compact discs. There may be other manifestations available for each of the expressions listed here (audio-cassettes, MP3 files, MP4 files, AIFF files, etc.), and there are in fact many other expressions of this 300-year-old work.

w₁: ***The Organization of Information*** by Arlene G. Taylor

 e₁: 1st edition English text

  m₁: print book by Libraries Unlimited in 1999

 e₂: 2nd edition English text

  m₁: print book by Libraries Unlimited in 2004

 e₃: Chinese translation of the 2nd edition

  m₁: print book by Ji xie gong ye chu ban she in 2006

$\mathbf{e_4}$: 3rd edition English text, co-written with Daniel N. Joudrey

$\mathbf{m_1}$: print book by Libraries Unlimited in 2009

$\mathbf{m_2}$: e-book by Libraries Unlimited in 2009

In some cases, resources are produced only as a single manifestation. Although one might associate this with materials such as *realia* (i.e., three-dimensional forms or objects) or works of art (where there may only be a single item as well), this can happen with print materials, too. A print edition of a book is generally considered one manifestation whether it is hardback or paperback. "New printings will not result in a new manifestation unless other changes are made. A manifestation may have different bindings (hardcover versus paperback), types of paper (regular or acid-free), or other variations (thumb-indexed) that do not significantly affect the printed image."[55] Some works never see subsequent editions, and some are not made available in other formats. A single manifestation is fairly common. That does not mean, however, that the work does not reach a large audience. For some widely disseminated resources (e.g., bestselling books), tens of thousands of individual items (or more) can be subsumed under a single manifestation. And, of course, some materials are republished, repackaged, and reformatted hundreds of times.

As the manifestation level is the usual starting point for the cataloging process, it is unsurprising that it has more attributes than the work and expression levels combined. There are 38 manifestation attributes in the FRBR model, some of which are specific to certain material types. The most frequently used of these attributes include the following:

- **Title of the manifestation**: title(s) found on a manifestation; it is often equivalent to *title proper*: the chief name of a resource; this title may or may not be the same as *title of the work* (e.g., the work generally known as *Hamlet* may have a manifestation title of *The Tragedy of Hamlet, Prince of Denmark*)

- **Statement of responsibility**: information from a manifestation regarding the parties responsible for the creation and/or realization of the content; may include more than one person, family, or corporate body

- **Edition/Issue designation**: word or phrase that helps to distinguish between manifestations by the same publisher (Third edition, American edition, Large-print edition, etc.); although edition statements are associated with manifestations, actual changes in content that reflect new editions are made at the expression level

- **Place of publication/distribution**: city or other site associated with the dissemination of a resource; home city/locality of the publisher or distributor; may include more than one place name

- **Publisher/Distributor**: name of a body responsible for the dissemination of a resource; may be a person, family, or corporate body; although one might expect a publisher to be treated as a separate entity with a *published/is published by* relationship to a manifestation, FRBR instead chooses to interpret publisher as an attribute of a manifestation

- **Date of publication/distribution**: date a manifestation was disseminated or released to the public; most commonly expressed as a year; likely to be more precise than *date of the work*; if this date is unavailable, other dates (such as copyright date or manufacture date) may be substituted
- **Fabricator/manufacturer**: body responsible for the manufacture of a resource
- **Series statement**: words or phrases that identify a series to which a manifestation belongs; may or may not include numbering; may include more than one series or subseries
- **Form of carrier**: category reflecting the physical form of a manifestation (volume, filmstrip, microfiche, computer disc, etc.); may include more than one carrier type
- **Extent of the carrier**: number of physical units comprising a carrier (pages, frames, sheets, discs, etc.)
- **Physical medium**: actual material used to produce a carrier (marble, plastic, metal, etc.)
- **Capture mode**: means used to record the content (analog, digital, ink on paper, etc.)
- **Dimensions of the carrier**: height, width, depth, diameter, or a combination of these
- **Manifestation identifier**: unique code associated with a manifestation (ISBN, ISSN, DOI, URI, etc.)

Other general attributes include *source of acquisition, terms of availability,* and *access restrictions on the manifestation.* There are also four attributes solely for books, two for serials, six for sound recordings, one for images, one for microforms, one for visual projections, two for microforms and visual projections, and four for electronic resources. See the full FRBR report to review all 38 of the attributes listed under manifestation.[56] It should be obvious that a description of a resource is going to contain quite a few characteristics associated with the manifestation level. Although the manifestation is the starting point for cataloging, relevant attributes associated with works, expressions, and items will also be included, if they are applicable, to have a comprehensive description.

Item—a physical object owned or held by an institution, individual, or family—is the final entity of the WEMI hierarchy. As such, it inherits all the attributes from the levels above it. Accordingly, what is true for the work, expression, and manifestation is true for the individual item in hand (or on the screen). An item is a single exemplar of a *manifestation,* which may be made up of one or more physical objects (e.g., an item may be a single DVD, a set of audio cassettes in a case, a two-volume biography). Item is identified in FRBR so that individual copies that are part of a manifestation may be identified as necessary. There are instances when a single item is the object of interest (e.g., if a library owns two copies of a resource, but one was owned by the resource's author and contains significant marginalia).

When thinking about library resources, it is obvious that institutions do not purchase works, expressions, or manifestations; libraries purchase items.

Only an item can be placed on a shelf or on reserve. An item, however, is an exemplar of the manifestation, and it does contain an expression of a work. Of course, an individual item may also contain more than one work (e.g., a collection of essays), more than one expression of the same work (e.g., original text and a translation side by side), and so on. Here are a few examples that include the item level:

w_1: *Twelfth Night* by Shakespeare

　　e_1: original English text

　　　　m_1: 1892 American Book Company edition

　　　　　　i_1: single copy held at PR2837.A1 in a particular library

　　　　m_2: microfiche of 1892 American Book Company edition

　　　　　　i_1: microform no. S-0411, which has two images upside-down

　　　　m_3: 2008 Arden Shakespeare edition

　　　　　　i_1: copy held at PR2837.A2 E43 2008 c.1

　　　　　　i_2: copy held at PR2837.A2 E43 2008 c.2

In this example, each item is represented by a call number, but it could also be represented by another form of item identifier such as a barcode. In the third manifestation, please note that there are two items. They are, as far as anyone can tell, identical copies from the same manifestation. There is nothing in particular to distinguish one from the other; they are completely and totally interchangeable. Despite this, they are still two different instances of item per the definitions in FRBR.

w_1: *The Organization of Information* by Arlene G. Taylor

　　e_3: 3rd edition English text

　　　　m_1: print book from 2009 published by Libraries Unlimited

　　　　　　i_1: copy signed by author at Z666.5 .T39 2009 c.1

　　　　　　i_2: copy at Z666.5 .T39 2009 c.2

This example also has two items found under the manifestation. These two items, however, are distinguishable. There is a difference between the two that may or may not be significant to most users, but the distinction is there nevertheless.

There are nine attributes associated with an item:

- **Item identifier**: unique number or code linked to an item; may be a barcode, RFID (radio-frequency identification) tag, a unique call number, accession number, etc.

- **Fingerprint**: identifier created from characters transcribed from specific pages in a printed book

- **Provenance of the item**: account of the ownership or custody of an item
- **Marks/inscriptions**: codes, numbers, signatures, or other marks assigned to an item by an artist, owner, manufacturer, etc.
- **Exhibition history**: account of public displays of an item including location(s), dates, institutions, and other such details
- **Condition of the item**: description of the physical condition of an item (missing pages, plates, brittleness, etc.)
- **Treatment history**: actions taken for conservation purposes
- **Scheduled treatment**: future actions to be taken for conservation purposes
- **Access restrictions on the item**: constraints on contact with an item (for use by staff only, not available until 25 years after the death of the creator, etc.)

As stated above, an item inherits all the attributes from the levels above it. That means that for each item, in addition to the nine item attributes, there are 38 manifestation attributes, 25 expression attributes, and 12 work attributes. This is a total of 84 attributes identified for Group 1 entities. But, until microforms of books of serially disseminated visually projected sound recordings of cartographic data are created, there will never be a single resource that requires all 84 attributes to be recorded, because too many of the attributes are used only with a single resource type.

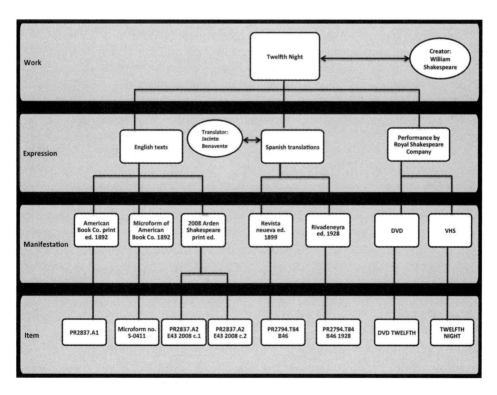

FIGURE 3.6 Expanded *Twelfth Night* Example as a FRBR Diagram.

FRBR Group 1 Entities (WEMI) in Action!

A library patron named Jesús recently read a review of Patty Griffin's *Silver Bell* in the "All Music" guide on the web. *Silver Bell* was created back in 2000, but it is considered a "lost album" because although it was recorded then, it was not released to the public until very recently. Jesús is very interested in listening to these songs, but he may need to be flexible about which version of the work he is able to access.

The *work* itself is titled *Silver Bell*, but that title refers to every expression of the work, and there are several in existence. The work refers to the overall artistic concept. The work was recorded in a particular *expression* in 2000, with fourteen specific tracks associated with it representing a particular mix of the album. That 2000 expression was not released to the public, but bootleg copies have surfaced over the years, but only as an electronic *manifestation*, usually in the form of MP3 files. Jesús, while interested in hearing this expression of the work, is not able to find a copy of this *item*, because most libraries generally do not collect illegal bootlegs. Another *expression* is the speculative version of the work that fans put together from MP3 files they have collected, based on unverified reports of track listings for *Silver Bell*. This, too, is something that Jesús would like to hear, but it is unlikely to be found in a library.

Jesús, however, is in luck, because in 2013 a new mix (*expression*) of the album (*work*) was released. It is considered a new expression because there have been some changes in the overall content. Twelve of the tracks were remixed by Glyn Johns to reflect the creator's updated vision of the work, and two of the fourteen tracks were replaced. Although these changes might be considered by some to be significant, the 2013 release still reflects the same artistic vision and a majority of the content. At times, different expressions of the same work do appear with additions, corrections, abridgements, and/or changes made as needed. In this case, Jesús is able to find two different formats (*manifestations*) in the catalog. It is available as an electronic music file through Hoopla and as a compact disc. Jesús, having reached his monthly download limit with the library, goes to the library building, searches the shelves for call number CD Pop G8523s c.2, and takes the CD (*item*) home to enjoy.

Group 2 Entities

The second group of FRBR entities comprises actors or agents in the bibliographic universe. Group 2 entities create content or contribute to it; they produce, disseminate, own, or provide access to resources. These entities, especially when acting as creators and contributors, are often recorded in metadata as AAPs or listed as names in statements of responsibility. As was mentioned earlier, in the FRBR model the Group 2 entities originally included only *person* and *corporate body*, but *family* was added when FRAD was written. According to the two models, PFCs *create* works, *realize* expressions, *produce* manifestations, and *own* items.[57]

A *person* is an individual, living or dead, who is "involved in the creation or realization of a work,"[58] or is the subject of a work. In the following examples, the first examples are formatted to show names as they might appear in the resources themselves or in statements of responsibility; the later examples (in bold) are formatted to show Group 2 entities as if they were AAPs.

p_1: William Shakespeare

p_2: Arlene G. Taylor

p_3: **Caroline, Queen, consort of George II, King of Great Britain, 1683-1737**

p_4: **Brunhoff, Jean de, 1899-1937**

A *family* is "two or more persons related by birth, marriage, adoption, civil union, or similar legal status, or who otherwise present themselves as a family."[59]

f_1: The Kennedys

f_2: The Gronkowski family

f_3: **Romanov (Dynasty : 1613-1917)**

f_4: **Borgia (Family : active 14th-18th centuries)**

A *corporate body* is a group, an institution, or a collection of two or more persons that act as a unit and are known by a particular name, "including . . . meetings, conferences, congresses, expeditions, exhibitions, festivals, fairs . . . . [and] organizations that act as territorial authorities [i.e., government bodies of all levels]."[60]

cb_1: The Commonwealth of Massachusetts

cb_2: The Smithsonian Institution

cb_3: **Neutral Milk Hotel (Musical group)**

cb_4: **Simmons College (Boston, Mass.). Graduate School of Library and Information Science**

FRBR lists four attributes for persons, five for corporate bodies, and no attributes for families. As these attributes are revisited in the next section in which FRAD is discussed, little detail is provided here; only the attributes appearing solely in FRBR are defined in this section. It is worth noting that FRAD, which focuses on the creation and use of authority data, includes different attributes in its model. For example, FRBR lists the following attributes for persons:

- **Name of person**: words, character strings, or phrases used to identify a person; may include full names, partial names, nicknames, etc.; there may be more than one name
- **Dates of person**
- **Title of person**
- **Other designation associated with the person**

FRAD lists 14 attributes for persons—only three of which are listed in FRBR. FRAD omits *name of person* entirely, because its approach to names is vastly different. FRBR identifies five attributes for corporate bodies:

- **Name of the corporate body**: words, character strings, or phrases used to identify a corporate body; may include full names, conventional names, shortened names, acronyms, or some other types of names; there may be more than one name
- **Number associated with the corporate body**: a number associated with certain types of corporate bodies, such as numbered meetings or conferences; any other number associated with a corporate body
- **Place associated with the corporate body**
- **Date associated with the corporate body**
- **Other designation associated with the corporate body**

FRAD has seven corporate body attributes, including three from the FRBR list. FRAD assigns six attributes to families. The FRBR attributes for these entities primarily reflect data included in bibliographic descriptions or access points; the attributes that are identified in FRAD are considerably more detailed and are primarily characteristics that would be included if one were creating an authority record. This is not surprising considering the purpose of each model. See the FRAD section below for more details on the attributes of Group 2 entities.

Group 3 Entities

The final group of FRBR entities represents the subjects of works. These are the things that subject headings and classification notations represent. The Group 3 entities include *concept, object, place,* and *event,* as well as the entities found in Groups 1 and 2, because a work can be about a work (e.g., literary criticism), a person (e.g., a biography), a corporate body (e.g., a corporate history), a particular expression (e.g., an analysis of a translation of *Don Quixote*), and so on. Group 3 entities are connected only to the work entity in Group 1. In other words, subjects are related only to works; the subject matter is not connected to or affected by the mode of expression or the physical embodiment.

The four subject-specific entities (COPE) are illustrated below. The first examples, again, are unauthorized forms; the latter bolded examples represent controlled forms of subject. *Concept* is an abstract idea. This can refer to almost anything that is immaterial or intangible. For example, the following are different forms of concepts.

c_1: Cataloging education

c_2: Fine dining

c_3: **Hellenism in literature**

c_4: **BF575 .A35**

An *object* is a physical article that can be seen or touched; it may be a manmade entity (e.g., jewelry) or a naturally occurring entity (e.g., amethyst). Objects are not humans or copies of information resources; those would fall under person or item instead.

> **o₁**: Cocker spaniel puppies
>
> **o₂**: DVRs
>
> **o₃**: **iMac (Computer)**
>
> **o₄**: **Prius automobile**

Place is a location; it includes regions, continents, geographic and water features, archeological sites, political jurisdictions, countries, states, provinces, cities, and other geographic locations.

> **pl₁**: Pangia
>
> **pl₂**: Plaza Mayor in Salamanca, Spain
>
> **pl₃**: the planet Venus
>
> **pl₄**: 42nd Street in New York City
>
> **pl₅**: **Ashur (Extinct city)**
>
> **pl₆**: **Güell Park (Barcelona, Spain)**
>
> **pl₇**: **Storm King Mountain (N.Y.)**
>
> **pl₈**: **Moosehead Lake (Me.)**

An *event* is an action, activity, incident, occurrence, time period, or some other proceeding; it may reflect something that happens, that will happen, or that has happened at some point in time.

> **ev₁**: The Renaissance
>
> **ev₂**: Maryland Day
>
> **ev₃**: Winter Olympic Games
>
> **ev₄**: **Salamanca, Battle of, Salamanca, Spain, 1812**
>
> **ev₅**: **979.461051**
>
> **ev₆**: **Harvard University—Riot, April 9, 1969**

When defining *event* and *place*, the FRBR model specifies that it is referring only to entities that are the subjects of works. This is notable because in some cases these entities may be considered to be corporate bodies and thus creators. The names of some places represent political jurisdictions, and political jurisdictions create works. Conferences, exhibitions, and meetings, which are corporate bodies that generate resources, might also be thought of as events.

As was the case when FRAD was published, thoughts about some of the FRBR entities changed when a later FR-family model, *Functional Requirements for Subject Authority Data* (FRSAD), was released. Although FRBR enumerates nearly a dozen entities that may represent the subjects of works, FRSAD models subject access in a more generalized, abstract approach. It states that works have subjects (referred to as *thema*); *thema* can be anything, including concepts, objects, families, works, any of the other FRBR or FRAD entities, and beyond; and thema are identified by particular labels or terms (referred to as *nomen*). In FRSAD, *thema* subsumes all the Group 3 entities and has relationships to only two other entities: *work* and *nomen*. To summarize, works have at least one *thema*, and each *thema* has at least one *nomen*.[61] This relationship is very similar to the relationship that *name* has to other entities in the FRAD model (see below). When the IFLA conceptual models (FRBR, FRAD, and FRSAD) are consolidated in the near future, changes in the approach to subject access may be included.[62] A simple illustration of the FRSAD entities can be seen in Figure 3.7, which is an extension of Figure 3.5 (on p. 67).

Term is the only attribute included for the four separate Group 3 entities that are listed in FRBR. The FRAD working group chose not to define attributes at all for the subject entities because by the time FRAD was written, work on FRSAD had already begun. They deferred to the FRSAD working group to determine whether more or different attributes were needed.[63]

> **Term for the Concept** [*Object, Place,* or *Event*]: word, phrase, or group of characters used to name or designate the *concept* . . . [*object, place,* or *event*]. A *concept* [*object, place,* or *event*] may be designated by more than one term, or by more than one form of the term. A bibliographic agency normally selects one of those terms as the uniform heading for purposes of consistency in naming and referencing the *concept* [*object, place,* or *event*]. The other terms or forms of term may be treated as variant terms for the *concept* [*object, place,* or *event*].[64]

A simple subject relationship is illustrated in Figure 3.8.

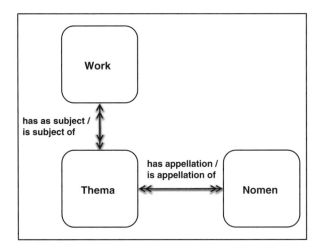

FIGURE 3.7 FRSAD's Entities and Their Inherent Relationships. (Based on FRSAD diagram, p. 15)

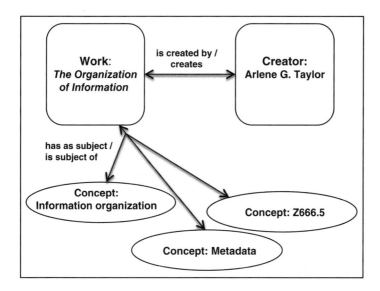

FIGURE 3.8 Connecting FRBR's Entities using *The Organization of Information*.

FRBR Relationships

Bibliographic relationships—those connections existing among the entities of the bibliographic universe—are not always immediately clear. Information resources may contain words such as *edition, version, translation, printing, adaptation, based on,* or other similar phrases and their translations, but relying on terms applied to a resource by its publisher or manufacturer can be problematic. "In many cases such terms or statements serve as a signal to the cataloguer that a relationship should be reflected in the bibliographic record. The problem with relying on commonly applied terms as a starting point for analyzing bibliographic relationships is that those terms are neither clearly defined nor uniformly applied."[65] The meaning of these common words or phrases is evident sometimes, but they do not always mean the same thing to different publishers or mean the same thing in different places around the world. At times, the Spanish word *edición* is equivalent to the English word *edition*—at other times, to the word *printing.* To increase clarity, FRBR attempts to identify precisely the relationships that exist among its entities and to ensure that those connections are evident in bibliographic descriptions. These relationships allow users to navigate the system and find derivative works, other works created by the same person, works on the same subject, and so forth. These relationships are not new, but in catalogs and other retrieval tools, the relationships have not always been explicitly named. The phrase "based on a play by Lanford Wilson" is not very precise, but the phrases "the second play of *The Talley Trilogy*" and "a prequel to Lanford Wilson's *5th of July*" are much clearer. Better indications of more specific relationships allow users to better understand the connection between related works.

In the FRBR document, two types of relationships are identified: (1) *generalized relationships* and (2) *specific relationships*.[66] Tillett refers to these as (1) *inherent relationships* and (2) *content relationships*.[67] The division between the two types is a logical one once the basic parameters are understood. The *generalized* or *inherent relationships* are based on a priori knowledge about the entities. Inherent relationships are those that have been built into the FRBR model by design. These relationships always exist because the three groups of FRBR entities have been defined in relation to each other. For example, between expressions and manifestations there will always be an embodiment relationship. That is just what expressions and manifestations do; that is how they interact. Inherent relationships are so fundamental that they are included in the diagrams used to explain the three groups of entities (see figures 3.3 to 3.5 to review these high-level relationships). They are also summarized in the following table.

TABLE 3.2 Inherent Relationships among FRBR Entities.

Entity	Inherent Relationships	Entity
Work	Is Realized through / Realizes	Expression
Expression	Is Embodied in / Embodies	Manifestation
Manifestation	Is Exemplified by / Exemplifies	Item
Group 2 (PFC)	Creates / Is Created by	Work
Group 2 (PFC)	Realizes / Is Realized by	Expression
Group 2 (PFC)	Produces / Is Produced by	Manifestation
Group 2 (PFC)	Owns / Is Owned by	Item
Group 3 (COPE, PFC, & WEMI)	Is Subject of / Has Subject	Work

The more specific *content relationships* are those that occur only among Group 1 entities. These are the relationships that must be deciphered by the cataloger if the catalog is going to be helpful for users to find related works, expressions, manifestations, and items. By clearly identifying these relationships in bibliographic metadata, users are able to determine the differences between two similarly named but distinct artistic or intellectual creations. Under content relationships, six categories are identified. Some are between two instances of the same entity (e.g., work-to-work relationships), and some are between entities of different types (e.g., manifestation-to-item relationships):

1. Work-to-Work relationships

2. Expression-to-Expression relationships

3. Expression-to-Work relationships

4. Manifestation-to-Manifestation relationships

5. Manifestation-to-Item relationships

6. Item-to-Item relationships

In addition to these six content relationship categories, whole-part relationships (discussed below) are identified under numbers 1, 2, 4, and 6. Each of the six categories contains one or more specific kinds of relationships. These relationship types are meant to represent some of the more common ones, but they are not exhaustive. All the relationships, like those inherent relationships at the higher level, are reciprocal in nature (i.e., the relationships flow in both directions between the two entities). In some cases, the relationship is between two independent or autonomous entities; in others, the relationship is with an entity that is dependent on the other (a referential relationship).

Work-to-Work Relationships

This type of relationship assumes that the works involved—though related in one of seven ways—are two separate works. That may seem obvious from the name of this relationship group, but it can be quickly forgotten when one is trying to determine whether something is a new work or simply a new expression. As discussed earlier, the line is not always clear between what is a derivative work and what is a derivative expression. For a relationship to be work-to-work, the content of the two connected works must be different enough to warrant labeling it a separate work. These are the types of relationships that were being addressed earlier in this chapter when the bibliographic family based on Barry's play *The Philadelphia Story* was used as an example. Describing the relationship between the play and the film version of *The Philadelphia Story* is fairly simple. Although their relationship cannot be conveyed using a hierarchical display, work-to-work relationships can be indicated using straightforward statements:

w_1 is the basis of w_2

w_2 is based on w_1

This, however, is still a bit too simplistic. It is more helpful to use precise indicators of the type of relationship:

w_1: Barry's *Philadelphia Story* has been adapted for the screen as w_2: *The Philadelphia Story* (film)

w_2: *The Philadelphia Story* (film) is a screen adaptation of w_1: Barry's *Philadelphia Story*

This is a more exact way to convey the relationship than by using an ambiguous phrase such as "based on" or "is a version of."

There are seven types of work-to-work relationships. Among those, some connect referential works and some connect autonomous works.

A referential *work* is one that is so closely connected to the other *work* in the relationship that it has little value outside the context of that other work. An <u>autonomous</u> *work* is one that does not require reference to the other *work* in the relationship in order to be useful or understood.[68]

An example of a referential work might be a teacher's guide to Orwell's *Animal Farm*, which is not particularly useful if *Animal Farm* is not accessible; the teacher's guide is so closely tied to the novel that it is somewhat useless without it. The relationship between the film versions of *The Philadelphia Story* and *High Society*, however, reflects autonomy; one need not be familiar with one to enjoy the other.

Three of the seven work-to-work relationships may involve either referential or autonomous works. For brevity's sake, only one of the reciprocal relationship statements will be presented in the following examples.

- **Successor relationship**: a work that involves a linear progression of content; examples include sequels (referential or autonomous) or succeeding works (autonomous)

    w_1: *American Documentation* is continued by w_2: *Journal of the American Society for Information Science*

- **Supplement**: a work that is used in combination with another; examples include indexes, teacher's guides, concordances, glosses (referential works), supplements, and appendices (referential or autonomous works)

    w_1: *Captors and Captives* has a supplement w_2: *Captive Histories: English, French, and Native Narratives of the 1704 Deerfield Raid*

- **Complement**: a work that is integrated into another work; examples include cadenzas, librettos, choreographies, endings for unfinished works (referential works), incidental music, musical settings for text, and pendants (autonomous)

    w_1: Verdi's score for *La Traviata* has a libretto w_2: Piave's libretto for *La Traviata*

    w_3: *The Buccanneers* by Edith Wharton was completed with w_4: an ending written by Marion Mainwaring

The other four work-to-work relationships involve only autonomous works:

- **Summarization**: a work that encapsulates or abridges another work; examples include digests and abstracts

    w_1: *Bookkeeping and Accounting* by Lerner is a summarization of w_2: *Schaum's Outline of Bookkeeping and Accounting*

- **Adaptation**: a work that is an alternate version, a reworking, or a significant modification of the content of another work; examples include adaptations, paraphrases, rewriting for children, free translations, musical variations, etc.

    w_1: *Tales from Shakespeare* by Charles and Mary Lamb is a paraphrase for children of w_2: *Plays. Selections* by Shakespeare

- **Transformation**: a work based on another work that is different in form or genre; examples include dramatizations, novelizations, versifications, screenplays, etc.

  w_1: *Blade Runner* is a screenplay written by Hampton Fancher and David Peoples loosely based on w_2: *Do Androids Dream of Electric Sheep?* by Philip K. Dick

  w_3: Tad Mosel's *All the Way Home* is a dramatization of the novel w_4: *A Death in the Family* by James Agee

  w_5: *Harry Potter and the Prisoner of Azkaban* (film) is a screen adaptation of w_6: J. K. Rowling's novel *Harry Potter and the Prisoner of Azkaban*

- **Imitation**: a work that mimics, caricatures, or lampoons another work; includes parodies, imitations, and travesties.

  w_1: *Goodnight Dune* is a parody of the children's book w_2: *Goodnight Moon* by Margaret Wise Brown and Clement Hurd

  w_1: *Goodnight Dune* is a parody of w_3: David Lynch's film *Dune*, which is a screen adaptation of the novel w_4: *Dune* by Frank Herbert

Expression-based Relationships

Expression-to-expression relationships come in two varieties: those involving expressions of the same work and those involving expressions of different works. Relationships between expressions of the same work entail a conversion or adaptation of one expression into a new expression; it is a direct modification. These include the following:

- **Abridgement**: a shortening or condensing of the expression; some content will be removed, but it does not change the content to the extent that it is a new work; includes abridgements, condensations, and expurgations

  e_1: Miller's original text of *The Gardener's and Botanist's Dictionary* has an abridgment e_2: *The Abridgement of the Gardener's Dictionary*

- **Revision**: an expression with changes, updates, corrections, improvements, or additions to the content, but the content is not changed to the extent that it is a new work; includes revised editions, enlarged editions, etc.

  e_1: Taylor's second edition of *The Organization of Information* has a revision e_2: the third edition of *The Organization of Information* by Taylor and Joudrey

  e_3: Goss's 29th American edition of Henry Gray's *Anatomy of the Human Body* has a revision e_2: Clemente's 30th American edition of Henry Gray's *Anatomy of the Human Body*

- **Translation**: a conversion of the expression from one language to another; includes literal translations and musical transcriptions

  e_1: Lewis Carroll's *Through the Looking Glass and What Alice Found There* has a translation e_2: by Jaime de Ojeda titled *A Través del Espejo y lo que Alicia Encontró al Otro Lado*

- **Arrangement (music)**: an adaptation of a previously written musical composition; a simplification or other modification of a musical work

    e₁: Robert Hazard's song *Girls Just Want to Have Fun* has multiple arrangements including **e₂**: an arrangement by Cyndi Lauper and **e₃**: an arrangement by Greg Laswell

The types of expression-to-expression relationships among different works are the same seven relationships that were identified for work-to-work relationships. The difference is that the relationship can be more precisely associated with a particular expression under each work (e.g., the third edition of *Tales from Shakespeare* by Charles and Mary Lamb is a paraphrase for children of some of the plays from Shakespeare's First Folio). These expression-to-expression relationships may involve issues specifically related to translations, performances, and revisions (e.g., identifying that a dramatic performance is based on a particular text of a play).

One might also encounter some expression-to-work relationships. These, too, reflect the same seven relationships found under work-to-work and expression-to-expression (between two different works). The difference is that a specific expression is being related to a more general work. This is done when the expression-to-expression relationship may not be determined easily. For example, it may be difficult to determine the exact expression of a literary work that was used as the basis for a dramatization or screenplay.

Whole-Part Relationships

As mentioned earlier, whole-part relationships can exist in four of the six types of content relationships. A whole-part relationship is between a larger entity and a component of it. For example, a single short story is a work, but it may also be a part of a collection of short stories, which is a work, too (an aggregate of individual works). To avoid confusion, it is important to understand exactly what is being described—the entire larger entity (e.g., the journal) or just a piece of it (e.g., an article from a journal)—before one proceeds to creating bibliographic metadata.

For work-to-work and expression-to-expression relationships, whole-part relationships may involve either *dependent* or *independent* parts. A dependent part, obviously, is one that is meant to be understood within the framework of the larger work or expression. A good example of a dependent part is a book chapter such as the one you are reading right now in a single, cohesive work (as opposed to a single chapter within a collection of independent essays that were collected or compiled to form a work). A chapter is a fundamental part of the complete expression of a work. It *could* be described separately, if deemed necessary, but it is not independent of the rest of the resource and consequently is an unlikely candidate for a separate description. Examples of dependent parts include chapters, sections, and parts of a work; volumes of a serial; a volume in a multi-part monograph; tables of contents, illustrations, and amendments of expressions; cinematography of film; and so on.

An independent part can be viewed as a separate work or expression, despite the relationship to the larger entity. A short story in a collection is an example of an independent work. It is a literary work unto itself. It is not necessarily related to any other short story in the collection (although it might be), and it can be described separately without much difficulty. Examples of independent parts include individual monographs in a series; screenplays or soundtracks for films; individual journal articles; discrete essays, poems, or stories in a collection; and so on. FRBR states that most often, dependent parts will not need to be separately identified and described. They are usually identified and described only in the context of the larger work. Independent parts of a whole are more likely to be identified and described separately, although there is certainly no requirement to do so unless it is deemed beneficial or necessary for users.[69]

Other Relationships

The other relationships identified in FRBR focus on manifestation-to-manifestation, manifestation-to-item, and item-to-item relationships. These relationships, which are generally focused on the physical carrier of the resource, involve manifestations of the same expression or items within the same manifestation. There is a great deal of duplication found among these categories; reproductions, micro-reproductions, macro-reproductions, and facsimiles appear in all three categories, and reprints appear in two of the three. Whole-part relationships also exist on the manifestation-to-manifestation and item-to-item levels. These relationships are not reviewed here, but a brief summary of these relationships is found in Table 3.3, and they can be read about in detail in the FRBR report.[70]

Conclusions of the FRBR Study

After identifying and describing the entities, attributes, and relationships, FRBR concludes by mapping all these components to the four user tasks. Through a series of tables, FRBR identifies what attributes and relationships are necessary to find, identify, select, and obtain entities using a scale of high-value, medium-value, and low-value. Without going into the tables in great detail, a few examples may help encapsulate this section of FRBR.

- **Title of work**: high value for finding, identifying, and selecting works
- **Translation relationship between expressions**: high value for selecting expressions; medium value for finding expressions; low value in identifying expressions
- **Title of manifestation**: high value for finding and identifying works, expressions, and manifestations; medium value for selecting works, expressions, and manifestations
- **Statement of responsibility**: high value for identifying and selecting expressions and manifestations; high value for obtaining manifestations; medium value for finding works, expressions, and manifestations; medium value for identifying and selecting works
- **Manifestation identifier**: high value for finding, identifying, and obtaining manifestations; medium value for identifying expressions
- **Typeface**: low value for identifying and selecting manifestations

For a thorough review of this mapping, see Tables 6.1-6.4 in the FRBR report.[71]

TABLE 3.3 Other FRBR Relationships.

FRBR Group	Relationship	Methods	Notes/Definitions
Manifestation-to-Manifestation	Reproduction	Reproduction Micro-reproduction Macro-reproduction	**Reproductions**: same content is presented, but reproductions do not preserve the look and feel of the original (e.g., microforms)
		Reprint Photo-offset reprint	**Reprints**: new versions of an existing manifestation; reissue the same content and may have some of the same physical attributes as the original (e.g., later printing)
		Mirror site Facsimile	**Mirror sites**: exact copies of a website hosted elsewhere
	Alternate	Alternate format Simultaneously released edition	**Alternates**: serve as substitutes for each other (e.g., the British and American versions of a book)
Manifestation-to-Item	Reproduction	Reproduction Micro-reproduction Macro-reproduction Reprint Photo-offset reprint Facsimile	**Facsimiles**: exact replicas of the original, without reduction or enlargement; preserve content, but also the look and feel of the original
Item-to-Item	Reconfiguration	Bound with	**Bound with**: two items sewn together and covered as a single volume
		Split into	**Split into**: item may be separated into two or more parts
		Extracted from	**Extracted from**: portion of an item may be separated and treated as another item
	Reproduction	Reproduction Micro-reproduction Macro-reproduction Facsimile	

What Relationships Do You See?

Here you find two different works, Shakespeare's *Hamlet* and a German-language retelling for children, *Hamlet für Kinder* (a nonexistent work imagined for this exercise). Each work has more than one expression. There are several persons involved in the creation of these works and expressions as well. The task is to identify the relationships you see. Include both the inherent and content relationships.

- w_1: *Hamlet* **created by William Shakespeare** (p_1)
    - e_1: Original English text
    - e_2: German translation by Christoph Martin Wieland (p_2)
    - e_3: French translation by Jean Marc Dalpé (p_3)
    - . . .

- w_2: *Hamlet für Kinder* **by Hans Schmidt** (p_4)
    - e_{27}: Original German text (based on Wieland's German translation)
    - e_{28}: French translation
    - e_{29}: English translation
    - . . .

If we are going to be thorough in identifying all the relationships, one must first consider the generalized *inherent relationships*. These are the easy ones. There are two works with multiple expressions. Therefore, w_1 *has been realized in* e_1, e_2, e_3, etc., and w_2 *has been realized in* e_{27}, e_{28}, e_{29}, etc. In addition, we know that w_1 *was created by* William Shakespeare (p_1) and w_2 *was created by* (the imaginary) Hans Schmidt (p_4).

After that, we must look at the specific *content relationships*. Although we could handle this very simply by stating this is a *work-to-work* relationship, w_2 *is a paraphrase or adaptation of* w_1, that relationship is not very precise. In this example, we know much more about the relationships that exist among these entities. This will not always be the case, but when the information is available, it can be used. So we know there are some *expression-to-expression* relationships within the same work: e_1 *has a translation* e_2, and e_1 *has a translation* e_3. We also know that e_{27} *has a translation* e_{28}, and e_{27} *has a translation* e_{29}. And some of the translations have relationships to specific contributors—e_2 *was translated by* p_2 and e_3 *was translated by* p_3.

These are not all the relationships, though. To get to one of the more important relationships, we need to add an *expression-to-expression* relationship among different works. This takes the place of the general *work-to-work* relationship we mentioned earlier. This relationship can be summarized as e_{27} *is a paraphrase or adaptation of* e_2. If we did not know that e_{27} was based on e_2 (it might have been based on e_1, the original English text, instead), then we would need to have a *work-to-expression* relationship (w_1 *is paraphrased as* e_{27}) or a *work-to-work* relationship (w_1 *is paraphrased as* w_2).

In the final chapter of the report, FRBR lists the basic requirements for bibliographic records. It identifies a basic level of functionality. FRBR has determined that bibliographic records must allow users to do the following:

- Find all manifestations embodying
  - the works for which a given person or corporate body is responsible
  - the various expressions of a given work
  - works on a given subject
  - works in a given series
- Find a particular manifestation
  - when the name(s) of the person(s) and/or corporate body(ies) responsible for the work(s) embodied in the manifestation is (are) known
  - when the title of the manifestation is known
  - when the manifestation identifier is known
- Identify a work
- Identify an expression of a work
- Identify a manifestation
- Select a work
- Select an expression
- Select a manifestation
- Obtain a manifestation[72]

Despite the presence of updated language, this list is reminiscent of Cutter's "Objects of a Catalog."[73]

Ultimately, FRBR provides a recommendation for the necessary descriptive elements in bibliographic records to ensure that the basic level of functionality is met. These basic data requirements are presented in a series of nine tables, but because these requirements are reinterpreted in RDA, they are only minimally presented here. For discussions of the core elements in RDA records, please see chapter 4 of this text. The basic requirements include the following descriptive elements:

- Titles proper, parallel titles, statements of responsibility
- Edition statements
- Numbering, mathematical data statements (coordinates and scale), musical presentation statements (type of score)
- Places, names, and dates of dissemination (production, publication, distribution, or manufacture)
- Carrier description: material designations, extent, and dimensions
- Series titles, parallel titles, statements of responsibility, and series numbering
- Notes of many kinds
- Standard numbers

The required access points (or organizing elements) include the following:

- Name headings (i.e., AAPs) for persons, families, and corporate bodies responsible for works and expressions
- Title headings for works and expressions
- Series headings
- Subject headings
- Classification numbers

After studying FRBR's list of elements needed for complete and useful bibliographic records, some have concluded that FRBR adds little to what was already being done in cataloging. The elements in the FRBR list are nearly identical to the core bibliographic elements found in the *International Standard Bibliographic Description* (ISBD), which from the mid-1970s until the implementation of RDA was the underlying framework of descriptive cataloging.[74] In other words, to some critics FRBR appears to have done little more than to justify what was already current cataloging practice. This is not a fair criticism, though. Despite the similarity of the metadata requirements to ISBD, FRBR has added a new layer to the profession's understanding of bibliographic control. It provides a conceptual foundation that was missing from previous approaches to cataloging. FRBR helps catalogers to understand the underlying reasons why information is organized and how individual descriptive metadata elements are effective in fulfilling the four user tasks. As an added bonus, the similarity of the lists of required FRBR and ISBD elements will help to make the transition from AACR2 to RDA smoother because data compatibility issues will be somewhat reduced.

FUNCTIONAL REQUIREMENTS FOR AUTHORITY DATA (FRAD)

As stated earlier, *Functional Requirements for Bibliographic Records* has reframed modern cataloging. FRBR, however, does not stand alone; it is part of the FR-family of conceptual models developed by IFLA. The second FR model is *Functional Requirements for Authority Data* (FRAD), which was developed by the Working Group on Functional Requirements and Numbering of Authority Records (FRANAR). FRANAR was formed in 1999, the year after FRBR was published, and the committee was charged with defining the functional requirements of authority records, studying the feasibility of an International Standard Authority Data Number, and serving as the IFLA liaison to other organizations working with authority files.[75] The final FRAD report—the outcome of the first charge—was approved by IFLA in early 2009.

What Is FRAD?

Functional Requirements for Authority Data is an abstract conceptual model designed as a companion to FRBR. It is "an extension and expansion of the FRBR model" and "has identified potential improvements to the FRBR model itself."[76] Instead of examining the basic metadata required to describe information resources, FRAD focuses on authority data, particularly on controlled access points used to represent persons, families, corporate bodies, and works (i.e., authorized and unauthorized forms of names or titles appearing in authority records). Subjects—which are commonly authority-controlled access points also—are not emphasized in FRAD but are discussed in the third FR model, FRSAD.

The purposes of FRAD are (1) to provide a framework for relating authority data to the needs of users (both external and internal to the library) and (2) to assist in an assessment of the potential for international sharing and use of authority data (within libraries and beyond).[77] As implied in the first purpose, there are two types of users identified in FRAD. One is the end user who encounters authority data in library catalogs. These are the everyday users whose convenience is placed first in the ICP and whose tasks are foundations of FRBR. The other user group comprises creators of authority data (catalogers, authority control librarians, database maintenance or data quality librarians, etc.). These are internal library users who create and maintain authority data to ensure successful retrieval, collocation, and disambiguation in the catalog. Their success is anchored to consistent authority work, which results in the production of comprehensive authority records. FRAD, however, models the relationships among entities found in authority data; it does not model an ideal authority record. Figure 3.9 provides an example of information that typically has been included in an authority record.

Name Authority Record: Taylor, Arlene G., 1941-

LC control no.:   n 80050006
LCCN permalink: http://lccn.loc.gov/n80050006

...
008   800519n| acannaab |a aaa
010 __ $a n 80050006
040 __ $a DLC $c DLC $d DLC
100 1_ $a Taylor, Arlene G., $d 1941-
400 1_ $w nna $a Dowell, Arlene Taylor, $d 1941-
670 __ $a Her Cataloging with copy, 1976: $b t.p. (Arlene Taylor Dowell)
670 __ $a Wynar, B.S. Introd. to cat. and class., 1985: $b CIP t.p. (Arlene G. Taylor)
...

Key to data:
008: Fixed field coded data
010: Identifier
040: Institutions that worked on authority record
100: Authorized access point
400: Variant form of name ($w nna indicates that it is a previously used name)
670: Source of data/Citation justifying the data in 400 field—Source is Taylor's first book, *Cataloging with Copy*
670: Source of data/Citation justifying the data in 100 field—Source is Wynar's 1985 edition of *Introduction to Cataloging and Classification*, on which Taylor worked

---

**FIGURE 3.9 An Excerpt from a MARC-encoded Authority Record.
(Based on the format used at: http://authorities.loc.gov/)**

FRAD User Tasks

The user tasks in FRAD are somewhat different from those found in the FRBR model. As you may recall, in FRBR the user tasks are *find, identify, select,* and *obtain.* In FRAD, the user tasks have been defined as follows:

- **Find**: Find an entity or set of entities corresponding to stated criteria . . . using an attribute or combination of attributes or a relationship of the entity as the search criteria . . . or . . . explore the universe of bibliographic entities using those attributes and relationships
- **Identify**: Identify an entity (i.e., to confirm that the entity represented corresponds to the entity sought, to distinguish between two or more entities with similar characteristics) or to validate the form of name to be used for a controlled access point
- **Contextualize**: Place an entity (a work, person, concept, etc.) in context; clarify the relationship between two or more entities; or clarify the relationship between an entity and a name by which that entity is known (e.g., name used in religion versus a secular name)
- **Justify**: Document the authority data creator's reason for choosing the name or form of name on which a controlled access point is based[78]

The first two functions are almost identical to those in found in FRBR. This is not surprising, for authority data is important to both searching for resources and identifying entities of interest in the catalog. Find and identify are tasks completed by both types of FRAD users.

The last two functions are unique to FRAD. *Contextualize,* as a user task, is performed by internal library users. Creators of authority data want to provide context, not only to other catalogers or authority control librarians but also to the general end user. In most of the better online catalog systems, some authority data is displayed to the public to provide additional information about the entity sought and to provide links to related names, titles, and terms. Contextualize allows everyone with access to the information to understand that

- S. R. Ranganathan's full name is Shiyali Ramamrita Ranganathan and that he was born in 1892 and died in 1972
- Sigur Rós is an Icelandic ambient pop band formed in 1994
- the person identified in the early 1980s as Arlene Taylor Dowell is better known as Arlene G. Taylor, and her works will be collocated under the later name
- *Battlestar Galactica* has three different authority-controlled title access points: one for the original series in the 1970s and two for the 21st-century reboot (one for the miniseries in 2003 and one for the 2004-2009 series)
- Stephen King, the horror novelist, was born in 1947 in Portland, Maine; Edwin is his middle name; he has published five novels as Richard Bachman; and many of his works will be located at PS3561.I483 on the shelves of libraries that use the Library of Congress Classification

The final FRAD user task, *justify*, is also performed by the creators of authority data. This task entails including citations for the decisions made while performing authority work. When creating authority data, one determines all the names used by an entity, chooses one name for the AAP based on the cataloging rules, and chooses which variant names to include in an authority record as references. In addition, other data elements are included to help understand the entity (see the task *contextualize* above). The authorized and variant names, and all the supporting data, must be documented in the authority record to justify their inclusion. This not only provides documentation, but also ensures that other catalogers will not need to duplicate efforts if further work must be performed on an authority record. The following are examples of authorized access points and accompanying citations justifying the inclusion of data in authority records.

AAP: **Ranganathan, S. R. (Shiyali Ramamrita), 1892-1972**

Note: Wikipedia, Oct. 1, 2008: (Shiyali Ramamrita Ranganathan; b. 1892; d. 1972)

AAP: **Sigur Rós (Musical group)**

Note: All music guide WWW site, Apr. 25, 2003: (Sigur Rós; Icelandic ambient pop band, formed 1994)

AAP: **Taylor, Arlene G., 1941-**

Note: Her Cataloging with copy, 1976: t.p. (Arlene Taylor Dowell)

Note: Wynar, B.S. Introd. to cat. and class., 1985: CIP t.p. (Arlene G. Taylor)

AAP: **Battlestar Galactica (Television program : 2003)**

Note: Internet movie database, Apr. 21, 2009: (Battlestar Galactica (2003) (TV), aka "Battlestar Galactica: The Miniseries" - USA (long title); has separate listing for: Battlestar Galactica (2004) (TV series))

AAP: **King, Stephen, 1947-**

Note: His Carrie, 1974.

Note: Washington post, 4/9/85: (Stephen King has written 5 novels using the pseudonym Richard Bachman)

Note: Stephen King.com, the official web site, viewed on Feb. 28, 2006: biography, etc. (Stephen Edwin King; b. Portland, Maine, 1947; site also includes listings of author's works) http://www.stephenking.com

Note: Collings, M.R. The work of Stephen King, 1993: CIP galley (b. Stephen Edward King, 9/21/47, Portland, Me.)

These citations justify the inclusion of various names and biographical details found elsewhere in the record. Generally, the citations are from manifestations of works created by the person, family, or corporate body being described, as well as from other reference sources to provide additional information. These citations include both print and online sources (and yes, nowadays, this includes Wikipedia). Some citations may include factual errors (e.g., "Edward" instead of "Edwin" in the last note of the Stephen King example above) despite the best efforts to include only verified information. In some records, there may be citations indicating that the information sought was *not* found in a particular resource despite looking for it.

FRAD Entities, Attributes, and Inherent Relationships

The three groups of entities in FRBR are absorbed into the FRAD conceptual model. For some of the entities and their attributes, definitions are expanded to incorporate aspects that were not considered in FRBR. In addition, five new entities are added to the model (*name*, *identifier*, *controlled access point*, *rules*, and *agency*). Also, there are changes in the attributes of the various FRBR entities (several were added, a few were removed, and many were not applicable). The order in which the entities are addressed has changed due to the shifting focus from bibliographic records to authority data. In FRAD, the Group 2 entities take more of the spotlight. As such, the new FRAD-specific entities and the Group 2 entities are reviewed first; then, a review of the other groups follows. The primary focus, in this section, is on the differences between the FRAD and FRBR approaches to entities and attributes.

FRAD's basic conceptual model continues the ideas established in FRBR but expands on them to include entities and relationships important in authority work. The most notable difference between the FRBR and FRAD approaches to entities and attributes is the exclusion of *name* as an attribute for any of the entities. This is due to a conceptual shift in how names are viewed in FRAD. In FRBR, a name is just a property or a characteristic of a person or a corporate body. In FRAD, a name becomes an entity itself, with which a person, a corporate body, or a family can have a relationship. This allows, for example, a person such as Stephen King to be a single person but to be known by more than one name. In the FRAD model, King does not have a name attribute; he has multiple relationships with name entities. This approach also allows for names to have relationships with each other (earlier name relationships, later name relationships, etc.). The role of names and controlled access points are central in the FRAD model. Figure 3.10 illustrates the basic points of the FRAD conceptual model, highlighting the inherent relationships that exist among the entities.

The following list enumerates and illustrates the key concepts found in the FRAD conceptual model:

1. Each of the FRBR entities—WEMI, PFC, and COPE—may be known by one or more names (e.g., one person is known by the names *George Sand*, *Amantine Dudevant*, and *Aurore Dupin*; the terms *Arch bridges* and *Arched bridges* refer to the same objects).

2. Names may represent one or more entities (e.g., the name *John Smith* refers to many different persons; the word *bridges* may refer to structures built over a ravine or a waterway, to dental apparatuses, to card games, to parts of ships, and also to the name of a publisher's series).

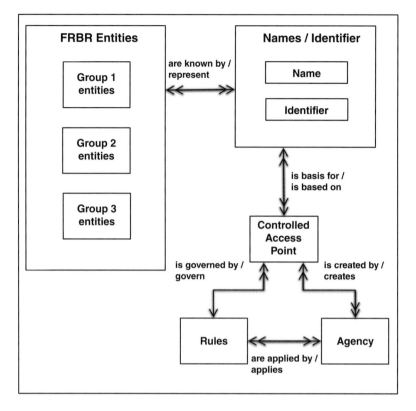

**FIGURE 3.10 FRAD Entities and Their Inherent Relationships.
(Based on figures in FRAD, pp. 4-7)**

3. Entities may be assigned one or more identifiers (e.g., Pablo Picasso
   has *n78086005* as an identifier in the Library of Congress (LC) name
   authority file, but is represented by *500009666* in the Getty's Union
   List of Artist Names; the concept *bridges* in Library of Congress
   Subject Headings has the identifier *sh85016829*, but in Getty's Art
   & Architecture Thesaurus it is *300007836*). It should be noted that
   identifiers generally refer to one entity only. Identifiers are unique (or
   are supposed to be) but names rarely are (e.g., the name *John Smith*
   can refer to several different people, but the identifier *nb91524207*
   refers only to the one who loves Scottish cheesemaking and was born
   on January 12, 1924).

4. A name and/or an identifier can be the basis for a controlled access
   point (e.g., the name *John Smith* is the heart of the authorized access
   point, **Smith, John, 1924 January 12-**).

5. Controlled access points are created/modified by agencies, which
   apply certain sets of cataloging rules in order to create access points
   consistently. (The *nb91524207* record for **Smith, John, 1924 January
   12-** was created by the British Library using AACR2, but was modified
   recently by the Library of Congress using RDA.)

Unique FRAD Entities

As already mentioned, FRAD, due to the nature of its content, has added five new entities to its conceptual model (i.e., *name, identifier, controlled access point, rules,* and *agency*). These entities are specific to authority data and allow the FRBR view of the bibliographic universe to be expanded to the realm of authority records, access points, and the processes involved in authority work.

Name is a word, a string of characters, several words, or a phrase that acts as a label or a designation for an entity. That is, an entity is known by its name. A name is used to identify any of the FRBR entities (WEMI, PFC, and COPE). A name could be a full name, initials, or a partial name. Names may involve given names, family names, birth names, royal names, changed names, earlier and later names, names assumed for various purposes (e.g., pseudonyms, religious names), corporate acronyms, patronymics, and so on. A name could also be a title or a subject term.

Although this entity may seem unnecessary to some (as evidenced by its exclusion from RDA), FRAD does offer a more faithful approach to an E-R model. It allows for the name entity to have its own set of attributes. When *name* is treated as an attribute (rather than as an entity), it is somewhat more difficult to bring out additional characteristics or properties of the name. Those would be characteristics of a characteristic. In fact, in RDA, the only name attributes from FRAD that are discussed at all are recorded only through notes in an authority record; they are not treated as individual bibliographic or authority metadata elements. Name has seven attributes assigned to it in FRAD.

- **Type of name**: category to which a name belongs; may be a personal, corporate, or family name; may be a title of a work, expression, or manifestation; may be a term used for a concept, object, place, or event
- **Name string**: string of alphanumeric characters, signs, or symbols used to signify a name
- **Scope of usage**: a type, genre, or form of creative or intellectual work associated with a name (e.g., Charles Lutwidge Dodgson wrote non-fiction; Lewis Carroll wrote children's fiction)
- **Dates of usage**: a period of time associated with the use of a name
- **Language of name**: language in which a name is expressed
- **Script of name**: set of characters and/or symbols used to present a name
- **Transliteration scheme**: scheme used to produce the transliterated form of the name[79]

Identifier, the second FRAD entity, is "a number, code, word, phrase, logo, device, etc.,"[80] that is uniquely associated with an entity (PFC, WEMI, and COPE) and is used to differentiate that entity from others. An identifier may be any of the following: International Standard Name Identifier (ISNI), International Standard Book Number (ISBN), International Standard Musical Work Code (ISWC), International Standard Recording Code (ISRC), International Standard Serial Number (ISSN), record numbers from the Library of Congress authority files, social security numbers, business registration numbers, shelf numbers, inventory control numbers, and so on. Identifiers have only one attribute defined in FRAD: *type of identifier*, which is a code or designation indicating the category or type to which the identifier belongs (e.g., ISSN, ISRC, undocs).

Controlled access point is a name, term, or code that is included in an authority record used to represent entities in the bibliographic universe (WEMI, PFC, and COPE). This entity may be based on a name or a title or both. It includes both AAPs and the variant forms that lead to them. The controlled-access-point entity has 13 attributes in FRAD. As so few of the attributes are applicable in the current cataloging rules, little time will be spent reviewing them in any great detail. There are a few attributes, though, that should be addressed:

- **Base access point**: basic name elements used to identify an entity; "all elements in a controlled access point that are integral to the name or identifier that forms the basis for the access point;"[81] it is an unadorned name that may need to be augmented with additions (e.g., it may be composed of nothing more than the family name and the given name of a person, the name of an organization, or the acronym for a corporate body)

- **Addition**: an element that enhances a base access point to differentiate it from others with the same base access point; sometimes called a *qualifier*; may be a fuller form of name, a date associated with an entity, a place name associated with an entity, a title of nobility, a language, and so on

- **Source of controlled access point**: a citation for a resource used when establishing the base access point for an entity

- **Undifferentiated access point**: a phrase or code used to indicate that the AAP established for an entity is not precise enough to differentiate between similarly named entities (e.g., a code in the authority record for **Smith, John** indicates that this is the AAP that will be used for all John Smiths who have too few details available to ensure a unique authorized access point)

The rest of the attributes for controlled access points—*type, status, designated usage, language of base access point, language of cataloguing, script of base access point, script of cataloguing, transliteration scheme of base access point,* and *transliteration scheme of cataloguing*—may be reviewed in the FRAD report as needed.[82]

The fourth new FRAD entity, *rules*, refers to a set of cataloging guidelines used to formulate the controlled access points found in an authority record. The attributes established for rules are *citation* and *rules identifier*. The meaning of citation is likely self-evident, but in case it is not, it is referring to identifying the rules used through a brief metadata statement similar to an entry in a bibliography (i.e., the names of responsible parties, title, edition, and publication information). Rules identifier is a code, acronym, or initialism referring to the rules used in authority work (e.g., RDA or AACR2).

Agency is the corporate body that is responsible for creating or modifying a controlled access point or an authority record. This includes libraries, archives, museums, bibliographic networks (e.g., OCLC or SkyRiver), and consortia. There are three self-explanatory attributes associated with agency: *name of agency, agency identifier,* and *location of agency.*

FRAD Entities in Context

To attain authority control (i.e., consistency, uniqueness, and connections) in library metadata, authority work must be performed. To achieve this, an *agency* applies cataloging *rules* when creating authority data in an authority record. Authority data contains, among other things, *controlled access points* (which include both *authorized access points* and *variant access points*). An *authorized access point* is based on the *name* most commonly associated with a FRBR entity (WEMI, PFC, and COPE). *Variant access points* are based on other forms of name associated with the entity, and are used as references to point to the authorized access point. Any *identifiers* associated with the entity are included in the authority record too. Authority work also involves recording other types of metadata about an entity (i.e., its various attributes, such as gender, the place associated with a corporate body, and so forth.). All these activities are documented in an authority record through various data elements, along with citations that justify the inclusion of the individual pieces of data.

For libraries to attain authority control, they must ensure that they consistently use a unique *authorized access point* to represent an entity in bibliographic records, as well as that they have references in the catalog that point from variant access points to authorized ones. Being able to search the catalog precisely and comprehensively is dependent on the standardization, connections, and uniqueness that come only from authority control.

Group 2 Entities: Person, Family, and Corporate Body

The entities in Group 2 take a greater focus in FRAD than they did in the FRBR model. This is because authority control, though it can be applied to works and expressions, is not as prevalent at the manifestation level, the level at which one starts creating bibliographic records (FRBR's *raison d'être*). With FRAD's emphasis on authority data, it is no wonder that attention has shifted from Group 1 entities to Group 2 entities, the agents responsible for the creation and realization of works and expressions.

Person is still defined as an individual, living or dead, but in FRAD several other characteristics are introduced into this concept. In the second FR-model, a person is defined as

> An individual or a persona or identity established or adopted by an individual or group. Includes real individuals. Includes personas or identities established or adopted by an individual through the use of more than one name . . . . Includes personas or identities established or adopted jointly by two or more individuals . . . . Includes literary figures, legendary figures, divinities, and named animals as literary figures, actors, and performers. . . .[83]

The revised definition of person is not restricted to real individuals only, but instead allows a person to be a *persona* or an *identity* as well (e.g., J.I.M.

Stewart writes contemporary fiction and literary criticism, but his other persona, Michael Innes, writes detective novels). It also states that a person can represent a pair or a group of individuals as well (e.g., a joint pseudonym). The definition also suggests that persons do not have to be actual human people. By including fictitious, literary, and legendary characters, as well as divinities and animals, the list of possible creators has expanded greatly. This means that Sherlock Holmes, Miss Piggy (the Muppet), and Socks (the Clintons' White House cat) are now persons, and therefore, can be considered the creators of works. Following the spirit of this change, there is already a record for *The Autobiography of Sherlock Holmes*, with a creator access point established for **Holmes, Sherlock**, with a relationship designator of *author*.

In FRAD, *person* has 14 attributes associated with it. It could have been 15, but as you are already aware, *name* is treated as a separate entity in FRAD rather than as an attribute of a person. Three of these attributes originated in FRBR (i.e., dates, titles, and other informational elements associated with the person), but the rest are new to FRAD. This allows persons to have multiple relationships with names, and the names can then have attributes of their own. (The FRAD approach to names was fundamentally rejected in RDA in favor of the approach found in FRBR whereby name of person *is* an attribute.) The 14 attributes for person are

- **Dates associated with the person**: period of time associated with a person; usually birth date, death date, or both; may reflect a period of activity instead; frequently represented by year, but months and days may be included to differentiate persons with same name and year designations; may be an approximate date
- **Title of person**: "word or phrase indicative of rank, office, nobility, honor, etc. (e.g., Major, Premier, Duke, [King, Bishop, Pope,] etc.), or a term of address (Sir, Mrs., [Professor, Abbot,] etc.) associated with the person"[84]
- **Gender**: gender associated with a person; values are not restricted; may be male, female, unknown, or another appropriate term or phrase (trans male, intersex, cisgender female, etc.); multiple values may be included as needed along with dates associated with those genders
- **Place of birth**: location where a person was born; may be a city, state, country, province, region, or some other geographic location
- **Place of death**: location where a person died; may be a city, state, country, province, region, or some other geographic location
- **Country**: a country associated with a person; yes, this is vague, but it allows for other locations to be added that do not fit place of birth, death, or residence
- **Place of residence**: location where a person lives or has lived; may be a city, state, country, province, region, or some other geographic location
- **Affiliation**: group to which a person is or has been connected or related (an employer, educational institution, a social or cultural organization, etc.)

- **Address**: current or former location associated with a person; may be a personal or professional address; may be a phone number or a street, postal, email, or web address
- **Language of person**: language used by a person to create or realize works and expressions
- **Field of activity**: a person's area of interest, endeavor, engagement, or expertise; may be different from a person's profession (e.g., a person's field of activity may be *cheesemaking*, whereas his or her profession may be *farmer*)
- **Profession/occupation**: what a person does or has done for work; may be different from a person's field of activity (e.g., a person's profession may be *professor*, while his or her field of activity is *library science*)
- **Biography/history**: a brief description of a person's life and activities
- **Other informational elements associated with the person**: a term that helps to distinguish a person from other persons with the same name; may include associations to a family, a creative work, another person, or a state of being; may include elements such as Sr., II, Spirit, Saint, Biblical figure, Demon, Ship captain's wife, the Wise, Professor of computer science, Author of *A Bride from the Rhineland*, Mythical animal, Vampire, Whale, and so forth

The next entity, *family*, did not appear in FRBR, so its definition and attributes originated with FRAD. A family is two or more people "related by birth, marriage, adoption, civil union, or similar legal status" or any group that presents itself as a family. This entity includes famous or notable family units, dynasties, royal and noble houses, clans, and so on.[85] The six attributes of a family are

- **Type of family**: category in which a group belongs such as family, dynasty, matriarchy, etc.
- **Dates of family**: period of time associated with a family; may include date ranges or centuries
- **Places associated with family**: location wherein a family resides or has resided; location otherwise associated with a family; may be a city, state, country, province, region, or some other geographic location
- **Language of family**: language associated with a family
- **Field of activity**: a family's area of interest, endeavor, engagement, or expertise
- **History of family**: a brief biographical description of a family and its members' lives and activities

Corporate body is a group, an institution, an organization, or a collection of two or more persons that act as a unit and are known by a particular name, including "meetings, conferences, congresses, expeditions, exhibitions, festivals, fairs. . . . [and] organizations that act as territorial authorities,"[86] such as countries, federations, states, regions, cities, counties, and other municipalities. Corporate bodies also include musical groups, theatre troupes, dance companies, and other artistic collectives; they may be active or defunct, real or fictitious, and independent of or subordinate to other corporate bodies.[87] Three of the attributes originated with FRBR (i.e., place, dates, and other information associated with a corporate body).

The seven attributes associated with corporate bodies are

- **Place associated with the corporate body**: location of a corporate body's headquarters or another location that is associated with a corporate body; may be a city, state, country, province, region, or some other geographic location; includes locations of conferences, meetings, exhibitions, and other such events
- **Dates associated with the corporate body**: period of time associated with a corporate body (date of incorporation, period in which a musical group was active, etc.); includes dates associated with conferences, meetings, exhibitions, and other such events (e.g., dates during which a conference was held); may include specific dates or date ranges
- **Language of the corporate body**: language used by a corporate body
- **Address**: current or former location associated with a corporate body; may be the address for a corporate body's headquarters or another location associated with the body; may be a phone number or a street, postal, email, or web address
- **Field of activity**: a corporate body's area of endeavor, engagement, or expertise; may include their area of responsibility or jurisdiction
- **History**: a brief corporate, organizational, or institutional history
- **Other information associated with the corporate body**: a term that helps to distinguish a corporate body from other corporate bodies with the same name (may include type of incorporation, type of organization, type of jurisdiction, etc.)

Group 1 and Group 3 Entities

In FRAD, the basic definitions of the FRBR Group 1 entities do not change significantly. There are some additional examples put forward in FRAD for the WEMI entities, but the core concepts remain the same in both models. The attributes, on the other hand, are somewhat different. In this section, only the additions and changes found in the FRAD report are addressed.

In the FRAD model, *work* has nine attributes listed (in FRBR there are 12). FRAD has eliminated one FRBR attribute, *title of the work*, because FRAD views names as entities instead of attributes. Titles are the names of works, so there is no need for a title attribute. FRAD also omits five additional attributes that were included in FRBR: *intended termination*, *intended audience*, *context for the work*, *coordinates*, and *equinox*. These five were excluded because they are not useful in the creation of access points or authority data. They are, however, still considered important for bibliographic records; their exclusion is not indicative of a change in the perception of their value. FRAD did keep the other six attributes from FRBR with only minor wording changes: *form of work*, *date of the work*, *key*, *numeric designation*, *medium of performance*, and *other distinguishing characteristic*. FRAD also adds three more attributes to work:

- **Subject of the work**: topical matter of a work; obviously, this is a *very* different approach from what is found in FRBR, where subjects are entities, and there is a relationship between a work and one or more Group 3 entities
- **Place of origin of the work**: location where a work was created; may be a city, state, country, province, region, or some other geographic location
- **History**: a brief history of the work

Expression, in FRBR, has 25 attributes associated with it. In FRAD, there are six attributes, all chosen from the FRBR model with no significant changes:

- **Form of expression**
- **Date of expression**
- **Medium of performance of expression** (music)
- **Language of expression**
- **Technique** (graphic and moving images)
- **Other distinguishing characteristic**

These six characteristics are considered to be the expression attributes that will play a role in the creation and use of authority data. Some of these attributes are addressed in the FRBR section above, but, as always, all the attributes are defined in the FRBR and FRAD reports.

Manifestation has 39 attributes that are important in bibliographic data. FRAD recognizes the importance of six attributes for possible use with authority data. All six are taken from FRBR with no real modifications:

- **Edition/issue designation**
- **Place of publication/distribution**
- **Publisher/distributor**
- **Date of publication/distribution**
- **Form of carrier**
- **Numbering** (for serials)

The final Group 1 entity, *item*, has nine attributes identified in FRBR. In FRAD, there are only three, two of which are new to the FR-family of conceptual models. One attribute, however, *custodial history of item*, seems to be a renamed version of an attribute from FRBR even though FRAD does not mention this at all. The definitions, of these two very similar attributes, are

- **Provenance of the item** (FRBR): a record of previous ownership or custodianship of the item[88]
- **Custodial history of item** (FRAD): the record of previous ownership of an item[89]

If there is a difference, other than the name of the attribute, it is a mystery. The other two item attributes in FRAD are *location of item* (a place where an item is held; may be a collection, library, museum, or other institution) and *immediate source of acquisition of item* (an institution, organization, or supplier of an item; may include a description of the circumstances of the acquisition).

In the FRBR model, the unique Group 3 entities had a single attribute under each one: *term*. Obviously, with its approach to separating name attributes from the entities and its creation of the attribute, *subject of the work*, FRAD has little to offer in terms of attributes for concept, object, place, and event. It includes a note under each entity that states, "No attributes are defined for the entity, Object, [Concept, Place, Event,] pending the work of the FRSAR Working Group."[90] As mentioned in the FRBR section above, the resulting work, FRSAD, took yet another approach to dealing with subject (see Figure 3.7). When the FR-family harmonization is complete, one of the three different approaches to subject will be chosen.

FRAD Relationships

Without a doubt, relationships are a critical part of the creation and use of bibliographic data; they are key in understanding the connections among the entities of the bibliographic universe. The importance of relationships, however, increases greatly when one begins to consider the processes of authority work. The concept of connections—among agents or names or terms—is one of the three foundations of authority control (along with standardization and uniqueness). Relationships are vital to the success of authority work, and FRAD offers an overview of the types of relationships that might be identified in the process. FRAD, like FRBR, discusses the types of relationships that exist among the Group 1 entities (see section on FRBR relationships above) but with somewhat different categories of relationships. The bulk of the FRAD section on relationships is focused on Group 2 entities and the relationships associated with *name* and *controlled access point*.

FRAD identifies three types of relationships: (1) *inherent relationships*, (2) *role relationships*, and (3) *specialized relationships*. Inherent relationships are those fundamental connections that exist at the highest levels of the conceptual

TABLE 3.4 Inherent Relationships among FRAD Entities.

Entity	Inherent Relationships	Entity
WEMI, PFC, COPE	Has appellation / Is appellation of	Name
WEMI, PFC, COPE	Is assigned / Is assigned to	Identifier
Name / Identifier	Is basis for / Is based on	Controlled Access Point
Controlled Access Point	Is governed by / Govern	Rules
Controlled Access Point	Is created (modified) by / Creates (modifies)	Agency
Agency	Applies / Are applied by	Rules

model. They are included in the diagram of the FRAD model in Figure 3.10; they are also summarized in Table 3.4.

FRAD also recognizes the presence of *role relationships*. Roles are more specific descriptions of the connections between Group 2 and Group 1 entities. They supplement the FRBR inherent relationships already identified among those entities (creates, realizes, produces, owns). Roles include designations, "such as editor, illustrator, translator, defendant, . . . previous owner, that may reflect the specific nature of the relationships between a person, family, or corporate body and a work, expression, manifestation, or item described or referred to in a bibliographic record. Such terms may be identifying data in bibliographic or authority records, but currently are typically added only to bibliographic records."[91] Role relationships are not described further in FRAD, nor are they in this section; they are, however, addressed in the chapters on RDA in discussions of relationship designators attached to AAPs.

The more specialized FRAD relationships are those that must be deciphered by the cataloger if the authority data is going to be helpful for users and other catalogers to find entities, to identify them unambiguously, and to navigate the catalog through linkages that are added based on authority data. By clearly identifying these relationships in authority records, users are able to determine the difference between two identical or similar, but distinct, entities (names, persons, corporate bodies, families, works, etc.). Under the specialized relationships, 12 categories are identified. Some are based on relationships between two instances of the same entity (e.g., person-to-person relationships) and some are between entities of different types (e.g., families-to-corporate body relationships). These categories are addressed in the following sections.

1. Relationships between Persons

2. Relationships between Persons and Families

3. Relationships between Persons and Corporate Bodies

4. Relationships between Families

5. Relationships between Families and Corporate Bodies

6. Relationships between Corporate Bodies

7. Relationships among Works, Expressions, Manifestations, and Items

8. Relationships between Names of Persons

9. Relationships between Names of Families

10. Relationships between Names of Corporate Bodies

11. Relationships between Names of Works

12. Relationships between Controlled Access Points

Each of the 12 categories contains one or more specific kinds of relationships. The relationships are representative but not exhaustive. All the relationships, like those inherent relationships at the highest levels, are reciprocal in nature, that is, the relationships flow in both directions between the two entities. These relationships may be identified through the use of links to other entities (with their own authority records) or through explanatory notes found in the authority record.

Relationships among Group 2 Entities

The first half of the list above reflects the categories of relationships that exist among the entities in Group 2. Each of these six categories is addressed in turn.

Person-to-Person: This category assumes that there are two persons involved in the relationship. It must be remembered that persons in FRAD may be dead or alive, human or animal, or may have several other characteristics such as being real or fictitious or legendary, being an actual person or a persona adopted by a person(s), and so on. There are seven relationship types in this category. Each is addressed briefly. In the FRAD documentation, stick-figure drawings are provided for each type to help readers better understand the nature of the relationships. Figure 3.11, which is not from FRAD, is an example created by the authors to reflect the kinds of illustrations found in FRAD.

Person-to-person relationships include the following:

- Pseudonymous relationship
- Religious relationship
- Secular relationship
- Official relationship
- Attributive relationship
- Collaborative relationship
- Sibling relationship
- Parent/child relationship

A *pseudonymous relationship* is between an individual person and a persona/ identity used by that person, as indicated by the use of another name. Pseudonymous relationships are documented in authority records. In some, where both the original name and the pseudonym are used to represent entities that create works, there should be a link or reference to another record for the related entity. When the relationship is between a person with a name that is generally unknown and that person's better-known persona, there should be a reference in the record indicating that the person is not known by their original name and primarily uses a pseudonym for creating works. Explanatory notes are necessary in the documentation to explain the relationships in either

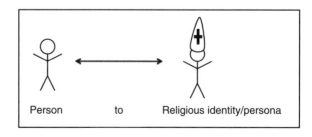

FIGURE 3.11 A FRAD Person-to-Person Relationship. (Based on the style of figures in FRAD, pp. 32-37)

situation. An example is Charles L. Dodgson, a real person who wrote works about mathematics, whereas his other bibliographic identity (persona) Lewis Carroll famously wrote about a little girl named Alice and her adventures. On the other hand, there is Patricia Neal, who publishes fiction, writes screenplays, and acts in motion pictures and television exclusively under her stage name Fannie Flagg. She is known by her pseudonym, and her original name is not associated with any of her works.

A *religious relationship* is between a person and that person's identity within a religious order, organization, life, or some other capacity. (See Figure 3.11.) Conversely, there is also a *secular relationship*, which is between a person and her or his identity outside of religious life. For example, Albino Luciani is not a well-known name, but his religious identity Pope John Paul the First is much more familiar. In other cases, it is the opposite. For example, an Irish folk singer/priest is known primarily as Charlie Coen rather than as Father Charlie or Father Coen. Another similar relationship is the *official relationship*, which is between a person and the identity assumed for an official capacity. For example, there is a person known as Juan Carlos de Borbón y Borbón, but that person is also the Spanish sovereign Juan Carlos, King of Spain, who ruled from 1975 to 2014.

An *attributive relationship* is "between one person and another person (either a "real" individual or a persona) or identity to whom one or more works by the former have been attributed, either erroneously or falsely."[92] An example of this is the relationships between William Henry Ireland and William Shakespeare. Ireland, in the 18th century, attributed his own terrible play *Vortigern and Rowena* to Shakespeare along with other documents that he forged.

A *collaborative relationship*, in this context, exists when two or more persons, who collaborate in intellectual or artistic endeavors, create works under a single identity. For example, Eando Binder is a joint pseudonym used by two science fiction authors, Earl Andrew Binder and his brother Otto Oscar Binder. Another example, from the non-fiction world, is L. T. F. Gamut, which is a collective pseudonym of five Dutch logicians: Johan van Benthem, Dick de Jongh, Jeroen Groenendijk, Martin Stokhof, and Henk Verkuyl.

The final two person-to-person relationships are *sibling* and *parent/child relationships*. They are rarely seen in either bibliographic or authority data. Until recently, this information was outside the realm of what one might include in an authority record. In recent years, though, more contextual information has been collected about the entities described in authorities, so these relationships are not illogical or unreasonable. They could be of interest to someone, so they are included as possible types of relationships. Although it is not recorded in authority data at LC at this time, it could be helpful to know that Liza Minnelli is the daughter of Judy Garland and Vincente Minnelli.

Person-to-Family and **Person-to-Corporate body**: These categories are lumped together because they share a single relationship type: *membership*. This relationship is between a person and a family (or corporate body) in which the person is a member or has an affiliation. Some examples include the following:

- Rob Gronkowski has a membership relationship with the Gronkowski family

- Mark Kozelek had a membership relationship with the musical group Red House Painters
- Steve Jobs had a membership relationship with Apple Computers
- Elizabeth Warren has a membership relationship with the U.S. Senate as well as with the Democratic Party

Family-to-Family: This category has only a single relationship type in FRAD: the *genealogical relationship*. This relationship recognizes that some families are descended from other families. This information may be important for understanding a family history or the context related to a family unit, clan, royal house, dynasty, matriarchy, and so on (e.g., the Yuan dynasty is descended from the Mongolian Borjigin clan).

Family-to-Corporate body: In this category, two types of relationships are identified. The first is the *founding relationship*. This occurs when a family is responsible for the creation of a corporate body. For example, in 1916, the Wegman family founded the grocery store chain Wegmans. Or, in 1923, four brothers, Albert, Harry, Sam, and Jack Warner, founded a movie studio and called it Warner Brothers. The other family-to-corporate body relationship type is the *ownership relationship* (e.g., the Walton family owns Wal-Mart Stores, Inc.).

Corporate body-to-Corporate body: In this category, two relationships are identified: *hierarchical* and *sequential* relationships. *Hierarchical* relationships occur when one corporate body entity is subordinate to another. This occurs when a corporate body is a department, committee, division, commission, or some other unit that is part of another larger body. For example, the School of Library and Information Science is part of (or a unit within) Simmons College in Boston. Another example is the American Red Cross Bay Area Chapter, which is subordinate to the national American Red Cross organization.

The other type, *sequential* relationships, occurs when the connection between two or more corporate bodies is based on time or order. For example, organizations can split apart into separate bodies or two individual corporate bodies may merge into one. An example is that the Standard Oil Company of New Jersey was formed in 1882; it changed its name 10 years later to the Standard Oil Company. In 1972, the company changed its name again, this time to Exxon Corporation. Then in 1999, Exxon Corporation and Mobil Corporation merged to form Exxon Mobil Corporation. Although the first two changes involve names only, the third change involves a corporate merger. Conventional wisdom, though, is that when there are formal name changes, the entities themselves have new identities along with new names; therefore they should be treated as brand new corporate bodies with their own authority records (although connected to their earlier incarnations). All these sequential changes are documented as part of the authority data for the corporate bodies involved.

Relationships among Group 1 Entities

FRAD, like FRBR, addresses the relationships that occur between Group 1 entities. In FRBR, six relationship categories were identified (including *Work-to-Work*, *Expression-to-Expression*, *Expression-to-Work*, etc.). In FRAD, a different approach was taken. There is only a single category—*Relationships among Works, Expressions, Manifestations, and Items*—and within it, seven

TABLE 3.5 Mapping of Group 1 Relationships in FRBR and FRAD.

FRAD Group 1 Relationships	FRBR Relationship Type	FRBR Categories
Equivalence	Reproduction	M2M, M2I, I2I
Equivalence	Alternate	M2M
Equivalence	Reconfiguration	I2I
Derivative	Summarization	W2W, E2E, E2W
Derivative	Adaptation	W2W, E2E, E2W
Derivative	Transformation	W2W, E2E, E2W
Derivative	Imitation	W2W, E2E, E2W
Derivative	Abridgement	E2E
Derivative	Revision	E2E
Derivative	Translation	E2E
Derivative	Arrangement	E2E
Descriptive	Subject relationships	W2W
Whole-Part	Whole-Part	W2W, E2E, E2W, M2M, I2I
Accompanying	Supplement	W2W, E2E, E2W
Accompanying	Complement	W2W, E2E, E2W
Sequential	Successor	W2W, E2E, E2W
Shared characteristic	n/a	n/a

Key: M2M = manifestation to manifestation, I2I = item to item, etc.

relationship types are identified, which are somewhat different than those seen in FRBR. The Group 1 relationship types found in FRAD are derived from the taxonomy of bibliographic relations developed by Barbara Tillett in her dissertation research from the late 1980s.[93] In Table 3.5, the Group 1 relationships in FRAD are mapped to those in FRBR.

The *equivalence relationship* exists among different types of carriers holding the same expression of a work. It includes copies, alternative formats (e.g., versions on CD and MP3), digital reproductions, facsimiles, reprinted material, photocopies, micro- and other reproductions. The key to equivalence relationships is that they share the same content (i.e., the same work and expression). FRAD acknowledges that this can be somewhat subjective depending on what exactly is meant by "the same."

w_1: Bach's *Wedding Cantata*

e_1: performance by Edith Mathis in 1960

m_1: Eterna LP in 1977

m_2: Corona compact disc in 2009

In the Bach example, m_1 and m_2 have an equivalence relationship. This type of relationship, however, is generally not expressed in authority data; it is more likely that this would be shared in a bibliographic record.

A *derivative relationship* is found when there are modifications to the work or expression. These may be somewhat minor or quite significant. Minor derivations include changes in the expression of the content, like those found in cases of different versions, editions, revisions, and strict translations. Major derivations are those where the work is transformed into something new, such as in cases of adaptations, changes of genre, free translations, paraphrases, parodies, and the like.

> e_1: Taylor's first edition of *The Organization of Information* has a revision e_2: the second edition of *The Organization of Information*
>
> w_1: Tad Mosel's *All the Way Home* is a dramatization of the novel w_2: *A Death in the Family* by James Agee

The Taylor example shows a minor derivation: a revision of an expression. The expression has been modified somewhat, but it has not changed into a new work. The Mosel example is a significant derivation, where the work has been transformed into a new, but related work.

A *descriptive relationship* is found between works and criticisms, evaluations, or reviews of that work. This type may include book reviews, annotated editions, commentaries, critiques, and so forth. It should be clear that a descriptive relationship between two works is really based on a subject relationship. If you have a commentary or a review of a scholarly work, what is that commentary about? It is about the original scholarly work.

> w_1: *Scout, Atticus, and Boo: A Celebration of Fifty Years of To Kill a Mockingbird* is commentary on the novel / is about w_2: *To Kill a Mockingbird* by Harper Lee

A *whole-part relationship* is acknowledged when there is a work that is or can be considered an independent component or a part of another larger work. These hierarchical relationships can also occur between a work and each of its various dependent components, whether or not each is considered a separate work in itself (e.g., a novel and its individual chapters). This relationship type can include a story (part) from an anthology (whole), papers in conference proceedings, an essay from a collection, articles from a journal, maps in an atlas, a publisher's series made up of independent works, and so on.

> w_1: *The Organization of Information* is part of w_2: Libraries Unlimited's *Library and Information Science Text Series*

The fifth type is the *accompanying relationship*, which can be found when a work is created to complement or supplement another work. In some cases, they complement equally, but in others, one work is the predominant item and the other is the dependent work. This relationship type includes text with supplements (e.g., teacher's manual for a textbook), software manuals or help programs, concordances, indexes, parts of a kit, and the like.

> w_1: Verdi's score for *La Traviata* has a libretto w_2: Piave's libretto for *La Traviata*

> w_3: *To Kill A Mockingbird in the Classroom: Walking in Someone Else's Shoes* by Louel C. Gibbons is a teacher's guide for w_4: *To Kill a Mockingbird* by Harper Lee

A *sequential relationship* is found in works that continue or precede other works, including successive titles of a serial, sequels to a novel, prequels of a movie, parts in a numbered series, among others types. This relationship is chronological in nature, focusing on time and the order in which entities appear.

> w_1: *American Documentation* is continued by w_2: *Journal of the American Society for Information Science*

> w_3: *The Dark Knight* (film) is a sequel to w_4: *Batman Begins* (film)

The seventh relationship type is the *shared characteristic relationship*, which is found in works that coincidentally share characteristics in common, such as common authors, titles, subjects, language, country of publication, color of binding, font size, and so on. This relationship may occur at any level in Group 1. An example is that Taylor's third edition of *The Organization of Information* and Universal Studio's Blu-Ray discs for the complete series of *Battlestar Galactica* were both released in 2009. Is this purely a coincidence or a real connection? With a *shared characteristic relationship* type available, it is a way to gather together what may seem to be random entities as long as they have some attribute in common. Because this relationship type is so broadly defined, it is not rigorously identified and included in either bibliographic or authority data. Gathering these entities together, instead, may occur as the result of a search in a retrieval tool (e.g., searching for all resources in the catalog that were published in Prague).

Relationships among the FRAD-Specific Entities

FRAD also introduces some relationship categories that relate to *names* and to *controlled access points*. These categories, and the types of relationship falling into each category, are addressed in turn. Many of the name relationships are reflected in *see* and *see also references* in authority records. A *see reference* informs users that a particular name is not authorized for use in the catalog, pointing instead to the AAP that is used. A *see also reference* informs users that they might also be interested in looking at another name or access point that is related to the one currently being viewed.

Names of Persons: This category begins with the assumption that there are two or more names related to a person and, therefore, must be addressed in the authority data. There are four types of relationships that might be encountered: *earlier name*, *later name*, *alternative linguistic form*, and *other variant name*. The first two types *earlier* and *later names* occur because persons do not always use the same names for their entire lives. For various reasons, names change.

> n_1: Cassius Clay has a later name n_2: Muhammad Ali
>
> n_4: Portia Degeneres is better known by her earlier name n_3: Portia de Rossi

Alternative linguistic form reflects the relationship between a person's preferred form of name and another form by which that person also may be known (e.g., a translated form of the name). The alternative linguistic form relationship type also applies to *Names of Families*, *Names of Corporate Bodies*, and *Names of Works* as well.

> n_1: Joan of Arc is the preferred form of name in the United States, but there are several alternative linguistic forms including n_2: Jeanne d'Arc, n_3: Juana de Arco, and n_4: Zhanna Dark
>
> n_1: Wuhan da xue is also known as n_2: Wuhan University in the United States, but in China it is best known as n_3: 武汉大学
>
> n_1: *Aesop's fables* is also known as n_2: *Aisōpou mythoi*, n_3: *Les fables d'Esope*, and n_4: *Ezoposi aṛaknerĕ*

Other variant name refers to other variations that may occur based on orthographic changes (e.g., differences in spelling, transliteration, punctuation, capitalization, etc.), word order variations, nicknames, epithets, and so on. Other variant names also apply to *Names of Corporate Bodies* and *Names of Works* as well.

> n_1: Mao Zedong is also known by other transliterated forms of his names n_2: Mao Tse-tung, n_3: Mao Ce-tung, n_4: Mao Tze-tung, as well as other variants based on other criteria, n_5: Maozedong, n_6: Mao Ze Dong, and n_7: Mao, Tsetung
>
> n_1: Pete Rodriguez, a musician in the 1960s was known by a nickname n_2: King of Boogaloo
>
> n_1: Sir Walter Raleigh has also been identified as n_2: Walter Ralegh, n_3: Walter Rauleigh, n_4: Walter Rawley, and n_5: W. R.
>
> n_1: College of Mount Saint Mary may also be referred to as n_2: Mt. St. Mary's College, n_3: Mount St. Mary's College, or n_4: Mount Saint Mary's College
>
> n_1: Al-Anon Family Group Headquarters, Inc. may also be referred to as n_2: Al-Anon, n_3: Al-Anon Family Groups, or n_4: Alateen
>
> n_1: *King Leir*, the anonymous play that may have served as a source for Shakespeare's play, may also be known as n_2: *True Chronicle History of King Leir and his Three Daughters, Gonorill, Ragan, and Cordella* or n_3: *Tragicall Historie of Kinge Leir and his Three Daughters*

Names of Families: This category has only a single relationship type: *alternative linguistic forms*. There is no real difference between what is found here and what is found under *Names of Persons*. It is a relationship between a family's preferred form of name and another form by which that family may be known (e.g., a translated form of the name).

Names of Corporate Bodies: There are four types of relationships found in this category: *expanded name, acronym/initials/abbreviations, alternative linguistic form*, and *other variant name* relationships. The first two types are related. An *expanded name* relationship is between the name of a corporate body and the larger, more explicit form of name by which it is also known. AFL-CIO is an example of a brief name that is the preferred form, but the body still has a fuller name, American Federation of Labor and Congress of Industrial Organizations, that appears occasionally. The *acronym/initials/abbreviations* is just the reverse where the full name is the preferred name, but an acronym, initialism, or abbreviation is also well known (e.g., International Federation of Library Associations and Institutions is the full name, but the body is frequently referred to as IFLA). The *alternative linguistic form* and *other variant name* relationships are the same as those identified under *Names of Persons* above.

Names of Works: In addition to *alternative linguistic form* and *other variant name*, this category adds a *conventional name* relationship. For some works, in addition to a formal name, a conventional name may be well known. For example, Bach's Cantata No. 202, "Weichet nur, betrübte Schatten," BWV 202 is widely known as "The Wedding Cantata." The *alternative linguistic form* and *other variant name* relationships are the same as those identified under *Names of Persons* above.

Controlled access points: This category has five different types reflecting the relationships that may exist between two controlled access points: *parallel language, alternate script, different rules, corresponding subject term or classification number*, and *identifier* relationships. Controlled access points are standardized character strings (authorized or not) that appear in authority records. These relationships are not about the names or the entities represented by them (i.e., persons, families, corporate bodies); the relationships address the access points themselves.

The first type is the *parallel language relationship*, which is having the same access point content exactly translated into another language. In its authority record, you will find access points for both **McGill University. Rare Books and Special Collections Division** and **McGill University. Division des livres rares et des collections spécialisées**. Related to this is the *alternate script relationship*, but it focuses on different scripts instead of languages (e.g., Roman alphabet versus the Greek alphabet). In addition, there is a *different rules relationship* to explain the connection between access points established using different rules. For example, **Baskin, H. Jack, Sr. (Henry Jack), 1940-** is the access point established under RDA, but the same access point under AACR2 is formulated as **Baskin, H. Jack**. Another relationship type identified is the *corresponding subject term or classification number relationship*. This is a "relationship between the controlled access point for the name of an entity (for a person . . . work . . . concept . . .) and a subject term in a controlled vocabulary, and/or a classification number for that entity.

Here the subject term and the classification number may also be viewed as parallel names/identifiers for the name of the same entity."[94] For example, this relationship may connect a personal name access point, **Faulkner, William, 1897-1962**, to a classification number **PS3511.A86**. Or, it might relate a subject heading (**Brigands and robbers**) to a classification number (**364.106**) that is similar, if not an exact match. The final relationship type is the *identifier relationship*, which is between a controlled access point for an entity and its identifier (e.g., the personal name AAP, **Schwartz, Candy**, has an identifier **n85819417**).

FRAD Mapping

After describing all the entities, attributes, and relationships, FRAD closes by mapping all the attributes and relationships identified throughout the model to the user tasks. Like FRBR, it is an attempt to demonstrate which elements of authority data help users to find and to identify, and which help catalogers to contextualize and to justify. For example, the mapping in FRAD's Table 4 shows that a person's name is useful for finding and contextualizing; a birth date helps with identifying, contextualizing, and justifying; a corporate body history helps with identifying and contextualizing; and so on. But unlike FRBR, there is "no attempt to assess or indicate the relative importance of each attribute or relationship to a given user task as was done in the FRBR model. Designations of which attributes and relationships are considered mandatory need to be determined on an application-specific basis." See Section 6 of the FRAD model to view the E-R/user tasks mappings.[95]

CONCLUSION

As stated at the beginning of this chapter, for better or for worse, the cataloging environment has changed dramatically over the past two decades. Practices have evolved, and will continue to evolve. Some long-held assumptions have been dismissed and some long-standing practices have been rejected. FRBR, FRAD, and the ICP have laid the groundwork for a new set of cataloging rules, *RDA: Resource Description & Access*. Despite some criticisms of FRBR and FRAD over the years, they are the conceptual models underlying the cataloging practices detailed in RDA. Not everything in these three foundational documents has been implemented in RDA (e.g., FRAD's name entities), but each has contributed to the development of a theoretical framework that has helped to structure these new guidelines. There is hope that this new set of "FRBR-ized" cataloging rules will improve the experience of using the catalog and will also lead to innovations in system design that incorporate linked data principles and Semantic Web technologies. It is hoped that with the foundations of FRBR, FRAD, and the ICP firmly in place, the cataloging community can increase efficiencies, avoid marginalization, cut costs, and make resulting bibliographic data more compatible with that of other communities.[96] There is great hope that RDA will transform cataloging and keep library bibliographic data relevant in the 21st century.

NOTES

1. For greater insight into the state of cataloging at the turn of the century, please see the variety of articles posted on "Library of Congress Professional Guild AFSCME Local 2910," accessed February 25, 2014, http://www.guild2910 .org/future.htm.

2. International Federation of Library Associations and Institutions (IFLA) Cataloguing Section and IFLA Meetings of Experts on an International Cataloguing Code, *The Statement of International Cataloguing Principles* (ICP) (The Hague: IFLA, 2009), http://www.ifla.org/publications/statement-of -international-cataloguing-principles.

3. International Conference on Cataloging Principles, Paris, 9th-18th October, 1961, *Report* (London: International Federation of Library Associations, 1963). Also known as the "Paris Principles."

4. Seymour Lubetzky, *Code of Cataloging Rules, Author and Title Entry: An Unfinished Draft for a New Edition of Cataloging Rules* (Chicago: American Library Association, 1960).

5. IFLA, *ICP*, 1.

6. Ibid., 1-2.

7. Ibid., 2.

8. Ibid., 10.

9. Library of Congress, "1.1F Statements of Responsibility," *Library of Congress Rule Interpretations*, 2nd ed. (Washington, D.C.: Library of Congress, 1989). Accessible through a subscription to "Cataloger's Desktop" at https:// desktop.loc.gov/ or through the "Cataloger's Reference Shelf" website, accessed February 25, 2014, http://www.itsmarc.com/crs/mergedprojects/ lcri/lcri/contents.htm; *Anglo-American Cataloguing Rules*, 2nd ed., prepared by the American Library Association, the British Library, the Canadian Library Committee on Cataloguing, the (British) Library Association, and the Library of Congress, ed. by Michael Gorman and Paul W. Winkler (Chicago: American Library Association, 1978).

10. Peter Pin-Shan Chen, "The Entity-Relationship Model: Toward a Unified View of Data." *ACM Transactions on Database Systems* 1, no. 1 (1976): 9-36.

11. IFLA, *ICP*, 3-4.

12. IFLA Study Group on the Functional Requirements for Bibliographic Records, *Functional Requirements for Bibliographic Records, Final Report* (München, Germany: K.G. Saur, 1998), 8, http://www.ifla.org/publications/functional -requirements-for-bibliographic-records.

13. Elaine Svenonius, *The Intellectual Foundation of Information Organization* (Cambridge, Mass.: MIT Press, 2000), 18-20.

14. Various discussions and comments on the merits of the FRBR user tasks have occurred on AUTOCAT. The AUTOCAT archives may be searched online by subscribers, accessed February 15, 2014, https://listserv.syr.edu/scripts/ wa.exe?A0=AUTOCAT. An example of discussions on this topic titled "FRBR Tasks" began on April 17, 2009.

15. IFLA, *ICP*, 9.

16. Ibid., 7.

17. Ibid.

18. Ibid.

19. Ibid., 7-8.

20. IFLA, *FRBR*, 5.

21. Charles A. Cutter, *Rules for a Dictionary Catalog*, 4th ed., rewritten (Washington, D.C.: GPO, 1904); S. R. Ranganathan, *The Five Laws of Library Science* (Bombay, India: Asia Publishing House 1963); S. R. Ranganathan, *Heading and Canons* (Madras, India: S. Viswanathan, 1955); Lubetzky, *Code of Cataloging Rules, Author and Title*; and "Paris Principles" among others.

22. IFLA, *FRBR*, 2.

23. Ibid., 8 and 79.

24. Ibid.

25. Ibid.

26. Ibid.

27. Svenonius, *The Intellectual Foundation of Information Organization*, 18-20; IFLA, *The Statement of International Cataloguing Principles*, 3-4.

28. *RDA: Resource Description & Access*, developed in a collaborative process led by the Joint Steering Committee for Development of RDA (Chicago: American Library Association, 2010). Also available as *RDA Toolkit: Resource Description & Access* (Chicago: American Library Association, 2010), accessed February 27, 2014, http://www.rdatoolkit.org/. See discussion of objectives at: *0.4.2.1 Responsiveness to User Needs*.

29. IFLA Working Group on Functional Requirements and Numbering of Authority Records (FRANAR), *Functional Requirements for Authority Data: A Conceptual Model (FRAD)*, edited by Glenn E. Patton (München, Germany: K.G. Saur, 2009). A more recent version, with corrections through 2013 and differing page numbers is available online. These endnotes will refer to the pagination of the electronic version. Accessed February 17, 2014, http://www.ifla.org/files/assets/cataloguing/frad/frad_2013.pdf. See p. 46 of the electronic version for the FRAD user tasks.

30. IFLA Working Group on the Functional Requirements for Subject Authority Records, *Functional Requirements for Subject Authority Data (FRSAD): A Conceptual Model* (München, Germany: De Gruyter Saur, 2011). The FRSAD report is also available online at the IFLA website. These endnotes will refer to the pagination of the electronic version. Accessed February 17, 2014, http://www.ifla.org/files/assets/classification-and-indexing/functional-requirements-for-subject-authority-data/frsad-final-report.pdf, 34.

31. IFLA, *FRBR*, 13.

32. In the archives field, some standards refer to corporate bodies, persons, and families in that order, and use the initialism CPF.

33. In the near future, all the *Functional Requirement* models (FRBR, FRAD, and FRSAD) will be harmonized and discrepancies such as this will be eliminated. For the sake of simplicity, the entity *family* will be described as being part of Group 2, even when referring to FRBR. *FRSAD—Functional Requirements for Subject Authority Data*—is addressed later in this chapter.

34. IFLA, *FRBR*, 31.

35. Ibid., 32.

36. For the latest on these activities, please see the IFLA "FRBR Review Group Reports," accessed March 06, 2014, http://www.ifla.org/frbr-rg.

37. IFLA, *FRBR*, 13.

38. Barbara Tillett, *What Is FRBR? A Conceptual Model for the Bibliographic Universe* (Washington, D.C.: Library of Congress Cataloging Distribution Service, 2004), 2-3, http://www.loc.gov/cds/downloads/FRBR.PDF.

39. Arlene G. Taylor gives an example, from the viewpoint of a creator, of how her conception of the teaching of information organization turned into her textbook *The Organization of Information* in "An Introduction to Functional Requirements for Bibliographic Records (FRBR)," in Arlene G. Taylor, editor,

Understanding FRBR: What It Is and How It Will Affect Our Retrieval Tools (Westport, Conn.: Libraries Unlimited, 2007), 5-6.

40. IFLA, *FRBR*, 17.
41. Richard Smiraglia, "The 'Works' Phenomenon and Best Selling Books," *Cataloging & Classification Quarterly* 44, no. 3/4 (2007): 180.
42. Thomas Brickhouse and Nicholas D. Smith, "Plato (427-347 BCE)," in *Internet Encyclopedia of Philosophy: A Peer-Reviewed Academic Resource*, edited by James Fieser and Bradley Dowden, accessed March 01, 2014, http://www.iep.utm.edu/plato/.
43. IFLA, *FRBR*, 33-35.
44. Ibid.
45. David Miller and Patrick Le Boeuf, " 'Such Stuff as Dreams Are Made On': How Does FRBR Fit Performing Arts?" *Cataloging & Classification Quarterly* 39, no. 3/4 (2005): 168-169.
46. IFLA, *FRBR*, 19.
47. Taylor, *Understanding FRBR*, 7-8.
48. IFLA, *FRBR*, 20.
49. Ibid., 37.
50. Ibid., 35-40.
51. Ibid., 17.
52. Tillett, *What Is FRBR?*, 4. This chart was originally published in: Barbara B. Tillett, "Bibliographic Relationships," in *Relationships in the Organization of Knowledge*, edited by Carol A. Bean and Rebecca Green (Dordrecht, The Netherlands: Kluwer Academic Publishers, 2001), 23.
53. Richard P. Smiraglia, "Bibliographic Families and Superworks," in Taylor, *Understanding FRBR*, 73-86.
54. IFLA, *FRBR*, 21.
55. Edward T. O'Neill, "FRBR: Functional Requirements for Bibliographic Records Application of the Entity-Relationship Model to *Humphry Clinker*." *Library Resources & Technical Services* 46, no. 4 (2002): 152.
56. IFLA, *FRBR*, 40-47.
57. Ibid., 14-15.
58. Ibid., 25.
59. IFLA, *FRAD*, 8.
60. IFLA, *FRBR*, 25-26.
61. IFLA, *FRSAD*, 15.
62. For the latest on these activities, please see the IFLA "FRBR Review Group Reports," Last update: 12 February 2015, http://www.ifla.org/frbr-rg.
63. IFLA, *FRAD*, 24.
64. IFLA, *FRBR*, 51-53.
65. Ibid., 55.
66. Ibid., 56.
67. Tillett, *What Is FRBR?*, 4.
68. IFLA, *FRBR*, 63-64.
69. Ibid., 67-68.
70. Ibid., 73-78.
71. Ibid., 79-92.
72. Ibid., 93-94.
73. Charles A. Cutter, *Rules for a Dictionary Catalog*, 4th ed. (Washington, D.C.: GPO, 1904), 12.
74. The latest version of which is: International Federation of Library Associations and Institutions, *ISBD: International Standard Bibliographic Description*, Consolidated ed. (Berlin: De Gruyter Saur, 2011).

75. IFLA, *FRAD*, i.
76. Ibid.
77. Ibid., 1.
78. Ibid., 46.
79. Ibid., 24-25.
80. Ibid., 14.
81. Ibid., 27.
82. Ibid., 25-28
83. Ibid., 8.
84. IFLA, *FRBR*, 50.
85. IFLA, *FRAD*, 8-9.
86. IFLA, *FRBR*, 25-26.
87. IFLA, *FRAD*, 9.
88. IFLA, *FRBR*, 48.
89. IFLA, *FRAD*, 24.
90. Ibid.
91. Ibid., 31.
92. Ibid., 33.
93. Barbara Tillett, "A Taxonomy of Bibliographic Relationships," *Library Resources & Technical Services* 30, no. 2 (1991): 156.
94. IFLA, *FRAD*, 45.
95. Ibid., 46-51.
96. Barbara Tillett, "Keeping Libraries Relevant in the Semantic Web with Resource Description and Access (RDA)." *Serials* 24, no. 3 (2011): 270-271.

SUGGESTED READING

IFLA Cataloguing Section and IFLA Meetings of Experts on an International Cataloguing Code. *The Statement of International Cataloguing Principles*. The Hague: IFLA, 2009.

IFLA Study Group on the Functional Requirements for Bibliographic Records. *Functional Requirements for Bibliographic Records, Final Report*. München, Germany: K.G. Saur, 1998.

IFLA Working Group on Functional Requirements and Numbering of Authority Records. *Functional Requirements for Authority Data: A Conceptual Model (FRAD)*. Edited by Glenn E. Patton. München, Germany: K.G. Saur, 2009.

IFLA Working Group on the Functional Requirements for Subject Authority Records. *Functional Requirements for Subject Authority Data (FRSAD): A Conceptual Model*. München, Germany: De Gruyter Saur, 2011.

Jin, Qiang. *Demystifying FRAD: Functional Requirements for Authority Data*. Santa Barbara, Calif.: Libraries Unlimited, 2012.

Maxwell, Robert L. *FRBR: A Guide for the Perplexed*. Chicago: American Library Association, 2008.

Taylor, Arlene G., ed. *Understanding FRBR: What It Is and How It Will Affect Our Retrieval Tools*. Westport, Conn.: Libraries Unlimited, 2007.

Zhang, Yin, and Athena Salaba. *Implementing FRBR in Libraries: Key Issues and Future Directions*. New York: Neal-Schuman Publishers, 2009.

Chapter 4

RDA Basics

INTRODUCTION

This chapter provides basic information about the latest descriptive-cataloging standard adopted by the Anglo-American library community and others—*RDA: Resource Description & Access*, developed by the Joint Steering Committee for Development of RDA (JSC).[1] This chapter, which is based in part on the introduction and chapter 1 of RDA, addresses the purpose, scope, objectives, and organization of the content standard, including an overview of RDA's 10 sections (which contain a total of 37 chapters). It discusses current terminology and how it relates to earlier vocabulary used for descriptive cataloging. It provides an overview of data types used in RDA and describes various features of the content standard that may be useful while cataloging, including alternatives, policy statements, and examples. It also addresses several pre-cataloging issues, such as mode of issuance, types of descriptions, bibliographic relationships, and technical reading.

Although it may be tempting to skip over this type of preliminary material, the successful use of the system is dependent on understanding the underlying structures of the content standard, what its features are, and how to get started. In short, this chapter is *about* RDA and how to approach it rather than about how to perform descriptive cataloging per se. Throughout this and the following chapters, whenever RDA instructions are cited, the information discussed is based on the text found in the RDA Toolkit, as it is the most up-to-date version of the cataloging guidelines. Not all instructions are discussed; the reader should examine the appropriate chapter of RDA for additional information, particularly on more complex problems. Because the rules are updated quarterly, RDA is a moving target. This text is a snapshot of the current version of the standard in 2015. Readers are cautioned that instructions may have changed since this text was published. Any particular discussion of the cataloging guidelines found in this text obviously should be confirmed in RDA itself.[2] Readers are encouraged to consult RDA frequently as they are exploring the content of this and the following chapters in Part II of this text.

RDA: A PROLOGUE

In this section of the text, some prefatory concepts are introduced. It begins with an overview of the content standard. Next is a discussion of different data types used in RDA. The section ends with a discussion of terminology used in contemporary descriptive cataloging.

What Is RDA?

RDA, produced primarily by the Anglo-American library community, is the latest in a long line of descriptive cataloging content standards, the history of which is described in chapter 2 of this text. RDA is based on the *Statement of International Cataloguing Principles* (ICP), *Functional Requirements for Bibliographic Records* (FRBR), and *Functional Requirements for Authority Data* (FRAD)—three international standards created by the International Federation of Library Associations and Institutions (IFLA) that are discussed in some detail in chapter 3 of this text. It also has a relationship with the second edition of the *Anglo-American Cataloguing Rules* (AACR2).[3] RDA is the intended replacement for AACR2 and is meant to be more inclusive than the previous standard in a number of ways.

> RDA is built on foundations established by the *Anglo-American Cataloguing Rules* (AACR) and the cataloguing traditions on which it was based. Instructions derived from AACR have been reworked to produce a standard that will be easier to use, more adaptable, and more cost-efficient in its application. A key factor in the design of RDA has been the need to integrate data produced using RDA into existing databases developed using AACR and related standards . . . . The metadata standards used in other communities (archives, museums, publishers, semantic web, etc.) were taken into consideration in the design of RDA. The goal was to attain an effective level of interoperability between those standards and RDA.[4]

RDA is a *content standard*, which is a set of rules or instructions to guide catalogers, indexers, metadata librarians, archivists, curators, and so on in the creation of data for a bibliographic record, an authority record, a metadata statement, or some other form of resource description. Content standards usually provide detailed instructions on how to record, order, and format the metadata to be included. The instructions at RDA 2.4.1 are representative examples of guidelines found in a content standard:

2.4.1.4 Recording Statements of Responsibility

Transcribe a statement of responsibility as it appears on the source of information

2.4.1.5 Statement Naming More Than One Person, etc.

Record a statement of responsibility naming more than one person, family, or corporate body as a single statement whether those persons, etc., perform the same function or different functions

2.4.1.6 More Than One Statement of Responsibility

If there is more than one statement of responsibility, record the statements in the order indicated by the sequence, layout, or typography of the source of information . . . . If the sequence, layout, and typography are ambiguous or insufficient to determine the order, record the statements in the order that makes the most sense[5]

The instructions at RDA 2.4.1 provide additional guidance, including a definition of the element, an indication of whether the element is required, a list of related elements, the source(s) from which the metadata should be transcribed or recorded, some optional omissions, some exceptions to the instructions, some additions for clarification, an instruction on how to address ambiguities, and so on.

The main text of RDA does *not* address how metadata is to be encoded or displayed in a catalog, although some encoding and display information is presented in appendices and mappings that appear in the RDA Toolkit. RDA is *schema neutral*; that is, it was not designed to be used with any particular encoding scheme or communication format, such as MAchine-Readable Cataloging (MARC),[6] Metadata Object Description Schema (MODS),[7] or the currently developing Bibliographic Framework Initiative (BIBFRAME).[8] The metadata created using RDA is compatible with any of these, as well as with other encoding formats, presentation standards, and metadata schemes. The focus of RDA is on the creation of metadata content rather than on where it goes or how it is displayed.

RDA supplants, or is intended to supplant, AACR2 as the content standard used by Anglo-American libraries. At the time of this writing, the three national libraries in the United States—the Library of Congress (LC), the National Library of Medicine (NLM), and the National Agricultural Library (NAL)—as well as numerous academic, special, and public libraries in this country, have implemented RDA. The national libraries of Australia, Canada, Great Britain, Malaysia, New Zealand, the Philippines, and Singapore have also adopted it; by the end of 2016, it is expected that the national libraries of Finland, Germany, Ireland, Latvia, the Netherlands, Scotland, and Switzerland will have implemented the new content standard as well.[9]

RDA is intended to be more widely applicable than earlier content standards. It is no longer focused solely on the Anglo-American library community. It is meant to be more international in scope—something that is enhanced by providing greater flexibility when it comes to the use of languages, scripts, numerals, dates, and units of measurement.[10] Wider international usage seems likely, considering the list of non-Anglo-American libraries that have implemented or that are interested in implementing the content standard.

RDA is also meant to be applicable to any and all resource types, and by communities other than libraries. A guiding force in the development of RDA was the awareness of the boundaries of the earlier content standard, AACR2, which divided cataloging instructions by a limited set of resource types typically collected by libraries (e.g., books, computer files, maps). As new resource types developed—especially in the area of electronic resources—the older content standard showed signs of strain attempting to accommodate these newer formats. RDA was designed to provide guidelines for describing resources no matter what carrier contains the work. RDA provides more instructions for handling non-book and unpublished resources, which could potentially lead to its adoption by metadata-creating institutions other than libraries. At the time of this writing, however, it is unknown how many, if any, non-library institutions are users of RDA.

The "RDA Prospectus," written in 2009 by the JSC, describes the intent behind the design of the new content standard:

> Digital technologies have significantly changed the environment in which libraries, archives, museums, and other information management organizations build and maintain the databases that describe and provide access to resources in their collections. The resources represented in those databases include a rapidly growing number that have been produced and disseminated using digital technologies. RDA is being designed to provide a flexible and extensible framework for both the technical and content description of such resources while also serving the needs of libraries organizing resources produced in non-digital formats. Database technologies are also undergoing significant change . . . . RDA is being developed to provide a better fit with emerging database technologies, and to take advantage of the efficiencies and flexibility that such technologies offer with respect to data capture, storage, retrieval, and display. . . . The FRBR and FRAD models provide RDA with an underlying framework that has the scope needed to support comprehensive coverage of all types of content and media, the flexibility and extensibility needed to accommodate newly emerging resource characteristics, and the adaptability needed for the data produced to function within a wide range of technological environments.[11]

From the beginning of the development process, the JSC was very clear that RDA would be different from and more forward-thinking than its predecessors while remaining compatible with the data created under those earlier standards.

When first encountering RDA, most students or new catalogers will need to spend some time getting to know the content standard. Like it or not, this is most likely going to involve some amount of reading the RDA text. Cataloging guidelines are not the most scintillating reading; though they are very informative, no one—not even the most ardent cataloger—is going to proclaim that the documentation and standards are exciting. In the actual cataloging process, the text of RDA is not meant to be read in a linear fashion. The primary way to access RDA is intended to be through the RDA Toolkit, an online resource. During the development process, there was some question of whether a print version of the content standard would even be produced (eventually it was). As an electronic tool—containing the text, but with built-in hyperlinks, browsing and search functionality, supplementary tools, content filters, personal profiles, bookmarking, and additional related resources—RDA Toolkit allows catalogers to consult only the text that is needed at any given moment. This can be both a benefit and a drawback. Students and new catalogers should be aware that although keyword searching and darting from instruction to instruction is helpful, it is no substitute for developing a deeper understanding of the content standard through thorough exploration and study (part of which includes using this text).

Data Types

When cataloging with RDA, sundry pieces of data in various forms may be employed as values to fill the various metadata elements. The following is a brief overview of the types of data that may be used:

- **Transcribed data**: data documenting exactly what was found on a resource. *Transcription* generally means the cataloger should accept the data as found, at least in terms of wording, spelling, and order; transcription, however, can contain slight changes for clarity or consistency (e.g., changes in capitalization, adjustments to spacing or punctuation). Examples of elements requiring transcribed data are the title proper and the edition statement.

- **Recorded data**: data elements that are recorded, but not copied *exactly*, from the source. It may be information about the resource but information that is not literally stated within it (e.g., extent, number of subunits, dimensions), or it may be information recorded following instructions that adjust the data in ways that are considered insignificant (e.g., date of publication, standard identifiers recorded using a specified display format, copyright dates).

RDA makes a distinction between *transcribing* and *recording* metadata. In various training sessions, forums, and meetings of the American Library Association (ALA), the phrase "Take what you see and accept what you get" has been used repeatedly to clarify *transcription* and how it relates to the ICP principle of *representation*. Many of the required RDA metadata elements for manifestations involve transcribed data, although not all.

For some metadata elements, controlled or standardized forms of data are required.

- **Standardized data**: data from a controlled list of values. For example, the media type and content type are chosen from a small list of options, and creator and contributor elements *usually* contain authorized access points for names taken from an authority file.

Some controlled vocabularies in RDA are open lists, whereas others are closed. An open list allows for the possibility of a cataloger adding other terms as needed. A closed list may suggest that if a term found within is not appropriate, a cataloger should use *other* or *unspecified*. Some lists are rather extensive, but others may contain only three or four values. There are approximately 70 controlled vocabularies in RDA, which are freely available online through the Open Metadata Registry.[12]

Some data elements require information that is provided by a cataloger.

- **Free text**: unstructured data supplied by a cataloger. The language reflects a cataloger's judgment as to what is required. Free-text descriptions are expected to be clear and concise. For example, many notes in a catalog record will be written using free text.

Although not specifically related to RDA, some metadata records might also include machine-assigned or machine-derived data.

- **Machine-assigned data**: data generated as part of automated metadata creation processes. For example, a control number or a creation date may be automatically generated when a record is created.
- **Machine-derived data**: information extracted from an electronic version of the resource being described or from another source. For instance, a table of contents may be imported directly into a record from publisher-supplied metadata.

Most resource descriptions entail a combination of these six data types.

Terminology

With a new cataloging standard comes new vocabulary. In addition to terms such as *entity* and *attribute*, which recently have been included in the cataloging lexicon based on new conceptual models (see chapter 3 of this text), there are terms that had equivalents in the previous cataloging standards. Although there was some debate over whether to include the older terminology in this text at all, it was realized that during this period of transition between AACR2 and RDA, it is useful to learn both the older and newer jargon. For the next decade or longer, it is likely that readers will be collaborating and conversing with librarians who learned to catalog using AACR2. For the sake of enhanced communication, this text includes some pre-RDA terminology so that it is not completely foreign, but for the most part, the text will employ current vocabulary.

Terms and Concepts in Bibliographic Description

In the area of descriptive cataloging, some terms or concepts have replaced older ones due to the adoption of RDA. Each has been replaced by one or more equivalent concepts. Some refer to specific metadata elements, whereas others are more general in nature.

The first is the concept of *resource*. In RDA and most other modern cataloging texts, the terms *resource* and *information resource* have replaced references to *library materials, information package, document,* and other words represent-ing individual formats such as *book, videotape, map,* and the like. *Resource* is an understandable neutral term that refers to either a *manifestation* or an *item* (as described in FRBR). Resources thus contain one or more *works* and *expressions* per the FRBR model.

Related to this is the replacement of the word *entry,* which was used to mean a record of an item in a catalog in previous content standards. Today, instead of speaking of *entries,* catalogers speak of *metadata, metadata state-ments, records, metadata records, surrogate records, bibliographic records,* or *bibliographic descriptions. Entry* is still used to refer to items in bibliographies, and may be used when discussing a record in a printed catalog. Entry may also be used to refer to certain access points (see below for that discussion).

Another concept included in RDA is *carrier*—the physical format of a manifes-tation in which the content is stored. Under previous cataloging rules, catalogers included a *physical description* of the resource as part of the overall bibliographic metadata; in RDA, catalogers describe the carrier. The carrier's characteristics are explicated through several metadata elements such as *media type, carrier type, extent* (with specific units), *dimensions,* and others.

Another element, *content type,* is often associated with *carrier type* and *media type,* because the three elements together replace an element of descrip-tion found in the *International Standard Bibliographic Description* (ISBD) and in AACR2 that was called the *general material designation* or *GMD.* A GMD told users: "This resource is a bit different from a book or other print item." It was found immediately after the title proper and acted as an "early warn-ing system" to let users know that the resource described was not a book or journal and that they might need special equipment to access the resource. The now defunct GMD was used only with certain material types. Although AACR2 listed 27 GMD values, in LC standard practice, fewer than 10 were rec-ommended for common use. As stated, *content type, carrier type,* and *media type* have replaced this single element and a physical description has been replaced by elements related to the carrier. Table 4.1 shows two examples comparing the use of the GMD/physical description approach in AACR2 to the more granular RDA approach (note that a small number of abbreviations are still allowable under RDA).

Two other concepts prevalent in AACR2 that have since been replaced or omitted in RDA are the *chief source of information* and *prescribed sources of information.* Only the first of these has a true counterpart in RDA. In earlier cataloging rules, *chief source of information* was an identified feature for each resource type that was to be the first source consulted when cataloging a resource of that type (e.g., a book's chief source of information was the title page or title page substitute). Information from the chief source was preferred to information found elsewhere. In RDA 2.2.2, a small set of *preferred sources of information* are identified for two specific groups of resources, plus a general group for all others:

1. resources comprising pages, leaves, sheets, or cards

2. resources consisting of moving images

3. all other resources

TABLE 4.1 Comparison of AACR2 and RDA Practices Related to Physical Description.

AACR2 Element	Value	RDA Element	Value
GMD	videorecording	Media type	video
		Carrier type	videodisc
		Content type	two-dimensional moving image
Extent/Specific Material Designation	1 videodisc (ca. 120 min.)	Extent/unit	1 videodisc *or* 1 DVD
		Running time	approximately 120 min.
Other physical details	sd., col.	Sound content	sound
		Colour content	color
Dimensions	4 3/4 in.	Dimensions	4 3/4 in.
GMD	electronic resource	Media type	computer
		Carrier type	online resource
		Content type	text
Extent/Specific Material Designation	n/a *or* viii, 68 p.	Extent / unit	1 online resource (viii, 68 pages)
		File type	text file *or* digital text file
		Encoding format	PDF
Other physical details	ill.	Illustrative content	illustrations
Dimensions	n/a	Dimensions	n/a

Each of these groups has at least two possible sources for information. For example, for a music CD, the preferred sources, in order of preference, are (1) a textual source on the resource itself or a label that is permanently printed on or affixed to the resource, (2) an internal source, and (3) a container or accompanying material issued with the resource.

AACR2's concept of *prescribed sources of information* does not have an exact equivalent concept in RDA. The prescribed sources were a set of locations from which to seek data for certain areas of description. For example, under AACR2, publication information for a book was to be sought from a title page, other *preliminaries* (i.e., title page verso, pages preceding the title page, and the cover), or a *colophon* (i.e., a statement of publication at the end of a resource). Information not taken from a prescribed source was enclosed in square brackets to indicate that it came from somewhere else. Square brackets continue to be used in RDA to indicate that the metadata comes from outside the resource itself (e.g., not printed on the CD, not found internally, and not on a container or accompanying material issued with the resource).

In RDA, prescribed sources for areas of description are not addressed; instead, every individual metadata element provides a statement about the source or a list of possible sources of information to be consulted. For example, the element *Place of Publication* indicates the cataloger should consult the same source where the publisher's name was found for the needed data (or another source within the resource itself or one of the other sources of information specified at RDA 2.2.4). Publisher's Name and Date of Publication both indicate that the cataloger should consult the same source as the Title Proper (or another source within the resource itself or one of the other sources of information specified at RDA 2.2.4). Under RDA, very little metadata is placed in square brackets, unless it was taken from outside the resource itself, or unless the metadata is in square brackets on the resource and it is being transcribed exactly. Even metadata obtained from outside the resource itself is not always placed in square brackets; if the metadata normally does not appear on the resource, it may be taken from anywhere and recorded without square brackets (e.g., a statement of responsibility for a photograph or a date associated with a hand puppet).

The final change is related to the concept of *levels of description* in AACR2. In the previous content standard, three levels of cataloging were identified. The first level was the bare minimum, which contained fewer than 10 bibliographic elements. The second level contained more metadata and was considered the standard approach to descriptive cataloging for most libraries using AACR2. The third level was employed only with special or rare materials and included every possible applicable descriptive element. In RDA, there is no exact match to this concept; in RDA, instead, there is a list of *core elements* that are to be included *if* applicable. Inclusion of no more than the core elements is considered minimal-level cataloging. It is up to the individual cataloger or the individual institution to decide how much additional detail is provided beyond the list of core elements; it is a matter of cataloger's judgment or local policy.

Terms and Concepts Related to Access Points and Authority Control

A number of terms related to access points and authority control have been replaced in RDA. Some of these changes reflect transformations of practice; others reflect only updated language. In either case the major changes are addressed below.

The first change is a simple but logical update: it is the emphasis on using the term *creator* rather than relying heavily on the term *author*. This does not mean that *author* is not used in cataloging; it is. It is just that when thinking about how to identify the persons, families, and corporate bodies (PFC) responsible for the existence of a work, the word *creator* is more encompassing of the diversity of roles that exists today. *Author* is fine to describe the creator of a textbook, but it does not work as well for art, musical compact discs, moving images, and so on.

When describing creators in RDA, an *authorized access point* (AAP) is used when authority control is being employed. This allows for all works by the same creator to be brought together by the same character string or identifier (e.g., **Joudrey, Daniel N.** is an AAP for one of the authors of this textbook, and the records for his works contain this string for the purpose of collocation). In earlier times, this string was referred to as a *heading*. A *heading* was a name or phrase placed at the head of a catalog record to provide an access point. In cataloging, one might find mention of a *name heading*, *genre/form heading*, or *subject heading*. Although *authorized access point* has replaced *name heading* as the term of choice, the other two phrases remain in common usage.

A *name heading*, under AACR2, was used to represent main and added entries. A *main entry* was the primary access point for a resource;[13] it was the access point that identified the primary (or the first-named) creator of the work. In some cases, a title was substituted as the primary access point (e.g., when no single creator could be identified as primary). Some catalogers have wondered why a main entry was chosen at all; the primary purpose for the distinction, among others, was so that there was a consistent way to refer to or to cite a work.[14] For example, in 2014, Wadsworth Cengage Learning published two textbooks with identical titles (*Introduction to Psychology*), one by Rod Plotnik and the other by James W. Kalat. A good way to avoid confusion with these two resources is to refer to them by their primary creators and their titles proper. In the form of an access point, one would be represented as **Kalat, James W. Introduction to psychology** and the other as **Plotnik, Rod. Introduction to psychology**. By identifying the main entry (i.e., the primary creator), it is understood that these are two different works and they can be consistently differentiated.

Under RDA, this naming function is still in place—catalogers construct access points to represent a work—but it does not use the term *main entry*. There are, of course, variations on this process depending on the entities involved in the creation of a resource, but, generally, catalogers combine the *authorized access point* for the creator that has principal responsibility for a work with the *preferred title of the work*. Together, these two components create a name/title access point to name a work. It is identical to the format of the two psychology examples used above.

Added entries were equivalent to other access points included in a metadata description. These might be access points associated with secondary or later-named creators. Or they might be for contributors or for any other PFCs associated with a work, expression, manifestation, or item. Added entries also included variant, series, and related work titles.

Another phrase that has changed with RDA is that of *uniform title*. A *uniform title* was a title chosen for cataloging purposes when a work has appeared under varying titles or in more than one form; it allows for the gathering together of all manifestations of a work, no matter what title proper was used. A *uniform title* was also used to distinguish between and among different works that have the same title. In RDA, the same function is fulfilled by the *preferred title of a work*, along with any differentiating information necessary such as the primary creator's authorized access point, dates of creation, form of work, place of origin, and so on. An example is *Hamlet* by William Shakespeare, which might be known as: *Hamlet; Hamlet, Prince of Denmark; The Tragical History of Hamlet, Prince of Denmark; Tywysog Denmarc; Tragedien om Hamlet, prins av Danmark*; and other titles. All these resources are brought together in the catalog under a single preferred title, *Hamlet*, which when combined with the authorized access point for Shakespeare provides a standard citation for the work: **Shakespeare, William, 1564-1616. Hamlet**. The resulting name/title access point is similar to what is discussed in a previous paragraph about *main entry*, but this is with a standardized/controlled title, not a transcribed title proper.

Some uniform titles in AACR2 were collective titles referring to the form of the work. They were used to collocate publications of a creator containing several works or extracts of works. For example, *The Complete Plays of William Shakespeare* would receive the uniform title *Plays* to create this access point: **Shakespeare, William, 1564-1616. Plays**. This function is also present in RDA, but it is referred to as a *conventional collective title*, not as a *uniform title*.

One feature of authority control is the presence of *references*—that is, pointers or directions from one access point to another (e.g., a link redirecting the user from Richard Melville Hall to **Moby** instead, because only the pseudonym *Moby* is used in the catalog). In AACR2, catalogers created *see* and *see also* references in authority data. A *see reference* pointed from an unauthorized name or term to one that was authorized for use (e.g., the Moby example). In the language of RDA, these are references from a *variant access point* to an *authorized access point*. A *see also reference* pointed from one authorized name heading or term to a related authorized name heading or term. For example, when searching for **Scamander, Newt** in the catalog, there is generally a note that says *See also* **Rowling, J. K.**, because the names are related. Using the terminology of RDA, this *see also reference* reflects a relationship between two different entities.

Differences in terminology are addressed occasionally in other places throughout this text. This list is not meant to be comprehensive, but illustrative of some of the major changes. As new terms are encountered (or, in some cases, older terms), please check the glossary of this text as well as the glossary provided in *The Organization of Information* by Arlene G. Taylor and Daniel N. Joudrey for more information.[15]

FEATURES OF RDA

In this section of the text, several features of RDA are discussed. These features include core elements, examples, exceptions, alternatives, and options. These features assist catalogers in understanding not only what is mandatory (if applicable), but also what is possible. Policy statements, which are created by specific institutions and organizations—such as the Library of Congress (LC), the National Library of Australia (NLA), the British Library (BL), the Music Library Association (MLA), and the Deutsche Nationalbibliothek, which has created policy statements for German-speaking countries

(*Anwendungsrichtlinien für den deutschsprachigen Raum* [DA-CH AWR])—are examined first because some of the features that are discussed later refer to policy statements.

Policy Statements

Policy statements (referred to as *best practices* by some organizations) are supplemental guidelines that clarify, explain, or interpret the instructions in RDA. They assist in matters such as how to consistently apply options, what information may be omitted from certain elements, and how to follow exceptions to policy. They also describe a particular institution's approach to core elements and how the catalogers at that institution have implemented particular guidelines. They describe best practices and policy decisions. In some cases, they might also provide examples that demonstrate how the metadata is recorded in MARC or how it is displayed using the punctuation conventions in ISBD.

The Library of Congress–Program for Cooperative Cataloging Policy Statements (LC-PCC PS or LC-PCC PSs when referring to more than one statement), provided by LC's Policy and Standards Division (PSD) and the Program for Cooperative Cataloging (PCC), clarify how catalogers, who follow the policy statements, are expected to approach certain RDA instructions that may be unclear, complex, or in need of consistent application. The LC-PCC PSs replace the Library of Congress Rule Interpretations (LCRIs), which performed the same function for AACR2. Not every instruction in RDA has an LC-PCC PS; that does not mean, however, that those instructions are abundantly clear. If an LC-PCC PS has not been provided, catalogers must rely on their own judgment or on a local policy if it has been established. In cases in which LC and the PCC disagree, have different priorities, or require different activities, there may be two separate policy statements for the same instruction with labels indicating which institution is responsible for which policy statement (e.g., *LC Practice:* or *PCC Practice:* or *LC/PCC Practice:*). The LC-PCC, BL, and NLA policy statements, as well as the "Application Guidelines for German-speaking Countries" (DA-CH AWR) and MLA's "Best Practices for Music Cataloging Using RDA and MARC21" can be accessed through the RDA Toolkit without a subscription.[16] Policy statements of other national libraries might be added to the Toolkit in the future as they are developed and become available.

Core Elements

As mentioned above, *core elements* are a new feature of RDA. Part of the purpose of restructuring the content standard was to add a formal metadata element set, which then allowed for certain metadata elements to be identified as *required* in the cataloging process. The core elements identified in RDA (*RDA Core*), however, define only the bare minimum of acceptable cataloging. The core comprises elements that fulfill the user tasks of find, identify, and select. It should be noted: "Only one instance of a core element is required. Subsequent instances are optional."[17] If all the core elements (that are applicable) are recorded and a resource is still indistinguishable from another resource(s), then additional metadata is necessary. Additional metadata elements, beyond the core, are included based on the necessity for differentiation, policy statements, cataloger's judgment, and/or local institutional policies.

Some of the elements identified as *Core* are always core, but others may be conditionally core (i.e., Core, *if* applicable; Core, *if* available). In addition, individual libraries may choose to expand on the core elements by requiring supplementary data elements that the institution deems important. Or they may leave the decision to include additional data to the individual cataloger. To ensure consistency, any local policies or exceptions to policies should be well documented and accessible. This is the approach taken by the Library of Congress and the PCC. In their policy statements, they identify additional elements as core for their catalogers (i.e., *LC Core* or *LC-PCC Core*). These additional core requirements include approximately 50 additional elements beyond RDA Core. Many libraries, which in the past were accustomed to following the LCRIs, may again choose to follow the LC-PCC PSs rather than creating their own local policy handbook. For some libraries, it is easier to follow LC's practices wholesale than to establish their own local interpretations of the guidelines or to leave it to an individual cataloger's judgment.

Even including RDA Core, Core-if, LC Core, and LC-PCC Core elements, the amount of metadata ultimately recorded in the description may seem somewhat slight. That is because instructions or policy statements may limit the number of values to be entered into any particular metadata element. For example, for the core element *Place of Publication* the RDA instruction states: "If more than one place of publication appears on the source of information, only the first recorded is required."[18] All catalogers should remember that *core* equals *minimal-level cataloging.* Catalogers should make reasonable and justifiable decisions about what additional elements or multiple values of a single element are necessary to make the catalog record understandable and the cataloged resource findable, rather than thoughtlessly following a set of rules or another organization's standard practices.

Core elements are identified in two ways in RDA. The first is that all core elements are listed together at RDA 0.6: Core Elements. They are also identified individually throughout the text of RDA by the *CORE ELEMENT* label, which in the RDA Toolkit is light blue. For example, the display in RDA looks similar to this:

2.3. Title

CORE ELEMENT

The title proper is a core element. Other titles are optional.

An excerpt of the core elements—the 19 core elements in RDA section 1: Recording Attributes of Manifestation and Item—is provided in Table 4.2. Of these, some are format-specific, and some are conditionally core.

TABLE 4.2 RDA Core Elements for Manifestations and Items.

Data type	Core elements for RDA section 1
Title	2.3.2 Title proper
Statement of responsibility	2.4.2 Statement of responsibility relating to title proper (if more than one, only the first recorded is required)
Edition statement	2.5.2 Designation of edition 2.5.6 Designation of a named revision of an edition
Numbering of serials	2.6.2 Numeric and/or alphabetic designation of first issue or part of sequence (for first or only sequence) 2.6.3 Chronological designation of first issue or part of sequence (for first or only sequence) 2.6.4 Numeric and/or alphabetic designation of last issue or part of sequence (for last or only sequence) 2.6.5 Chronological designation of last issue or part of sequence (for last or only sequence)
Production statement	2.7.6 Date of production (for a resource in an unpublished form)
Publication statement	2.8.2 Place of publication (if more than one, only the first recorded is required) 2.8.4 Publisher's name (if more than one, only the first recorded is required) 2.8.6 Date of publication
Series statement	2.12.2 Title proper of series 2.12.9 Numbering within series 2.12.10 Title proper of subseries 2.12.17 Numbering within subseries
Identifier for the manifestation	2.15 Identifier for the manifestation (if more than one, prefer an internationally recognized identifier if applicable)
Carrier type	3.3 Carrier type
Extent	3.4 Extent (only if the resource is complete or if the total extent is known)

Section 2 of RDA, which focuses on works and expressions, has 16 core elements (some of which are format specific and some of which are conditionally core). Other sections of RDA have various numbers of core elements: Section 3 has 31 core elements; sections 5 and 6 have two each; section 7 has one; and

TABLE 4.3 LC Core Elements for Manifestations and Items.

Data type	LC Core elements for RDA section 1 (*in addition* to RDA Core)
Title	2.3.2 Parallel title proper 2.3.4 Other title information 2.3.7 Earlier title proper 2.3.8 Later title proper 2.3.9 Key title 2.3.10 Abbreviated title
Series Statement	2.12.8 ISSN of series 2.12.16 ISSN of subseries
Mode of Issuance	2.13 Mode of Issuance
Frequency	2.14 Frequency
Notes	2.17.2 Note on title
	2.17.13 Note on issue, part, or iteration used as the basis for identification of the resource
Carriers	3.2 Media type 3.5 Dimensions 3.11 Layout 3.19 Digital file characteristic 3.21.4 Note on changes in carrier characteristics
Acquisition/Access	4.5 Restrictions on use 4.6 Uniform Resource Locator

sections 4, 8, 9, and 10 have none at this time. In each section containing core elements, some of these elements are conditionally core. The full lists of core elements for these sections can be viewed at RDA 0.6.5 to 0.6.12. For more information about the organization of RDA see the structural overview later in this chapter.

A list of the 19 LC Core elements for RDA section 1—current as of April 2015—is provided in Table 4.3. LC and PCC libraries use these elements to supplement the 19 RDA Core elements in the same section. The LC Core elements can be found by perusing the individual LC-PCC PSs, or the full list can be found in a document at the LC Acquisitions and Bibliographic Access (ABA) website along with other cataloging documentation from the Library of Congress.[19]

Examples

Throughout RDA numerous examples are provided to illustrate how instructions are generally applied. Most examples do not contain MARC encoding, ISBD punctuation, or additional data elements; they are presented in isolation

---

2.3.1.6 Introductory Words, etc.

Do not transcribe words that serve as an introduction and are not intended to be part of the title.

> **EXAMPLE**
>
> Sleeping Beauty
>
> Source of information reads: Disney presents Sleeping Beauty
>
> Selections from The desert song
>
> Source of information reads: Decca Records presents selections from The desert song

---

FIGURE 4.1 An Example of RDA Examples.

(i.e., they illustrate the data created using *only* that instruction). The examples are not meant to be comprehensive; they are illustrative, not restrictive or prescriptive. Some examples include additional information that provides context, as can be seen in Figure 4.1. In these examples, RDA clarifies exactly what appears on the actual resources.[20]

The examples in RDA stand out from the rest of the text because they are placed within textboxes throughout the content standard. In the RDA Toolkit, these textboxes have a yellow background.

Alternatives, Options, and Exceptions

Within the text of RDA there are guidelines that are marked as *alternatives*, *options*, and *exceptions*. Each of these is clearly identified by an italicized label, which in the RDA Toolkit is colored green. In the Toolkit, a green vertical bar also appears in the left margin next to an alternative, optional, or exceptional instruction.

Alternatives provide another approach to what is specified in the immediately preceding instruction. For example, at RDA 7.15.1.3: Recording Illustrative Content, the general instruction states: "If the resource contains illustrative content, record *illustration* or *illustrations*, as appropriate. . . ." Immediately after a simple example, the cataloger is given an alternative way to approach recording a statement of illustration.[21] This is illustrated in Figure 4.2.

Observe in Figure 4.2 that immediately after the label *Alternative* there are icons in the RDA Toolkit that link to various policy statements. Clicking a link takes the cataloger to the institution's corresponding policy statement for that rule. The LC-PCC PS states: "*LC practice for Alternative*: Generally do not record the type of illustrative content in place of or in addition to the term *illustration* or *illustrations*."[22] Note that this is a policy statement only for the Library of Congress; there is no PCC practice listed. The alternative

Alternative LC-PCC PS   NLA PS   BL PS   MLA   D-A-CH

Record the type of illustrative content in place of or in addition to the term *illustration* or *illustrations* if considered important for identification or selection. Use one or more appropriate terms from the following list:

charts
coats of arms
facsimiles
forms
genealogical tables
graphs
illuminations
maps
music
photographs
plans
portraits
samples

EXAMPLE

coats of arms
facsimiles
portraits

Resource contains all three types of illustrative content

If none of the terms in the list is appropriate or sufficiently specific, record details of illustrative content (see 7.15.1.4).

FIGURE 4.2 An Alternative Instruction in RDA.

instruction in RDA and the list of potential values are followed by an example illustrating the alternative approach.

Options appear in two forms in RDA: *Optional additions* and *Optional omissions*. The purpose of the first is to supplement what is required in the immediately preceding instruction with additional metadata. For example, following the instruction at RDA 7.15.1.3: Recording Illustrative Content, one finds the optional addition seen in Figure 4.3.[23] Although there is no LC-PCC PS, the NLA PS states: "Apply if considered important for identification or selection."[24] The BL PS states: "Cataloguer's judgement. Exception for Early Printed Resources: Apply the optional addition."[25] The German PS states: "Das Anwenden der optionalen Ergänzung liegt in Ihrem Ermessen," which roughly translates to "Applying the optional addition is at your discretion."[26]

Optional omissions indicate that certain metadata may be excluded from what is applicable to the immediately preceding instruction. For example, the instruction at RDA 2.4.1.5: Statement Naming More Than One Person, etc., says, "Record a statement of responsibility naming more than one person, family, or corporate body as a single statement whether those persons, etc., perform the same function or different functions."[27] After several examples, one finds the optional omission illustrated in Figure 4.4.[28]

Optional Addition NLA PS BL PS D-A-CH

Record the number of illustrations if the number can be readily ascertained (e.g., when the illustrations are numbered).

EXAMPLE

48 illustrations

100 maps

1 form
2 maps
10 photographs
15 plans
Resource contains all four types of illustrations with numbers stated

FIGURE 4.3 An Optional Addition in RDA.

Optional Omission LC-PCC PS NLA PS BL PS MLA D-A-CH

If a single statement of responsibility names more than three persons, families, or corporate bodies performing the same function (or with the same degree of responsibility), omit any but the first of each group of such persons, families, or bodies. Indicate the omission by summarizing what has been omitted in a language and script preferred by the agency preparing the description. Indicate that the summary was taken from a source outside the resource itself (see 2.2.4).

EXAMPLE

Roger Colbourne [and six others]

Source of information reads: Roger Colbourne, Suzanne Bassett, Tony Billing, Helen McCormick, John McLennan, Andrew Nelson and Hugh Robertson

by Raymond Queneau, Jacques Jouet [and 4 others]

Source of information reads: by Raymond Queneau, Italo Calvino, Paul Fournel, Jacques Jouet, Claude Berge & Harry Mathews

FIGURE 4.4 An Optional Omission in RDA.

The LC-PCC PS states: "*LC practice/PCC practice for Optional omission*: Generally do not omit names in a statement of responsibility."[29]

Unlike alternatives and options, *exceptions* are not subordinate to general instructions. An exception, which applies to a specific resource type or to a particular situation, is an instruction that takes precedence over the immediately

---

Exception

If there is reason to believe that an earlier name will persist as the name by which the person is better known, choose that name as the preferred name.

> **EXAMPLE**
>
> Benjamin Disraeli
> *not* Benjamin Disraeli, Earl of Beaconsfield
> Title acquired late in life; better known by earlier name
>
> Caroline Kennedy
> *not* Caroline Kennedy Schlossberg
> Better known by name before marriage

FIGURE 4.5 An Exception in RDA.

preceding instruction. If the condition or format type applies to the resource in hand, then the exception is applied rather than the general guideline. For example, at 9.2.2.7 it states: "If a person has changed his or her name, choose the latest name or form of name as the preferred name. . . ." Immediately after the examples, one sees the exception shown in Figure 4.5.[30]

Libraries and other metadata-generating institutions faced with alternatives and options have choices before them. To handle them, they may choose one or more of the following approaches:

- Create local policies for all options and alternatives.
- Create local policies for some, but not all, options and alternatives.
- Follow the policy statements of others, such as the LC-PCC PSs, if they are available.
- Relinquish responsibility for the decisions to the individual catalogers who are creating the metadata.

Because of their general reason for existence, RDA exceptions often do not necessitate policy statements, although some exceptional situations may require some additional clarification.

RDA INTRODUCTION

Purpose and Scope

RDA provides a set of guidelines to describe and to provide access to information resources of any type collected by libraries and other information institutions. Per RDA 0.0: Purpose and Scope, these instructions have been designed to create data that supports the user tasks described in FRBR and FRAD (see chapter 3 of this text for discussions of the user tasks). As stated earlier, FRBR and FRAD are two of the conceptual underpinnings for RDA, but not everything in these conceptual models has been included in RDA.

TABLE 4.4 The FRBR and FRAD User Tasks in RDA.

FRBR	FRAD	FRAD (in RDA)
find	find	find
identify	identify	identify
select	contextualize	clarify
obtain	justify	understand

For example, the attributes associated with the specific FRAD entities *name*, *identifier, controlled access point*, and *rules* are "covered selectively." FRAD's "attributes and relationships associated with the entities *concept, object*, and *event* . . . [and its] relationships between *controlled access points*" are currently considered "out of scope."[31]

In looking at the user tasks presented in RDA (see Table 4.4), it should be noted that those identified for FRAD do not represent exactly the user tasks found in IFLA's FRAD conceptual model. The RDA versions of the FRAD user tasks are variations on the same ideas. In the actual FRAD report, the final two user tasks are defined as follows:

- **Contextualize**: to place a person, corporate body, work, etc., in context; clarify the relationship between two or more persons, corporate bodies, works, etc.; or clarify the relationship between a person, corporate body, etc., and a name by which that person, corporate body, etc., is known (e.g., name used in religion versus secular name).

- **Justify**: to document the authority data creator's reason for choosing the name or form of name on which a controlled access point is based.[32]

RDA replaces the terms *contextualize* and *justify* with the somewhat more prosaic *clarify* and *understand*, and simplifies their definitions:

- **Clarify**: to clarify the relationship between two or more such entities, or to clarify the relationship between the entity described and a name by which that entity is known

- **Understand**: to understand why a particular name or title, or form of name or title, has been chosen as the preferred name or title for the entity[33]

Although the basic meaning of *contextualize/clarify* has not changed dramatically, the language used in RDA is cleaner. The transition from *justify* to *understand*, however, is greater. The basic idea has transformed from one of simply providing documentation of choices made during the authority control process to a broader goal of comprehending why a name has been chosen, which may or may not occur through that documentation.

One other thing to note about RDA 0.0: Purpose and Scope is the presence of the very first LC-PCC PS. It addresses what is referred to as *pre-cataloging decisions*. These are addressed later in this chapter.

Implementation Scenarios

It is stated in RDA 0.1: Key Features that "RDA is designed to take advantage of the efficiencies and flexibility in data capture, storage, retrieval, and display made possible with new database technologies. RDA is also designed to be compatible with the legacy technologies still used in many resource discovery applications."[34] This statement is most notable not for its content, which has been stated in other places, but for its footnote. Its footnote refers to a document that is not mentioned elsewhere in RDA, but is an important piece of RDA history that explains the thinking behind the development of the content standard and its creators' hopes for future implementations. This foundational document, "RDA Database Implementation Scenarios," by Tom Delsey (former editor of RDA), outlines how RDA metadata content can be implemented in three different ways.[35] It provides an overview of how it can be implemented in a low technology environment as well as in the typical online catalog environment of today. But first it offers a vision of an implementation scenario that utilizes technologies not currently employed in library catalogs.

In the first scenario, addressing future implementations, Delsey describes how RDA data could be "stored in a relational or object-oriented database structure that mirrors the FRBR and FRAD conceptual models."[36] In other words, each entity type in FRBR and FRAD (WEMI, PFC, and COPE, as identified in chapter 3) could have their own records and the relationships between entities would be reflected in links. For example, the record for George R. R. Martin (a person record) would be linked to the work record for *A Dance with Dragons*. The work record would in turn be linked to various expression records for *A Dance with Dragons* (e.g., for translations in Bulgarian, Catalan, etc., and for formats, such as text, audiobook, e-book, etc.). Manifestation records, for each individual resource (e.g., the Bantam publication, the Harper Voyager publication, the Random House Audio sound recording, etc.) would be linked to a work record and appropriate expression records. After just a few years, this scenario already seems somewhat dated considering that discussions of the future of bibliographic data tend to eschew approaches based on record structures in favor of a vision based on individual metadata statements formatted as linked data on the web. Of course, that vision may *also* evolve rapidly into something else as the profession and its technology advance.

The second implementation scenario reflects a linked record structure—basically what occurs in most contemporary catalogs today. Authority records are created to describe creators, contributors, series, subjects, and preferred titles of works. Bibliographic records are created containing descriptive metadata elements related to manifestations and items, as well as authorized access points for works, expressions, persons, corporate bodies, families, and subjects. There are links, in many ILS systems, between bibliographic records and authority records. The mixture of bibliographic and authority-controlled data about the various FRBR entities, all within a single somewhat simple record structure, is often confusing to new catalogers. It does not reflect the benefits of using the RDA/FRBR approach to metadata. If all the metadata is comingled in one record, some might ask, "Why bother to distinguish the different FRBR entities at all?" The answer is that it is for the future. The profession has hopes that as information and communication technology progresses it will allow for greater machine processing of the data. In the future, catalogs (or whatever replaces them) may be able to take greater advantage of the more granular data and the links beginning to be produced today. However, in this period of transition, when systems, data, instructions, and personnel are at various levels of development simultaneously, it can seem as if progress is non-existent rather than just slow.

The third implementation scenario is the simplest. It is a flat-file database structure. It is best represented by the card catalog, where metadata resides in two distinct files (the bibliographic and authority files), between which there is no interaction (i.e., they are not linked). This approach, though dated, is still valid. It can be easy to forget that some institutions, or some collections within institutions, still use card catalogs to manage their bibliographic data, or that some online catalogs are still somewhat unsophisticated and lack internal links between the files.

Objectives and Principles Governing RDA

RDA 0.4 states that four objectives guided the development of the new content standard: (1) responsiveness to user needs, (2) cost efficiency, (3) flexibility, and (4) continuity. They are based, in part, on ICP, FRBR, and FRAD. The first objective, *responsiveness to user needs*, reflects more explicit versions of the user tasks found in FRBR and FRAD.[37] It states that the metadata created using RDA should enable users to accomplish 15 specific tasks. The following list is adapted from RDA 0.4.2.1:[38]

1. *Find* resources based on a user's search criteria.

2. *Find* all resources that reflect a specific work/expression.

3. *Find* all resources linked to a specific PFC.

4. *Find* all resources on a specific subject.

5. *Find* related WEMI entities.

6. *Find* PFCs based on a user's search criteria.

7. *Find* PFCs related to the PFC retrieved based on a user's search criteria.

8. *Identify* the resource described (i.e., confirm it is the resource sought, or distinguish it from others with similar characteristics).

9. *Identify* the PFC represented by the data (i.e., confirm that it is the PFC sought, or distinguish it from entities with similar names and other characteristics).

10. *Select* the physical form/electronic formatting and encoding of the resource based on a user's needs.

11. *Select* a resource based on a user's needs with respect to content, form, audience, language, and so on.

12. *Obtain* a resource through electronic or physical means (e.g., purchase, loan, an online connection, etc.).

13. *Understand* the relationship between or among two or more entities.

14. *Understand* the relationship between the entity and a name used by that entity.

15. *Understand* why a name or title has been chosen to be used for the entity.

The second objective, *cost efficiency*, is equivalent to the ICP's *economy* principle (discussed in chapter 3 of this text). *Flexibility*, the third objective, states that data should be format-neutral and usable in a variety of environments. The fourth objective, *continuity*, states that the data should be backward-compatible and should easily integrate with records created using AACR2.

These four objectives are followed by eight principles,[39] which are based, in part, on IFLA's *Statement of International Cataloguing Principles.*[40] Numbers 2, 4, 5, and 7 below have equivalent principles listed in the ICP (see chapter 3 in this text):

1. **Differentiation**: the metadata created for an entity should be sufficient to distinguish it from other similarly identified entities (e.g., differentiating Plotnik's *Introduction to Psychology* from Kalat's).

2. **Sufficiency**: the metadata created should be enough to support the user tasks.

3. **Relationships**: significant connections among and between entities should be identified through the metadata.

4. **Representation**: names and resource descriptions should reflect the ways that entities (resources, creators, etc.) represent themselves; involves significant transcription of data directly from resources.

5. **Accuracy**: the metadata created should authentically depict resources or the names associated with resources as they are; the cataloger should provide "supplementary information to correct or clarify ambiguous, unintelligible, or misleading representations."[41]

6. **Attribution**: the roles and relationships among PFCs and resources should reflect the designation of responsibilities identified in resources for each entity.

7. **Common Usage or Practice**: terminology used when describing information resources should align itself with the vocabulary of the majority of the users.

8. **Uniformity**: "The appendices on capitalization, abbreviations, order of elements, punctuation, etc., should serve to promote uniformity in the presentation of data describing a resource or an entity associated with a resource."[42]

Structural Overview

Unlike the previous content standard, AACR2, which was structured around resource types, RDA uses the FRBR entities (WEMI, PFC, COPE) as the foundation for its arrangement. RDA is divided into 10 sections, with sections 1-4 focusing on the attributes defined in FRBR and FRAD for the entities and with sections 5-10 focusing on their relationships. Each RDA section begins with a general chapter providing guidelines for recording the type of information discussed in that section, followed by specific chapters for the major entities within it. Each of the general-guideline chapters contains a set of similar features to set the stage for the rest of the chapters in the section (e.g., scope, terminology). The individual chapters in each section of RDA also begin with a similar structure (e.g., purpose and scope, general guidelines) before diverging into their entity-specific content. Because the content is not meant to be read in a linear fashion, a certain amount of repetition is found in the RDA chapters—in structure, if not exactly in content.

Describing Entities

Section 1 of RDA focuses on the attributes of manifestations and items that are used to identify an information resource. It includes separate chapters on carriers and the attributes used for acquisition or access. This section includes four chapters:

Section 1: Recording Attributes of Manifestation & Item

1: General Guidelines on Recording Attributes of Manifestations and Items

Summary: This chapter provides background information on how to record metadata about manifestations and items. It discusses terminology used in the section; the objectives and principles applicable to manifestations and items; core elements; a list of section 1 elements that are to be recorded in the language and script found in the resource; the three types of descriptions possible (comprehensive, analytical, and hierarchical); a list of circumstances that result in requiring a new metadata description (related to serials, multipart monographs, and integrating resources); transcription issues (including capitalization, punctuation, diacritical marks, symbols, spacing, abbreviations, and inaccuracies); how to record numbers, dates, and notes; and a brief statement on the approach to facsimiles and reproductions.

2: Identifying Manifestations and Items

Purpose: to help users to find and identify resources

Summary: This chapter provides instructions on how to record the attributes of manifestations and items. Similar to the approach taken in AACR2 before it, the RDA cataloging process starts with the manifestation (as represented by a particular item). It begins with general information about the differences between resources issued as a single unit (e.g., monographs), resources issued in more than one part (e.g., serials, multipart monographs), and integrating resources (e.g., some loose-leaf publications). It is followed by a discussion of sources of information and then by instructions addressing individual metadata elements and their sub-elements.

Instructions/Elements: [To give the reader an idea of the kinds of elements included in each of the RDA chapters, the element numbers and identifying captions are listed here for RDA chapter 2. The descriptions for the remaining RDA sections and chapters outlined below do not list the elements, as the numbers and captions carry little meaning until the content of each guideline can be read in context. Major elements for all RDA chapters are listed in appendix A of this text.]

   2.3 Title, including many sub-elements such as Title Proper, Parallel Title, Other Title Information, Parallel Other Title Information, Variant Title, Earlier Title Proper, Later Title Proper, Key Title, and Abbreviated Title

   2.4 Statement of Responsibility

   2.5 Edition Statement

   2.6 Numbering of Serials

   2.7 Production Statement

   2.8 Publication Statement

   2.9 Distribution Statement

   2.10 Manufacture Statement

   2.11 Copyright Date

   2.12 Series Statement

   2.13 Mode of Issuance

   2.14 Frequency

   2.15 Identifier for the Manifestation

   2.16 Preferred Citation

   2.17 Note on Manifestation

   2.18 Custodial History of Item

   2.19 Immediate Source of Acquisition of Item

   2.20 Identifier for the Item

   2.21 Note on Item

3: Describing Carriers

Purpose: to help users to select appropriate resources based on physical description and format

Summary: This chapter provides instructions on how to record the attributes of the resource's carrier. This chapter addresses physical characteristics and the formatting/encoding of the information held within the carrier.

4: Providing Acquisition and Access Information

Purpose: to help users to obtain resources

Summary: This chapter provides a few instructions on how to record attributes that are used to support acquisition and access, among which are instructions for providing URLs.

Section 2 concentrates on the attributes of works and expressions (including a separate chapter on the content of the resource). Although much of the metadata created using these chapters will appear in bibliographic records (as data elements or as access points), some of the metadata will be entered into authority records for works and expressions.

Section 2: Recording Attributes of Work & Expression

5: General Guidelines on Recording Attributes of Works and Expressions

Summary: This chapter provides background information on how to record metadata about works and expressions. It discusses terminology used in the section; the objectives and principles applicable to works and expressions; core elements; a note that titles of works are to be recorded in the language and script as found in the resource; and an overview of the creation of authorized and variant access points representing works and expressions, status of authority data, sources consulted, and cataloger's notes.

6: Identifying Works and Expressions

Purpose: to help users to find and identify the works and expressions contained within resources

Summary: This chapter provides instructions on how to choose and record the preferred title of works and expressions, choose and record variant titles, record other attributes of works and expressions, and construct access points for works and expressions. In addition, the chapter addresses four forms of material that require special attention (official communications and musical, legal, and religious works).

7: Describing Content

Purpose: to help users to select resources based on the content within them

Summary: This chapter provides instructions on how to record the attributes of works and expressions that are related to the content of a resource. This chapter does *not* address issues of subject access.

At the end of RDA chapter 6 instructions for creating access points to represent works and expressions are provided. This is a shift from the approach found in section 1, which is primarily focused on descriptive metadata elements. Of the data generated in section 2 about works and expressions, some may be used for descriptive metadata, some for authority metadata, and some for use as part of authorized access points.

Section 3 moves on to the Group 2 entities. As with section 2, this section also contains instructions that can be used to produce metadata that belongs in authority records. Some of the instructions guide catalogers in creating access points for PFCs. Authorized access points appear in individual bibliographic records in addition to appearing in authority records.

Section 3: Recording Attributes of Person, Family, & Corporate Body

8: General Guidelines on Recording Attributes of Persons, Families, and Corporate Bodies

Summary: This chapter provides background information on how to record metadata about PFCs. It discusses terminology used in the section; the objectives and principles applicable to PFCs; core elements; a note that names are to be recorded in the language and script as found in the resource; general guidelines for recording names (including a discussion of capitalization, numbers, accents and diacritical marks, hyphens, spacing, and abbreviations); an overview of the creation of authorized and variant access points representing PFCs; instructions on scope and dates of usage of names; and status of authority data, undifferentiated name indicators, sources consulted, and cataloger's notes.

9: Identifying Persons

Purpose: to help users to identify persons

Summary: This chapter provides instructions on choosing and recording preferred and variant names for persons, recording other attributes for persons, and constructing access points. It provides instructions on recording names and other attributes as separate elements (e.g., in authority records), as parts of access points (e.g., appearing in both authority records and bibliographic records), or as both. It refers the reader to appendix F for additional instructions on recording names in certain languages.

10: Identifying Families

Purpose: to help users to identify families

Summary: This chapter provides instructions on choosing and recording preferred and variant names for families, recording other attributes for families, and constructing access points. It provides instructions on recording names and other attributes as separate elements (e.g., in authority records), as parts of access points (e.g., appearing in both authority records and bibliographic records), or as both.

11: Identifying Corporate Bodies

Purpose: to help users to identify corporate bodies

Summary: This chapter provides instructions on choosing and recording preferred and variant names for corporate bodies, recording other attributes for corporate bodies, and constructing access points. It provides instructions on recording names and other attributes as separate elements (e.g., in authority records), as parts of access points (e.g., appearing in both authority records and bibliographic records), or as both. The chapter begins with a definition and some examples of corporate bodies.

Section 4 addresses Group 3 entities (i.e., subjects). Except for RDA chapter 16, at the time of this writing the chapters in this section are blank save for the statement, "To be developed after the initial release of RDA."

Section 4: Recording Attributes of Concept, Object, Event, & Place

12: General Guidelines on Recording Attributes of Concepts, Objects, Events, and Places—Currently empty.

13: Identifying Concepts—Currently empty.

14: Identifying Objects—Currently empty.

15: Identifying Events—Currently empty.

16: Identifying Places

Purpose: to help users to identify places

Summary: This chapter provides instructions on choosing and recording preferred and variant names for geographic locations, recording other attributes for places, and constructing access points. It introduces the reasons why place names are found in access points (e.g., as the name of a government, and as additions to titles of works, corporate body names, and conference names).

Describing Relationships

Starting with section 5 (Recording Primary Relationships between Work, Expression, Manifestation, & Item), RDA shifts to describing relationships. Section 5 contains only chapter 17: General Guidelines on Recording Primary Relationships. At this time, RDA chapter 17 is *not* being applied by the Library of Congress or by PCC libraries in accordance with the LC-PCC PS for RDA 17.0: Purpose and Scope. This may change in the future, but for now LC and the PCC require neither of the two core elements from this chapter—Work Manifested and Expression Manifested.

Section 6 addresses the relationships between Group 1 and Group 2 entities. In other words, it describes creator relationships, contributor relationships, and other relationships between PFCs and resources.

Section 6: Recording Relationships to Persons, Families, & Corporate Bodies

18:   General Guidelines on Recording Relationships to Persons, Families, and Corporate Bodies Associated with a Resource

Summary: This chapter provides background information on how to record relationships between PFCs and resources. It discusses terminology used in the section, the objectives and principles reflected by these relationships, core elements, the use of identifiers or authorized access points to represent relationships, and the use of relationship designators and notes to provide more details about the relationships.

19:   Persons, Families, and Corporate Bodies Associated with a Work

Purpose: to help users to find works through persons, families, or corporate bodies as creators or others associated with a work

Summary: This chapter provides instructions on recording relationships between works and PFCs (i.e., creators and others associated with a work). These may include authors, composers, compilers, and artists, as well as honorees, addressees, directors of films, sponsoring bodies, and so on.

20:   Persons, Families, and Corporate Bodies Associated with an Expression

Purpose: to help users to find expressions through persons, families, or corporate bodies as contributors

Summary: This chapter provides instructions on recording relationships between expressions and PFCs (i.e., contributors). These may include illustrators, editors, translators, musicians, actors, and other performers.

21:   Persons, Families, and Corporate Bodies Associated with a Manifestation

Purpose: to help users to find manifestations through persons, families, or corporate bodies

Summary: This chapter provides instructions on recording relationships between manifestations and PFCs (e.g., publishers, manufacturers, designers, lithographers).

22:   Persons, Families, and Corporate Bodies Associated with an Item

Purpose: to help users to find items through persons, families, or corporate bodies

Summary: This chapter provides instructions on recording relationships between items and PFCs (e.g., owners, custodians, collectors, binders).

Section 7 addresses recording relationships between works and their subjects (i.e., terms, phrases, and classification numbers that represent what the resource is about). It contains only Chapter 23: General Guidelines on Recording the Subject of a Work. This chapter briefly explains the nature of subject relationships. It allows for the description of these relationships through the use of identifiers, access points from identifiable subject systems, textual descriptions (e.g., summaries or abstracts), and relationship indicators. The chapter is painted in the very broadest of brushstrokes. This chapter, and other subject-related content in RDA, may be expanded further in the future.

Section 8 addresses recording relationships between WEMI entities. It may come as a bit of surprise, but this is the section that contains *contents notes*. Contents notes may reflect a relationship to related works, expressions, or manifestations (RDA chapters 25, 26, or 27).

Section 8: Recording Relationships between Works, Expressions, Manifestations, & Items

24: General Guidelines on Recording Relationships between Works, Expressions, Manifestations, and Items

Summary: This chapter provides background information on how to record metadata about the relationships between WEMI entities. It discusses terminology used in the section, the objectives and principles applicable to WEMI, core elements, techniques for representing these relationships (authorized access point, identifier, or description), the use of relationship designators, instructions on part numbering, sources consulted, and cataloger's notes.

25: Related Works

Purpose: to help users to find related works

Summary: This chapter provides instructions on recording relationships between works (e.g., transformations, critical works, supplements, prequels, reviews, parodies, dramatizations, paraphrases).

26: Related Expressions

Purpose: to help users to find related expressions

Summary: This chapter provides instructions on recording relationships between expressions (e.g., translations, illustrated versions, revised editions, expanded versions).

27: Related Manifestations

Purpose: to help users to find related manifestations

Summary: This chapter provides instructions on recording relationships between manifestations (e.g., electronic versions, reprints, reproductions).

28: Related Items

Purpose: to help users to find related items

Summary: This chapter provides instructions on recording relationships between items (e.g., microform versions, items bound together).

Section 9 discusses relationships among the Group 2 entities, which might include other bibliographic identities, pseudonyms, related persons, subordinate corporate bodies, and so on.

Section 9: Recording Relationships between Persons, Families, & Corporate Bodies

29: General Guidelines on Recording Relationships between Persons, Families, and Corporate Bodies

Summary: This chapter provides background information on how to record metadata about the relationships between PFC entities. It discusses terminology used in the section, the objectives and principles applicable to PFCs, core elements, techniques for representing these relationships (authorized access point or identifier), the use of relationship designators, sources consulted, and cataloger's notes.

30: Related Persons

Purpose: to help users to find related persons

Summary: This chapter provides instructions on recording relationships between persons and related PFCs (e.g., collaborators, family members, founders, separate bibliographic identities, group members).

31: Related Families

Purpose: to help users to find related families

Summary: This chapter provides instructions on recording relationships between families and related PFCs (e.g., a person's family, a family that founded a corporate body entity, descendants, progenitors).

32: Related Corporate Bodies

Purpose: to help users to find related corporate bodies

Summary: This chapter provides instructions on recording relationships between corporate bodies and related PFCs (e.g., performing groups and its members, companies that merge to form a new company).

The final section (Recording Relationships between Concepts, Objects, Events, & Places) comprises five chapters, all of which are empty save for the phrase "To be developed after the initial release of RDA."

> ### Section 10: Recording Relationships between Concepts, Objects, Events, & Places
>
> **33: General Guidelines on Recording Relationships between Concepts, Objects, Events, and Places**—Currently empty.
>
> **34: Related Concepts**—Currently empty.
>
> **35: Related Objects**—Currently empty.
>
> **36: Related Events**—Currently empty.
>
> **37: Related Places**—Currently empty.

At the time of this writing, the future of these subject chapters is unclear.

These 10 RDA sections are followed by 13 appendices labeled A-M. They contain supplementary information and instructions:

> **A: Capitalization**: capitalization rules for English and 23 other languages
>
> **B: Abbreviations**: guidelines for the limited use of abbreviations using Latin, Cyrillic, Greek, Hebrew, and Yiddish characters
>
> **C: Initial Articles**: a list of initial articles in a limited number of languages
>
> **D: Record Syntaxes for Descriptive Data**: written instructions for presenting RDA metadata with ISBD punctuation
>
> **E: Record Syntaxes for Access Point Control**: guidance in the form of mappings and written instructions for presenting RDA access points and authority data using guidelines developed in AACR2
>
> **F: Additional Instructions on Names of Persons**: detailed instructions on how to choose and record names in 10 specific languages; instructions on how to record surnames that include articles and/or prepositions in 11 specific languages
>
> **G: Titles of Nobility, Terms of Rank, etc.**: a list of titles from France, the Iban people of Borneo, Indonesia, and the United Kingdom
>
> **H: Dates in the Christian Calendar**: guidelines on recording dates in the Christian calendar—that is, the use of B.C. and A.D. (and no, it is not B.C.E. and C.E.)
>
> **I: Relationship Designators: Relationships between a Resource and Persons, Families, and Corporate Bodies Associated with the Resource**: a list of terms used as relationship designators and their definitions; focuses on the creator, contributor, and other roles in the creation, expression, production, dissemination, or ownership of a resource—for example, dedicator, defendant, degree granting institution, degree supervisor, director, and so on
>
> **J: Relationship Designators: Relationships between Works, Expressions, Manifestations, and Items**: a list of terms used

as relationship designators and their definitions; focuses on the relationships that may exist among the WEMI entities; for example, abridgement of (work), choreography for (expression), translated as, mirror site, bound with, and so on

K: Relationship Designators: Relationships between Persons, Families, and Corporate Bodies: a list of terms used as relationship designators and their definitions; focuses on the relationships that may exist among the PFC entities; for example, employee, family member, alternate identity, product of merger, descendants, and so on

L: Relationship Designators: Relationships between Concepts, Objects, Events, and Places: Not yet created; to be developed after the initial release of RDA

M: Relationship Designators: Subject Relationships: a list of terms used as relationship designators and their definitions; focuses on the relationships that may exist between subjects and the WEMI entities; for example, analyzed in (work), critique of (work), and so on

At the end of the appendices, a glossary is provided.

PRE-CATALOGING DECISIONS AND CONSIDERATIONS

As mentioned earlier, before beginning to describe a resource, a cataloger must first address several pre-cataloging issues. To describe a resource accurately and efficiently, the cataloger needs to understand what it is that is in hand. In other words, the cataloger should explore the resource and determine what exactly is being cataloged. The cataloger must ask:

- What is this resource? How is it issued? Is it one unit? Is it composed of parts?
- Is it updated? If so, how is it updated?
- Is it a new resource, a new version of an existing resource, or a new copy of a previously existing version?
- Is it a part of another resource? Is it related to another resource? Does it require a separate description?
- What parts of the resource should be examined? What attributes are important?

The answers to these questions can affect which RDA instructions are followed. Making these determinations *before* beginning the cataloging process is helpful. Questions related to the mode of issuance, bibliographic relationships, the need for a new record, the type of description required, and the examination of the resource are addressed in the remainder of this chapter.

Mode of Issuance

As mentioned in a previous section of this chapter, before one even gets to the first cataloging instruction, RDA 0.0: Purpose and Scope has an LC-PCC PS that

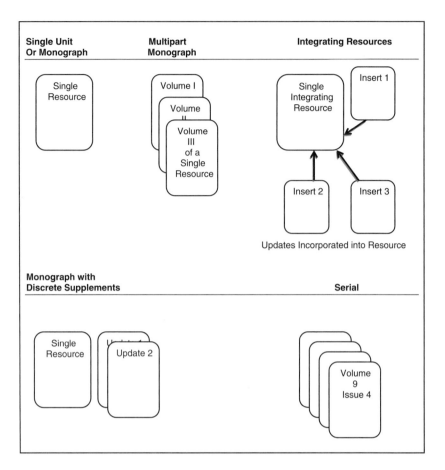

FIGURE 4.6 Modes of Issuance.

addresses some pre-cataloging decisions.[43] The first part of the policy statement addresses *mode of issuance*, "a categorization reflecting whether a resource is issued in one or more parts, the way it is updated, and its intended termination."[44] Figure 4.6 illustrates differences among the various modes of issuance.

In Figure 4.6, the following modes are illustrated:

- **Single unit**: a resource issued as a solitary component (e.g., a DVD, a book, a PDF); sometimes referred to as a *monograph* (a complete bibliographic unit or resource); note that some monographs may be updated with discrete supplements at a later time (e.g., a supplement to a genealogical work, an update to a volume of legal statutes), but these are not specifically addressed under *mode of issuance*

- **Multipart monograph**: a finite resource issued in multiple parts (e.g., a three-volume biography; a set of general encyclopedias in 24 volumes); it may be issued concurrently or in successive parts at regular or irregular intervals, but it is not intended to be continued indefinitely

- **Integrating resource**: a resource that is added to or changed by means of updates that are integrated into the whole resource (e.g., an updating loose-leaf manual, a website with content that updates occasionally or regularly)

- **Serial**: a publication (physical or electronic) that is issued in successive parts at regular or irregular intervals, usually bearing numbering and intended to continue indefinitely (e.g., a periodical, a newspaper, conference proceedings, an annual report, some monographic series)

In LC-PCC PS 0.0, there is information to help catalogers determine just what is in hand when there is uncertainty. The policy statement addresses situations such as

- **Serial versus Integrating Resource**: Is the word *edition* on the resource? Does it represent numbering or an edition statement?
- **Monograph versus Integrating Resource**: What is the likelihood of updates?
- **Monograph versus Serial**: Frequency of distribution? Is there numbering? Is there a pre-determined conclusion?
- **Other Situations Requiring Further Consideration**: These include a variety of resource types and formats:
  - Electronic resources
  - Loose-leaf documents
  - Conference proceedings
  - Supplements
  - Republications
  - Printed travel guides
  - Others
- **Changes in Cataloging Decisions—Monograph/Serial**: When should a repeatedly issued monographic resource be treated as a serial?[45]

Understanding what a resource is and how it is issued prepares the cataloger to follow the appropriate instructions in RDA and to apply exceptions when necessary. Whether a resource is a monograph, an integrating resource, a serial, or a multipart monograph changes how catalogers approach the description, the source from which the information is taken, and even how inaccuracies and typos are addressed. These categories reflecting mode of issuance are addressed primarily in RDA section 1 (i.e., attributes of manifestations and items), although they do appear sporadically in later sections of RDA. In RDA chapter 2, an element has been established to record the mode of issuance in the description.

Bibliographic Relationships

When a resource is added to the collection, another issue that must be addressed is whether (1) the resource is a new work, (2) the resource is a new version of a previously issued resource, or (3) the resource is a new copy or reissue of a previously cataloged resource. In other words, the cataloger must consider whether there are bibliographic relationships to be addressed and whether a new record is needed. It is recommended that the reader, before proceeding further, review the flowchart for bibliographic relationships (see Table 3.1), along with its accompanying discussion.

The cataloger must consider whether the resource to be cataloged is a new work. Another consideration is determining whether this work is related to other works. To find out, catalogers may consult a variety of resources, including their own local catalogs, but because institutions do not collect every resource on a topic or every resource by an author, the cataloger should also consult a bibliographic network, such as OCLC or SkyRiver; a catalog of a national library, such as LC's catalog; or some other bibliographic tool. In these retrieval tools, catalogers may wish to search for the title and the creator. Below are some questions that should be asked while examining the search results:

1. **Title**: Are there other resources with the same title? Are they by the same creator? Are they disseminated by the same publisher? Are they part of the same series? Do they contain the same work? Do they contain a new expression of the work? Are there earlier editions? Are there records for the same edition? Is the title similar to the titles of other works? Are there related works (e.g., supplements, sequels, transformations)? Remember, titles do not always remain unchanged, nor are titles proper always unique!

2. **Creator**: Has the creator produced other works? Are these works similar or related to the resource in hand? Are there resources that appear to be the same work but that have another title? Has the creator worked with others? Have these other creators or contributors produced similar or related works? Are any of these resources earlier editions of the same work?

The cataloger certainly wants to determine whether this is a new work, but it is also helpful to do a little detective work to find out whether there are any other bibliographic relationships about which the cataloger and the users should be aware. It is important to understand a resource's place in the bibliographic universe and to get a sense of what relationships might exist (i.e., whether the resource is part of a bibliographic family). This allows the cataloger to make as many connections to other related resources as needed. If the resource is examined, considered, and described in isolation, important links to other resources may be omitted.

If, in this process, it is learned that previously published resources containing the same work exist (whether it is the same or a different expression), the cataloger must then determine whether a new record is needed. LC-PCC PS 0.0 starts the discussion with determining whether a resource is a new edition or a new copy/reprint of an edition already in existence. The information is summarized and enhanced in Table 4.5.

The LC-PCC PS goes on to address other circumstances that may or may not require a new record, including sections on supplementary materials, serial supplements to other serials, indexes to serials, serial cumulations, serials

TABLE 4.5 Determining Whether a New Description is Needed.

If the resource is ...	Then ...	
a new work (e.g., completely original content, criticism, an adaptation of a work)	a new description is needed, and	if the work is related to another work, then a link to/access point for the related work should be considered.
an existing work, but with a new expression (e.g., a new edition, changed content, a translation)	a new description is needed, and	if the expression is related to another, then a link to/access point for the related expression or work should be considered. A link to/access point for an earlier edition should also be considered.

an existing work with an existing expression (a new printing, no real changes in the content, a reproduction)	a new description is *not* needed, if	• the resource is a
		  ○ copy
		  ○ reproduction
		  ○ facsimile
		  ○ reissue
		  ○ reprint
		• there are only minor changes, such as
		  ○ a difference in printing or copyright dates when there is a publication date
		  ○ a minor variation in a publisher name
		  ○ an addition, deletion, or change of an ISBN
		  ○ a difference in binding, and so on

an existing work, but it is unclear whether or not it is a new expression (e.g., a publication with no indication of changes or updates)	a new description is needed, if	there are explicit changes in • title • edition statement • publication information • carrier description (extent, illustrative content, dimensions, etc.) • series

issued in parts, reprinted issues of non-newspaper serials, newspapers, and loose-leaf services. These sections of the LC-PCC PS should be consulted as needed.

In RDA 1.6: Changes Requiring a New Description, situations in which new descriptions may be needed are addressed (e.g., changes in a resource's mode of issuance, changes in title proper). These are listed in Table 4.6.

TABLE 4.6 Circumstances Requiring a New Description.

If the resource is ...	And the change is related to ...	Then ...
a multi-part monograph	mode of issuance (i.e., resource changes to a serial or an integrating resource)	create a new description
	media type (e.g., resource changes from a projected medium to a computer medium)	create a new description
a serial	mode of issuance (i.e., resource changes to a multipart monograph or an integrating resource)	create a new description
	media type (e.g., resource changes from unmediated to a computer medium)	create a new description
	carrier type (e.g., changes to/from online resource from/to another computer carrier)	create a new description
	the title proper, and it is a *major* change, such as	create a new description
	1) a change in the first five non-article words,	
	2) a change that affects the title's meaning or indicates a change of topic, or	
	3) the name of a corporate body in the title changes	
	the title proper, and it is a *minor* change (as listed in RDA 2.3.2.13)	**do not** create a new description
	responsibility for the serial that changes its identification as a work	create a new description
	the edition statement indicating a significant change to the scope or coverage of a serial	create a new description
an integrating resource	mode of issuance (i.e., changes to a multipart monograph or a serial)	create a new description
	media type (e.g., unmediated to a computer medium)	create a new description
	base volume (e.g., if an updating loose-leaf resource starts over with new base volumes)	create a new description
	the edition statement indicating a significant change to the scope or coverage of a serial	create a new description

Types of Description

After determining mode of issuance, exploring bibliographic relationships, and establishing whether a new description is needed, the cataloger should determine the type of description required. In RDA 1.5: Type of Description, the content standard enumerates three different approaches that may be taken: *comprehensive, analytical,* and *hierarchical* descriptions.

A *comprehensive description* is a description of a resource as a whole. It can be used to describe single units (e.g., a DVD, a PDF), multipart monographs (e.g., a three-volume biography; a set of 24 general encyclopedias), serials (e.g., periodicals, newspapers, proceedings), integrating resources (e.g., updating loose-leaf materials, updating websites), and collections of "two or more units assembled by a private collector, a dealer, a library, an archive, etc."[46] (e.g., a private collection of antique bottle caps, a library's database of local digital images). If the resource being described comprehensively has individual parts, those parts may be described in the carrier description (e.g., 4 filmstrips and 1 audiocassette), as a related work (e.g., the individual short stories in a volume of collected works), or as a related manifestation (e.g., a description of each volume in a two-volume set).

An *analytical description* is a description of one part of a larger resource. It can be used to describe a part of a single unit (e.g., a single digital image from a collection of 500 images, a short story in a collection), a part of a multipart monograph (e.g., a DVD issued as part of a kit that contains a DVD, a workbook, and a set of finger puppets), a part of a serial (e.g., a conference paper in proceedings, a single volume of a series, a single issue of a periodical, an article in a magazine or online journal), a part of an integrating resource (e.g., a posting in a blog), and a "part of a collection assembled by a private collector, a dealer, a library, an archive, etc. (e.g., a set of lithographs in a collection of art prints, a digital recording of a performance in a database compiled by a repertory theatre). It is possible to prepare separate analytical descriptions for any number of parts of a larger resource (i.e., for one part only, for two or more selected parts, or for all parts of the resource)."[47] If the part is being described, the larger resource may be referred to in a series statement (i.e., the series to which the resource belongs), as a related work (e.g., the collection containing the short story), or as a related manifestation (e.g., a reference to the set containing the single volume).

A *hierarchical description* is "used to describe a resource consisting of two or more parts. It combines both a comprehensive description of the whole and analytical descriptions of one or more of the parts. If parts of the resource are further subdivided into their own parts, analytical descriptions can be created for those further subdivisions."[48] This is the equivalent of the *multilevel description* concept in ISBD.[49] The LC-PCC PS for RDA 1.5.4: Hierarchical Description states: "*LC practice for general cataloging/PCC practice*: Do not create hierarchical descriptions."[50]

Most standard cataloging entails creating a comprehensive description. For materials deemed to be of greater importance, catalogers might consider analytical descriptions for some or all parts of a larger resource (e.g., a particular document or file of items in an archival collection). Hierarchical description is rarely employed in catalogs in the United States, as the Library of Congress discourages its use in the LC-PCC PS; this continues the policy found in the LCRIs that said, "Do not employ the technique of multilevel description in any case."[51]

Technical Reading of a Resource to Be Cataloged

To identify conventional elements of an information resource so that they can be described on a catalog record or some other form of metadata, it is necessary to know not only what to look for, but also how to look. Technical reading in this manner is scarcely the same as reading for information or for entertainment when the entire resource may be read, seen, or heard. Obviously, the cataloger will have no time for reading of this sort and thus must learn to read technically. Reading technically involves recognizing certain devices peculiar to the particular type of information resource being cataloged. In this way, the cataloger can quickly determine its contents and how it can be described uniquely in such a way that this information can be passed on to potential users. The following discussion contains concepts useful to the cataloger in both descriptive cataloging and subject cataloging.

The first part of an information resource that the cataloger examines in detail is the *preferred source(s) of information* (discussed briefly above). These sources vary according to the type of material. If the first-listed preferred source of information is absent for any reason, the cataloging instructions prescribe alternate sources. The preferred sources of information are listed in RDA 2.2.2-2.2.4.

Usually the preferred source(s) of information provides the most complete bibliographic information about the resource: the fullest form of the title; the creator(s) or other person(s) responsible for the work; the name and/or number of the version; the name of the publisher, producer, manufacturer, and/or distributor; the place and date of publication, production, manufacture, and/or distribution; and other significant information. Figures 4.7 and 4.8 show examples of preferred sources of information. One is from a book (i.e., the title page); the other is from a set of stereographic discs (i.e., the View-Master reels themselves). Figure 4.9 shows the container that holds the discs.

Titles

The first element that the cataloger ordinarily notices is the title. The title from the preferred source of information (minus any subtitle or other title information) is called the *title proper*; as such, it is used in all library records, in trade catalogs, and in bibliographies. It may or may not adequately describe the contents of a resource. The book title *A Short History of the United States* is fairly self-evident, but the title of the serial, *Toward Freedom*, needs an explanation. A glance through an issue will reveal that the serial discusses the

THE ORGANIZATION OF
INFORMATION
Third Edition

Arlene G. Taylor and Daniel N. Joudrey

Library and Information Science Text Series

U N L I M I T E D
A Member of the Greenwood Publishing Group
Westport, Connecticut • London

FIGURE 4.7 An Example of a Preferred Source of Information (Book).

development of new nations; this will be indicated as a subject heading on the catalog record or in the metadata statements.

In addition to the major part of the title, some resources have additional titles. An *alternative title* is introduced by the word *or* and was widely used in manifestations published before the 20th century. As in Gilbert and Sullivan's *Patience, or, Bunthorne's Bride*, it amplifies the title by telling the reader that *Patience*, in this case, is a woman's name rather than the name of a specific virtue. A *parallel title* is the title proper of a resource repeated in another language or in another script. For instance, a bilingual book on snowmobiles in the province of Quebec has its title proper in French, *La motoneige au Québec*, and its parallel title in English, *Snowmobiling in Quebec*. Parallel titles may or may not reflect the language(s) appearing in the resource itself. For instance, *La motoneige au Québec* may be presented in both languages or it may not have a word of English in it other than the parallel title. Parallel titles are not necessarily reliable indicators of the language of the content. *Other title information* is often used to qualify the title proper. Such qualifications are often

FIGURE 4.8 An Example of a Preferred Source of Information (View-Master Reels).

called *subtitles*. For example, *Behavior Control: The Psychologist as Manipulator* is the complete title of a recorded lecture. *The Psychologist as Manipulator* is the subtitle. It explains the aspect of behavior control covered in the talk. There is also other title information that is not a subtitle, but does give further explanatory information. In the title, *Barbara Morgan Photography: Trisolini Gallery of Ohio University, Athens, Ohio, January 9-February 3, 1979*, the other title information tells where and when the exhibit was held.

The title proper and other titles in the preferred sources of information, however, are not the only possible ones. Other titles exist, and the cataloger must note those that vary significantly from the title proper. When such titles are noted, the patron who knows a work only by a *variant title* can be directed to it. For example, Haydn's Symphony 94 in G Major is also known as the "Surprise Symphony," and some patrons would look for this popular form

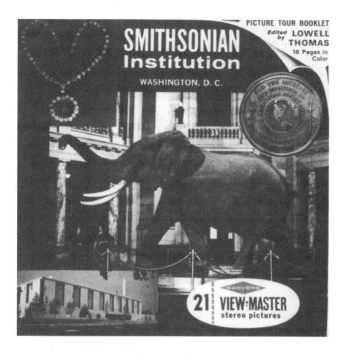

FIGURE 4.9 An Example of a Secondary Source of Information (Container for View-Master Reels).

of the title instead of the title proper. Books and other resources may carry a *cover title* (i.e., title printed on the cover), a *binder's title* (i.e., title lettered on the original spine of the book), or a *running title* (i.e., title repeated at the top of each page or each alternate page of the book) that differs from the title proper. Sound recordings, video recordings, graphic materials, and software may have titles on their containers that differ slightly from those on the preferred sources of information. Websites may display different titles on the main body of the page from those in the title bar. Serials may have title variations on the cover or on an added title page, as well as earlier and later titles proper. A series title, however, is not a title variation, but rather indicates a series to which an information resource belongs.

It should be noted that *serials* and *series* in the library and publishing world have definitions that vary from their literary connotations, in which the words are separated on the basis of the story told (i.e., one story told in several installments versus several stories about the same characters but that do not have to be read or seen in order). In library parlance, serials and series are both issued successively, and usually the successive parts come from the same issuing agency. Serials, though, often appear at regular intervals, and are intended to continue indefinitely, whereas series often, though not always, are issued irregularly and are planned to be issued in finite numbers. Serials include periodicals, journals, newspapers, annual reports, and the like. Series usually comprise separate resources that are related in subject or form, are published in a uniform style, and all have a collective title separate from their individual titles. However, some series are numbered, in which case the collective group may be cataloged as a serial.

A *series* may consist of several works all written by the same person or persons, as is the case with Will and Ariel Durant's *The Story of Civilization*, which consists of several uniform volumes. This is called an *author's series*. A series may also be issued by a publisher who commissions several authors to write one or more volumes on a specified subject. Such is the case with the Rinehart *Rivers of America* series of many volumes. Or perhaps an author is not commissioned but submits a work that happens to fit into a category established by the publisher. An example is the *Library and Information Science Text Series*, published by Libraries Unlimited. Such series are called *publishers' series*.

The *monographic series* is a series that is usually issued with some regularity; each title in a monographic series ordinarily is given a number, usually in chronological order (e.g., *Luis Ugarte* by Alison Hermosillo Bagwell is volume 19 of the series *Monografías de arquitectos del siglo XX*). For many patrons, the name of the series and the number of a title in it are the important identifying elements. Patrons may not remember individual authors and titles but look for these resources under the series name. Thus although author and title of an individual resource are major identifying elements, a series title in a monographic series assumes a significant role.

Statements of Responsibility

Often the second element to be identified by the cataloger is the *statement of responsibility*. This is also usually found in the preferred sources of information, although not always. A statement of responsibility generally contains the names of persons, families, and/or corporate bodies responsible for creating and/or contributing to the content of the resource. It may or may not contain words to indicate the roles of the entities, the levels of responsibility, the nature of the contribution, and so on (e.g., *by, and, with the assistance of, translated by*).

Depending on the type of resource being cataloged, those named in a statement of responsibility might include authors, compilers, illustrators, editors, composers, cartographers, artists, photographers, directors, production companies, movie studios, performers, and so on. In addition to the primary statement of responsibility for the manifestation, when examining the resource, a cataloger might also see statements of responsibility for editions and for series as well. In some resources, a statement of responsibility may not be immediately evident, or it may not be present at all.

As discussed above, the name of one of the creators—usually the one primarily responsible for the work, or the one listed first on the source—also may be used to create an access point for naming the work. This is done to create a standard form of citation. For example, if a resource has four creators, one creator is consistently used in the name/title access point to ensure collocation, rather than having four inconsistent forms of access points on various records for the resource.

It may be necessary to locate some information about an unfamiliar creator. For example, if a textual work is imaginative in nature, the author's nationality must be known, because most classification schemes use nationality to classify novels, drama, and poetry. This is discussed in the chapters on classification in this text. It is also sometimes necessary to know an author's nationality to know how to form the AAP for the name.

Editions or Versions

The *edition* (or *version*), if named, is often found in the preferred sources of information but may also be found in other places, such as the preliminaries in a book, on a container or a label, in a preface or introduction, in a colophon, or in another part of the resource. In the print world, the edition is distinguished from a printing or issue in that a new edition indicates that certain specific changes—additions, deletions, modifications—have been made from earlier versions of the item. By contrast, a new printing or new issue means that more copies of the work were manufactured to keep up with demand. In the case of books and most book-like materials, printings may have minor corrections or revisions, usually incorporated into the original type image. For other materials, a new issue may have slight variations from the original.

Editions may be named (e.g., revised and enlarged edition, abridged edition, expurgated edition) or numbered (e.g., Fifth edition, 3rd revised edition). Any of these statements indicates to the cataloger and the user that some change in content or in form has been made. This information is very important to a scholar. To study the development of a poet, the literary scholar must have early and late editions of the poet's work. A physicist might want only the latest edition of a book on thermodynamics. General users, also, find this information useful. They may want only the latest software release, a director's cut of a film, or the widescreen version of a film.

Dissemination Information

Because the name of the publisher, producer, manufacturer, or distributor might indicate the type or quality of a work, this information might be important to a user who must choose one resource from several on a specific subject. If the publisher is noted for excellence in a certain area (e.g., Skira Rizzoli in art, McGraw-Hill in technology), dissemination information has some value to the user. This information, including places and dates, is generally found in the preferred sources of information but may also be found in the same "other" locations as the edition statement. If the content is copyrighted, the copyright date and the holders of the copyright must be listed in or on it. This information is important when the publication date and the copyright date differ. In such a case, both dates may be recorded.

Other Characteristics

The cataloger must be quick to identify other important and useful pieces of information about a resource and must learn to assess quickly the details of a physical carrier or characteristics of a remote-access resource. These metadata elements include the media type, carrier type, extent of the resource (e.g., number of maps, cassettes, reels, discs, sheets, leaves, pages, volumes, slides, prints, pieces), dimensions (e.g., height, length, diameter), other physical data (e.g., sound characteristics such as type of recording, recording medium, playing speed, groove characteristics, and so on), system requirements, and the like. *Accompanying materials*—which are dependent parts of a resource (such as answer booklets, slides, and teacher's manuals) that accompany and are cataloged with the main component of the resource—must be identified for inclusion in the description. Information such as language, edition history, intended audience, contents of multi-volume items, and the presence of bibliographies should often be noted in the description. Standard identifiers, such as an International Standard Book Number (ISBN), International Standard Serial Number (ISSN), Uniform Resource Locator (URL), or Uniform Resource Identifier (URI), are of major importance as a means of unique international identification. They are also recorded in the metadata description.

If there is a preface, the cataloger should read it as an aid to determining the author's plan or objective and as an aid in identifying the edition. It also provides a key to subject matter. Similar aids are introductions, forewords,

---

```
    OCLC 236328585    No holdings in DD0 - 374 other holdings; 5 other IRs

Books Rec Stat c      Entered 20080822  Replaced 20150626112449.2
  Type  a    ELvl        Srce         Audn        Ctrl          Lang  eng
  BLvl  m    Form        Conf  0      Biog        MRec          Ctry  ctu
             Cont  b     GPub         LitF   0    Indx   1
  Desc  i    Ills   a    Fest  0      DtSt   s    Dates  2009,

010       2008037446
040       DLC $b eng $e rda $c DLC $d BTCTA
020       9781591585862 $q (alk. paper)
020       9781591587002 $q (pbk. ; $q alk. paper)
050   00  Z666.5 $b .T39 2009
082   00  025 $2 22
100   1_  Taylor, Arlene G., $d 1941- $e author.
245   14  The organization of information / $c Arlene G. Taylor and Daniel N. Joudrey.
250       Third edition.
264    1  Westport, Connecticut : $b Libraries Unlimited, $c [2009]
264   _4  $c ©2009
300       xxvi, 512 pages : $b illustrations ; $c 26 cm.
336       text $b txt $2 rdacontent
337       unmediated $b n $2 rdamedia
338       volume $b nc $2 rdacarrier
490   1_  Library and information science text series
504       Includes bibliographical references (pages 479-498) and index.
505   0_  Organization of recorded information -- Retrieval tools -- Development of the
          organization of recorded information in Western civilization -- Metadata -- Encoding
          standards -- Systems and system design -- Metadata : description -- Metadata : access and
          authority control -- Subject analysis -- Systems for vocabulary control -- Systems for
          categorization -- Conclusion.

520   1_  "As with previous editions, it begins with strong justification for the continued importance
          of organizing principles and practice. Following a broad overview of the concept and its
          role in human endeavors, Taylor and Joudrey provide a detailed and insightful discussion
          of such basic retrieval tools as inventories, bibliographies, catalogs, indexes, finding aids,
          registers, databases, major bibliographic utilities, and other organizing entities. They then
          trace the development of the organization of recorded information in Western civilization
          from 2000 B.C.E. to the present. [This book is] ... for students and professionals eager to
          embrace the heritage, immediacy, and future of this fascinating field of study." -- $c Back cover.

650    0  Information organization.
650   _0  Metadata.
650    7  Information organization. $2 fast $0 (OCoLC)fst00972595
650   _7  Metadata. $2 fast $0 (OCoLC)fst01017519
700   1_  Joudrey, Daniel N. $e author.
830   _0  Library and information science text series.
856   41  $3 Table of contents only $u http://catdir.loc.gov/catdir/toc/ecip0826/2008037446.html
```

FIGURE 4.10 An Excerpt from a MARC Record for the Resource Shown in Figure 4.7 (Source: OCLC Connexion, WorldCat—record number 236328585).

Visual Materials	Rec Stat	c	Entered	20150102	Replaced	20150806004650.2
Type g	**ELvl**	I	**Srce** d	**Audn** g	**Ctrl**	**Lang** eng
BLvl m	**Form**		**GPub**	**Time** nnn	**MRec**	**Ctry** oru
Desc i	**TMat**	s	**Tech** n	**DtSt** q	**Dates**	1962, 1966

007	g $b s $d c $e u $h z $i c
024 8_	A 792
040	SCL $b eng $c SCL $e rda
043	n-us-dc
090	Q11.S8 $b S65
092	069.09753 $b S664 $2 23
245 00	Smithsonian Institution.
264 _1	Portland, Oregon : $b Sawyer's Inc., $c [between 1962 and 1966]
300	3 stereograph discs (7 pairs of frames each) : $b color ; $c 3 1/2 in.
300	16 pages : $b color illustrations ; $c 11 cm.
336	still image $2 rdacontent $3 reels
336	text $2 rdacontent $3 booklet
337	stereographic $2 rdamedia $3 reels
337	unmediated $2 rdamedia $3 booklet
338	stereograph disc $2 rdacarrier $3 reels
338	volume $2 rdacarrier $3 booklet
490 0_	Sawyer's view-master guided picture tour ; $v packet no. A 792
500	Picture tour booklet edited by Lowell Thomas.
500	For use with View-master.
500	Publication date is estimated between 1962 and 1966. The earlier date is based on content on Reel 1 dated 1962. The later date is based on date that Sawyer was purchased by General Aniline & Film (GAF) Corporation, after which the reels bore the registered trademark of GAF.
520 2_	Shows and describes some of the major exhibits housed in three of the buildings of the Smithsonian Institution in Washington, D.C.
505 00	$g Reel one. $t Air and space exhibits A7921 -- $g Reel two. $t Natural history exhibits A7922 -- $g Reel three. $t History & technology exhibits A7923.
610 20	Smithsonian Institution $v Pictorial works.
655 _0	View-Master reels.
700 1_	Thomas, Lowell, $d 1892-1981 $e editor. $3 booklet

FIGURE 4.11 A MARC Record for the Resource Shown in Figure 4.8 (An Original Record based on the OCLC format).

accompanying printed materials, and containers. The table of contents, with its listing of chapter titles, headings, and subheadings, is a valuable indication of the scope of a work. An index is a source for determining subject content and special emphases. A bibliography may also serve as an aid by providing important resources on the subject from the author's point of view. For more on subject analysis, see chapter 11 of this text.

During the process of technical reading the cataloger may take notes of relevant elements of information as they are found, so that they can be formed into a coherent description for the bibliographic record or into a set of metadata statements that will represent the information resource in the catalog or beyond. Figures 4.10 and 4.11 show RDA metadata entered into MARC records for the resources shown in Figures 4.7 and 4.8.

CONCLUSION

This chapter is an introduction to RDA. It is an overview of the features of the content standard and some of the issues that need to be addressed before beginning the process of actually cataloging a resource. Cataloging typically begins with description of a resource, which involves recording information about the resource in such a way that it will be identified exactly and cannot be confused with any other resource. Discussions of this descriptive cataloging process proceed through the next five chapters.

NOTES

1. *RDA: Resource Description & Access*, developed in a collaborative process led by the Joint Steering Committee for Development of RDA (Chicago: American Library Association, 2010). Also available through paid subscriptions to *RDA Toolkit* (Chicago: American Library Association, 2010), accessed July 27, 2015, http://www.rdatoolkit.org/. In lieu of page numbers, any references to specific parts of RDA are made using instruction numbers.
2. *RDA Toolkit* (Chicago: American Library Association, 2010), http://www.rdatoolkit.org/.
3. *Anglo-American Cataloguing Rules, Second Edition*, 2002 Revision, prepared under the direction of the Joint Steering Committee for Revision of AACR (Ottawa: Canadian Library Association; Chicago: American Library Association, 2002).
4. RDA, 0.3.1: Relationship to Other Standards for Resource Description and Access: General.
5. RDA, 2.4.1.4–2.4.1.6.
6. Library of Congress, *MARC Standards*, accessed August 11, 2015, http://www.loc.gov/marc/.
7. Library of Congress, *Metadata Object Description Schema (MODS)*, accessed June 19, 2015, http://www.loc.gov/standards/mods/.
8. Library of Congress, *Bibliographic Framework Initiative*, accessed June 23, 2015, http://www.loc.gov/bibframe/.
9. "Who's Cataloging in RDA" *RDA Toolkit*, accessed May 30, 2015, http://www.rdatoolkit.org/RDA_institutions; European RDA Interest Group, "EURIG Survey on Adoption of RDA—2013: Report," accessed June 19, 2014, http://www.slainte.org.uk/eurig/docs/EURIG_Survey-2013_v1_0.pdf.
10. RDA, 0.11: Internationalization.
11. Joint Steering Committee for Development of RDA, "RDA: A Prospectus," accessed June 20, 2015, http://www.rda-jsc.org/rdaprospectus.html.
12. "The RDA (Resource Description and Access) Vocabularies," *Open Metadata Registry*, accessed June 20, 2014, http://rdvocab.info/.
13. In earlier times, before the transition to RDA, the term *main entry* also had another meaning. *Main entry* referred not only to the primary creator (or first-named creator) or the primary access point (sometimes a title), but also to the record that had the main entry as the heading. For example, in the card catalog, the card with the heading for the primary author was the *main entry card*. The primary access point and the record containing it were conflated in the term *main entry*. After the move to online catalogs, main entry (the record) was no longer applicable, there being only one copy of a MARC record for the resource in the catalog. The use of *main entry* to distinguish between the primary creator and other creators (or the primary access point and secondary access points) was, and is, still applicable in the online catalog.
14. For other uses of main entry, *see* Arlene G. Taylor and Daniel N. Joudrey, *The Organization of Information* (Westport, Conn.: Libraries Unlimited, 2009), 262–271.
15. Taylor and Joudrey, *The Organization of Information*, 441–478.

16. "Library of Congress–Program for Cooperative Cataloging Policy Statements (LC-PCC PS)" and the other policy statements are available in *RDA Toolkit: Resource Description & Access* (Chicago: American Library Association, 2010), accessed June 22, 2014, http://access.rdatoolkit.org/. Free access to the LC-PCC PS is available through the *Resources* tab. Copies of the LC-PCC PSs and MLA's "Best Practices for Music Cataloging Using RDA and MARC21" are also available with a paid subscription in *Cataloger's Desktop*.

17. RDA, 0.6.3: Core Elements: Cardinality.

18. RDA, 2.8.2: Place of Publication.

19. "Resource Description and Access (RDA): Information and Resources in Preparation for RDA," Library of Congress, accessed June 24, 2014, http://www.loc.gov/aba/rda/.

20. RDA, 2.3.1.6: Introductory Words, etc.

21. RDA, 7.15.1.3: Recording Illustrative Content.

22. Library of Congress, LC-PCC PS for 7.15.1.3.

23. RDA, 7.15.1.3: Recording Illustrative Content.

24. National Library of Australia, NLA PS for 7.15.1.3.

25. British Library, BL PS for 7.15.1.3.

26. Deutsche Nationalbibliothek, D-A-CH AWR für 7.15.1.3 Optionale Ergänzung.

27. RDA, 2.4.1.5: Statement Naming More Than One Person, etc.

28. Ibid.

29. Library of Congress, LC-PCC PS for 2.4.1.5.

30. RDA, 9.2.2.7: Change of Name.

31. RDA, 0.2.3: Alignment with FRAD.

32. IFLA Working Group on Functional Requirements and Numbering of Authority Records (FRANAR), *Functional Requirements for Authority Data: A Conceptual Model (FRAD)*, edited by Glenn E. Patton (München, Germany: K.G. Saur, 2009). A more recent version, with corrections through 2013 and differing page numbers is available online. These endnotes will refer to the pagination of the electronic version. Accessed February 17, 2014, http://www.ifla.org/files/assets/cataloguing/frad/frad_2013.pdf, 46.

33. RDA, 0.0: Purpose and Scope.

34. RDA, 0.1: Key Features.

35. Tom Delsey, "RDA Database Implementation Scenarios," 1 July 2009, http://www.rda-jsc.org/docs/5editor2rev.pdf.

36. Ibid.

37. RDA, 0.4.2: Objectives.

38. RDA, 0.4.2.1: Responsiveness to User Needs.

39. RDA, 0.4.3: Principles.

40. IFLA Cataloguing Section and IFLA Meetings of Experts on an International Cataloguing Code, *The Statement of International Cataloguing Principles* (ICP) (The Hague: IFLA, 2009), http://www.ifla.org/publications/statement-of-international-cataloguing-principles.

41. RDA, 0.4.3.5: Accuracy.

42. RDA, 0.4.3.8: Uniformity.

43. Library of Congress, LC-PCC PS for 0.0.

44. RDA, 2.13: Mode of Issuance.

45. Library of Congress, LC-PCC PS for 0.0.

46. RDA, 1.5.2: Comprehensive Description.

47. RDA, 1.5.3: Analytical Description.

48. RDA, 1.5.4: Hierarchical Description.

49. International Federation of Library Associations and Institutions, *ISBD: International Standard Bibliographic Description*, Consolidated ed. (Berlin: De Gruyter Saur, 2011), Appendix A.

50. Library of Congress, LC-PCC PS for 1.5.4.
51. Library of Congress, "13.6. Multilevel Description," *Library of Congress Rule Interpretations*, 2nd ed. (Washington, DC: Library of Congress, 1989). Accessible through a subscription to "Cataloger's Desktop" at https://desktop.loc.gov/ or through the "Cataloger's Reference Shelf" website, accessed February 25, 2014, http://www.itsmarc.com/crs/mergedprojects/lcri/lcri/contents.htm.

SUGGESTED READING

El-Sherbini, Magda. *RDA: Strategies for Implementation.* Chicago: American Library Association, 2013.

Hart, Amy. *RDA Made Simple: A Practical Guide to the New Cataloging Rules.* Santa Barbara, Calif.: Libraries Unlimited, 2014.

Kincy, Chamya Pompey, with Sara Shatford Layne. *Making the Move to RDA: A Self-Study Primer for Catalogers.* Lanham, Md.: Rowman & Littlefield, 2014.

Maxwell, Robert L. *Maxwell's Handbook for RDA, Resource Description & Access: Explaining and Illustrating RDA: Resource Description and Access Using MARC21.* Chicago: American Library Association, 2013.

Mering, Margaret, editor. *The RDA Workbook: Learning the Basics of Resource Description and Access.* Santa Barbara, Calif.: Libraries Unlimited, 2014.

Oliver, Chris. *Introducing RDA: A Guide to the Basics.* Chicago: American Library Association, 2010.

Chapter 5

Manifestations and Items

INTRODUCTION

Description is the part of the cataloging process concerned with the identification of a resource. It entails recording information about a manifestation in such a way that it can be found easily and identified exactly. The information resource, after being documented, should not be confused with any other resource no matter how similar some of the metadata elements might be (e.g., identical titles proper). Many elements contribute to the identification of a resource. A title is almost always the first identifying element, followed by the names of persons, families, and/or corporate bodies (PFC) responsible for the content in the resource. Information identifying a version or an edition of the resource is also very helpful, as are names of other persons associated with that expression (e.g., revisers, illustrators, translators, editors). Standard identifiers, such as International Standard Book Numbers (ISBNs), also help identify the resource. In addition to those responsible for the content, the names of corporate bodies associated with the resource (e.g., those acting as manufacturers, distributors, producers, publishers) are useful information, as are dates, series information, and various kinds of numbering. Even the size, the type and number of illustrations, and the extent of the manifestation (e.g., number of pages for a book, number of discs in a DVD set) may be helpful information for a patron seeking a particular version of the resource. When found, all of these elements help users to understand exactly what the resource is. In this chapter, the elements of RDA[1] that are useful in describing and identifying manifestations and items are reviewed. Readers are reminded to consult RDA frequently as they are exploring the content of this and the following chapters on descriptive cataloging. Reading this text is not a substitute for consulting RDA directly.

In this chapter, as well as in those following it, most examples of bibliographic metadata are presented using a format-neutral approach. A small number of examples, however, may be formatted using a specific encoding or presentation scheme. These exceptions are clearly identified as such. For a more comprehensive overview of MARC-formatted RDA cataloging, see chapter 9 of this text.

RECORDING METADATA ELEMENTS

Before the cataloging of a manifestation can begin in earnest, a few more concerns must be addressed. These issues, outlined in RDA chapter 1, include discussions related to terminology, objectives, transcription, and other issues. The chapter's structure is presented in Textbox 5.1.

1: General Guidelines on Recording Attributes of Manifestations and Items

1.0 Scope
1.1 Terminology
1.2 Functional Objectives and Principles
1.3 Core Elements
1.4 Language and Script
1.5 Type of Description
1.6 Changes Requiring a New Description
1.7 Transcription
1.8 Numbers Expressed as Numerals or as Words
1.9 Dates
1.10 Notes
1.11 Facsimiles and Reproductions

Textbox 5.1 RDA Chapter 1 Structure.

Each section of RDA begins with a chapter of general guidelines. Section 1's general guidelines set out some baseline instructions that apply to the other chapters in the section on manifestations and items (i.e., RDA chapters 2-4). The general guidelines in RDA section 1 are fully listed in this text, but in the discussions of later sections, the general guidelines are covered minimally—focusing only on content specific to those particular sections. As much as possible, repetition is kept to a minimum, though doing so is somewhat difficult as RDA repeats information frequently.

RDA chapter 1 begins with a discussion of the scope of the chapter (i.e., an overview of its own contents). It then moves on to discuss key terminology used in section 1, including terms such as *resource*; *mode of issuance*: *comprehensive, analytical,* and *hierarchical descriptions*; and *work, expression, manifestation,* and *item*. It then lists four objectives (of the 15 identified in "Responsiveness to User Needs" in the RDA Introduction) that are applicable to the metadata created in section 1:

- To find resources based on a user's search criteria
- To identify the resource described

- To select the physical form/electronic formatting and encoding of the resource based on a user's needs
- To obtain a resource through electronic or physical means

The chapter then addresses the principles from the RDA Introduction that are relevant to section 1:

- Differentiation
- Sufficiency
- Representation
- Accuracy
- Common usage

Following that, the chapter provides a reminder to catalogers to include, at a minimum, all applicable core elements when describing a manifestation (see Table 4.2 on p. 142 for a list of elements found in RDA section 1 considered to be RDA Core). It is followed by a note that instructs the cataloger to go beyond the basic core elements as needed: "Include any additional elements that are required in a particular case to differentiate the manifestation or item from one or more other manifestations or items with similar identifying information."[2] It also covers the three types of descriptions possible in RDA (comprehensive, analytical, and hierarchical descriptions) and various changes in resources that necessitate new descriptions. These are all topics discussed in more detail in chapters 3 and 4 of this textbook.

RDA chapter 1 also contains some guidelines that have not been addressed in this text up to this point. These include guidelines on language and script; details about transcription; how to record numerals, dates, and notes; and issues related to facsimiles and reproductions. Each is addressed in the following sections.

RDA 1.4 Language and Script

RDA 1.4 addresses issues of language and script. The instruction provides a list of 61 metadata elements that are to be transcribed in the language and the script in which they appear in the resource. Those 61 elements include every metadata element established for a manifestation, *except* for copyright date, International Standard Serial Number (ISSN), mode of issuance, frequency, identifier, preferred citation, and notes. Item-level (2.18-2.21) and carrier-related (3.2-3.22) metadata elements are excluded from the list also. The elements on the list are to be recorded as found; the other elements (i.e., those not on the list) are to be recorded in the language(s) and script(s) preferred by the cataloging agency. The phrase *preferred language and script* always refers to the language and script used to record the metadata, *not* to the language and script of the content of the resource. In the United States, the preferred language is English, and the preferred script is Latin (or Roman). Other countries—especially those where two or more national languages coexist (e.g., Belgium, Canada, Switzerland)—may have more than one preferred language and script.

In the instructions for the alternatives and optional addition for RDA 1.4, transliteration is mentioned. *Transliteration* is the representation of the characters of one alphabet by those of another. *Romanization* is transliteration specifically into the Roman script. As an alternative, RDA suggests for some elements in the list it may be necessary to transliterate the data if transcription is not possible. Within the Library of Congress–Program for Cooperative Cataloging policy statements (LC-PCC PSs) it is stated that one should provide the information in the non-Roman script if the language/script is Perso-Arabic script (e.g., Arabic, Persian, Pushto, Urdu), Hebrew, Yiddish, Chinese, Japanese, Korean, a Cyrillic-based script, or Greek. It also states that Romanized equivalents may be provided for some elements on the list.[3]

RDA 1.7 Transcription

Another important issue addressed in RDA chapter 1 is transcription. *Transcription* is the process of documenting exactly what is found on the resource; it is a specific method of logging the data. It generally means that the cataloger should take the data as found in terms of wording, spelling, and order, but it can entail slight changes for clarity or consistency. These allowable changes may appear in several areas, including capitalization and punctuation among others.

The paramount principle regarding transcription of bibliographic metadata is to "take what you see." On the surface, this seems like a shift from the approach found in the previous content standard, the second edition of the *Anglo-American Cataloguing Rules* (AACR2),[4] which included procedures for using abbreviations, formatting numbers, changing capitalization, punctuating data, and so on. At times, AACR2 required the cataloger to change data taken from the resource (e.g., replace square brackets used in a title with parentheses) or to add or correct data as needed (e.g., clarifying statements, typos). Catalogers using RDA are expected to preserve the information found on the resource when transcribing it for particular elements (i.e., those elements with instructions that begin with the word *transcribe* rather than with the word *record*). This, however, does not mean that every aspect of the data will be documented exactly. RDA 1.7.1 indicates that while transcribing the information for certain elements, the cataloger should apply the general guidelines provided by RDA for the following:

1.7.2 Capitalization

1.7.3 Punctuation

1.7.4 Diacritical marks

1.7.5 Symbols

1.7.6 Spacing of initials and acronyms

1.7.7 Letters or words intended to be read more than once

1.7.8 Abbreviations

1.7.9 Inaccuracies

Some of the guidelines point to appendices that provide additional instructions and data (e.g., RDA 1.7.8 leads the cataloger to RDA appendix B: Abbreviations and Symbols). The general guidelines at 1.7.1 also provide two alternatives that may be chosen by individual libraries.

The first alternative states that instead of applying RDA 1.7.2 to 1.7.9, the individual cataloging agency may choose to use an in-house or a formally published style manual (e.g., *Chicago Manual of Style*[5]). The LC-PCC PS for this alternative requires LC and PCC catalogers to follow RDA 1.7.3 to 1.7.9 and their appendices; it encourages their catalogers to follow 1.7.2 as well, although it acknowledges that for capitalization, catalogers may "take what they see" instead.[6]

The second alternative states that catalogers can accept metadata as it is if they are copy cataloging (i.e., another institution originally created the descriptive metadata), or if the data came from digital sources through automated processes (e.g., scanning, downloading). The LC-PCC PS for the second alternative encourages catalogers to "accept data derived from digital sources (e.g., ONIX data for CIP resources); make any adjustments to the supplied information judged appropriate," including capitalization modifications.[7]

In short, when it comes to transcription, catalogers and individual institutions may limit how it is applied. Although it is permissible to transcribe exactly what is found on the resource, RDA still encourages catalogers to adjust the data in many of the same ways as found in AACR2—just not as prevalently (e.g., the drastic reduction in the use of cataloger-supplied abbreviations). Even though the authors can see the great benefit in simply transcribing what is found on the resource, it is difficult to discard the long-standing and deeply instilled tenet that it is important to standardize presentation, capitalization, abbreviations, spacing, and so on. The authors, for the sake of consistency in cataloging, encourage catalogers to apply RDA 1.7.2-1.7.9, though they acknowledge that the days of being complete sticklers about things such as this are now over.

Capitalization

The capitalization guideline found at RDA 1.7.2 is quite simple. It says, when transcribing or recording data, to apply the instructions found in RDA appendix A. In the appendix, a general guideline states that catalogers are to capitalize words according to the instructions of the language being recorded and should record in lowercase letters any words that are not covered in RDA appendix A. Following that, the appendix provides some specific instructions for the capitalization of particular parts of the description (A.2-A.9), capitalization in English (A.10-A.30), and capitalization in other languages (A.31-A.55). As stated, even though it encourages the use of the capitalization instructions for transcribed elements, the LC-PCC PS acknowledges that they may or may not be adhered to in favor of the "take what you see" dictum:

> *LC practice/PCC practice for Alternative*: For capitalization of transcribed elements, catalogers are encouraged (but not required) to follow Appendix A; it is permitted to "take what you see" on the resource. For other elements, follow this appendix. If supplying information in brackets or providing a Romanized form, apply cataloger's judgment to follow this appendix or not.[8]

Names

RDA A.2 instructs catalogers to capitalize the names of persons, families, corporate bodies, and places. The instruction is to capitalize the first letter in names except for those entities that are typically identified using unusual capitalization. The examples of different types of names provided below show a mix of authority-controlled forms of names and those found in statements of responsibility or elsewhere. The capitalization in these examples does not vary based on whether they are controlled or uncontrolled forms of name; the differences between controlled and uncontrolled forms of names are the order of the name elements and the presence of qualifying information, such as dates and explanatory terms:

- Dolly Parton
- hooks, bell, 1952-
- Gentleman in distress
- Ibrāhīm al-Wāfī
- Felipe VI, King of Spain, 1968-

- AAA
- Sun Kil Moon (Musical group)
- eBay for Charity
- Spacecraft and Launch Vehicle Dynamic Environments Workshop (2012 : El Segundo, Calif.)

- Blomstrand (Family : Sweden)
- Berryman family
- Sakakibara (Clan : active 14th century- : Jōetsu-shi, Japan)

- Cambridgeport (Mass.)
- São Paulo
- Ibiza Island (Spain)

The guidelines for names state that catalogers should *not* capitalize the articles in names beginning with Arabic articles (e.g., al, el, es) or Hebrew articles (e.g., ha, he), but they should capitalize

- words or phrases used in place of a name, including any proper names or titles used within it (e.g., Lady at Dublin, Author of Miss Grey's text);
- titles and other terms treated as part of a name, designations associated with a person, a field of activity, or an occupation or profession (e.g., Aunt Abbie; Acharya, Pushpa Raj (Poet); Mrs. Allen Tickle; Seuss, Dr.);
- acronyms or initialisms used by a corporate body (e.g., NATO Headquarters, UNICEF); and
- terms associated with a family type or a corporate body designation (e.g., Romanov (Dynasty : 1613-1917); The The (Musical group); Apollo 11 (Spacecraft)).

Capitalize other words by applying the guidelines at A.10-A.55, as applicable to the language involved.

Titles

The capitalization guidelines for titles are divided into two sections, those for titles of works and those for titles of manifestations. The basic instruction is to capitalize the first word (or abbreviation) of a title, whether it is the title of the work or the manifestation (i.e., title proper). Capitalize other words as appropriate to the language of the title (e.g., capitalize all proper nouns in English, capitalize all nouns in German). Also, capitalize the first word of a part title, section title, or a supplement title, but do not, generally, capitalize the first word of other title information. As it is with names, if unusual capitalization of the title is present, it may be transcribed as found on the source. If there are other terms associated with the title of a work (a qualifier indicating form, language, etc.), capitalize the first word. There are exceptions for certain terms associated with music (e.g., medium of performance) and serials (e.g., terms associated with numbering of a part), which are not capitalized. Also, do not capitalize the first word of a title following punctuation that indicates that words have been omitted (e.g., ellipses).

- Everything is perfect when you're a liar
- Romeo and Juliet
- Excellent conceited tragedie of Romeo and Juliet
- Weichet nur, betrübte Schatten
- Using informational text to teach To kill a mockingbird
- Plays. Selections
- British writers. Supplement XX
- Understanding international law through moot courts : genocide, torture, habeas corpus, chemical weapons, and the responsibility to protect
- Art Smith's healthy comfort : how America's favorite celebrity chef got it together, lost weight, and reclaimed his health!
- From notepad to iPad : using apps and web tools to engage a new generation of students
- 5/15/45-the last dance (Choreographic work : Watanabe)
- Sextet in E-flat major for transverse flute, oboe, violin, viola, violoncello or bassoon and basso continuo, op. 5
- . . . and then there were none

Other Elements

From the instructions found in RDA A.5-A.9, catalogers are to capitalize the first word or abbreviation of the edition statement, the numbering for a serial, each sentence within notes, and statements describing the details of an element. Catalogers do not capitalize terms for the numbering of a series or subseries. Following these element-specific instructions, there are general instructions for capitalization in English, which are primarily derived from *The Chicago Manual of Style*. The reader is encouraged to consult RDA's appendix A for a greater understanding of the guidelines and for many more examples.

Punctuation

RDA 1.7.3 instructs catalogers to transcribe the punctuation that they see on the resource, but to add punctuation for clarity as needed (e.g., adding commas between two names in a statement of responsibility when they are

TABLE 5.1 List of Punctuation Topics in LC-PCC PS 1.7.1.

Section	Topics
Access Points in Name Authority and Bibliographic Records (General)	• Punctuation/spacing within access points (associated with periods, ampersands, parentheses, quotation marks, and open dates) • Ending marks of punctuation (which include periods, closing parentheses, closing brackets, quotation marks, question marks, exclamation points, and hyphens) in bibliographic and authority records
Access Points for Persons in Name Authority and Bibliographic Records	• Initials/letters (periods and spaces) • Abbreviated or missing portions of preferred names • Prefixes in certain names • Subfield $i in authority records
Access Points for Corporate Names, Including Meetings, in Name Authority and Bibliographic Records	• Quotation marks • Initials • Abbreviations • Place names at the end • Subfield $i in authority records
Bibliographic Linking Entries	Follows the instructions outlined in the sections above
Punctuation at the End of MARC Fields	Addresses the 245, 246-247, 250, 264, 300, 310/321, 362, and 490 MARC fields
Punctuation in Subfield $3 in MARC Fields 264, 490	$3 indicates the issues, parts, or iterations applicable to the field
Punctuation in Subfield $x in MARC 8XX Fields	Placement of $x
Punctuation in Notes	• When additional information is expected • Ending marks of punctuation • Use of square brackets
Temporary/Uncertain Data	Use of temporary data

presented on two separate lines on the resource). Two exceptions are listed in the instruction. The first is to remove punctuation when that punctuation is used to separate two different data elements (e.g., a comma between a publisher's name and its location). The second is to remove punctuation when that punctuation is used to separate two or more instances of the same element (e.g., a hyphen or centered dot used to separate multiple instances of publishers' names). RDA says little else on the issue of punctuation. The same, however, cannot be said about LC-PCC PS 1.7.1: General Guidelines on Transcription.

LC-PCC PS 1.7.1 addresses topics related to punctuation and spacing. Much of this information specifically addresses punctuation for MARC records rather than for the actual metadata being created. As most of the LC-PCC PS is addressing formatting issues, little detail is included here other than Table 5.1, which provides a list of the topics covered in the policy statement.

RDA provides a discussion of *International Standard Bibliographic Description* (ISBD) punctuation in appendix D. ISBD is used to display cataloging data in a consistent manner in MARC records and on catalog cards. For more information about ISBD punctuation, see chapter 23 of this text.

Abbreviations

Although one of the major changes in RDA is eliminating many of the cataloger-supplied abbreviations (e.g., ed., et al., s.l.), not every abbreviation is gone. In transcribed elements, catalogers record exactly what is seen. If an abbreviation appears on the source, that is what is transcribed; if it is a completely spelled-out word or phrase, then the complete version is transcribed. The guidelines no longer instruct catalogers to abbreviate many of the common terms that they once did, such as *edition*, *publishing*, and *company*. Many of the Latin abbreviations used, such as *et al.* (for *et alia*) and *s.n.* (for *sine nomine*), have been replaced by modern-language equivalents, such as *and 3 others* or *publisher not identified* respectively.

For some recorded elements, though, abbreviations or symbols are still required (e.g., the units of measurement used in dimensions). For these, RDA 1.7.8 tells catalogers to apply the instructions found in appendix B, which provides a list of the abbreviations used in various alphabets and scripts following four sets of instructions:

- **Names of Persons, Families, Corporate Bodies, and Places**
  - Use abbreviations that are integral parts of a name, but only if used by the PFC (e.g., Chas, Jos).
  - Use abbreviations for larger places when recorded as qualifiers for a local geographic name; for example, the heading **Boston (Mass.)** uses a state abbreviation found in RDA appendix B; please consult RDA chapter 16 for additional instructions related to identifying places.

- **Titles of Works**
  - Use abbreviations that are integral parts of a title (e.g., *ALA bulletin*).
  - Catalogers may use the abbreviation *etc.* in titles such as *Laws, etc.*

- **Transcribed Elements**
  - For transcribed elements, record what is seen on the source. Catalogers should not impose abbreviations.

- **Other Elements**
  - Use the appropriate symbols or abbreviations found in RDA appendix B for the following elements:
    - Dimensions (e.g., 12 in. or 9 cm)
    - Extent of Storage Space (e.g., 20 m or 32 linear ft.)
    - Duration (e.g., 75 min. or approximately 2 hr.)
    - Numeric Designation of a Musical Work (e.g., op. 112 or no. 4)
    - Numbering of Part (e.g., v. 3-6 or no. 3)
    - Medium of Performance of Musical Content (e.g., B or Bar)
    - Additional Scale Information (e.g., 1 in. to 2 miles)
    - Right Ascension (e.g., Right ascension 2 hr. 00 min. to 2 hr. 30 min./Declination -30° to -45°)
    - Date (e.g., A.D. and/or B.C.)
    - Other Distinguishing Characteristic of a Legal Work: The abbreviation *etc.* is used with terms such as *Protocols, etc.*
  - Do *not* use abbreviations in other elements.

Following these instructions, there are lists of abbreviations used with the Latin, Cyrillic, and Greek alphabets, as well as Hebrew and Yiddish abbreviations and abbreviations for certain countries, states, provinces, and territories.

Other Transcriptions Issues

Diacritical marks (i.e., accent marks) are to be transcribed as found on the resource. In short, when it comes to accent marks, "Ŭše thém i̇́ theẏ aȑe øñ ţhe ṛěšoûrçe!" Optionally, they may be added if they are absent from the source but are commonly used in the standard spelling of a word.

If there is a word or letter that is meant to be read more than once, repeat the word or letters as necessary. The example provided in RDA illustrates this issue. On the source of information, the title page contains *Canadian citations canadiennes*. It is intended to be read as *Canadian citations* as the title proper, with *Citations canadiennes* as a parallel title. The transcription is

> Canadian citations
> Citations canadiennes

If a symbol is on the source of information, and it can be reproduced in the metadata description, transcribe it as it is seen on the source. Some symbols, however, cannot be reproduced. When a symbol cannot be entered into a description, a word or phrase replaces the symbol, and catalogers are to add notes to explain. For example, if the information in Figure 5.1 were seen on

Please!

by David P. Miller

Curry College Press
Milton, MA
2015

FIGURE 5.1 Faux Title Page Containing a Non-Reproducible Symbol.

a title page, it would need to be translated as "Please! [No smoking]." A note would be added stating, "The title page contains an image of a lit cigarette with a *no* or a *prohibition* symbol over it indicating *No smoking*." There is a somewhat lengthy LC-PCC PS at 1.7.5 that goes into detail about how to handle particular situations with signs and symbols.

If an acronym or initialism is present on the source—with or without periods (i.e., full stops) between the letters—the initialism or acronym is to be transcribed without spaces. For example, *ALA Bulletin* is transcribed exactly as seen, but *I. F. D. S. A. Handbook* gets transcribed as "I.F.D.S.A. handbook." Additional information about the spacing for initials used as parts of access points is found in LC-PCC PS 1.7.1: General Guidelines on Transcription.

If there is a misspelling or inaccuracy on the resource—in a transcribed element—catalogers are to transcribe the inaccuracy as found on the source, unless there is an exception to this guideline (e.g., catalogers are instructed to correct obvious typographic errors in the titles proper of serials and integrating resources). Catalogers may make a note if it is important to explain the situation. If the inaccuracy appears in a title, catalogers also have the ability to add a variant title access point for the corrected form. Catalogers generally do not correct typos in transcribed elements, but they *may* rectify them in other places.

RDA 1.8-1.9 Numbers and Dates

When recording numbers—as numerals, words, or dates—there are several instructions in RDA 1.8 and 1.9 to consider. These guidelines particularly apply to the sub-elements under 2.6 Numbering of Serials, to the dates found in the dissemination instructions (2.7-2.10), to series numbering (2.12.9 and 2.12.17), and to a year that a degree was granted (7.9.4)—elements that, in whole or in part, are meant to be recorded, not transcribed. For elements that are intended to be transcribed, numbers are documented as they are found on the source of information (e.g., as *50* from the title *50+ Best Books on Texas* and as *Fifty* from the title *Fifty Shades of Chicken*). This should once again remind catalogers that they should learn which elements are recorded and which are transcribed.

The basic instruction for numbers is to record numerals in the form preferred by the cataloging agency; the alternative is "to take what you see." LC practice is to follow the alternative and to take what is seen. For example, if on a series title page one finds *No. XII*, then a cataloging agency that prefers Arabic numerals would record it as *No. 12*, but catalogers at LC would record it as *No. XII*. There is a second alternative: "to take what you see" *and* to record the same data in the agency's preferred form as well (e.g., No. XII [No. 12]). LC does not apply the second alternative; PCC, however, does not take a position on this alternative. Until computer technology is advanced enough to interfile 1, 2, X, 12, XIII, XLIII, LX, 61, 120, DL, and 1005 into one correctly ordered sequence, it might be best to continue to record these numbers in the preferred form of the cataloging agency—generally, Arabic numerals in the United States and Canada.

RDA instructions say to substitute numerals for any numbers expressed as words. So if the last issue of a serial is listed on the source as *volume ten, number six*, then according to this guideline, it will be recorded as *volume 10, number 6*. For numbers that reflect inclusive dates or other spans, the numerals should be recorded in full. For example, if the resource states that it covers the period 1976-79, then the numerals *1976-1979* are recorded instead. For ordinal numbers—no matter how they are presented on the source—the cataloger records them as numerals and indicates order/ranking through the standard approach used in the appropriate language (in English 1st, 44th, 272nd; in Spanish 1°, 44°, 272°; in German 1., 44., 272., etc.).

If a date appears on the resource itself, then catalogers use the instructions found for numerals in RDA 1.8. The instructions at RDA 1.9 are specifically for cataloger-supplied dates that are related to the dissemination of the resource (2.7-2.10). Catalogers supply dates only when dates are unavailable on the source of information. They are to indicate that supplied dates are from a source outside of the resource itself by placing them in square brackets. Question marks are used to indicate that the date is a *probable date* rather than a confirmed date. According to RDA 1.9.2, there are five types of supplied dates:

- **Actual Year Known**: if the year is known, record it (e.g., [2015])

- **Probable Year**: if the date is not confirmed, a likely year is offered along with a question mark (e.g., [1965?])

- **Either One of Two Consecutive Years**: if it can be narrowed down to a small range of two years, then record that range (e.g., [1941 or 1942])

- **Probable Range of Years**: if it cannot be narrowed down, then a likely period of time is offered (e.g., [between 1990 and 1999?])
- **Earliest and/or Latest Possible Date Known**: if the latest or earliest dates are known, they should be provided (e.g., [not before 1962], [not after June 30, 1966], [between August 20, 1999 and December 31, 1999]); a date such as this is *always* possible, because the resource has to have been disseminated *before* the date of cataloging

RDA 1.10 Notes

When it comes to recording notes as part of the bibliographic description (in RDA chapters 2-7), there are four guidelines to follow:

- Apply to the notes the cataloging agency's standard approach to capitalization (i.e., follow RDA appendix A, follow an in-house style manual, or follow an established style manual).
- Record quotations in quotation marks followed by the source, except when the source is the preferred source of information.
- Refer to passages in the resource if such a reference supports information in the description or if it eliminates some repetition of information.
- If a note is applicable to a portion of the resource only, make that understood.

RDA 1.11 Facsimiles and Reproductions

"When describing a facsimile or reproduction, record the data relating to the facsimile or reproduction in the appropriate element. Record any data relating to the original manifestation as an element of a related work or related manifestation, as applicable." In short, this instruction states that the cataloger describes fully what is in hand and refers to the original as needed.

Although this was standard practice in the past, there was a notable exception in all rules through AACR—microforms that were created for the purpose of reproducing books or journals (instead of being for the production of new works) were cataloged as if they were the originals; all other details of the reproduction were presented in notes. For example, the physical description referred to the number of pages and so on, rather than to the number of microfiche sheets or microfilm reels. AACR2, however, abandoned the exception for microforms that are reproductions. After much discussion in ALA committees in 1980-1981, LC issued a policy decision not to follow AACR2 in this regard, and cataloging of microform reproductions continued to be cataloged as if they were the originals, with microform details being given in notes. The one exception, as a nod to AACR2, was that the GMD *microform* was to be placed after the title proper. At the time of this writing, there is some suggestion that RDA may revert to the former LC practice for microforms. This is a topic to watch.

ADDITIONAL PRE-CATALOGING CONSIDERATIONS

To describe a manifestation, catalogers use RDA chapter 2, the contents of which are enumerated in Textbox 5.2.

2: Identifying Manifestations and Items

2.0 Purpose and Scope

2.1 Basis for Identification of the Resource

2.2 Sources of Information

2.3 Title

2.4 Statement of Responsibility

2.5 Edition Statement

2.6 Numbering of Serials

2.7 Production Statement

2.8 Publication Statement

2.9 Distribution Statement

2.10 Manufacture Statement

2.11 Copyright Date

2.12 Series Statement

2.13 Mode of Issuance

2.14 Frequency

2.15 Identifier for the Manifestation

2.16 Preferred Citation

2.17 Note on Manifestation

2.18 Custodial History of Item

2.19 Immediate Source of Acquisition of Item

2.20 Identifier for the Item

2.21 Note on Item

Textbox 5.2 RDA Chapter 2 Structure.

Before beginning to describe a manifestation, though, there is yet *another* set of pre-cataloging guidelines. These guidelines appear at the beginning of every completed RDA chapter and, at minimum, contain a statement about the purpose and scope of that chapter. In RDA chapter 2, the purpose and scope discuss how the elements found in the chapter reflect elements that are needed to identify resources by users and by the producers of the resources themselves. It also discusses how not all the elements in the chapter are applicable to all resources but that the applicable core elements should be included at the very least. If the core elements are insufficient to uniquely identify the resource, then additional metadata is required.

The introductory section continues with RDA 2.1: Basis for Identification of the Resource. It instructs catalogers to choose a source of information that is appropriate for identifying the resource as a whole based on the mode of issuance (i.e., a single unit, a resource in more than one part, or an integrating resource) and the type of description desired (i.e., comprehensive or analytical).[9] In general for monographic works, catalogers use the resource as a whole as the basis of the description; for multipart monographs and serials, the description is based on the first or earliest part available; and for integrating resources, the latest version of the resource is used as the basis for the description. For serials, multipart monographs, and integrating resources, the basis for identification of the resource is usually included in the metadata description (e.g., "Identification of the resource based on: Vol. 1, no. 2."). More detailed information is found at RDA 2.1.2-2.1.3.

RDA 2.2: Sources of Information addresses where in the resource to find the information that is needed: it focuses on determining *preferred sources of information*. The preferred source is the first stop in the process of bibliographic description; it is the source favored above other possible sources of information. For example, the title proper of a resource might appear on several different sources, such as on a title page, a cover, a colophon, and at the top of each page or screen. The metadata found on one source may or may not be identical to that found on one of these other sources. By having one source favored over the others, catalogers know which metadata to record if there are differences among the sources. Usually the preferred source(s) of information provides the most complete bibliographic information about the resource. These sources vary according to the type of material. If the resource is issued with a container, catalogers are to treat the container as a part of the resource; if a container has been added after production (publication, etc.), it is considered a separate component.

If the first-listed preferred source of information is absent for any reason, the cataloging instructions prescribe alternate sources. Table 5.2 summarizes the guidelines for preferred sources of information. If there is more than one preferred source of information present in the resource, use the one that comes first in the resource, unless these sources have differences in language and script, differences in dates, or reflect differences between a reproduction and an original item. See RDA 2.2.3.1 to 2.2.3.3 for more guidance on these exceptional situations.

If the information needed to describe a resource is not found on the resource itself, it may be taken from any of the following (in the order of preference): (1) accompanying material not treated as part of the resource, such as an answer booklet or a *readme file*; (2) other published metadata for the resource; (3) a container *not* issued with the resource (e.g., a case created by the owner); or (4) any other source (e.g., a reference work, such as a biographical dictionary). When the metadata element is one that is meant to be transcribed, an indication that the data has been supplied from another source is required. This may be in the form of notes (e.g., "Edition statement from back cover."), special coding, or, most commonly, by placing the data in square brackets (e.g., [1975]). RDA 2.2.4 concludes by stating: "Do not indicate that the information was taken from a source outside the resource itself if the resource is of a type that does not normally carry identifying information (e.g., a photograph, a naturally occurring object, a collection)."[10]

TABLE 5.2 Preferred Sources of Information.

Category of resource types	Examples	Preferred sources of information	If those are unavailable, then...
Resources comprising **pages, leaves, sheets,** or **cards** (or images of these)	Books, printed music, maps, manuscripts, posters, printed serials, sheets of microforms, flashcards, etc.	Title page, title sheet, or title card (or an image of these)	A cover/jacket issued with resource, a caption, a masthead, or a colophon (or an image of these) or, if those are unavailable, then another source within resource
Resources comprising **moving images**	Film reel, a DVD, a video game, an MPEG video file, etc.	Title frame(s) or title screen(s)	*If a tangible moving image resource:* 1) a label permanently printed on or affixed to resource, 2) a container or accompanying material issued with resource, 3) an internal source forming part of a tangible digital resource (e.g., a DVD menu), or 4) another source within resource *If an online moving image resource:* 1) textual content, 2) embedded metadata that contains a title (e.g., metadata embedded in an MPEG video file), or 3) another source within resource
Other resources	Digital images, databases, globes, CDs, MP3 files, audio cassettes, objects, puppets, kits, websites, etc.		*If a tangible resource:* 1) a textual source on resource itself or a label permanently printed on or affixed to resource (e.g., a label on an audio CD or a model), 2) an internal source, such as a title screen, 3) a container or accompanying material issued with resource, or 4) another source within resource *If an online resource:* 1) textual content, 2) embedded metadata in textual form that contains a title, or 3) another source within resource

DESCRIBING MANIFESTATIONS AND ITEMS

With all these pre-cataloging considerations in mind, the descriptive cataloging process can begin. In the next sections of this text, the various elements needed to describe manifestations and items are reviewed in the order in which they appear in RDA chapters 2-4. Throughout RDA, there are instructions that specifically address the description of facsimiles and reproductions; RDA also provides numerous instructions addressing changes occurring over the lifespan of multipart monographs, serials, and integrating resources throughout its chapters. These instructions are mentioned occasionally in this text, but the focus is on the elements that apply to the majority of manifestations. Also in this text are brief mentions of particular sub-instructions for certain resource types, but these are infrequent. For each of the major manifestation elements, the authors have included a textbox containing definitions, sub-elements, core elements, and sources of information.

Relevant LC-PCC PSs are reviewed throughout the following sections and chapters of this text. On occasion, when the authors disagree with a policy statement, believe an element should be required, or have opinions on the application of certain guidelines or policy statements, these thoughts are shared with readers as well. They are—in a way—the *Introduction to Cataloging and Classification*, 11th edition policy statements (ICC11 PSs). Unless otherwise stated, the authors of this textbook agree with the LC and PCC list of supplementary elements to enhance the minimal core elements identified in RDA. Additional elements that fall outside of RDA Core and LC Core but that are still recommended for inclusion by the authors of this text are referred to as ICC11 Core.

RDA 2.3 Titles

2.3 Title

Definition: The name of a work, expression, or manifestation, usually identified from the preferred source of information for a resource.

Sub-elements and Their First Sources of Information: There are specific instructions that discuss the sources of information for each title element. Please consult the more complete instructions that discuss the sources of information in RDA.

> **2.3.2 Title Proper** – Follow the instructions from 2.2
> **2.3.3 Parallel Title Proper** – Any source within resource
> **2.3.4 Other Title Information** – Same source as title proper
> **2.3.5 Parallel Other Title Information** – Same source as parallel title proper
> **2.3.6 Variant Title** – Any source
> **2.3.7 Earlier Title Proper** – Same source as title proper in an earlier iteration
> **2.3.8 Later Title Proper** – Same source as title proper from a later part or issue
> **2.3.9 Key Title** – The ISSN Register, a source within resource itself, or any other source
> **2.3.10 Abbreviated Title** – Any source

> **RDA Core**: Title Proper
>
> **LC Core**: Parallel Title Proper; Other Title Information; Earlier Title Proper; Later Title Proper; Key Title; Abbreviated Title
>
> **ICC11 Core**: Variant Title, if applicable

A *title*, according to RDA 2.3.1, "is a word, character, or group of words and/or characters that names a resource or a work contained in it."[11] Titles come in different forms. The following contains some examples of different types of titles that one may encounter:

- a title proper, such as *The days of Anna Madrigal*
- a translated title proper for a particular language expression, such as *Pikaruokakansa*, the Finnish title for *Fast food nation*
- a preferred title of a work, such as *Introduction to functional grammar*, which in later editions is known by the title proper *Halliday's introduction to functional grammar*
- a parallel title, such as *Doctrine aérospatiale des Forces canadiennes*, which appears on the title page after the title proper *Canadian Forces aerospace sense doctrine*
- a collective title, such as *Complete full-length plays, 1975-1995*
- a conventional collective title, such as *Plays. Selections*
- other title information, such as *the rise of the American novel*, which is the subtitle for *Truth's ragged edge*
- a variant title, such as a distinctive portion of other title information (e.g., *Animal tales from Rajasthan*) that is different from the title proper (e.g., *The pious cat*)

Titles may appear in many places in or on the same resource. For example, one may encounter a title on or in

- a title page, title card, title screen, title frame, or title bar in a browser
- a cover, spine, or jacket
- the top or bottom margin of each page of a book
- the largest heading at the top of a document
- a metadata description inside an electronic document
- a case, label, or container
- accompanying material

and so on.

The basic instruction at RDA 2.3.1.4: Recording Titles states that a title is to be transcribed as found on the preferred source of information, using the transcription guidelines found at RDA 1.7.1. This instruction applies to all the title sub-elements under RDA 2.3. In addition, an optional omission, four exceptions, and three clarifying instructions follow (RDA 2.3.1.5-2.3.1.7).

The optional omission allows for catalogers to abridge an extensive title proper, parallel title, other title information, and so on, but *only* if it can be done without a loss of essential information. The ellipsis (. . .), used as a mark of omission, indicates that some metadata has been removed. Catalogers, however, are warned never to exclude the first five words of a title. There is *not* an LC-PCC PS for this optional omission, but the authors of ICC11 think that a policy statement may be helpful.

> **ICC11 PS for Optional Omission at RDA 2.3.1.4 Recording Titles**: Be cautious and thoughtful about omitting any information from title statements (title proper, other title information, parallel titles, etc.). Generally, do not abridge a title unless it is excessively long or it obscures essential information. If abridging the title removes its distinctiveness from other titles, it is not to be a candidate for abridgment. If transcribing the complete title can be done without undue effort and time or ill effects, record the complete title.

In some resources—particularly those from the 17th century to the late 19th century, in which publishing customs and practices led to what today would be considered overly crowded title pages—lengthy titles, other title information, statements of responsibility, illustrations, and other information may fill the virtual entirety of the title pages.[12] An example of a verbose title page is found in Figure 5.2.

From this example, it should be clear that not everything must be transcribed fully in every case. Cataloger's judgment must come into play. For this particular item, *The Life and Strange Surprizing Adventures of Robinson Crusoe*, is probably more than enough to identify the resource uniquely; the other title information could be omitted completely without a loss of understanding. Others, however, may disagree with this assessment and decide that all this information is key to understanding the resource. So although catalogers are encouraged to record the fullest information possible for most resources, there are exceptions.

In addition to the basic instruction on recording titles, there are four exceptions listed at RDA 2.3.1.4:

- **Introductory words**: This is a reference to a later instruction on introductory words (addressed below).
- **Inaccuracies**: For most resources, inaccuracies are transcribed exactly as found on the resource, but for serials and integrating resources, the process is different. For these two resource types, catalogers are expected to correct any obvious typos in the title proper, and to make a note explaining the situation. Catalogers may also create a variant title access point if judged necessary.
- **Date, name, number, etc., that varies from issue to issue**: If the title of a serial or of a multipart monograph includes dates, names,

THE

L I F E

AND

STRANGE SURPRIZING

ADVENTURES

OF

R O B I N S O N   C R U S O E
O F   *Y O R K,* MARINER:

Who lived Eight and Twenty Years,
all alone in an un-inhabited Island on the
Coast of AMERICA, near the Mouth of
the Great River of OROONOQUE;

Having been cast on Shore by Shipwreck, wherein
all the Men perished but himself
WITH
An Account how he was at last as strangely
deliver'd by PYRATES.

Written by Himself.

L O N D O N
MDCCXIX

FIGURE 5.2 A Representation of a Verbose Title Page.

or numbers that vary from issue to issue, catalogers omit these and indicate the omission with ellipses. An example is *Report of Governor . . . for the year . . . .*

- **Earlier title, etc.**: If the title of a serial or an integrating resource indicates that there was an earlier title, or that this resource has absorbed another resource, catalogers should not transcribe any indications of the relationship, even if they are grammatically linked to the title. Catalogers do not use ellipses to indicate an omission. The earlier titles, titles absorbed, etc., are recorded as the titles of related works.

As these four instructions are exceptions to the general instruction to transcribe titles as found and, as explained in the preceding chapter, exceptions are not *options*, each of the four must be applied if relevant to the resource. Complying with them is not a matter of cataloger's judgment.

If a title is simply the name of person, family, or corporate body, the cataloger records the name as the title of the resource. This situation is most likely to occur with biographies, critical works, conference proceedings, and corporate or family histories. More frequent than this situation, however, is finding a name of a PFC as *part* of a title, rather than as the entire title. In these cases, if the name is an integral part of the title, such as through the use of a case ending, then the name is recorded as part of the title. For example, in the *Annual report of the National Archives of Canada*, the name and the title are inextricably linked. If it is *not* integral to the title, then the name will be recorded elsewhere (e.g., in the statement of responsibility or the publisher's name). Catalogers should recognize that there is a difference between the two resources found in Figure 5.3. The first involves the use of a possessive, which grammatically connects the name and the title; the second is simply the name of the creator placed before the title proper. These two preferred sources would result in different titles proper (i.e., the first is *William Shakespeare's Hamlet*, the second is *Hamlet*).

FIGURE 5.3 Examples of Titles and Names.

If the title contains introductory words that are not intended to be part of the title, they are not transcribed as part of the title. Introductory words may be more commonly found on certain types of resources (e.g., moving images, sound recordings).

> **~~Nut Family presents~~ The Nuts: bedtime at the Nut house**
>
> **~~Welcome to~~ Oil City confidential**
>
> **~~Storyville presents~~ Duke Ellington: the original piano transcriptions**
>
> **~~Welcome to~~ The official web site of the state of Maine.**

If there were ever an instruction calling for cataloger's judgment, this would be it. It can be difficult to determine whether some words are merely introductory words or if they are considered significant, and it is often questionable what was *intended* by an author, a movie studio, a record company, or a publisher. There is an optional addition for this instruction at RDA 2.3.1.6; it allows catalogers to record the introductory words with the remainder of the title as a variant title in the description.

> **ICC11 PS for Optional Addition at RDA 2.3.1.6 Introductory Words, etc.:** If there is doubt about whether the introductory words are intended to be part of the title, apply the option and create a variant title. Most likely it will not affect retrieval negatively, and it could be helpful to some users.

The final instruction in the basic guidelines for titles discusses situations involving the titles of parts, sections, and supplements. If the separately issued part, section, or supplement has only a title for itself (i.e., lacking the common title shared by all parts or sections), the title of the part, section, or supplement is recorded as the primary title (e.g., The two towers). The common title is recorded as a series statement or as a related work, whichever is most appropriate. If the resource contains both the common title and the individual title, then a cataloger must determine if the section, part, or supplement title is sufficient to identify the resource uniquely. If it is sufficient, then the section, part, or supplement title is recorded as the primary title (e.g., Tigh me up, Tigh me down, *not* Battlestar Galactica. Tigh me up, Tigh me down); if not, then it is recorded after the common title shared by all the parts or sections (e.g., Merrily we roll along. Vocal score).

Title Proper

Title proper, an RDA Core element, is the title that is the principal name of an information resource. It is the main title that is used to cite or name a resource. It excludes any parallel titles, other title information, and parallel other title information, but it includes alternative titles. An *alternative title* is a second title introduced by the word *or* (or its equivalent in another language). Alternative titles were widely used in manifestations published before the twentieth century, but occasionally they are used today (e.g., *Breakfast of champions, or, Goodbye blue Monday!*). As a second separate title *within* the title proper, the capitalization instructions are applied to the second title as well. A file name for an electronic document (e.g., Chapter05-ICC11-DescCat-Manif-Item-DNJ.docx) is not considered a title proper, unless it is the only title appearing in the resource.

The title proper is to be transcribed as it appears on the preferred source (see RDA 2.2.2-2.2.4), according to the basic instructions at RDA 2.3.1 (e.g., transcribe the title but without introductory words; make no corrections unless the resource is a serial or integrating resource). If the title appears on the preferred source in more than one language or script, the cataloger is to choose the title in the language that most closely matches the primary content of the resource. If that does not apply, then the title proper is chosen based on the sequence, layout, or typography of the titles presented on the preferred source. If there are two or more forms of title in the same language or script on the preferred source of information, then, again, catalogers should choose the title proper based on the sequence, layout, or typography of the titles presented on the preferred source and record the other titles as parallel titles, other title information, or variant titles as appropriate.

Some titles proper are collective titles. *Collective titles* are inclusive titles that represent a compilation that contains two or more individually titled parts (see Figure 5.4). If the resource is being described as a whole (i.e., a comprehensive description), and there is a collective title as well as individual titles for the parts, then catalogers record the collective title as the title proper. There is a note that instructs catalogers to record the titles of the

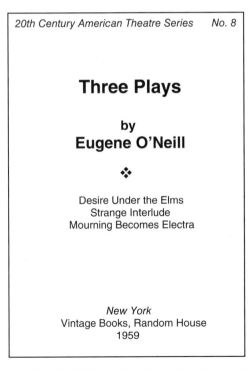

FIGURE 5.4 Example of Title Page For a Compilation.

individual works in the description if they are considered important for access or identification.

> **Title proper**:   Three plays
>
> **Contents notes**: Desire under the elms
>
> Strange interlude
>
> Mourning becomes Electra

There is no LC-PCC PS for this instruction, but the PCC considers collective titles and the titles of individual contents to be core for some types of resources.[13]

> **ICC11 PS for Optional Addition at RDA 2.3.2.6.1 Comprehensive Description [Collective Titles]**: Create contents notes listing the individual titles or create individual name/title access points for each work, or both.

If a compilation is to be described comprehensively but *lacks* a collective title, then the cataloger records the titles of the parts as they appear on the resource, in the order presented on the resource, as the title proper. If there is no single source of information listing all the titles of the parts, then the individual sources identifying the parts are considered to be one collective source of information. For example, if the resource in Figure 5.4 lacked the collective title *Three plays*, then the title proper would be

> **Title**: Desire under the elms ; Strange interlude ; Mourning becomes Electra

This example, by the way, uses ISBD punctuation and spacing (space semicolon space) to make clear it contains three separate part titles strung together to create a single title proper. An RDA alternative states that a cataloger may supply a collective title if one is lacking, but both the LC-PCC PS and the authors of this text agree that it is not a good idea.[14]

If an analytical description is preferred (i.e., each part of the compilation is described separately), the title proper will reflect the individual part being described. The collective title for the larger resource *may* be recorded as a series title or as a title of a related manifestation.

> **Title proper**: Strange interlude
>
> **Related manifestation**: *Contained in*: Three plays

If, however, the title of the part is insufficient to identify the resource adequately, then the collective title followed by the title of the part being described is recorded as the title proper (e.g., Three plays. 2nd Play).

For some resources, additional elements may be included as part of the title proper. These reflect the needs of certain resource types (i.e., musical works and cartographic materials). The list of additional elements for musical works includes type of composition, medium of performance, key, date of composition, opus number, and so on. Scale may be added to the title proper of a cartographic resource. More detail on these situations may be found in RDA 2.3.2.8.

If a title does not appear on the resource itself, the cataloger is to take a title proper from another source. It may come from accompanying material, other metadata descriptions, a supplied container, or any other source, such as a reference work. If that is ineffective, then the cataloger may supply a title. In these cases, a note explaining the title's source is appropriate.

If the cataloger must devise a title because one cannot be found elsewhere, then a concise description of the resource should be used as the title proper. A devised title may entail a description of the type or nature of the resource (photograph, public service announcement, diary, poster, untitled manuscript, etc.), its subject matter (names of topics, entities, dates, locations, etc.), or both. RDA 2.3.2.11 states that the devised title should reflect the language and script of the content, but the LC-PCC PS advises to apply the alternative and record the devised title in the preferred language or script of the cataloging agency (e.g., in English in the United States).

> **Devised title**: Photograph of old stagecoach in Yellowstone
> National Park, Wyoming in 1913

Additional instructions for creating devised titles for musical works, cartographic resources, moving image resources, and archival collections are listed at RDA 2.3.2.11.1-2.3.2.11.4.

Instructions for recording any changes in the title proper follow at RDA 2.3.2.12. These instructions are specifically for three modes of issuance, each reflecting the basis of the description discussed in RDA 2.1: Basis for Identification of the Resource:

- **Multipart monographs**: If the title proper changes, the original title proper is kept, and the changed title is recorded as a *later title proper*.

- **Serials**: If the title proper changes, a new description is created *if* it is a major change. A related work relationship should be indicated between descriptions. If the change is only minor, the changed title is recorded as a *later title proper*.

- **Integrating resources**: If the title proper changes, the latest form is given as the title proper and the replaced title is recorded as an *earlier title proper*.

The discussion of what entails a major versus a minor change in the title proper of a serial appears at RDA 2.3.2.13. Major changes include any of the following:

- changes (e.g., additions, deletions, reordering) in the first five words of the title proper (not including initial articles)
- differences in the rest of the title that change the meaning of the title or indicate a change in topic or coverage
- changes in the name of a corporate body that is included in the title

- changes in any component of the title when it is expressed through the use of characters or groups of characters rather than through the use of words (e.g., a change in the Chinese characters used in a title) that affect the meaning of the title or indicate a difference in topic or coverage

Major changes entail creating a new description; minor changes do not. The nine types of minor changes in RDA 2.3.2.13.2 are listed here:

- differences in how a word, character, group of words, or group of characters is represented (e.g., spelling variations; abbreviations, signs, or symbols added or removed; changes in numbering, such as Arabic, Roman, spelled-out forms; singular versus plural forms; changes in the form of the character)
- changes in articles, prepositions, or conjunctions (or analogous parts of speech in other languages) in the title
- differences in how the name of a corporate body is presented
- changes in punctuation
- differences in the order of titles when they appear in more than one language or script
- changes in the words or other characters used to indicate numbering
- alternating titles proper, reflecting a pattern
- changes in the order of words in a list in the title
- differences in the words or characters reflecting resource type (e.g., journal versus magazine)

If it is unclear whether a change is major or minor, the cataloger is to treat it as a minor change.

Parallel Titles

A *parallel title* is a title proper written in another language and/or in another script. The *parallel title* element does not include other title information in any language or script, but it does include alternative titles, if present. A parallel title may be transcribed from anywhere on the resource. If the title proper is recorded from another source of information (other than the resource itself), the parallel title should be taken from that same source. *Parallel title* is not a core element in RDA, but it is a core element for LC and PCC libraries.

> **ICC11 PS for RDA 2.3.3 Parallel Title**: Consider *parallel title* a core element. Even though RDA states, "Only one instance of a core element is required. Subsequent instances are optional,"[15] the PCC states that a cataloger should "Record all."[16] ICC11 recommends recording all parallel titles that appear on the preferred sources of information (as opposed to *anywhere* on the resource), unless there is an excessive number of them. In that

case, record only those deemed most likely to enhance access in the local catalog.

If more than one parallel title is found on the resource, then they should be recorded in the order presented, considering sequence, layout, and typography. For example, if the resource is in Spanish but there are titles in Spanish, French, and English, then the Spanish title is the title proper (per the guidelines for the title proper), and the French and English titles should be recorded in the order in which they appear on the title page (sheet, card, screen, frame, etc.).

> **Title proper**: Algunos problemas de interpretación de la religión Chané
>
> **Parallel title**: Quelques problèmes d'interprétation de la religion Chané
>
> Some problems in the interpretation of Chané religion

Additional instructions for specific formats (e.g., changes in a serial, music titles) are found in RDA 2.3.3: Parallel Title Proper.

Other Title Information and Parallel Other Title Information

Other title information (OTI) is words or phrases (e.g., a subtitle) that appear in conjunction with and are subordinate to the title proper of an information resource.

> **Title proper**: Ghost ship
>
> **OTI**: a novel from the NUMA files

It is to be transcribed from the same source as the title proper. Based on a definition that includes the words *in conjunction with* and *subordinate to*, OTI generally should not be taken from any source other than where the title proper is found (e.g., if there is a title page that supplies the title proper, other title information should not be taken from the cover or a colophon).

As is the case with titles proper, OTI may be quite lengthy. In some cases, it is helpful to abridge overly long OTI. The instructions and warnings about abridging titles apply to instances of OTI as well. An example of abridged OTI follows.

> **On Source**: Federal Reserve Act Amendments: Hearings Before The Subcommittee On Domestic Monetary Policy Of The Committee On Banking, Finance, And Urban Affairs, House Of Representatives, Ninety-Eighth Congress, First Session, On H.R. 3868, A Bill To Amend The Federal Reserve Act To Provide For A New Class Of Directors For Federal Reserve Banks, H.R. 3869, A Bill To Retire Federal Reserve Bank Stock, H.R. 4009, A Bill To Modernize The Federal Reserve System, September 15 And October 18, 1983

> **Title proper**: Federal Reserve Act Amendments
>
> **Abridged OTI**: hearings before the Subcommittee on Domestic Monetary Policy of the Committee on Banking, Finance, and Urban Affairs, House of Representatives, Ninety-eighth Congress, first session, on H.R. 3868 . . . H.R. 3869 . . . H.R. 4009 . . . September 15 and October 18, 1983

Parallel other title information is OTI in another language or script. It is to be transcribed from the same source as the parallel title proper. If there is no parallel title proper, but parallel other title information is presented, only the parallel other title information from the same source as the title proper is transcribed.

Other title information does not include titles proper, parallel titles, alternative titles, part titles, section titles, cover titles, binder's titles, and so on. It may include other words or phrases appearing with the title proper that indicate the resource's form (e.g., a biography), genre (e.g., a romance novel), contents (e.g., conference papers), or reasons for existence (e.g., a festschrift). OTI is not a core element in RDA, but it is a core element for LC and ICC11; it is not currently listed as a core element for PCC libraries. Parallel other title information is not considered core by any of these entities.

> **ICC11 PS for RDA 2.3.4 Other Title Information**: Consider *other title information* a core element, if present. Be cautious about including extraneous information that does not help to identify, retrieve, or select the resource.

There may be more than one instance of OTI, and generally they should be recorded in the order in which they appear on the source.

> **Title proper**: Cure for the future
>
> **OTI 1**: the real options approach in corporate real estate management
>
> **OTI 2**: an exploratory study in Dutch health care

It becomes more complex, however, when there are several instances of parallel information (e.g., two OTI statements and their parallel counterparts, or, one OTI statement, but with several parallel versions of it). If there are two instances of OTI, as seen in Figure 5.5, then they are clustered together in the appropriate elements. For example, if the content of the resource in Figure 5.5 were evenly split between English and French, then the data would be transcribed in an RDA template as follows, because English comes first.

> **Title proper**: African Universities Congress
>
> **OTI**: interaction and interrelation in Africa academic conference abstracts
>
> **Parallel title**: Congrès des universités africaines
>
> **Parallel OTI**: l'interaction et la corrélation en Afrique résumés de la conférence académique

> **African Universities Congress:**
> Interaction and Interrelation in Africa
>
> **Congrès des Universités Africaines:**
> L'interaction et la Corrélation en Afrique
>
>
> Academic Conference Abstracts
> Résumés de la Conférence Académique
>
>
>
>
> Khartoum, Sudan
> International University of Africa
> 2006

FIGURE 5.5 Example of Parallel Other Title Information Found on a Title Page.

The result is that the two languages are neatly separated among the elements. If, however, there were only the first instance of other title information, but all the title elements appeared in English, French, and Spanish, then the transcription would look somewhat different, with the languages mixed together in the parallel elements.

Title proper: African Universities Congress
OTI: interaction and interrelation in Africa
Parallel title: Congrès des universités africaines
Congreso de universidades de África
Parallel OTI: l'interaction et la corrélation en Afrique
interacción e interrelación en África

In today's MARC-based cataloging environment, situations such as these can be difficult to encode in a manner comprehensible by the public.

OTI is typically found on the resource itself. The cataloger does not devise OTI for resources, other than for some cartographic resources lacking an indication of the geographic area or subject matter (e.g., adding [Paris, France] when the title proper is *Street map*) and for the trailers for moving image resources (e.g., adding [trailer] when the title proper indicates only *The hunger games*). The cataloger should indicate that these additions were not found on the resource, either through notes or by placing the metadata in square brackets. Additional instructions for OTI and parallel other title information can be found at RDA 2.3.4 and 2.3.5.

Variant Titles

According to RDA 2.3.6, a *variant title* is a title associated with an information resource, but one that is not the title proper, other title information, a parallel title, or any of the other specific title sub-elements identified in RDA. A variant title may be transcribed from the resource itself or recorded from elsewhere. *Variant title* is not a core element in RDA, for LC, or for PCC libraries, but it is a core element for ICC11.

> **ICC11 PS for RDA 2.3.6 Variant Title**: Consider *variant title* a core element, if applicable. Add the variant titles discussed below that are judged most likely to support the user tasks. "When in doubt, be liberal in making variant titles but generally do not make a variant title that is not sufficiently distinctive to be a useful access point."[17]

Variant titles include the following:

- titles found on or near the resource itself, such as
  - caption, masthead, colophon, half title page, added title page, and running titles
  - cover, spine, jacket, sleeve, container, and binder's titles
  - titles found in accompanying material
  - other titles found on the title page, title screen, title card, and elsewhere
  - other permutations of titles found on the resource
- titles found in reference works or outside the resource itself
- titles assigned by a cataloger or a cataloging agency while cataloging, such as
  - additional titles assigned by a repository
  - translations of titles performed by a cataloger
  - transliterations of titles performed by a cataloger
  - titles containing spelled-out versions of numbers, abbreviations, etc., in title
  - corrected titles, when a title contains an inaccuracy
- additional titles assigned by the creator or by previous owners or custodians
- a portion of a title, such as an alternative title, section title, part title, and so on
- variations in parallel titles proper, other title information, or parallel other title information appearing on an earlier iteration of an integrating resource or on a later issue or part of a multipart monograph or serial

Although variant titles are not an RDA, LC, or PCC Core element, there is a lengthy and useful LC-PCC PS for 2.3.6.3: Recording Variant Titles. Although it is placed in the context of encoding this metadata into MARC bibliographic records, the overall content provides helpful information about various kinds of variant titles the cataloger should consider. The LC-PCC PS begins by specifically addressing 16 types of permutations related to the title proper.

Title Proper Variations presented in LC-PCC PS for RDA 2.3.6.3

- **Abbreviations**: If an abbreviation appears in the first five words of a title, a variant title with the spelled-out word in its place is created:
  - **Title proper**: *St. James encyclopedia of popular culture*
  - **Variant title**: *Saint James encyclopedia of popular culture*

- **Ampersands**: If an ampersand (or a plus sign (+) or another symbol representing the word *and*) appears in the first five words of a title, a variant title with the word *and* (or its foreign language equivalents) in its place is created:
  - **Title proper**: *Joys & concerns*
  - **Variant title**: *Joys and concerns*

- **Initials, Acronyms, and Letters**: When a series of letters appear in the first five words of a title *with separating punctuation* (hyphen, period, slash), a variant title without the separating punctuation is created:
  - **Title proper**: *A.L.A. cataloging rules for author and title entries*
  - **Variant title**: *ALA cataloging rules for author and title entries*

- **Arabic Numbers**: If Arabic numerals are used in the title proper (especially in the first five words), a variant title that substitutes the spelled-out form for the numerals using the language of the title proper is created:
  - **Title proper**: *Addicted to company, pt. 1*
  - **Variant title**: *Addicted to company, part one*

- **Dates Representing a Single Year or Span of Years**: Generally catalogers do *not* substitute a spelled-out version for the Arabic numerals used in a single-year date or for a span of years in a title. If a date is presented in Roman numerals, however, a variant title with Arabic numerals representing the date is created:
  - **Title proper**: *MCMLXXXVI: newsletter of the Johannesburg Publicity Association*
  - **Variant title**: *1986*

- **Other Dates**: If other types of dates are represented by Roman numerals, a variant title with Arabic numerals representing the dates is created. Catalogers make additional variant titles for spelled-out versions, if deemed useful:
  - **Title proper**: *A master plan for XXI century Havana*
  - **Variant title**: *A master plan for 21st century Havana*
  - **Variant title**: *A master plan for twenty-first century Havana*

- **Roman Numerals**: If a title contains Roman numerals, a variant title substituting them with Arabic numerals is created. Catalogers make additional variant titles for the spelled-out versions, if deemed useful:
  - **Title proper**: *XIV biennale internazionale d'arte della citta di Venezia*
  - **Variant title**: *14. biennale internazionale d'arte della citta di Venezia*
  - **Variant title**: *Quattordicesimo biennale internazionale d'arte della citta di Venezia*

- **Spelled-out Form of Numbers**: If a title contains the spelled-out form of numbers, a variant title substituting them with Arabic numerals is created, if deemed useful:
  - **Title proper**: *Fifty & counting*
  - **Variant title**: *50 and counting.*

  Note: Two more permutations of the title, *Fifty and counting* and *50 & counting*, could be added but generally catalogers have not been encouraged to create variants of variants. Under RDA, there is no restriction on variants; catalogers must use their judgment. One variant title addressing both components (i.e., *fifty* and *&*) may be enough.

- **Signs and Symbols**: If a title contains a sign or a symbol in the first five words of the title proper, a variant title with the name or a description of the sign or symbol as a substitute for it is created, if deemed useful:
  - **Title proper**: *I ♥ Huckabees*
  - **Variant title**: *I [heart] Huckabees* or *I [heart symbol] Huckabees*

  Note: If the heart symbol cannot be recorded in the title proper, then *I [heart] Huckabees* will be recorded as the title proper with a note explaining the use of the symbol and no variant title is needed.

- **Other**: If a title proper contains a term within the first five words for which there could be an alternate form that would be filed differently, a variant title under that form is created, if deemed useful:
  - **Title proper**: *Benson Family Cook Book*
  - **Variant title**: *Benson Family Cookbook*

- **Corrected titles proper (monographs)**: If a typo or an inaccuracy is found in the title proper, generally it is not corrected—unless it is for a serial or an integrating resource. The corrected title proper is recorded as a variant title:
  - **Title proper**: *Particle emission from a bench-scale fluidized-bed comsustor*
  - **Variant title**: *Particle emission from a bench-scale fluidized-bed combustor*

  Note: For a serial or an integrating resource, the inaccurate title is recorded as a variant title.

- **Alternative titles**: If the title proper contains an alternative title, variant titles are created for each part of the title both before and after the word *or*:
  - **Title proper**: *Oliver Twist, or, The parish boy's progress*
  - **Variant title**: *Oliver Twist*
  - **Variant title**: *The parish boy's progress*

- **Part or Designation of Part**: If the title proper contains a part or a designation of a part, a variant title for the part is created, if deemed useful:
  - **Title proper**: *The walking dead. Part two: The fall of the governor*
  - **Variant title**: *The fall of the governor*

- **Partial titles**: If the title proper contains a long or complex title, and a cataloger judges a portion(s) of it to be useful for retrieval and identification, then a variant title for the portion is created:
  - **Title proper**: *The New York Times book of great chess victories and defeats.*
  - **Variant title**: *Book of great chess victories and defeats*
  - **Variant title**: *Great chess victories and defeats*

- **Statements of Responsibility**: If a title proper contains what is or appears to be a statement of responsibility, a variant title for the title without it is created, if deemed useful:
  - **Title proper**: *Dar Williams live at Bearsville Theater*
  - **Variant title**: *Live at Bearsville Theater*

- **Introductory words**: If a title proper is preceded by introductory words that were not transcribed as part of the title proper, a variant title for the title with introductory words reinserted is created, if deemed useful:
  - **Title proper**: *Duke Ellington: the original piano transcriptions*
  - **Variant title**: *Storyville presents Duke Ellington: the original piano transcriptions*

Other Title Variations

In addition to the title proper variations detailed in the previous section, other types of variant titles may be associated with a resource. LC-PCC PS 2.3.6.3 states that catalogers are encouraged to create, more or less automatically, variant title access points for cover titles, parallel titles, and added title-page titles when they are different from the title proper. It also suggests providing variant titles for caption titles, half titles, running titles, and other title information when the work was, at some point, known by one of these titles, when the work has been cited in reference works with one of these titles, or when those titles are given prominence through typography, sequencing, or layout. Also, when other title information contains an acronym or initialism, then a variant title with the spelled-out version is recommended. Consult the LC-PCC PS for further discussions on the titles of accompanying material, words or phrases found at the head of the title, binder's titles, corrected titles (other than title proper), parallel titles, and independent titles in a compilation.

Additional Title Elements

The instructions at RDA 2.3.7-2.3.10 address titles primarily used with integrating resources and serials:

- **Earlier Title Proper**: This LC Core element is recorded when a new title proper for an integrating resource has replaced the original title in the description. It is transcribed from the same source as a title proper. The basis for the description of an integrating resource is the latest iteration. The instructions are found at RDA 2.3.7.

> **Title proper**: Baldwin's Kentucky revised statutes annotated
>
> **Earlier title proper**: Baldwin's Kentucky revised statutes, with rules of practice, annotated

- **Later Title Proper**: This LC-PCC Core element is recorded when the title proper for a multipart monograph or a serial has changed from the original title, but the original remains the title proper in the description. It is transcribed from the same source as a title proper. The basis for the description of a serial or a multipart monograph is the first, lowest numbered, or earliest part available. The instructions are found at RDA 2.3.8.

> **Title proper**: Some eminent Indian mathematicians of the twentieth century
>
> **Later title proper**: Eminent Indian mathematicians of the twentieth century

- **Key Title**: This LC Core element contains the unique name assigned to a serial resource by an ISSN registration agency. In order of preference, it is recorded from the ISSN Register, transcribed from anywhere on the resource, or recorded from another source. The instructions are found at RDA 2.3.9.

- **Abbreviated Title**: This LC Core element contains a serial title abbreviated for the purposes of indexing or identification. Transcribe it from anywhere on the resource. The instructions are found at RDA 2.3.10.

> **Title proper**: Cataloging & classification quarterly
>
> **Key title**: Cataloging & classification quarterly
>
> **Abbreviated title**: Cat. classif. q.

RDA 2.4 Statements of Responsibility

2.4 Statement of Responsibility

Definition: A statement in an information resource that names persons, families, and corporate bodies responsible for the intellectual or artistic content. It may include those responsible for creating the work, contributing to the expression, and so on.

Sub-elements and Their First Listed Sources of Information: Please consult the more complete instructions that discuss the sources of information in RDA.

> **2.4.2 Statement of Responsibility Relating to Title Proper** – Same source as the title proper
> **2.4.3 Parallel Statement of Responsibility Relating to Title Proper** – Same source as the parallel title proper

RDA Core: Statement of Responsibility Relating to Title Proper *(but only the first of which is required)*

ICC11 Core: Statement of Responsibility Relating to Title Proper (record *all* statements of responsibility that support discovery, identification, and selection)

A *statement of responsibility* (SOR), according to RDA 2.4.1, is "a statement relating to the identification and/or function of any persons, families, or corporate bodies responsible for the creation of, or contributing to the realization of, the intellectual or artistic content of a resource."[18] In other words, it includes not only creators, such as authors and composers, but also illustrators, translators, editors, and other types of contributors. Some responsible parties, however, are not included in the SOR. For example, the names of producers, publishers, distributors, and manufacturers are recorded according to later instructions.

> **Title proper**: Six suites for violoncello solo
> **OTI**: BWV 1007-1012
> **SOR**: Johann Sebastian Bach
>
> **Title proper**: Breakfast on Mars and 37 other delectable essays
> **SOR**: edited by Rebecca Stern & Brad Wolfe
>
> **Title proper**: Ancoratus
> **SOR**: St. Epiphanius of Cyprus
> **SOR**: translated by Young Richard Kim

An SOR may include personal, family, and/or corporate body names; it may include epithets that act as names (e.g., A.N. Other; a lady), references to the creators of other works (e.g., by the author of The Spanish brothers), and so on. It may also include linking words (e.g., *by, and, in collaboration with*) as well as other types of words or phrases that explain something about a role or relationship.

> **SOR**: by a practical housewife
>
> **SOR**: by the author of Little Ella
>
> **SOR**: second cello part composed by Anthony Arnone
>
> **SOR**: English reversioned by FUNimation Entertainment

There are actually several types of SORs. The most common are those associated with titles proper, but there are also those associated with parallel titles, edition statements, and series statements—in this text, the latter two are addressed with those particular elements. There are also statements of responsibility, usually associated with the title proper, that specifically address the names of performers, narrators, and presenters, as well as those associated with the technical and artistic credits for a resource (e.g., those involved with the production of a film); these SORs are described below.

The basic instruction at RDA 2.4.1.4: Recording Statements of Responsibility asserts that the SOR should be transcribed as it appears on the resource. This means that wording, spelling, and order should reflect what appears on the source, and that catalogers should not insert words such as *by* or *and* to the SOR—transcribing them if they appear on the source is fine, but adding them is generally unnecessary. There is, as with titles and other title information, an option that allows catalogers to abridge parts of an SOR. This is to be applied *only* if it can be done without a loss of essential information. For this element, however, marks of omission are *not* to be used. This allows catalogers to remove unnecessary information such as degrees, affiliations, qualifications, dates of founding, mottoes, and so on. The following example illustrates this option:

> **Source**: by Rev. Egbert Watson Smith, D.D.
>
> **Transcribed SOR**: by Rev. Egbert Watson Smith, D.D.
>
> **Abridged SOR**: by Egbert Watson Smith
>
> **Abridged SOR**: by Rev. Egbert Watson Smith
>
> **Abridged SOR**: by Egbert Watson Smith, D.D.

The LC-PCC PS states, "Generally do not abridge a statement of responsibility."[19] Although this is very much in keeping with a "take what you see" approach to cataloging and has little negative effect most of the time, it may not always be the appropriate answer for all situations. In the following examples, the SORs are somewhat longer and more convoluted.

> **Source**: by William Whiston, M.A. sometime professor of the mathematicks in the University of Cambridge and Humphry Ditton, master of the new mathematick school in Christ's Hospital, London.
>
> **Abridged SOR**: by William Whiston and Humphry Ditton.
>
> **Source**: William Jones, lecturer in physics, the University of Sheffield, Norman March, professor of theoretical

> solid state physics, Imperial College of Science and
> Technology, University of London
>
> **Abridged SOR**: William Jones, Norman March.

In both of these examples, the metadata in the abridged SOR is more easily
understood because it is uncluttered. And both resources are still identifiable
without the unnecessary information being included. It does lose some of the
charm of statements like "sometime professor of the mathematicks," but that
is a relatively small price to pay for clarity. Besides, much of the data removed
would be more useful in an authority record for the creators than in the bibliographic records for the resources.

> **ICC11 PS for Optional Omission for RDA 2.4.1.4 Record-
> ing Statements of Responsibility**: Although abridgement is not
> generally recommended, use, judiciously and thoughtfully, the
> option that allows catalogers to abridge SORs when needed. This
> may prove to be useful if a statement of responsibility is cluttered
> with extraneous data. Be careful not to remove essential identify-
> ing information.

Some SORs are quite simple with only a single name. Some, however, may
contain two, three, or many more names of PFCs performing identical or different tasks. In either case, the SOR is recorded as found on the resource.

> **SOR**: Lois Mai Chan

> **SOR**: by Charles Dickens, edited by Angus Easson, with an
> introduction by Malcolm Andrews, and original illustrations
> by George Cattermole and Hablot K. Browne ('Phiz'),
> Samuel Williams, and Daniel Maclise

Some resources may contain more than one statement of responsibility, each
with one or more names contained within it.

> **SOR**: starring Gillian Anderson, Jamie Dornan, Archie Panjabi,
> John Lynch, Bronagh Waugh, and Colin Morgan
> **SOR**: created, written and directed by Allan Cubitt

> **SOR**: produced by John DeLuca, Rob Marshall, Marc Platt,
> Callum McDougall
> **SOR**: screenplay by James Lapine
> **SOR**: music and lyrics by Stephen Sondheim
> **SOR**: directed by Rob Marshall

It can, at first, be somewhat difficult to determine if what one is viewing is a
single SOR or multiple statements. Often making this determination involves
cataloger's judgment based on layout and typography. For example, the two
title pages in Figure 5.6 contain the same information, but they may be interpreted very differently.

The Organization of Information Ninth Edition by Meryl Streep & Glenn Close with illustrations by M.C. Escher & H.R. Giger and edited by Maxwell Perkins New Pittsburgh Libraries Unlimited 2050	The Organization of Information Ninth Edition by Meryl Streep and Glenn Close with illustrations by M.C. Escher and H.R. Giger and edited by Maxwell Perkins New Pittsburgh Libraries Unlimited 2050

FIGURE 5.6 Two Title Pages Displaying the Same Information.

For the first title page, it seems quite likely that only a single SOR would be transcribed.

> **SOR**: by Meryl Streep & Glenn Close with illustrations by M.C. Escher & H.R. Giger and edited by Maxwell Perkins

For the second, however, two or three statements are likely to be recorded.

> **SOR**: by Meryl Streep & Glenn Close
>
> **SOR**: with illustrations by M.C. Escher & H.R. Giger
>
> **SOR**: and edited by Maxwell Perkins

If there is more than one SOR, the cataloger is to record them in the order in which they appear on the source, considering sequence, layout, and typography. If it is still unclear, the cataloger should record the statements in the order that makes the most sense.

When it comes to recording SORs, RDA 2.4.1.5 provides another optional omission. It states that a cataloger may omit some of the names in an SOR, *if* there are more than three names listed, and *if* these entities performed the same function. If applying this option, the cataloger can be selective as to which names to include and which to omit. The cataloger is warned, however, never to exclude the first name listed on the source. Following the names that *are* transcribed, the cataloger should summarize what has been omitted with a phrase such as *[and six others]*. The phrase is placed in square brackets to indicate that it does not appear on the resource itself. This option replaces a rule in AACR2 that was known as the *rule of three*. It stated that for a resource with *more* than three names listed in the SOR, the cataloger should record: (1) only the first name, (2) a mark of omission, and (3) "[et al.]" to indicate that others were involved in the creation. The LC-PCC PS for RDA 2.4.1.5 indicates that catalogers generally should *not* omit names from SORs. The authors concur but acknowledge that if a resource includes an overly long list of creators (e.g., a paper with nearly 3,000 researchers sharing authorship),[20] it may be necessary to abridge the SOR.

> **ICC11 PS for RDA 2.4.1.5 Statement Naming More Than One Person, etc.**: Generally do not omit names in a statement of responsibility, unless under extraordinary circumstances. It may be something to consider if there are twenty or more names listed in a statement of responsibility.

The guidelines at RDA 2.4.1 contain several sub-instructions for situations that might occur when recording a statement of responsibility. These include issues related to groups of people, explanatory words or phrases, and SORs without names. If the SOR includes both the names of a group and its members (e.g., a band's name as well as the names of the individual musicians), the cataloger is to omit the individual members' names from an SOR, in favor of placing them in a note. If a statement of responsibility is unclear about the roles and responsibilities of those named within it, the cataloger may add a brief description in the SOR if judged necessary.

> **SOR**: [compiled by] Jesús Alonso Regalado
> **SOR**: [narrated by] John De Lancie
> **SOR**: [edited by] Allan W. Atlas

This is reserved for relationships that go beyond typical creation relationships (e.g., writing a book, composing a musical work), which is implied when only a name is recorded. If a noun (e.g., research) or a noun phrase (e.g., dramatized adaptations) occurs in conjunction with the name of a person, family, or corporate body and (1) it is indicative of the role played by the PFC and (2) the sequence, layout, or typography supports that the noun or noun phrase is part of the SOR, then include it as part of the statement of responsibility (e.g., a story and drawings by Gabrielle Beverakis; a novelization by Max Allan Collins). If the cataloger finds that names are absent from the SOR on the source, but instead contains a phrase describing the responsibility, record that phrase instead (e.g., authored by a collaborative of consumers, families, and private & state agency partners on behalf of the Honorable M. Jodi Rell, governor). In other cases, there may be no statement of responsibility at all. Unlike titles proper, a statement of responsibility is not essential to a description, so if one is not found in the preferred sources of information, the cataloger does not devise one.

There are two specific elements listed in RDA 2.4: the Statement of Responsibility Relating to Title Proper (SOR-TP) and its parallel counterpart. According to RDA, the SOR-TP is a core element that is to be transcribed from the same source as the title proper, from another part of the resource, or elsewhere as listed in RDA 2.2.4. If the SOR-TP is transcribed from somewhere outside the resource itself, it should be placed in square brackets and a note about its source should be given. Even though RDA states that if there is more than one SOR-TP, only the first is core, it *also* states that if not all SORs are being transcribed, the cataloger should ensure that those of bibliographic significance are included (i.e., those identifying the creators of the intellectual or artistic content). The PCC states, "Catalogers are encouraged to transcribe any other SORs that aid in resource discovery, identification, and selection."[21] In case of doubt, the cataloger should always transcribe, at least, the first statement. The Parallel SOR-TP is not considered a core element in RDA, by LC, or by the PCC, but if it is to be included, it is transcribed according to the guidelines found at RDA 2.4.3.

Performers, Narrators, Presenters, and Those Listed in Artistic or Technical Credits

This type of data is generally presented in the form of a list of contributors to a resource. Performers, narrators, presenters, and those receiving artistic or technical credit may be recorded in either a statement of responsibility (see RDA 2.4) or a note on statement of responsibility (see RDA 2.17.3). In previous versions of RDA, separate elements had been established in chapter 7 to record these contributors. As of the April 2015 update to RDA, these elements were removed from the content standard.

In either an SOR or a note, the list includes individual contributors as well as groups of contributors that act as corporate bodies (e.g., comedy troupes, musical groups). The names of entities performing these roles (e.g., actors, vocalists, designers) are recorded if they are considered important for identifying, accessing, or selecting a resource (e.g., identifying a film version of *Hamlet* where the title role is played by Kenneth Branagh and not by Laurence Olivier). For musicians, the cataloger also records the instruments they play, if available. For those contributors listed as part of technical or artistic credits, the cataloger records a statement of each PFC's function along with each name.

> **SOR**: produced, directed, and written by Werner Bundschuh; producers, Werner Bundschuh, Christie Taylor; executive producer, Henry Hampton.
>
> **Performer note**: Narrated by Lynne Thigpen.
>
> **Credits note**: Director of photography, Rick Malkames; editor, James Rutenbeck; music, Nik Bariluk.
>
> **SOR**: Paramount Pictures and Lakeshore Entertainment present a Lorne Michaels production; director, Kelly Makin.
>
> **Performer note**: Kids in the Hall: Dave Foley, Bruce McCulloch, Kevin McDonald, Mark McKinney, Scott Thompson.
>
> **Credits note**: Producer, Lorne Michaels; writers, Norm Hiscock, Bruce McCulloch, Kevin McDonald, Mark McKinney, Scott Thompson; director of photography, David A. Makin; music, Craig Northey.

SOR: produced by George Roy Hill, Robert L. Crawford; based on the novel by John Irving; screenplay by Steve Tesich; directed by George Roy Hill.

Note: Cast: Robin Williams, Mary Beth Hurt, Glenn Close, John Lithgow, Hume Cronyn, Jessica Tandy, Swoosie Kurtz.

SOR: Sigur Rós.

Note: Composed and performed by Sigur Rós (Jón Þór Birgisson, vocals, guitars, keyboards; Kjartan Sveinsson, guitar, keyboards; Georg Hólm, keyboards, bass, glockenspiel; and Orri Páll Dýrason, keyboards, drums) with additional musicians.

RDA 2.5 Edition Statement

2.5 Edition Statement

Definition: A statement identifying a specific edition or version of a work. The edition statement indicates that a manifestation contains a particular expression of the work.

Sub-elements and Their First Listed Sources of Information: Please consult the more complete instructions that discuss the sources of information in RDA.

2.5.2 Designation of Edition – Same source as title proper

2.5.3 Parallel Designation of Edition – Same source as designation of edition

2.5.4 Statement of Responsibility Relating to the Edition – Same source as designation of edition

2.5.5 Parallel Statement of Responsibility Relating to the Edition – Same source as parallel designation of edition

2.5.6 Designation of a Named Revision of an Edition – Same source as designation of edition

2.5.7 Parallel Designation of a Named Revision of an Edition – Same source as designation of a named revision of an edition

2.5.8 Statement of Responsibility Relating to a Named Revision of an Edition – Same source as designation of a named revision of an edition

2.5.9 Parallel Statement of Responsibility Relating to a Named Revision of an Edition – Same source as parallel designation of a named revision of an edition

RDA Core: Designation of Edition and Designation of a Named Revision of an Edition

ICC11 Core: Statement of Responsibility Relating to the Edition and Statement of Responsibility Relating to a Named Revision of an Edition, if applicable

---

An *edition* is a particular version of a resource. AACR2 states the edition (for a book) is "all copies produced from essentially the same master copy and issued by the same entity."[22] It reflects a particular expression of intellectual content. In RDA an *edition statement* is "a statement identifying the edition to which a resource belongs."[23] Although *edition* is a concept reflecting an expression, the edition statement contains metadata that can only be found on a manifestation (i.e., because the expression is a non-tangible entity). The edition statement contains a *designation of edition*, which is "a word, character, or group of words and/or characters, identifying the edition to which a resource belongs."[24]

In the instructions for edition statements, there are four basic elements:

- **Designation of Edition**
- **Statement of Responsibility Relating to the Edition**
- **Designation of a Named Revision of an Edition**
- **Statement of Responsibility Relating to a Named Revision of an Edition**

In addition to these four elements, there are the four *parallel* versions of these elements (i.e., the same four elements but specifically used to record the information presented in another language or script). A designation of edition may appear in many forms on a manifestation. It may be presented simply with ordinal numbers and little else except a word or a phrase representing the concept of *edition*. Others may be more complex, with phrases involving numerals, letters, or spelled-out versions of numbers and using words in either spelled-out or abbreviated forms. Some edition designations have accompanying SORs. All this and more may appear in one or more languages (e.g., parallel edition statements). Some edition statements include information about revised versions of particular editions, referred to in RDA as a *Named Revision of an Edition* (e.g., 2nd edition, revised and enlarged). For unpublished resources, a statement of version, iteration, or issue, may be treated as an edition statement. Examples of edition statements include the following:

- 4th edition
- Fifth edition
- Twelfth ed.
- 2nd rev. ed.
- 44th standard ed.
- New edition
- Game of the year edition
- Fully revised second edition
- Eighth edition by Stephen E. Lucas
- First American edition, reprinted with revisions
- International version
- Draft
- Director's cut
- Nouvelle version
- MAPP digital edition
- PS3 version
- Ver. 7
- 2e éd. du recueil noté
- Wydanie I
- 6. Aufl.
- 9an edizioa
- 4de uitgawe

The basic instruction for edition statements is to transcribe them as they appear on the resource. If an abbreviation appears on the source itself, it should be transcribed, but the cataloger should not impose abbreviations on the edition statement. An RDA optional addition allows the cataloger to devise an edition statement if the resource lacks one, but is known to contain significant changes from other editions. There is no LC-PCC PS for this optional addition. As an edition statement is not found on all resources, it would be fairly common for this particular element to be empty.

> **ICC11 PS for Optional Addition for RDA 2.5.1.4 Recording Edition Statements**: Generally, do not apply optional addition allowing the cataloger to devise an edition statement.

If the option *is* applied, the cataloger should be certain that changes are manifest in the new version of the resource.

Designation of an Edition

The *designation of an edition*—generally, the first component of an edition statement (e.g., 9th edition)—is a core element in RDA. If it is present, it should be transcribed as found on the source of information (usually the same source as the title proper). The instruction at RDA 2.5.2.1 reminds the cataloger that in some languages, the same word may be used for both a new edition and a new printing; generally, for widely available resources, new printings are not recorded in metadata descriptions. A statement of the number of copies reflects information about a new printing; it is not an indication of edition information. If the cataloger is unsure whether the version in hand is a new edition or a new printing, then the words *edition, issue, release, level, state,* or *update* (or their equivalents in other languages) may be an indication of a new edition. In making this decision, the cataloger should also take into consideration statements indicating changes in content, geographic coverage, language, audience, format or presentation, dates associated with the content, and voice range or format for musical works.

Under RDA 2.5.2: Designation of Edition, several sub-instructions address issues that may be encountered when recording edition metadata, such as missing words, multiple edition designations, designations in multiple languages, and so on. Some of the more commonly encountered issues are addressed here. If the edition designation consists of solo letters or numbers (i.e., without words like *edition* or *issue*), then the cataloger is instructed to add an appropriate word to clarify the metadata. This additional information must indicate it came from a source outside the resource itself (e.g., [Version] 1.1). If there is more than one edition designation, then the cataloger records them in the order in which they appear on the source. If the designation appears in more than one language or script, then the cataloger records the statement in the language of the title proper, and the others may be recorded as parallel edition designations. If a designation of edition is an integral part of (or is grammatically linked to) a title proper, OTI, or SOR, then the cataloger transcribes the edition designation as part of the title proper, OTI, or SOR as appropriate (e.g., Eleventh edition of The ills of life and how to cure them); the information is *not* repeated in the edition element.

Statement of Responsibility Relating to the Edition

In some resources, the cataloger will encounter a statement of responsibility related to the particular edition of the resource in hand. This occurs when responsibility for the content of a resource changes over editions (e.g., updated editions, revised editions, editions with new editors, newly illustrated editions). When the responsibility is limited to a particular edition, and that resource has a designation of edition, then the cataloger records a statement of responsibility listing those PFCs responsible for the edition. If the cataloger is unsure of whether an SOR applies to all or just to some editions, or if there is no edition designation, then the names of those responsible are recorded as part of the SOR-TP. Statements of responsibility are transcribed as instructed at RDA 2.4.1: Statements of Responsibility:

> **Title Proper**: Fowler's dictionary of modern English usage
>
> **SOR for Title Proper**: first edition [by] H.W. Fowler
>
> **Designation of Edition**: Fourth edition
>
> **SOR for Edition**: edited by Jeremy Butterfield

> **Title Proper**: Little Dorritt
>
> **SOR for Title Proper**: Charles Dickens
>> edited by John Holloway

The SOR associated with an edition and the SOR associated with a named revision of an edition are not core elements in RDA or at LC. The PCC considers them core for rare materials only. ICC11 considers them to be core if the entities responsible for the content have changed and if an edition designation is present.

> **ICC11 PS for RDA 2.5.4 Statement of Responsibility Relating to the Edition**: Consider *statement of responsibility relating to the edition* a core element, if applicable and if an edition designation is present.

Designation of a Named Revision of an Edition

Designation of a Named Revision of an Edition, an RDA Core element, is a word or phrase that is used to identify a particular revision of an edition (e.g., "a named reissue of a particular edition containing changes from that edition").[25] If it is present, it should be transcribed as found on the source of information (*usually* the same source as the designation of edition). The type of information found in this element is better understood by viewing some examples:

> **Designation of Edition**: First American edition
>
> **Designation of a Named
> Revision of an Edition**: reprinted with revisions

Designation of Edition: 2nd edition

**Designation of a Named
Revision of an Edition**: corrected impression

Designation of Edition: Rev. ed.

Edition SOR: with revisions, an introduction, and a chapter on
writing by E.B. White

Designation of a Named Revision of an Edition: 2nd ed.

Named Revision of an Edition SOR: with the assistance of
Eleanor Gould Packard

For other instructions related to edition, including those for the elements in
parallel edition statements, the reader should consult RDA directly.

RDA 2.6 Numbering of Serials

2.6 Numbering of Serials

Definition: Numbering that indicates the volumes, issues, or parts of a serial.

Sub-elements and Their First Listed Sources of Information: Please consult
the more complete instructions that discuss the sources of information in RDA.

**2.6.2 Numeric and/or Alphabetic Designation of First Issue or Part of
Sequence** – Same source as title proper on first issue or part
2.6.3 Chronological Designation of First Issue or Part of Sequence –
Same source as title proper on first issue or part
**2.6.4 Numeric and/or Alphabetic Designation of Last Issue or Part of
Sequence** – Same source as title proper on last issue or part
2.6.5 Chronological Designation of Last Issue or Part of Sequence –
Same source as title proper on last issue or part

**2.6.6 Alternative Numeric and/or Alphabetic Designation of First Issue
or Part of Sequence** – Same source as title proper on first issue or part
**2.6.7 Alternative Chronological Designation of First Issue or Part of
Sequence** – Same source as title proper on first issue or part
**2.6.8 Alternative Numeric and/or Alphabetic Designation of Last Issue
or Part of Sequence** – Same source as title proper on last issue or part
**2.6.9 Alternative Chronological Designation of Last Issue or Part of
Sequence** – Same source as title proper on last issue or part

RDA Core: Numeric and/or Alphabetic Designation of First Issue or Part of
Sequence, Chronological Designation of First Issue or Part of Sequence,
Numeric and/or Alphabetic Designation of Last Issue or Part of Sequence, and
Chronological Designation of Last Issue or Part of Sequence

The *numbering of serials*, a category that contains four sub-elements and four alternative forms of these sub-elements, is metadata that obviously applies to serials only. These sub-elements contain data to identify the issues or parts of a serial. This may entail the use of numbers, letters, dates, or some other symbol or character to indicate the issues or parts. These characters may or may not be combined with words such as *volume, issue, part, number*, and the like. On some serials, there may be more than one concurrent form of numbering appearing on the resource (e.g., a numerical designation and a chronological one). For some serials, the numbering sequence may change over time leading to more than one system of numbering being recorded in the metadata description.

The basic instruction at 2.6.1.4 is to *record* the numbers but to *transcribe* the words as they are found on the source of information, applying the general guidelines in RDA chapter 1. There is an exception, however, that allows for slashes to be substituted for hyphens, if it helps with clarity (e.g., 2013-14 becomes 2013/2014). In general, the cataloger always records the numbering for the first issue or part of the serial (e.g., Vol. 1, no. 1); if the serial is no longer active, then the cataloger also records the number of the last issue or part (e.g., volume 14, number 12). If the sequence of numbering changes during the lifetime of a serial (one or more times), the cataloger should add the numbering for the first issue of each new sequence in addition to the numbering for the very first issue. This also applies to serials that have ceased publication (i.e., one should record the final issue for each sequence of numbering). The sequences should be recorded in the order in which they were used on the serial. The cataloger should also create a note to describe any slight variations that are judged important for identification and selection of the resource. If the serial has more than one concurrent form of numbering on the resource, the cataloger records the second and later sequences as *alternative* number systems, using the elements in RDA 2.6.5-2.6.9.

Numeric and/or Alphabetic Designation of First Issue or Part of Sequence and Numeric and/or Alphabetic Designation of Last Issue or Part of Sequence

The basic instructions for these RDA Core elements are nearly identical except for words such as *first* and *last*, *subsequent* and *previous*, and so on. There are a few additional sub-instructions for a first issue, but those are mentioned separately after the general guidelines that apply to both first and last issues. For the sake of brevity, this section presents the instructions only in the context of *first issues* (rather than *first parts, last issues*, or *last parts*). For example, the text might say "take the designation from the first issue" instead of "take the designation from the first and last issues or parts of sequence."

A *numeric/alphabetical designation of first issue* is numbering presented on the first issue for a serial. The metadata is recorded from the source of information, on the first issue or the first available issue, that has a title proper. If that is not possible, the cataloger should use another source within the first issue, or as a last resort, any of the sources listed in RDA 2.2.4 (i.e., accompanying material, other published descriptions, a container not issued with resource, or any other source).

The basic instructions state that if the first issue is identified by a numeric designation, the cataloger should record it in the serial's description (e.g., number 1; Vol. 1, issue 1; part A). The corresponding instruction is that if publication has ceased, the numeric designation of the last issue should also be recorded (e.g., volume 10, number 12; Pt. Q). There is, however, an alternative instruction to provide a note on the numbering instead. As this is common practice, LC and PCC have adopted the alternative approach. For example, instead of entering *Vol. 1, no. 1-* into the metadata element, it is formulated as a note, such as "Began with Vol. 1, no. 1."

If either of these designations is formatted as a year and a number that represents a division of the year (e.g., week, month, quarter), the cataloger should record the year first, followed by the division (e.g., 1987-1, 2014-12, 2009-52). If the first issue has no numbering, but subsequent issues do, then the cataloger should supply a numeric designation based on the pattern established (e.g., [Vol. 1, no. 1] or [Vol. 14, no. 365]) with a note explaining how this information was derived. If the identification of a serial is based on an issue other than the first, and the numeric designation can be ascertained, then the cataloger should supply a numeric designation for the first issue (e.g., [number 1]), with a note describing the issue or part used as the basis for identification (e.g., Identification of the resource based on issue no. 3). The three sub-instructions that only apply to first issues address situations such as when the numbering continues from previous serials, when there are phrases included such as *new series*, and when the numbering restarts but phrases such as *new series* or *2nd series* are missing. The reader should consult RDA 2.6.2.3 for more information. The alternative versions of the same elements apply the same general instructions.

Chronological Designation of First Issue or Part of Sequence and Chronological Designation of Last Issue or Part of Sequence

The basic instructions for these RDA Core elements are nearly identical except for words such as *first* and *last, subsequent* and *previous,* and so on. For the sake of brevity, this section presents the instructions only in the context of *first issues* (rather than *first parts, last issues,* or *last parts*). For example, the text might say "take the chronological designation from the first issue" instead of "take the chronological designation from the first and last issues or parts of sequence."

A *chronological designation of first issue* is numbering presented on the first issue of a serial in the form of a date. For these elements, a date may consist of a year by itself; a year and a month in combination; a year, month, and day together; or some other configuration. The metadata is recorded from the source of information, on the first issue, that contains a title proper. If that is not possible, the cataloger should use another source within the first issue, or as a last resort, any of the sources listed in RDA 2.2.4 (i.e., accompanying material, other published descriptions, a container not issued with resource, or any other source).

The basic instructions state that if the first issue is identified by a chronological designation, the cataloger should record it in the serial's description (e.g., 1982; August 1965; spring 2015). The corresponding idea is that if the publication has ceased, the chronological designation of the last issue should also be recorded (e.g., Dec. 31, 1999). There is, however, an alternative instruction to provide a note on the numbering instead. As this is common practice, LC and the PCC have adopted the alternative approach.

Chronological Designation
of First Issue: October/December 1966-

Following LC-PCC PS: Began with October/December 1966.

Numeric *and* Chronological Designation of First *and* Last Issues: Volume 1, number 1 (1997) - volume 9, number 2 (2008)

Following LC-PCC PS: Began with volume 1, number 1 (1997); ceased publication with volume 9, number 2 (2008).

If the first issue has no chronological designation, but subsequent issues do, then the cataloger should supply a chronological designation based on the pattern established (e.g., [January 31, 2003]) with a note explaining how this information was derived. If the identification of the serial is based on an issue other than the first, and the chronological designation can be ascertained, then the cataloger should supply one for the first issue (e.g., [1975]), with a note describing the issue or part used as the basis for identification. There is an optional addition stating that if the chronological designation includes dates from calendars other than the Gregorian or Julian calendar, the cataloger may add the corresponding Gregorian/Julian date (e.g., 4308 [1975]). The alternative versions of the same elements apply the same general instructions. For more information about serials cataloging, more specialized resources, such as the CONSER documentation provided by the Program for Cooperative Cataloging,[26] should be consulted.

RDA 2.7-2.10 Dissemination Information

In RDA, from 2.7 to 2.10, four modes of dissemination are addressed: *production, publication, distribution,* and *manufacture.* Each mode refers to individual statements (e.g., production statement, publication statement). The four statements comprise one or more individual elements. The four areas share an identical pattern of elements within them: *place of . . . , name of . . . , date of . . . ,* and parallel versions of the place and name elements. In this section, the instructions for the major publication elements are covered fully. The instructions for production, distribution, and manufacture statements are very similar to those found under publication statement, and are covered only to discuss the basic concept and to point out differences in approach. The parallel elements are not addressed, because they show little difference from their standard counterparts.

2.7-2.10 Dissemination Information

Definition: The part of the description that includes information about the production of unpublished resources, and the publication, distribution, and/or manufacture of published resources.

Sub-elements:
> **2.7** Production Statement
>> **2.7.2** Place of Production
>> **2.7.3** Parallel Place of Production
>> **2.7.4** Producer's Name
>> **2.7.5** Parallel Producer's Name
>> **2.7.6** Date of Production
>
> **2.8** Publication Statement*
> **2.9** Distribution Statement*
> **2.10** Manufacture Statement*

* Each follows the pattern established under *Production Statement*.

RDA Core:
> **Production**: Date of production, if an unpublished resource
> **Publication**: Places, Names, and Dates, *if* applicable

First Listed Sources of Information: Please consult the more complete instructions that discuss the sources of information in RDA.
> **Place of Publication/Distribution** – Same source as publisher's/distributor's name
> **Parallel Place** – Same source as place of publication/distribution
> **Publisher's/Distributor's Name** – Same source as title proper
> **Parallel Name** – Same source as publisher's/distributor's name
> **Date of Publication/Distribution** – Same source as title proper

> **Place of Production/Manufacture** – Same source as producer's/manufacturer's name
> **Parallel Place** – Same source as place of production/manufacture
> **Producer's/Manufacturer's Name** – Same source as title proper
> **Parallel Name** – Same source as producer's/manufacturer's name
> **Date of Production/Manufacture** – Any source

RDA 2.8 Publication Statements

According to RDA 2.8.1, a publication statement is "a statement identifying the place or places of publication, publisher or publishers, and date or dates of . . . publication, release, or issuing of a resource. Consider all online resources to be published."[27] A publication statement may contain up to five elements: *place of publication, parallel place of publication, publisher's name, parallel publisher's name,* and *date of publication*. Of these, place of publication, publishers' name, and date are the RDA Core elements. When these three elements are complete, no further dissemination information is needed, because the core requirements have been met. If there is more than one instance for these elements, RDA states that only the first is required.

> **ICC11 PS for 2.8 Publication Statements**: If more than one publisher's name or place of publication is found on the preferred source of information, record all, *unless* there is an excessive number, it would create confusion, or it could obscure the primary information.

The basic instruction for recording publication statements points out that some parts of the statement are transcribed according to the guidelines at RDA 1.7 (i.e., places, names, words associated with dates, and their parallel counterparts) and some are recorded using the instructions at RDA 1.8 (i.e., numbers used as dates).

Place of Publication

This RDA Core element contains metadata about places associated with the publication of a resource (i.e., the location of the publisher or the releasing or issuing body). The information should be sought from the same source as the publisher's name, although if it is not present, it may be taken from elsewhere in the resource, or, as a last resort, from an outside source. The basic instruction states that the metadata is transcribed as found, including both the local place (e.g., city, village, borough, town) and the larger jurisdiction(s) in which it falls (e.g., country, state, province) if both are present on the resource. Abbreviations are used if they are found on the source of information.

> **Place of publication**: New York
>
> **Place of publication**: München
>
> **Place of publication**: Chapel Hill, North Carolina
>
> **Place of publication**: Cambridge, Mass.
>
> **Place of publication**: Pittsburgh, Pa.

There are two optional additions listed at 2.8.2.3. The first states that the full address of the publisher may be recorded if it appears on the source. Generally, this option should not be applied. The second states that if only a local place name is listed on the source, the cataloger may add the larger jurisdiction if it is judged helpful to identify the place. For example, a place called *Albany* is found in New York, but also in Georgia, California, and 18 more states in the United States, as well as in Nova Scotia, Western Australia, New Zealand, South Africa, and England.

> **Source**: Albany
>
> **Place of publication**: Albany [New York]
>
> **Source**: Albany
>
> **Place of publication**: Albany [New Zealand]

Some local place names may seem to stand on their own (e.g., New York, London, Toronto), but fewer place names than one might expect are actually unique. For example, there are places called New York, Kentucky; New York, Texas; and New York, England. On the other hand, one can generally be confident that most publishers listing *New York* as their location are referring to New York, New York. If a resource is disseminated from New York, Kentucky, the exact location—one hopes—should be made clear on that resource.

> **ICC11 PS for Optional Additions to RDA 2.8.2.3 Recording Place of Publication**: Generally, do not apply the first option to supply full address of the publisher. Do, however, apply the second option to supply the name of the larger jurisdiction if it is not on the source. Do not assume the local place name is identifiable around the world without a qualifier (e.g., Dublin [Ohio] and Dublin [Ireland]).

If the place name is known to be fictitious (e.g., Gotham City, Braavos), the cataloger should create a note giving the actual place name.

> **Source**: Lake Wobegon, Minnesota
>
> **Place of publication**: Lake Wobegon, Minnesota
>
> **Note**: Actual publication location is Saint Paul, Minnesota.

If there is more than one place of publication listed on the source, RDA requires only that the first be recorded. The instructions state that if more than one place is being recorded, the cataloger should transcribe them in the order indicated by the sequence, layout, or typography on the resource. The choice of how many and which additional locations to include, if any, is the cataloger's or the cataloging agency's.

> **Source**:
>
> Oxford University Press
>
> Oxford • New York • Auckland • Cape Town • Dar es Salaam
> Hong Kong • Karachi • Kuala Lumpur • Madrid • Melbourne
> Mexico City • Nairobi • New Delhi • Shanghai • Taipei • Toronto
>
> 2011

> **Abridged place of publication**: Oxford

> **Abridged place of publication**: Oxford
> New York

> **Abridged place of publication**: Oxford
> Hong Kong

> **Transcribed place of publication**: Oxford
> New York
> Auckland
> Cape Town
>
> . . .

A policy statement for RDA 2.8.2 instructs LC catalogers creating Cataloging-in-Publication (CIP) data also to record the first place in the United States if the first place listed on the source is not in the United States. It would not be surprising if other catalogers in the United States followed this policy statement for their own (non-CIP) cataloging.

If the place of publication is not found on the source, there are five options for the cataloger. All should be recorded in square brackets to indicate that the metadata does not appear on the resource itself.

- **Known place of publication**: If the place of publication is known, but it is not on the source, the cataloger may supply it from another source.

    Place of publication: [London, Ontario]

- **Probable place of publication**: If the cataloger is uncertain of the place, a probable local place name may be supplied, using a question mark to indicate it is probable but not certain. If a larger jurisdiction is included, the placement of the question mark depends on what is probable and what is certain. If the local place is probable, but the larger jurisdiction is certain, the question mark follows the local place. If the larger jurisdiction is uncertain or both are uncertain, the question mark follows the larger jurisdiction.

    Place of publication: [Montreal?]
    Place of publication: [Rockville?, Maryland]
    Place of publication: [Cambridge, Massachusetts?]

- **Known country, state, province, etc., of publication**: If a probable place is unknown, a known country, state, or province may be recorded.

    Place of publication: [Morocco]

- **Probable country, state, province, etc. of publication**: If a country, state, or province is unknown, a probable country, state, or province may be supplied, using a question mark to indicate it is probable but not certain.

    Place of publication: [Comoros?]

- **No place of publication identified**: If probable information cannot be determined, the cataloger may record the statement *Place of publication not identified* as part of the description. Catalogers at LC and in PCC libraries are encouraged to provide, if at all possible, a probable place rather than use this statement.[28]

    Place of publication: [Place of publication not identified]

Publisher's Name

Publisher's name is an RDA Core element that contains the name of a corporate body, person, or family responsible for publishing or issuing the information resource (i.e., making it available or releasing it for public use). A name should be understood to include characterizing words or phrases in addition to more traditional names. The information should be sought in the same source as the title proper, although if it is not present, it may be taken from elsewhere within the resource, or, as a last resort, from an outside source. The basic instruction states to transcribe the name as found on the source. An optional omission at RDA 2.8.4.3 allows the cataloger to eliminate some levels in a corporate hierarchy. The LC-PCC PS, however, states it is not a good idea to omit this information, and the authors agree that, in most cases, the information should be transcribed as seen.

> **Source**: Academic Press, an imprint of Elsevier B.V.
>
> **Transcription**: Academic Press, an imprint of Elsevier B.V.

Exceptions, however, may be made for long, convoluted statements.

> **Source**: Doubleday, an imprint of Transworld Publishers, a Random House Group Company
>
> **Transcription**: Doubleday

If the name of the publisher is fictitious, include a note to provide clarifying information.

If the function of the PFC responsible for issuing the resource is unclear, transcribe words or phrases from the source indicating their function:

- Manufactured and marketed by Deutsche Grammophon & Decca Classics, US
- Distributed in the United States by Lerner Publishing Group, Inc.
- Printed and published by Lois Bet Print & Publication on behalf of Tribal Research Institute, Art & Culture Department
- Produced, manufactured and distributed by Platinum Records

If such words or phrases are not found on the resource, an optional addition at RDA 2.8.4.4 allows the cataloger to add an explicit statement of function if needed for clarity:

- [Manufactured and distributed by] Findaway World

If there is more than one publisher's name listed on the source, RDA requires only that the first be recorded. If more than one name is being transcribed, the cataloger should record the names in the order indicated by the sequence, layout, or typography on the resource itself. If a publisher is not listed anywhere on the resource, and one cannot be identified through other sources, then the statement "[publisher not identified]" is recorded in that element. There is no policy statement urging catalogers to avoid this phrase, because no one wants them to guess a *probable* publisher.

Date of Publication

Date of publication is an RDA Core element that contains a date associated with publishing or issuing the resource (i.e., the date the publisher released the resource or made it available for public use). The date—usually just a year, but it can be more specific if needed—should be sought from the same source as the title proper, although if it is not present, it may be taken from elsewhere within the resource, or, as a last resort, from an outside source (e.g., consulting a publisher's catalog or even contacting the publisher directly).

The date is recorded (not transcribed) in the form of numerals preferred by the cataloging agency, although an option at RDA 1.8.2 allows the cataloger to transcribe dates in the form that is on the source instead (e.g., using Roman instead of Arabic numerals). The LC-PCC PS says to apply this option. Although most Anglo-American catalogers will encounter publication dates from the Gregorian calendar primarily, some resources may display dates from other calendar systems. If the date on the source is not of the Gregorian (or Julian) calendar, the cataloger may add a corresponding date from the Gregorian calendar in square brackets (e.g., 2545 B.E. [2002]); the LC-PCC PS supports applying this option. If multiple dates are recorded (i.e., from different calendars), record them in the order indicated by the sequence, layout, or typography, but remember only the date in the calendar preferred by the cataloging agency is required. If the date appears to be fictitious or incorrect, a note of explanation that provides the correct date should be added.

If no date appears on the resource, the cataloger is to supply a known date (e.g., [2015]) or an approximate date of publication (e.g., [2009?]) following the instructions on how to record supplied dates at RDA 1.9.2 (see discussion of numbers and dates on pp. 190-191). If this is not possible, the cataloger may, as a last resort, record the phrase "[date of publication not identified]." There is a somewhat lengthy, but useful LC-PCC PS that guides catalogers on issues related to missing dates. The LC-PCC PS for 2.8.6.6: Date of Publication Not Identified in a Single-Part Resource is summarized in Table 5.3.

It is clear from the LC-PCC PS that a supplied date is greatly preferred to "[date of publication not identified]"—a phrase that can be avoided completely if one uses the instruction at RDA 1.9.2.5 along with the date of cataloging (generally, a resource must be published *before* it reaches a cataloger). For example, if a cataloger were describing a locally released music CD on August 3, 2015 and no dates were found anywhere on or about the resource, then the cataloger can always record "[not after August 3, 2015]" in the date element.

TABLE 5.3 Alternatives When Date of Publication Is Missing.

If there is no publication date, but	Then	On source	Recorded Date of Publication
... there is a copyright date	... use the copyright date in square brackets, if the date seems a probable publication date	©2015	[2015]
... there is a copyright date, but for the year *after* the resource is received	... use the copyright date in square brackets	©2016	[2016]
... there is a copyright and manufacture date (and the year is the same for both)	... use that year in square brackets, if the date seems a probable publication date	©2015 2015 printing	[2015]
... there is a copyright date and a date of manufacture but the years differ	... use the copyright date in square brackets, if the date seems a probable publication date; a manufacture date may also be recorded	©2012 2015 printing	[2012] *Also*, Date of Manufacture: 2015
... there is a distribution date and it seems reasonable as a publication date	... use the date of distribution in square brackets; a distribution date may also be recorded	Distributed in 2015	[2015] *Also*, Date of Distribution: 2015
... there is a distribution date, but it does not seem reasonable as a publication date	... supply a date in square brackets based on the information provided	Distributed in 2004; in introduction author refers to creating the work in 1999	[between 1999 and 2004]
... there is only a date of manufacture and it seems reasonable as a publication date	...use the date of manufacture in square brackets; a manufacture date may also be recorded	First Printing 2015	[2015] *Also*, Date of Manufacture: 2015
... there is only a date of manufacture, but it does not seem reasonable as a publication date	... supply a date in square brackets based on the information provided; a manufacture date may also be recorded	34th printing 2015	[not after 2015]

RDA 2.7 Production Statements

According to RDA 2.7.1, "A production statement is a statement identifying the place or places of production, producer or producers, and date or dates of production of a resource in an unpublished form. Production statements . . . [address] inscription, fabrication, construction, etc., of a resource in an unpublished form."[29] In other words, it addresses making or assembling unpublished resources (e.g., objects, works of art, a locally assembled kit, a manuscript). Parts of a production statement are transcribed (e.g., places and names), and others are recorded (e.g., dates).

The biggest difference between production statements and publication statements is that only *date of production* is an RDA Core element and it may be taken from *any* source—meaning that square brackets are not used for this element. *Name of producer* and *place of production* are not required and are first sought from the same source as the title proper. Although the date of production is the only core element, it does not preclude place and name from being included if the information is available. In addition, there are some guidelines specifically for archival collections in this section.

RDA 2.9 Distribution Statements

According to RDA 2.9.1, "A distribution statement is a statement identifying the place or places of distribution, distributor or distributors, and date or dates of distribution of a resource in a published form."[30] The three major elements of a distribution statement were, at one time, considered RDA Core-if, meaning that they could be core under certain circumstances, particularly when the corresponding elements in the publication statement were missing (e.g., if the place of publication was not identified, then place of distribution was treated as a core element). This, however, is no longer the case as of the April 2015 RDA update. Now, distribution statements are included in a description solely based on cataloger's judgment regardless of what is recorded in the publication statement. The LC-PCC PS for RDA 2.9 states that a distribution statement is considered core for rare materials in PCC libraries if the data is available. The authors of this text, however, continue to encourage catalogers to include a complete distribution statement if the publication statement is incomplete or if the statement appears useful for discovery, identification, or selection.

> **ICC11 PS for RDA 2.9 Distribution Statement**: If any of the elements of the publication statement (i.e., place, name, or date of publication) are missing, then include a complete distribution statement if considered useful for access, identification, and/or selection. For other resources, distribution statements are included based on cataloger's judgment.

RDA 2.10 Manufacture Statements

According to RDA 2.10.1, "A manufacture statement is a statement identifying the place or places of manufacture, manufacturer or manufacturers, and date or dates of manufacture of a resource in a published form. Manufacture statements include statements relating to the printing, duplicating, casting, etc., of a resource in a published form."[31] The three major elements in manufacture statements, like those of distribution statements, were once considered RDA Core-if. Now, manufacture statements are included solely based on cataloger's judgment regardless of what is recorded in the publication and distribution statements. The LC-PCC PS for RDA 2.10 states that a manufacture statement is considered core for rare materials in PCC libraries, if the data is available. The authors of this text, however, continue to encourage catalogers to include a complete manufacture statement if the publication and distribution statements are incomplete or if the statement appears useful for discovery, identification, or selection.

> **ICC11 PS for RDA 2.10 Manufacture Statement**: If any of the elements (i.e., place, name, or date) of the publication or distribution statements are missing, then include a complete manufacture statement if considered useful for access, identification, and/or selection. For other resources, manufacture statements are included based on cataloger's judgment.

RDA 2.11 Copyright Date

A copyright date is "a date associated with a claim of protection under copyright or a similar regime. Copyright dates include phonogram dates (i.e., dates associated with claims of protection for audio recordings)."[32] This element, until April 2015, was considered core if publication and distribution dates were absent. Now, they are added solely based on cataloger's judgment, regardless of what is recorded in the date of publication element. Copyright dates may be recorded from any source—which means square brackets are never needed when the copyright date is recorded *as a copyright date* (i.e., recording it in the copyright date element rather than recording it as a probable publication date, where it would take square brackets).

When recording the copyright date, insert the appropriate copyright symbol (© or ℗) before the date (e.g., ℗1978). If the symbol cannot be reproduced, then insert an appropriate term (*copyright* or *phonogram copyright*) before the date (e.g., copyright 1988). Specific instructions on various aspects of a copyright date can be reviewed at RDA 2.11.

> **ICC11 PS for RDA 2.11 Copyright Date**: Record the copyright date in the description when dates of publication and distribution are unavailable, if there is a significant difference between the copyright and publication dates, or if considered useful for access, identification, and/or selection.

RDA 2.12 Series Statements

2.12 Series Statement

Definition: The part of the description that includes information about the series. A series is a number of separate works, usually related in subject or form that are issued successively. They are usually issued by the same entity and are in uniform style, with a collective title.

Sub-elements and Their First Listed Sources of Information: Please consult the more complete instructions that discuss the sources of information in RDA.

> **2.12.2 Title Proper of Series** – Series title page
> **2.12.3 Parallel Title of Series** – Any source
> **2.12.4 OTI of Series** – Same source as title of series
> **2.12.5 Parallel OTI of Series** – Same source as parallel title of series
> **2.12.6 SOR Relating to Series** – Same source as title of series
> **2.12.7 Parallel SOR Relating to Series** – Same source as parallel title of series
> **2.12.8 ISSN of Series** – Series title page
> **2.12.9 Numbering within Series** – Series title page
>
> **2.12.10 Title Proper of Subseries** – Series title page
> **2.12.11 Parallel Title of Subseries** – Any source
> **2.12.12 OTI of Subseries** – Same source as title of subseries
> **2.12.13 Parallel OTI of Subseries** – Same source as parallel title of subseries
> **2.12.14 SOR Relating to Subseries** – Same source as title of subseries
> **2.12.15 Parallel SOR Relating to Subseries** – Same source as parallel title of subseries
> **2.12.16 ISSN of Subseries** – Series title page
> **2.12.17 Numbering within Subseries** – Series title page

RDA Core: Title Proper of Series, Numbering within Series, Title Proper of Subseries, and Numbering within Subseries

LC Core: ISSN of Series and ISSN of Subseries

A *series* is a number of separate works, usually related in subject or form that are issued successively. They are generally issued by the same publisher (producer or distributor), and are in uniform style, with a collective title. RDA defines *series* as "a group of separate resources related to one another by the fact that each resource bears, in addition to its own title proper, a collective title applying to the group as a whole. The individual resources may or may not be numbered."[33] The term *series* may refer to an *author's series*, a *publisher's series*, or a *monographic series* (see chapter 4 of this text). In this text, *series* in archival collections are *not* being addressed. A *series statement* is:

a statement identifying a series to which a resource belongs and the numbering of the resource within the series. A series statement some-times includes information identifying one or more subseries to which the resource belongs. Series statements sometimes include statements of responsibility relating to a series or subseries. The information relating to one series, or one series and one or more subseries, constitutes one series statement.[34]

It is important to note that this section refers specifically to *series statements* (i.e., transcriptions of the series information found on the resource for the purpose of identification), not to *series access points* (i.e., authority-controlled series titles established for the purpose of collocation in retrieval). These instructions also address *subseries*, which is a series within a series (e.g., *Benjamins translation library. EST subseries*). As the structure of the elements are identical for series and subseries, and the instructions are nearly so, the elements are discussed in tandem in this text (e.g., numbering of series and numbering of subseries are discussed together).

At RDA 2.12, there is an LC-PCC PS that discusses various aspects of series, including the following:

- distinguishing between true series and phrases that might appear to be series
- series for republished resources
- series for selected issues of periodicals that have been published separately
- supplements and special numbers to serials
- series titles that are grammatically connected to the title of a resource
- source of instructions for series for motion pictures, television programs, and video recordings

Consult this policy statement—especially the 10 circumstances discussed in the section on *Series versus Phrases*—for a better grasp of these issues and on the nature of series statements.

The basic instruction states that most series elements should be transcribed as they appear on the preferred source of information, with the exceptions being numbering associated with series and subseries, which have specific instructions at 2.12.9 and 2.12.17. If the resource belongs to more than one series, subseries, or a series and a subseries, then the cataloger is to record each series statement separately.

Title Proper of Series (and Subseries)

This and the following sections include information on the instructions applicable to both series and subseries. For the sake of brevity, the text refers only to *series. Subseries* elements are mentioned specifically when there is something of note or the approach is somewhat different. Examples include metadata for both series and subseries.

A *title proper of series*, an RDA Core element, is the collective name given to volumes or parts issued in a series. It is the principal name of the series; it is the title used when citing a series.

> **Series title proper**: Library and information science text series
> **Series title proper**: Masterworks of Tibetan painting
> **Series title proper**: Divergent trilogy
> **Series title proper**: Neuroscience seminar series
> **Series title proper**: Global music series
>
> **Series title proper**: Lecture notes in mathematics
> **Subseries title proper**: Mathematical biosciences subseries
>
> **Series title proper**: Lecture notes in mathematics
> **Subseries title proper**: CIME Foundation subseries

The guidelines for a title proper, found at RDA 2.3.1 (such as those for abridgements, introductory words, inaccuracies), apply to a title proper of series as well. For example, if an alternative title is present (i.e., a second title proper introduced by the word *or*), the cataloger is to record it as part of the series title proper. There are other instructions that differ from those under 2.3.1; for example, if the series numbering for the resource is integrated into the series title, the cataloger records such numbering as part of the series title proper.

> **Series title proper**: No. 44 of the Posthumous works. Second series
> **Series title proper**: 9th event of the 2012-2013 concert series

If the series title appears in multiple languages on the source, the cataloger should choose as the series title proper the one that is in the language of the title proper of the resource; the others may be transcribed as parallel titles proper of the series. If the series title appears on the source in more than one form (e.g., Buckendale lecture series, L. Ray Buckendale lectures, the L. Ray Buckendale lecture series), then the cataloger must make a choice based on sequence, layout, and typography; if it is still unclear, the cataloger should choose the most comprehensive title for the series.

> **Series title proper**: the L. Ray Buckendale lecture series

If the resource contains both a series and a subseries, the source of information chosen should be one that contains both series titles. At RDA 2.12.10: Title Proper of Subseries, an LC-PCC PS discusses situations where what appears to be a subseries does not actually represent a subseries. In case of doubt as to whether a series statement is a subseries or a second separate series, the cataloger should treat it as a separate series. There are also some specific instructions related to subseries that should be noted.

ISSN of Series (and Subseries)

An *International Standard Serial Number* (ISSN) is a distinctive and unique number assigned to a serial by the International Serials Data System, a network of national and international centers sponsored by UNESCO. The centers develop and maintain registers of serial publications; this includes the assignment of ISSNs and key titles. An *ISSN of a Series* is an ISSN assigned to a series title. It is an LC-PCC Core element. Not all series, however, are assigned ISSNs.

The instruction for recording an ISSN for a series states to transcribe the ISSN as it appears on the source. If the ISSN for a subseries is also present, *both* should be transcribed; the cataloger should never omit the ISSN for the main series, per the LC-PCC PSs for RDA 2.12.8.3 and 2.12.16.3.

> **Series title proper**: Lecture notes in mathematics
>
> **Subseries title proper**: CIME Foundation subseries
>
> **ISSN of series**: ISSN 0075-8434

Numbering within Series (and Subseries)

The RDA Core element *Numbering within series* represents an indication of the sequencing of parts within a series. "Numbering within series can include a numeral, a letter, any other character, or the combination of these. Numbering is often accompanied by a caption (volume, number, etc.) and/or a chronological designation."[35] The numbering within a series can come from anywhere within the resource itself, with the words transcribed following the instructions at RDA 1.7 and the numbers being recorded using the instructions at RDA 1.8.

- 5
- 27-50
- C
- 2007/05, 28 August 2007
- v. 6
- no. IV
- album 2
- new series, number 2

- L-510-01
- suplemento 2, 1997
- grāmata 2
- Heft 90 (August 2009)
- volym 233
- 6. Bd.
- broj 15

Additional specifications for recording this element are found at RDA 2.12.9.3-2.12.9.8; these guidelines address issues such as chronological designations, new sequences of numbering, alternative numbering systems, and separately numbered issues or parts.

Other Series Elements

A *parallel title proper* is recorded only if the series title appears in multiple languages or scripts. *Other title information* for series and subseries, *statements of responsibility* for series and subseries, and their parallel counterparts are transcribed only if considered important to identify the series. In some cases, these additional elements will be important to identify and understand the resource and should be included. For example, a series title *Occasional papers* is virtually meaningless unless the SOR is included as well. Shown here, using ISBD to combine the two elements, the series statement begins to make more sense:

> **Series with SOR**: Occasional papers / American Association of Law
> Libraries

For each of these elements, the instructions refer back to the comparable metadata elements under the instructions at RDA 2.3: Title and RDA 2.4: Statement of Responsibility.

RDA 2.13-2.17 Other Manifestation Elements

RDA 2.13 Mode of Issuance

As discussed in chapter 4 of this text, *mode of issuance* is "a categorization reflecting whether a resource is issued in one or more parts, the way it is updated, and its intended termination."[36] It is not only a pre-cataloging decision, but it is also an RDA metadata element. It is determined by examining the resource itself, from accompanying materials, or from any source. This element requires the use of a controlled vocabulary. The cataloger, when recording *mode of issuance*, has four values to choose from: *single unit*, *multipart monograph*, *serial*, and *integrating resource*. This is a core element for LC and PCC. In the MARC environment, this is recorded as coded data for *Bibliographic Level*—the 07-byte in the MARC leader (see chapter 21 of this text) using the following values: *m* = single unit/multipart monograph, *s* = serial, and *i* = integrating resource.

RDA 2.14 Frequency

Frequency, an LC-PCC Core element, is a description of the publishing interval for the issues/parts of a serial or the updates for an integrating resource. The information is taken from any source within or outside of the resource itself. This element is to be recorded from a closed controlled vocabulary list provided at RDA 2.14.1.3:

- daily
- three times a week
- biweekly
- weekly
- semiweekly
- three times a month
- bimonthly
- monthly
- semimonthly
- quarterly
- three times a year
- semiannual
- annual
- biennial
- triennial
- irregular

If none applies, the cataloger should create a note to explain the nature and details of the frequency. If the frequency changes, that, too, may be recorded in the description as a note.

RDA 2.15 Identifier for the Manifestation

An *identifier for the manifestation* is a unique character string associated with a resource that differentiates that manifestation from others. This identifier may include internationally recognized standard numbers such as an International Standard Book Number (ISBN) or an ISSN (mentioned above), a Universal Resource Name (URN),[37] other character strings assigned by agencies responsible for disseminating resources (e.g., publishers, manufacturers, government printing offices and publishing agencies), document fingerprints, and so on. Identifiers may be taken from any source within or outside of the resource itself. It is a core element in RDA. If more than one type of identifier is present, RDA instructs the cataloger to prefer ones that are used internationally, if applicable.

If there is a particular display format commonly used with the identifier, the cataloger should record it using that format.

> **Identifier for Manifestation**: ISSN 1049-0434
>
> **Identifier for Manifestation**: doi: 10.1080/01639374.2014.
> 911236

If no particular format is associated with the type of identifier, then the cataloger records the identifier as it appears on the source of information, preceding it with the name of the agency responsible for assigning the number.

> **Identifier for Manifestation**: A&M Records: B0016562-02

If the manifestation displays more than one of the same type of standard identifier (e.g., if the resource has more than one part and there are identifiers for the whole set and the individual parts), then the cataloger records the identifier appropriate for the resource being described. If it is a comprehensive description, the number for the set should be recorded, but if it is an analytical description, only the number for the part being described is recorded. An optional addition allows the cataloger to record the identifiers for both the whole and the parts on both comprehensive and analytical descriptions.

> **Identifier for Manifestation**: ISBN 0521295319 (set of six
> paperback volumes)
>
> **Identifier for Manifestation**: ISBN 0521295262 (volume 2)

Additional instructions are provided for issues such as the use of qualifiers for incorrect identifiers such as *(invalid)* or *(incorrect)*; the use of qualifiers for physical characteristics or location, such as *(paperback)*, *(hbk.)*, *(e-book)*, *(loose-leaf)*, or *(U.S.)*; and the use of qualifiers for parts, such as *(v. 2)* or *(volume 6)*. These are followed by specific instructions for two music elements: *publisher's number for music* and *plate number for music*.

RDA 2.16 Preferred Citation

A *preferred citation* is a citation for the resource being described in the form preferred by the creator, publisher, custodian, and so on. This element may be recorded from anywhere. The basic instruction states that the citation should be recorded in the form in which it appears on the source of information. At this time, the *preferred citation* element is used infrequently in bibliographic metadata.[38]

RDA 2.17 Note on Manifestation

Many resources require description beyond that which is presented formally in the RDA elements. This is provided through notes. Notes qualify or amplify the formal description. They contribute to the intelligibility of the description by providing additional information or context. A *note on manifestation*, as one might expect, is not a single element, but is instead a category containing any number of notes that might be useful and necessary.

Notes are not usually transcribed data. In general, a cataloger composes a note using his or her own choice of words to clearly and concisely communicate information to users and to other catalogers, formulated using the general guidelines at RDA 1.10: Notes. For some notes, however, there are standard phrases that have long been used to communicate certain information (e.g., *Title from cover* versus *Cover title*).

In RDA 2.17: Note on Manifestation, there are 12 sub-instructions related to the major manifestation elements. Of these, only *Note on Title* and *Note on Issue, Part or Iteration Used as Basis for Identification of Resource* are core elements for LC and PCC libraries; none are RDA Core.

2.17.2	**Note on Title**
2.17.3	**Note on Statement of Responsibility**
2.17.4	**Note on Edition Statement**
2.17.5	**Note on Numbering of Serials**
2.17.6	**Note on Production Statement**
2.17.7	**Note on Publication Statement**
2.17.8	**Note on Distribution Statement**
2.17.9	**Note on Manufacture Statement**
2.17.10	**Note on Copyright Date**
2.17.11	**Note on Series Statement**
2.17.12	**Note on Frequency**
2.17.13	**Note on Issue, Part, or Iteration Used as Basis for Identification of Resource**

Note on Title

A *note on title* seems fairly self-explanatory, but a few examples might help to illustrate the types of information that may be shared in these notes. The most common types of title notes are those indicating its origins when a title is transcribed from an atypical source of information. There are also notes explaining title variations, inaccuracies, deletions, and anything else about a title that is judged necessary by the cataloger. According to LC and PCC practices, *note on title* is considered core when needed to identify the source from which a title was taken. The instruction at RDA 2.17.2.3: Title Source states that the cataloger creates this type of note whenever the title is taken from a source other than a title page, card, or sheet, if the resource consists of pages, leaves, sheets, or cards (or images of them), or a title frame or screen for a moving image resource. The LC-PCC PS also indicates that it should appear in every CONSER-compliant record to indicate the source of the serial title. Examples include:

- Title from cover.
- Title from spine.
- Title from container.
- Title from home page.
- Title from title screen.
- Title from booklet.
- Title from flute part.
- Title from panel.
- Title from menu.

- Spanish and French titles from cover.
- Earlier title: Financial elements of contracts.
- Cover has subtitle: vocal one step.
- Guide has subtitle: An agenda for language and culture centered school reform.

Notes on title variations are needed when there have been minor changes in the titles across various parts of a multipart monograph, iterations of an integrating resource, or issues of a serial. Variations can occur in any number of the title elements (title proper, parallel title, etc.). If differences have little impact on retrieval, a note suffices (e.g., Title varies slightly; Subtitle may vary; Additional Dutch title varies).

In accordance with the transcription guidelines, if a typo or an inaccuracy appears in a title on the source of information, the cataloger is to transcribe it as is. The instructions also allow for creating a note to provide the corrected form of title, if considered necessary or useful.

> **Title proper**: Exhaustive commentaries with uptodate case laws on the Partnership Act, IX of 1932
>
> **Note**: Title should read: Exhaustive commentaries with up-to-date case laws on the Partnership Act, IX of 1932.
>
> **OTI**: Rwanda's match to growth and stability
>
> **Note**: Other title information should read: Rwanda's march to growth and stability.

> **Part Title**: Elements of ordinary differntial equations
>
> **Note**: Typographical error in title on title page for volume 4. Title should read: Elements of ordinary differential equations.

Notes for other aspects related to titles are to be made by the cataloger as needed.

Note on Issue, Part, or Iteration Used as the Basis for Identification of the Resource

"A *note on issue, part, or iteration used as the basis for identification of the resource* is a note identifying what was used to identify the resource: the issue or part of a multipart monograph or serial or the iteration of an integrating resource. For an online resource, the note . . . can also include the date on which the resource was viewed for description."[39] This note is core according to LC and PCC practices. It is used when the identification of a multipart monograph or a serial is not based on the earliest or lowest numbered part or issue or when the iteration used for identifying an integrating resource is not the latest version. If this happens, the cataloger makes a note to indicate the part or issue that was used instead. Specific sub-instructions are given for numbered and unnumbered serials, multipart monographs, integrating resources, and the date of viewing of online resources. Examples include:

> **Note**: Identification of the resource based on: Vol. 1, no. 3 (Aug. 1999).
>
> **Note**: Latest issue consulted: no. 12 (Jan./June 1999).
>
> **Note**: Identification of the resource based on version consulted: Oct. 26, 2000.
>
> **Note**: Title from home page (viewed June 14, 2015).

Other Types of Notes

Of the other 10 types of notes, none are considered core by RDA, LC, or PCC. A few notes falling into these 10 types are important to point out. Under *note on statement of responsibility*, the cataloger might create notes about attribution of the work, variant names, different forms of names, or performers, narrators, presenters, and other PFCs found in the technical or artistic credits of a resource who are not listed in an SOR.

> **Note**: Comoedia divina is generally attributed to Aloys Wilhelm Schreiber.
>
> **Note**: At head of title: 113th Congress, 2d session, Senate.
>
> **Note**: Author's initials represented by musical notes on title page.
>
> **Note**: Cast: Divine, David Lochary, Mary Vivian Pierce, Mink Stole, Edith Massey.
>
> **Note**: Field collection made by Lowell Lybarger in Pakistan.
>
> **Note**: As told to the Ladies of the Club.
>
> **Note**: Music by Miles Davis; transcribed by Rob DuBoff, Mark Vinci, Mark Davis, and Josh Davis.

Under *note on numbering of serials*, the cataloger might create notes about numbering of first and/or last issue or part, complex or irregular numbering, or the periods covered.

> **Note**: Began with vol. 1, no. 2 (Apr. 19, 1968); ceased with issue 445 (Dec. 3, 1987).
>
> **Note**: Numbering begins each year with no. 1.
>
> **Note**: Numbering erratic.
>
> **Note**: Irregular numbering in beginning: no issues for Jan. 13, 20 ; Jan. 27 is no. 2 ; no. 3 also Jan. 27, and unlike Jan. 27, no. 2, no. 3 has a small no. 8 on title page ; no. 4 and no. 5 both labeled Feb. 3 ; no. 6 begins Feb. 10 and is regular through no. 17, April 28 ; no. 18, May 12 ; no. 19, May 26 ; and no. 20, June 9.

Under *note on series statement*, the cataloger might create notes about complex series statements or incorrect numbering.

> **Note**: The ISSN printed on the t.p. verso is for the parent series, Saguntum. The correct ISSN for the Extra subseries is 2253-7295.
>
> **Note**: Subseries statement from volume detail webpage.
>
> **Note**: Vols. also bear the series numbering used in the census (e.g. "Series 1, India" for vols. covering all of India, the state series numbering for vols. about an individual state).
>
> **Note**: Numbering irregular: series numbering most often retained through series title changes; however, some numbers reused on different analytic titles.

Under *note on frequency*, the cataloger might create notes about the details of or changes in frequency of serials or integrating resources.

> **Note**: Semimonthly
>
> **Note**: Frequency varies. Irregular until 1991. Now quarterly.

For instructions and examples of other types of notes on manifestations, consult RDA 2.17.

RDA 2.18-2.21 Item Attributes

The primary focus of RDA chapter 2 is on the manifestation-level elements. There are, however, four elements that specifically address the item:

- **RDA 2.18 Custodial History of Item**: a record of the provenance of an item; discusses ownership and/or custody; years of ownership may be added after names, if available.

  > **Custodial History of Item**: Previously owned by Robert Illing, who was given these clapsticks while visiting the Northern Territory in the 1950s.

> **Custodial History of Item**: Though the individuals pictured are not named, the collection's provenance indicates it belonged to the Mingo family of Port Allen, West Baton Rouge Parish, Louisiana.

- **RDA 2.19 Immediate Source of Acquisition of Item**: a record of the source and circumstances of acquiring the item; the source, date, and method of acquisition should be described, if available.

> **Immediate Source of Acquisition of Item**: Gift of the estate of Sue Adams Boyer (3rd wife of Porter H. Adams), 9 September 1985.

> **Immediate Source of Acquisition of Item**: This collection was purchased from Professor Michael Zwettler after his death, Ohio State University, Department of Near Eastern Languages and Cultures.

- **RDA 2.20 Identifier for the Item**: a unique character string associated with an item; a specified display format should be used, if applicable; the identifier is preceded with the name of the agency responsible for the identifier; incorrect identifiers are recorded, but identified as such.

> **Identifier for the Item**: Wellcome Library no. 44769i.
>
> **Identifier for the Item**: Beatley Library: Z666.5 .T39 2009 c.3.

- **RDA 2.21 Note on Item**: a note used to supplement the description of the item.

> **Note on Item**: This is copy number 3 of 200 copies – t.p. verso.
>
> **Note on Item**: Schomburg has author's autographed copy, dated Feb. 15, 1989.

RDA, LC, and PCC consider all these elements as optional (i.e., none are core). The information for them may be taken from any source. If more information about describing the item is needed, RDA 2.18-2.21 may be consulted directly.

DESCRIBING CARRIERS

Chapter 3 of RDA addresses another aspect of manifestations and items—the description of carriers through their attributes or characteristics. A *carrier* is the "physical medium in which data, sound, images, etc., are stored."[40] In some cases, however, the media are not always tangible (e.g., an electronic resource such as a web page, a PDF, a streaming video, an .MP4 file). The carrier description, therefore, addresses not only the physical characteristics of a resource, but also the formatting and encoding of electronic media. It replaces the *physical description* that was a key part in ISBD and AACR2 cataloging. Many of the AACR2 descriptive elements are included in the carrier description, although some have been moved to RDA chapter 7: Describing Content (e.g., statements of illustration, running time).

To describe carriers, a cataloger uses RDA chapter 3. Its contents are enumerated in Textbox 5.9.

3: Describing Carriers

3.0 Purpose and Scope
3.1 General Guidelines on Describing Carriers
3.2 Media Type
3.3 Carrier Type
3.4 Extent
3.5 Dimensions
3.6 Base Material
3.7 Applied Material
3.8 Mount
3.9 Production Method
3.10 Generation
3.11 Layout
3.12 Book Format
3.13 Font Size
3.14 Polarity
3.15 Reduction Ratio
3.16 Sound Characteristic
3.17 Projection Characteristic of Motion Picture Film
3.18 Video Characteristic
3.19 Digital File Characteristic
3.20 Equipment or System Requirement
3.21 Note on Carrier
3.22 Note on Item-Specific Carrier Characteristic

Textbox 5.9 RDA Chapter 3 Structure.

Not all elements in RDA chapter 3 are examined closely in this text. Many of them are format specific. This text covers the major elements that apply to the majority of resources (e.g. carrier type, media type, extent, and dimensions) and provides brief overviews of format-specific elements.

RDA 3.1 General Guidelines on Describing Carriers

RDA 3.1 begins by discussing the source of information for a carrier description. RDA 3.1.1 states that the cataloger bases the description on the resource itself, any accompanying material, or its container. It does, however, allow that sometimes the cataloger may need to use another source for additional information. When that is the case, the cataloger may use any source available.

The same resource may be disseminated in more than one form or carrier. For example, a single textual work may be manifested as a book, an e-book, a PDF, a facsimile or reproduction of the original book, a web resource, a microform, and so on. One of the basic principles underpinning RDA is *representation* (see chapter 3 of this text). Representation requires that the description created for a resource reflect the most accurate picture of it. This means that the cataloger should record the carrier elements that apply to the manifestation being described. In other words, the cataloger should describe exactly what is in hand, because a description of a book should look somewhat different from a description of a PDF or that of a microform. This has not always happened in the past, but RDA 3.1.2 and RDA 3.1.3 are clear that this should be the case.

Resources Consisting of More Than One Carrier Type

Some resources entail more than one carrier type (e.g., a kit, a book with an accompanying DVD). RDA 3.1.4 offers three approaches to address this situation when it occurs while creating a comprehensive, rather than an analytical, description. The first approach is to record only two elements (carrier type and extent) for each carrier that is part of the resource:

Carrier type: volume

audio disc

Extent: xii, 238 pages

1 sound disc (*or* 1 CD or 1 compact disc)

This approach may be used if a detailed carrier description is judged unnecessary. An optional addition allows for a container holding the multi-part resource to be described along with its dimensions; for example, the phrase *in suitcase box (74 × 63 × 6 cm)* may be included if it is deemed useful.

The second approach is to record a full description of each carrier that is part of the resource, including carrier type, extent, and other relevant characteristics. This option provides the most detail about the carriers. The same optional addition as from the first approach allows for a container holding the multi-part resource to be described along with its dimensions.

Carrier type: volume

Extent: xii, 238 pages

Dimensions: 21 cm

Carrier type: audio disc

Extent: 1 sound disc

Dimensions: 4 3/4 in.

Type of recording: digital

Playing speed: 1.4 m/s

Configuration of playback channels: stereo

Optional container information: 1 box (16 × 30 × 24 cm)

The third option is to describe the predominant carrier and the extent of the resource in very general terms, describing the units as *various pieces*. The details of the pieces may be included in a note on carrier if judged to be useful in identification or selection.

> **Carrier type**: sheet
>
> **Extent**: 27 various pieces

If the number of units cannot be specified or approximated, then the cataloger may omit the number of pieces (e.g., "various pieces"). The same optional addition as from the first approach allows for a container holding the multi-part resource to be described along with its dimensions.

RDA states that the cataloger should choose the approach that is most appropriate for the resource being described. In some cases, that may entail a simple description with little detail. In others, each component may be described completely. RDA, being schema neutral, explains what can be recorded, but not where and how. Other standards (e.g., MARC and ISBD) try to make these approaches clearer by explaining how the descriptions of these components can be documented in bibliographic records.

LC-PCC PS 3.1.4, which addresses resources consisting of more than one carrier type, discusses the Library of Congress's implementation of the three approaches. It states that for resources consisting of several carrier types—often referred to as *kits* or *multimedia items*—LC catalogers are to treat one part of the resource as the primary component, with the others treated as accompanying materials. *Accompanying materials* are dependent parts of a resource that accompany and are cataloged along with the primary component (e.g., 10 small laminated maps that accompany a geography textbook). When it comes to handling accompanying materials, LC and PCC offer three basic approaches that are enumerated in the policy statement: (1) detailed descriptions, (2) simple descriptions, and (3) no carrier description. When a detailed description is required or desired, the cataloger creates complete metadata for the separate carrier descriptions. For example, if a cataloger were working with the resource used in some of the examples above—the book with a compact disc—the information is recorded as two separate carrier descriptions:

> **Carrier type**: volume
>
> **Extent**: xii, 238 pages
>
> **Dimensions**: 21 cm

> **Carrier type**: audio disc
>
> **Extent**: 1 sound disc
>
> **Dimensions**: 4 3/4 in.
>
> **Type of recording**: digital
>
> **Configuration of playback channels**: stereo

When it is time to enter this metadata into a particular encoding scheme, such as MARC, additional choices may be necessary. For example, in MARC the cataloger might record two separate physical description statements, one for each carrier, or the cataloger might record all the metadata for both carriers as a single statement. If neither of these approaches is needed, then the accompanying material can be recorded in a note, such as: "Issued with one accompanying compact disc." For more information on how to encode accompanying material in the MARC format, see chapter 9 of this text.

Online Resources

RDA 3.1.5 highlights some issues related to online resources. Its basic instructions are fairly straightforward:

- **Carrier type**: For remote-access online resources, *online resource* is used (RDA 3.3).
- **Extent**: If the resource is complete, the extent is recorded (RDA 3.4).
- **Other characteristics**: If considered important, other characteristics of the online resource are recorded as applicable (3.6-3.20).

If the resource is made up of more than one file type, the details for all components are recorded as deemed appropriate. For example, if one had an online resource, the following elements *could* be recorded, although RDA, LC, and the PCC require very few details for most online resources.

Carrier type: online resource

Extent: 1 online resource (10 pages)

File type: text file

Encoding format: PDF

File size: 118 KB

Resolution: 792 × 612 pixels

RDA 3.2 Media Type

Media type, an LC-PCC Core element, is a category "reflecting the general type of intermediation device required to view, play, run, etc., the content of a resource."[41] In other words, it provides basic information about how users interact with the resource; it tells them when equipment is needed or not (i.e., *unmediated*). The source of information for this element is the resource itself. This element, along with *carrier type* (see below) and *content type* (see chapter 6), replaces the *general material designation* (GMD) found in ISBD and AACR2. The basic instruction is to record one or more terms from a closed controlled vocabulary list provided at RDA 3.2.1.3:

- audio
- computer
- microform
- microscopic
- projected
- stereographic
- unmediated
- video

Each of these is explained in Table 3.1 in RDA. If none apply, then the cataloger may use *other* instead. If the media type cannot be ascertained, then the cataloger may use the term *unspecified* instead. There is an alternative that allows the cataloger to record only one media type, but in general, it should not be applied.

> **ICC11 PS for Alternative for RDA 3.2.1.3: Recording Media Types**: Do not apply. Record as many media types as needed.

RDA 3.3 Carrier Type

Carrier type, an RDA Core element, is a category "reflecting the format of the storage medium and housing of a carrier in combination with the type of intermediation device required to view, play, run, etc., the content of a resource."[42] It is an element that provides a basic understanding of the physical format of the resource and is one of the three elements that replace the GMD. The source of information for this element is the resource itself. The basic instruction is to record one or more terms from the closed 46-term controlled vocabulary list provided at RDA 3.3.1.3. The list is based on the eight media types listed at RDA 3.2: Media Type. Some of the terms are carrier types that a modern cataloger will encounter very infrequently, if ever (e.g., microfiche cassette, audio cylinder).

TABLE 5.4 RDA Carrier Types.

Media types	Carrier types
Audio	Audio cartridge, audio cylinder, audio disc, audio roll, audiocassette, audiotape reel, and sound-track reel
Computer	Computer card, computer chip cartridge, computer disc, computer disc cartridge, computer tape cartridge, computer tape cassette, computer tape reel, and online resource
Microform	Aperture card, microfiche, microfiche cassette, microfilm cartridge, microfilm cassette, microfilm reel, microfilm roll, microfilm slip, and micro-opaque
Microscopic	Microscope slide
Projected	Film cartridge, film cassette, film reel, film roll, filmslip, filmstrip, filmstrip cartridge, overhead transparency, and slide
Stereographic	Stereograph card and stereograph disc
Unmediated	Card, flipchart, object, roll, sheet, and volume
Video	Video cartridge, videocassette, videodisc, and videotape reel

If none apply, then the cataloger may use *other* instead. If the media type cannot be ascertained, then the cataloger may use the term *unspecified* instead. There is an alternative that allows the cataloger to record only one carrier type, even if two or more apply, but in general, the alternative should not be applied.

> **ICC11 PS for Alternative for RDA 3.3.1.3: Recording Carrier Types**: Do not apply. Record as many carrier types as needed.

RDA 3.4 Extent

Extent, an RDA Core element, is "the number and type of units and/or subunits making up a resource. A *unit* is a physical or logical constituent of a resource (e.g., a volume, audiocassette, film reel, a map, a digital file). A *subunit* is a physical or logical subdivision of a unit (e.g., a page of a volume, a frame of a microfiche, a record in a digital file)."[43]

- **Unit**: 1 volume
- **Subunit**: 336 pages

Extent is an element that contains several sets of instructions for different types of resources. It provides a basic understanding of the length, size, amount, or scope of the resource. It is an RDA Core element, but only if the resource is complete or the total extent is known. If the resource is incomplete or the total number of units is not known, the cataloger may record the unit type, but without a number preceding it (e.g., volumes). This, however, is not required; an alternative allows the cataloger to leave the extent element empty in these cases.

The source of information for this element is the resource itself. The following lists the basic instructions:

1. Record the extent by providing a number and the type of unit into which the resource is divided (e.g., 2 volumes, 1 film reel, 18 slides).
2. For the type of unit, record a term from the list of carrier types (see Table 5.4 above). Make the term plural, if appropriate. If considered important, an applicable trade name may be substituted as a term for the type of unit (e.g., 1 Windows-compatible computer disc).
3. If there is more than one carrier type included, record the extent for each (e.g., 1 video cartridge, 1 booklet).
4. Specify the number and type of subunits, as needed (e.g., xii, 238 pages).

There is an alternative that states the cataloger may use a commonly found term for the type of unit if it is not found in the list of carrier types (e.g., 1 igneous rock, 25 specimens) or if the cataloging agency prefers terms in common usage (e.g., 1 CD-ROM, 1 DVD).

In addition to the basic instructions (RDA 3.4.1), five exceptions are listed. Each is for a specific category of resources: cartographic materials, notated music, still images, text, and three-dimensional forms. Each exception points to a set of instructions that take precedence over the general instructions (e.g., if the resource is text, the cataloger uses the RDA *exceptions* instructions [RDA 3.4.5] instead of the basic ones).

If the exact number of units cannot be determined, the cataloger is instructed to approximate the number of units and to record it preceded by the word *approximately* (e.g., approximately 350 microfiche).[44] If an approximation is not possible, the cataloger may omit the number according to the LC-PCC PS for RDA 3.4.1.4 (e.g., microfiche). If the exact name of the unit cannot be concisely relayed in the description, the cataloger is instructed to record the number of units followed by the phrase *various pieces* (e.g., 15 various pieces). If the number of these unnamed pieces is not ascertainable, the cataloger may omit the number per the LC-PCC PS for RDA 3.4.1.5 (e.g., various pieces). If the individual units of the resource have identical content, the cataloger may add the word *identical* before the name of the unit (e.g., 24 identical stereograph discs). If there are identical sets of units involved, that, too, can be brought out in the extent (e.g., 30 identical sets of 5 stereograph discs).

For some resources, subunits are also recorded as part of the extent. RDA 3.4.1.7: Number of Subunits lists the resource types (excluding the five exception categories mentioned previously and detailed below) that may include subunits in parentheses following the term for the primary unit. These resource types are listed in Table 5.5.

For some resource types that reproduce or duplicate print, manuscript, or graphic resources (i.e., microforms, some computer files, online resources), the subunits are determined using the exception instructions for the extent of cartographic resources, notated music, still images, or text (RDA 3.4.2-3.4.5), as applicable. If the subunits are unnumbered and the actual number is not easily determined, then the cataloger may record *approximately* in front of the number (e.g., 1 computer disc (approximately 90 pages)).

Following the general guidelines on extent, there are instructions for the five exceptional resource types:

3.4.2 Extent of Cartographic Resource

3.4.3 Extent of Notated Music

3.4.4 Extent of Still Image

3.4.5 Extent of Text

3.4.6 Extent of Three-Dimensional Form

In the following section, text is reviewed fully, as it is the most complex and the most common of the exceptions, and the other four are mentioned briefly.

TABLE 5.5 Subunits for Certain Resource Types.

Resource types	Subunits	Examples
Computer discs, cartridges, etc.	Audio files, video files, and data files.	1 computer disc (12 audio files) 1 computer disc (14 audio files, 1 video file, JPG files, PDF files, and Word documents)
	If it contains text, images, etc., it may include pages, maps, icons, drawings, etc.	4 computer discs (1,913 maps) 1 computer disc (184 aerial photographs)
Filmstrips and filmslips	Frames or double frames	1 filmstrip (36 frames) 1 filmstrip (81 double frames)
Flipcharts	Sheets	2 flip charts (112 sheets)
Microfiches and microfilm	Frames	1 microfiche (240 frames)
	If containing text, etc., it may include pages, etc.	2 microfiches (165 leaves) 1 microfilm reel (1 vocal score (80 unnumbered pages))
Online resources	Audio files, video files, and data files.	1 online resource (2 video files) 1 online resource (1 program file) 1 online resource (2 audio files, 1 video file)
	If containing text, etc., it may include pages, etc.	1 online resource (ix, 46 pages) 1 online resource (1 score (viii, 99 pages))
Overhead transparencies	Overlays or attached overlays	23 overhead transparencies (10 overlays) 9 transparencies (3 attached overlays, 2 moveable masks)
Stereographs	Pairs of frames	1 stereograph disc (7 pairs of frames) 1 stereograph reel (7 pairs of frames)
Videodiscs of still images	Frames	1 videodisc (10,680 video still frames)

Extent of Text: Single Units

The RDA Core element, *extent of text*, is used if a resource is a book, manuscript, updating loose-leaf manual, serial, or any other text-based resource housed in volumes, sheets, portfolios, or cases. There are 22 sub-instructions that address a wide variety of issues a cataloger might encounter when describing a resource's extent. They are divided into two sections; the instructions from RDA 3.4.5.2 to 3.4.5.15 are for resources that are a single unit (e.g., a novel), and the guidelines in RDA 3.4.5.16 to 3.4.5.22 are for resources that are spread across more than one unit (e.g., multi-volume reference work). Throughout these instructions, there are special exceptions for early printed resources (e.g., rare books), which should be consulted as needed.

3.4.5: Extent of Text

3.4.5.1   Application

Single unit
3.4.5.2   Single Volume with Numbered Pages, Leaves, or Columns
3.4.5.3   Single Volume with Unnumbered Pages, Leaves, or Columns
3.4.5.4   Change in Form of Numbering within a Sequence
3.4.5.5   Misleading Numbering
3.4.5.6   Incomplete Volume
3.4.5.7   Pages, etc., Numbered as Part of a Larger Sequence
3.4.5.8   Complicated or Irregular Paging, etc.
3.4.5.9   Leaves or Pages of Plates
3.4.5.10   Folded Leaves
3.4.5.11   Double Leaves
3.4.5.12   Duplicated Paging, etc.
3.4.5.13   Pages Numbered in Opposite Directions
3.4.5.14   Single Sheet
3.4.5.15   Single Portfolio or Case

More than one unit
3.4.5.16   More Than One Volume
3.4.5.17   Continuously Paged Volumes
3.4.5.18   Individually Paged Volumes
3.4.5.19   Updating Loose-Leafs
3.4.5.20   More Than One Sheet
3.4.5.21   More Than One Portfolio or Case
3.4.5.22   Units and Sets of Units with Identical Content

Textbox 5.10 Instructions for Extent of Text.

The basic instruction for a single volume is that the cataloger should record the number of the last numbered page, leaf, or column (PLC), whichever is appropriate for the resource. A *column* is "one of two or more vertical sections of text appearing on the same page or leaf."[45] A *leaf* consists of "a single bound or fastened sheet as a subunit of a volume; each leaf consists of two pages, one on each side, either or both of which may be blank."[46] A *page*, therefore, is one side of a leaf. The front of the leaf is known as the *recto* and the back of the leaf as the *verso.*

The cataloger records the number or letter of the last-numbered PLC in the resource, followed by the appropriate term. The cataloger records the extent in *pages* if the leaves contain numbering on both sides. If the leaves contain numbering on only one side, the extent is recorded in *leaves.* The cataloger uses numerals, rather than numbers presented as words (e.g., 300 pages, *not* three hundred pages) in the extent even if the pagination is spelled-out numbers. If the volume has sequences of pages *and* leaves (or some other PLC combination), the cataloger records each sequence. A *sequence* of pages, leaves, or columns is "a) a separately numbered group of pages, etc. or b) an unnumbered group of pages, etc., that stands apart from other groups in the resource, or c) a number of pages or leaves of plates distributed throughout the resource." [47]

> **Extent**: 300 pages
>
> **Extent**: ix, 688 pages
>
> **Extent**: 202 leaves
>
> **Extent**: 182 columns
>
> **Extent**: 14 pages, 240 leaves
>
> **Extent**: A-N pages (*not* N pages)

Exceptions exist for early printed resources, updating loose-leaf resources, and serials.

If the volume is unnumbered, then the cataloger has three options: (1) record the actual number of PLCs if it can be readily determined (e.g., 50 unnumbered pages); (2) record an approximation, if the exact number is not easily determined (e.g., approximately 1,200 unnumbered columns); or (3) record *1 volume (unpaged)*. LC (but not PCC) practice is to follow the third option. The authors believe that the decision, based on the resource in hand, should be left to the cataloger. When it comes to unnumbered volumes, how does the cataloger determine whether it should be recorded in terms of pages or leaves? If the text appears on both sides of the leaves, then the extent is recorded in terms of *pages*; if the text appears on only one side of the leaves, the extent is recorded in terms of *leaves*.

If the resource contains both numbered and unnumbered sequences, the cataloger should disregard the unnumbered sequences unless they are substantial in size or unless some information in the unnumbered sequence is mentioned elsewhere in the description (e.g., in a note). When recording an unnumbered sequence, then the cataloger has three options again: (1) record the actual number of PLCs if it can be readily determined; (2) record an approximation, if the exact number is not easily determined; or (3) record the phrase "unnumbered sequence of" followed by the term *leaves*, *pages*, or *columns*, whichever is most appropriate.

> **Extent**: 153 leaves, 47 unnumbered leaves
>
> **Extent**: ix, 450, approximately 150 pages
>
> **Extent**: 202 pages, unnumbered sequence of leaves

If the unnumbered sequences of PLCs are not substantial or contain inessential content (e.g., advertising, blank pages), then the cataloger should not record those sequences.

If the type of numbering system changes (e.g., going from Roman numerals to Arabic) within a single sequence of numbering in the resource, the cataloger does not record the first part of the sequence.

> **Resource**: preliminary pages numbered i-ix followed by one blank page, and then by the main text that contains numbering from 11-522
>
> **Extent**: 522 pages

If there are two sequences, with or without different systems of numbering, the cataloger records them according to the general guidelines already
discussed.

> **Resource**: preliminary pages numbered i-xiii followed by the
> main text with numbering 1-274
>
> **Extent**: xiii, 274 pages
>
> **Resource**: preliminary pages numbered 1-14 followed by the
> main text with numbering 1-274
>
> **Extent**: 14, 274 pages

As is the case with titles and other elements, inaccuracies in the sequences
of numbering are recorded as found on the resource. If considered important
for understanding and identifying the resource, the cataloger may add the
correct information. The cataloger should first record the misleading number,
insert the words *that is*, and then record the correct figure.

> **Resource**: preliminary pages numbered i-xxviii followed by
> the main text that contains numbering from 1-407,
> then a page numbered 408, then *another* page
> numbered 407
>
> **Extent**: xxviii, 407, that is, 409 pages

If the resource being described is part of another resource, and the numbering within continues the numbering from another volume, then the cataloger
records the numbering of the first and last PLC preceded by the term appropriate for the resource.

> **Extent**: pages 410-782

If, however, the resource also has its own separate numbering system, the
cataloger should record the numbering for the individual volume rather than
that of the larger sequence. Instead a note should be included for the pagination reflecting the larger sequence.

> **Resource**: Pages 1-373 are also numbered 410-782.
>
> **Extent**: 373 pages
>
> **Note on extent**: Pages also numbered as part of larger resource:
> 410-782

If the pagination is complicated or irregular—beyond what has already been
discussed in this text—the cataloger again has a choice as to how to record the
number of PLCs. The cataloger may: (1) record the total number of PLCs with
an appropriate phrase following the number (i.e., "in various pagings," "in various foliations," *or* "in various numberings"); (2) record the numbering of the
main sequences with the total number of the other PLC numbering sequences
following; or (3) record "1 volume (various pagings)."

> **Resource**: The resource contains 400 pages total but involving various sequences
>
> **Extent**: 400 pages in various pagings
>
> **Extent**: x, 150, 123 pages, 117 variously numbered pages
>
> **Extent**: 1 volume (various pagings)

LC (but not PCC) practice, again, is to follow the less detailed third option. The authors believe that the decision, based on the resource in hand, should be left to the individual cataloger.

If the resource contains leaves or pages of *plates*—illustrative leaves that are not included in the pagination of the main text—the number of leaves or pages of plates is recorded immediately after the numbering sequence(s) for the volume, whether the plates are presented as a single unit or scattered throughout the volume. Additional instructions on plates are found at RDA 3.4.5.9 and should be consulted as needed. There are also instructions for variations such as folded leaves, double leaves, missing pages or leaves, duplicated paging, pages numbered in opposite directions, and resources on a single sheet or in a portfolio or case. The reader should consult these instructions as needed.

> **Extent**: 246 pages, 32 pages of plates
>
> **Extent**: 122 folded leaves
>
> **Extent**: xii, 35, 35 pages
>
> **Extent**: iv, 127, 135, vii pages
>
> **Extent**: 1 sheet
>
> **Extent**: 1 folded sheet (8 pages)
>
> **Extent**: 1 portfolio
>
> **Extent**: 1 case (30 pages, 2 sheets)

Extent of Text: Multiple Units

The basic instruction for resources in more than one volume states that the cataloger should record the number of volumes followed by the word *volumes* (e.g., 22 volumes). If the volumes are continuously paged, the number of PLCs in parentheses may supplement the extent; but separate sequences of preliminary text should not include any but the first volume. This instruction, according to the LC-PCC PS, should never be applied to serials and integrating resources.

> **Extent**: 27 volumes (xi, 7941 pages)
>
> **Resource**: Volume 1: i-xxi, 1-393, Volume 2: i-xxviii, 394-909
>
> **Extent**: 2 volumes (xxi, 909 pages)

If the volumes are individually paged—not continuously paged—the cataloger may record only the number of volumes (e.g., 2 volumes) and omit the pagination. An optional addition, however, allows the cataloger to include the pagination for each volume in parentheses.

> **Resource**: Volume 1: i-xx, 1-221, Volume 2: i-xxv, 1-521
>
> **Extent**: 2 volumes (xx, 221; xxv, 521 pages)

LC catalogers do not apply the option.

There are also a few simple instructions addressing other variations. If the resource is an updating loose-leaf publication, the cataloger is to record the number of the volumes with a qualifier following it (e.g., 51 volumes (loose-leaf)). If the resource consists of more than one sheet or more than one portfolio or case, the cataloger records the number of units and an appropriate term.

> **Extent**: 4 sheets
>
> **Extent**: 2 portfolios
>
> **Extent**: 2 cases (iv pages, 16 leaves; iii pages, 20 leaves)

Extent for the Other Exceptional Categories

For cartographic materials (maps, atlases, globes, etc.), the cataloger records the number of units followed by one of the terms below, using a singular or plural form as appropriate.

- atlas
- diagram
- globe
- map
- model
- profile
- remote-sensing image
- section
- view

If these terms are not sufficient, the cataloger may use a concise term or phrase that applies to the resource being described, including those found under still images and three-dimensional forms. More than one term may be applied if the resource comprises multiple components. If the exact number of units is unknown, the term *approximately* may be inserted.

> **Extent**: 1 globe
>
>   2 maps
>
> **Extent**: approximately 100 maps

RDA 3.4.2 also contains specific instructions on multiple cartographic units on one or more sheets (e.g., 6 maps on 1 sheet), on single cartographic units on more than one segment or sheet (e.g., 1 section in 4 segments, 1 map on 4 sheets), and on the volumes and pagination of atlases (e.g., 1 atlas (2 volumes), 1 atlas (xvii, 37 pages, 74 leaves of plates)).

For notated music, the cataloger records the number of units followed by an appropriate term for the format, using a singular or plural form as needed.

More than one term may be applied if the resource comprises multiple components. The cataloger should specify the number of volumes and/or PLCs in parentheses, following the format of notated music.

> **Extent**: 1 score (368 pages)
>
> **Extent**: 1 vocal score (5 pages, 1 unnumbered page)
>
> **Extent**: 1 choir book (110 unnumbered pages)
>
> **Extent**: 1 score (24 pages)
>
> 1 piano conductor part (8 pages)
>
> 35 parts

For still images (drawings, paintings, prints, photographs, etc.), the cataloger records the number of units followed by one of the terms below, using a singular or plural form as appropriate. More than one term may be applied if the resource comprises multiple components. If the exact number of units is unknown, the term *approximately* may be inserted.

- activity card
- chart
- collage
- drawing
- flash card
- icon
- painting
- photograph

- picture
- postcard
- poster
- print
- radiograph
- study print
- technical drawing
- wall chart

If these terms are not sufficient, the cataloger may use a concise term or phrase that applies to the resource being described.

> **Extent**: 1 painting
>
> **Extent**: 4 wall charts
>
> **Extent**: approximately 500 flash cards

RDA 3.4.4 also contains specific instructions on multiple images on one or more carriers (e.g., 2 collages on 1 sheet), on single still image on more than one carrier (e.g., 1 poster in 16 sheets), and on portfolios and albums of images (e.g., 2 sketchbooks, 1 portfolio (40 prints)).

For three-dimensional forms, formerly known as *realia*, the cataloger records the number of units followed by one of the terms below, using a singular or plural form as appropriate. More than one term may be applied if the resource comprises multiple components. If the exact number of units is unknown, the term *approximately* may be inserted.

- coin
- diorama
- exhibit

- game
- jigsaw puzzle
- medal

- mock-up
- model
- sculpture
- specimen
- toy

If these terms are not sufficient, the cataloger may use a concise term or phrase that applies to the resource being described. For some types of realia, the number and type of subunit may be recorded in parentheses after the type of unit. If the names of subunits cannot be listed concisely, the cataloger may use the phrase *various pieces*.

> **Extent**: 1 teapot
>
> **Extent**: 1 jigsaw puzzle (750 pieces)
>
> **Extent**: approximately 500 specimens
>
> **Extent**: 1 game (various pieces)

RDA 3.5 Dimensions

Dimensions, an LC Core element for non-serial tangible resources, are the measurements of a resource, specifically of the carrier or the container. Dimensions may include height, length, width, diameter, and gauge. The source of information for this element is the resource itself. The basic instruction is to record dimensions in terms of the number of centimeters followed by *cm*—a metric symbol (not an abbreviation) that does not require an ending period. When recording dimensions, the cataloger generally rounds up the measurement to the next whole centimeter. If for example, the spine of a book measures 22.36 centimeters, then *23 cm* is recorded as the dimensions for that resource.

There is an alternative at RDA 5.3.1.3: Recording Dimensions that states the cataloger may record the dimensions using another system if it is the policy of the cataloging agency. LC applies this alternative for discs and for all types of audio carriers (although this has not always been consistently applied). For example, in the United States, the dimensions of DVDs are generally recorded as *4 3/4 in.* (which has been rounded up to the nearest quarter-inch) but sometimes they are recorded as *12 cm*; long-playing record albums and singles are usually recorded as *12 in.* or *7 in.*, but audiocassettes sometimes have no dimension listed at all, sometimes they are recorded as *10 × 7 cm, 4 mm tape*, and sometimes they appear as *3 7/8 × 2 1/2 in., 1/8 in. tape*.

The sub-instructions for dimensions include dimensions of carrier, dimensions of container, resources with more than one carrier or container, and changes in dimensions for serials, multipart monographs, and integrating resources. There are also separate sets of instructions for maps and still images. A basic overview of the dimensions of carriers is found in Table 5.6.

If the resource comprises more than one carrier, how the dimensions are recorded depends on whether the carriers are of the same type and size. If the carrier types and the sizes are the same, then the cataloger records the

TABLE 5.6 Dimensions of Carriers and Containers.

Carrier type	Dimensions	Examples
Cards (e.g., flash, aperture, computer cards)	Height × width	15 × 31 cm
Cartridges		
Audio cartridges	Length × height, followed by a comma and width of tape in mm	14 × 10 cm, 7 mm tape
Computer cartridges	Length of side of cartridge inserted into machine	10 cm
Film, filmstrip, or video cartridges	Gauge (i.e., width) in mm. For 8 mm, indicate if single, standard, super or Maurer. Length *may* be added.	16 mm super 8 mm 35 mm
Microform cartridges	Width in mm	35 mm
Cassettes		
Audio cassettes	Length × height, followed by a comma and width of tape in mm	10 × 7 cm, 4 mm tape 3 7/8 × 2 1/2 in., 1/8 in. tape *(per LC-PCC PS)*
Computer and microfiche cassettes	Length × height	10 × 7 cm 12 × 17 cm
Film or video cassettes	Gauge (i.e., width) in mm. For 8 mm, indicate if single, standard, super or Maurer. Length *may* be added.	standard 8 mm 13 mm
Microfilm cassettes	Width in mm	16 mm
Discs (e.g., LPs, compact discs, DVDs, CD-ROMs)	Diameter	12 cm 30 cm 4 3/4 in. *(per LC-PCC PS)*
Filmstrips and filmslips	Gauge (i.e., width) in mm.	35 mm
Flipcharts	Height × width	23 × 18 cm
Microfiches	Height × width	11 × 15 cm
Overhead transparencies	Height × width excluding frame or mount	28 × 22 cm 9 × 9 cm
Reels (i.e., audio, computer, film, video, and microfilm reels)	Diameter of reel, followed by a comma and width of the tape or film in mm For 8 mm film, indicate if single, standard, super or Maurer. Length *may* be added.	18 cm, 13 mm tape 31 cm, 13 mm tape 18 cm, 16 mm 37 cm, 35 mm

TABLE 5.6 Dimensions of Carriers and Containers. (*continued*)

Carrier type	Dimensions	Examples
Rolls (e.g., film and microfilm)	Gauge (i.e., width) in mm. For 8 mm, indicate if single, standard, super or Maurer. Length *may* be added.	super 8 mm
Sheets (e.g., sheet, folded sheet, scroll) *Does not apply to maps or still images.*	Height × width excluding frame or mount	28 × 22 cm 54 × 42 cm folded to 27 × 21 cm 27 × 471 cm rolled to 27 × 7 cm in diameter
Slides (e.g., photographic, microscope)	Height × width	5 × 5 cm 3 × 8 cm
Three-dimensional forms	The dimensions of the form. Use words to indicate dimension as needed	23 cm high 14 × 28 × 7 cm
Globe	Diameter	12 cm in diameter
Volumes (e.g., books)	Height	22 cm
	If height is less than 10 cm, record in mm.	75 mm
	If the width is less than half the height, or width is greater than the height, record height × width.	20 × 8 cm 20 × 32 cm
	For *significant* differences in binding and text block, record both.	20 × 8 cm in binding 22 × 12 cm
Containers	Name the container and record height × width × depth in addition to the dimensions of the carrier.	case 17 × 34 × 6 cm box 30 × 25 × 13 cm

common size as dimensions. If the types are the same, but the sizes differ, the cataloger describes the dimensions of the smallest and the largest carriers (e.g. 24-28 cm). An alternative allows that if all the carriers are one of two sizes, the cataloger may record (1) the dimensions of both (e.g., 8 × 13 cm and 10 × 15 cm) or (2) the size of the largest followed by the phrase *or smaller* (e.g., 26 × 21 cm or smaller). LC applies this alternative. The guidelines for resources in more than one container follow suit. For instructions on the dimensions of maps and still images, the reader should consult RDA 3.5.2 and 3.5.3.

Format-specific Elements

The following is a brief description of the many format-specific elements included in RDA chapter 3. Each description contains a definition, lists of vocabulary terms used, any specific sub-instructions, and examples. For each of these elements, the preferred source of information is the resource itself (or its accompanying material or container). RDA instructions 3.6-3.22 provide much more detail on these elements. For each of these characteristics, more detail may be added than is presented here.

RDA 3.6-3.8 Base Material, Applied Material, and Mount

Base material is the matter or substance used as a foundation for a physical resource. The basic instruction is to use one or more of the following terms:

- acetate
- aluminum
- Bristol board
- canvas
- cardboard
- ceramic
- diacetate
- glass
- hardboard
- illustration board
- ivory
- leather
- metal
- nitrate
- paper
- parchment
- plaster
- plastic
- polyester
- porcelain
- rubber
- safety base
- shellac
- skin
- stone
- synthetic
- textile
- triacetate
- vellum
- vinyl
- wax
- wood

Another appropriate term(s) may be used if none of these are appropriate. Additional details may be added to the base material as appropriate. This element may be used with a diverse set of resources, such as manuscripts, films, globes, microscopic slides, microfiche, paintings, models, and the like. In general, one would not expect to see this or the following elements applied to books, serials, integrating resources, or other widely distributed print resources.

> **Base material**: ceramic tile
> **Base material**: goat leather

Applied material is the physical matter or substance applied to the base material. The basic instruction is to use one or more of the following terms or another appropriate term:

- acrylic paint
- chalk
- charcoal
- crayon
- dye
- gouache
- graphite
- ink
- lacquer
- magnetic particles
- nitrate
- oil paint
- pastel
- plaster
- plastic
- tempera
- watercolour
- wax

If there is more than one applied material, the cataloger records the predominant one first, followed by others as appropriate. The phrase *mixed materials* may be used if more than one applied material is used and they are not readily ascertained. A separate list of emulsions for microfilm is provided (i.e., diazo, mixed, silver halide, and vesicular).

> **Applied materials**: gouache and gold leaf
> **Applied materials**: graphite, ink, and wash

A *mount* is the material used as a support or backing for the base material. For example, a chalk drawing (i.e., the applied material) on paper (i.e., the base material) may be affixed to a piece of wood or some type of board (i.e., the mount). This element uses the same open vocabulary list established for *base material*.

> **Mount**: Mounted on starched linen
> **Mount**: On brass stand

RDA 3.9 Production Method

Production method is the procedure used to make or generate the resource. The basic instruction is to use one or more of the following terms or another appropriate term:

- blueline
- blueprint
- collotype
- daguerreotype
- engraving
- etching
- lithograph
- photocopy
- photoengraving
- photogravure
- print
- white print
- woodcut

There are separate sub-instructions, each with its own vocabulary, provided for manuscripts (e.g., holograph, manuscript, printout, and typescript) and tactile resources (e.g., embossed, solid dot, swell paper, and thermoform).

> **Production method**: lithograph
> **Production method**: embossed
> **Production method**: typescript (photocopy)
> **Production method**: ambrotype

RDA 3.10 Generation

"*Generation* is the relationship between an original carrier and the carrier of a reproduction made from the original (e.g., a first generation camera master, a second generation printing master)."[48] Five sets of sub-instructions have been developed for different types of carriers: audio recordings, digital resources, microforms, motion picture films, and videotapes. Each has its own vocabulary lists. The basic instruction is to use one of the following terms, or to supply another appropriate term:

- **Audio**: master tape, tape duplication master, disc master, mother, stamper, and test pressing.
- **Digital**: original, master, and derivative master.
- **Microform**: first generation, printing master, service copy, and mixed generation.
- **Motion picture**: original, master, duplicate, reference print, and viewing copy.
- **Videotape**: first generation; second generation, master copy; and second generation, show copy.

RDA 3.11-3.13 Layout, Book Format, and Font Size

Layout reflects the arrangement of content (text, images, etc.) in a resource. This is a core element for LC and the PCC if the resource is a form of cartographic material. Each type of layout has its own vocabulary list. The basic instruction is to use one or more of the following terms or another appropriate term:

- **Cartographic materials**: both sides and back to back.
- **Sheets**: double sided and single sided.
- **Tactile music notation**: bar by bar, bar over bar, line by line, line over line, melody chord system, open score, outline, paragraph, section by section, short form scoring, single line, and vertical score.
- **Tactile text**: double sided, single sided, and double line spacing.

Book format is the size of a book based on the folding of printed sheets to form leaves. The basic instruction is to use one of the following terms: *folio, 4to* (i.e., quarto), *8vo* (i.e. octavo), *12mo, 16mo, 24mo, 32mo, 48mo*, and *64mo*. The element *book format* is most often used for the description of rare and early printed books.

Font size reflects the size of the typeface used to present text in a resource. This metadata may be expressed generically (e.g., *large-print*) or specifically (e.g., *18 point*) or both. It may be used with braille resources as well as with large-print books and other text resources. The basic instruction is to use one of the following terms, or to supply another appropriate term: *large print, giant print*, and *jumbo braille*. If more detail is needed, then the cataloger should describe font size(s) specifically and concisely (e.g., Font size varies from 12 point to 24 point).

RDA 3.14 Polarity

Polarity is "the relationship of the colours and tones in an image to the colours and tones of the object reproduced . . . . For a photograph, motion picture film, or microform, record the polarity if considered important for identification or selection."[49] The basic instruction is to use one term from the closed vocabulary list: *positive*, *negative*, and *mixed polarity*. For motion picture film, additional information about the form of print may be recorded (e.g., fine grain duplicating negative).

RDA 3.15 Reduction Ratio

Reduction ratio is the ratio between the size of an original resource and a micro-image produced from it. This element is used to describe microfilm, microfiche, and aperture cards. There are five values from which to choose:

- **Low reduction**: for ratios less than 16×
- **Normal reduction**: between 16× and 30×
- **High reduction**: between 31× and 60×
- **Very high reduction**: between 61× and 90×
- **Ultra high reduction**: over 90×

RDA 3.16-3.19 Various Format Characteristics: Sound, Projected Motion Picture, Video, and Digital

The element, *sound characteristics*, includes descriptions of eight technical specifications associated with audio resources. More than one sound characteristic may be necessary to fully describe the resource. It includes sub-instructions for the following data elements.

- **Type of Recording**: "the method used to encode audio content for playback."[50] The cataloger should record *analog*, *digital*, or another appropriate term.
- **Recording Medium**: "the type of medium used to record sound on an audio carrier."[51] The cataloger should record *magnetic*, *magneto-optical*, *optical*, or another appropriate term.
- **Playing Speed**: the optimal operating speed for the resource; Most commonly recorded with analog discs (i.e., 33 1/3 rpm, 45 rpm, 78 rpm), but it may also be recorded for digital discs (i.e., 1.2 m/s-1.4 m/s), analog cylinders (144.4 rpm), analog tapes (e.g., 4.75 cm/s, 9.5 cm/s, 19 cm/s, 38 cm/s; if using inches, 1 7/8 ips, 3 3/4 ips, 7 1/2 ips, 15 ips), and sound-track films (e.g., 24 fps).

- **Groove Characteristic**: width of the groove on an analog audio carrier. It is used with analog discs (e.g., a phonograph record) and the choice of term is *coarse groove* or *microgroove*. It is also used for phonograph cylinders, where the terms are *fine* or *standard*.
- **Track Configuration**: configuration of the audio portion of a sound-track film. The cataloger should record either *centre track* or *edge track*.
- **Tape Configuration**: the number of tracks on an audiotape recording (e.g., 8 track, 12 track).
- **Configuration of Playback Channels**: number of sound channels. The cataloger should record one or more of the following: *mono, stereo, quadraphonic, surround*, or another appropriate term. The terms *mono* and *stereo* are no longer considered abbreviations and do not require a full stop (i.e., a period) at the end.
- **Special Playback Characteristics**: includes additional characteristics related to noise reduction and equalizing systems. The cataloger should record one or more of the following: *CCIR standard, CX encoded, dbx encoded, Dolby, Dolby-A encoded, Dolby-B encoded, Dolby-C encoded, LPCM, NAB standard*, or another appropriate term.

Additional characteristics, generally associated with digital files, are addressed in RDA 3.19: Digital File Characteristic.

The *projection characteristic of motion picture film* element includes description of two technical specifications associated with projected moving image resources. It includes sub-instructions for the following data elements.

- **Presentation Format**: the format used in the creation of the motion picture. The cataloger should record one or more of the following: *Cinerama, Cinemiracle, Circarama, IMAX, multiprojector, multiscreen, Panavision, standard silent aperture, standard sound aperture, stereoscopic, techniscope, 3D*, or another appropriate term.
- **Projection Speed**: the optimal operating speed for projection motion picture carrier (e.g., 20 fps).

The element *video characteristic* includes a description of two technical specifications associated with video recordings:

- **Video Format**: the encoding formatting for analog video recording. The cataloger should record one of the following: *Beta, Betacam, Betacam SP, CED, D-2, EIAJ, 8 mm, Hi-8 mm, Laser optical, M-II, Quadruplex, Super-VHS, Type C, U-matic, VHS*, or another appropriate term.
- **Broadcast Standard**: the video formatting used for television broadcasting. The cataloger should record one of the following: *HDTV, NTSC, PAL, SECAM*, or another appropriate term.

The *digital file characteristic* element, which is LC Core *if* the resource is a form of cartographic materials, includes descriptions of the technical specifications associated with the encoding of digital resources of various types (text, image, audio, video, and so on). The instructions state that any general digital file characteristic, such as recording density or sectoring, should be recorded if they are considered useful. This element includes sub-instructions for the following:

- **File Type**: the type of data encoded in the file. The cataloger should record one or more of the following: *audio file, data file, image file, program file, text file, video file*, or another appropriate term.

- **Encoding Format**: the approach used to encode the content. This element includes six separate lists of terms. One or more terms from a list may be used; if none are suitable, another appropriate term may be used. The cataloger should record the version of the encoding format if it affects or restricts use.

  ○ **Audio Encoding Formats**: *CD audio, DAISY, DVD audio, MP3, RealAudio, SACD*, and *WAV*.

  ○ **Data Encoding Formats**: *Access, Excel, Lotus*, and *XML*.

  ○ **Image Encoding Formats**: *BMP, GIF, JPEG, JPEG2000, PNG*, and *TIFF*.

  ○ **Spatial Data Encoding Formats**: *ArcInfo, BIL, BSQ, CAD, DEM, E00*, and *MID/MIF*.

  ○ **Text Encoding Formats**: *ASCII, HTML, Megadots, MS Word, PDF, RTF, SGML, TeX, Word Perfect, XHTML*, and *XML*.

  ○ **Video Encoding Formats**: *Blu-Ray, DVD video, HD-DVD, MPEG-4, QuickTime, RealVideo, SVCD, VCD*, and *Windows media*.

- **File Size**: the number of bytes comprising the file. The size is recorded if it is readily accessible and judged to be useful (e.g., 202 MB, 3.3 GB).

- **Resolution**: the number of pixels in an image. It addresses the level of detail in an image. The resolution is recorded if it is readily accessible and judged to be useful (e.g., 2048 × 1536 pixels, 1024 × 768 pixels).

- **Regional Encoding**: "a code identifying the region of the world for which a DVD videodisc has been encoded"[52] to operate, and is prevented from playing on players from another region. The regional encoding is recorded if it is judged to be useful (e.g., region 1, all regions).

- **Encoded Bitrate**: the number of bits that are conveyed or processed over a given unit of time. It indicates the optimal speed of streaming audio and video. The bitrate is recorded if it is readily accessible and judged to be useful (e.g., 6.0 Mbps, 3,000 Kbps).

- **Digital Representation of Cartographic Content**: technical specifications associated with the encoding of geospatial information. This element includes three types of information: *data type* (i.e., raster, vector, or point), *object type* (e.g., string, point, line), and the *number of objects* used to represent spatial information (e.g., 20171).

RDA 3.20 Equipment or System Requirement

This element includes a specification of the equipment or system required for the operation of the resource. The cataloger should record the make or model of equipment or hardware, the operating system needed, memory requirements, the programming language, and/or other necessary software, plug-ins, or peripherals. Some examples help illustrate the range of information that might be recorded:

- **System requirements**: Wii U console.
- **System requirements**: XBox 360 console; 256 KB to save game; HDTV 720p/1080i/1080p.
- **System requirements**:
  - *Operating System*: PC Windows 2000+, Mac OSX+
  - *Browser Compatibility*: IE6+, Firefox 2+, Opera 9+, Safari 2+
  - *Browser settings*: enable JavaScript, enable popups from the Henry Stewart Talks site
  - *Required Browser Plug-ins & Viewers*: Adobe (Macromedia) Flash Player 7+, Adobe Acrobat Reader 6.0+

RDA 3.21 Carrier Notes

At the end of RDA chapter 3, it discusses the use of notes related to carriers. A *note on carrier*, as one might expect, is not a single element, but is instead a category containing any number of notes that might be useful and necessary. In RDA 3.21: Note on Carrier, there are several sub-instructions:

3.21.2	**Note on Extent of Manifestation**
3.21.2.3	Describing Various Pieces
3.21.2.4	Resource Issued in More Than One Unit Not to Be Continued
3.21.2.5	Score and Parts in a Single Physical Unit
3.21.2.6	Pagination Forming Part of a Larger Sequence
3.21.2.7	Duplicated Paging
3.21.2.8	Number of Bibliographic Volumes Differing from Number of Physical Volumes
3.21.2.9	Early Printed Resources
3.21.2.10	*[Empty instruction]*
3.21.2.11	Other Details of Extent
3.21.3	**Note on Dimensions of Manifestation**
3.21.4	**Note on Changes in Carrier Characteristics**

Of these, only *Note on Changes in Carrier Characteristics* is a core element for LC; none are RDA Core. Notes may be taken from any source. Examples for various types of notes on carrier follow.

Describing Various Pieces

- Includes photographs, advertisements, newsletters, articles, and newspaper clippings related to advertising.
- Contains 1 map (2 sheets of 11 × 17"), 1 set of 280 die cut 1/2" playing pieces (printed on 2 sheets), 1 set of charts and tables (2 sheets), rules of play (8 sheets).

Volumes and Pagination

- 2 bibliographic volumes in 4 physical volumes.
- Opposite pages bear duplicate numbering.
- Appendix separately paged; letter A appears as part of the page numbering.
- Pagination in reverse order, starts from 450 to 401.

Dimensions

- Size varies: XXIV. évf., sz. 4 (1938:apr.)- : 25 cm
- Maximum Height: 72 in., Minimum Height: 8 in.; Folded Length: 27 in.
- Size of frame: 44 × 105 cm
- Measurements given are those of plate-mark. Printed area measures 31 × 94 cm

Changes in Carrier Characteristics

- Some issues have accompanying CD-ROM.
- Periodic supplements issued online only, in between annual editions.
- After issue no. 160 available online only.

Other Notes on Carriers

- The accordion-type binding allows the viewer to flip through the pages just like a normal book, but also gives the option to unfold it in its entirety.
- Gold-tooled morocco binding by Benjamin West, approximately 1840.
- Late 16th century blind-tooled centrepiece binding, dark brown calf.
- Extensive paper damage and wormholes throughout, affecting text. Very fragile.
- Author's autograph and dedication on endpapers.
- Altered books: 4 unmatched book cases; pencil drawings on endpapers; binder clips attached.
- Several of the items are torn or missing pieces, and the material is very brittle.
- Missing pages 353-368.
- Library's copy missing pages 173-174. Page 175 is blank.

PROVIDING ACQUISITION AND ACCESS INFORMATION

RDA chapter 4, the final chapter in section 1: Recording Attributes of Manifestation & Item, is a brief one. It contains some general instructions and metadata elements to consider in the description of the resource. The focus of the chapter is on creating metadata to assist in the process of acquiring or accessing a resource. The metadata recorded may be taken from any source of information. The five acquisition/access elements are addressed below.

Terms of availability are the stipulations or conditions by which a resource is available for purchase or use. The basic instruction is that the cataloger should record the price, if the resource is for sale, or a brief description of other conditions, if the resource cannot be purchased.

> **Terms of Availability**: $24.95
>
> **Terms of Availability**: $12.99 USA/$15.99 CAN
>
> **Terms of Availability**: rental material
>
> **Terms of Availability**: free to members

Qualifiers may be added to the terms of availability if needed, for example: (£15.00 to libraries; £10.00 to association members). The LC-PCC PS for this element states: "*LC practice*: Generally do not provide prices or other availability information except for rental scores or rental performance materials. Give the note 'Rental material' as a term of availability as appropriate to indicate to other libraries that the item is not available for purchase."[53]

Contact information is fairly self-explanatory. It is the phone number, web address, email, physical address, and so on for a publisher or an archives. The cataloger is to record the information if considered important.

> **Contact information**: http://www.loc.gov/cds
>
> **Contact information**: ABC-CLIO, P.O. Box 1911, Santa Barbara, CA 93116-1911
>
> **Contact information**: 617-555-2863

Restriction on access is also self-explanatory. The cataloger is to record, very specifically, any limitations on access to the resource, including the nature of the restrictions as well as dates, times, or duration associated with the restrictions.

> **Restrictions on Access**: No restrictions on access to materials.
>
> **Restrictions on Access**: Some family correspondence is restricted during Patricia de Man's lifetime. Access to student record material is restricted for 75 years from the latest date of the materials in those files. Restrictions are noted at the file level.
>
> **Restrictions on Access**: Access restricted to subscribers via a username and password or IP address authentication.

> **Restrictions on Access**: There are no restrictions on access, except that the collection can only be seen by prior appointment. Some materials may be stored off-site and cannot be produced on the same day on which they are requested.

Restrictions on use, another element addressing limits, is focused on how a resource may be used. The cataloger is to record, very specifically, any limitations on use, including the nature of the restrictions as well as dates, times, or duration associated with the restrictions. *Restrictions on use* is an LC-PCC Core element.

> **Restrictions on Use**: Research copy reel–cannot be reproduced for purchase.
>
> **Restrictions on Use**: Researchers may consult the oral history interview, but must secure permission to cite or quote its contents from Columbia University, Oral History Research Office, New York, NY 10027.
>
> **Restrictions on Use**: Written permission required for public use.
>
> **Restrictions on Use**: Information on literary rights available in the repository.
>
> **Restrictions on Use**: This film is restricted to classroom use.

The *Uniform Resource Locator* (URL) is the final element in RDA chapter 4. It is an LC-PCC Core element, which contains the address of a remote-access electronic resource.

> **URL**: https://twitter.com/dnjoudrey
>
> **URL**: http://www.pitt.edu/~agtaylor/
>
> **URL**: http://www.origamipoems.com/poets/93-david-p-miller

If a URL has changed, the URL in the description should be updated. There is an LC-PCC PS describing what to do if the URL is no longer active or if the address is active but the original resource is no longer there.

CONCLUSION

This chapter is focused on the initial process of describing a resource, particularly on the metadata elements that are necessary for identifying and describing a manifestation. It discusses the recording of bibliographic metadata, such as title, statements of responsibility, and edition statement, but also examines the major elements addressing the physical nature of the resources and/or its encoding of the content. Elements related to the individual item and to access issues are also reviewed. In the next chapter, the process of describing works and expressions is explored. Unlike this chapter, the next not only discusses problems of description, but also discusses issues related to access points and authority control.

NOTES

1. *RDA: Resource Description & Access*, developed in a collaborative process led by the Joint Steering Committee for Development of RDA (Chicago: American Library Association, 2010). Also available through paid subscriptions to *RDA Toolkit* (Chicago: American Library Association, 2010), accessed July 24, 2015, http://www.rdatoolkit.org/. In lieu of page numbers, any references to specific parts of RDA are made using instruction numbers.
2. RDA, 1.3: Core Elements.
3. Library of Congress, "LC-PCC PS for 1.4," in "Library of Congress–Program for Cooperative Cataloging Policy Statements (LC-PCC PS)" *RDA Toolkit: Resource Description & Access* (Chicago: American Library Association, 2010), accessed July 2, 2015, http://access.rdatoolkit.org/. Free access to the LC-PCC PS is available through the Resources tab. Copies of the LC-PCC PS are also available with a paid subscription in *Cataloger's Desktop*.
4. *Anglo-American Cataloguing Rules, Second Edition*, 2002 Revision, prepared under the direction of the Joint Steering Committee for the Revision of AACR (Chicago: American Library Association, 2002).
5. *The Chicago Manual of Style*, 16th ed. (Chicago: University of Chicago Press, 2010).
6. Library of Congress, "LC-PCC PS for 1.7.1 First Alternative."
7. Library of Congress, "LC-PCC PS for 1.7.1 Second Alternative."
8. Library of Congress, "LC-PCC PS for A.1 Alternative."
9. Hierarchical descriptions are omitted because they are rarely seen in American library catalogs, and the LC-PCC PS states that they are not to be created.
10. RDA, 2.2.4: Other Sources of Information.
11. RDA, 2.3.1.1: Scope [of Recording Title].
12. Theodore Low De Vinne, *The Practice of Typography: A Treatise on Title-pages* (New York: The Century Co., 1902), 203; Janine Barchas, *Graphic Design, Print Culture, and the Eighteenth-Century Novel* (Cambridge, UK: Cambridge University Press, 2003), 61-66.
13. Program for Cooperative Cataloging (PCC), "PCC RDA BIBCO Standard Record (BSR) Metadata Application Profile," page 6, April 14, 2015 revision, http://www.loc.gov/aba/pcc/bibco/bsr-maps.html.
14. Library of Congress, "LC-PCC PS for 2.3.2.9 Alternative."
15. RDA, 0.6: Core Elements.
16. PCC, "BSR," 6.
17. Library of Congress, "LC-PCC PS for 2.3.6.3 Recording Variant Titles."
18. RDA, 2.4.1.1: Scope [of Recording Statements of Responsibility].
19. Library of Congress, "LC-PCC PS for 2.4.1.4 Option."
20. For example, The ATLAS Collaboration, "A Particle Consistent with the Higgs Boson Observed with the ATLAS Detector at the Large Hadron Collider," *Science* 338, no. 6114 (2012): 1576-1582, which comes with a complete author list as supplementary material for this paper: http://www.sciencemag.org/content/338/6114/1576/suppl/DC1.
21. PCC, "BSR," 7.
22. *Anglo-American Cataloguing Rules, Second Edition*, 2002 Revision, appendix D-3.
23. RDA, Glossary D-F.
24. RDA, 2.5.2.1: Scope [of Recording Designation of Edition].
25. RDA, 2.5.6.3: Recording Designations of a Named Revision of an Edition.
26. Program for Cooperative Cataloging, "CONSER–Cooperative Online Serials Program," accessed August 6, 2015, http://www.loc.gov/aba/pcc/conser/.

27. RDA, 2.8.1.1: Scope [of Recording Publication Statements].
28. Library of Congress, "LC-PCC PS for 2.8.2.6 Place of Publication Not Identified in the Resource."
29. RDA, 2.7.1.1: Scope [of Recording Production Statements].
30. RDA, 2.9.1.1: Scope [of Recording Distribution Statements].
31. RDA, 2.10.1.1: Scope [of Recording Manufacture Statements].
32. RDA, 2.11.1.1: Scope [of Recording Copyright Dates].
33. RDA, Glossary S.
34. RDA, 2.12.1.1: Scope [of Recording Series Statements].
35. RDA, 2.12.9.1: Scope [of Recording Numbering within Series].
36. RDA, 2.13.1: Scope [of Recording Modes of Issuance].
37. This does *not* include Uniform Resource Locators (URLs) or Uniform Resource Identifiers (URIs), which are addressed in RDA chapter 4.
38. Karen Smith-Yoshimura et al., *Implications of MARC Tag Usage on Library Metadata Practices* (Dublin, Ohio: OCLC, 2010). http://www.oclc.org/research/publications/library/2010/2010-06.pdf.
39. RDA, 2.17.13.1: Scope [of Note on Issue, Part, or Iteration Used as the Basis for Identification of the Resource].
40. RDA, Glossary C.
41. RDA, 3.2.1.1: Scope [of Recording Media Type].
42. RDA, 3.3.1.1: Scope [of Recording Carrier Type].
43. RDA, 3.4.1.1: Scope [of Recording Extent].
44. Formerly, under AACR2, *ca.* (*circa*) was used.
45. RDA, Glossary C.
46. RDA, Glossary L.
47. RDA, 3.4.5.2: Single Volume with Numbered Pages, Leaves, or Columns.
48. RDA, 3.10.1.1: Scope [of Recording Generation].
49. RDA, 3.14.1: Basic Instructions on Recording Polarity.
50. RDA, 3.16.2.1 Scope [of Recording Type].
51. RDA, 3.16.3.1 Scope [of Recording Medium].
52. RDA, 3.19.6.1 Scope [of Regional Encoding].
53. Library of Congress, "LC-PCC PS for 4.2.1.3 Recording Terms of Availability."

SUGGESTED READING

El-Sherbini, Magda. *RDA: Strategies for Implementation.* Chicago: American Library Association, 2013.

Hart, Amy. *RDA Made Simple: A Practical Guide to the New Cataloging Rules.* Santa Barbara, Calif.: Libraries Unlimited, 2014.

Kincy, Chamya Pompey, with Sara Shatford Layne. *Making the Move to RDA: A Self-Study Primer for Catalogers.* Lanham, Md.: Rowman & Littlefield, 2014.

Maxwell, Robert L. *Maxwell's Handbook for RDA, Resource Description & Access: Explaining and Illustrating RDA: Resource Description and Access Using MARC21.* Chicago: American Library Association, 2013.

Mering, Margaret, editor. *The RDA Workbook: Learning the Basics of Resource Description and Access.* Santa Barbara, Calif.: Libraries Unlimited, 2014.

Oliver, Chris. *Introducing RDA: A Guide to the Basics.* Chicago: American Library Association, 2010.

Chapter 6

Works and Expressions

INTRODUCTION

This chapter reviews the elements of RDA[1] that are useful in describing and identifying works and expressions. RDA chapters 5-7 not only describe the characteristics of works and expressions that may appear as part(s) of a bibliographic description (e.g., language, illustrative content), but also provide basic instructions for creating access points. In addition, these chapters include elements that are generally recorded as authority data rather than as bibliographic data. RDA chapter 5 provides general instructions for recording this metadata, chapter 6 covers identifying works and expressions, and chapter 7 provides guidelines on describing content. For quick reference, RDA chapter 6 is primarily about establishing authority data for works and expressions, whereas chapter 7 is about recording work- and expression-level elements in bibliographic data.

With this chapter, ICC11 begins a discussion of establishing authority data using RDA. Some basic concepts of authority control are introduced in the chapter, but for a fuller picture, the reader should review chapter 8 in *The Organization of Information* by Arlene G. Taylor and Daniel N. Joudrey.[2] Readers also may read chapter 10 of this text to learn more about authority control, although the chapter addresses implementing authority control in the MAchine-Readable Cataloging (MARC) environment rather than in the schema-neutral environment of chapters 4-8 of this text.

Another concern that the authors want to point out is that they considered placing the RDA chapters on identifying persons, families, and corporate bodies (PFC) before those on works and expressions. The primary reason for considering this is that the names of creators are often combined with titles to create an authorized access point (AAP) for a work. Ultimately, it was decided

277

not to separate the FRBR Group 1 entities (i.e., WEMI) by placing PFCs in between. Some readers, however, may wish to read the chapter on persons, families, and corporate bodies first. Either approach to the content is valid. In the examples in this chapter, authorized forms of names for PFCs are included to create complete access points.

In this chapter, the examples of AAPs for works are presented without initial articles in the preferred titles of works. Although RDA states that initial articles are to be recorded, long-standing standard American cataloging practice is to remove initial articles; this is due to limitations associated with the current encoding standard, MARC. At this time, established AAPs for works in the Library of Congress Name Authority File (also known as the LC/NACO Authority File or the LCNAF)[3] omit initial articles; the examples provided in this chapter have been taken from that source and thus do not include initial articles.

RECORDING ATTRIBUTES OF WORKS AND EXPRESSIONS

Before works and expressions can be discussed, a few background concerns must be addressed. Each section of RDA begins with a chapter of general guidelines. The guidelines outlined in RDA chapter 5 include some baseline instructions that also apply to the other chapters in RDA section 2 (i.e., RDA chapters 6 and 7), and contain discussions related to terminology, objectives, core elements, and several other issues. Its structure is presented in Textbox 6.1.

5: General Guidelines on Recording Attributes of Works and Expressions

5.0 Scope
5.1 Terminology
5.2 Functional Objectives and Principles
5.3 Core Elements
5.4 Language and Script
5.5 Authorized Access Points Representing Works and Expressions
5.6 Variant Access Points Representing Works and Expressions
5.7 Status of Identification
5.8 Source Consulted
5.9 Cataloguer's Note

Textbox 6.1 RDA Chapter 5 Structure.

RDA 5.1 Terminology

RDA 5.1 discusses general terminology used throughout RDA section 2, including terms such as *work* and *expression*, which should be somewhat familiar concepts after reading chapter 3 of this text. It reminds catalogers that these entities can refer to single units (e.g., a novella, a map, a biological specimen, a piece of software), aggregates (e.g., a series, a collection of nine short stories, a set of five individual posters), and parts or components of these entities (e.g., each one of the nine short stories is a work, but each is also a part of the larger work).

RDA 5.1 also defines *access points*, a term previously mentioned throughout this text. It is helpful to remember that access points appear in both authorized and variant forms. An access point for a work or expression is a name, term, or character string associated with a particular work or an expression of a work. Access points are discussed in more detail below.

Terminology addressed in 5.1 also includes *title*, pointing out that the terms *title of the work*, *preferred title*, and *variant title* are used in these chapters. Although the guidelines do not specify it, it should be remembered that work titles and titles proper (i.e., manifestation titles) are not the same things. Of these terms, *preferred title for the work* may reflect a new concept for readers. In RDA, *title of work* refers to *any* word, phrase, or string that names a work—including the one that is chosen to identify the work (i.e., the preferred title for the work), as well as ones that are considered less common, less useful, or nonstandard in some way (i.e., variant titles for the work). A preferred title is used as the basis for an authorized access point for a work.

RDA 5.2 Functional Objectives and Principles

RDA 5.2 lists five objectives (of the 15 identified in "Responsiveness to User Needs" in the RDA Introduction) that are relevant to the metadata that is created using RDA section 2. By creating metadata related to works, expressions, and content, catalogers increase users' abilities to do the following:

- Find works and expressions based on their search criteria
- Identify the work and/or expression described
- Understand relationships among titles associated with the work or expression
- Understand why a title was chosen as preferred or as a variant
- Select a work or expression appropriate for their needs in regard to content

The chapter then addresses the two relevant principles from the RDA Introduction. In the context of works and expressions, *differentiation* is self-evident; the metadata should allow the user to distinguish between similarly named works or expressions. *Representation* means that the title, chosen as the preferred title for the work (i.e., the basis of the authorized access point), should be the title most frequently used in resources containing the work in its original language. If that is not possible, then the title found most frequently in reference sources or the title found most frequently in resources (in any language) should be chosen as the preferred title. Other titles associated with the work or expression and other forms of the titles are considered variants.

RDA 5.3 Core Elements

RDA 5.3 provides a short reminder that a list of core elements for works and expressions may be found at RDA 0.6. The list is somewhat confusing, partly because the instructions do not explicitly state in what form or where these elements are to be recorded. Table 6.1 explains the general core requirements for section 2 of RDA. It should be noted that although there is an element for the preferred title for the work, there is not an equivalent element for the expression level. This is because when identifying an *expression*, one always begins with the title of the *work*. Differentiation of a specific expression occurs through one or more additions to the preferred title for the work. It is important to remember that the preferred title for the work is recorded as part of an authorized access point, which generally is recorded as authority data and then can be used, in its authorized form, in bibliographic records, bibliographic descriptions, or metadata statements. For a particular expression of a work, the elements *content type* and *language of expression* are required. When additional data elements are necessary to uniquely identify the work or expression, additional information representing form, place, dates, or some other distinctive characteristics are used. These might be recorded as separate data elements (e.g., entries in an authority record), as part of the access point (e.g., appending language onto the preferred title), or in both places (e.g., adding it to the access point, but also placing it in the appropriate field in the authority record). Not every morsel of metadata about an entity is useful in an access point.

An LC-PCC PS for RDA 0.6.6 states that when attempting to differentiate the AAPs of two or more entities with identical preferred titles, then the cataloger should always add one or more differentiating elements to the access point. Cataloger's judgment is used to decide whether "to also record these elements as separate elements and whether to record additional identifying elements (those not needed for differentiation) as separate elements."[4] LC practice also includes adding expression attributes to an AAP for a work when the resource being cataloged is in one of the following categories:

- music resources
- sacred scriptures
- translations
- language editions

For example, if an LC cataloger were describing a Spanish translation of Lanford Wilson's *5th of July*, then he or she would search for the authorized access point for that Spanish expression to include in the bibliographic metadata. If an AAP for the expression does not yet exist, the cataloger would search for the original work, and then append the language of the translation onto its AAP. This creates a new access point: **Wilson, Lanford, 1937-2011. 5th of July. Spanish**. The cataloger, if trained in authority work, could then create a new authority record for this particular language expression.

TABLE 6.1 RDA Core Elements for Works and Expressions.

Category	Core elements, *if applicable and ascertainable*	How is the data recorded?	Generally where the cataloger places the metadata
Works	Preferred title	As an AAP. Title is preceded by the name of the creator (sole, primary, or first-named, whichever is applicable). If no creator is associated with the work, the AAP is the preferred title alone.	In bibliographic data *and* authority data
	Identifier	Separate data element	Authority data—but in the future, it may appear in bibliographic data (e.g., replacing or supplementing the text string in the AAP)
Works, *if needed for differentiation*	Form, date, place of origin, and other characteristics of works	Separate data elements *and/or* part of the AAP	Separate elements appear in authority data; *some* of the elements may also appear as part of the AAP in bibliographic and authority data
Expressions	Content type Language of expression	Separate data elements *and/or* part of the AAP	Authority data and/or bibliographic data *(as described above)*
	Identifier for the expression	Separate data element	Authority data—but in the future, it may appear in bibliographic data (e.g., replacing or supplementing the text string in the AAP)
Expressions, *if needed for differentiation*	Date and other characteristics of expression	Separate data elements *and/or* part of the AAP	Authority data and/or bibliographic data *(as described above)*
Other	Certain types of content, such as musical works and cartographic expressions, may require other elements. Additional elements are included based on policy statements (e.g., LC-PCC PS), local institutional policies, and cataloger's judgment.		

RDA 5.4 Language and Script

RDA 5.4 informs catalogers that titles for works are to be recorded as found in resources being used to establish the title. If the work is originally in English, then an English title gets recorded as the title of the work in Latin script. If the work is in Urdu and written in Perso-Arabic script, then the title for the work should be recorded in Urdu and Perso-Arabic script in the authority data. An alternative states that the cataloger may record a transliterated form of the title, and it may be used either as a substitute for, or in addition to, the form that appears on the source. LC and PCC practice is to use the transliterated form in the AAP in the authority data. See the LC-PCC PS for more details as needed. The elements in RDA chapter 6 are recorded according to the specific instructions for each element in that chapter; those in chapter 7 are to be recorded in the language preferred by the cataloging agency (e.g., generally in English in the United States).

RDA 5.5-5.6 Authorized and Variant Access Points: Titles for Works and Expressions

Authorized access points are established strings of alphanumeric characters chosen to represent an entity. *Variant access points* (VAPs) are also strings that represent an entity, but they are not authorized for use in bibliographic metadata; they are used to point to the AAP (i.e., they are references). For works and expressions, an AAP entails either (1) a name/title access point or (2) a title-only access point. In both of these cases the title portion is based on the best-known title of the work and/or expression in the original language. Some works are known by many titles, but only one is chosen as the *preferred title*; other titles may be recorded as VAPs in the authority data for the work. Sometimes these title access points are referred to as *authority-controlled titles*, *standardized titles*, or, formerly, *uniform titles*; references might be called *variant titles* or *unauthorized titles*.

Authorized access points are established for different purposes and they accomplish a variety of tasks. Obviously they are primarily used to identify a work contained within a resource (i.e., a manifestation or item), but their presence also allows for another important function of cataloging: *collocation,* the bringing together of like resources. An AAP can be used to retrieve all versions of a work no matter what their titles proper might be. Manifestation titles can vary greatly, but a secondary purpose of the AAP for a work is to provide some consistency and standardization. For example, the title of Shakespeare's play *The Merchant of Venice* varies in its appearance in different published versions containing the work.

AAP for work: Shakespeare, William, 1564-1616. Merchant of Venice

Title proper: Shakespeare's The merchant of Venice

Title proper: Marchand de Venise

Title proper: Most excellent historie of the merchant of Venice

> **Title proper**: Shakespeare's comedy of The merchant of Venice
>
> **Title proper**: Shakspere's The merchant of Venice
>
> **Title proper**: William Shakespeare's The merchant of Venice

If a user performs a title search for *The Merchant of Venice* by Shakespeare and the AAP for the work is not present in the record, he or she might not retrieve *The Most Excellent Historie of the Merchant of Venice* (although it *could* be retrieved in a keyword search). In some cases, the title proper may be so far removed from the AAP that it might not be recognizable as the same work unless the AAP is present in the description:

> **AAP for work**: Wodehouse, P. G. (Pelham Grenville), 1881-1975. Aunts aren't gentlemen
>
> **Title proper**: Cat-nappers

In addition to identifying the work found in a manifestation (or in many different manifestations), an AAP for a work or an expression may be used for identifying related works and related expressions, including subject relationships.

> **Title proper**: To kill a mockingbird: teacher's guide
>
> **AAP for related work**: Harper, Lee. To kill a mockingbird.

> **Title proper**: Hamlet closely observed
>
> **AAP as subject heading**: Shakespeare, William, 1564-1616. Hamlet.

Another important function of an AAP is disambiguation (i.e., removing ambiguity by separating two or more entities known by the same name or title). Titles are not unique. For example, many resources have the title *Introduction to Psychology*. Many of those types of common titles can be distinguished through the creators' names, but other resources—particularly those containing works where a creator is not identified—may need an authorized access point to separate them. For example, many resources have the title *Bulletin*. Without an authorized access point to distinguish between them, it could be quite difficult to find the resource needed and to identify which work is which.

> **AAP for work**: Bulletin (Connecticut Arboretum)
>
> **AAP for work**: Bulletin (Connecticut. Department of Agriculture)
>
> **AAP for work**: Bulletin (Connecticut. Department of Farms and Markets)

An authorized access point for a work or for an expression generally contains the following elements in this order:

1. An authorized access point for the primary (or first-named) creator (i.e., the entity responsible for the work), *if applicable*

2. A preferred title for the work
3. Additional data elements necessary to uniquely identify the work or expression

Sometimes the AAP entails little more than just a title (e.g., when creators associated with the work are unknown). This creator-less preferred title may or may not be followed by additional data elements or qualifiers. Additional qualifiers include elements such as the form, date, and place of origin of the work, as well as other characteristics that may be useful for disambiguation among various works sharing a title and possibly other attributes.

Not every work or expression is identified in the form of an AAP, although many certainly are. Not every cataloger in every library is able to create nationally shareable authority data, nor does every cataloger have the time or willingness to do authority work. Although RDA does have core requirements for work and expression-level elements, they may not necessarily be added to the bibliographic description in today's MARC environment. For example, if the work has a unique title and it is identical to the title proper for the manifestation that contains the work, an AAP is just not necessary on a very practical level (although it is required by RDA). It is assumed that the work is represented by the combination of the creator's AAP and the title proper in the bibliographic metadata and can remain in this form until there is a more urgent need to create an authorized access point for the work. Another example may be a work that has only been disseminated under a single title, in a single form, and in a single language, but the title is the same as another work. In this case, a work AAP should be established, but the need to identify an expression is not necessarily there.

When an expression of a work does need to be specifically identified, the AAP for the expression always begins with the AAP for the work. It is then augmented by one or more additional data elements to represent the particular expression (e.g., content type, language). This does not mean, however, that all possible additional data elements should be added to the AAP for works or for particular expressions. They may, instead, be more appropriate as part of the authority data for the entity. In many cases, additional metadata is unnecessary and/or undesirable in the access point itself because only the metadata that serves to uniquely identify the entity is required. Although additional metadata elements provide greater context for understanding the entity, as mentioned above, not everything known about a creator or a title is necessary in its AAP. For example, no one wants to use the following as an access point:

Shakespeare, William, 1564-1616, Stratford-upon-Avon (England), male, English-language dramatist, poet, actor. Taming of the shrew (play : comedy : written in England).

This amount of additional information is unnecessary in the access point; a less embellished form, **Shakespeare, William, 1564-1616. Taming of the**

shrew, certainly suffices. All this additional information, though, should be recorded as part of the authority data, which in today's cataloging environment lives in a MARC-encoded authority record (see chapters 10 and 21 of this text). Here are some examples of AAPs for works and expressions:

> **AAP for work**: Inge, William. Picnic
>
> **AAP for work**: Beatles. Sgt. Pepper's Lonely Hearts Club Band
>
> **AAP for work**: Sir Gawain and the Green Knight
>
> **AAP for work**: Scribe, Eugène, 1791-1861. Comte Ory (Play)
>
> **AAP for work**: Scribe, Eugène, 1791-1861. Comte Ory (Libretto)
>
> **AAP for work**: Boorstin, Daniel J. (Daniel Joseph), 1914-2004. Image
>
> **AAP for work**: Shakespeare, William, 1564-1616. As you like it
>
> **AAP for expression**: Shakespeare, William, 1564-1616. As you like it. Panjabi
>
> **AAP for expression**: Shakespeare, William, 1564-1616. Works. 2007. Focus/R. Pullins
>
> **AAP for expression**: Sontag, Susan, 1933-2004. Against interpretation, and other essays. German

Variant access points for a work or an expression entail the same basic structure (AAP for creator and a title). The difference is that the title is not the preferred one; it is a variation on the title or on the form of title (e.g., spelling variations, language variations, different wording). On occasion the name portion might also be different. Another difference is that additions to the name/title form of access point are added only if considered important for identification:

> **VAP for work**: Inge, William. Summer brave
>
> **VAP for work**: Beatles. Sergeant Pepper's Lonely Hearts Club Band
>
> **VAP for work**: Gawayne and the Grene Knight
>
> **VAP for work**: Delestre-Poirson, C.-G. (Charles-Gaspard), 1790-1859. Comte Ory (Play)
>
> **VAP for work**: Boorstin, Daniel J. (Daniel Joseph), 1914-2004. What happened to the American dream
>
> **VAP for work**: Shakespeare, William, 1564-1616. Shakespeare's comedy, in five acts, As you like it
>
> **VAP for expression**: Shakespeare, William, 1564-1616. Oki ni mesu mama
>
> **VAP for expression**: Shakespeare, William, 1564-1616. New Kittredge Shakespeare. 2007
>
> **VAP for expression**: Sontag, Susan, 1933-2004. Kunst und Antikunst

Authorized and variant access points may be constructed for compilations and for one or more parts of a work following specific RDA guidelines.

General Elements for Authority Data

In RDA chapter 5, there are three elements that are used specifically while creating authority data. These are *status of identification, source consulted,* and *cataloguer's note.* All three are necessary when a cataloger or authority control librarian is doing authority work. None of these elements is RDA Core, but each is core for LC and PCC libraries.

RDA 5.7 Status of Identification

Status of identification refers to a code or term associated with the level of authentication of the authority data related to the work or expression. The element provides a short list of controlled vocabulary terms:

- **Fully established**: This is used when the authority data conforms to the cataloging instructions and the process has been completed and documented. In other words, the steps necessary to create the authorized access point have been taken, and sufficient evidence to support the choice of access points has been recorded.
- **Provisional**: This is used if the evidence for establishing the authorized access point is insufficient and further work on the authority data is required.
- **Preliminary**: This is used if the access point recorded has been taken from another bibliographic description because the resource is not available at the time the access point is being established. Further verification is required once the resource is in hand.

In today's cataloging environment, this information is provided as coded data in the MARC authority record's fixed field (see chapter 21 of this text). The goal is for all authority data to be fully established.

RDA 5.8 Source Consulted

Source consulted refers to any source of information used when creating authority data. Each resource that is consulted during the process of establishing authority data should be cited as a source. This process provides documentation demonstrating that the cataloger/authority control librarian performed the necessary steps to make decisions. The basic instruction is to cite the sources used when establishing the preferred and variant titles and other data elements recorded; this includes sources that provide useful information, but also sources that contain no information about the entity at all. When the information is not found in a source, the cataloger may record *No information found* following the citation. Citing a source where no information is found helps document the authority work process and saves the time of other catalogers/authority control librarians.

The citation for the resource consulted generally starts with the name of the creator, the title proper, and a date. After the minimal citation, a brief statement of the information found is recorded, as is the location of that information (e.g., title page).

Source consulted: Adamo, M. Little women, 2001, c1998: t.p. (Little women : opera in two acts)

Source consulted: His Henry V, 1982.

Source consulted: His The chronicle historie of Henry the Fift, 1993.

Source consulted: Encyclopedia Britannica, via WWW, Aug. 31, 2012: (Henry V; chronicle play in five acts; written by William Shakespeare; first performed in 1599, published in 1600).

Source consulted: Wikipedia, via WWW, Aug. 31, 2012: (Henry V; two major film adaptations, Laurence Olivier film in 1944 and Kenneth Branaugh film in 1989).

Source consulted: Barab, S. Autumn song, between 1955 and 1970?: title page (Autumn song; text, Dante Rossetti; for voice and piano).

Source consulted: Moore, J.K. The songs of Seymour Barab, 2000: (No information found).

Source consulted: Seymour Barab WWW site, April 9, 2013: (No information found).

RDA 5.9 Cataloguer's Note

In addition to the documentation already discussed, other notes in authority data are needed. In RDA, a *cataloguer's note* is "an annotation that might be helpful to those using or revising the authorized access point representing a work or expression, or creating an authorized access point representing a related work or expression."[5] These notes justify or clarify the reasoning for choosing the preferred name/title or the form of name/title chosen; they explain limits on the use of access points, help to differentiate between entities with similar names/titles, cite the instruction used to create the data, and provide any other information that might be useful.

Cataloguer's Note: Preferred title selected according to RDA 6.14.2.3, first exception (Better known title in the same language).

Cataloguer's Note: AACR2 authority record represents both the work and all Greek expressions of the work. In RDA this access point represents the work only.

Cataloguer's Note: Editions of this author's version are entered under Aesop's fables, with added entry under Anonymus Neveleti.

Cataloguer's Note: Since this discarded movement is now performed/published separately, consider it a separate work.

Cataloguer's Note: Heading for the group of works with the collective titles "Foundation series" or "The foundation novels." Do not treat as a bibliographic series.

Cataloguer's Note: Authorized access point represents the textual contents of the manuscript; for the manuscript as a physical entity, use: Rohan hours (no2008129601); for the illustrative matter of the manuscript with commentaries by Millard Meiss and Marcel Thomas, published in French, use: Rohan Master, active 15th century. Heures de Rohan (no2008129603).

DESCRIBING WORKS AND EXPRESSIONS

Chapter 6 of RDA is where the cataloger finds instructions to begin the process of describing works and expressions that are contained within resources. Its focus is primarily on establishing authority data, including an authorized access point. Once the work or expression is established in an authority file or its equivalent, the AAP—created as part of the authority work—may be used in bibliographic descriptions.

As can be seen in Textbox 6.2, the chapter provides guidelines on choosing and recording preferred and variant titles and for recording other metadata elements associated with works and expressions. The guidelines state that the elements related to works and expressions may be used in the creation of access points, that they may be recorded as separate elements in authority data, or that they may be used in both. The instructions provide flexibility as to where and in what form the data is recorded.

The chapter also includes sections on specific types of works (i.e., musical, religious, and legal works, and official communications) and on constructing access points (authorized and variant) for works and expressions. This text does not address special types of materials; instead, it focuses on the general guidelines for establishing works and expressions and on the associated instructions for constructing access points for them. For more details on describing musical works, legal works, religious works, and official communications, catalogers may consult the appropriate guidelines in RDA chapter 6 (and supplementary cataloging resources, if available). If the cataloger is working with multipart monographs, serials, and/or integrating resources, RDA 6.1.3 provides instructions on addressing changes in responsibility and/or titles that affect identification of works in these forms. For example, in cases in

---

6: Identifying Works and Expressions

Textbox 6.2. RDA Chapter 6 Structure.

which an integrating resource has a change in the title or in the entity responsible for the work, then the authorized access point should be revised to reflect the latest iteration. These instructions and accompanying policy statements may be consulted as needed.

Please note that in today's MARC environment, serials (e.g., journals, magazines, newspapers) typically do not have authority records. Instead, they are described in bibliographic records. In the future, it could be possible that authority data for serials could be created, although no plans for such activities have been announced. Series—some of which are serials—are usually controlled through the use of authority records, although the Library of Congress no longer provides this form of authority work. PCC members and other libraries, however, still create, consult, and update series authority records. For more information on how to create series authority records in today's MARC environment, please see LC's *Descriptive Cataloging Manual* (Section Z1: Name And Series Authority Records).[6]

RDA 6.2 Title of the Work

Unlike the title instructions under manifestations, which contain nine different types of titles, RDA chapter 6 only identifies two types: *preferred title for the work* and *variant title for the work*. Of these, preferred title for the work is an RDA Core element. The discussion of these elements is preceded by general guidelines that include nearly 10 instructions addressing how to record work and expression titles.

The first instruction states that the cataloger may take titles from any source. This is followed by several guidelines on how to record those titles. Unlike the instructions for titles proper and other manifestation titles, RDA 6.2.1.4 instructs the cataloger to apply the capitalization guidelines in instruction A.3 in appendix A. There is no alternative listed saying to "take what you see," and therefore catalogers must understand that they should capitalize the first word of the title and any other word that is generally capitalized in the language involved. For example, if the title of the work is *The New Adventures of Mary-Kate & Ashley*, the title would be recorded as *The new adventures of Mary-Kate & Ashley*, capitalizing only the first word and the proper nouns because the title is in English.

The section goes on to state that numbers should be recorded as they appear on the source of information, whether that is in the form of numerals or words, and that the same should be done with diacritical marks. An alternative allows for diacritical marks to be added, even if they don't appear on the source, following the standard usage in the language of the title. RDA 6.2.1.7 specifically states that initial articles, if present, should be recorded in titles of works, but the alternative immediately following— omit an initial article unless it is an important part of a name or phrase— is applied by LC, NLA, PCC, and most other libraries. It is important to remember that this is referring to authority-controlled titles used as access points in authority data; it does *not* refer to titles proper in bibliographic records.

> **ICC11 PS for Alternative for 6.2.1.7 Initial Articles**: Apply the alternative. Do not record initial articles in the authority data for titles of works or expressions as long as cataloging is done in the current MARC environment.

If initialisms or acronyms appear in the title, no spaces are inserted between the letters whether or not full stops (i.e., periods) are used (e.g., A.L.A. or ABC). Abbreviations are used only if the abbreviation is part of the actual title, it represents the word *number* at the beginning of the title of a musical work (e.g., Nr. 14, Kleine Studie), or it is part of the title *Laws, etc.*, which is the preferred title assigned to compilations of laws.

Choosing the Preferred Title for the Work

Titles may be taken from any source of information, but for the preferred title for a work that was created *after* 1500 (i.e., modern works), the cataloger consults resources that contain the work (e.g., a printed book containing Shakespeare's *Hamlet*), or the cataloger may consult reference sources. If the work is from an earlier period (before 1501), the first sources to consult are modern reference sources. If those are inadequate to establish the preferred title for the work, then the following should be consulted (in order of preference): (1) modern editions of the work, (2) early editions of the work, and (3) manuscript copies.

There are four instructions for choosing the preferred title. They are for different types of situations: (1) works created after 1500, (2) works created before 1501, (3) works for which titles in the original language are not found or are not applicable, and (4) works for which the title found is in a non-preferred script. These situations are examined below. The reader should consult the specific instructions in RDA for more information about the latter two situations and for specific instructions related to musical, legal, and religious works, and official communications.

For the preferred title for works created after 1500, the cataloger is to choose the best-known title in the work's original language, that is, the title that is most commonly found in actual resources (or in surrogates for those resources) or in reference sources. The best-known title, however, is not necessarily the original title in the original language, because the very first title may not be the one that survives (e.g., the original title for Swift's *Gulliver's Travels* was *Travels into Several Remote Nations of the World*). So, how does a cataloger determine which title is the best known? The cataloger must gather data from individual resources (or their surrogates) and from reference sources and use his or her best judgment to make the determination. If there is seemingly no title that is best known or if the cataloger is uncertain as to which title in the original language is best known, then the cataloger can choose the title proper of the original edition of the resource (i.e., the first title in the original language). If the work is published in different languages at the same time, and an original language cannot be determined, or if the work is published simultaneously in same language but under different titles, the cataloger may choose the title proper of the first resource received as the preferred title (e.g., *Harry Potter and the Philosopher's Stone* and *Harry Potter and the Sorcerer's Stone*).

In the following example, the preferred title is the original title in the original language. It is the best known internationally (if not in the United States).

> **Item in hand**: J.K. Rowling's Harry Potter & de Steen der Wijzen
>
> **Preferred title**: Harry Potter and the Philosopher's Stone

In the following example, the best-known title is in the original language, but it is not the original title.

> **Item in hand**: Shakespeare's Tragicall Historie of Hamlet, Prince of Denmarke
>
> **Preferred title**: Hamlet

In this example, the best-known title is the original title in the original language.

> **Item in hand**:   Simone de Beauvoir's Second sex
>
> **Preferred title**: Deuxième sexe

For the preferred title for works created before 1501, the cataloger is to choose the title in the work's original language that is most commonly found in modern reference sources. In other words, the cataloger does not spend time looking at manifestations containing the work; instead the focus is on the information derived from researching the work in reference materials. Actual versions of the work are consulted only if the results of the research in reference sources prove to be inconclusive. An exception for Classical Greek and Byzantine Greek works is provided. The exception states that for these works, a cataloger should choose a well-established title in the preferred language of the cataloging agency. For example, the established access point is **Aristotle. On the generation of animals** *not* Aristotle. Peri zōōn geneseōs or Aristotle. Περὶ ζῴων γενέσεως. If there is not a well-established title in the preferred language of the cataloging agency, then the cataloger chooses the Latin title (**Aristotle. Categoriae**, *not* Aristotle. Katēgoriai or Aristotle. Κατηγορίαι). If that is unavailable, the Greek title is chosen (**Menander, of Athens. Dyscolus**).

If the title proper of the original edition is unknown and/or unobtainable and reference sources do not have a title in the original language, the cataloger applies RDA 6.2.2.6: Titles in the Original Language Not Found or Not Applicable. This guideline—which applies to individual works of art, choreographic works, and other works that do not necessarily have well-known formal titles—allows the cataloger to choose a well-known title in the agency's preferred language *if* one has been established. If one has *not* been established, the cataloger may devise a title instead.

If the title is in a script that is not the preferred script of the cataloging agency, the cataloger may transliterate the title after consulting RDA 6.2.2.7: Titles Found in a Non-Preferred Script, unless its alternative applies. The alternative guideline states that the cataloger may use a well-established title found in reference sources that is in the agency's preferred language. The LC-PCC PS applies the alternative, but only for certain types of resources.

Recording the Preferred Title for the Work

There are four sets of instructions for recording the title once it has been chosen. The first, RDA 6.2.2.8, includes guidelines for (1) single works and (2) compilations of different works by different creators. The basic instruction states that the cataloger is to record the preferred title by applying the general guidelines at RDA 6.2.1, which were mentioned above (i.e., following the instructions for capitalization, numbers, diacritical marks, and so on). The cataloger should also apply the rules found at RDA 2.3.1.4–2.3.1.6, which address issues related to inaccuracies, introductory words, words that vary from issue to issue, and so on. Nothing else is required.

   The second set of instructions, RDA 6.2.2.9, provides guidance for the cataloger on how to record titles for works that involve one or more parts. For a single part of a larger work (including multipart monographs and author's series), the cataloger records the preferred title for that part *if* the part title is useful for identification. For example, *Oedipus Rex* is the preferred title for a distinctively named part of *The Theban plays*, a trilogy by Sophocles. *A Dance with Dragons* is the preferred title for book five of George R. R. Martin's series *A Song of Ice and Fire*.

> **Part**: *Oedipus Rex*
> **Part**: *A Dance with Dragons*

Even if the part is known only by a generic name, the cataloger should record that designation as the preferred title for the part:

> **Part**: Season 5
> **Part**: Part F

If there are two or more parts, the cataloger must first determine if they are (1) consecutively numbered parts, (2) non-consecutively numbered parts, or (3) unnumbered parts. If the work consists of consecutively numbered parts that are identified by generic terms and numbers, then the cataloger records the common term in the singular and follows it by the inclusive numbers for the parts recorded as numerals:

> **Part**: Book 1-4
> **Part**: Chapter 7-14

If the parts are unnumbered, then the cataloger records the preferred title for each of the parts:

> **Part**: *Agamemnon*
> **Part**: *Eumenides*

If the parts are non-consecutively numbered, then the cataloger records, for each part, the common term in the singular and the numbers. For example, if a work comprises three parts, three titles would be recorded:

> **Part**: Chapter 6-7
> **Part**: Chapter 9-11
> **Part**: Chapter 14

   An alternative for this instruction states that if two or more unnumbered or non-consecutively numbered parts of a work are being identified, the cataloger may record the conventional collective title *Selections* as the preferred title for the parts along with or instead of the names of the parts.

      Part: Book 7-8, Book 12, Selections
      Part: Selections

A *conventional collective title* is a title used for a compilation or collection containing two or more works by a person, family, or corporate body (e.g., *Plays*, *Works*, *Speeches*), or it may be used for two or more parts of a work (e.g., *Selections*). LC practice is to record *Selections* instead of identifying each part, unless one or more of the parts is especially important, in which case the part title can also be added. Although it might seem strange to record *Selections* or *Chapter 7-14* as the title of a part, it will become clearer when this is placed in the context of creating AAPs (see below). The conventional collective title *Selections* is never used on its own in an access point. *Book 7-14* is also fairly meaningless without additional title metadata. When AAPs are created for parts of a work, these part titles are combined with the title of a larger work to ensure that the access point identifies the work entirely.

> **ICC PS for Alternative for 6.2.2.9.2 Two or More Parts**: In authority data, prefer recording *Selections* rather than identifying the assorted numbering of individual parts. For parts with titles, consider establishing each with an authorized access point. If that is not possible, consider including individual part titles in the bibliographic description (e.g., in contents notes).

    The third set of instructions addresses how the cataloger records the preferred titles for compilations by a single creator. If that compilation has a unique title (e.g., Walt Whitman's collection of poems entitled *Leaves of Grass*), which is used in resources embodying that work, then the cataloger applies the instructions for works created before 1501 or after 1500, whichever is appropriate. Frequently, however, compilations do not have unique titles, in which case the cataloger applies the sub-instructions found at RDA 6.2.2.10. These are divided into instructions for complete works, for complete works in a single form, and for other compilations of two or more works.

    If the work being identified is or purports to be the complete works of a PFC (up to the date of publication of the original manifestation containing the compilation), then the cataloger records the conventional collective title *Works* as the preferred title. If the complete works in the compilation are in one particular form only, then the cataloger may use one of the following terms:

- Correspondence
- Essays
- Librettos
- Lyrics
- Novels
- Plays
- Poems
- Prose works
- Short stories
- Speeches

If none of these are applicable, the cataloger may supply a more specific term instead.

If the compilation consists of two or more, but not all, works by a PFC (in the same or in different forms), then the cataloger establishes the preferred title for each work in the compilation as authority data.

> **Compilation**: Four plays by Lillian Hellman
>
> **Work contained in compilation**: *Days to come*
>
> **Work contained in compilation**: *The children's hour*
>
> **Work contained in compilation**: *The little foxes*
>
> **Work contained in compilation**: *Watch on the Rhine*

If the compilation is large, however, this could get quite unwieldy; so an alternative states that the parts may be identified collectively (e.g., Speeches, Poems), followed by the term *Selections*. LC has adopted this alternative. For example, for the collection of plays by Hellman, the cataloger would record "Plays. Selections" as the preferred title for this compilation.

> **ICC11 PS for Alternative for 6.2.2.10.3 Other Compilations of Two or More Works**: Do not apply the alternative unless the number of works is quite large. If all titles have not been established in authority data, and they cannot be established easily, consider including the titles of the individual works in the bibliographic description (e.g., in contents notes).

The fourth and final set of instructions addresses preferred titles for compilations of works by *different* PFCs. With a resource of this type, the cataloger must determine whether the compilation has been given a collective title in either (1) manifestations of the compilation or (2) reference sources. If a collective title is identified, it is used as the preferred title for the compilation. If there is no collective title associated with the compilation, the cataloger records the preferred title for each work in the compilation. Although an alternative allows for a devised title to be used instead, the LC-PCC PS at RDA 6.2.2.11.2 suggests that this is not a good option; the authors of this text concur.[7]

Variant Titles for the Work

A *variant title for a work* is a title associated with the work but one that is different from the one chosen as the preferred title. Variant titles may be taken from any source. They are recorded according to the guidelines for titles of works already discussed (e.g., capitalization, acronym spacing). Variant titles include any title that is different from the preferred one, especially a title that has been used in an actual distributed resource, has been cited in reference sources, or is the result of transliteration using a different scheme. RDA does caution catalogers against recording as a variant title every title that is different from the title proper of the work. Only those that are significantly different from the preferred title should be included in the authority data as variants, and that is only if they seem like strings for which users might search. Most title variations will be recorded in bibliographic descriptions rather than in authority data. The key types of variants most likely to be included in the authority record involve alternative linguistic forms of the title for the work (i.e., different languages, different scripts, different spellings, and different transliterations), although other variant titles for the work may be included based on cataloger's judgment.

Preferred title for the work: Evgeniĭ Onegin

Variant title for the work: Anyegin

Variant title for the work: Eugenijus Oneginas

Variant title for the work: Eugene Onegin

Variant title for the work: Yevgeny Onegin

Preferred title for the work: Bury my heart at Wounded Knee

Variant title for the work: Na rŭl Undidŭ Ni e mudŏ chuo

Variant title for the work: 나 를 운디드 니 에 묻어 주오

Preferred title for the work: Hamlet

Variant title for the work: First edition of the tragedy of Hamlet

Variant title for the work: First quarto of Hamlet

Variant title for the work: Gamlet

Variant title for the work: Hamlet, Prince of Denmark

Variant title for the work: Shakespeare's Hamlet

Variant title for the work: Tragedy of Hamlet, Prince of Denmarke

Variant title for the work: Tragicall historie of Hamlet Prince of Denmarke

Preferred title for the work: Two towers

Variant title for the work: 2 towers

Variant title for the work: Lord of the rings. Two towers

Work-related Elements

In the following section of this text, some of the elements listed are recorded as separate metadata elements in the authority data, and a subset of those may be recorded as part of the authorized access point. Next to each heading the reader will find (B) for *both* or (S) for *separate element only*. Note that among the following metadata elements, there is no need to create a code for *access point only*. This is because all the elements described may be included in authority data for a work or an expression. In the examples that follow, some show the element being used in both the authority data and the access point, some in the authority data only, and some in the AAP only. This illustrates that even though all the elements are allowed to be recorded in the authority data, catalogers might not always do so.

RDA 6.3 Form of Work (B)

Form of work, an RDA Core element when needed for disambiguation, is an indication of the work's genre or class. It is taken from any source and it is recorded as a separate element in the authority data, but also may appear as part of access points for works, if necessary to distinguish the title of the work from an entity with the same name or title. There is no controlled list of terms, but some examples of terms used as forms of work include the following:

- Poem
- Play
- Novel
- Television program
- Radio program

- Computer file
- Motion picture
- Choreographic work
- Series
- Tapestry

The cataloger should choose a term that precisely and concisely describes the nature of the work.

> **AAP for work**:   Gale, Zona, 1874-1938. Miss Lulu Bett (Play)
> **Separate element for Form of work**: Play
>
> **AAP for work**:   Dryden, John, 1631-1700. All for love
> **Form of work**:   Play
>
> **AAP for work**:   Charlemagne (Play)
> **Form of work**:   [element not recorded]

RDA 6.4 Date of Work (B)

Date of work, an RDA Core element for treaties, is also core when needed for disambiguation. It is the earliest date associated with the creation of a work. As works in the FRBR model are abstract entities, it can be very difficult to pinpoint an exact date that a work was created. For example, is *date of work* the date an author conceived the idea, the date(s) associated with creating the first expression for the work, the date it was first manifested as a physical object, or something else? Recognizing that this is somewhat problematic, the instructions state that the cataloger may consider the date of the earliest known manifestation embodying the work as its creation date (i.e., date of work). The date of work may be taken from any source and recorded according to the calendar preferred by the cataloging agency (e.g., the Gregorian calendar in the United States). The date is recorded as a separate element in the authority data, but also may appear as part of an access point for a work if necessary to distinguish a work from an entity with the same name or title. The source for the date should be included in the documentation for the sources consulted.

AAP for work: Dayton Peace Accords (1995)
Separate element for Date of work: 1995

AAP for work: Blackwood, Algernon, 1869-1951. Wendigo
Date of work: 2014

AAP for work: Alaska (Motion picture : 1944)
Date of work: [element not recorded]

RDA 6.5 Place of Origin of Work (B)

Place of origin of work—an RDA Core element when needed for disambiguation—is the geographic location in which the work was created. The metadata is taken from any source, and it is recorded as a separate element in the authority data, but also may appear as part of access points for works if necessary to distinguish a work from an entity with the same name or title. The instruction says to record the place name according to the instructions found in RDA chapter 16; in short, to record the name of the local place in the language preferred by the cataloging agency, followed by a comma, and then by a larger place (i.e., country, state, province, territory, and so on). It allows for the names of countries, states, provinces, territories, and so on, to be abbreviated as instructed in RDA appendix B. LC and PCC catalogers, following the instructions for Name and Series Authority Records in LC's *Descriptive Cataloging Manual* (DCM),[8] will instead record place names in authority data as they appear in the LCNAF. As the DCM is not followed everywhere, either of these forms may be seen in authority data:

RDA Place: Salamanca, Spain   *or*   **DCM Place**: Salamanca (Spain)
RDA Place: London, England   *or*   **DCM Place**: London (England)
RDA Place: Cambridge, Mass.   *or*   **DCM Place**: Cambridge (Mass.)

The source for the place of origin should be included in the documentation for the sources consulted.

AAP for work: Discovery series (Cambridge, Mass.)
Separate element for Place of work: Cambridge, Mass.

AAP for work: National Gang Center bulletin
Place of work: Washington (D.C.)

AAP for work: Labor bulletin (Boston, Mass.)

Place of work: [element not recorded]

RDA 6.6 Other Distinguishing Characteristic of the Work (B)

Other distinguishing characteristic of the work—an RDA Core element when needed for disambiguation—is a catchall phrase for other useful attributes that may help to identify a work. These characteristics are taken from any source, and they are recorded as separate elements in the authority data, but also may appear as parts of access points for works if necessary to distinguish a work from an entity with the same name or title. The sources of these other characteristics are included in the documentation for the *source consulted* element. There is no list of exactly what these characteristics might be, but the examples used in RDA include the following:

- corporate bodies
- issuing bodies
- owners
- production companies
- surnames of the directors of motion pictures
- anything else that helps to differentiate between entities

AAP for work: Agreement under Article VI of the Treaty of Mutual Cooperation and Security between Japan and the United States of America, regarding Facilities and Areas and the Status of United States Armed Forces in Japan (1960 January 19)

Place of work: Washington (D.C.)

Separate element for Other characteristic: United States Japan

AAP for work: Counselor (Motion picture)

Other characteristic: Scott

Source consulted: Internet Movie Database, Oct. 10, 2013 (The Counselor, 2013, directed by Ridley Scott, genres: crime, drama, thriller)

AAP for work: American literature (Auburn University. Educational Television Department)

Other characteristic: [element not recorded]

RDA 6.7 History of the Work (S)

History of the work is fairly self-explanatory; it is a narrative description of the work's history. It is recorded from any source, and obviously, it is only recorded as a separate element in the authority data.

AAP for work: Lily, William, 1468?-1522. Introduction of the eyght partes of speche, and the construction of the same

History of the work: 'Lily's Grammar' was the most famous Latin grammar in England. A proclamation of 1542 issued by Henry VIII established it as the only authorized grammar to be used by schoolmasters. It dominated the teaching of Latin for more than three centuries. Although first printed twenty years following his death and Lily's name never appeared on the earliest printings, it was generally attributed to him and was referred to as 'Lily's grammar.' Originally issued separately, then bound with two other titles.

The description may be compiled by the cataloger from more than one source or recorded directly from a single source of information. Documentation for the history should be included in the list of sources consulted while creating the authority data.

RDA 6.8 Identifier for the Work (S)

Identifier for the work, an RDA Core element, is a unique character string associated with a work that differentiates that work from others. It may be taken from any source. As works are abstract entities, the identifier may be associated with a surrogate for the work instead, such as an authority record. When recording the identifier, RDA 6.8.1.3 indicates that a name or an identification of the agency should be included before the identifier (e.g., LCCN: n 80020646 or Library of Congress control number: n 80020646).

Expression-related Elements

RDA 6.9 Content Type (B)

Content type is a category "reflecting the fundamental form of communication in which the content is expressed and the human sense through which it is intended to be perceived."[9] It is an RDA Core element and is the third element, along with carrier type and media type, designed as a replacement for the general material designation (GMD) of ISBD[10] and AACR2.[11] Content type may be identified using any source, but the one or more terms used to describe it must be taken from the closed controlled vocabulary presented at RDA 6.9.1.3. The content type(s) is recorded as a separate element in the authority data but may also appear as part of an access point for an expression, if necessary. The list of content types contains the following terms:

- cartographic dataset
- cartographic image
- cartographic moving image
- cartographic tactile image
- cartographic tactile three-dimensional form
- cartographic three-dimensional form
- computer dataset
- computer program
- notated movement
- notated music

- performed music
- sounds
- spoken word
- still image
- tactile image
- tactile notated movement
- tactile notated music

- tactile text
- tactile three-dimensional form
- text
- three-dimensional form
- three-dimensional moving image
- two-dimensional moving image

If none of the specific content types listed is appropriate, then the cataloger may record *other* as the content type; if it is unknown and cannot be readily ascertained, the cataloger may record *unspecified*.

RDA 6.10 Date of Expression (B)

Date of expression—an RDA Core element when needed to distinguish between two or more expressions of the same work—is the earliest date associated with the expression. As expressions are also abstract entities, it can be very difficult to pinpoint an exact date. the date of a live performance used as the basis for a sound recording, the year a textbook was written, the date of the director's cut of a movie, the broadcast date for a TV program, and so on. Because learning of such dates may not be possible, the instructions allow the cataloger to consider the date of the earliest known manifestation embodying the expression as its date of expression. The date of expression may be taken from any source and recorded according to the calendar preferred by the cataloging agency (e.g., the Gregorian calendar in the United States) in the form of a year or a range of years, unless a more specific date is necessary. The date is recorded as a separate element in the authority data but also may appear as part of access points for expressions if necessary to distinguish one expression of a work from another. Although it does not state this in RDA, the source of the date should be documented in the authority data.

RDA 6.11 Language of Expression (B)

Language of expression, an RDA Core element, is the language used to express a work. It may be taken from any source and is recorded in the language preferred by the cataloging agency from a standard list of names of languages (e.g., the MARC Code List for Languages, which is the preferred list for LC and PCC libraries). The language is to be recorded as a separate element in the authority data and it is very often added to access points for works to indicate a specific language expression (e.g., **Rowling, J. K. Harry Potter and the Chamber of Secrets. Marathi**).

Some expressions contain more than one language. This should not be confused with a work that has multiple expressions, each in a different language with its own access point. In a case in which a single work is expressed in multiple languages (e.g., a film with some dialogue in English, some in Hindi, and some in Hinglish), the languages may be recorded in the authority data for the expression and also in the bibliographic description for the resource containing the expression. The original expression, containing more than one language, would *not* require a language to be included as part of the access point. A language would not be added until a translation or a dubbed expression of the work is created, at which point the translated language would be appended to the access point. Another example of multi-language expression would be *Bron* or *Broen*, a Scandinavian television program in which the dialogue is in both Swedish and Danish, or its American remake, *The Bridge*, which is in both English and Spanish.

RDA 6.12 Other Distinguishing Characteristic of the Expression (B)

Other distinguishing characteristic of the expression—an RDA Core element when needed for disambiguation—includes other useful attributes that may help to identify an expression. These characteristics are taken from any source, and they are recorded as separate elements in the authority data, but also may appear as parts of access points for expressions if necessary to distinguish one expression from another of the same work. The sources of these other characteristics are documented in the authority data. As is the case with works, there is no list of what these characteristics might be, but examples include the following:

- names of translators
- names of choreographers
- names of publishers
- names of narrators

- indications of different versions, cuts, or editions
- anything else that helps to differentiate between expressions

RDA 6.13 Identifier for the Expression (S)

Identifier for the expression, an RDA Core element, is a unique character string associated with an expression that differentiates that expression from others. It may be taken from any source. As expressions are abstract entities, the identifier may be associated with a surrogate instead, such as an authority record. When recording the identifier, RDA 6.13.1.3 indicates that a name or an identification of the agency should be included before the identifier (e.g., LCCN: n 00077119 or Library of Congress control number: n 00077119).

Examples of Expression-level Metadata

AAP for expression:	Bible. Old Testament. Hawaiian. 1838
Identifier for expression:	LCCN: n 00077119
Date of the expression:	1838
Language of expression:	haw [MARC code for Hawaiian]

AAP for expression:	Bradley, C. Alan, 1938- Flavia de Luce mystery. Spoken word
Identifier for expression:	LCCN: no2010106062
Date of expression:	2010
Content type:	spoken word
Language of expression:	eng

AAP for expression:	Bible. Gospels. English. New Millennium Spoken Word. 2002
Identifier for expression:	Library of Congress control number: nr2003018044
Date of expression:	2002
Language of expression:	eng
Other distinguishing characteristic (version):	New Millennium Spoken Word

RDA 6.27 Constructing Access Points

Access points are names, terms, or codes through which bibliographic or authority data is searched and identified. Access points, as described in chapter 3 of this text, may be controlled or uncontrolled. *Uncontrolled access points* are those not appearing as part of authority data. *Controlled access points* are those appearing in an authority record or some other container of authority data, including both authorized access points (AAPs) and variant access points (VAPs). *Authorized access points* are the names, titles, terms, or codes that have been established as the preferred or authoritative ones. VAPs are the others that were not chosen as preferred; in other words, a variant access point is a reference.

In RDA 6.27, there are four different sets of instructions provided for constructing access points for works and expressions:

- Authorized access point for works
  Parton, Dolly. 9 to 5 (Musical)
- Authorized access point for parts of works
  Apollonius, of Perga. Conics. Book 1-4
- Authorized access point for expressions
  Gramsci, Antonio, 1891-1937. Marxismo e letteratura. Selections. Serbo-Croatian
- Variant access point for works and expressions
  Baum, L. Frank (Lyman Frank), 1856-1919. Maravilloso mago de Oz

Authorized Access Points for Works

The guidelines at RDA 6.27.1 for creating AAPs for works are divided into different sets of instructions based on different kinds of works:

- Works created by a single PFC
- Collaborative works
- Compilations of works by different PFCs
- Adaptations and revisions
- Commentaries, annotations, illustrative content, etc., added to a previously existing work
- Works where the creator has more than one identity
- Works of uncertain or unknown origin

Works by a Single Creator

The simplest of the instructions is for works created by a single PFC. In this case, the cataloger creates an authorized access point by appending the preferred title for the work (see discussion above) onto the AAP for the person, family, or corporate body. The title, generally, follows a full stop or period if following the punctuation designated in appendix E of RDA, although exceptions may occur if the AAP for the PFC ends in an open date.

> **AAP for work**: Sondheim, Stephen. Sunday in the park with George
>
> **AAP for work**: Voltaire, 1694-1778. Candide
>
> **AAP for work**: Taylor, Patrick, 1941- Apprenticeship of Doctor Laverty
>
> **AAP for work**: Wilson, Lanford, 1937-2011. Works
>
> **AAP for work**: Henley, Beth. Plays. Selections
>
> **AAP for work**: United States. 21st Century Language Act of 2012
>
> **AAP for work**: Lonely Planet Publications (Firm). Lonely Planet city map series
>
> **AAP for work**: Weir (Family : Weir, Robert Walter, 1803-1889). Weir family papers (Archival collection : 1765-1929)

Collaborative Works

If the work is the result of a collaborative process between two or more PFCs, the cataloger must determine which entity was *primarily* responsible for it. Although only one creator is included in the AAP for a work, the other creators will be included in the bibliographic description of the resource containing the work in the statement of responsibility and/or in name access points. The approaches to determining which creator's name is used in the AAP are summarized in Table 6.2.

TABLE 6.2. Flowchart for Determining Responsibility for a Collaborative Work.

1. Is there a single person, family, or corporate body identified as having principal responsibility for the work?	**Yes**	Then that PFC is used in the first half of the authorized access point for the work.
	No	Then go to #2.
2. Does the collaboration involve one or more corporate body creators?	**Yes**	Then the corporate body with principal responsibility (or the first-named) is used in the first half of the AAP, *if* the work falls within the categories at RDA 19.2.1.1.1. If those instructions do *not* apply, then go to #3.
	No	Then go to #3.
3. Is the work a motion picture? **Note**: *A small number of films do have single creators; if that is the case, please use RDA 6.27.1 instead.*	**Yes**	Use title alone, and do not concern yourself with a primary creator.
	No	Then go to #4.
4. Is this a musical, legal, or religious work or an official communication?	**Yes**	See specific instructions at RDA 6.28-6.31
	No	Then go to #5.
5. Are two or more PFCs represented as having principal responsibility for the work?	**Yes**	Use the *first-named* creator in the first half of the AAP.
	No	Then go to #6.
6. Is principal responsibility indicated at all?	**Yes**	Start over! Something went wrong in the process.
	No	Then go to #7.
7. Does the order of the names fluctuate in resources and in reference sources?	**Yes**	Use the *first-named* creator from the resource you received first in the first half of the AAP.
	No	Use the *first-named* creator in the first half of the AAP.

There is an alternative that allows the access point to include the authorized names for *all* the creators, but LC and the PCC instruct catalogers not to apply the option; the authors of ICC11 concur—particularly in the current MARC 21 environment.

Compilations

If the work is a compilation (i.e., an aggregation of different works) by different creators (e.g., some monographic series, an edited volume of short stories), then the AAP is based on a collective title that is chosen as the preferred title. The name of a person, family, or corporate body does *not* precede it.

AAP for compilation: Norton anthology of world masterpieces

AAP for compilation: Innovative technology summary report

AAP for compilation: Far horizons (Short story collection)

This can be problematic, of course, if the compilation does not have a collective title. In this case, the cataloger is instructed to provide name/title AAPs for each work in the compilation.

AAP for 1st work: Shufeldt, Robert W. (Robert Wilson), 1850-1934. Scientific taxidermy for museums

AAP for 2nd work: Goode, G. Brown (George Brown), 1851-1896. Report upon the condition and progress of the U.S. National Museum during the year ending June 30, 1893.

An alternative allows the cataloger to devise a title representing the compilation for the authorized access point (e.g., *Two museum reports*), but LC and the PCC instruct catalogers not to apply the option; the authors of ICC11 concur.

Adaptations and Revisions

If the work is an adaptation or a revision of a previously existing work, and the changes in the content and nature of the work are substantial, then it is considered to be a new work. Thus, an authorized access point must be established for the new work, comprising the AAP for the creator of the new work (i.e., the reviser or the adaptor) and the preferred title for the adaptation or revision. (See Table 3.1 and accompanying discussion on new works and expressions in chapter 3 of this text.) In some cases, the creator may remain the same, but the preferred title or another characteristic changes along with the content, as shown in the Schwalbe example.

AAP for original work: Millholland, Charles Bruce. Napoleon of Broadway

AAP for adaptation: Hecht, Ben, 1894-1964. Twentieth century

AAP for original work: Adams, Douglas, 1952-2001. Hitchhiker's guide to the galaxy (Radio plays)

AAP for adaptation: Adams, Douglas, 1952-2001. Hitch-hiker's guide to the galaxy (Novel)

AAP for original work: Schwalbe, Kathy. Introduction to project management

AAP for revised work: Schwalbe, Kathy. Revised introduction to project management

If the work is presented as an edition of a previously existing work, it should not be considered a new work; it is instead a new expression of a previously existing work. For a new expression of an existing work, the cataloger should use the AAP representing the existing work.

AAP for first edition: Taylor, Arlene G., 1941- Organization of information

AAP for second edition: Taylor, Arlene G., 1941- Organization of information

If necessary to specify the existence of this particular expression, an authorized access point for the expression should be constructed using the instructions at RDA 6.27.3.

Works with Supplementary Content Added

If the work is a previously existing work with commentary (annotations, illustrations, etc.) added at a later time, but it is presented as the intellectual or creative work of those responsible for the additional content (rather than the original creator), then the cataloger constructs the AAP using the later creator and the preferred title for the commentary, annotations, and so on. For example, Jeffrey Caminsky is considered the primary author of *The Sonnets of William Shakespeare*, a volume of Shakespeare's sonnets with extensive commentary, annotations, and analysis; it is considered to be Caminsky's work.

If the work, however, is treated as a new edition of the earlier work with new commentary supplementing it, the cataloger treats this as a new expression and the AAP for the original work is used. For example, *Shakespeare's Sonnets*, a volume edited by Alfred Rowse, is considered a new expression of an existing work and would therefore be assigned the AAP: **Shakespeare, William, 1564-1616. Sonnets**. If there is a specific need to identify a new expression with its own AAP, the instructions at RDA 6.27.3 are followed.

Works with Creators Using Multiple Identities

If the creator of a work has multiple bibliographic identities (e.g., the man known as Mark Twain, Samuel Clemens, Louis de Conte, and Quintus Curtius Snodgrass), and a work has been distributed in various manifestations with different identities associated with that work, then the cataloger should use the identity of the creator most frequently used on manifestations of that work in the AAP. To determine which is most frequently used, a quick search of OCLC's bibliographic network or the catalog of a large institution is helpful.

Work: *Absent in the Spring*

SOR in manifestations: Mary Westmacott

SOR in manifestations: Agatha Christie

SOR in manifestations: Agatha Christie writing as Mary Westmacott

For this example, both Mary Westmacott (the original name associated with the work) and the phrases, "Mary Westmacott also known as Agatha Christie" or "Agatha Christie writing as Mary Westmacott," are fairly evenly split as to the number of records using those statements of responsibility. Manifestations with only Agatha Christie listed in the statement of responsibility are many fewer. Considering that the phrases use both names, then the greater presence of the name Mary Westmacott should take precedence.

AAP based on frequency: Westmacott, Mary, 1890-1976.
Absent in the spring

RDA advises that if the identity most frequently used cannot be readily determined, then the cataloger should construct the AAP using the creator's name found in the most recent resource containing the work, which at the time of this writing would lead to a different access point than the one that was chosen above.

AAP based on
most recent work: Christie, Agatha, 1890-1976. Absent in the spring

Anonymous and Attributed Works

The creator or creators of a work are not always known. Over time, the identity of a creator might be forgotten, or perhaps, the identity of the creator was kept secret or was not considered terribly important. Whatever the circumstance, there are works whose creators are unknown or uncertain.

AAP for work by unknown creator: Beowulf

If a work has been attributed to one or more creators, but there is still uncertainty as to the responsibility for the work, the cataloger creates an access point using the preferred title of the work alone.

AAP for work (uncertain attribution): Apius and Virginia
not Bower, Richard, -1561. Apius and Virginia

If reliable reference sources proclaim that one entity is the probable creator of the work, the authorized access point for the PFC to whom the work is attributed should precede the preferred title. If the work is truly anonymous, then the cataloger, again, uses only the preferred title.

AAP for work (traditional attribution): Aneirin. Gododdin

Additions to Authorized Access Points for Works

If the authorized access point established for a work is not unique, then what is commonly referred to as a *conflict* exists. Conflicts are not allowed among AAPs, because the goal in authority work is to create a unique identifying character string for each entity. This means that if an access point is not unique, then it must be differentiated from other identical access points. For example, the various works known as *Battlestar Galactica* must be disambiguated:

> **AAP for work**: Battlestar Galactica (Motion picture)
>
> **AAP for work**: Battlestar Galactica (Television program :
>   1978-1979)
>
> **AAP for work**: Battlestar Galactica (Television program : 1980)
>
> **AAP for work**: Battlestar Galactica (Television program : 2003)
>
> **AAP for work**: Battlestar Galactica (Television program :
>   2004-2009)

Additional data elements, called *qualifiers*, are used to create distinctive access points. The standard qualifiers include the four core elements in RDA 6.3-6.6: form of work, date of work, place of origin of work, and other distinguishing characteristic of the work (see discussion above). These are not listed in order of preference; the cataloger or authority control librarian chooses the qualifiers that work best. According to LC-PCC PS 6.27.1.9, qualifiers are recorded in parentheses and separated by a space-colon-space if more than one is needed. Some examples follow:

> **AAP for work**: Loos, Anita, 1893-1981. Gentlemen prefer
>   blondes
>
> **AAP for work**: Loos, Anita, 1893-1981. Gentlemen prefer
>   blondes (Play)
>
> **AAP for work**: Psycho (Motion picture : 1960)
>
> **AAP for work**: Psycho (Motion picture : 1998)
>
> **AAP for work**: American music series
>
> **AAP for work**: American music series (Austin, Tex.)

RDA 6.27.1.9 does not go beyond the instruction to make the additions if needed to resolve a conflict among access points. However, a lengthy LC-PCC PS provides guidelines both for general practices and for specific types of resources. The general guidelines point out that a cataloger must search through bibliographic and authority data in order to establish when conflicts exist. The LCNAF, the LC catalog, and the large bibliographic networks (such as OCLC WorldCat or SkyRiver) are authoritative sources for that bibliographic and authority data; they provide good snapshots of resources already cataloged and of authority data already established. The policy statement also points out that when adding information to the AAP to break a conflict, the cataloger should make additions to the *new* access point rather than to the AAP that is already established, and that qualifiers should not be added based on predictions of future conflicts; decisions should be based on the data available at the time that an authorized access point is being established.

The policy statement also uses additional examples to clarify that elements, beyond those already listed as qualifiers (form, date, and place of work), may be used as other characteristics of a work. These may include the following:

- Issuing bodies, publishers, and other corporate bodies
- Dates of publication (if different from date of work)
- Descriptive data elements (e.g., edition statements, carrier types)
- Places of publication (if different from place of origin of work)
- Other appropriate terms

For some resource types (e.g., choreographic works and expressions, works of art), more specialized characteristics might be necessary. The specific resource types covered in LC-PCC PS 6.27.1.9 include the following:

- Numbered and unnumbered monographic series/Serials
- Monographs
- Integrating resources
- Choreographic works and expressions
- Named individual works of art
- Motion pictures
- Television and radio programs

A lengthy appendix on motion pictures, television programs, and radio programs discusses the use of specific qualifiers useful for those resource types. It mentions dates, languages, names of directors, production companies, episode titles, episode numbers, seasons, and other distinguishing elements for use in both bibliographic descriptions and authority data. When establishing access points for works that fit into any of these resource types, catalogers should consult LC-PCC PS 6.27.1.9 for extensive guidance.

> **AAP**: Abbott and Costello show (Radio program)
> **AAP**: Abbott and Costello show (Television program)
>
> **AAP**: Grey Gardens (Motion picture : 1975)
> **AAP**: Grey Gardens (Motion picture : 2009)

AAP: Leonardo, da Vinci, 1452-1519. Virgin of the rocks (Musée du Louvre)

AAP: Leonardo, da Vinci, 1452-1519. Virgin of the rocks (National Gallery (Great Britain))

AAP: Out of the ordinary

AAP: Out of the ordinary (Choreographic work : Boyce)

AAP: Out of the ordinary (Hingham Historical Society)

AAP: Occasional paper (African Capacity Building Foundation)

AAP: Occasional paper (Biological Field Station (Cooperstown, N.Y.))

AAP: Occasional paper (Development Workshop (Firm : Luanda, Angola))

AAP: Occasional paper (Monetary Authority of Singapore : Online)

AAP: Occasional paper (University of Auckland. Department of Geography)

Authorized Access Points for a Part or Parts of Works

RDA 6.27.2, which addresses AAPs for parts of works, is divided into two subsections: instructions for creating an AAP for one part of a work (6.27.2.2) and those for two or more parts (6.27.2.3). The instructions for a single part are very similar to those discussed above for an entire work. The basic rule is to create the AAP by combining, in this order, (1) the authorized access point for the creator responsible for the part and (2) the preferred title for the part. This applies to parts of works that have distinctive titles.

AAP for entire work: Sophocles. Theban plays

AAP for part: Sophocles. Oedipus Rex

AAP for part: Sophocles. Antigone

AAP for part: Sophocles. Oedipus at Colonus

AAP for entire work: Bell, Larry, 1952- Seasons

AAP for part: Bell, Larry, 1952- Fall

AAP for part: Bell, Larry, 1952- Winter

AAP for part: Bell, Larry, 1952- Spring

AAP for part: Bell, Larry, 1952- Summer

If the part title is not distinctive, or the AAP is for a serial, integrating resource, television program, or radio program, then the cataloger creates an AAP from the authorized access point representing the work as a whole, plus the preferred title for the part appended onto the end.

AAP for part: Williams, Kenneth P. (Kenneth Powers), 1887-1958. Lincoln finds a general. Volume 3

AAP for part: Aristotle. Physics. Book 3

> **AAP for part**: Fringe (Television program). Season 3
>
> **AAP for part**: Advances in geophysics. Supplement

If the AAP established for the work as a whole is a title-only access point, then the cataloger also would expect to use a title-only access point for a separately described part of that work. The only exceptions are those described above (part title is not distinctive, serials, etc.), in which case, the AAP for the whole work precedes the preferred title for the part.

If the work being described entails consecutively numbered parts of a work, and the parts use generic terms (e.g., Book, Chapter) and numbers or letters to identify them, then the cataloger creates the AAP by combining the access point for the whole work and the preferred title for the consecutive parts using the singular form of the generic term and the appropriate numbers.

> **AAP for parts**: Apollonius, of Perga. Conics. Book 1-4.
>
> **AAP for parts**: Melville, Herman, 1819-1891. Moby Dick. Chapter 7-9

If the parts are unnumbered or non-consecutively numbered, the cataloger may construct an AAP for each of the parts.

> **AAP for part**: Tye, Christopher, 1497?-1572. Actes of the Apostles. Chapter 1
>
> **AAP for part**: Tye, Christopher, 1497?-1572. Actes of the Apostles. Chapter 4
>
> **AAP for part**: Aeschylus. Agamemnon
>
> **AAP for part**: Aeschylus. Eumenides

There is an alternative, however, which states that instead of creating AAPs for each part, the cataloger may record the conventional collective title *Selections* as the preferred title for the parts, following the AAP for the work as a whole.

> **AAP for parts**: Tye, Christopher, 1497?-1572. Actes of the Apostles. Selections
>
> **AAP for parts**: Aeschylus. Oresteia. Selections

LC practice is to record *Selections* instead of creating an AAP for each part.

> **ICC11 PS for Alternative for 6.27.2.3 Two or More Parts**: Always apply the alternative when a generic term and a number are used to identify non-consecutively numbered parts. Also, apply the alternative when there are unnumbered parts that have their own titles. Catalogers are *also* encouraged to create individual access points for the individual parts, unless the number of parts makes this cost prohibitive:
>
> > **AAP for parts of the work**: Aeschylus. Oresteia. Selections
> >
> > **AAP for individual part**:   Aeschylus. Agamemnon
> >
> > **AAP for individual part**:   Aeschylus. Eumenides

Authorized Access Point Representing an Expression

An authorized access point for an expression begins with the authorized access point for the work (or part(s) of the work). Following the AAP for the work, the cataloger adds one or more of the expression-related elements in RDA 6.9-6.12 designated for use in access points (see discussion above):

- Content type (e.g., spoken word, performed music, cartographic image)
- Date of expression in the form of yyyy or yyyy-yyyy (e.g., 1965, 1974-1975)
- Language of expression in the language of the cataloging agency (e.g., Spanish, *not* español)
- Another distinctive characteristic of the expression (e.g., translator, version, choreographer, publisher)

These qualifiers are not listed in order of preference; the cataloger or authority control librarian chooses the qualifier(s) that works best to distinguish between expressions of the same work.

AAP for work:	Rowling, J. K. Harry Potter and the goblet of fire.
AAP for expression:	Rowling, J. K. Harry Potter and the goblet of fire. Hebrew
AAP for expression:	Rowling, J. K. Harry Potter and the goblet of fire. Hindi
AAP for expression:	Rowling, J. K. Harry Potter and the goblet of fire. Italian
AAP for work:	Blade runner (Motion picture)
AAP for expression:	Blade runner (Motion picture : Director's cut)
AAP for expression:	Blade runner (Motion picture : Final cut)
AAP for work:	Swan lake (Choreographic work)
AAP for expression:	Swan lake (Choreographic work : Barra)
AAP for expression:	Swan lake (Choreographic work : Ivanov and Petipa)
AAP for expression:	Swan lake (Choreographic work : Gruber after Gorski)
AAP for work:	Catholic Church. Ordo lectionum Missae
AAP for expression:	Catholic Church. Ordo lectionum Missae (2nd ed., 1981)

The guidelines in RDA do not go beyond the instruction to make additions to the AAP for the work if they are needed to differentiate between expressions of the same work. However, a policy statement provides further guidance on translations and language editions. This LC-only policy discusses, among other things, the idea that if the reason for establishing a particular expression is due to language differences or translations, the LC cataloger should *not* attempt to differentiate between translations in the same language. In other words, for an LC cataloger, the translation by Marina Astrologo and the translation by Beatrice Masini are both represented by the same AAP: **Rowling, J. K. Harry Potter and the goblet of fire. Italian**. It notes that other elements in the bibliographic data provide users with enough information to be able to make their selection of translations. A cataloger who is not at LC has the ability—and some might say an obligation—to create a unique expression-level AAP for each translation. Therefore, if the cataloger is strictly following RDA and is not following LC practice, two AAPs should be established:

> **AAP**: Rowling, J. K. Harry Potter and the goblet of fire. Italian
> (Astrologo)
>
> **AAP**: Rowling, J. K. Harry Potter and the goblet of fire. Italian
> (Masini)

The LC-PCC PS also states that if a resource contains both the original language expression and a translation of the work (or two language editions of the same work), an AAP for each expression should be added to the metadata describing the resource. If it also contains additional translations or language editions, the cataloger should use judgment in deciding how many AAPs are added (the authors of ICC11 recommend adding them all). The LC-PCC PS also refers catalogers to RDA 6.28.3 if they are working with an expression of a musical work and to RDA 6.30.3 for sacred scriptures.

Variant Access Point Representing a Work or Expression

Variant access points for works and expressions are unauthorized words or character strings used to represent works and expressions; they are sometimes referred to as *references*, *cross-references*, or *unauthorized titles*. The reason catalogers establish VAPs in authority data is to ensure that users searching for works are pointed in the right direction no matter which title they use in their title searches. The authorized access point is used to collocate all versions of a work when that work has been represented by two or more titles over the years, more than one form of the same title, or when there are two or more expressions of the work. All the variations are potential VAPs. The basis for the VAP is a variant title. The other aspects of an access point remain the same—that is, the name of the creator (single, primary, or first-named) precedes the variant title and necessary qualifiers follow it:

> **AAP for work**: Leonardo, da Vinci, 1452-1519. Virgin of the
> rocks (Musée du Louvre)
>
> **VAP for work**: Leonardo, da Vinci, 1452-1519.
> Felsgrottenmadonna (Musée du Louvre)

PCC policy, as described at LC-PCC PS 6.27.4, is that a VAP should never conflict with an AAP for another work (i.e., qualifiers should be added to make them unique), but a VAP for one work may be identical to the VAP for another work (i.e., qualifiers are not necessary to distinguish between them). If the AAP does not contain the name of a creator, then the variant access point *generally* will not have one either.

AAP for work: Bulletin (Connecticut. Department of Agriculture)

VAP for work: Bulletin (Connecticut. Dept. of Agriculture)

VAP for work: Connecticut. Department of Agriculture. Bulletin

AAP for work: Shakespeare, William, 1564-1616. Merchant of Venice

VAP for work: Shakespeare, William, 1564-1616. Marchand de Venise

VAP for work: Shakespeare, William, 1564-1616. Most excellent historie of the merchant of Venice

AAP for work: Wodehouse, P. G. (Pelham Grenville), 1881-1975. Aunts aren't gentlemen

VAP for work: Wodehouse, P. G. (Pelham Grenville), 1881-1975. Cat-nappers

AAP for work: Rowling, J. K. Harry Potter and the philosopher's stone

AAP for expression: Rowling, J. K. Harry Potter and the philosopher's stone. Dutch

VAP for expression: Rowling, J. K. Harry Potter & de steen der wijzen

AAP for expression: Rowling, J. K. Harry Potter and the philosopher's stone. Luxembourgish

VAP for expression: Rowling, J. K. Harry Potter an den Alchimistesteen

Additional variant access points may be constructed based on cataloger's judgment. For example, the cataloger might add a VAP

- for a title without the creator's name preceding it, even though the AAP contains a creator's name;
- for varying forms of a title, such as replacing an ampersand with the word *and*;
- for a creator and title even though the AAP is title only;
- that includes the name for a person previously attributed with responsibility for the work but who is no longer viewed as a credible possible creator;

- for works where the creator's name is combined with the title in some form in the AAP;
- with varying forms of the qualifier, for example, a case in which the issuing bodies' name varies or the place has changed;
- with a different creator name, such as when a pseudonym has been used, there are multiple creators for the work, a creator's name has changed, and so on.

LC-PCC PS 6.27.4 can be consulted if the cataloger needs additional guidance on establishing VAPs for series titles. The extensive policy statement addresses nearly a dozen topics related to series. If working with librettos, lyrics, or other texts for musical works, the cataloger should consult RDA 6.27.4.2 and 6.28.

For VAPs for a part of a work with a distinctive title, the cataloger first must know the form of the authorized access point for the work. Some possible configurations are outlined in Table 6.3, but the core idea is that the cataloger may construct any VAP if it is considered necessary for access.

TABLE 6.3. Configurations of Variant Access Points for a Part of a Work.

If the AAP is formulated as:	Then the VAP may be formulated as:	Examples
Creator AAP + Preferred Title of Work + Preferred Title of Part	Creator AAP + Preferred Title for Part	**AAP:** Albert, Stephen, 1941-1992. Distant hills coming nigh (Orchestra version). Flower of the mountain **VAP:** Albert, Stephen, 1941-1992. Flower of the mountain (Orchestra version)
Creator AAP + Preferred Title for Part	Creator AAP + Preferred Title of Work + Preferred Title of Part	**AAP:** Martin, George R. R. Storm of swords. **VAP:** Martin, George R. R. Song of ice and fire. Storm of swords.
Preferred Title of Work + Preferred Title of Part	Preferred title for part only	**AAP:** Bible. Song of Solomon **VAP:** Song of Solomon (Book of the Old Testament) *qualifier added because it was considered important for identification*
Preferred title for part only	Preferred Title of Work + Preferred Title of Part	**AAP:** Lancelot (Prose romance) **VAP:** Lancelot (Prose cycle). Lancelot

If the work is a compilation of works by a single PFC, and the preferred title is a conventional collective title, such as *Essays* or *Plays. Selections*, and the dissimilar title proper on the resource is referred to in reference sources, then the cataloger may construct a VAP using the title proper of that resource.

> **AAP**: Henley, Beth. Plays. Selections
>
> **VAP**: Henley, Beth. Four plays
>
> **VAP**: Henley, Beth. Three plays

If additions are needed, the cataloger may add them.

> **AAP**: Durang, Christopher, 1949- Works. Selections. 1995
>
> **VAP**: Durang, Christopher, 1949- 27 short plays. 1995
>
> **VAP**: Durang, Christopher, 1949- Twenty-seven short plays. 1995
>
> **AAP**: Durang, Christopher, 1949- Works. Selections. 1997
>
> **VAP**: Durang, Christopher, 1949- Complete full-length plays, 1975-1995. 1997

The basic approaches to VAPs for expressions are fairly simple. The first approach entails using the AAP for the work as the baseline from which the cataloger starts. Variants in these access points appear only in the additions that are used for expressions, (e.g., version, edition, language).

> **AAP for expression**: Stockhausen, Karlheinz, 1928-2007. Momente (1965)
>
> **VAP for expression**: Stockhausen, Karlheinz, 1928-2007. Momente (Donaueschinger version)
>
> **AAP for expression**: Stockhausen, Karlheinz, 1928-2007. Momente (1972)
>
> **VAP for expression**: Stockhausen, Karlheinz, 1928-2007. Momente (Europa version)

If, however, a particular variant title is only used with a particular expression, that, too, may be used as a VAP.

> **AAP for expression**: Shakespeare, William, 1564-1616. Coriolanus. Spanish
>
> **VAP for expression**: Shakespeare, William, 1564-1616. Coriolano
>
> **AAP for expression**: Hellman, Lillian, 1905-1984. Scoundrel time. Spanish
>
> **VAP for expression**: Hellman, Lillian, 1905-1984. Tiempo de canallas

Additional data elements (i.e., qualifiers) may be added as necessary.

Instructions for Special Materials

As stated, these elements are not reviewed in this text. If the reader is interested in works and expressions for *musical works*, including discussions of the title of a musical work, medium of performance, numeric designation of a musical work, key, and other distinguishing characteristic of the expression of a musical work, RDA 6.14-6.18 should be consulted. For those interested in *legal works*, including discussions of the title of a legal work, the date of a legal work, the date of promulgation of a law, the date of a treaty, other distinguishing characteristic of a legal work, and the participants in a treaty, RDA 6.20-6.22 may be consulted. For *religious works*, including the title of a religious work, the date of expression of a religious work, and other distinguishing characteristic of the expression of a religious work, RDA 6.23-6.25 provide guidelines. For the instruction on *official communications*, such as those by a pope, a ruler, a government, and so on, RDA 6.26 may be consulted. For information on constructing access points for these types of materials, see the following:

6.28 Musical Works and Expressions

6.29 Legal Works and Expressions

6.30 Religious Works and Expressions

6.31 Official Communications

DESCRIBING CONTENT

Chapter 7 of RDA addresses another aspect of works and expressions, the description of content. *Content* refers to the intellectual or artistic substance of the work and expression. RDA chapter 7 addresses certain types of content characteristics, but it does not address the subject of a work, which is also a characteristic of content. Approaches to subject are not yet a major part of RDA. Discussion of subject matter may be found in section IV of this text. This chapter instead looks at a variety of other content features, outlined in Textbox 6.3.

Generally, content-related elements are important parts of the bibliographic description, because they allow users to select a version of the resource that works best for them based on the characteristics of the work and/or expression. Not all elements in RDA chapter 7 are examined closely, however. Several of them are format-specific, such as equinox and format of notated music; they are not reviewed here, because they do not apply to multiple types of works and expressions. Instead, this text covers the more widely applicable metadata elements. None of the elements in the chapter are RDA Core except for *scale*, which applies only to cartographic materials; several, however, are LC Core.

RDA 7.1 General Guidelines on Describing Content

This section begins by discussing the source of information for content elements. It states that the cataloger bases the description of content on the

Textbox 6.3. RDA Chapter 7 Structure.

resource itself. It does, however, acknowledge that sometimes the cataloger may need to use another source for additional information. When that is the case, the cataloger may use sources outside the resource itself. More specific guidance is provided for each element throughout the RDA chapter.

Work-related Elements

RDA 7.2 Nature of the Content

The *nature of the content* is "the specific character of the primary content of a resource (e.g., legal articles, interim report)."[12] This brief narrative account may be taken from any source. It is recorded if other content elements do not provide an adequate picture of the resource. The *nature of the content* element may contain additional information about the metadata provided for RDA 6.3: Form of work or it may provide a brief summary of the resource's contents.

Nature of the content: Diaries

Nature of the content: Songs and instrumental music

Nature of the content: Data set

Nature of the content: Quarterly technical progress report

RDA 7.3 Coverage of the Content

Coverage of the content addresses a time period and/or a location associated with the content of the resource. This brief narrative account may be taken from any source. It is recorded if other content elements do not provide an adequate picture of the resource. This element is very similar to the *coverage* element in the Dublin Core metadata element set (see chapter 22 of this text).

Coverage of the content: Bangkok road maps in 1998

Coverage of the content: Originally produced in France as a television program in 1998

Coverage of the content: Based on Myanmar survey map 1998

Coverage of the content: 1998

RDA 7.7 Intended Audience

Intended audience reflects the group of users for whom a resource was created or for whom it is suitable. The groups are typically defined by age (e.g., ages 4-6, adolescents, MPAA rating: NC-17) or educational level (e.g., remedial, preschool), but other categories may be used (e.g., specialized audiences, general audience). The audience for a resource may not be readily apparent, nor is it always recorded in the bibliographic description. If audience information is not presented on the resource, catalogers are not expected to make judgments as to its intended audience. It is most often used when a specific audience is targeted (e.g., materials for children).

Intended audience: Ages 9-13.

Intended audience: Grades 4-6.

Intended audience: "This book is intended for mature audiences due to gore, explicit sexual situations and language"—Back cover.

Intended audience: An international magazine for gay men.

Intended audience: Written for doctoral students.

LC considers *intended audience* a core element for children's materials.

ICC11 PS for 7.7 Intended Audience: Include whenever the intended audience of a resource is explicitly stated. Otherwise, include only when the cataloger is confident that there is a specific target audience. Consult readily available sources to make this determination, but if this requires in-depth research, it should not be undertaken.

RDA 7.9 Dissertation or Thesis Information

Dissertation or thesis information—a core element for LC and PCC libraries—is an indication that a work was created in connection with the requirements for an academic degree (e.g., M.S., Ph.D.). This element is made up of three separate sub-elements that are to be recorded: (1) academic degree, (2) granting institution, and (3) year degree granted.

Academic degree: Ph.D.

Granting institution: University of Pittsburgh

Year degree granted: 2005

This information may be taken from any source, but the cataloger should not record this metadata for every resource *based on* a dissertation or a thesis. This element is included *only* if the resource itself is a dissertation or thesis. Many dissertations and theses are later revised by their authors into books. These related derivative works are new works (or perhaps new expressions if the revisions are not extensive). Such a new work receives a new bibliographic description, which would not contain the dissertation/thesis elements. Instead a statement, such as one of the following, would be included as a note:

Note: Revision of the author's dissertation.

Note: Originally presented as the author's thesis at UNC-Chapel Hill in 1981.

Expression-related Elements

RDA 7.10 Summarization of the Content

A brief summary, abstract, or synopsis is generally what is provided in the *summarization of the content* element. This element does not, however, include tables of contents or contents notes; they are discussed in RDA chapter 25: Related Works (see ICC11 chapter 8) as whole-part relationships. Summary information, an LC Core element for children's materials, may be taken from any source. The basic instruction at 7.10.1.3 on summarizing the content states that the cataloger is to provide a brief objective summary of the content if (1) it is considered important for identification or selection, and (2) sufficient information is not found elsewhere in the bibliographic description. In general, summaries are not provided for most text-based non-fiction resources for adults or a general audience. For example, it would be rather unusual to find a summary for the latest *Introduction to Psychology* textbook.

An LC-PCC PS provides information about LC's practices for summarizing content. It states that summaries, abstracts, and reviews from both external and internal sources may be included as part of this element. If the information is from an outside source, its source must be noted; if a cataloger creates the information, the source of the summary does not need to be identified. LC catalogers generally create summaries for foreign language, children's, moving image, and electronic resources. Summaries obtained from other sources should be enclosed in quotation marks and followed by the name of the source. Catalogers do not write reviews or abstracts of resources for bibliographic descriptions, but in some cases external reviews and abstracts may be included, though only in quotations and with attribution. For some resources, links to publisher descriptions, reviews, and summaries may be included.

> **Summary**: Based on Frank Wedekind's controversial 1891 drama, Decca Broadway presents the cast recording for the acclaimed new Broadway production. Written by pop music composer Duncan Sheik, and starring Lea Michele, the musical explores emotions, violence, and suicide.

> **Summary**: "This is the comprehensive guide to all things Game of Thrones and beyond. From the prehistory to the coming of the First Men, through the reign of the Targaryen kings and Robert's Rebellion, this guide—co-written by George R.R. Martin and the immensely knowledgeable founders and keepers of the www.westeros.org site—will tell series readers old and new all they might want to know about the history and culture of Westeros and the lands beyond the Narrow Sea—a tapestry of all new history that George has invented solely for this volume."—Provided by publisher.

> **Review**: "His work has been praised by his significant contemporaries, including Jonathan Franzen, Thomas Pynchon, Jeffrey Eugenides, and George Saunders, who described The Verificationist as 'one of the most pleasure-giving, funny, perverse, complicated, addictive novels of the last twenty years.' And here, at last, is the story collection we have been waiting for, The Emerald Light in the Air, Antrim's best book yet."—Provided by publisher.

RDA 7.11 Place and Date of Capture

These elements hold the places and dates associated with the creation of the content of the resource through the recording or filming of an activity, an event, or a performance. These data elements may be taken from any source. *Place of capture* may reflect a specific studio or concert hall, if known, and the geographic location associated with it. The *date of capture* contains the date or a range of dates, including year, month, day, and time.

Place and date of capture: Recorded in the Chapel of New College, Oxford, on July 28-31, 1996.

Place and date of capture: CD recorded live, Jan. 30, 2003, at the Ryman Auditorium, Nashville.

Place and date of capture: Final work recorded 1990, New York City.

Place and date of capture: Recorded in New York between March 2, 1936 & June 5, 1944.

Place of capture: Recorded in New York City, Nashville, Minneapolis.

Date of capture: Recorded August 1998.

RDA 7.12 Language of the Content

This LC-PCC Core element captures the language or languages of the content in a resource. Catalogers should note that this element is different from the element *language of the expression*, which is recorded as a type of authority data. It identifies the language used to express the work or to express a translation of that work; it is recorded as part of an authorized access point established for a particular language expression of a work. The element *language of the content*, on the other hand, is part of the bibliographic description of a resource; it is used to reflect one or more languages found within that resource. The metadata recorded for this element may or may not include languages beyond the language of the expression. For example, if the cataloger were describing a subtitled version of Pedro Almodóvar's film *All About My Mother* the following information would be included in the bibliographic description of the resource:

> **Title of the manifestation**: All about my mother
>
> **AAP for work**: Todo sobre mi madre (Motion picture)
>
> **Language of content**: Spanish dialogue; English and French subtitles.

If authority data were also being created for the work, then the following elements would be recorded:

> **AAP for work**: Todo sobre mi madre (Motion picture)
>
> **VAP for expression**: All about my mother (Motion picture)
>
> **VAP for expression**: Tout sur ma mère (Motion picture)
>
> **Language of expression**: Spanish

Other examples for language of the content include:

> **Language of content**: Program notes in Norwegian by F.G. in container.
>
> **Language of content**: Chiefly sung in a made-up language based on Icelandic called Hopelandic.

> **Language of content**: Parallel text in Swedish and English.
>
> **Language of content**: Dialogue in English, Spanish, Portuguese, or Thai. Subtitles also in English, Spanish, Portuguese, or Thai.

RDA 7.13 Form of Notation

The instructions for *form of notation* comprise four separate sets of sub-instructions, each addressing the symbols or character sets used in expressions. Under RDA 7.13, there are instructions for: (1) the script used to express the language content (e.g., Latin, Cyrillic, Pahawh Hmong); (2) the form of musical notation (e.g., letter notation, staff notation); (3) the form of tactile notation (e.g., braille code, Moon code); and (4) the form of notated movement (e.g., Labanotation, DanceWriting). In each case, one or more terms is taken from the lists provided in RDA. There is also latitude for more detail to be added to each form of notation (e.g., Partly reconstructed from a video of the first performance; Contains print, braille, and tactile images). Script and form of musical notation are both LC-PCC Core elements.

RDA 7.14 Accessibility Content

Accessibility content is used if the expression of the work contains "content that assists those with a sensory impairment in the greater understanding of content which their impairment prevents them fully seeing or hearing. Accessibility content includes accessible labels, audio description, captioning, image description, sign language, and subtitles. Accessibility content does not include subtitles in a language different from the spoken content."[13] Information may be taken from any source.

> **Accessibility content**: Closed-captioned.
>
> **Accessibility content**: English SDH (subtitled for the deaf and hearing impaired).
>
> **Accessibility content**: An American Sign Language translation of select articles from the printed edition.

RDA 7.15 Illustrative Content

Illustrative content, an LC Core element for children's materials, is a statement that indicates the presence and/or type of illustrations used to enhance and expand the primary content of the resources. Inherent in this definition is the subordinate nature of illustrative content. If a work consists *primarily* of illustrative materials (which under former practices would have been identified as *all ill.* or *chiefly ill.*), then other RDA elements (e.g., content type, form of work, nature of the content) play a larger role in communicating the nature of the content than does *illustrative content.*

The cataloger may record information about the supplementary illustrative content from any source. The basic instruction states to record *illustration* or *illustrations*, whichever is more fitting. Generally, tables and numerical data are not considered illustrations, and illustrated title pages and minor illustrations are ignored.

RDA does not go beyond this instruction, but an alternative at 7.15.1.3 provides that the cataloger may record specific forms of illustrations in place of or in addition to *illustration* or *illustrations*, if judged to be helpful for identification or selection. The terms include the following:

- charts
- coats of arms
- facsimiles
- forms
- genealogical tables
- graphs
- illuminations

- maps
- music
- photographs
- plans
- portraits
- samples

If none of these terms is appropriate, the cataloger may include specific details in the bibliographic description (e.g., Color map of Vienna on front endpapers; Detailed sketches accompanying each page of text). LC generally does *not* apply this alternative; LC catalogers are to record only *illustration* or *illustrations* (a practice that is less informative and less fun).

> **ICC11 PS for Alternative for 7.15.1.3 Recording Illustrative Content**: Apply the alternative and provide more specific information about the illustrative matter if applicable.

There is also an optional addition that allows the cataloger to record the number of illustrations if it can be determined easily (e.g., the illustrations are numbered). LC has no policy for the optional addition.

> **ICC11 PS for Optional Addition for 7.15.1.3 Recording Illustrative Content**: Include the optional addition if it can be done without undue effort.
>
> **Illustrative content**: illustrations
>
> **Illustrative content**: 10 maps
>
> **Illustrative content**: illustrations
> **Illustrative content**: 4 maps
> **Illustrative content**: 2 portraits
>
> **Illustrative content**: 15 illustrations
> **Details of illustrative content**: the illustrations are woodcuts
>
> **Illustrative content**: illustrations (some color)
> **Illustrative content**: facsimile

Illustrative content: plans

Illustrative content: portraits

Information related to color in the resource is recorded according to instructions at RDA 7.17.

RDA 7.16 Supplementary Content

The element *supplementary content* describes additional materials that are intended to enhance the primary content of a resource. Certain types of supplementary content—indexes and bibliographical references in monographic works—are considered core requirements by LC. The information about supplementary content may be taken from any source and the data recorded should discuss the type of content, its extent, and its location within the resource (e.g., the pages containing the content).

Supplementary content: Includes index.

Supplementary content: Includes bibliographical references (pages 345-378).

The policy statement for RDA 7.16.1.3: Recording Supplementary Content describes LC practices for supplementary content. It states that the cataloger generally should include a note about bibliographies, bibliographical references, discographies, filmographies, indexes, appendices, or errata slips if they are present in the resource because these features are considered important for users in terms of selection. It also states that catalogers should generally use standardized forms of notes that have developed over the decades, such as the following:

Supplementary content: Includes index.

Supplementary content: Includes indexes.

The choice, obviously, depends on the number of indexes found in the content of the resource.

Supplementary content: Includes bibliographical references.

Supplementary content: Includes bibliographical references (pages 310-325).

The first of these is used for bibliographical citations in any form (e.g., endnotes for each chapter, footnotes on each page); the second form of note is used if there is a single bibliography in a particular location in the resource, rather than references that are scattered throughout. And note that the term traditionally used to describe these references is "bibliographi*cal*," not "bibliographic."

Supplementary content: Includes bibliographical references and index.

Traditionally, an index note and a bibliographical reference note are combined if both types of content appear in the resource. Many catalogers add pagination to this combined note if there is only a single bibliography.

> **Supplementary content**: Includes bibliographical references (pages 310-325) and index.

> **ICC11 PS for 7.16.1.3: Recording Supplementary Content**: Use a standardized form, as outlined by the LC-PCC PS, for these common notes.

RDA 7.17 Colour Content

Colour content (or *Color content* in the United States) is a statement that indicates the presence of color or tone in the content of resources. For this information the cataloger is to consult the resource itself, although other sources may be consulted as needed. The basic instruction at RDA 7.17.1.3 states that the cataloger is to record colour content if considered relevant to identifying or selecting the resource. The cataloger is to use either *monochrome* or *polychrome* as the value in this element. An alternative instruction allows for using other terms from a substitute vocabulary. The LC policy statement states, "If recording colour content, generally use a substitute term (e.g., color), or record a phrase such as "some color" or "chiefly color" as details of colour content."[14] Additional details may be added when necessary for identification or selection. In the current cataloging environment, colour content and illustrative content may be combined in a single statement.

> **Illustrative and color content**: illustrations (some color)
>
> **Illustrative and color content**: chiefly color illustrations
>
> **Illustrative and color content**: color illustrations
>
> **Color content**: Shows a purple and white textual poster advertising a performance of Barrie Ingham's one-man show, "The Actor" at the Opera House.
>
> **Color content**: Artwork arranged on purple and red background depicts various circus acts.
>
> **Color content**: The images are hand-colored in orange, green, and yellow. Each card is mounted on plain pastepaper backed with red-speckled lilac-colored paper.

RDA 7.18 Sound Content

Sound content is an indication of the presence of sound in resources. It is, however, only used for resources that are *not* sound recordings. For example, a description of a music compact disc does not contain this element; it provides values for the sound characteristic listed in RDA 3.16 instead (e.g., digital, stereo). The cataloger takes this information from the resource itself, but other sources may be consulted as needed. In general, catalogers simply record the term *sound* when it is present in a resource other than a sound recording. For moving images, however, the options are *sound* and *silent*.

> **Sound content**: sound
>
> **Sound content for a moving image**: silent

RDA 7.22 Duration

Duration, an LC Core element, reflects the running time, performance time, or playing time of the resource. The information may be taken from any source. The basic instruction states that if the resource has a playing time, the cataloger should record duration as (1) a number and the units of time represented by that number or (2) in the form of *hh:mm:ss*. Duration is one of the few metadata elements where the cataloger is instructed to use abbreviations; in this case, the units of time should be abbreviated according to RDA appendix B.

The instructions state that if the exact duration is provided or readily ascertainable, the cataloger records the time in the form preferred by the agency.

> **Duration**: 75 min.
>
> **Duration**: 01:15:00
>
> **Duration**: 9 min., 15 sec.
>
> **Duration**: 00:09:15

If the exact duration is not provided and not easily determined, an approximation is recorded.

> **Duration**: approximately 45 min.
>
> **Duration**: approximately 16 hrs.

If duration cannot be approximated, the cataloger does not record it. If duration is being recorded for a resource made up of more than one part, the duration of each component may be recorded.

> **Duration**: 00:45:00
>
> 00:23:00
>
> 01:07:00

If, however, the cataloging agency prefers to record the total duration instead, they may do so in place of, or in addition to, recording the duration of the individual components.

> **Total duration**: 02:15:00
>
> **Duration of components**: 00:45:00
>
> 00:23:00
>
> 01:07:00

Additional details about duration may be included as necessary.

RDA 7.28 Award

The *award* element is an indication that the expression of the work has been formally recognized for excellence. This information applies to all sorts of resource types and may be taken from any source.

> **Award**: Academy Awards: Best Screenplay, Paddy Chavefsky; Best Actor, Peter Finch; Actress, Faye Dunaway; Supporting Actress, Beatrice Straight. Academy Award nominations: Best Picture; Best Director, Sidney Lumet; Best Cinematography, Owen Roizman; Best Actor, William Holden; and Supporting Actor, Ned Beatty.
>
> **Award**: Man Booker Prize, 2013.
>
> **Award**: Boston Globe/Horn Book Fiction Award Winner, 2014.
>
> **Award**: Winner of a 1995 Peabody Award.

RDA 7.29 Note on Expression

The element *note on expression* contains additional information that the cataloger believes to be important to understanding the content of the resource. Catalogers may record notes based on information found in any source. RDA 7.29.2 identifies one particular type of note that may be included; this is the Note on Changes in Content Characteristics. This is particularly relevant to serials, integrating resources, and multipart monographs. It addresses differences between earlier and later versions of those resources.

CONCLUSION

In this chapter, the description of bibliographic resources has continued, particularly in the latter part of the chapter with the discussions of content-related elements. This chapter, however, also has introduced the recording of metadata for the purpose of authority control. It has looked at the metadata required for establishing separate data elements that are to be recorded in authority data and also the components required for creating authorized access points and variant access points for works and expressions. The exploration of authority data continues in the next chapter where metadata required for persons, families, and corporate bodies is discussed in detail.

NOTES

1. *RDA: Resource Description & Access*, developed in a collaborative process led by the Joint Steering Committee for Development of RDA (Chicago: American Library Association, 2010). Also available through paid subscriptions to *RDA Toolkit* (Chicago: American Library Association, 2010), accessed July 28, 2015, http://www.rdatoolkit.org/. In lieu of page numbers, any references to specific parts of RDA are made using instruction numbers.
2. Arlene G. Taylor and Daniel N. Joudrey, *The Organization of Information* (Westport, Conn.: Libraries Unlimited, 2009), 245-301.

3. Library of Congress, "Library of Congress Authorities," accessed October 15, 2014, http://authorities.loc.gov.

4. Library of Congress, "LC-PCC PS for 0.6.6," in "Library of Congress-Program for Cooperative Cataloging Policy Statements (LC-PCC PS)" *RDA Toolkit: Resource Description & Access* (Chicago: American Library Association, 2010), accessed July 28, 2015, http://access.rdatoolkit.org/. Free access to the LC-PCC PS is available through the Resources tab. Copies of the LC-PCC PS are also available with a paid subscription in *Cataloger's Desktop.*

5. RDA, 5.9.1.1: Scope [for Making Cataloguer's Notes].

6. Library of Congress, "Z1: Name And Series Authority Records," *Descriptive Cataloging Manual*, prepared by the Policy and Standards Division, Library of Congress (Washington, D.C.: Library of Congress, 2014), http://www.loc.gov/catdir/cpso/dcmz1.pdf.

7. Library of Congress, "LC-PCC PS for 6.2.2.11.2: Alternative."

8. Library of Congress, "Z1: Name And Series Authority Records," *Descriptive Cataloging Manual*, http://www.loc.gov/catdir/cpso/dcmz1.pdf.

9. RDA, 6.9.1.1: Scope [of Recording Content Type].

10. International Federation of Library Associations and Institutions, Cataloguing Section Standing Committee, *ISBD: International Standard Bibliographic Description*, Consolidated ed. (Berlin: De Gruyter Saur, 2011). Also available online at the IFLA website: http://www.ifla.org/files/assets/cataloguing/isbd/isbd-cons_20110321.pdf.

11. *Anglo-American Cataloguing Rules, Second Edition*, 2002 Revision, prepared under the direction of the Joint Steering Committee for Revision of AACR (Ottawa: Canadian Library Association; Chicago: American Library Association, 2002).

12. RDA, 7.2.1.1: Scope [of Recording the Nature of the Content].

13. RDA, 7.14.1.1: Scope [of Recording the Accessibility Content].

14. Library of Congress, "LC-PCC PS for 7.17.1.3: Alternative."

SUGGESTED READING

El-Sherbini, Magda. *RDA: Strategies for Implementation.* Chicago: American Library Association, 2013.

Hart, Amy. *RDA Made Simple: A Practical Guide to the New Cataloging Rules.* Santa Barbara, Calif.: Libraries Unlimited, 2014.

Kincy, Chamya Pompey, with Sara Shatford Layne. *Making the Move to RDA: A Self-Study Primer for Catalogers.* Lanham, Md.: Rowman & Littlefield, 2014.

Maxwell, Robert L. *Maxwell's Handbook for RDA, Resource Description & Access: Explaining and Illustrating RDA: Resource Description and Access Using MARC21.* Chicago: American Library Association, 2013.

Mering, Margaret, editor. *The RDA Workbook: Learning the Basics of Resource Description and Access.* Santa Barbara, Calif.: Libraries Unlimited, 2014.

Oliver, Chris. *Introducing RDA: A Guide to the Basics.* Chicago: American Library Association, 2010.

Chapter 7

Persons, Families, Places, and Corporate Bodies

INTRODUCTION

In this chapter, the elements of RDA[1] that are useful in identifying and describing *persons*, *families*, and *corporate bodies* (PFC) are reviewed. The entity *place*, from Group 3 of the FRBR conceptual model (i.e., subjects), is also discussed. Places are addressed in this chapter because geographic names very often represent the government that controls the territory or jurisdiction represented by the name. In other words, places are often, but not always, corporate bodies that create works or contribute to expressions. The RDA discussion of place is covered in its entirety in this ICC11 chapter, because at the time of this writing, the other Group 3 entities are not discussed in RDA; the Joint Steering Committee for Development of RDA (JSC) has not yet declared to what extent RDA will address subjects.

This chapter of ICC11 continues the conversation about establishing authority data that began in the previous chapter. RDA section 3: Recording Attributes of Person, Family, and Corporate Body contains four chapters that describe the characteristics of PFCs that may appear as part of an authority record or some other form of authority data, and they provide basic instructions for creating access points for each entity. RDA chapter 8 covers the general guidelines for recording the metadata elements related to PFCs. Chapter 9 is about describing persons, chapter 10 looks at families, and chapter 11 is for corporate bodies. These topics are covered in this order in this ICC11 chapter, except that RDA chapter 16 (i.e., place names) is covered before corporate bodies. As some corporate bodies are made up of place names, and

331

some corporate bodies require geographic qualifiers added after their names, it is helpful to cover place names first.

Some basic concepts of authority control are re-introduced in this chapter in the context of names, but for a fuller picture, the reader should review chapter 8 in *The Organization of Information* by Arlene G. Taylor and Daniel N. Joudrey.[2] Readers also may read chapter 10 of this text to learn more about authority control, although the chapter addresses implementing authority control specifically in the MARC environment. The authors considered placing the RDA chapters on identifying persons, families, and corporate bodies (PFC) before those on works and expressions. The primary reason for considering this is that the names of creators are often combined with titles to create authorized access points (AAPs) for works. Ultimately, it was decided not to separate the FRBR Group 1 entities (i.e., work, expression, manifestation, and item, also known as WEMI). This chapter was written without the expectation that readers have become familiar with ICC11 chapter 6 beforehand.

RECORDING ATTRIBUTES OF PERSONS, FAMILIES, AND CORPORATE BODIES

Before PFCs can be discussed, a few background concerns must be addressed. Each section of RDA begins with a chapter of general guidelines. RDA chapter 8 includes not only baseline instructions that apply to the other chapters in the section (i.e., RDA chapters 9-11), but also discussions related to terminology, objectives, and core elements. Its structure is presented in Textbox 7.1.

8: General Guidelines on Recording Attributes of Persons, Families, and Corporate Bodies.

  8.0   Scope
  8.1   Terminology
  8.2   Functional Objectives and Principles
  8.3   Core Elements
  8.4   Language and Script
  8.5   General Guidelines on Recording Names
  8.6   Authorized Access Points Representing PFCs
  8.7   Variant Access Points Representing PFCs
  8.8   Scope of Usage
  8.9   Date of Usage
  8.10   Status of Identification
  8.11   Undifferentiated Name Indicator
  8.12   Source Consulted
  8.13   Cataloguer's Note

Textbox 7.1 RDA Chapter 8 Structure.

RDA 8.1 Terminology

RDA chapter 8 discusses general vocabulary terms used throughout section 3, including terms such as *persons*, *families*, and *corporate bodies*, which should be familiar concepts after reading earlier chapters of this text (although it might be a good idea to review the discussion in chapter 3 of this text of what a *person* is in the post-FRBR cataloging environment—for example, fictitious characters are now persons). Chapter 8 also discusses *access points*, a term previously mentioned throughout this text. An access point for a PFC is a name, term, or character string associated with a particular PFC. It is helpful to remember that access points appear as authorized access points (AAPs) and as variant access points (VAPs, also known as *references*). RDA chapter 8 also addresses *name*, "a word, character, or group of words and/or characters by which a person, family, or corporate body is known,"[3] pointing out that it also comes in two forms: preferred and variant. A *preferred name* is the name or form of name chosen to represent a PFC; it is used as the basis for the AAP representing that PFC. A *variant name* is another name or a different form of name by which a PFC is known.

RDA 8.2 Functional Objectives and Principles

The chapter lists four objectives (of the 15 identified in "Responsiveness to User Needs" in the RDA Introduction) that are relevant to the metadata that is created using section 3. By creating metadata related to PFCs, catalogers help users to (1) find PFCs based on their search criteria, (2) identify the PFC described, (3) understand relationships among names associated with the PFC, and (4) understand why a name was chosen as preferred or as a variant.

The chapter addresses the two relevant principles from the RDA Introduction that apply to names. In the context of PFCs, *differentiation* is self-evident; the metadata should allow the user to distinguish between identically (or similarly) named persons, families, or corporate bodies. *Representation* means that the name chosen as the preferred name for a PFC (i.e., the basis of the AAP) should be the name most frequently used in resources associated with the PFC or a well-accepted name in the language and script preferred by the cataloging agency creating the metadata. Other names associated with a PFC are considered variants, including other names found in resources, names found in reference sources, and any other name users might expect to be associated with the PFC.

When choosing a name as preferred, it should be a name (or a form of name) that is found in resources, in the original language and script, associated with the PFC. These sources could entail resources by a PFC, about a PFC, in honor of a PFC, and so on. The instructions specifically use the words "associated with that person . . ." rather than "works by that person . . .", which were the words used in the previous set of descriptive cataloging rules. It states that the preferred name should be one found in resources in the original language and script, but in some exceptional cases, a name may be chosen in the language and script preferred by the cataloging agency. If the name chosen has more than one part (e.g., two surnames), the entry element chosen (i.e., the part that comes first in alphabetical lists of names) should reflect the practices of the country and/or language associated with the person or family.

RDA 8.3 Core Elements

RDA 8.3 reminds catalogers of a long list of RDA section 3 core elements found in RDA 0.6. The list is somewhat confusing, partly due to its structure. The list contains more than one part, and more than one type of entity is covered in each part of the list. The instructions also do not explicitly state in what form or where these elements are to be recorded (i.e., as part of the AAP, as an entry in the authority data, or as both). Table 7.1 lists and explains the use of the core elements for this section of RDA.

When a name identifying a PFC needs to be distinguished from another, additional data elements beyond the core name are used. These might be recorded as separate data elements (e.g., including field of activity in an authority record), as part of the access point (e.g., inserting family type after a family name), or in both places (e.g., adding a geographic name to the access point, but also as a separate data element in the authority record for a corporate body). Remember, though, that not every morsel of metadata about an entity is useful in an access point. It is also important to remember that if a name cannot be differentiated, no matter how much effort is put forth, there is a *last-resort* option to allow for undifferentiated names (e.g., creating an access point for **Smith, John** that applies to several persons with the name who cannot be disambiguated). This option should not be, and generally is not, taken lightly. Every reasonable attempt to do effective authority work should be made first before resigning oneself to using an undifferentiated name. An LC-PCC PS at RDA 8.3 states that when attempting to differentiate the AAPs of two or more entities with identical names, the cataloger should always add one or more differentiating elements to the access point.[4]

RDA 8.4 Language and Script

This section informs catalogers that names are to be recorded as found in resources being used to establish the names. If the resource is originally in English, then an English name gets recorded in Latin script. If the resource is in Urdu and written in Perso-Arabic script, then the name should be recorded in Urdu and in the Perso-Arabic script in the authority data. An alternative states the cataloger may record a transliterated form of the name and it may be used either as a substitute for, or in addition to, the form that appears on the source. LC and PCC practice is to use a transliterated form in the AAP in the authority data. Non-Latin forms are used as VAPs. How non-Latin names are recorded as bibliographic data is discussed in the LC-PCC PS, which the reader should see for more details as needed.

TABLE 7.1 RDA Core Elements for Persons, Families, and Corporate Bodies.

Category	Core Elements, *if applicable and ascertainable*	How is the data recorded?	Generally where the cataloger places the metadata
For all entities (PFCs)	• Preferred name for person, family, or corporate body	As an AAP	In authority *and* bibliographic data
	• Identifier for person, family, or corporate body	Separate data element	Authority data—but in the future, it may appear in bibliographic data (e.g., replacing or supplementing the text string in the AAP)
Persons	• Title of the person • Dates of birth and/or death • Other designation • Profession or occupation (for names not conveying the idea of a person)	Separate data elements *and/or* part of the AAP	In authority data *and* bibliographic data
if needed for differentiation	• Additional titles of the person (other than those considered core) • Fuller form of name • Profession or occupation • Period of activity of the person • Other designation (additional designations not considered core)	Separate data elements *and/or* part of the AAP	Separate elements appear in authority data; *some* of the elements may also appear as part of the AAP in bibliographic and authority data
Families	• Type of family • Date associated with the family	Separate data elements *and/or* part of the AAP	In authority data *and* bibliographic data
if needed for differentiation	• Place associated with the family • Prominent member of the family	Separate data elements *and/or* part of the AAP	Separate elements appear in authority data; *some* of the elements may also appear as part of the AAP in bibliographic and authority data

(continued)

TABLE 7.1 (*continued*)

Category	Core Elements, *if applicable and ascertainable*	How is the data recorded?	Generally where the cataloger places the metadata
Corporate Bodies	• Location of conference, etc. • Date of conference, etc. • Number of a conference, etc. • Associated institution (for conferences, etc.) • Type (for names not conveying the idea of a corporate body)	Separate data elements *and/or* part of the AAP	In authority data *and* bibliographic data
if needed for differentiation	• Date of establishment • Date of termination • Period of activity • Associated institution • Other place or designation associated with the corporate body	Separate data elements *and/or* part of the AAP	Separate elements appear in authority data; *some* of the elements may also appear as part of the AAP in bibliographic and authority data

RDA 8.5 General Guidelines on Recording Names

As with any section of RDA, basic instructions that apply to all the chapters in the section are provided in one place, in this case at RDA 8.5. They may be summarized as follows:

- **Capitalization**: RDA appendix A is applied to the capitalization of names. In short, one is instructed to capitalize the first word of each name, following the sub-instructions at A.2.1-A.2.6, but if a name has unusual capitalization, one uses the form that is found on resources.
  - Alvarez de la Torre, Guillermo B.
  - hooks, bell, 1952-
  - IUCC (Group)
- **Numbers**: If a number is part of a name, the cataloger records the form (i.e., as numerals or as words) as it is found in resources.
  - 7L (Disc jockey)
  - Nine (Rapper)
  - 4 1/2 Film (Firm)
- **Accents and Other Diacritical Marks**: These marks are recorded as seen on the sources of information. They may be added if missing, but only if they are considered integral to the name.

  - ◦ Aarún Ramé, Jesús Lorenzo
  - ◦ Ágúst Þór Ámundason
  - ◦ Björk
- **Hyphens**: Hyphens are retained between given names as appropriate, and are also included in transliterated names as appropriate.
- **Spacing of Acronyms and Initials**: There are two instructions: one for persons and families and one for corporate bodies.
  - ◦ **Corporate bodies**: For corporate bodies, the cataloger is to remove spacing between letters or initials, whether full stops are present or not (e.g., BBC Engineering, J.D. Sullivan Center for In-Situ Mining Research)
  - ◦ **Personal or family names**: For personal or family names, one is to leave spaces after letters or initials, whether full stops are present or not (e.g., Reighly, R. C., -1864; A. R. B.)
- **Abbreviations**: The basic instruction is to apply B.2 in RDA appendix B.
  - ◦ Abbreviations that are integral parts of a name are used, but only if used by the PFC (e.g., Chas, Jos)
  - ◦ Abbreviations for larger places are used when recorded as qualifiers for a local place name; for example, the heading **Boston (Mass.)** uses a state abbreviation found in appendix B

RDA 8.6 Access Points Representing Persons, Families, and Corporate Bodies

When a cataloger creates an AAP for a person, family, or corporate body, the preferred name for the PFC is the basis of the access point. If a conflict exists for the name (i.e., two or more PFCs have the same name), qualifiers (i.e., additional data elements) are added to break the conflict. Traditionally, AAPs cannot conflict with another AAP or a VAP. If the name cannot be disambiguated, the name should be identified as undifferentiated.

When a cataloger creates a VAP for a person, family, or corporate body, a variant name for the PFC is the basis of the access point. Qualifiers are added if considered important for identification. Traditionally, VAPs cannot conflict with AAPs, but they may be identical to the VAP for another entity. For example, "RDA" is a variant access point for several names, including **New Zealand Resident Doctors' Association** and **Germany (East)** (which was called República Democrática Alemana in Spanish), and it is a variant access point for the titles **Resource description & access**, and **Révolution démocratique africaine**, among others.

General Elements for Authority Data

Similar to RDA chapter 5, chapter 8 contains some metadata elements that are used specifically while creating authority data. These are *scope of usage*, *date of usage*, *status of identification*, *undifferentiated name indicator*, *source consulted*, and *cataloguer's note*. Most are necessary when a cataloger or authority control librarian is doing authority work. Some are particularly important when working with certain kinds of entities or types of names (e.g., entities who change their names). None of these elements is RDA Core, but four out of the six are core elements for LC and PCC libraries (all except for *scope of usage* and *date of usage*).

RDA 8.8-8.9 Scope and Date of Usage

These two elements provide context for how and when a name has been used. *Scope of usage* looks at the types of works associated with a preferred name:

> **AAP**: Adjei, Mawuli
>
> **Scope of Usage**: Name used for writing critical works.

> **AAP**: Adzei, Mawuli
>
> **Scope of Usage**: Pen name used for writing fiction and poetry.

Date of usage looks at the period of time associated with a preferred name.

> **AAP**: Exxon Corporation
>
> **Date of Usage**: 1973-2000.

> **AAP**: Standard Oil Company
>
> **Date of Usage**: 1892-1972

The data may be taken from any source.

RDA 8.10 Status of Identification

Status of identification refers to a code or term associated with the level of authentication of the authority data for a person, family, or corporate body. The element provides a short list of controlled vocabulary terms:

- **Fully established**: This is used when the authority data conforms to the cataloging instructions and the process has been completed and documented. In other words, the steps necessary to create the AAP have been taken and sufficient evidence to support the choice of access points has been recorded.

- **Provisional**: This is used if the evidence for establishing the AAP is insufficient and further work on the authority data is required.

- **Preliminary**: This is used if the access point recorded has been taken from another bibliographic description because the resource is not available at the time the access point is being established. Further verification is required once the resource is in hand.

In today's cataloging environment, this information is provided as coded data in the MARC authority record's fixed field (see chapter 21 of this text). The aim is for all authority data to be fully established.

RDA 8.11 Undifferentiated Name Indicator

An *undifferentiated name indicator* is a code or category that signifies that the core metadata elements associated with names of persons are insufficient to distinguish one person from another with an identical name. If the name must remain undifferentiated, the cataloger records the term or a code for *undifferentiated* in the record. In today's cataloging environment, this information is provided as coded data in the MARC authority record's fixed field (see chapter 21 of this text).

RDA 8.12 Source Consulted

Source consulted refers to any source of information (individual resources, catalogs, websites, personal communications with a PFC, bibliographic databases such as OCLC, etc.) used when creating authority data. Each resource that is consulted during the process of establishing names and other metadata elements should be cited. This process provides documentation that the cataloger/authority control librarian performed the necessary steps to make choices and decisions about the entity.

The basic instruction is to cite the sources used when establishing the preferred and variant names and the other data elements recorded; this includes sources that provide useful information, but also sources that contain no information about the entity at all. When information is *not* found in a source, the cataloger may record *No information found* following the citation. Citing a source where no information is found helps document the authority work process and saves the time of other catalogers/authority control librarians.

This citation generally starts with the name of the creator (although it is not absolutely necessary), the title proper of the resource consulted, and a date. Traditionally, if the name being established is the creator of the resource being cited, the name of the creator may be replaced by terms such as *His*, *Her*, or *Its*. After the minimal citation, a brief statement of the information found is recorded, as is the location of that information.

> **Source consulted**: Taylor, Arlene G. Wynar's introduction to cataloging and classification, 2000: t.p. (David P. Miller) galley (Levin Library, Curry College)
>
> **Source consulted**: Email from author, May 23, 2000: (David Peter Miller; b. 1955)
>
> **Source consulted**: Its Bread and circus [SR] p1988: label (Toad the Wet Sprocket)
>
> **Source consulted**: AMG, Jan. 9, 2009 (Toad the Wet Sprocket; American alternative rock band; formed 1986, Santa Barbara, Calif. by singer Glen Phillips, guitarist Todd Nichols, bassist Dean Dinning (the nephew of '50s hitmaker Mark "Teen

Angel" Dinning), and drummer Randy Guss; split in July 1998; a British band of the same name also listed)

Source consulted: Wikipedia, July 15, 2014 (Toad the Wet Sprocket; origin: Santa Barbara, Calif.; genre: alternative rock; years active: 1986-1998, 2002, 2006-present)

RDA 8.13 Cataloguer's Note

In addition to the documentation already discussed, other notes in authority data are needed. In RDA, a *cataloguer's note* is "an annotation that clarifies the selection and recording of identifying attributes, relationship data, or access points for the entity."[5] These notes justify or clarify the reason for choosing the preferred name or the form of name chosen; they explain limits on the use of access points, help to differentiate between entities with similar names, cite the instruction used to create the data, and provide any other information that might be useful.

Cataloguer's Note: Under AACR2 Limerno Pitocco was considered not to be a pseudonym, but a character that Teofilo Folengo had created. In RDA, as a fictitious character, he is treated as a person entity.

Cataloguer's Note: Given name is Clarence D. but prefers Jimmy.

Cataloguer's Note: For works of this author entered under other names, search also under: Hyman, Jackie, 1949- Jade, Jacqueline. Topaz, Jacqueline.

Cataloguer's Note: Do not confuse with: Ames, John (Vocalist) (n 2001065125)

Cataloguer's Note: Data provided by the ESTC/BL

Cataloguer's Note: Variants in 670 not considered name changes

RDA chapter 8 provides a general context for establishing authority data for persons, families, and corporate bodies. In the following sections, more specific metadata elements that are used to describe these Group 2 entities are explored.

IDENTIFYING PERSONS

The instructions in chapter 9 of RDA focus on the description of persons, primarily on the creation of authority data for persons (including the establishment of authorized access points). Once persons are established in an authority file or its equivalent, the AAPs that are created as part of the authority work may be used in bibliographic descriptions to represent creators, contributors, and others associated with works, expressions, manifestations, or items. For persons who are the subjects of works, please see chapter 13 of this text.

As can be seen in Textbox 7.2, the chapter provides guidelines on choosing and recording preferred and variant names. A preferred name is the basis for the AAP associated with a person; a variant form of name is the basis for a VAP (i.e., a reference).

9: Identifying Persons

9.0 Purpose and Scope
9.1 General Guidelines on Identifying Persons
9.2 Name of the Person
9.3 Date Associated with the Person
9.4 Title of the Person
9.5 Fuller Form of Name
9.6 Other Designation Associated with the Person
9.7 Gender
9.8 Place of Birth
9.9 Place of Death
9.10 Country Associated with the Person
9.11 Place of Residence, etc.
9.12 Address of the Person
9.13 Affiliation
9.14 Language of the Person
9.15 Field of Activity of the Person
9.16 Profession or Occupation
9.17 Biographical Information
9.18 Identifier for the Person
9.19 Constructing Access Points to Represent Persons

Textbox 7.2 RDA Chapter 9 Structure.

The instructions for individual metadata elements found in RDA 9.3 through 9.18 may be used in the creation of (1) access points, (2) separate metadata elements in authority data, or (3) both. The chapter also includes specific sections of instructions for constructing access points (authorized and variant). RDA also reminds catalogers that the concept *persons* includes deities, biblical and other religious figures, fictional and legendary characters, and real non-human entities (e.g., named animals). RDA appendix F provides additional instructions on how to record names from various places around the world (see Textbox 7.3).

RDA 9.2 Names of Persons

A *name of a person* is the word, letters, symbols, or strings used to identify a person. It is the appellation or appellations by which the person is known— and a person can be known by many names. When identifying a person, RDA

For the following types of names, consult RDA appendix F:

- Names in the Arabic alphabet
- Burmese and Karen names
- Chinese names containing a non-Chinese given name
- Icelandic names
- Indic names
- Indonesian names
- Malay names
- Roman names
- Romanian names containing a patronymic
- Thai names
- Names in various languages that include an article and/or preposition (e.g., de la, zur, van):
  - Afrikaans
  - Czech and Slovak
  - Dutch and Flemish
  - English
  - French
  - German
  - Italian
  - Portuguese
  - Romanian
  - Scandinavian (Danish, Norwegian, Swedish)
  - Spanish

Textbox 7.3 Languages and Scripts Addressed in Appendix F.

is concerned with two categories of names: (1) preferred names, which are RDA Core elements, and (2) variant names, which RDA treats as optional elements. The cataloger may take names of persons from any source, but generally a preferred name is determined by consulting the following (in order of preference):

1. the preferred sources of information (e.g., title page, title screen, title card) in resources associated with the person;
2. other formal statements appearing in those resources (e.g., a name attached to an introduction or preface); and
3. any other resource (e.g., reference sources).

Variant names are taken from resources associated with the person or from reference works.

Preferred Name for the Person

The *preferred name for the person*, an RDA Core element, "is the name or form of name chosen to identify the person. It is also the basis for the authorized access point representing that person."[6] When catalogers or authority control librarians establish preferred names for persons, they may have no actual choices to make. Sometimes persons identify themselves with only a single name or a single form of name. In other cases, some may use different names at different points in their lives, some may have two or more bibliographic identities, and some may use only one name but are known by different forms of that name (e.g., Katherine, Kathy, Kate, Katie, Kat). For example, one of your textbook authors—in terms of published resources—is known only as Daniel N. Joudrey; there is no other name associated with his works. One of his writing partners, however, has been known by two names. Although some of her early works were published under the name Arlene Taylor Dowell, she is better known as Arlene G. Taylor.

The basic instruction at RDA 9.2.2.3: Choosing the Preferred Name is that the cataloger generally chooses the most commonly known name of a person. Which name that is could be a matter of cataloger's judgment based on evidence gathered from resources (i.e., from the preferred sources of information), catalogs, bibliographic databases, and reference sources; sometimes the information comes from the person directly or from her or his institution, publisher, producer, and the like. A preferred name might be a person's real name, initials, nickname, or epithet; it might be a name used only for creating works (e.g., a pen name, *nom de plume*, alias, pseudonym), a title of nobility, or another word or phrase representing the person. Some examples of preferred names follow:

Preferred name: Tony Blair
Variant name: Anthony Charles Lynton Blair

Preferred name: George Edward Novack
Variant name: William F. Warde

Preferred name: Minnie Pearl
Variant name: Sarah Ophelia Cannon

Preferred name: B. J. Thomas
Variant name: Billie Joe Thomas

Preferred name: Bill Clinton
Variant name: William Jefferson Clinton

Preferred name: H. D.
Variant name: Hilda Doolittle

Preferred name: Lady Gaga
Variant name: Stefani Germanotta

> **Preferred name**: Duke of Wellington
>
> **Variant name**: Arthur Wellesley

While the cataloger is recording the names, the general guidelines, discussed above, are to be applied (e.g., capitalization, hyphenation, spacing of initials). If a person's preference is known, that should take precedence in how the name is recorded, but if the preference is unknown, then the cataloger applies the instructions, including those found in RDA appendix F, as needed.

If the name consists of more than one part, the cataloger must determine which part is to be recorded as the first (or entry) element. The entry element depends on the person's language, country of residence, or country of activity. For example, in the United States, most individuals are entered under a single surname (i.e., a last name or family name). In Spain and other Spanish-speaking countries, however, individuals are entered under the first part of a compound surname; in Portugal, Brazil, and other Portuguese-speaking countries, the entry element is most often the second part of a compound surname. A person associated with certain other locations may be entered under a given name (i.e., first name) rather than under a surname or a patronymic.

> **Last name first**: Berman, Sanford
>
> **First of compound surname**: Alonso Regalado, Jesús
>
> **Second of compound surname**: Lobo, Francisco Rodrigues
>
> **Entry under given name**: Alda Björk Valdimarsdóttir

The instructions for personal names are many. There are specific sets of instructions established for different aspects of choosing a name and recording the names of persons. These are outlined in Table 7.2.

TABLE 7.2 Sub-instructions for Choosing and Recording Names of Persons.

Activity	RDA instructions
Choosing the preferred name	9.2.2.5 to 9.2.2.8
Recording names with a surname	9.2.2.9 to 9.2.2.13
Recording a name with a title of nobility	9.2.2.14 to 9.2.2.17
Recording names without a surname or title of nobility	9.2.2.18 to 9.2.2.20
Recording names with initials, letters, or numerals	9.2.2.21
Recording phrases or characterizing words as names	9.2.2.22 to 9.2.2.26

Choosing the Preferred Name: Different Forms of the Same Name

If a person is or has been known by two or more forms of the same name (their real name, shortened forms of that name, nicknames, married name, etc.), then the choice of the preferred name is based on four criteria—whichever are applicable:

- **Fullness**. If a person's form of name has varied in terms of fullness, choose the most commonly found form. If no form predominates, choose the latest form of name (e.g., the form used on the most recent resources). If the cataloger is unsure about the latest form, choose the fullest. The other forms may be recorded as variant names.

  > **Predominant and latest form**: J. P. H. Shield
  >
  > **Occasional form**: Julian P. H. Shield
  >
  > **Occasional form**: Julian Hamilton-Shield
  >
  > **Occasional form**: J. P. Hamilton-Shield
  >
  > **Fullest form**: Julian P. Hamilton-Shield
  >
  > **Preferred name**: J. P. H. Shield

- **Language**: If a person's form of name has varied because of language differences, choose the form that appears in the language used in most of the resources. In case of doubt, choose the form most commonly found in reference sources in the person's country of residence or activity. There is an alternative instruction to choose the name in the language preferred by the cataloging agency, but LC and PCC libraries do not apply it. The other forms of name may be recorded as variant names.

  > **Name found on resource**: Josep Gudiol i Cunill
  >
  > **Name found on resource**: José Gudiol y Cunill
  >
  > **Name found on resource**: Joseph Gudiol i Cunill
  >
  > **Language of most works**: Catalan
  >
  > **Country of residence**: Catalonia (Spain)
  >
  > **Preferred name**: Josep Gudiol i Cunill

Two exceptions for language have been made:

- **Greek/Latin forms versus those in the person's language**: If the name of the person is found in Greek or Latin as well as in the person's native or adopted language, then choose the form most commonly found in reference sources. In case of doubt, use the Greek or Latin form only for those who created resources before A.D. 1400; the others are to be established in the person's native or adopted language.

- **Established form in a language preferred by cataloging agency**: If the name consists of a given name and a phrase, choose a well-established form in the language of the cataloging agency (e.g., John of Avila, *not* Juan de Ávila). In case of doubt, use the form established in the person's native or adopted language.

- **Non-preferred Script**: If the person's name appears in a script that is not the preferred script of the cataloging agency, then the cataloger is to transliterate the name. See RDA 9.2.2.5.3 for additional instructions on names in non-preferred scripts, including an alternative to the basic instruction. The other forms of name may be recorded as variant names.

> **Name in non-preferred script**: 郭小櫓
>
> **Preferred name**: Xiaolu Guo

- **Spelling**: If spelling variations appear among different resources or different versions of a resource, the cataloger is to choose the form of name found in the first resource received. The other forms of name may be recorded as variant names.

> **Name in first resource received**: Thomas Dekker
>
> **Name in other resources**: Thomas Deckar
>
> **Name in other resources**: Thomas Decker
>
> **Name in other resources**: Thomas Dicker
>
> **Preferred name**: Thomas Dekker

Choosing the Preferred Name: Different Names

If a person has used two or more names, the cataloger chooses the name that is most commonly known in resources associated with the person. If that is not clear, then the cataloger chooses the most common name found in reference works. If that proves inconclusive, the cataloger chooses the latest name. These instructions do *not* apply if a person has changed names or the person has more than one identity; there are separate guidelines for these situations. As is generally the case, the names not chosen may be included as variant names.

> **Predominant name**: Billy Mumy
>
> **Less common name**: Charles William Mumy
>
> **Preferred name**: Billy Mumy

If there has been a name change, the cataloger chooses the latest name as the preferred name for a person.

> **Earlier name**: Victoria Adams
>
> **Alternative name**: Posh Spice
>
> **Latest/Preferred name**: Victoria Beckham
>
> **Earlier name**: Warren Wilhelm, Jr.
>
> **Later name**: Warren De Blasio-Wilhelm
>
> **Latest/Preferred name**: Bill De Blasio

This instruction is not applied, however, if "there is reason to believe that an earlier name will persist as the name by which the person is better known."[7]

In this case the cataloger is instructed to choose that better-known name as the preferred name.

> **Earlier name**: Portia de Rossi
>
> **Latest name**: Portia DeGeneres
>
> **Preferred name**: Portia de Rossi

If a person has more than one bibliographic (literary, artistic, etc.) identity (e.g., the person uses a real name and/or one or more pseudonyms), each identity is established following the instructions at RDA 9.2.2.8. For each identity, the cataloger must determine a preferred name (i.e., the most commonly known name associated with that identity). The cataloger records other names not chosen as variant names. Relationships among names should also be recorded (see ICC11 chapter 8):

> **Pseudonym**: Mark Twain
>
> **Real name**: Samuel Langhorne Clemens
>
> **Another Identity**: Quintus Curtius Snodgrass
>
> **Another Identity**: Louis de Conte

> **Real name**: Joyce Carol Oates
>
> **Pseudonym**: Rosamond Smith

If a person uses *only* a pseudonym and does not use a real name as a creator, the cataloger is to choose the pseudonym as the preferred name and to record the real name as a variant name.

> **Pseudonym**: Lady Gaga
>
> **Real name**: Stefani Germanotta

Even though this textbook, generally, is not using the MARC format to illustrate data being created with RDA, the authors have chosen to include Figure 7.1 that contains an excerpt from a MARC authority record for a person with multiple identities to illustrate an extreme case of multiple bibliographic identities.

Recording the Preferred Name: Surnames

Not every name includes a surname, so the instructions in RDA are divided into sets of instructions for names that contain one or more surnames (RDA 9.2.2.9-9.2.2.13) and those that do not contain a surname (RDA 9.2.2.14-9.2.2.26). The basic instruction at RDA 9.2.2.9 for recording a name includes the following steps:

1. Record the surname as the first element.
2. Follow it with a comma.
3. Follow the comma with the other parts of the preferred name in direct order.
4. Omit any terms of honor or terms of address.

Rec stat c	**Entered** 19800404	**Replaced** 20131212100823.0	
Type z	**Upd status** a	**Enc lvl** n	**Source**
Roman l	**Ref status** a	**Mod rec**	**Name use** a
Govt agn l	**Auth status** a	**Subj** a	**Subj use** a
Series n	**Auth/ref** a	**Geo subd** n	**Ser use** b
Ser num n	**Name** a	**Subdiv tp** n	**Rules** z

```
010    n 80038417
040    DLC $b eng $c DLC $e rda $d DLC $d OCoLC $d DLC $d OCoLC $d Uk $d DLC $d Uk $d DLC $d
       UkOxU $d IEN
053 _0 PS3566.A34
100 1_ Paine, Lauran
500 1_ Ainsworthy, Roy, $d 1916- $w nnnc
500 1_ Carrel, Mark, $d 1916- $w nnnc
500 1_ Thompson, Russ, $d 1916- $w nnnc
500 1_ Andrews, A. A., $d 1916-2003 $w nnnc
500 1_ Ashby, Carter, $d 1916- $w nnnc
500 1_ Benton, Will, $d 1916- $w nnnc
500 1_ Bishop, Martin, $d 1916- $w nnnc
500 1_ Bond, Lewis H., $d 1916- $w nnnc
500 1_ Bonner, Jack, $d 1916- $w nnnc
500 1_ Bradford, Will, $d 1916- $w nnnc
500 1_ Bradley, Concho, $d 1916- $w nnnc
500 1_ Bradshaw, Buck, $d 1916- $w nnnc
500 1_ Brennan, Will, $d 1916- $w nnnc
500 1_ Burnham, Charles, $d 1916- $w nnnc
500 1_ Carter, Nevada, $d 1916- $w nnnc
500 1_ Stuart, Margaret, $d 1916- $w nnnc
500 1_ Hunt, John, $d 1916- $w nnnc
500 1_ Martin, Bruce, $d 1916- $w nnnc
```

[... PLUS 67 OTHER IDENTITIES]

```
663    For works of this author entered under other names, search also under: $b Ainsworthy, Roy, 1916- ,
       $b Allen, Clay, 1916- , $b Almonte, Rosa, 1916- , $b Andrews, A. A., 1916-2003, $b Archer, Dennis,
       1916- , $b Armour, John, 1916- , $b Ashby, Carter, 1916- , $b Bartlett, Kathleen, 1916- , $b Batchelor,
       Reg, 1916- , $b Beck, Harry, 1916- , $b Bedford, Kenneth, 1916- , $b Benton, Will, 1916- , $b Bishop,
       Martin, 1916- , $b Bond, Lewis H., 1916- , $b Bonner, Jack, 1916- , $b Bosworth, Frank, 1916- ,
       $b Bovee, Ruth, 1916- , $b Bradford, Will, 1916- , $b Bradley, Concho, 1916- , $b Bradshaw, Buck,
       1916- , $b Brennan, Will, 1916- , $b Burnham, Charles, 1916- , $b Carrel, Mark, 1916- , $b Carter,
       Nevada, 1916- , $b Cassady, Claude, 1916- , $b Cassidy, Claude, 1916- , $b Clark, Badger, 1916- ,
       $b Clarke, Richard, 1916- , $b Clarke, Robert, 1916- , $b Custer, Clint, 1916- , $b Dana, Amber,
       1916- , $b Dana, Richard, 1916- , $b Davis, Audrey, 1916- , $b Drexler, J. F., 1916- , $b Duchesne,
       Antoinette, 1916- , $b Durham, John, 1916- , $b Fisher, Margot, 1916- , $b Fleck, Betty, 1916- ,
       $b Flynn, George, 1916- , $b Foster, Harry, 1916- , $b Frost, Joni, 1916- , $b Glendenning, Donn,
       1916- , $b Glenn, James, 1916- , $b Gordon, Angela, 1916- , $b Gorman, Beth, 1916- , $b Harrison,
       Fred, 1916- , $b Hart, Francis, 1916- , $b Hartley, Travis, 1916- , $b Hayden, Jay, 1916- , $b Hill,
       Roger, 1916- , $b Holt, Helen, 1916- , $b Houston, Will, 1916- , $b Howard, Elizabeth, 1916- ,
       $b Howard, Troy, 1916- , $b Hunt, John, 1916- , $b Ingersol, Jared, 1916- , $b Kelley, Ray, 1916- ,
       $b Kimball, Frank, 1916- , $b Kimball, Ralph, 1916- , $b Koehler, Frank, 1916- , $b Morgan, Angela,
       1916- , $b Morgan, Frank, 1916- , $b O'Conner, Clint, 1916- , $b Sharp, Helen, 1916- , $b Slaughter,
       Jim, 1916- , $b St. George, Arthur, 1916- , $b Standish, Buck, 1916- , $b Stuart, Margaret, 1916- ,
       $b Thomas, Bruce, 1916- , $b Thompson, Buck, 1916- , $b Thompson, Russ, 1916- , $b Thorn,
       Barbara, 1916-
670    His Arrowhead rider, 1956.
670    The gunsight affair, 2004: $b CIP t.p. (Lauran Paine)
670    LC/NAF, Sept. 24, 2008 $b 678 info (b. 1916)
```

FIGURE 7.1 A MARC Authority Record Containing a List of Every Identity Established for Lauran Paine. (Source: OCLC Connexion, Authorities—record number 420510)

In other words, the general pattern for names entered under a surname is as follows:

> **Pattern**: [Family name/surname], [First/given name] [Rest of name]

The cataloger, however, should not remove terms of honor or address if the name consists of the term and a surname only (e.g., Dr. Berg), or consists of the term of address and a spouse's name (e.g., Mrs. L. G. Abell).

> **Surname as first element**: Blair, Tony
>
> **Surname as first element**: Novack, George Edward
>
> **Surname as first element**: Thomas, B. J.
>
> **Surname as first element**: Clinton, Bill

If the preferred name contains a surname and other parts of the name that *follow* it, then the cataloger records the name in that order but places a comma after the surname.

> **Preferred name**: Jin Shengtan
>
> **Surname as first element**: Jin, Shengtan
>
> **Preferred name**: Phan Chu Trinh
>
> **Surname as first element**: Phan, Chu Trinh

If the name consists only of a surname, the cataloger records only the surname.

> **Preferred name**: Morrissey
>
> **Full name**: Morrissey, Steven Patrick
>
> **Surname as only element**: Morrissey

There are six specific sub-instructions for names containing single surnames or elements that function as surnames.

1. **Surname represented by an initial**: If the person's surname is no more than an initial, but there are other parts represented in full, then the cataloger records the initial as the first element, followed by a comma, and then the rest of the name.

   > **Initial as first element**: D., Alexa Estelle

2. **Part of name treated as surname**: If the person's name does not contain a surname, but contains a part of a name that essentially functions as a surname, then the cataloger records that part as a surname, followed by a comma and the rest of the name.

   > **Part acting as a surname**: Bāyirlī, Muḥammad Saʿīd
   >
   > **Part acting as a surname**: X, Malcolm

3. **Persons known only by a surname**: If a person is known primarily by a surname and a term associated with it, then the cataloger treats the

term as part of the name. The cataloger records the surname, followed by a comma, and then the term. The name in direct order should be recorded as a variant name.

> **Surname and term**: Quaritsch, Dr.
>
> **Surname and term**: Moses, Grandma
>
> **Surname and term**: Kellaway, Mrs.

4. **Married person identified by partner's name**: If a married person is known by a partner's names plus a term of address, the cataloger records the partner's name followed by a comma, and then the term of address to specify that this is the spouse or partner of the person named.

> **Surname as first element**: Hayes, Jasper, Mrs.
>
> **Surname as first element**: Bolduc, Édouard, Mme

5. **Words indicating relationships following surnames**: For Portuguese surnames, the cataloger may record the following as part of the surname: *Filho, Junior, Neto, Netto,* or *Sobrinho.*

> **Portuguese name**
> **indicating relationship**: Coelho Neto, Marcos

If the name is any other language, the cataloger records *Jr., Sr., fils, pére, II, III,* and so on, following the other parts of the person's name.

> **Name indicating relationship**: Baez, Joan, Sr.
>
> **Name indicating relationship**: Jadin, Valentin, fils

6. **Saints**: If the name of a canonized person contains a surname, do not include the term *Saint* in the name. It is recorded as a designation associated with a person, not as part of the name.

If the name of a person contains or appears to contain a *compound surname*—a surname comprising two or more proper names separated by a space or a hyphen—and the person has a preference as to which part of the name is entered first, the cataloger follows the person's preference. A personal preference may be easier to detect if the person is living, still creates works, has a web presence, and so on; determining the preferences of non-contemporary authors may prove to be more challenging. The cataloger should record alternate forms of compound surnames as variant names for the person.

> **Person's name**: Andrew Lloyd Webber
>
> **Prevalent usage by person**: Lloyd Webber, Andrew
>
> **Occasional usage by person**: Lloyd-Webber, Andrew
>
> **Variant name**: Webber, Andrew Lloyd

> **Person's name**: George Iain Duncan Smith
>
> **Prevalent usage by person**: Duncan Smith, Iain
>
> **Occasional usage by others**: Smith, Iain Duncan

If the person's preference is unknown, the cataloger enters the name under the surname under which that person is listed in reference works in that person's language or in the places where the person has lived or worked.

> **Compound surname (Spain)**: Alonso Regalado, Jesús
>
> **Compound surname (Portugal)**: Lobo, Francisco Rodrigues

If the established usage in a person's country or language is unclear, then the cataloger consults the reference work, *Names of Persons: National Usages for Entry in Catalogues,* for more information.[8] If the usage for the country is not covered in this source, the guideline is to enter under the first part of the surname.

Compound surnames—or what appear to be compound surnames—can be challenging. The difficulty is not so much recording them, but identifying which names are actual compound surnames and which names simply have the appearance of one. For example, without further investigation it is difficult to tell whether Frances Smith Johnson should be entered under *Johnson* or *Smith Johnson*. Is it *Doyle, Arthur Conan* or *Conan Doyle, Arthur?*

Some surnames contain separately written prefixes consisting of articles, prepositions, or other types of prefixes. If the prefix is *not* an article or a preposition, the cataloger simply records the prefix as the first element of the surname. If the prefix is hyphenated or has been combined with the surname, the cataloger also records the prefix as the first element. If a person's surname contains an article (e.g., le, la), a preposition (e.g., de, à), or combination of both (e.g., de la, du), the cataloger records as the first element the part under which the name is generally entered in alphabetical lists in that person's language or in the places where the person lived or worked. In order to determine this, the cataloger should consult RDA appendix F for instructions for names in particular languages (see Textbox 7.3 for the list of languages). The cataloger records alternate forms of name as variant names.

> **Name with prefixes (English)**: De la Mare, Albinia C.
>
> **Name with prefixes (English)**: Van Doren, Mark
>
> **Name with prefixes (Dutch)**: Geer, Peter van der
>
> **Name with prefixes (French)**: Le Jay, Guy Michel
>
> **Name with hyphenated
> prefix (in the United States)**: El-Sherbini, Magda
>
> **Compound surname with a
> combined prefix in first surname**: MacDonald Quiceno, Jessica
>
> **Name with combined prefix**: FitzGerald, Katy
>
> **Name with hyphenated prefix**: Mac-Daniell, Alexander

Recording the Preferred Name: Titles of Nobility

RDA 9.2.2.14 addresses names containing a title of nobility. This instruction applies to persons who (1) have more than one type of name (i.e., a personal name and a title of nobility) and (2) use their titles rather than their personal names in their works (or, if there are no textual works to consult, to those persons who are listed by title in reference sources). If a person is commonly known by a title of nobility, the proper name in that title should be the entry element. (Reference sources that list all members of the nobility under title should not be used for this decision.) The proper name in the title is followed by a comma and then the personal name in direct order. The personal name is followed by a comma and then the term of rank. In other words, the general pattern for names entered under a title of nobility is

> **Pattern**: [Title of nobility's proper name], [First/given name] [Rest of name] [Family name/surname], [Rank/title]

Unused forenames are not included. A reference is made from the personal surname unless it is the same as the proper name in the title. Additional instructions for other aspects of titles of nobility are found at RDA 9.2.2.14-9.2.2.17. RDA appendix G provides several lists of titles of nobility, terms of rank, and so on, for several locations around the world.

> **Title of nobility**: Byron, George Gordon Byron, Baron
>
> **Title of nobility**
> **(fictitious character)**: Grantham, Robert Crawley, Earl of
>
> **Title of nobility**: Moore of Drogheda, Alice Moore, Viscountess

Recording the Preferred Name: Names without Surnames or Titles of Nobility

If a person is identified by a name that does not include a surname (and that person does not have a title of nobility), then the cataloger records the name that is used to identify that person—whatever the name happens to be. This may be a person's given name, a single-name pseudonym, a nickname, or something else. If the person is associated with a place (e.g., place of birth, place of activity), has a notable profession or occupation (e.g., rector, doctor), or is identified by some other term, these designations are included as part of the name after a comma. Roman numerals, such as those associated with monarchs, popes, and the like, are treated as part of a name. The term *Saint*, however, is not to be recorded as part of the name; it is recorded as an addition to the name for a person (as discussed in later instructions).

> **Name without a surname**: Cher
>
> **Name without a surname**: Björk
>
> **Name without a surname**: Moby
>
> **Name without a surname**: Leonardo, da Vinci

Name without a surname: John, the Baptist
Name without a surname: Benedict XVI

The entry element for the name is the part used in reference sources. If the choice is still unclear, the last part is recorded as the first element. Alternate forms are recorded as variant names.

Appropriate entry element: Leonardo, da Vinci
In case of doubt: Vinci, Leonardo da

If the name includes a patronymic—which is not a surname, but instead is a name derived from a person's father's given name—the cataloger is instructed to record the first given name as the entry element. It is followed by other names in direct order. See specific instructions for patronymics in Arabic, Icelandic, and Romanian names in RDA appendix F. Alternate forms are recorded as variant names.

Name with a patronymic: Lorenzo, di Tebaldo
Name with a patronymic: Alemayehu Hailu Gebre
Name with a patronymic: Abraham ben David, of Sokolow
Name with a patronymic: Helga Jónsdóttir

If the name belongs to a royal person, the instructions are to include the name of a royal house, dynasty, territorial designation, and so on, recorded in direct order. Titles are added to the name according to later instructions.

Name for a royal person: Charles XIV John
Name for a royal person: Elizabeth, of France
Name for a royal person: Johan Willem Friso

Recording the Preferred Name: Other Types of Names

If a person primarily uses initials, letters, or numerals as a name, the cataloger should record as the preferred name those initials, letters, or numerals representing the person. Initials (letters and numerals) and words or phrases associated with them are recorded in direct order. In some cases, typographic symbols may be included as part of the name.

Name comprising letters: A. B. C. D. E.
Name comprising initials: A. D. G.
Name comprising letters: Dr. K.
Name comprising numerals: 1.8.7
Name comprising a numeral and a term: 4-Tree
Name comprising numerals and a letter: 10C

If a person is primarily known (1) by a name or appellation that does not contain a given name or (2) by a phrase that has a given name but is preceded by words other than a term of address or a title of office, then the name or phrase should be recorded in direct order. Alternate forms are recorded as variant names.

>**Phrase as name**: Lady Gaga
>
>**Phrase as name**: Mother Hen
>
>**Phrase as name**: Little Louie
>
>**Phrase as name**: Brother Bones

If the name has the appearance of a surname along with a given name or initials, record the surname-like element first.

>**Name with pseudo-surname**: Mouse, Minnie
>
>**Name with pseudo-surname**: Girl, Christian
>
>**Name with pseudo-surname**: Other, A. N.

If a person is primarily known by a given name preceded by a term of address or a title of position or office, then the phrase should be used as the preferred name for the person. The given name is recorded first, followed by a comma, and the term or phrase. Alternate forms are recorded as variant names.

>**Phrase with given name**: Abbie, Aunt
>
>**Phrase with given name**: Frank, Doctor
>
>**Phrase with given name**: Lala, Chef
>
>**Phrase with given name**: Nina, Miss

If the person is primarily known by a characterizing word or phrase or a name that places the person in association with another work, the cataloger records that word or phrase as the preferred name in direct order. An alternative, which is applied by LC and PCC, eliminates any articles that precede the phrases or words.

>**Characterizing phrase as name**: Advocate for the poor
>
>**Characterizing phrase as name**: Wildman of the woods
>
>**Characterizing phrase as name**: Father of a family
>
>**Characterizing phrase as name**: Lady of distinction [*not* A lady of distinction]
>
>**Associated work as part of name**: Author of A bride from the Rhineland
>
>**Associated work as part of name**: Author of Letters from Scotland
>
>**Associated work as part of name**: Author of Modes of life, or, Town and country

If the person is also known by a real or another name as well as this characterizing word or phrase, the cataloger should prefer the actual name and record the phrase as a variant name instead. The cataloger should also record the title of the work as an entry element—followed by the rest of the phrase after a comma—as a variant form of name (e.g., Letters from Scotland, Author of).

Variant Name for the Person

A *variant name for the person* is another name or another form of name that is associated with a person; it is one that differs from the preferred name. The cataloger records variant names following the same general guidelines that are followed when recording preferred names. A variant name should be recorded if the name is one used by the person, one found in references works, or one resulting from differing systems of transliteration. Candidates for variant names include the following:

- **Real names**: If the preferred name is a pseudonym and the real name is known but unused in works, the cataloger is instructed to record the real name as a variant (see discussion of separate bibliographic identities above).

    Preferred name: Moby

    Real name: Hall, Richard Melville

- **Secular names**: If the preferred name is a religious name, the cataloger records the secular name as a variant.

    Preferred name: John Paul I

    Secular name: Luciani, Albino

- **Names in religion**: If the preferred name is a secular name, the cataloger is instructed to record the religious name as a variant.

    Preferred name: Bessette, André

    Religious name: André, frère

    Religious name: André, Brother

- **Earlier names**: If the preferred name is a later name, the cataloger records the earlier name as a variant.

    Preferred name: Cochrane, Pauline A.

    Earlier name: Atherton, Pauline

    Fuller form: Cochrane, Pauline Atherton

- **Later names**: If the preferred name is an earlier name, the cataloger is instructed to record the later name as a variant.

> **Preferred name**: Longoria, Eva
>
> **Later name**: Parker, Eva Longoria

- **Alternative Linguistic Forms of Names**: The cataloger also records names with alternative language forms, alternative scripts, alternative spellings, or alternative transliterations if found in resources and reference sources.

> **Preferred name**: Twain, Mark
>
> **Alternative linguistic form**: Tvėn, Mark
>
> **Alternative linguistic form**: Tuĕĭn, Mark
>
> **Alternative linguistic form**: Tuwayn, Mārk
>
> **Alternative linguistic form**: Tʻu-wen, Ma-kʻo
>
> **Alternative linguistic form**: Touen, Makū
>
> **Alternative linguistic form**: Twain, Marek
>
> **Alternative linguistic form**: Tuwen, Make
>
> **Alternative linguistic form**: Make Teviin
>
> **Alternative linguistic form**: Твен, Марк
>
> **Alternative linguistic form**: 馬克吐温
>
> **Preferred name for other identity**: Clemens, Samuel Langhorne
>
> **Preferred name for other identity**: Snodgrass, Quintus Curtius
>
> **Preferred name for other identity**: Conte, Louis de

- **Other variant names**: If other variants are considered useful for identification or access, the cataloger is instructed to record as variant names anything else described as alternatives to the general instructions for preferred names (e.g., record in inverted order rather than in direct order, different forms of fullness, entering under full name instead of initials).

> **Preferred name**: A. E.
>
> **Other variant**: Ellis, A.
>
> **Other variant**: E., A.
>
> **Other variant**: Layman
>
> **Preferred name**: Alonso Regalado, Jesús
>
> **Other variant**: Regalado, Jesús Alonso
>
> **Other variant**: Alonso-Regalado, Jesús
>
> **Other variant**: Alonso, Jesús
>
> **Preferred name**: Rice, Anne
>
> **Real name**: O'Brien, Howard Allen Frances
>
> **Other variant**: O'Brien, Anne
>
> **Alternative linguistic form**: Raĭs, Ėnn

Alternative linguistic form: Райс, энн
Preferred name for other identity: Rampling, Anne
Preferred name for other identity: Roquelaure, A. N.

Additional Elements for Persons

A name, obviously, is the key element to identifying a person, but other elements are also needed. Names are not unique, so additional metadata may be required in cases of conflict (i.e., where the two names are indistinguishable without more information). In the following section, some of the attributes listed are recorded as separate metadata elements in the authority data, and a subset of those may be recorded as part of the AAP. Next to each heading readers will find (S) for *separate element only* and (B) for *both*. Note that among the following metadata elements, none is identified as for *access point only*. This is because each attribute may be included as a separate element in the authority data about the person.

RDA 9.3 Dates Associated with Persons (B)

In RDA 9.3, three types of dates are associated with persons: date of birth, date of death, and period of activity. *Date of birth* and *date of death* are RDA Core elements and should be recorded whenever the dates are available; *period of activity* is an RDA Core-if element, meaning it is core *if* certain circumstances are in place. In this case, the element is core if needed for disambiguation.

Dates are taken from any source and are recorded in the calendar preferred by the cataloging agency. For information on the use of B.C. (before Christ) and A.D. (*anno Domini*, a Latin abbreviation for *in the year of the Lord*) in connection with dates, the cataloger should consult RDA appendix H. In a somewhat surprising turn, RDA opted not to use C.E. (common or current era) and B.C.E. (before the common era) instead of the more Christian-centric abbreviations.

Date elements may be recorded as part of an AAP, part of the authority data, or both. In general, the form of date is simply the year (1972), but in some cases where additional information is needed to distinguish between persons, the cataloger may include a more complete date as part of the authority data and/or in the AAP. An alternative at RDA 9.3.1.3 allows for the inclusion of a month or a month and date in the form of *yyyy Month dd* (e.g., 1972 January 15) or *yyyy Month* (1972 January), where the month is written in the language of the cataloging agency. The instructions also provide information on variations that may occur in dates.

- **Probable Date**: If the date is likely but not confirmed, then the probable year is offered with a question mark as an indicator that the date is not certain (e.g., 1965?).

- **Either One of Two Consecutive Years**: If the date can be narrowed down to a range of two years, then the range is recorded with the word *or* between the two years (e.g., 1941 or 1942).

- **Approximate Date**: If the date can only be approximated (i.e., the date is uncertain by several years), then the inexact date is recorded, preceded by the word *approximately* (e.g., approximately 664).

- **Period of Activity**: If a single date does not suffice to reflect dates of activity, a range of dates is added in the form *yyyy-yyyy* or *century-century* (e.g., 1593-1615; 13th century-14th century; 1816-approximately 1837; approximately 365 B.C.-352 B.C.).

- **Expanded Date**: If needed for disambiguation or for identification, a month or a month and a day may be added to the date in a format preferred by the cataloging agency (e.g., 1965 August 20; 1965-08; 19431023).

Dates of Birth and Death

These two RDA Core elements provide the year a person was born, the year a person died, or both. In each case, months (or months and days) may be added if needed. The LC-PCC PSs for 9.3.2.3 and 9.3.3.3 provide instructions on using a hyphen to indicate whether the date refers to date of birth or a date of death when adding one of these elements to an AAP. A date followed by a hyphen and a space is a date of birth (e.g., 1973- or 1965?-); a date preceded by a hyphen is a date of death (e.g., -1641 or -approximately 1529). In an AAP, both dates may appear separated by a hyphen (e.g., 1922-2010; 1964 or 1965-1998). If the information is also recorded as part of the person's authority data, there is generally no need for hyphens; they will be recorded as separate elements.

Period of Activity of the Person

Period of activity is a range of dates or a single date that is associated with the active period of a person's career, occupation, profession, or field of endeavor. This information may be taken from any source (including reference works). The element is considered RDA Core-if; it is required only when needed to make a distinction between two or more persons with the same name. It is generally recorded in years or centuries—whichever is applicable—when birth and death dates are unknown. An LC-PCC PS for RDA 9.3.4.3 specifies that the terms *active* and *century* are used rather than the abbreviations used in previous cataloging rules (i.e., *fl. for* "flourished" and *cent.*). They may be included as part of the access point or as part of the authority data for a person.

- active approximately 365 B.C.-352 B.C.
- active 1816-approximately 1837
- active 1593-1615
- active 13th century-14th century

RDA 9.4 Titles Associated with Persons (B)

RDA 9.4 contains instructions for titles of royalty and nobility; terms for popes, bishops, and others with religious vocations; and terms of rank, honor, or office, including the use of initials or abbreviations for academic degrees or organizational memberships. It does not include terms of address that indicate gender or marital status (e.g., Mrs. or Mr.). The basic instruction indicates that a title for a person should be recorded from any source. The titles may be recorded as parts of access points, separate elements in authority data, or both.

- **Titles of Royalty**
  - **Highest Royal Status**: Royal persons are generally known by their given names. Thus their titles are key elements in the identification of the person. Highest royal titles include: king, queen, emperor, empress, and other equivalent terms. Instructions are to record the person's title and the name of the country or people ruled in the language preferred by the cataloging agency.

Preferred name: Aba Sámuel	**Title**: King of Hungary
Preferred name: Anna	**Title**: Empress of Russia
Preferred name: Vytautas	**Title**: Grand Duke of Lithuania

  - **Royal Consorts**: A royal consort is the spouse of the person with the highest royal status. The cataloger should record, in the language preferred by the cataloging agency, the consort's title followed by the phrase *consort of* and the preferred name and title for the royal person.

Preferred name: Aelfgifu	**Title**: Queen, consort of Edwy, King of England
Preferred name: Mara	**Title**: consort of Murat II, Sultan of the Turks
Preferred name: Philip	**Title**: Prince, consort of Elizabeth II, Queen of Great Britain

  - **Children and Grandchildren of Royalty**: Instructions are to record the title of the child or grandchild of a royal person in the language of the cataloging agency.

    - Princess of Bohemia
    - Prince, Duke of Connaught
    - Infanta of Portugal

    If the title is brief (Prince, Princess, or an equivalent term), then the cataloger may include an additional title or a phrase (e.g., *daughter of, son of, grandson of* along with the preferred name and title of the royal person) to supplement the title.

    - Princess, daughter of Tomohito, Prince of Mikasa
    - Czarevitch, son of Nicholas II, Emperor of Russia
    - Prince, grandson of Mongkut, King of Siam

- **Titles of Nobility**: These instructions are for persons with a title of nobility whose title is *not* an element of the preferred name for the person. For example, some noblepersons create works and are known primarily by the name associated with their titles and not their surnames or family names.

- Byron, George Gordon Byron, Baron
- Burlington, Dorothy Boyle, Countess of

For cases such as these, see RDA 9.2.2.14 and the discussion of it in this text. Others create works and are primarily known by their given names and surnames.

- Balfour, Arthur James

  not Balfour, Arthur James Balfour, Earl of
- Bacon, Francis

  not St. Albans, Francis Bacon, Viscount

In these cases, the title of nobility *may* be recorded as an addition to the name or it may be recorded only in the authority data as a separate data element or as a variant name.

- **Religious Titles**: Instructions for religious titles are to record *Pope* as the title of a pope and *Antipope* for an antipope. For a bishop, cardinal, archbishop, abbot, or another high-ranking religious official known primarily by a given name, the cataloger records, in the language preferred by the cataloging agency, the title that the person holds. More than one title may be recorded as necessary. Names of dioceses, archdioceses, or patriarchates may be added as needed. Other terms of address (e.g., Sister, Mother, fra, Mullah, Rabbi) and, if applicable, initials of a Christian religious order (e.g., F.S.C., O.S.B.), may be added as needed after a given name. For more specific instructions on religious titles, the reader should see RDA 9.4.1.6-9.4.1.8.

- **Other Terms of Rank, Honor, or Office**: The cataloger may record other titles if they appear with the preferred name (e.g., Lady, Reverend, M.L.I.S., Venerable, Major General).

RDA 9.5 Fuller Form of Name (B)

This RDA Core-if element is required when needed to distinguish between two or more people with the same name. The element contains "a) the full form of a part of a name represented only by an initial or abbreviation in the form chosen as the preferred name, or b) a part of the name not included in the form chosen as the preferred name."[9] Fuller forms may be taken from any source. The basic instruction states that if the fuller form of name is known, but the preferred name does not include all of the parts, then the cataloger may record the fuller form as part of authority data, an AAP, or both. The fuller form may reference the given names, middle initials, surnames, and other name elements as appropriate. The name containing the fuller form should be recorded as a variant form in the authority data.

Preferred name: Smith, John E.   **Fuller form**: John Edward

Preferred name: Smith, John E.   **Fuller form**: John Edwin

Preferred name: Smith, John E.   **Fuller form**: John Eliphalet

Preferred name: Cabrera R., Augusto G.

Fuller form: Cabrera Rodríguez, Augusto Giraldo

Preferred name: Bloom, Bobby

Other name *not* a fuller form of name: Bloom, Robert

RDA 9.6 Other Designations Associated with Persons (B)

This section of RDA (9.6) contains instructions for designations judged useful for identifying a person not already covered in the previous instructions (i.e., dates, titles, and fuller forms of names). These *other designations* are considered RDA Core if they are for Christian saints, spirits, and persons named in sacred scripture or an apocryphal book. These designations are also core for fictitious characters, legendary figures, and real non-human entities. Any additional designations are required only to prevent a conflict. The information used to create these other designations may be taken from any source; the element may be recorded in authority data, as part of the AAP, or both.

- **Saints**: The term *Saint* is used.
- **Spirits**: *Spirit* is used if the person being described is purported to be a ghost or a spirit.
- **Persons Named in Scripture**: For a person named in sacred scripture or in an apocryphal book, instructions are given to record a designation that is appropriate for the person (e.g., Biblical priest, Biblical figure, Biblical patriarch, Book of Mormon figure, Prophet, Archangel, Angel, Demon).
- **Fictitious and Legendary Persons**: The cataloger should use *Fictitious character*, *Legendary character*; terms for mythological gods, goddesses, and heroes (e.g., Mythological character, Greek deity, Egyptian deity, Norse deity, Roman deity); or another appropriate designation.
- **Real Non-human Entities**: The guidelines suggest using a designation appropriate for the type, species, or breed of non-human entity (e.g., Dog, Border collie, Cat).
- **Other designations**: If needed, the cataloger may choose another designation that helps to disambiguate the persons. The term chosen should be sufficiently specific to distinguish between the entities (e.g., Wife of Vidyānanda Jhā, True son of the Church of England, Son of Jacob).

RDA 9.7 Gender (S)

Gender—which is recorded only as a separate element in authority data—has been a controversial addition to RDA. Commonly, in Western society, gender is treated as a binary concept. Currently RDA 9.7 reflects that bias by providing only a small list of values for the element: *female*, *male*, and *not known*.

> **AAP**: Eliot, George, 1819-1880
> **Gender**: female

> **AAP**: Abramson, Leslie W.
> **Gender**: male

> **AAP**: Ababurka, A. V.
> **Gender**: not known

Gender, however, is a more multifaceted concept than that; it goes beyond the experiences of those who are gender normative or *cisgendered* (i.e., persons whose identity and biological sex closely correspond) to take into account those with different experiences of gender identity and gender expression. It is something that goes beyond the surface-level clues—such as a name or what one sees in an image—on which catalogers must base their decisions about a person's gender. Even with additional biographical information about the person being described, the cataloger is still making assumptions. The need for greater inclusiveness in RDA's list of values will seem obvious to many readers, but even today, some readers may never consider the concept beyond their own gender-normative experiences.

RDA's implementation of *gender* has been rather disappointing to those who are aware of the hegemony of gender binarism. Its approach is simplistic and some believe it "reinforces regressive conceptions of gender identity."[10] The instruction does state that if none of the three options is adequate, another term may be added.

> **AAP**: Bornstein, Kate, 1948-
> **Gender**: transgender

> **AAP**: Nicholson, Serge
> **Gender**: transgender male

The onus to come up with an alternative term, however, is placed on the cataloger who, again, may make assumptions. With a few small additions, such as *transgender* and *intersex*, the list of terms in RDA could be more inclusive, which would be a step in the right direction, but the basic problems of determining gender from a distance (i.e., a cataloger making assumptions rather than acquiring the data from the person directly) is not easily resolved. As a result, some catalogers may opt not to address this problematic element in authority data. If this information is included, the source(s) should be documented in the *source consulted* element.

In the following example, the cataloger has attempted to provide additional contextual information about the person (i.e., note the dates associated with the gender values and the documentation provided).

AAP: Bono, Chaz

Gender: female 1969-2008?

Gender: male 2008?-

Source consulted: Wikipedia, Feb. 14, 2011 (Chaz Bono; Chaz Salvatore Bono (born Chastity Sun Bono; March 4, 1969); American transgender advocate, writer, actor, and musician; female-to-male transgender man; around age 39, Bono underwent female-to-male gender transition. A two-part Entertainment Tonight feature in June 2009 explained that Bono's transition had started a year before; Bono legally changed gender and name in May 2010.

RDA 9.8-9.11 Places Associated with Persons (S)

These mostly self-explanatory elements at RDA 9.8-9.11 address place of birth, place of death, and places of residence, as well as countries associated with a person. Generally, places of birth, death, and residence are provided as cities or towns followed by a larger jurisdiction—a state, province, or country, depending upon the specific location—but states, provinces, and/or countries may be substituted for the city if the more exact location is unknown. These elements provide contextual information about the person and are recorded in the authority data if the information is available. The data may be obtained from any source. The information is recorded following the instructions in RDA chapter 16 (see discussion later in this chapter), including the use of abbreviations found in RDA appendix B. In the United States, established place names are found in the LC Name Authority File (LCNAF); the cataloger usually consults the authorities database rather than establishing the place name from scratch. In some cases, place name associated with a person may be a non-jurisdictional location; if so, the place name is found in the Library of Congress Subject Headings (LCSH) instead of the LCNAF (see discussion of geographic names in chapter 13 of this text). If these place-related elements are included in the authority data, the source(s) should be documented in the *source consulted* element.

AAP: Friedman, Veronica M., 1945-1986

Date of birth: 19451015

Date of death: 19861012

Place of birth: Calif.

Place of death: Alameda (Calif.)

Country associated with person: U.S.

Gender: transsexual woman

ICC11 PS for RDA 9.8 Place of Birth of Person: Do not include local place of birth of a living person below the level of state, province, and so on. Local place of birth along with specific date of birth, and other such information, can be used for identity theft. Use cataloger's judgment when providing detailed personal information.

RDA 9.12 Address (S)

In RDA, *address* may refer to a physical home address, a business or an employer's address, an email address, or an Internet address, such as a URL. The data element may be obtained from any source. If address is included, the source(s) should be documented in the *source consulted* element.

> **ICC11 PS for RDA 9.12 Address of Person**: Do not include physical addresses for persons, even if they are readily available from widely accessible sources. Concerns for privacy and safety should prevail. Use cataloger's judgment when providing other types of addresses.

RDA 9.13 Affiliation (S)

An affiliation is an associated group, organization, or institution. One or more affiliations may be included in the authority data. The connection to the person may be through employment, membership, cultural identity, or some other means. The information may be taken from any source. The cataloger records the preferred name for the affiliated group in the element. If affiliation is included, the source(s) should be documented in the *source consulted* element.

> **AAP**: Kozelek, Mark
>
> **Associated group**: Sun Kil Moon (Musical group)
>
> **Associated group**: Red House Painters (Musical group)

> **AAP**: Warren, Elizabeth
>
> **Date of birth**: 19490622
>
> **Associated group**: United States. Congress. Senate 2013-
>
> **Associated group**: George Washington University 1966-1968
>
> **Associated group**: University of Houston 1970
>
> **Associated group**: Rutgers University 1976
>
> **Associated group**: Democratic Party (U.S.)

RDA 9.14 Language of the Person (S)

This element records the language(s) the person uses or used in language-based expressions of works. The information may be taken from any source and recorded in the language preferred by the cataloging agency. Recommended best practice is to take the name of the language from a standard list of languages (e.g., the MARC Code List for Languages, which is the preferred list for LC and PCC libraries for other RDA elements). If language is included, the source(s) should be documented in the *source consulted* element.

RDA 9.15-9.16 Field of Activity (S) and Profession/Occupation (B)

These two elements, although related, are not identical. *Field of activity* addresses a person's area of interest and expertise (*not* necessarily what she or he does to make money); *profession or occupation* is a category describing what a person does for a living—a vocation or an avocation. Unlike *field of activity*, the element *profession or occupation* is an RDA Core-if element and it may be used as part of the AAP for the name if appropriate. Profession is required when the name of the person does not convey the notion that a person is being described (e.g., Final Fantasy (Musician) is a person, not a musical group or a title). *Profession/occupation* is also core if there is a conflict between two or more persons with the same name. The information in these elements is taken from any source, but best practice for both elements is to record the data using controlled vocabulary from a source such as LCSH or *Medical Subject Headings* (MeSH).[11] If these elements are included in the authority record, the source(s) should be documented.

> **Preferred Name**: Smith, Mary
>
> **AAP**: Smith, Mary (Educator)
>
> **Field of Activity**: Education
>
> **Profession**: Educators

> **Preferred Name**: Smith, Mary
>
> **AAP**: Smith, Mary (Poet)
>
> **Field of Activity**: Poetry
>
> **Field of Activity**: Fiction
>
> **Field of Activity**: Journalism
>
> **Profession**: Poets
>
> **Profession**: Novelists
>
> **Profession**: Journalists

> **Preferred Name**: Smith, Mary
>
> **AAP**: Smith, Mary (Social worker)
>
> **Field of Activity**: Social work with children
>
> **Profession**: Social worker
>
> **Profession**: College teachers

RDA 9.17 Biographical Information (S)

This element contains a brief narrative describing a person's life, in whole or in part. Biographical information may come from any source; if it is included in the authority data, the source(s) should be documented in the *source consulted* element.

> **Biographical information**: Stephanie Yuen is a publisher, editor, food, wine and travel writer, and a self-taught chef.

> **Biographical information**: Gary McKenzie, from Chicago, has illustrated comic books, comic strips, and children's books and ran his own theatre company, Hi-Volt Theatre Company, from 1999-2003.

Biographical information: Suchen Christine Lim was born in 1948 in Malaysia. In 1963, her family moved to Singapore. Lim obtained her BA (Honours in English) from the University of Singapore. She is the first winner of the Singapore Literature Prize (Fiction) in 1992. Lim, who has four novels to her name, is also the writer of short stories, children's stories, students' textbooks and a play. In addition to being an acclaimed writer, Lim has also taught at Catholic Junior College, and contributes towards curriculum development at the Ministry of Education, Singapore.

RDA 9.18 Identifier for the Person (S)

The *identifier for the person*, an RDA Core element, is a unique character string associated with a person that differentiates that person from others. It may be taken from any source. Because persons are not objects nor are they resources with bar codes or unique numbers stamped on or inside them, they tend to have few identifiers (public or otherwise), and most cannot be used for bibliographic purposes (e.g., a Social Security number in the United States). Instead, an identifier is generally associated with a surrogate for the person, such as an authority record. When recording an identifier, RDA 9.18.1.3 indicates that a name or an identification of the agency should be included before the identifier (e.g., LCCN: no2012104917 or Library of Congress control number: no2012104917).

RDA 9.19 Creating Access Points for the Person

Access points are names, terms, or codes through which bibliographic or authority data is searched and identified. Access points may be controlled or uncontrolled. *Uncontrolled access points* are those not appearing as part of authority data; *controlled access points* are those appearing in an authority record or some other container of authority data, including both *authorized access points* (AAPs) and *variant access points* (VAPs). An AAP for a person is based on the name that has been established as the preferred or authoritative one. Most standardized AAPs are unique and, thus, applicable to only one person (see, however, the discussion of undifferentiated names earlier in this chapter). If the preferred name is not unique, the conflict must be resolved by adding additional data elements as part of the AAP. VAPs are based on other names that were not chosen as the preferred one; in other words, a variant access point is a reference.

Authorized Access Points for Persons

RDA 9.19.1.1 provides general guidelines for creating AAPs for persons. The basic instruction states that the AAP for a person is based on the preferred name that is established using the guidelines at RDA 9.2.2: Preferred Name for the Person.

> **Preferred name**: Sobule, Jill
>
> **Preferred name**: Woolf, Virginia
>
> **Preferred name**: Harper-Scott, J. P. E.
>
> **Preferred name**: John Paul
>
> **Preferred name**: Aelfgifu

Qualifiers (i.e., additional data elements) are added to the name according to the instructions at RDA 9.19.1.2-9.19.1.8. Some qualifiers will be added if the information is readily available (e.g., terms such as *Queen, Saint, Spirit*); others are added to the name only if needed to break a conflict (e.g., elements such as fuller form of name or profession). An RDA option allows catalogers to add *any* qualifier even if it is not needed. LC and PCC libraries do not apply this option absolutely; instead, they prefer to look at each qualifier individually to determine which they will add. Another LC-PCC PS for 9.19.1.1 states that if an LC or PCC cataloger is establishing a new AAP, but no additions can be found to differentiate it from an existing identical AAP, qualifiers may be added to the name that has already been established in order to prevent a conflict.

> **AAP**: Sobule, Jill
>
> **AAP**: Woolf, Virginia, 1882-1941
>
> **AAP**: Harper-Scott, J. P. E. (John Paul Edward), 1977-
>
> **AAP**: John Paul I, Pope, 1912-1978
>
> **AAP**: Aelfgifu, Queen, consort of Edwy, King of England, active 956

If the preferred name for a person is a phrase or appellation not conveying the idea of a person (e.g., the musician named Iron & Wine), then the cataloger adds an appropriate qualifier, even if it is not needed to break a conflict. The cataloger adds one of the following elements:

- the person's profession or occupation
    > **AAP**: Iron & Wine (Musician)

- a term indicating that the person is a fictitious or legendary character
    > **AAP**: Bunt (Fictitious character)

- a term indicating the "person" is a real non-human entity (e.g., a type, species, or breed of animal).
    > **AAP**: Socks (Cat), 1989-2009

If no suitable qualifiers are found to disambiguate two or more entities, an undifferentiated name may be used as the access point for more than one entity. This situation was more common under the previous set of cataloging rules, which did not have as many options for qualifiers, but it may still occur under RDA. Very common names, such as Margaret Smith or John Jones, are likely to result in undifferentiated name AAPs.

Additions to the Access Points

Titles Associated with a Person

If a person's preferred name contains a title or another designation (as determined using the instructions at RDA 9.4 and 9.6), that title is included as an addition to the AAP for the person. If the addition is a title of royalty or nobility, a religious rank, or the term *Saint*, then it follows the name, but precedes any dates that are to be added. If the qualifier is *Spirit*, then it is included as the last element in the AAP. If the qualifier is another form of designation (e.g., terms such as *Biblical figure, Greek mythological character*), it follows the name and precedes the dates, but it is entered in parentheses; if more than one *other designation* is used, each is entered in its own set of parentheses.

- **Titles of Royalty**: When dealing with the names of royal persons that include a title, the cataloger adds the title of royalty to the AAP even if it is not needed for disambiguation. It is a key part of identifying these persons and it should be entered after the preferred name.

  AAP: Aba Sámuel, King of Hungary, -1044

  AAP: Anna, Empress of Russia, 1693-1740

  AAP: Aishwarya Rajya Laxmi Devi Shah, Queen, consort of Birendra Bir Bikram Shah Deva, King of Nepal, 1949-2001

  AAP: Arthur, Prince, Duke of Connaught, 1850-1942

  AAP: Akiko, Princess, daughter of Tomohito, Prince of Mikasa, 1981-

- **Titles of Nobility**: If a person's title of nobility generally appears in the resources associated with that person, then the cataloger adds the title of nobility to the AAP for the person, even if it is not needed for disambiguation. The title should follow the preferred name and fuller forms of names if present.

  AAP: Byron, George Gordon Byron, Baron, 1788-1824

  AAP: Astor, Nancy Witcher Langhorne Astor, Viscountess, 1879-1964

  If the title is *not* used in a person's works, then it is to be omitted:

  AAP: Balfour, Arthur James, 1848-1930

- **Religious Titles**:
  - **Popes**: *Pope* or *Antipope* is added after the preferred name.
  - **Saints**: *Saint* is added after the preferred name, fuller forms of name, titles of nobility, or titles of religious rank. The cataloger does not add *Saint* if the AAP represents a person who was also a pope or of the highest royal ranks.

○ **Bishops and Titles of Religious Vocation**: If the preferred name used with works contains a religious title and a given name, then the given and fuller forms of name are followed by the title, even if it is not needed for disambiguation.

> **AAP**: John Paul I, Pope, 1912-1978
>
> **AAP**: Adalbert I, Archbishop of Mainz, -1137
>
> **AAP**: Alfred, Mother, 1829-1899
>
> **AAP**: Agathon, Brother, F.S.C., 1731-1798
>
> **AAP**: Barbara, Saint
>
> **AAP**: Nicetas, of Remesiana, Saint, -approximately 414
>
> **AAP**: Celestine V, Pope, 1215-1296
> (*not* Celestine V, Pope, Saint, 1215-1296)

• **Spirits**: If the person responsible for a work is a spirit (as a reminder, the category *persons* now includes fictitious characters, deities, animals, etc.), then the AAP must contain the term *Spirit* at the end in parentheses. If the entity represented is the spirit of a real person, the AAP for the actual person is used as the base for the new AAP.

> **AAP**: Wilde, Oscar, 1854-1900 (Spirit)
>
> **AAP**: Poppaea Sabina, Empress, consort of Nero, Emperor of Rome, -65 (Spirit)
>
> **AAP**: Zoosh (Spirit)

• **Other Designations**: One or more other designations may be added to the AAP if needed for disambiguation. These may include terms for persons in sacred scriptures or apocryphal works; characters in fictional works, legends, etc.; and types, species, and breeds of real non-human entities (i.e., animals). These other designations are added after fuller forms of name, titles, and/or the term *Saint*. An option states that these designations may be added even if they are not needed for disambiguation.

> **ICC11 PS for Optional Addition to RDA 9.19.1.2.6 Other Designations**: Apply the option. This type of clarifying addition helps with the identification of persons who are fictional, legendary, non-human, etc. For some users, this information can be essential.
>
> **AAP**: Watson, John H.
>
> **AAP**: Watson, John H., 1939-
>
> **AAP**: Watson, John H. (Fictitious character)
>
> **AAP**: Moses, 1978-
>
> **AAP**: Moses (Biblical leader)

AAP: Moses (Biblical leader) (Spirit)

AAP: Moses, Brother, 1949-1987

AAP: Moses, Chief, approximately 1829-1899

AAP: Moses, Grandma, 1860-1961

AAP: Berry (Dog)

AAP: Berry, duchesse de (Marie Louise Élisabeth d'Orléans), 1695-1719

AAP: Berry (Musician)

Dates of Birth and/or Death

Catalogers add dates of birth and/or death if there is a need to distinguish between two or more identical AAPs. In general, the date is in the form of a year, but in some cases, where additional information is required, a month and day may be needed.

AAP: Adams, John, approximately 1670-1740

AAP: Adams, John, 1735-1826

AAP: Adams, John, 1750?-1814

AAP: Adams, John, -1757

AAP: Adams, John, 1938-

AAP: Adams, John, 1938 August 13-

AAP: Adams, John, 1939-

AAP: Adams, John, 1940-

AAP: Adams, John, 1940 May 13-

An optional addition states that dates may be added even if there is no need for disambiguation. LC and PCC practice is to add dates to new AAPs if the dates are available; for existing authority data, their catalogers have the option to add dates, although it is not encouraged unless other changes are required in the AAP.

ICC11 PS for Optional Addition to RDA 9.19.1.3 Dates:
Apply the option.

Fuller Forms of Names

Catalogers may add fuller forms of name to distinguish between two or more identical AAPs. In general, fuller forms are used as part of the access point if dates of birth or death are not available. If a fuller form of name is not used as an element in the AAP, it can still be recorded as part of the authority data. An optional addition states that a fuller form of name may be added to the AAP, before the dates, even if there is no need for disambiguation. LC and PCC catalogers apply the option *if* part of the name in the AAP is an initial or an abbreviation and the cataloger considers it important for identification of the person.

> **AAP**: Byatt, A. S. (Antonia Susan), 1936-
>
> **AAP**: Mansfield, M. (Mildred), 1862-
>
> **AAP**: Queen, Tara L. (Tara Licciardello)
>
> **AAP**: Hernández G., María Gabriela (Hernández González)

Periods of Activity

If dates of birth and/or death are not available, the cataloger may add the period of activity of the person. These dates are added if needed to distinguish between two or more identical AAPs.

> **AAP**: A. F. R.
>
> **AAP**: A. F. R., active 18th century
>
> **AAP**: A. F. R., active 19th century
>
> **AAP**: Cui, Hong
>
> **AAP**: Cui, Hong, active 496-525
>
> **AAP**: Cui, Hong, 1972-

As with the other qualifiers, there is an option to add these dates even if they are not needed for disambiguation. LC and PCC libraries generally do not apply this option.

> **ICC11 PS for Optional Addition to RDA 9.19.1.5 Period of Activity**: Do not apply the option. Add only when dates of birth and/or death are unavailable and another distinguishing qualifier cannot be not found.

Professions or Occupations

If dates of birth and/or death are not available, the cataloger may add profession or occupation to the AAP, if it is needed to distinguish one access point from another. If a profession or occupation is to be included, the singular form of the term is used (e.g., *Librarian*, not *Librarians*).

> **AAP**: Jin, Qiang (Librarian)
>
> **AAP**: Dixon, Patricia (Aboriginal Australian political activist)
>
> **AAP**: Cannon, Scott (Videographer and anti-fracking activist)
>
> **AAP**: Marais (Dancer), active 17th century

As with the other qualifiers, there is an option to add these terms even if they are not needed for disambiguation. LC and PCC libraries do not apply the option.

ICC11 PS for Optional Addition to RDA 9.19.1.6
Profession or Occupation: Do not apply the option. Add profession or occupation to the AAP only for disambiguation. Profession/occupation, however, should be recorded among the metadata elements in the authority record, if applicable and ascertainable.

Other Terms of Rank, Honor, or Office

To distinguish between two or more identical AAPs, catalogers may add terms of rank, honor, or office to the name if dates of birth and/or death are not available.

> **AAP**: Moore, Edwin (Reverend)
>
> **AAP**: Cheng, Yizheng (Major General)
>
> **AAP**: Arnold, Suzanne, Ph. D.

There is an option to add these terms even if they are not needed for disambiguation. LC and PCC libraries apply the option when the term is considered important for identification.

Other Designations

If dates of birth and/or death are not available and the qualifiers listed in RDA 9.19.1.2.6 are not applicable, the cataloger may add another term or phrase to disambiguate identical AAPs.

> **AAP**: Jhā, Saroja (Wife of Vidyānanda Jhā)
>
> **AAP**: A. A. (True son of the Church of England)
>
> **AAP**: Joseph (Son of Jacob)

There is an optional addition of other designations even if there is no need to disambiguate, but the LC-PCC PS advises generally not to apply the option.[12]

Variant Access Points for Persons

Variant access points are created when a person has been represented by more than one name or form of name in resources. A variant name is the basis for a variant access point (see discussion of variant names above), and may include any of the following:

- Real names
- Secular names
- Names in religion
- Earlier names
- Later names

- Alternative language forms
- Alternative scripts
- Alternative spellings
- Alternative transliterations

AAP: Bessette, André, Saint, 1845-1937

VAP: André, Brother, 1845-1937

VAP: André, Brother, Saint, 1845-1937

VAP: André, frère, Saint, 1845-1937

VAP: Bessette, Alfred, Saint, 1845-1937

AAP: A. E. (A. Elllis), active 1855

VAP: E., A. (A. Elllis), active 1855

VAP: Ellis, A., active 1855

VAP: Layman, active 1855

AAP: Rice, Anne, 1941-

VAP: O'Brien, Howard Allen Frances, 1941-

VAP: O'Brien, Anne, 1941-

VAP: Raïs, Ėnn, 1941-

VAP: Райс, энн, 1941-

IDENTIFYING FAMILIES

Chapter 10 of RDA presents the cataloger with instructions to describe families. Its focus is primarily on establishing authority data and access points for family entities that are responsible for creating works, contributing to expressions, producing manifestations, or owning items (or providing access to them). There are two separate processes for establishing family names: the first is for families as subjects, and the second is for families as FRBR's Group 2 entities. The family access points created through subject heading work cannot be used to represent a creator and the family access points created through authority work cannot be used as a subject (see discussion of families as subjects in chapter 13 of this text).

> **AAP for family as creator (RDA)**: Jones (Family : Douglas
> County, Colo.)
> **AAP for family as subject (LCSH)**: Jones family

Once a family is established in the LCNAF or its equivalent, the AAP may be used in bibliographic descriptions as creators, contributors, and others associated with works, expressions, manifestations, or items.

As can be seen in Textbox 7.4, the chapter provides guidelines on choosing and recording names for families. It also provides instructions for other metadata elements associated with families that may be used in the creation of (1) access points, (2) separate metadata elements in authority data, or (3) both. The chapter also includes a specific section on constructing access points (authorized and variant) for families.

Textbox 7.4 RDA Chapter 10 Structure.

RDA 10.2 Name of the Family

The chief identifying element associated with a family is its name. The *name of the family* is a word, letters, symbols, or strings used to identify a family. It is the appellation by which the family is known. Names associated with a family fall into two categories: (1) preferred names, which are RDA Core, and (2) variant names, which RDA treats as optional. One name, generally the most common name associated with the family, is chosen as the preferred name; any others used by the family are treated as variants. If a family name changes at a later time, new access points and authority data are created; both names are used in bibliographic metadata.

The preferred name for the family, which is an RDA Core element, is used as the basis for the AAP for the family. The cataloger may take names of families from any source, but generally a preferred name is determined by consulting: (1) the preferred sources of information (e.g., title page, title screen, title card) in resources associated with the family; (2) other formal statements appearing in those resources (e.g., a name attached to an introduction or preface); and (3) any other resource (e.g., reference sources). Variant names are taken from resources associated with the family or from reference works.

The most commonly known name for the family is chosen as the preferred name. That name can be a surname or its equivalent, a royal or dynastic name, the name of clan, and so on. It is recorded following the instructions at RDA 8.5, which discuss issues of capitalization, numbers, diacritical marks, hyphens, spacing, and abbreviations (see discussion above). If the name contains two or more parts, the cataloger records "as the first element that part of the name under which the family would normally be listed in authoritative alphabetic lists in its language, country of residence, or country of activity. Record the other part or parts of the name following the first element."[13] This instruction is to be followed unless the preference of the family is different from standard usage. If the family's preference is known, or is ascertainable, the cataloger uses that instead.

When choosing a preferred name, several issues may be encountered. The first is when a family is known by more than one form of the same name. If there are different forms, the cataloger applies the same guidelines that apply to persons (RDA 9.2.2.5.1-9.2.2.5.4) for variations.

- **Fullness**: Choose, in order of preference, (1) the most common, (2) the latest, or (3) the fullest form of name.
- **Language**: Choose the form that is (1) in the language used in most of the resources associated with the family or (2) most commonly found in reference sources from the family's country of residence or activity.
- **Non-preferred Script**: Transliterate the name.
- **Spelling**: Choose the form in the first resource received. The other forms of name may be recorded as variant names.

> **Preferred name**: Romanov
>
> **Variant name**: Romanoff
>
> **Variant name**: Romanof
>
> **Variant name**: Романовых
>
> **Variant name**: Romanovykh
>
> **Variant name**: Holstein-Gottorp-Romanov

If the same family is known by two or more different names, the cataloger chooses the name most commonly associated with the family (i.e., the better known name). If that is unclear, the cataloger should choose the name that appears most frequently in resources associated with the family. If that is still unclear, then the cataloger uses the name that appears most commonly in reference works. The others may be recorded as variant names.

As stated above, if a family has changed its name, both names are established as authorized access points, and authority data is collected on both family names. The earlier name is used as the preferred name with any resources associated with the earlier name; the later name is used with resources created after the name change. Both names are treated as separate, but related, entities.

When recording the preferred name, the approach depends on the type of family name. For a name that contains a surname (or its equivalent), the surname is recorded as the family's name according to the instructions found for surnames in RDA chapter 9: Identifying Persons. The guidelines from that chapter that apply to families include those listed in Textbox 7.5. For names of dynasties, royal houses, and clans, simply record the name according to the general instructions for recording names in RDA 8.5 (e.g., capitalization, accents marks, hyphens).

Variant Name for the Family

A *variant name for the family* is another name or another form of name that is associated with a family. A variant name should be recorded if it is one used by the family, one found in reference works, or one resulting from differing systems of transliteration. Candidates for variant names include those

---

Rules for Surnames that Also Apply to Names of Families

9.2.2.9 General Guidelines on Recording Names Containing a Surname
    9.2.2.9.1 Surname Represented by an Initial
    9.2.2.9.2 Part of the Name Treated as a Surname
    9.2.2.9.3 Persons Known by a Surname Only
    9.2.2.9.4 Married Person Identified Only by a Partner's Name
    9.2.2.9.5 Words, etc., Indicating Relationship Following Surnames
    9.2.2.9.6 Saints

9.2.2.10 Compound Surnames
    9.2.2.10.1 Established Usage
    9.2.2.10.2 Established Usage Not Determined

9.2.2.11 Surnames with Separately Written Prefixes
    9.2.2.11.1 Articles and Prepositions
    9.2.2.11.2 Other Prefixes

9.2.2.12 Prefixes Hyphenated or Combined with Surnames

Textbox 7.5 RDA Instructions that Apply to Surnames for Persons and Families.

appearing in different languages or different scripts and those with different spellings or different transliterations. If the family has a hereditary title associated with it, that title also may be recorded as a variant name for the family. Any other variants, not addressed in the instructions, may be recorded if the cataloger believes they are useful for identification or access.

Additional Elements for Families

The family name, obviously, is the key element to identifying a family, but other elements are also needed. Names are not unique, so additional metadata elements may be required in cases of conflict (i.e., where two names are indistinguishable without more information). In the following section, some of the elements listed are recorded as separate metadata elements in authority data, and a subset of those may be recorded as part of the AAP. Next to each heading readers will find (B) for *both* and (S) for *separate element only*. Note that among the following metadata elements, none is identified as for *access point only*. This is because each element may be included in the authority data about the family.

RDA 10.3 Type of Family (B)

Type of family is an RDA Core element. The values in this element reflect kinds or types of families. The metadata may be taken from any source, but the values are typically limited to *family, clan, royal house, dynasty,* or another appropriate term determined by the cataloger.

RDA 10.4 Date Associated with the Family (B)

Another RDA Core element, which should be fairly self-explanatory, is *date associated with the family*; it is an element that may be taken from any source. As is the case with some of the instructions for names, the instructions for dates refer the reader back to the previous RDA chapter to apply RDA 9.3 to family entities (e.g., record dates according to the preferred calendar of the cataloging agency, use question marks for uncertain dates). The source(s) of the date(s) is to be documented in the *source consulted* element.

RDA 10.5 Place Associated with the Family (B)

Place associated with the family, an RDA Core element, is a location where a family lives, has lived, or with which the family is otherwise associated. The element is core if two or more families share the same name and additional metadata is required to break a conflict. Guidelines are to record one or more locations following the instructions for place names in RDA chapter 16 and the list of abbreviations found in RDA B.11 (see discussion below). The source(s) of places associated with the family are to be documented in the *source consulted* element.

RDA 10.6 Prominent Member of the Family (B)

This RDA Core element contains the name of a well-known person who is part of the family. The element is core if two or more families share the same name and additional metadata is required to break a conflict. Instructions are to add the name of one or more prominent family members to the family's AAP and authority data. Catalogers should use AAPs when determining the form of name of the individual(s) to be added. Catalogers use the *source consulted* element to document the process and the choices that were made.

RDA 10.7 Hereditary Title (B)

A *hereditary title* is a title of nobility that is connected to a family. The cataloger records a hereditary title in direct order in the plural form (e.g., Earls of Grantham). The source(s) of information is documented in the *source consulted* element.

RDA 10.8 Language of the Family (S)

This element records the language(s) used by the family in its works. The information may be taken from any source and recorded in the language preferred by the cataloging agency. Recommended best practice is to take the name of the language from a standard list of languages (e.g., the MARC Code List for Languages, which is the preferred list for LC and PCC libraries for other RDA elements). If language of the family is included, the source(s) should be documented in the *source consulted* element.

RDA 10.9 Family History (S)

This element contains a brief narrative describing biographical information about the family or about some of its members' lives. Family history may come from any source; if it is included in the authority data, the source(s) should be documented in the *source consulted* element.

RDA 10.10 Identifier for the Family (S)

The *identifier for the family*, an RDA Core element, is a unique character string associated with a family that differentiates that family from others. It may be taken from any source. The identifier may be associated with a surrogate for the family, such as an authority record. When recording an identifier, RDA 10.10.1.3 indicates that a name or an identification of the agency should be included before the identifier (e.g., LCCN: no2012067728 or Library of Congress control number: no2012067728).

RDA 10.11 Creating Access Points for the Family

Controlled access points are names, terms, or codes identified in authority data, through which entities are searched and identified. These include both authorized access points (AAPs) and variant access points (VAPs). An AAP for a family is based on the name that has been established as the preferred or authoritative one. VAPs include other names that were not chosen as preferred; in other words, a variant access point is a reference.

RDA 10.11.1.1 provides general guidelines for creating AAPs for families. The basic instruction states that the AAP for a family is based on the preferred name that is established using the guidelines at RDA 10.2.2: Preferred Name for the Family.

> **Preferred name**: Cunningham
>
> **Preferred name**: Romanov
>
> **Preferred name**: Koteda
>
> **Preferred name**: Knox
>
> **Preferred name**: Chichibu no Miya

Qualifiers (i.e., additional data elements) are added to the name according to the instructions at RDA 10.11.1.2-10.11.1.5. There are four types of additions or qualifiers (in the order of preference): *type of family, date associated with the family, place associated with the family,* and *prominent member of the family.* The first two are added routinely; the latter two are added to the name only if needed to break a conflict. Options, however, allow for both place and prominent member to be added even if no conflict exists. All qualifiers are placed in parentheses following the preferred name.

> **AAP**: Cunningham (Family : 1795- : Trigg County, Ky.)
>
> **AAP**: Romanov (Dynasty : 1613-1917)
>
> **AAP**: Koteda (Clan : active 15th century-17th century : Hirado-shi, Japan)

AAP: Knox (Family : Knox, Thomas Fitzhugh, 1807-1890)

AAP: Chichibu no Miya (Royal house)

Variant access points are based on the names *not* chosen as the preferred name for the family. The type of family is added in parentheses to the variant name, but adding other qualifiers to the VAP is based on cataloger's judgment. They should be added if considered necessary to identify the family.

IDENTIFYING PLACES

Place names are discussed in RDA chapter 16. Although it comes after corporate bodies in RDA, the authors have chosen to address this topic before corporate bodies because certain types of corporate bodies use places names as their names or as part of their names. Traditionally, governments are identified by the conventional name of the territory under their jurisdiction, and many subordinate government agencies (e.g., departments, ministries) are entered under the geographic name used to represent that government. Other corporate bodies also have a place name within their names or as a qualifier to prevent conflicts. Due to the prevalence of geographic information found in corporate names, it seems reasonable to address *places* first. Place names are discussed in connection with corporate bodies later in this chapter of the text. Textbox 7.6 provides an overview of the instructions found in RDA chapter 16.

16: Identifying Places

16.0 Purpose and Scope
16.1 General Guidelines on Identifying Places
16.2 Name of the Place
16.3 Identifier for the Place
16.4 Constructing Access Points to Represent Places

Textbox 7.6 RDA Chapter 16 Structure.

The purpose of chapter 16 is to provide guidelines on establishing authority data for geographic names. Once established in an authority file or its equivalent, place names may be used as any of the following:

- names of governments and their subordinate bodies as creators, contributors, and others associated with works, expressions, manifestations, or items
- additions to access points to disambiguate the following entities:
  - titles of works
  - families

- ○ corporate bodies
- ○ conference names
- ○ meeting names

- • separate metadata elements in authority records or their equivalents to provide context for the following entities:

- ○ persons
- ○ families
- ○ corporate bodies
- ○ works

Some place names, but not all, may also be used as the subjects of works; at the time of this writing, however, RDA does not fully address subject relationships. See, instead, the discussion of geographic subject headings in chapter 13 in this text. The reader should also note that unlike the instructions for persons, families, and corporate bodies, there is no section focused on the creation of access points for place names. There are only notes (1) referring readers to the relevant instructions for AAPs for governments and (2) presenting a general note about AAPs for other places that says, "[To be added in a later release]."[14]

RDA 16.2 Name of the Place

Geographic locations may be known by multiple names (e.g., Munich, München, Minga), and so one of the first choices to make is which name is to be identified as the preferred name. "The *preferred name for the place* is the name or form of name chosen to identify a place. The preferred name for the place is also used: (a) as the conventional name of a government, etc.; (b) as an addition to the name of a family, a corporate body, a conference, etc., or a work; (c) to record a place associated with a person, family, or corporate body."[15] This is an LC Core element when establishing place names that are used to represent governments and jurisdictions.

Sources for geographic names are very different from those for any other entity in RDA. Instead of using resources associated with the entity, the preferred sources are (1) gazetteers and other reference works in the language of the cataloging agency and (2) those same resources but in the language of the actual jurisdiction; the first source is preferred over the second source. For libraries in the United States, the resources used for geographic names are listed in Table 7.3.

According to the basic instruction at RDA 16.2.2.4, when establishing place names, catalogers simply record the most frequently found form in gazetteers and reference works, unless the instructions at RDA 16.2.2.8-16.2.2.14 are relevant. It states that place names include initial articles if present (e.g., The Bahamas, El Paso), but an alternative instruction follows immediately saying that these initial articles may be omitted (e.g., Bahamas), unless the article is a significant part of the name (e.g., El Paso). LC and PCC libraries apply this alternative to remove unnecessary initial articles.

TABLE 7.3 Sources for Geographic Names.

For names located in . . .	Source
the United States	U.S. Board on Geographic Names (BGN) Geographic Names Information System (GNIS): http://geonames.usgs.gov/pls/gnispublic
Australia	Geoscience Australia: http://www.ga.gov.au/place-names/index.xhtml
Canada	Natural Resources Canada's Canadian Geographical Names Data Base: https://www.nrcan.gc.ca/earth-sciences/geography/place-names/search/9170
Great Britain	The Ordnance Survey gazetteer of Great Britain: http://leisure.ordnancesurvey.co.uk
New Zealand	Several sources. Please see LC-PCC PS 16.2.2.2 for detailed information.
other places	Consider the form found in the resource along with the form found on the GEOnet Names Server (GNS): http://geonames.nga.mil/gns/html/

The basic instruction also states that the cataloger records, as part of the preferred name, the name of a larger place or jurisdiction containing the location being established (although there are exceptions for names of countries and some specific jurisdictions; see below). These larger jurisdictions are recorded in parentheses (sometimes using the abbreviations found in RDA appendix B) if the place name being established is a conventional name for a government. A comma precedes the larger jurisdiction if the place name is being used as any of the following:

- a conference location
- other place associated with the corporate body
- the place of origin for a work
- a place associated with a person
- a place associated with a family
- a place associated with a corporate body

For example, the city of Cambridge, Massachusetts, may be found in either of the following forms depending on its use:

> **Jurisdiction**: Cambridge (Mass.)
>
> **Qualifier**: (Cambridge, Mass.)

An LC-PCC PS provides additional guidance on the following situations:

- choice of the name of the larger place (e.g., use the *current* AAP for the larger place in most cases—but there are exceptions)
- form of name for the larger place (e.g., use the name in its AAP, but generally omit qualifiers for *type of jurisdiction* or *other designations*)
- islands and island groups (e.g., the distance from the local place to the larger jurisdiction plays a role in the name chosen for a qualifier)

See the LC-PCC PS for more details. RDA 16.2.2.4 also notes that special instructions at RDA 16.2.2.8-16.2.2.14 should be applied if relevant.

If the name appears in a script other than the preferred script of the cataloging agency, the cataloger must transliterate the name. There is an alternative for the cataloger to use a transliterated form found in references sources, but LC and PCC advise not to apply the alternative. Other forms, however, can be recorded as variant names.

Choosing the Preferred Name

When a place is known by different names (e.g., in different languages or different scripts), the cataloger is to choose the name in the form of the language used by the cataloging agency, if that form is available and that form is in general use. For example, in the United States the preferred name for the Bavarian capital would be Munich (Germany), not München (Germany), Minga (Germany), or München (Deutschland). Otherwise, the cataloger is to choose the form in the official language of the jurisdiction in which the place is located (e.g., Kemijärvi (Finland), which has no English language form). If there is more than one official language, the cataloger chooses the most common form found in sources preferred by the cataloging agency. An LC-PCC PS at RDA 16.2.2.3 provides additional information about choosing the preferred name, including a list of terms in which LC's choice of name may be different from that found in the preferred source of information. It also provides instructions on the use of *Mount* and *Saint* in names, and an instruction to use the name *Great Britain* rather than *United Kingdom*.

If the name of a place has changed, RDA refers readers to other instructions to assist with making decisions on which name to choose. For the names of governments or jurisdictions, all of the sequential names used by the entity are likely to be established as separate AAPs, *if* they produced works. When cataloging a resource, the instruction at RDA 11.2.2.6 applies:

> If the name of a corporate body has changed . . . choose the earlier name as the preferred name for use with resources associated with the earlier name. Choose the later name as the preferred name for use with resources associated with the later name.[16]

When establishing the names of local places, another type of name change is of concern: the names of the larger jurisdictions that are added in parentheses as qualifiers may change over time. In such cases, entirely new authority records are *not* created. Instead, only the qualifier for the larger place used with the name is changed. For example, Galle (Sri Lanka) is the preferred name for the city, while its former name, Galle (Ceylon), has been relegated to variant-name status. In some cases, the cataloger will find that both the local and the larger place names have changed over time. For example, Leningrad (R.S.F.S.R.) is now known as Saint Petersburg (Russia)—its earlier and its later name; both names, however, are established, because the local place name represents a different entity. For choosing additions to family names, corporate names, and conferences involving place names that have changed, see the appropriate instructions in RDA.

Recording the Preferred Name

As mentioned above, there are some specific instructions in RDA, each of which may be applied to a place name when the instruction is relevant. Each falls under the guidelines for recording the preferred name of a place. Some of these instructions address the type of place, some address particular locations in the world, and others address the resolution of conflicting names.

At RDA 16.2.2.8, the instruction for *terms indicating type of jurisdictions* focuses on place names that include terms indicative of the type of jurisdiction (e.g., State, Commonwealth, County). It states that if the place name begins with a term that indicates jurisdiction and the place is commonly listed in reference works or lists of places under the latter part of the name (rather than the jurisdictional term), then the cataloger is to enter the place under the more specific name and to omit the type of jurisdiction from the name. For example, County Armagh in Northern Ireland is listed under the letter *A* in alphabetical lists of places; therefore, the preferred name should be:

> **Place name**: Armagh (Northern Ireland)
> *not* County Armagh (Northern Ireland)

Another example is:

> **Place name**: Virginia
> *not* Commonwealth of Virginia

For all other situations, the jurisdictional term is recorded.

> **Place name**: Ciudad Hildalgo (Mexico)
> **Place name**: District of Columbia

The type of jurisdiction may be included as part of the authority data collected about the entity whether it is omitted from or is included in the name.

For most locations in the world, the recording of place names is not complicated. The names of the largest political jurisdictions or governments (i.e., countries) are not recorded with a qualifier. That leads to establishing place names such as Laos rather than Laos (Asia).

Local place names within most countries also are quite simple; the basic instruction at RDA 16.2.2.12 states that the cataloger records only the name of the country as a qualifier for the preferred name, unless (1) it is one of the exceptional situations addressed in RDA 16.2.2.9-16.2.2.11 (see the following discussion of Australia, Canada, the United States, the former U.S.S.R., and the former Yugoslavia) or (2) it is in need of additional data elements in its qualifiers in order to break a conflict. LC-PCC PS 16.2.2.13 also provides further guidance regarding other areas of the world where jurisdictional responsibility might be unclear or questionable.

> **Place name**: Salamanca (Guanajuato, Mexico)
> [there are also other towns named Salamanca in the Mexican states of Chihuahua, Durango, and Nuevo León]
>
> **Place name**: Salamanca (N.Y.)
> **Place name**: Salamanca (Spain)
> **Place name**: Salamanca (Spain : Province)

Applicable abbreviations may be used if found in RDA appendix B. An alternative instruction—to add the name of a state, province, or another highest-level division between the local place name and the country name—is applied by LC and PCC libraries only for Malaysia.

RDA provides special instructions for places in Australia, Canada, the United States, the former U.S.S.R., or the former Yugoslavia. For the states, territories, and provinces of the United States, Australia, and Canada, those units are entered on their own without a larger place name attached to them as a qualifier; for example the name is established as "Nebraska" and *not* as "Nebraska (U.S.)" with a qualifier. For the constituent republics of the former U.S.S.R. and the former Yugoslavia, the republics (and now independent nations) are named without qualifiers. RDA 16.2.2.10 provides similar instructions for England, Northern Ireland, Scotland, and Wales. Catalogers do not record a larger jurisdiction for these places: Use Scotland, *not* Scotland (Great Britain).

For local place names within the areas listed above, the name of a larger body is added for identification and disambiguation. For places within the United States, Australia, and Canada, the abbreviations for their states, territories, and provinces (as found in RDA appendix B.2) are added as qualifiers. For example, the cataloger establishes Lincoln (Neb.) rather than Lincoln (U.S.). For the former U.S.S.R. and Yugoslavia, the qualifiers should reflect the latest form of name for their former republics. For example, the cataloger would create Bishkek (Kyrgyzstan) for the city, not Bishkek (Kirghiz S.S.R.). However, the earlier name for that city would look somewhat different: Frunze (Kirghiz S.S.R.). The older name for Bishkek—Frunze—is established using the Soviet republic as its qualifier, because the name Frunze was used only in the Soviet era; it never existed in what is now known as Kyrgyzstan. For local places in England, Northern Ireland, Scotland, and Wales, the cataloger records the name of the constituent country as the larger jurisdiction.

> **Place name**: Aberdeen (Scotland)
> *not* Aberdeen (Great Britain)

Examples of establishing place names in these locations are provided in Table 7.4. See RDA 16.2.2.11 for additional instructions on overseas territories, dependencies, and other similar situations.

TABLE 7.4 Examples of Exceptional Geographic Areas.

Country	Jurisdiction type	Examples of larger places	Examples of local places
Australia	State or territory	**New South Wales**	**Aberdeen (N.S.W.)**
Canada	Province	**Ontario**	**Toronto (Ont.)**
United States	State	**Pennsylvania**	**Pittsburgh (Pa.)**
Former U.S.S.R.	Constituent Country	**Uzbek S.S.R.** (Name for government 1924-1991.)	**Tashkent (Uzbekistan)** (Use "Uzbekistan" as qualifier for places within the country.)
		Uzbekistan (Name for the independent nation 1992-)	
Former Yugoslavia	Constituent Country	**Croatia**	**Zagreb (Croatia)**
Great Britain	Constituent Country	**Wales**	**Abbeycwmhir (Wales)**

In most cases, if there are two or more local places with the same name, the name of the larger place as a qualifier resolves the conflict. If the name of the larger place, however, is not enough to distinguish between the two places, another term or phrase should be added. If there is no commonly used term that can be used to distinguish between the places, the name of an intermediate place may be entered before the name of the larger place. An LC-PCC PS provides additional guidance on resolving conflicts.

> **Place name**: Edgewood (Bell County, Ky.)
>
> **Place name**: Edgewood (Kenton County, Ky.)
>
> **Place name**: Waimea (Hawaii Island, Hawaii)
>
> **Place name**: Waimea (Kauai, Hawaii)

If the place name is for a part or a section of a city, the local place name is qualified by the name of the city or town as well as the larger place containing the city.

> **Place name**: Chinatown (San Francisco, Calif.)
>
> **Place name**: Adams Morgan (Washington, D.C.)

Variant names are recorded for the place when there are names that vary significantly from the place name chosen as the preferred name. The cataloger also records other place names or forms of names found in reference works. There are specific instructions in RDA addressing initial articles, expanded names, initialisms and abbreviations, and alternative linguistic forms of place names (i.e., different languages, different scripts, different spellings, different transliterations, and different forms in which numbers are expressed).

At the time of this writing, the instructions for recording identifiers for places and for constructing access points for places are not included in RDA. They are expected to be included in later releases. Despite the lack of instructions, or perhaps because of it, there are several LC-PCC PSs on various topics related to access points. They provide specific instructions on (1) constructing access points related to Berlin, Great Britain, London, Taiwan, U.S. Townships, and Washington, D.C.; (2) addressing ambiguous entities (such as city sections, communes, park districts, water districts, and so on), military installations, and the relationship between Native American tribes in the United States and place names; and, (3) the choice of larger places for variant access points.

IDENTIFYING CORPORATE BODIES

RDA chapter 11, the instructions for describing corporate bodies, focuses primarily on establishing authority data and authorized access points. Once the corporate body is established in an authority file or its equivalent, the AAP—created as part of the authority work—may be used in bibliographic descriptions to represent creators, contributors, or other roles associated with resources. For corporate bodies as the subjects of works, please see chapter 13 of this text.

11: Identifying Corporate Bodies

11.0 Purpose and Scope
11.1 General Guidelines on Identifying Corporate Bodies
11.2 Name of the Corporate Body
11.3 Place Associated with the Corporate Body
11.4 Date Associated with the Corporate Body
11.5 Associated Institution
11.6 Number of a Conference, etc.
11.7 Other Designation Associated with the Corporate Body
11.8 Language of the Corporate Body
11.9 Address of the Corporate Body
11.10 Field of Activity of the Corporate Body
11.11 Corporate History
11.12 Identifier for the Corporate Body
11.13 Constructing Access Points to Represent Corporate Bodies

---

Textbox 7.7 RDA Chapter 11 Structure.

As can be seen in Textbox 7.7, the chapter provides guidelines on corporate body names. It also provides instructions for other metadata elements associated with corporate bodies that may be used in the creation of (1) access points, (2) separate metadata elements in authority data, or (3) both.

The chapter also includes specific sections on constructing access points (authorized and variant). A preferred name is the basis for the AAP associated with a corporate body; a variant form of name is the basis for a VAP. The discussion on the scope and purpose of the chapter also reminds catalogers that the term *corporate body* is not just referring to corporations. It has a much broader definition than that:

A body is considered to be a corporate body only if it is identified by a particular name and if it acts, or may act, as a unit. A particular name consists of words that are a specific appellation rather than a general description. Typical examples of corporate bodies are associations, institutions, business firms, nonprofit enterprises, governments, government agencies, projects and programs, religious bodies, local church groups identified by the name of the church, and conferences. Ad hoc events (e.g., athletic contests, exhibitions, expeditions, fairs, and festivals) and vessels (e.g., ships and spacecraft) are considered to be corporate bodies.[17]

To new catalogers it is sometimes surprising to see some of the entities included in the definition of *corporate body*. Organizations and institutions of all types are intuitively good fits for the category; one does not, however, usually think of a ship or a space expedition as a corporate body. Conferences, meetings, fairs, festivals, exhibitions, contests, and events (henceforth represented by the single term *conferences* throughout this chapter) also can appear inappropriate for the corporate body label, but they are, indeed, included. One might not think of a circus troupe, a theatre company, a musical group, or a band of wandering troubadours as corporate bodies, but as long as they are an organization or group, have a collective name for that group, and act (or may act) as a unit, they fit the definition.

RDA 11.2 Names of Corporate Bodies

A *name of a corporate body* is the word(s), letters, symbols, or strings used to identify a corporate body. It is the appellation by which that body is known. When identifying a corporate body, RDA is concerned with two categories of names: (1) preferred names, which are RDA Core and (2) variant names, which RDA treats as optional. The cataloger may take names of corporate bodies from any source, but generally a preferred name is determined by consulting the preferred sources of information (e.g., title page, title screen, title card) in resources associated with the corporate body; if that proves insufficient, then the cataloger consults other formal statements appearing in those resources (e.g., a name in a logo). If that is not productive either, then other resources (e.g., reference sources) may be consulted. Variant names are taken from resources associated with the corporate body or from reference works.

Preferred Name for the Corporate Body

The *preferred name for the corporate body*, an RDA Core element, "is the name or form of name chosen to identify the corporate body. It is also the basis for the authorized access point representing that body."[18] When catalogers establish preferred names for corporate bodies, they may have no real choices to make in regard to the name. Sometimes corporate bodies identify themselves with only a single name or a single form of name throughout their entire history. On the other hand, corporate bodies may use different names during different periods. Some may use varying forms of the same name during the same period or across time periods. Mergers, acquisitions, separations, and changes of identity may occur that result in new names being used. Corporate body names can be quite challenging for both catalogers and users.

The basic instruction at RDA 11.2.2.3: Choosing the Preferred Name is that the cataloger generally chooses the most commonly known name of a corporate body. Which name that is could be a matter of cataloger's judgment based on evidence gathered from resources, catalogs and other bibliographic databases, and reference sources; sometimes that information comes from the corporate body directly.

RDA 11.2.2.4 states that the cataloger should record the name in the form that appears in resources associated with the corporate body, while the general guidelines on recording names (e.g., capitalization, hyphens, spacing of initials) are applied. If the name of the corporate body does not appear in that corporate body's own resources, or if the cataloger is uncertain about the most common form of name, then the cataloger records the name as commonly found in reference sources.

There are specific instructions established for different aspects of choosing and recording names of corporate bodies. The cataloger follows only those instructions that are relevant to the name of the corporate body being established. Discussions of these instructions follow in the next sections of this text.

Choosing Among Different Forms of the Same Name

If a corporate body is known by two or more forms of the same name in resources associated with that body, the choice of the preferred name is based on a set of general guidelines at RDA 11.2.2.5; these are outlined in Table 7.5. Following these guidelines, there are instructions for special circumstances.

- **Spelling variations**: If there are variations in the spelling of the name in the resources associated with the corporate body, the cataloger chooses the form found in the first resource received. The others may be used as variant names. An LC-PCC PS at 11.2.2.5.1 discusses situations involving orthographic reform; consult it as needed.

  Preferred form: Berks Summer Theatre

  Variant spelling: Berks Summer Theater

- **Language variations**: If the name appears in different languages, the cataloger chooses the name in the official language of the body as the preferred form of name. An alternative states that the form in the language of the cataloging agency may be chosen instead of an official language of the body, but LC and PCC libraries do not apply the alternative.

TABLE 7.5 General Instructions for the Choice of Preferred Name for a Corporate Body.

If	then
. . . there is only one name found in resources associated with the corporate body,	. . . that name is chosen as the preferred name.
. . . more than one form of that name is found in resources associated with the corporate body,	. . . the name found in the preferred source of information is chosen as the preferred name.
. . . more than one form of the name appears in the preferred source of information,	. . . the name presented formally in the preferred source of information (e.g., in the statement of responsibility) is chosen as the preferred name.
. . . more than one name or no name is presented formally in the preferred source of information,	. . . the name that appears most frequently is chosen as the preferred name.
. . . it is unclear which form of name is most frequently found,	. . . the brief form of name is chosen as the preferred name (e.g., an initialism or acronym) if it is sufficient to identify the body.
. . . there is no brief form that is specific enough to identify the body,	. . . use the form of name found in reference sources.
. . . the cataloger wishes to ensure appropriate access for the user,	. . . all the other possible choices should be recorded as variant forms of the corporate body name.
. . . the corporate body has changed its name,	. . . these rules do not apply. See RDA 11.2.2.6 instead.

If there is *more than one* official language, and one of them coincides with the preferred language of the cataloging agency, the cataloger chooses that form for the preferred name (e.g., in the United States, the cataloger would choose the English name, if there is one). If there is more than one official language, but none is the preferred language of the cataloging agency, the cataloger chooses the name in the language that is predominantly used by the body (e.g., if most resources are published in French, then the cataloger chooses the French name). If there is no clear choice, the cataloger chooses the form of name that is found in the resource received first. The others may be used as variant names.

> **Preferred form**: MeteoSchweiz
>
> **Variant language form**: MétéoSuisse
>
> **Variant language form**: MeteoSvizzera
>
> **Variant language form**: MeteoSwiss

- **International bodies**: If the corporate body is international in scope, and its name (in resources associated with it) appears in the language of the cataloging agency, the cataloger chooses that name as the preferred one. If not, apply the instructions at 11.2.2.5.2 for language variations (above). The others may be used as variant names.

> **Preferred form**:   International Labour Organisation
>
> **Variant language form**: Organização Internacional do Trabalho
>
> **Variant language form**: Organisation internationale du travail
>
> **Variant language form**: Organismo Internacional del Trabajo

- **Conventional names**: A *conventional name* is "a name, other than the real or official name, by which a corporate body has come to be known."[19] If the corporate body is better known in reference sources in its own language by a conventional name, choose it rather than an official name as the preferred form.

> **Preferred form**:   Westminster Abbey
>
> **Variant language form**: Collegiate Church of St. Peter in Westminster

The instructions for conventional names have several exceptions for particular types of corporate bodies:

- **Ancient and international bodies**: If there is a name in the language of the cataloging agency, prefer that form.
- **Autocephalous patriarchates, archdioceses, etc.**: Enter under the name of the place by which it is identified. Add the type of ecclesiastical jurisdiction in parentheses.
- **Religious orders and societies**: If there is a best-known form of name in the language of the cataloging agency, prefer that form.
- **Governments**: Enter under the name of the place that is governed (e.g., Massachusetts, *not* Commonwealth of Massachusetts). If an official name is in common usage, choose that instead. (See discussion of RDA chapter 16 above.)
- **Conferences, congresses, meetings, etc.**: In general choose the fuller form or more specific form of the conference name. (See separate discussion on conference names below.)
- **Local places of worship**: "The name of a local place of worship is the name of a church, cathedral, monastery, convent, abbey, temple, mosque, synagogue, etc."[20] If the name appears in different forms, prefer the predominant form. If the predominant form cannot be determined, choose (in preference order):

> i. a name containing a person, object, place, or event
>
> ii. a name containing a word or phrase descriptive of the type of institution
>
> iii. a name beginning with the place where the institution is located

The reader is advised to consult these instructions further, as needed.

Name Changes

In the world of cataloging, when a corporate body changes its name, a new entity is created. Even though those responsible for the body, the focus of the organization, and the types of resources produced may remain exactly the same, it is treated as a new entity. In many ways, this is the easiest way to address name changes for corporate bodies. The cataloger creates new authority data and a new AAP to use. It is not a completely fresh start, though; the new entity is linked to the older name and authority data. The names have a relationship between them; recording that relationship is addressed in chapter 8 of this text and in RDA chapter 32. Both the earlier and later names may be used with resources. Descriptions of resources will include the corresponding name of the corporate body (i.e., only the name that was used by the body during the period when the resource was created).

According to the LC-PCC PS for 11.2.2.6, some name changes—those considered "minor"—do not result in a new entity being established:

A difference is minor if the existing authorized access point and the name in the resource being cataloged differ only in one or more of the following ways:

1. the representation of words (abbreviation, acronym, initialism, or symbol and the spelled out form; two different spellings of the same word; a word in the form of a single word and in the form of a compound);
2. a change in a preposition, article, or conjunction;
3. a change in punctuation.[21]

Recording the Preferred Name

As mentioned above, RDA 11.2.2.4 instructs the cataloger to record the name in the form that appears in resources associated with the corporate body, while the general guidelines on recording names (e.g., capitalization, hyphens, spacing of initials) are applied. There are, however, some specific instructions related to particular aspects of a name that may apply.

- **Initials**: If the name consists of or contains initials, the cataloger records those initials with or without punctuation between the letters, depending on the form of name used most frequently by the corporate body. For example, Frente de Unidad Nacional, a political party in Guatemala, most frequently uses the initials F.U.N. to identify itself in its own resources. Unesco, on the other hand, most frequently omits full stops from its name and capitalizes only the first letter.

> **Preferred name**: F.U.N.
>
> **Variant name**: FUN
>
> **Variant name**: Frente de Unidad Nacional
>
> **Preferred name**: Unesco
>
> **Variant name**: U.N.E.S.C.O.

> **Variant name**: United Nations Educational, Scientific, and
> Cultural Organization

- **Initial articles**: If the preferred name for a corporate body includes an
  initial article, it should be recorded as part of the name. An alternative,
  which is applied by LC and PCC catalogers, allows for the initial
  article to be dropped unless the initial article is a key part of the name
  (e.g., one would not remove *El* from the name El Paso Historical Society).
  For a list of initial articles in various languages, see RDA appendix C.
- **Citations of honors**: Omit any phrases of this type.
- **Terms indicating incorporation and certain other terms**: Catalogers
  are to omit the following terms unless they are deemed necessary for
  identification of the entity as a corporate body or they represent an
  essential part of the name:

    a) an adjectival term or abbreviation indicating incorporation
       (e.g., *Incorporated, Inc., E.V., Ltd.*)
    b) a term indicating state ownership of a corporate body
    c) a word or phrase, abbreviated or in full, indicating the type of
       incorporated entity (e.g., *Aktiebolaget, Gesellschaft mit beschränkter
       Haftung, Kabushiki Kaisha, Società per azione*)[22]

See the instruction at RDA 11.2.2.10 for specific examples and additional
instructions for other terms to omit (e.g., U.S.S. before the names of ships).

- **Number or year of convocation of a conference, etc.**: Omit the
  number or year of a conference (see the discussion of conferences at the
  end of this chapter).
- **Names found in a non-preferred script**: If the name appears in a
  script that is not the preferred script of the cataloging agency, the
  cataloger is instructed to transliterate the name. An alternative allows
  the cataloger to take a transliterated form of name directly from
  resources associated with the corporate body. LC and PCC catalogers
  are not to apply the option; they prefer to have catalogers transliterate
  the names themselves.

Recording the Preferred Name of Subordinate and Related Bodies

Some organizations, departments, groups, and the like are subordinate
corporate bodies. A subordinate corporate body represents a unit, a part, or a
portion of a larger body (e.g., a school within a university, a ministry within a
government). The names of some subordinate corporate bodies are distinctive,
but other bodies may require the name of the larger entity (in full or in part) as
part of its name to ensure identification. In the state of Montana, for example,
the Highway Planning Committee was a corporate body entity in the mid-20th
century. Because it was involved in the creation of a work, its name had to
be established as an AAP. In choosing its preferred name, the name of the

larger body (i.e., the state of Montana) was included to ensure complete identification of the corporate entity: **Montana. Highway Planning Committee**.
The name *Highway Planning Committee*, in itself, is not unique. For example,
another Highway Planning Committee was part of the American Association of
State Highway Officials. Its name also reflects a subordinate relationship to a
larger entity: **American Association of State Highway Officials. Highway
Planning Committee**. In both cases, the corporate body is fully identified
through the use of the larger entity's name along with the specific name of the
subordinate unit.

Subordinately entered names are not necessary for many corporate bodies,
but in some circumstances they are essential. For most corporate bodies having a distinctive, recognizable, and unique name, the corporate body name is
recorded independently.

> **Preferred name**: Library of Congress
>
> **Preferred name**: Wharton School
>
> **Preferred name**: XTO Energy Inc.

If a name is entered independently, then a subordinate form of the name may
be included as a variant in the authority data.

> **Variant name**: United States. Library of Congress
>
> **Variant name**: University of Pennsylvania. Wharton School
>
> **Variant name**: Exxon Mobil Corporation. XTO Energy Inc.

If, however, the corporate body falls within one of the following categories,
its name is recorded as a subdivision of the AAP for the larger entity. If the
name is entered subordinately, the cataloger should remove any occurrences
of the name or any abbreviation related to the name of the larger entity if it is
presented in the form of a noun (unless the omission would impair identification of the entity).

> **Preferred name**: Simmons College (Boston, Mass.). Alumnae
>   Association
>
>   *not* Simmons College (Boston, Mass.). Simmons Alumnae
>   Association.

The direct form of the names (e.g., Simmons Alumnae Association or Highway
Planning Committee) may occasionally be helpful as a reference. If the cataloger
is unclear whether the corporate body's name should be entered subordinately,
or whether the entity falls within one of the categories below, then the cataloger
should enter the body under its own name directly. The categories for subordinate corporate bodies, RDA 11.2.2.14.1-11.2.2.14.18, are described below.

- **Body whose name implies it is part of another body**: If the name
  contains a term denoting that the entity is part of another body (e.g.,
  department, division, section, branch), then it should be entered under
  the name of the higher body.

> **Preferred name**: Association for Library Collections & Technical Services. Cataloging and Metadata Management Section

- **Body whose name implies administrative subordination**: If the name contains a term (e.g., *committee, commission*) that denotes administrative subordination, then it should be entered under the name of the higher body. Do not apply if the name of the higher body is *not* needed for identification. The LC-PCC PS at RDA 11.2.2.14.2, in addition to discussing the category's application to government bodies, provides three lists (English, French, and Spanish) of additional words that may indicate that the body falls within this category. The English list contains the following terms:

  - administration
  - administrative [board, group, . . .]
  - advisory . . .
  - agency
  - authority
  - board
  - bureau
  - directorate
  - executive
  - . . . group
  - inspectorate
  - office
  - panel
  - secretariat
  - service
  - task force
  - working party

  > **Preferred name**: Association for Library Collections & Technical Services. Subject Analysis Committee

- **Body whose name is general in nature or simply indicates a geographic, chronological, or numbered or lettered subdivision of a parent body**: If the name contains only general terms (e.g., no proper nouns, subject words, or identifying adjectives) or only terms indicating a local branch, a chronological grouping, or a lettered or numbered division, then it should be entered under the name of the higher body.

  > **Preferred name**: Concord Free Public Library (Concord, Mass.). Friends
  >
  > **Preferred name**: Academy of Talented Scholars. Class 1-208
  >
  > **Preferred name**: American Red Cross. Boston Metropolitan Chapter

- **Body whose name does not convey the idea of a corporate body and does not contain the name of the higher body**: If the name does not provide an indication that the entity is a corporate body, then it should be entered under the name of the higher body.

  > **Preferred name**: South Africa. Technology for Women in Business

- **University faculty, school, college, institute, laboratory, etc., with name that simply indicates a particular field of study**: If the name of the entity simply indicates the field of study, rather than a specifically named school, then it should be entered under the name of the higher body.

   Preferred name: Simmons College (Boston, Mass.). Graduate School of Library and Information Science

- **Non-governmental body with name that includes the entire name of the higher or related body**: If the corporate body is a non-governmental agency, and the name contains the entirety of the higher body's name, then it should be entered under the name of the higher body. A lengthy LC-PCC for RDA 11.2.2.14.6 goes into detail about LC and PCC practices regarding what is meant by the terms "includes" and "entire name." It also lists some exceptions. The reader should consult the LC-PCC PS as needed.

   Preferred name: Harvard University. Board of Overseers

   Variant name: Board of Overseers of Harvard University

- **Ministry or similar major executive agency**: If the corporate body is a high-level governmental agency, and has no superior agency above it (i.e., it is a ministry or major executive agency), then it should be entered under the name of the government.

   Preferred name: United States. Central Intelligence Agency

- **Government or religious officials**: If the office of a government or religious official is responsible for a resource, then the official/office is entered under the name of the higher body. Additional information may be added to the preferred name to make the AAP more specific.

   Preferred name: Canada. Prime Minister

   Preferred name: Canada. Prime Minister (1980-1984 : Trudeau)

- **Others entered subordinately**: The following types of corporate body entities (described in RDA 11.2.2.14.9-11.2.2.14.18) are also entered subordinately under their higher bodies.
  - Legislative bodies
  - Constitutional conventions
  - Courts
  - Principal services of the armed forces of a government
  - Embassies, consulates, etc.
  - Delegations to an international or intergovernmental body
  - Councils, etc., of a single religious body

- ○ Religious provinces, dioceses, synods, etc.
- ○ Central administrative organs of the Catholic Church
- ○ Papal diplomatic missions, etc.

If the corporate body is to be entered subordinately under a larger organization (as described in the immediately preceding discussion), then the name of the corporate body is recorded as a subdivision that is appended to the AAP for "the lowest organizational unit in the hierarchy that is recorded directly under its own name."[23] In other words, it is entered under the unit closest above it in its hierarchy that is entered under its own name. If there are units in the hierarchy that fall between the subdivision and the name that is to be the entry element, those units are omitted *unless* they are needed to distinguish this body from another that does or might have the same form of name. For example, within the government of Missouri, multiple corporate body entities have the name *Office of Public Affairs*.

> **Corporate body name**: Office of Public Affairs
>
> **Lowest body in hierarchy
> entered under its own name:** Missouri
>
> **Intervening unit in the hierarchy**: Department of Mental Health
>
> **AAP**: Missouri. Department of Mental Health. Office of Public
>   Affairs

> **Corporate body name**: Office of Public Affairs
>
> **Lowest body in hierarchy
> entered under its own name**: Missouri
>
> **Intervening unit in the hierarchy**: Department of Natural
>   Resources
>
> **AAP**: Missouri. Department of Natural Resources. Office of Public
>   Affairs

If the intervening units are not included (i.e., both are recorded as *Missouri. Public Affairs Office*), there is a conflict between the access points. For names where there is no conflict, then the name is presented without the intervening unit.

> **Corporate body name**: Office of the Public Counsel
>
> **Lowest body in hierarchy
> entered under its own name**: Missouri
>
> **Intervening unit in the hierarchy**: Department of Economic
>   Development
>
> **AAP**: Missouri. Office of the Public Counsel

In this example, no other body in the Missouri government has an Office of the Public Counsel (at least not in the name authority file), so the intervening unit is unnecessary. Omission of elements of a hierarchy is an area where the results of different catalogers' judgments may vary. RDA states: "Omit intervening units in the hierarchy, unless the name of the subordinate or related body has been, or is likely to be, used by another body recorded as a subdivision of the authorized access point representing the same higher or related body."[24] A phrase such as "or is likely to be" can lead to differences in judgment. Common sense must dictate the inclusion of other parts of the hierarchy for most corporate bodies. The cataloger should consider whether the name would be appropriate for another subordinate body within the same higher body structure and whether some word or phrase in a name in the hierarchy expresses an idea necessary for the identification of the subordinate body. Whatever the decisions made, the other forms of name may be recorded as variant names.

The instructions at RDA 11.2.2.16-11.2.2.29 contain guidelines for recording names for specific kinds of corporate bodies. Some may be entered under their own names, while others must be entered subordinately. These instructions focus on government agencies, legislative bodies, and religious organizations. They also include additional instructions for religious and government leaders acting in an official capacity. A list of these types, along with examples, is provided in Table 7.6. The reader should consult the instructions in RDA for further guidance.

TABLE 7.6 RDA Instructions for Specific Kinds of Corporate Bodies.

RDA instruction	Type of corporate body	Example(s)
11.2.2.16	Joint Committees, Commissions, etc.	Joint Committee on Reducing Maternal and Neonatal Mortality in Indonesia
11.2.2.17	Conventionalized Names for State and Local Units of United States Political Parties	Democratic Party (Mass.). State Committee
Government officials		
11.2.2.18.1	Heads of State, Heads of Government, etc.	Mexico. President United States. President (1893-1897 : Cleveland) Bohemia (Kingdom). Sovereign (1740-1780 : Maria Theresa)
11.2.2.18.2	Ruling Executive Bodies	Aragon (Spain). Junta Superior
11.2.2.18.3	Heads of International Intergovernmental Bodies	United Nations. Secretary-General (1992-1996 : Boutros-Ghali)
11.2.2.18.4	Governors of Dependent or Occupied Territories	Tobago (Colony). Governor (1816-1827 : Robinson)

(continued)

TABLE 7.6 (*continued*)

RDA instruction	Type of corporate body	Example(s)
11.2.2.18.5	Other officials (for some enter under the ministry; for others under the position)	Pakistan. Ministry of Communications England. Exchequer

Legislative bodies

RDA instruction	Type of corporate body	Example(s)
11.2.2.19.1	Legislatures	Mali. Assemblée nationale Norway. Stortinget United States. Congress. House
11.2.2.19.2	Legislative Committees and Subordinate Units	Rwanda. Parliament. Chamber of Deputies United States. Congress. House. Committee on Education and Labor. Ad Hoc Subcommittee on Discrimination Against Women
11.2.2.19.3	Successive Legislatures	United States. Congress (1st : 1789-1791). House United States. Congress (113th, 2nd session : 2014)
11.2.2.20	Constitutional Conventions	Micronesia (Federated States). Constitutional Convention (2001) Delaware. Constitutional Convention (1791-1792)
11.2.2.21	Courts	Dublin (Ireland). Metropolitan Children Court United States. Circuit Court (7th Circuit) Great Britain. Royal Navy. Court-martial (Crookshanks : 1748)
11.2.2.22	Armed Forces	Spain. Ejército del Aire United States. Army. New York Infantry Regiment, 86th (1861-1865) United States. Marine Corps. Amphibious Tractor Battalion, 5th Massachusetts. Air National Guard
11.2.2.23	Embassies, Consulates, etc.	Bhutan. Embassy (Kuwait) United States. Consulate (Buchanan, Liberia)

TABLE 7.6 (*continued*)

RDA instruction	Type of corporate body	Example(s)
11.2.2.24	Delegations to International and Intergovernmental Bodies	Australia. Delegation to the United Nations Conference on the Law of the Sea Portugal. Delegação (Paris Peace Conference (1919-1920))
Religious bodies		
11.2.2.25	Councils, etc., of a Single Religious Body	Mennonite Church. Washington County, Maryland, and Franklin County, Pennsylvania, Conference
11.2.2.26.1	Bishops, Rabbis, Mullahs, Patriarchs, etc.	Catholic Church. Diocese of Verona (Italy). Bishop Church of the Province of New Zealand. Diocese of Wellington. Bishop (1895-1911 : Wallis)
11.2.2.26.2	Popes	Catholic Church. Pope Catholic Church. Pope (2013- : Francis)
11.2.2.27	Religious Provinces, Dioceses, Synods, etc.	Presbyterian Church (U.S.A.). Synod of Lakes and Prairies.
11.2.2.28	Central Administrative Organs of the Catholic Church (Roman Curia)	Catholic Church. Signatura Apostolica Catholic Church. Poenitentiaria Apostolica
11.2.2.29	Papal Diplomatic Missions, etc.	Catholic Church. Apostolic Nunciature (Spain)

Variant Name for the Corporate Body

A *variant name for the corporate body* is another name or another form of name that is associated with the body; it is one that differs from the preferred name. A variant name should be recorded if the name is used by the corporate body, is found in reference works, or results from differing systems of transliteration. Candidates for variant names include:

- **Alternative forms of names for subordinate corporate bodies**: If the preferred name for the body has been created as a subdivision of a higher body, then the cataloger records a variant name for the direct form of name if it is judged likely to enhance access or identification.

Preferred name: United States. Central Intelligence Agency

Variant name: Central Intelligence Agency

- **Subordinated forms of name for independent corporate bodies**:
If the preferred name is the name of the corporate body entered by
itself, but the body is part of a larger or higher body, then the cataloger
records a variant name for the name as a subdivision of the larger body.

Preferred name: Smithsonian Folklife Festival

Variant name: Smithsonian Institution. Folklife Festival

Variant name: Smithsonian Institution. Center for Folklife Programs and Cultural Studies. Smithsonian Folklife
Festival

- **Expanded names**: If the preferred name is or contains an acronym,
initialism, or an abbreviation, then the cataloger records the expanded
form of the body's name as a variant name.

Preferred name: AFL-CIO

Variant name: American Federation of Labor and Congress of
Industrial Organizations

Preferred name: Mount St. Mary's Seminary of the West

Variant name: Mount Saint Mary's Seminary of the West

- **Acronyms, initialisms, and abbreviations**: If the body is primarily
known by a fuller form of name, the cataloger records acronyms,
initialisms, and abbreviated forms as variant names.

Preferred name: United States. Federal Bureau of Investigation

Variant name: FBI

Preferred name: Federation of British Industries

Variant name: FBI

Preferred name: Ethnikē Epitropē Galaktos

Variant name: E.E.G.

Variant name: EEG

Variant name: National Dairy Committee of Greece

Variant name: N.D.C.

Variant name: NDC

- **Alternative linguistic forms of names**: Any names in other languages,
in alternative scripts, with alternative spellings, or that are the result of
alternative transliterations should be recorded as variant names.

Preferred name: United Nations

Variant name: Naciones Unidas

Variant name: Vereinigte Nationen

Variant name: Vereinten Nationen

Variant name: Förenta nationerna

Variant name: Sāzmān-i Milal-i Muttafiq

Variant name: Kula Samagga

Variant name: U.N.

Variant name: ONU

Variant name: VN

Variant name: או״מ

Variant name: 国際連合

Variant name: الـم تحدة الأمم

- **Other variant names**: Any other names that are described as alternatives to the general instructions for preferred names in RDA are recorded as variant names, if considered useful for identification or access.

  Preferred name: 77 Gallery

  Variant name: Seventy-seven Gallery

  Preferred name: Alabama College

  Variant name: Alabama Girls Technical Institute

Additional Elements for Corporate Bodies

A name, obviously, is the key element to identifying a corporate body, but other elements are also needed. Names are not unique, so additional metadata elements may be required in cases of conflict (i.e., where the two names are indistinguishable without more information). In the following section, some of the elements listed are recorded as separate metadata elements in the authority data, and a subset of those may be recorded as part of the AAP. Next to each heading readers will find (B) for *both* and (S) for *separate element only*. Note that among the following metadata elements, none is identified for *access point only*, because each element may be included in the authority data about the corporate body.

RDA 11.3 Place Associated with the Corporate Body (B)

Place associated with the corporate body is an element that contains an important location linked to the corporate body. Place is an RDA Core element, but only for conference names (see separate discussion of conferences at the end of this chapter); for all other corporate bodies, it is considered core only if two or more corporate bodies share the same name, and additional metadata is required to break a conflict. The LC-PCC PS at RDA 11.3 provides additional details about the use of geographic names to break conflicts. In general, the cataloger records one or more locations following the instructions for place names in RDA chapter 16 (see discussion above) and the list of abbreviations found in RDA appendix B.11.

The element *other place associated with the corporate body* may contain (1) a geographic location where a corporate body's headquarters is situated, (2) a jurisdiction associated with a corporate body, (3) an area in which the body operates or is active, or (4) some other setting for the corporate body (other than the location of a conference). The geographic area may contain a country, state, local place, and so on. If the corporate body has a national profile or reach, the place should reflect the country in which it operates (e.g., India; U.S.); if it is a statewide or provincial body, the location should be at an appropriately matched level (e.g., Karnataka, India; Ohio; Ont.); if the body is a local organization or group, specific location information should be added (e.g., Bangalore, India; Toronto, Ont.). Local places (i.e., cities, towns, villages, etc.) may also be added to statewide or national bodies, if a conflict requires additional place names to break it. On occasion, a city section or neighborhood may be included in the place name.

If there is a change of name for the jurisdiction or local place, the cataloger should record the latest name in use during the corporate body's period of activity. The name of the earlier jurisdiction may be recorded in the authority data, if judged important. If the name of the place changes after the body is no longer functional, nothing in the metadata needs to change.

Corporate body: National Committee on the Status of Women
Place: India
Corporate body: National Committee on the Status of Women
Place: Kenya

Corporate body: Whig Party
Place: Md.
Corporate body: Whig Party
Place: Mass.

Corporate body: Washington Library
Place: Camden, N.J.
Corporate body: Washington Library
Place: Washington, D.C.

Corporate body: Eliot School
Place: Jamaica Plain, Boston, Mass.
Corporate body: Eliot School
Place: Portland, Or.

RDA 11.4 Date Associated with the Corporate Body (B)

The RDA element, *date associated with the corporate body*, does not reflect just a single concept, but actually entails several types of dates that may be encountered when establishing a corporate body's AAP and its accompanying authority data. This element may contain a date of establishment or termination, period of activity, or the date range for a conference. A date is an RDA Core element for conferences (see separate discussion of conferences below). For other corporate bodies, the element is core only if it is needed for disambiguation. In general, these dates may be taken from any source.

Dates are recorded in the calendar preferred by the cataloging agency. For information on the use of B.C. (before Christ) and A.D. (*anno Domini*, a Latin abbreviation for *in the year of the Lord*) in connection with dates, the cataloger should consult RDA appendix H. Date elements may be recorded as part of an AAP, part of the authority data, or both. In general, the form of date is simply the year (e.g., 1972) or a range of years (e.g., 1972-1981). If the year can only be estimated (i.e., the date is uncertain by several years), then the cataloger records the date preceded by the word *approximately* (e.g., approximately 1972). If a single date does not suffice to reflect the dates of activity, a range of dates is added in the form *yyyy-yyyy* or *century-century* (e.g., 1993-2005, 19th century-20th century).

A *date of establishment* is a date that a corporate body was founded or began. A *date of termination* is the date that a corporate body was dissolved, disbanded, or otherwise ended. This data may be recorded under any circumstances, but they are considered RDA Core only when they are necessary to distinguish between two or more corporate bodies.

Period of activity of the corporate body is a date or range of dates indicating the period in which the corporate body operated or is/was active. It is recorded when the dates of establishment and termination are both unknown. If specific years are unknown, centuries may be recorded instead.

> **Corporate body**: Book Publishers Bureau
> **Date of establishment**: 1938
> **Date of termination**: 1945
>
> **Corporate body**: Apollo [a vessel]
> **Period of activity**: 1970-1988

RDA 11.5 Associated Institution (B)

An *associated institution* is another organization or body related or connected to a corporate body being established. It is an RDA Core element for conferences if the associated institution provides better identification of the conference than does a geographic location (see separate discussion of conferences below). It is also considered core for other corporate bodies, if two or more bodies have the same name and the associated institution provides better identification than a geographic location. The information may be taken from any source, but it should be recorded using the preferred name for the institution.

> **Corporate body**: B'nai B'rith Hillel Foundation
> **Associated institution**: Brandeis University
>
> **Corporate body**: B'nai B'rith Hillel Foundation
> **Associated institution**: Brown University

RDA 11.7 Other Designations Associated with the Corporate Body (B)

This element is accompanied by sets of instructions for: (1) types of corporate bodies, (2) types of jurisdictions, and (3) other designations. The content for the element should contain a word, phrase, or term intended to indicate that the entity is a corporate body and to distinguish the body from other entities with the same name. For corporate bodies that have names that do not readily convey the idea of a corporate body (e.g., Creative Design; &Son), *other designation associated with the corporate body* is an RDA Core element. The designation is recorded in the language preferred by the cataloging agency, but if there is no term in that language, a term from the official language of the corporate body should be used.

Corporate body: 2 GRRRLS
Type: Firm

Corporate body: Civil Wars
Type: Musical group
Associated place: Nashville (Tenn.)

Corporate body: Apollo
Type: Frigate
Period of activity: 1799-1804
Associated place: Great Britain
Associated institution: Great Britain. Royal Navy

Corporate body: Apollo
Type: Frigate
Period of activity: 1970-1988
Associated place: Great Britain
Associated institution: Great Britain. Royal Navy

For a government body, the cataloger records the *type of jurisdiction* in the language preferred by the cataloging agency, but if there is no appropriate term in that language, then a term from the official language of the jurisdiction should be used. Using this instruction, the example used above in the section on place names would be transformed from Armagh (Northern Ireland) to Armagh (Northern Ireland : County).

Government body: Lippe
Type (in the language of the cataloging agency): Principality

Government body: Lippe (Germany)
Type (in the language of the jurisdiction): Kreis

If places, dates, associated institutions, types of bodies, and types of juris-dictions, are not enough to distinguish between the corporate bodies, the cata-loger must record another designation—one that is appropriate to distinguish between the bodies.

> **Government body**: Germany
>
> **Other designation**: East
>
> **Government body**: Germany
>
> **Other designation**: Territory under Allied occupation, 1945-1955
>
> **Government body**: Germany
>
> **Other designation**: West
>
> **Corporate body**: U.S. Open
>
> **Other designation**: Golf tournament
>
> **Corporate body**: U.S. Open
>
> **Other designation**: Tennis tournament

RDA 11.8 Language of the Corporate Body (S)

This element reflects the language used by the corporate body in resources associated with the body. The information may be taken from any source and recorded in the language preferred by the cataloging agency. Recommended best practice is to take the name of the language from a standard list of lan-guages (e.g., the MARC Code List for Languages, which is the preferred list for LC and PCC libraries for other RDA elements). If language is included, the source(s) should be documented in the *source consulted* element.

RDA 11.9 Address of the Corporate Body (S)

In RDA, *address* may refer to a physical headquarters' address, an email address, or an Internet address, such as a URL. The data element may be obtained from any source. If address is included, the source(s) should be doc-umented in the *source consulted* element.

> **Corporate body**: Liberty Mutual Insurance Company
>
> **Address**: 175 Berkeley Street, Boston, MA 02116
>
> **Corporate body**: Cardiff Metropolitan University
>
> **Address**: Cardiff, Wales
>
> **Address**: http://www3.cardiffmet.ac.uk

RDA 11.10 Field of Activity of the Corporate Body (S)

Field of activity documents a corporate body's area of engagement, respon-sibility, jurisdiction, or proficiency. The information may be taken from any source. If it is included, the source(s) should be documented in the *source consulted* element.

> **Corporate body**: Liberty Mutual Insurance Company
> **Field of activity**: Insurance

> **Corporate body**: Cardiff Metropolitan University
> **Field of activity**: Education, Higher

> **Corporate body**: Apollo
> **Type**: Frigate
> **Period of activity**: 1970-1988
> **Field of activity**: Warships

RDA 11.11 Corporate History (S)

This element contains a brief narrative describing historical information about the corporate body. It may come from any source; if it is included in the authority data, the source(s) should be documented in the *source consulted* element.

> **Corporate body**: Exxon Corporation

> **Corporate history**: The Standard Oil Company of New Jersey was incorporated in 1882. In 1892 its name was changed to Standard Oil Company. In 1972 the name Exxon Corporation was adopted. Works by this body published before the change of name in 1972 are found under Standard Oil Company. Works published after that change of name are found under Exxon Corporation. SUBJECT ENTRY: Works about this body are entered under the name used during the latest period covered. In the case where the required name is represented in this catalog only under a later form of the name, entry is made under the later form.

RDA 11.12 Identifier for the Corporate Body (S)

The *identifier for the corporate body*, an RDA Core element, is a unique character string associated with a body that differentiates that body from others. It may be taken from any source. The identifier may be associated with a surrogate for the corporate body, such as an authority record. When recording an identifier, RDA 11.12.1.3 indicates that a name or an identification of the agency should be included before the identifier (e.g., LCCN: n 79053084 or Library of Congress control number: n 79053084).

RDA 11.13 Creating Access Points for the Corporate Body

Controlled access points are names, terms, or codes identified in authority data, through which entities are searched and identified. These include both authorized access points (AAPs) and variant access points (VAPs). An AAP for a corporate body is based on the name that has been established as the preferred or authoritative one. VAPs include other names that were not chosen as preferred; in other words, a variant access point is a reference.

RDA 11.13.1.1 provides general guidelines for creating AAPs for corporate bodies. The basic instruction states that the AAP for a corporate body is based on the preferred name that is established using the guidelines at RDA 11.2.2: Preferred Name for the Corporate Body. The punctuation used in the examples follows the instructions in RDA appendix E: Record Syntaxes for Access Point Control.

> **Preferred name**: Apollo
>
> **Preferred name**: Eliot School
>
> **Preferred name**: B'nai B'rith Hillel Foundation
>
> **Preferred name**: U.S. Open
>
> **Preferred name**: Book Publishers Bureau

Qualifiers (i.e., additional data elements) are added to the name according to the instructions at RDA 11.13.1.2-11.13.1.8 and in that order. Seven types of additions or qualifiers (in the order of preference) are outlined in Table 7.7. If the name does not obviously indicate that the entity is a corporate body, then either *type of corporate body* or *other designation associated with the body* must be added to the AAP.

The LC-PCC PS for 11.13.1.1 states that if there is a conflict between two (or more) preferred names or AAPs, the cataloger should make an addition to each name, not just the one being established at the moment (i.e., add a qualifier

TABLE 7.7 Qualifiers Used with Corporate Bodies.

Qualifier	When to apply
Type of corporate body	The entity's name does not convey the notion of a corporate body, or in case of conflict
Place associated with the corporate body	In case of conflict
Associated institution	In case of conflict
Date associated with the corporate body	In case of conflict
Type of jurisdiction	In case of conflict
Other designations associated with the corporate body	The entity's name does not convey the notion of a corporate body, or in case of conflict
Number, date, and location of a conference	When the body is a conference, meeting, etc.

to the name that is already established). The LC-PCC PS uses an example to show how qualifiers might be added to resolve conflicts:

Arlington Development Center (Arlington, Tex.)

Independent non-government body

Arlington Development Center (Arlington, S.D.)

Government body belonging to the city of Arlington

Arlington Development Center (Infodata, Inc.)

Subordinate non-government body

Arlington Development Center (S.D.)

Government body belonging to the state of South Dakota

Type of corporate body should be added to the AAP if there is a conflict between names. It may also be added if the preferred names are not identical but are so similar that they may be confused (a determination that, obviously, depends on cataloger's judgment!).

AAP: 2 GRRRLS (Firm)

AAP: Civil Wars (Musical group)

AAP: Common Ground (Arts event)

The LC-PCC PS for RDA 11.13.1.2 discusses the approach by LC and PCC libraries to initials and acronyms, which is to always include a qualifier; this might entail adding the type of corporate body after the initialism or including the spelled-out version of the name as an *other designation associated with the body*.

A *place associated with the body* is added in cases of conflict. The cataloger adds the name of a geographic location at the country, state, province, or local level as appropriate.

AAP: National Committee on the Status of Women (India)

AAP: National Committee on the Status of Women (Kenya)

AAP: Whig Party (Mass.)

AAP: Whig Party (Md.)

AAP: Eliot School (Jamaica Plain, Boston, Mass.)

AAP: Eliot School (Portland, Or.)

An optional addition states that the name of a place may be added to the preferred name, even if there is no conflict, if it helps users identify the corporate body entity.

ICC11 PS for Optional Addition at 11.13.1.3 Place Associated with the Body: Use cataloger's judgment. If it seems useful for identification, add a place name even if there is no conflict.

If the body is a chapter or branch of a larger corporate body entity that is entered subordinately under the name of the higher body, but the name does not include a place name, the place name associated with that branch or chapter may be added to the name as a qualifier.

> **AAP with place added as qualifier**: Aleph Zadik Aleph. Nathan Henry Miller Lodge, Chapter 674 (Oakland, Calif.)
>
> **AAP with place as part of the name**: Aleph Zadik Aleph. Cleveland Chapter

For churches, temples, mosques, radio stations, or television stations that do not include a place name as part of the name, it may be added as a qualifier.

> **AAP**: Adina Mosque (Pandua, India)
>
> **AAP**: WDVM-TV (Television station : Washington, D.C.)

If the name of the place changes, use the latest name that was in use during the period in which the corporate body was operational. The LC-PCC PS at 11.13.1.3 instructs catalogers to update the AAP to reflect the later form of place name in the qualifier whenever appropriate. If *date associated with the body, name of an associated institution,* or another designation seems to be a better qualifier, the cataloger may choose to use one of those additions instead of a place name.

If there is a conflict, the name of an *associated institution* may be needed to disambiguate the two corporate body names. If the name of an associated institution is commonly connected to the body, it should be the preferred qualifier (rather than a local place name). An optional addition allows for associated institutions to be recorded at any time if it helps users identify the body.

> **AAP**: B'nai B'rith Hillel Foundation (Brandeis University)
>
> **AAP**: B'nai B'rith Hillel Foundation (Brown University)

Dates may be added as qualifiers to corporate body AAPs if there is a conflict and place and associated institution are not available or are not sufficient to distinguish between two or more bodies.

> **AAP**: Apollo (Frigate : 1799-1804)
>
> **AAP**: Apollo (Frigate : 1970-1988)

An optional addition allows the cataloger to include dates even if no conflict exists, if it is considered useful for identification purposes.

> **AAP**: Book Publishers Bureau (1938-1945)

Type of jurisdiction may be used to distinguish between two or more governments represented by a place name. In general, type of jurisdiction is not added for cities or towns; they receive the name of the immediately larger jurisdictions as their qualifiers. Type of jurisdiction is used to qualify larger jurisdictional place names or to address conflicts.

> **AAP**: Clinton (Ark.)
>
> **AAP**: Clinton (B.C.)
>
> **AAP**: Clinton (Butler County, Pa. : Township)
>
> **AAP**: Clinton (Lycoming County, Pa. : Township)
>
> **AAP**: New York (N.Y.)
>
> **AAP**: New York (State)
>
> **AAP**: New York (Colony)
>
> **AAP**: Lippe (Germany)
>
> **AAP**: Lippe (Germany : Kreis)
>
> **AAP**: Lippe (Principality)

If the additions mentioned in this section are not useful in distinguishing between the AAPs for two or more corporate body entities, then some other useful designation must be added. The cataloger must find a fitting designation. An optional addition allows the cataloger to include one of these *other designations* if it is useful for identification of or understanding the corporate body.

> **AAP**: Germany (East)
>
> **AAP**: Germany (Territory under Allied occupation, 1945-1955)
>
> **AAP**: Germany (West)
>
> **AAP**: U.S. Open (Golf tournament)
>
> **AAP**: U.S. Open (Tennis tournament)

Variant access points are based on the names that were not chosen as the preferred name for the corporate body. As is the case with persons and families, variations may include spelling differences, differences in language, differences in transliteration, and so on. Qualifiers may be added to the VAPs if they are needed for identification. The VAP may include qualifiers that are not needed in the authorized access point.

> **AAP**: Air Force Space Museum (U.S.)
>
> **VAP**: Cape Canaveral Air Force Station (Fla.). Air Force Space Museum

Names and Access Points for Conferences, Meetings, etc.

Conferences can provide a real challenge to new catalogers. At first, one might not even realize that conferences, meeting names, events, fairs, festivals, exhibitions, and the like are considered corporate bodies. For the time that a conference is running, that conference is a group or organization known by a particular name and it acts as a unit; it may also create works. This section of the text provides an overview of this unusual type of corporate body.

Despite some specific qualifiers or additional data elements, the process for establishing conference names is identical to that of other corporate bodies. The process begins by identifying the preferred and variant forms of name. Choosing the preferred form of name entails identifying the most commonly known name for the conference if the conference is known by more than one. The name is taken from the preferred sources of information on resources associated with the conference, other formal statements in the resources, or other sources, such as reference works. The instructions for recording the preferred name and choosing among different forms of the same name are identical to the instructions for any other corporate body (e.g., capitalization, numbers, spelling and language differences), but an exception for conferences is included. For a conference name, RDA 11.2.2.5.4 states that if there is more than one form of name used in the preferred source of information, the cataloger is to choose the form of name that includes the name of an associated or sponsoring body (in full or abbreviated form).

> **Preferred name**: Ada-Europe International Conference on Reliable Software Technologies
>
> **Variant name**: International Conference on Reliable Software Technologies

This instruction is not applied to a conference that has a name that is subordinate to the name of a corporate body associated with the conference. The cataloger goes to RDA 11.2.2.14.6 instead (see further discussion below).

> **Preferred name**: American Society for Reproductive Medicine. Annual Meeting
>
> **Variant name**: Annual Meeting of the American Society for Reproductive Medicine

If the conference has a specific name as well as a more general name as an on-going event, choose the specific name as the preferred name.

> **Preferred name**: KM 150
>
> **Variant name**: Kirkpatrick Macmillan 150
>
> **Variant name**: International Veteran Cycle Rally
>
> **Note**: KM150—to celebrate the 150th Anniversary of the invention of the pedal-driven bike by Kirkpatrick Macmillan in about 1840.

> **Preferred name**: Atomic-Scale Imaging of Surfaces and Interfaces
>
> **Variant name**: Materials Research Society. Fall Meeting

Another instruction specifically related to conferences is found at RDA 11.2.2.11: Number or Year of Convocation of a Conference, etc. This instruction states that if the name of a conference contains a year of convocation or the number of the conference, the cataloger is to omit the number or year from the preferred name. In previous practice, indications of the frequency (e.g., biennial, annual) were also omitted, but that is not required in RDA.

> **Preferred name**: Cold Spring Harbor Symposium on Quantitative Biology
>
> **Variant name on source**: 77th Cold Spring Harbor Symposium on Quantitative Biology, May 30-June 4, 2012
>
> **Preferred name**: Phytochemical Society of North America. Annual Meeting
>
> **Variant name on source**: Forty-first Annual Meeting of the Phytochemical Society of North America, Oklahoma City, Okla., Aug. 2001.

This does *not* mean the number and year of the conference will not be recorded elsewhere (i.e., as qualifiers for the name); they are simply not included as part of the preferred name. The last example above, therefore, would have these additional elements associated with it:

> **Preferred name**: Phytochemical Society of North America. Annual Meeting
>
> **Number**: 41st
>
> **Year**: 2001
>
> **Location**: Oklahoma City (Okla.)

RDA specifically discusses conferences again at RDA 11.2.2.14.6: Non-Governmental Body with Name That Includes the Entire Name of the Higher or Related Body, which states that if the corporate body is a non-governmental body, and the name contains the entirety of the superior body's name within it, then it should be entered subordinately under the name of the higher body. This applies to conference names as well. The LC-PCC PS for this instruction states, "if a named meeting contains the entire name of a [higher or superior] corporate body . . . treat the meeting subordinately to the authorized access point for the body if the name contains, in addition to the name of the body, no more than a generic term for the meeting or no more than a generic term plus one or more of the following elements: the venue of the meeting; number, date, or other sequencing element."[25]

> **Preferred name**: Astronomical Society of the Pacific. Annual Meeting
>
> **Other name on source**: 125th annual conference of the Astronomical Society of the Pacific, a conference held at San Jose State University, San Jose, California, USA, 20-24 July 2013

If the name, however, contains more than just generic designations, then the cataloger records a fuller name for the preferred name.

> **Preferred name**: Annual Northwestern University Vascular Symposium
>
> *not* Northwestern University. Vascular Symposium, Annual

Once the conference's preferred name has been established, other forms of the name may be recorded as variant names.

As with other corporate bodies, additional metadata about a conference may be recorded as part of its authority data. Place names, dates, associated institutions, and the number of the conference are the primary elements needed to supplement the name of the conference for the purpose of identification. These elements may be recorded as parts of the AAP for the conference, as separate metadata elements in the authority data, or both. In addition, some conferences, meetings, and the like may have names that do not convey the idea of a conference (e.g., a conference with a name comprising letters and/or numbers). In these cases, *type of corporate body* may be added to help users understand the nature of the entity.

> **Preferred name**: ABZ
>
> **Type of corporate body**: Conference
>
> **Variant name**: International Conference on Abstract State Machines, Alloy, B, VDM and Z

The instructions for places associated with a corporate body include guidelines for the RDA Core element *Location of conference, etc.* It contains the name of the local place where the conference was held and follows the basic instructions for recording place names found in RDA chapter 16. Because some conferences may be held in more than one place, more than one local place name may be recorded.

> **Conference name**: Columbia Conference on International Economic Development
>
> **Location of conference**: Williamsburg, Va.
>
> **Location of conference**: New York, N.Y.

An exception is provided in the instructions. It states that instead of recording the name of the local place, the cataloger can record the name of an associated institution, if the institution is better known or the local place name is not well known. In the following example, both associated institution and place are recorded in the authority data.

> **Conference name**: Tiananmen Conference
>
> **Associate institution**: Harvard University
>
> **Location of conference**: Cambridge (Mass.)

If the conference has been held online, then the cataloger records the term *Online* as the location.

> **Event name**: Global Development Goals and Linkages to Health and Sustainability
>
> **Type of corporate body**: Workshop
>
> **Location of conference**: Online

Date of Conference, etc. is another RDA Core element. It reflects the "date or range of dates on which a conference, congress, meeting, exhibition, fair, festival, etc. was held."[26] The basic instructions state that the cataloger records the year or years of the conference.

> **Conference name**: Conference on Medical Aspects of the Chernobyl Accident
>
> **Date of conference**: 1988
>
> **Location of conference**: Kiev, Ukraine

In some cases, however, more information can be included to specify the actual dates that a conference was held in the form *Year Month Day(s)* (e.g., 1984 September 12-13) with the month spelled out in the language of the cataloging agency. This level of specificity is included in rare cases when there is a need to distinguish between two or more conferences with the same name that were held in the same year.

An *associated institution* is another organization related or connected to a corporate body. It is an RDA Core element for conferences if the associated institution provides better identification of the conference than does a geographic location.

> **Conference name**: Symposium on Sex and Sexuality in Hispanic Film and Letters
>
> **Associated institution**: University of Pittsburgh

Number of a Conference, an RDA Core element, is a designation of a particular conference's place in the sequence of a series of conferences (e.g., 2nd, 31st, 102º). This data may be taken from any source, and it should be recorded as an ordinal number according to the preferences of the cataloging agency.

> **Conference name**: ABZ
>
> **Conference number**: 3rd
>
> **Date of conference**: 2012
>
> **Place of conference**: Pisa, Italy

With this data in hand, the cataloger can create an AAP for the conference. Two different types of conference access points can be established following the instructions in RDA: (1) access points for single instances of a conference and (2) access points for a series of ongoing conferences. The LC-PCC PS for 11.13.1.8 informs the cataloger:

> For ongoing conferences, separate authority records may be created for the collective conference [i.e., for the entire series of conferences, not an individual conference] (typically made when cataloging a serial), an individual instance of an ongoing conference (typically made when cataloging a monograph), or both. These records may coexist in the LC/NACO

authority file. A record for the collective conference should always be made to connect the earlier and later names of the collective conference.[27]

The instructions for access points for a single instance of a conference (RDA 11.13.1.8.1) address (1) one-time only conferences, (2) a single conference in a series of conferences, and (3) conferences that are recorded subordinately. For all these types, the cataloger adds three forms of qualifiers to the preferred name of the conference, if applicable, in the following order: the number of the conference, the date of the conference, and the location of the conference. The punctuation used in the examples adheres to the instructions in RDA appendix E: Record Syntaxes for Access Point Control.

The following are examples of single instances of continuing uniquely named conferences:

- Ada-Europe International Conference on Reliable Software Technologies (18th : 2013 : Berlin, Germany)
- KM 150 (Festival) (1990 : Drumlanrig Castle)
- Cold Spring Harbor Symposium on Quantitative Biology (77th : 2012 : Cold Spring Harbor, N.Y.)
- Annual Northwestern University Vascular Symposium (38th : 2013 : Chicago, Ill.)

The following are examples of single instances of continuing subordinately named conferences.

- American Society for Reproductive Medicine. Annual Meeting (69th : 2013 : Boston, Mass.)
- Phytochemical Society of North America. Annual Meeting (41st : 2001 : Oklahoma City, Okla.)
- Astronomical Society of the Pacific. Annual Meeting (125th : 2013 : San Jose, Calif.)

The following examples are of one-time-only conferences (i.e., not part of a continuing series of conferences):

- Atomic-Scale Imaging of Surfaces and Interfaces (Symposium) (1992 : Boston, Mass.)
- Conference on Medical Aspects of the Chernobyl Accident (1988 : Kiev, Ukraine)

The following examples illustrate single conferences that are not part of a continuing conference. They also illustrate the exception at RDA 11.13.1.8.1 that allows the cataloger to include the name of an associated institution, rather than a local place name, if it provides better identification or if the place name is unknown.

- Tiananmen Conference (2014 : Harvard University)
- Symposium on Sex and Sexuality in Hispanic Film and Letters (1991 : University of Pittsburgh)

This example is for a workshop that was held online.

- Global Development Goals and Linkages to Health and Sustainability (Workshop) (2012 : Online)

This example includes more than one place name in the qualifier.

- Columbia Conference on International Economic Development (1970 : Williamsburg, Va., and New York, N.Y.)

In addition to the records for single conferences and single instances of conferences, AAPs and accompanying authority data can be created for an entire series of conferences. In this case, no qualifiers are added to the preferred name for the conference.

- Ada-Europe International Conference on Reliable Software Technologies American
- Society for Reproductive Medicine. Annual Meeting
- International Veteran Cycle Rally
- Cold Spring Harbor Symposium on Quantitative Biology (Cold Spring Harbor, N.Y.)
- Phytochemical Society of North America. Annual Meeting
- Astronomical Society of the Pacific. Annual Meeting
- Annual Northwestern University Vascular Symposium

The final examples in this section illustrate a set of AAPs established for both the entire series of a conference and for each instance of the individual meetings.

- ABZ (Conference)
- ABZ (Conference) (1st : 2008 : London, England)
- ABZ (Conference) (2nd : 2010 : Orford, Québec)
- ABZ (Conference) (3rd : 2012 : Pisa, Italy)
- ABZ (Conference) (4th : 2014 : Toulouse, France)

CONCLUSION

This chapter has introduced the basics of authority data and access points for persons, families, corporate bodies, and places. It has reviewed the major elements that are used to identify those entities acting as creators, contributors, and others associated with resources. In the next chapter, issues related to relationships between resources and the FRBR Group 2 entities are addressed. Other forms of relationships (among works, among persons, etc.) are also addressed in the next chapter.

NOTES

1. *RDA: Resource Description & Access*, developed in a collaborative process led by the Joint Steering Committee for Development of RDA (Chicago: American Library Association, 2010). Also available through paid subscriptions to *RDA Toolkit* (Chicago: American Library Association, 2010), accessed July 28, 2015, http://www.rdatoolkit.org/. In lieu of page numbers, any references to specific parts of RDA are made using instruction numbers.
2. Arlene G. Taylor and Daniel N. Joudrey, *The Organization of Information* (Westport, Conn.: Libraries Unlimited, 2009), 245-301.
3. RDA, 8.1.3: Name.
4. Library of Congress, "LC-PCC PS for 8.3: Core Elements," in "Library of Congress-Program for Cooperative Cataloging Policy Statements (LC-PCC PS)" *RDA Toolkit: Resource Description & Access* (Chicago: American Library Association, 2010), accessed July 28, 2015, http://access.rdatoolkit.org/. Free access to the LC-PCC PS is available through the Resources tab. Copies of the LC-PCC PS are also available with a paid subscription in *Cataloger's Desktop*.
5. RDA, 8.13.1.1: Scope [for Making Cataloguer's Notes].
6. RDA, 9.2.2.1: Scope [for Preferred Name for the Person].
7. RDA, 9.2.2.7: Change of Name [Exception].
8. *Names of Persons: National Usages for Entry in Catalogues*, 4th revised and enlarged edition (München, Germany: K.G. Saur, 1996). Also available online via IFLA, http://www.ifla.org/files/assets/cataloguing/pubs/names-of-persons _1996.pdf.
9. RDA, 9.5.1.1: Scope [for Fuller Forms of Names].
10. Amber Billey, Emily Drabinski, and K. R. Roberto, "What's Gender Got to Do with It? A Critique of RDA 9.7," *Cataloging & Classification Quarterly* 52, no. 4 (2014): 412.
11. LC-PCC PS for 9.16.1.3: Recording Professions or Occupations; Library of Congress, "Z1: Name and Series Authority Records," *Descriptive Cataloging Manual*, prepared by the Policy and Standards Division, Library of Congress. (Washington, D.C.: Library of Congress, 2014), http://www.loc.gov/catdir/ cpso/dcmz1.pdf.
12. LC-PCC PS for 9.19.1.8: Other Designation: Alternative.
13. RDA, 10.2.2.4: Recording the Preferred Name.
14. RDA, 16.4: Constructing Access Points to Represent Places.
15. RDA, 16.2.2.1: Scope [for Preferred Name for the Place].
16. RDA, 11.2.2.6: Change of Name.
17. RDA, 11.0: Purpose and Scope [Identifying Corporate Bodies].
18. RDA, 11.2.2.1: Scope [for Preferred Name for the Corporate Body].
19. RDA, 11.2.2.5.4: Conventional Name.
20. Ibid.
21. LC-PCC PS for 11.2.2.6: Change of Name.
22. RDA, 11.2.2.10: Terms Indicating Incorporation and Certain Other Terms.
23. RDA, 11.2.2.15: Direct or Indirect Subdivision.
24. Ibid.
25. LC-PCC PS for 11.2.2.14.6: Non-governmental Bodies with Name That Includes the Entire Name of the Higher or Related Body.
26. RDA, 11.4.2: Scope [for Date of Conference, etc.].
27. LC-PCC PS for 11.13.1.8: Number, Date, and Location of a Conference, etc.

SUGGESTED READING

El-Sherbini, Magda. *RDA: Strategies for Implementation*. Chicago: American Library Association, 2013.

Hart, Amy. *RDA Made Simple: A Practical Guide to the New Cataloging Rules*. Santa Barbara, Calif.: Libraries Unlimited, 2014.

Kincy, Chamya Pompey, with Sara Shatford Layne. *Making the Move to RDA: A Self-Study Primer for Catalogers*. Lanham, Md.: Rowman & Littlefield, 2014.

Library of Congress. "Z1: Name And Series Authority Records," In *Descriptive Cataloging Manual*, prepared by the Policy and Standards Division, Library of Congress (Washington, D.C.: Library of Congress, 2014). http://www.loc.gov/catdir/cpso/dcmz1.pdf.

Maxwell, Robert L. *Maxwell's Handbook for RDA, Resource Description & Access: Explaining and Illustrating RDA: Resource Description and Access Using MARC21*. Chicago: American Library Association, 2013.

Mering, Margaret, ed. *The RDA Workbook: Learning the Basics of Resource Description and Access*. Santa Barbara, Calif.: Libraries Unlimited, 2014.

Oliver, Chris. *Introducing RDA: A Guide to the Basics*. Chicago: American Library Association, 2010.

Chapter 8

Relationships and the Use of Access Points

INTRODUCTION

In this chapter, the sections of RDA[1] that are useful in describing and recording relationships are discussed. Cataloging has always been concerned with relationships. There have always been creators, contributors, and other agents included in the bibliographic descriptions contained in catalogs. With a different content standard in place (i.e., RDA) that has two entity-relationship models as its underpinnings (i.e., FRBR and FRAD), it is of little surprise that more emphasis has been placed on identifying and recording relationships. RDA dedicates six of its 10 sections (or 21 of its 37 chapters) to relationships. At this point in time, however, little has changed in how these relationships are actually recorded in bibliographic data. Catalogers are still using access points and notes to indicate the relationships that exist among entities. In some cases, the type of relationship is identified only through the MAchine-Readable Cataloging (MARC) encoding typically used in today's cataloging environment, although some additional relationship indicators have been developed to bypass and/or supplement this approach.

One purpose of relationships in RDA is to link a resource to the important entities associated with it. For example, a typical record begins by describing a resource (i.e., a manifestation). The description includes links to entities associated with the resource, such as the creator or creators of the work; contributors to its expression; and any person, family, or corporate body (PFC) responsible for the intellectual or artistic content of the resource (i.e., those entities of bibliographic significance). These relationships are those primarily described in RDA section 6 (RDA chapters 19-22). A resource, according to the FRBR conceptual model, contains within it a work and an expression. In some cases, the relationship between the resource and the work and/or expression must be described (usually after the work has been expressed and manifested many times). These relationships are generally

---

Section 5: Recording Primary Relationships Between Work, Expression, Manifestation, & Item

17: General Guidelines on Recording Primary Relationships

Section 6: Recording Relationships to Persons, Families, & Corporate Bodies

18: General Guidelines on Recording Relationships to Persons, Families, and Corporate Bodies Associated with a Resource
19: Persons, Families, and Corporate Bodies Associated with a Work
20: Persons, Families, and Corporate Bodies Associated with an Expression
21: Persons, Families, and Corporate Bodies Associated with a Manifestation
22: Persons, Families, and Corporate Bodies Associated with an Item

Section 7: Recording Relationships to Concepts, Objects, Events, & Places

23: General Guidelines on Recording Relationships between Works and Subjects

Section 8: Recording Relationships between Works, Expressions, Manifestations, & Items

24: General Guidelines on Recording Relationships between Works, Expressions, Manifestations, and Items
25: Related Works
26: Related Expressions
27: Related Manifestations
28: Related Items

Section 9: Recording Relationships between Persons, Families, & Corporate Bodies

29: General Guidelines on Recording Relationships between Persons, Families, and Corporate Bodies
30: Related Persons
31: Related Families
32: Related Corporate Bodies

Section 10: Recording Relationships between Concepts, Objects, Events, & Places

[Currently empty]

Textbox 8.1 RDA Structure for Relationship Sections.

those found in RDA section 5 (RDA chapter 17). The resource also has subject relationships, but these are not yet fully addressed in RDA (a preliminary overview of subject relationships was added to RDA section 7 in April 2015). The bibliographic description contains links (i.e., access points) to PFCs, works, expressions, and subjects that formally establish these existing relationships.

Another purpose of relationships in RDA is to link entities to other related entities. In a typical authority record, connections among related entities are recorded in order to provide users with a greater understanding of the nature of the relationships that exist. For example, when describing a person, a cataloger typically includes links to other related persons or personae per the instructions in RDA section 9. When describing a work according to RDA section 8, a wide variety of relationships might be represented in the authority data (e.g., a derivative relationship). In Textbox 8.1 an overview of the relationship sections of RDA is provided.

RECORDING PRIMARY RELATIONSHIPS BETWEEN WORK, EXPRESSION, MANIFESTATION, & ITEM

RDA chapter 17 discusses the inherent, fundamental relationships found among the Group 1 entities: works, expressions, manifestations, and items (WEMI). Group 1 comprises the components of a bibliographic resource; it represents what is collected in libraries and other information institutions. The four entities are hierarchically connected, as can be seen in Figure 3.3 (p. 66), which illustrates their innate relationships. These are as follows: (1) a single work may be realized through one or more expressions (e.g., the content of a novel may be translated into many different languages); (2) one or more expressions may be embodied in one or more manifestations (e.g., a translated work and its original version may appear in a printed book together, and they may be distributed on microform or as an e-book as well); and (3) a manifestation is exemplified by one or more items (e.g., thousands of copies of the latest best-selling novel are published because more than one institution or person will purchase a copy).

The purpose of RDA chapter 17 is to ensure that the relationships between a resource and its work and expression(s) are clearly identified so that users are able to find (1) all resources that embody a particular work or expression and (2) all items that exemplify a particular manifestation. In RDA 17.0: Purpose and Scope, it states that in some cases, "for practical purposes, it is possible to declare a relationship . . . between a work and a manifestation with an implied expression. In such cases, the expression is understood to exist, but is not identified explicitly."[2] For most bibliographic descriptions, this approach could be taken easily, particularly for new resources, resources that have been disseminated only in one language (i.e., those that have never been translated), and resources expressed in only one form (e.g., as text).

In the United States, the Library of Congress (LC) believes that RDA chapter 17 is not implementable or necessary in today's cataloging environment.

This is made clear in the LC-PCC PS associated with RDA 17.0, which states: "*LC practice/PCC practice for Chapter 17*: Do not apply chapter 17 in the current implementation scenario."[3] This constraint is based on the use of the MARC bibliographic format for encoding cataloging data and on its duplication of content. Without going into great detail about MARC records (see instead chapters 9 and 21 of this text), the problems with implementing RDA chapter 17 are (1) no MARC fields have been established to contain these particular relationships and (2) the metadata, in many cases, is identical to metadata already found in the bibliographic description. For example, if a work has only been known by one title during its existence and it has been used as the title of each manifestation, then the work and the expression titles are redundant. As can be seen in the following example, the user does not need to see all of this information in the same record:

> **Creator**: Brown, Daniel, 1951-
>
> **Title of manifestation**: The boys in the boat
>
> **Title of work**: The boys in the boat
>
> **Title of expression**: The boys in the boat. English

As stated above, on a practical level the expression is often not needed, particularly if the resource embodies the original expression or if there is only one expression. The title of the work also is not always needed in the bibliographic description of the resource, particularly if the work and manifestation titles are identical. With the creator and the title of the manifestation included, all the metadata necessary to identify the FRBR Group 1 entities is already present. On the other hand, if the work and/or expression title is different, additional metadata becomes necessary. For example, it can be helpful to the user to see this information in a bibliographic record:

> **Creator**: Wilder, Thornton, 1897-1975
>
> **Title of manifestation**: Nuestra ciudad
>
> **Title of work and expression**: Our town. Spanish

There is, however, a mechanism in the MARC 21 bibliographic format for entering that work/expression title as a "uniform title" and an additional RDA data element is not necessary at this time. In other implementation scenarios (i.e., a non-MARC implementation), none of this may be applicable and RDA chapter 17 may be needed. Therefore, the content is reviewed in the next few pages of this chapter.

RDA chapter 17 identifies three different techniques that may be used to record primary relationships. These techniques center on the use of the following metadata components:

- **Identifiers**: As discussed in chapter 5 of this text, an *identifier* is a unique character string associated with a work, expression, manifestation, or item that differentiates it from other works, expressions, manifestations, and items. In theory, although not common in today's cataloging practice, it is possible to include an identifier in the bibliographic description to identify works, expressions, manifestations, and items. Identifiers might include URIs, authority record numbers, ISBNs, and so on.

- **Authorized access points (AAPs)**: AAPs may be established for some, but not all, works and expressions per the instructions in RDA chapter 6; they are not, however, created for manifestations or items (at least not yet). This approach is similar to what is done in today's cataloging practice—that is, adding MARC *main entry* and *uniform title* fields to a bibliographic record to represent the work (and sometimes the expression). This practice is fairly effective, at least in the MARC environment, because both components of a work/expression AAP— the creator's controlled name and the preferred title for the work—are present in the record, even if they are not combined into a single AAP. For a discussion of the MARC implementation of RDA, see chapter 9 of this text.

- **Composite description**: The third option is the composite description, which entails a "description that combines one or more elements identifying the work and/or expression embodied in a manifestation with the description of that manifestation."[4] This option shows similarities to the descriptions that can be created when using the *International Standard Bibliographic Description* (ISBD).[5] In other words, it is an amalgamation of metadata elements organized into a formal description. For more on ISBD, see chapter 23 of this text.

Elements for Primary Relationships among WEMI

The elements covered in RDA chapter 17 are listed in Table 8.1. As mentioned above, this RDA chapter has not been implemented in the United States at this time; consequently, the authors do not delve too deeply into the eight metadata elements presented in RDA chapter 17 beyond basic definitions and examples. The reader should consult RDA for more details on the elements as needed.

17.5 Expression of Work

An *expression of work* is "a realization of a work in the form of alphanumeric, musical or choreographic notation, sound, image, object, movement, etc., or any combination of such forms."[6]

> **Expression of work**: Hugo, Victor, 1802-1885. Notre-Dame de Paris. English

This element identifies the expression of a work contained in the resource. As the reader can see, it contains nothing more than an AAP for an expression that was created using the instructions in RDA chapter 6 (e.g., combining the creator's AAP, the preferred title of the work, and an expression-level

TABLE 8.1 Primary Relationships in RDA Chapter 17.

RDA instructions	Focal Entity	Explanation
17.5 Expression of Work	Expression	This is the expression of the work (with no indication of a particular manifestation).
17.6 Work Expressed	Work	This is the work being expressed (with no indication of a particular manifestation).
17.7 Manifestation of Work	Manifestation	This is the resource (i.e., manifestation) containing a particular work (but without reference to any particular expression).
17.8 Work Manifested	Work	This is the work found in a resource (but without reference to any particular expression).
17.9 Manifestation of Expression	Manifestation	This is the resource containing one or more expressions of a work.
17.10 Expression Manifested	Expression	This is the expression or expressions of a work found in a particular resource.
17.11 Exemplar of Manifestation	Item	This is an item that represents the manifestation.
17.12 Manifestation Exemplified	Manifestation	This is the manifestation represented by an individual item.

qualifier such as language). A difficulty in presenting this in today's MARC-based cataloging environment is that the data is separated into different fields. The AAP must be split apart until additional MARC fields are developed specifically to contain these elements or cataloging moves beyond the MARC environment in favor of something else (e.g., a linked data approach to bibliographic resources). The following is an example of how the components of the *expression of work* element are currently implemented in the MARC format.

> 100 1_ $a Hugo, Victor, $d 1802-1885.
>
> 240 10 $a Notre-Dame de Paris. $l English
>
> 245 14 $a The hunchback of Notre Dame / $c Victor Hugo ; translated by Walter J. Cobb ; with a new introduction by Bradley Stephens and an afterword by Graham Robb.

17.6 Work Expressed

The *work expressed* is the "work realized through an expression";[7] it is the work or works contained within the manifestation. It is different from *expression of work* in that *work expressed* is identifying which work is contained in a manifestation being described, but *expression of work* is identifying which expression of a work is being described. Again, an AAP is used, this time to identify the work. Similar to the previous element, the elements in the AAP are split apart in today's MARC-based catalog records.

Work expressed: Hugo, Victor, 1802-1885. Notre-Dame de Paris

17.7 Manifestation of Work

A *manifestation of work* is "a physical embodiment of an expression of a work."[8] It identifies the resource that contains a particular work. In the following example, the International Standard Book Number (ISBN) is used, because authorized access points are not created for manifestations.

Manifestation of work: ISBN: 9782895380009

A composite description could also be used to identify this element. This description is formatted using traditional ISBD order, punctuation, and spacing:

Manifestation of work: Notre-Dame de Paris / Victor Hugo ; introduction, notes et chronologie par Jacques Seebacher ; collection dirigée par Michel Simonin. — Paris : Librairie Générale Française, 1999.

In today's cataloging practices, the identifier used for the manifestation of the work is the same as the element found at RDA 2.15: *Identifier for the Manifestation*; there is no reason to enter it twice in the same record. A composite description would simply be the descriptive elements already used to describe the manifestation. In other words, elements such as title proper, statement of responsibility, publication location, publisher, and publication date do not need to be entered twice in the same record.

17.8 Work Manifested

A *work manifested* is the work or works found in a manifestation. Whereas *manifestation of work* identifies which resource contains a particular work, this element identifies which work is found in this resource. *Work manifested* is an RDA Core element, but only the primary or the first-named work in the resource is required. In very practical terms, this element is no different from the *work expressed* element, although the element definitions represent two different aspects of the primary relationships among the FRBR Group 1 entities (see the explanations in Table 8.1). Once again, in today's MARC-based cataloging, this element would be split into two different fields.

Work manifested: Hugo, Victor, 1802-1885. Notre-Dame de Paris

17.9 Manifestation of Expression

A *manifestation of expression* is "a physical embodiment of an expression."[9] It identifies the resource that contains a particular expression of a work. In the following example, the International Standard Book Number (ISBN) is used because authorized access points are not yet created for manifestations.

Manifestation of expression: ISBN: 9780451531513

A composite description could also be used to identify this element. This description is formatted using traditional ISBD order, punctuation, and spacing:

> **Manifestation of expression**: The hunchback of Notre Dame / Victor Hugo ; translated by Walter J. Cobb ; with a new introduction by Bradley Stephens and an afterword by Graham Robb. — New York : Signet Classics, c2010.

The same concerns about duplication that applied to the *manifestation of work* apply to this element as well.

17.10 Expression Manifested

An *expression manifested* is the expression(s) found in a manifestation. Whereas *manifestation of expression* identifies which resource contains a particular expression of a work, this element identifies which expression is found in a resource. *Expression manifested* is an RDA Core element if there is more than one expression in the manifestation; only the primary or the first expression in the resource is required. In very practical terms, this element is no different from the *expression of the work* element, although the element definitions represent two different aspects of the primary relationships among the FRBR Group 1 entities.

> **Expression manifested**: Hugo, Victor, 1802-1885. Notre-Dame de Paris. English

If more than one expression is included in a resource, more than one AAP would be necessary. For example, for a book that contains both an English and an Estonian translation of *The Hunchback of Notre Dame*, two instances of the relationship would be necessary.

> **Expression manifested**: Hugo, Victor, 1802-1885. Notre-Dame de Paris. English
>
> **Expression manifested**: Hugo, Victor, 1802-1885. Notre-Dame de Paris. Estonian

17.11 Exemplar of Manifestation

An *exemplar of manifestation* is a "single exemplar or instance of a manifestation."[10] In other words, it identifies an item that represents the manifestation. In most cases, a call number or a bar code suffices.

Exemplar of manifestation: PQ2288.A33 2010

17.12 Manifestation Exemplified

A *manifestation exemplified* is the manifestation represented by the item. Whereas *exemplar of manifestation* identifies "which item," this element identifies which manifestation this item is representing. A standard identifier, such as an ISBN, is appropriate for this element. Again, the data in this element does not look different from what is found in the *manifestation of work* and *manifestation of expression* elements, although conceptually the elements are quite different.

Manifestation exemplified: ISBN: 9780451531513

As mentioned already, the Library of Congress and PCC libraries have not implemented RDA chapter 17. That does not mean, however, that other libraries may not try to implement these elements or that these elements will not be implemented in the future. Readers should be attentive to any future changes regarding the implementation of RDA chapter 17.

RELATIONSHIPS BETWEEN PFCs AND THE GROUP 1 ENTITIES

RDA section 6 describes the types of relationships that may exist between PFCs and works, expressions, manifestations, and items. There is a chapter for each of the FRBR group 1 entities following the chapter of general guidelines for recording these relationships. Textbox 8.1 (at the beginning of this chapter) provides an overview of the structure of RDA section 6. It is in this section that the most common bibliographic relationships found in cataloging data begin to appear (i.e., creators and contributors).

RDA Chapter 18 General Guidelines

The general guidelines begin with an overview of the purpose and scope of the chapter: to discuss terminology used; to identify the principles and objectives associated with RDA section 6; to list the RDA core elements; to discuss the use of AAPs and identifiers to record relationships; to describe the use of relationship designators; and to discuss the role of notes. In general, the terminology introduced at the beginning of chapter 18 is already familiar from earlier RDA chapters:

- Person
- Family
- Corporate body
- Work

- Expression
- Manifestation
- Item
- Access point

The use of the term *resource* is, however, somewhat different in the context of the chapters in RDA section 6. Instead of referring to manifestations and items only (as the concept was defined in RDA chapter 1), now *resource* can refer to works and expressions also. One new term is introduced: *relationship designator*. A relationship designator is a device (i.e., a label, phrase, or term) that indicates the kind or type of relationship that exists between a PFC and a resource. The relationship designator provides context; it offers users additional information to help them understand the nature of the relationship being described. Relationship designators may be recorded with AAPs or with identifiers associated with PFCs. Lists of relationship designators are provided in RDA (in appendices I through M). Catalogers may choose one or more terms from these lists, or, if needed, they may supply terms of their own. The examples in this chapter include both RDA and cataloger-supplied relationship designators.

At RDA 0.6, two core elements are identified for RDA section 6: *creator* and *other person, family, or corporate body associated with a work*. If more than one creator is associated with a work, then only the principal or the first-named creator is required (whichever is appropriate). The second core element, *other person, family, or corporate body associated with a work*, is required only if the AAP for the work is to be built using the preferred name of a PFC performing a role other than that of a creator; an example of this is a defendant in a trial, whose name is a part of the AAP for the trial transcript. Each of the core elements is discussed further below.

RDA 18.4 identifies two methods of recording the relationship between a PFC and a resource: (1) through an identifier or (2) through an authorized access point; each of which may be followed by one or more relationship designators. If an identifier is to be used (which is not common practice today, as an access point is still the preferred method), then the cataloger is to follow specific instructions found in earlier chapters based on the type of Group 2 entity (for persons, the cataloger consults RDA 9.18; for families, RDA 10.10; for corporate bodies, RDA 11.12).

Creator (using identifier only): LCCN: no2005003010

As can be seen from the example above, it is not immediately clear to the human eye just who or what is responsible for the work if only an identifier is used to represent the creator. The LC-PCC PS for RDA 18.4.1.1: Identifier for the Person, Family, or Corporate Body states that catalogers should not use an identifier alone. This leads the authors of this text to infer that an identifier should be used only in conjunction with an authorized access point. In the near future, it may become common practice to enter identifiers into bibliographic descriptions instead of AAPs—with the idea being that the AAP or the name associated with the identifier can be automatically displayed for users as needed.

> **Creator (using AAP only)**: Songs: Ohia (Musical group)

As stated, contemporary cataloging practices involve the use of AAPs to identify the PFCs responsible for resources. The guidelines for using AAPs to represent a relationship also refer the cataloger to follow specific instructions found in earlier chapters based on the type of Group 2 entity (for persons, the cataloger consults RDA 9.19.1; for families, RDA 10.11.1; for corporate bodies, RDA 11.13.1).

RDA 18.5 Relationship Designators

As stated above, a *relationship designator* is a device (i.e., a label, phrase, or term) that indicates the kind or type of relationship. The designators are used to indicate the specific function(s) performed by a PFC in relation to a resource. Although there has been little use of relationship designators over the past several decades, they are not a new idea. Before the *Anglo-American Cataloguing Rules*, 2nd edition (AACR2)[11] were implemented in 1981, relationship designators were used extensively. Although relationship designators *were* included in AACR2 as optional additions, the Library of Congress discouraged their use (save for a few small exceptions). Also, in the MARC format, a particular subfield ($4) for relator codes has been available for decades to indicate the role played by a PFC associated with a resource. This MARC feature has not necessarily been used extensively, but it has been available.

In RDA, the practice of indicating the role or relationship of a PFC to a resource has now been codified in the cataloging guidelines. It must be noted, however, that relationship designators are not considered RDA Core elements, and thus their inclusion in a bibliographic description is still determined by individual catalogers or cataloging agencies. In other words, they may or may not be included despite the following instruction: "Record a relationship designator to indicate the specific function performed by a person, family, or corporate body in relation to the resource."[12]

Information about the nature of the relationship may be taken from any source. The general instruction states that following the AAP or the identifier for the PFC, the cataloger is to record one or more of the relationship designators found in RDA appendix I. As many designators as necessary may be used if more than one role is performed by the PFC. If none of the terms in the appendix are appropriate, the cataloger can use a term that specifically and concisely summarizes the nature of the relationship.

> **AAP for creator**: Sun Kil Moon (Musical group)
> **Relationship designators**: composer, performer
>
> **AAP for others associated with a work**: Buck, Chris
> **Relationship designators**: film director, screenwriter.
>
> **AAP for contributor**: Menzel, Idina
> **Relationship designator**: voice actor

At the time of this writing, there are 25 relationship designators for creators, 32 for others associated with a work, 58 for contributors, and 29 for relationships between PFCs and manifestations or items. Following RDA 18.5, there is an instruction stating that if more explanation of the relationship is needed, notes may be used to expand on the relationship designators used.

RELATIONSHIPS BETWEEN PFCs AND WORKS

According to RDA, creation relationships occur *only* at the work level. This is in accordance with the defined relationships outlined in the FRBR and FRAD conceptual models. RDA clearly states that at the work level, Group 2 entities only fill two particular roles: *Creator* and *Other Person, Family, or Corporate Body Associated with a Work* (henceforth known as *Others* in this chapter of ICC11). These two categories of relationships that exist between works and PFCs are specifically addressed in RDA chapter 19.

According to the general guidelines at RDA 19.1, catalogers should record information about the relationships between PFCs and works based on what is found in the preferred sources of information in resources containing the work. If the information found there is unclear, the cataloger may consult (in order of preference) the following:

1. other statements appearing prominently in the resources
2. information appearing only in the content of the resources (e.g., the text of a book, the sound content of an audio recording)
3. other sources[13]

RDA 19.2 Creator

Creator, an RDA Core element, is a PFC responsible for making, generating, or originating a creative or intellectual work. This may be an author, an artist, a choreographer, a musician, a composer, an architect, a cartographer, an enacting jurisdiction, a programmer, and so on. A work may have more than one responsible party involved in its creation, but according to RDA 19.2, only one creator is required in the bibliographic description. Creators who are jointly responsible for a work may perform the same activity (e.g., three authors writing together) or different activities (e.g., a musician and a visual artist working on an art installation). In general, the single *required* creator would be the most appropriate of the following:

- the creator with principal responsibility
- the first-named creator, if principal responsibility is shared with other creators
- the first-named creator, if principal responsibility is unclear

Principal responsibility is not always readily evident when examining a collaboratively created resource; so, having the instruction to record the first-named creator in those cases is practical and timesaving, even if it may seem a bit arbitrary.

Just because RDA states that only one creator is required that does not mean that catalogers will follow that suggestion. Unless the number of creators is large and burdensome, it is likely that catalogers will record *all* creators, especially now that catalogers are free from the shackles of the so-called *rule of three* that appeared in earlier cataloging rules, which restricted the number of creators recorded. An LC-PCC PS states that additional creators may be included based on cataloger's judgment.

> **ICC11 PS for 19.2 Creator**: Record the names of all PFCs involved in the creation of the work, if the number is not burdensome. Always include the name of the first creator.
> If the number of creators is 20 or greater, or if the number of creators is restricted by local policy, be thoughtful as to which creators are included.

At RDA 19.2.1.1, after defining *creator*, the scope statement offers a few descriptions of two less common types of creators. First mentioned are *creators of compilations*. In some cases, a PFC may create a new work through the activities of selecting, arranging, and aggregating, and sometimes soliciting individual works to be included in a compilation. The cataloger must judge whether a compilation represents a new work, and thus the compiler performed an act of creation, or whether the compiler's functions were centered on gathering and editing activities (which do not reflect a creator's role, but instead suggest the undertakings of an editor). When a compilation is considered a new work, the compiler is treated as its creator (rather than as a contributor). Also mentioned are *creators of revised works*. In some cases, a PFC may create a new work through the revision of a previously existing resource. The cataloger must determine whether the modifications to the revised resource are substantial enough to be considered a new work or just a new expression of the original work. When the revisions are substantial (e.g., an extensively revised textbook), then the reviser is considered this new work's creator. As discussed in chapters 3 and 6 of this text, determining whether a resource contains a new work or simply a new expression of an existing work can be challenging, and it may be dependent on cataloger's judgment.

RDA 19.2.1.1.1 *Corporate Bodies Considered to Be Creators*

Another type of creator discussed extensively is the corporate body creator. Historically, there has been much angst expressed about whether a corporate body can write or author (i.e., create) a work, or is it only persons who can create (at the time, families were not considered to be creators). Even though persons constitute corporate bodies, some in the international cataloging community opposed acknowledging any form of corporate body authorship. The debate was settled in previous sets of cataloging rules by limiting the notion of corporate body creation to only a small list of categories of works that reasonably could be generated by corporate bodies (e.g., annual reports, legislation, church documents). Similar restrictions continue in the RDA guidelines for the types of situations when a corporate body can be a considered a creator. Corporate bodies are treated as creators only when they are responsible for

TABLE 8.2 Categories of Works for Which Corporate Bodies May Be Deemed to be Creators.

Types of Works that can be Entered Under Corporate Bodies	Examples
a. Works that deal with the body itself in terms of management, administration, and internal functioning	Administrative reports, policy or procedure manuals, reports on finances or operations, directories of members or staff, catalogs of the body's resources, etc.
b. Works that address the body's views or official pronouncements on external matters (as opposed to internal matters, which are the focus of the first category)	Reports of commissions, working groups, committees, etc.; standards developed for particular issues or activities; etc.
c. Works containing hearings conducted by government bodies or other corporate bodies	Legislative hearings, judicial hearings, executive body hearings, etc.
d. Works of a collective nature that report on the activities of conferences, expeditions, or events	Expedition reports, conference proceedings, collected papers from an event, etc.
e. Works—in the form of sound recordings, films, video recordings, or written records of performances—resulting from the collective activity of a performing group in which the responsibility of the group for the existence of the work is more than a just a performance or execution of a previously existing script, score, etc.	Improvised jazz performances, improvisational comedy performances, sound recordings where the musical group is responsible for the composition as well as the performance, etc.
f. Works of a cartographic nature for which the body does more than merely publish or distribute the work	An atlas of maps created by a corporate body
g. Certain legal works	Laws, decrees, bills, and other forms of legislation, regulations, constitutions, charters, judicial documents and decisions, etc.
h. An art work created by two or more collaborating artists acting as a named group or entity	A named work of art created by an art collective, etc.

creating or issuing works that fall into one or more of the eight categories listed in Table 8.2.

In general, for a corporate body to be considered a creator, it must be responsible for the intellectual or artistic content of the work. If, for example, the corporate body is only responsible for publishing and/or distribution, it does not support a case for identifying the corporate body as the creator. It should also be remembered that at RDA 6.27.1.3 an exception reminds catalogers that if one or more corporate bodies and one or more persons or families are responsible for creating a collaborative work, and that work falls within the categories listed at RDA 19.2.1.1.1, then the corporate body is to be treated as the primary creator of the work rather than the person(s) or family(s). Additional guidance in applying the instructions is provided in the LC-PCC PS for RDA 19.2.1.1.1.

Other Creators

RDA also provides instructions on two other types of creators:

- **Government and Religious Officials**: The cataloger should consider religious and governmental leaders (chief executives, heads of state, popes, bishops, etc.) to be creators of works, if those works are considered official communications (e.g., decrees, executive orders, declarations, bulls, orders) from the offices they represent.

- **Persons or Families Considered to be Creators of Serials**: If they are responsible for the entire serial rather than just a particular issue or volume, a person or family may be considered the serial's creator. A person or a family is generally not identified as the creator of a serial, but it must be considered in cases where any of the following are applicable:

  ◦ a personal or family name appears in the title

  ◦ a person or family is the publisher

  ◦ the serial contains content based on personal opinions or observations

  ◦ no others appear to be involved in the creation of the serial

  In case of doubt, the cataloger should not consider a person or a family to be the creator of the serial.

RDA 19.2.1.3 Recording Creators

The instruction in RDA for recording creators is straightforward. It says: "Record a creator by applying the general guidelines on recording relationships to persons, families, and corporate bodies associated with a resource (see 18.4)."[14] Consulting RDA 18.4, the cataloger finds the instructions for recording the relationship between the PFC and the resource through the use of either identifiers (which, at this time, is not standard practice) or authorized access points (a long-standing practice). Both methods allow for the inclusion of one or more relationship designators. The rest of RDA 19.2.1.3 entails numerous lists of examples representing a variety of situations one may encounter when choosing, identifying, and recording creators. It should be noted that creators are not only recorded in bibliographic records, but also in the AAPs for works and expressions (see chapter 6 of this text for more information). Because some readers who may be new to cataloging may struggle with choosing creators, the flowchart in Table 8.3 is offered to help clarify the process.

TABLE 8.3 Choosing Creators.

A Flowchart for Recording Creators		
1. Is the creator of the work unknown?	**Yes**	Then go to #2.
	No	Then go to #3.
2. Do reference sources suggest a *probable* creator(s) for the work?	**Yes**	Then go to #3.
	No	Then a creator access point is not required in the bibliographic description/record.
3. Is there a single person, family, or corporate body identified with having lone responsibility for the work?	**Yes**	Then that PFC is identified as the sole creator of the work. The AAP for the creator is required in the bibliographic description/record.
	No	Then it is a collaborative effort; go to #4.
4. Does the collaboration involve one or more corporate body creators (even if there is also a person or a family)?	**Yes**	Then the AAP for the corporate body with principal responsibility (or the first-named body) is recorded as the creator—*if* work falls within the categories at RDA 19.2.1.1.1. If those instructions do *not* apply, then go to #5.
	No	Then go to #5.
5. Has sole principal responsibility been indicated for the collaborative work?	**Yes**	Then that PFC is identified as the primary creator of the work. The AAP for the primary creator is required in the bibliographic description/record; other creators are included based on cataloger's judgment.
	No	Then go to #6.
6. Are two or more PFCs represented as having principal responsibility for the work?	**Yes**	Then the AAP of the *first-named* creator is required in the bibliographic description/record; other creators are included based on cataloger's judgment.
	No	Then go to #7.

7. Are there two or more PFCs involved in the creation of the work, but none is identified as having principal responsibility?	**Yes**	Then the AAP of the *first-named* creator is required in the bibliographic description/record; other creators are included based on cataloger's judgment.
	No	Then go to #8.
8. Is the work a compilation with the works of multiple creators included?	**Yes**	Then go to #9.
	No	Start again in the flowchart *or* review the instructions in RDA carefully for an appropriate instruction that fits the situation.
9. Is there a collective title?	**Yes**	Then a creator access point is not required. Consider including name/title AAPs for each work in the compilation.
	No	Although there is no primary creator, construct name/title AAPs for each work in the compilation.

The examples provided below are indicative of the categories of examples found in RDA. Some ISBD punctuation has been added to the title and statements of responsibility for clarity.

- **One Person Responsible for the Creation of the Work**

   Title and Statement of responsibility (SOR): Cold mountain / Charles Frazier

   Creator AAP: Frazier, Charles

   Relationship designator: [Not recorded]

   Title and SOR: Morning phase / Beck

   Creator AAP: Beck

   Relationship designators: composer, performer

   Title and SOR: The adventures of Huckleberry Finn / by Samuel L. Clemens

   Creator AAP: Twain, Mark, 1835-1910

   Relationship designator: author

   Note: Samuel Clemens is the real name of the author known as Mark Twain

- **One Family Responsible for the Creation of the Work**

  Title and SOR: Warmed by the hearthstone / the Moran family and friends

  Creator AAP: Moran (Family : Cloone, Ireland)

  Relationship designator: [Not recorded]

  Title and SOR: Correspondance des Borgia : lettres et documents choisis / préfacés et traduits de l'italien, du catalan et du latin par Guy Le Thiec

  Creator AAP: Borgia (Family : active 14th century-18th century)

  Relationship designator: author

- **Two or More Persons, Families, or Corporate Bodies Responsible for the Creation of the Work Performing the Same Role**

  Title and SOR: Systems analysis for librarians and information professionals / Larry N. Osborne, Margaret Nakamura

  Creator AAP: Osborne, Larry N.

  Relationship designator: [Not recorded]

  Creator AAP: Nakamura, Margaret

  Relationship designator: [Not recorded]

  Title and SOR: Cheek to cheek / Tony Bennett & Lady Gaga

  Creator AAP: Bennett, Tony, 1926-

  Relationship designator: singer

  Creator AAP: Lady Gaga

  Relationship designator: singer

  Title and SOR: Toasts! : the perfect words to celebrate every occasion / [compiled] by June Cotner and Nancy Tupper Ling

  Creator AAP: Cotner, June, 1950-

  Relationship designator: compiler

  Creator AAP: Tupper Ling, Nancy

  Relationship designator: compiler

- **Two or More Persons, Families, or Corporate Bodies Responsible for the Creation of the Work Performing Different Roles**

  Title and SOR: Legion of Super-Heroes. Enemy manifest / Jim Shooter, writer ; Francis Manapul, penciller

  Creator AAP: Shooter, Jim

  Relationship designator: [Not recorded]

  Creator AAP: Manapul, Francis

  Relationship designator: [Not recorded]

Title and SOR: Hedwig and the Angry Inch : original Broadway cast recording / music and lyrics by Stephen Trask ; book by John Cameron Mitchell

Creator AAP: Trask, Stephen

Relationship designators: composer, lyricist

Creator AAP: Mitchell, John Cameron

Relationship designator: librettist

- **Persons, Families, or Corporate Bodies Responsible for Creating a New Work Based on a Previously Existing Work**

    Title and SOR: Introduction to cataloging and classification / Daniel N. Joudrey, Arlene G. Taylor, and David P. Miller

    Creator AAP: Joudrey, Daniel N.

    Relationship designator: author

    Creator AAP: Taylor, Arlene G., 1941-

    Relationship designator: author

    Creator AAP: Miller, David P. (David Peter), 1955-

    Relationship designator: author

In addition, RDA provides examples for each of the categories allowing for corporate body creators. The following additional examples illustrate the categories:

- **Works of an Administrative Nature**

    Title: Personnel directory, March 15, 1946

    Creator AAP: United States. Radio Research Laboratory, Harvard University

    Relationship designators: compiler, publisher

- **Works Recording the Collective Thought of the Body**

    Title and SOR: State Party report on the state of conservation of the Great Barrier Reef World Heritage Area (Australia) / Australian Government

    Creator AAP: Australia. Department of the Environment

    Relationship designator: author

- **Works Recording Hearings Conducted by Legislative, Judicial, Governmental, and Other Bodies**

    Title and SOR: 2012 accountability hearing with the Nursing and Midwifery Council : Government and Nursing and Midwifery Council responses to the Committee's ninth report of session 2012-13 : third special report of session 2013-14 / Health Committee

    Creator AAP: Great Britain. Parliament. House of Commons. Health Committee

    Relationship designator: [Not recorded]

- **Works Reporting the Collective Activity of a Conference, Expedition, or Event**

  Title and SOR: Fifth UNESCO/WMO International Conference on Hydrology : final report (Geneva, 8-12 February 1999) / United Nations Educational, Scientific and Cultural Organization ; World Meteorological Organization

  Creator AAP: International Conference on Hydrology (5th : 1999 : Geneva, Switzerland)

  Relationship designator: [Not recorded]

  Creator AAP: Unesco

  Relationship designator: sponsor

  Creator AAP: World Meteorological Organization

  Relationship designator: sponsor

- **Works Resulting from the Collective Activity of a Performing Group**

  Title and SOR: Benji / Sun Kil Moon

  Creator: Sun Kil Moon (Musical group)

  Relationship designators: composer, performer

- **Cartographic Works Originating with a Corporate Body Responsible for More than Just Publication or Distribution**

  Title: Sawtooth National Forest firewood map : for personal use firewood permits : Minidoka Ranger District

  Creator AAP: United States. Forest Service

  Relationship designator: cartographer

- **Various legal works, including:**
  - **Laws of a Political Jurisdiction**
  - **Decrees of a Head of State, Chief Executive, or Ruling Executive Body**
  - **Bills and Drafts of Legislation**
  - **Administrative Regulations, etc.**
  - **Constitutions, Charters, etc.**
  - **Court Rules**
  - **Charges to Juries, Indictments, Court Proceedings, and Court Decisions**

    Title: An Act to Authorize the Peace Corps Commemorative Foundation to Establish a Commemorative Work in the District of Columbia and Its Environs, and for Other Purposes

    Creator AAP: United States

    Relationship designator: enacting jurisdiction

- **Individual Works of Art by Two or More Artists Acting as a Corporate Body**

  Title and SOR: 4 × 4 screens / Wrights & Sites ; conceived and edited by Stephen Hodge

  Creator AAP: Wrights & Sites

  Note: Wrights & Sites are Stephen Hodge, Simon Persighetti, Phil Smith and Cathy Turner

- **Official Communications**

  Title: An alternative plan for locality pay increases : communication from the President of the United States transmitting an alternative plan for locality pay increase payable to civilian federal employees covered by the General Schedule (GS) and certain other pay systems in January 2013, pursuant to 5 U.S.C. 5305(a)(3)

  Creator AAP: United States. President (2009- : Obama)

  Relationship designator: author

RDA 19.3 Other Person, Family, or Corporate Body Associated with a Work

In addition to the creator relationship that might exist between a PFC and a work, RDA does acknowledge that Group 2 entities might play other roles in relation to a work. These roles can be generically described as *Others*, but RDA does provide some specific examples in the instructions at RDA 19.3; it also provides a list of these other roles in RDA appendix I. This element represents a PFC associated with a work in a non-creator role. This may include, for example, the following:

- PFCs to whom a collection of correspondence is addressed
- PFCs honored by festschrifts
- directors, cinematographers, producers, productions companies, etc., working on motion pictures, televisions programs, audio recordings, radio programs, etc.
- sponsoring bodies for events, research, reports, and so on
- institutions hosting events, exhibitions, conferences, and the like

Others are recorded in the bibliographic description if they are helpful for identification and access. It should be noted that others associated with a work are not only recorded in bibliographic records, but also in the authority records for works (see chapter 6 of this text). In addition to the general category of *Others*, RDA provides two specific sub-categories with their own sets of guidelines: (1) *Other Person, Family, or Corporate Body Associated with Legal Works* and (2) *Other Person, Family, or Corporate Body Associated with a Religious*

Specific Types of *Others* Associated with Works

19.3.2 Other PFCs Associated with Legal Works

19.3.2.1   Application
19.3.2.2   Jurisdiction Governed by a Law, Regulation, etc.
19.3.2.3   Issuing Agency or Agent
19.3.2.4   Court Governed by Rules
19.3.2.5   Body Governed by a Constitution, etc.
19.3.2.6   Person or Corporate Body Prosecuted in a Criminal Trial, etc.
19.3.2.7   Person or Corporate Body Indicted
19.3.2.8   Person or Corporate Body Bringing the Action in Noncriminal Proceedings
19.3.2.9   Person or Corporate Body on the Opposing Side in Noncriminal Proceedings
19.3.2.10 Judge
19.3.2.11 Parties to a Case
19.3.2.12 Lawyer Representing a Party
19.3.2.13 Participants in a Treaty

19.3.3 Other PFCs Associated with a Religious Work

19.3.3.1   Application
19.3.3.2   Denominational Body Associated with a Creed, etc.
19.3.3.3   Church or Denominational Body Associated with a Liturgical Work
19.3.3.4   Body within a Church, etc., Associated with a Liturgical Work

---

Textbox 8.2 Sub-instructions Regarding Legal and Religious Works Under RDA 19.3.2 and 19.3.3.

Work. Both are RDA Core-if elements. The reader should consult RDA 19.3.2 and 19.3.3 for more information as needed. Textbox 8.2 provides a list of the instructions found under these two elements.

RELATIONSHIPS BETWEEN PFCs AND EXPRESSIONS

According to RDA chapter 20, the relationship between a PFC and an expression is a *contributor* relationship. Contributors help to realize an expression of a work—sometimes in the original creation of the work and sometimes in later expressions of the work with supplementary content (e.g., illustrations, commentary) that was not present in the original expression. Among many others, typical contributor roles include the following:

- Abridgers
- Actors
- Animators
- Arrangers
- Conductors
- Dancers
- Editors
- Illustrators
- Musicians

- Narrators
- Puppeteers
- Production designers
- Singers
- Stage directors
- Surveyors
- Translators
- Writers of supplementary textual content (afterword, preface, introduction, etc.)

In accordance with the general guidelines at RDA 20.1, catalogers should record information about the relationships between PFCs and expressions based on what is found in the preferred sources of information in resources containing the expression. If the information found there is unclear, the cataloger may consult (in order of preference) the following:

1. other statements appearing prominently in the resources
2. information appearing only in the content of the resources (e.g., the text of a book, the sound content of an audio recording)
3. other sources[15]

If a resource contains more than one expression of a work and different PFCs are associated with different expressions, then the cataloger should record the contributors associated with each expression found in the resource. Contributors are recorded according to the general guideline for recording relationships (RDA 18.4).

The examples provided below are indicative of some of the contributor types found in RDA. Some ISBD punctuation has been added to the title and statements of responsibility for clarity.

- **Editor**

    Title and SOR: A new companion to Victorian literature and culture / edited by Herbert F. Tucker

    Contributor AAP: Tucker, Herbert F.

    Relationship designator: editor

    Title and SOR: Peter Orlovsky, a life in words : intimate chronicles of a beat writer / Peter Orlovsky, edited by Bill Morgan

    Creator AAP: Orlovsky, Peter, 1933-2010

    Relationship designator: author

    Contributor AAP: Morgan, Bill, 1949-

    Relationship designator: editor

- **Writer of Added Commentary, etc.**

   Title and SOR: Centrado en Jesús / Marcos Baker ; prólogo por César García

   Creator AAP: Baker, Mark D. (Mark David), 1957-

   Relationship designator: author

   Contributor AAP: García, César, 1972-

   Relationship designator: author of foreword

   Title and SOR: Canadian federal budget

   Creator AAP: Canada. Department of Finance

   Relationship designator: [Not recorded]

   Contributor AAP: Stikeman, Elliott (Firm)

   Relationship designator: writer of added commentary

   Title and SOR: Freycinet National Park : map & notes / TASMAP ; produced by Information and Land Services, Department of Primary Industries, Parks, Water and Environment

   Creator AAP: TASMAP

   Relationship designator: cartographer

   Others AAP: Tasmania. Department of Primary Industries, Parks, Water and Environment. Information and Land Services

   Relationship designator: issuing body

   Contributor AAP: Tasmania. Parks and Wildlife Service

   Relationship designator: writer of added text

- **Illustrator**

   Title and SOR: Alice's adventures in Wonderland / by Lewis Carroll ; illustrations by John Tenniel

   Creator AAP: Carroll, Lewis, 1832-1898

   Relationship designator: [Not recorded]

   Contributor AAP: Tenniel, John, 1820-1914

   Relationship designator: illustrator

   Title and SOR: Bad Kitty drawn to trouble / Nick Bruel

   Creator AAP: Bruel, Nick

   Relationship designators: author, illustrator

   Contributor AAP: [Not applicable]

- **Translator**

   Title and SOR: The seagull / by Anton Chekhov ; translated and with an introduction by Stephen Mulrine

   Creator AAP: Chekhov, Anton Pavlovich, 1860-1904

   Relationship designator: author

Contributor AAP: Mulrine, Stephen

Relationship designator: translator

• **Arranger, Performer, and Other Types of Contributors**

Title and SOR: Kubic's monk / music composed by Thelonious Monk ; arrangements by Pierrick Pédron Trio and Vincent Artaud

Creator AAP: Monk, Thelonious

Relationship designator: composer

Contributor AAP: Artaud, Vincent, 1970-

Relationship designator: arranger of music

Contributor AAP: Pierrick Pédron Trio

Relationship designators: arranger of music, performer

Title and SOR: The big chill / Columbia Pictures presents a Carson Productions Group, Ltd. production of a Lawrence Kasdan film ; written by Lawrence Kasdan & Barbara Benedek ; directed by Lawrence Kasdan . . .

Contributor AAP: Kasdan, Lawrence, 1949-

Relationship designators: screenwriter, film director

Contributor AAP: Benedek, Barbara

Relationship designator: screenwriter

Contributor AAP: Columbia Pictures Corporation

Relationship designator: production company

Contributor AAP: Carson Productions

Relationship designator: production company

Contributor AAP: Berenger, Tom, 1950-

Relationship designator: actor

Contributor AAP: Close, Glenn, 1947-

Relationship designator: actor

Contributor AAP: Goldblum, Jeff, 1952-

Relationship designator: actor

RELATIONSHIPS BETWEEN PFCs AND MANIFESTATIONS/ITEMS

RDA chapters 21 and 22 provide instructions for recording the relationships that exist between PFCs and manifestations and items. RDA suggests that the cataloger may record the relationships identified in these chapters in the form of access points or unique identifiers (see discussion of RDA 18.4 above). This, however, is not standard practice in today's cataloging environment. In the description of rare, unique, or non-print materials, these relationships may be considered important for identification and, thus, recorded as part of the description. In general practice, though, these relationships are typically reflected only as part of the transcribed descriptive data created for a resource (see the chapters in RDA section 1), rather than as authorized access points. Until standard cataloging practice begins to create separate AAPs for publishers and their staff members, distributors, manufacturers, producers of unpublished resources, owners and custodians of items, and other PFCs associated with manifestations or items, the authors advise readers to consult these chapters and their examples only as needed.

> **ICC11 PS for RDA Chapters 21 and 22**: Until standard cataloging practices change to either: (1) include access points for those PFCs responsible for manifestations and items or (2) evolve to more adequately reflect entity-relationship models, do not apply the instructions in RDA chapters 21 and 22. Instead record publishers, distributors, manufacturers, producers, etc., in the appropriate elements in the bibliographic description (e.g., publications statements, custodial history of item).

RELATIONSHIPS AMONG GROUP 1 ENTITIES

Section 8 of RDA is labeled "Recording Relationships between Works, Expressions, Manifestations, & Items." In addition to chapter 24, which discusses general guidelines, there are short individual chapters in RDA on related works, related expressions, related manifestations, and related items. Each of these chapters is discussed in turn below. The instructions provided in these chapters may be applied to bibliographic descriptions, authority data, or both.

RDA Chapter 24 General Guidelines

The general guidelines in RDA chapter 24 begin with an overview of the purpose and scope of the chapter: to discuss terminology used; to identify the principles and objectives associated with RDA section 8; to discuss the use of AAPs, identifiers, and descriptions to record relationships; to describe the use of relationship designators; to provide instructions on numbering of parts within works; and to provide instructions on including citations and notes about relationships in the authority data. In general, the terminology listed in RDA chapter 24 is already familiar from earlier chapters of this text:

- Work
- Expression
- Manifestation
- Item
- Access point
- Relationship designator

TABLE 8.4 Definitions and Examples of Basic Relationships Among the Group 1 Entities.

Type	Definition	Examples
Related work	another work that is connected in some way to the work being described	a sequel, a supplement, a complement, an adaptation, etc.
Related expression	another expression that is connected in some form to the expression being described	an abridgement, a revision, a translation, etc.
Related manifestation	another manifestation that is connected in some form to the manifestation being described	a reproduction, a reprint, a simultaneously released edition, etc.
Related item	another item that is connected in some form to the item being described	a reconfiguration, a micro-reproduction, etc.

Although the terms in Table 8.4 (*Related work*, *Related expression*, *Related manifestation*, and *Related item*) are already somewhat familiar to readers of this text from its discussion of the FRBR conceptual model in ICC11 chapter 3, RDA only now in chapter 24 introduces these concepts. In chapters 25-28, these relationship concepts are addressed in turn.

The functional objectives and principles in this RDA section concern the need to enable users (1) to find related WEMI entities when they retrieve a resource and (2) to understand the nature of the relationships that exist. The cataloger is instructed that the data created should reflect all significant bibliographic relationships that exist among Group 1 entities. There are, however, no core elements identified in RDA section 8.

RDA 24.4 identifies three methods of recording the relationship between a resource and a related WEMI entity: (1) through an identifier for any of the four entities, (2) through an authorized access point for a work or an expression only, or (3) through a description of any of the four types of related entities. All three methods may be used in combination with one or more relationship designators. If an identifier is to be used, then the cataloger is instructed to follow specific instructions found in earlier chapters based on the particular type of Group 1 entity (for works, the cataloger consults RDA 6.8; for expressions, RDA 6.13; for manifestations, RDA 2.5; and for items, RDA 2.19).

> **Work identifier**: LCCN: n 98092274
>
> **Manifestation identifier**: ISBN 9781849462426

The LC-PCC PS for 24.4.1: Identifier for the Related Work, Expression, Manifestation, or Item states that the cataloger should not use an identifier alone.

This leads the authors of this text to infer that an identifier should be used only in conjunction with an AAP or a description.

Common long-standing cataloging practice is to use an AAP to identify related works and expressions. The guidelines for using AAPs to represent a relationship also refer the cataloger to specific instructions found in earlier chapters based on the type of entity (for works, the cataloger consults RDA 6.27.1-6.27.2; for expressions, RDA 6.27.3). An AAP cannot be used to identify a related manifestation or a related item because the process of creating authority data (which leads to the establishment of an AAP) is not performed at the manifestation and item levels.

> **Work AAP**: Leonardo, da Vinci, 1452-1519. Mona Lisa
>
> **Expression AAP**: Albright, Rosie. Pig detectives. Spanish

The third approach is to provide a structured or an unstructured description of the related resource. A *structured description* is "a full or partial description of the related resource using the same data that would be recorded in RDA elements for a description of that related resource."[16] RDA states that the cataloger should present structured descriptions in the order specified by a recognized display standard, such as ISBD.

> **Related manifestation**: *Reprint of*. The whole life nutrition cookbook / Alissa Segersten, Tom Malterre. Bellingham, WA : Whole Life Press, [2008]
>
> **Related manifestation (partial description)**: *Reprint of*. 3rd. ed. — New York : McGraw-Hill, [1970]

An *unstructured description* is a note that includes a full or partial description of the related resource.

> **Related manifestation**: *Facsimile of*. Lettres de Monsieur Le Marquis de Montcalm, Gouverneur-General en Canada, a messieurs de Berryer & de la Molé, ecrites dans les Années 1757, 1758, & 1759 avec une version Angloise
>
> **Related manifestation (partial description)**: Reprint of the original edition published in 1999 by Frances Lincoln

As stated above, a *relationship designator* is a device (i.e., a label, phrase, or term) that indicates the kind or type of relationship that exists. In RDA section 8, this refers to relationships between a resource and another related resource. They may be used with AAPs, identifiers, or descriptions of related resources. It must be noted, however, that relationship designators are not considered RDA Core, and thus their inclusion in a bibliographic description is still determined by individual catalogers or cataloging agencies. In other words, they may or may not be included despite an instruction to "Record an appropriate term . . . to indicate the specific nature of the relationship between related works, expressions, manifestations, or items."[17] In the RDA examples of relationship designators for related works, expressions, manifestations, and items, the designators are presented in italics in front of the AAP, identifier, or structured description.

A list of relationship designators for related works, expressions, manifestations, or items is found in RDA appendix J. The general instruction states that along with an AAP, an identifier, or a structured description for the related resource, the cataloger records one or more relationship designators. With an unstructured description, however, the cataloger is to include information about the nature of the relationship as part of the description. As many relationship designators as necessary may be used. If none of the terms in RDA appendix J are appropriate, the cataloger can record as a designator a term that specifically and concisely summarizes the nature of the relationship.

> **Title and SOR**: The little mermaid / produced by Howard Ashman, John Musker ; written and directed by John Musker, Ron Clements
>
> **AAP for related work**: *Motion picture adaptation of (work)*: Andersen, H. C. (Hans Christian), 1805-1875. Little mermaid
>
> **Title and SOR**: Hamlet II : Ophelia's revenge : a novel / by David Bergantino
>
> **Unstructured description (with indication of relationship)**: Based on the tragedy of Hamlet, Prince of Denmark by William Shakespeare

At the time of this writing, there are approximately 150 relationship designators for related works (including separate lists for derivative, whole-part, accompanying, and sequential relationships). There are about the same number of relationships listed for related expressions (using the same categories as related works). There are approximately 25 for related manifestations and approximately 20 for related items (both groups are divided into categories based on equivalent, whole-part, and accompanying relationships).

RDA 24.6 addresses *numbering of part*, which is "a designation of the sequencing of a part or parts within a larger work. Numbering of part may include: (a) a numeral, a letter, any other character, or a combination of these (with or without a caption (volume, number, etc.)) and/or (b) a chronological designation."[18] This topic is typically related to series, although it may be applied to any type of resource divided into numbered parts. The reason this topic appears in RDA section 8 is because it reflects whole-part relationships within a series. Numbering is recorded as it is found on the preferred sources of information, while applying the instructions for numbers found in RDA 1.8. Abbreviations from RDA appendix B may be used in association with the numbering of parts. An LC-PCC PS reminds catalogers that the Library of Congress no longer creates controlled access points or performs authority work for series, and that the PCC considers these activities optional. The policy statement, however, provides additional information on numbering issues for libraries that are still performing these activities. These issues include: how to record numbering that is grammatically connected to a series title; how to record series numbering when more than one system of numbering is present; how to address numbering errors; how to record numbers preceded by one or more letters; and so on. For more information about creating and revising MARC-based series authority records, please see "Z1: Name and Series Authority Records" in LC's *Descriptive Cataloging Manual*.[19]

When information about relationships between resources is described as part of authority data (e.g., identifying an original source when the work being described is an adaptation), additional information must be included besides the related work and its relationship designator. *Source consulted* and *cataloguer's notes* are included to clarify the relationship and to justify its inclusion in the record. *Source consulted*, an LC-PCC Core element, refers to any source of information consulted while the cataloger performed the authority work. Each resource that is consulted during the process is cited as a source. This process provides documentation demonstrating that the cataloger/authority control librarian performed the necessary steps to make decisions about the access point, references, and additional authority data elements. The basic instruction is to cite the sources used when establishing the relationship; this includes sources that provide useful information, and also sources that may contain no information about the relationship at all.

In addition to the documentation already discussed, other notes in authority data are needed. In RDA, a *cataloguer's note* is "an annotation that might be helpful to those using or revising the relationship data, or creating an authorized access point representing a related work or expression."[20] These notes perform a variety of functions:

- justifying or clarifying the reasons for choosing the preferred name or title in the AAP or a particular form of the name or title
- explaining limits on the use of access points
- helping to differentiate between entities with similar names/titles
- citing the instruction used to create the data
- providing any other information that might be useful to users (including other catalogers)

> **AAP for work**: Adams, Douglas, 1952-2001. Hitchhiker's guide to the galaxy (Novel)
>
> **AAP for related work**: *Novelization of (work):* Adams, Douglas, 1952-2001. Hitchhiker's guide to the galaxy (Radio plays)
>
> **Source consulted**: The hitchhiker's guide to the galaxy : the original radio scripts, 2003, Kindle edition, via Amazon.com, viewed on April 28, 2014 . . .
>
> **Source consulted**: Wikipedia, April 28, 2014: The Hitchhiker's Guide to the Galaxy (novel) (The Hitchhiker's Guide to the Galaxy is the first of five books in the Hitchhiker's Guide to the Galaxy comedy science fiction "trilogy" by Douglas Adams [with the sixth written by Eoin Colfer]. The novel is an adaptation of the first four parts of Adams' radio series of the same name . . .
>
> **AAP for work**: Kapp, Richard. Teddy and Alice
>
> **AAP for related work**: *Based on (work):* Sousa, John Philip, 1854-1932. Works. Selections
>
> **Source consulted**: Philharmonia Virtuosi of New York. Sousa for orchestra [SR] p1989: label (Teddy and Alice; musical) container

(music by John Philip Sousa; adaptations and original music by Richard Kapp; lyrics by Hal Hackady) insert ([Richard Kapp] was asked to exhume works from Sousa's repertoire that might serve as the score of a new musical to be based on the special relationship of Theodore Roosevelt and his daughter, Alice; adaptation; some songs were retained intact; others were new songs)

Cataloguer's note: Consider an adaptation of works by John Philip Sousa

RDA Chapters 25-26 Related Works and Expressions

In descriptive cataloging, the terms *related work* and *related expression* may be used to describe a variety of more specific relationships. These terms encompass all the FRBR work-to-work, work-to-expression, and expression-to-expression relationships. Readers are advised to review these relationships, outlined in chapter 3 of this text, before proceeding in this chapter. These relationships include, but are not limited to sequels, continuations, supplements, complementary works, summarizations, paraphrases, adaptations, transformations (dramatizations, novelizations, screenplays, etc.), parodies, translations, arrangements, revisions, and abridgements. These relationships may also entail whole-part relationships, such as a work within a series (another work) or individual works found within a compilation or a collection. The parameters of related works and expressions are not specifically defined in RDA other than to say that a *related work* is "a work, represented by an identifier, an authorized access point, or a description, that is related to the work being described (e.g., an adaptation, commentary, supplement, sequel, part of a larger work)."[21] The related expression definition is almost identical. It says that a *related expression* is "an expression, represented by an identifier, an authorized access point, or a description, that is related to the expression being described (e.g., a revised version, a translation)."[22]

The LC-PCC policy statements indicate that for compilations, *related work* is an LC Core element and that *related expression* is an LC-PCC Core element. The LC-PCC PS for RDA 25.1 (*related work*) enumerates some specific LC practices regarding compilations. It states that the cataloger is to enumerate the works contained within the compilation as contents notes, unless these works appear elsewhere in the description (e.g., in a title element). There are no limitations on the number of works that may be listed as contents notes, unless the number is "burdensome." LC practice also calls for an AAP for the predominant or first work in the compilation if that work represents a considerable portion of the resource. In short, LC catalogers are not required to create access points for each work held within a compilation.

The application of LC-PCC PS 25.1 is slightly different for PCC libraries. It begins by stating that the cataloger should give "complete" contents notes, unless the number of works is burdensome or they appear elsewhere in the description. It recommends an AAP for the predominant work in the collection, but also suggests the possibility of additional AAPs for works other than the predominant or first work, if considered important for access. Additionally, this LC-PCC PS states that *related work* is a core element for serials when there is a *continues* or *continued by* relationship (e.g., the journal *American Documentation* was continued by the *Journal of the American Society for Information Science*).[23] Furthermore, it states that if the work is a commentary, the cataloger should include an AAP for the related work being commented upon. LC does not consider *related work* core for anthologies of poetry, hymnals, conference proceedings, most journals, collections of interviews or letters, and similar resources.

The LC-PCC PS for RDA 26.1 states that *related expression* is considered core for compilations for both LC and PCC libraries. It addresses situations in which more than one expression might be found in a compilation. When the original expression and one translation appear in a resource, the cataloger is to include AAPs for each expression in the bibliographic description. If more than one translation is included, only an AAP for one of the translations is required, but others may be included based on cataloger's judgment.

According to LC and PCC practices, formal contents notes entail recording the titles proper and the statements of responsibility for the works contained within the compilation. Prefatory materials are generally omitted from the contents notes, as are chapter and section numbers. Works are recorded with a space-dash-space between them to demarcate one work from another. If the resource is manifested in more than one volume, volume designations should also be included among the chapters.

> **ICC11 PS for 25.1 Related Work**: Create contents notes for all works found in compilations in all cases. A listing of works is often available electronically from publishers and electronic retailers; copy and paste as much as possible. If some of the works are already established in the authority file, include their AAPs in the bibliographic description. For those that are not yet established, create AAPs and accompanying authority data for each work if the number is not extensive. If the number is burdensome, create AAPs and authority data as time and resources permit.

RDA chapters 25 and 26 provide numerous examples using identifiers, AAPs, structured descriptions, and unstructured descriptions. As identifiers are not yet commonly used in contemporary cataloging practice to indicate related works and expressions, the examples in this text focus instead on the use of AAPs and descriptions of both varieties.

• **Using Structured Descriptions**

> **Title and SOR**: Robot uprisings / edited by Daniel H. Wilson and John Joseph Adams
>
> **Contents notes (structured description)**: Complex God / Scott Sigler — Cycles / Charles Yu — Lullaby / Anna North — Eighty miles an hour all the way to Paradise / Genevieve Valentine — Executable / Hugh Howey — The omnibot incident / Ernest Cline — Epoch / Cory Doctorow — Human intelligence / Jeff Abbott — The

golden hour / Julianna Baggott — Sleepover / Alastair Reynolds — Seasoning / Alan Dean Foster — Nanonauts! in battle with tiny death-subs! / Ian McDonald — Of dying heroes and death-less deeds / Robin Wasserman — The robot and the baby / John McCarthy — We are all misfit toys in the aftermath of the velveteen war / Seanan McGuire — Spider the artist / Nnedi Okorafor — Small things / Daniel H. Wilson

AAPs for related works: [Not recorded]

Title and SOR: Diagnostic imaging. Cardiovascular / Suhny Abbara [and 14 others]

Edition statement: Second edition

Structured description of expression: *Revision of:* Diagnostic imaging. Cardiovascular. Salt Lake City, Utah : Amirsys, 2008

- **Using Structured Descriptions and AAPs**

  Title and SOR: Seven famous Greek plays / edited with introductions by Whitney J. Oates and Eugene O'Neill, Jr.

  Contents notes (structured description): Prometheus bound / Aeschylus ; translated by P.E. More — Agamemnon / Aeschylus ; translated by E.D.A. Morshead — Oedipus the king / Sophocles ; translated by R.C. Jebb — Antigone / Sophocles ; translated by R.C. Jebb — Alcestis / Euripides ; translated by R. Aldington — Medea / Euripides ; translated by E.P. Coleridge — The frogs / Aristophanes ; translated by G. Murray

  AAP for work & expression: Aeschylus. Prometheus bound. English (More)

  AAP for work & expression: Aeschylus. Agamemnon. English (Morshead)

  AAP for work & expression: Sophocles. Oedipus Rex. English (Jebb)

  AAP for work & expression: Sophocles. Antigone. English (Jebb)

  AAP for work & expression: Euripides. Alcestis. English (Aldington)

  AAP for work & expression: Euripides. Medea. English (Coleridge)

  AAP for work & expression: Aristophanes. Frogs. English (Murray)

  Title and SOR: Introduction to cataloging and classification / Arlene G. Taylor ; with the assistance of David P. Miller

  Structured description: *Revised edition of:* Wynar's introduction to cataloging and classification. Revised 9th edition. 2004

> **AAP for related expression**: Taylor, Arlene G., 1941- Wynar's introduction to cataloging and classification

- **Using AAPs**

  Title and SOR: Tarzan / Walt Disney Pictures, Edgar Rice Burroughs . . .

  AAP for related work: *Motion picture adaptation of (work):* Burroughs, Edgar Rice, 1875-1950. Tarzan of the apes

  AAP in work authority record: Alcott, Louisa May, 1832-1888. Little women

  AAP for related work: *Sequel:* Alcott, Louisa May, 1832-1888. Little men

  AAP for related work: *Adapted as motion picture (work):* Little women (Motion picture : 1933)

  AAP for related work: *Adapted as musical theatre (work):* Wolf, Beatrice, 1931- Little women

  AAP for related work: *Adapted as opera (work):* Adamo, Mark. Little women

  AAP for related work: *Dramatized as (work):* De Forest, Marian, 1864-1935. Little women

  AAP in expression authority record: Miller, Raine. Blackstone affair. Spanish

  VAP for expression: Miller, Raine. Affaire Blackstone

  AAP for related expression: *Translation of:* Miller, Raine. Blackstone affair

- **Using Unstructured Descriptions**

  Title and SOR: China online : locating society in online spaces / edited by Peter Marolt and David Kurt Herold

  Unstructured description: The book is a sequel to the editors' earlier work, Online Society in China (Routledge, 2011)

  Title and SOR: Baudelaire's revenge / Bob van Laerhoven ; translated from the Dutch by Brian Doyle

  Unstructured description of expression: *Translation of:* De wraak van Baudelaire

- **Using Unstructured Descriptions and AAPs**

  Title and SOR: Moonrise kingdom : original screenplay / by Wes Anderson & Roman Coppola

  Unstructured description: Screenplay for the motion picture Moonrise Kingdom

  AAP for related work: Moonrise kingdom (Motion picture)

Title and SOR: Report / Scottish Plant Breeding Station

Unstructured description: *Continues*: Scottish Plant Breeding Station. Annual report. *Continued by*: Scottish Plant Breeding Station. Record

AAP for earlier related work: Scottish Plant Breeding Station. Annual report

AAP for later related work: Scottish Plant Breeding Station. Record

Title and SOR: Khrushchev in power : unfinished reforms, 1961-1964 / Sergei Khrushchev ; translated by George Shriver

Unstructured description for expression: Translation of the first volume of the author's trilogy, "Nikita Khrushchev"

AAP for original expression: *Translation of (work):* Krushchev, Sergei. Nikita Khrushchev, volume 1

Following the examples, RDA 25.2 introduces a new element, *explanation of relationship*, which is a statement that is recorded in an authority record to elaborate on or further clarify the relationships among related works or related expressions. These types of explanatory statements are presented to other catalogers, but may also be shown to users of the catalog as general references.

AAP in work authority record: Blake, William, 1757-1827. Songs of innocence

AAP for related work: Blake, William, 1757-1827. Songs of innocence and of experience

Explanation of relationship: When *Songs of innocence* is published together with *Songs of experience* under the title *Songs of innocence and of experience*, use that as a collective title. If they appear without the collective title, treat them as separate works

RDA Chapters 27-28 Related Manifestations and Items

These chapters contain information about related manifestations and items. Both elements, *related manifestation* and *related item*, are considered core elements for reproductions (e.g., reprints, republications, facsimiles, micro-reproductions). *Related manifestation* is considered LC-PCC Core, while *related item* is LC Core only (and only when it is considered important to identify exactly which item was reproduced as a related item). A related manifestation or item generally addresses issues related to resources available in more than one form. Some examples include the following:

- a book and a book-on-tape containing the same work and expression
- a print and online version of a serial
- a web-based reproduction of a pamphlet and the original
- a PDF and the print-version of a document
- a moving image resource released as a streaming video and as a DVD

- a map and its reproduction
- a rare book and its reprint
- the individual components of a kit, a multipart resource, or a set of resources (e.g., posters, slides, volumes)
- an autographed still image and a reproduction of it
- four individual pieces of sheet music that have been bound together by a library
- a finding aid for an archival collection that is in both paper and electronic forms

As is the case with related works and expressions, related manifestations and items can be represented using different methods. In this case, they may be denoted by structured descriptions, unstructured descriptions, or identifiers; authorized access points are not used, as mentioned several times previously.

- **Structured descriptions**

   Title of manifestation and SOR: A history of the Inquisition of the Middle Ages / by Henry Charles Lea

   Related manifestation: *Facsimile reprint of:* Harper & Brothers ed., published in New York, 1887

   Title of manifestation and SOR: The whole life nutrition cookbook : over 300 delicious whole foods recipes, including gluten-free, dairy-free, soy-free, and egg-free dishes / Alissa Segersten and Tom Malterre

   Dissemination information: New York : Grand Central Life & Style, 2014

   Related manifestation: *Reprint of:* The whole life nutrition cookbook / Alissa Segersten, Tom Malterre. — Bellingham, WA : Whole Life Press, [2008]

   Title of manifestation: The art of Julian Bream

   Related manifestation: *Reproduction of (manifestation):* Bream, Julian. The art of Julian Bream. New York : RCA Victor, [1960]

   Title of manifestation and SOR: Bubalus antiquus / par A. Pomel

   Carrier of manifestation: 1 online resource (94 pages, 10 leaves)

   Dissemination information: Electronic reproduction. Chicago : University of Chicago Library, [2014]

   Related manifestation: *Print version:* Pomel, Nicolas Auguste, 1821-1898. Bubalus antiquus. Alger : Impr. P. Fontana et cie, 1893

- **Unstructured description**

   Title of manifestation: Let's square dance!

   Carrier of manifestation: 5 audio discs

   Sound characteristics of manifestation: analog, 33 1/3 rpm, mono

Related manifestation: Also issued as 78-rpm albums E-3000--E-3004 and as 45-rpm sets EEB-3000--EEB-3004

Title of manifestation and SOR: Molecular control of vertebrate limb development / Lee Ann Niswander

Carrier of manifestation: 1 videocassette

Related manifestation: Also issued as an audio cassette

Title of manifestation and SOR: A history of Old Gilead Church House, 1860-1960 / Eugenia Blakey Hayes

Related item: *Bound with*: Green River Baptist Church minutes, 1803-1827. Bound together subsequent to publication

- **Identifier**

Title of manifestation and SOR: Breek vry! : 5 maniere om struikelblokke te oorkom vir 'n buitengewone lewe / Joel Osteen

Related manifestation: *Also issued online:* ISBN 9781415320983 (ePub), ISBN 9781415320990 (PDF)

Title of manifestation and SOR: What garden pest or disease is that? : organic and chemical solutions for every garden problem / Judy McMaugh

Publication statement: Miller's Point, NSW : Lansdowne, 1994

Related manifestation: *New Holland reprint:* ISBN 1864366990

The reader should consult RDA chapters 27 and 28 and accompanying LC-PCC PSs for more information on and examples of related manifestations and items.

RELATIONSHIPS AMONG GROUP 2 ENTITIES

Section 9 of RDA is labeled "Recording Relationships between Persons, Families, & Corporate Bodies." In addition to RDA chapter 29, which discusses general guidelines, there are short individual chapters on related persons, related families, and related corporate bodies. Each of these chapters is discussed in turn. The instructions provided in these chapters are typically applied to authority data rather than to bibliographic descriptions.

The general guidelines in RDA chapter 29 begin with an overview of the scope of the chapter: to discuss terminology used; to identify the principles and objectives associated with RDA section 9; to discuss core elements; to discuss the use of AAPs and identifiers to record relationships; to describe the use of relationship designators; and to discuss notes used to clarify and justify relationships included in the authority data. In general, the terminology listed is already familiar from earlier RDA chapters:

- Person
- Family
- Corporate body
- Access point
- Authorized access point
- Relationship designator

TABLE 8.5 Definitions and Examples of Basic Relationships Among the Group 2 Entities.

Type	Definition	Examples
Related person	a person who is connected in some form to the PFC being identified in the authority data	two separate identities associated with a person, a person who is part of a performing group or a family, etc.
Related family	a family that is connected in some form to the PFC being identified in the authority data	a family who founded a corporate body, a family with a famous progenitor, etc.
Related corporate body	a corporate body that is connected in some form to the PFC being identified in the authority data	a comedy troupe to which a person belongs, a company with which another company has merged, etc.

The terms *related person*, *related family*, and *related corporate body* are introduced. Their meanings, listed in Table 8.5, are fairly self-evident.

The functional objectives and principles in this RDA section concern the need to enable users (1) to find PFCs related to persons, families, or corporate bodies represented in the data they retrieve and (2) to understand the nature of the relationships that exist among PFCs. The cataloger is instructed that the data created should reflect all significant relationships that exist among Group 2 entities. There are, however, no core elements identified in RDA section 9.

RDA 29.4 identifies two methods of recording the relationship between related PFCs: (1) through an identifier or (2) through an authorized access point; both of which are followed by one or more relationship designators. If an identifier is to be used, which is not common practice today, then the cataloger is instructed to follow specific instructions found in earlier chapters based on the type of Group 2 entity (for persons, the cataloger consults RDA 9.18; for families, RDA 10.10; for corporate bodies, RDA 11.12).

Related person (using identifier only): LCCN: n 2003080230

As can be seen from this example, it is not immediately clear to the human eye just who or what the related entity is if only an identifier is used to represent it. The LC-PCC PS for 28.4.1: Identifier for the Related Person, Family, or Corporate Body states that the cataloger should not use an identifier alone. This leads the authors to infer that an identifier should be used only in conjunction with an authorized access point.

Common long-standing cataloging practice is to use an AAP to identify related PFCs. The guidelines for using AAPs to represent a related PFC also refer the cataloger to follow specific instructions found in earlier chapters based on the type of Group 2 entity (for persons, the cataloger consults RDA 9.19.1; for families, RDA 10.11.1; for corporate bodies, RDA 11.13.1).

Related person (using AAP only): *Group member:* Kozelek, Mark

As previously stated, a *relationship designator* is a device (i.e., a label, phrase, or term) that indicates the kind or type of relationship that exists. In RDA section 9, this refers to relationships between a PFC and another related PFC. Designators may be used with AAPs or identifiers. It must be noted, however, that relationship designators are not considered RDA Core, and thus their inclusion in a bibliographic description is still determined by individual catalogers or cataloging agencies. In other words, they may or may not be included despite an instruction to "Record an appropriate term . . . to indicate the specific nature of the relationship between related persons, families, or corporate bodies."[24] In the examples that follow, relationship designators for related PFCs are presented in italics in front of the AAP. Identifiers are not shown in the examples because that method is rarely used in contemporary cataloging practice.

A list of relationship designators for related PFCs is found in RDA appendix K. The general instruction states that along with an AAP or an identifier, the cataloger records one or more of the relationship designators. As many relationship designators as necessary may be used. If none of the terms in RDA appendix K are appropriate, the cataloger can record a term that specifically and concisely summarizes the nature of the relationship.

> **AAP for person**: Puzo, Mario, 1920-1999
>
> **AAP for related person**: *Alternate identity:* Cleri, Mario, 1920-1999
>
> **AAP for corporate body**: Albert Barg Photography
>
> **AAP for related person**: *Founder:* Barg, Albert, 1944-
>
> **AAP for related person**: *Employee:* Weisberg, Jeff, 1961-
>
> **AAP for person**: Miskin, A. R. (Arthur Richard), 1876-1960
>
> **AAP for related family**: *Descendants:* Miskin (Family : Miskin, A. R. (Arthur Richard), 1876-1960)

At the time of this writing, there are 42 relationship designators for related PFCs. The 10 related-person relationships comprise the following:

- **Person to Person Relationships**: *alternate identity* and *real identity*
- **Person to Family Relationships**: *family member* and *progenitor*
- **Person to Corporate Body Relationships**: *employee, founder, graduate, incumbent, member,* and *sponsor*

The lists for families and corporate bodies are found in RDA appendix J.

Because the information about relationships among PFCs is described as part of authority data, additional information must be included besides the related PFC and its relationship designator. *Source consulted* and *cataloguer's notes* are included to clarify the relationship and to justify its inclusion in the authority data. *Source consulted*, an LC-PCC Core element, refers to citations to sources of information consulted during the process of establishing authority data. This process provides documentation demonstrating that the cataloger/authority control librarian performed the necessary steps to make decisions regarding access points, additional elements, and relationships. The basic instruction is to cite the sources used when establishing the relationship; this includes sources that provided useful information, but also sources that contained no information about the relationship at all.

In addition to the documentation already discussed, other notes in authority data are needed. In RDA, a *cataloguer's note* is "an annotation that might be helpful to those using or revising the relationship data, or creating an authorized access point representing a related person, family, or corporate body."[25] These notes may clarify the relationship, explain limits on the use of access points, help differentiate between entities, cite the instruction used to create the data, and provide any other information that might be useful.

AAP for corporate body: Binghamton Asylum for the Insane

AAP for related corporate body: *Predecessor:* New York State Inebriate Asylum

AAP for related corporate body: *Successor:* Binghamton State Hospital

Source consulted: Annual report of the trustees, 1889: t.p. (Binghamton Asylum for the Insane)

Source consulted: Thirty-third annual report, 1912: cover (Binghamton State Hospital at Binghamton, N.Y.); Asylums of New York State, via WWW, Jan. 4, 2012: [Binghamton history] chronology page (1854: "The United States Inebriate Asylum for the Reform of Poor and Destitute Inebriates" is chartered by the New York State Legislature; 1857: The institution is renamed "The New York State Inebriate Asylum"; 1879: May: "Binghamton Asylum for the Insane" est.; 1890: The institution is renamed "Binghamton State Hospital")

AAP for person: Twain, Mark, 1835-1910

AAP for related person: Clemens, Samuel Langhorne, 1835-1910

AAP for related person: Snodgrass, Quintus Curtius, 1835-1910

AAP for related person: Conte, Louis de, 1835-1910

Cataloguer's note: Pseudonym not established: Jean François Alden

Source consulted: DAB [Dictionary of American Biography], 1930 (Clemens, Samuel Langhorne, 1835-1910; better known under pseud. Mark Twain; also used name Quintus Curtius Snodgrass)

AAP for family: Cunningham (Family : 1795- : Trigg County, Ky.)

AAP for related person: *Progenitor:* Cunningham, William, 1765-1823

AAP for related person: *Progenitor:* Cunningham, Nancy, 1776-1830

Cataloguer's note: The Cunningham family consists of descendants of William and Nancy Cunningham, who married in 1795 and later settled in Trigg County, Kentucky

Source consulted: The Cunningham family cookbook, 1997: pages 5-6 (descendants of William and Nancy Cunningham. William emigrated from Scotland some time after 1785 and married Nancy Carr in 1795. The family eventually settled in Trigg County, Ky.)

RDA Chapter 30-32 Related Persons, Families, and Corporate Bodies

Chapters 30-32 in RDA are *almost* identical; the difference being, of course, each chapter focuses on a different Group 2 entity. Each chapter begins with a statement of its purpose: to provide catalogers with information about recording relationships between a person [family or corporate body] and related PFCs. There are no RDA Core elements in RDA section 9, but *related person* is considered core by LC and PCC libraries for persons with multiple bibliographic identities (see Mark Twain example). *Related corporate body* is LC-PCC Core for corporate bodies with sequential relationships with an immediately preceding corporate body and an immediately succeeding corporate body (see Binghamton example).

The instructions in these chapters are minimal. They each state: "Record a relationship to a related person [family or corporate body] by applying the general guidelines at [RDA] 29.4."[26] They are followed by an instruction for providing an *explanation of relationship*, if considered important. An *explanation of relationship* contains a statement that is recorded in the authority data to elaborate on or clarify the relationships among related PFCs. These types of explanatory statements can be presented to the users of the catalog as general references.

AAP for person: Twain, Mark, 1835-1910

Explanation of relationship: For works of this author written under other names, search also under: Clemens, Samuel Langhorne, 1835-1910; Snodgrass, Quintus Curtius, 1835-1910; and Conte, Louis de, 1835-1910

Many examples are provided in RDA to illustrate the relationships among PFCs. The following examples are meant to supplement those in RDA chapters 30-32.

- **Related Persons**

  AAP for person: Bachman, Richard

  AAP for related person: *Real identity:* King, Stephen, 1947-

AAP for person: Lessing, Doris, 1919-2013

AAP for related person: *Alternate identity:* Somers, Jane, 1919-2013

AAP for person: Steadman, Sage

AAP for related person: *Alternate identity:* Hippie with Anger Issues

AAP for family: Borgia (Family : active 14th century-18th century)

AAP for related person: *Family member:* Callistus III, Pope, 1378-1458

AAP for related person: *Family member:* Alexander VI, Pope, 1431-1503

AAP for corporate body: Darwin Correspondence Project

AAP for related person: *Founder:* Burkhardt, Frederick, 1912-2007

AAP for related person: *Founder:* Smith, Sydney, 1911-1988

AAP for related person: *Incumbent:* Secord, James A.

AAP for corporate body: 10,000 Maniacs (Musical group)

AAP for related person: *Member:* Lombardo, John, 1952-

AAP for related person: *Member:* Merchant, Natalie

AAP for related person: *Member:* Ramsey, Mary

AAP for corporate body: Smart Brain Training Solutions

AAP for related person: *Sponsor:* Stanek, William R.

• **Related Families**

AAP for person: Fowler, Robert, 1829-1903

AAP for related family: *Descendants:* Fowler (Family : 1829-2009 : Crawford County, Kan.)

AAP for corporate body: Berith Salom (Organization)

AAP for related family: *Founding family:* Spanjaard (Family)

• **Related Corporate Bodies**

AAP for person: Wyckoff, Elizabeth, 1915-1994

AAP for related corporate body: *Employer:* Bryn Mawr College

AAP for related corporate body: *Employer:* Mount Holyoke College

AAP for person: Snodgrass, Kate

AAP for related corporate body: *Officiated corporate body:* Boston Playwrights' Theatre

AAP for related corporate body: *Founded corporate body:* Boston Theater Marathon

AAP for person: Miskin, A. R. (Arthur Richard), 1876-1960

AAP for related corporate body: *Founded corporate body:* Miskin Scraper Works

AAP for corporate body: Penguin Random House

AAP for related corporate body: *Component of a merger:* Penguin Group

AAP for related corporate body: *Component of a merger:* Random House (Firm)

AAP for corporate body: National Council on Public Polls (U.S.)

AAP for related corporate body: *Corporate member:* ABC News

AAP for related corporate body: *Corporate member:* Annenberg Public Policy Center

AAP for related corporate body: *Corporate member:* Behavior Research Center

AAP for related corporate body: *Corporate member:* CBS News

AAP for corporate body: Northwestern Terra Cotta Works

AAP for related corporate body: *Founding corporate body:* True, Brunkhorst & Co.

AAP for related corporate body: *Successor:* Northwestern Terra Cotta Company

AAP for corporate body: University of South Carolina. Libraries

AAP for related corporate body: *Hierarchical superior:* University of South Carolina

AAP for related corporate body: *Hierarchical subordinate:* McKissick Memorial Library

AAP for related corporate body: *Hierarchical subordinate:* South Caroliniana Library

AAP for related corporate body: *Hierarchical subordinate:* Thomas Cooper Library

AAP for corporate body: John Cabot International College

AAP for related corporate body: *Predecessor of split:* American University of Rome

AAP for related corporate body: *Successor:* John Cabot University

Explanation of relationship: Email from librarian at John Cabot University, September 16, 2014 (John Cabot International College is a name . . . found on the oldest catalogs (1972-1991) of

John Cabot University. JCU originated in 1972 as a little schism from the American University of Rome . . . .)

AAP for corporate body: Metro-Goldwyn-Mayer

AAP for related corporate body: *Mergee:* Metro Pictures Corporation

AAP for related corporate body: *Mergee:* Goldwyn Pictures Corporation

AAP for related corporate body: *Mergee:* Louis B. Mayer Pictures

AAP for corporate body: Louis B. Mayer Pictures

AAP for related corporate body: *Product of a merger:* Metro-Goldwyn-Mayer

SUBJECT-BASED RELATIONSHIPS IN RDA

As stated previously, most of the subject-related chapters in RDA are empty. Chapter 23 was added in April 2015, but RDA section 10 is still empty, as are RDA chapters 12-15 and 33-37. Chapter 23 is very straightforward and contains little detail on how to use subject access standards. It simply states that works have subjects, and at least one subject relationship should be identified in a bibliographic description. Subjects may be represented by an identifier, by an AAP from a controlled vocabulary or a classification scheme, or by a subject description (such as an abstract or summary). There is little else to discuss at this time. For a full description of subject access, readers are advised to consult chapters 11-20 of this text instead. These chapters provide a full introduction to subject cataloging and classification.

CONCLUSION

This chapter has introduced the use of access points (and, in some cases, other devices) to represent the relationships important to understanding resources and the entities involved in their creation, realization, and dissemination. It has discussed how relationships are important aspects of both bibliographic and authority data. It has reviewed the major roles and elements that are used to identify those entities acting as creators, contributors, and others associated with resources, as well as the types of relationships that exist among and between the various groups of FRBR entities.

NOTES

1. *RDA: Resource Description & Access*, developed in a collaborative process led by the Joint Steering Committee for Development of RDA (Chicago: American Library Association, 2010). Also available through paid subscriptions to *RDA Toolkit* (Chicago: American Library Association, 2010), accessed June 28, 2015, http://www.rdatoolkit.org/. In lieu of page numbers, any references to specific parts of RDA are made using instruction numbers.
2. RDA, 17.0: Purpose and Scope.

3. Library of Congress, "LC-PCC PS for 17.0," in "Library of Congress-Program for Cooperative Cataloging Policy Statements (LC-PCC PS)," *RDA Toolkit: Resource Description & Access* (Chicago: American Library Association, 2010), accessed June 28, 2015, http://access.rdatoolkit.org/. Free access to the LC-PCC PS is available through the Resources tab. Copies of the LC-PCC PS are also available with a paid subscription in Cataloger's Desktop.
4. RDA, 17.4.2.3: Composite Description.
5. International Federation of Library Associations, *ISBD: International Standard Bibliographic Description*, recommended by the ISBD Review Group; approved by the Standing Committee of the IFLA Cataloguing Section, Consolidated ed. (München, Germany: De Gruyter Saur, 2011). Also available online at the IFLA website: http://www.ifla.org/files/assets/cataloguing/isbd/isbd-cons_20110321.pdf.
6. RDA, 17.5.1.1: Scope [of Expression of Work].
7. RDA, 17.6.1.1: Scope [of Work Expressed].
8. RDA, 17.7.1.1: Scope [of Manifestation of Work].
9. RDA, 17.9.1.1: Scope [of Manifestation of Expression].
10. RDA, 17.11.1.1: Scope [of Exemplar of a Manifestation].
11. *Anglo-American Cataloguing Rules*, 2nd ed., prepared by the American Library Association, the British Library, the Canadian Library Committee on Cataloguing, the (British) Library Association, and the Library of Congress, ed. by Michael Gorman and Paul W. Winkler (Chicago: American Library Association, 1978).
12. RDA, 18.4.1: Recording Relationships to Persons, Families, and Corporate Bodies Associated with the Resource.
13. RDA, 19.1.1: Sources of Information [of General Guidelines on Recording Persons, Families, and Corporate Bodies Associated with a Work].
14. RDA, 19.2.1.3: Recording Creators.
15. RDA, 20.1.1: Sources of Information [of General Guidelines on Recording Persons, Families, and Corporate Bodies Associated with an Expression].
16. RDA, 24.4.3: Description of the Related Work, Expression, Manifestation, or Item.
17. RDA, 24.5.1.3: Recording Relationship Designators.
18. RDA, 24.6.1.1: Scope [of Numbering of Part].
19. Library of Congress, "Z1: Name and Series Authority Records," *Descriptive Cataloging Manual*, prepared by the Policy and Standards Division, Library of Congress (Washington, D.C.: Library of Congress, 2014), http://www.loc.gov/catdir/cpso/dcmz1.pdf.
20. RDA, 24.8.1.1: Scope [for Making Cataloguer's Notes].
21. RDA, 25.1.1.1: Scope [for Related Work].
22. RDA, 26.1.1.1: Scope [for Related Expression].
23. Library of Congress, LC-PCC PS for 25.1: Related Work.
24. RDA, 29.5.1.3: Recording Relationship Designators.
25. RDA, 29.7.1.1: Scope [for Making Cataloguer's Notes].
26. RDA, 30.1.1.3: Recording Relationships to a Related Person; 31.1.1.3 Recording Relationships to a Related Family; and 32.1.1.3 Recording Relationships to a Related Corporate Body.

SUGGESTED READING

El-Sherbini, Magda. *RDA: Strategies for Implementation*. Chicago: American Library Association, 2013.
Hart, Amy. *RDA Made Simple: A Practical Guide to the New Cataloging Rules*. Santa Barbara, Calif.: Libraries Unlimited, 2014.

Kincy, Chamya Pompey, with Sara Shatford Layne. *Making the Move to RDA: A Self-Study Primer for Catalogers.* Lanham, Md.: Rowman & Littlefield, 2014.

Maxwell, Robert L. *Maxwell's Handbook for RDA, Resource Description and Access: Explaining and Illustrating RDA: Resource Description and Access Using MARC21.* Chicago: American Library Association, 2013.

Mering, Margaret, ed. *The RDA Workbook: Learning the Basics of Resource Description and Access.* Santa Barbara, Calif.: Libraries Unlimited, 2014.

Oliver, Chris. *Introducing RDA: A Guide to the Basics.* Chicago: American Library Association, 2010.

Chapter 9

RDA Metadata in the MARC Format

INTRODUCTION

In this chapter, the authors provide an example to help make the process of cataloging more concrete. It is an illustration of how to perform original cataloging using *Resource Description & Access* (RDA),[1] *International Standard Bibliographic Description* (ISBD),[2] and MAchine-Readable Cataloging (MARC).[3] See chapters 4-8, 21, and 23 of this text for more information about each of these standards. This chapter does not cover subject cataloging and classification; see chapters 11-20 for discussions of those aspects of the cataloging process.

In this chapter, the authors take a somewhat different approach to explaining the content. Because the focus is on providing step-by-step cataloging instructions to the readers (i.e., taking them through each decision and choice), the authors decided that these processes are best communicated through the use of the first-person and second-person pronouns. In this chapter, therefore, "we" speak directly to "you," the reader. Although this may not conform to "formal writing" standards, we believe that it will make the following narrative easier to read and digest.

ORIGINAL CATALOGING EXAMPLE

As we discussed in chapter 4 of this text, we begin the cataloging process by determining exactly what it is that we have in hand. This means starting with an examination of the resource to identify the various entities, attributes, and relationships that need to be included in the description. It is during this examination that you begin to think about the pre-cataloging considerations that were identified in chapter 4 of this text.

The resource that we are going to use for this example is a fictitious book conceived by the authors of this text. This resource does not exist, so there is no record for it in bibliographic databases or catalogs; there is no actual copy of the resource that you can see or hold. For the purposes of this illustration, we have created a title page for the imaginary resource (see Figure 9.1). We have also created a title page verso (see Figure 9.2) and an additional page of information (see Figure 9.3) to better understand this make-believe resource. With the data found in Figures 9.1-9.3, there should be enough information for you to create a bibliographic record using RDA, MARC, and ISBD.

In addition, in appendix B of this text, there is an RDA template (which can be downloaded by readers). We designed it to hold the initial descriptive cataloging data that is created while using RDA. It can be used for MARC-based and non-MARC-based cataloging approaches. The template contains five columns. In the first three columns, you find RDA instruction numbers, RDA element names, and a place for the content. In the final two columns, you see MARC fields and subfields and the ISBD punctuation typically used with the data. In cases in which non-MARC and/or non-ISBD metadata is going to be created, the final two columns may be eliminated or ignored.

The template in appendix B is provided for quick reference. Due to publishing constraints, it is presented in a format that is unusable for actual cataloging purposes because the empty column in which to place metadata content has been greatly reduced in size so that the other columns can be read more easily. A more functional version of the template is available online in PDF, RTF, and DOC formats.[4]

Initial Steps

As mentioned earlier, the first step is to conduct a thorough examination of the resource with certain pre-cataloging conditions in mind. This entails asking questions, such as the following:

- What is the resource?
- How is it issued? Is it one unit? Does it have parts?
- Is it updated or to be updated? If so, how is it updated?

THE ORGANIZATION OF INFORMATION:

A Teacher's Guide to the Third Edition

by
Daniel N. Joudrey, Ph. D.,
Associate Professor, School of Library and Information Science,
Simmons College

and
Arlene G. Taylor, Ph. D.,
Professor Emerita, School of Information Sciences,
University of Pittsburgh

Illustrations by David P. Miller, MA, MSLIS

Edited by Lois Chan, Ph. D.

Library and Information Science Text Series

LIBRARIES
U N L I M I T E D
Santa Barbara, California

FIGURE 9.1 Title Page for the Faux Resource Used in the Cataloging Example.

First edition

Copyright ©2013 by Daniel N. Joudrey.

All rights reserved. No portion of this book may be reproduced,
by any process or technique, without the express written consent
of the publisher.

ISBN: 978-1-59158-998-2-X (alk. paper)
        978-1-59158-999-X (pbk. : alk. paper)

Libraries Unlimited, an imprint of ABC-CLIO
130 Cremona Drive, Santa Barbara, California 93117
http://www.abc-clio.com/LibrariesUnlimited.aspx

Distributed by ABC-CLIO, Santa Barbara, California

Printed in the United States of America
by Deluxe Quick-E Printing, Pasadena, California
        First printing, 2014.
        Second printing, 2015.

CD-ROMs manufactured 2014 by Alternative Digital Printing, Santa Barbara, California.

The paper used in this book complies with the Permanent Paper Standard issued by the National
Information Standards Organization (Z39.48–1984).

10 9 8 7 6 5 4 3 2 1

FIGURE 9.2 Verso of the Title Page for the Faux Resource.

Additional information about the resource:

- In the book, there are introductory pages that are numbered iii-ix. The main text of the book has pages numbered 1-378.

- There are leaves of plates in the book, each containing a single illustration, a graph, or a form; all are by David Miller and all are in color. The leaves are unnumbered, but the illustrative matter is numbered 1-22.

- The book measures 25.4 centimeters.

- There is a bibliography on pages 351-368.

- There is an index in the back of the book.

- On the spine, it reads: *Oofl3: A Teacher's Guide.*

- This book is a companion to the third edition of the textbook *The Organization of Information* by Arlene G. Taylor and Daniel N. Joudrey, published by Libraries Unlimited in 2009 (ISBN: 9781591585862).

- The book contains strategies, tips, and tricks for teaching a graduate-level course on Information Organization in a library and information science program.

- **Table of Contents**:
  - Introduction
  - Chapter 1 Providing Context: Organization of Recorded Information
  - Chapter 2 What Students Need to Know About Retrieval Tools and Systems
  - Chapter 3 Make the History of Information Organization Come Alive!
  - Chapter 4 Metadata: What's That?
  - Chapter 5 Teaching Encoding in 5 Easy Steps
  - Chapter 6 Introducing Students to Description
  - Chapter 7 Authority Control Basics
  - Chapter 8 Teaching Subject Access: The Most Fun EVER!
  - Bibliography
  - Index

- In the inside back cover there is a compact disc titled *Teaching Information Organization*, which contains materials for teaching with *The Organization of Information*. Materials on the CD-ROM include: 15 sets of lecture slides (PPT), 15 files containing lecture notes (PDF), 15 in-class exercises with answer keys (PDF), and 6 assignments and answer keys (DOCX). The authors of the teacher's guide created all the contents.

FIGURE 9.3 Additional Information About the Faux Resource.

Through our examination, we can quickly determine that the resource is not a serial, an integrating resource, or a multi-volume set; it is a book—more specifically, it is a single-part monograph. It is not issued over time in pieces or parts; it is not an updating resource (e.g., with new pages to be inserted quarterly). It is a single unit, *but* it does have accompanying material; there is a CD-ROM that must be addressed.

We also need to ask some questions about relationships that might exist:

- Is the resource a new resource, a new version of an existing resource, or a new copy of a previously existing version? Is it a part of another resource?

- Are there other resources with the same title? Are they by the same creator(s)? Are they disseminated by the same publisher? Are they part of the same series? If there are other resources with the same title, do the resources contain the same work? Do they contain a new expression of the work?

- Are there earlier editions of the resource? Are they by the same creator?

- Has the creator produced other works? Are these works similar or related to the resource in hand? Are there resources that appear to be the same work but that have another title? Has the creator worked with others? Have these other creators or contributors produced similar or related works?

- Is the title of the work being cataloged similar to the titles of other works? Are there related works (e.g., supplements, sequels, transformations) that contain the title or share the title?

From the title page, it is obvious that our book does have some relationships to consider. To begin exploring relationships, you may check the resource itself and one or more of the following sources: (1) your own catalog, (2) the Library of Congress (LC) catalog, and (3) a bibliographic database such as OCLC's WorldCat. For this exercise, we chose to go to the OCLC database of bibliographic records. From that source, we determined that there is a work with the same title—*The Organization of Information*—but it does not have the subtitle found on the book we are cataloging. The subtitle on this resource—*A Teacher's Guide to the Third Edition*—provides a great deal of information about the relationships that exist. Our resource is connected to the third edition (i.e., an expression) of a work that shares the same title. We also found that (1) the two works are by the same creators, (2) the two resources are published by the same company, (3) the two works are part of the same series, and (4) the two works contain different content. Based on what we found in the database and in the book itself, the resource we are cataloging is a new work, but it is a supplement to the third edition of *The Organization of Information*. As such, it requires its own description. It is clear that our resource is also related to a series, *The Library and Information Science Text Series*. To summarize what we have determined, we would make notes that say:

> **Mode of issuance**: single unit/monograph
>
> **Type of description needed**: comprehensive (including the accompanying material)
>
> **Bibliographic relationship**: related to another work/ expression—the third edition of *The Organization of Information* by Taylor and Joudrey (expression-to-work/supplemental relationship)
>
> **Bibliographic relationship**: related to the Libraries Unlimited publisher's series *The Library and Information Science Text Series* (work-to-work/whole-part relationship)
>
> **Record status**: a new record is needed, because it is a new work

The next step is a thorough technical reading of the resource (see chapter 4 in this textbook). Because this is an exercise rather than a real-life experience, we do not have the full resource to examine, but if we did, we would start by looking at the preferred source of information. According to RDA 2.2.2, the preferred source would be the title page, because this is a single unit made up of pages, and there is a title page that conveys information about the resource as a whole (not just a part of the resource). On that source, we begin looking for our bibliographic data (titles, statements of responsibility (SOR) information, dissemination information, series information, etc.). Because the preferred source does not contain all the information that we need, we must consult other parts of the resource (e.g., the verso, other preliminaries, the text, the physical carrier) to find additional information. We also need to record the data according to the instructions in RDA. In the subsequent sections, we will follow the individual RDA instructions to start framing the raw data from the resource into a metadata record.

RDA Instructions for Manifestations and Items

To ensure consistency and compatibility, the authors have decided that the instructions provided in RDA 1.7 regarding transcription are to be followed closely. That means the guidelines for capitalization, punctuation, diacritical marks, symbols, abbreviations, and so on will be followed faithfully. Although most of these guidelines simply instruct us to transcribe what we see, capitalization is the big exception. For capitalization, we are following the explicit instructions in RDA appendix A rather than transcribing it as is. This means the data recorded for title proper and other title information must be transformed when added to our bibliographic record.

The first elements we need to concern ourselves with are the title elements, for which we consult RDA 2.3 for guidance. On our preferred source, we see both a *title proper* (i.e., the main title) and *other title information* (e.g., the subtitle). From this resource's typography and layout, it seems apparent that this is a title proper and its subtitle, rather than one lengthy title proper that contains punctuation. If the title and subtitle were presented in equal-sized fonts and were not divided by space, we might need to consider it a single title. The title is not overly long, appears only in one language and in one script, and is not a collective title; there are no introductory words to consider, and there are no inaccuracies to address. Thus there is little to do to the title proper other than to transcribe it (i.e., there are no real decisions or judgments to make). You record it as you see it, following the instructions for transcription at RDA 1.7, and capitalizing it according to RDA appendix A. The same approach applies to the subtitle. The one thing that is omitted is the punctuation that appears between the title proper and the subtitle. This is owing to the exception found at RDA 1.7.3, which states that catalogers should omit punctuation marks that are used to separate different metadata elements. In this case the colon is used to separate title proper and subtitle; it is not recorded in either element.

> **Title proper**: The organization of information
>
> **Other title information**: a teacher's guide to the third edition

The only other title element that is needed is a variant title—actually, two of them are needed. In our examination of the resource, we recognize that the spine title is somewhat different than the title on the title page. It reads, *Oofl3: A Teacher's Guide*. *Oofl3* appears to be an acronym for the full title plus the edition number (i.e., *The Organization of Information*, 3rd edition). The spine title is recorded, as found, in the *variant title* element. The other variant title comes from the CD-ROM. While the CD-ROM is part of our resource, it has a unique title, *Teaching Information Organization*, which should also be included in our description, as someone somewhere may search for it. Some catalogers, also, might be concerned about the phrase "third edition" that is part of the other title information. In general, if a spelled-out number is found in a title, a variant title with an Arabic numeral is created to ensure access. In this case, though, the spelled-out number is in other title information, not the title proper. Because other title information is usually not indexed with the main titles, a variant title containing "3rd edition" is not particularly necessary. It will not hurt, mind you, but it is not vital.

> **Spine title**: Oofl3: a teacher's guide
>
> **Related component title**: Teaching information organization

The next element to record is the *statement of responsibility related to the title proper* (SOR) at RDA 2.4. Unless it is overly long or burdensome, we generally transcribe the statement of responsibility exactly as it appears on the preferred source. There is an optional omission, however, that states that inessential information may be removed in some cases. If we do not apply the optional omission, the SORs are transcribed as follows:

> **SOR**: by Daniel N. Joudrey, Ph. D., Associate Professor, School of Library and Information Science, Simmons College and Arlene G. Taylor, Ph. D., Professor Emerita, School of Information Sciences, University of Pittsburgh
>
> **SOR**: illustrations by David P. Miller, MA, MSLIS
>
> **SOR**: edited by Lois Chan, Ph. D.

If the option is applied, then the SORs are transcribed as:

> **SOR**: by Daniel N. Joudrey and Arlene G. Taylor
>
> **SOR**: illustrations by David P. Miller
>
> **SOR**: edited by Lois Chan

In this case, we actually prefer using the optional omission for the sake of clarity. The relevant information is unmistakable and not obscured by extraneous information.

For this resource, three statements of responsibility have been recorded. This is an interpretation based on the information seen on the title page. Although it can be frustrating to new catalogers that typographical and design features (such as font size and page layout) can play a role in determining how we interpret title page data, there is simply no possible way to design specific instructions that can be applied to every case. Other catalogers may have recorded two SORs (e.g., one for the creators and one for the illustrator and editor); others might have recorded only one (i.e., incorporating the three statements into one statement), but we believe the layout (i.e., the separation of Joudrey and Taylor from Miller and Chan) and the wording (i.e., there are no connecting words between Miller and Chan) lend themselves to three separate statements of responsibility.

The next thing that we will do is look for information about an edition statement (RDA 2.5). For this resource, nothing appears in the preferred source of information. The word *edition* does appear on the title page (*A Teacher's Guide to the Third Edition*), but it is used as part of the subtitle, and it refers to the edition of the related resource. If the title information had said "A Teacher's Guide, Third Edition," it would mean that this is the third edition of the teacher's guide, and it would be handled differently. Even though an edition statement for this resource is not on the same source of information as the title proper, we are not thwarted; according to RDA 2.5.2.2, we may also seek this information from other locations within the resource itself or, if necessary, from accompanying material, other published descriptions of the resource, a container, or any other source. When you look at the resource closely, you see that on the verso of the title page there is a reference to the edition. This information is transcribed, as it appears on the source, in the *edition statement* element.

Edition statement: First edition

After transcribing the edition statement we are going to look for any indications of statements of responsibility for the edition (e.g., updated by John F. Smith), parallel edition statements (e.g., 1. edizioa), and designations of named revisions of the edition (e.g., revised and enlarged). Spotting none, we can move on. We can skip over the next two elements (RDA 2.6: Numbering of Serials and RDA 2.7: Production Statement) because they are not applicable; this resource is not a serial and does not comprise unpublished material.

Next we are going to look at RDA 2.8 for instructions on publication statements. The three core elements that concern us are *place of publication*, *publisher's name*, and *date of publication*. We start by looking at the preferred source of information for *publisher's name*: the same source as the title proper. On the title page, we find both the publisher's name and the location of the publisher. This is helpful because the preferred source for *place of publication* is the same source as *publisher's name*. We transcribe both as they appear on the preferred source of information.

Place of publication: Santa Barbara, California
Publisher's name: Libraries Unlimited

What we are missing on the title page is a date of publication. We are going to need to determine the publication date to complete our dissemination information. The first place we should look is the verso of the title page.

Often when you look at the verso of a title page, you will see additional information related to the dissemination of the resource. For this resource, you find a copyright date, manufacturing information (including various dates), distribution information, and even some additional publication information. The publisher's name, for example, is provided in a fuller form: *Libraries Unlimited, an imprint of ABC-CLIO*. Despite this additional information, we record "Libraries Unlimited" only, because it is the form found on the preferred source of information. What do we do with the other dissemination information? We need to examine it carefully to determine what is useful and what is not. According to RDA, distribution information (RDA 2.9), manufacturing information (RDA 2.10), and copyright dates (RDA 2.11) are not required and are included only in accordance with cataloger's judgment. The names and locations of the distributor and the manufacturers are not required, but if we believe these data elements are helpful or necessary, we can add them to our description anyway. For the sake of thoroughness, we will add them all.

> **Place of distribution**: Santa Barbara, California
>
> **Distributor's name**: ABC-CLIO
>
> **Place of manufacture**: Pasadena, California
>
> **Manufacturer's name**: Deluxe Quick-E Printing
>
> **Place of manufacture (CD-ROM)**: Santa Barbara, California
>
> **Manufacturer's name**: Alternative Digital Printing

After reviewing the title page verso, the date of publication has still not been identified. We do, however, have several possibilities to consider. We have a copyright date of 2013. We have no distribution date, but we have three dates of manufacturing: The first printing of the text and the production of the CD-ROMs both occurred in 2014, whereas a second printing occurred in 2015. The evidence overwhelmingly points to 2014 as a likely publication date, but we will use the LC-PCC PS for RDA 2.8.6.6: Date of Publication not Identified in the Resource to be sure we are being logical about the choice. This LC-PCC PS instructs us first to consider the copyright date (2013), but only if it seems like a viable publication date. For this resource, it does not seem to be a likely publication date, because according to the information on the title page verso, the first printing of the resource did not occur until 2014. The second printing, which occurred in 2015, would not reflect the publication date, obviously because the original publication of the resource occurred before the date of the second printing. In this particular case, the best choice for date of publication is 2014. The date is recorded in square brackets to indicate that this data (being entered into *date of publication*) did not come from the resource itself (or a note could be used instead of square brackets). Because the date was inferred from the date of manufacture, that provides some justification for including the complete manufacture statement in our description. The copyright date may also be included if considered important.

> **Date of publication**: [2014]
>
> **Copyright date**: ©2013

The next element to consider is the series statement (RDA 2.12). This information is located on the title page; it is transcribed exactly as it is found. There are no subseries, no International Standard Serial Numbers, no statements of responsibility for the series, and no parallel series information; nothing more than the following statement is needed at this time.

> **Title proper of series**: Library and information science text series

Mode of Issuance (RDA 2.13), an LC Core element, is recorded next. It is fairly straightforward because the value must come from RDA table 2.1. In this case, we are dealing with a single unit, not a multipart monograph, a serial, or an integrating resource. The following element, *Frequency* (RDA 2.14), is not applicable so we can skip over that.

> **Mode of issuance**: single unit

An identifier for the manifestation (RDA 2.15) appears on this resource on the title page verso. Actually, more than one identifier appears there. Two International Standard Book Numbers (ISBNs) are present. Both of these are recorded, but because the resource bears more than one identifier of the same type, we must add a brief qualification to each of the ISBNs.

> **ISBN**: 978-1-59158-998-2 (alk. paper)
>
> **ISBN**: 978-1-59158-999-X (pbk. : alk. paper)

Looking ahead in RDA chapter 2, it appears that we have covered all the elements needed to describe the manifestation. So next we will turn to the carrier (RDA chapter 3).

RDA Instructions for Carriers

We, again, will follow RDA order in describing the elements related to the physical carriers that comprise this resource. For this part of the exercise, we are relying on the information found in Figure 9.3, as we do not have an actual resource with which to work. For the sake of verisimilitude, we will proceed as if the resource were in front of us.

The resource we have in hand has multiple carriers. It is a book that has its own physical characteristics, but it also has a CD-ROM that comes with it. This means we must make a decision about how we will describe these carriers. RDA 3.1.4 addresses situations in which the resource consists of more than one carrier type and offers three approaches: (1) recording only the number of units and the carrier type for each; (2) recording full details for each of the carriers; and (3) recording a predominant carrier and describing the others using a very general phrase (e.g., *various pieces*). To provide a more complete picture of the resource, we are going to use the second approach and describe each carrier in some detail. This means we may record two instances for each element that applies to carriers.

The first elements to record are *Media Type* (RDA 3.2) and *Carrier Type* (RDA 3.3). Both of these elements take their values from controlled lists found in RDA chapter 3.

> **Media type**: unmediated
>
> **Carrier type**: volume

> **Media type**: computer
> **Carrier type**: computer disc

After recording these elements, we move on to more specific elements, such as *Extent* (RDA 3.4) and *Dimensions* (RDA 3.5). The instructions for *Extent of Text* (RDA 3.4.5) tell us to record the extent in terms of the appropriate subunit, rather than using the unit identified in the carrier type. This means that we record the pagination (or the number of leaves or columns, if appropriate). Our resource has introductory pages (title page, verso, table of contents, etc.) that are numbered iii-ix. The main text of the book has pages numbered 1-378. In other words, we have two separate sequences of pages that must be recorded as such. The book also includes unnumbered leaves of plates. Whenever leaves or pages of plates are included in a textual resource, but are not included in the pagination, their sequence should also be recorded. Even if the leaves are unnumbered, each illustration (one per leaf) is numbered, so it is easy to ascertain the number of leaves of plates.

> **Extent**: ix, 378 pages, 22 unnumbered leaves of plates

For the CD-ROM, the extent is going to be somewhat simpler because computer discs do not fall in one of the exceptional categories of carriers that have their own sets of instructions. The extent starts with the number of units and the carrier type (e.g., 1 computer disc). There is an option, however, that allows for the usage of more common terms (e.g., CD-ROM). The decision on which term to use comes down to the individual cataloger or their institution, but in this case we are going to use the more common term, because it expands the users' understanding of the carrier type rather than just repeating the terminology used in that element. In addition, the number and type of subunits found on the computer disc may be added in parentheses according to RDA 3.4.1.7.1.

> **Extent**: 1 CD-ROM (15 MS PowerPoint files, 36 text files)

Obtaining the dimensions of a book involves the use of a ruler. It is typically no more complicated than measuring the spine in centimeters and then rounding up to the next whole centimeter. The resource we are describing is 10 inches (in.) or 25.4 centimeters (cm) tall; thus we record "26 cm" as the dimensions of the book. The dimensions of a disc reflect the diameter of that disc. It is recorded in inches (to the next 1/4 inch up) rather than centimeters, if we are following standard LC-PCC practices. The dimensions for the two components of the resource are recorded as follows:

> **Dimensions (book)**: 26 cm
> **Dimensions (disc)**: 4 3/4 in.

No other carrier-related elements are required in the description except perhaps a note that describes the location of the CD-ROM.

Note: In the inside back cover there is a compact disc titled *Teaching Information Organization*, which contains materials for teaching with the third edition of *The Organization of Information*.

RDA Instructions for Works and Expressions

In this section, we address some of the elements related to works and expressions, but not all. Many of the elements in RDA chapter 6 are not relevant to bibliographic records, but are instead appropriate for authority records only. A resource just published in its first edition generally would not require an authority record for the work unless it has been published in another language or with another title. The resource we are using for our example is somewhat unusual in that it contains a title that is also a title of a separate but related work, which is *also* by the same authors. Because it is by the same authors and its title proper is identical to the title of the resource it supplements, the potential for confusion is high. In this case, an authorized access point (AAP) for the work and accompanying authority data might prove useful to other catalogers and users.

The first element we concern ourselves with is *Title of the Work*. Because we are following LC-PCC practices (for the most part), we will record the title without an initial article (RDA 6.2.1.7). We might also record a variant title that includes the subtitle to ensure that this information is found somewhere in the authority record.

> **Preferred title for the work**: Organization of information
>
> **Variant title for the work**: Organization of information: a teacher's guide to the third edition

Because the title is identical to that of a related resource by the same creators, *Form of Work* becomes a required element (it is an RDA Core-if element). There is no standardized list of forms provided in RDA, so we must supply one. Perhaps it could be "Teacher's guide," "Teacher's manual," or "Teaching aid." All may work equally well, so it comes down to choosing whichever might provide additional insight or nuance. We have chosen one that we believe provides the most clarity.

> **Form of work**: Teacher's manual

The other work/expression elements relevant to this resource can be recorded fairly easily. There are only a few that are appropriate for this resource. If the resource had been expressed in multiple languages or forms, then additional characteristics might be necessary.

- **Date of work** (RDA 6.4): It can be assumed that the value for this element can be inferred from the date of publication, or in this case the copyright date, which was the year before (2013).
- **Place of origin of work** (RDA 6.5): It can be assumed that this work was created in the United States based on each author's location found on the title page.

- **History of the work** (RDA 6.7): A note that states, "This book is a companion to the third edition of the textbook *The Organization of Information* by Arlene G. Taylor and Daniel N. Joudrey, published by Libraries Unlimited in 2009 (ISBN: 9781591585862)" should suffice.

- **Content type** (RDA 6.9): This element requires values from the controlled list found in RDA chapter 6. The values would be *text* and *still image*.

- **Language of expression** (RDA 6.11): This would be *English* or *eng*.

From this data collected about the work and expression, an AAP can be constructed (RDA 6.27), which could then be placed into an authority record to ensure that references to this work are standardized. The AAP for this work is constructed using (1) the authorized AAP for the name of the primary or the first-named creator, (2) the preferred title for the work, and (3) any necessary additions (i.e., qualifiers) to ensure that the access point is unique and that it distinguishes this work from any others.

> **First-named creator**: Daniel N. Joudrey
>
> **Second-named creator**: Arlene G. Taylor
>
> **Preferred title**: Organization of information
>
> **Preliminary AAP**: Joudrey, Daniel N. Organization of information

Due to Joudrey's association with another work with an identical title, it is best to add a qualifier to the AAP to distinguish it from expressions of the work it supplements, *The Organization of Information* by Taylor and Joudrey. Although its AAP would be different, because Taylor is the primary creator of the various expressions of the original work (i.e., **Taylor, Arlene G., 1941- Organization of information. 2009**), there is yet room for confusion, particularly if future editions of the textbook will have Joudrey's name listed as the first author. The choices for additional data elements to add to the AAP for the teacher's manual are: form, date, place of origin, and other distinguishing characteristic of the work. As neither place nor date is useful in separating this work from its related work, the only helpful choices are *form of work* or finding some other distinguishing characteristic or phrase. Because the forms of the works are different, this is a reasonable choice for a qualifier.

> **Final AAP**: Joudrey, Daniel N. Organization of information (Teacher's manual)

The authority data for this resource, coded in the MARC authorities format, would look similar to the record found in Figure 9.4.

After our little detour into authority work, we need to get back to our bibliographic record. We still have work and expression-related elements to describe, specifically those related to content. The first elements to consider are the *Summarization of the Content* (RDA 7.10) and *Intended Audience* (RDA 7.7). Although neither element is mandatory, they may be helpful to the user of the catalog in understanding the nature of the resource. Values for these

Rec stat	c	Entered	20140120	Replaced	20150205073943.0		
Type	z	Upd status	a	Enc lvl	n	Source	
Roman	l	Ref status	a	Mod rec		Name use	a
Govt agn	l	Auth status	a	Subj	a	Subj use	a
Series	n	Auth/ref	a	Geo subd	n	Ser use	b
Ser num	n	Name	a	Subdiv tp	n	Rules	z

010	n XXXXXXXX
040	DLC $b eng $e rda $c DLC
046	$k 2013
100 1_	Joudrey, Daniel N. $t Organization of information (Teacher's manual)
336	text $a still image $2 rdacontent
370	$g United States
377	eng
380	Teacher's manual
400 1_	Joudrey, Daniel N. $t Organization of information: a teacher's guide to the third edition
670	His Organization of information: a teacher's guide to the third edition, 2014: $b t.p. (Organization of information: a teacher's guide to the third edition) introduction p. vii (This book is a companion to the third edition of the textbook The Organization of Information by Arlene G. Taylor and Daniel N. Joudrey.)
670	His Organization of information: a teacher's guide to the third edition $b t.p. (Daniel N. Joudrey, Ph. D., Associate Professor, School of Library and Information Science, Simmons College) t.p. (Arlene G. Taylor, Ph. D., Professor Emerita, School of Information Sciences, University of Pittsburgh)
687	This book is a companion to the third edition of the textbook The Organization of Information by Arlene G. Taylor and Daniel N. Joudrey, published by Libraries Unlimited in 2009 (ISBN: 9781591585862)

FIGURE 9.4 MARC-encoded Authority Record for this Work (An Original Record Based on the OCLC Format).

metadata elements are often taken from a resource itself (e.g., from the back cover, from the introduction).

> **Summarization of the content**: This book is a companion to the third edition of the textbook *The Organization of Information* by Arlene G. Taylor and Daniel N. Joudrey, published by Libraries Unlimited in 2009 (ISBN: 9781591585862). It contains strategies, tips, and tricks for teaching a graduate-level course on Information Organization in a library and information science program.

> **Intended audience**: Instructors of graduate-level courses on Information Organization.

Language of the Content (RDA 7.12), *Illustrative Content* (RDA 7.15), *Supplementary Content* (RDA 7.16), and *Colour Content* (RDA 7.17) should all be added to the description as well. Language of the content is very straightforward; for the resource we are cataloging, we record "English"; nothing else is needed. There are multiple forms of illustrative content in our resource. Standard LC practice for illustrative matter is to record nothing beyond

"Illustrations." We, however, feel that more information about the content can help our patrons and that it takes only a few extra seconds to type other terms into the field. For this resource, we can record additional terms to inform our users of the nature of those illustrations. One aspect we may bring out in the description is the use of color for these illustrations. Following the LC policy statement for the alternative at 7.17.1.3, we only need to record "color" as part of our metadata rather than indicating *monochrome* or *polychrome* as RDA instructs. Supplementary content is also found in this resource; it contains an index and a bibliography. This information should be included in any bibliographic record. We are formatting this information according to long-standing cataloging practices that are illustrated in the LC-PCC PS for RDA 7.16.1.3.

> **Language of the content**: English
>
> **Illustrative content**: illustrations, graphs, forms
>
> **Supplementary content**: Includes bibliographical references (pages 351-368) and index.
>
> **Colour content**: color

Relationships and Access Points

At this point, we jump ahead in RDA, because the sections on describing Group 2 and Group 3 entities are not relevant to the cataloging that we are doing at this moment. We have no particular need to create authority data for a person, family, or corporate body (PFC) because AAPs for the creators and contributors are already present in the LC Name Authority File (LCNAF). Instead, we are looking to the chapters on relationships for our next steps. We are not spending time on RDA chapter 17 (General Guidelines on Recording Primary Relationships), however, because it is not being implemented in the current MARC cataloging environment in the United States. Instead we are focusing on the relationships between Group 2 entities and the resource (i.e., creator and contributor relationships). These relationships are indicated by the inclusion of AAPs for the related entities in the bibliographic record. Also, per RDA chapter 18 (General Guidelines on Recording Relationships to Persons, Families, and Corporate Bodies Associated with a Resource), we want to make sure that these access points contain relationship designators in order for our users to understand the roles that the PFCs played.

The creator relationship is obviously the primary focus. Although RDA requires only the first-named creator, it is almost impossible to believe that a cataloger would not record a second or even a fifth or sixth author. As long as there are fewer than 20 or so PFCs related to the resource, we feel that they should all be recorded (beyond 20 can be considered burdensome). We, therefore, are recording all creators of this work, others who may be involved in the work, and any contributors to the expression. To ensure consistency in our bibliographic records, we consistently use AAPs that have been established previously for each entity. To find an AAP, you must search an authority file. Here in the United States, we look to the LCNAF, or in some cases we might search the Virtual International Authority File (VIAF). After searching the authority file, we are able to copy and paste the AAP directly into the bibliographic data, but that is not all that we need. We also need to record appropriate relationship designators from RDA appendix I.

> **First-named creator**: Joudrey, Daniel N.
> **Relationship designator**: author
> **Additional creator**: Taylor, Arlene G., 1941-
> **Relationship designator**: author

In addition to creators, others who have added to the content of the resource (i.e., contributors) are recorded. There are two obvious choices presented to us on the title page: the illustrator and the editor. Although RDA chapter 20 does not require *any* contributors to be added to a bibliographic record, we believe anyone who has made bibliographically significant contributions to the content (on the work and the expression levels) should be included as an access point.

> **Contributor**: Miller, David P. (David Peter), 1955-
> **Relationship designator**: illustrator
> **Contributor**: Chan, Lois Mai
> **Relationship designator**: editor

In addition to indicating creation and contribution relationships, we are expected to describe any relationships that may exist between Group 1 entities (e.g., work-to-work relationships, manifestation-to-manifestation relationships). These relationships are addressed in RDA chapters 24-28. There are four fairly obvious relationships that must be included in our bibliographic description. There are two work-to-work relationships, one expression-to-work relationship, and one manifestation-to-manifestation relationship. As discussed in earlier chapters of this text and in RDA chapter 18, these relationships can be described using a variety of techniques. We are using the approaches that are most commonly seen in contemporary cataloging practice. In some cases we use AAPs; in others, we use structured or unstructured descriptions. The relationship designators, from RDA appendix J, are in italic type in the examples below; the designators are presented directly in front of the AAPs or the descriptions for greater clarity.

The first work-to-work relationship is a whole-part relationship between the resource in hand and the series to which it belongs. To indicate the relationship between these two related works, an AAP for the series should be added to the record in addition to the series statement that is transcribed as part of the descriptive data. Sometimes these data elements are identical; sometimes they are not. Adding the AAP (from the LCNAF) makes all works in the series quickly findable in the catalog because the AAP acts as a link for each of those records, and they can be retrieved together.

> **Series AAP (work-to-work relationship)**: *in series*: Library and information science text series

The second work-to-work relationship is one that many catalogers would not think of as a work-to-work relationship: providing information about the table of contents. Each chapter in the larger resource can be considered a work of its own (a whole-part relationship). To provide this information, we create contents notes in the form of a structured description.

> **Contents notes**: *container of (work)*: Providing context: organization of recorded information — What students need to know about retrieval tools and systems — Make the history of information organization come alive! — Metadata: what's that? — Teaching encoding in 5 easy steps — Introducing students to description — Authority control basics — Teaching subject access: the most fun EVER!

The third relationship is that of an expression-to-work relationship. It is the supplemental relationship between our resource and the third edition (i.e., a particular expression) of *The Organization of Information* by Arlene G. Taylor and Daniel N. Joudrey. If the work we are describing applied to all editions of the work, *The Organization of Information*, this would be another work-to-work relationship, but it is evident that the teacher's manual is only related to the third edition of the textbook.

> **Related work/expression**: *supplement to (expression)*: Taylor, Arlene G., 1941- Organization of information. 2009

The last of the relationships is a manifestation-to-manifestation relationship. In this case we can use an unstructured description:

> **Note**: In the inside back cover there is a compact disc titled *Teaching Information Organization*, which contains materials for teaching with the third edition of *The Organization of Information*. Materials on the CD-ROM include: 15 sets of lecture slides (PPT), 15 files containing lecture notes (PDF), 15 in-class exercises with answer keys (PDF), and 6 assignments and answer keys (DOCX). The authors of the teacher's guide created all the contents.

Or a structured description could be used:

> **Related manifestation**: *issued with:* Teaching information organization / Daniel N. Joudrey and Arlene G. Taylor. — Santa Barbara, California : Libraries Unlimited, 2014. — 1 CD-ROM (15 MS Power Point files, 36 text files) : color illustrations, PDF ; 4 3/4 in.

Whichever approach is used, it is important that it is clear that there are two physical components to this resource: the book and the CD-ROM. At the end of this process, the bibliographic data for this resource, entered into our RDA Book Template, would look like the preliminary record found in Figure 9.5.

RDA	Element	Metadata Content	MARC	ISBD
ICC11 RDA Book Template (for single-part monographs)				
Manifestations and Items				
2.3.2	Title proper (T)	The organization of information	245 $a	n/a
2.3.4	Other title information (T)	a teacher's guide to the third edition	245 $b	:
2.3.6	Variant titles	Oofl3: a teacher's guide [spine title]	246 $a	
2.4.2	Statement of responsibility for title proper (T)	by Daniel N. Joudrey and Arlene G. Taylor	245 $c	/
	Subsequent statements of responsibility (T)	illustrations by David P. Miller edited by Lois Chan	245 $c	;
2.5	Designation of edition (T)	First edition	250 $a	n/a
2.8.2	Place of publication (T)	Santa Barbara, California	264 #1 $a	n/a
2.8.4	Publisher's name (T)	Libraries Unlimited	264 #1 $b	:
2.8.6	Date of publication	[2014]	264 #1 $c	,
2.9.2	Place of distribution (T)	Santa Barbara, California	264 #2 $a	n/a
2.9.4	Distributor's name (T)	ABC-CLIO	264 #2 $b	:
2.10.2	Place of manufacture (T)	Pasadena, California Santa Barbara, California	264 #3 $a	n/a
2.10.4	Manufacturer's name (T)	Deluxe Quick-E Printing Alternative Digital Printing	264 #3 $b	:
2.10.6	Date of manufacture	2014	264 #3 $c	,
2.11	Copyright date	©2013	264 #4 $c	n/a
2.12.2	Title proper of series and subseries (T)	Library and information science text series	490 $a	n/a
2.13	Mode of issuance	single unit	Ldr/07	
2.15	Identifier for manifestation	ISBN: 978-1-59158-998-2 (alk. paper) ISBN: 978-1-59158-999-X (pbk. : alk. paper)	020 $a	n/a
Carriers				
3.2	Media type	unmediated computer [for accompanying material]	337	n/a
3.3	Carrier type	volume computer disc [for accompanying material]	338	n/a
3.4	Extent	ix, 378 pages, 22 unnumbered leaves of plates	330 $a	n/a
3.5	Dimensions	26 cm	300 $c	;
	Carrier description of accompanying material	Extent: 1 CD-ROM (15 MS PowerPoint files, 36 text files) Dimensions: 4 3/4 in.	300 $e	+
Works and Expressions				
6.2.2	Preferred title for the work or expression	Organization of information	130 $a 240 $a 7XX $t	n/a n/a .
6.9	Content type	text still image	336	n/a
	Other work or expression level information	Form of work: Teacher's manual AAP for work: Joudrey, Daniel N. Organization of information (Teacher's manual)		

FIGURE 9.5 A Preliminary Record for this Resource in an RDA Book Template.

(*continued*)

Content

7.7	Intended audience	**Instructors of graduate-level courses on Information Organization.**	008/22 521 $a	n/a
7.10	Summarization of the content	**This book is a companion to the third edition of the textbook *The Organization of Information* by Arlene G. Taylor and Daniel N. Joudrey, published by Libraries Unlimited in 2009 (ISBN: 9781591585862). It contains strategies, tips, and tricks for teaching a graduate-level course on Information Organization in a library and information science program.**	520 $a	n/a
7.12	Language of the content	**English**	008/35-7 546	n/a
7.15	Illustrative content	**illustrations, graphs, forms**	300 $b	:
7.16	Supplementary content	**Includes bibliographical references (pages 351-368) and index.**	500 $a 504 $a	n/a
	Other content elements	**Color**		

Persons, Families, and Corporate Bodies (PFCs) Associated with Resource

19.2	Principal or First-named Creator	**Joudrey, Daniel N., author**	1XX $a	n/a
19.2	Additional creators	**Taylor, Arlene G., 1941- , author**	7XX $a	n/a
20.2	Contributors	**Miller, David P. (David Peter), 1955- , illustrator** **Chan, Lois Mai, editor**	7XX $a	n/a

Related Resources

25.1	Related work	***in series*: Library and information science text series** ***container of (work)*: Providing context: organization of recorded information — What students need to know about retrieval tools and systems — Make the history of information organization come alive! — Metadata: what's that? — Teaching encoding in 5 easy steps — Introducing students to description — Authority control basics — Teaching subject access: the most fun EVER!**	500/505/ 7XX/490/ 8XX	
26.1	Related expression	***supplement to (expression)* : Taylor, Arlene G., 1941- Organization of information. 2009**	500/7XX	
27.1	Related manifestation	***issued with:* Teaching information organization / Daniel N. Joudrey and Arlene G. Taylor. — Santa Barbara, California : Libraries Unlimited, 2014. — 1 CD-ROM (15 MS PowerPoint files, 36 text files) : color illustrations, PDF ; 4 3/4 in.** **In the inside back cover there is a compact disc titled Teaching Information Organization, which contains materials for teaching with the third edition of The Organization of Information. Materials on the CD-ROM include: 15 sets of lecture slides (PPT), 15 files containing lecture notes (PDF), 15 in-class exercises with answer keys (PDF), and 6 assignments and answer keys (DOCX). The authors of the teacher's guide created all the contents.**	500/7XX	

FIGURE 9.5

(*continued*)

PLACING THE ORIGINAL CATALOGING EXAMPLE INTO MARC

At this point, we have all our descriptive data. What we need to do next is to encode it in some format so that it is accessible in the electronic environment of the catalog. For illustration purposes, we are going to use the MARC bibliographic format. Before reading further in this chapter, you may wish to review (or read for the first time) the chapter on MARC encoding (see chapter 21). Without a basic knowledge of MARC, the subsequent paragraphs may be difficult, if not impossible, to follow. Other electronic formats are discussed in chapter 22.

If I am cataloging in my local integrated library system (or library services platform), I will enter the data into the cataloging module's template; if I am cataloging in a bibliographic network such as OCLC, then I will use the RDA workform for the resource's particular format (e.g., a book). Because there is no guarantee that the readers of this textbook will be familiar with any particular template or form, we are going to use a generic workform based on the OCLC template in which to record our data (Figure 24.2, on p. 929).

Fixed Field Data Elements

We start by entering data into the fixed field. The fixed field block in OCLC, which contains elements from both the leader and the MARC 008 field, contains 21 data elements. To make sure that we are filling in these data elements appropriately, we consult either (1) the LC MARC documentation[5] or (2) OCLC's "Bibliographic Formats and Standards."[6] Because we are using a template similar to that of OCLC, it makes sense to use their MARC documentation, especially because their information about the fixed field is organized according to mnemonic labels used for the various data elements included. Each of the fixed field elements is addressed here:

- **Type of Record (Type)**: This element reflects the kind of resource described in the record. Because we are dealing with text in book form, we record "a," which is for *language materials.*

- **Bibliographic Level (BLvl)**: Bibliographic level contains a value reflecting the mode of issuance. Our resource is a single-part monograph, so we record "m" for *monograph/item.* Had our resource been a serial or an integrating resource, then we would have recorded an "s" or an "i."

- **Descriptive Cataloging Form (Desc)**: This element contains a code for the form of descriptive cataloging performed. Until recently, many records were coded "a" for *AACR2*[7]; now, using RDA, we code our records as "i" for *ISBD* if that standard is being used in the MARC record (as happens in most RDA records in the United States). If ISBD were *not* included, a "c" would be recorded for *ISBD punctuation omitted.* To supplement the information provided by the "i" in **Desc**, additional data ("rda") is recorded in the MARC 040 field in subfield $e.

- **Encoding Level (ELvl)**: This data element reflects the record's degree of completeness. Because we are not creating a complete record (with subject headings and classification numbers) we use "K" for *Less-than-full input by OCLC participants*. If this were a complete record, we would code it "1" for *Full-level input by OCLC participants*.

- **Form of Item (Form)**: Form indicates the form of material described in the record. The values generally represent variations on a standard print resource; in this case, it is left blank for *none of the following* [values].

- **Nature of Contents (Cont)**: This data element provides information about significant parts of the item containing certain types of content or material. Our resource contains a bibliography and is a handbook; we thus need two codes (we can supply up to four). We enter "bf" for *bibliographies* and *handbooks*, respectively.

- **Illustrations (Ills)**: The illustrations data element can contain up to four values for various kinds of illustrative content in the resource. Our resource contains three types of illustrations (i.e., illustrations, graphs, and forms), which are on plates within the resource. So we try to bring out all of these aspects. Looking at the OCLC documentation, however, it appears that graphs are not coded in the data element; but there is a code for plates, even though it is not a type of illustration. We thus record only "afk" for *illustrations*, *plates*, and *forms*.

- **Cataloging Source (Srce)**: This byte indicates the original cataloging source. A "d" for *other* is recorded, because we are not a national bibliographic agency (blank) or a PCC library ("c").

- **Conference Publication (Conf)**: This resource is not the proceedings, a report, or a summary of a conference, so "0" is the appropriate value.

- **Government Publication (GPub)**: It is also not a government publication, so **GPub** is left blank.

- **Festschrift (Fest)**: This resource is not a *festschrift* (a resource published in honor of a person, an institution, or a society on the occasion of an anniversary celebration), so we enter "0" for *not a festschrift*.

- **Audience (Audn)**: Although we have entered a very specific audience for this teacher's manual (or handbook), none of the values are an appropriate fit. There is no value for teachers, instructors, cataloging professors, etc. We can instead enter "f" for a *specialized* audience. A note may be useful in explaining the audience in the record.

- **Biography (Biog)**: There is no biographical material, so **Biog** is left blank.

- **Literary Form (LitF)**: This resource is non-fiction, so "0" is entered for *not fiction (not further specified)*.

- **Type of Date/Publication Status (DtSt)**: This element, obviously, indicates the type of date for the resource. This data element, however, can be somewhat difficult to determine for new catalogers. For our item we have three manufacture dates (two are 2014, and the third is 2015), a copyright date (2013), and a supplied publication date ([2014]). In looking at the list of date types and their preference order, it quickly becomes clear that our value for Type of Date should be "s" for a single date (the supplied publication date). For single items, the choices, in order of preference, are B.C. date (which is n/a to our book), reprint/original date (n/a), detailed date with month and day included (n/a), single date, and so on. Because

TABLE 9.1 Fixed Field Values Used (Based on the OCLC Format).

Type	a	**ELvl**	k	**Srce**	d	**Audn**	f	**Ctrl**		**Lang**	eng
BLvl	m	**Form**		**Conf**	0	**Biog**		**MRec**		**Ctry**	cau
		Cont	bf	**GPub**		**LitF**	0	**Indx**	1		
Desc	i	**Ills**	afk	**Fest**	0	**DtSt**	s	**Dates**	2014,		

single date (i.e., the publication date) comes before anything else that might be applicable, we choose it. This means that only a single date gets entered into the **Dates** element in the fixed field (see below).

- **Type of Control (Ctrl)**: The resource is not described using archival descriptive principles and standards, so **Ctrl** is left blank.
- **Modified Record (MRec)**: The metadata was not modified for machine-readable encoding, so MRec is left blank.
- **Index (Indx)**: There is an index in the resource, so we enter "1" for *Index present.*
- **Dates (Dates)**: Our supplied publication date, 2014, is entered into the field. Nothing else is needed, and the square brackets are omitted.
- **Language Code (Lang)**: This contains a code for the *Language of the content* (RDA 7.12); "eng" is used in this element of the fixed field. If more than one language were included in the expression of the work, then the MARC 041 and 546 fields might be required.
- **Country of Publication (Ctry)**: This is a code that indicates the country (and sometimes state or province) in which the resource was published. We enter "cau" for *California-United States.*

A view of the complete fixed field is provided in Table 9.1.

MARC Fields for Manifestation and Item Elements

After the fixed field is finished, we begin to enter our RDA bibliographic data into the MARC template following the order of elements in RDA or ISBD (although they are not exactly identical, they do have a *somewhat* similar order for many of the basic elements). This means that we start with the title and statement of responsibility.

Before the process can continue in earnest, we must make sure we know what documentation to consult. Again, we may consult either the LC or the OCLC documentation. For the variable content fields, we like both sources. One benefit to using the LC documentation for this part of the process is that the webpage for each MARC field has "Input Conventions," which provide information on punctuating and spacing a MARC record appropriately (beyond the ISBD punctuation discussed in RDA appendix D). For example, on the page for the MARC 245 field (Title Statement), it says, "Field 245 ends with a period, even when another mark of punctuation is present, unless the last word in the field is an abbreviation, initial/letter, or data that ends with final punctuation."[8] This information is very helpful for new catalogers. For the process of encoding our data in MARC, we can use the minimal information provided in the RDA Book Template as a starting point to get an idea of which MARC field to consult. You must remember that the template only provides the most common MARC field for a data element; there are so many exceptional cases in cataloging, though, that you should never rely on the template alone (which may be out of date sooner rather than later). You should use the template to find an initial MARC field(s), but follow that up by consulting whichever form of documentation you prefer to ensure that it is, or is not, the field that you need.

Within each MARC field, there are *tags,* *indicators,* and *subfields.* A tag is a main numerical code assigned to a field in a MARC record to designate the type of content held in the field (e.g., a 245 field contains titles and statements of responsibility). The two digits that follow the tag are called *indicators.* Each indicator position has a certain meaning in the context of its particular field, allowing for correct processing of the metadata contained within the field. Subfields are the distinct elements within fields; they are containers for a more granular level of data. They are designated by a delimiter—a symbol such as the dollar sign ($), the pipe character (|), or the double dagger (‡)—followed by an alphanumeric code to indicate the type of content contained within the subfield.

So, if we are following RDA or ISBD order, then we start with the title and statement of responsibility. This means we must first examine the MARC 245 field. The 245 field appears in every MARC record in OCLC because any resource that can be cataloged must be called *something* (i.e., there must be a title). Thus a title, whether it is on the resource itself or is supplied, must be included in the record. In the 245, there are two indicators and several major subfields. These are:

- **Indicator 1—Title Added Entry**: This indicator tells the system that there should be an access point for the title.

- **Indicator 2—Nonfiling Characters**: This indicator tells the system to skip over a number of alphanumeric characters when recording the title in the catalog's indexes (e.g., the value 4 may mean to skip over *T, h, e,* and a space to get to the first non-article word of the title).

- **$a—Title**: This subfield contains the main title for the resource.

- **$b—Remainder of Title**: This subfield contains subtitles, parallel titles, and other title information associated with the resource. More than one piece of data may appear in $b.

- **$c—Statement of Responsibility, etc.**: This subfield contains the names of those responsible for the resource. More than one element may be recorded in $c.

Placing the data for our resource in this field looks like this:

> **245 14** The organization of information : $b a teacher's guide to the third edition / $c by Daniel N. Joudrey and Arlene G. Taylor ; illustrations by David P. Miller ; edited by Lois Chan.

The two variant titles that we have do not fit anywhere in our 245 field. They belong instead in MARC 246 fields (Varying Form of Title). This field's first indicator asks us if we want a note about the variant title to appear in the record, if we want an access point for the variant title, both, or neither. In this case, it is important to have access points for variant titles; whether notes are needed is a little less important, but they probably should be included. It would be strange to have users search and retrieve the resource by a variant title without actually seeing it mentioned in the search result. We will go for both a note and an access point, which is the value "1." The second indicator is for the specific type of title. With our resource, we have a spine title, which is represented by the value "8." For the title of the accompanying CD-ROM, the second indicator does not offer a specific value that fits. We could use "3" for *other title*, but we could also choose to leave it blank for no type specified. If we leave it blank, we can use $i to provide specific relationship information preceding the access point.

246 18 Oofl3 : $b a teacher's guide

246 1_ $i Title of accompanying CD: $a Teaching information organization

The major subfields in the 246 field ($a and $b) are the same as in the 245 field. (You must remember, however, that this will not always be the case. Subfield codes are contextual; they change from MARC field to MARC field.) No ending punctuation is used in a 246 field, unless the last word is an abbreviation or the like.

You have probably noticed that there are punctuation symbols and spaces inserted in the MARC fields we have completed. This is the ISBD punctuation that has been mentioned several times above (and in chapter 23 of this textbook). In RDA-based descriptive cataloging, ISBD is used to connect the elements in MARC subfields. It helps pull discrete chunks of data into a fuller statement. In the 245 and the 246, the colon (just before $b) states, "This is a subtitle or other title information." The slash in the MARC 245 field indicates that what follows is an SOR and the semicolons let us know that what follows are additional SORs. The punctuation is predictive; it precedes its accompanying element and announces what type of data will appear. The punctuation is also contextual; most of the time, a punctuation symbol in one MARC field represents something different in another MARC field (or ISBD area). Throughout the rest of the examples in this section of the textbook, we will not stop to explain every MARC subfield or piece of ISBD punctuation. Please consult chapters 21 and 23 in this textbook and the formal MARC and ISBD documentation for more information on these details.

With the title statements now complete, we want to focus on the next metadata element: the edition. There is only the designation of the edition, so it is fairly simple. It belongs in the MARC 250 field. There is no preceding punctuation because the edition statement in ISBD is only preceded by the area-separating punctuation (i.e., point-space-dash-space); in MARC this area-separating punctuation is not applicable.

250 _ _ First edition.

Next we move to our dissemination area. It belongs in the MARC 264 field (which is a fairly recent replacement for the 260 field, which is still seen in older, non-RDA records). The question is how much of the dissemination data to include in the record. In our RDA template, we transcribed publication data, distribution data, manufacture data, and a copyright date. If we are following RDA practices exactly, no more than the publishing data is required, which looks like this:

> **264 _1** Santa Barbara, California : $b Libraries Unlimited, $c [2014]

This field, similar to the MARC 260 field that it replaces, typically contains subfields for the place of the disseminating body, the name of the disseminating body, and the date that the resource was disseminated. The field ends in either a period or another piece of punctuation (i.e., period, hyphen, bracket, or parenthesis), although there are some cases where no punctuation is used (e.g., when some subfields are missing). Because we have a square bracket, no period is required. The internal punctuation is standardized. A colon precedes the body responsible for disseminating the resource, and a comma precedes the date of dissemination (except for a copyright date). Please note that there are spaces on both sides of the colon and most other ISBD punctuation marks. For commas and full-stops (i.e., periods), however, there is only a space following the punctuation mark. This is standard ISBD spacing practice that is explained more fully in the formal ISBD documentation.[9]

If we decide to include all the dissemination metadata, then we must take advantage of the repeatable 264 field and be sure that the values in the second indicator are appropriately coded. The values for the second indicator are: 0=Production Statement, 1=Publication Statement, 2=Distribution Statement, 3=Manufacture Statement, and 4=Copyright Notice Date. A much fuller recording of the dissemination data looks like this:

> **264 _1** Santa Barbara, California : $b Libraries Unlimited, $c [2014]
>
> **264 _2** Santa Barbara, California : $b ABC-CLIO
>
> **264 _3** Pasadena, California : $b Deluxe Quick-E Printing, $c 2014.
>
> **264 _3** Santa Barbara, California : $b Alternative Digital Printing, $c 2014.
>
> **264 _4** $c ©2013

Note that the distribution statement (i.e., 264 _2) contains no ending punctuation because the field is incomplete. And, when the field contains only a copyright date, no ending punctuation is used at all.

The next element we must address is the series information. For this item, we transcribe exactly what we find on the resource itself. The series title is found on the title page, but there are no additional pieces of series data found there or anywhere else on the item (i.e., no ISSN, no SOR, no series numbering). Before we can complete the MARC 490 field we need to determine the answer to a question: Are we going to treat this series as an access point (representing a whole-part work-to-work relationship) or treat it only as a transcribed statement reflecting the manifestation? Although the Library of Congress no longer traces series metadata (i.e., tracks an access point in order to find all records containing it), other libraries do. We are not only going to transcribe the data, but also we are going to create an access point so that all resources that are part of the same series can be brought together by that access point. This answer gives us the appropriate value in the first indicator of our 490. By coding it *1*, it says we are tracing the series and, therefore, we have an access point in the 8XX fields. The 490 has no ending punctuation, but the 830 field ends with a punctuation mark.

> **490 1**_ Library and information science text series
>
> **830** _**0** Library and information science text series.

It is quite obvious that the data in the 830 field is identical to that found in the 490, but for other resources being cataloged, this may not always be the case. With our resource, the series title on the resource itself matches perfectly the AAP that has been established in the authority record for the series in the LCNAF. Even though they match exactly, the data is processed differently by most catalog systems, so both MARC fields—at least for the time being—are needed if we wish to collocate by series titles in the catalog. (See chapter 21 for further discussion of what might seem like duplicate data in MARC.)

An identifier is the final manifestation element required for this item. We identified two ISBNs for this resource. We are going to record both. The ISBNs are recorded in separate MARC 020 fields. The digits are recorded without hyphens and the qualification is recorded as part of $a (in the following examples $a *is* present, but the delimiter and the subfield code are not displayed).

> **020** _ _ 9781591589982 $q (alk. paper)
>
> **020** _ _ 978159158999X $q (pbk. ; $q alk. paper)

MARC Fields for Carrier Elements and Accompanying Materials

Carrier information is the next thing to be added to the record. The first carrier element is the media type. It, along with content type and carrier type, recently replaced the GMD (245 $h) in MARC records. The three MARC fields created for these elements (336, 337, and 338) are recorded together even though one of the three elements (content type) is not related to carriers but is instead associated with the expression of the work. In $2, we specify the source of the term used. Because our resource is made up of two carriers, both are described in these elements. We can use the $3 in MARC to specify which fields are associated with which type of carrier. For the 336, $3 is unnecessary because both types of content appear in both carriers (and $3 is not repeatable).

> **336** _ _ text $2 rdacontent
>
> **336** _ _ still image $2 rdacontent

337 _ _ unmediated $2 rdamedia $3 book

337 _ _ computer $2 rdamedia $3 CD-ROM

338 _ _ volume $2 rdacarrier $3 book

338 _ _ computer disc $2 rdacarrier $3 CD-ROM

The carrier description continues with the extent of the resource. The extent, the first element of the physical description, is recorded in $a of the MARC 300 field. For our resource, it contains pagination and leaves of plates. As was the case in the 33X fields, we find a mixture of carrier and expression-level metadata appearing in the MARC 300 field. In $b, which is preceded by a colon, other physical details are recorded; for our resource this contains an extensive statement of illustrative matter (a content element). You record the dimensions (e.g., a carrier element) in $c, following a semicolon separating it from $b. Although not required, we decided it is more helpful to the patron to have a fuller picture of the illustrative content than the brief "Illustrations" statement required by the LC-PCC PS for RDA 7.15.1.3. In $b, we also add our color statement. It is traditionally combined with the statement of illustration. Because all the illustrations are in color, we simply state, "color illustrations." If there were variations among the illustrations, the statement would necessarily be more complex. In addition, the 300 field contains a $e, which is used for *accompanying materials*, a concept that, despite being used in the instructions for sources of information, is not actually defined in RDA.

The concept of accompanying materials is best explained in the context of LC-PCC PS 3.1.4: Resources Consisting of More than One Carrier Type, which discusses the Library of Congress's approach to describing resources with multiple carriers. It states that for resources consisting of several carrier types (e.g., a book with a CD-ROM, a game cartridge with a booklet), we are to treat one part of the resource as the primary component, with the other component(s) treated as accompanying materials. *Accompanying materials* are dependent parts of a resource that accompany (and are cataloged along with) the primary component (e.g., a small set of maps that accompany a geography textbook). LC and the PCC offer three basic approaches that are enumerated in the policy statement: (1) detailed descriptions, (2) simple descriptions, and (3) no carrier description.

When a detailed description is required or desired, we can create either two separate carrier descriptions or a single complex carrier description. For our resource, the information could be recorded as two separate carrier descriptions:

300 _ _ ix, 378 pages, 22 unnumbered leaves of plates : $b color illustrations, graphs, forms ; $c 26 cm

300 _ _ 1 CD-ROM (15 MS PowerPoint files, 36 text files) : $b color illustrations, PDF ; $c 4 3/4 in.

Or, the carrier description could be recorded as a single statement, using the $e for accompanying material in the 300 field:

300 _ _ ix, 378 pages, 22 unnumbered leaves of plates : $b color illustrations, graphs, forms ; $c 26 cm + $e 1 CD-ROM (15 MS PowerPoint files, 36 text files : color illustrations, PDF ; 4 3/4 in.)

If a simpler carrier description is all that is needed, then the same two approaches may be followed. Two separate physical description fields:

300 _ _ ix, 378 pages, 22 unnumbered leaves of plates : $b color illustrations, graphs, forms ; $c 26 cm

300 _ _ 1 CD-ROM

Or, a single 300 field:

300 _ _ ix, 378 pages, 22 unnumbered leaves of plates : $b color illustrations, graphs, forms ; $c 26 cm + $e 1 CD-ROM

If neither of these approaches is needed, then the accompanying material can be recorded in a note, such as: *Issued with one accompanying compact disc.*

For our resource, we will use a detailed single statement using $e. For this item, we will end the 300 field with a period. The LC-PCC documentation for RDA 1.7.1: Transcription states that whenever a 490 field (series statement) appears in a bibliographic record, we must ensure that the 300 field ends with a period.

300 _ _ ix, 378 pages, 22 unnumbered leaves of plates : $b color illustrations, graphs, forms ; $c 26 cm + $e 1 CD-ROM (15 MS PowerPoint files, 36 text files : color illustrations, PDF ; 4 3/4 in.).

MARC Fields for Content Elements

Following the physical description, there are a few additional content elements to be recorded (beyond illustrative matter). We have summary information readily accessible, so that gets recorded in a MARC 520 field. We have an understanding of the supplementary material found in the resource. The resource includes both an index and bibliographical references, thus the combined statement is entered into a 504 note. Had there only been an index (and no bibliography), the note would be recorded in a 500 field. Because the fixed field element for audience does not allow for much specificity, we should include a Target Audience note (521 field) as well. This data is recorded as follows:

504 _ _ Includes bibliographical references (pages 351-368) and index.

520 _ _ This book is a companion to the third edition of the textbook *The Organization of Information* by Arlene G. Taylor and Daniel N. Joudrey, published by Libraries Unlimited in 2009

(ISBN: 9781591585862). It contains strategies, tips, and tricks for teaching a graduate-level course on Information Organization in a library and information science program.

521 _ _ Instructors of graduate-level courses on Information Organization.

MARC Fields for Access Points and Notes Representing Relationships

Now that the basic descriptive data has been entered into the MARC record, we need to begin addressing access points and relationships. We know that we have a work title, four persons involved with the development of the resource, and a number of other relationships that must be addressed.

As discussed above, a work title is necessary because of the similarity of the title proper to the title proper of the related work and the fact that the two creators are identical for both resources. This means we should add the work title to provide some clarity. We do this in a MARC 240 field (Uniform Title). There are a few small quirks associated with the MARC 240 and the recording of a work and expression title. Even though the MARC field provides a second indicator that specifies non-filing characters (e.g., skipping over 4 spaces for *T*, *h*, *e*, and a space), the LC-PCC PS for RDA 6.2.1.7: Initial Articles [in work titles] states that we are to omit the initial article. The work title, therefore, is recorded as follows:

240 10 Organization of information (Teacher's manual)

The access points for the creators are recorded differently in MARC. At this time, the MARC format still uses the 1XX field to identify the primary creator of the work (e.g., the creator with principal responsibility or the first-named creator). In this case, the authors shared responsibility for the content, so the one named first is placed in a 100 field (Main Entry—Personal Name). The second creator is placed in a 700 field (Added Entry—Personal Name). In both access point fields, the appropriate relationship designator for roles should be added in a $e (Relator Term). The two contributors are also entered in 700 fields.

100 1_ Joudrey, Daniel N., $e author.

700 1_ Taylor, Arlene G., $d 1941- $e author.

700 1_ Miller, David P. $q (David Peter), $d 1955- $e illustrator.

700 1_ Chan, Lois Mai, $e editor.

The final pieces of our MARC puzzle that we need to address are the four remaining relationships. One relationship, the work-to-work relationship with the series, has already been addressed. Now we need to look at the other work-to-work relationship: the contents. For this we create a 505 field (Formatted Contents Notes) in the record. Because we have the complete contents listed, the first indicator is "0" rather than a value reflecting incomplete or partial contents notes. The second indicator tells our catalogs whether the notes are basic (all data in one $a) or enhanced (with separate subfields for titles ($t), statements of responsibility ($r), and other components). For our resource, we only need basic notes, so the second indicator is left blank. If, however, we felt that each chapter title needed to be searchable (and our catalog is programmed to include $t in the general title index), then we might have chosen to create enhanced contents notes instead.

> **505 0_** Providing context: organization of recorded information — What students need to know about retrieval tools and systems — Make the history of information organization come alive! — Metadata: what's that? — Teaching encoding in 5 easy steps — Introducing students to description — Authority control basics — Teaching subject access: the most fun ever!

In addition to this relationship, we want to relate this resource to the expression of the work it supplements. This is done using a 700 field, but this time the 700 field contains a name/title access point and not just a personal name. We add the title (again, without an initial article) in $t. For this particular expression, the date associated with the edition is added in a $f; without it, users might assume that the resource being cataloged could be used with other editions of *The Organization of Information*.

> **700 1_** $i supplement to (expression): $a Taylor, Arlene G., 1941- $t Organization of information. $f 2009.

These are not the only relationships we need to address; there is still a manifestation-to-manifestation relationship and some additional information about the accompanying material. Both can be recorded as notes.

> **500 _ _** Issued with: Teaching information organization / Daniel N. Joudrey and Arlene G. Taylor. — Santa Barbara, California : Libraries Unlimited, 2014. — 1 CD-ROM (15 MS PowerPoint files, 36 text files) : color illustrations, PDF ; 4 3/4 in.

> **500 _ _** In the inside back cover there is a compact disc titled "Teaching Information Organization," which contains materials for teaching with the third edition of "The Organization of Information." Materials on the CD-ROM include: 15 sets of lecture slides (PPT), 15 files containing lecture notes (PDF), 15 in-class exercises with answer keys (PDF), and 6 assignments and answer keys (DOCX). The authors of the teacher's guide created all the contents.

Both help the user to understand more fully the accompany material, its contents, and its location in the resource.

The preliminary MARC record that we have created is provided in Figure 9.6.

Rec Stat	n	Entered	20150108	Replaced	20150819103849.20				
Type	a	**ELvl**	k	**Srce**	d	**Audn**	f	**Ctrl**		**Lang**	eng
BLvl	m	**Form**		**Conf**	0	**Biog**		**MRec**		**Ctry**	cau
		Cont	bf	**GPub**		**LitF**	0	**Indx**	1		
Desc	i	**Ills**	afk	**Fest**	0	**DtSt**	s	**Dates**	2014,		

040		SCL $e rda $c SCL
020		9781591589982 $q (alk. paper)
020		978159158999X $q (pbk. ; $q alk. paper)
041	0	eng
049		SCL
100	1	Joudrey, Daniel N., $e author.
240	1 0	Organization of information (Teacher's manual)
245	1 4	The organization of information : $b a teacher's guide to the third edition / $c by Daniel N. Joudrey and Arlene G. Taylor ; illustrations by David P. Miller ; edited by Lois Chan.
246	1 8	Oofl3 : $b a teacher's guide
246	1	$i Title of accompanying CD: $a Teaching information organization
250		First edition.
264	1	Santa Barbara, California : $b Libraries Unlimited, $c [2014]
264	2	Santa Barbara, California : $b ABC-CLIO
264	3	Pasadena, California : $b Deluxe Quick-E Printing, $c 2014.
264	3	Santa Barbara, California : $b Alternative Digital Printing, $c 2014.
264	4	$c ©2013
300		ix, 378 pages, 22 unnumbered leaves of plates : $b color illustrations, graphs, forms ; $c 26 cm + $e 1 CD-ROM (15 MS PowerPoint files, 36 text files : color illustrations, PDF ; 4 3/4 in.).
336		text $2 rdacontent
336		still image $2 rdacontent
337		unmediated $2 rdamedia $3 book
337		computer $2 rdamedia $3 CD-ROM
338		volume $2 rdacarrier $3 book
338		computer disc $2 rdacarrier $3 CD-ROM
490	1	Library and information science text series
500		Issued with: Teaching information organization / Daniel N. Joudrey and Arlene G. Taylor. — Santa Barbara, California : Libraries Unlimited, 2014. — 1 CD-ROM (15 MS PowerPoint files, 36 text files) : color illustrations, PDF ; 4 3/4 in.
500		In the inside back cover there is a compact disc titled "Teaching Information Organization," which contains materials for teaching with the third edition of "The Organization of Information." Materials on the CD-ROM include: 15 sets of lecture slides (PPT), 15 files containing lecture notes (PDF), 15 in-class exercises with answer keys (PDF), and 6 assignments and answer keys (DOCX). The authors of the teacher's guide created all the contents.
504		Includes bibliographical references (pages 351-368) and index.
505	0	Providing context: organization of recorded information — What students need to know about retrieval tools and systems — Make the history of information organization come alive! — Metadata: what's that? — Teaching encoding in 5 easy steps — Introducing students to description — Authority control basics — Teaching subject access: the most fun EVER!
520		This book is a companion to the third edition of the textbook *The Organization of Information* by Arlene G. Taylor and Daniel N. Joudrey, published by Libraries Unlimited in 2009 (ISBN: 9781591585862). It contains strategies, tips, and tricks for teaching a graduate-level course on Information Organization in a library and information science program.
521		Instructors of graduate-level courses on Information Organization.
700	1	Taylor, Arlene G., $d 1941- $e author.
700	1	Miller, David P. $q (David Peter), $d 1955- $e illustrator.
700	1	Chan, Lois Mai, $e editor.
700	1	$i supplement to (expression): $a Taylor, Arlene G., 1941- $t Organization of information. $f 2009.
830	0	Library and information science text series.

FIGURE 9.6 A Preliminary MARC Record for this Resource (An Original Record Based on the OCLC Format).

CONCLUSION

In this chapter, we have provided a step-by-step overview of the descriptive cataloging process using a fabricated resource to help guide you along the way. It does not address every issue that could arise while cataloging a resource, but it is an illustration of many of the most common decisions we might make. The second half of the chapter illustrated encoding the description in the MARC bibliographic format. For more on MARC 21 and alternative approaches to encoding, please see Part V of this text. In chapter 10, you find an overview of authority control issues and processes.

NOTES

1. *RDA: Resource Description & Access*, developed in a collaborative process led by the Joint Steering Committee for Development of RDA (Chicago: American Library Association, 2010). Also available through paid subscriptions to *RDA Toolkit* (Chicago: American Library Association, 2010), accessed June 28, 2014, http://www.rdatoolkit.org/.
2. International Federation of Library Associations, *ISBD: International Standard Bibliographic Description*, recommended by the ISBD Review Group; approved by the Standing Committee of the IFLA Cataloguing Section, Consolidated ed. (München, Germany: De Gruyter Saur, 2011). Also available online at the IFLA website: http://www.ifla.org/files/assets/cataloguing/isbd/isbd-cons_20110321.pdf.
3. Library of Congress, Network Development and MARC Standards Office, *MARC 21 Format for Bibliographic Data*, accessed May 26, 2014, http://www.loc.gov/marc/bibliographic/ecbdhome.html.
4. The template is available at http://web.simmons.edu/~joudrey/ICC11/ in .PDF, .RTF, and .DOC formats.
5. Library of Congress, *MARC 21 Format for Bibliographic Data*.
6. OCLC, *Bibliographic Formats and Standards*, 4th edition, accessed November 2, 2014, http://oclc.org/bibformats/en.html.
7. *Anglo-American Cataloguing Rules, Second Edition*, 2002 Revision, prepared under the direction of the Joint Steering Committee for Revision of AACR (Ottawa: Canadian Library Association; Chicago: American Library Association, 2002).
8. Library of Congress, "245 – Title Statement," *MARC 21 Format for Bibliographic Data*, October 2008, http://www.loc.gov/marc/bibliographic/bd245.html.
9. IFLA, *ISBD*, Consolidated ed., Section A.3.2.1.

Part III

Authority Control

Chapter 10

Authority Control

INTRODUCTION

Authority control, as currently practiced, is the result of the process of maintaining consistency in the verbal form used to represent an access point in a catalog and the further process of showing the relationships among names, works, expressions, and subjects. The goal is to make possible the identifying, collocating, and evaluating functions of the catalog, described in chapter 1 of this text, and further explicated in this chapter. The following discussion includes authority control of subject headings in addition to authority control of names and works, although introduction to subject analysis and creation of subject headings follows in the next chapters.

As mentioned in several earlier chapters, international authority control is increasingly of concern. This is true because of the need to allow the creators of catalogs in various countries using various languages to designate their own "authorized" forms (i.e., character strings) of names and subject terms. Everyone should not be required to use English-language "authorized" forms, but we all should be able to use the same authority control. In order to accomplish international authority control the Virtual International Authority File (VIAF) has been established, originating at the Library of Congress (LC) but now under the aegis of OCLC, to draw together authority data from many different national libraries and to provide links between equivalent entities.[1]

AUTHORITY CONTROL AND FUNCTIONS OF THE CATALOG

As described in chapter 1 of this text, understanding the functions of a catalog has been developing for well over a century. Among the more recent statements is the IFLA document, published in 1998, called *Functional*

Requirements for Bibliographic Records (FRBR),[2] which maps the relationships it identifies to four *user tasks*:

- to *find* entities that correspond to the user's stated search criteria . . .
- to *identify* an entity . . .
- to *select* an entity that is appropriate to the user's needs . . .
- to acquire or *obtain* access to the entity described . . .[3]

These tasks form the basis for the functions of a catalog that are presented in another IFLA document that came into being after a decade of discussion by cataloging specialists from all over the world. This document, published in 2009, is the *Statement of International Cataloguing Principles* (ICP).[4] As outlined in chapter 3 of this text, the ICP presents the functions of a catalog as assisting a user to find, identify, select, and acquire bibliographic resources, and to navigate through an arrangement of bibliographic and authority data. The ICP functions clearly reflect the user tasks of FRBR. A companion document to FRBR is *Functional Requirements for Authority Data* (FRAD), first published in 2009, with amendments in 2013.[5] FRAD, like FRBR, maps the relationships it identifies to four user tasks:

- **Find**: Find an entity or set of entities corresponding to stated criteria . . . using an attribute or combination of attributes or a relationship of the entity as the search criteria . . . or . . . explore the universe of bibliographic entities using those attributes and relationships.
- **Identify**: Identify an entity (i.e., to confirm that the entity represented corresponds to the entity sought, to distinguish between two or more entities with similar characteristics) or to validate the form of name to be used for a controlled access point.
- **Contextualize**: Place an entity (a work, person, concept, etc.) in context; clarify the relationship between two or more entities; or clarify the relationship between an entity and a name by which that entity is known (e.g., name used in religion versus a secular name).
- **Justify**: Document the authority data creator's reason for choosing the name or form of name on which a controlled access point is based.[6]

These user tasks specifically address the activity of authority control. Two groups of users are defined: authority data creators, and users of authority data as presented in catalogs, bibliographies, and other such tools. *Find* and *identify* are also used in FRBR, but in FRAD their definitions are extended to include the exploration of all entities matching a user's criteria and also to include the process of distinguishing between similar entities and using the authority data to confirm that the entity is the one sought. The two additional user tasks, *contextualize* and *justify*, speak directly to the process that is followed for authority control: providing data to explain an entity's place in the relationship structure of the catalog and data to explain the sources of information that validate the use of a particular form of controlled access point. Whatever the terminology used, authority control greatly enhances a user's ability to have success in using a catalog.

FUNDAMENTALS OF AUTHORITY CONTROL

As described in chapter 3 of this text, the foundations of authority control are *standardization* (i.e., using the same form of name consistently), *uniqueness* (i.e., ensuring that authorized access points are distinctive), and *connections* (i.e., relationships are identified so that variant forms of names or terms point to the chosen authorized access point).

Standardization

Authority control provides standardization through the use of consistent forms of access points with references from forms not used. In a system under authority control, a user can assume that all works related to a name or a concept will be found together or will at least be connected with references. Once one determines, for example, that records are found under **Cochrane, Pauline A.**, and not under Atherton, Pauline, one can assume that everything by this person will be found under this authorized access point (AAP). It is not necessary to look under Cochrane, P. A., or the alternate spelling, Cochran, or to try to think of other possible spellings or forms. Typically, catalogs provide references to point users to the authorized name used in the catalog. Such a reference, for example, might say

> Bordensky (Family : Md.)
> *See* **Borden (Family : Md.)**

It is also possible to find titles through use of a consistent AAP for works that have different titles proper. A particular edition of the Bible, for example, can be found under **Bible**. One need not remember an exact title such as *Holy Bible* or *Good News for Modern Man*, although specific editions can also be found under these titles if one remembers them.

Likewise, once one determines that works about psychological help for families are found under **Family psychotherapy** and not under the term *Family therapy*, one can assume that everything on that topic will be found there. Identification of works on a particular subject is made easier by using only one of the terms when there are two or more synonyms or by always using the words of a phrase in the same order, for example, **Serials control systems**, not *Control systems for serials* or *Control systems, Serials*.

Uniqueness

Authority control provides for disambiguating similar entities by providing character strings that are unique for each entity. If, for example, a user is searching for an agronomist named Margaret Smith and finds that there are more than 100 people in a catalog who are named Margaret Smith, it can be helpful to learn that the majority of them are distinguished from each other by dates of birth, middle names or initials, or some form of qualifier (i.e., a distinguishing data element). Identifying the agronomist could, one hopes, be done by using keyword searching of bibliographic or authority data and finding that her AAP is **Smith, M. A. (Margaret Anne)**, a character string that could then be used to find all of her writings together. In similar fashion, common titles such as *Annual Report* that are under authority control are distinguished from each other, usually by the name of the organization that has created the report. A third kind of disambiguation occurs with words such as *Mercury*, which can be a name, a title, a musical group, a basketball team, a planet, a metal, and so on. The AAPs and variant access points (VAPs) for these various entities distinguish them and help to identify them. For example:

Mercury Acting Company

Mercury (Basketball team)

Mercury, Bruce

Mercury (Choreographic work : Ashton)

Mercury (Firm : Aylesford, England)

Mercury, Freddie

Mercury, Freddie (Spirit)

Mercury (Planet)

Mercury (Roman deity)

Mercury (Ship)

Mercury Theatre

Connections

Authority control provides connections in a catalog through the linking of consistent character strings for access points in a syndetic structure. *Syndetic* is an adjective meaning "connective, connecting." It is used to characterize the nature of a catalog under authority control because of the connecting that is brought about by using consistent access points and by providing references to and among those access points.

Names are collocated by bringing everything by and about a person, family, or corporate body (PFC) together under the same form of name; or in some cases where a PFC actually has used two or more different *names* (not just different forms of a name), collocation may be accomplished by connecting the names with references. Examples of the latter are:

University of North Carolina at Chapel Hill. School of Information and Library Science

Earlier name: **University of North Carolina at Chapel Hill. School of Library Science.**

Dodgson, Charles Lutwidge, 1832-1898

See also: Carroll, Lewis, 1832-1898

Works are collocated by creating a standardized title for every work that has appeared under more than one title and by providing references from the titles not chosen for the authorized access point. In this way, for example, all manifestations of the various expressions of the Bible can be found together; as another example, Dickens's *Life and Adventures of Nicholas Nickleby* can be found with editions of the same work titled *Nicholas Nickleby*. Choosing preferred titles for works also aids in showing relationships among works. Bibliographic records for the musical stage play and the film version of *Nicholas Nickleby* contain access points for the preferred title for Dickens's original work, and can be found collocated with it. References also can help to show relationships among works. An example of such a reference is:

> Tolkien, J. R. R. (John Ronald Reuel), 1892-1973. Lord of the rings. 2. Two towers
>
> *See* **Tolkien, J. R. R. (John Ronald Reuel), 1892-1973. Two towers.**

The preferred title chosen for the work in this example collocates the bibliographic records for the work under the title of the part, but the reference collocates with the title of the whole larger work, letting the user know that parts of the whole work are available in addition to the whole work.

Authority control ensures that subjects are connected by providing consistent headings for discrete concepts, by assuring that there are references to those headings from terms not used, and by providing a network of references to and among broader terms, narrower terms, and related terms. For example, let us suppose that someone is using a catalog in which the subjects are from the *Library of Congress Subject Headings* (LCSH) and in which appropriate references have been provided. If this person looks up *heart attack*, a reference will show that this term is not used but that **Myocardial infarction** is used instead. At **Myocardial infarction**, in addition to finding bibliographic records representing works on the subject, the user will find a reference to the narrower term **Cardiogenic shock**. In an ideal world, there would also be a reference to the broader term **Coronary heart disease**, although, traditionally, library catalogs have referred only to narrower and related terms because it was felt that to refer to broader terms made an impossibly complicated network. (This was true in manual systems. Many libraries even gave up providing related and narrower term references in manual catalogs.) If the broader term reference *is* made, however, the user can follow up with a search under **Coronary heart disease** and be referred to the related term **Type A behavior** and three other narrower terms besides the one that led to this term: **Angina pectoris**, **Coronary artery stenosis**, and **Silent myocardial ischemia**. There could also be a reference to the broader term **Heart—Diseases**.

SYSTEM DESIGN

It should be emphasized that authority control of names, works, and subject terminology does not ensure that everything by and about a PFC or everything on a subject will be found together. The design of the system in which the names, titles, and subject headings are displayed is a major factor. A discussion of how system design can supplement and enhance authority control can be found in Martha M. Yee and Sara Shatford Layne's *Improving Online Public Access Catalogs.*[7] In addition, the Subject Analysis Committee of the American Library Association has published recommendations for system design for the best use and display of subject reference structures. This work is aptly described by David Miller, Tony Olson, and Sara Shatford Layne.[8] Finally, a chapter in *The Organization of Information* addresses issues of system design that can assist or deter users in their successful use of a catalog.[9]

It should also be pointed out that many search terms thought of by users will not match either authorized access points or references. For example, a user of an authority-controlled online catalog who searches for *heart attacks* will likely be told there are no matches, because the reference is from *heart attack* in the singular. Or a person may search for a name spelled as it sounds (e.g., Kirshenbaum, Baruk instead of Kirschenbaum, Baruch). Systems can be designed with enhanced search capabilities to supplement authority control in such situations.

LACK OF AUTHORITY CONTROL

In systems without authority control, it is up to the user to try to think of all possible ways that a name, work, or subject could be verbally represented, while at the same time eliminating all possible representations that will not satisfy the need. For example, a user wanting material on **Mercury** as a metal must eliminate that which concerns the planet or the Roman god; and a user wishing to consult works by John F. Murphy on cash management (see Figure 10.1) must sort out these from works by other John F. Murphys who write about chemical engineering, education, geology, law, parenting, and other subjects, and who do not always use titles that are descriptive of their contents.

In fact, in many of today's supposedly authority-controlled online catalogs, users must do this same sorting, because works by all John F. Murphys, regardless of variant qualifiers or birth dates, are interfiled in the mélange of keyword search results that prevails in today's retrieval tools. In keyword search results, users see no references to this or that John F. Murphy. (See Figure 10.2.) This is a step backward from card catalogs, in which all works by the person whose AAP is **Murphy, John F., 1913-1985** were filed together before works by the person whose AAP is **Murphy, John F., 1922-**.

It has been argued by some that users have for some time now been finding material in uncontrolled online databases that index papers and articles. This is true, but the process is not without some frustration. And the free text searching in search engines on the Internet can yield hundreds of thousands of hits, many completely unrelated to the desired search. A series of articles in 1985 and 1986 in *DATABASE* and *ONLINE* addressed the problem of searching for names in such databases.[10] Even though these articles are now three decades old, they still have much to offer in explaining many of the difficulties encountered in searching any database that is not under authority control. Upon reading these articles the reader may be struck by the immense number of complications waiting to sabotage the uninitiated, and may wonder how any searcher could possibly remember all the tricks necessary for a complete

```
010      n 83175165
040      DLC $b eng $c DLC $d DLC
100  1_  Murphy, John F.
670      Murphy, A.M. Successful parenting, c1983 (a.e.) $b CIP t.p. (John F. Murphy, Ed. M.)


010      n 80072584
040      DLC $b eng $c DLC
100  1_  Murphy, John F., $d 1922-
400  1_  Murphy, Jack, $d 1922-
670      His Mary's immaculate heart, 1951.


010      n 83016187
040      DGPO $b eng $e rda $c DLC $d OkU
100  1_  Murphy, John F. $q (John Francis), $d 1913-
374      Bankers $2 lcsh
375      male
378      $q John Francis
670      His Sound cash management and borrowing, 1981: $b t.p. (John F. Murphy, retired bank
         exec. and member Manasota SCORE Chapter, Sarasota, Fla.)


010      no 90025472
040      DGPO $b eng $e rda $c DGPO $d RPB $d DLC $d OkU
100  1_  Murphy, John F. $q (John Francis), $d 1922-2006
375      male
400  1_  Murphy, J. F. $q (John Francis), $d 1922-2006
670      Richmond, G.M. Preliminary quaternary geologic map of the Dinwoody Lake area,
         Fremont County, Wyoming [MI], 1989?: $b t.p. (John F. Murphy; U.S. Geological Survey)
670      Phone call to author, 11/26/90 $b (John Francis Murphy, b. 8/27/22)


010      n 78011669
040      DLC $b eng $c DLC $d MoSpS-AV
100  1_  Murphy, John Francis, $d 1937-
400  1_  Murphy, John F. $q (John Francis), $d 1937-
670      American Society of International Law. Legal aspects ... 1978 (a.e.) $b t.p. (John F.
         Murphy)
670      International criminal law [VR] 1995: $b guide (Professor John F. Murphy, Villanova
         University School of Law; speaker)
```

FIGURE 10.1 Partial Authority Records for Five Authors Who Use the Name "John F. Murphy." (Source: OCLC Connexion, Authorities)

name search. These articles are mini-lessons in performing authority work, except that it is up to the user, not the cataloger, to do the work over and over as searches are performed.

AUTHORITY WORK

Authority control, of course, cannot be achieved automatically. It requires authority work to be done by catalogers and indexers. First, it is necessary to discover all available evidence related to the naming of a PFC, geographic body, work, topic, or genre/form, and then to choose the form of name to use as the AAP and the forms to use as references according to the instructions and/or cataloger's judgment. Then there must be creation of authority records. A carefully prepared authority record contains the form of name or term chosen for use as the AAP, a list of variant forms or terms that may be

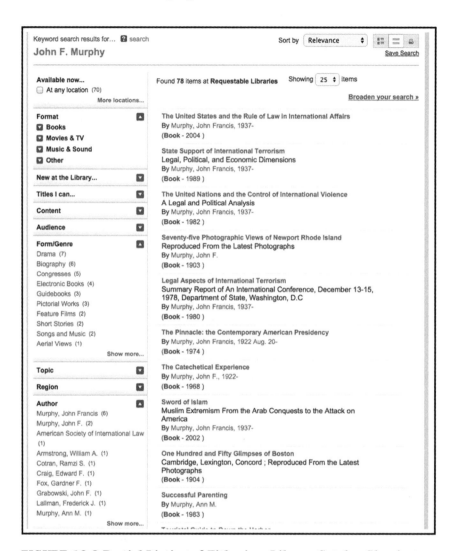

FIGURE 10.2 Partial Listing of Titles in a Library Catalog Showing the Result of a Keyword Search for Authors Named "John F. Murphy." (Source: Boston Public Library Catalog)

used as references, a list of sources consulted in the process of deciding on the access points, and additional metadata to better identify and understand the entity being described in the authority data.

Name and Title Authority Work

The process followed for names, preferred titles for works, and series is somewhat different from that used for subjects. The first step in the process used for names, titles, and series is verification, which means determining the existence of an entity and the accepted form of authorized access point to use.

A PFC name or a title is first recorded as it appears in the work being cataloged. The next step usually is to check the library's catalog and authority files to determine if an AAP for this PFC name or title already has been established for the library. If it has, the authorized form is noted and used in the cataloging in hand, unless the form and/or the recorded data needs to be updated based on new available data. If the authorized form is not already established or it needs to be updated, the cataloger checks the LC Name Authority File (LCNAF) either online at LC's authorities website[11] or through a bibliographic network in which the library holds membership. If the name or title is in the LCNAF and is coded as being in RDA form, the record is copied for the local file. This may be accomplished by downloading the authority record from the bibliographic network to the local system.

For example, suppose a cataloger is cataloging an album of photographs taken by a local patron who was attending the Smithsonian Folklife Festival. The cataloger checks the LCNAF and finds the record shown in Figure 10.3. This is an authority record created in the MARC 21 format (MAchine-Readable Cataloging format for the United States, Canada, and Great Britain) by a Name Authority Cooperative (NACO) Program library and updated by LC and other NACO libraries (as shown in the 040 field). Most libraries try to use LCNAF records as much as possible in order to reduce their local authority work. In addition to being coded according to the MARC 21 authorities format, the record is formatted as found in the OCLC system. (Fields in records formatted in OCLC do not show the delimiter and subfield code "$a" if the first subfield is *subfield a*; second or later instances of $a in a field, however, do show the code; and all subfield codes after *a* in the English alphabet are shown, wherever they appear.) The record in Figure 10.3 is created using RDA instructions, which is noted by *rda* appearing in $e of the 040 field. In the MARC 21 authorities format the AAP is given in a field beginning with "1" (100, 110, 111, 130, 150, 151, etc., usually abbreviated 1XX to designate the whole group), and any variant access points are given in fields beginning with "4" (400, 410, etc., usually abbreviated 4XX) or "5" (500, 510, etc., usually abbreviated 5XX). Catalogs built around the MARC format are programmed to create references from forms of name appearing in 4XX or 5XX fields. The contents in 4XX fields are forms of names or titles that do not appear as AAPs on bibliographic or authority records. A reference made from a 4XX field to a 1XX field is called a *see from* reference in MARC. The contents in 5XX fields are forms of names or titles that do appear as AAPs on authority records. A reference made from a 5XX field to a 1XX field is called a *see also from* reference. Notes are given in 6XX fields (667, 670, 675, 678, 680, 681, 682, 690). Series information appears in the 64X fields (i.e., 640–646); special kinds of references are given in fields 663 through 666. MARC records, of course, can be displayed however a system programmer chooses.

The record in Figure 10.3 shows *Smithsonian Folklife Festival* in a 111 field, which is for a conference or meeting name. The OCLC documentation states: "Conference or meeting names are the names of athletic contests, conferences, exhibitions, expositions, festivals, meetings and scientific expeditions."[12] There are three 4XX fields from which *see* references will be made (e.g., Folklife Festival, Smithsonian *see* Smithsonian Folklife Festival). A *see also from* reference will be made from the former name of the festival in the 511 field. Two 670

ARN	4779096				
Rec stat c		Entered 19980724	Replaced 20131221073738.0		
Type	z	Upd status	a	Enc lvl	n	Source	c
Roman	l	Ref status	a	Mod rec		Name use	a
Govt agn	l	Auth status	a	Subj	a	Subj use	a
Series	n	Auth/ref	a	Geo subd	n	Ser use	b
Ser num	n	Name	n	Subdiv tp	n	Rules	z

010	no 98098828
040	DSI $b eng $e rda $c DSI $d IEN $d DLC $d CU-A
046	$s 1998
111 2	Smithsonian Folklife Festival
368	Festivals $2 lcsh
411 2	Folklife Festival, Smithsonian
410 2	Smithsonian Institution. $b Center for Folklife Programs and Cultural Studies. $b Smithsonian Folklife Festival
410 2	Smithsonian Institution. $b Folklife Festival
511 2	$i Predecessor: $a Festival of American Folklife $w r
670	Smithsonian Folklife Festival on the National Mall, Washington, D.C., 1998: $b t.p. (1998 Smithsonian Folklife Festival ... June 24-28 & July 1-5) cover (Smithsonian Folklife Festival 1998)
670	Phone call to Center for Folklife Programs and Cultural Studies, July 24, 1998 $b (The Festival of American Folklife changed its name to Smithsonian Folklife Festival in 1998; the festival is produced by the Smithsonian Institution Center for Folklife Programs and Cultural Studies)

FIGURE 10.3 MARC Name Authority Record. (Source: OCLC Connexion, Authorities—record number 4779096)

fields provide justification for the cataloger's choices by giving sources consulted with the information learned from each source.

If a name or title is not in the LCNAF or is not coded as being in RDA form, then RDA is consulted for the appropriate instructions for identifying PFCs or works. If verification problems emerge, such as the existence of different names or different forms of the same name, further sources of information must be consulted. Such sources that might be consulted include other works by the same person or family, additional works issued by the same corporate body, publisher sites on the Internet, reliable directories, biographical dictionaries, or other reference sources. It is also possible to contact publishers (using contact data found at their websites) and/ or creators (often through an institution with which they are associated, or through a website with which they might be connected) for additional information. Then an authority record must be made or updated. The one or more sources of authoritative information that have been used are cited in the authority record. Pertinent references are listed. References also should be made, along with a revised authority record, for any conflicting AAP that had to be changed in the process of creating the authorized access point for the name or title in hand.

If the record found is not coded as being in RDA form, a cataloger may decide to add to the record to provide new justification that is readily available. Suppose, for example, that the new edition of *Introduction to Cataloging and Classification* has the information found in Figure 10.4. A search for the author, Arlene G. Taylor, in the LCNAF finds a record last edited in 1985, shown in Figure 10.5.

About the Author

Dr. ARLENE G. TAYLOR is Professor Emerita, School of Information Sciences, University of
Pittsburgh, and author of several works on cataloging and classification and authority control.
Born in Kansas, USA, in 1941, she spent most of her childhood and teen years in Oklahoma. She
attended Oklahoma Baptist University, receiving a B.A. in 1963. She received an MSLS from
the University of Illinois in 1966, after which she worked as a cataloger at the Library of
Congress (Washington, DC), Christopher Newport College (Newport News, VA), and Iowa
State University (Ames, IA) through 1975. Experience in these positions, along with
opportunities to teach as an adjunct lecturer in the Graduate School of Library and Information
Science at the University of Illinois, led to a desire to teach library science full time. She earned
her Ph.D. in the School of Information and Library Science, University of North Carolina at
Chapel Hill, in 1981. While a doctoral student, Dr. Taylor taught at North Carolina Central
University (1975-1976, 1979) and since then has taught at the University of Chicago (1981-
1986), Columbia University (1986 -1993), and University of Pittsburgh (1993-2007). She
received the 1996 Margaret Mann Citation in Cataloging and Classification from the Cataloging
and Classification Section of ALA, the 2000 ALA Highsmith Library Literature Award, and the
2011 Distinguished Alumnus Award from the Graduate School of Library and Information
Science of the University of Illinois. More information about Dr. Taylor may be found on her
web page: http://www.pitt.edu/~agtaylor. She may be contacted at: ataylor@sis.pitt.edu.

FIGURE 10.4 Information About an Author Provided on a Faux "About the Author" Page in a Book.

ARN	431885							
Rec stat	c	**Entered**	19800519	**Replaced**	19851002111141.3			
Type	z	**Upd status**	a	**Enc lvl**	n		**Source**	c
Roman	l	**Ref status**	a	**Mod rec**			**Name use**	a
Govt agn	l	**Auth status**	a	**Subj**	a		**Subj use**	a
Series	n	**Auth/ref**	a	**Geo subd**	n		**Ser use**	b
Ser num	n	**Name**	a	**Subdiv tp**	n		**Rules**	c
010		n 80050006						
040		DLC $b eng $c DLC $d DLC						
100	1_	Taylor, Arlene G., $d 1941-						
400	1_	Dowell, Arlene Taylor, $d 1941- $w nna						
670		Her Cataloging with copy, 1976: $b t.p. (Arlene Taylor Dowell)						
670		Wynar, B.S. Introd. to cat. and class., 1985: $b CIP t.p. (Arlene G. Taylor)						

**FIGURE 10.5 Authority Record Found in LCNAF for Arlene G. Taylor.
(Source: OCLC Connexion, Authorities—record number 431885)**

The cataloger may decide to update the authority record to RDA standards,
adding some of the new information from the faux "About the Author" page. An
obvious new field is 046 for Dates that are associated with the entity described
in the record, which has subfields for birth and death dates for persons, beginning and ending dates for corporate bodies, and so on. This field is illustrated
in a faux updated authority record shown in Figure 10.6.

In addition to the new 046 field, a set of new fields that were created to
accommodate the RDA guidelines is the 37X set of fields. In Figure 10.6 field
370 includes $a Kansas, for the place of birth, $c USA, for an associated
country, and five *e* subfields for places of residence; $c and $e are repeatable,

```
ARN      431885

     Rec stat c      Entered 19800519   Replaced 20150802111141.3
     Type      z       Upd status a          Enc lvl    n          Source     c
     Roman     l       Ref status  a          Mod rec               Name use a
     Govt agn  l       Auth status a          Subj       a          Subj use  a
     Series    n       Auth/ref    a          Geo subd   n          Ser use   b
     Ser num   n       Name        a          Subdiv tp  n          Rules     z

010      n 80050006
040      DLC $b eng $e rda $c DLC $d DLC
046      $f 1941
100   1_ Taylor, Arlene G., $d 1941-
370      Kansas $c USA $e Oklahoma $e Chapel Hill (N.C.) $e Chicago (Ill.) $e New York
         (N.Y.) $e Pittsburgh (Pa.)
371      $m ataylor@sis.pitt.edu $u http://www.pitt.edu/~agtaylor
372      Information organization $a Cataloging $a Authority files (Information retrieval) $2
         lcsh
373      University of North Carolina at Chapel Hill. School of Information and Library
         Science $t 1981
373      University of Chicago. Graduate Library School $s 1981 $t 1986
373      Columbia University. School of Library Service $s 1986 $t 1993
373      University of Pittsburgh. School of Information Sciences $s 1993 $t 2007
374      Librarians $a Catalogers $s 1966 $t 1975 $2 lcsh
374      Library science teachers $a College teachers $a Authors $2 lcsh
375      female
377      eng
400   1_ Dowell, Arlene Taylor, $d 1941- $w nne
670      Her Cataloging with copy, 1976: $b t.p. (Arlene Taylor Dowell)
670      Wynar, B.S. Introd. to cat. and class., 1985: $b CIP t.p. (Arlene G. Taylor)
670      Introd. to cat. and class., 2015: $b t.p. (Arlene G. Taylor) About the author (Professor
         Emerita, School of Information Sciences, University of Pittsburgh; b. 1941 (Kan.);
         MSLS, Graduate School of Library and Information Science, University of Illinois,
         1966; cataloger at the Library of Congress (Washington, DC), Christopher Newport
         College (Newport News, VA), and Iowa State University (Ames, IA) through 1975;
         Ph.D., School of Information and Library Science, UNC-Chapel Hill, 1981; University
         of Chicago (1981-1986); Columbia University (1986-1993); University of Pittsburgh
         (1993-2007); Web page: http://www.pitt.edu/~agtaylor. Email: ataylor@sis.pitt.edu).
670      Email from author, Aug. 2, 2015: $b ("I would prefer NOT to share what my middle
         initial G. stands for.")
```

FIGURE 10.6 Faux Updated Authority Record for Arlene G. Taylor. (An Original Record Based on OCLC Connexion, Authorities—record number 431885)

which means there can be as many listed as are appropriate. Field 371 is for address(es); $m is for an electronic mail address and $u is for a uniform resource identifier. Field 372 is for a field of activity, field of endeavor, or area of expertise associated with the person; in this case three areas are listed. Field 373 is a repeatable field for a group, institution, and so forth, associated with the person; $s and $t are for the starting and ending dates of the person's association with the institution. In this example four institutions have been listed, even though nine different institutions were mentioned in the "About the Author" information. It is up to cataloger's judgment to determine how many related institutions are included in an authority record. Field 374 is for occupation with repeatable $a allowed for overlapping occupations; because this person changed occupations, two 374 fields are given. The first 374 field includes starting and ending dates which are easily determined. The occupations identified in the second 374 field, however, have less well-defined start and end dates; consequently, the cataloger chose not to include dates in that field. Also found in field 374 is $2, which is for the source of the terms used in this field, in this case "lcsh," the designation for *Library of Congress Subject Headings*. Field 375 represents gender of the person. Field 377 is for the language the person uses when writing for publication or other public communication. Other 37X fields that are not illustrated in this example are 376 – Family information used with family names and 378 – Fuller form of personal name (not given in this example because of the last 670 note field). Some 38X fields were also created for use in RDA authority records, but are not applicable to persons: 380 – Form of work; 381 – Other distinguishing characteristics of work or expression; 385 – Audience characteristics; and 386 – Creator/Contributor characteristics.

The 400 field in Figure 10.6 is a *see from* reference, like the 410 and 411 fields in Figure 10.3. In this case the reference is from a name previously used by the author and refers to her current name. The first 670 field provides justification for this reference. The $w in the 400 field was changed from *nna*, as it appears in Figure 10.5, to *nne*. The *a* in *nna* stands for "Pre-AACR2 form of heading," which was technically correct in 1985 when the record was last replaced. But the more accurate designation really is *e*, which means that this was an earlier form of name used by this author, and this earlier form of name would have been established this way either before or after implementation of the *Anglo-American Cataloguing Rules*, 2nd ed. (AACR2), if Dr. Taylor had still been using the earlier form of name after AACR2 implementation (it just happened to be established the year before AACR2 was implemented).

If a library is a NACO participant, the cataloger submits a new or updated authority record to the international database through the NACO program. NACO is the name authorities program of the Program for Cooperative Cataloging (PCC), an international program operating out of LC, but consisting of a cooperative group of several hundred institutions. NACO participants receive special training upon joining NACO.[13] Following training, participants submit newly created or modified authority records to a liaison at LC who provides feedback for three to six months, after which the participants become independent. Independent catalogers enter the records directly into OCLC or SkyRiver.[14]

Subject Authority Work

Subject authority work is almost always done by verifying a heading as being the latest terminology given in the official list used by the library. The online version of the *Library of Congress Subject Headings* (LCSH), for example, can be searched through a bibliographic network, through *Classification Web*, or in the latest PDF version on LC's Cataloging and Acquisitions homepage. In most libraries with online catalogs, the subject authority file is linked with the bibliographic file so that all recommended references are presented to users who search for those terms.

If a subject string is being constructed for original cataloging, and the cataloger is using LCSH, it is necessary also to consult the *Subject Headings Manual*, either in PDF form or through *Cataloger's Desktop*. Subject Authority Cooperative (SACO) Program participants may submit proposals to LC for either new subject headings not found in LCSH, or proposals to change headings that are found in LCSH but are deemed to be outdated, incomplete, or exhibit other deficiencies.[15] SACO, like NACO, is part of the PCC. NACO institutions are automatically members of SACO, and in addition, any institution may apply to become a SACO-only member. Such membership requires an institutional commitment to an annual goal of 10–12 proposals for new or changed LCSH headings and/or new or changed LC Classification numbers.[16] It is expected that a cataloger making a proposal is using the latest versions of LCSH and its manual. It is also expected that research be performed to assure that the proposed heading is not a duplicate and that the necessary sources be cited to demonstrate that the term is used in writing and is needed. It is also possible to propose a new classification number. Persons making classification proposals should be using the latest available LC classification schedules and the *Classification and Shelflisting Manual.*

Figure 10.7 shows a subject authority record in the MARC 21 format as displayed in OCLC. Terms coded 450 are *used for* terms from which *see* or *use* references should be made. Terms coded 550 can be either related terms or broader terms. The difference is made known through the use of $w in the field. When $w contains the value "g" in the first of its four positions, the term in the field is a broader term. Both related and broader terms should have references made from them to *see also* the term in the 150 field. MARC 21 authority records do not show narrower terms, working on the assumption that the narrower terms are automatically taken care of when the system is programmed to display all the references from broader terms on every record.

ARN	02110833			
Rec stat c	**Entered** 19860211	**Replaced** 19980416155519.3		
Type z	**Upd status** a	**Enc lvl** n	**Source**	
Roman l	**Ref status** a	**Mod rec**	**Name use** b	
Govt agn l	**Auth status** a	**Subj** a	**Subj use** a	
Series n	**Auth/ref** a	**Geo subd** i	**Ser use** b	
Ser num n	**Name** n	**Subdiv tp** n	**Rules** n	

010	sh 85018276
040	DLC $b eng $c DLC $d DLC
053	HD69.C6
150	Business consultants
450	Efficiency engineers
450	Management advisory services
450	Management consultants
550	Consultants $w g
550	Interim executives
670	UMI business vocab. $b (Management advisory services)

FIGURE 10.7 Sample MARC Subject Authority Record. (Source: OCLC Connexion, Authorities—record number 02110833)

CREATION OF AUTHORITY FILES

After creation of authority records, the next step in authority work is the addition of the records into an authority file. In order for the authority file to serve its purpose it must be linked in some way to the bibliographic file. In card or paper systems the link was implicit. That is, the link was in the mind of a human who perceived the presence of an identical form on both the authority record and the catalog record and also perceived the presence in both files of the appropriate reference(s).

In some online systems the authority system linkage is still implicit. In such systems the authority file is a completely separate file from the bibliographic file, and authority control of new records is dependent on the cataloger finding the correct form of an AAP in the authority file and then entering it correctly into the bibliographic record. There are no references in these files, although the authority files may be searched under the forms from which references are authorized. In such systems, changes in form of AAPs mean that unless there are strict procedures for checking AAPs already in a file against every new name, title, or subject entered, two or more forms of a name, title, or subject may appear simultaneously with different bibliographic records displayed at each different form. A recent catalog search returned the following character strings with numbers of bibliographic records to the right of each:

> Williams, Tennessee, 1911-1983, 1
>
> Williams, Tennessee, 1911-1983. 83
>
> Williams, Tennessee, 1911-1983 47

The first has a comma after the death date, the second has a period after the death date, and the third has no punctuation after the death date. A sophisticated automated linked authority control system should "catch" these as being equivalent (and, perhaps, either new to the system or in error) and would identify them so that a catalog manager could check their validity.

Subject headings also can cause display problems when authority control is only implicit. Changes are made to LCSH headings with some frequency. In March 2014, for example, **English sparrow** was changed to **House sparrow**. In an authority file with only implicit authority control, the cataloger first using the new heading must notice the change and take steps to have the records with the former heading changed to the current one. In such situations, it is possible occasionally to run the bibliographic file against the authority file to check for headings that match references and to change any matches found to the new form; but it is not feasible to do this often, and in the meantime, multiple forms exist unless someone notices and changes them individually.

In more sophisticated systems the linkage between authority file and bibliographic file is explicit. That is, a direct internal linkage exists between a heading stored in the authority file and the same heading stored in the bibliographic file. In such systems the headings for every new record are checked against the authority file, and new or changed headings are flagged for review. In these systems also, references are displayed from unused terms to used ones and from used terms to narrower terms and usually also to related terms. References to broader terms are often not displayed, however (as discussed earlier in this chapter).

In the most sophisticated systems there is a linkage that uses relational file techniques to link a bibliographic record using only identification numbers in place of AAPs to a system of authority records that store all the AAPs linked to an identification number for each. The advantage here is that each AAP is stored only once; so matching of bibliographic and authority AAPs is unnecessary. In addition when an AAP has to be changed, the change is made only in the authority record. What the user sees in such a system is the AAP character string that is no different from what is seen in the previously described linked systems.

MAINTENANCE OF AUTHORITY SYSTEMS

In order to maintain an authority system, it is necessary to have routine error checking between authority and bibliographic files. There must also be routine error checking among authority records for consistency. For example, if a changed heading authority record does not replace the older heading record properly, it would be possible to have a response to a search for one term refer to another term only to have a reference at that term referring back to the first (e.g., **English sparrow** *see* **House sparrow** and **House sparrow** *see* **English sparrow** in the same catalog).

Updating is necessary when a library is using LC authority data as the basis of its authority system. Names are changed to reflect new usages by some authors; subjects are constantly changed to update terminology, add references, and so on; and new headings are added. There must be procedures for replacing the changed records and adding the new ones. Changed records are particularly difficult because there is not yet a mechanism for notifying a library that has used a bibliographic record in the past that its terminology or name form has now been changed. One problem in such a case is that the titles of works of an author whose AAP has changed may appear in two or more separate alphabetical subsets—the same problem that can result when no authority work was done in the first place. Some systems (e.g., OCLC) now routinely run new authority records from LC against the bibliographic file on a regular basis, although it is not difficult to find catalogs in which this has not been done; and therefore, old forms of names and subjects abound.

CONCLUSION

There are several potential uses for authority control that have not yet been realized. One is the idea mentioned earlier of providing access to broader subject terms. Another is the potential for controlling elements of records not now perceived as access points (e.g., names of publishers). A third potential lies in further control of works. Editions of works, for example, are now related only by either the fact of their having identical author and/or title access points or the provision of notes on bibliographic records giving earlier titles or authors. Now that authority control of works under RDA can be extended to such relationships as editions and other derivative works, identifying works in fields such as music and literature can be greatly enhanced.[17]

NOTES

1. Thomas Hickey, *Cooperative Authority Control: Virtual International Authority File (VIAF)*, NISO/DCMI Webinar, December 4, 2013, http://www.slideshare .net/oclcr/niso-dcmiviafwebinar2013.
2. International Federation of Library Associations and Institutions (IFLA) Study Group on the Functional Requirements for Bibliographic Records, *Functional Requirements for Bibliographic Records, Final Report* (München, Germany: K.G. Saur, 1998), http://archive.ifla.org/VII/s13/frbr/frbr_current_toc.htm or http://www.ifla.org/files/assets/cataloguing/frbr/frbr_2008.pdf.
3. *FRBR*, 82.
4. IFLA Cataloguing Section and IFLA Meetings of Experts on an International Cataloguing Code, *Statement of International Cataloguing Principles* (The Hague: IFLA, 2009), http://www.ifla.org/files/assets/cataloguing/icp/ icp_2009-en.pdf.
5. IFLA Working Group on Functional Requirements and Numbering of Authority Records, *Functional Requirements for Authority Data: A Conceptual Model* (FRAD) (München, Germany: K.G. Saur, 2009), amended and corrected through July 2013, http://www.ifla.org/files/assets/cataloguing/frad/frad_2013.pdf.
6. Ibid., 46.
7. Martha M. Yee and Sara Shatford Layne, *Improving Online Public Access Catalogs* (Chicago: American Library Association, 1998). For additional discussion of how system design can supplement authority control, *see*: Christine L. Borgman, "Why Are Online Catalogs *Still* Hard to Use?" *Journal of the American Society for Information Science* 47, no. 7 (July 1996): 493–503.
8. David Miller, Tony Olson, and Sara Shatford Layne, "Promoting Research and Best Practices in Subject Reference Structures: A Decade of Work by the Subject Analysis Committee," *Library Resources & Technical Services* 49, no. 3 (July 2005): 154–166, http://www.ala.org/alcts/sites/ala.org.alcts/files/ content/resources/lrts/archive/49n3.pdf.
9. Arlene G. Taylor and Daniel N. Joudrey, *The Organization of Information*, 3rd ed. (Westport, Conn.: Libraries Unlimited, 2009), Chapter 6.
10. Catherine E. Pasterczyk, "Russian Transliteration Variations for Searchers," *DATABASE* 8 (February 1985): 68–75; Anne B. Piternick, "What's in a Name? Use of Names and Titles in Subject Searching," *DATABASE* 8 (December 1985): 22–28; David M. Pilachowski and David Everett, "What's in a Name? Looking for People Online—Social Sciences," *DATABASE* 8 (August 1985): 47–65; David M. Pilachowski and David Everett, "What's in a Name? Looking for People Online—Current Events," *DATABASE* 9 (April 1986): 43–50; David Everett and David M. Pilachowski, "What's in a Name? Looking for People Online— Humanities," *DATABASE* 9 (October 1986): 26–34; Bonnie Snow, "Caduceus: People in Medicine: Searching Names Online," *ONLINE* 10 (September 1986): 122–127.
11. Library of Congress Authorities, [last updated] February 20, 2015, http:// authorities.loc.gov/.
12. OCLC Bibliographic Formats and Standards (Dublin, OH: OCLC, ©2015) http://www.oclc.org/bibformats/en/1xx/111.html.

13. "NACO – Name Authority Cooperative Program" accessed November 22, 2014, http://www.loc.gov/aba/pcc/naco/.
14. "Frequently asked questions about joining the NACO Program," accessed November 22, 2014, http://www.loc.gov/aba/pcc/naco/nacoprogfaq.html#5.
15. "SACO – Subject Authority Cooperative Program," accessed November 24, 2014, http://www.loc.gov/aba/pcc/saco/index.html.
16. "About the SACO Program," accessed November 24, 2014, http://www.loc.gov/aba/pcc/saco/about.html.
17. Richard Smiraglia, "Authority Control of Works: Cataloging's Chimera?" *Cataloging & Classification Quarterly* 38, no 3/4 (2004): 291–308; also published in *Authority Control in Organizing and Accessing Information: Definition and International Experience*, edited by Arlene G. Taylor and Barbara B. Tillett (New York: Haworth Information Press, 2004), pp. 291–308.

SUGGESTED READING

Jin, Qiang. *Demystifying FRAD: Functional Requirements for Authority Data.* Santa Barbara, Calif.: Libraries Unlimited, 2012.

Library of Congress. "Z1: Name and Series Authority Records." In *Descriptive Cataloging Manual,* prepared by the Policy and Standards Division, Library of Congress. (Washington, D.C.: Library of Congress, 2014), available at http://www.loc.gov/catdir/cpso/dcmz1.pdf.

Smiraglia, Richard. *The Nature of "A Work": Implications for Knowledge Organization.* Lanham, Md.: Scarecrow Press, 2001.

Taylor, Arlene G., and Barbara B. Tillett, eds. *Authority Control in Organizing and Accessing Information: Definition and International Experience.* New York: Haworth Information Press, 2004.

Taylor, Arlene G., and Daniel N. Joudrey. *The Organization of Information.* 3rd edition. Westport, Conn.: Libraries Unlimited, 2009. Chap. 8, "Metadata: Access and Authority Control."

Tillett, Barbara B. "Authority Control: State of the Art and New Perspectives." *Cataloging & Classification Quarterly* 38, no. 3/4 (2004): 23–42; also published in *Authority Control in Organizing and Accessing Information: Definition and International Experience,* edited by Arlene G. Taylor and Barbara B. Tillett. New York: Haworth Information Press, 2004.

Part IV

Subject Access

Chapter 11

Subject Access

INTRODUCTION

Subject analysis—one of the most intellectually challenging aspects of information organization—is the part of cataloging that deals with identifying and describing the intellectual or artistic contents of an information resource. Why do catalogers perform subject analysis? Comparable to the goals of descriptive cataloging, it is carried out to enable users to find, identify, select, and obtain resources, and to navigate within library catalogs. Specifically, it is performed to

- **Identify the subjects of works**
  By performing subject analysis, catalogers formally associate specific topics with works. The process results in concise subject statements (e.g., subject headings and call numbers) that briefly describe the resource. These subject statements allow users to evaluate and select the resources that best meet their needs.

- **Find works according to subjects**
  Users may not always know what resources they need or which authors to read, but they typically know which topics or subjects interest them. By performing subject analysis, catalogers provide users with the ability to retrieve individual resources in library catalogs by matching those concise subject statements against users' search strings.

- **Collocate works of a like nature**
  Subject analysis allows for finding not only individual resources, but also sets of resources. Assigning subjects to works creates shared-characteristic relationships among individual resources that are about the same topics. This allows the catalog to bring together (i.e., collocate) materials of a like nature. If users conduct a subject search for a particular topic, their search results will include all the resources in the catalog

521

containing that subject heading. Or if users retrieve a resource that meets their information needs through other means (e.g., keyword searching), they can click on relevant subject links to find all the other resources on those topics.

- **Provide a logical location for similar resources**
  Collocation not only occurs in catalogs but also in the stacks. Classification is another way that materials are collocated. Subject analysis allows resources with identical or similar subjects to be shelved together based on their call numbers (i.e., a classification number plus a Cutter/item number).

- **Save the users' time**
  In the spirit of S. R. Ranganathan's fourth law in his *Five Laws of Library Science*,[1] subject analysis helps to save time. It helps users winnow away thousands, hundreds of thousands, or even millions of resources in the pursuit of needed information. If there were no subject analysis, in order to understand what a resource is about, users would rely on titles, words from tables of contents (if present), and other descriptive cataloging data, which are not always the most reliable indicators of subject matter. This would be a time-consuming process. Or users would have to rely on full-text access, if it were available, which comes with its own host of problems, including *infoglut* (i.e., information overload). Subject analysis makes finding resources on a given subject and understanding the nature of the resources both easier and more efficient.

Thomas Mann, a reference librarian at the Library of Congress (LC), refers to subject access systems as "the standardized intellectual gridwork that makes the literature of the world—in all subject areas and in all languages—identifiable and retrievable in a systematic and predictable manner."[2] Promoting and maintaining that predictable and reliable gridwork is exactly why catalogers perform subject analysis. Besides, no one else (and nothing else) provides this beneficial service. Despite predictions to the contrary over the past 20 years, Arlene G. Taylor and Daniel N. Joudrey note:

> Machines are not yet good at identifying the aboutness of information resources and they still cannot assign controlled vocabulary and classification with any satisfactory degree of accuracy. While a computer can determine what words are used in a document and the frequency of those words, at this time it cannot understand the multifaceted or nuanced concepts represented by those words. Even the most sophisticated algorithms cannot replace the human mind for its efficiency in understanding the deeper meaning of texts and being able to represent those meanings through the use of subject languages.[3]

SUBJECT ANALYSIS PROCESS

Subject analysis comprises two principal activities: (1) *conceptual analysis* and (2) *translation*. The process begins with an examination of the physical carrier and an analysis of the intellectual content of the resource. This conceptual analysis is done to determine what the work is *about* (i.e., its subject matter), but also to understand what the work *is* (i.e., its form or genre). In the case of visual materials, it might also involve identifying what the image is *of* (i.e., the chief elements of an image). For example, a cataloger might identify that a particular resource is *about* mass consumption and mundane consumerism, that it *is* a print of an artwork, and that it is *of* 32 cans of Campbell's Soup. These facets of analysis are sometimes individually referred to as *aboutness*, *is-ness*, and *of-ness*. In this chapter, for the sake of brevity, all three facets are subsumed under the term *aboutness* unless otherwise noted.

Joudrey, in his dissertation research, found that a group of untrained analysts used multiple approaches to aboutness determination, and also used various strategies for examining resources. Each participant in Joudrey's study used a different combination of techniques to gain an understanding of aboutness. These findings led to the conclusion that there is no single analysis method that will work for everyone for every resource.[4] Although there is no "correct" way to determine aboutness, a suggested method is presented in Taylor and Joudrey's *Organization of Information*.[5] The book provides an overview of aboutness-related challenges, strategies, and approaches. It offers guidelines on what to look for when performing conceptual analysis. It also includes, in Appendix A, a workform that lists steps to follow and concepts to consider in the process; the workform is accompanied by an illustration of its use.[6]

Even though there is no one approach to conceptual analysis, there are some suggestions that help to ensure that aboutness data can be found. For example, when examining a resource, one should, at least, inspect the following components:

- **Physical carriers**
  - the item itself
  - covers, jackets, labels, etc.
  - containers, cases, etc.

- **Visual information**
  - cover art and other design elements
  - illustrations, photographs, prints, etc.
  - diagrams, tables, charts, etc.

- **Bibliographic and/or document features**
  - title pages, other preliminaries, opening screens, homepages, title bars, page sources, etc.
  - tables of contents, chapter titles, section titles or headings, hyperlinks, etc.
  - introductions, prefaces, forewords, summaries, abstracts, etc.
  - conclusions, concluding paragraphs, final sections, final sentences, etc.
  - end features such as indexes, appendices, and bibliographies, as well as site maps, credits, etc.

In addition to examining the physical aspects of a resource, the process entails analyzing the content. Whereas the process begins with a search for main topics and genre/form (and *of-ness*, if applicable), one is also looking for the overall discipline or branch of knowledge; names of persons, families, and corporate bodies featured heavily in the content; the names of jurisdictions, geographic areas, or geographic features that play a significant role in the content, either as a main topic or as context; the names of other entities, concepts, objects, and events; as well as time periods or other chronological elements. One might also be on the lookout for purpose, audience, point of view, language, tone, methods used to create the content, and intellectual level, if they notably affect the content.

Over the years, a number of approaches have been offered for examining content. Patrick Wilson identifies four approaches in his seminal work, *Two Kinds of Power: An Essay on Bibliographic Control.*[7] These and other approaches to analyzing content are discussed in more detail in *The Organization of Information* by Taylor and Joudrey.[8] Two other works that are also helpful for someone faced with the need to determine aboutness are *Documentation: Methods for Examining Documents, Determining Their Subjects and Selecting Indexing Terms* published by the International Organization for Standardization,[9] and *Subject Analysis: Principles and Procedures* by Derek W. Langridge.[10]

The understanding gained during the conceptual analysis leads to the translation phase. But before jumping directly into a list of controlled vocabulary terms or classification schedules, it is helpful to organize one's thoughts about the resource first. These thoughts should be expressed in natural language as a written *aboutness statement* to identify: (1) the work's subject matter, (2) relationships among those topics, (3) applicable forms or genres, and (4) other key concepts related to the work (prominent names, geographic areas, time periods, etc.). One or two sentences or a short paragraph beginning with, "This resource is about . . ." will suffice to summarize ideas and to prioritize words or concepts to be searched in the controlled vocabulary. If one is also classifying the resource, this process may entail determining the disciplines, sub-disciplines, topics, subtopics, places (i.e., geographic areas in which the subject is set), periods, and genres/forms (e.g., fiction, historical treatment, dictionary) in order to sketch out a rudimentary hierarchy to assess where the aboutness concepts fall in a classification scheme. A. G. Brown gives an excellent introduction to the process of learning to place one's subject into a conceptual framework necessary for classification.[11]

Once an aboutness statement is composed, then it can be used for the translation phase. The cataloger assigns subject headings from a controlled list of terms, which may have rules for using the list, as is the case with *Library of Congress Subject Headings* (LCSH), which is discussed in chapter 13, or with the *Sears List of Subject Headings*, discussed in chapter 14. The cataloger also assigns symbols from the particular classification scheme being used, discussed in chapters 16–20. The subject term(s) most often appear as access points for the resource in the library's catalog. The classification notation is usually used as the basis for a call number for a physical information resource that will determine the position of the resource on the library's shelves.

CHALLENGES IN SUBJECT ANALYSIS

Subject analysis is not always a simple task. Either or both of the two principal activities can be taxing. Sometimes conceptual analysis can be rather easy (e.g., examining a standard *Introduction to Psychology* textbook), but for some resources the process may take concerted effort to determine what they are about. Some resources are quite complex and what they address is not always clear at first. The question "What is this work about?" can have many answers; it depends on who is asking the question, and the answers may be affected by issues such as background, education, cultural identity, and so on. The translation process, following the determination of aboutness, also has its own pitfalls. Sometimes, there is an easily found, concise, exact match to the aboutness concept in the controlled vocabulary. Other times, however, the rules for applying the controlled terminology may prevent adding what seems to be a logical subject heading string. This may result in the translation phase becoming a convoluted process that never results in a completely satisfying match. This, of course, may have more to do with the limitations or boundaries of the individual vocabulary itself. To facilitate the process as much as possible, there are some aspects of subject analysis that should be kept in mind.

Before analyzing resources, one must have a clear idea about the level of exhaustivity that is to be applied. *Exhaustivity* is the number of concepts that will be considered. Brown identifies two basic degrees of exhaustivity: *depth indexing* and *summarization*.[12] Depth indexing aims to extract all the main concepts dealt with in an information resource, recognizing many subtopics and subthemes. If one is doing depth indexing, then many topics that are covered in only small parts of the resource will be noted. Summarization identifies only a dominant, overall subject of the resource, recognizing only concepts embodied in the main theme. In library cataloging, traditionally, subject analysis has been carried out at the summarization level, reserving depth indexing for other enterprises such as periodical or back-of-the-book indexes. A good rule of thumb for the summarization approach—based on a policy associated with the application of LCSH—is that any topic representing approximately 20% of a resource should be identified in the aboutness statement.[13]

Determining what a resource is about at the summarization level can be a difficult matter. In chapter 1, Charles A. Cutter's statement of the basic functions of a catalog was quoted, including "To show what the library has . . . on a given subject." This implies that it is obvious what being "on a given subject" means. Wilson has discussed this matter at some length and has suggested that part of the problem is that catalogers and others are taught to look for *the* subject of a resource.[14] He observes that if a person is writing a book or paper, and you ask what the person is writing about, he or she can tell you. If you go further and ask what is the subject about which the person is writing, this seems to be an equivalent question; but using the definite article *the* in front of *subject* implies that there will be just one thing to mention in answer to the question. Wilson's further explication demonstrates the fallacy of this assumption.[15]

Although some information resources *seem* to have an easily determined subject, that may not always be so. Some examples might help to illustrate this point.

- A work titled *History of Mathematics* is about the discipline of mathematics, but it is more specifically about mathematics from a historical perspective. It is not, however, about the discipline of history; it is in the form of a history. This distinction has a certain subtlety that is learned through education in our present-day Western tradition. It is possible that in another place or another time *history* would be considered to be the subject of anything that is historical, regardless of the specific topic of the work.

- A website for an event, a project, or an organization, such as Planned Parenthood, can be complicated. On one hand, if you ask what is *the* subject of the website, there is a simple, clear answer that could suffice: it is about the corporate body entity **Planned Parenthood Federation of America**. Is this useful and completely satisfying? No, probably not. Though the website is about the organization, it is also helpful to highlight some of the topics that are addressed by the organization. One assumes that if a user is interested in an organization, an event, or a project but he or she does not know the name of that entity, then this user will attempt to find it through terms reflecting the organization's activities, roles, interests, or services. Terms reflecting these will be necessary in describing this resource. So, in some cases, catalogers may need to describe multiple levels of aboutness (i.e., the subject of the subject). For the Planned Parenthood website, in addition to a subject access point for the organization itself, a cataloger may include concepts such as *birth control*, *reproductive* or *sexual health*, *family size* or *family planning*, and *community health services*.

- Let us take another example, *Nature in Italian Art: A Study of Landscape Backgrounds from Giotto to Tintoretto*. This work is about landscape painting—specifically in Italian art during a set period of time. Is it *about* Italian art? In the very specific sense of the subject, no—it is much more specific than *Italian art*. But who is to say that it would not be useful to someone searching for information on Italian art? Is it about Giotto and Tintoretto and all the landscape artists in between? Yes, of course it is, and if one were doing depth indexing, each one of those artists would be indexed; but if one is looking for *the* subject, a listing of names of numerous artists will not do.

In some cases, the subject of a work may take effort to uncover. Determining aboutness may depend, to some extent, on specialized knowledge or the ability to quickly grasp unfamiliar material. Some resources may be very general in nature (e.g., a set of encyclopedias), some may not have an obvious topical thread (e.g., a collection of short stories by Bostonians about anything or nothing), some may be very involved (e.g., a doctoral dissertation on a highly technical complex topic), and some may never overtly state exactly what they are about. In these situations, the cataloger must interpret what the resource is about from the information that is presented. One must remember, however, that aboutness is more than just the sum of a work's parts (i.e., individual sentences, paragraphs, or chapters). For example, many people could read a list of names that includes Giotto and Tintoretto but not know that it is a list of Italian artists, not to mention that they were landscape painters. Moreover, a person could read and understand each individual sentence in Foucault's *Order of Things: An Archaeology of the Human Sciences* but still not understand what the writing as a whole is about. The determination of aboutness depends greatly on a cataloger's intellect, knowledge, judgment, attentiveness, analytical skills, and interpretive skills. Henry Evelyn Bliss has discussed this problem:

> If [a] book on Scotland is not mainly geographic and historical, but consists of descriptive and narrative chapters together with a mélange of literary and scientific observations and reflections on the national traits and institutions, also considerable social philosophy in the last chapters, the judgment [of what the book is about] is indeed complex and the decisions may be uncertain.[16]

Bliss sees a complex problem that requires judgment. On the other hand, W. C. Berwick Sayers, when faced with this same example, quipped, "But surely, from first to last, this is a book on Scotland."[17] It all depends on who is asking and answering the question, "What is this work about?"

By now, it should be fairly obvious that catalogers themselves play a role in determining the aboutness of some resources. Despite the best efforts of those involved, subject analysis is never going to be an altogether objective process. Even with the most straightforward materials, the process "can only be performed through the lens of the analyst's own background, knowledge, culture, responsibilities, and even mood . . . . [It is] a highly subjective, interpretive process that is dependent on human skills of observation, interpretation, and analysis."[18] Whereas *objectivity*—or more accurately, *neutrality*—is certainly something to strive for, human beings are the ones performing these analyses. Although humans bring tremendous assets to the process (reading between the lines, finding deeper meaning, understanding subtext, appreciating nuance, etc.), they also can bring preconceptions (conscious or otherwise), inconsistency, their cultural and societal biases, educational backgrounds, emotions, and so forth. Though the process is an interpretive one, and therefore somewhat subjective, as long as it is approached with knowledge of the potential pitfalls and more than a modicum of self-awareness, it is hoped that catalogers will be able to embrace a position of impartiality and balance by using good cataloger's judgment and by reining in their more obvious preconceptions, prejudices, and antipathies.

Because it is difficult to define what "on a given subject" means, and because determining aboutness depends upon the indexer's or cataloger's knowledge, opinions, experiences, and judgment, Marcia Bates has observed, "it is practically impossible to instruct indexers or catalogers [on] how to find subjects when they examine documents. Indeed, we cataloging instructors usually deal with this essential feature of the skill being taught by saying such vague and inadequate things as 'Look for the main topic of the document.'"[19]

ATTITUDES TOWARD SUBJECT ACCESS

Holly Yu and Margo Young state, in their literature review for an article on the impact of search engines on subject searching, "For more than twenty years, research has demonstrated that subject or topical searches are both popular and problematic. Tolle and Han found that subject searching is [the] most frequently used and the least successful. Moore reported that 30 percent of searches were for subject, and . . . . Hunter found that 52 percent of all searches were subject searches and that 63 percent of these had zero hits."[20] Prior to the 1980s there was considerable aversion toward subject access in the United States based in part on studies that showed that academic library card catalog users used a subject approach only about 30 percent of the time. However, Karen Markey constructed a grid of card catalog use studies in several types of libraries completed between 1967 and 1981 that showed that subject approaches in card catalogs varied from 10 percent to 62 percent and the median was about 40 percent.[21] Studies of online catalog users have demonstrated that subject access in online catalogs is quite popular—one study of many types of libraries with different online systems showed that subject approaches accounted for about 59 percent of all catalog uses.[22] Another study proposed that the popularity of subject searching depends on the population using the catalog.[23] In the early 1990s, Larson stated that subject searching was declining,[24] but he and others like Bates recognized that "the interest in subject access had not declined, but increasingly, that need was met by keywords."[25] In fact, in a case study from 2006, Eng Pwey Lau and Dion Hoe-Lian Goh found that the "use of keyword searches contributed to 68.9% of all queries while other options such as title, author and subject accounted for 16.5%, 8.2% and 6.4% of all searches respectively."[26] With such variations among the results of research, it is certainly easy enough to cherry-pick the research that supports one's position.

In more recent years, there has been an occasional call to abandon some aspects of subject access. In "The Changing Nature of the Catalog," a 2006 report commissioned by LC, Karen Calhoun recommends that libraries "abandon the attempt to do comprehensive subject analysis manually with LCSH in favor of subject keywords" and urged "LC to dismantle LCSH."[27] This led to a number of vehement responses from those who support the continued use of subject access systems, particularly subject headings.[28] Later in 2006, LC convened its Working Group on the Future of Bibliographic Control to examine if and how cataloging activities supported the management of and access to resources in an evolving information and technology landscape (i.e., a landscape highly reminiscent of the Google search engine approach to information advocated for by Calhoun). In 2008, the Working Group report, in a somewhat surprising twist, rejected Calhoun's subject analysis recommendations, stating, "Subject analysis—including analyzing content and creating and applying subject headings and classification numbers—is a core function of cataloging; although expensive, it is nonetheless critical."[29] Markey, in a provocative think piece in *D-Lib Magazine*, reviews the history of subject access in online catalogs and concludes that there are many possible directions that the profession can take in building future catalogs in regard to subjects. Even though the idea of eliminating subjects is among the possibilities on her list, there are many more options presented that take advantage of subject data.[30] Others believe that the catalog itself is not the concern, but instead the focus should be on using discovery layers with a catalog to present the existing subject data in new ways. "The collective investment libraries have made in subject and name authorities is leveraged with the faceted navigation features" of a discovery layer interface.[31] (See chapter 24 for more on discovery environments.)

From all the passionate interest, it must be assumed that subject analysis has been done well enough that people find it useful, if not perfect. In fact there is evidence that subject headings add considerable value to bibliographic metadata. In research into the role of subject headings in the online catalog, Tina Gross and Arlene G. Taylor found that "if subject headings were to be removed or no longer included in catalog records, users performing keyword searches would miss more than one third of the hits they currently retrieve. On average 35.9% of hits would not be found."[32] That is, for one third of records retrieved by users conducting keyword searches, the keyword(s) being sought appear in the record *only* in subject headings. Recently Gross, Taylor, and Joudrey replicated the research on the same catalog, but now with tables of contents and summaries added to catalog records.

With the addition of tables of contents and summaries or abstracts, an average of 27 percent of hits would be lost if the subject headings were not present in the records. Although the proportion of hits that would be lost in the absence of subject headings is reduced with the addition of contents and summary data, it still represents a significant proportion of total hits (more than one fourth). This study also found that when limited to English [language materials only], the loss is 24.8 percent, demonstrating that subject headings in English are, indeed, helpful in locating materials in other languages.[33]

ALPHABETICAL AND CLASSIFIED APPROACHES TO SUBJECTS

During subject analysis, the cataloger must take into account the dual nature of the resources to be added to the collection. Information resources are both intellectual and physical entities. In descriptive cataloging, the carrier description addresses the physical entity, and authorized access points for titles and names are constructed to allow for access to the intellectual work. For access to the intellectual and creative content, subject catalogers choose one or more subject terms to insert into the bibliographic metadata. However, they traditionally choose only one classification notation. Classifiers strive for the optimum location in view of the content, the accepted classification schedule, and the needs of the users. Such decisions are not always easy to make. For instance, as was seen in the Scotland example above, the same treatise might go equally well into political science, economic history, social history, or the general history of a place, among other classes. In the choice of subjects to be represented in the catalog or index for this hypothetical treatise, all the aspects can be brought out through the choice of multiple subject access points. And, of course, virtual resources (e.g., web pages) are not limited to only one place on any shelf. As discussed in chapter 2 of this text, classified catalogs allow several classification notations to be assigned, but few catalogs in the United States are classified. However, categorization of websites allows classifying each one in more than one category.

Each approach in a catalog requires a different pattern of communication. The alphabetical catalog gives a horizontal approach through its random scattering of access points throughout the entire linguistic finding apparatus. The classified catalog offers a vertical (hierarchical) approach through its closely related classes and categories, under which materials can be identified by means of logical, orderly sequences from general to specific. With online catalogs it is possible to have both approaches in the same catalog, and some experimentation with this has been done.[34] In the United States, for the most part, access by classification notation in online catalogs is nothing more than a shelflist approach—that is, there is only one classification notation for any one physical resource.

Users who want information on a certain subject usually approach a catalog with questions formulated in their own words. These words must be translated into the predetermined access terminology of the catalog. The connection between users and subject headings (the alphabetical approach) has been facilitated by the use of keyword searching. Instead of the user's terminology having to coincide with that of a controlled list, the user may enter her or his own terminology. If one record can be identified that seems to match the user's subject need, subject headings in the record can be searched specifically to find other records on the subject (e.g., by clicking the hyperlink or by performing a subject search). In most catalogs, performing a subject heading search allows users to find the subject's reference structure of narrower and related terms. Likewise, classification notations in a relevant record can be searched to find other records that have been given the same classification or to browse other resources in the immediate area of the classification number.

Although it has yet to come to pass, it has been suggested that keyword searching will be enhanced by the power of effective linguistic tools. The field of natural language processing (NLP) uses a variety of linguistic tools, such as lexical ontologies, to analyze language. A lexical ontology may include an analysis of each term as to its usage as different parts of speech; and within each part of speech, it may give the various senses in which a term may be used. For example, a *fence* may be a structure built to set off a particular area or a receiver of stolen goods. Then within each sense, synonyms, antonyms, related terms, broader terms, narrower terms, and so on, may be given. The use of sophisticated linguistic tools in catalogs, if implemented, could greatly benefit users. For example, when a user searches the catalog for a particular keyword, the system could present the user with the various senses of that word, from which the user could choose the one wanted. A further step could be to ask the user whether he or she wishes to search for all synonyms of the sense chosen.[35] This is somewhat similar to the *explode* function found in some online indexes by which, with a click of a checkbox, one can search not only the term itself, but also all of its narrower terms. The future of subject access is a bright one, especially since the discussions have turned to how technology can be used to enhance and supplement human subject analysis expertise, rather than focusing on how technology can replace it.

CONCLUSION

This chapter has discussed the topic of subject analysis and arrangement of library materials both by verbal/alphabetical approaches and by classification. In the chapters that follow, these two approaches are considered separately along with systems and schemes for implementing each approach. The reader should remember, however, that these are two sides of the same coin and that both are attempts to provide users with access to the intellectual or artistic contents of the resources being analyzed. For more discussion of controlled vocabularies and classification concepts, the reader is referred to *The Organization of Information* by Taylor and Joudrey.[36]

NOTES

1. S. R. Ranganathan, *The Five Laws of Library Science*, 2nd ed. (Bombay: Asia Pub. House, 1963), 287–325.
2. Thomas Mann, *Cataloging Quality, LC Priorities, and Models of the Libraries Future* (Washington, D.C.: Cataloging Forum, Library of Congress, 1991), 21.
3. Arlene G. Taylor and Daniel N. Joudrey, *The Organization of Information*, 3rd ed. (Westport, Conn.: Libraries Unlimited, 2009), 304.
4. Daniel N. Joudrey, "Building Puzzles and Growing Pearls: A Qualitative Exploration of Determining Aboutness" (PhD diss., University of Pittsburgh, 2005), http://d-scholarship.pitt.edu/10357/.
5. Taylor and Joudrey, *The Organization of Information*, Chapter 9: Subject Analysis.
6. Ibid., 419–427.
7. Patrick Wilson, *Two Kinds of Power: An Essay on Bibliographic Control* (Berkeley: University of California Press, 1968), 69–92. The chapter in which this appears, "Subjects and the Sense of Position" is also published in *Theory of Subject Analysis: A Sourcebook*, edited by Lois Mai Chan, Phyllis A. Richmond, and Elaine Svenonius (Littleton, Colo.: Libraries Unlimited, 1985).
8. Taylor and Joudrey, *The Organization of Information*, 317–327.
9. International Organization for Standardization, *Documentation: Methods for Examining Documents, Determining Their Subjects and Selecting Indexing Terms* (Geneva, Switzerland: International Organization for Standardization, 1985).
10. D. W. Langridge, *Subject Analysis: Principles and Procedures* (London: Bowker-Saur, 1989).
11. A. G. Brown, in collaboration with D. W. Langridge and J. Mills, *An Introduction to Subject Indexing*, 2nd ed. (London: Bingley, 1982), frames 91–130.
12. Ibid., frames 48 and 51.
13. Library of Congress, *Subject Headings Manual*, 1st ed. (Washington, D.C.: Cataloging Distribution Service, Library of Congress, 2008). "H 180: Assigning and Constructing Subject Headings," 1. Also available in Cataloger's Desktop through a subscription or available freely on the web in PDF form, accessed July 18, 2015, http://www.loc.gov/aba/publications/FreeSHM/freeshm.html.

14. Wilson, *Two Kinds of Power*, 70–71.
15. Ibid., 309–320.
16. Henry Evelyn Bliss, *The Organization of Knowledge in Libraries and the Subject-Approach to Books* (New York: H.W. Wilson, 1933), 118.
17. W. C. Berwick Sayers, *Manual of Classification for Librarians and Bibliographers*, 2nd ed. rev. (London: Grafton, 1944), 222.
18. Taylor and Joudrey, *The Organization of Information*, 313.
19. Marcia J. Bates, "Subject Access in Online Catalogs: A Design Model," *Journal of the American Society for Information Science* 37, no. 6 (November 1986): 360.
20. Holly Yu and Margo Young, "The Impact of Web Search Engines on Subject Searching in OPAC," *Information Technology in Libraries* 23, no. 4 (2004): 169, in which they refer to: John E. Tolle and Sehchang Hah, "Online Search Patterns: NLM CATLINE Database," *Journal of the American Society for Information Science* 36 no. 2 (Mar. 1985): 82–93; Carol Weiss Moore, "User Reaction to Online Catalogs: An Exploratory Study," *College and Research Libraries* 42, no. 4 (1981): 295–302; and Rhonda N. Hunter, "Success and Failures of Patrons Searching the Online Catalog at a Large Academic Library: A Transaction-Log Analysis," *RQ* 30 (Spring 1991): 399.
21. Karen Markey, *Subject Searching in Library Catalogs: Before and After the Introduction of Online Catalogs* (Dublin, Ohio: OCLC, 1984), 75–77.
22. Joseph R. Matthews, Gary S. Lawrence, and Douglas K. Ferguson, eds., *Using Online Catalogs: A Nationwide Survey*, sponsored by the Council on Library Resources (New York: Neal-Schuman, 1983), 144.
23. Lynn Silipigni Connaway, Debra Wilcox Johnson, and Susan E. Searing, "Online Catalogs from the Users' Perspective: The Use of Focus Group Interviews," *College & Research Libraries* 58, no. 4 (1997): 411.
24. Ray R. Larson, "The Decline of Subject Searching: Long-term Trends and Patterns of Index Use in an Online Catalog," *Journal of the American Society for Information Science* 42, no. 3 (1991): 207.
25. Marcia J. Bates, "Task Force Recommendation 2.3 Research And Design Review: Improving User Access to Library Catalog and Portal Information, Final Report (Version 3)," accessed April 4, 2014, http://www.loc.gov/catdir/bibcontrol/2.3BatesReport6-03.doc.pdf.
26. Eng Pwey Lau and Dion Hoe-Lian Goh, "In Search of Query Patterns: A Case Study of a University OPAC," *Information Processing and Management* 42, no. 5 (2006): 1320.
27. Karen Calhoun, "The Changing Nature of the Catalog and Its Integration with Other Discovery Tools: Final Report, Prepared for the Library of Congress. March 17 2006," Library of Congress, accessed April 3, 2014, http://www.loc.gov/catdir/calhoun-report-final.pdf.
28. *See* (1) Library of Congress, Cataloging Policy and Support Office, "Library of Congress Subject Headings Pre- vs. Post-Coordination and Related Issues," accessed April 4, 2014, http://www.loc.gov/catdir/cpso/pre_vs_post.html; and (2) a whole series of papers written in response to questions about the future of cataloging found at the Library of Congress Professional Guild website, accessed April 4, 2014, http://guild2910.org/future.htm.
29. Library of Congress Working Group on the Future of Bibliographic Control, "On the Record: A Report of the Library of Congress Working Group on the Future of Bibliographic Control," accessed April 4, 2014, http://www.loc.gov/bibliographic-future/news/lcwg-ontherecord-jan08-final.pdf.
30. Karen Markey, "The Online Library Catalog: Paradise Lost and Paradise Regained?" *D-Lib Magazine* 13, no. 1/2 (Jan./Feb. 2007), http://www.dlib.org/dlib/january07/markey/01markey.html.

31. Kristin Antelman, Emily Lynema, and Andrew K. Pace, "Toward a Twenty-First Century Library Catalog," *Information Technology and Libraries* 25, no. 3 (Sept. 2006): 136.

32. Tina Gross and Arlene G. Taylor, "What Have We Got to Lose? The Effect of Controlled Vocabulary on Keyword Searching Results," *College & Research Libraries* 66, no. 3 (May 2005): 212–230.

33. Tina Gross, Arlene G. Taylor, and Daniel N. Joudrey, "Still a Lot to Lose: The Role of Controlled Vocabulary in Keyword Searching," *Cataloging & Classification Quarterly* 53, no. 1 (2015): 1–39.

34. For an example of research using terminology associated with classification in keyword searches, *see*: Karen Markey and Anh Demeyer, *Dewey Decimal Classification Online Project: Evaluation of a Library Schedule and Index Integrated into the Subject Searching Capabilities of an Online Catalog: Final Report to the Council on Library Resources* (Dublin, Ohio: OCLC, 1986).

35. For more about ontologies *see*: Natalya F. Noy and Deborah L. McGuinness, *Ontology Development 101: A Guide to Creating Your First Ontology* (Knowledge Systems Laboratory, Stanford University, 2000), http://www.ksl.stanford.edu/people/dlm/papers/ontology-tutorial-noy-mcguinness-abstract.html.

36. Taylor and Joudrey, *The Organization of Information,* "Systems for Vocabulary Control," Chapter 10, and "Systems for Categorization," Chapter 11.

SUGGESTED READING

Brown, A. G., in collaboration with D. W. Langridge and J. Mills. *An Introduction to Subject Indexing.* 2nd ed. London: Bingley, 1982.

Chan, Lois Mai, Phyllis A. Richmond, and Elaine Svenonius, eds. *Theory of Subject Analysis: A Sourcebook.* Littleton, Colo.: Libraries Unlimited, 1985.

Chan, Lois Mai, with the assistance of Theodora L. Hodges. *Cataloging and Classification: An Introduction.* 3rd ed. Lanham, Md.: Scarecrow Press, 2007. Chapter 7: Principles of Controlled Vocabularies and Subject Analysis.

Foskett, A. C. *The Subject Approach to Information.* 5th ed. London: Library Association Publishing, 1996.

Fugmann, Robert. *Subject Analysis and Indexing: Theoretical Foundation and Practical Advice.* Frankfurt am Main, Germany: Indeks Verlag, 1993.

Hider, Philip, with Ross Harvey. *Organising Knowledge in a Global Society: Principles and Practice in Libraries and Information Centres.* Revised edition. Wagga Wagga, NSW, Australia: Centre for Information Studies, Charles Sturt University, 2008. Chapter 6: Subject Access Concepts.

International Organization for Standardization. *Documentation: Methods for Examining Documents, Determining Their Subjects and Selecting Indexing Terms.* Geneva, Switzerland: International Organization for Standardization, 1985.

Joudrey, Daniel N. "Building Puzzles and Growing Pearls: A Qualitative Exploration of Determining Aboutness." PhD diss., University of Pittsburgh, 2005.

Langridge, D. W. *Subject Analysis: Principles and Procedures.* London: Bowker-Saur, 1989.

Subject Indexing: Principles and Practices in the 90's: Proceedings of the IFLA Satellite Meeting Held in Lisbon, Portugal, 17–18 August 1993. München, Germany: K.G. Saur, 1995.

Taylor, Arlene G., and Daniel N. Joudrey. *The Organization of Information.* 3rd ed. Westport, Conn.: Libraries Unlimited, 2009. Chapter 9: Subject Analysis.

Wilson, Patrick. *Two Kinds of Power: An Essay on Bibliographic Control.* Berkeley: University of California Press, 1968.

Chapter 12

Verbal Subject Access

INTRODUCTION

After conceptual analysis, there are two common means of providing access to the intellectual or artistic contents of information resources: a verbal approach and a notational approach. The verbal approach entails using a list of controlled vocabulary terms and references to provide an alphabetical approach to the concepts. The other traditional approach to subject access is classification, which provides a linear hierarchical approach. These two techniques—offering alternative, and to some extent complementary, modes of access to library collections and resources—constitute the aspect of information organization known as *subject cataloging*.

Controlled vocabularies are important tools in the subject cataloging process. A *controlled vocabulary* is an authority-controlled or standardized list in which subject terms or classification notations are enumerated in a browsable and/or searchable location (in paper or electronic format). It is a mechanism to identify the preferred term for each subject concept, to control synonyms or nearly synonymous terms, to distinguish between homographs and homonyms, and to link concepts that are related in some fashion. In other words, it is a list of terms that provides connections, standardization, and uniqueness to the subject concepts therein. There are different senses of the term *controlled vocabulary*, some more restrictive than others; it may refer to simple term lists, subject heading lists, and thesauri alone, or it may include ontologies, synonym rings, classification schemes, and taxonomies as well.[1] In this text, the term generally refers to verbal subject languages, whereas notational approaches are referred to as *classification*. In chapters 12–15, verbal approaches to subject representation are covered, primarily through the use of subject heading lists. In chapters 16–20, classification is discussed.

Why are controlled vocabularies necessary? It is because people do not use the same words to describe the same concept. This is due to the variety of options found in the English language. In general, people like to use synonyms while communicating; they appreciate different ways to convey the same idea. This affects the writing of materials by authors, the describing of resources by catalogers, and the searching of information by users. Because there are many ways to express an idea, controlled vocabularies have been developed to help gather together resources about the same topics no matter what words are used in the resources themselves. In these lists, one term is chosen as a preferred term to represent the concept, and its synonyms are used as references that point to the preferred term. For example, in describing a book about human beings between the ages of 18 and 25, the cataloger would apply **Young adults** to that resource, because that term is the authorized form used in the *Library of Congress Subject Headings* (LCSH), a popular controlled vocabulary for libraries. That term would be assigned even if its two references, *Young people* and *Young persons*, were the words predominantly used throughout the resource.

Despite the usefulness of controlled vocabularies, they are not necessarily appropriate for all information environments. They tend to work best in contained systems, like catalogs, indexes, and other closed database systems where it is feasible to create, maintain, and apply them. "A controlled approach to terminology does not work well for a large-scale, distributed system like the Internet, where no one is responsible for identifying the subjects of works and assigning authorized descriptors, and where the number of resources is simply enormous."[2]

BASIC CONCEPTS AND STRUCTURE OF SUBJECT HEADINGS

A *subject heading* is a term or phrase used to represent a topic, which is found in a list and is used in bibliographic metadata; therefore a *subject heading list* is a collection of authorized subject headings alongside "any references, scope notes, and subdivisions associated with each term or phrase."[3] The purpose of subject headings is to serve as access points by which works can be searched. They act as points of collocation where works on the same topics can be retrieved and displayed together in a catalog. In some subject heading systems, terms may also represent bibliographic forms (e.g., encyclopedia) or literary forms and genres (e.g., Spanish epic poetry). Potentially, anything that can be written about could be a subject heading. Subject headings are used to represent concepts, objects, places, events, philosophies, disciplines, activities and processes, organisms, classes of people, ethnic groups, and so forth.

Information professionals distinguish *pre-coordinate indexing*—in which appropriate terms are chosen and coordinated into phrases or subject-subdivision combinations at the time of indexing or cataloging—from *post-coordinate indexing* using single concept terms, which are then coordinated by users after the encoded metadata descriptions have been stored. Most subject headings in library catalogs are pre-coordinated, whereas their counterparts in indexes (called *descriptors*, *index terms*, or *thesaurus terms*) are meant to be used in post-coordinated systems. All standard published lists of subject headings were developed with pre-coordinate indexing techniques. Lists of descriptors, called *thesauri*, are typically used in post-coordinate systems.

Subject headings have dual objectives: (1) to identify pertinent material on a given subject or topic and (2) to enable users to find material on related subjects. Both objectives pose problems of communication; both demand a set of terms that match, as far as possible, the terms likely to be in the minds of users wishing to locate material on a given topic or in a given discipline. A number of years ago, E. J. Coates warned:

> This would be fairly simple to achieve if there were an uncomplicated, one-to-one relationship between concepts and words: that is to say, if there were a single word corresponding to each separate concept and a single concept corresponding to each separate word. In fact, we have on the one hand concepts that can be rendered by any one of a number of words, and on the other hand, concepts for which no single word equivalent exists in the natural language.[4]

Modern subject heading practice has its roots in Charles A. Cutter's *Rules for a Dictionary Catalog*, first published in 1876.[5] Later theorists refined and expanded Cutter's work in various ways. In the early 1950s, David Judson Haykin, former Chief of the Library of Congress (LC) Subject Cataloging Division, enumerated the principles that he believed were the underpinnings for the choice of terms for a subject list. His principles may be summarized as follows:

1. *The Reader as the Focus*: Haykin, like Cutter before him, believed that "the reader is the focus in all cataloging principles and practice . . . . The heading, in wording and structure, should be that which the reader will seek in the catalog, if we know or can presume what the reader will look under." This, of course, is very similar to what was later professed in IFLA's 21st century *Statement of International Cataloguing Principles* (ICP).

2. *Unity*: "A subject catalog must bring together under one heading all the books which deal principally or exclusively with the subject, whatever the terms applied to it by the authors of the books and whatever the varying terms applied to it at different times. The cataloger must, therefore, choose with care the term to be used and apply it uniformly to all the books on the subject. [The cataloger] must choose a term which is unambiguous and does not overlap in meaning other headings in the catalog, even where that involves defining the sense in which it is used as compared with, or distinguished from, other closely related headings. Obviously, the cataloger must guide the reader who might be more familiar with other synonymous terms by making references from all synonyms. As a corollary, the same term must not be used for more than one subject."

In more recent times, these ideas have been expressed as two principles:

- *Uniform heading:* a subject should be represented by only one heading, so that materials that are about that topic (and that use variant terminology) can be gathered and retrieved together.
- *Unique heading:* each heading must represent only one subject.

In other words, the principle of *uniform heading* is about collocation and the principle of *unique heading* is about disambiguation.

3. *Usage:* "The heading chosen must represent common usage or, at any rate, the usage of the class of reader for whom the material on the subject within which the heading falls is intended . . . . [The cataloger] must use the term in the sense in which it is currently used . . . [to keep] the catalog up to date . . . . Whether a popular term or a scientific one is to be chosen depends on several considerations. If the library serves a miscellaneous public, it must prefer the popular to the scientific term."

4. *English vs. Foreign Terms:* "Foreign terms should be used [in an English language catalog] only . . . when the concept is foreign to Anglo-American experience and no satisfactory term for it exists . . . and . . . when the foreign term is precise and the English one is not."

5. *Specificity:* "The heading should be as specific as the topic it is intended to cover. As a corollary, the heading should not be broader than the topic; rather than use a broader heading, the cataloger should use two specific headings which will approximately cover it . . . . [In] a subject catalog employing subject headings . . . the headings are not merely specific, but are both direct and specific, naming the topic without the interposition of the broader subject."[6]

The following discussion touches on some of the most important problems encountered in construction and use of subject headings.

The Choice of Subject Headings

Linguistic usage determines correctness of form in natural language, as all grammarians and lexicographers well know. Language changes constantly, not only in response to new discoveries and formulations of knowledge, but also in response to dynamic forces of its own, some but not all of which have been codified by linguists. In choosing subject terms, librarians and other creators of controlled vocabularies (sometimes referred to as *taxonomists*) try to consider both the author's usage and the users' needs and preferences; but authors and users are likely to use different terms for the same subject. Without a record of choices (e.g., an authority controlled list of headings), the cataloger may enter the same subject under two or more different headings. For example, an oblivious cataloger could place some works about persons being put to death by the state as a punishment for a crime under *death penalty* and others under *capital punishment*. This situation is problematic. It scatters works on the same topic, and in order to retrieve all materials on the topic, a user would have to perform multiple searches using every possible synonym of *capital punishment*. This certainly would not save the user's time, nor does it consider the convenience of the user.

Any number of decisions must be made when creating a controlled list of terms. For instance, at the most basic level, the taxonomist must determine which terms to include, which to exclude, and how terms will be presented (singular versus plural, abbreviations versus spelled-out forms, use of qualifiers, use of subdivisions, and so on).[7] Two types of decisions are especially likely to miscarry: those for which more than one adequate term is available and those for which no adequate term is available.

Synonymous Concepts

The taxonomist must sometimes choose one subject term from among several synonyms or very similar terms. As the English language rarely has true synonyms, first one must decide when one term is needed instead of two or more. For example: Are *dinners*, *dining*, *eating*, and *meals* all necessary in the same list? The decision must be based on whether there is enough of a distinction among the meanings or nuances to warrant adding more than one term. If it is deemed that no more than one term is necessary, one must choose among the various possibilities to represent the concept. Cutter suggested the following sequence of preferences when selecting from synonymous or nearly synonymous headings:

1. *The term most familiar to the general public.* Cutter no doubt was thinking of the local library's public. One of the major differences between LCSH and the *Sears List of Subject Headings* (*Sears*) is that LCSH, being designed for use in a comprehensive research library, favors scientific terminology (e.g., **Felidae** with a reference from *Wildcats*), whereas *Sears* tends to use more popular terms (e.g., **Wild cats** with a reference from *Felidae*).

2. *The term most used in other catalogs.* Since users frequently change libraries or consult more than one library catalog, it is comforting to find that terminology remains stable, even standardized, so long as it does not violate the usage of the local library's public. Far-reaching bibliographic networks make reliably standardized terminology even more desirable. A different, but related, argument is that new concepts and terms are often introduced into the periodical literature before they form the topics of books. If a library's subject heading list does not yet include such a term, the cataloger might consult other thesauri, the *New York Times Index*, or commonly used periodical indexing and abstracting tools, to discover what usage, if any, has been established. For example, if one were choosing a term to represent the concept *carcinoma* or *malignancy*, one might check other subject heading lists to see what term is used. LCSH uses **Cancer**, Sears uses **Cancer**, but the Medical Subject Headings (MeSH) uses **Neoplasms**.

3. *The term that has fewest meanings.* The clear intent here is to avoid ambiguity wherever possible. For instance, if one were choosing between *ghosts* and *spirits*, Cutter's suggestion points to using *ghosts* as the choice for the heading, because *spirits* can refer to a number of other things (e.g., alcoholic beverages).

4. *The term that comes first in the alphabet.* This is the type of arbitrary, procedural decision that can be invoked when semantic considerations have been exhausted (e.g., if *false teeth* and *dentures* are both well-known, widely used, and have an equal number of additional meanings, then one might choose *dentures* because it comes first in the alphabet).

5. *The term that brings the subject into the neighborhood of other, related subjects.* It was previously noted that a serious drawback of alphabetic arrangement is its fragmentation of subject matter. As a result, some alphabetic subject heading lists indulge in some ways of bringing together these scattered concepts (using subdivisions to collocate ideas, using inverted forms of terms, choosing less familiar terms, etc.). Here is Cutter's recognition that these techniques may be valid, but only after all other modes for choosing among synonymous terms have been exhausted. An example is if the term **Magician** has already been established in the subject heading list, and one must choose among *Prestidigitation*, *Magic tricks*, and *Sleight of hand* as the heading for the activity, then it is fairly clear which term should be chosen if the term for the performer and the term for the activity are to be brought together.[8]

Supplying Phrases

Some concepts must be expressed by combinations of words, although phrase headings present certain disadvantages. Coates, speaking about card catalogs, indicated that most catalog users try to formulate search topics in single words, even when a phrase would be used in natural language.[9] Research in online catalogs has tended to verify this observation. Various uncertainties shadow the introduction of phrases into a controlled vocabulary. In determining the order of words, should a heading always retain the order of natural language, or should modifications and transpositions be allowed in the interests of brevity and clarity? Should a variety of syntactic forms be used, or should the syntax of phrase headings be confined to a few simple forms that occasionally make them seem awkward and artificial? Some theorists feel that, lacking cleanly enunciated rules, phrase-makers have produced a number of troublesome headings. Modern usage condones several varieties, which different subject lists usually adapt to their own uses. The specific rules printed in *Sears* and in LCSH simplify but do not solve this problem, since they are purely arbitrary.[10] The problem of communication still exists. Many information resources are listed under subject headings that users would not immediately think of as the appropriate ones under which to search. For the most part phrase headings can be roughly categorized as follows in Table 12.1. All examples are taken from LCSH.

TABLE 12.1 Structural Categories of Subject Headings.

Category	Notes	Examples
Modified nouns	Modifiers can take different syntactic forms:	
	Nouns preceded by adjectives or other modifiers	**Regional planning** **Fur-bearing animals** **Country life**
	Nouns followed by adjectives or other modifiers	**Art, Assyro-Babylonian** **Names, African** **Bears (Gay culture)**
Conjunctive phrases	The conjunction is nearly always *and*	**Mills and mill-work** **Right and left (Political science)** **Truth or dare (Game)**
Prepositional phrases	*In* and *of* are most common, but other prepositions may be used to form phrases	**Segregation in education** **Freedom of information** **Boating with dogs** **Names, Geographical, in literature**
Serial phrases	Phrases that indicate more than one concept, possible qualification, additional term, etc.	**Plots (Drama, novel, etc.)** **Comic books, strips, etc.** **Associations, institutions, etc.**
Complex phrase forms	Phrases involving several concepts or more than one facet of a topic	**Fortune-telling by tea leaves** **African American women chief executive officers** **Library orientation for minority college students**
Subdivided topical phrases	To avoid overly complex phrasing, some topical facets may be established as subdivisions to be used with a variety of headings	**Book industries and trade—Exhibitions** **Boats and boating— Maintenance and repair** **Banks and banking— Records and correspondence—Law and legislation**

The Number of Subject Headings

The number of subject headings entered into a description for a single resource depends on many factors—none of which should be an arbitrary number blindly applied to every resource. When library catalogs were in card form, rapidly increasing bulk was both an economic and a use hazard. Maintenance costs (housing, filing, revising) were high, and users grew confused or wasted considerable time moving from one point to another in a roomful of several thousand trays.

The conventional wisdom has been that the larger the number of subject headings provided, the greater the cost of cataloging a title. On the other hand, limiting the number of subjects to one or two per record can be even more expensive, because the cataloger must take longer to determine what should be the *best* heading to represent the content in question. A major consideration should be that the assignment of more headings per resource makes the total resources of the library more available and may bring out special aspects and bits of unusual or significant information.

In the early 1980s LC was adding about two subject headings per cataloged item. This was up from fewer than two entries per record prior to the implementation of the *Anglo-American Cataloguing Rules, Second Edition* (AACR2). The tendency over the decades prior to 1980 was to reduce the average number of subject access points. However, this trend has reversed, and more entries per record are being made. Indexes and abstracting tools in science and technology, by contrast, tend to use specific subject access points to a point of minute analysis. The use of 20 to 40 subject terms for one brief article is not unheard of. Subject analysis of library titles expanded with the increased use of automated bibliographic and authority control. Online catalogs have made increasing the number of subject headings proportionately less expensive in time, effort, and cost of retrieval.

Technology is facilitating more, and better, studies of library use, to discern optimum types and quantities of subject headings for full subject retrieval. A 1983 Council on Library Resources (CLR) study of online catalog use of 15 online catalogs showed that in catalogs with subject access, about 59 percent of all searches were for subject information rather than for known items (i.e., title or author searches).[11] This was quite different from earlier studies of card catalog use, many of which showed that more than two-thirds of searches in academic libraries were known-item searches (although the percentage of subject searches in public libraries was often higher).[12] The CLR researchers recommended that system designers implement keyword searching for subjects and browsing of the subject index or thesaurus, which have now been almost universally accomplished. The researchers also recognized that such systems can only find subject terms that exist in bibliographic records, and therefore they recommended increased subject information in bibliographic records along with strict authority control to restrict the number of synonymous and related terms.[13] More recently, Tina Gross and Arlene G. Taylor[14] and Gross, Taylor, and Daniel N. Joudrey[15] show that even among searches using keyword-based strategies only, subject headings still play a significant role in providing access. Without controlled subject headings, between a quarter and a third of search results would be lost, because a keyword is found only in a subject heading on those records.

Relationships among Subject Terms

Consistency is one of the most important criteria for assigning subject headings. The cataloger should choose one subject term, and one alone, to index all materials on the same topic. In addition to the authorized terms, references are also important to subject access. References are made to the chosen subject heading from all other likely related terms. These references help the user to locate available material on a topic, plus collateral topics, at the level of specificity and from the point of view most useful for a particular need. References are based primarily on three types of relationships: equivalence relationships (references from unused terms to the authorized heading), associative relationships (coordinate references among related concepts), and hierarchical relationships.

Equivalence Relationships

An equivalence relationship is between a term that is used and one or more terms that are not. An unused term is one under which no resources are entered. Instead, a reference is made from that term to the one that is used:

> Lunar expeditions
> > USE **Space flight to the moon.**

In the controlled vocabulary, reciprocal **USE** and **UF** (used for) indicators are employed to represent equivalence relationships. Equivalence relationships may reflect true synonymy (I.D. bracelets, USE **Identification bracelets**), near synonymy (e.g., Ocean water, USE **Seawater**), lexical variants (e.g., Paediatrics, USE **Pediatrics**), or terms so closely related that they are hard to separate (e.g., Desegregation, USE **Segregation**). For example, in LCSH one sees:

> Flight to the moon
> > USE **Space flight to the moon**
>
> . . .
>
> Lunar expeditions
> > USE **Space flight to the moon**
>
> . . .
>
> Lunar flight
> > USE **Space flight to the moon**
>
> . . .

Space flight to the moon

UF Flight to the moon

Lunar expeditions

Lunar flight

The instruction given may be something other than the word *USE*; for example, it may state *For material on this subject search under . . .* or *See . . . .* It is also possible for an online catalog to give no reference in a situation where a *see* reference would be given in a manual catalog, but instead to automatically send the user to the used term. For example, a user searching under *lunar expeditions* might be automatically given a list of the library's material that had been assigned the heading **Space flight to the moon**. This practice is called *invisible referencing*.

Hierarchical Relationships

Hierarchy is the backbone of a controlled vocabulary. "Hierarchical relationships are based on degrees or levels of superordination and subordination, where the superordinate term represents a class or a whole, and subordinate terms refer to its members or parts."[16] Hierarchical references move vertically, leading the user to topics at different levels of specificity. The associations between individual terms are reflected in the relationship indicators **BT** (broader term) and **NT** (narrower term). They often reflect a genus-species or parent-child relationship (e.g., a parrot is a type or kind of bird; therefore **Birds** is a broader term of **Parrots**, and **Parrots** is a narrower term under **Birds**). In addition to genus-species relationships, the connection among BTs and NTs might reflect whole-part relationships (e.g., **Brain stem** is a narrower term under **Brain**) or instance relationships (e.g., **Mediterranean Sea** is a narrower term under **Seas**). See Figure 12.1 for an example of a simplified hierarchy in a subject heading list.

In this figure, the *top term* (**TT**) in the hierarchy is seen: **Life (Biology)**. Within the hierarchy there are many BT-NT relationships (e.g., between **Animals** and **Domestic animals** or between **Domestic animals** and **Cats**). This demonstrates how the broader term and narrower term labels are relative to the term's immediate neighbors. It should also be noted that these relationships do not extend past one level. For example, **Cats** is *not* a narrower term of **Organisms**; in this simplified hierarchy, **Cats** is a narrower term of **Domestic**

```
Life (Biology)
     Organisms
          Animals
               Domestic animals
                    Cats
                         Longhair cats
                              Persian cat
                                   Himalayan cat
```

FIGURE 12.1 Simplified Hierarchy in a Subject Heading List.

animals only. In LCSH, the term **Cats** is actually a narrower term under two different headings (LCSH is *polyhierarchical*); its two broader terms are **Domestic animals** and **Felis**. The hierarchies in some controlled vocabularies can become quite complex. A more accurate rendering of the **Himalyan cat** hierarchy is displayed in Figure 12.2.

In current library practice, hierarchical references of this type nearly always move downward from a general term to one or more specific topics subsumed under it:

Cruelty

    NT Atrocities

    NT Torture

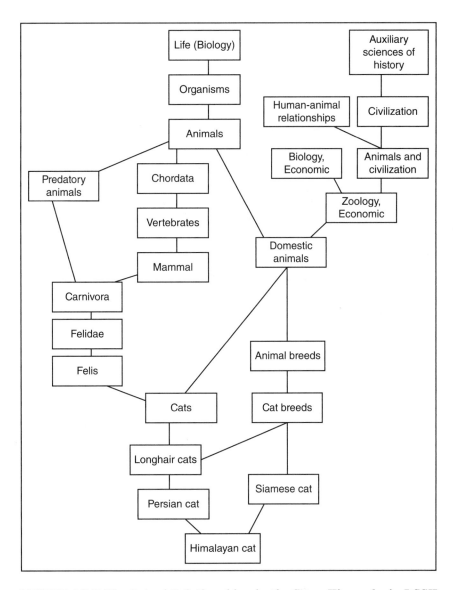

FIGURE 12.2 The Actual Relationships in the Same Hierarchy in LCSH.

In indexing practices, however, many systems provide for moving either up or down the hierarchy.

While the unused term references mentioned above are mostly between synonymous terms, they are occasionally hierarchical in their relationship to the used term. A few of them move upward from a specific term that is not used to the broader term that contains it.

> Comic operas
>> Use **Operas**

This happens more often in *Sears* than in LCSH, because *Sears* is intended for smaller collections, and there is a need to collocate concepts at a broader level. A small number of other unused term references show an illustrative relationship:

> Economic entomology
>> Use **Beneficial insects**

Associative Relationships

Associative relationships are "between terms that are neither equivalent nor hierarchical, yet the terms are semantically or conceptually associated to such an extent that the link between them should be made explicit in the controlled vocabulary, on the grounds that it may suggest additional terms for use in indexing or retrieval."[17] These coordinate references are most often referred to as *related term* (**RT**) relationships that suggest to the user that if the material already located is more or less relevant, there are other related headings that might also yield some relevant material. In the catalog, the instruction given is often displayed as: *See also . . .* or *Related material on this topic may be found under. . . .*

> **Hearing**
>> See also **Deafness**

> or

> **Deafness**
>> Related material on this topic may be found under **Hearing**

The connections and relationships shown by coordinate references are horizontal rather than vertical. They usually overlap in such ways that reciprocal or multilateral entries are deemed to be necessary:

> **Reforestation**
>> See also **Tree planting**

> **Tree planting**
>> See also **Reforestation**

Other coordinate references suggest associative rather than overlapping relationships:

Police misconduct
See also **Police—Complaints against**

Police—Complaints against
See also **Police misconduct**

Scope Notes

Besides simple references, subject heading lists sometimes include scope notes to define and delimit a subject term. These may or may not suggest further terms for the user to consult. Some catalog systems allow these notes or guides to be displayed preceding all subject entries given under those terms in their catalogs. Other systems, however, do not allow such displays and may not even present hierarchical or associative relationships in the catalog. The following two examples of scope notes come from LCSH:

Community and school
Here are entered works on ways in which the community at large, as distinct from government, may aid the school program.

Light art
Here are entered works on art that uses light as an artistic medium. Works on the portrayal of light in art are entered under **Light in art**.

Some lists include key headings or pattern headings, with instructions to the cataloger on how to construct other headings of similar form that have been omitted from the list for reasons of brevity. The following example is from *Sears*:

Hijacking of airplanes
Use same form for the hijacking of other modes of transportation.

To assure maximum consistency, a careful, up-to-date record of all subject term selections and references should be kept, by checking the terms used and the additions made in the vocabulary's database or printed list or by maintaining a separate subject authority file as part of the integrated library system (ILS), or both.

General Principles of Controlled Vocabularies

There are a number of principles that should be kept in mind when approaching a controlled vocabulary. Some are related to the creation of the subject heading list or thesaurus; others are related to the process of applying controlled vocabulary terms to information resources. Both are reviewed in the sections that follow.

Principles of Creation

Three principles related to the creation of controlled vocabularies are important: *specificity*, *literary warrant*, and *direct entry*. Understanding these concepts will assist in searching and navigating the authorized list of subject terms. *Specificity* is the level of subject analysis that is addressed by a particular controlled vocabulary. In *The Organization of Information*, Taylor and Joudrey refer to it as "the level of semantic depth."[18] The level of specificity is a decision made by the taxonomist(s) at the initial stages of creation. Some vocabularies are more specific than others. Some are focused on a single discipline or area of knowledge, and therefore include greater depth, at least in their subjects. Some vocabularies are more general in nature and cover topics at varying levels of specificity. LCSH, a vocabulary attempting to cover the entire universe of knowledge, displays more specificity than *Sears*, another broad vocabulary used with smaller collections, which collocates concepts at a more general level. For example, the creators of a vocabulary must decide whether to include (1) the concept *dogs* only or (2) the concept *dogs*, but also *types of dogs* (such as hairless dogs or toy dogs) and *individual dog breeds* (such as the Golden Retriever or the Chinese Crested Powderpuff). The level of specificity determines how much gets collocated into those more general concepts and how much gets distributed into more specific subtopics.

If one examines the concept of *dreams* in both LCSH and *Sears*, one will find the following hierarchies (see Figure 12.3), which reflect their relative amounts of specificity. This concept should not be confused with *specific entry* (see below) even though some librarians writing about cataloging may use the terms interchangeably. Specificity may be expressed in various ways, such as through additional narrower terms (e.g., adding **Nightmares** and **Children's nightmares** as further levels in the hierarchy) or through the use of subject subdivisions to sharpen or narrow the focus of the term (e.g., creating the subject heading strings **Dogs—Barking** and **Dogs—Food—Recipes** to add additional layers of meaning).

Literary warrant—the principle that new terminology is added to a controlled vocabulary only after resources about a new concept exist—was developed by E. Wyndham Hulme in the early 20th century. "A class [or subject] heading is warranted only when a literature in book form has been shown to exist, and the test of the validity of a heading is the degree of accuracy with which it describes the area of subject-matter common to the class."[19] Literary warrant prevents taxonomists from creating terms based on a theoretical combination

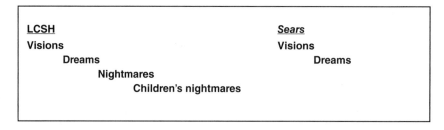

FIGURE 12.3 Comparing Specificity Between Subject Heading Lists.

of ideas (e.g., adding a subdivision to every possible heading even if there is no need). Thus, controlled vocabularies are expanded only as needed, in some cases based on subject proposals submitted by catalogers who recognize omissions in a list. This bottom-up approach (i.e., working from the literature in hand) is currently the typical method for controlled vocabulary construction. Policies and approaches, though, have changed over time. For example, in the late 20th century, it was expected that three resources would be in existence before a concept could be included in LC's subject access tools, but in more recent years subject heading and classification proposals may be submitted after a single resource becomes available. For most LC subject headings, besides the work being cataloged, it is expected that the concept will appear in a standard reference source such as a dictionary or a general encyclopedia. At this time, LC does not accept Wikipedia as the only source for a subject proposal.

> While Wikipedia can be useful, more authoritative reference sources are usually readily available and should be consulted and cited instead of, or in addition to, Wikipedia. One method for finding such authoritative sources is to examine the bibliographies at the end of Wikipedia articles, which often provide links to official web sites, standard online dictionaries and encyclopedias, and so forth. When the original source of the information is freely available, it is best to consult and cite the original source because information sometimes becomes abbreviated or garbled in the retelling.[20]

Some vocabularies, like LCSH, are very strict and only add new topics through a closed editorial process; others, like *Sears*, allow for the adding of terms by individual catalogers at any time. An example of this latter approach from *Sears* is:

Art
SA [See also] . . . art of particular countries, regions, or ethnic groups, e.g. **American art**; **Greek art**; **Native American art**; etc. [to be added as needed]

The principle of *direct entry* stipulates the entry of a concept directly under the term that names it, rather than as a subdivision of a broader concept. In contemporary cataloging practice, any approach other than direct entry is out of favor. In previous centuries, however, it was more common first to divide the subject catalog into sections based on broad headings, which were then subdivided further with more specific concepts falling within them. Direct entry leads to simple direct forms of subject headings rather than elaborate indirect constructions involving broader terms as might be found in the alphabetico-classed catalogs of the past:

Passion fruit	versus	**Food—Fruit—Passion fruit**
Time perception	versus	**Humanities—Philosophy—Psychology— Cognition—Perception—Time perception**

Electrocution	versus	**Criminal law—Criminal justice, Administration of—Corrections— Punishment—Capital punishment—Electrocution**

While the indirect approach provides collocation in a different way, users could not always predict the broader categories (e.g., Is it **Birds— Nightingale** or **Animals—Nightingale** or **Vertebrates—Nightingale**?). Over time, the direct entry approach made the alphabetical subject catalog more predictable, and therefore, more useable. Both Cutter and Haykin favored specific, direct entries over the alphabetico-classed approach.[21]

Principles of Application

When it comes to the application of controlled vocabularies, two principles must be discussed: *specific entry* and *coextensive entry*. As mentioned earlier, *specific entry* is not the same as *specificity*, despite some terminological conflations. It is also important not to confuse the concepts of *specific entry* and *coextensive entry*.

Specific Entry versus Specificity

The reason for these warnings is that over the years, and still to this day, some have used the term *specificity* in multiple ways. Some have used it to refer to the property of a controlled vocabulary or to a subject term (as is used in the section above). Some have used it to refer to the application of terms to individual resources (discussed here as *specific entry*). Some have used the term to refer to both ideas.

Taylor and Joudrey describe *specific entry* as the principle that "an aboutness concept should be assigned the most specific term that is available for that concept in the controlled vocabulary."[22] The notion started with Cutter (although some believe it may have its origins in Robert Watt's *Bibliotheca Britannica*).[23] In his *Rules for a Dictionary Catalog*, Cutter defined *specific entry* as "registering a book under a heading which expresses its special subject as distinguished from entering it in a class which includes that subject."[24] He explains:

> Enter a work under its subject-heading, not under the heading of a class which includes that subject. *Ex.* Put Lady Cust's book on "the cat" under **Cat**, not under **Zoölogy** or **Mammals**, or **Domestic animals** . . . . This rule of "specific entry" is the main distinction between the dictionary-catalog and the alphabetico-classed. Some subjects have no name. They are spoken of by a phrase or by several phrases not definite enough to be used as a heading . . . . Possible matters of investigation . . . must attain a certain individuality as objects of inquiry and be given some sort of *name*, otherwise we must assign them class-entry. And it is not always easy to decide what is a distinct subject.[25]

Based on Figure 12.3, if a cataloger were adding to the catalog a YouTube video about how to comfort children after they have nightmares, he or she would assign **Children's nightmares** to the resource if LCSH were the chosen controlled vocabulary; if the cataloger were using *Sears*, however, she or he would assign **Dreams**. In both cases, the cataloger would be assigning the most specific term available from the vocabulary in use and, therefore, the principle of specific entry would be followed.

David Haykin[26] and John Metcalfe, too, are careful in making the distinction between the two concepts using the term *specific entry* as Cutter intended for the application of controlled vocabulary. Metcalfe also speaks of *specification* for increasing the levels of specificity found among the terms in a subject list through the use of certain types of subdivisions.[27] Not everyone, however, is as precise as Cutter, Haykin, and Metcalfe in their use of terminology.

In the opening to her article, "Specificity in Subject Headings," Hilda Steinweg speaks of the concept of *specific entry* without using the phrase; the rest of the article, however, is about the level of specificity within LCSH as might be expected from the use of the word in the title.[28] Patrick Wilson in "The End of Specificity" begins by stating, "The Library of Congress (LC) appears to be abandoning the Rule of Specific Entry in subject cataloging." This appears to conflate the ideas of *specificity* (as seen in the misleading title) and *specific entry*, which is the topic of the entire article and a phrase frequently seen throughout. He defines *specific entry*: "Enter a work under a heading that describes its topic specifically, and not also under a broader, generic heading."[29]

Elaine Svenonius explores the concept of *specific entry* and how it is connected to the concept of *specificity*. She writes, "the specific entry principle is both vague and ambiguous. There are claims, perhaps misinterpreting Cutter, that the principle is relative. In any case, there seems to be a substantial amount of consensus that the specific entry principle is difficult to interpret and apply."[30] She also states, "The oldest and most debated of such specifications . . . is Cutter's injunction to assign to a work the most specific heading possible. This . . . [is] the only application principle common to a number of different subject heading languages."[31] Svenonius, in several other articles, addresses the topic of *specificity*; in some of the earlier pieces she treats the two concepts somewhat separately, but in later writings she enfolds *specific entry* into discussions of *specificity*,[32] having determined it fits within the definition of *operational specificity*, one of seven types of specificity she identifies.[33] John Balnaves also identifies different uses of the word *specificity*; one of his five uses is Cutter's *specific entry*. Although Balnaves uses the phrase *specific entry*, like Svenonius, he sees it as connected to *specificity*.[34]

Today, much of the confusion about the terms lies with the LC *Subject Headings Manual* (SHM), which has the following entry in its instruction sheet H 180 Assigning and Constructing Subject Headings:

4. **Specificity**. Assign headings that are as specific as the topics they cover. Specificity is not a property of a given subject heading; instead,

it is a relative concept that reflects the relationship between a subject heading and the work to which it is applied. For example, a seemingly broad heading like **Psychology** is specific when it is assigned to an introductory textbook on psychology. The method through which specificity is achieved depends on the nature of the available headings. In many cases, specificity can be achieved by assigning a basic heading consisting of one word or a phrase; in other cases, specificity can be achieved by subdividing a heading.[35]

With an instruction such as this it is not difficult to see why people might get the two concepts mixed up. Although the authors see the connection between the two principles, for clarity, it is helpful to distinguish between the two: using *specificity* when talking about the qualities of the controlled vocabulary list as a whole and *specific entry* when discussing the application of vocabulary terms to resources.

Specific Entry versus Coextensive Entry

It should be noted that the concept of *specific entry* is also not the same as the concept of *coextensive entry*. Systems for subject analysis attempt to make subject headings coextensive, as much as possible, with the concept/topics covered in the information resource analyzed. That is, the subject heading(s) will cover all, but no more than, the concepts or topics covered in the information resource. Svenonius states, "A coextensive heading is one that summarizes a book's topic, fits it like a cap that is neither too loose, nor too tight."[36] Sometimes, however, to get that perfect fit, a cataloger may need more than one heading to achieve coextensive entry.

A great weakness of the concept of *specific entry* is that subjects must be described in terms that are constantly changing. Materials very often have to be cataloged before a suitable term has been added to any standard list. Many subjects now represent a cross-fertilization among once traditional disciplines, and new concepts are being generated rapidly. In addition, particular terms can fluctuate in meaning. There is also a tendency for any alphabetical subject list based on the ideal of *specific entry* to develop sequences of topical subdivisions or modifications that convert true random alphabetical access into an inadvertent categorizing device. All such lists show marks of a split personality in this respect.

The two most popular American subject heading lists, *Library of Congress Subject Headings* and *Sears List of Subject Headings*, are reviewed in the next two chapters. Chapter 15 presents some other indexing systems that are used as modes of subject access to organized library collections.

Coextensive and Specific Entry in Action!

If we had a book about **cats** and **dogs**, what terms would we assign if we wanted to fulfill both coextensive and specific entry as we are supposed to do? First, we would consult our controlled vocabulary to find out how it expresses these concepts. In LCSH, we find the following authorized headings in three different hierarchies:

There is no single term to cover the topic of this resource. None of the pos-

Canis	Domestic animals	Felidae
Gray wolf	Cats	Felis
Dogs	Dogs	Cats

sibilities brings these two animals together. Assigning **Domestic animals** is not an option, even though both headings fall under this concept, because the heading **Domestic animals** is far too broad for a work about cats and dogs. When you look at the other NTs under **Domestic animals** you realize the concept also encompasses **Animal breeds**, **Horses**, **Livestock**, **Pets**, **Rabbits**, and **Working animals** as well as **Cats** and **Dogs**. In order to have a single heading that is coextensive with the subject of the resources, the heading would have to be **Cats and dogs**, but that heading does not exist. To be coextensive with the aboutness of the resource, we need to apply two separate headings.

To meet the requirement of **specific entry**, we would choose the headings that best reflect the level of meaning found in the resource itself. If the work is about cats and dogs, then choosing **Cats** and **Dogs** makes the most sense. Their level of semantic depth is a perfect match for that of the resource. We would not use broader terms such as **Felis** or **Gray wolf** because those terms are not as specific as what is found in the resource. To fulfill the principles of **coextensive entry** and **specific entry**, this work would require two separate subject headings:

Cats
Dogs

NOTES

1. *Z39.19: Guidelines for the Construction, Format, and Management of Monolingual Controlled Vocabularies*, approved July 25, 2005 by the American National Standards Institute; reaffirmed May 13, 2010 (Baltimore, Md.: National Information Standards Organization, 2010), http://www.niso.org/apps/group_public/download.php/12591/z39-19-2005r2010.pdf.
2. Arlene G. Taylor and Daniel N. Joudrey, *The Organization of Information*, 3rd ed. (Westport, Conn.: Libraries Unlimited, 2009), 334.
3. Ibid., 472–473.
4. E. J. Coates, *Subject Catalogues: Headings and Structure* (London: Library Association, 1960), 19.

5. Charles Ammi Cutter, *Rules for a Dictionary Catalog*, 4th ed. (Washington, D.C.: GPO, 1904; republished, London: Library Association, 1972). The original version of this work was Charles A. Cutter, "Rules for a Printed Dictionary Catalogue," in *Public Libraries in the United States of America: Their History, Condition, and Management*, U.S. Bureau of Education (Washington, D.C.: GPO, 1876), Part II.

6. David Judson Haykin, *Subject Headings: A Practical Guide* (Washington, D.C.: GPO, 1951), 7–11.

7. These and other controlled vocabulary challenges are described in detail in Taylor and Joudrey, *The Organization of Information*, 336–340.

8. Cutter, *Rules for a Dictionary Catalog*, 70.

9. Coates, *Subject Catalogues*, 19.

10. For the development of phrase heading forms in *Library of Congress Subject Headings* and in *Sears List of Subject Headings*, *see* chapters 13 and 14 of this text.

11. Joseph R. Matthews, Gary S. Lawrence, and Douglas K. Ferguson, eds., *Using Online Catalogs: A Nationwide Survey* (New York: Neal-Schuman, 1983), 144–146.

12. Karen Markey, *Subject Searching in Library Catalogs: Before and After the Introduction of Online Catalogs* (Dublin, Ohio: OCLC Online Computer Library Center, 1984), 75–87.

13. *Using Online Catalogs*, 177–179.

14. Tina Gross and Arlene G. Taylor, "What Have We Got to Lose? The Effect of Controlled Vocabulary on Keyword Searching Results," *College & Research Libraries* 66, no. 3 (May 2005): 212–230.

15. Tina Gross, Arlene G. Taylor, and Daniel N. Joudrey, "Still a Lot to Lose: The Role of Controlled Vocabulary in Keyword Searching," *Cataloging & Classification Quarterly* 53, no. 1 (2015): 1–39.

16. *Z39.19: Guidelines for the Construction, Format, and Management of Monolingual Controlled Vocabularies*, 46.

17. Ibid., 51.

18. Taylor and Joudrey, *The Organization of Information*, 341.

19. E. Wyndham Hulme, "Principles of Book Classification," *Library Association Record* 13 (1911): 447.

20. "Summary of Decisions, Editorial Meeting Number 23," LC Policy and Standards Division, accessed April 23, 2014, http://www.loc.gov/aba/pcc/saco/cpsoed/psd-110815.html.

21. Cutter, *Rules for a Dictionary Catalog*, 17–18; Haykin, *Subject Headings*, 3–4.

22. Taylor and Joudrey, *The Organization of Information*, 343–344.

23. John Metcalfe, *Subject Classifying and Indexing of Libraries and Literature* (New York: Scarecrow Press, 1959), 31.

24. Cutter, *Rules for a Dictionary Catalog*, 22.

25. Ibid., 66–67.

26. Haykin, *Subject Headings*, 9–11.

27. John Metcalfe, *Information Indexing and Subject Cataloging* (New York: Scarecrow Press, 1957), 84, 222–223; Metcalfe, *Subject Classifying and Indexing*, 46, 179; John Metcalfe, *Alphabetical Subject Indication of Information* (New Brunswick, N.J.: Graduate School of Library Service, Rutgers, 1965): 30–35.

28. Hilda Steinweg, "Specificity in Subject Headings," *Library Resources & Technical Services* 23, no. 1 (1979): 55.

29. Patrick Wilson, "In the End of Specificity," *Library Resources & Technical Services* 23, no 2 (1979): 116.

30. Elaine Svenonius, "Metcalfe and the Principles of Specific Entry," in *The Variety of Librarianship: Essays in Honour of John Wallace Metcalfe*, edited by W. Boyd Rayward (Chicago: ALA, 1976), 172.

31. Elaine Svenonius, "LCSH: Semantics, Syntax and Specificity," *Cataloging & Classification Quarterly* 29, no. 1–2 (2000): 19.

32. Elaine Svenonius and Helen F. Schmierer, "Current Issues in the Subject Control of Information," *Library Quarterly* 47, no. 3 (1977): 333, 347; Elaine Svenonius, *The Intellectual Foundation of Information Organization* (Cambridge, Mass.: MIT Press, 2000), 188–189.

33. Svenonius, "Metcalfe and the Principles of Specific Entry," 186–187.

34. John Balnaves, "Specificity," in *The Variety of Librarianship: Essays in Honour of John Wallace Metcalfe*, edited by W. Boyd Rayward (Chicago: ALA, 1976), 49, 54–55.

35. *Subject Headings Manual*, 1st ed. (Washington, D.C.: Cataloging Distribution Service, Library of Congress, 2008). "H180: Assigning and Constructing Subject Headings," 2. Also available in Cataloger's Desktop through a subscription or available freely on the web in PDF form, accessed April 10, 2014, http://www.loc.gov/aba/publications/FreeSHM/freeshm.html.

36. Elaine Svenonius, "LCSH: Semantics, Syntax and Specificity," 27.

SUGGESTED READING

Chan, Lois Mai, Phyllis A. Richmond, and Elaine Svenonius, eds. *Theory of Subject Analysis: A Sourcebook*. Littleton, Colo.: Libraries Unlimited, 1985.

Coates, E. J. *Subject Catalogues: Heading and Structure*. London: Library Association, 1960.

Foskett, A. C. *The Subject Approach to Information*. 5th ed. London: Library Association Publishing, 1996. Chapter 8: Alphabetical Subject Headings: Cutter to Austin.

Haykin, David Judson. *Subject Headings: A Practical Guide*. Washington, D.C.: GPO, 1951.

Mann, Thomas. *Library Research Models: A Guide to Classification, Cataloging, and Computers*. New York: Oxford University Press, 1993. Chapter 4: The Traditional Library Science Model. Part 2: The Vocabulary-Controlled Catalog.

Pettee, Julia. *Subject Headings: The History and Theory of the Alphabetical Approach to Books*. New York: H. W. Wilson, 1946.

Taylor, Arlene G., and Daniel N. Joudrey. *The Organization of Information*. 3rd ed. Westport, Conn.: Libraries Unlimited, 2009.

Chapter 13

Library of Congress Subject Headings (LCSH)

INTRODUCTION

Library of Congress Subject Headings (LCSH) is a system of authority-controlled, multidisciplinary terminology that is used to represent the topical, geographic, chronological, and form elements of the contents of resources. Unlike discipline-specific thesauri, it attempts to cover the entire universe of knowledge. The official list, *Library of Congress Subject Headings*, consists of terms, with references, that have been established since 1898 for use in the subject catalogs of the Library of Congress (LC); it also contains subdivisions that may be used to make headings more specific. LCSH is the most comprehensive list of English-language subject headings in existence and the only subject headings list accepted as a worldwide standard.[1] "LCSH has been translated into many languages and is used around the world by libraries large and small."[2] Although developed to give subject access to the vast collections of one particular library, this list can be, and has been, adopted by libraries of all sizes, including many that do not use the *Library of Congress Classification* (LCC). For example, many public libraries use LCSH as their controlled vocabulary but *Dewey Decimal Classification* (DDC) as the basis for their call numbers.

Many libraries use LCSH as their primary vocabulary, but some augment it by using other, more specific, thesauri for particular collections or for specific types of resources. For example, some libraries use *Medical Subject Headings* (MeSH) for their medical and health-related materials. Library and Archives Canada (LAC, the Canadian national library and archives) uses LCSH as its basic list but supplements it with a special set of vocabulary terms for Canadian materials, *Canadian Subject Headings* (CSH).[3] LC also produces several of its own supplementary thesauri to be used along with LCSH. Authorized genre/form terms are found in the *Library of Congress Genre/Form Terms for Library and Archival Materials* (LCGFT); headings for the Children's and Young Adults' Cataloging (CYAC) Program are provided in *Children's Subject Headings* (CSH); and for music cataloging there is the *Library of Congress Medium of Performance Thesaurus for Music* (LCMPT).

LCSH is used in the United States by most large public, academic, and special libraries that do not have technical subject lists of their own. Because bibliographic records created by LC often carry DDC numbers[4] as well as LC call numbers but have only LC subject headings, some smaller libraries also use LCSH. Others use the shorter, less frequently revised *Sears List of Subject Headings* (*Sears*) as their primary subject list, but consult LCSH for suggestions when *Sears* cannot provide the specificity or the diversity they want.[5] (*Sears* is discussed in chapter 14.)

BACKGROUND

Library of Congress subject headings come from a long tradition of theory and practice that is generally held to begin with Charles A. Cutter's *Rules for a Dictionary Catalog*.[6] A brief review of Cutter's approach and of the major developments stemming from his work can be found in chapter 12. The purpose of the present chapter is to highlight trends leading directly to the current manifestations of LC subject headings.[7]

On July 1, 1909, J. C. M. Hanson, chief of the Catalog Division of LC, addressed the Catalog Section of the American Library Association (ALA) at its Bretton Woods Conference. In his paper, "The Subject Catalogs of the Library of Congress,"[8] he alluded to a two-volume subject catalog published by LC in 1869, *Catalogue of the Library of Congress: Index of Subjects*, but called the subject heading developments of the intervening 40 years too radical to permit a meaningful comparison. The many changes brought about by a new classification scheme (see chapter 18 for the history of LCC) and the move into a new building required a new approach to subject indexing. LC catalogers agreed to start from the ALA's *List of Subject Headings for Use in Dictionary Catalogs* (1895),[9] which embodied much of Cutter's theory and which originally formed an appendix to his rules. The ALA list was designed for smaller libraries of "generally popular character," but with LC's printed card distribution plans, such an orientation was advantageous.

When LC began to print and sell catalog cards, subject terms were provided only if an LC classification number was also printed. Because schedules for many of the main classes of LCC were still undeveloped, the list of subject headings grew slowly in the first decade. Proposed new headings were compared to those in the ALA list before final selection. Separate publication of the new subject heading list did not start until 1909, when the annotated and interleaved copies of the ALA's *List of Subject Headings for Use in Dictionary Catalogs* grew unwieldy. It was assumed from the first that cumulations of additions and changes would be issued periodically to supplement the main list, which itself appeared in parts until March 1914.

The practice of subordinating place to subject in scientific and technical headings, as well as under many economic and educational topics, was established at this time. But other subjects—historical, political, administrative, social, and descriptive—were to be subordinated to place, although Hanson admitted to "a number of subjects so nearly on the border line, that it has been difficult in all cases to preserve absolute consistency in decisions."[10] Besides the place/subject versus subject/place precedents, other syntactic forms evolved. "There is undeniably a strong tendency in the Library of Congress catalog to bring related subjects together by means of inversion of headings, by combinations of two or more subject-words, and even by subordination of one subject to another."[11] Hanson recognized that subordination within the dictionary arrangement of his new subject list was a concession to the alphabetico-classed or systematic organization of the 1869 catalog. He argued, "the student and the investigator . . . are best served by having related topics brought together so far as that can be accomplished without a too serious violation of the dictionary principle."[12] The practice of inversion of certain types of modified headings was firmly established by 1951 when David Judson Haykin wrote:

> It is unlikely that the reader will look under an adjective denoting language, ethnic group, or place for material on a subject limited by language, ethnic group, or place, although, in the case of ethnic groups particularly, the interest in the group may outweigh that in the subject. On this basis it has been assumed, although it has not been demonstrated, that a reader interested in French art or French anonyms and pseudonyms would be much more likely to look under *Art, French* (or *Art—France*) and *Anonyms and pseudonyms, French* than under the respective uninverted forms, that is, the linguistic, ethnic, or local adjective, which may be considered the more specific approach to the subject.[13]

These and other practices have been questioned and modified in recent years but were basic premises in the establishment of subject headings at LC for many years and are still reflected in the list.

FORMATS AND SUPPLEMENTARY TOOLS

LC subject headings are made available in several formats. The longest-running format was the printed and bound version. For many years these lists were published in new editions every five years or so, but starting in 1988 with the 11th edition, they were published annually with only one exception (no edition was published in 2008 due to production problems).[14] Beginning with the ninth edition, it was necessary to publish the list in two volumes, which quickly expanded, and the last several editions were published in six volumes. The volumes have for many years been published in red bindings and are affectionately known as "The Big Red Books." In 2013, however, LC revealed its plan to change its approach to providing access to cataloging documentation.

> The Library of Congress has announced a transition to online-only publication of its cataloging documentation. As titles that are in production

are released, the Library's Cataloging Distribution Service (CDS) will no longer print new editions of its subject headings, classification schedules and other cataloging publications. The Library will instead provide free downloadable PDF versions of these titles. For users desiring enhanced functionality, the Library's two web-based subscription services, *Cataloger's Desktop* and *Classification Web*, will continue as products from CDS.[15]

As a result, the 35th edition published in 2013 is the last of "The Big Red Books." It contains approximately 332,500 headings spread over 6,845 pages. A fully updated version of LCSH is still available through LC's online subscription product *Classification Web* (informally known as *ClassWeb*).[16] At the time of this writing, the PDF version of LCSH currently offered is the 37th edition from 2015. It is freely available through LC's Acquisitions and Bibliographic Access (ABA) Directorate website and contains more than 337,000 headings spread over 27 separate files (one each for the letters *A* to *Z* and one for numerals).[17] Currently, LC plans to post a new edition in print-ready PDF files every January; older PDF editions of LCSH are archived on the ABA website.[18] In other words, in January 2016, the 38th edition becomes available, and the 37th edition is archived alongside the 34th, 35th, and 36th editions.

MARC (MAchine-Readable Cataloging) authority records for LC subject headings (or their equivalents) are available through several services or sites:

1. **OCLC**: subject authority records have been available through this subscription-based service since 1987[19]
2. **Library of Congress Authorities**: LC's official and freely available authority data website[20]
3. ***ClassWeb***: authority records are available in this subscription-based product by choosing the MARC record view for each subject heading[21]
4. **LC MARC Distribution Service**: records are available in MARC 21 and MARCXML formats for direct input into a local catalog through this subscription-based service[22]
5. **LC Linked Data Service**: a freely available website that provides URIs for the standards and vocabularies promulgated by the Library of Congress[23]

See ICC11 chapter 21 to review the MARC fields relevant to subject headings in both the bibliographic and authorities formats (e.g., the 6XX fields in bibliographic records).

Several supplementary tools have been developed for use with LCSH. The instructions that guide LC catalogers when applying LCSH have been published as the *Subject Headings Manual* (SHM). The SHM is an essential tool to consult for anyone who wishes to apply subject headings correctly. It consists of nearly 300 numbered memos (or *instruction sheets*) all prefixed with the letter *H* (e.g., H 1095, H 180). It was formerly issued in loose-leaf form with periodic updates,[24] but is now freely available in PDF at LC's ABA website.[25] The SHM is also available through LC's web-based documentation service, *Cataloger's Desktop*, by subscription.[26] A question one might ask is: Why would a cataloging department subscribe to *Cataloger's Desktop* when the resources are freely available on the web? It is because *Cataloger's Desktop* gathers these and many other resources into one convenient location and makes them all keyword searchable and fully browsable.

LCSH is supplemented by the *Library of Congress Subject Headings Monthly List*, available on the ABA website.[27] These lists are LC's formal mechanism to announce changes within the subject heading system. They provide catalogers around the world with the very latest information about new and altered subject headings, references, and scope notes in one convenient location. In years past, there were often delays in updating the official LCSH authority file that is represented in *ClassWeb*, the print volumes, and other sources of subject authority data; these (then-weekly) lists provided advanced notice of all imminent changes. In today's more technologically advanced environment, in *ClassWeb* most changes to LCSH are effected the same days that the lists are published. There are, however, slight delays in the updates to some of the other sources for subject authority data. For example, it may take up to 24 hours for the LC Authorities website to be updated and up to one week for the data in OCLC to be updated.

In years past, catalogers stayed up-to-date on LCSH through the *Cataloging Service Bulletin* (CSB). The CSB provided information about changes to the SHM, listed some newly established subject headings and headings that had been changed, and provided information about new publications that may be useful to the subject cataloger. LC stopped publishing the CSB in 2010, but over 30 years' worth of issues are freely available on the LC ABA website and can be useful for understanding changes that occurred during the periods covered.[28] The ABA website also contains summaries of the monthly editorial meetings, in which the Policy and Standards Division (PSD) specialists explain decisions about LCSH and LCC proposals, list newly approved free-floating subdivisions, and make announcements about—and sometimes clarify—policy. In short, it provides insights into the very latest issues related to subject cataloging.[29]

A final resource that was very helpful, but sadly is no longer being published, is the *Free-floating Subdivisions: An Alphabetical Index*. At the time of this writing, it is no longer being updated. If one encounters a published edition of this resource or finds a version of it online: *caveat emptor*! Fortunately, the current lists of free-floating subdivisions appear in the electronic, print, and PDF versions of LCSH, as well as in SHM memos H 1095-H 1145.5.

APPLYING SUBJECT HEADINGS

Subject headings are assigned to represent the aboutness of the work contained within a resource. An aboutness statement is developed during the course of subject analysis to identify the key concepts that are to be translated into subject headings. In most library settings, the level of exhaustivity for subject analysis (see chapter 11) is at the summarization level (i.e., the subject description of the work summarizes the overall contents of the work instead of providing an exhaustive list of the minute individual topics covered within). In some cases, a single subject heading might suffice (e.g., **Embalming**), but in others, a complex subject heading string (i.e., a main heading plus one or more subdivisions) might be necessary to represent the aboutness of the resource (e.g., **Embalming—Law and legislation—Greece—Crete—Popular works**). In some cases, a single heading is inadequate and an array of headings—perhaps a mixture of solo main headings and lengthy complex strings—is necessary to coextensively represent the subject of the work. When using LCSH, it is important to consider the authorized terms, but it is also necessary to use the syndetic structure of references and the scope notes to navigate the list and to find the most appropriate headings available. Catalogers also must remember to take advantage of the supplementary tools described above, particularly the SHM. Accurate subject heading work depends on reliably consulting and applying the instructions found in the SHM.

SHM H 180, "Assigning and Constructing Subject Headings," enumerates over a dozen points to consider when applying subject headings to a work. The first several provide a framework for the activity. H 180 states that the subject headings assigned to a work should cover the most important topics and summarize the overall content of the resource (i.e., the summarization level of exhaustivity). LC practice is to "assign headings only for topics that comprise at least 20% of the work."[30] This is commonly referred to as the *twenty-percent rule*, and it can be very helpful in keeping the subject headings focused on the major topical components of a work. The twenty-percent rule may also apply to supplemental content or notable bibliographic features, such as bibliographies, maps, images, and so on.

The subject headings applied should reflect the nature of the resource being cataloged. For example, if a cataloger is describing only a part of the whole work, then the subjects should reflect the part rather than the whole. There should be no arbitrary limit to the number of subject headings assigned to a work, but LC points out that although some items may need only one, others may be described using up to six. LC practice, though, is to use no more than 10 headings. In other words, one to six is fairly standard, but a cataloger may go up to 10 headings if necessary. If more than one heading is assigned to a work, the headings should be ordered according to their importance. In short, assign the predominant topic(s) first, followed by secondary topics. See SHM H 80 (*not* H 180) for information about the ordering of subject headings.

The principles of *specific entry* and *coextensive entry*, as described in the previous chapter, are both employed in LCSH. To put it simply, catalogers assign the most specific LC subject headings that are appropriate for the work being cataloged. They also attempt to match the scope of the subject matter of the work as closely as possible through the subject headings used. For example, a work on the use of puppies in combating depression in teenagers is entered under the headings **Puppies—Therapeutic use** (*not* **Dogs—Therapeutic use** or **Animals—Therapeutic use**) and **Depression in adolescence—Treatment** (*not* **Depression, Mental—Treatment**). Specific entry keeps the terms from being too broad; coextensive entry tries to get a close match between the headings and the subject matter in the resource. Both are key to successfully applying subject headings to works.

Several of the guidelines in H 180 address the choice among several related subject headings. Although the key H 180 instructions are reviewed in this section, additional instructions are found in the complete memo. Please consult H

180, H 80, and the other SHM instruction sheets referred to throughout this chapter for more information.

The first of these instructions in H 180, regarding choices among related headings, addresses the topic of *bi-level indexing*, which occurs when both a broader term and one or more of its narrower terms are assigned to a work. This usually occurs when a broader topic is discussed, but a more specific subtopic is used to illustrate it. In these cases, LC recommends assigning headings for both the broader topic and the illustrating subtopic as long as the subtopic meets the twenty-percent rule. If, for example, there were a work primarily on the use of animals in therapy, which addresses the use of dogs, rabbits, cats, kittens, puppies, and ferrets, but pays special attention to puppies (and puppies represent at least a fifth of the resource), then a cataloger would assign both **Animals—Therapeutic use** and **Puppies—Therapeutic use** to the record.

The memo also addresses the *rule of three* and the *rule of four*. In the rule of three, LC states that if there is a topic that includes more than three subtopics, but the resource being cataloged is only focused on two or three of those subtopics, it is best to apply the two or three individual topics as subject headings rather than the broader one. For example, if you have a work about traveling in Uruguay, Argentina, and Chile, it is best to assign the three individual headings **Uruguay—Description and travel**, **Argentina—Description and travel**, and **Chile—Description and travel**, rather than assigning **South America—Description and travel**. LC favors the individual headings because the broader heading covers so much more content than just the three. H 180 goes on to state that this might also be expanded to four headings, if necessary. The rule of four states, "In certain circumstances it may be preferable to assign headings for four subtopics of a broad concept. If a heading covers a broad range and each subtopic forms only a small portion of that whole range, assign the four subtopics instead . . . . LC practice: *Do not exceed four subtopics under any circumstances*."[31] So if that work were instead about traveling in Paraguay, Uruguay, Argentina, and Chile, then the cataloger *could* assign the four individual strings *if* he or she deems the broader topic is still too far-reaching for the work in hand. But, if the work were about traveling in *five* South American countries, then, if the cataloger is diligently following the rules, **South America—Description and travel** is the only option left because the work reflects more than four subtopics.

After all the subject headings have been assigned to a resource, it is important for catalogers to assess their work. This can happen by comparing the resource being described to others in the catalog and by thinking about the searching process from the point of view of the users. Asking these few simple questions should help:

1. Do the headings assigned appropriately collocate the work with similar works? Is this work a good fit with the others already placed under these headings?
2. Do the headings adequately communicate what the work is about? Do they provide a brief description of the overall contents of the work?
3. Do the headings capture what is important, new, unique, or significant about the resource?

4. Are the headings something a user would search for in order to find this work? Do these headings make sense as search terms for the work in hand?

5. If a user were to search these terms, would that user be satisfied with this resource? Would the user be happy to get it as a result of a search for these headings?

If the answer to one or more of these questions is *no*, then there might be a problem, and additional thought may be advisable.

TOPICAL SUBJECT HEADINGS

(MARC 21 bibliographic field 650, 2nd indicator 0; MARC 21 authority field 150)

Structure

Topical subject headings in LCSH are constructed in a variety of ways, ranging from a single noun to complex descriptive phrases. In his *Rules for a Dictionary Catalog*, Cutter enumerated six varieties of subject headings according to their grammar or syntax.[32] They covered only primary headings (i.e., headings without further subdivision). The categories below are his, but the examples come from the current edition of LCSH:

Cyberbullying	[A single word]
Ugly contests	[A noun preceded by an adjective]
Space tourism	[A noun preceded by another noun used like an adjective]
Children of blind parents	[A noun connected with another noun by a preposition]
Libraries and society	[A noun connected with another noun by *and*]
Butch and femme (Lesbian culture) in motion pictures	[A phrase or sentence]

Although Cutter tolerated modifier inversions "only when some other word is decidedly more significant or is often used alone with the same meaning as the whole name," he made no explicit provision for parenthetical qualifiers or other complex forms, which, like subdivisions, are usually reminiscent of the alphabetico-classed approach. Some examples of these unusual forms of headings include:

Etching, Anonymous	[simple inverted heading]
Damn (The English word)	[parenthetical qualifiers]
Architecture, Medieval, in art	[inverted heading as part of a phrase]

Topical headings in LCSH can also be grouped in other ways; this discussion follows that of Lois Mai Chan in her treatise on subject headings.[33]

Single Noun Headings

Cutter's Rule No. 172 reads: "Enter books under the word which best expresses their subject, whether it occurs in the title or not."[34] He worked primarily in terms of the simple concept-name relationship on which the noun forms of all languages are based. Over the years, LC has experimented with slight variations of this single-word heading, for example the inclusion of an initial article (e.g., **The West**), which is sometimes inverted in the interests of clarity (e.g., **State, The**). Subject headings are no longer established with an English article in the initial position. **The West** has been changed to **West (U.S.)**.[35]

Another variation was the distinction drawn, particularly in literature and art, between singular nouns (denoting the activity or the form, e.g., **Essay** and **Opera**) and plural nouns (denoting the objects, e.g., **Essays** and **Operas**). Guidelines in SHM H 285 delineate when to use a plural form of heading (e.g., count nouns, brands of products) and when to use a singular form of noun as the heading (e.g., abstract concepts, parts of the body).[36] Some older plural headings (e.g., **Paintings**) have been canceled in favor of the singular form. **Painting**, for example, is now used for both the activity and the object.

Adjectival Headings

Adjectival headings start with a modifier that is followed by a noun or noun phrase (e.g., **Minority-owned engineering firms**). The modifier may be an adjective or it may be a noun used as an adjective:

- Common adjective
  - **Bad news**
  - **Crazy quilts**
  - **Frozen apples**
  - **Psychological games**

- Ethnic, national, or geographic adjective
  - **Basque drama**
  - **Hispanic American accountants**
  - **Israeli periodicals**
  - **Southern sky (Astronomy)**

- Participial modifiers
  - **Applied ethics**
  - **Hearing aids**
  - **Running races**

- Common noun used as a modifier
  - **City dwellers**
  - **Dogsled mail**
  - **Plant fibers**

- Proper noun used as a modifier
  - **Apple computer**
  - **Bernstein polynomials**
  - **Boeing airplanes**

Conjunctive Phrase Headings

Headings composed of two or more nouns, with or without modifiers, connected by *and* or ending with *etc.* belong in this group. Those that are additive may comprise similar elements:

Books and reading	**Rogues and vagabonds**
Brigands and robbers	**Formulas, recipes, etc.**
Questions and answers	**Church work with tourists, travelers, etc.**

Or, the elements may be contradictory or they may be related in some other way:

Good and evil	**Drinking and boating accidents**
Right and wrong	**Libraries and communism**

Headings that are related in "some other way" are now established—and should be assigned—only when a work being cataloged discusses a relationship between two topics from both perspectives and in such broad terms that the relationship could not be described by use of a main heading with a subdivision.[37] Many older additive headings have been separated. For example, the heading **Buddha and Buddhism** has been replaced by two separate headings: **Buddha (The concept)** and **Buddhism**.

Prepositional Phrase Headings

Prepositions sometimes enable the subject cataloger to express single but complex ideas for which there is not a single word. Some express relationships for which an "and phrase" would be artificial (e.g., **Photography in psychiatry**, **Shelving for nonbook materials**, or **Police services for juveniles**). Some are inverted (e.g., **Justice, Administration of** and **Knowledge, Theory of**). Examples of other prepositions used are found in Table 13.1. Many of these circumlocutions are replaced when a simpler expression gains currency (e.g., **Psychoanalysis in historiography** was replaced by **Psychohistory**). *As* headings for classes of persons have been restricted to certain situations where the resulting connotation will not be seen as disparaging (e.g., **Buddhist monks as soldiers**, **African American artists as teachers**, or **Musicians as dandies**). Old headings in which men or women were identified as professionals or in some other role (e.g., **Men as collectors** and **Women as astronauts**) have been replaced by less marginalizing phrases (e.g., **Antique collecting for men** and **Women astronauts**).[38]

Parenthetical Qualifiers

Nouns or phrases in parentheses following primary terms have in the past resulted in a variety of linguistically inept headings. LC no longer adds them to designate special applications of a general concept, although it has no

TABLE 13.1 Prepositions Used in LCSH.

Preposition	Examples
Against:	Offenses against the person
	Crimes against peace
	Sex discrimination against men
	Claims against decedents' estates (Roman law)
As:	Sorghum as food
	Invertebrates as carriers of plant disease
	Aluminum foil as art material
	Apes as pets
From:	Theft from motor vehicles
	Muslim converts from Zoroastrianism
	Fugitives from justice
	Benefitting from a wrongful act (Jewish law)
On:	Counterculture on television
	Advertising on postal stationery
	Atlases on microfilm
	Ability, Influence of age on
To:	Aids to air navigation
	Access to the sea (International law)
	Impediments to marriage
	Admission to the bar
With:	Altars with pulpits
	Castanets with chamber orchestra
	Trading with the enemy
	Animals with disabilities

plans to change established headings such as **Vibration (Marine engineering)**, **Cooking (Frozen foods)**, and **Excavations (Archaeology)**. For newly established situations, three techniques are available:

- *In* and *of* headings:
  - **Information theory in biology**
    not **Information theory (Biology)**
  - **Abandonment of automobiles**
    not **Abandonment (Automobiles)**

- Phrase headings:
  - **Combinatorial enumeration problems**
    not **Enumeration problems (Combinatorial analysis)**

- Subdivisions under a primary heading:
  - **Public health—Citizen participation**
    not **Citizen participation (Public health)**

A few situations in which it may be necessary to use parenthetical qualifiers are recognized. If the term or phrase has more than one dictionary definition, qualifiers may be added to specify a discipline, especially if the heading represents a concept:

Semantics (Philosophy)

Chaos (Christian theology)

Or, they may be added to identify the category of the object designated by the heading:

Bridges

Bridges (Computer networks)

Bridges (Dentistry)

Bridges (Graph theory)

It is also LC practice to use parenthetical qualifiers to remove ambiguity or to make an obscure word or phrase more explicit, such as **Cluttering (Speech pathology)**, or to identify the category for a named entity, such as **Arulo (Artificial language)**.[39] Parenthetical expressions are also used in headings for buildings and other structures and for musical works.

Empire State Plaza (Albany, N.Y.)

Cantatas, Secular (Women's voices)

Inverted Headings

Inversions, although awkward syntactically, serve the alphabetico-classed function of subordinating specific descriptors under their broad generic categories. Here, too, there has been much inconsistency.

Older people's writings, Peruvian

Education, Bilingual

Asylum, Right of (Islamic Law)

In the course of its efforts to modernize and systematize LCSH, LC has attempted to set policy for the creation of new inverted headings. For example, topical headings modified by adjectival qualifiers referring to ethnic groups, languages, or nationalities are to be established in the inverted form:

One-act plays, Catalan

Cooking, Chinese

Proverbs, Korean

There are, however, a few exceptions, one of which is for headings qualified by ethnic groups of the United States; they are established in direct order.

Ethiopian American teenagers

Mexican American proverbs

Another exception is for certain high-level literary or language forms listed in SHM H 306.

> **Catalan drama**
>
> **Chinese fiction**
>
> **Korean newspapers**[40]

LC occasionally changes an existing heading, especially in cases where every instance of the concept but one is in direct order.

Semantics

Not only have syntactic forms of subject headings come under close scrutiny and revision in recent years, but LCSH terminology also has been reconsidered. Word meanings, particularly their connotative aspects, mutate rapidly; social and political upheavals cause many changes, and scientific and technological developments account for many more. The problem of shifting terminology is particularly troublesome for a subject access list that was originally designed for use with card or printed book catalogs, which is based on specific entry, avoidance of synonyms, and controlled references.

A ringing complaint that LCSH terminology was obsolete and prejudicial came from Sanford Berman.[41] In his 1971 magnum opus, *Prejudices and Antipathies*, he identified more than 200 subject headings as being problematic for various reasons. As the head of the cataloging department at the Hennepin County Library (HCL) in Minnesota, Berman edited the *HCL Cataloging Bulletin*, a bimonthly publication that contained lists of subject headings and references added to the HCL catalogs.[42] Many new concepts were added as headings at HCL before being added to LCSH. Unfortunately, after Berman's retirement, HCL discontinued this service, but the awareness that Berman raised is still at work at LC. In a review of Berman's criticism of LCSH 30 years later, Stephen Knowlton found that nearly two-thirds of the problematic headings that Berman identified in *Prejudices and Antipathies* have been partially or fully revised to address Berman's concerns.[43]

Other writers have also criticized LC's stance on conceptual and linguistic shifts. Doris Clack's 1975 analysis of African-American literature resources started from a critique of LC subject analysis. She observed, "Inadequate subject analysis is not just a problem with black literature—though admittedly there the level of adequacy is critically low—nor has it only in recent years been brought to the attention of the library world."[44] Clack devoted the bulk of her treatise to various lists of LC class numbers and subject terms from the African-American perspective. Since her book was published, LC has made many changes. The one cited below involved changing approximately 12,000 cards:

> A basic function in the maintenance of a subject heading system is that of updating headings to conform to changing terminology or altered concepts. In general, the Library of Congress is and has been conservative in making changes since it involves altering reference structures

surrounding a given heading as well as accommodating the change in both the card catalogs and the machine-readable database. However, after a long period of great reluctance in effecting major changes, the Library has recently been involved in a number of changes represented in the following list . . .

> **Negroes.** This heading discontinued February 1976.
> See **Afro-Americans** for later materials on the permanent residents of the United States. See **Blacks** for later materials on persons outside the United States. . . .[45]

It can be seen in this statement that a major deterrent to LC's making changes was the card catalog. Since they closed the card catalog in 1981 and have had only machine-readable records to update, terminology changes have been made more readily; but because LC's home-grown computer system did not have global search and replace capabilities, changes still had to be made record by record. This made it difficult to consider massive changes such as changing **Afro-Americans** to the more popular **African Americans** of the 1990s. At the end of 1999, the implementation of a new integrated library system (ILS) made such changes easier, and all headings that began with or contained *Afro-American* were changed to *African American* in 2000.

Reflecting another socio-linguistic revolution was Joan K. Marshall's 1977 critique of gender bias in LCSH.[46] She used six principles developed by ALA's Social Responsibilities Round Table Task Force Committee on Sexist Subject Headings to replace logically and consistently the guesswork that had evolved from Cutter's concern for the convenience of the public. Basing her work on the six principles, she submitted an alphabetical, annotated *Thesaurus for Nonsexist Indexing and Cataloging*. As in the case of the subject concepts for people of African descent, LC has overhauled most of its more obsolete or offensive sexist headings.

These issues, however, are not just relics of an earlier time; criticism of LCSH's treatment of marginalized groups continues. In the late 1990s, in a content analysis of the literature of subject access, Hope Olson and Rose Schlegl found 93 resources that showed evidence of "biases of gender, sexuality, race, age, ability, ethnicity, nationality, language, and religion."[47] Olson continues to explore these issues, and in 2009, discussed some major exclusions and some examples of marginalization and distortion that are still found in LCSH. Under exclusions, she lists the concepts of *Wicca* and *corporate welfare* as examples. Both concepts have since found a home in LCSH: **Wicca** and **Wiccans** are now both authorized headings and *corporate welfare* is a reference to the heading **Subsidies**. Under marginalization, she used **Handicapped**, **Poor**, and **Aged** as examples of how some headings reflect the quality of being *other*, rather than focusing on similarities to mainstream culture. In LCSH, two of these three have changed: LCSH now uses **People with disabilities** and **Older people** as headings; **Poor** remains as it was. Olson uses the heading **Feminism** to explain the concept of distortion—how the subject heading's relationships (e.g., narrower and related terms) can provide a misleading, inaccurate, or biased picture of the overall topic.[48] Although LC continues to address as many of these issues as it can, in as timely a manner as it can, the rather small staff of subject cataloging policy specialists usually have their hands full; changes sometimes must wait until there are resources and adequate time to address them. Olson, however, points out that information professionals should not expect LC to be the panacea to all the problems of subject access. She points out, "Each individual librarian is responsible for LCSH in its standard form and, to an even greater degree, in its application. We cannot foist off responsibility onto the Library of Congress or onto the singular public or the literature. We must take responsibility along with the Library of Congress and use it according to the long-standing ethic of our profession to promote universal access."[49]

PROPER NAME HEADINGS

Any proper name that has been established in the name authority file and has been designated as LCSH-compatible can be used as a subject heading in the LC system. Names are not generally included in the subject list or given subject authority records. The current policy is to provide subject authority records only for those names that are used as examples or as pattern headings (see discussion below), or those that need special subject subdivisions or instructions printed under them (e.g., **Presley, Elvis, 1935-1977—Sightings**).

Personal, Family, and Corporate Names, and the Titles of Works
(MARC 21 bibliographic fields 600, 610, 611, 630; MARC 21 authority fields 100, 110, 111, 130)

The authorized forms of personal names, names of corporate bodies, names of jurisdictions, names of conferences and meetings, and titles of works are found in the Library of Congress Name Authority File (also known as the LC/NACO Authority File and the LCNAF), and most, *but not all*, can be used as subject headings. For example, the authorized access point (AAP) for President Obama as the head of state—**United States. President (2009- : Obama)**—cannot be used as a subject heading. In the authority record it states: "SUBJECT USAGE: This heading is not valid for use as a subject. Works about this person are entered under **Obama, Barack**." This means that only the authorized access point for his personal name can be used as a subject heading. It is common for persons with multiple identities or roles (e.g., pseudonyms, individuals who are also heads of states, high ranking religious leaders) to have only a single AAP used in subject cataloging. This ensures the collocation of works about a person under a single heading.

When a name that is authorized for subject usage is the subject of a work, the correct form is taken from LCNAF and placed in a subject field in the bibliographic record. These names are established in accordance with the instructions in the descriptive cataloging standard,

RDA: Resource Description & Access, and its accompanying LC-PCC Policy Statements. Some examples of names that may be used as subjects include the following:

> **Twain, Mark, 1835-1910**
>
> **State (Comedy group)**
>
> **Charlotte Hall (Md.)**
>
> **American Library Association. Annual Conference**
>
> **Irving, John, 1942- Hotel New Hampshire**
>
> **Guardians of the Galaxy (Motion picture)**

Family names are handled in a somewhat different manner from personal names. They appear in two places, being split between LCSH and LCNAF. Family names are relatively recent additions to the LCNAF because the former descriptive cataloging standard, the *Anglo-American Cataloguing Rules, Second Edition* (AACR2), did not allow them to be used as creator access points. RDA now does: "RDA permits family names to be used as descriptive access points if the family is credited with the creation of a work. They may therefore be established in the name authority file."[50] These RDA-created AAPs for families, however, cannot be used as subject headings. If there are works about that family, a heading should be sought in LCSH. If it is not there, it should be proposed as an addition to LCSH. The names of individual members of that family may also be assigned from the LCNAF if appropriate for the work. These family names are generally used for genealogical and biographical works. Some family names established in LCSH include examples such as:

> **Benson family**
>
> **Miller family**
>
> **Taylor family**

In response to other changes implemented in RDA, another type of name is being handled differently as well. As of 2013, individual fictitious, literary, and legendary characters; deities and mythological figures; and individually named animals are now considered to be persons.[51] Owing to their new "personhood," and the possibility that they may be credited with creating works, members of these groups are now established in the LCNAF according to RDA instructions, rather than being established in LCSH following the rules in the SHM, as had been the practice until 2013. As a result, these names may be formulated differently than they were in LCSH. For example, in LCSH the heading for the fictional British detective Sherlock Holmes was **Holmes, Sherlock (Fictitious character)** and it was coded as a topical heading in MARC (i.e., a 650 field in the bibliographic record). Now, as part of the LCNAF, the heading has been changed to an unqualified AAP—**Holmes, Sherlock**—and it is coded as a personal name instead (i.e., a 600 field in a MARC bibliographic record). See the discussion of qualifiers below.

TABLE 13.2 Comparing Fictional Name Headings in LCSH and the LCNAF.

LCSH	LCNAF
150 $a Marvel, Captain (Fictitious character)	100 1_ $a Marvel, $c Captain
150 $a Keiko (Whale)	100 0_ Keiko, $d approximately 1976-2003
150 $a Aphrodite (Greek deity)	100 0_ $a Aphrodite $c (Greek deity)
150 $a Medea (Greek mythology)	100 0_ Medea, $c consort of Aegeus, King of Athens (Mythological character)
150 $a Socks (Cat)	100 0_ $a Socks $c (Cat), $d 1989-2009

At the time of this writing, only a portion of the headings for these new persons has been transferred to the LCNAF with many remaining in LCSH for the time being—for example, **Miss Baker (Monkey)** and **Liyongo (Legendary character)**. When time and resources permit, all these new persons (fictitious characters, deities, named animals, etc.) will be moved to the LCNAF. In the meantime, it is best to check both sources. Some examples, encoded for MARC authority records, are provided in Table 13.2.

In RDA, the approach to this type of person is handled exactly as it would be for a real person. Some types of qualifiers (i.e., additional metadata elements used to identify persons) are added in every case where a qualifier is applicable. For example, dates of birth and/or death and titles associated with royal persons are always added if available and if applicable. That is why the AAP for Medea, as seen in Table 13.2, is rather extensive now that it is formulated according to the RDA instructions. Other designations associated with a person, such **(Fictitious character)** or **(Whale)**, are not mandatory because they are added only when needed to resolve conflicts with other identical names in the LCNAF. In the cases of Captain Marvel, Keiko the whale, and Sherlock Holmes, there were no conflicts (*but* Dr. John H. Watson is another story!). There is an option to add these sorts of qualifiers based on cataloger's judgment, but the RDA instructions do not require them at the time of this writing. It should also be noted that headings for groups of fictitious, legendary, and mythological characters and deities, (e.g., Justice League of America, Hardy Boys, Smurfs, Nymphs, Valkyries) will remain in LCSH for the time being because they cannot currently be created using RDA. The headings receive qualifiers in plural form, as appropriate:[52]

> **Justice League of America (Fictitious characters)**
> **Nymphs (Greek deities)**
> **Valkyries (Norse mythology)**

Fictitious Character Headings in Action!

Under the new approach to creating a heading for fictional characters using RDA, the basic heading used to represent the fictional character Sherlock Holmes is **Holmes, Sherlock**, not **Holmes, Sherlock (Fictitious character)**. Does this change how one approaches applying the headings to a variety of resources? No, not really.

> If you have a nonfiction work about the character, then the heading is:
> **Holmes, Sherlock**.

> If you have *A Study in Scarlet* by Conan Doyle, then the heading is:
> **Holmes, Sherlock—Fiction**.

> If you have *Sherlock Season 1*, the BBC/Masterpiece Theater series starring Benedict Cumberbatch and Martin Freeman, then the heading is:
> **Holmes, Sherlock—Drama**.

> If you have *A Poetic Tribute to Baker Street* collected, compiled, and readings by Philip R. Brogdon, then the heading is:
> **Holmes, Sherlock—Poetry**.

In fact, the headings themselves are not very different (just the possible removal of the qualifier); the differences lie in the MARC coding for a bibliographic record (e.g., now coding each in a 600 field for a personal name, rather than in a 650 for a topical heading).

Geographic Names
(MARC 21 bibliographic field 651; MARC 21 authority field 151)

Geographic, jurisdictional, and physiographic names form a large part of any library's subject network. Prior to the mid-1970s, only key examples to illustrate modes of entry and types of subdivision were listed in LCSH. Since most were not listed, catalogers had to search for bibliographic records to verify the proper form of entry. With the adoption of AACR2 in 1981, it was decided to create subject heading authority records for *non-jurisdictional* geographic names in a form consistent with the *jurisdictional* forms controlled by the descriptive cataloging rules (at that time AACR2; now RDA). Some examples of jurisdictional names established in the LCNAF include the following:

Andorra	**Toronto (Ont.)**
Wales	**Salamanca (Spain)**
Arkansas	**Eräjärvi (Finland)**

Subject authority records are created for all non-jurisdictional geographic and physiographic names, except for those few that are created as free-floating phrase headings (see discussion below). These non-jurisdictional geographic headings typically include geographic features (mountains, lakes, caves, forests, etc.), geologic basins and formations, undersea features, celestial bodies, continents, regions, conceptual groupings of countries, man-made features and designated areas (parks, reservoirs, farms, roads, bridges, etc.), archaeological sites, and ancient cities:[53]

Antarctica	**Nile River Valley**
New England	**Ankhu River (Nepal)**
Glen Canyon (Utah and Ariz.)	**Bear Island (Md.)**
Eräjärvi (Finland : Lake)	**Bear Island (Norway)**
Dolly Varden Mines (B.C.)	**Plaza Mayor (Salamanca, Spain)**
Pluto (Dwarf planet)	**Cloisters Gardens (New York, N.Y.)**
Communist countries	**Tikal Site (Guatemala)**
Maryland, Southern	**Babylon (Extinct city)**

The form of jurisdictional names is taken from the LCNAF, but subject authority records are created when needed in order to add a topical and/or chronological subdivision to them.

> **Chicago (Ill.)—History—To 1875**
> **Hawaii—Annexation to the United States**
> **Germany—Civilization—Italian influences**

In addition, within the LCNAF the names of subordinate bodies and titles of works may be added to jurisdictional names to identify specific corporate bodies or documents; these may also be used as the subjects of works:

> **New York (N.Y.). Police Department**
> **Honolulu (Hawaii). Charter (1973)**
> **Colorado. Barber and Cosmetologist Act**

In quite a few of the examples above, the geographic names contain one or more qualifiers.[54] As is the case with personal names, qualifiers are used to distinguish between entities with the same name (see Bear Island examples above). They may also be used to identify the larger jurisdiction of the geographic name (see Chicago example) or to add an explanatory word or phrase (see Babylon and Pluto examples). For most local place names (cities, towns, boroughs, etc.), a country is used as the qualifier. For five exceptional areas, however, the qualifier is the *first-order political division* (i.e., the level of political jurisdiction just below the country level such as state, province, or constituent country). The five exceptional locations are given in Table 13.3.

TABLE 13.3 Geographic Locations Using First Order Political Divisions.

Country	First-Order Political Division
Australia	State
Canada	Province
Great Britain	Constituent country
Malaysia	State
United States	State

This results in the use of the heading **Chicago (Ill.)**, rather than **Chicago (United States)**. In some cases, a geographic feature or region will cross one or more jurisdictional boundaries; this results either in a qualifier that contains more than one jurisdiction or no qualifier at all.

Batten Kill (Vt. and N.Y.)
Nile River

Place names reflecting political or jurisdictional changes are treated somewhat differently as subject headings than they are as descriptive cataloging access points. In descriptive cataloging, the name used for the place at the time of the creation of the work is used as the access point. In subject cataloging, however, when the name of a jurisdiction (country, state, city, etc.) has been changed without substantially affecting the territory covered, it is LC's policy to make all subject entries under the new name regardless of the time period covered. Subject entries under an old name are changed to the new name. These changes are referred to as "linear jurisdictional name changes."[55] This policy is followed regardless of whether the government changed the jurisdiction's name or if the change was made to accommodate cataloging rules. Examples of these types of name changes are given in Table 13.4.

When jurisdictions have merged or split, various headings may be appropriate depending on the time period covered by the work in hand. In general, the headings should correspond to the area and time period being discussed.

TABLE 13.4 Examples of Changed Geographic Names.

Older Form	Latest Form
Argentine Republic	Argentina
British Honduras	Belize
Ceylon	Sri Lanka
Zaire	Congo (Democratic Republic)
Formosa	Taiwan

Example: The state of Virginia originally included the area now comprising the state of West Virginia. The heading **Virginia** is used for works on the pre-split period discussing the area corresponding to the present Virginia and West Virginia collectively. The heading **Virginia** is also used for works on the pre-split period discussing the area corresponding to the present state of Virginia. The heading **West Virginia** is used for works on the pre-split period discussing the area now included in the present state of West Virginia.[56]

This is a fairly straightforward example. More complex situations, however, do exist. Listed below are the SHM instruction sheets related to specific places that require additional documentation.

H 925	China and Taiwan
H 928	Congo
H 945	Germany
H 955	Great Britain
H 975	Hawaii
H 978	Hong Kong
H 980	Jerusalem, Gaza Strip, Golan Heights, West Bank, and Palestine
H 985	Latin America
H 987	Malaysia and Malaya
H 990	New York (N.Y.)
H 1023	Soviet Union
H 1045	Vatican City
H 1050	Washington (D.C.)
H 1055	Yugoslavia

It was stated above that subject authority records have been created for all non-jurisdictional geographic and physiographic names. There is one exception: the few place names that are created as free-floating phrase headings. They are formulated by taking the name of a city or a geographic feature (such as a lake or mountain chain) and interpolating a predetermined word or phrase between the main part of the heading and the qualifier. The types of free-floating geographic name phrase headings listed in Table 13.5 are from SHM memo H 362.[57]

For new catalogers, geographic subjects can pose difficulty because they are handled in two different ways in LCSH: (1) as main headings, the topic of this section; and (2) as subdivisions in topical subject heading strings, which are discussed later in this chapter. In short, the cataloger must determine if the subject is to be represented using a **Place—Topic** or a **Topic—Place** approach. Each concept in LCSH falls into one of these two available patterns. This determination, however, is not up to the cataloger; the editors of LCSH have already made the decision. The easiest way to determine whether a place name should be a primary heading or a subdivision of a topic is to go to the topical heading representing the concept to see if it allows for geographic

TABLE 13.5 Free-floating Phrase Heading Patterns for Geographic Names.

Pattern	Established Heading	Example(s)
[name of city] **Metropolitan Area** ([geographical qualifier])	Boston (Mass.)	Boston Metropolitan Area (Mass.)
[name of city] **Region** ([geographical qualifier])	Worcester (Mass.)	Worcester Region (Mass.)
[name of city] **Suburban Area** ([geographic qualifier])	Boston (Mass.)	Boston Suburban Area (Mass.)
[name of geographic feature] **Region** ([geographic qualifier, if part of name as established])	Berkshire Hills (Mass.) Hanscom AFB (Mass.)	Berkshire Hills Region (Mass.) Hanscom AFB Region (Mass.)
[name of river] **Region** ([geographic qualifier, if part of name as established])	Charles River (Mass.) Hoosic River	Charles River Region (Mass.) Hoosic River Region

subdivision. If it does, then **Topic—Place** is the pattern the cataloger will follow. If it does not, then the cataloger must look at the *see also* (SA) notes and the list of topical subdivisions to determine how a **Place—Topic** approach will be handled. For example, the following headings display different approaches for handling geographic aspects.

> **Antiques** (May Subd Geog)
>
> . . .
>
> **SA**   particular kinds of antique objects, especially the subdivisions **Catalogs, Collectors and collecting** or **Exhibitions** when they occur under such objects, e.g. **Kitchen utensils; United States—Centennial celebrations, etc.—Collectibles; Pharmacy paraphernalia; Glassware—Catalogs; Pewter— Collectors and collecting; Furniture—Exhibitions**

> **Antiquities** (Not Subd Geog)
>
> . . .
>
> **SA**   subdivision **Antiquities** under names of countries, cities, etc., ethnic groups existing in modern times, e.g. **Aboriginal Australians—Antiquities**, and individual wars, e.g. **United States—History—Civil War, 1861-1865—Antiquities**

The first heading, **Antiques**, allows for geographic subdivision as evidenced by the notation (*May Subd Geog*). If there were a work about antiques in

Pennsylvania, it would be entered under **Antiques—Pennsylvania**. It cannot be entered under the name of the location because the concept *antiques* is not a subdivision in LCSH. On the other hand, if there were a work about the antiquities of Greece, this resource must be entered under **Greece—Antiquities**, because it cannot be entered using the other pattern, per the *(Not Subd Geog)* instruction. The *see also* reference, in this case, is key to understanding how to structure the subject heading string. One way to become familiar with the types of subdivisions that are entered under a geographic name heading is to review the list of topical and form subdivisions in H 1140. Any subdivision in that list can be used after a place name, if applicable. The subdivisions primarily focus on, among other things, the history, economics, social conditions, customs, or politics of a place. The cataloger can also review the established subdivisions listed under a specific geographic area's heading in LCSH, if present. In addition to *(May Subd Geog)* and *(Not Subd Geog)*, headings are also placed into one more category of geographic subdivision: no decision. Headings belonging to this category are not explicitly labeled, and the lack of a label indicates that geographic subdivision may not be applied, just as if it said *(Not Subd Geog)*.

> **Children** (May Subd Geog)
> **Children and philosophy**
> **Children in art** (Not Subd Geog)

Because only headings notated *(May Subd Geog)* may be geographically subdivided, **Children and philosophy** and **Children in art** cannot be followed by a place name, although **Children** can. For more on geographic issues, please consult SHM instruction sheets H 690-H 1055.

HEADINGS FORMERLY OMITTED FROM LCSH

A troublesome corollary of the principle of specific entry is the inevitable, and seemingly endless, proliferation of subject terms for individual members of certain subject categories. Until the early 1980s, LC omitted from its printed list a wide variety of such terms. These terms were included in the library's official records but were not spelled out in the printed editions of LCSH. They included such categories as names of sacred books, fictitious and legendary characters, works of art, chemicals, geographic regions, parks, archaeological sites, and buildings. In some cases an SA reference was provided (see below for a discussion of SA references), but catalogers were usually left without any specific guidance about the style or syntax that an individual heading should have.

Authority records are now made for the individual names in such groups. They may appear in either the subject headings list or in the LCNAF depending on the type of concept (e.g., the titles of sacred books are established in the name authority file, while the names of buildings are found in the subject heading list). In some cases, these individual headings are added as narrower terms for a heading, but in others the headings are not necessarily included in the hierarchical reference structure of LCSH. For example, the titles of individual sacred books are not going to be included as NTs under the subject heading **Sacred Books** because they belong to two different authority files.

LC also formerly used some free-floating phase headings. For example, **[. . .] in [. . .]** phrase headings, where the first ellipses represented topics that could be filled in as needed (e.g., **[Topic] in art** and **[Topic] in literature** were heavily employed). These phrase headings are no longer free-floating and must be individually established, meaning that the editors of LCSH must formally create them. The free-floating phrase **[Name heading] in art** (e.g., **Manhattan (New York, N.Y.) in art**) has been replaced by the free-floating subdivision **—In art** used under names of Christian denominations, corporate bodies, and countries, cities, states, or other geographic areas (e.g., **Manhattan (New York, N.Y.)—In art**). LC's former phrase **[Activity/Topic] as a profession** (e.g., **Medicine as a profession**) has been replaced with the free-floating subdivision **—Vocational guidance** used after occupations, fields of endeavor, industries, names of corporate bodies, and individual military services (e.g., **Medicine—Vocational guidance**).

Other examples of discontinued practices include free-floating watershed and valley headings, among others based on headings for bodies of water. Previously, headings such as **Potomac River Watershed** and **Allegheny River Valley (Pa. and N.Y.)** did not appear in LCSH but could be created on the fly by catalogers. Since the early 1990s, every heading of that type has to be individually established in LCSH by the LC subject cataloging policy specialists.

Today, all primary headings are specifically authorized, meaning that they must explicitly appear in either the subject heading list or in the LCNAF, with the single exception of some region headings that are based on names of cities and geographical features (see above). It should be pointed out that this discussion of categories of headings formerly omitted from LCSH refers only to main headings. In the discussion under *Subdivisions* below, it can be seen that there are *many* heading/subdivision combinations that are not listed in the subject authority file.

GENERAL CHARACTERISTICS OF LCSH

The appearance of LCSH differs depending upon whether one is dealing with a print-style version of the list (i.e., *ClassWeb*, the Big Red Books, or the print-ready PDFs) or with a MARC version. In the print-style versions, all authorized subjects, including subjects with subdivisions, appear in boldface type, while reference tracings and references that are alphabetically interfiled with the main headings are in lightface type. References interfiled with authorized subjects are followed by the instruction USE, which is in turn followed by the preferred heading. The instruction SA (*see also*) is given in some entries and precedes terms or phrases that show related headings or subdivisions. The notations UF (used for), BT (broader term), RT (related term), and NT (narrower term) precede reference tracings in printed entries. In *ClassWeb*, the terms following BT, RT, and NT are hyperlinked so that a click on one of these terms takes the user to that term with its associated references. Figure 13.1 presents an example of a print-style entry in the subject heading list.

Social networks (May Subd Geog)
[HM741 (Sociology)]
Here are entered works on the system of personal relationships in which an
    individual is involved, including neighborhood, friendship, kinship,
    occupational and economic connections, etc.
UF   Networking, Social
      Networks, Social
      Social networking
      Social support systems
      Support systems, Social
BT   Interpersonal relations
RT   Cliques (Sociology)
      Microblogs
SA   subdivision **Social networks** under classes of persons and ethnic groups
NT   Business networks
      Online social networks
      Policy networks

FIGURE 13.1 *ClassWeb* **Entry for a Subject Heading.**

In the MARC 21 authorities format, numeric codes identify the functions of
the terms. The authorized terms are given a three-digit code beginning with the
number *one* (e.g., 150, 151). As a category or a group, these are referred to as
the 1XX fields. Equivalent or *used for* terms are assigned codes beginning with
the number *four* (e.g., 450, 451; the 4XX fields); general *see also* references are
coded 360; and broader and related terms are assigned codes beginning with
the number *five* (e.g., 550, 551; the 5XX fields). Narrower terms are *not* shown
in LC's implementation of the MARC 21 authorities format.

Syndetic (Reference) Structure

Figures 13.1 and 13.2 illustrate the usages of the abbreviations in the print-style
formats and of the codes in the MARC format. In Figure 13.1, the five terms following UF serve as tracings to indicate that there are references that read:

> Networking, Social
>   USE Social networks
>
> . . .
>
> Support systems, Social
>   USE Social networks

In the days of the card catalog, this also served as an instruction that when
the heading **Social networks** was first entered into the catalog, these five
references were also to be added to the catalog. In online catalogs, which generally have linked authority files, downloading the authority record into the
system not only adds the authorized heading, but also adds the references
more-or-less automatically.

The BT line not only indicates that the term following BT is a broader term in the hierarchy of the concept, but also serves as a tracing to indicate that there should be a reference in the catalog that reads:

Interpersonal relations

Search also under the narrower term Social networks

In traditional library practice, it has been considered improper to provide a reference from a narrower term to its broader term, on the assumption that there would be no place to stop until one arrived at an imaginary top term of *General knowledge*, and the catalog would be overflowing with references. Now that catalogs are mostly online, however, there is no reason to limit references, and there is some suggestion that users would like to be able to browse up a hierarchy to the broader terms in addition to being able to browse narrower and related terms.

The terms following RT are related terms. Neither is hierarchically above the other. The instruction here is to make references both from and to these terms:

Social networks

Search also under Cliques (Sociology)

Microblogs

Cliques (Sociology)

Search also under Social networks

Microblogs

Search also under Social networks

The terms following NT are narrower in the concept hierarchy, and there is an implicit instruction to make a reference that reads

Social networks

Search also under the narrower terms

Business networks

Online social networks

Policy networks

In some catalogs, NT references may be interfiled with RTs in the reference display. Unless the wording of the instruction in the catalog refers specifically to *related terms* or *narrower terms*, then a user may not have an understanding of the relationships between the terms when displayed in this manner:

Social networks

Search also under:

Business networks

Cliques (Sociology)

Microblogs

Online social networks

Policy networks

The MARC 21 format version of the same record (see Figure 13.2) shows the authorized subject heading coded 150. The UF terms are coded 450. In some records a term coded 450 may be followed by **$w nne** (see Figure 13.9, p. 593). This is the *control subfield* ($w), which provides additional instructions about the term and its relationship to the authorized heading. In this case, the value *e*, in the third position, means *earlier*; this indicates that the now unused term was once the authorized heading for the concept, but the current authorized heading is the one in the 150 field.

Broader and related terms are both coded 550. The broader term is distinguished from the two related terms by **$w g** following the term. One way to remember this means *broader term* is to associate the value *g*, in the first position of the control subfield, with the concept *general* because a broader term is more general than its NTs. The special instructions about the concept used as a subdivision are coded 360. Narrower terms are not included in MARC 21 authority records on the assumption that if all references are made from broader terms listed in all of the authority records in an online system, references to the narrower terms will automatically be taken care of. This does in fact work, as can be seen in the sample screen display from the LC catalog (see Figure 13.3), in which all terms that have **Social networks** in a 550 field in their records are displayed.

ARN	2062210						
Rec stat	c	Entered	20001220	Replaced	20110330133409.0		
Type	z	Upd status	a	Enc lvl	n	Source	
Roman	l	Ref status	a	Mod rec		Name use	b
Govt agn	l	Auth status	a	Subj	a	Subj use	a
Series	n	Auth/ref	a	Geo subd	i	Ser use	b
Ser num	n	Name	n	Subdiv tp	n	Rules	n

010	sh 87002172
040	DLC $b eng $c DLC $d DLC
053 _0	HM741 $c Sociology
150	Social networks
360	$i subdivision $a Social networks $i under classes of persons and ethnic groups
450	Networking, Social
450	Networks, Social
450	Social networking
450	Social support systems
450	Support systems, Social
550	Interpersonal relations $w g
550	Cliques (Sociology)
550	Microblogs
670	Work cat.: Research on support for parents and infants in the postnatal period, 1987 $b (Social networks)
670	LC database, Mar. 18, 1987.
670	Soc. systems & family patterns $b (Social network)
670	Hennepin $b (Networks)
675	Web. 3; $a Penguin dict. soc.; $a Fairchild dict. soc.; $a BDNE2
670	Google search, Sept. 22, 2006 $b (social networks; social networking)
680	$i Here are entered works on the system of personal relationships in which an individual is involved, including neighborhood, friendship, kinship, occupational and economic connections, etc.

FIGURE 13.2 MARC 21 Subject Authority Record as Formatted in OCLC. (Source: OCLC Connexion, Authorities—record number 2062210)

Social networks. (464)   Library of Congress subject headings

> *Search Also Under*: subdivision Social networks under classes of persons and ethnic groups
> *Note*: Here are entered works on the system of personal relationships in which an individual is involved, including neighborhood, friendship, kinship, occupational and economic connections, etc.
> *Narrower Term*: Business networks.
> *Narrower Term*: Online social networks.
> *Narrower Term*: Policy networks.
> *See Also*: Cliques (Sociology)
> *See Also*: Microblogs.

FIGURE 13.3 Display of Narrower Terms and Related Terms in the LC Catalog.

The instructions for references imbedded in the abbreviations and MARC codes are not to be followed blindly, but should be applied where useful and needed. If, for example, a catalog lacks entries under the narrower terms **Policy networks**, **Business networks**, and the related term **Microblogs**, then the reference from **Social networks** would omit these and read only

Social networks

Search also under

Cliques (Sociology)

Online social networks

If all five headings are lacking, then references should not be made at all. Online systems can be programmed to display only references to headings that actually appear in the catalog. *Blind references* in the catalog help no one.

The related and broader term references to **Social networks** present a complicated problem. If there were no entries in the catalog under **Microblogs**, strictly speaking it would be inaccurate to make a reference reading:

Microblogs

Search also under

Social networks

Some theorists argue that it is nonetheless justifiable to make such references on the assumption that the term referred from will eventually be activated. Even if it is not, they say, the reference serves to move users from a term not included in the catalog to one where there may be pertinent resources. Some libraries may convert such ambiguous references into USE references in their own local catalogs:

Microblogs

USE Social networks

If the term referred from is later activated, the instruction on the reference can be changed back to *Search also under* or an equivalent phrase. This system is difficult to handle, and in online catalogs it is necessary to write unambiguous programs that create references only as authorized in the authority file. The problem can be solved by using *Broader terms*, *Narrower terms*, and other standardized relationship indicators in catalogs instead of the more generic *See also* or *Search also under* (phrases used in numerous systems). There should be no semantic problem with telling a user that a related term for **Microblogs** is **Social networks**, even if there are no entries under **Microblogs**. In fact, the traditional ban on referring users from narrower terms to broader terms should also be lifted. The problem is also being solved in some systems by listing the number of bibliographic records beside each term. Listing a referred-to term with zero records alerts the user to the term's presence in the subject heading list, but indicates that the particular database in use does not have any resources with the term.

A number of writers have criticized LCSH's syndetic structure and its lack of ability to show hierarchical relationships in a traditional *tree structure* (a way to represent a hierarchical structure in a graphical form that resembles a tree). See Figure 12.2 (p. 545) in the previous chapter for an example of a rather un-treelike graphical display of an LCSH hierarchy. The first 10 editions of LCSH had a very different syndetic structure, which still has an effect on LCSH today. Instead of the familiar BTs, RTs, and NTs, there were only *See* and *See also* references.

Commenting on that earlier structure, E. J. Coates wrote in 1960 that LCSH merely linked an "indeterminate selection" of related terms—that at times there was more than one level of hierarchy in a list under one primary term, while at other times intermediate hierarchical terms were omitted from the chain of references.[58] George Sinkankis demonstrated in his 1972 study, in which he followed the *See also* references under the heading **Hunting**, that a user was quickly led away from the subject. By following the references he was led to **Migrant labor**, **Pimps**, **Liturgy and drama**, and **Panic**, among other terms.[59] Even in 2015, the headings **Pimps** and **Hunting** can be connected in just five steps. Toni Petersen wrote in 1983, around the time that the LCSH editors were moving to today's hierarchical structure, that during the project to create the *Art and Architecture Thesaurus* (AAT), the designers chose to keep LCSH terms as a base and to modify and expand them. Some LCSH references had to be ignored, though, because they could not be automatically converted to broader, narrower, and related terms without human intervention. There were too many types of references present.[60] Mary Dykstra was critical of the format LC began using in the 11th edition of LCSH, published in 1985. It was the first edition to use today's standardized relationship indicators (BT, RT, etc.), instead of the previous system that used *x* and *xx* to trace *See* and *See also* references. Dykstra believed that LC was trying to make LCSH look like a true thesaurus, which it is not because of its use of headings instead of descriptors.[61]

LC recognizes that there are still some problems with the syndetic structure of LCSH, but has not been able to eliminate all the inappropriate references that were created in the past; staff time is not always available for cleanup projects. Beginning in the mid-1980s, however, subject catalogers at LC put into effect a fairly strict policy for creating new references for all new headings created. The general rule is to make a broader term reference from the class of which the heading is a class member (i.e., genus-species relationships), to make a reference for a whole-part relationship, and/or to make a reference for cases in which a specific heading is an instance or example of a broader category, as appropriate to the heading. Examples of these three parts of the general rule are illustrated in Table 13.6.

Broader term references are made only from the next broader level in a hierarchy. Related terms are used to link two headings that are not in the same hierarchy (e.g., a concept and an object). For related term references, one of the headings should be strongly implied whenever the other is considered (e.g., **Boats and boating** has a related term **Ships**).[62] Although this reference policy moves LCSH toward answering its critics, the problem will not be solved completely until all cleanup projects have been completed.

General References

Two types of general references frequently appear in LCSH and provide guidance to both the cataloger and the user.

A general reference is a reference made not to specific individual headings but to an entire group of headings, frequently listing one or more headings by way of example. It was formerly considered impractical to list as specific references all individual headings encompassed by a broader heading, even though such specific references would have been theoretically logical and proper and even though the individual headings were printed in LCSH. Instead, general see also references have been made, retaining the code SA . . . . It is expected that each library will make specific references to each individual [subject] about which the library has works. Many general references will gradually be replaced by specific references to narrower headings.[63]

TABLE 13.6 Types of Hierarchical Relationships.

Type of hierarchical relationship	Example
Genus-species	**Military cinematography** BT Cinematography Photography, Military
Whole-part	**Toes** BT Foot
Instance	**Erie, Lake** BT Lakes—United States

The first type of general reference is the *see also* (SA) reference that is used to (1) indicate groups of terms or names that are related to the subject heading but are not formally coded as NTs or RTs and (2) provide special instructions concerning how the concept embodied in the heading may be used as a subdivision. The following examples illustrate how the SA is used to provide information about other types of headings that are informally related to the authorized term.

Structural engineering

SA specific kinds of structures, e.g. **Bridges**; **Buildings**; specific structural forms, e.g. **Girders**; **Plates (Engineering)**; and specific systems of construction, e.g. **Building, Iron and steel**; **Concrete construction**

Heart

SA headings beginning with the words **Cardiac** or **Cardiogenic**

The next example illustrates the use of the SA for explaining how the concept may be used as a subdivision. This leads to subject heading/subdivision combinations that are valid, but not necessarily found in the formal LCSH list (e.g., **Graduate students—Psychology**).

Psychology

SA subdivision **Psychology** under titles of individual sacred works, and under religions, religious topics, classes of persons, ethnic groups, and names of individual persons; and subdivision **Psychological aspects** under other topics for works that discuss the influence of particular conditions, activities, objects, etc., on the mental condition or personality of individuals

The second type of reference is the general *see* reference. "A general *see* reference is a 'use' reference made not to specific individual headings but to a category of subject headings or subdivisions, frequently listing one or more individual headings or subdivisions as examples."[64] A single general *see* reference is often used instead of numerous individual UF references, as in the case of this reference:

Judaic . . .

USE subject headings beginning with or qualified by the word Jewish, e.g. Jewish art and symbolism; Short stories, Jewish

Including this general *see* reference means that a specific UF for *Judaic* does not need to be included in every authority record that includes the word

Jewish. Other general see references point only to authorized subdivisions that might be of interest, such as this example:

> Pictorial works
>
>> USE subdivision **Pictorial works** under names of countries, cities, etc., individual persons, families, and corporate bodies, and under classes of persons, ethnic groups, individual literary works entered under author, individual wars, and topical headings

Like headings, general see references are coded as 150s in the MARC authority format, but they are *not* authorized headings. They can sometimes be recognized through the ellipsis at the end of the 150 field (as in Judaic . . ., above), but they *always* have a 260 field (a field that only appears in the records for general see references). They also have some distinctive coding in the fixed field in MARC authority records. In the print-style versions of LCSH, general see references are in lightface type, with the usage information being provided after the notation USE. Both SA and general see references are intended to serve as guidance for users, and should be displayed in the public catalog.

Scope Notes

Scope notes are sometimes included in subject authority records to specify the range of application for a term or to draw distinctions between related terms.[65]

- Scope notes explain single headings that may be unfamiliar or unclear.

    Ecofemimism: Here are entered works on feminist theory that emphasizes the interdependence of all living things and the relationship between social oppression and ecological domination.

- They explain the difference between a heading and one or more overlapping headings.

    Homophobia: Here are entered works on active discrimination against, or aversion to, homosexuals. Works on prejudicial attitudes or assumptions held by heterosexuals concerning homosexuals or homosexuality as well as works on the presumption that everyone is heterosexual and that heterosexuality is the only normal sexual orientation are entered under **Heterosexism**.

- They differentiate between two headings that may have similar structures.

    Art—Radiography: Here are entered works on radiography techniques in examining works of art. Works on the relationship between art and radiography are entered under **Art and radiography**.

- They provide special instructions, explanations, or referrals when needed.

  Remixes: Here are entered recorded musical works derived from one or more existing sound recordings through processes known as remixing. This heading is applied to sound recordings that are entirely remixes, prominently identified as remix(es), mixes, or expressions such as dance mix and club mix, but not to recordings where mix(es) means only medley, mixture, or miscellaneous.

In the past, a few libraries with card catalogs copied these notes onto cards and filed them in the catalog just ahead of the subject entries under the pertinent heading. Most libraries, though, simply provided one or more copies of LCSH near the catalog for reference use by patrons doing subject searches. With the advent of online catalogs, it was not possible at first to display scope notes; now many, but not all, online catalogs have this capability, and there is encouragement to provide more of that kind of information to users. In print-style versions of LCSH, a scope note is displayed between a heading and its references. A typical example of a heading with a scope note is in Figure 13.4. In the MARC 21 authorities format the scope note is in a MARC 680 field as can be seen in Figure 13.5—the authority record for **Sexism** (as displayed in the OCLC database).

Subdivisions
(MARC 21 subfields $x, $y, $z, and $v)

It was mentioned earlier that the practice of establishing subdivisions for headings was firmly set in Hanson's time as a concession to the alphabetico-classed organization of catalogs. The introduction to LCSH states, "The application of Library of Congress subject headings requires extensive use of subject subdivisions as a means of combining a number

Sexism (May Subd Geog)

Here are entered works on sexism as an attitude as well as works on attitude and overt discriminatory behavior. Works dealing solely with discriminatory behavior directed toward both of the sexes are entered under Sex discrimination

UF	Sex bias
BT	Attitude (Psychology)
	Prejudices
	Sex (Psychology)
	Social perception
RT	Sex role
NT	Heterosexism
	Sex discrimination

FIGURE 13.4 Printed Entry for a Subject Heading with a Scope Note.

ARN	02102436				
Rec stat	c	Entered 19860211	Replaced	19870326163626.7	
Type	z	Upd status a	Enc lvl n	Source	
Roman	l	Ref status b	Mod rec	Name use b	
Govt agn	l	Auth status a	Subj a	Subj use a	
Series	n	Auth/ref a	Geo subd i	Ser use b	
Ser num	n	Name n	Subdiv tp n	Rules n	

010	sh 85120678
040	DLC $b eng $c DLC $d DLC
150	Sexism
450	Sex bias
550	Attitude (Psychology) $w g
550	Prejudices $w g
550	Sex (Psychology) $w g
550	Social perception $w g
550	Sex role
680	$i Here are entered works on sexism as an attitude as well as works on attitude and overt discriminatory behavior. Works dealing solely with discriminatory behavior directed toward both of the sexes are entered under $a Sex discrimination.
681	$i Note under $a Sex discrimination

FIGURE 13.5 MARC 21 Authority Record Showing a Scope Note in the 680 Field. (Source: OCLC Connexion, Authorities—record number 2102436)

of different concepts into a single subject heading. Complex topics may be represented by subject headings followed by subdivisions. Some subdivisions are printed in *LCSH* but a greater number of subdivisions may be assigned according to rules specified in the [*Subject Headings*] *Manual*. Only a fraction of all possible heading-and-subdivision combinations are listed in *LCSH*."[66] Subdivisions are used to make a main heading more specific, that is, to narrow the scope of the subject heading. They fall into several broadly defined categories: topical and chronological subdivisions specific to particular headings; geographic subdivisions; form subdivisions; free-floating subdivisions; and subdivisions under pattern headings. Guidance on the application of subdivisions in LCSH is found in the SHM, particularly in H 1075-H 1200.

Topical Subdivisions Specific to Particular Headings
(MARC 21 bibliographic and authority subfield $x;
MARC 21 subdivision authority record field 180)

Topical subdivisions represent an additional aspect, action, attribute, or subtopic of the main heading (e.g., **Monsters—Symbolic aspects**). They are not used to represent narrower terms, as that form was disposed of when the principle of direct entry was embraced (e.g., catalogers use **Cats**, not **Domestic animals—Cats**). In some cases, up to two topical subdivisions may be assigned to make the heading as specific as the topic being addressed in the work (e.g., **Shinto shrines—Organization and administration—Law and legislation**).

Lumber *(May Subd Geog)*
  [TS800-TS837]
    BT   Forests and forestry
           Wood products
    RT   Timber
    SA   *kinds of lumber, e.g.* Cypress; Walnut
    NT   Hardwoods
           Pit-wood
           Planing-mills
  —Advertising
    USE Advertising—Lumber
  —**Drying** *(May Subd Geog)*
    [TS837]
    UF   Lumber—Seasoning
           Lumber drying
           Seasoning of lumber
           Wood—Drying
    BT   Wood—Preservation
  —**Law and legislation** *(May Subd Geog)*
  —**Measurement**
    UF   Lumber—Mensuration *[Former heading]*
           Scaling (Forestry)
  —Mensuration
    USE Lumber—Measurement
  —**Rate-books**
    [HE2116.L8]
  —Seasoning
    USE Lumber—Drying
  —**Transportation** *(May Subd Geog)*
    [HE199.5.L84 (Freight)]
    [HE595.L8 (Ships)]
    [HE2321.L8 (Railroads)]

  — —**Law and legislation** *(May Subd Geog)*

FIGURE 13.6 Printed Entry for a Subject Heading and its Subdivisions.

Some subdivisions are specific to the concept in the heading and must therefore be authorized specifically for the heading. Those editorially established subdivisions that appear in printed versions of LCSH are introduced by a long dash (i.e., — an *em* dash); if a second subdivision is subordinate to a first subdivision, then there are two long dashes, separated by a space. Figure 13.6 shows the subdivisions established for the heading **Lumber**, as found in the book and PDF versions of LCSH. Figure 13.7 shows the same information, but as displayed in *ClassWeb*. The greatest difference between the two is that *ClassWeb* does not omit main headings before the dashes to indicate subdivision use.

In the MARC version of LCSH, each string containing **Lumber** and a subdivision has a separate authority record. The MARC records for the main heading and four of its subdivision records are shown as Figures 13.8 to 13.12. In the records, the dashes that appear in the printed list are represented by the code $x.

Lumber (May Subd Geog)
    [TS800-837]
    BT   Forests and forestry
          Wood products
    RT   Timber
    SA   kinds of lumber, e.g. **Cypress; Walnut**
    NT   Hardwoods
          Pit-wood
          Planing-mills
Lumber—Advertising
    USE   Advertising—Lumber
Lumber—Drying (May Subd Geog)
    [TS837]
    UF   Lumber—Seasoning
          Lumber drying
          Seasoning of lumber
          Wood—Drying
    BT   Wood—Preservation

Lumber—Law and legislation (May Subd Geog)

Lumber—Measurement
    UF   Lumber—Mensuration [Former heading]
          Scaling (Forestry)

Lumber—Mensuration
    USE   Lumber—Measurement

Lumber—Rate-books
    [HE2116.L8]

Lumber—Seasoning
    USE   Lumber—Drying

Lumber—Transportation (May Subd Geog)
    [HE199.5.L84 (Freight)]
    [HE595.L8 (Ships)]
    [HE2321.L8 (Railroads)]

Lumber—Transportation—Law and legislation (May Subd Geog)

FIGURE 13.7 A Subject Heading and Its Subdivisions in *ClassWeb*.

ARN 02070743			
Rec stat c Entered 19860211 Replaced 20100506085941.0			
Type z	Upd status a	Enc lvl n	Source
Roman l	Ref status a	Mod rec	Name use b
Govt agn l	Auth status a	Subj a	Subj use a
Series n	Auth/ref a	Geo subd i	Ser use b
Ser num n	Name n	Subdiv tp n	Rules n
010 sh 85078804			
040 DLC $b eng $c DLC $d DLC $d WaU			
053 TS800 $b TS837			
150 Lumber			
360 $i kinds of lumber, e.g. $a Cypress; Walnut			
550 Forests and forestry $w g			
550 Wood products $w g			
550 Timber			
670 Plank, M.E. Lumber recovery from ponderosa in western Montana, 1981.			

FIGURE 13.8. MARC Record for a Subject Heading. (Source: OCLC Connexion, Authorities—record number 2070743)

```
ARN 03645412
Rec stat  c   Entered  19940607   Replaced  19961004125910.7
Type        z      Upd status   a        Enc lvl    n        Source
Roman       l      Ref status   a        Mod rec             Name use  b
Govt agn    l      Auth status  a        Subj       a        Subj use  a
Series      n      Auth/ref     a        Geo subd   i        Ser use   b
Ser num     n      Name         n        Subdiv tp  n        Rules     n
010      sh 94004017
040      DLC $b eng $c DLC $d DLC
053      HF6161.L9
150      Advertising $x Lumber
450      Advertising $x Lumber trade $w nne
450      Lumber $x Advertising
670      Work cat.: NUCMC data from Forest History Soc. for Laughead, W.B. Papers,
         1897-1958 $b (William B. Laughead, advertising manager for Red River
         Lumber Company, popularizer of folk hero Paul Bunyan through advertising
         pamphlets of the company)
```

FIGURE 13.9 MARC Record that Generates a USE Reference (see second 450 field). (Source: OCLC Connexion, Authorities— record number 3645412)

```
ARN 02070757
Rec stat  c   Entered   19860211   Replaced  19950918171534.2
Type        z      Upd status   a        Enc lvl    n        Source
Roman       l      Ref status   b        Mod rec             Name use  b
Govt agn    l      Auth status  a        Subj       a        Subj use  a
Series      n      Auth/ref     a        Geo subd   i        Ser use   b
Ser num     n      Name         n        Subdiv tp  n        Rules     n
010      sh 85078805
040      DLC $b eng $c DLC $d DLC
053      TS837
150      Lumber $x Drying
450      Lumber $x Seasoning
450      Lumber drying
450      Seasoning of lumber
450      Wood $x Drying
550      Wood $x Preservation $w g
```

FIGURE 13.10 MARC Record for a Subject Heading and Its Subdivision. (Source: OCLC Connexion, Authorities—record number 2070757)

```
ARN 02070790
Rec stat  c   Entered  19860211   Replaced  19960305120606.5
Type        z      Upd status   a        Enc lvl    n        Source
Roman       l      Ref status   n        Mod rec             Name use  b
Govt agn    l      Auth status  a        Subj       a        Subj use  a
Series      n      Auth/ref     a        Geo subd   i        Ser use   b
Ser num     n      Name         n        Subdiv tp  n        Rules     n
010      sh 85078810
040      DLC $b eng $c DLC $d DLC
053      HE199.5.L84 $c Freight
053      HE595.L8 $c Ships
053      HE2321.L8 $c Railroads
150      Lumber $x Transportation
```

FIGURE 13.11 MARC Record for a Subject Heading and Its Subdivision. (Source: OCLC Connexion, Authorities—record number 2070790)

```
ARN 02070794

  Rec stat   n Entered   19860211    Replaced    19860211000000.0
  Type       z      Upd status   a       Enc lvl   n        Source
  Roman      l      Ref status   n       Mod rec            Name use   b
  Govt agn   l      Auth status  a       Subj      a        Subj use   a
  Series     n      Auth/ref     a       Geo subd  i        Ser use    b
  Ser num    n      Name         n       Subdiv tp n        Rules      n

  010     sh 85078811
  040     DLC $b eng $c DLC
  150     Lumber $x Transportation $x Law and legislation
```

FIGURE 13.12 MARC Record for a Subject Heading and Its Subdivisions. (Source: OCLC Connexion, Authorities—record number 2070794)

Chronological Subdivisions Specific to Particular Headings

*(MARC 21 bibliographic and authority subfield $y;
MARC 21 authority record field 182)*

In LCSH, chronological subdivisions are sometimes assigned to bring out the time period reflected in the content of the work (as opposed to the publication or creation date). Only a small percentage of headings are established with chronological subdivisions, and the most common are those associated with the historical, social, or political periods of individual jurisdictions (e.g., **Zimbabwe—Economic conditions—To 1965**) and those established with arts-related headings (e.g., **Rock music—2001-2010, Drama—20th century—History and criticism**). Time periods may also be established under individual topical headings (e.g., **Libraries—History—400-1400**). The assignment of century subdivisions is allowed in the free-floating approach to subdivisions and is discussed below (e.g., **Political campaigns—United States—History—21st century**).

Chronological subdivisions are designed to reflect only broad periods under a topic; they are not expected to be an exact match to the content of an individual resource, nor do catalogers have the ability to tailor chronological headings to suit specific content. For example, if the cataloger had a book about conditions in Boston around the time of the midnight ride of Paul Revere (1775) and another about Boston during the deadly hurricane season of 1780, both would receive the subject heading, **Boston (Mass.)—History—Revolution, 1775-1783**. This string is the closest fit for both resources. This approach collocates works about the same general time period, without separating them into chronological periods that are too narrow. For some resources, two or more separate strings may be needed if the topic spans more than one chronological period. For example, a work on Boston's politics from its founding until the U.S. Civil War would require both **Boston (Mass.)—Politics and government—To 1775** and **Boston (Mass.)—Politics and government—1775-1865** to adequately represent the subject matter. Chronological subdivisions appear in the printed versions of LCSH as seen in Figure 13.13. In MARC 21 authority records, chronological subdivisions are preceded by the code $y. Again, every heading/subdivision combination has its own separate authority record. MARC records for **Papua (Indonesia)** and its chronological subdivisions are shown in Figures 13.14 to 13.17.

Papua (Indonesia) *(Not Subd Geog)*

. . .

—Politics and government

— —To 1963

— —1963-

FIGURE 13.13 Printed Entry (Partial) for a Place with Established Chronological Subdivisions.

ARN 05786797			
Rec stat c	Entered 20020614	Replaced 20140327045720.0	
Type z	Upd status a	Enc lvl n	Source
Roman l	Ref status a	Mod rec	Name use a
Govt agn l	Auth status a	Subj a	Subj use a
Series n	Auth/ref a	Geo subd n	Ser use b
Ser num n	Name n	Subdiv tp n	Rules z

```
010    no2002052215
040    DLC-OI $b eng $e rda $c DLC-OI $d DLC $d WaU $d DLC $d OCoLC $d DLC $d OCoLC
       $d WaU $d DLC
034    $d E1380000 $e E1380000 $f S0050000 $g S0050000 $2 geonet
043    a-io---
046    $s 2002
151    Papua (Indonesia)
368    $b Province
377    ind
451    Tanah Papua (Indonesia)
451    West New Guinea (Indonesia)
451    Provinsi Papua (Indonesia)
451    Papua Province (Indonesia)
451    Province of Papua (Indonesia)
551    Irian Jaya (Indonesia) $w a
551    Irian Jaya Barat (Indonesia)
670    Papua menggugat, 2002: $b t.p. (Papua; Tanah Papua)
670    Undang-Undang Republik Indonesia nomor 21 Tahun 2001 Tentang Otonomi Khusus Bagi
       Provinsi Papua, 2001: $b p. 5 (art. 1: Provinsi Papua adalah Provinsi Irian Jaya yang diberi
       Otonomi Khusus dalam kerangka Negara Kesatuan Republik Indonesia)
670    GEOnet, June 3, 2003 $b (Papua [short form], Provinsi--ADM1,05°00' S 138°00' E, variants:
       West New Guinea; West Irian; Tanah Papua; Nieuw-Guinee; Nieuw-Guinea; Netherlands New
       Guinea; Netherland New Guinea; Nederlands Nieuw-Guinea; Nederlandsch Nieuw-Guinee;
       Irian Jaya, Propinsi; Irian Barat, Propinsi; Irian Barat, Daerah Tinghat I; Irian Barat; Irian;
       Dutch New Guinea; ID09)
670    West Papua action Web site, Jan. 19, 2005 $b (West Papua, the western half of New Guinea
       island, termed "Irian Jaya province," or, more recently, "Papua" under Indonesian control)
670    Peluang investasi Papua, 2008: $b cover p.4 (Provinsi Papua; Papua Province)
670    Wikipedia, Dec. 13, 2011: $b Papua (province) (Papua comprises most of the western half of
       the island of New Guinea and nearby islands. Its capital is Jayapura. It's the largest and
       easternmost province of Indonesia. The province originally covered the entire western half of
       New Guinea. In 2003, the Indonesian government declared the westernmost part of the island,
       around Bird's Head Peninsula, a separate province--its name was first West Irian Jaya and is
       now West Papua; Since its annexation in 1969, it became known as "West Irian" or "Irian
       Barat" until 1973, and thereafter renamed "Irian Jaya". This was the official name until the
       name "Papua" was adopted in 2002; ....
781    _0  $z Indonesia $z Papua
```

FIGURE 13.14 MARC Name Authority Record for a Place.
(Source: OCLC Connexion, Authorities—record number 5786797)

```
ARN 02121129
Rec stat  c  Entered  20030421   Replaced   20030529125830.0
Type        z        Upd status  a        Enc lvl    n       Source
Roman       l        Ref status  n        Mod rec            Name use   b
Govt agn    l        Auth status a        Subj       a       Subj use   a
Series      n        Auth/ref    a        Geo subd   l       Ser use    b
Ser num     n        Name        n        Subdiv tp  n       Rules      n
010      sh 85068061
040      DLC $b eng $c DLC $d DLC
151      Papua (Indonesia) $x Politics and government
```

**FIGURE 13.15 MARC Subject Authority Record for a Place and Its
Subdivision. (Source: OCLC Connexion, Authorities—record number
2121129)**

```
ARN 02121131
Rec stat  c  Entered  20030421  Replaced   20030529125802.0
Type        z        Upd status  a        Enc lvl    n       Source
Roman       l        Ref status  n        Mod rec            Name use   b
Govt agn    l        Auth status a        Subj       a       Subj use   a
Series      n        Auth/ref    a        Geo subd   l       Ser use    b
Ser num     n        Name        n        Subdiv tp  n       Rules      n
010      sh 85068062
040      DLC $b eng $c DLC $d DLC
151      Papua (Indonesia) $x Politics and government $y To 1963
```

**FIGURE 13.16 MARC Record for the First Chronological Subdivision.
(Source: OCLC Connexion, Authorities—record number 2121131)**

```
ARN 02121132
Rec stat c  Entered  20030421   Replaced   20030529125900.0
Type        z        Upd status  a        Enc lvl    n       Source
Roman       l        Ref status  n        Mod rec            Name use   b
Govt agn    l        Auth status a        Subj       a       Subj use   a
Series      n        Auth/ref    a        Geo subd   l       Ser use    b
Ser num     n        Name        n        Subdiv tp  n       Rules      n
010      sh 85068063
040      DLC $b eng $c DLC $d DLC
151      Papua (Indonesia) $x Politics and government $y 1963-
```

**FIGURE 13.17 MARC Record for the Second Chronological Subdivision.
(Source: OCLC Connexion, Authorities—record number 2121132)**

Geographic Subdivisions

*(MARC 21 bibliographic and authority subfield $z; MARC 21
subdivision authority record field 181; MARC 21 authority
record field 781 in records for geographic headings)*

The instruction *(May Subd Geog)* found in parentheses after a subject heading in the print-style versions of LCSH tells catalogers that place names may
be added to the heading in order to relate the topic to a particular geographic

location or to its place of origin. It can be done without the **[Topic]—[Place]** combination being spelled out in the list and without separate MARC authority records being created. It should be noted, however, that not every heading in LCSH allows geographic subdivisions (e.g., **Women in literature** *(Not Subd Geog)*). Geographic subdivisions may contain no more than two levels and cannot consist of places below the city level. For geographic elements below the city level, an additional heading may be available for use. For example, a work about the restaurants in the Central Square neighborhood in Cambridge, Massachusetts will be assigned **Restaurants—Massachusetts—Cambridge**, but it will also be assigned the heading **Central Square (Cambridge, Mass.)**.

In a MARC authority record, the code for geographic subdivision is given in byte 06 of the 008 fixed field. The letter *i* indicates that geographic subdivision is allowed. In the OCLC system the fixed field byte is labeled *Geo subd*. The print-style and MARC versions of this are illustrated in Figures 13.18 and 13.19. Each figure has the relevant information highlighted.

Lumbering   (May Subd Geog)

    [TS800-837 (Manufactures)]
    Here are entered works on the manufacturing of logs into lumber.
    Works on the felling of trees through the transporting of logs to
    sawmills or to a place of sale are entered under Logging.
    BT Forest products industry
    RT Lumber trade
    NT Communication in lumbering
         Explosives in lumbering
         Logging
         Lumbermen

FIGURE 13.18 Printed Entry Showing a Heading That May Be Subdivided Geographically.

ARN 02070847						
Rec stat c	Entered 19860211		Replaced	19970902143428.1		
Type	z	Upd status	a	Enc lvl	n	Source
Roman	l	Ref status	b	Mod rec		Name use b
Govt agn	l	Auth status	a	Subj	a	Subj use a
Series	n	Auth/ref	a	**Geo subd i**		Ser use b
Ser num	n	Name	n	Subdiv tp	n	Rules n
010	sh 85078820					
040	DLC $b eng $c DLC $d DLC					
053	TS800 $b TS837 $c Manufactures					
150	Lumbering					
550	Forest products industry $w g					
550	Lumber trade					
680	$i Here are entered works on the manufacturing of logs into lumber. Works on the felling of trees through the transporting of logs to sawmills or to a place of sale are entered under $a Logging.					
681	$i Note under $a Logging					

FIGURE 13.19 MARC Record Showing a Heading That May Be Subdivided Geographically. (Source: OCLC Connexion, Authorities—record number 2070847)

It should be noted that in the example shown in Figure 13.15 for the heading **Papua (Indonesia)—Politics and government**, geographic subdivision is not permitted. The code shown following *Geo subd* in that record is a fill character, shown in the example as | (i.e., the vertical bar or pipe).

The code *i* (as seen in Figure 13.19) stands for the word *indirect*, which indicates that geographic subdivision is allowed. It describes the manner in which LCSH goes about providing geographic subdivision. Indirect subdivision means that the two elements of the geographic name are to be arranged hierarchically, with a broader place name preceding the local place.

The geographic subdivision is created by removing the state, province, or country (i.e., the larger jurisdiction) from the qualifier in the geographic heading (established for the place in the authority file) and putting it in the first $z after the subject heading. The remaining portion of the geographic heading is placed into the second $z. For example, if a cataloger has a book on lumbering activities in Portland, Oregon, the subject and the geographic headings must first be located. The subject heading **Lumbering** is appropriate for the work and it may be geographically subdivided. The LCNAF also includes the authorized geographic heading **Portland (Or.)**. In order to formulate an appropriate subject heading string, the abbreviation "Or." is removed from the qualifier, it is spelled out, and it becomes **$z Oregon**, following the subject heading. Since the parentheses are now empty, they can be removed altogether and the remaining portion of the heading (i.e., **Portland**) becomes the second $z. The full heading is thus **Lumbering—Oregon—Portland**, *not* **Lumbering—Portland (Or.)**. The latter would be an example of *direct subdivision.*

Formerly, *direct subdivision* was allowed in LCSH (and is still used in *Sears*, as explained in chapter 14). This meant that the local place name was added immediately after the subject heading. Thus, a work about Opera in Santa Fe would be assigned the following subject string: **Opera—Santa Fe (N.M.)**. In 1976, direct geographic subdivision was abandoned by LC, although there are still a few well-defined exceptions. The advantage of indirect subdivision is that materials on one topic are collocated first at the country or state (province, etc.) level, before being divided into cities or local areas; direct subdivision separates such material by the first letters of the names of cities. On the other hand, indirect subdivision cannot be applied in some cases (e.g., when a geographic entity falls within three countries), whereas direct subdivision allows the use of the established name without alteration. Table 13.7 gives a list of exceptional geographic entities that still use direct subdivision.[67]

The following list shows examples of geographic subdivisions that conform to the policies discussed in this section:

> **Catholic Church—France—Paris**
>
> **Children—Ontario—Toronto**
>
> **Children—Australia—New South Wales**
>
>> *Note:* Only two geographic levels are allowed; so, a city in New South Wales would follow Australia.
>
> **Children—Australia—Newcastle (N.S.W.)**

Education—Washington (D.C.)

Geology—Aegean Islands (Greece and Turkey)

Geology—Indonesia—Ambon Island

Lumbering—Pyrenees

TABLE 13.7 Exceptional Entities Using Direct Geographic Subdivisions.

Exceptions	Notes	Examples
Names of countries or continents	These are used as the first level of geographic information for most parts of the world.	**Library schools—Mexico** **Library schools—Africa** **Library schools—Spain** (*not* Library schools— Europe—Spain)
Names of first-order political divisions for certain countries	In the USA, Canada, and Great Britain, the first level of geographic subdivision is the state, province, or constituent country.	**Library schools— Massachusetts** **Library schools—Ontario** **Library schools—England**
Inverted headings for regions	Regions identified by a directional qualifier and the name of a continent, country, state, etc., are not divided through that continent, country, state, etc. first.	**Library schools—Spain, Northern** **Library schools— California, Southern** **Library schools—Europe, Eastern** (*not* Library schools—Europe— Europe, Eastern)
Names of geographical entities not wholly within one country, state, etc.	One does not attempt to subdivide these locations through a single jurisdiction.	**Birds—Appalachian Mountains** **Birds—Mississippi River**
Two exceptional cities	Jerusalem and Washington, D.C. are entered directly. They are not subdivided through a larger entity.	**Birds—Jerusalem** **Birds—Washington (D.C.)**
Names of certain disputed territories	Gaza Strip, Golan Heights, Palestine, and the West Bank are entered directly because of their contested status	**Birds—Gaza Strip** **Birds—Golan Heights** **Birds—Palestine** **Birds—West Bank**
Some islands	Islands at a distance from owning land masses	**Birds—Canary Islands** **Birds—Greenland**
Antarctica	Entities on the continent are divided through the continent.	**Birds—Antarctica** **Birds—Antarctica— Weddell Sea Region**

For geographic subdivisions, as for geographic headings, local name changes are observed. For instance, works that formerly would have received the heading **Banks and banking—Leopoldville, Belgian Congo** are now found under **Banks and banking—Congo (Democratic Republic)—Kinshasa**. In card catalogs it was very difficult to keep up with such subdivision changes because of the difficulty of finding all occurrences of, for example, **Belgian Congo** used as a subdivision. In online catalogs, keyword searching has made such changes easier, although some critics objected to making such changes "regardless of the form of the name used in the work cataloged."[68]

Since 1999, MARC 21 authority records for geographic headings that are established in the LCNAF or LCSH have included a 781 field that indicates the way that the heading should be used as a geographic subdivision. If a heading cannot be used as a geographic subdivision, a note to that effect is provided instead in a 667 field: "SUBJECT USAGE: This heading is not valid for use as a geographic subdivision."

If both geographical and topical subdivisions are established in the same heading, the last provision for geographic subdivision prevails. For example, the subject heading **Children** may be subdivided geographically. The subdivision **Quotations**, however, cannot be. Therefore, the correct form of subject heading string for a work on quotations of children in Illinois would be **Children—Illinois—Quotations**. The topical subdivision **Dental care**, however, may be geographically subdivided. Thus, the correct heading structure for the dental care of children in Illinois is **Children—Dental care—Illinois**.

Other explanations and illustrations of geographic headings and subdivision practices are issued from time to time. The current policies on geographic subdivisions and other LCSH-related topics are found in the *Subject Headings Manual*, with the most recent developments being announced on the Library of Congress ABA website.[69]

Form Subdivisions
(MARC 21 bibliographic and authority subfield $v;
MARC 21 authority record field 185)

Although form subdivisions have been assigned in subject heading strings from the beginning of LCSH, they have been uniquely coded in the MARC format only since 1999. In LCSH, quite often the same word is used to indicate that the work is *about* a particular form and that a work is *an example of* a particular form. The subdivision is coded in MARC according to its function in the subject string, resulting in the possibility of identical subject string constructions being coded differently. For example, **Science $x Periodicals** represents a work about science periodicals, while **Science $v Periodicals** represents a work that is a periodical that deals with scientific subjects. To determine whether a subdivision is topical, form, or both, catalogers must consult *ClassWeb*, individual MARC authority records, or the PDF version of the list of free-floating subdivisions.

Free-Floating Subdivisions

(MARC 21 bibliographic and authority subfield $x and/or $v)

In the LCSH system, there are subdivisions (mostly topical and form) that can be combined with specific categories of subject headings, on the fly, without being formally established by the editors of LCSH. The resulting combinations of subject headings and subdivisions do not have separate authority records made for each one; they are combined as needed. These are collectively designated as *free-floating* subdivisions, but catalogers should take note: they are not completely free in their application. Most free-floating subdivisions are used only in carefully defined situations, with headings that fall into a very limited set of categories. The rules for application of these subdivisions are enumerated in the SHM. There are six groups of free-floating subdivisions, and each has one or more instruction sheets that explain relevant policies and practices.

1. general free-floating subdivisions
   a. SHM H 1095 Free-Floating Subdivisions
2. subdivisions used under classes of persons and ethnic groups
   a. H 1100 Classes of Persons
   b. H 1103 Ethnic Groups
3. subdivisions used under names of corporate bodies, persons, and families
   a. H 1105 Corporate Bodies
   b. H 1110 Names of Persons
   c. H 1120 Names of Families
4. subdivisions used under place names
   a. H 1140 Names of Places
   b. H 1145.5 Bodies of Water
5. subdivisions controlled by pattern headings
   a. H 1146 Subdivisions Controlled by Pattern Headings
   b. H 1147 Animals
   c. H 1148 Art
      and 25 additional patterns, the instructions for which are contained in SHM memos H 1149-1200
6. multiple subdivisions
   a. H 1090 Multiple Subdivisions

Each group is explained briefly in the following pages.

Before applying subdivisions, there are several things catalogers must consider. The first is whether the concept represented by a heading-and-subdivision combination already exists in LCSH. For example, a cataloger cannot (or rather, *should* not) create the subject heading strings **Libraries—Administration** and **Libraries—Management** because those two strings are

UFs for the authorized heading **Library administration**. The second is determining whether the focus of the subdivision is already present in the main heading. For example, the strings **Codependency—Psychological aspects** and **Job stress—Psychological aspects** should not be assembled because the concept *psychological aspects* is already implicit in the primary topics.

If there is more than one subdivision to be used, the correct order of the components must be determined. There are two basic patterns into which most subject heading strings fall.

1. Topic—Place—Period—Form:
    Pear industry—Oregon—History—19th century—Maps

2. Place—Topic—Period—Form:
    England—Civilization—16th century—Sources

The first is used for topics that can be geographically subdivided. The second is for topics that begin with a place name where the topic may be an aspect of that place's history, social life, culture, and so forth. An additional topical subdivision may be added to either of these constructions; its placement is dependent upon whether the additional topical subdivision may be geographically subdivided. These two patterns are based on a recommendation from the Airlie House conference in 1991.

> If the cataloger chooses to apply subdivisions, the subdivisions should always appear in the following order: topical, geographic, chronological, form. This is not to suggest that each type of subdivision shall always be present under each heading; it is simply to specify a standard order for them when they are assigned.[70]

After the subdivisions are ordered appropriately, the subdivision coding must conform to the practices of the encoding scheme in use (e.g., if the data elements are being entered into MARC, the topical subdivisions should be coded in $x, the form subdivisions belong in $v, chronological elements in $y, and geographic elements in $z). These and other subdivision practices are articulated in H 1075 and H 1095.

General Free-Floating Subdivisions

General free-floating subdivisions comprise the topical and form subdivisions listed in H 1095. Along with each subdivision there is a scope note, followed by *See also* references to other subdivisions when applicable.

$x **Political aspects** *(May Subd Geog)* *(H 1942)*
> Use under individual religious sects and denominations and topical headings for works on the political dimensions or implications of nonpolitical topics.
>
> > See also **—Politics and government** under names of countries, cities, etc., and under ethnic groups.

Scope notes provide information about the specific categories of headings with which the subdivision may be used (e.g., with individual religious sects and denominations), as well as general categories of headings (e.g., topical headings). They may provide conditions of use for the subdivision (e.g., for works on the political dimensions or implications of nonpolitical topics). Scope notes generally specify or narrow the subdivision's application. For some subdivisions, though, such as **—Computer games**, the scope note states, "Use under subjects." This means that the subdivision is truly free-floating because it can be used under *any* type of subject heading. There are also sometimes references to other memo numbers in the SHM (e.g., H 1942), often because the concept represented by the subdivision has an instruction sheet addressing it; catalogers should always consult that other memo for full information on assigning the subdivision. Some entries in H 1095 also include the instruction *(May Subd Geog)*. An example of a heading combined with a general free-floating subdivision is **Environmental education—Political aspects**.

Subdivisions Used under Classes of Persons and Ethnic Groups

These subdivisions are listed in memos H 1100 (Classes of Persons) and H 1103 (Ethnic Groups). The primary headings under which the list in H 1100 may be used entail various classes of persons, including headings such as: **Mothers**; **Teenagers**; **Catholics**; **Baseball coaches**; **African American dentists**; **Children of women prisoners**; **Alien labor, Turkish**; **Divorced people**; **Community college athletes**; **Lungs—Cancer—Patients**; and **Simmons College (Boston, Mass.). Graduate School of Library and Information Science—Faculty**. Many of the subdivisions in this list carry the instruction *(May Subd Geog)* but only a few have scope notes. SHM memo H 1100 does *not* include social classes (e.g., **Working class**) or collective social groupings (e.g., **Families**). It also does not include ethnic groups and nationalities, which are covered in H 1103.

> **$x Supervision of** *(May Subd Geog)*
> Use under occupational groups and types of employees.

An example of a heading using this subdivision is **Student teachers—Supervision of**.

H 1103 is used with headings for ethnic and national groups, "including preliterate groups, historic peoples no longer in existence, races, and ethnic groups in the United States."[71] Examples of ethnic groups are: **Greek Americans**; **Galicians (Spain)**; **French-Canadians**; **Germanic peoples**; **Nyahkur (Thai people)**; **Koma (Nilo-Saharan people)**; **Jews**; and **Navajo Indians**. Headings for nationalities or for people from a geographic region (e.g., **East Timorese, Europeans, Ghanaians**) are included when they designate those nationalities or regional inhabitants *outside* their native countries or regions. Many of the subdivisions in this list carry the instruction *(May Subd Geog)*, but only a few have scope notes.

> **$x Kinship** *(May Subd Geog)*
> Use for works on the group's system of rules governing descent, succession, marriage, etc., and determining the relationships of individuals.

An example of a heading using this subdivision is **Tuaregs—Kinship**.

Subdivisions Used under Names of Corporate Bodies, Persons, and Families

Subdivisions to be used under names of corporate bodies are given in H 1105. H 1110 lists subdivisions used under names of persons, and H 1120 lists those for family names. The subdivisions in H 1105 may be used under names of all types of corporate bodies, including "businesses and corporations, nonprofit institutions, voluntary associations, cultural institutions, religious organizations, political parties, fraternal groups, labor organizations, professional societies, clubs, international agencies, government agencies on all levels, etc. The category also includes names of individual exhibitions, fairs, expositions, but excludes" the names of conferences, congresses, meetings, or names of jurisdictions.[72] Some terms in H 1105 have scope notes, the *(May Subd Geog)* instruction, and references to other subdivisions.

$x Employees

Use under names of individual nongovernmental corporate bodies. Use **—Officials and employees** under names of individual international, government, or quasi-governmental agencies.

See H 1100 for further subdivisions used under classes of persons.

An example of a heading using this subdivision (plus an additional subdivision following it) is: **Microsoft Corporation—Employees—Biography**. In this example, with the addition of the subdivision **Employees**, a corporate body name has been transformed into a class of persons. This means that H 1100, the list of subdivisions for classes of persons, may now be applied to the subject heading string as needed. In addition, subdivisions from the general list of free-floating subdivisions also may be applied as needed.

Subdivisions listed in H 1110 may be used under the names of persons established in the LCNAF. A separate list that once existed for literary authors was discontinued in 1998. Similar to previous lists, H 1110 contains some scope notes and references to other subdivisions. Unlike the other lists, this one has a number of unused terms with *see* references to the terms that should be used instead.

$x Relations with men

Use for works on intimate associations. For works on relations with an individual man, assign an additional heading for the man.

An example of a heading using this subdivision is **Conrad, Joseph, 1857-1924—Relations with men**.

Despite the recent change that designates fictitious, literary, and legendary characters, deities, and individually named animals as persons, they are *not* covered by the H 1100 memo. Only subdivisions provided in H 1095 may be applied to these new types of "persons" (e.g., **Holmes, Sherlock—Art**). If it is necessary to use a subdivision from H 1100 after the name of a deity, for example **Zeus (Greek deity)—Homes and haunts**, it must be individually established by the editors of LCSH.

The list of subdivisions to be used under family names (H 1120) is relatively short with no scope notes or references. Example: **Candolle family—Herbarium**.

Subdivisions Used under Place Names

These subdivisions are presented in two SHM memos: H 1140 lists subdivisions used under names of places and H 1145.5 lists those to be used with names of bodies of water. Like the list for subdivisions under corporate bodies, the list of subdivisions in H 1140 includes some scope notes that limit the use of some of the subdivisions. It is applied to the following types of places:

> continents; regions; islands; countries; states, provinces, and equivalent jurisdictions; counties and other local jurisdictions larger than cities; and headings for metropolitan areas, suburban areas, and regions based on names of cities. They may also be used, except as noted, under names of cities . . . , under names of extinct cities . . . , and under names of city sections, districts, or quarters . . . . Appropriate subdivisions may also be used under headings for geographic features and designated areas, including parks, reserves, gardens, streets and roads, refugee camps, etc., or regions based on geographic features.[73]

H 1140 does *not* apply to extraterrestrial locations, such as celestial bodies and other astronomical features.

> **$v Charters, grants, privileges**
>
> > Use only under countries, etc., other than the United States, and under cities other than those of the United States.

An example of a heading using this subdivision is **Great Britain—Charters, grants, privileges**. Other examples illustrating the use of H 1140 include **Chicago (Ill.)—Ethnic relations** and **Klondike River Valley (Yukon)—Gold discoveries**.

The list of subdivisions in H 1145.5, those used with names of bodies of water, is very short. Examples include **Allegheny Reservoir (Pa. and N.Y.)—Water rights** and **Rio Grande (N.M.)—Channelization**. An instruction states that appropriate subdivisions from the list in H 1140, those used under names of places, may also be used under names of bodies of water (e.g., **Okmulgee Lake (Okla.)—Maps**).

Subdivisions Controlled by Pattern Headings

Pattern headings are examples of a particular category of subject heading. They are explained in the instruction sheet in SHM H 1146:

> Standardized sets of topical and form subdivisions were developed for use under particular categories of subject headings or name headings

used as subjects. To avoid repeating these subdivisions under all possible headings, only one or a few representative headings from each category are established in the subject authority file with a [full] set of the subdivisions appropriate for use under other headings belonging to the category. Such headings are called *pattern headings* for their respective categories.[74]

Several specific categories of subjects have distinctive sets of subdivisions applicable to all examples of their type. These include such categories as *educational institutions, religious and monastic orders, languages, musical instruments, industries, military services, animals, diseases*, and *chemicals*. Pattern headings are represented by examples in the printed LCSH and in the online authority file, but one must have a table or previous knowledge to find them. A table of all the pattern headings, in alphabetical order by category, is found in the introduction to the printed and PDF versions of LCSH, and it is also in the "Library of Congress Subject Headings: Introduction" in *Cataloger's Desktop*. A table grouped by subject fields is found in H 1146. For each pattern heading there is also a separate memo in the SHM that (1) provides the pattern heading(s) for the category, (2) explains what is included in the category, and (3) lists all allowable subdivisions for that category. Table 13.8 shows pattern headings used in LCSH.

TABLE 13.8 LCSH Pattern Headings.

Category	Pattern Heading(s)
Animals	**Fishes** and **Cattle**
Art	**Art, Chinese** **Art, Italian** **Art, Japanese** **Art, Korean**
Chemicals	**Copper** and **Insulin**
Colonies	**Great Britain—Colonies**
Diseases	**Cancer** and **Tuberculosis**
Educational institutions	
Individual	**Harvard University**
Types	**Universities and colleges**
Industries	**Construction industry** and **Retail trade**
Languages and groups of languages	**English language** **French language** **Romance languages**
Legal topics	**Labor laws and legislation**

Category	Pattern Heading(s)
Legislative bodies	**United States. Congress.**
Literary authors (Groups)	**Authors, English**
Literary works entered under author	**Shakespeare, William, 1564–1616. Hamlet.**
Literary works entered under title	**Beowulf**
Literatures (including individual genres)	**English literature**
Materials	**Concrete** and **Metals**
Military services	**United States—Armed Forces** **United States. Air Force** **United States. Army** **United States. Marine Corps** **United States. Navy**
Musical compositions	**Operas**
Musical instruments	**Piano, Clarinet,** and **Violin**
Organs and regions of the body	**Heart** and **Foot**
Plants and crops	**Corn**
Religious bodies	
Religious and monastic orders	**Jesuits**
Religions	**Buddhism**
Christian denominations	**Catholic Church**
Sacred works	**Bible**
Vehicles, Land	**Automobiles**
Wars	**World War, 1939–1945** **United States—History—Civil War, 1861–1865**

Following the pattern, if one were cataloging a work about kidneys, for example, it would be appropriate to find **Heart** in LCSH and choose appropriate subdivisions found there to be used with the heading **Kidneys**. General free-floating subdivisions found in H 1095 (discussed above) are not usually repeated under pattern headings, but they may also be used as appropriate.

Multiple Subdivisions

A *multiple subdivision* is one that incorporates bracketed terms and the abbreviation *etc.* to indicate that the cataloger is permitted to add specific details as needed, following the basic pattern shown in the example. This structure is employed to allow for the creation of numerous similar subdivisions without each being established in the authority file. For example, the multiple subdivision **Translations into French, [German, etc.]** allows for the following strings to be created:

> **Shakespeare, William, 1564-1616—Translations into Arabic**
>
> **Shakespeare, William, 1564-1616—Translations into Belarusian**
>
> **Shakespeare, William, 1564-1616—Translations into Bengali**
>
> **Shakespeare, William, 1564-1616—Translations into Bulgarian**
>
> **Shakespeare, William, 1564-1616—Translations into Catalan**
>
> **Shakespeare, William, 1564-1616—Translations into Chinese**
>
> **Shakespeare, William, 1564-1616—Translations into Croatian**
>
> **Shakespeare, William, 1564-1616—Translations into Czech**
>
> **Shakespeare, William, 1564-1616—Translations into Danish**
>
> . . .

Multiple subdivisions most frequently allow for the insertion of specific aspects of a topic that are based on religions, individual religious denominations, language, nationalities, individual wars, and, on occasion, general topics. Some additional examples include the following;

> **Abortion—Religious aspects—Buddhism, [Christianity, etc.]**
>
> **Alcoholism—Religious aspects—Baptists, [Catholic Church, etc.]**
>
> **America—Discovery and exploration—Dutch, [British, French, etc.]**
>
> **Christian literature, Early—Greek authors, [Latin authors, Syriac authors, etc.]**
>
> **United States. Army—History—Civil War, 1861-1865, [World War, 1914-1918, etc.]**
>
> **Subject headings—Aeronautics, [Education, Latin America, Law, etc.]**

Subdivision Authority Records

In 1999, LC began distributing subdivision records for the more than 3,000 topical, form, and chronological free-floating subdivisions in LCSH. These records contain subdivision data in 18X fields. Codes in 073 fields identify the location in the *Subject Headings Manual* of instructions for using

```
ARN  04933911
Rec stat  c  Entered     19990225      Replaced  20130513103119.1
  Type       z       Upd status  a          Enc lvl     n        Source
  Roman      l       Ref status  a          Mod rec              Name use  b
  Govt agn   l       Auth status  n         Subj        a        Subj use  b
  Series     n       Auth/ref     d         Geo subd    l        Ser use   b
  Ser num    n       Name         n         Subdiv tp   b        Rules     n
010      sh 99001477
040      IEN $b eng $c DLC $d DLC
073      H 1095 $a H 1100 $a H 1103 $a H 1105 $a H 1110 $z lcsh
185      $v Indexes
485      $v Bibliography $v Indexes
485      $v Dictionaries, indexes, etc. $w nne
680      $i Use as a form subdivision under subjects.
681      $i Reference under the heading $a Indexes; Electronic indexes
```

FIGURE 13.20 MARC Authority Record for a Subdivision. (Source: OCLC Connexion, Authorities—record number 4933911)

each of the subdivisions. Each record includes a basic usage statement, and some records have references. A typical subdivision record is shown in Figure 13.20.

Classification Aids

(MARC 21 bibliographic field 053)

Many subject headings, including some with subdivisions, are accompanied by *Library of Congress Classification* (LCC) notations. Sometimes more than one LCC notation is given, with a term from the schedule to show the various aspects of classification represented by the subject heading (see Figure 13.21). Frequently a range of notations is supplied (see Figure 13.18, p. 597). In the MARC 21 authorities format, the classification numbers are given in a field with the tag 053 as shown in Figure 13.22. When a term is used to identify the particular aspect the classification notation represents, that term is coded $c in the 053 field.

Classification notations are usually supplied when a term is first established. Occasionally they are added at a later time, but there is no systematic checking or revision of these notations. Thus, a classification notation could be changed or its meaning revised in the LCC schedules, but it might not be changed in LCSH. Thus these notations are only a guide and should not be assigned without verification.

Filing Arrangement

The list of subject headings in printed versions is given in alphabetical order. Filing rules were revised in 1980 to facilitate computer manipulation, and the revised rules continued to be used for the book versions of LCSH until the last edition was published. The current PDF version of the subject headings still uses those filing rules.

Chestnut *(May Subd Geog)*
    [QK495.F14 (Botany)]
    [SB401.C4 (Nut trees)]
    [SD397.C5 (Forestry)]
  UF Castanea sativa
      Castenea vesca
      Castanea vulgaris
      Chestnut tree
      Common European chestnut
      English chestnut
      European chestnut
      Italian chestnut
      Spanish chestnut
      Sweet chestnut
  BT Castanea

**FIGURE 13.21 Printed Entry Showing LCC Notations
for the Subject Heading.**

ARN 02140296							
Rec stat	c	Entered	19860211	Replaced	20100614171134.0		
Type	z	Upd status	a	Enc lvl	n	Source	
Roman	l	Ref status	b	Mod rec		Name use	b
Govt agn	l	Auth status	a	Subj	a	Subj use	a
Series	n	Auth/ref	a	Geo subd	i	Ser use	b
Ser num	n	Name	n	Subdiv tp	n	Rules	n

010	sh 85023154
040	DLC $b eng $c DLC $d DLC
053	**QK495.F14 $c Botany**
053	**SB401.C4 $c Nut trees**
053	**SD397.C5 $c Forestry**
150	Chestnut
450	Castanea sativa
450	Castanea vesca
450	Castanea vulgaris
450	Chestnut tree
450	Common European chestnut
450	English chestnut
450	European chestnut
450	Italian chestnut
450	Spanish chestnut
450	Sweet chestnut
550	Castanea $w g
681	$i Example under $a Nuts

**FIGURE 13.22 MARC Authority Record Showing LCC Notations in 053
Fields. (Source: OCLC Connexion, Authorities—record number 2140296)**

Basic arrangement is word by word. Numbers given in digits precede alphabetical characters in the order of increasing value. Initials separated by punctuation file as separate words. Abbreviations without interior punctuation file as single whole words:

1 Chase Manhattan Plaza (New York, N.Y.)

4-H clubs

8-Ball (Game)

63rd Street Tunnel (New York, N.Y.)

480 Greenwich Street/502 Canal Street House (New York, N.Y.)

666 in the Bible	USE Six hundred and sixty-six (The number) in the Bible
A-36 Apache (Fighter planes)	USE Mustang (Fighter planes)
A.J.S. motorcycle	USE AJS motorcycle

A priori

A3D bomber	USE Skywarrior bomber
A4D (Jet attack plane)	USE Skyhawk (Jet attack plane)
Aage family	USE Agee family
ACI test	USE Adult-child interaction test

ACTH

AJS motorcycle

AK 8 motion picture camera

Alaska—History

ALGOL (Computer program language)

In the book and PDF versions of LCSH, punctuation of subject terms affects filing order more immediately than it does in lists such as *Sears*, which only sacrifices some categorical arrangement to straight alphabetical order. Subject headings from LCSH that contain subordinate elements preceded by one or more dashes fall into three groups:

1. period subdivisions (MARC subfield $y), arranged chronologically according to explicit dates, regardless of whether a descriptive term is used,
2. topical and form subdivisions (MARC subfield $x and subfield $v), arranged alphabetically, and
3. geographical subdivisions (MARC subfield $z), arranged alphabetically.

The secondary subdivisions under **United States—Foreign relations** illustrate all three groups in order:

1. United States—Foreign relations—To 1775
   United States—Foreign relations—To 1865
   United States—Foreign relations—1775-1783
   United States—Foreign relations—1783-1815
   United States—Foreign relations—1783-1865
   United States—Foreign relations—1789-1797
   United States—Foreign relations—1789-1809
   United States—Foreign relations—1797-1801

      United States—Foreign relations—19th century
      United States—Foreign relations—1801-1809
      United States—Foreign relations—1801-1815
      United States—Foreign relations—1809-1812
      United States—Foreign relations—1809-1817
      United States—Foreign relations—1812-1815

      • • •

      United States—Foreign relations—21st century
      United States—Foreign relations—2001-2009
      United States—Foreign relations—2009-

2. United States—Foreign relations—Executive agreements
      United States—Foreign relations—Historiography
      United States—Foreign relations—Juvenile literature
      United States—Foreign relations—Law and legislation

      • • •

      United States—Foreign relations—Treaties

3. United States—Foreign relations—Iran
      United States—Foreign relations—Japan
      United States—Foreign relations—Latin America
      United States—Foreign relations—Middle East
      United States—Foreign relations—Soviet Union

In *ClassWeb*'s default display, though, these three groups generally collapse into two: numerals first, followed by words in alphabetical order. And, in fact, period subdivisions beginning with a word are found alphabetically and centuries are placed after the end of the *following* century due to the machine's processing of numbers:

      United States—Foreign relations
      United States—Foreign relations—1775-1783
      United States—Foreign relations—1783-1815
      United States—Foreign relations—1783-1865

      • • •

      United States—Foreign relations—1993-2001
      United States—Foreign relations—19th century   ←
      United States—Foreign relations—2001-2009
      United States—Foreign relations—2009-
      United States—Foreign relations—20th century   ←
      United States—Foreign relations—21st century
      United States—Foreign relations—Executive agreements

United States—Foreign relations—Iran

United States—Foreign relations—Japan

•••

United States—Foreign relations—Speeches in Congress

United States—Foreign relations—To 1775   ←

United States—Foreign relations—To 1865

United States—Foreign relations—Treaties

In the PDF and book versions of LCSH, all subject subdivisions (identified by dashes) file ahead of inverted modifiers, which are punctuated by commas. Inverted modifiers, in turn, file ahead of parenthetical qualifiers. Last of all come phrases that start with the primary term. In *ClassWeb's* default display, and in the OCLC display of authority records, the main heading with its subdivisions comes first (with all subdivisions interfiled no matter the type), but following those, all other headings beginning with that main heading (e.g., phrases, inverted forms, parenthetical terms) are in alphabetical order without regard for punctuation. Both filing sequences are presented together in Table 13.9 for comparison. Table 13.10 summarizes the order (i.e., the filing arrangement) in which the headings appear. *ClassWeb* does include an option to display the subject headings in the order in which they appear in printed versions. This feature can be quite useful, particularly when scanning to find the appropriate chronological subdivision for the history of a place such as Egypt, which has numerous period subdivisions, some including a descriptive term and some without.

GENRE/FORM TERMS

(MARC 21 bibliographic field 655; MARC 21 authority field 155)

Form is a concept that has been associated with subject analysis from the inception of the idea that books could be entered in catalogs and placed on shelves according to the category to which they belonged. Early categories included such things as *encyclopedias*, *biographies*, and *histories*, as well as *chemistry* and *religion*. Later, as subject headings evolved to refer to what an item was about instead of a category to which the book belonged, the idea of *form* remained part of the subject heading assignment process. Because it was often difficult to separate the ideas of aboutness and form (as in the case of *history*, which seems to incorporate elements of both), the concept of form has only recently been given its own treatment in bibliographic records.

A definition, created by a subcommittee of ALA's Subject Analysis Committee, was approved by appropriate ALA bodies in January 1993:

Form data are those terms and phrases that designate specific kinds or genres of materials. Materials designated with these terms or phrases may be determined by an examination of:

their physical character (e.g., videocassettes, photographs, maps, broadsides)

TABLE 13.9 Side-by-Side Comparison of LCSH Filing Sequences.

Order of Headings in Print-style Versions of LCSH	Order of Headings in Online Versions of LCSH
Children	Children
Children—Age determination	Children—Age determination
Children—Anthropometry	Children—Alabama
Children—Attitudes	Children—Alaska
...	Children—Andes Region
Children—Writing—Examinations	Children—Anthropometry
Children—Alabama	...
Children—Alaska	Children—Attitudes
Children—Andes Region	...
...	Children—Writing—Examinations
Children—Zimbabwe	...
Children, Aboriginal Australian	Children—Zimbabwe
Children, Ashanti	Children, Aboriginal Australian
Order of Headings in Print-style versions of LCSH	Order of Headings in online versions of LCSH
...	Children and adults
Children, Yoruba	...
Children (Assyro-Babylonian law)	Children and war
Children (Canon law)	Children as air pilots
...	Children, Ashanti
Children and adults	Children (Assyro-Babylonian law)
...	...
Children and war	Children (Canon law)
Children as air pilots	...
...	Children in literature
Children in literature	Children of miners
...	...
Children of miners	Children with visual disabilities
...	...
Children with visual disabilities	Children, Yoruba
Children's accidents	Children's accidents

TABLE 13.10 LCSH Filing Orders.

Print-style Versions (Books and PDFs)	Online Versions (*ClassWeb* and MARC)
Heading	Heading
Heading—Chronological subdivisions	Heading—Subdivisions (of any kind)
Heading—Topical subdivisions	Heading as part of a phrase (inverted, direct, or with a qualifier)
Heading—Geographic subdivisions	
Heading, Inverted	
Heading (Qualified)	
Heading as the beginning of a phrase	

the particular type of data that they contain (e.g., bibliographies, questionnaires, statistics)

the arrangement of information within them (e.g., diaries, outlines, indexes)

the style, technique, purpose, or intended audience (e.g., drama, romances, cartoons, commercials, popular works)

or a combination of the above (e.g., scores)

A single term may be modified by other terms, in which case the whole phrase is considered to be form data (e.g., aerial photographs, French dictionaries, conversation and phrase books, wind ensemble suites, telephone directories, vellum bound books, science fiction).[75]

In recent years, LC began establishing genre/form terms, which are treated differently from the topical headings in LCSH (e.g., they are coded 655 in the MARC format instead of 650). In 2007, LC began a project led by Janis L. Young of LC's Policy and Standards Division to create a new thesaurus, *Library of Congress Genre/Form Terms for Library and Archival Materials* (LCGFT). By 2010, it contained genre/form terms for moving images (films, television programs, and video recordings), spoken-word recorded sounds (including radio programs), legal materials, and cartographic materials. This was only the first phase of an ongoing project that will continue to develop and expand this vocabulary list. In 2015, approximately 175 general genre/form terms (i.e., terms that are not specific to a particular discipline) were added to the list (e.g., **Databases**, **Diaries**, **Dictionaries**), as were nearly 600 genre/form terms for musical works (e.g., **Fight songs**, **Finales (Music)**, **Fingering charts**, **Flamenco music**) and almost 400 terms for literary genres and forms (e.g., **Nonfiction comics**, **Novels in verse**, **Nursery rhymes**).

LCGFT contains entries that look very similar to those in LCSH. It employs the same relationship indicators (i.e., BT, NT, RT, UF, and USE) and other features (e.g., scope notes) found in LCSH. A major difference between LCSH and LCGFT is that it was developed using a post-coordinated approach to

Western films   (Not Subd Geog)
This heading is used as a genre/form heading for films that feature the American West during the period of westward expansion.

UF Cisco Kid films [Former heading]
   Cowboy and Indian films
   Cowboy films
   Horse operas (Motion pictures)
   Horse opries (Motion pictures)
   Horse pics (Motion pictures)
   Lone Ranger films [Former heading]
   Oaters (Motion pictures)
   Oats operas (Motion pictures)
   Sagebrushers (Motion pictures)
   Westerns (Motion pictures)
   Zorro films [Former heading]
BT Motion pictures
NT Singing cowboy films
   Spaghetti Westerns

FIGURE 13.23 An Example from *Library of Congress Genre/Form Terms for Library and Archival Materials* (LCGFT).

ARN 8866712							
Rec stat c	Entered 20110509		Replaced 20120822155924.1				
Type z	Upd status a		Enc lvl n		Source		
Roman l	Ref status a		Mod rec		Name use b		
Govt agn l	Auth status a		Subj z		Subj use a		
Series n	Auth/ref a		Geo subd		Ser use b		
Ser num n	Name n		Subdiv tp n		Rules n		

010	gf2011026735 $z sh2007025276 $z gf2011026135 $z gf2011026371 $z gf2011026750
040	DLC $b eng $c DLC $f lcgft $d WaU $d DLC
155	Western films
455	Cisco Kid films $w nne
455	Cowboy and Indian films
	. . .
455	Westerns (Motion pictures)
455	Zorro films $w nne
555	Motion pictures $w g
670	Moving image genre-form guide via WWW, July 19, 2007 $b (western: Fictional work set in the period of American westward expansion. In the name of civilization, the wilderness is conquered and nature subordinated. Key thematic oppositions are between civilization and nature, law and anarchy, settler and nomad, and the new arrivals and the Native American. The hero is a person of integrity and principle, who tames the land, stands alone, faces danger, and is the fastest draw)
670	López, D. Films by genre, c1993 $b (Western (Cowboy Film, Western Film). Westerns are an amalgam of myth, history and legend--fantasy and reality intertwine. Set on the North American continent (movies set in Latin America, Australia, South Africa, or other lands are not authentic Westerns), they are based on tradition and a solid historical heritage. Many western heroes existed in real life ... and some of the Western sagas describe real historical episodes of the conquest of the American West; peopled by a profusion of colorful and familiar types--cowboys, Indians, U.S. marshals, rangers, bounty hunters, Mexicans, half-breeds, saloon girls, homesteaders, carpetbaggers and John Wayne who appeared in 153 movies; fall under seven basic plot types; the terms oater, oats opera, horse opera or horse opry are synonymous with Western; they also have a derogatory meaning indicating a cheaply made film about cowboys--a B-Western. A sagebrusher is another slang term for a Western)
670	A history of early film, 2002: $b p.lxi, v. 3 (cowboy and Indian films)
	. . .
680	$i This heading is used as a genre/form heading for films that feature the American West during the period of westward expansion.

FIGURE 13.24 Abbreviated MARC Record for a Heading in LCGFT. (Source: OCLC Connexion, Authorities—record number 8866712)

Term	Western films
SN	Consult LCSH for particular kinds of western films: e.g., Hopalong Cassidy films, Lone Ranger films.
UF	Westerns
BT	Adventure films
BT	Adventure television programs
BT	Historical drama

FIGURE 13.25 An Example from *Guidelines on Subject Access to Individual Works of Fiction, Drama, etc.* (GSAFD).

indexing. "The chief difference between genre/form terms and subject headings in the LCSH system lies in their application. Unlike most subject headings, genre/form terms are intended to be used as facets without further subdivision."[76] Figure 13.23 shows a genre/form term from LCGFT as seen in *Classification Web*. Figure 13.24 shows an abbreviated authority record for the same concept (some references and source-consulted notes were omitted to save space). In the authority record, the source of the term is indicated by the code in 040 $f.

As stated, the LCGFT project is ongoing; genre/form terms from religion, art, and other disciplines may be added in the future. At the time of this writing there are some SHM instruction sheets for certain types of materials covered by the terms found in LCGFT (i.e., moving images, legal materials, non-music sound recordings, radio programs, maps, and atlases);[77] in time, additional documentation will be provided.

In 2014, the *Library of Congress Medium of Performance Thesaurus for Music* (LCMPT) was published to help music catalogers describe the instruments used to perform musical works. In 2015, LC announced plans for an additional vocabulary—*Library of Congress Demographic Group Terms* (LCDGT)—"to describe the creators of, and contributors to, resources, and also the intended audience of resources."[78] All three of these thesauri (LCGFT, LCMPT, and LCDGT) are meant to supplement LCSH; they do not and cannot replace it. For the latest news on the progress of these and other supplementary vocabulary projects, please consult the LC ABA website.[79]

There are also a number of specialized lists of genre/form terms in the rare books, art and architecture, audio-visual, and map communities, among others. One commonly used list is the *Guidelines on Subject Access to Individual Works of Fiction, Drama, etc.* (GSAFD). Terms from GSAFD are added to the 655 fields of catalog records by many libraries to provide genre and subject access to individual works of fiction, drama, poetry, humor, and folklore (as opposed to collections).[80] There is some overlap between GSAFD and LCGFT. Some terms are identical, but others differ (compare Figures 13.23 and 13.25). Although the authorized headings in the GSAFD and LCGFT examples are the same, it is not difficult to see the differences in the equivalence and hierarchical relationships identified in each of the vocabularies.

TABLE 13.11 Comparison of LCSH and CYAC Headings.

LCSH	Children's Subject Headings
Cliff-dwellers	Cliff dwellers
Enuresis	Bedwetting
Navel	Belly button
Phytogeography	Plant distribution
Zoogeography	Animal distribution

SUBJECT HEADINGS FOR CHILDREN'S AND YOUNG ADULTS' MATERIALS

(MARC 21 bibliographic field 650, 2nd indicator 1;
MARC 21 authority field 150, fixed field 008/11 code b)

Since 1965 LC has provided a special service for children's catalogers. Known originally as the Annotated Card Program, and now referred to as Children's and Young Adults' Cataloging Program (CYAC), it originated in order to provide "more appropriate and in-depth subject treatment of juvenile titles and to offer easier subject access to those materials."[81] The "Introduction to Children's Subject Headings," a supplementary vocabulary to LCSH, gives a description of the program, a history, an explanation of application, a review of commonly used subdivisions, and general instructions for applying and modifying standard LC subject terms. In the MARC 21 bibliographic format, CYAC terms are tagged specifically as subject terms for children with a second indicator of "1" in 6XX fields. Some comparative examples are shown in Table 13.11. For more information on cataloging for children, please see specialized resources, such as the latest edition of *Cataloging Correctly for Kids*—a compilation of essays on the topic by various authors.[82]

FACETED APPLICATION OF SUBJECT TERMINOLOGY (FAST)

(MARC 21 bibliographic fields 600, 610, 611, 630, 648, 650, 651, 655,
2nd indicator 7, subfield $2 fast; MARC 21 authority fields
100, 110, 111, 130, 148, 150, 151, 155)

The complex syntax and rules for constructing LCSH headings tend to limit the effectiveness of automated authority control and also to limit the application of LCSH to situations in which highly skilled personnel are available. Recent calls have therefore been made for simplification to enable easier use, clear understanding, straightforward application, and uncomplicated automated adaptation. Rebecca Dean states, "The purpose of adapting the LCSH with a simplified syntax to create FAST (Faceted Application of Subject Terminology) headings is to retain the very rich vocabulary of LCSH while making the schema easier to understand, control, apply and use."[83]

After a subcommittee of the Subject Analysis Committee of the American Library Association determined that a new subject access system was needed for Internet resources and other non-traditional materials, it studied the issue of semantic interoperability and reported in 1999 that a controlled vocabulary should be simple and easy to apply, should be intuitive enough to not require sophisticated training to use, should be logical, and should be scalable from the simplest implementation to the most sophisticated.[84] A research group at OCLC, working with Lois Mai Chan of the University of Kentucky and Lynn El-Hoshy of LC's Cataloging Policy and Support Office, explored the issue and decided to develop a new schema derived from LCSH, but specifically designed for applications that go beyond the traditional library catalog. They determined that a "subject vocabulary suitable for the Web environment should be: (1) simple; (2) easy for catalogers and indexers to assign and maintain; (3) easy for searchers to understand and search; and (4) flexible enough for use across disciplines and in various knowledge discovery and access environments, not the least of which is the OPAC."[85] Their approach takes advantage of the vocabulary control exercised by LC catalogers but does not require development of new terminology. FAST is defined by Edward T. O'Neill and Lois Mai Chan to have the following characteristics:

- A controlled vocabulary with all headings established in the authority file, with the exception of headings containing numeric values only
- Based on the LCSH vocabulary
- Designed for an online environment
- A post-coordinated faceted vocabulary
- Usable by people with minimal training and experience
- Compatible with automated authority control[86]

FAST is a faceted vocabulary, while LCSH is pre-coordinated. A faceted vocabulary is one where the concepts represented are divided into defined categories representing particular facets (i.e., aspects or angles of the subject matter). For example, some terms are topical, some are chronological, some are names, and so on. This means that in FAST, the LCSH string **Microsoft Corporation—Employees—Biography** is converted to three separate headings, each representing a separate facet. FAST has eight facets:

1. Topical: general subject matter, (e.g., **Cataloging**)
2. Geographic: place names (e.g., **Europe**)
3. Chronological: time periods (e.g., **2001-2009**)
4. Event: an occurrence or historical incident (e.g., **Cannes Film Festival**; **War of 1812**)
5. Personal name: the name of a person (e.g., **Pelosi, Nancy, 1940-**)
6. Corporate name: the name of an organization or group that may act together and have a name (e.g., **Magnetic Fields (Musical group)**)
7. Title: the name associated with the work in a resource (e.g., **Beowulf**; **Hamlet (Shakespeare, William)**; **Qur'an**)

8. Genre/form: a type or kind of bibliographic structure, literary or artistic form, etc. (e.g., **Science fiction television programs**)

FAST does allow *some* subdivision, but each facet's main headings can be subdivided only by subdivisions from the same facet. Topical headings may be subdivided by topical subdivisions (e.g., **Hospitals—Administration**) but not by a chronological or any other type of subdivision; geographic headings may be subdivided only by geographic subdivisions (e.g., **Massachusetts—Somerville**); and so on. Each of the heading-with-subdivision combinations is established with its own authority record in the FAST authority file. Therefore, instead of a list of free-floating subdivisions that one would consult to find appropriate subdivisions for a particular main heading, there is an authority record for each permitted combination. Thus an authority record can be found for the strings **Education—Dictionaries—Spanish** and **Chemistry—Dictionaries—Spanish**. It may be surprising to see three components strung together in a faceted vocabulary, but as long as the individual topics are part of the same facet, they remain connected to preserve the context provided by the authorized strings.

In the geographic facet, geographic names are established and used in indirect order. For example, Pittsburgh, Pennsylvania is always represented as **Pennsylvania—Pittsburgh** in FAST instead of **Pittsburgh (Pa.)**, as it appears when it is a main heading in LCSH. The indirect approach to geographic headings is also applied to bodies of water (e.g., **Atlantic Ocean—Chesapeake Bay**). The chronological facet goes against LC policy, and follows some earlier recommendations (rejected by LC for LCSH) that chronological headings should consist of the actual time periods of coverage reflected in the resources being described. Thus chronological headings in FAST consist of a single date or a beginning date and an ending date covering the time period of the resource. The event facet contains any activity that occurs during a limited period of time. This may be a single event or one that is repeated.

The personal name facet (including family names) and the corporate name facet use names as they are established in the LC Name Authority File. A name is included in the FAST authority file only if it has been used as a subject in at least one record in the OCLC database and only if the name is valid for subject use. The headings for the title facet are established using the preferred title for the work and may be qualified by the name of the primary creator. The form facet consists of terms that have been identified as those that appear in either a 655 MARC field or would be coded as a subfield *v* in other 6XX fields.

OCLC has been developing additional products and tools to work in coordination with the FAST vocabulary. In recent years, it has developed tools such as:

- **mapFAST**: a mashup with Google Maps that provides map-based access to bibliographic records using FAST geographic authorities[87]
- **searchFAST**: a user interface for identifying and accessing FAST authority records that can also be used to retrieve bibliographic records from WorldCat that have the selected FAST heading[88]

- **FAST Linked Data**: an experimental linked open data service that provides access to the FAST data set[89]
- **FAST Converter**: a web interface for the conversion of LCSH headings to FAST headings[90]
- **assignFAST**: a web service for FAST subject selection; it explores automating the manual selection of headings based on autosuggest technology[91]

New uses of FAST are being explored. Readers should monitor the progress of new developments on the OCLC Research website.

CONCLUSION

In spite of perennial criticisms on grounds of its outdated terminology, illogical syntax, and general inefficiency for precise subject retrieval, LCSH is the most widely accepted controlled vocabulary list in use in English-language libraries today. LC, with prompting and assistance from interested bystanders, now and again assesses its virtues and disadvantages. Intensive efforts continue the work toward maintaining this tool. The Subject Authority Cooperative Program (SACO) is one way that libraries assist LC with improving LCSH.[92] Being a member of SACO allows a library's catalogers to submit proposals for new and revised subject headings and classification numbers to LC via the Program for Cooperative Cataloging (PCC). For the foreseeable future, this enduring subject list gives every sign of retaining its vitality and preeminence for subject access to library collections, either through traditional cataloging processes or through its imminent use in the linked data environment.

NOTES

1. James D. Anderson and Melissa A. Hofmann, "A Fully Faceted Syntax for Library of Congress Subject Headings," *Cataloging & Classification Quarterly* 43, no. 1 (2006): 8-9.
2. Library of Congress Cataloging Policy and Support Office, "Library of Congress Subject Headings Pre- vs. Post-Coordination and Related Issues," accessed April 14, 2014, http://www.loc.gov/catdir/cpso/pre_vs_post.pdf.
3. Library and Archives Canada, *Canadian Subject Headings*, accessed April 14, 2014, http://www.collectionscanada.gc.ca/csh-bin/search/l=0.
4. Melvil Dewey, *Dewey Decimal Classification and Relative Index*, 23rd ed., edited by Joan S. Mitchell et al. (Dublin, OH: OCLC Online Computer Library Center, 2011); *Abridged Dewey Decimal Classification and Relative Index*, 15th ed., edited by Joan S. Mitchell et al. (Dublin, OH: OCLC Online Computer Library Center, 2012). DDC, Dewey, Dewey Decimal Classification, and WebDewey are registered trademarks of OCLC.
5. *Sears List of Subject Headings*, 21st ed., Barbara A. Bristow, editor; Christi Showman Farrar, associate editor (Ipswich, Mass.: H. W. Wilson, a division of EBSCO Information Services; Armenia, N.Y.: Grey House Publishing, 2014).
6. Charles Ammi Cutter, *Rules for a Dictionary Catalog*, 4th ed., rewritten (Washington, D.C.: GPO, 1904; republished, London: The Library Association,

1972). The original version of this work was: Charles A. Cutter, "Rules for a Printed Dictionary Catalogue," in *Public Libraries in the United States of America: Their History, Condition, and Management*, U.S. Bureau of Education (Washington, D.C.: GPO, 1876), Part II.

7. For fuller information on the origin and development of the LC subject headings list, *see* Lois Mai Chan, *Library of Congress Subject Headings: Principles and Application*, 4th ed. (Westport, Conn.: Libraries Unlimited, 2005); Richard S. Angell, "Library of Congress Subject Headings—Review and Forecast," in *Subject Retrieval in the Seventies: New Directions*, edited by Hans (Hanan) Wellisch and Thomas D. Wilson (Westport, Conn.: Greenwood Publishing Co., 1972), 143-163.

8. J. C. M. Hanson, "The Subject Catalogs of the Library of Congress," *Bulletin of the American Library Association* 3 (September 1909): 385-397.

9. American Library Association, *List of Subject Headings for Use in Dictionary Catalogs* (Boston: Library Bureau, 1895).

10. Hanson, "Subject Catalogs," 387.

11. Ibid., 389.

12. Ibid., 390.

13. David Judson Haykin, *Subject Headings: A Practical Guide* (Washington, D.C.: GPO, 1951), 11.

14. *Subject Headings Used in the Dictionary Catalogues of the Library of Congress*, [1st]-3rd eds. (Washington, D.C.: Library of Congress, Catalog Division, 1910-1928); *Subject Headings Used in the Dictionary Catalogs of the Library of Congress*, 4th-7th eds. (Washington, D.C.: Library of Congress, Subject Cataloging Division, 1943-1966); *Library of Congress Subject Headings*, 8th-12th eds. (Washington, D.C.: Library of Congress, Subject Cataloging Division, 1975-1989); *Library of Congress Subject Headings*, 13th-35th eds. (Washington, D.C.: Library of Congress, Office for Subject Cataloging Policy, 1990-2013).

15. Library of Congress, "Library of Congress Transitions to Free, Online-Only Cataloging Publications," *News from the Library of Congress*, accessed April 14, 2014, http://www.loc.gov/today/pr/2013/13-121.html.

16. *Classification Web* (Washington, D.C.: Library of Congress, Cataloging Distribution Service), accessed August 12, 2015, http://classificationweb.net/ [requires ID and password]. For subscription information: http://www.loc .gov/cds/classweb/.

17. "Library of Congress Subject Heading PDF Files," Library of Congress, accessed August 12, 2015, http://www.loc.gov/aba/cataloging/subject/.

18. "Update on Subject and Classification Documentation Plans," Library of Congress, accessed June 10, 2014, http://www.loc.gov/catdir/cpso/ catdocplans.html.

19. Subject authorities are available through OCLC Connexion, accessed August 12, 2015, http://connexion.oclc.org/. Subscription required.

20. "Library of Congress Authorities," Library of Congress, accessed August 12, 2015, http://authorities.loc.gov/. Freely available on the web.

21. *Classification Web* (Washington, D.C.: Library of Congress, Cataloging Distribution Service), accessed August 12, 2015, http://classificationweb. net/. Subscription required.

22. "MARC Distribution Services (databases)," Library of Congress, accessed April 14, 2014, http://www.loc.gov/cds/products/marcDist.php.

23. "LC Linked Data Service: Authorities and Vocabularies," Library of Congress, accessed April 14, 2014, http://id.loc.gov/.

24. *Subject Headings Manual*, 1st ed. (Washington, D.C.: Cataloging Distribution Service, Library of Congress, 2008). Also available in *Cataloger's Desktop*.

25. "Subject Heading Manual PDF Files," Library of Congress, accessed August 12, 2015, http://www.loc.gov/aba/cataloging/subject/.

26. *Cataloger's Desktop* (Washington, D.C.: Library of Congress, Cataloging Distribution Service), accessed August 10, 2015, http://desktop.loc.gov/ [requires ID and password]. For subscription information: http://www.loc .gov/cds/desktop/.
27. "Library of Congress Subject Headings Approved Lists," Library of Congress, accessed August 12, 2015, http://www.loc.gov/aba/cataloging/subject/.
28. "List of the Cataloging Service Bulletin PDF Files," Library of Congress, accessed April 14, 2014, http://www.loc.gov/aba/publications/FreeCSB/ freecsb.html.
29. "Summary of Decisions from the Monthly Editorial Meeting," Library of Congress, accessed April 24, 2014, http://www.loc.gov/aba/pcc/saco/ cpsoed/cpsoeditorial.html.
30. *Subject Headings Manual*, H 180.
31. Ibid.
32. Cutter, *Rules*, 71-72.
33. Chan, *Library of Congress Subject Headings*, 48-59.
34. Cutter, *Rules*, 71.
35. *Subject Headings Manual*, H 290; H 690, 7.
36. *Subject Headings Manual*, H 285.
37. *Subject Headings Manual*, H 310.
38. *Subject Headings Manual*, H 360.
39. *Subject Headings Manual*, H 357.
40. *Subject Headings Manual*, H 306, H 320, H 350, H 351.
41. Sanford Berman, *Prejudices and Antipathies: A Tract on the LC Subject Heads Concerning People* (Metuchen, N.J.: Scarecrow Press, 1971).
42. Hennepin County Library, Cataloging Section, *Cataloging Bulletin*, May 1973-Nov./Dec. 1999.
43. Steven A. Knowlton, "Three Decades since *Prejudices and Antipathies*: A Study of Changes in the Library of Congress Subject Headings," *Cataloging & Classification Quarterly* 40, no. 2 (2005): 127-128.
44. Doris H. Clack, *Black Literature Resources: Analysis and Organization* (New York: Marcel Dekker, 1975), 10.
45. *Cataloging Service*, bulletin 119 (Fall 1976): 22, 24.
46. Joan K. Marshall, *On Equal Terms: A Thesaurus for Nonsexist Indexing and Cataloging* (Santa Barbara, Calif.: American Bibliographical Center-CLIO Press, 1977).
47. Hope A. Olson and Rose Schlegl, "Bias in Subject Access Standards: A Content Analysis of the Critical Literature," in *Information Science: Where Has It Been, Where Is It Going?*, edited by James Turner, *Proceedings of the 27th Annual Conference of the Canadian Association for Information Science* (Montréal: CAIS/ACSI, 1999), 236.
48. Hope A. Olson, "Difference, Culture and Change: The Untapped Potential of LCSH," *Cataloging & Classification Quarterly* 29, no. 1/2 (2009): 60-61.
49. Ibid., 70.
50. *Subject Headings Manual*, H 1631.
51. "Summary of Decisions, Editorial Meeting Number 07," LC Policy and Standards Division, accessed April 18, 2014, http://www.loc.gov/aba/pcc/ saco/cpsoed/psd-130715.html.
52. Ibid.
53. *Subject Headings Manual*, H 690.
54. Ibid.
55. Ibid.
56. Ibid.
57. *Subject Headings Manual*, H 362.

58. E. J. Coates, *Subject Catalogues: Headings and Structure* (London: Library Association, 1960).

59. George M. Sinkankis, "A Study in the Syndetic Structure of the Library of Congress List of Subject Headings." PhD diss., University of Pittsburgh, 1972.

60. Toni Petersen, "The AAT: A Model for the Restructuring of LCSH," *Journal of Academic Librarianship* 9, no. 4 (September 1983): 207-210.

61. Mary Dykstra, "LC Subject Headings Disguised as a Thesaurus," *Library Journal* 113 (March 1, 1988): 42-46.

62. *Subject Headings Manual*, H 370.

63. "Introduction," *Library of Congress Subject Headings*, 37th ed. (Washington, D.C.: Library of Congress, 2015), xi, http://www.loc.gov/aba/publications/FreeLCSH/lcshintro.pdf.

64. *Subject Headings Manual*, H 374.

65. *Subject Headings Manual*, H 400.

66. "Introduction," *Library of Congress Subject Headings*, accessed August 12, 2015, http://www.loc.gov/aba/publications/FreeLCSH/lcshintro.pdf.

67. *Subject Headings Manual*, H 830, H 807, H 980, H 1045, H 1050.

68. *Cataloging Service*, bulletin 120 (Winter 1977): 10.

69. "Subject Headings & Genre/Form Terms," Library of Congress, accessed August 12, 2015, http://www.loc.gov/aba/cataloging/subject/.

70. The Airlie House Conference recommendations are recounted as part of Appendix 4 of "Library of Congress Subject Headings Pre- vs. Post-Coordination and Related Issues," Library of Congress Cataloging Policy and Support Office, accessed April 23, 2014, http://www.loc.gov/catdir/cpso/pre_vs_post.pdf.

71. *Subject Headings Manual*, H 1103.

72. *Subject Headings Manual*, H 1105.

73. *Subject Headings Manual*, H 1140.

74. *Subject Headings Manual*, H 1146.

75. American Library Association, Subject Analysis Committee, 1993, "Definition of Form Data," http://www.pitt.edu/~agtaylor/ala/form-def.htm.

76. "Introduction to Library of Congress Genre/Form Terms for Library and Archival Materials," Library of Congress, accessed August 12, 2015, http://www.loc.gov/aba/publications/FreeLCSH/gftintro.pdf.

77. *Subject Headings Manual*, H 1913, H 1705, H 2230, H 1969.5, H 1865.

78. "Library of Congress Requests Comments on Pilot Demographic Group Vocabulary," Library of Congress, accessed June 5, 2015, http://www.loc.gov/catdir/cpso/lcdgt-announcement.html.

79. "Genre/Form Headings at the Library of Congress," Library of Congress, accessed August 12, 2015, http://www.loc.gov/catdir/cpso/genreformgeneral.html.

80. Subject Analysis Committee, Subcommittee on the Revision of the Guidelines on Subject Access to Individual Works of Fiction, Drama, etc., *Guidelines on Subject Access to Individual Works of Fiction, Drama, etc.*, 2nd ed. (Chicago: American Library Association, 2000).

81. "Introduction to Children's Subject Headings," Library of Congress, accessed August 12, 2015, http://www.loc.gov/aba/publications/FreeLCSH/cshintro.pdf.

82. Sheila S. Intner, Joanna F. Fountain, and Jean Weihs, eds. *Cataloging Correctly for Kids: An Introduction to the Tools*, 5th ed. (Chicago: American Library Association, 2011).

83. Rebecca J. Dean, "FAST: Development of Simplified Headings for Metadata," in *Authority Control in Organizing and Accessing Information: Definition and International Experience*, edited by Arlene G. Taylor and Barbara B. Tillett (New York: Haworth Information Press, 2004), 331-332.

84. *Subject Data in the Metadata Record: Recommendations and Rationale: A Report from the [ALA/ALCTS/SAC] Subcommittee on Metadata and Subject Analysis*, July 1999, http://www.ala.org/alcts/resources/org/cat/subjectdata_record.

85. Lois Mai Chan and Edward T. O'Neill, *FAST: Faceted Application of Subject Terminology: Principles and Application* (Santa Barbara, Calif.: Libraries Unlimited, 2010), 21.

86. Edward T. O'Neill and Lois Mai Chan, "FAST (Faceted Application of Subject Terminology): A Simplified LCSH-Based Vocabulary," World Library and Information Congress: 69th IFLA General Conference and Council, 1-9 August 2003, Berlin, http://archive.ifla.org/IV/ifla69/papers/010e-ONeill_Mai-Chan.pdf.

87. "mapFAST," OCLC Research, accessed April 25, 2014, http://oclc.org/research/activities/mapfast.html.

88. "searchFAST," OCLC Research, accessed April 25, 2014, http://fast.oclc.org/searchfast/.

89. "FAST Linked Data," OCLC Research, accessed April 25, 2014, http://experimental.worldcat.org/fast/.

90. "FAST Converter," OCLC Research, accessed April 25, 2014, http://oclc.org/research/activities/fastconverter.html.

91. "assignFAST," OCLC Research, accessed April 25, 2014, http://oclc.org/research/activities/assignfast.html.

92. "SACO Program Description: Program for Cooperative Cataloging," accessed April 17, 2014, http://www.loc.gov/aba/pcc/saco/.

SUGGESTED READING

Berman, Sanford. *Prejudices and Antipathies: A Tract on the LC Subject Heads Concerning People.* Metuchen, N.J.: Scarecrow Press, 1971.

Broughton, Vanda. *Essential Library of Congress Subject Headings.* New York: Neal-Schuman Publishers, 2012.

Chan, Lois Mai. *Library of Congress Subject Headings: Principles and Application.* 4th ed. Westport, Conn.: Libraries Unlimited, 2005.

Chan, Lois Mai, and Edward T. O'Neill. *FAST: Faceted Application of Subject Terminology: Principles and Applications.* Santa Barbara, Calif.: Libraries Unlimited, 2010.

Foskett, A. C. *The Subject Approach to Information.* 5th ed. London: Library Association Publishing, 1996. Chapter 23: Library of Congress Subject Headings.

Fountain, Joanna F. *Subject Headings for School and Public Libraries.* Bilingual 4th ed. Santa Barbara, Calif.: Libraries Unlimited, 2012.

Intner, Sheila S., Joanna F. Fountain, and Jean Weihs, eds. *Cataloging Correctly for Kids: An Introduction to the Tools.* 5th ed. Chicago: American Library Association, 2011.

Intner, Sheila S., and Jean Weihs. *Standard Cataloging for School and Public Libraries.* 5th ed. Santa Barbara, Calif.: Libraries Unlimited, 2014. Chapter 8: Library of Congress Subject Headings.

Mann, Thomas. *Doing Research at the Library of Congress: A Guide to Subject Searching in a Closed Stacks Library.* 2nd ed. Washington, D.C.: Library of Congress, Humanities and Social Sciences Division, 2005.

Olson, Hope A., and John J. Boll. *Subject Analysis in Online Catalogs.* 2nd ed. Englewood, Colo.: Libraries Unlimited, 2001. Chapter 6: Subject Headings and Descriptors.

Chapter 14

Sears List of Subject Headings (Sears)

INTRODUCTION

The *Sears List of Subject Headings* (*Sears*), now in its 21st edition, is widely used by small and medium-sized public libraries and by school libraries. It is very much smaller in scope and more general in treatment than *Library of Congress Subject Headings* (LCSH), which is commonly used in academic and research libraries. Its history of continuous publication is not as long-standing as that of the Library of Congress (LC) list. The preface states:

> Minnie Earl Sears prepared the first edition of this work in response to demands for a list of subject headings that was better suited to the needs of the small library than the existing American Library Association and Library of Congress lists. Published in 1923, the *List of Subject Headings for Small Libraries* was based on the headings used by nine small libraries that were known to be well cataloged.[1]

For many years *Sears* followed LCSH fairly closely, differing mainly in level of specificity—although its principles encourage specific entry and creation of headings of greater specificity by the local cataloger when needed. In its earlier editions *Sears* used the broader headings from LCSH. However, in the most recent editions, *Sears* has shown more independence.

From 1978 through 2001, six editions of a special-interest companion volume for Canadian libraries were published.[2] This companion has been incorporated into the 21st edition of *Sears*.[3] The idea behind this is to provide

627

efficiency for catalogers by gathering, in alphabetical order, all the vocabulary into one volume. This gives one inclusive vocabulary that reflects the increasing international use of the *Sears* list. Another companion is a Spanish language translation, which includes a history of the relationship between *Sears* and some former Spanish subject heading lists, written by Tina M. Gross, and an English-Spanish index.[4]

TERMINOLOGY

New headings for recent editions of *Sears* "were suggested by librarians representing various sizes and types of libraries, by commercial vendors of bibliographic records, and by the catalogers, indexers, and subject specialists at EBSCO Information Services."[5] The 21st edition is the first to have the advice and assistance from a new group called the Sears Advisory Board. The Board is composed of public and school librarians, many of whom have also served on committees of the American Library Association. The board meets several times a year both in person during relevant conferences and digitally.[6]

Examples of completely new headings in the 21st edition of *Sears* are **Arctic sovereignty**, **Deportation**, **Flash mobs**, and **Web-based instruction**. It is easy to see the need for these concepts that have come into more common usage since the publication of the 20th edition in 2010. Some new headings, however, such as **Animal rescue**, **Back pain**, **Ice storms**, **Retirement planning**, and **Salt** seem less obviously new concepts, and one may wonder at their not having been included in earlier editions. *Sears*, like LCSH, follows the principle of literary warrant; so it is possible that these concepts were not written about before 2010 in the resources acquired by libraries that use *Sears*. Also, users might not have asked for resources on these subjects much until the last few years, in which case suggestions to the *Sears* editors for these additions would have been made more recently.

Some new headings in the 21st edition of *Sears* align the terms with the principles in the latest descriptive cataloging standard *RDA: Resource Description & Access* (e.g., **Bible. N.T.** updated to **Bible. New Testament**). Quite a few new headings were added in order to address the growing literature in the areas of science, technology, engineering, and mathematics (referred to as "STEM" in public education circles where more education in these areas is recommended to address the perceived lack of candidates for positions in these fields). Examples of such new headings are: **Cloud forests**, **Cubic equations**, **Electrophysiology**, **Extinction (Biology)**, **Factorials**, **Hydraulic fracturing**, and **Near-Earth objects**. A specific STEM field that has had considerable advances since the previous edition is computing. Among the new headings here are **Broadband internet**, **Cloud computing**, **Digital rights management**, **Electronic book readers**, and **Linked data (Semantic web)**.

Expanded literature in economics has followed the financial crisis of 2008 and the subsequent worldwide recession. New headings have been established to meet this need, such as **Economic indicators**, **Gross domestic product**, **Money supply**, and **Refinancing**. Education also has been expanding recently with new approaches to teaching/learning. Headings to accommodate these innovations are: **American College Testing assessment**, **Block scheduling (Education)**, **Flipped classrooms**, and **Massive open online courses** (which has MOOCs as a *used for* term). Sports headings were given special attention in the 21st edition of *Sears*, resulting in such new headings as **Iditarod (Race)**, **NBA Finals (Basketball)**, **Paralympic games, 2014 (Sochi, Russia)**, and **World Cup (Soccer)**.

Lastly, a number of new headings have to do with the changing demographics of library users and their search expectations. **Bullying** was a reference to **Bullies** in the 20th edition, but is now a heading. **Hispanic Americans** was canceled in favor of **Latinos (U.S.)**. The term *Gays* appeared only in references to **Gay men** and **Lesbians** and in the heading **Gays and lesbians in the military**, but now **Gays** is a broader term for all those concepts. **Transgender people** and **LGBT people** are new headings with no usage even in references in previous editions. **Human trafficking** has replaced the former **Trafficking in persons**. **Racial profiling in law enforcement** is a new heading under the broader term **Race discrimination**.

LCSH may be consulted when new terminology is being considered, but modifications of LCSH terms are often made to meet the needs of smaller collections. Included among the terms in *Sears* are some terms that originated in LC's *Children's Subject Headings*. The editors of *Sears* try to keep revisions to existing headings to a minimum, so that *Sears* users will not be faced with large numbers of updates when they start using a new edition. Some linguistic change will always occur regardless of the social climate. However, formal subject lists have tended to be conservative in their response to new terminology. In attempting to retain the goodwill of their constituents, they are understandably sensitive to the disruptions caused to a library's cataloging routines when an unduly large number of new subject forms are mandated at one time. Still, the argument that an obsolete form reflects usage in the bulk of the literature indexed is specious. Furthermore, it becomes misleading as new materials with new terminology are added. On the other hand, librarians with card catalogs feared not only the time and effort required to change subject headings on large numbers of cards, but also the stresses placed on the filing apparatus when revised cards had to be moved from one section of the catalog to another. As online catalogs have become the norm, this problem has eased, and as more small libraries and school libraries acquire online catalogs with the capability for global updating, the problem will become virtually nonexistent. EBSCO offers MARC authority records to cataloging companies and subscribing customers for ease of updates.

A comparison of *Sears* headings with comparable ones from LCSH can be helpful in understanding the differences between the lists. Table 14.1 shows several types of differences with examples of the *Sears* headings and the LCSH headings in each case.

Modernization of Terminology

Through the years, *Sears* has undergone the same attempts to eliminate racist, sexist, and pejorative headings that have been made with LCSH. For example, the heading **Negro actors** was replaced by **Black actors** and its narrower term, **African American actors**, while **Air lines—Hostesses** became **Flight attendants**, and **Man (Theology)** was changed to **Human beings (Theology)**. Other headings with prejudicial connotations disappeared or underwent purification

TABLE 14.1 Examples of Some Types of Differences Between Sears and LCSH.

Type of Difference	*Sears*	LCSH
Brevity and simplicity	**Litigation**	**Actions and defenses** **Complex litigation** **Government litigation**
Broader concepts	**Hallucinogens**	**Hallucinogenic drugs** **Hallucinogenic plants**
	Silk screen printing	**Screen process printing** **Serigraphy**
Less technical terms	**Heart attack**	**Myocardial infarction**
Common phraseology	**Lung cancer**	**Lungs—Cancer**

rites. The 10th edition's **Jewish question** disappeared along with **Women in aeronautics** and most other **Women in . . .** and all **Women as . . .** headings. **Underdeveloped areas** was downgraded into a USE reference to **Developing areas** in the 11th edition, changed to a USE reference to **Third World** in the 12th edition, and then became a USE reference to **Developing countries** in the 13th edition. **Insanity** was converted into a USE reference to **Mental illness— Jurisprudence** in the 14th edition, which, in turn, became **Insanity defense** in the 16th edition. **Man, Primitive** became **Nonliterate man** in the 14th edition, followed by becoming **Primitive societies** in the 16th edition. A major feature of the 17th edition was the revision for the native peoples of the Western Hemisphere. Headings beginning with **Indians . . .** were canceled in favor of **Native Americans**. A considerable change in the 21st edition is that almost half of the canceled headings deal with changing headings containing the word *handicapped* to headings containing the word *disabilities* (e.g., **Handicapped** became **People with disabilities**; **Physically handicapped children** became **Children with physical disabilities**; **Architecture and the handicapped** became **Architecture and people with disabilities**).

Modernization has also occurred with time periods. *Renaissance*, used as an adjective, has been replaced by the subdivision **—15th and 16th centuries** (e.g., **Renaissance decoration and ornament** became **Decoration and ornament—15th and 16th centuries**). The adjective *Modern*, meaning a particular time period, has been eliminated. The former **Modern art** is now either **Modernism in art**, **Art—19th century**, **Art—20th century**, **Art—21st century**, or all four. In the same manner **Modern architecture** followed by a time period is now found under **Architecture** subdivided by centuries (e.g., **Modern architecture—1800–1899 (19th century)** has been replaced by **Architecture—19th century**).

Sears has, for many editions, deleted certain headings of decreasing interest. For example, **Iran-Contra Affair, 1985–1990** was deleted from the 18th edition. **Olympic games, 1996 (Atlanta, Ga.)** was replaced with **Olympic games, 2012 (London, England)** in the 21st edition. Such deleted headings are still valid and may be used in catalogs, however. Other deleted headings are no longer valid; in this case, they are given as references to other headings.

USE OF SUBJECT HEADING THEORY IN *SEARS*

The general philosophy of *Sears* is contained in two phrases, both of which the cataloger should remember as he or she makes specific application of the list to the individual materials in the library's collection: the principle of specific entry and the principle of unique heading.[7]

The principle of *specific entry* means that a specific heading is preferred to a general one. For a book about cats alone, **Cats** is preferred to **Domestic animals**. On the other hand, the headings **Siamese cats** or **Seal-point Siamese cats** might be too specific for some libraries; although the principle of specific entry would place a work on Siamese cats under that heading, and *Sears* has a general reference under **Cats** that reads: "SA names of specific breeds of cat [to be added as needed]." The cataloger must know the collection, know its emphases, and know something of the way people use it to be prepared to assign subject headings to it. Are users likely to look for very specific headings, or do they expect to find information under a more general collocating category?

The principle of *unique heading* means that one subject heading, and one alone, is chosen for all items on that subject. The choice of subject headings must be logical and consistent. References should be inserted in the catalog wherever it is anticipated that patrons are likely to approach the topic through different terminology. A few general principles or guidelines are useful for constructing unique subject headings that are logical and consistent:

- Prefer the English word or phrase unless a foreign one best expresses the idea. *Sears*, for example, carries the reference: Laissez faire. USE **Free enterprise**.
- Try to use terms that are used in other libraries as well, unless the library in question is highly specialized or otherwise unique.
- Try to use terms that will cover the field (i.e., terms that will apply to more than one item).

References

Sears breaks down references into three main categories, and the introduction discusses each in some detail: specific *see* references; specific *see also* references; and general references.[8] References in *Sears* carry the same designations as in LCSH, that is, USE, UF, SA, BT, NT, and RT; however, the *Sears* introduction still identifies these as *see*, *see also*, and general references, possibly because of the number of smaller catalogs that still contain references designated in this way rather than *search also under* or other newer reference forms.

See references are considered essential to the success of the catalog. Yet the cataloger in a local library may not find necessary every *see* reference suggested in the list. For example, *Sears* proposes "Plants, Edible USE **Edible plants**." There is also a narrower term reference under **Plants** to **Edible plants**, and in a small catalog, the inverted reference could be superfluous. The most frequent and helpful varieties of *see* references direct the user from

- Synonyms or terms so nearly synonymous that they would cover the same kind of material:
  Chemical geology
  USE **Geochemistry**

  Pay equity
  USE **Equal pay for equal work**

- The second part of a compound heading:
  Illusions
  USE **Hallucinations and illusions**

  Motels
  USE **Hotels and motels**

- Variant spellings or initialisms to the accepted spelling or full form:
  Koran
  USE **Qur'an**

  ESP
  USE **Extrasensory perception**

- Opposites when they are included without being specifically mentioned:
  Disobedience
  USE **Obedience**

  Truth in advertising
  USE **Deceptive advertising**

- The singular to the plural when the two forms would not file together:
  Goose
  USE **Geese**

See also references pose theoretical and practical problems that jeopardize their efficacy. Yet both *Sears* and LCSH make heavy use of them. The above warning against making references simply because they are suggested in a standard list holds as true for *see also* references as it does for *see* references.

It was stated in chapters 12 and 13 that *see also* references normally move downward from a general term to a more specific term or terms:

Conservation of natural resources

See also **Energy conservation; Nature conservation**

In this example the general term refers to two more specific terms. The user who pursues the reference by looking under **Nature conservation** will find a still more specific downward reference to more headings:

Nature conservation

See also **Endangered species; Landscape protection; Natural monuments; Plant conservation; Wildlife conservation**

Although the reference in the catalog may appear as just shown, the designation in the *Sears* list for these terms is NT, for *narrower term(s)*. The list also includes terms designated BT, for *broader term(s)*. As mentioned in chapter 13, most catalogs do not make *see also* references to broader terms.

Sears also indulges in a high number of bilateral or reciprocal references, where the movement is horizontal, between related subjects of more or less equal specificity. These terms are designated RT, for *related term(s)*, in the list. The following examples have been pruned of extraneous terms to make their reciprocity more visible:

> **Gods and goddesses**
>> *See also* **Mythology**; **Religions**
>
> **Mythology**
>> *See also* **Gods and goddesses**
>
> **Religions**
>> *See also* **Gods and goddesses**
>
> **Mollusks**
>> *See also* **Shells**
>
> **Shells**
>> *See also* **Mollusks**

In the case of general *see* and *see also* references, the terms being referred to are not specific headings, but instead are general groups or categories of things that may be established as headings as needed. Examples:

> Faculty
>> USE   types of educational institutions and names of individual educational institutions with the subdivision *Faculty*, e.g. **Colleges and universities—Faculty** [to be added as needed]
>
> **Furniture**
>> SA   furniture of particular countries, e.g. **American furniture**; types of furniture, and names of specific articles of furniture, e.g. **Tables**; **Chairs**; etc. [to be added as needed]

The results of these general references may be so diverse or numerous that it is suggested that specific references be made from a broader term to all narrower terms on the next level of specificity:

> **Furniture**
>> *See also* **Beds**
>>   **Bookcases**
>>   **Chairs**
>>   **Desks**
>>   **Tables**

Only those headings that actually appear in the catalog would be included in such a specific list.

General references to terms with subdivisions present another problem. For example, when the list gives

> Illustrations
> USE   subjects, names, and uniform titles with the subdivision *Pictorial works*; e.g., **Animals—Pictorial works**; **United States—History—1861–1865, Civil War—Pictorial works**; etc. [to be added as needed]

and the library that has subject entries for both referrals adds a book consisting largely of pictures of children, should the cataloger revise the reference entry by inserting **Children—Pictorial works** as a third illustration? Or can he or she depend on the "etc." to cover all subsequent examples? Most libraries follow the second option, thus throwing the burden of search on the user, who probably either will not understand the instructions or, after a bit of desultory searching, will give up, unless the catalog is online *and* the system allows the possibility of doing a search on just the *Pictorial works* segment of headings. However well the user copes, valuable materials may be overlooked.[9]

The following list enumerates some major types of general references, giving an example for each:

- Common names of various members of a class:
  Dogs SA types of dogs, e.g. **Guide dogs**; and names of specific breeds of dogs [to be added as needed]

- Names of individual persons, etc.:
  Presidents—United States SA names of presidents [to be added as needed]

- Names of particular institutions, buildings, structures, societies, etc.:
  Bridges SA types of bridges and names of individual bridges [to be added as needed]

- Names of particular geographic features:
  Natural monuments SA names of individual natural monuments [to be added as needed]

- Names of places subdivided by subject:
  Defenses
      USE types of defenses, e.g. **Air defenses**; and names of continents, regions, countries, and individual colonies with the subdivision *Defenses*, e.g. **United States—Defenses** [to be added as needed]

- Subjects followed by form subdivisions:
  Case studies
      USE subjects with the subdivision *Case studies*, e.g. **Juvenile delinquency—Case studies** [to be added as needed]

- Subjects with national adjectives:
  Essays
      . . . Collections of literary essays by American authors are entered under **American essays**; by English authors, under **English essays**; etc. . . .

STRUCTURE OF SUBJECT HEADINGS

Like LCSH, *Sears* terms consist of a variety of forms, ranging from a single noun to different kinds of complex descriptive phrases:[10]

- **Single noun**: The single noun is the most desirable form of subject heading if it is specific enough to fit the item at hand and the needs of the library. In general, if there is a significant difference between the singular and plural forms, the plural is preferred (e.g., Mouse USE **Mice**). However, there are situations where the singular form is used to cover abstract ideas or general usage (e.g., **Essay** as a literary form), while the plural designates individual examples of the form.

- **Modified noun**: The modified noun takes at least two forms: (1) normal word order (e.g., **Health maintenance organizations**), and (2) explanatory modifier added in parentheses (e.g., **Hotlines (Telephone counseling)**). Formerly, inverted word order was used, but now it only appears as a *used for* term from which a reference is made to the normal word order (e.g., Technical assistance, American USE **American technical assistance**).

- **Compound heading**: The compound heading is usually two nouns joined by *and*, but the nouns are sometimes also modified (e.g., **Coal mines and mining**). The terms in a compound heading are conjoined for various reasons:
  - To link related topics. Usually both ideas are covered in a single treatise, e.g., **Anarchism and anarchists**, **Clocks and watches**, and **Puppets and puppet plays**.
  - To link opposites. Again, the pairs are often discussed together, e.g., **Corrosion and anticorrosives**, **Good and evil**, and **Joy and sorrow**.

  In most cases, usage dictates the order of terms, but when that fails, alphabetical order is preferred. If a library should acquire enough materials under one of two such terms to make searching difficult or tiresome, the cataloger might consider splitting the subject heading into its two components, with linking references. For example, LCSH has broken its former heading **Antigens and antibodies** into **Antigens** and **Immunoglobulins**.

- **Phrase heading**: The phrase heading may be prepositional (e.g., **Cost and standard of living**), serial (e.g., **Stories, plots, etc.**), or an intriguing combination of forms (e.g., **Superhero comic books, strips, etc.** or **Life support systems (Medical environment)**).

TYPES OF SUBDIVISIONS

Subject subdivisions indicate a specialized aspect of a broad subject or point of view (e.g., **Artificial satellites—Orbits**). They are set off from the primary heading by a dash. Like the print-ready PDF version of LCSH, *Sears* separates the category from references that are inverted with commas (e.g., Artificial satellites, American USE **American artificial satellites**) and from phrases beginning with the same words (e.g., **Artificial satellites in tele-communication**). However, following the section of subdivisions, the inverted forms and the phrases are interfiled in straight alphabetical order, letter by letter to the end of each word, disregarding punctuation, as instructed in the American Library Association (ALA) filing rules.[11]

A primary purpose of the subject subdivision is to subdivide topics that are broad in scope or that have much written about them (e.g., **Education**). Without subdivision, there would be many entries under such headings sub-arranged only by, perhaps, author or by date. Headings with large numbers of entries can be tedious for a catalog user to search. Subdivision allows grouping of the entries in meaningful ways; for example:

> **Education—Aims and objectives**
> **Education—Curricula**
> **Education—Experimental methods**

There are several types of subdivisions, including topical subdivisions, geographic subdivisions, chronological subdivisions, and form subdivisions, and some or all of these may be compounded under a given topic. Three of the subdivision types are used to show subtopics in the example:

> **United States—History—1861–1865, Civil War—Pictorial works**

Subdivisions of Broad Application

Some subdivisions are of broad application and may be used by the cataloger to divide practically any subject heading in the list, if local policy allows the cataloger to add such subdivisions even if they are not established in the list. Form subdivisions fall into this category, as do many general and topical subdivisions that may be used under subjects as appropriate. These are given in the main list with instructions for their use as subdivisions with appropriate subject headings. There is also a list in the front of the volume that gives all subdivisions in the list except geographic or chronological.[12] This is a simple alphabetical list for handy reference only. The cataloger should always check the main list for instructions for the use of each subdivision.

Sears, like LCSH, has a group of headings that serve as patterns for the subdivisions that may be used under all headings of the same type. A list of these, with explanations of each, may be found in the front of the *Sears* volume. Some of these *key headings*, as described in the list, are:[13]

- *Authors*: **Shakespeare, William, 1564–1616** (to illustrate the subdivisions that may be used under any voluminous author, and in some cases other individual persons)
- *Languages*: **English language** (to illustrate subdivisions that may be used under any language or group of languages)
- *Literature*: **English literature** (to illustrate subdivisions that may be used under any literature)

- *Places*: **United States**
  Ohio
  Chicago (Ill.)
  (to illustrate subdivisions—except for historical periods—that may be used under any country, state, or city)
- *Public figures*: **Presidents—United States** (to illustrate subdivisions that may be used under the [official headings for] presidents, prime ministers, governors, and rulers of any country, state, etc., and in some cases under the names of individual presidents, prime ministers, etc.)

To use the subdivisions under the key headings, one finds the appropriate example (e.g., **English language—Idioms**) and then applies the subdivision to the heading for the item in hand (e.g., **French language—Idioms**).

Subdivisions of Limited Application

Some special topic subdivisions cannot readily be transferred from one heading to another because they are specially tailored to bring out important aspects of individual topics, e.g., **Deaf—Means of communication** or **Airplanes—Piloting**. One could not reasonably use **Deaf—Piloting** or **Airplanes—Means of communication**. Such subdivisions are listed both in the alphabetical reference list and in the main list. A cataloger is expected to use common sense in applying them.

Chronological Subdivisions

Time subdivisions, which apply most frequently to history, define a specific chronology for the primary topic. Some consist merely of dates (e.g., **Europe—History—1789–1900**). Often the date or dates are followed by a descriptive phrase (e.g., **Church history—30–600, Early church**). Prior to the 12th edition, the descriptive phrase preceded the dates in such headings. The change in position facilitates filing in chronological order both manually and by machine. Occasionally the chronological designation is an inverted qualifier rather than a subdivision (e.g., **Gettysburg (Pa.), Battle of, 1863**).

Geographic Headings and Subdivisions

Geographic locations are of two forms: (1) area—subject, e.g., **Chicago (Ill.)—Census**, and (2) subject—area, e.g., **Geology—Bolivia**. *Sears* adds parenthetical instructions to those headings in its list that may be divided by place, e.g., **Geology** (May subdiv. geog.). Under some headings the instructions are more detailed, e.g., **American hostages** (May subdiv. geog. except U.S.).

Unlike LCSH, *Sears* does not dictate the form of geographic subdivisions. The introduction specifies that *Sears* uses, in the main list, direct place subdivision (in which the name of the place discussed in the work is used directly as the subdivision) rather than indirect place subdivision (in which the name of a larger geographic area is interposed between the subject and a smaller area discussed in the work). *Sears* uses the RDA form of a place name in using direct subdivision (i.e., **—Chicago (Ill.)**, not just **—Chicago**), but it does not mandate this usage for the libraries using its list. Some libraries may wish to follow LCSH practice and use indirect place subdivision (i.e., **—Illinois— Chicago**). If direct place subdivision is chosen, it is wise to use RDA forms of place name for the sake of consistency.

Geographic area names with subject subdivisions are less conspicuous in the list, but play an important role in most library catalogs. Instructions may take the form: "**Italy** . . . May be subdivided like **United States** except for *History*." Then specific subdivisions for Italy follow, including the *History* subdivision with chronological subdivisions specifically appropriate for Italy.

Subject headings in various fields, especially in the fields of science, technology, and economics, usually are subdivided by place. Those in history, geography, and politics usually are made subdivisions under place.[14] It is assumed that the real subject of a book about Colorado history, and the subject term the patron will most likely consult, is **Colorado**, not **History**. In *Sears*, the main subject heading **History** is used only for general works on history as an intellectual discipline.

HEADINGS FOR BELLES-LETTRES

Individual works of *belles-lettres* (e.g., novels, plays, and poetry) are not always assigned subject headings. It has often been assumed that patrons are more likely to seek access to these materials through author or title. However, there are many themes of literature that may be used as subject headings. In the list of form subdivisions supplied by *Sears*, **—Fiction** appears as a suggested option for libraries that prefer to make subject headings for fictionalized history or biography. Thus, a novel about conflicts between Israel and the Arab countries in the Middle East might be given the subject heading, **Israel-Arab conflicts—Fiction**. In addition other genre headings, such as **Mystery fiction** or **Science fiction**, can be assigned to these works. The 18th edition of *Sears* was the first to include in its "Principles of the Sears List" guidance to libraries that choose to assign topical and geographic headings to individual works of fiction, drama, and poetry—guidance that continues in the 21st edition.[15]

For literary anthologies it is common to give a genre heading with the subdivision **—Collections** (e.g., **Poetry—Collections**; **American drama— Collections**), but *Sears* sometimes uses the plural noun (e.g., **Essays**) rather than using the subdivision.[16] Topical headings reflecting themes of the work as a whole are also common (e.g., **Love poetry**; **Dogs—Fiction**).

PHYSICAL CHARACTERISTICS AND FORMAT OF *SEARS LIST OF SUBJECT HEADINGS*

The 21st edition of *Sears* opens with a preface that gives its historical setting and identifies the authoritative sources and the new features incorporated in it. It is followed by an explanatory essay that has become a *Sears* tradition, undergoing considerable expansion in scope and detail over the years. This essay is called "Principles of the Sears List of Subject Headings."[17] It treats both the theoretical and practical aspects of subject heading work. It merits careful reading, not only by those planning to use the *Sears* list, but also by anyone wishing to gain knowledge of traditional subject list usage. The discussion of principles is followed by an explanation of what kinds of headings are expected to be added by the cataloger, the list of key headings mentioned above, a list of canceled headings with their replacements, explanations of the use of subdivisions in *Sears*, the list of every subdivision (except geographic or chronological subdivisions) for which there is specific provision in *Sears*, an explanation of the symbols used, and finally the list proper.

In the list proper, subject entries are printed in boldface type. USE references appear in lightface type in the same alphabetical sequence. Filing in *Sears* has already been discussed under "Types of Subdivisions." The excerpt in Figure 14.1 shows the various elements that may be included under a subject entry, although not every entry requires all of these elements.

DDC numbers from the *Abridged Dewey Decimal Classification* are given with the permission of the publisher, OCLC.[18] The example in Figure 14.1 shows the associated DDC number in its customary place, on the same line with the subject entry. Two or three numbers may be specifically included to remind the user that he or she might profitably seek further in the DDC to find the best number for the particular need.

Scope notes have been used more extensively in each new edition of *Sears*. The one in Figure 14.1 is typical. The reader receives first a positive instruction on appropriate use of the entry. Then comes a negative instruction (albeit stated positively) on the kinds of material that should be placed under a different entry.

The initials UF (standing for *used for*) normally follow the scope note or, if there is no scope note, the entry proper. The letters UF before one or more terms mean that a USE reference is recommended from each such term to the

---

Children's poetry   808.81
> Use for individual poems, collections, or materials about poetry written for children. Individual works and collections of poetry written by children are entered under **Children's writings**. Materials about poetry written by children are entered under **Child authors**.

UF	Poetry for children
SA	subjects and personal, corporate, and place names with the subdivision *Juvenile poetry*; e.g. **Christmas—Juvenile poetry** [to be added as needed]
BT	**Children's literature** **Poetry**
NT	**Children's songs** **Lullabies** **Nonsense verses** **Nursery rhymes** **Tongue twisters**

FIGURE 14.1 An Example of a Subject Heading in the Print Version of Sears.

heading under which the UF appears. Terms preceded by UF are never used as subject headings. Next come the letters SA (standing for *see also*) followed by an explanation of general kinds of terms that may be related. Then we see the letters BT (standing for *broader terms*) followed by terms that represent concepts broader than the concept represented in the heading. Next come the letters NT (standing for *narrower terms*). They precede a list of more specific headings that the user might like to explore. Although not present in the example, many entries end with a list of terms of related significance that follow the letters RT (standing for *related terms*). Each boldface entry in the lists following BT, NT, and RT is a legitimate subject heading. Reference to these headings might very well lead to further headings that could help expand or modify the search to reveal the full range of materials available in the particular collection. But a reference is not usually made in the catalog unless the catalog actually has material under the heading referred to (see discussion of this issue as related to LCSH in chapter 13).

Thus *Sears* suggests the following references for the subject entry **Children's poetry** (shown in Figure 14.1), but the local cataloger is expected to consider each on its merits, in view of the terminology used by the library's clientele and the presence of other subject entries in the catalog:

> Poetry for children
> > USE **Children's poetry**
>
> **Children's literature**
> > *See also* **Children's poetry**
>
> **Poetry**
> > *See also* **Children's poetry**
>
> **Children's poetry**
> > *See also* **Children's songs**
> > > **Lullabies**
> > > **Nonsense verses**
> > > **Nursery rhymes**
> > > **Tongue twisters**

The cataloger should also consider whether a *see also* reference needs to be made in response to the SA instruction under **Children's poetry**.

Sears includes a list of "Headings to Be Added by the Cataloger."[19] Several varieties of proper names and common names are identified for which there is no attempt to include all possibilities in the printed list. One or two obvious names of each variety can be found in the list proper, to serve as examples or because important or typical subdivisions have been given. The cataloger is also reminded that general *see also* references imply other specific names that the cataloger is to add as needed, using available reference sources to establish correct entry forms.

In addition to the print volume of *Sears*, there is another version of the subject heading list that is available electronically. From around the time they acquired H.W. Wilson (the former publisher of *Sears*) in 2011, EBSCO

<table>
<tbody>
<tr><td colspan="2">**Children's poetry**</td></tr>
<tr><td>**Dewey Classification:**</td><td>808.81</td></tr>
<tr><td>**Scope Note:**</td><td>Use for individual poems, collections, or materials about poetry written for children. Individual works and collections of poetry written by children are entered under Children's writings. Materials about poetry written by children are entered under Child authors.</td></tr>
<tr><td>**Use For:**</td><td>Poetry for children</td></tr>
<tr><td>**See Also:**</td><td>subjects and personal, corporate, and place names with the subdivision Juvenile poetry; e.g. Christmas/Juvenile poetry [to be added as needed]</td></tr>
<tr><td>**Broader Terms:**</td><td>Children's literature
Poetry</td></tr>
<tr><td>**Narrower Terms:**</td><td>Children's songs
Lullabies
Nonsense verses
Nursery rhymes
Tongue twisters</td></tr>
<tr><td>**AN:**</td><td>151131</td></tr>
</tbody>
</table>

FIGURE 14.2 An Example of a Subject Heading in the Online Version of Sears.

Information Services has made the *Sears* list available through their EBSCO-host database service.[20] The same basic information is provided in the online version, but the formatting of the entries is somewhat different; for example, the labels SA and BT are spelled out as *See Also* and *Broader Terms*. The same heading that appears in Figure 14.1 is used in Figure 14.2 to show the format used online. Searching in the database, obviously, is also quite a different experience than browsing through the print volume. In the print version, *use* references are presented in their appropriate places in the alphabetical sequence as independent entries; in the database, a search on an equivalent term simply takes the searcher to the authorized term without an intermediary step. The database tends to operate using keyword search approaches; as a result some searches that should be straightforward and immediate are cluttered with extraneous results, often with the needed term far down the list.

UPDATING

Sears updates its usage by successive editions. New print editions are published every few years. The online version, available by subscription through EBSCOhost, is updated annually. The relatively limited scope of *Sears*, for use in small and medium-sized libraries, makes comprehensive revision manageable for both editors and users. The results are more coherently integrated than the ad hoc revisions issued for LCSH. In addition, it is not necessary

to wait one to three years for updated terminology in today's rapidly changing environment, because catalogers using *Sears* are encouraged to use the
existing patterns and principles to create, for immediate use, headings that
fit their needs. Although LC provides monthly updates of LCSH that permit (if
they do not always ensure) professional response on the part of one enormous
library to inevitable, but generally unpredictable, shifts in publishing interests
and emphases, they regularly have a backlog of requests for headings. Neither
approach monopolizes all the advantages. What matters is that every viable
subject access mode should remain under constant surveillance and revision,
offering a dynamic compromise between rigid custom and assimilative change.

CONCLUSION

The assigning of subject headings is an activity that inevitably seems complicated and bewildering to the neophyte cataloger. Unlike other cataloging
activities, it has no logical progression other than the linguistic development
of knowledge itself. Even the assigning of a classification number to a book is
less forbidding, for the novice usually has some sort of previous orientation
to the Dewey system, at least, and can see, if dimly, the divisions of knowledge and why they should exist. Subject headings are, however, not difficult
once the cataloger learns to handle them. Both *Sears* and LCSH are quite
explicit in their directions; both contain lists of general subdivisions with specific instructions for their use. If followed consistently, they will provide useful
reference guides for the user, including the reference librarian.

A beginning cataloger should study the subject list used in the local library.
It would be helpful to choose a subject in which he or she is personally interested, tracing it throughout the list and observing the interrelation of references. There are other aids, such as the reference tools in the library and the
Internet. They amplify subjects and clarify aspects not immediately understood, especially in an age when no one can expect to know everything. The
library's online public catalog is also helpful. A classification number search
can suggest subject headings that have been used before with a particular
classification. A subject search in the catalog can suggest classification numbers if the cataloger has a subject heading in mind. Neither is a completely
reliable crutch. Books are very often written about new subjects and about
more than one subject. The vagaries of past and present individual catalogers, however experienced, may mislead. Yet both resources are generally helpful; both serve to characterize the practices of the local library. To become a
successful cataloger, one must know what is current local practice and work
within that frame of reference. Major changes should not be put into effect
until the reasons for what is done are fully understood and the reactions of
users and fellow librarians can be anticipated.

NOTES

1. *Sears List of Subject Headings*, 21st ed., Barbara A. Bristow, editor; Christi
   Showman Farrar, associate editor (Ipswich, Mass.: H. W. Wilson, a division of
   EBSCO Information Services; Armenia, N.Y.: Grey House Publishing, 2014), viii.

2. Lynne Isberg Lighthall, ed., *Sears List of Subject Headings: Canadian Companion*, 6th ed., with the assistance of Shana Bystrom, et al. (New York: H. W. Wilson, 2001).
3. B. A. Bristow and C. S. Farrar, "Preface," *Sears List of Subject Headings*, vii.
4. *Sears: Lista de Encabezamientos de Materia: Nueva Traducción y Adaptación de la Lista Sears*, Iván E. Calimano, editor; Ageo García, editor asociado; Judy Medina, Carmen Torres, traductores; incorporando el trabajo de 1984 de Carmen Rovira (New York: H. W. Wilson, 2008).
5. Bristow and Farrar, "Preface," vii.
6. Ibid.
7. For more detailed discussion of the theory of subject headings, refer to chapter 12, "Verbal Subject Access."
8. The list of reference types is adapted from *Sears*, xxxvii-xxxix, but the examples are changed to give alternative insights.
9. *Sears*, xxxviii-xxxix, also discusses this problem.
10. For a review of the structure of LCSH and further comment on some of the points mentioned here, *see* "Types of Topical Subject Headings" in chapter 13 and "The Choice of Subject Headings" in chapter 12.
11. *See* the section on "Filing Arrangement" in chapter 13 of this text to compare the filing used in the book version of LCSH with that found in *Sears*.
12. *Sears*, xlvii-liii.
13. Ibid., xliii.
14. Ibid., xxv-xxvi.
15. Ibid., xxx-xxxii.
16. Ibid., xxix-xxx.
17. Much of the foregoing discussion is based on this essay.
18. Melvil Dewey, *Abridged Dewey Decimal Classification and Relative Index*, 15th ed., edited by Joan S. Mitchell, et al. (Dublin, OH: OCLC, 2012). DDC, Dewey, Dewey Decimal Classification, and WebDewey are registered trademarks of OCLC.
19. *Sears*, p. xlii.
20. The online version of *Sears* is available through EBSCOhost. See https://www.ebscohost.com/ for more information on subscriptions to this online product. The introduction to the vocabulary, "Principles of the Sears List of Subject Headings," can be accessed at http://support.ebsco.com/downloads/resources/SearsFM.pdf.

SUGGESTED READING

Ferguson, Bobby. *Subject Analysis: Blitz Cataloging Workbook.* Englewood, Colo.: Libraries Unlimited, 1998. Chapter 2: Sears List of Subject Headings.

Foskett, A. C. *The Subject Approach to Information.* 5th ed. London: Library Association Publishing, 1996, 348–353.

Fountain, Joanna F. *Subject Headings for School and Public Libraries: An LCSH/Sears Companion.* Englewood, Colo.: Libraries Unlimited, 2001.

Intner, Sheila S., and Jean Weihs. *Standard Cataloging for School and Public Libraries.* 5th ed. Santa Barbara, Calif.: Libraries Unlimited, 2014.

"Principles of the Sears List of Subject Headings." In *Sears List of Subject Headings.* 21st ed., Barbara A. Bristow, editor; Christi Showman Farrar, associate editor. Ipswich, Mass.: H. W. Wilson, a division of EBSCO Information Services; Armenia, N.Y.: Grey House Publishing, 2014, xv–xli.

Satija, M. P., and Elizabeth Haynes. *User's Guide to Sears List of Subject Headings.* Lanham, Md.: Scarecrow Press, 2008.

Chapter 15

Other Verbal Access Systems

INTRODUCTION

For well over a century, libraries have provided subject retrieval of items from their collections through the use of pre-coordinate lists of integrated and cross-referenced topical headings. The preceding chapters have discussed *Library of Congress Subject Headings* (LCSH) and *Sears List of Subject Headings* (*Sears*), which remain the most universally recognized linguistic tools for analyzing library collections. Developments in information science offer additional modes of indexing that throw both practical and theoretical light on traditional subject lists. Some of the techniques are offered as supplements, or substitutes, for traditional subject catalogs. This chapter reviews those enterprises most pertinent to library subject retrieval and explains briefly the applications of the more successful ones.

DOCUMENT INDEXING

The word *index* still connotes back-of-the-book and periodical indexes more often than it does subject catalogs for library collections. However, library indexes and catalogs are nearly as old as alphabets, being present in some form with almost every organized collection of written records as far back as the early Mesopotamian and Egyptian archives. In the final years of the 19th and the early years of the 20th centuries, catalogers frequently made numerous *analytics* for significant informational works in their libraries. Books were expensive. The high cost of acquisitions and the relative scarcity of printed materials were countered with efforts to exploit collections intensively. Librarians were a captive labor force, often with "disposable time" on the job. And what more profitable "pick-up work" could there be than making analytic indexes to anthologies and treatises? If the cards followed standard cataloging practices they were filed into the official catalog. If they were less carefully constructed, they might be kept in a desk drawer or a shoebox in the reference department. John Rothman wrote about a continuing reciprocity between library classification and indexing:

> Although indexing is often clearly differentiated from cataloging and classification, there is considerable overlapping in practice, and the development of new cataloging techniques or new classification systems is bound to affect indexing practices. Thus the development of the Dewey and other decimal classification systems for library catalogs was paralleled by the development of decimal, coded, and faceted topical indexing systems.[1]

HIERARCHICAL CONTROLLED VOCABULARIES

Controlled vocabularies, with their systematized language that subsumes narrower terms or subdivisions under broader terms, are familiar to librarians in many contexts. In previous chapters their use in library subject catalogs is discussed. The commercial arena, where indexes are created to analyze periodical articles, anthologies, report literature, patents, and the like for rapid retrieval in nearly all disciplines, has also turned to controlled vocabularies, usually called *thesauri*.

The terms *thesaurus* and *subject heading list* are often used interchangeably in the literature, but they are not really the same. There are several notable differences between the two concepts. Since 1974, when ANSI Z39.19 *Guidelines for Thesaurus Structure, Construction and Use* was published, there have been international standard guidelines for thesauri.[2] There were, however, no such standards for subject heading lists. In 2005, a revision of ANSI/NISO Z39.19, *Guidelines for the Construction, Format, and Management of Monolingual Controlled Vocabularies,* was approved; this revision was subsequently reviewed and reaffirmed in 2010.[3] Its title was changed from the 1974 edition to reflect a shift in focus from a standard for thesauri to one for controlled vocabularies, including subject heading lists, synonym rings, taxonomies, and thesauri.

Another difference between thesauri and subject heading lists is that thesauri are composed of individual terms, while subject heading lists are composed of subject headings, which may entail complex phrases or a series of terms strung together. This difference has been described by Mary Dykstra.[4] She says that in general a term denotes a single concept, while a subject heading may consist of composites of terms, although a subject heading may also consist of a single concept. Yet another difference lies in the way terms and subjects are related to each other (i.e., the syndetic structure). The guidelines for thesauri give rules for establishing hierarchical relationships and for assigning related (or associative) terms. While LCSH also has rules that are used when establishing new headings, composite headings are more difficult to relate than terms, and there remain many headings and relationships that were established before the rules were made. Dykstra argues that by adopting the abbreviations used by thesauri to show these relationships (e.g., BT, RT), LCSH exacerbated the confusion that already existed.[5]

A final difference is that a thesaurus is likely to cover only a limited discipline or cross-disciplinary area, whereas subject heading lists tend to be designed for subject application to general or multidisciplinary collections. The scope of each vocabulary is very different. One aims for depth, while the other is more focused on breadth. This means that the levels of specificity vary greatly; a discipline-specific thesaurus is able and expected to delve deeper into the subject matter, whereas a subject heading list is somewhat more general, but more widely inclusive.

In the following sections, two additional subject heading lists and four thesauri from different disciplines are discussed to illustrate the range of other controlled vocabularies that are available to supplement the standard vocabularies used in the information professions (i.e., LCSH and *Sears*). These vocabularies began their availability in print form, but with the rapid growth in online information in the 21st century, most controlled vocabulary lists have moved online. The forms in which these resources are available vary. For example, half can still be purchased in book format, but half cannot. In some cases, the book versions are woefully out of date. Some are freely available on the Web, while others required a subscription for access.

Medical Subject Headings (MeSH)

A controlled vocabulary widely used in libraries is *Medical Subject Headings* (MeSH), created at the National Library of Medicine (NLM). It is used in most medical libraries as well as being used as a thesaurus for the MEDLINE database. MeSH was first available in print beginning in 1960 and in electronic form in 1975. Since 2008 MeSH has been kept up to date only online. The 2015 MeSH contains 27,455 terms plus more than 220,000 *entry terms* (i.e., references).[6] Additionally, there are more than 224,000 Supplementary Concept Records (SCRs) in a separate thesaurus. SCRs are headings for substances in the literature that are not currently MeSH headings (e.g., oxycodone terephthalate). This file is updated weekly; MeSH itself is updated annually.[7] MeSH is used by NLM for indexing articles from biomedical journals for the MEDLINE database (also called *PubMed*). Catalogers at NLM also use MeSH for cataloging the resources acquired by the library.[8]

The format of MeSH differs considerably from that of LCSH or *Sears*. When a term is searched in the MeSH Browser[9] and a record is retrieved, there are three possible views. The default view is the *Standard View*, but a user may instead choose either *Concept View* or *Expanded Concept View*. An example of a record from MeSH in the *Concept View* is shown in Figure 15.1.

The introduction to MeSH explains how to use the vocabulary, giving explanations of such things as the labels used in a heading display.[10] For example, it explains: "Terms in a MeSH record which are strictly synonymous with each other are grouped in a category called a 'Concept.' (Not to be confused with Supplementary Concept Records.)"[11] In Figure 15.1, for example, the concept represented by the preferred term **Communicable Diseases** has a synonym "Infectious Diseases" that will also bring up this same record if this term is searched from the MeSH Browser search box. The

MeSH Heading	Communicable Diseases
Tree Number	C01.539.221
Annotation	/ prev = COMMUNICABLE DISEASE CONTROL for GEN only; do not confuse X ref INFECTIOUS DISEASES with INFECTION: see note there
Concept 1 (Preferred)	**Communicable Diseases**
	Term Communicable Diseases
	Term Infectious Diseases
See Also	Disease Reservoirs
Allowable Qualifiers	BL CF CI CL CN CO DH DI DT EC EH EM EN EP ET GE …
Entry Version	COMMUNICABLE DIS
Entry Combination	prevention & control:Communicable Disease Control
Date of Entry	19990101
Unique ID	D003141

FIGURE 15.1 A Subject Heading from the MeSH Browser. (Courtesy of the National Library of Medicine)

Annotation for **Communicable Diseases** has instructions for the user not to confuse "Infectious Diseases" with "Infection" and to see the note there. In the record for **Infection** there is a lengthy annotation, much of which is aimed at indexers, that notes several terms that might be differentiated by the indexer (see Figure 15.2). This record (presented in the *Standard View*) has, in addition, a *Scope Note*, meant for the user of the index or catalog, that defines **Infection**.

The label *Allowable Qualifiers* is followed by a list of two-letter codes for terms that are called *subheadings* (i.e., subdivisions in other subject heading lists). In both records shown in Figures 15.1 and 15.2 the first three allowable qualifiers are BL, CF, and CI, standing for *blood, cerebrospinal fluid*, and *chemically induced*, respectively. Each of these can be used as a subheading with **Communicable Diseases** and also with **Infection**. The combinations cannot be found in the MeSH Browser, but individual qualifiers can be found in the database (see Figure 15.3). Every qualifier record has a *Record Type* identified as *Q*. Once the headings and subheadings are identified, and it has been determined which ones can be used together, the combined headings may be added to a bibliographic record. For example:

650 _2 $a Communicable Diseases $x chemically induced

650 _2 $a Infection $x blood

The label *Entry Version* in a MeSH record is for a term in all upper case that gives the custom short form of a heading used by indexers for NLM indexing and searching.[12] *Entry Combination* is used where certain descriptor/ qualifier combinations are prohibited, and the term that is to be used

MeSH Heading	Infection
Tree Number	C01.539
Annotation	general only as concept of disease caused by microorganisms; many texts saying "infection" & many saying "sepsis" mean BACTERIAL INFECTIONS: check text but note that SEPSIS is available; "infectious disease" can be INFECTION but is more likely COMMUNICABLE DISEASES; policy: Manual 22.12-.19, 23.12+; relation to microorganisms: Manual 22.11-.19 & TN 209; / drug therapy: consider also ANTI-INFECTIVE AGENTS & its specific groups; / prev = INFECTION CONTROL but see note there
Scope Note	Invasion of the host organism by microorganisms that can cause pathological conditions or diseases.
See Also	Anti-Infective Agents
Allowable Qualifiers	BL CF CI CL CN CO DH DI DT EC EH EM EN EP ET GE ...
Entry Version	INFECT
History Note	/prevention & control was INFECTION/prevention & control 1966-91
Entry Combination	prevention & control:Infection Control
Date of Entry	19990101
Unique ID	D007239

FIGURE 15.2 A Related Subject Heading from MeSH. (Courtesy of the National Library of Medicine)

Subheading	chemically induced
Record Type	Q
Entry Version	CHEM IND
Abbreviation	CI
Scope Note	Used for biological phenomena, diseases, syndromes, congenital abnormalities, or symptoms caused by endogenous or exogenous substances.
Annotation	subhead only; for biol phenomena or diseases induced by endogenous or exogenous substances; indexing policy: Manual 19.8.14; DF: /chem ind or /CI
Online Note	search policy: Online Manual; use: main heading/CI or CI (SH) or SUBS APPLY CI
History Note	1967; used with Category C & F 1967-1974; C & F3 1975-2000; C, F, & G 2001 forward
Date of Entry	19731227
Revision Date	20030722
Date Established	19670101
Unique ID	Q000139

FIGURE 15.3 A Subdivision Record from MeSH. (Courtesy of the National Library of Medicine)

instead is given. Hence, the heading **Communicable Diseases** and the subheading *prevention & control* are not to be used together. Instead one should use the heading **Communicable Disease Control**. Other labels that may be encountered are *Note*, which gives free-text information about the biological properties of a substance, and *History Note*, which gives free-text information about the term's past history deemed helpful to the online searcher.[13]

MeSH is hierarchical and every term is assigned a *Tree Number*, which for **Communicable Diseases** is "C01.539.221." Its tree structure looks like this:

> **Bacterial Infections and Mycoses** [C01]
>> **Infection** [C01.539]
>>> **Communicable Diseases** [C01.539.221]
>>>> **Communicable Diseases, Emerging**
>>>> [C01.539.221.500]

There are 16 broad categories for tree structures (e.g., category A for anatomic terms, category B for organisms, C for diseases). MeSH tree structures "should not be regarded as representing an authoritative subject classification system but rather as arrangements of descriptors for the guidance and convenience of persons who are assigning subject headings to documents or are searching for literature."[14] Also, the numbers have no significance beyond arrangement in a hierarchy. Each heading appears in at least one place in the trees, and may also appear in as many other places as are appropriate. This structure allows users to find additional subject headings which are more specific than, or broader than, a given heading.

Use of MeSH by catalogers is explained in "Using Medical Subject Headings (MeSH) in Cataloging."[15] After the tutorial modules that cover main heading concepts and subheadings, there are modules for geographic headings, publication types, names as subjects, and a discussion of deconstructed headings versus heading strings. *Geographic* headings are all found in the *Z* tree. For example, the hierarchy for North Carolina is:

> **Geographic Locations** [Z01]
>> **Americas** [Z01.107]
>>> **North America** [Z01.107.567]
>>>> **United States** [Z107.567.875]
>>>>> **Appalachian Region** [Z107.567.875.075]
>>>>>> **North Carolina** [Z107.567.875.075.475]

Geographic headings are used when a resource is related to a geographic area, *if* the geographic area is important to the subject of the resource. For example, if research is conducted in North Carolina but results are considered widely applicable (i.e., not limited to North Carolina), then **North Carolina** would not be assigned. When terms are used, they are used exactly as found in the MeSH Browser and the most specific applicable term should be used, unless there are more than three specific terms, in which case the next most general term is used. For example, a research study specific to four states in the Appalachian Region (which contains a total of 12 states) should be assigned *Appalachian Region*, whereas a study specific only to North Carolina, Virginia, and West Virginia would be assigned the names of the three states. Topical headings and subheadings may also be used with geographic headings, although there are some restrictions that may be found in the teaching and introductory web pages cited above.

Examples of *publication types* are: *Abstracts, Clinical Trial, Legal Cases*, and *Statistics*. Such terms indicate what a resource type *is* rather than what it is *about*. Publication types are found in the *V* tree. Scope notes provide guidance for their use. At least 20 percent of a resource must be of the particular publication type in order to use the term on a cataloging record; but more than one term may be used for a record, if appropriate. Personal names, corporate names, and uniform titles for works also may be used as subject headings, if they are discussed in the resource being cataloged, but these are not in MeSH. They are taken from the NLM Name Authority File (NAF).

NLM typically records its subject headings in a deconstructed form. Whereas the Library of Congress traditionally records topic, geographic, chronological, and form elements into one long subject string, NLM records each of these in faceted form, each in its own field. However, at the request of their constituent user libraries, they distribute MARC records with the subject headings in a form that matches the traditional LCSH subject string. Computer programs have been written to create the strings. For example, if the following headings are on a record in the NLM catalog:

> **650 12 $a Aged**
>
> **650 12 $a Geriatrics**
>
> **650 22 $a Delivery of Health Care**
>
> **651 _2 $a United States**
>
> **655 _2 $a Directory**

They would appear as follows in MARC 21 distribution:

> **650 12 $a Aged $z United States.**
>
> **650 12 $a Geriatrics $z United States $v Directory.**
>
> **650 22 $a Delivery of Health Care $z United States $v Directory.**[16]

In addition to being used with medical collections, MeSH may also be used in catalogs of general collections. A collection indexed with LCSH may have more specific terms from MeSH applied to its medical and health-related resources.

BISAC Subject Headings List

The list prepared by the Book Industry Study Group (BISG) for subject coding of books is called the *BISAC Subject Headings List*. BISAC stands for *Book Industry Standards and Communications*. Developed mainly for use by bookstores for trade books, BISAC has now become a requirement for ONIX records used in the publishing industry, and some systems will not load a record if it does not contain a BISAC code.[17] (ONIX stands for *ONline Information eXchange* and is a standard format that publishers use to distribute electronic information about their publications.)

BISAC has a top level of 52 major areas, such as Art, Cooking, Gardening, Medical, Religion, and Photography. After choosing one of the 52 broad subjects, the user of the system goes to the second level by looking at the listing under that broad category. At the second level are listed all the possibilities for two, three, or four levels of headings, or alternatively, a reference to the terminology that should be used in place of the term first chosen (e.g., RELIGION / Muslim *see headings under* Islam). Once the heading is chosen (e.g., RELIGION / Islam / History), the code for that selection (i.e., REL037010) is recorded as the BISAC code for the book being prepared for publication. The following example shows an excerpt from the religion section of the BISAC list.[18]

REL000000	RELIGION / General
REL001000	RELIGION / Agnosticism
REL114000	RELIGION / Ancient
REL072000	RELIGION / Antiquities & Archaeology
	RELIGION / Archaeology *see* Antiquities & Archaeology
	. . .
REL036000	RELIGION / Inspirational
REL016000	RELIGION / Institutions & Organizations
REL037000	RELIGION / Islam / General
REL037010	RELIGION / Islam / History
REL041000	RELIGION / Islam / Koran & Sacred Writings
REL037020	RELIGION / Islam / Law
REL037030	RELIGION / Islam / Rituals & Practice
REL037040	RELIGION / Islam / Shi'a
REL090000	RELIGION / Islam / Sufi
REL037050	RELIGION / Islam / Sunni
REL037060	RELIGION / Islam / Theology
REL038000	RELIGION / Jainism
	RELIGION / Jewish Life *see* Judaism / Rituals & Practice
	. . .

The codes begin with a mnemonic three-character alpha segment, which is followed by six numerals. The code has no hierarchical significance. The English-language heading itself is used to reference the subject of the book.

BISAC has a simplicity that is attractive, particularly to small general collections such as public or school libraries. Recognizing this, the managers of the

Dewey Decimal Classification (DDC) have incorporated BISAC mappings into WebDewey 2.0.[19] The BISAC-to-Dewey mappings allow one to search or browse DDC numbers and see, along with the DDC area represented, BISAC headings that fit that number. For example at DDC number 025.04252 (Search Engines) one can see the BISAC heading "COMPUTERS--Web--Search Engines."

In 2007, the Maricopa County Library District in Arizona replaced the DDC class numbers assigned to its non-fiction resources with language-based BISAC headings for the purpose of rearranging its collection—essentially taking a bookstore approach to shelving its non-fiction materials. In a *Library Journal* article from 2010, Barbara Fister states, "Many librarians feel BISAC's relative simplicity and user-friendly language have an advantage over Dewey's complexity . . . . Categories for a book are typically determined by the publisher . . . and are used throughout the distribution chain by companies like Amazon, Baker & Taylor, Barnes & Noble, . . . and others. In many ways, it fuses the functions of subject headings with classification."[20] A few other public libraries have since followed suit.

Thesaurus of Psychological Index Terms

The *Thesaurus of Psychological Index Terms* is used to index the American Psychological Association's (APA) databases, particularly the PsycINFO database, which contains "approximately 3 million citations and summaries dating as far back as the 1600s."[21] The thesaurus contains over 8,200 terms. Although the most recent print version was the 11th edition, published in 2007, updates from as recent as 2012 are posted on the APA website.[22] The online version of the *Thesaurus of Psychological Index Terms* is available only with a subscription to PsycINFO or another APA database through vendors such as EBSCO or Proquest, among others.

Most thesauri have introductory material that explains how to use them. Introductory material from the *Thesaurus of Psychological Index Terms*[23] is available on the APA website. The introduction provides a typical explanation:

> The Relationship Section is the most powerful section of the Thesaurus because it provides all the information about each term, including its definition, hierarchical relationship to other terms, and other data to help you decide whether or not to use the term in your search.
>
> The Thesaurus lists each term alphabetically and cross-references and displays each term with its broader, narrower, and related terms.
>
> PsycINFO periodically updates the indexing vocabulary with new terms. The year of the term's addition in the Thesaurus appears as a four-digit superscript.[24]

The introduction then goes on to explain several features that may be unfamiliar. They include:

- **Subject codes** (SC): five digit identifiers associated with a term

- **Posting notes** (PN): the number of times the term has been used in indexing records in the PsycINFO database
- **History notes** (HN): explanations of how the term has evolved and the periods associated with previous terms
- **Scope notes** (SN): definitions and comparisons to other terms

Term relationships are then explained, and include the familiar USE and UF indicators. The thesaurus, however, shortens the relationship indicators for broader, narrower, and related terms to the letters *B, N,* and *R.*

It can be seen that such designations of terms and term relationships influenced the usages now found in LCSH. What follows is an example of an entry from the print version of this thesaurus:

Communication Skills[1973]

PN	4117	**SC**	10540

SN   Individual ability or competency in any type of communication. Limited to human populations.

    UF   Communicative Competence

    B   Ability [1967]

    N   Language Proficiency [1988]

           Rhetoric [1991]

           Writing Skills [1985]

    R ↓ Communication [1967]

           Communication Barriers [2006]

      ↓ Communication Disorders [1982]

           Communication Skills Training [1982]

           Pragmatics [1985]

           Social Cognition [1994]

      ↓ Verbal Communication [1967]

Use of a down arrow in front of any narrower or related term indicates that that term has narrower terms itself.

Entries found in online versions of this thesaurus appear somewhat differently than entries in the print edition. In the online versions, headings are not always presented in boldface type, added hyperlinks allow searchers to navigate the vocabulary efficiently, and the PNs and SCs are not always present. Also, in some of the online versions, the relationship indicators are replaced by fully written phrases (e.g., *Broader Terms* instead of *B*), the superscript four-digit year appearing after the heading is a separate element labeled *Year Term Introduced*, and the indication that a term has narrower terms itself is a plus sign (+) instead of a down arrow. An illustration of how the term *Communication Skills* may be presented in an online version of the thesaurus follows:

Communication Skills

Year Term Introduced	1973
Scope Note	Individual ability or competency in any type of communication. Limited to human populations.
Broader Terms	Ability
Narrow Terms	Language Proficiency
	Rhetoric
	Writing Skills
Related Terms	Communication +
	Communication Barriers
	Communication Disorders +
	Communication Skills Training
	Pragmatics
	Social Cognition
	Verbal Communication +
Used For	Communicative Competence

Thesaurus of ERIC Descriptors

The *Thesaurus of ERIC Descriptors* is the controlled vocabulary used to index the Education Resources Information Center's (ERIC) digital library of educational research and other education-related materials (e.g., tests, lesson plans, guides, reports, proceedings). The database contains approximately 1.5 million citations from 1966 to the present; its thesaurus contains nearly 12,000 terms: approximately 4,500 descriptors, 7,000 synonyms, and 150 former descriptors. The database, with its thesaurus fully integrated into the retrieval tool, is available on the web at no cost.[25] A print version of the 14th edition of the thesaurus was last published in 2001.[26] At the time of this writing, the online thesaurus had been last updated in May 2015. The thesaurus, encoded in an XML format, is also available to download for local use.[27]

The *Thesaurus of ERIC Descriptors* uses the standardized abbreviations for the relationships that were also adopted by LCSH: UF—*Used for*; NT—*Narrower term*; BT—*Broader term*; RT—*Related term*. The term *USE* is the mandatory reciprocal of UF, putting a *non-postable term* (i.e., unauthorized synonym) into place. Unlike LCSH, however, SN precedes a *scope note*, which is a note that discusses the usage or meaning of a term. Some terms may also have parenthetical qualifiers to help distinguish them from identical terms with different usages (i.e., homograph control).

Under *postable terms* (i.e., authorized descriptors) other kinds of information are also given. An *add date* (i.e., date of first entry) is included. Search strategies for materials entered into the database prior to that time should in most instances use different terminology. For some concepts, a prior term is listed among the UFs; a date range next to a USE or UF reference indicates that it was previously a postable term. A posting count (the number of citations available when the current edition of the print version of the *ERIC Thesaurus* was published) is given for the number of times the term has been used as a descriptor or identifier in *Current Index to Journals in Education* (*CIJE*) and *Resources in Education* (*RIE*). A Group Code (GC) number is given to assist the user in identifying other descriptors that are conceptually related to the term.

A few examples from the *ERIC Thesaurus* entries follow:

Drill Presses

USE Machine Tools

Drills (Practice)   *MAR. 1980*

Postings: 675   GC: 310

SN   Repetition of tasks or procedures

NT   Pattern Drills (Language)

BT   Teaching Methods

RT   Memorization

Rote Learning

Study

Drinking   *MAY 1974*

Postings: 2,154   GC: 210

SN   Consumption of alcoholic beverages

UF   Alcohol Consumption

Alcohol Use

Social Drinking

NT   Alcohol Abuse

BT   Behavior

RT   Alcohol Education

Alcoholic Beverages

Drug Use

Health Behavior

Health Education

Recreational Activities

Drinking Drivers

USE Driving While Intoxicated

The print version contains more than just the alphabetical display of thesaurus terms; it also contains a rotated display, a two-way hierarchical term display, and a descriptor group display.[28]

Again, the online version, an example of which is shown below, is different in structure and appearance.[29]

Drinking

Scope note: Consumption of alcoholic beverages

Category: Health and Safety

Search collection using this descriptor

Broader Terms	**Related Terms**
Behavior	Alcohol Education
	Drug Use
Narrower Terms	Health Behavior
Alcohol Abuse	Health Education
	Recreational Activities

Use this term instead of

Alcohol Consumption

Alcohol Use

Alcoholic Beverages (2004)

Drinking Drivers (2004)

Driving While Intoxicated (2004)

Drunk Driving (2004)

Social Drinking

Some of the differences are related to changes in the terms that have occurred between 2001 and 2015 (e.g., four authorized terms are no longer in use, including **Driving While Intoxicated** and **Alcoholic Beverages**). Other changes are due to formatting choices made for the online environment. Interestingly, the postings note, date added, and the group code are not displayed at all. The various relationship indicators have been converted to spelled-out labels.

Inspec Thesaurus

A more complex example comes from the *Inspec Thesaurus* of the Institution of Engineering and Technology (IET).[30] The *Inspec Thesaurus* is used to index IET's Inspec database. "The Inspec database contains 15 million bibliographic and indexed records to physics and engineering global research literature."[31] The 2012 print edition of the *Inspec Thesaurus* contains "18,755 terms of which 9,722 terms are preferred terms . . . [and] 9,033 terms are lead-ins,"[32] related to physics, electrical engineering, electronics, communications, information technology, and allied disciplines. The full *Inspec Thesaurus* is available through subscription to the Inspec database, but is also available in PDF and XML formats for downloads.[33] (INSPEC was once an acronym for Information Services for the Physics and Engineering Communities, but has now evolved into the name *Inspec*.) The print version uses abbreviations as shown in Table 15.1.

TABLE 15.1 Abbreviations Used in the *Inspec Thesaurus*.

Indicator	Meaning	Definition
UF	*Used for*	indicates a lead-in term from which a reference is made
NT	*Narrower Term(s)*	indicates one or more specific terms, one level lower in the hierarchy
BT	*Broader Term(s)*	indicates one or more general terms, one level higher in the hierarchy
TT	*Top Term(s)*	indicates the most general term(s) in the hierarchy
RT	*Related Term(s)*	indicates conceptual relationships between terms, not related hierarchically
CC	*Classification Code(s)*	one or more *Inspec* classification codes used to indicate subjects related to that represented by the thesaurus term
DI	*Date of Input*	indicates the date the term was first used in the thesaurus
PT	*Prior Term(s)*	indicates terms used for the concept before establishment of the current preferred term

The following is a brief excerpt from the *Inspec Thesaurus*, in which a somewhat unusual approach to capitalization is illustrated.[34]

dynamic nuclear polarisation
UF	dynamic nuclear polarization
	solid effect
BT	magnetic double resonance
TT	resonance
NT	CIDNP
	Overhauser effect
RT	nuclear polarisation
CC	A0758
	A3335D
	A7670E
DI	January 1977
PT	magnetic double resonance

dynamic nuclear polarization
USE	dynamic nuclear polarisation
DI	January 1979

The online display of terms, again, depends on the formatting used in the database being searched. Online, the abbreviations may not be used and the categories are often in a different order.

Art & Architecture Thesaurus (AAT)

The *Art & Architecture Thesaurus* (AAT) is a controlled vocabulary designed to index "art, architecture, decorative arts, material culture, and archival materials. The target audience includes museums, libraries, visual resource collections, archives, conservation projects, cataloging projects, and bibliographic projects."[35] AAT currently contains over 353,000 terms and other information about concepts. It was first created in the late 1970s, but the vocabulary began to flourish greatly in the 1980s and 1990s—a development that continues through today. Although print editions were published in 1990 and 1994, the *Art & Architecture Thesaurus* (AAT) is now available online at no cost, in a searchable database hosted at the Getty Research Institute's vocabulary website. The database of terms is refreshed every fortnight. The raw data files may also be leased for use and are currently available in XML and relational tables, which are released in July annually.[36]

AAT is arranged in eight facets or categories: Associated Concepts, Physical Attributes, Styles and Periods, Agents, Activities, Materials, Objects, and Brand Names. Each facet is subdivided into sub-facets, called *hierarchies*. In the hierarchies, *descriptors* (representing the key concepts) are displayed to show their broader term/narrower term relationships. Also present are *guide terms* (i.e., placeholders in angle brackets) that create logical structures within the hierarchies. The AAT has strict rules for the establishment of hierarchical relationships and for related terms, which it calls *associative relationships*. It has attempted to resolve much of the subjectivity that has plagued other thesauri. In Figure 15.4, an example from the furnishings hierarchy provides an overview of the concept *outdoor furniture* as well as the guide terms helping to structure the hierarchy (e.g., <outdoor furniture by general type>).[37]

At any concept in the hierarchy, one can look at the concept record to see synonyms and spelling variants listed simply as terms (one or more of which may be preferred), related concepts, documentation of the sources used, and a scope note. A partial record for *outdoor furniture* is shown in Figure 15.5. In 2014, AAT began offering their vocabulary as linked open data (LOD). The terms can be downloaded in the following LOD formats: RDF, N3/Turtle, JSON, and N-Triples. For additional information on linked data, see chapter 22 of this text.

COORDINATE INDEXING

The post-World War II information explosion dramatized the values of good indexing. Older methods that had gone into eclipse were revived and improved. New theories sprang up to support other techniques. A major departure from the relatively simple hierarchical use of subordinate divisions and inverted modifiers in traditional subject heading lists was the idea

```
⚒  Top of the AAT hierarchies
⚒  .... Objects Facet
⚒  ........ Furnishings and Equipment (Hierarchy Name)
⚒  ............ Furnishings (Hierarchy Name)
⚒  ................ furnishings (artifacts)
⚒  ................... <furnishings by form or function>
⚒  ....................... furniture
⚒  ........................... <furniture by location or context>
   ............................... outdoor furniture
⚒  ................................... <outdoor furniture by general type>
   ...................................... garden furniture
   ...................................... patio furniture
   ...................................... porch furniture
⚒  ................................... <outdoor furniture by specific type>
   ...................................... Adirondack chairs [N]
   ...................................... deck chairs [N]
   ...................................... gliders (furniture) [N]
   ...................................... picnic benches [N]
   ...................................... picnic tables [N]
   ...................................... Westport chairs [N]
```

FIGURE 15.4 Hierarchical View of a Concept in *Art & Architecture Thesaurus* Online. (Courtesy J. Paul Getty Trust)

of post-coordinate searching, in which the searcher could play a more active role. A coordinate index consists of a list of subject terms in a standard format. Each term is independent of all others, except for cross references, and is designed to retrieve all documents for which it is specifically relevant. A user can stop at the single-term level of search if he or she is satisfied with the results. True post-coordinate searching, however, moves on to a second level. Taking two or more terms that together delimit a still more specific search topic, and requesting the records indexed with both or all of them, the searcher retrieves only those items that have been indexed under all the chosen terms.

Suppose the searcher is looking for material on the use of solar energy for drying grain. The index might offer the terms **Solar energy**, **Heat engines**, and **Grain**. Perhaps five document citations emerge because those five documents are indexed with all three terms. In a traditional printed subject catalog, this type of post-coordinate searching is awkward and difficult. The underlying assumption is that the list itself is pre-coordinate. That is, the assimilation and matching of concepts has already been done by the cataloger and is implicit in the terminology of the list. For example, *LCSH* offers the subject headings **Solar energy in agriculture** and **Grain—Drying** as subject identifiers for the above items. In a printed catalog, there would be no way of matching the two concepts to specify the available items except by comparing subject entries under each heading or examining full

---

ID: 300165810   **Record Type**: concept

outdoor furniture (<furniture by location or context>, furniture, ... Furnishings and Equipment (Hierarchy Name))

Note: Term generally applied to a great variety of furniture specially designed for use outdoors.

Terms:

 outdoor furniture (preferred,C,U,LC,English-P,D,U,PN)
 furniture, outdoor (C,U,English,UF,U,N)
 戶外家具 (C,U,Chinese (traditional)-P,D,U,U)
 hù wài jiā jù (C,U,Chinese (transliterated Hanyu Pinyin)-P,UF,U,U)
 hu wai jia ju (C,U,Chinese (transliterated Pinyin without tones)-P,UF,U,U)
 hu wai chia chü (C,U,Chinese (transliterated Wade-Giles)-P,UF,U,U)
 buitenhuismeubilair (C,U,Dutch-P,D,U,U)
 tuinmeubilair (C,U,Dutch,UF,U,U)
 mobiliario para jardín (C,U,Spanish-P,D,U,SN)
 mueble de jardín (C,U,Spanish,AD,U,SN)
 mobiliario del jardín (C,U,Spanish,UF,U,SN)
 mueble para jardín (C,U,Spanish,UF,U,SN)

Facet/Hierarchy Code: V.TC

Hierarchical Position:

⚲ Objects Facet
⚲ .... Furnishings and Equipment (Hierarchy Name) (G)
⚲ .... Furnishings (Hierarchy Name) (G)
⚲ .... furnishings (artifacts) (G)
⚲ .... <furnishings by form or function> (G)
⚲ .... furniture (G)
⚲ .... <furniture by location or context> (G)
⚲ .... outdoor furniture (G)

Additional Notes:
. . .
Sources and Contributor:
. . .
Subject:
. . .
Note:
. . .

FIGURE 15.5 Partial Record from the *Art & Architecture Thesaurus Online*. (Courtesy J. Paul Getty Trust)

bibliographic records to find those on which both headings were traced. (It should be noted that with the availability of more sophisticated search methods that exist in the online catalog, this particular difficulty was, to a certain extent, eradicated—at least for those who can formulate a more complex search string.)

In post-coordinate indexing, the coordination of terms is the responsibility of the searcher, rather than of the subject cataloger. The terms are usually single nouns, and the specific documents may be identified with accession numbers rather than hierarchical classification or call numbers. In 1953 Mortimer Taube introduced the *Uniterm Index*—called by that name to emphasize its post-coordinate use of single terms as opposed to composite headings.[38] It was primarily a manual system, using cards with headings displayed at the top and 10 columns in which document accession numbers could be entered according to the number's final digit. For example, documents 56A, 306, 96, 1176, and 1006 might all be listed in column 6 of each of the three cards bearing the Uniterms: **Solar energy**, **Heat engines**, and **Grain**. The technique, known as terminal digit posting, has been most successful in its computerized applications, where some of the tediousness and error-proneness of manual listing is forestalled.

To overcome the disadvantages of a visual search, other modes of post-coordinate indexing were soon developed. Mechanical scanning devices were based on the fact that cards could be precisely gridded for punched holes to replace the columns of written or printed numbers. Two or more of these punched cards (e.g., the three carrying the headings **Solar energy**, **Heat engines**, and **Grain**) could be laid together and held up to the light, or otherwise probed, to extract the reference numbers that they indexed in common. Several brands of these cards were marketed, variously called *optical coincidence cards*, *peek-a-boo cards*, or *feature cards*.

A newer form of coordinate indexing is that created by keyword access in online catalogs and other databases. This is described by Marcia J. Bates (emphasis in the original):

> In fact, *online search capabilities themselves constitute a form of indexing.* Subject access to online catalogs is thus a combination of original indexing and what we might call "search capabilities indexing." . . . Typical online search capabilities are keyword searching, Boolean searching, truncation, and multi-index searching (that is, combining query terms from more than one index, e.g., "FIND TITLE Grapes AND FIND AUTHOR Steinbeck") . . . .When an online catalog simply possesses the capability of being searched by title keyword, in effect a whole new index is added to the catalog, with every title word an index term, even though the whole index is not seen printed out.[39]

Typically, online catalogs with keyword access allow the user to input several search terms to be searched at once with an implicit Boolean *AND* in operation. That is, a keyword search may be *solar energy grain*, which the system interprets to mean "Find bibliographic records that have the words *solar* AND *energy* AND *grain*." While this method can yield false drops (e.g., "Electrical energy characterization of grain boundaries in gallium arsenide and their relationship to solar cell performance"), it can also yield a number of useful retrievals in much less time than that needed for manual indexing. It cannot be a complete substitute for manual indexing, however, because keyword vocabulary is not controlled (i.e., no connections are made between synonyms, variant word forms, related terms, etc.), not all titles contain subject-content words, and authors writing on the same concepts use different words to express those concepts.

The commands used to retrieve information from databases nearly all make use of the Boolean logic operators *and*, *or*, and *not*. With these instructions, search commands that are highly sophisticated and very powerful examples of post-coordinate searching can be executed. For example, someone using the ERIC database might want to examine material on the consumption of alcohol in clubs, at social gatherings, and the like, but not have to wade through all those discussing related problems of health. Using the *ERIC Thesaurus*, he or she could construct the search command "(Drinking *or* Alcoholic Beverages) *and* ((Behavior *or* Recreational Activities) *not* (Health *or* Health Education))." Since the commands within parentheses are executed first, all documents indexed under the following rubrics would be retrieved:

> **Drinking *and* Behavior *but not* Health**
>
> **Drinking *and* Behavior *but not* Health Education**
>
> **Drinking *and* Recreational Activities *but not* Health**
>
> **Drinking *and* Recreational Activities *but not* Health Education**
>
> **Alcoholic Beverages *and* Behavior *but not* Health**
>
> **Alcoholic Beverages *and* Behavior *but not* Health Education**
>
> **Alcoholic Beverages *and* Recreational Activities *but not* Health**
>
> **Alcoholic Beverages *and* Recreational Activities *but not* Health Education**

AUTOMATIC INDEXING METHODS

Indexers, like other human beings, are fallible, often are inconsistent, are subject to extraneous influences on their work, operate at a slow pace, and are therefore the most expensive component of an indexing operation. The idea of replacing human indexers by feeding part or all of a text into a machine that would assign index terms automatically, impartially, and with unfailing consistency and accuracy arose, therefore, quite early in the computer age. Success has, however, largely eluded the best efforts of many investigators and inventors.

KWIC and KWOC Indexing

The earliest automatic indexing method relying on the power of computers to perform repetitive tasks at high speed was invented by Hans Peter Luhn, an IBM engineer, who in 1958 produced what became known as *KWIC* (Key Word In Context) indexing. Luhn reported his system in 1960.[40] On the assumption that titles of scientific and technical articles generally include words indicating the most significant concepts dealt with, he wrote a program that printed strings of title words, each word appearing once in alphabetical order in the center of a page, with all other words to the left or right of the center word printed in the order in which they appeared in the title; when the right-hand margin was reached, the rest of the title (if any) was wrapped around to the left-hand margin and continued inward. A user had only to scan the left-justified middle column for a desired keyword and could, when the word was found, read the rest of the title in context. The method worked indeed fully automatically (i.e., without any human intervention other than the data entry) and resulted in a quickly and inexpensively produced display of potentially sought terms. Most KWIC programs also employ so-called stop lists to

---

Titles of resources to be indexed:
- *Cataloging and Classification: A Review of the Literature*
- *Introduction to Cataloging and Classification*
- *A Practicum in Cataloging and Classification*
- *The Use of the Internet for Cataloging and Classification*

KWIC (Key Word In Context) Index

	Cataloging	and Classification: A Review of the Literature
Introduction to	**Cataloging**	and Classification
A Practicum in	**Cataloging**	and Classification
The Use of the Internet for	**Cataloging**	and Classification
Cataloging and	**Classification**	A Review of the Literature
Introduction to Cataloging and	**Classification**	
A Practicum in Cataloging and	**Classification**	
The Use of the Internet for Cataloging and	**Classification**	
The Use of the	**Internet**	for Cataloging and Classification
	Introduction	to Cataloging and Classification

...

KWOC (Key Word Out of Context) Index

Cataloging	Cataloging and Classification: A Review of the Literature
Cataloging	Introduction to Cataloging and Classification
Cataloging	A Practicum in Cataloging and Classification
Cataloging	The Use of the Internet for Cataloging and Classification
Classification	Cataloging and Classification: A Review of the Literature
Classification	Introduction to Cataloging and Classification
Classification	A Practicum in Cataloging and Classification
Classification	The Use of the Internet for Cataloging and Classification
Internet	The Use of the Internet for Cataloging and Classification
Introduction	Introduction to Cataloging and Classification

...

KWAC (Key Word And Context) Index

Cataloging and Classification: A Review of the Literature
Cataloging and Classification. Introduction to
Cataloging and Classification. A Practicum in
Cataloging and Classification. The Use of the Internet for
Classification: A Review of the Literature. Cataloging and
Classification. Introduction to Cataloging and
Classification. A Practicum in Cataloging and
Classification. The Use of the Internet for Cataloging and
Internet for Cataloging and Classification. The Use of the
Introduction to Cataloging and Classification

...

FIGURE 15.6 An Illustration of KWIC, KWOC, and KWAC Indexes.

eliminate common words such as articles, prepositions, and conjunctions from the middle column where they presumably would not be sought. This earlier and rather crude form of automatic indexing has, ironically, remained the only one that has proven itself to be practical and is still being used.

An adaptation of the KWIC method, known as *KWOC* (Key Word Out of Context), simply prints the sought words in the left-hand margin instead of in the middle of the page, the rest of the title (or the entire title, including the keyword itself) being printed to the right or beneath the keyword. Another adaptation, known as *KWAC* (Key Word And Context), combines the two other approaches providing the keyword in the left-hand margin, but also still placed in context. All three types are illustrated in Figure 15.6.

KWIC, KWOC, and KWAC indexing have, however, some severe limitations. For example, only words that appear in titles can be sought, while the article itself may deal with many other concepts not mentioned in the title. Since there is absolutely no vocabulary control (other than the elimination of stop-list words), synonymous terms are not available to users as potential access points for searching (for example, there are no references, say, from **Agriculture** to a related term such as **Farming**, or between the synonyms **Sodium Chloride** and **Salt**). Also, many titles are not representative of the subject dealt with or are purposely written to catch the attention of prospective readers without indicating the subject at all, for example, "On the Care and Construction of White Elephants" (which is about cataloging) or "The Money-eating Machines" (on computer management).

In addition, lengthy KWIC indexes were tiresome to scan, especially when they were printed in small type and in all capitals, as was often the case. Thus, contrary to the pun intended by the acronym KWIC, such indexes were neither quick for the user nor really indexes to concepts dealt with in texts but rather were listings of words that authors happened to put into titles. On the other hand, after the introduction of KWIC indexes, titles of scientific and technical articles became more indicative of their contents because authors and editors became aware of the fact that inexpressive titles would be overlooked in KWIC and similar indexing techniques.[41] In the social sciences and humanities, however, the custom of authors giving catchy and uninformative titles to their papers continues unabated.

Extraction of Words

KWIC indexing was only the first of the so-called derivative indexing methods, all of which are based on the principle of extracting words from machine-readable text—a title, an abstract, or the full text of a document. Automatic extraction of words is generally coupled with *truncation* in searching, that is, the possibility of searching for a word stem without regard to its prefixes or suffixes, in order to retrieve a maximum of potentially useful occurrences of that word. Thus, a physicist looking for the presence of the concept *pressure* may search for *PRESS* (the asterisks indicating that prefixes and suffixes are also to be searched), which may return the following results:

COM   PRESS
COM   PRESSION

IM   PRESSION

SUP   PRESSION

PRESS

PRESSER

PRESSES

PRESSURE

PRESSURIZE

PRESSURIZATION

PRESSWORK

While truncation (or stemming) does increase recall, it lowers precision because it may result in unwanted and irrelevant items being retrieved (the latter known as *false drops*). At least two phenomena dictate this. First, homonyms cannot be detected by mere extraction methods—that is, in the example just cited, IMPRESSION, SUPPRESSION, and PRESSWORK do not pertain to *pressure* in the physical sense, while PRESS may pertain both to mechanical equipment and to newspapers, the latter being of no research interest to a physicist. Second, the elimination of common words by a stop list may also result in false drops whenever relationships are of importance; for example, a Boolean search for TEACHERS *and* STUDENTS *and* EVALUATION will retrieve both teachers' evaluation of students and students' evaluation of teachers, because the elimination of the crucial words *of* and *by* makes it impossible to know who does what for whom.

For a time it was tried to correct the lack of indicators of relationships in derivative indexing by so-called *links* and *roles*, the former making explicit which words were linked to each other in a relationship, while the latter indicated functions (e.g., acting *as* or *for* something). These devices led indeed to higher precision, but they had to be assigned at the input stage by human beings. As that greatly diminished any gains made by automatic extraction of terms, the method was soon abandoned.

Term Frequency and Linguistic Methods

On the assumption that terms (other than common words) to be indexed are those occurring either very frequently in a text (and therefore indicating concepts dealt with) or very seldom (indicating a topic mentioned expressly only once or twice in the title or first paragraph but then being referred to by *it* or *this* and the like), methods were designed to perform automatic indexing on the basis of frequency of occurrence and co-occurrence of terms, using probabilistic models. Some investigators tried to couple such methods of determining how often a term is used (term frequency methods) with term weighting—that is, assigning different degrees of importance to terms on the basis of what terms are used in a search request or on the basis of where and how terms appear (e.g., in the title, in an abstract, or in the first or last paragraph of a text, and whether they are italicized or capitalized), all of which can to some extent be determined automatically.

Another approach is by syntactic and semantic analysis. Syntactic analysis is concerned with the automatic recognition of significant word order in a phrase or sentence and with inflections, prefixes, and suffixes that indicate grammatical relationships, while the semantic analysis approach seeks to analyze noun phrases automatically with the aid of stored dictionaries and other linguistic aids. The two methods are often used in conjunction. Research in the field of Natural Language Processing (NLP) has proliferated in recent years, and progress has been made; although the dream of information retrieval systems that can respond to a user's need through use only of natural language queries in full text databases analyzed only by computer has not been realized.

Searching the full text of websites by search engines such as Google makes use of linguistic methods when returning responses such as "Did you really mean . . . ?" when a misspelled word has been used in a search. Such search engines do not yet have sophisticated lexical tools that pull together synonyms, suggest hierarchical relationships, or distinguish among several meanings for the same word.

Ontologies

Linguistic or lexical ontologies are used in NLP to assist in the analysis of natural language text. Ontologies in the field of artificial intelligence are formal representations of what, to a human, is common sense. Linguistic ontologies must formalize the reality of using language for communication, and include the realities of grammar, semantics, and syntax. Linguistic ontologies are similar to subject heading lists and thesauri in that they organize words into sets of synonyms, and then use relationships like broader, narrower, and related terms to organize the synonym sets. They are unlike subject lists and thesauri in their analysis of categories such as nouns, verbs, adjectives, and adverbs. They also do not necessarily designate preferred terms in the synonym sets.

Not all ontologies are linguistic ontologies. Some have strong underpinnings of categorization or classification. Others emphasize vocabulary and definitions. Most are designed to represent the entities of particular areas of knowledge. The OWL Web Ontology Language defines ontology as that which "defines the terms used to describe and represent an area of knowledge." The OWL document further states, "Ontologies include computer-usable definitions of basic concepts in the domain and the relationships among them."[42] The W3C states:

> On the Semantic Web, vocabularies define the concepts and relationships (also referred to as "terms") used to describe and represent an area of concern. Vocabularies are used to classify the terms that can be used in a particular application, characterize possible relationships, and define possible constraints on using those terms. In practice, vocabularies can be very complex (with several thousands of terms) or very simple (describing one or two concepts only). There is no clear division between what is referred to as "vocabularies" and "ontologies". The trend is to use the word "ontology" for more complex, and possibly quite formal collection of terms, whereas "vocabulary" is used when such strict formalism is not necessarily used or only in a very loose sense. Vocabularies are the basic building blocks for inference techniques on the Semantic Web.[43]

The vision for the Semantic Web requires that computers and humans share knowledge. Ontologies provide the definitions of basic concepts, which allow such sharing of meaning and thus are the building blocks of the Semantic Web. For brief overviews of NLP, ontologies, and the Semantic Web readers are referred to *The Organization of Information* by Arlene G. Taylor and Daniel N. Joudrey.[44] More detailed information on the Semantic Web and ontologies can be found in the technical documentation provided by the World Wide Web Consortium (W3C).[45]

Computer-Aided Indexing

As indicated above, except for KWIC, KWOC, and KWAC indexing, none of the other automatic indexing methods has been applied on a large scale. For the time being, the large access services and databases still use human indexers and abstractors, even though their work is far from perfect or consistent, because none of the methods of automatic indexing invented so far has shown itself to be able to compete in terms of indexing quality or economic viability. Focus in research is no longer on automatic indexing methods, but computers, as discussed above, are increasingly aiding information retrieval in various other ways. In addition, computers are now widely used by indexers in computer-aided indexing, relying on stored dictionaries of synonyms and homonyms, lists of authors' names for automatic verification, lists of trade names and names of chemical compounds, plants and animals, and so forth. They are also used to take the drudgery out of indexing by automatically arranging entries in alphabetical order or subordinating subheadings and cross references in exact sequence under a heading, and by performing many other functions that previously had to be done manually and therefore were quite expensive and often subject to errors.

SWITCHING LANGUAGES

The preceding discussion has been a cursory examination of a number of systems available to provide subject access in addition to library subject cataloging activities. Most are self-contained, providing their own categories and terminology, with syntactical rules designed to express complex or multi-faceted concepts. Each exhibits both strengths and weaknesses. Not one has yet proved sufficient to meet all needs, nor is one demonstrably better than all others in every situation.

The information explosion, together with rapid developments in automation, has made inter-communication among subject disciplines, libraries, and nations both a possibility and a growing necessity. Several possible solutions to this problem have been proposed. One has been a movement toward switching languages. A *switching language* has been defined as a "mediating language used to establish equivalencies among various indexing languages."[46] It is "the idea that a user could use the same indexing language to search in information systems that are indexed with different indexing languages."[47] With a multilateral translation program, materials already indexed would be more readily available, while libraries and information centers could avoid future duplication by joining systems of shared cataloging without discarding or revamping their own catalogs and indexes.

A number of attempts, such as umbrella classifications, have been tried and failed. A somewhat different approach was that of the BRS/TERM database, which was created to enhance online searching.[48] The vocabularies of six thesauri were organized into concept records that included hierarchical information and free-text searching suggestions. This kind of approach has an inherent linguistic interest that has led researchers to reexamine the structure and properties of indexing languages.

Another such project is the Unified Medical Language System (UMLS).[49] Started in 1986 by the National Library of Medicine, the UMLS, through the development of software and vocabulary control tools, improves the ability of health professionals and researchers to retrieve biomedical information from a variety of sources. Promoting interoperability is crucial, because relevant health and biomedical information is scattered across many databases that use very different controlled vocabularies and/or classifications. The UMLS comprises three knowledge sources: the Metathesaurus, the SPECIALIST lexicon, and a semantic network. The Metathesaurus brings together in a uniform format more than 100 different vocabularies in multiple languages and links different terminology used for the same concepts. It does not attempt to make judgments about the best terminology to use—the usages in the source vocabularies are preserved; but it does establish new relationships among terms from different vocabularies. The SPECIALIST lexicon consists of NLP tools, and the semantic network contains a set of broad subject categories and the semantic relationships that exist among them.[50] Projects in specialized subject areas like the one covered by the UMLS show that technological solutions to difficult lexical problems can be found, but generally only with a great deal of time, effort, financial support, technological sophistication, and human involvement.

CONCLUSION

A number of approaches for providing access to information resources by their subject matter have been discussed in this chapter. Subject headings have traditionally been used in library catalogs, but indexes that provide access to journal articles, patents, and documents being published on the Internet have been making use of thesauri specific to specialized subject areas, and more recently have used ontologies and various automatic indexing techniques. Given the explosion of information and its availability, research into and development of new ways to provide subject access quickly must continue.

NOTES

1. John Rothman, "Index, Indexer, Indexing," in *Encyclopedia of Library and Information Science*, Vol. 11 (New York: Marcel Dekker, 1974), 289.

2. International Organization for Standardization, *Documentation: Guidelines for the Establishment and Development of Monolingual Thesauri*, 2nd ed. ISO 2788 (Geneva: ISO, 1986, first edition published in 1974); British Standards Institution, *British Standard Guide to Establishment and Development of Monolingual Thesauri*, BS 5723 [Rev. ed.] (London: BSI, 1987); American National Standards Institute, *American National Standard Guidelines for Thesaurus Structure, Construction, and Use*, ANSI Z39.19-1980 (New York: ANSI, 1980).

3. National Information Standards Organization, *Guidelines for the Construction, Format, and Management of Monolingual Controlled Vocabularies*, ANSI/NISO Z39.19-2005 (R2010) (Bethesda, Md.: NISO Press, 2010).

4. Mary Dykstra, "LC Subject Headings Disguised as a Thesaurus," *Library Journal* 113 (March 1, 1988): 42-46.

5. Ibid., 43.

6. National Library of Medicine, "Fact Sheet: Medical Subject Headings (MeSH)," accessed July 16, 2015, http://www.nlm.nih.gov/pugs/factsheets/mesh.html.

7. National Library of Medicine, "What Are Supplementary Concept Records?" accessed July 16, 2015, http://www.nlm.nih.gov/bsd/disted/drugs/scrs.html.

8. National Library of Medicine, "Fact Sheet."

9. National Library of Medicine, "MeSH Browser (2015 MeSH)," http://www.nlm.nih.gov/mesh/2015/mesh_browser/MBrowser.html

10. National Library of Medicine, "Introduction to MeSH—2015," http://www.nlm.nih.gov/mesh/introduction.html.

11. National Library of Medicine, "Concept Structure in MeSH," accessed July 16, 2015, http://www.nlm.nih.gov/mesh/concept_structure.html.

12. National Library of Medicine, "XML MeSH Data Elements," accessed July 16, 2015, http://www.nlm.nih.gov/mesh/xml_data_elements.html.

13. Ibid.

14. National Library of Medicine, "MeSH Tree Structures," accessed July 16, 2015, http://www.nlm.nih.gov/mesh/intro_trees.html.

15. National Library of Medicine, "Using Medical Subject Headings (MeSH) in Cataloging," last reviewed 23 June 2015, http://www.nlm.nih.gov/tsd/cataloging/trainingcourses/mesh/intro_010.html.

16. National Library of Medicine, "Module 8—Deconstructed Headings vs. Subject Strings," accessed July 16, 2015, http://www.nlm.nih.gov/tsd/cataloging/trainingcourses/mesh/mod8_070.html.

17. National Book Network, "Frequently Asked Questions: What Is a BISAC Code?" accessed August 25, 2014, http://www.nbnbooks.com/about/faq.shtml?answer8=T.

18. Book Industry Study Group, "Complete BISAC Subject Headings, 2014 Edition," https://www.bisg.org/complete-bisac-subject-headings-2014-edition.

19. OCLC, Dewey Services, "WebDewey," accessed September 4, 2014, https://www.oclc.org/dewey/features.en.html.

20. Barbara Fister, "The Dewey Dilemma," *Library Journal*, October 1, 2009, http://lj.libraryjournal.com/2010/05/public-services/the-dewey-dilemma/.

21. "American Psychological Association (APA) Online Resources," APA, accessed June 5, 2015, http://www.ebscohost.com/promoMaterials/APA_Online_Resources_Flyer.pdf.

22. "Thesaurus of Psychological Index Terms," American Psychological Association, accessed June 5, 2015, http://www.apa.org/pubs/databases/training/thesaurus.aspx.

23. *Thesaurus of Psychological Index Terms*, 11th ed. (Washington, D.C.: American Psychological Association, 2007). A 2012 update is available.

24. "Introductory Material from the Thesaurus of Psychological Index Terms," American Psychological Association, accessed June 5, 2015, http://www.apa .org/pubs/databases/training/thesaurus-intro.aspx.

25. "ERIC," Institute of Education Sciences, accessed July 16, 2015, http://eric. ed.gov/.

26. *Thesaurus of ERIC Descriptors*, 14th ed. (Phoenix, Ariz.: Oryx Press, 2001).

27. "Downloads," ERIC, accessed July 16, 2015, http://eric.ed.gov/?download.

28. *Thesaurus of ERIC Descriptors*, xxx-xxxi.

29. Online version of the ERIC thesaurus, accessed June 5, 2015, http://eric .ed.gov/.

30. *Inspec Thesaurus*, 2012 [ed.] (London: Institution of Engineering and Technology, 2012).

31. "About Inspec," IET, accessed July 17, 2015, http://www.theiet.org/resources/ inspec/about/index.cfm.

32. "Inspec Thesaurus," IET, accessed July 17, 2015, http://www.theiet.org/ resources/inspec/about/records/ithesaurus.cfm.

33. Ibid.

34. *Inspec Thesaurus*, 2012 [ed.] (London: Institution of Engineering and Technology, 2012).

35. "About the AAT," The Getty Research Institute, accessed June 6, 2015, http:// www.getty.edu/research/tools/vocabularies/aat/about.html.

36. "Obtain the Getty Vocabularies," The Getty Research Institute, accessed June 7, 2015, https://www.getty.edu/research/tools/vocabularies/obtain/index.html.

37. *Art & Architecture Thesaurus Online*, accessed June 6, 2015, http://www .getty.edu/research/tools/vocabularies/aat/index.html.

38. Mortimer Taube and Associates, *Studies in Coordinate Indexing* (Washington, D.C.: Documentation, Inc., 1953).

39. Marcia J. Bates, "Rethinking Subject Cataloging in the Online Environment," *Library Resources & Technical Services* 33, no. 4 (October 1989): 401.

40. Hans Peter Luhn, "Keyword in Context Index for Technical Literature (KWIC Index)," *American Documentation* 11 (1960): 288-295.

41. J. J. Tocatlian, "Are Titles of Chemical Papers Becoming More Informative?" *Journal of the American Society for Information Science* 21 (1970): 345-350.

42. "OWL Web Ontology Language: Use Cases and Requirements," W3C, accessed May 12, 2014, http://www.w3.org/TR/webont-req/.

43. "Vocabularies" W3C, accessed May 12, 2014, http://www.w3.org/standards/ semanticweb/ontology.

44. Arlene G. Taylor and Daniel N. Joudrey, *The Organization of Information*, 3rd ed. (Westport, Conn.: Libraries Unlimited, 2009), Chapter 10.

45. "Semantic Web," W3C, accessed June 7, 2015, http://www.w3.org/standards/ semanticweb/; "Vocabularies," W3C, accessed June 7, 2015, http://www .w3.org/standards/semanticweb/ontology.

46. "Usage Guide Glossary," DCMI, accessed May 12, 2014, http://dublincore. org/documents/usageguide/glossary.shtml.

47. Jens-Erik Mai, "The Future of General Classification," *Cataloging & Classification Quarterly* 37, no. 1-2, (2003): 6.

48. Sara D. Knapp, "Creating BRS/TERM, a Vocabulary Database for Searchers," *Database* 7, no. 4 (December 1984): 70-75.

49. National Library of Medicine, "Unified Medical Language System (UMLS)," accessed July 16, 2015, http://www.nlm.nih.gov/research/umls/.

50. National Library of Medicine, "UMLS Quick Start Guide," accessed July 16, 2015, http://www.nlm.nih.gov/research/umls/quickstart.html.

SUGGESTED READING

Anderson, James D., and José Pérez-Carballo. *Information Retrieval Design: Principles and Options for Information Description, Organization, Display, and Access in Information Retrieval Databases, Digital Libraries, Catalogs, and Indexes*. St. Petersburg, Fla.: Ometeca Institute, 2005. Chapter 8: "Analysis and Indexing Methods."

Foskett, A. C. *The Subject Approach to Information*. 5th ed. London: Library Association Publishing, 1996. Part IV (Chapters 25-27): Post-coordinate Indexing Languages.

Hider, Philip, with Ross Harvey. *Organising Knowledge in a Global Society: Principles and Practice in Libraries and Information Centres*. Revised ed. Wagga Wagga, NSW: Centre for Information Studies, 2008. Chapter 8: "Alphabetical Subject Access Mechanisms" and Chapter 9: "Subject Access to Web Content."

Lancaster, F. W. *Indexing and Abstracting in Theory and Practice*. 3rd ed. Champaign: University of Illinois, Graduate School of Library and Information Science, 2003.

Chapter 16

Classification

INTRODUCTION

Collections in libraries of any appreciable size are arranged according to some system, and the arrangement is generally referred to as *classification*. *Classification* is the art of grouping together like things and separating the unlike. Arlene G. Taylor and Daniel N. Joudrey define classification as "the placing of subjects into categories . . . the process of determining where an information resource fits into a given hierarchy and often then assigning the notation associated with the appropriate level of the hierarchy to the information resource and to its surrogate."[1] Classification is more than just finding the right notation or category; it is about relationships. It provides a logical arrangement of topics and subtopics from the general to the specific that can be translated into a linear arrangement for materials in a library. Classification traditionally provides formal, orderly access to the shelves, but it is also a mechanism by which to collocate materials in information retrieval tools. Classification allows for browsing resources both on the shelves and in the catalog.

Subject headings and classification share a common purpose. Both are attempts to translate the aboutness of a resource into a controlled subject language, but they take very different approaches to accomplishing it. Whereas subject headings give an alphabetical verbal approach to the concepts inherent in documents, classification schemes provide a logical (or at least a methodical) notational or categorical approach to the arrangement of those documents. There is no one-to-one correlation between subject headings and classification; subject headings are organized around individual topics, but classification schemes begin with a discipline-based approach to knowledge in which every topic fits in one or more places. For example, while *Library of Congress Subject Headings* (LCSH) provides a single subject heading for **Cows**,

673

the *Dewey Decimal Classification* (DDC) provides at least four classification numbers related to the concept, because cows appear in different disciplines (zoology, animal husbandry, etc.).

Classification, as a human activity, is inherently connected to both philosophy and cognitive psychology. Grouping like entities—a large part of classification—is a basic human cognitive function; one that is understood through the lens of one of cognitive psychology's major research areas, *categorization*. Categorization provides an understanding of the formulation of classes that are based on similar characteristics among individual entities (i.e., categories based on *likeness*). From philosophy (particularly logic), the notion of *division* is introduced. Logic provides an understanding of the need for a rigorous, modulated, and exhaustive process for systematically dividing classes into smaller subclasses. Classification is an activity of *both* gathering (i.e., grouping, categorizing, or lumping) and sorting (i.e., dividing, separating, or splitting). In actual practice, these two activities tend to blur, but conceptually they are distinct functions within classification. In other words, the classifier uses a classification scheme to collocate and order similar resources, and as a result, to separate the unlike.

Classification is a construct. It is a creation, not a discovery. There are no essential or absolute classifications. Even the famous Linnaean taxonomy of living things is only one perspective on living entities. There are alternatives to Linnaeus, such as cladistics, evolutionary systematics, and phenetics. There are no right or wrong classifications; there are only those that do or do not meet their intended purposes. A classification scheme is only as good as its choices of appropriate, thoughtfully selected *characteristics of division* (i.e., attributes or properties chosen to help sort members of a class into subclasses), the order of which determines the ultimate shape of the final classification. For example, when a scheme is being designed, a typical choice in a literature class is how to handle properties such as *authorship, form, language*, and *chronological period*. The order in which these characteristics are addressed is called the *citation order* and it determines what is collocated and what is scattered. If one chooses a citation order of (1) language, (2) form, (3) period, and (4) author, then all literature in the same language will be brought together in the classification. The consequences of this choice, however, are that literary forms, such as poetry or speeches, are separated throughout the class among the different languages; that works of a particular century are scattered even more, first divided by language and then by form; and that works by the same author might be separated if there are differences in language, form of writing, or chronological period. Each classification scheme, having been constructed by one or more creators who made myriad choices, handles topics differently; no two classifications are identical in their approaches.

No matter what scheme is chosen, the purpose of classification is to bring related materials together in a helpful sequence. Ease of access is especially important if the collection is heterogeneous. It is convenient and desirable—particularly in the open-shelf collections to which most libraries in the United States are committed—to have, for example, all histories of the United States or all symphony scores together, so that users, who may or may not have one title in mind, can find related works in one location (or, at least, in a small number of them).

The ultimate aim of any classification system is to lead users to the documents they require. Traditionally in the United States this has been accomplished either through direct search of the shelves (open stacks) or through the help of a library attendant whose duty is to retrieve the materials on demand (closed stacks). Each system has its virtues. The use of open stacks encourages browsing, and thus stimulates intellectual awareness and fosters unexpected discovery. This works best with a logical, fairly comprehensible system of classification that encourages the patron's self-reliance in seeking resources on a particular subject or its specific aspects. The closed stacks approach lessens the chances that materials will be mishandled, misplaced, or stolen, but it forces a user to limit his or her own searching to the catalog and to wait for library staff to bring the materials specifically requested. Closed stacks are valuable in a storage library situation where resources may not be shelved in subject groups at all, but in fixed locations arranged by size or date of accession, with consecutive numbers assigned as shelf addresses. *Fixed location* means that each item has one specific, stationary position on a particular shelf in the library, as was the case in many libraries prior to the late 19th century. *Relative location* is a fluid, constantly changing arrangement of items according to their relationship to one another and resulting from the addition of new materials or the removal of old, weeded, or lost materials. In a system using relative location, items may be moved from shelf to shelf without altering or disturbing their classified sequence. Now, in addition to the traditional approaches, some libraries offer classified access to electronic resources through the catalog.

LIBRARY CLASSIFICATION

Organized documentary collections have existed since early civilizations learned to convert their spoken languages to written forms. Even before the codex book appeared, early record depositories received some form of utilitarian arrangement. Groupings were made by title, by broad subject, by chronology, by author, by order of acquisition, by size, and so on. One of the earliest catalogs was the one known as *Pinakes*, compiled for the great Alexandrian library by the poet Callimachus in the third century B.C. Although this catalog did not survive, it is known that it arranged the entries in at least 10 (and possibly more) main classes, subdivided alphabetically by author. In the Middle East and in the Byzantine Empire it served as a model for other catalogs and bibliographies until the early Middle Ages. The monastery libraries of that time in western Europe were mostly small and had almost no need for classification, but the university libraries of the late Middle Ages arranged books corresponding to the Trivium (grammar, logic, rhetoric) and Quadrivium (arithmetic, music, geometry, astronomy), the traditional seven subject fields taught. Within the classes, books had fixed locations on the shelves.

Beginning in the 16th century, librarians devised many different classification schemes for the arrangement of books, but fixed locations predominated in most European and early American libraries until the mid-19th century. The most substantive developments in the arrangement of library collections were concurrent with the rapid growth of libraries and their use during the

19th century. At that time, librarians felt a definite need for better methods of arrangement so that the content of their holdings would be available, and more apparent, to the user.

The history of modern library classification corresponds to the various attempts to adapt and modify existing philosophical systems of knowledge to the arrangement of materials and to users' needs. One of the best-known early American classifiers was Thomas Jefferson, third president of the United States. He adapted certain elements of Francis Bacon's outline of knowledge not only to his own library, but also to his plans for the organization of the University of Virginia and the reorganization of the College of William and Mary.

Bacon's system classified materials as functions of the three basic faculties: history (natural, civil, literary, ecclesiastical) as the function of memory; philosophy (including theology) as that of reason; and poetry, fables, and the like as that of imagination.[2] Its influence was widespread. Jean Le Rond d'Alembert used the Baconian system for the arrangement of the famous *Encyclopédie ou dictionnaire raisonné des sciences des arts et des métiers* of the French Enlightenment (1751-1765). Jefferson's classification was based on that modification, as was the *Catalogue* of Benjamin Franklin's Library Company of Philadelphia (1789). Three years before Jefferson's *Catalogue of the Library of the United States* was installed at the Library of Congress (LC), a variant of the Philadelphia scheme was used to produce the 1812 *Catalogue of the Library of Congress.*[3]

Among other early followers of the Baconian system were Thaddeus Mason Harris, librarian at Harvard (1791-1793); Edward William Johnson, librarian of the College of South Carolina and later of the St. Louis Mercantile Library; and, finally, Johnson's successor, William Torrey Harris, a Hegelian who inverted the Baconian system, creating an independent American classification. At the same time, various adaptations of J. C. Brunet's utilitarian classification scheme existed in several American libraries as a direct result of its use to arrange parts of the British Museum and the Bibliothèque Nationale.

In 1876 Melvil Dewey devised his famous classification, now known as the *Dewey Decimal Classification* (DDC), based in large part on W. T. Harris's system, with a decimal notation.[4] Soon DDC was spreading its influence throughout the world. At about the same time, Charles A. Cutter began his work at the Boston Athenaeum. Cutter sought to achieve, not a classification of knowledge, but a practical, useful method for arranging library materials. Nevertheless, his *Expansive Classification* (EC) shows the definite influence of the progressive order in the classifications of the sciences of Herbert Spencer and August Comte, especially in the development of its subordinate classes.[5]

Toward the end of the 19th century, when LC had grown from several thousand books to nearly one million, it was apparent that the library would need a new classification system. After much deliberation, J. C. M. Hanson and Charles Martel decided to design an independent system governed by the actual content of the collection (i.e., the concept of *literary warrant,* which is discussed in chapter 12). This form of classification differed from a purely philosophical approach in that it was based on the books as entities. For this reason *Library of Congress Classification* (LCC) is more enumerative than many other schemes.

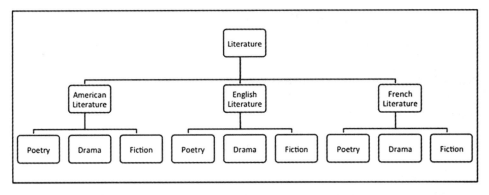

FIGURE 16.1 Illustration of a Very Simple Hierarchical Classification.

For the purpose of providing a simple classification of classifications, schemes are often referred to as *enumerative, hierarchical*, or *faceted*. These categories are not mutually exclusive. An *enumerative classification* attempts to assign designations for (i.e., to enumerate) all the single and composite subject concepts required in the system. *Hierarchical classification* is based on the assumption that the process of subdivision and collocation must exhibit, as much as possible, the natural organization of the subject, proceeding from classes to divisions to subdivisions and following, at least in part, the rules of division as set down by logic. It reflects a series of ordered groups going from broader to more specific categories as it develops. The two types can be somewhat similar in appearance because the result of a minutely sub-divided, hierarchical classification is extensive enumeration resulting in the listing of topic after topic. Illustrations of hierarchical classification schemes, however, typically have the familiar *tree of knowledge* structure (see Figure 16.1.), whereas a purely enumerative system is more of a list. A *faceted classification* (also known as *analytico-synthetic classification*) confines its explicit lists of designations to single concepts, giving the local classifier generalized rules with which to construct notations for composite subjects (see the section on faceted classification below). Within its lists of concepts, however, some hierarchy may be found.

In summary, established philosophical systems of knowledge, with various modifications, underlie most traditional library classifications. The frequent distinction between classification of knowledge and classification of materials seems to have confused the thinking of many librarians. The two processes have important interactions. Even cursory examination of any library clas-sification (including those purporting to organize the resources themselves) reveals an intellectual concept of the resource as an illustration of certain ideas in one of many available media. Philosophical classification organizes knowledge itself—registering, evaluating, and classifying thoughts, ideas, and concepts for the universal purpose of adequately representing the field of human learning. Library classification arranges resources that express and preserve knowledge, making adjustments as needed because of the physical format of such materials. For more discussion of classification, readers are referred to Taylor and Joudrey's *Organization of Information*.[6]

TRADITIONAL CLASSIFICATION SCHEMES

Most traditional classification systems are both hierarchical and enumerative. By contrast, more recent schemes tend to be faceted. In this text, the discussion includes all three types of classification schemes. It is good to remember that materials on shelves or in physical files are arranged in a single, linear order. Most resources can be requested by author, title, subject, or form, but they can be organized by only one of these at a time. Linear arrangement imposes certain limitations on the classifier. Over the years efforts to meet such limitations have resulted in features that are characteristic of nearly every library classification.

Each classification scheme comprises three components: *schedules, notation,* and an *index.* The schedules are the heart of the scheme; they are the list of subjects, in classified order, that shows the relationships among concepts. The schedules contain main classes, which may number anywhere from 10 to 50 or more depending on the scheme, and subclasses, which may number in the thousands. All the major intellectual/academic disciplines are represented by main classes or by a combination of main classes and subclasses. Within the schedules, disciplines and their major subtopics are arranged according to their similarity. The goal, of course, is that related topics are placed closer together than unrelated topics. In other words, proximity demonstrates relationships. The space in the classification for a particular discipline or a topic should be approximately proportional to the size of the literature of that discipline. Some classifications have a limited amount of space and therefore must be economical in how they distribute their notation.

One common feature of classification schedules is a general works class, which accommodates resources that are too broad in scope for inclusion in any single class. Such works usually overlap several traditional disciplines or classes (e.g., encyclopedias, dictionaries, general periodicals). In addition, genre classes organize materials according to their form of presentation rather than their subject content. Literary works (e.g., poetry, drama, fiction) are the most obvious, but books of etchings, photographs, musical scores, and so on also fall into this group. Form divisions group resources in a class according to their form or mode of treatment. For example, notations for outlines, dictionaries, or periodicals are used to pull together those presentations; and notations for philosophical treatments, such as research in a subject, histories, and biographies show the inner form of works.

Notation is shorthand code for the class, division, and subdivisions chosen for an information resource. It may be composed of letters, numerals, arbitrary signs, or a mixture of these. Notation can be of two types: *pure* or *mixed.* Pure notation employs only one kind of symbol. As a pure notation system, DDC uses only numbers. For example, 152.46 represents the concept *fear.* Mixed notation uses two or more kinds of symbols. LCC, for example, uses both letters and numbers, and it represents *fear* as BF575.F2. The choice of notation affects how classification schemes accommodate new concepts. For example, the editors of DDC must be very thoughtful about how their notation is used because the system's base is pure and also numerical; both of which limit how much can fit in the upper levels of its hierarchies. Using the notation

0-9 is naturally more limiting than using A-Z or using A-Z *and* 0-9. For more on the qualities necessary for useful notation (such as uniqueness, simplicity, brevity, hospitality, flexibility, and expressiveness), readers should consult Eric Hunter's *Classification Made Simple*.[7]

A final feature of traditional classification schemes is the index. The index provides an alphabetical approach to the classified part of the scheme. It is indispensible for locating concepts within a classification scheme. As most classifications are discipline-based, individual topics may be scattered in various parts of the scheme (e.g., cows in zoology, cows in animal husbandry, cows in agricultural economics). The index allows the classifier to find all places where the topic may appear and choose the one that best fits the disciplinary approach of the work itself. In multicultural communities, the same index may be produced in several languages, taking full advantage of the scheme's use of symbols (rather than words) to represent concepts.

FACETED CLASSIFICATION

While it shares the same basic components of a traditional classification scheme (i.e., the schedules, notation, and index), a faceted classification differs from a traditional one in that it does not assign fixed slots to subjects in sequence, but instead lists clearly defined, mutually exclusive, and collectively exhaustive aspects of a subject. The premise is that any subject or class can be analyzed into its component parts (i.e., its aspects, properties, or characteristics). These pieces or aspects of a subject are called *facets*, a term introduced into classification theory by the Indian librarian and classificationist, S. R. Ranganathan in his *Colon Classification* (CC) in the early 1930s.[8] In order to represent both simple and complex subjects, a classification number is built by combining facets according to specific patterns developed for different disciplines.

Although the term *facet* was then new to classification, the idea was not (as Ranganathan freely admitted). It had its roots in Dewey's device of place—that is, using a standard number to represent a geographic location (e.g., the United States is 73) and appending it to any eligible classification number. This is done by means of the digits 09, which in DDC act as a device now known as a *facet indicator*. This allows catalogers to append 0973 onto the end of many DDC numbers to represent the United States as the geographic aspect of a topic. Dewey recognized three things:

- Certain characteristics, such as geographic location, form/genre, and some others, are general and should be applicable to most subjects (i.e., DDC's standard subdivisions).

- Such numbers must be clearly distinguished from the class notation for the main subject to avoid confusion (i.e., the use of identifiable facet indicators such as 0 or 1).

- Two or more facets can be combined to express a more complex subject (i.e., number building). See Figure 16.2 for an example of simple number building in DDC.

Topic: *Frost damage to oranges*

<u>634.31</u>   Base notation for the concept *Oranges*
634.31<u>9</u>   Facet indicator for *Injuries, diseases, pests*
634.319<u>11</u>   Two digits taken from the subject *Frost injury* (632.<u>11</u>)
                              in another part of the schedules

---

FIGURE 16.2 A Brief Example of Number Building in DDC.

Most other classification schemes designed after DDC provide widely applicable facets for places, time periods, and forms. Even LCC, which is a more enumerative scheme, includes such facets, although they are specially developed for each class as a part of the enumerative structure and are not uniformly applicable to all classes. The *Universal Decimal Classification* (UDC) expanded DDC's standard subdivisions to its 10 generally applicable *auxiliary tables* (see the section on UDC in chapter 17). Finally, Ranganathan's *Colon Classification* introduced a fully faceted approach by means of class notations constructed entirely from individual facets in a prescribed sequence from the most specific to the most general.

Originally, Ranganathan proposed five basic facets, *PMEST*, consisting of *personality*, the focal or most specific concept; *matter* or *material*, a property, component, or element of that concept; *energy*, an activity, operation, or process; *space*, a place or location; and *time*, a chronological element. These basic facets were used to analyze a class or subject and to construct a composite class notation for it (hence the name *analytico-synthetic classification*). For example, the topic, *the design of metal ploughshares in the 19th century United States*, shows all five facets from the most specific to the most general:

ploughshares	personality
metal	matter
design	energy
United States	space
19th century	time

It was soon found that these five basic facets were too broad and that most classes or disciplines needed tailor-made facets; for example, the field of education can be broken down into facets for students, educators, teaching methods, subjects taught, level of instruction, and so on; agriculture needs facets for crops, operations (sowing, harvesting, etc.), implements and tools, and so forth. These more specific facets, however, still fall within the boundaries of the original five (PMEST), which are now referred to as the *five fundamental categories*. Each facet, no matter how specific or narrowly defined, is an exemplar of P, M, E, S, or T. The notion of multiple rounds and multiple levels of the fundamental categories was included in later editions of CC. In the 21st century, one could refer to the role of the fundamental categories as that of being *meta-facets* (i.e., facets for the facets), although Ranganathan never did so.

In the CC schedules, established lists of concepts are found under each main class. The concepts themselves are referred to as *isolates*, and they are grouped according to the facets in which they may be used. Each isolate is assigned a specific notation. Once a concept is established, it does not need to be repeated again in the classification schedules; it can be reused, whenever needed, with any applicable subjects. When an isolate is chosen for a facet, the isolate is said to become the *focus* of the facet.

To synthesize a classification number, the process begins with the notation representing the main class. What follows are the facets chosen specifically for that class in a set citation order (i.e., its *facet formula*). To create a complete classification number, the classifier strings together the notations from the main class and the individual foci representing each facet. This is done in accordance with the established facet formula and any additional instructions provided in the schedules.

Each facet must have a distinctive notation and a *facet indicator* to show the sequence of the facets unambiguously. The facet indicators used in CC are punctuation marks. Each piece of punctuation shows exactly what facet is coming next. The following are the facet indicators for the five fundamental categories:

,	(comma)	personality
;	(semicolon)	matter
:	(colon)	energy
.	(period, full stop, or dot)	space
'	(inverted comma)	time

For example, a classifier with a resource on the eradication of viruses in rice plants in Japan in the 1970s would first identify the disciplinary focus of the work in order to determine the sequence of facets needed to represent the topic fully. This topic is an agricultural one; therefore, the classifier would consult the Agriculture schedules (the J class) to find its facet formula. The next step would be to identify the individual foci for each facet and the notation for each:

J	(agriculture)	main class
381	(rice plant)	personality
423	(disease/virus)	matter
5	(eradication/prevention)	energy
42	(Japan)	space
N7	(1970s)	time

Once the notations are identified, they are compiled, along with the appropriate facet indicators, to create a composite class number. The final classification number, built according to the seventh edition of CC, is **J,381;423:5.42'N7**.[9] Number building in CC or in DDC is similar to putting together a puzzle; the process involves finding the right pieces and putting them together in the correct sequence. An exploration of number building in the literature class of CC is found in the textbox on the next page.

A faceted structure relieves a classification from a rigid hierarchical arrangement and from having to create thousands of fixed pigeonholes for subjects that happened to be known or were foreseen when a system was designed.

Further Exploration of Faceted Classifications

A helpful example of how faceted classification works can be found in the literature schedules (the *O* class) of the 6th edition of the *Colon Classification* (CC6). In the literature class, CC6 has identified four specific facets that relate to most, if not all, works of literature: *language, form, author,* and *work.* According to Ranganathan, each of these facets represents the fundamental category *personality,* because they are primary aspects of the subject (and also because they do not fit in *matter, energy, space,* or *time!*).

The established facet formula in CC6 for works of literature is **O [P], [P2], [P3], [P4]** with each [P] representing one of the four specific facets ([P] = language, [P2] = form, [P3] = author, and [P4] = work). In the schedules, each facet will have either:

(1) an established list of concepts (i.e., isolates) for a particular class that may be used within a particular facet (e.g., the list of forms established for [P2]);
(2) a reference to another established list found in another part of the schedules (e.g., for [P], use the language divisions in Chapter 5); or,
(3) a specific instruction for filling that facet (e.g., for [P3] typically create a notation reflecting the year of birth via the time isolate).

The following examples are excerpts from two different lists of isolates from the schedules:

Language Isolate (used in [P])
1	Indo-European
11	Teutonic
111	English
112	Dutch
...	

Form Facet [P2]
1	Poetry
2	Drama
3	Fiction
4	Letters
...	

To create a class number for a work of literature, a classifier would piece together the four individual notations representing the appropriate isolates and the facet indicators according to the established formula. He or she would also follow any additional instructions provided in the scheme. So, if one had an English-language play, *The 5th of July* by Lanford Wilson (b. 1937), the class number would start with the main class (O). The first two facets are fairly straightforward: [P]=111 and [P2]=2. The latter two facets, however, are more involved; they entail additional instructions because neither playwrights nor individual titles are listed in the schedules. For [P3], CC6 instructs one to use a chronological device, generally based on an author's birth year; in this case, the value is N37 (N is for the 20th century and 37 is for the specific year). For [P4], CC6 suggests the number of the work if all the author's works were ordered chronologically. The instructions, based on how many total works have been created by that author, are somewhat complex. Because there are fewer than 64 plays by Wilson, *The 5th of*

July (his 25th play) is represented by the digits 41 (it is the first play of the fourth group of eight plays). Pulled together the classification number for this work is:

O111,2,N37,41

Notes:

- Since it is used in a [P] facet in the literature class, N37 is preceded by a comma, not an apostrophe.
- In CC6, there is no comma before the first [P]. This is not the case in CC7 (published 17 years after Ranganathan's death). Many prefer CC6 to the more complex and flawed CC7.

Rigid systems often left no room for future developments and made no provision for the expression of complex relationships. Enumeration is, however, not entirely absent from faceted schemes: CC has some 50 main classes, largely corresponding to traditional disciplines.

All traditional schemes are essentially based on the strictly hierarchical genus-species relationship for most of their subdivisions. Faceted schemes recognize this relationship where warranted, but also display others, such as whole-part, operations and processes, agents and tools, substances, physical forms, organizational aspects, and many more as needed, for each specific field or subject. The design of faceted classification schemes is treated in detail by B. C. Vickery.[10] An example of a small faceted classification scheme, designed to meet the needs of a specific subject area, is found in the next textbox.

A faceted class number, such as those in the examples above, is not necessarily meant to serve as a *call number* (i.e., a shelving device or address discussed in detail in chapter 19 of this text). Although all or part of a faceted class number may be used for a call number, it may be more commonly used for the arrangement of resources in bibliographies and databases, where the faceted notation provides a helpful sequence, and the individual facets can be accessed and retrieved either alone or in any desired combination. This feature is or could be especially important for online retrieval as a complement to verbal retrieval methods by subject headings or keywords. Yet in the United States, unlike in other parts of the world, retrieval by classification is often ignored. In the United States, when available, it is often based on left-anchored searching, which means that the retrieval mechanism does not look beyond the first digits for individual sequences within a classification number. In most modern American catalogs, little has been done to leverage the potential power of a faceted classification approach. In some, however, individual facets *may* be retrievable through keyword searching. In other parts of the world, where classification is thought of as an access point and a retrieval mechanism, some catalogs may be better suited for searching faceted classification notations, but many are as limited as American catalogs in this respect.

Faceted Classification in Action!

T: Travel

Purpose of Travel	Mode of Transportation	Geographic Elements	Time Period	Form
10 Bereavement	W Airplane	1 United States	a 18th cent.	001 Encyclopedia
11 Business	X Boat	2 China	b 19th cent.	002 Guidebook
12 Family Vacation	Y Car	3 Honduras	c 20th cent.	003 Road atlas
13 Recreation	Z Train	4 India	d 21st cent.	004 Serial

The table above contains a portion of an imaginary *analytico-synthetic* classification scheme. It could be used to classify a small travel library. For example, if you were given the classification number **T13Y1c003**, you should be able to discern that the resource assigned this number is a road atlas for 20th century recreational car travel in the United States. Because the notation is fairly different in each facet of this scheme, no facet indicators are needed; if all the notations were numbers or capital letters, it would be a different story.

Just to give you an idea of how different this would be for an enumerative, hierarchical scheme, you would need 1024 individual classes (which would take up pages and pages of the schedules) to accomplish what is seen in this one small table.

Try a few on your own. What numbers would you use for the following? How would they be organized on the shelves if the filing order is numbers, then lower-case letters then uppercase letters?

1. business air travel in India
2. beginnings of train travel in 19th century China
3. a serial about travel
4. a guide for 21st century boating tours for family vacations in Honduras
5. an encyclopedia about travel in the 20th century

Answers are at the end of this chapter.

The faceted approach is, indeed, not limited to the construction and assignment of class notations. It is also clearly discernible in verbal subject representations (e.g., a subject heading such as **Newspapers—United States—Bibliography** shows **United States** in the place facet and **Bibliography** in the form facet). The list of subdivisions in the *Sears List of Subject Headings* is actually a list of facets, although it is not arranged systematically as it would be in a faceted classification (see discussion of *Sears* subdivisions in chapter 14).

Since the 1960s all major classification schemes (with the exception of LCC) either have been partially restructured on a faceted basis or display a fully faceted structure. The influence of faceted classification theory has been most conspicuous in DDC, which now offers facets not only for its traditional standard subdivisions and geographic areas, but also for individual literatures and languages, for ethnic and national groups, and in completely revised schedules for such areas as music and biology that rely heavily on faceting in their internal structures. Special faceted classifications have been designed for broad fields such as education or business management, as well as for more specialized ones such as occupational safety, the diamond industry, library and information science, and many others (see discussion of special classification schemes in chapter 20).

CRITERIA FOR A SUCCESSFUL CLASSIFICATION SCHEME

Classification schemes, as indicated earlier, vary widely. Besides providing for the subject organization of the collection, a successful classification scheme may also contain devices for indicating method of treatment or form of materials treated, time periods, places, peoples, various types of persons, and other special categories. Any or all of these devices may be justifiably and successfully used for a special situation such as a rare book collection or a collection concerned with a particular subject area or period. The following is a list of criteria that may be used to judge a classification system.

- **Inclusive and Comprehensive**: A classification scheme must encompass the whole area of knowledge in the field(s) that it claims to represent. It must therefore include all subjects that are, have been, or may be recognized, allowing for possible future additions to the particular body of knowledge being covered. It must make provision, not only for the resources themselves, but also for every actual and potential use of the resources.

- **Systematic**: Not only must the division of subjects be exhaustive, but a classification must also bring together related topics in a logical, comprehensible fashion, allowing its users to locate easily whatever they want that is available. It must be arranged so that each aspect of a subject can be considered a separate, yet related, part of the scheme, and it must be arranged so that new topics and aspects can be added in a systematic manner.

- **Flexible and Expansible**: A classification system must be constructed so that any new subject in its knowledge area may be inserted without dislocating the general sequence of the classification. It must allow for recognized knowledge in all its ramifications, and it must be capable of admitting new topics or new aspects of well-established topics. The flexibility of the notation is of first importance if the classification scheme is to be expansive and hospitable in the highest degree. It should also be current. DDC and LCC, for example, are kept up to date via electronic updates to their web-based classification tools as soon as changes are approved. These revisions are especially important in subject areas in which a great deal of new work is being done.

- **Understandable**: Classifications must employ terminology that is clear and descriptive, with consistent meanings that reflect significant distinctions between classes for both the user and the classifier. The arrangement of terms in the schedule and the index should help reveal the significance of the arrangement. The terms themselves should be unambiguous and reasonably current, correctly identifying the concepts and characteristics present in the materials being classified.

BROAD AND CLOSE CLASSIFICATION

Close classification means classing each work as specifically as possible, using all available subdivisions in the classification scheme. Broad classification collocates works under the main divisions and main subdivisions of the scheme, without using its breakdowns into narrower concepts. When a library has relatively few resources in a given subject area, broad classification might actually be more useful than isolating each resource under its own specific classification notation. A library using the DDC with a large collection of Bibles, for example, may need to classify the King James Version in 220.5203, whereas a smaller collection might cut back to the broad number 220. Generally speaking, DDC provides small libraries with more opportunities to cut back to broader notations than does LCC, because DDC's enumeration stresses hierarchies of subject matter, while LCC has relatively few notations that signify broad categories.

GENERAL PRINCIPLES OF CLASSIFYING

Most of this chapter has been directed to the broad principles, methods, and problems of constructing classification systems. Some attention should now be given to choosing the optimum location for each resource. When classifying an information resource with respect to a particular collection, it is often tempting to arrange resources with local needs in mind, but classification schemes vary in their hospitality to local manipulation. It is assumed that such possibilities and difficulties were considered when the choice was made of one scheme over all others for use in a particular setting. Once the particular system of arrangement is chosen, certain general precepts enable the classifier to apply it meaningfully to the information resources being organized. The following summary is designed to aid that process. These principles apply primarily to both the DDC and the LCC schemes.

- **In general, classify the material first according to subject, then by the form in which the subject is represented.** There are exceptions, of course. For example in DDC, in literature, classification is first by country/language, then by form, then by time period, then by author; in LCC, classification is first by country/language, then by time period, then by author, then by form. Subject does not figure into the classification in either case.

- **Classify an information resource where it will be most useful.** The classifier has to consider the nature of the collection and the needs of the user. For example, should a sports biography be classified with sports or with a general biography class number? The answer to this question might be quite different in a school library than in a large public library or a library that specializes in sports materials.

- **Place the resource in the most specific subject subdivision that will contain it, rather than with a more general topic.** This principle, of course, may be affected by a decision to use broad rather than close classification. Most libraries, for example, classify general French histories together and then subdivide the rest of the resources dealing with the history of France by the specific time periods or local places they cover. To assign the same notation to all would result in a discouragingly large assortment of volumes under one notation. On the other hand, small libraries might prefer to classify their few volumes dealing with this subject in a general classification number for French history.

- **When an information resource deals with two or three subjects, place it with the predominant subject.** Although it is fairly straightforward, this principle requires a little explanation. The subject that is treated most fully, generally, should take precedence over secondary subjects. There are some refinements to this general principle. For example, if the work covers two subjects, one of which is represented as acting upon or influencing the other, such a work should be classified with the subject influenced or acted upon. Thus a work discussing French influences on English literature should be classified with English literature. On similar grounds, a work such as *Religious Aspects of Philosophy* should be classed in philosophy, not in religion, since a treatment of some particular aspect of a subject should be classed with the subject, not with the aspect.

- **When an information resource deals with two or three subjects, and none is predominant, place it with the one treated first.** If two subjects are coordinate (e.g., electricity and magnetism treated equally in the same volume) the information resource should be classified with whichever topic comes first (in LCC, with which comes first in the text; in DDC, with which comes first in the DDC schedules).

- **When an information resource deals with more than three subjects, place it in the general class that combines all of them.** For four or more topics, all part of a broader class, assign the broader class. Another, perhaps more involved difficulty arises with a monographic series or collected set. Winston Churchill's *History of the English-Speaking Peoples* can be classified as an author's collection of four related volumes under a broad history number. Or the classifier can place volume 1 with other works on very early Britain, volume 2 with those on discovery and growth of the New World, and so on. LC, at one time, often classified series and collected sets together but has in recent years moved to classify series volumes separately in many cases. When series are classified together, LC catalogers may provide, for optional use by other libraries, an alternative, volume-specific classification notation.

CONCLUSION

Critics have noted limitations in existing classification systems used by most libraries today.[11] A few are summarized here only as a basis for further study. There is a long-standing argument over the logical arrangement of various systems. Although a scheme may be logical within itself, it can also have inconsistencies. For example, in DDC, language (400s) is separated from literature (800s), and history (900s) is separated from the social sciences (300s). In LCC, language is classified with literature (classes P-PZ), and history (classes D-F) is relatively closer to the social sciences (class H). Arguments can be advanced for both approaches. Language is closely related to literature, but it is also essential to all disciplines. History throws much light on the social sciences, but every discipline and every literature has its own history that influences, and is influenced by, general social history. There is some evidence that the current trend toward faceting has lessened concern about achieving the one incontestably correct logical arrangement.

As mentioned above, DDC and LCC, the two most popular library classifications in the United States, are both linear and, therefore, one-dimensional. Concepts found in works are multi-dimensional, but because classification is most often used to arrange resources on shelves, only one number is assigned to each title whether it covers one subject or many. Classified catalogs address this problem to a certain extent because they allow the classifier to assign as many numbers to the catalog record as are appropriate. But classified catalogs have not gained acceptance in the United States. Instead, the many subject relationships among resources and works are shown through a verbal, alphabetical approach (i.e., subject headings with references; see chapters 12-15).

Other limitations include problems of reorganization and relocation arising from the need to keep any classification scheme up to date. Both DDC and LCC are revised regularly with new numbers being added for new concepts and with some concepts being moved to more logical locations in the scheme (e.g., computer science in DDC was moved from 001.6 to 004-006, and in LCC a new class, ZA, was created for information resources, to give this rapidly growing area room to expand). Occasionally, a section of a scheme is completely reorganized so that the old numbers are reused with new meanings (e.g., 560-590 for life sciences was completely reorganized for the 21st edition of DDC). These are sometimes referred to as *phoenix schedules* (i.e., the schedule is "burned" only to have a new schedule rise from its ashes). While such reorganizations and relocations are very logical from a theoretical point of view, they may wreak havoc for orderly browsing in libraries. Most libraries cannot afford to reclassify older resources, so they either push all resources belonging to a reorganized section together on the shelves and start a new section for the new resources, or they simply give up and say that the number is only a location address in any case (an approach known as "Mark it and park it"). A more in-depth discussion of this problem may be found in *Subject Analysis in Online Catalogs* by Hope A. Olson and John J. Boll,[12] and in *The Organization of Information* by Taylor and Joudrey.[13]

Another problem arising from the process of keeping a classification scheme up to date is that the notation tends to become more complex and awkward as the schedules are expanded to include new subjects and to define old topics more specifically. In LCC, for example, digits are added after decimal points to place a new concept with older equivalent concepts. For example, in library and information science, Z666 is for the concept *bibliography* and Z667 is for the concept *information retrieval systems*. When *information organization*, an equivalent concept to *information retrieval*, was added to the classification scheme, it was placed at Z666.5.

Related to the problem of keeping up with revisions in classification schemes is the fact that in most libraries, most of the classification numbers are taken from cataloging provided by an outside agency (e.g., a centralized processing facility or LC). These numbers are only as current as the time period in which they were assigned. A more in-depth discussion of this problem may be found in Taylor's *Cataloging with Copy*.[14]

In an international context, classification is taken much more seriously than it has been in the United States. In a setting in which many languages are involved it has been found that numerical and other symbols can transcend the language barriers imposed upon verbal subject approaches. As information technology becomes more sophisticated many of the limitations mentioned above have the potential to be overcome, and even though it seems unlikely to happen, classification has the potential to become an international switching language for subject communication.[15]

In chapters 17-20, some of the better-known modern classifications devised by librarians and used in various contexts are discussed. Their resemblances and differences are briefly examined to show their actual and possible uses, strengths, and limitations.

Answers for Faceted Classification in Action

1. T11W4
2. TZ2b
3. T004
4. T12X3d002
5. Tc001

If these notations were to be used for shelving the resources, the books would appear in the following order (numbers *0-9* before letters *a-z* before letters *A-Z*):

1. T004 - a serial about travel
2. T11W4 - business air travel in India
3. T12X3d002 - a guide for 21st century boating tours for family vacations in Honduras
4. Tc001 - an encyclopedia about travel in the 20th century
5. TZ2b - beginnings of train travel in 19th century China

NOTES

1. Arlene G. Taylor and Daniel N. Joudrey, *The Organization of Information*, 3rd ed. (Westport, Conn.: Libraries Unlimited, 2009), 448.
2. Cf. Bacon's *Advancement of Learning* (1605) and his Latin translation of it: *De augmentis* (1621).
3. Leo E. LaMontagne, "Historical Background of Classification," in *The Subject Analysis of Library Materials* (New York: Columbia University School of Library Service, 1953), 20.
4. Melvil Dewey, *A Classification and Subject Index for Cataloguing and Arranging the Books and Pamphlets of a Library*, Amherst, Mass., 1876. Latest edition is *Dewey Decimal Classification and Relative Index*, Edition 23, edited by Joan S. Mitchell, et al. (Dublin, OH: OCLC, 2011). DDC, Dewey, Dewey Decimal Classification, and WebDewey are registered trademarks of OCLC.
5. Thomas M. Dousa, "Evolutionary Order in the Classification Theories of C. A. Cutter & E. C. Richardson: Its Nature and Limits," *NASKO* 2, no.1 (2009): 76-90. doi:http://dx.doi.org/10.7152/nasko.v2i1.12810.
6. Taylor and Joudrey, *The Organization of Information*, 375-415.
7. Eric Hunter, *Classification Made Simple*, (Burlington, Vt.: Ashgate, 2009), 73-84.
8. S. R. Ranganathan, *Colon Classification*. (Madras, India: Madras Library Association; London: Goldston, 1933).
9. S. R. Ranganathan, *Colon Classification*, 7th ed., revised and edited by M. A. Gopinath. (Bangalore: Ranganathan Endowment for Library Science, 1989), 14-17.
10. B. C. Vickery, *Faceted Classification: A Guide to the Construction and Use of Special Schemes*, 1st ed. reprinted with additional material (London: Aslib, 1968).
11. A helpful list of articles and books on classification theory can be found in the brief bibliography: Phyllis A. Richmond, "Reading List in Classification Theory," *Library Resources & Technical Services* 16 (Summer 1972): 364-382.
12. Hope A. Olson and John J. Boll, *Subject Analysis in Online Catalogs*, 2nd ed. (Englewood, Colo.: Libraries Unlimited, 2001), 192-193.
13. Taylor and Joudrey, *The Organization of Information*, 392-394.
14. Arlene G. Taylor, with the assistance of Rosanna M. O'Neil, *Cataloging with Copy*, 2nd ed. (Englewood, Colo.: Libraries Unlimited, 1988), 170-246.
15. Russell Sweeney, "The Atlantic Divide: Classification Outside the United States," in *Classification of Library Materials*, edited by Betty G. Bengtson and Janet Swan Hill (New York: Neal-Schuman, 1990), 40-51.

SUGGESTED READING

Bowker, Geoffrey C., and Susan Leigh Star. *Sorting Things Out: Classification and Its Consequences*. Cambridge, Mass.: MIT Press, 1999.

Broughton, Vanda. *Essential Classification*. U.S. edition. New York: Neal-Schuman, 2004.

Chan, Lois Mai, with the assistance of Theodora L. Hodges. *Cataloging and Classification: An Introduction*. 3rd ed. Lanham, Md.: Scarecrow Press, 2007. Chapter 12: Classification and Categorization.

Foskett, A. C. *The Subject Approach to Information.* 5th ed. London: Library Association Publishing, 1996. Chapter 10: General Classification Schemes. Chapter 21: The Colon Classification.

Hider, Philip, with Ross Harvey. *Organising Knowledge in a Global Society: Principles and Practice in Libraries and Information Centres.* Rev. ed. Wagga Wagga, NSW, Australia: Centre for Information Studies, Charles Sturt University, 2008. Chapter 7: Classification.

Hunter, Eric J. *Classification Made Simple: An Introduction to Knowledge Organisation and Information Retrieval.* 3rd ed. Burlington, Vt.: Ashgate, 2009.

Langridge, D. W. *Classification: Its Kinds, Elements, Systems and Applications.* London: Bowker-Saur, 1992.

Mann, Thomas. *Library Research Models: A Guide to Classification, Cataloging, and Computers.* New York: Oxford University Press, 1993. Chapter 3: The Traditional Library Science Model. Part I: The Classification Scheme.

Olson, Hope A., and John J. Boll. *Subject Analysis in Online Catalogs.* 2nd ed. Englewood, Colo.: Libraries Unlimited, 2001. Chapter 7: Bibliographic Classification.

Richardson, Ernest Cushing. *Classification, Theoretical and Practical: Together with an Appendix Containing an Essay towards a Bibliographical History of Systems of Classification.* 3rd ed. New York, H. W. Wilson, 1930.

Taylor, Arlene G., and Daniel N. Joudrey. *The Organization of Information.* 3rd ed. Westport, Conn.: Libraries Unlimited, 2009. Chapter 11: Systems for Categorization.

Chapter 17

Decimal Classification

INTRODUCTION

Of the modern library classification schemes, the *Dewey Decimal Classification* (DDC)[1] is both the oldest and the most widely used in the United States. It also has a substantial following abroad and has been published in both full and abridged editions for more than a century.[2] Until recently, the classification system had always been available in print form, but in 2015 it was announced that the 23rd full edition and the 15th abridged edition would be the last print editions in English. From this point forward, the online subscription-based service known as *WebDewey*[3] will be the primary way to access the full classification. Abridged versions of the classification will also be available online through WebDewey and, to a lesser extent, at the dewey.info website (formatted in 12 languages for use as linked data).[4]

The DDC has more than 40,000 explicit assignable numbers in its schedules, more than 12,000 facets in its tables, and more than 103,000 terms in its index; DDC numbers are mapped to more than 40,000 terms in *Library of Congress Subject Headings* (LCSH), Book Industry Standards and Communications (BISAC) subject headings, *Sears List of Subject Headings* (*Sears*), and *Medical Subject Headings* (MeSH).[5] According to OCLC, the DDC "has been translated into more than 30 languages and serves library users in over 200,000 libraries in 135+ countries worldwide, making it the world's most widely used library classification system. More than 60 of these countries use the DDC to organize their national bibliographies."[6]

Such widespread use is a tribute to Melvil Dewey, whose original plan was adaptable enough to incorporate new subjects as they emerged and flexible enough to withstand the changes imposed by the passage of time. Melville Louis Kossuth Dewey was born on December 10, 1851, and graduated in 1874 from Amherst College, where he became assistant college librarian. He actually began developing the first draft of his system for arranging books while working as a student assistant in the college library in 1873. He soon became a leader in American librarianship, helping to found both the American Library Association (ALA) and the first American library school at Columbia University. Being a man of many interests, he was also an advocate of spelling reform. He shortened his forename to *Melvil*, dropped his two middle names, and even attempted to change the spelling of his surname to *Dui*. Throughout his career he promoted librarianship by his teaching, writing, and speaking. In recognizing and acting upon the need to systematize library collections for effective use, he knew of various previous attempts, but found them inadequate.[7]

Dewey never claimed to have originated decimals for classification notation, but earlier systems used them merely as shelf location devices with no significant relation to the subject matter. What Dewey did claim as original, and with some justification, was his *relative index*, compiled as a key to the diverse material included in his schedules and tables. His most significant contribution was perhaps the use of purely decimal notation to represent hierarchical relationships. The digits 0 to 9, used as decimals, result in a pure notation that can be subdivided indefinitely. In the system, a minimum of three digits is mandatory for the notation. Some digits may act as placeholders (e.g., the two zeros in 700) or as facet indicators (e.g., 0 or 1 in certain classes). If the notation is longer than three digits, a decimal point is placed after the third digit as a visual device: "The dot is not a decimal point in the mathematical sense, but a psychological pause to break the monotony of numerical digits and to ease the transcription and copying of the class number. A number should never end in a 0 anywhere to the right of the decimal point."[8] It may be surprising to learn that the decimal point has no real significance in the system, but it does not; every digit, even the first, is treated as a decimal.

The first edition of Dewey's scheme, prepared for the Amherst College Library, was issued anonymously in 1876 under the title *A Classification and Subject Index for Cataloguing and Arranging the Books and Pamphlets of a Library*. It included schedules to 1,000 divisions numbered 000-999, together with a relative index and prefatory matter—a total of 44 pages. The 2nd, revised and greatly enlarged edition was published under Dewey's name in 1885. Since that time over 20 more full editions and 15 abridgments have appeared. The 14th full edition, published in 1942, remained the standard edition for many years because an experimental index to the 15th edition, published in 1951, was unsuccessful. In 1958 the 16th edition appeared with many changes and additions, including a complete revision of **546 Inorganic chemistry** and **547 Organic chemistry**. Since that time, besides other less sweeping changes, most successive editions have carried totally new developments of one or more targeted portions of the system. The 23rd edition (DDC23) was published in 2011; the associated 15th abridged edition was published in 2012.

DDC notations are assigned the tag 082 in metadata records that are encoded in MARC 21 (the current MAchine-Readable Cataloging format used by Canada, Great Britain, and the United States). The 082 field is used when DDC numbers have been created for a particular item by the Library of Congress (LC) or another national cataloging agency; it may also be used by local libraries if the second indicator is coded "4." In OCLC and other bibliographic networks, a DDC notation created by a local library participating in the network may instead be placed in MARC field 092—a field that is not part of the standard MARC 21 bibliographic format, but that has been established for local use to contain full DDC call numbers (see chapter 19 of this text for more information on assigning full call numbers). The 092 is used when a library still needs to print catalog cards with DDC numbers, as MARC field 082 is a non-printing field (see chapter 21 of this text for more on the MARC formats).

Closely related to DDC is the *Universal Decimal Classification* (UDC), which was originally based on the 5th edition of the DDC. Paul Otlet and Henri La Fontaine developed UDC into a faceted classification (at least to a certain degree) using a wide variety of facet indicators to create compound classification numbers. It was originally designed to represent the complex subjects of the world's published information in the Institut International de Bibliographie. Although it is used in libraries around the globe, it is not widely seen in the United States. It is discussed briefly at the end of this chapter.

BASIC CONCEPTS

The system arranges all knowledge, as represented by library materials, into 10 broad subject classes (see "Summary of the 10 Main DDC Classes" below). Using Arabic numerals for symbols, DDC is flexible to the degree that numbers can be expanded in linear fashion to cover special aspects of general subjects. Theoretically, expansions may continue indefinitely. The more specific the work being classified, the longer the number combination tends to grow. LC records have been known to carry suggested Dewey numbers containing 21 digits, that is, 18 places past the decimal point. Such long numbers, however accurate, are unwieldy; it is hard to crowd them onto book spines and containers of audio-visual resources, and the dangers of mistakes in copying and shelving are multiplied. For these and related reasons many larger libraries have turned from DDC to some other system, such as *Library of Congress Classification* (LCC), which has a more economical notation.

Nevertheless, the DDC system has many advantages. Its content is compact, consisting in DDC23 of the following: a volume for introductory matter, the manual, tables of additional digits used to supplement the main classification schedules, and lists of relocations, discontinuations and reused numbers; two volumes for summaries and the schedules themselves; and a fourth volume for the index. The DDC incorporates many mnemonic devices that may be transferred from one class to another (e.g., –03 at the end of a classification number of any length often indicates a dictionary of the subject). The classifier, once familiar with the system, can apply it to incoming materials quite rapidly. It provides a limited number of optional alternative locations and allows for great detail of specification. Patrons are likely to be familiar with it, because it is the system most frequently used in school and public libraries—at least in the United States. Furthermore, it arranges subjects from the general to the specific in a logical order, which often can be traced by analogy through more than one class. It is philosophical in conception, being based on a systematic outline of knowledge that allows for subjects not yet known. Even so, the overall arrangement is not preemptively theoretical or logical. Dewey's intent was to provide a practical system for classifying books in the libraries of the United

TABLE 17.1 Some DDC Class Numbers Pertaining to *Families*.

DDC Notation	Aspects of the Topic *Families*
158.24	Interpersonal relations with *family* members
173	Ethics of *family* relationships
201.7628292	*Family* violence—Social theology
259.12	*Family* counseling
261.8327	Abuse within the *family*
304.666	*Family* planning [Demography]
306.85	*Family*
306.859	Matriarchal *family*
346.015	Domestic relations (*Family* law)
362.82	*Families* [with specific social problems]
363.96	*Family* planning [Overpopulation]
392.36	Dwelling places [including those for *families*]
591.563	*Family* behavior [in Animal behavior]
616.89156	*Family* psychotherapy
796	*Families*—Recreation—Outdoors
929.2	*Family* histories

States. The resulting American focus of the classification remains one of its notable limitations, although efforts have been made in later editions to rectify its biases, especially its Christocentric approach to the religion class.

A basic premise of the Dewey approach is that there is no one class for any given subject. The primary arrangement is by discipline. Any specific topic may appear in any number of disciplines. Various aspects of such a topic are usually brought together in the relative index to offset the scattering of topics across the scheme. For example, a work on *families* may be classified in one of several places depending on its emphasis, as can be seen in Table 17.1. In addition to the aspects shown there, other material on families may be found in still different DDC numbers. Use of the relative index would lead the classifier to some of them.

The basic concepts of the system are covered in two places in DDC: the introduction and the manual. The introduction gives detailed explanations of the schedules and tables and detailed instructions in classifying and building numbers with DDC. It is required reading for anyone working or planning to work with the DDC. The manual is devoted to a discussion of the tables and schedules by number, pointing out areas of difficulty and explaining what should or should not be included in certain numbers. Sometimes classifiers do not realize that there is another possible solution or another choice until they find a note that refers them to the manual (e.g., *See Manual at 391 vs. 646.3, 746.92.*). Manual notes may refer to an individual schedule or table number, spans of numbers, or two or more competing numbers. The following is an example from the manual:

571-573 vs. 610

Results of research in biology and medicine

Use 571-573 for results of physiological and anatomical research with animal models in 571-573. Use 615-618 for results of pharmacological, therapeutic, and pathological research if the medical relevance for humans is either stated or implied. If in doubt, prefer 571-573.

In addition to the manual, a few outside sources provide guidance. There are several helpful web resources, including OCLC's Dewey Services website[9] and *025.431: The Dewey Blog*.[10] There are some print resources available, but most were not updated for the 23rd edition; *caveat emptor*! One of these resources is *Dewey Decimal Classification: Principles and Application* by Lois Mai Chan and Joan S. Mitchell, the former DDC Editor-in-Chief; this resource was a very helpful resource for understanding the 22nd edition of the DDC; it is, however, more than 10 years old and thus of only limited use today. Chapters 1 and 4 are useful general discussions of the foundations of DDC.[11]

SCHEDULE FORMAT

Summaries

At the beginning of volume 2 and on the Dewey Services website, DDC provides three summaries, showing successively the 10 main classes, the 100 divisions, and the 1,000 sections of the basic scheme.[12] The same information also can be found by browsing each main class in WebDewey, but it involves many more steps. Each main class consists of a group of related disciplines.

Summary of the 10 Main DDC Classes

000	**Computer science, information & general works**
100	**Philosophy & psychology**
200	**Religion**
300	**Social sciences**
400	**Language**
500	**Science**
600	**Technology**
700	**Arts & recreation**
800	**Literature**
900	**History & geography**

Each main class is separated into 10 divisions, although a few of these, as well as some further subdivisions, may seem to be rather artificially located within the class. The hundred divisions are shown in the Second Summary, from which the following numbers are taken:

Summary of the Divisions of a Typical DDC Class

600	**Technology**
610	**Medicine & health**
620	**Engineering**
630	**Agriculture**
640	**Home & family management**
650	**Management & public relations**
660	**Chemical engineering**
670	**Manufacturing**
680	**Manufacture for specific uses**
690	**Construction of buildings**

Each division is subdivided into 10 sections. Again, some of these may seem artificially located. The 1,000 sections are shown in the Third Summary, from which the following numbers are taken:

Summary of the Sections of a Typical DDC Division

610	**Medicine & health**
611	**Human anatomy, cytology & histology**
612	**Human physiology**
613	**Personal health & safety**
614	**Incidence & prevention of disease**
615	**Pharmacology & therapeutics**
616	**Diseases**
617	**Surgery & related medical specialties**
618	**Gynecology, obstetrics, pediatrics & geriatrics**
619	**[Unassigned]**

In some cases, the captions in the summaries are abbreviated forms of what appears in the actual schedules. For example, in the schedules, 614 reads as *Forensic medicine; incidence of injuries, wounds, disease; public preventive medicine*, and 617 is *Surgery, regional medicine, dentistry, ophthalmology, otology, audiology*.

Volume 2 presents in detail the subjects placed in 000 through 599. Fully detailed schedules for subjects placed in 600 through 999 are in volume 3. In the full schedules, each of the DDC numbers that has subdivisions extending over more than four pages gives a summary of the first digits past the decimal point.

612	**Human physiology**

SUMMARY

612.001–.009	Standard subdivisions
.01–.04	[Biophysics, biochemistry, control processes, tissue and organ culture, physiology of specific activities]

.1	Circulatory system
.2	Respiratory system
.3	Digestive system
.4	Hematopoietic, lymphatic, glandular, urinary systems
.6	Reproduction, development, maturation
.7	Musculoskeletal system, integument
.8	Nervous system
.9	Regional physiology

At the main classes and the 100 divisions, multilevel summaries are provided. An example of this can be found at **610 Medicine and health**.

Entries in Schedules

In the full schedules the 1,000 sections are listed separately, followed in detail by any subdivisions they may have. There are often irregularities, attesting that the phenomena of the world cannot always be subdivided and re-subdivided into groups of 10:

Extended Decimal Subdivision of a DDC Topic

612	Human physiology
612.1	Circulatory system
612.11	Blood
612.12	Blood chemistry
612.13	Blood vessels
612.14	Blood pressure
612.17	Heart
612.18	Vasomoters

In the preceding example, the relationships are well represented. The hierarchical relationships between *human physiology* and the *circulatory system* and between the *circulatory system* and its six subdivisions are made clear by the notation (i.e., each level of specificity is represented by an additional digit) and by the captions through their indentions.

The preceding display also shows the presence of coordinate classes (i.e., siblings classes), where the notation of the siblings is of equal length. This example, while common, is not representative of the entire classification scheme. As just mentioned, not every concept can be neatly divided into 10 components. If the number of coordinate classes is greater than 10, then some siblings may require additional digits or other notational adjustments to fit in the class. In other words, there may be differences between a conceptual structure and a notational structure. See Figures 17.1 and 17.2 for two different views of the same set of concepts.

In Figure 17.1, a group of related concepts is presented without notation. Most of these domestic animals are on the same level of hierarchy in this

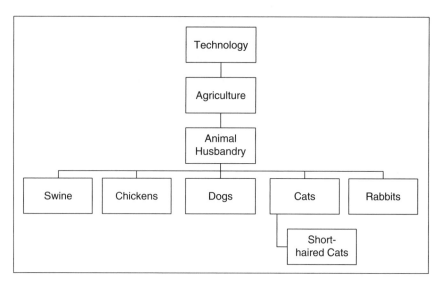

FIGURE 17.1 A Conceptual Hierarchy in DDC.

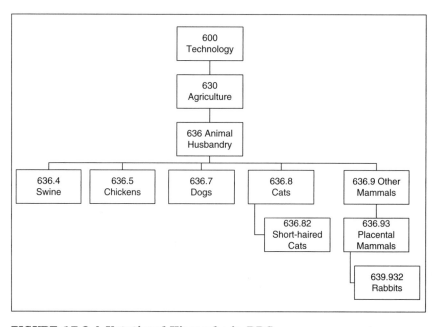

FIGURE 17.2 A Notational Hierarchy in DDC.

diagram; except for a particular type of cat, they are all equal in placement. But due to the purely numerical base for the classification, the notation cannot duplicate exactly that same conceptual structure. Instead, notational adjustments are made in Figure 17.2 to accommodate all the concepts.

Successive lengthening of the base number by a digit (or occasionally more than one digit) achieves step-wise division. This pyramidal structure, demonstrated here, means that in subject relationships, what is true of the whole is true of the parts. For instance, agriculture is a branch of technology; animal husbandry is an aspect of agriculture, and so forth.

A Typical DDC Hierarchical Sequence

600	Technology
630	Agriculture & related technologies
636	Animal husbandry
636.6	Birds other than poultry
636.68	Ornamental birds, songbirds, hawks
636.686	Finches, parrots, hawks
636.6865	Parrots
636.68656	Cockatiels

As the notation expands beyond the decimal point, DDC editors introduce a space after every third number in the print volumes (in WebDewey long sequences are unbroken). The spaces are inserted merely to facilitate reading the closely listed digits. On library materials and bibliographic records the spaces should be omitted, so that the number will occupy no more space than is absolutely necessary. The final number in the preceding example would be written 636.68656 in a bibliographic record. The schedules rarely display numbers with more than four decimal places, although the relative index sometimes expands numbers to eight or even nine decimals. In the relative index, one finds the caption *Radiation injuries—Animals—Veterinary medicine*, which is represented by the number 636.08969897. Yet the schedules proper expand the section for animal husbandry only as far as **636.089 Veterinary medicine**. Instructions at 636.089 in the schedules allow the building of the longer number found in the index. The concept of *number building* is explained later in this chapter.

Certain places in the schedules where fully symmetrical expansion cannot be maintained are given *centered entries*, which represent concepts for which there is no specific number in the notational hierarchy and which, therefore, cover an abbreviated span of numbers. These appear with centered lines immediately above them and with the *greater-than* symbol (>) at their left margins. Centered entries are always followed by a note that tells where to class comprehensive works that cover the subject represented by the centered entry.

> **439.6-439.8 Specific North Germanic languages**

Class comprehensive works in 439.5

Other useful formatting devices are the section numbers and running titles at the top of each page of volumes 2 and 3 (the schedules), the use of bold-face and lightface type in various sizes, and left-hand marginal indentions to indicate hierarchical structure. The schedules also employ square brackets for numbers from which a topic has recently been shifted (or relocated) and parentheses to indicate numbers that are considered alternatives to standard DDC practice (i.e., optional numbers).

> **355 [.6068]**   **Management [of Military Administration]**
>
> Do not use; class in 355.6

> **(789)**   **Composers and traditions of music**
>
> (Optional number and subdivisions; prefer 780 for music as a whole; prefer 781-788 for principles, forms, ensembles, voices, instruments)

Typographic symbols, such as asterisks (*) and daggers (†), are used to indicate footnotes at the bottom of the pages of the schedules (or in the *Notes* box within WebDewey); these footnotes usually contain important number building instructions or restrictions.

Notes

Perhaps the most helpful sources of information for the DDC classifier are the notes. They are essential in forming an accurate, appropriate, and well-built classification number. They can, however, be somewhat difficult to understand for students and librarians unaccustomed to the DDC. After becoming somewhat familiar with the system, users can interpret the notes more easily. There are several major kinds of notes:

- notes that tell what is found at a classification
- notes that tell what is found at other classifications
- *including* notes (i.e., notes that identify topics in *standing room*)
- notes that explain changes in schedules and tables
- notes that instruct the classifier in number building
- notes that prescribe citation and preference order
- notes that explain options

Notes found in the first two groups have what is called *hierarchical force*. This means that they are applicable to all the subdivisions under the number that has the note, as well as to the number with the note.

Notes That Tell What Is Found at a Classification

These notes provide a basic overview of what belongs in a classification number. They include scope notes, definition notes, number-built notes, former heading notes, variant name notes, and class-here notes. Each is explained below.

A *scope note*, as discussed in the context of subject headings in chapter 12, is a note that delimits or explains the usage of a concept, term, or notation.

070.172   Newspapers
Limited to comprehensive works on newspaper journalism

643   Housing and household equipment
Works for owner-occupants or renters covering activities of members of household

A *definition note* provides an explanation of the meaning of a term.

641.5   Cooking
Preparation of food with and without use of heat

A *number-built note* explains the source of built numbers that are included in the schedules.

559.9   Earth sciences of extraterrestrial worlds
Number built according to instructions under 554-559

In this case, the classifier should consult the instructions at 554-559 to learn how the number was created. At 554-559, there are number-building instructions that state:

Add to base number 55 notation 4- 9 from Table 2, e.g., geology of Japan 555.2, of moon 559.91

A *former heading note* indicates when there has been a change in the caption associated with a particular DDC notation. Similar to LCSH and other controlled vocabularies, there is a constant need to update terminology as language evolves. Some examples include:

362.74   Troubled young people
Former heading: Maladjusted young people

687.165   Sleepwear and loungewear
Former heading: Nightclothes

A *variant name note* lists one or more synonyms for the terms used in the DDC caption.

305.235   Young people twelve to twenty
Variant names: adolescents, teenagers, young adults, youth

599.633   Suidae
Variant names: pigs, swine

Of all the notes describing what is found at a classification notation, the *class here note* is probably the most important. This note is used to identify major topics or aspects of those topics that are considered coextensive or nearly coextensive with the topic represented in the caption. These listed topics are said to *approximate the whole* of the class. In other words, the topics enumerated under a class notation are considered roughly equivalent to the heading. A class-here note also indicates where comprehensive and interdisciplinary works are to be classified. A *comprehensive work* is a resource that addresses multiple aspects of a subject from *within* the same disciplinary approach. According to the introduction, a *comprehensive number* is one that "covers all the components of the subject treated within that discipline. The components may be in a span of consecutive numbers or distributed throughout the schedule or table."[13] An *interdisciplinary work* is a resource that approaches a subject from multiple disciplines or perspectives. An *interdisciplinary number* is "used for works covering a subject from the perspective of more than one discipline, including the discipline where the interdisciplinary number is located."[14] Without indication in the schedules of the interdisciplinary and comprehensive numbers, it would be much more difficult to classify such works consistently. Identifying them is an important function of class-here notes.

305.5   **People by social and economic levels**

Class here class struggle, people by level of cultural development, social classes

170.42   **Metaethics**

Class here comprehensive works on moral realism, moral anti-realism

336.2   **Taxes**

Class here taxation, internal (inland) revenue, interdisciplinary works on taxes

Notes That Tell What Is Found at Other Classifications

These notes, which point the classifier to other places within the classification scheme, begin with the words *for*, *see also*, or *class* (as opposed to *class here*). The following *plagiarism* example, which begins with a class-here note, also provides a class-elsewhere note (beginning with the word *class*) and a see note (beginning with the word *for*).

808.025   **Plagiarism**

Class here works that focus on avoiding unintentional plagiarism, interdisciplinary works on plagiarism

Class citation style in 808.027

> *For a specific aspect of plagiarism, see the aspect, e.g., plagiarism in the context of copyright law 346.0482, plagiarism as a kind*

> *of student cheating 371.58, plagiarism in the*
> *work of an American fiction writer of the late*
> *20th century 813.54*

In the following *Folk music* example, six notes are presented, including a definition note, two class-elsewhere notes (although it might appear as one), a see also note, and two see manual notes (discussed below).

781.62   Folk music

Music originating within and associated with an ethnic or national group

Class folk rock in 781.66172. Class a specific style of music provided for in 781.64-781.66 with the style, e.g., reggae 781.646, Afro-Cuban jazz 781.6572687291

See also 780.9 for music of and performed in a specific location

See Manual at 781.62 vs. 780.89; also at 781.62 vs. 781.63-781.66

Obviously, encountering multiple notes is not uncommon in DDC.

Including Notes

These notes provide a location for topics that do not yet have enough works about them to justify a separate number. It is assumed that there may be more works in the future, in which case the topics could be assigned their own number. Therefore, the rules for applying DDC do not allow number building of any kind (including additions of standard subdivisions) for topics in *standing room* (a metaphor taken from "standing room only" where a person may stand in the back of a theater if there are no seats available at that time). The assumption is that the number in which the topic stands may be subdivided at a later time to create a number for the topic, and so, if no number building has been done, all items on that topic can be classified in the new number for the topic simply by adding new digits to the general number. Standing-room notes begin with the word *including*.

394.14   Use of drugs

Including marijuana, narcotics, tobacco

For alcoholic beverages, see 394.13

792.028   Acting and performance

Including impersonation, improvisation, use of expression and gestures

794.12   Chess—Strategy and tactics

Including specific strategies and tactics, e.g., combinations, sacrifices, traps, pitfalls, attack, counterattack, defense

In the third example, there are already some subdivisions established under this number.

794.1	Chess
794.12	Strategy and tactics
794.122	Openings
794.123	Middle games
794.124	End games

It is certainly possible that in the future individual subdivisions for specific combinations, traps, defenses, and so on, could be made.

Notes That Explain Changes in Schedules and Tables

These notes tell a classifier that there have been changes at a particular number since the last edition. There may have been revisions of contents covered, a discontinuation of coverage either for a whole number or for a part of its contents, or a relocation of all or part of the contents:

363[.3497]   **Disasters induced by human activity**
Number discontinued; class in 363.34

Explosions relocated to 363.1798; civil disorder relocated to 363.32; riots relocated to 363.323

Notes That Instruct the Classifier in Number Building

Number-building instructions provide ways to gain greater depth of analysis at a particular classification. These instructions usually begin with the word *Add*, indicate a *base number* with which to start (i.e., the kernel on which a fuller number will be built), and where in the classification schedule to go for additional digits to append onto the base number. In some cases, additional instructions are given for further additions to the number. A fairly simple example of a number-building note follows:

057   **General serial publications in Slavic languages**
Add to base number 057 the numbers following 037 in 037.1-037.9 for language only, e.g., Polish-language serial publications 057.85

Number building is discussed in detail below.

Notes That Prescribe Citation and Preference Order

These notes help a classifier decide which of more than one aspect or characteristic to use for classification. Preference order establishes the order in which one chooses a facet when only one can be chosen. For example:

305.9   **People by occupation and miscellaneous social statuses; people with disabilities and illnesses, gifted people**

. . .

Unless other instructions are given, class a subject with aspects in two or more subdivisions of 305.9 <u>in the number coming last</u>, e.g., unemployed librarians 305.9092 (*not* 305.90694)

. . .

Citation order allows the use of two or more characteristics (i.e., facets) in a *specified* order:

930-990   **History of specific continents, countries, localities; extraterrestrial worlds**

. . .

Add to base number 9 notation 3-9 from Table 2, e.g., general history of Europe 940, of England 942, of Norfolk, England 942.61; then add further as follows:

001	Philosophy and theory
002	Miscellany
00223	Maps, plans, diagrams
003	Dictionaries, encyclopedias, concordances
004	Ethic and national groups

. . .

In the history example, the citation order is clearly defined by the system: begin with the history base number (i.e., 9), add geographical information from Table 2 (e.g. 42 for England), and then add from an internal list of subdivisions as needed (e.g., 00223 Maps). If the instructions are followed exactly, then the facets comprising the completed notation are placed in the correct order (e.g., 942.00223). This is part of the number building process that is discussed in more detail later in this chapter.

Notes That Explain Options

Such notes are usually given in parentheses and may be of benefit in providing alternative methods for handling certain situations. International users find that options for religions, languages, and literatures allow them to give preferred treatment for local needs.

016   **Bibliographies and catalogs of works on specific subjects or in specific disciplines**

. . .

(Option: Class with the specific discipline or subject, plus notation 016 from Table 1, e.g., bibliographies of medicine 610.16)

In this example, classifiers are made aware of the option of placing a bibliography of medicine in the 610s with other medical topics, rather than organized with other bibliographies on various other subjects.

COMPLETELY REVISED SCHEDULES IN RECENT EDITIONS

In DDC21, there were three significant areas that underwent complete remodeling: **350-354 Public administration**, **370 Education**, and **560–590 Life sciences**. For two of these areas, public administration and life sciences, facets and facet indicators became a basic part of the design. Faceting in this form was introduced in the music schedule that was completely revised for DDC20. It allows for the building of numbers through the use of the facet indicators 0 and 1. In addition to those complete revisions, DDC21 began a two-edition plan to reduce Christian bias in the religion class.

DDC22 completed the relocations and expansions that were planned for **200 Religion**. It had no completely revised schedules but nonetheless had some major changes including: updated developments and terminology for social groups and institutions in 305-306; improvements to the 340 schedule that relate to laws of nations, human rights, and intergovernmental organizations; substantial updating of **510 Mathematics** and **610 Medicine and health**; movement of numbers for facilities for travelers from 647.94 into the 910-919 area with other travel-related concepts; and updating of numerous geographic areas in Table 2. Perhaps the most striking change in DDC22 was the removal of Table 7 (Groups of Persons), which was largely a duplication of the broad outline of the schedules themselves. Classifiers now use notations available in the schedules and in —08 from Table 1 in place of the former Table 7.

Similar to DDC22, there were no completely revised schedules in DDC23. Instead, many of the changes to the content were adjustments to how some fairly ubiquitous concepts were handled, and some changes were more structural in nature. One of the more significant revisions was the handling of groups of people, especially the terminology applied to them. For example, the terminology *groups of people* replaced the phrases *kinds of persons* and *social groups*. Also, the more understandable term *biography* replaced the long-standing but confusing phrase *persons treatment*. These changes affected the schedules in various ways but were particularly noticeable in the Table 1 Standard Subdivisions that begin with –08 and in the **305 Groups of People** section. DDC23 had additional updates in its other tables as well. For example, there were significant expansions within Table 2 for the ancient world, Italy, Switzerland, Sweden, Finland, Turkey, Indonesia, Vietnam, and Canada, and there were more possibilities to represent specific themes and subjects in literature through an expanded Table 3C. In the schedules 000-999, updates included a modernization of **004-006 Computer science**; an initial restructuring of the Orthodox Church and Islam portions of the religion schedules; and, new developments in logic, political parties, law, criminology, medicine, as well as myriad additions and changes throughout the rest of DDC.

The structural changes found in DDC23 included the elimination of dual headings. The term *dual heading* refers to a caption for a DDC number made up of two separate terms, the first being the main topic and the second being an important component or subordinate topic. For example, the caption **570 Life sciences Biology** has been replaced by the simpler **570 Biology**, with the phrase *Life sciences* being placed in a class-here note. The other structural change was the removal of any span of numbers that was unbalanced in terms of the number of digits on either side of the hyphen. For example, the number span 305.805–.89 has been replaced by two spans: 305.805–.809 and 305.81–.89.

NUMBER BUILDING

A premise in working with DDC is that all possible numbers are not specifically included in the schedules, but more precise numbers than those listed can be built or synthesized using tables or other parts of the schedules. This idea is introduced in chapter 16 in a discussion of faceted classification. In this section, the idea as applied to DDC is explored further.

Adding from Tables

Tables 1 through 6 (referred to as T1-T6) are found in volume one of the print DDC23; in WebDewey, links to the tables are provided at the bottom of the initial search screen. Tables give the classifier ways to expand existing numbers in the schedules. Each number in these tables is preceded by a dash to show that it cannot stand alone as a classification number. The dash should be omitted when the number is appended to a classification notation. For some concepts, tables may refer the classifier to one or more additional tables in order to complete the number. For example, some instructions in T5 require the use of T6.

Table 1. Standard Subdivisions (T1)

All shelf classifications provide a dual approach to organization. Some items are grouped on the basis of their subject content; others are placed according to their form or genre. The standard subdivisions supplied in T1 are derived from what was called a table of *form divisions* in the earliest editions of the DDC. The present-day *standard subdivisions* include concepts other than form. Some actually do denote form (dictionaries, biographies, serials, etc.); others represent modes of treatment, covering theoretical or historical aspects of the subject, such as philosophy and theory, history, and so on. The following are the main categories found in T1.

> **–01** **Philosophy and theory.** An exposition of any subject treated from the theoretical point of view. *Examples:*
>
> 701   Philosophy and theory of fine and decorative arts
>
> 720.1   Architecture—Philosophy and theory
>
> 722.701 Roman architecture—Philosophy and theory

–02   Miscellany. An assortment of treatments and form subdivisions. *Examples:*

702.78	Artist marks
725.40222	Industrial buildings—Architectural drawings

–03   Dictionaries, encyclopedias, concordances. A straightforward subdivision. Its meaning is unambiguous. No further subdivisions are enumerated. *Examples:*

703	Dictionaries, encyclopedias, or concordances of fine and decorative arts
720.3	Architecture—Dictionaries
727.803	Library buildings—Encyclopedias

–04   Special topics. Undefined in T1. A space reserved for topics that have no other place in the schedules. *Examples:*

704.9	Iconography in the fine and decorative arts
720.44	Architecture of portable and temporary buildings

–05   Serial publications. Used for publications (print or electronic) in which the subject is treated in journal articles, newspapers, magazines, and yearbooks. No further subdivisions are enumerated. *Examples:*

705	Serial publications of fine and decorative arts, such as *Art Journal*
720.5	Architecture magazines, such as *Architectural Record*
720.9505	*Journal of Asian Architecture and Building Engineering*

–06   Organization and management. Assortment of subdivisions covering organizations, societies, and assorted management issues. Used for management treatises, marketing, personnel management, charters, histories of societies, administrative reports, membership lists, and the like. *Examples:*

706.8	Management of a fine and decorative arts organization
720.6041	Membership directory for a British organization of architects, such as the Royal Institute of British Architects

–07   Education, research, related topics. Addresses education (including its various levels), study programs, resources for education and research, various kinds of research, museums and exhibits, instructional methods, awards, and so on. *Examples:*

707.9	Fine arts awards
720.711	Graduate education in architecture
722.11074	A guidebook to a museum of ancient Chinese architecture, such as Beijing's Museum of Ancient Architecture

–08 **Groups of people.** Includes groups based on gender, age, relationships, abilities, occupations, ethnic or national associations, and miscellaneous social attributes. *Examples:*

704.086942	Homeless artists
727.8083	Library building adaptations for young people

–09 **History, geographic treatment, biography.** A frequently used subdivision that includes provisions for adding historical treatment (including specific chronological periods), geographic treatment (primarily through the use of Table 2; see below), and biographies of individuals, pairs, or groups of people. *Examples:*

720.9	Fletcher's *History of Architecture*
727.840973	Architecture of branch library buildings in the United States
720.92	A biography of Frank Lloyd Wright

As can be seen in many of these examples, most of the standard subdivisions are further subdivided in T1. For example, under T1-01 Philosophy and theory the following subtopics are listed:

–011	Systems
–012	Classification
–014	Communication
–014 1	Discourse analysis
–014 8	Abbreviations, acronyms, symbols
–015	Scientific principles
(–016)	Bibliographies, catalogs, indexes *(optional number)*
–019	Psychological principles

The T1-09 subdivision is used frequently in DDC because it contains several universal concepts. It can be divided by historical periods, indicate biographical form, or be geographically divided through the addition of area digits from T2. The main –09 subdivisions include the following:

–09	History, geographic treatment, biography
–0901-0905	Historical periods
–091	Areas, regions, places in general
–092	Biography
–093-099	Specific continents, countries, localities; extraterrestrial worlds

For example, the addition of –0973 onto the end of 727.84 changes the subject matter from the architecture of branch libraries *anywhere* to the architecture of branch library buildings *in the United States*. This is explained in more detail below, in the section on Table 2.

Unless specific instructions indicate otherwise, standard subdivisions may be used with any number if such application is meaningful. Standard subdivisions may only be used once in number building activities. For some subdivisions, however, excerpts from Table 1 are repeated along with specific number-building instructions. If these excerpts are present, it is because they are allowable after using a particular subdivision. Without explicit instructions and/or a list of selected subdivisions, further number building is prohibited. If the classifier must choose between competing T1 subdivisions, the table of preference located at the beginning of T1 provides guidance on which to choose.

One specific instruction not to add standard subdivisions is found only in the introduction in volume 1 and is often overlooked. When a work does not "approximate the whole of the subject of the number," the standard subdivision usually should not be added.[15] This was mentioned already in the discussion of *Including notes* that identify topics that are *in standing room*. If, for example, a resource is about the history of the NACO program (which assists in the development of the LC name authority file), it should be placed in **025.35 Cooperative cataloging, classification, indexing**. Because the resource is not about all forms of cooperative cataloging, and because there is no specific number for collectively developing just the name authority file, the standard subdivision –09 for history should not be attached to the number.

Although in the table each subdivision's number is preceded by a single zero that acts as a facet indicator, it is sometimes necessary in the schedules to apply a double or triple zero to introduce the subdivision (e.g., instead of using –03 for dictionaries, one may be required to use –003 or –0003 instead). This happens only when single zero subdivisions are already appropriated in the schedules for special purposes. The instructions that cover such situations are explicit and a pattern showing double or triple zeroes will be enumerated in the schedules and section summaries. All notes or instructions should be read carefully before proceeding. A few examples will illustrate certain basic principles:

a) **Standard subdivisions listed in the schedules**
   In some parts of the schedules, a concept that is ordinarily expressed as a standard subdivision is included with its own number. For example, **805 Serial publications** is listed directly in the schedules of the literature class:

800	Literature (Belles-lettres) and rhetoric
801	Philosophy and theory
802	Miscellany
803	Dictionaries, encyclopedias, concordances
[804]	[Unassigned]
805	Serial publications
806	Organizations and management
807	Education, research, related topics
808	Rhetoric and collections of literary texts from more than two literatures
809	History, description, critical appraisal of more than two literatures

Thus 805 is the number used for a serial about literature, not 800.5 or 800.05. In this class, nearly every section within this division is identical to the standard subdivisions. The only exceptions are 808, which has nothing to do with groups of people, and 804, which is unassigned rather than holding a special topic. Likewise, **501 Philosophy and theory** is listed after **500 Natural sciences and mathematics**. None of the subtopics under T1-01, such as –012 Classification, are included after 501, but one can use these subtopics if appropriate. For example, a work on classification in the natural sciences would be classified 501.2.

b) **Standard subdivisions not listed and no instructions given**
The most common situation is one in which standard subdivisions are not included in the schedules and no instructions are given. In such cases a single-0 introduces the standard subdivision. For example, the schedules give the number 371.4 for student guidance and counseling. A work on the philosophy and theory of student guidance and counseling would be given the classification number 371.401.

c) **Single-0 subdivisions used for a specific purpose; standard subdivisions introduced by a double-0**
An example of the double-0 appears at **271 Religious congregations and orders**. Single-0 subdivisions are used for specific kinds of religious congregations, such as **271.01 Contemplative religious orders**, **271.03 Teaching orders**, **271.04 Preaching orders**, and so on. Here the instruction is to use 271.001-271.009 for standard subdivisions. Thus an encyclopedia of religious congregations and orders is classified in 271.003.

d) **Single-0 and double-0 subdivisions used for special purposes; standard subdivisions introduced by a triple-0**
An example of the triple-0 appears at **946 Spain, Andorra, Gibraltar, Portugal**. Single-0 numbers 946.01-946.08 are reserved for historical periods of Spain *alone*. Double-0 numbers 946.001-946.009 are reserved for standard subdivisions of Spain *alone*. Therefore, 946.0001-946.0009 (triple-0) are used for standard subdivisions of Spain, Andorra, Gibraltar, Portugal *together*. An encyclopedia of the Iberian Peninsula, therefore, would be classified as 946.0003.

Table 2. Geographic Areas, Historical Periods, Biography (T2)

When a given heading can be subdivided geographically and the library has many books dealing with that subject, it is recommended that the classifier use T2 (the geographic area table), which allows expansion of the number systematically by region or site. It is by far the bulkiest of the six tables accompanying the DDC schedules. Its general arrangement is as follows:

–01-05	Historical periods
–1	Areas, regions, places in general; oceans and seas
–2	Biography
–3	Ancient world
–4	Europe
–5	Asia
–6	Africa
–7	North America
–8	South America
–9	Australasia, Pacific Ocean islands, Atlantic Ocean islands, Arctic islands, Antarctica, extraterrestrial worlds

Area –1 (which also may be referred to as T2-1) is used for the treatment of any subject geographically, but not limited by continent, country, or locality. It allows diverse elements that have natural ties to regions or groups (e.g., frigid zones, temperate zones, land forms, or types of vegetation) to be brought together under certain subjects. T2-2 permits subdivision by biography (which includes diaries, reminiscences, correspondence, etc.) of persons associated with any subject for which the schedule instructions say to add geographic notation directly instead of adding standard subdivisions. T2-3 offers specific subdivisions for ancient countries and areas during associated periods of ancient history. The date of demarcation between ancient and modern history varies among regions and countries; those dates are provided in the captions for each subdivision. Area notations –4 through –9 are for specific continents and modern countries. For example, area number –4 Europe has the following summary subtopics:

–41	British Isles
–42	England and Wales
–43	Germany and neighboring central European countries
–44	France and Monaco
–45	Italy, San Marino, Vatican City, Malta
–46	Spain, Andorra, Gibraltar, Portugal
–47	Russia and neighboring east European countries
–48	Scandinavia and Finland
–49	Other parts of Europe

Area notations may be added directly to schedule numbers where so instructed. For example, a general treatise on higher education in Dundee, Scotland, is classified in **378 Higher education**. The schedule at **378.4–.9 Higher education in specific continents, countries, localities in modern world** instructs the classifier to add to base number 378, the notation 4-9 from T2. In T2, –412 7 is listed as the number for Dundee City (under –412 Northeastern Scotland). This number is therefore appended to 378, resulting in 378.4127 as the following analysis shows:

300	Social sciences
370	Education
378	Higher education (Tertiary education)
378.4	Europe
378.41	British Isles
378.412	Northeastern Scotland
378.4127	Dundee City

Where specific instructions (as in 378.4–.9) are not given for geographical treatment in the schedules, the classifier can apply geographic locations through the use of T1-09 to any number that lends itself to that approach. For example, the specific DDC number for savings banks is 332.21. To classify a work on savings banks in London, the schedule gives no specific direction to use T2, nor does it give any specific directions for proceeding further. So the standard subdivision –09 may be used directly because as long as the topic is not *in standing room* or there are no instructions that forbid applying standard subdivisions, a classifier can always use T1. In T1, a note under –093-099 says to add to base number –09 notation 3-9 from Table 2. So resources on savings banks in London are classified in 332.2109421 as shown here:

300	Social sciences
330	Economics
332	Financial economics
332.2	Specialized banking institutions
332.21	Savings banks
332.210	*Facet indicator*
332.2109	Standard subdivision for geography
332.21094	In Europe
332.210942	In England and Wales
332.2109421	In Greater London

Although these examples result in fairly long numbers, they are actually quite simple to construct.

Table 3. Subdivisions for the Arts, for Individual Literatures, for Specific Literary Forms (T3)

Table 3 is actually three tables:

- T3A: Subdivisions for Works by or about Individual Authors
- T3B: Subdivisions for Works by or about More than One Author
- T3C: Notation to be Added Where Instructed in Table 3B, 700.4, 791.4, 808-809

The titles of these tables are descriptive of their uses. They are never used alone but are used following specific instructions for literature; notations from Table 3 may also be used where instructed in 700.4 and 791.4, which are numbers in the arts class. The notation –1 through –8 in T3A and T3B develop and expand the form divisions that appear in the full schedules under 810, 820, 830, 840, 850, and 860.[16] These mnemonic form divisions for kinds of literature are found in Table 17.2 below.

Flow charts for building literature numbers can be found at the T3 instructions in the manual in volume 1 of DDC23. These are of great assistance in following the massive amount of instructions found in the literature schedules and with T3. Two examples of built literature numbers follow:

Lanford Wilson's *5th of July* (1978)

800	Literature
810	American literature in English
812	American drama in English
812.5	1900-1999
812.54	1945-1999

TABLE 17.2 DDC Form Divisions in the Literature Classes.

Notation	Description	Examples
–1	Poetry	**831 German poetry**
–2	Drama	**839.12 Yiddish drama**
–3	Fiction	**839.313 Dutch fiction**
–4	Essays	**869.4 Portuguese essays**
–5	Speeches	**891.865 Czech speeches**
–6	Letters	**895.16 Chinese letters**
–7	Humor and satire	**896.3927 Swahili humor and satire**
–8	Miscellaneous writings	**899.2118 Tagalog miscellaneous writings**

[–7 Humor and satire does not appear in Table 3-A; it is not used for individual authors.]

In the Wilson example, the base number (810) is determined through the list of languages found in the literature class, but despite the presence of specific section numbers there as well, the classifier is instructed to use T3 to complete the number because additional instructions are found there. In this example, T3A is employed because the work is by a single author. T3 instructs the classifier to add a form division and then a chronological period number (based on publication dates), which is provided back in the American literature schedules at 811-818. Compiling this number in the correct citation order is not difficult *if* the instructions are consulted.

The second example, a work by many authors, uses T3B and T3C instead. Its instructions are somewhat more elaborate and must be followed carefully. This example incorporates language, form, and period as do many literature numbers, but it also includes a standard subdivision to indicate that this is a *collection* of works and some notation representing a subject or theme.

A collection of 20th century Indonesian humor and satire about river travel

800	Literature
890	Literature of other specific languages
899	Literature of Austronesian languages
899.2	Austronesian languages *(from T6)*
899.22	Malayo-Polynesian languages of Indonesia
899.221	Indonesian literature
899.2217	Humor and satire *(from T3B)*
899.22172	1900-1999
899.221720	*Facet indicator*
899.2217208	Collections of literary texts
899.22172080	*Facet indicator*
899.221720803	Literature with specific themes
899.2217208032	Travel *(from T3C)*
899.22172080321	Places in general *(from T2)*
899.221720803216	Air and water
899.2217208032169	Fresh and brackish waters
899.22172080321693	Rivers and streams

Table 4. Subdivisions of Individual Languages and Language Families (T4)

Table 4 is used with base numbers for individual languages to break down the various components or facets of a language as explained under 420-490. Similar to the approach used in T3, it provides mnemonic form divisions for languages (see Table 17.3).

TABLE 17.3 DDC Form Divisions Used with Languages.

Notation	Description	Examples
−1	Writing systems, phonology, phonetics	**431 German writing systems**
−2	Etymology	**439.12 Yiddish etymology**
−3	Dictionaries	**439.313 Dutch dictionaries**
−5	Grammar	**491.865 Czech grammar**
−7	Historical and geographic variations, modern nongeographic variations	**496.3927 Swahili dialects**
−8	Standard usage of the language (Prescriptive linguistics)	**499.2118 Tagalog usage guides**

Table 5. Ethnic and National Groups (T5)

Table 5 is used according to specific instructions at certain places in the schedules or in other tables, or through the interposition of T1-089 the standard subdivision for specific ethnic or national groups. These applications are exactly parallel to the use of Table 2, which is used either on direct instruction in the schedules or on interposition of T1-09 for history, geographic treatment, or biography. The T5 summary includes the following top-level categories:

−05	Persons of mixed ancestry with ethnic origins from more than one continent
−09	Europeans and people of European descent
−1	North Americans
−2	British, English, Anglo-Saxons
−3	Germanic peoples
−4	Modern Latin peoples
−5	Italians, Romanians, related groups
−6	Peoples who speak, or whose ancestors spoke, Spanish, Portuguese, Galician
−7	Other Italic peoples
−8	Greeks and related groups
−9	Other ethnic and national groups

Table 6. Languages (T6)

Table 6 is a basic mnemonic table used to indicate the particular language of a work or the language that is the subject matter of a work. It is used as instructed in the schedules or other tables.

-1 Indo-European languages

-2 English and Old English (Anglo-Saxon)

-3 Germanic languages

-4 Romance languages

-5 Italian, Dalmatian, Romanian, Rhaetian, Sardinian, Corsican

-6 Spanish, Portuguese, Galician

-7 Italic languages

-8 Hellenic languages

-9 Other languages

For example, in order to classify a Bible in French, one would start with the entry given in both the index and the schedules, **220.5 Modern versions and translations** [of the Bible]. For **220.53-59 Versions in other languages**, the schedule direction says to "Add to base number 220.5 notation 3-9 from Table 6, e.g., the Bible in German 220.531." The notation for French in T6 is -41. The resulting whole number for a modern French Bible may be analyzed as follows:

220   The Bible

220.5   Modern versions and translations

220.54   In the Romance languages

220.541   In modern French

Adding from Other Parts of the Schedules

There are a number of places where the classifier is instructed to find a number elsewhere in the schedules and to add it whole to the number at hand, as demonstrated by the following example:

000   Computer science, information & general works

010   Bibliographies

016   Bibliographies and catalogs of works on specific subjects

> Add to base number 016 notation 001-999, e.g., bibliographies of computer programs and software 016.0053, of general encyclopedic works 016.03, of philosophy 016.1, of novels 016.80883 . . .

If one wanted to classify a bibliography of works on the architecture of libraries, the number for the architecture of library buildings, 727.8, would be attached to 016 for bibliographies, resulting in 016.7278.

In many other places the classifier is instructed to take only a part of another number and add it to a base number given in the instruction. The following example illustrates this kind of instruction:

300	Social sciences
390	Customs, etiquette & folklore
398	Folklore
398.3	Real phenomena as subjects of folklore
398.36	Scientific themes
398.369	Animals

> Add to base number 398.369 the numbers following 59 in 592-599, e.g., rabbits 398.369932

At 599.65 one finds

599	Mammalia (Mammals)
599.6	Ungulates
599.65	Cervidae (Deer)

So, for a work on deer as the subject of folklore, the classifier would take the digits *following* 59 (i.e., 59<u>9.65</u>) and append it (965) to the base number (398.369). The final notation would be 398.369965.

More complicated instructions may give more than one directive for building a number. For example, a classifier with a resource about deaths related to cancer of the heart would start with the number for cancers.

600	Technology
610	Medicine & health
616	Diseases
616.9	Other diseases
616.99	Tumors and miscellaneous communicable diseases
616.994	Cancers
616.9941	Cancers of cardiovascular organs and blood
616.99411–.99415	Cancers of cardiovascular organs

> Add to base number 616.9941 the number following 611.1 in 611.11-611.15, e.g., cancer of heart 616.99412; then add further as instructed under 618.1-618.8, e.g., therapy for cancer of heart 616.9941206

At 611.1 the subdivisions for organs of the cardiovascular system are found:

.1	Cardiovascular organs
.11	Pericardium
.12	Heart
.13	Arteries
.14	Veins
.15	Capillaries

This results in the number 616.99412 for cancer of the heart. Then, per the instruction that states "add further as instructed under 618.1-618.8," digits from the table found at 618.1-.8 are added as needed:

001-009	Standard subdivisions
01-03	Microbiology, special topics, rehabilitation
04	Special classes of diseases
05	Preventive measures and surgery
052	Preventive measures
059	Surgery
06	Therapy
07	Pathology
075-079	Diagnosis, prognosis, death, immunity
	Add to 07 the numbers following 616.07 in 616.075-616.079, e.g., physical diagnosis 0754
08	Psychosomatic medicine
09	Case histories

This results in the number 616.9941207, but more information is still needed to complete the process. At 616.07, the following breakdown is provided:

616.07	Pathology
616.071	Etiology
616.075	Diagnosis and prognosis
616.078	Death
616.079	Immunity

So for a work on death from cancer of the heart, the final classification number is 616.99412078, that is, 616.9941 (base number), followed by 2 for the heart, followed by 07 for pathology, and followed by 8 for death. Internal *add tables*, such as the one at 618.1-618.8 are found in many places in the schedules and must be used only as instructed. Notice that in this example, four different parts of the same class were used to build this number (i.e., 616.99411-616.99415, 611.1, 618.1-618.8, and 616.075-616.079). This can be quite common with complex topics.

When a single work treats multiple aspects of a subject, such as age, gender, and physical characteristics, the classifier must be careful to observe citation and preference order. As mentioned earlier, citation order allows a number to be built that takes into account two or more of the aspects. Instructions are given in such cases as to the order in which the aspects may be represented in the number (e.g., add to base number . . . then add further as instructed . . .). If a citation order is not given, then one must choose among the aspects according to instructions for preference.

Sometimes the classifier is instructed to prefer the aspect that comes first (or last) in the schedule, while at other times there may be a table of preference given. For example:

704.942   Human figures

Unless other instructions are given, observe the following table of preference, e.g., groups of children 704.9425 (*not* 704.9426):

Erotica	704.9428
Nudes	704.9421
Specific groups of people	704.9423-704.9425
Groups of human figures	704.9426

The important point to remember is to follow instructions. More detail about number building can be found in the introduction to DDC23 and in training materials provided by OCLC's Dewey Services.[17]

THE RELATIVE INDEX

The *relative index* is so called because it shows relationships of each specific topic to one or more disciplines and to other topics. It contains terms found in the schedules and tables, as well as synonyms for those terms; names of countries, states, provinces, major cities, and important geographic features; and some names of persons. It does not have phrases that contain concepts represented by standard subdivisions (e.g., art education, medical laboratories). Many *see also* references are given (e.g., Medicines, *see also* Drugs). Geographic name entries usually refer the user to the appropriate area table number as well as to the history number for the place if it has been established (e.g., Massachusetts 974.4 and T2-744). The index includes a variety of geographic places: large areas such as continents and countries (e.g., Thailand T2-593), well-known local places such as cities and towns (e.g., Halifax, Nova Scotia T2-716225), and sometimes quite small and remote locations from around the world (e.g., Bouvet Island T2-9713). A few referrals to the standard subdivisions and to other tables (e.g., Repairs 620.0046 and T1--028 8; Abandoned children—arts T3C–3526945) are also included.

The DDC relative index enumerates alphabetically all the main headings in the classification schedules, plus certain other specific entries not actually listed in the schedules. One such instance is the entry for *Radiation injuries—Animals—Veterinary medicine* discussed earlier in this chapter. In other places, the index terminology varies from that found in the schedules for the same class number, although the general meanings coincide. For example, in the schedules the notation 612.793 has the caption *Glands of skin* but that number is also associated with the entry *Sebaceous*

Seasons	508.2
arts	T3C--33
astronomy	525.5
biological adaptation	578.43
effect on natural ecology	577.23
folklore	398.236
history and criticism	398.33
influence on crime	364.22
literature	808.8033
history and criticism	809.9333
specific literatures	T3B--08033
history and criticism	T3B--0933
music	781.524
natural history	508.2

FIGURE 17.3 A Typical DDC Relative Index Entry.

glands–Human physiology in the relative index. An example of a typical index entry is provided in Figure 17.3.

Note in the figure that there is a single classification number across from the main heading. This is the *interdisciplinary number*. An interdisciplinary number, as explained in the section on "Notes That Tell What Is Found at a Classification," is useful for works that address a topic from a wide range of perspectives when one discipline alone cannot be chosen as the primary one. This number is given a position of prominence in the relative index to ensure that it is spotted easily.

The classifier should, of course, consult the index, especially in cases in which the location of the desired topic, or the precise nature of its relation to other topics, is in doubt. Yet the relative index should never become a substitute for the schedules. It is coordinated with them, but is limited for reasons of space and cannot show hierarchical progressions or topical groupings. It will guide the classifier to some, but not necessarily all, aspects of a given subject. The next important step in the classification process is to consult the schedules for verification, perspective, and possible further instructions. Only by using the two types of display together can the full potential of the scheme be realized.

BROAD AND CLOSE CLASSIFICATION

Because it offers a wide variety of techniques and nearly limitless expansions in number building, DDC is hospitable to all the titles that a large library might add in any subject. It also offers various ways to meet the limited needs of smaller libraries. The classifier must remember that, in general, when there are relatively few works in a given subject area, DDC encourages broad classification. Digits in class notations after decimal points may be cut off at any appropriate place.

Broad versus Close Classification

If you have been asked to classify the work The Hunter's Guide to White Tail Deer, you have a number of options as to where to place this resource. By default, the classification system generally expects you to choose the most specific number available, but local needs may trump standard practice.

If your collection in this subject is fairly small, an 8-digit number may be more than you need.

Instead, you could put it at **799.2**, which covers all hunting.

Or, you could put it at **799.26** for *big game hunting* or **799.27** for *specific kinds of big game*.

Or, you could put it at **799.276** for *hunting hoofed animals*.

Or, you could put it at **799.2765** for *hunting all kinds of deer*.

Or, you could put it at **799.27652** for *hunting white tail deer*.

The final determination is up to you and your institution, based on the size and scope of your collection.

Formerly, LC provided two segmentation marks (slashes) in the DDC numbers provided in its MARC records to show where the abridged version of the number would end and/or to show the beginning of a standard subdivision. As of 2005, only one segmentation mark is given in a number to indicate the end of an abridged number. An example of the former practice is 940.53/18/092, which stands for *World War II—Holocaust—Biographies*. A small library with a limited collection of materials on World War II might prefer to keep them all together under 940.53. If the library has several dozen items on the war, it might keep the ones on the Holocaust together by using 940.5318. If it maintains a separate resource collection for use by researchers, it could add the standard subdivision –092 to distinguish the biographies. In today's practice, this number is now given only one segmentation mark, where the abridged DDC number would end: 940.53/18092. When a library decides to retain entire numbers to achieve close classification at particular points in the collection, it omits the slash marks, which are used in LC records merely to suggest breaking points.[18]

In catalog records created by other members of a network, the DDC classification numbers do not have slash marks. If a shorter number is desired, one must consult the schedules to find an appropriate point of abridgement. For example, in the World War II Holocaust number just discussed, breaking the number at 940.531 places the item with other works on the social, political, and economic history of the war—not a very logical option. Breaking it at 940.5318 places it with items on the Holocaust, but not subdivided by a standard subdivision—quite logical. The classifier needs to check the schedules and not just cut the number at an arbitrary number of digits past the decimal point.

UPDATING

Over the last several decades, new editions of the DDC had been published approximately every seven years. Between editions, updating was and is accomplished via publication of new and changed entries on the Dewey website.[19] It contains corrections of errors, clarifications, updating, and expansions. For example, a recent addition to the DDC is a note at **025.0427 Semantic web**, which states, "Class here linked data." *Linked data* is not found in the printed DDC23 schedules or its index, but it has been added to the "Updates to DDC23" website and to both the relative index and the schedules in WebDewey. Also available on the Dewey Services home page are other kinds of updating tools such as LCSH/DDC mappings, as well as links to discussion papers and the Dewey blog.[20] A policy for continuous revision has been adopted by OCLC, which means that each revision is released when it is completed rather than waiting for a single release date for an entire group of revisions.

ABRIDGED EDITIONS

The first *Abridged Decimal Classification and Relativ Index for Libraries, Clippings, Notes, etc.*, appeared in 1894, the year in which the fifth edition of the full schedules was published. The last abridged edition (Ed. 15) was based on DDC23 and published in 2012. Like its predecessors, it was designed primarily for general collections of 20,000 titles or fewer, such as are found in small public and school libraries. It contained many fewer entries than the full edition; and the tables, schedules, index, and manual all appeared in one volume. The numbers used were compatible with DDC23 so that growing libraries could expand from the abridged to the full edition as their collections increase. As stated at the beginning of the chapter, there will be no more print editions of the DDC schedules in English in either full or abridged form. Currently, the 15th abridged edition is available on the WebDewey site in the form of PDF files. As time goes on, the format provided for abridged versions of DDC may change.

WEBDEWEY

WebDewey offers online searching and browsing access to the *Dewey Decimal Classification*. In addition, it maps DDC to LCSH and links the mapped LCSH terms to their corresponding authority records. Mappings to BISAC headings and to the *Sears List of Subject Headings* have been added to WebDewey. Selected MeSH headings are also mapped to DDC numbers. WebDewey offers two work areas where a cataloger may build a number during the process of reading the number-building instructions. The first is simply an empty textbox that allows manually building the notation digit by digit. The second is an automated number building function that works with the specific number building instructions that begin with the phrase "Add to base number. . . ." Local notes can also be added; they are displayed in context so that local classification practices are appropriately available. WebDewey is available as an add-on service to OCLC Connexion, OCLC's cataloging service.

It is considered difficult by some to learn DDC by starting with WebDewey instead of the print volumes, because one cannot get a sense of the big picture on just one screen versus being able to look at two or more pages of text at once. However, for the experienced user, WebDewey can offer advanced means of display that are found to be quite desirable. For example, searching can be done using one or multiple indexes and by using Boolean operators, proximity searches, right and left truncation, and character masking. There are browsable Key Word in Context (KWIC) indexes of the Relative Index and LCSH, and browsable sequential indexes of DDC numbers. Classification and table numbers are presented in hierarchical displays that show the position in relation to broader and narrower classes. Extensive use of hyperlinks gives fast access to related records and to entries in the manual that are cited in notes for particular numbers. Top-down navigation through DDC is possible starting with a display of the 10 main classes. A tutorial assists in introducing new users to the best approaches for using WebDewey.[21]

In addition, OCLC has started providing free access to the dewey.info website with the idea of contributing to the growing web of linked data. "Dewey.info is an experimental space for linked DDC data. The intention of the dewey.info prototype is to be a platform for Dewey data on the Web."[22] It provides URIs for and access to each of the 1000 sections in the DDC summaries; the information about each section appears in 12 different languages. More about this budding service can be found at the OCLC website.[23]

DIFFICULTIES: LONG NUMBERS, RELOCATIONS, AND DISSATISFACTION

Among the difficulties built into the DDC system are its long numbers, which increase rather than diminish as the system grows, nullifying some of the mnemonic character of the basic system. For example, the number 636.08969897, which was cited earlier as coming from the relative index entry for radiation injury in veterinary medicine, is so long that any mnemonic associations between it and the number 616.9897 (from which it was built) are obscured. Librarians who wish to retain these long numbers because of extensive holdings in one or more fields could print them on item labels in several lines. The foregoing number could be written in shorter segments as follows:

636		**636.089**
.089	or	**69897**
698		
97		

Related to the long number difficulties are the topical relocations that occur from one edition to another. Such surgery is forced upon the system by its limited notational base and the swift growth and change in the world of knowledge and of publication. An article by Pat Thomas written soon after publication of DDC20 gives pointers on adjusting to DDC's expansions, reductions, relocations, and revised schedules.[24] No library can afford to ignore all efforts to keep shelf arrangement contemporary with the shifts in knowledge as reflected first in the literature and then in the updates to DDC. Decisions about updating DDC are made by an editor-in-chief and assistant editors in consultation with the DDC Editorial Policy Committee (EPC). The DDC EPC, a 10-member international board, represents interests of librarians in various kinds of libraries and advises the DDC editors and OCLC concerning the ongoing development of DDC.

In the mid-20th century, there was a big rush, particularly among academic libraries, to switch from DDC to LCC. It was based on a number of factors: lower costs associated with classifying with LCC;[25] more readily available LCC call numbers in copy cataloging; shorter LCC notation; fewer revisions in LCC; and some dissatisfaction with certain editions of DDC. These switches seem to have run their course; in more recent years, however, some public and school libraries have begun looking at alternatives to DDC.[26] Some libraries have turned to BISAC headings (see discussion of BISAC in chapter 15). "Unlike Dewey, which categorizes related knowledge systematically, BISAC is an alphabetical list of categories ranging from *Antiques and Collectibles* to *True Crime*. Many librarians feel BISAC's relative simplicity and user-friendly language have an advantage over Dewey's complexity. The BISAC system is maintained by the Book Industry Study Group, which classifies books into 52 broad categories, each with additional levels of specificity. Categories for a book are typically determined by the publisher . . . and are used throughout the distribution chain by companies like Amazon, Baker & Taylor, . . . and others. In many ways, it fuses the functions of subject headings with classification."[27]

UNIVERSAL DECIMAL CLASSIFICATION (UDC)

The development of the *Universal Decimal Classification* (UDC) was begun in 1895 by two Belgian lawyers, Paul Otlet and Henri LaFontaine, who founded the International Institute of Bibliography. It was designed for the classification of a huge catalog of the world's published information in all fields of knowledge known as the Universal Bibliographic Repertory. Otlet wrote in 1897 that "this repertory will consist of an inventory of all that has been written at all times in all languages, and on all subjects."[28] It is "something which could be described as a kind of artificial brain."[29] Otlet and LaFontaine, both utopian, socialist pacifists, dreamed of universal peace coming through the help of systematic documentation. Although they did not see either world peace or completion of an inventory of knowledge, their dream of a repertory of the world's knowledge may be coming to pass on the World Wide Web.

UDC was based on DDC5, but was, with Dewey's permission, expanded by the addition of many more detailed subdivisions and the use of typographical symbols (i.e., UDC's auxiliary signs) to indicate complex subjects and what is known today as *facets*. DDC's decimal notation was retained (except for final zeros), but for long numbers a decimal is placed after every third digit:

5	Mathematics. Natural sciences
59	Zoology
599	Mammalia (mammals)
599.7	Ungulata (ungulates / hoofed mammals)
599.73	Artiodactyla (even-toed ungulates)
599.731	Suiformes / Nonruminantia
599.731.1	Suidae
599.731.11	Sus (genus)
599.731.111	Wild boars

The discipline-based main classes, as well as some subdivisions, are still the same in UDC as they are in DDC, but class 4 (i.e., DDC 400) has been amalgamated with class 8 and is currently vacant. Many major and almost all minor subdivisions are now quite different from those in DDC.

Similar to DDC, the UDC comprises enumerative, hierarchical, and faceted elements. As can be seen in the preceding example, hierarchy is built directly into the system, as is the inevitable enumeration that comes from identifying each element within those hierarchies. The main difference between the two schemes, however, lies in the enhanced analytico-synthetic structure of UDC. Although DDC does provide for some number building, its ability to combine more than one classification element is somewhat limited.

UDC's faceted structure has its roots in DDC's device for indication of place—namely, the insertion of T1-09 followed by notation for a country or region from T2 (e.g., –0973 for the United States). UDC uses many of the same place notations as DDC but encloses them in parentheses instead of using the facet indicator –09. For example, *plant propagation in the United States* is 631.530973 in DDC but is 631.53(73) in UDC (note that the main class notation is the same in both). UDC has expanded upon the types of facets that can be added to a base number. In addition to place, UDC also has specific facets for the language of a work, its physical form, nationalities and peoples, time periods, materials, relationships, processes, operations, persons, and properties (including points of view), all of which can be appended to basic notations either alone or in combination. These facets are added from UDC's six *common auxiliary tables*, which are similar to T1-T6 in DDC. In addition to the common auxiliaries, *special auxiliaries* are distributed throughout the classification at the beginning of the class in which they are applicable. These are similar to the internal tables scattered throughout the DDC that have limited applicability, and, hence, do not belong in T1-T6 in volume 1. The common auxiliaries are listed in the following table.

TABLE 17.4 UDC Common Auxiliaries.

Notation	Description	Examples
=...	Table 1c: Common auxiliaries of language	=111 English =852 Andean languages
(0...)	Table 1d: Common auxiliaries of form	(03) Reference works (047.2) Travel reports
(1/9)	Table 1e: Common auxiliaries of place	(236.51) Ethiopian Highlands (735.214.4) Charles County, MD
(=...)	Table 1f: Common auxiliaries of human ancestry, ethnic grouping and nationality	(=622.82) Polynesians (=017) American native continental ancestry group
"..."	Table 1g: Common auxiliaries of time	"20" Twenty-first century CE "363.5" Time of emergency
	Table 1k: Common auxiliaries of general characteristics:	
-02	Common auxiliaries of properties	-024.68 Touching. Tangential -028.71 Biased. Slanted
-03	Common auxiliaries of materials	-032.26 Salt water. Brine -037.75 Ribbon. Tape. Webbing
-04	Common auxiliaries of relations, processes, and operations	-043.62 Starting -048.47 Conformity
-05	Common auxiliaries of persons and personal characteristics	-056.233 Persons of average size or height -057.177.4 First-line managers. Supervisors

Some examples using these auxiliaries include:

631.53=162.1	Plant propagation—written in Polish
631.53(038)	—Dictionary
631.53(37)	—in Italy
631.53(=1:37)	—by Ancient Romans
631.53"323"	—in Autumn (fall)

That UDC allows the classifier to represent multifaceted subjects with more granularity, through its complex notation, is a considerable difference from DDC. UDC allows for two or more separate classification numbers to be combined using the system's auxiliary signs. The common auxiliary signs are listed in Table 17.5.

TABLE 17.5 Common Auxiliary Signs.

Notation	Description	Examples
	Table 1a: Connecting symbols:	
+	Coordination. Addition	**622+669 Mining and Metallurgy**
/	Consecutive extension	**643/645 The home and household equipment**
	Table 1b: Relating symbols:	
:	Simple relationship	**17:7 Ethics in relation to art**
::	Order-fixing	**77.044::355.4 War photography**
[ ]	Subgrouping	**[622+669](485) Mining and metallurgy in Sweden**
	Table 1h: Subject specification by notations from non-UDC sources:	
*	General non-UDC notation	**62-97*C150 Temperature of 150 degrees Centigrade**
A/Z	Direct alphabetical specification	**(492.83UTR) City of Utrecht 929NAP1 Biography of Napoleon I**

Some examples using these auxiliary signs include:

631.53+634.653	Plant propagation—Avocados
631.532/.535	—Vegetative propagation
631.53:635.9	—Ornamental plants
631.53::911.52	—Natural landscapes
[631.53+634.653](72)	—Avocados—Mexico

Some resources, in order to have their subjects fully represented through the notation, may require multiple classification numbers along with one or more auxiliary signs and one or more facets. For example, a work about the use of computers in the management of hospital personnel can be created by linking two UDC class notations with a colon (the most commonly used of the auxiliary signs) and appending a facet from the common auxiliaries of properties in Table 1k:

614.21:658.3-027.44	Hospitals—Personnel management—Computer aided

Another example shows just how challenging assembling the classification can become if the subject is more complex. If a classifier had a tourist map of Grafton County, New Hampshire from the 1970s in the form of a PDF, then the final UDC notation would be something like this:

338.48(734.211.4)"197"(084.3)(0.034.2PDF)

3	Social sciences
33	Economics
338	Economic situation. . . . Production. Services. Prices
338.4	Production and services according to economic sectors
338.48	Tourism
338.48(7	Place—North America
338.48(73	United States of America (USA)
338.48(734	States of the north-eastern USA
338.48(734.2	New Hampshire
338.48(734.211.4)	Grafton County
338.48(734.211.4)"1	Second millennium CE
338.48(734.211.4)"19	Twentieth century CE
338.48(734.211.4)"197"	1970s
338.48(734.211.4)"197"(0	Common auxiliary of form
338.48(734.211.4)"197"(08	Illustrations
338.48(734.211.4)"197"(084	Images. Graphic documents
338.48(734.211.4)"197"(084.3)	Cartographic images.
338.48(734.211.4)"197"(084.3)(0.0	Special auxiliaries
338.48(734.211.4)"197"(084.3)(0.03	Documents according to production
338.48(734.211.4)"197"(084.3)(0.034	Machine-readable documents
338.48(734.211.4)"197"(084.3)(0.034.2	Digital documents
338.48(734.211.4)"197"(084.3)(0.034.2PDF)	Specific document type, A-Z

Such class notations, however, are not always used as *call numbers* (i.e., shelf addresses; see chapter 19); instead, they may be intended for a classified catalog in which each component of the class notations may serve as an access point. If the UDC notation is to be used for shelf classification, a part of the notation may be chosen as the call number if the string is lengthy or complex, or the entire string may be used, however unwieldy it might be. To ensure consistency in shelving, UDC provides a table explaining their set filing order (e.g., simple numbers precede numbers with colons, which precede numbers with double colons, and so on).[30] Due to this highly faceted structure and largely expressive notation the UDC has been used successfully in computerized information retrieval.[31]

UDC schedules were first published from 1904 to 1907 in French, followed later by full editions in English. UDC has since been published in whole or in part in 40 languages. It is widely used in many countries where English is the main or a co-official language (e.g., the British Isles, Canada, Australia, New Zealand, India) and in countries using other languages (e.g., Germany, Japan, Brazil, Spanish-speaking countries).[32] Based on Aida Slavic's survey of UDC users from 2006, of the more than 110 countries in which the UDC was employed at that time, approximately 28% of those countries used UDC as their primary classification scheme.[33] A list of countries currently using the scheme is presented on the UDC website.[34]

Until 1992 UDC was managed by the International Federation of Documentation (FID) in The Hague (Netherlands). When it became apparent in the 1980s that a more broadly based organization was needed to administer UDC, FID and the publishers of the Dutch, English, French, Japanese, and Spanish editions combined to found a new body, the UDC Consortium (UDCC). An early action of the UDCC was to create an international database that would be a master file. The database, called the UDC Master Reference File (MRF), now containing more than 70,000 entries, is updated once a year. An editor-in-chief and an editorial board of international membership oversee the continuous revision and expansion.[35]

Since 1992, UDCC has maintained the scheme by reviewing its content and initiating revisions and extensions. The results are published in *Extensions and Corrections to the UDC*.[36] A two-volume, easy-to-use edition of UDC was published in a "complete" edition by the British Standards Institution in 2005.[37] It is derived from the MRF. Supplements are issued each year, each one cumulating all previous ones so that one has only to look in two places for the latest notations. An abridged edition, containing about 4,100 entries, was published in 2003.[38] UDC Online is an electronic version of the complete edition of UDC and is available by subscription; its features are similar to features of WebDewey.[39] In the United States UDC is used mainly in some scientific and technical libraries and by one abstracting database.[40] More detailed descriptions of the UDC, its development, and its application may be found in a number of publications.[41]

NOTES

1. Melvil Dewey, *Dewey Decimal Classification and Relative Index*, 23rd ed., edited by Joan S. Mitchell et al. (Dublin, OH: OCLC, 2011). DDC, Dewey, Dewey Decimal Classification, and WebDewey are registered trademarks of OCLC.
2. Melvil Dewey, *Abridged Dewey Decimal Classification and Relative Index*, 15th ed., edited by Joan S. Mitchell et al. (Dublin, Ohio: OCLC, 2012).
3. "WebDewey," accessed June 12, 2015, http://dewey.org/webdewey/. Users must have a paid subscription to access this resource.
4. "Dewey Decimal Classification / Linked Data," accessed May 15, 2014, http://dewey.info/. As of July 2015, the dewey.info website has been off-line for several months. OCLC and the Dewey Team have stated several times that it will return shortly.
5. "Dewey by the Numbers," *025.431: The Dewey blog*, June 02, 2015, http://ddc.typepad.com/025431/2015/06/dewey-by-the-numbers.html.

6. "Dewey Translations," OCLC, accessed June 6, 2015, http://www.oclc.org/dewey/resources/translations.en.html.

7. "How One Library Pioneer Profoundly Influenced Modern Librarianship," OCLC, accessed May 15, 2014, http://www.oclc.org/dewey/resources/biography.en.html. A longer biography is also available: Wayne A. Wiegand, *Irrepressible Reformer: A Biography of Melvil Dewey* (Chicago: American Library Association, 1996).

8. Dewey, *Dewey Decimal Classification*, 23rd ed., xlvi.

9. "Dewey Services," OCLC, accessed May 15, 2014, http://www.oclc.org/dewey/.

10. *025.431: The Dewey blog*, accessed June 18, 2015, http://ddc.typepad.com/.

11. Lois Mai Chan and Joan S. Mitchell, *Dewey Decimal Classification: Principles and Application*, 3rd ed. (Dublin, Ohio: OCLC, 2003).

12. "Dewey Summaries," OCLC, accessed June 7, 2015, http://www.oclc.org/content/dam/oclc/dewey/DDC%2023_Summaries.pdf.

13. Dewey, *Dewey Decimal Classification*, 23rd ed., lxxv.

14. Ibid., lxxviii.

15. Ibid., lx.

16. The schedules for 870 and 880 are for classic Latin and Greek literature and the sections within are somewhat different; the 890 division, which focuses on literatures in other languages is structured very differently. 890 attempts to fit all of the literature of the world, except for those specified in 810-880, in 10 sections, and the digits representing the form divisions appear after the decimal point.

17. OCLC, "Dewey Services," accessed May 22, 2014, https://oclc.org/dewey.en.html.

18. OCLC, "Segmentation Marks in Dewey Numbers," accessed May 22, 2014, http://oclc.org/content/dam/oclc/dewey/news/newsletter/ddcnews_ifla2005.pdf.

19. OCLC, "Updates to DDC23," accessed May 22, 2014, http://www.oclc.org/en-US/dewey/updates/ddc23.html.

20. OCLC, "Stay Current with Ongoing Updates to the DDC," accessed May 22, 2014, http://www.oclc.org/en-US/dewey/updates.html.

21. OCLC, "WebDewey 2.0: An Overview," accessed June 6, 2015, http://www.oclc.org/support/training/portfolios/cataloging-and-metadata/webdewey/tutorials/webdewey-overview.en.html.

22. OCLC, "Dewey Decimal Classification/Linked Data," accessed May 28, 2014, http://dewey.info.

23. OCLC, "Dewey Services: Dewey Summaries as Linked Data," accessed May 28, 2014, http://www.oclc.org/dewey/webservices.en.html.

24. Pat Thomas, "Implementing *DDC20*," *DC&* 5, no. 1 (March 1990): 7-8.

25. "Report on the Use of Exceptional Dewey Classification Scheme for Literature including a Recommendation for Reclassification," July 11, 2010, http://www.library.illinois.edu/committee/exec/supplement/S2009-2010/Report_on_the_Use_of_Exceptional_Dewey_Classification.html. In this report, the committee refers to a study done at Duke University in which it was determined that the cost of classifying a resource using DDC was considerably more expensive than classifying with LCC.

26. Amy B. Wang, "County Library Embraces Dewey-less World," *The Arizona Republic*, September 9, 2009, http://www.azcentral.com/arizonarepublic/news/articles/2009/09/09/20090909deweyless0909.html; Cassidy Charles, "Is Dewey Dead?" *Public Libraries Online*, December 18, 2012, http://publiclibrariesonline.org/2012/12/is-dewey-dead/; Nate Hill, "New Classification System for Public Libraries?" *The PLA blog*, January 19, 2009, http://plablog.org/2009/01/new-classification-system-for-public-libraries.html.

27. Barbara Fister, "The Dewey Dilemma," *Library Journal*, October 1, 2009, http://lj.libraryjournal.com/2010/05/public-services/the-dewey-dilemma/.

28. W. Boyd Rayward, *The Universe of Information: The Work of Paul Otlet for Documentation and International Organisation*, FID520 (Moscow: FID, 1975), 113, https://www.ideals.illinois.edu/handle/2142/651. The original quotation by Paul Otlet is found in "Compte-rendu Sommaire des Deliberations: Conference Bibliographique Internationale, Deuxieme Session, Bruxelles, 1897," *IIB Bulletin*, II (1897): 225.

29. Ibid., 30.

30. "Using UDC: Practical Guide," accessed May 28, 2014, http://edu.udc-hub.com/en/intro.php. Available only through a subscription to the UDC Online.

31. Ibid.

32. "About Universal Decimal Classification," UDC Consortium, accessed May 28, 2014, http://www.udcc.org/index.php/site/page?view=about.

33. Aida Slavic, "Use of the Universal Decimal Classification: A World-wide Survey," *Journal of Documentation* 64, no. 2 (2008): 218.

34. "UDC Users Worldwide," UDC Consortium, accessed May 28, 2014, http://www.udcc.org/index.php/site/page?view=users_worldwide.

35. "About Universal Decimal Classification," UDC Consortium, accessed May 28, 2014, http://www.udcc.org/index.php/site/page?view=about.

36. *Extensions and Corrections to the UDC* (The Hague: FID, 1951-). Annual.

37. British Standards Institution, *Universal Decimal Classification, Complete Edition* (London: BSI, 2005).

38. British Standards Institution, *Universal Decimal Classification*, 2nd ed., abridged (London: BSI, 2003).

39. "UDC Online," accessed May 27, 2014, http://udc-hub.com/index.php.

40. *Meteorological and Geoastrophysical Abstracts* (Boston: American Meteorological Society, 1950-).

41. I. C. McIlwaine, *The Universal Decimal Classification: A Guide to Its Use*, revised edition (The Hague: UDC Consortium, 2007); I. C. McIlwaine, "Universal Decimal Classification (UDC)," in *Encyclopedia of Library and Information Sciences*, 3rd ed. (New York: Taylor & Francis, 2010); Aida Slavic et al., "Maintenance of the Universal Decimal Classification: Overview of the Past and Preparations for the Future," *International Cataloguing and Bibliographic Control* 37, no. 2 (2008): 23-29; W. Boyd Rayward, "The UDC and FID: A Historical Perspective," *Library Quarterly* 37 (July 1967): 259-278.

SUGGESTED READING

Chan, Lois Mai, and Joan S. Mitchell. *Dewey Decimal Classification: Principles and Application*. 3rd ed. Dublin, Ohio: OCLC, 2003.

Intner, Sheila S., and Jean Weihs. *Standard Cataloging for School and Public Libraries*. 5th ed. Santa Barbara, Calif.: Libraries Unlimited, 2014.

McIlwaine, I. C. *The Universal Decimal Classification: A Guide to Its Use*. Revised edition. The Hague: UDC Consortium, 2007.

Miksa, Francis L. *The DDC, the Universe of Knowledge, and the Post-Modern Library*. Albany, N.Y.: OCLC Forest Press, 1998.

Olson, Hope A., and John J. Boll. *Subject Analysis in Online Catalogs*. 2nd ed. Englewood, Colo.: Libraries Unlimited, 2001. Chapter 8: Online Catalogs and the Dewey Decimal and Library of Congress Classifications.

Rayward, W. Boyd. *The Universe of Information: The Work of Paul Otlet for Documentation and International Organisation.* Moscow: FID, 1975.

Satija, M. P. *The Theory and Practice of the Dewey Decimal Classification System.* Oxford: Chandos, 2007.

Wiegand, Wayne A. *Irrepressible Reformer: A Biography of Melvil Dewey.* Chicago: American Library Association, 1996.

Chapter 18

Library of Congress Classification (LCC)

INTRODUCTION

The Library of Congress (LC) was founded in 1800 as part of President John Adams's "Act to Make Further Provision for the Removal and Accommodation of the Government of the United States." In Section 5 of the act, $5,000 was allotted for the purchase of books and for establishment of a library space. By 1802, the Library of Congress had 740 books, a space in the Capitol, and a librarian to oversee the collection. Its earliest classification system was by size (folios, quartos, octavos, etc.), subarranged by accession numbers. By 1812 the collection had grown to more than 3,000 volumes, and a better method of classification was needed. The solution was to arrange the works under 18 broad subject categories similar to the Bacon-d'Alembert system used in the 1789 *Catalogue* of Benjamin Franklin's Library Company of Philadelphia. Soon after, in 1814, British soldiers burned the Capitol, where the collection was housed. To re-establish it, Thomas Jefferson offered to sell Congress his library of 6,487 volumes. Jefferson had cataloged and classified the works himself using 44 main classes and divisions based on a different interpretation of the Bacon-d'Alembert system. Its overarching structure was based on a tri-part division of knowledge: *Memory* (i.e., history), *Imagination* (i.e., the fine arts), and *Reason* (i.e., philosophy). After some debate, Congress agreed to purchase the Jefferson books for $23,950, or $3.69 per item. Although many were destroyed in a later fire, the classification that came with them was used until the end of the 19th century. By that time, Librarian of Congress Ainsworth Rand Spofford had made so many ad hoc modifications to the scheme, largely based on shelving and other physical limitations, that it was barely recognizable and completely inadequate for a collection that had grown to nearly 1.5 million volumes.

Many significant changes occurred at LC near the turn of the century. In 1897, John Russell Young, the Librarian of Congress from 1897-1899, "instructed James C. M. Hanson, Head of the Catalogue Division, and Charles Martel, the newly appointed Chief Classifier, to study the possibilities of adopting a new classification system."[1] Hanson and Martel examined existing classification schemes as options for the LC collection. There were already in existence the first five editions of the *Dewey Decimal Classification* (DDC) and the first six expansions of Charles A. Cutter's *Expansive Classification* (EC). LC classifiers studied both, as well as the German *Halle Schema* devised by Otto Hartwig. Young's time at LC was short and a new classification was not adopted during his tenure.

In 1899, Dr. Herbert Putnam, the new Librarian, with many new staff appointments and a brand new building, also decided it was important to reorganize and reclassify his rapidly growing collection. Since it was to be moved into more adequate shelving areas, the time was right to make some changes and leave the Jeffersonian classification system behind. Although Hanson and Martel rejected the other proposed schemes and instead worked intensively to develop ideas for a new classification system, Putnam did not immediately accept their work; "he questioned whether the Library of Congress should develop its own system instead of adopting a nationally accepted scheme such as the *Dewey Decimal Classification*. Because of his doubts, reclassification was held up for two years. In the end, it was decided that a new system was needed, and that Hanson's proposal to develop a scheme along the lines of Cutter's EC should be accepted."[2]

The experience Hanson and Martel gained exploring other classification systems was invaluable, and their debt to Cutter is implicit in the basic structure of their system. While the outline and notation of their 21 main classes are very similar to those of EC, there are no main classes for I, O, W, X, or Y as there are in Cutter's system.[3] All five letters do appear, however, as second or third symbols in the notation for various LC subclasses. The other major similarity to the EC is in the structure of class **Z-Bibliography. Library Science. Information Resources (General)**, which was the first class devised and was adopted from Cutter with only minor variations.

After Putnam and his Chief Cataloger, Charles Martel, determined the broad outlines of the new classification, various subject specialists were asked to develop each individual schedule, or portion of the system. Within a broad general framework set up to ensure coordination (known as Martel's seven points), each topic or form of presentation identified as a class or subclass was further organized to display the library's holdings and to serve anticipated research needs.

The original organization of the classification was according to broad disciplines as seen a century ago. Since interdisciplinary topics were difficult to accommodate in this system, many arbitrary choices have been made over the years. Each schedule was developed separately, following its own internal logic. The order of topics, types of captions, level of detail, form of notes, etc., reflects the material being classified and the style of those involved in its creation, application, and development. As a result, each schedule has unique features, and it is difficult to generalize about the schedules as a whole.[4]

Schedules comprising single classes or parts of classes were separately published as they were completed. Except for the **K-Law** schedules, most parts of the classification system had been published at least once between 1899 and 1950. Many have since gone through several editions. In one sense, the scheme represents a series of special classifications. Yet special libraries, with narrowly defined collecting and service goals, often find the *Library of Congress Classification* (LCC), which serves broader, more interdisciplinary uses, unsatisfactory for their purposes.

New classification numbers are approved every month, and to keep the system functionally up to date, individual schedules, or parts thereof, are reviewed as circumstances dictate and time allows. Revisions, reallocations, and additions keep LCC flexible and hospitable to new subjects or points of view. For example, in the 1960s interest in eastern religions and the increase in materials from Asia occasioned a re-allocation in 1972 of the topic *Buddhism* from the span BL1400-1495 into a whole new subclass, BQ. Revisions were likewise made in subclass **PL-Languages and Literatures of Eastern Asia, Africa, Oceania**, particularly in the sections for Chinese, Japanese, and Korean literatures.

Number spans are also updated on an as-needed basis to reflect political changes around the world. In 2010, a revision to the classification numbers in the DS schedule for the Iraq War was released. The previous classification array for that event was insufficient for the volume and variety of works published about it.

In recent years, some of the few remaining unpublished schedules have been released. Many of these classes have been in the **K-Law** schedules. For example, in the 2000s, schedules for Jewish, Islamic, and canon law have been developed and published. In 2014, the latest LCC schedules, **KIA-KIK-Law of Indigenous Peoples in North America**, were released online in *Classification Web* (see discussion below), but are not yet available in printed form.

New revisions of schedules continued to be printed until 2013. Among the most recent editions are revisions of General Works (A class), Philosophy, Psychology (B-BJ), History of Asia, Africa, Australia, New Zealand, etc. (DS-DX), Political Science (J), several law classes (K, KF, KX), Education (L), English and American Literature. Juvenile Belles Lettres (PR, PS, PZ), Science (Q), Medicine (R), and Agriculture (S); all were published in 2012. In 2013, however, LC announced a change in its approach to providing access to cataloging documentation.

The Library of Congress has announced a transition to online-only publication of its cataloging documentation. As titles that are in production are released, the Library's Cataloging Distribution Service (CDS) will no longer print new editions of its subject headings, classification schedules and other cataloging publications. The Library will instead provide free downloadable PDF versions of these titles. For users desiring enhanced functionality, the Library's two web-based subscription services, *Cataloger's Desktop* and *Classification Web*, will continue as products from CDS.[5]

At the time of this writing, the plan is to produce new PDF versions of each classification schedule annually. The first new PDF versions were produced in May 2015. Older PDF versions will be archived online for research purposes.[6]

Hundreds of number-letter combinations compatible with the notation have not yet been employed or have been retired in favor of new locations. The scheme will continue to accommodate for a long time the many new subjects and aspects of subjects not yet anticipated. The scheme is particularly useful for large university and research collections because of its hospitality and inherent flexibility. It has been used effectively in smaller academic and public libraries, although its adaptability for broad classification is limited. Even special libraries frequently base their own more technical constructs on it, extending its schedules or parts of schedules to cover their unique materials. Some foreign libraries also use the system even though, in spite of LC's large foreign holdings, it is primarily designed from an American perspective.

In records that are encoded in the MARC bibliographic format (see chapter 21), call numbers based on LCC that are assigned by LC or the British Library are placed in field 050. Those assigned by Library and Archives Canada or other contributing Canadian libraries, the National Library of Medicine, or the National Agricultural Library are entered in field 055, 060, or 070, respectively. In the OCLC system, members are asked to enter locally assigned call numbers based on LCC in field 090, although acknowledgment is made that 050, with the appropriate indicator values set, can also be used.

CLASSIFICATION TOOLS AND AIDS

The schedules are contained in more than 40 separate volumes or PDF files. Besides the basic schedules, there are some separately published tables to be used with specific schedules and a short general *Outline*, now in its seventh edition, which gives the secondary and tertiary subclass spans for most classes. Several volumes are devoted to subclass coverage of broad areas, such as related language and literature groups. A list of the available schedules is found in Table 18.1.

The schedules are also all available via LC's online subscription product *Classification Web* (hereafter referred to as *ClassWeb*).[7] *ClassWeb* offers a number of advantages over the print versions. In addition to access to the classification scheme and the *Library of Congress Subject Headings* (as discussed in chapter 13), it provides correlations between LCC numbers and LCSH. There are advanced search and navigation tools, and many hypertext links exist within and among the schedules. A notes file allows addition of local institutional or personal comments.

Similar to those for subject headings, instructions for classifying with LCC and arranging resources on the shelves are available in LC's *Classification and Shelflisting Manual* (CSM).[8] Until 2014, the CSM was available in print, but as of July 2014, it is offered only as free PDFs on the LC Policy and Standards Division (PSD) website.[9] It is also available as part of *Cataloger's Desktop*.

TABLE 18.1 Outline of LCC Schedules in Printed Form.

Notation	Title	Latest version
A-Z	Outline	n/a
A	General Works	2012
B-BJ	Philosophy, Psychology	2012
BL-BQ	Religion (General). Hinduism. Judaism. Islam. Buddhism	2008
BR-BX	Christianity. Bible	2008
C	Auxiliary Sciences of History	2008
D-DR	History (General) and History of Europe	2011
DS-DX	History of Asia, Africa, Australia, New Zealand, etc.	2012
E-F	History: America	2011
G	Geography. Maps. Anthropology. Recreation	2007
G Tables	Geographic Cutter Number Tables http://www.loc.gov/catdir/cpso/GCutter.pdf	2013
H	Social Sciences	2008
J	Political Science	2012
K	Law (General)	2012
K Tables	Form Division Tables For Law (apply to all K subclasses except KD, KE, and KF)	2010
KB	Religious Law	2008
KD	Law of the United Kingdom & Ireland	2008
KDZ, KG-KH	Law of the Americas, Latin America, & the West Indies	2008
KE	Law of Canada	2008
KF	Law of the United States	2012
KJ-KKZ	Law of Europe	2008
KJV-KJW	Law of France	2008
KK-KKC	Law of Germany	2008
KL-KWX	Law of Asia & Eurasia, Africa, Pacific Area & Antarctica	2008
KZ	Law of Nations	2012
L	Education	2012
M	Music and Books on Music	2010
N	Fine Arts	2010
P-PZ Tables	Language and Literature Tables	2010

(continued)

TABLE 18.1 (*continued*)

P-PA	Philology and Linguistics (General). Greek Language and Literature. Latin Language and Literature	2010
PB-PH	Modern European Languages	2009
PJ-PK	Oriental Philology and Literature, Indo-Iranian Philology and Literature	2008
PL-PM	Languages of Eastern Asia, Africa, Oceania. Hyperborean, Indian, and Artificial Languages	2010
PN	Literature (General)	2010
PQ	French, Italian, Spanish, and Portuguese Literatures	2008
PR, PS, PZ	English and American Literatures. Juvenile Belles Lettres	2012
PT	German, Dutch, and Scandinavian Literatures	2009
Q	Science	2012
R	Medicine	2012
S	Agriculture	2012
T	Technology	2010
U-V	Military Science. Naval Science	2008
Z	Bibliography. Library Science. Information Resources (General)	2009

Updating

ClassWeb is a dynamic interface; minor corrections are made available the same day they are approved, and new classification numbers are added monthly. Updating of the print versions, on the other hand, is accomplished by several publications, most of which are available directly from LC.[10]

- **Revised editions of individual schedules.** As seen in the list of volumes in Table 18.1, revised editions of the various schedules have been published at different times. All schedules and the *Outline* were sold individually by LC's CDS until July 2014. Access is now provided through the free PDF versions and the subscription-based *ClassWeb*.

- *Library of Congress Classification Monthly List*. Additions and changes are available on the LC Acquisitions and Bibliographic Access website. PSD posts new and revised classification numbers, as well as summaries of decisions and tentative (i.e., as-yet unapproved) lists of changes.[11] At the same site one can find the Web version of the LC

Classification Outline, the PDF versions of the classification schedules and the CSM, and various memos about policy changes.

- *SUPERLCCS: Gale's Library of Congress Classification Schedules Combined with Additions and Changes*. These cumulations of the schedules, combined with LC's monthly *Additions and Changes,* have been published annually since 1988 by Gale Research Company, now known as just Gale, a business of Cengage Learning. SUPERLCCS is available in print with added "Gale notes" to the text to clarify some LCC instructions and explain the terminology used in the schedules.[12]

- *Cataloging Service Bulletin* (CSB). This channel for decisions and experiments in technical processing at LC was published quarterly from 1945 until 2010.[13] It provided valuable data on LCC and shelflisting practice, as well as other aspects of subject and descriptive cataloging. Although the publication has ceased, it is still useful for understanding previous changes in the classification scheme. The full run of the modern CSB (1978-2010) is available through *Cataloger's Desktop,* or it may be downloaded in PDF format for free.[14] Pre-1978 editions have not been digitized, but copies of them are maintained at LC and elsewhere.

Indexing

There is no official comprehensive index to the print versions of LCC. Rather, each volume has its own index, and an index in one volume only rarely refers to a concept in another volume. This lack has been satisfied online in *Class-Web,* where one can search in various ways for words associated with all classification notations.

If one is using the print versions of LCC, one needs to consider the various disciplines that might have notations for a topic and search in the index of the schedule for each of those disciplines. The captions used to describe the same concept may be different in various disciplines; so, one might need to be persistent and creative in attempting to locate the topic of interest. For example, the index to class **T-Technology** provides the following entries under *Baths, Public*:

Baths, Public
    Building construction: TH4761
    Plumbing: TH6518.B3

but the class **N-Fine Arts** index entry reads:

Bath houses:
    Architecture: NA7010

the class **R-Medicine** entry reads:

Public baths:
    Public health: RA605+

the class **H-Social Sciences** has two entries that read:

Bathhouses:
Gay culture: HQ76.965.B38

Baths, Public:
Employees: HD8039.P86+

and among the various volumes of the K classes, there are entries that read:

Baths, Public:
Islamic law: KBP184.47.P82

Bath houses
Tang and post-Tang China: KNN345.B37
Bath houses (Ancient China): KNN195.B37

The best indexing is in *ClassWeb* where one can do a *caption search*, an *index search*, or a *keyword search*, and also some combinations of them. Each type of search returns different results. To find some of the classification numbers above, one could search for *public baths* (or some variant) in one or more of the search boxes or employ truncation (e.g., public bath*) to retrieve more results. A caption search for *public bath** returns classification numbers or ranges associated with *Public bath employees* (HD), *Public baths* (KBP), and *Public baths, comfort stations, etc.* (RA) only. The index search for *public bath** returns only a single classification number—the one for *Public bath employees*. Using the keyword search, however, *ClassWeb* returns 16 results, some of which are relevant; some of which are not.

KBP184.47.P82	Public baths (Ablutions) [Islamic law]
KNN345.B37	Bath houses (Tang and post-Tang China) [Law]
HD8039.P86-.P862	Public bath employees [Labor. Working class]
TH4761	Baths [Building construction]
TH6518.B3	Baths, Public [Plumbing]
[RA605-607]	Public baths, comfort stations, etc. [Public health]
RA605	Public baths, comfort stations, etc. —General works
RA606	Bathing beaches. Baths and swimming pools
RA607	Comfort stations
RA780	Cleanliness. Bathing [Public health]
RA794	Health resorts, spas, etc. [Medical tourism]
RA850.B3	Bath, England. Hot Springs [Medical geography]
RA969.33	Bathing facilities [Hospital services]

NA5471.B3	Bath Abbey [Architecture—Religious buildings]
NA7010	Baths and washhouses [Architecture]
KNN195.B37	Bath houses (Ancient China) [Law]

Presented in this fashion, it can be difficult to determine exactly what is meant by each caption. Explanatory phrases have been added in this text using square brackets to help the readers with context, but these do not appear in *ClassWeb*. One must examine each number to determine which ones might be useful. This is not a terribly burdensome approach when there are only 16 results; when there are 104,432 keyword results, however, it is not helpful. Another option is to change the settings under "Search tips and options" to allow either a partial or full hierarchy to be displayed. That, too, can be problematic as it provides a great deal more text for each entry, as seen below:

RA794	Public aspects of medicine—Medical geography. Climatology. Meteorology—Medical tourism—Health resorts, spas, etc.
KNN345.B37	Asia (South Asia. Southeast Asia. East Asia): China—General—By period—618 A.D. to 1644 A.D. Tang and post-Tang periods—Public order and welfare—Social legislation. Social (urban) services—Particular, A-Z—Bath houses
HD8039.P86-.P862	Industries. Land use. Labor—Labor. Work. Working class—By industry or trade, A-Z—Public bath employees
TH4761	Building construction—Buildings: Construction with reference to use—Other public buildings—Baths

. . .

Another possible way to find notations from more than one discipline is to search LCSH.[15] While it was never designed to function as an index to LCC, many entries and subdivisions refer in brackets to one or more class numbers, often including terminology used in the schedules. For example, under the heading **Public Baths** one finds the following:

> **Public baths** (May Subd Geog)
> [RA605-RA606 (Public health)]
>> UF Baths, Public [Former heading]
>> BT Baths
>>   Public buildings
>> NT Bathhouses
>>   Baths, Roman

The narrower terms **Bathhouses** and **Baths, Roman** have no classification notations associated with them. The broader term **Baths** has only notations for school hygiene, personal hygiene, and therapeutics. The broader term **Public buildings** lists [NA4170-4510 (Architecture)], but this does not include the **NA7010 Bath houses** notation. It can be seen that under the heading, **Public baths** one would miss the entries from the N and T schedules. The classification numbers printed in LCSH are not intended to be comprehensive. Current policy states that the notations may be provided only when the scope and language of the heading are identical, or nearly identical, in scope to the caption in the schedules.[16] Notations are added as time and resources permit, but are often spotty, as the above example indicates. Since former practices were uneven, the notations should always be double-checked for accuracy in the schedules.

Sometimes LCC notations relating to a given concept can be grouped more quickly through LCSH than through the many individual schedule indexes, as shown in the following example:

LCC indexes:

B-BJ-Philosophy; Psychology
Hypnotism (Parapsychology): BF1111-1156

BL, BM, BP, BQ-Religion: Religions, Hinduism, Judaism, Islam, Buddhism
Hypnotism: BL65.H9

H-Social Sciences
Hypnotism and crime: HV6110

KK-Law of Germany
Hypnosis (Force)—Criminal law: KK8020.F67
Hypnotism and criminal law: KK8014

Q-Science
Hypnotic conditions—Physiology: QP425-427

R-Medicine
Hypnotherapy: RJ505.H86
Hypnotic age regression: RC499.H96

Hypnotics: RM325
Hypnotism and hypnosis
    Anesthesiology: RD85.H9
    Dentistry: RK512.H95
    Forensic medicine: RA1171
    Psychiatry: RC490-499

LCSH:

Hypnotic susceptibility (May Subd Geog)
[BF1156.S83]
. . .

Hypnotics   (May Subd Geog)
[RM325]
. . .

Hypnotism

[BF1111-BF1156 (Parapsychology)]

[HV6110 (Hypnotism and crime)]

[RC490-RC499 (Psychiatry)]

. . .

Hypnotism and crime

[HV6110]

Hypnotism in dentistry   (May Subd Geog)

[RK512.H95]

. . .

Hypnotism in surgery   (May Subd Geog)

[RD85.H9]

One would miss the entries at BL, QP, RA, and others, when using LCSH as an index to LCC, but its use can still be helpful, especially if one is having difficulty finding a starting point in the classification schedules. In the LCC index in *ClassWeb* when performing a caption search for *hypnotic*, one retrieves the results shown in Table 18.2.

In 1978 the United States Historical Documents Institute, Inc., and University Microfilms International jointly sponsored the filming of 6.8 million cards of the LC shelflist, arranged by call number, covering 1968-1979.[17] This tool, which is still available, was used by some libraries as a kind of index, but of course the materials in the shelflist and the classification notations used to order them are more than 35 years old, so it is of little use in contemporary subject cataloging, although it makes for an interesting historical artifact.

Just as the Gale cumulations and the LC shelflist reproductions are commercial aids based on official, publicly accessible LC data, so too a number of indexing ventures have reflected similar trade manipulation of publications or automated processing available from LC. Their problem has been in keeping up to date. A publication that can serve as a kind of index is Scott's *Conversion Tables: LC-Dewey, Dewey-LC, and LC Subject Headings-LC and Dewey*.[18] Again, age is a factor, and this resource, published in 2005, cannot be expected to accurately reflect the latest version of the classification scheme. It should also be noted that these correlations are also available as part of a subscription to *ClassWeb*. The following is a list of the correlations that *ClassWeb* provides:

1. LCC to DDC
2. LCC to National Library of Medicine Classification (NLM)
3. LCC to LCSH
4. LCC to LCSH including names (LCSH+)
5. LCSH to LCC
6. LCSH to DDC
7. LCSH to NLM
8. LCSH+ to LCC
9. LCSH+ to DDC
10. LCSH+ to NLM
11. Creator names to LCC

12. Creator names to DDC

13. Creator names to NLM

14. DDC to LCC

15. DDC to LCSH

16. DDC to LCSH+

17. NLM to LCC

18. NLM to LCSH

19. NLM to LCSH+

TABLE 18.2 Example of Search Results for *Hypnotic* in ClassWeb.

Hypnotic age regression
   RC499.H96   Hypnotic age regression
Hypnotic conditions: Physiology
   [QP425-427]   Sleep. Hypnotic conditions, etc.
Hypnotics
   RM325   Hypnotics. Sedatives
Hypnotism: Bibliography: Medicine
   Z6675.H9   Hypnotism
Hypnotism: Criminal law
   K5028   Criminal law and hypnotism
Hypnotism: Psychiatry
   [RC490-499]   Hypnotism and hypnosis. Suggestion
                             therapy
Hypnotism and crime
   HV6110   Hypnotism and crime
Hypnotism and criminal law
   KK8014   Criminal law and hypnotism
Hypnotism and hypnosis: Anesthesiology
   RD85.H9   Hypnosis
Hypnotism and hypnosis: Anesthesiology: Dentistry
   RK512.H95   Hypnotism
Hypnotism and hypnosis: Forensic medicine
   RA1171   Other special
Hypnotism and religion
   BL65.H9   Hypnotism
Hypnotism in literature: General: Literary history
   PN1059.H8   Hypnotism
Hypnotism in motion pictures
   PN1995.9.H95   Hypnotism
Hypnotism (Parapsychology)
   [BF1111-1156]   Hypnotism. Animal magnetism. Odylic
                             force. Biomagnetism. Mesmerism.
                             Subliminal projection

BASIC FEATURES

Because LCC was developed over a century ago as a utilitarian scheme to shelve books at LC, it is a highly enumerative system. It is based on the idea of literary warrant, which means it greatly reflects the collection development priorities of the library that was used as its basis (e.g., it is heavily weighted toward the social sciences, politics, literature, and history). While not based entirely on Cutter's EC, it did borrow some characteristics. Among the basic features derived from Cutter are its order of main classes, its use of capital letters for main and subclass notation, its use of Arabic numerals for further subarrangement, and its modification of the Cutter author-mark idea (i.e., *Cutter numbers*) to achieve alphabetic sub-arrangements of various kinds.

All the LC schedules have similar, but not identical, sequencing arrangements and appearance. Within each sequence of class numbers the order proceeds, as a rule, from general aspects of the topic or discipline to its particular divisions and subtopics. Chronological sequences may trace historical events, publication dates, or other useful time frames. Geographical arrangements are frequently alphabetical but just as frequently are given in a preferred order, starting with the Western Hemisphere and the United States. Class **G-Geography. Maps. Anthropology. Recreation** is distinct from the history classes, although located next to them. This distribution is similar to the DDC location of **910 Geography and Travel** within class **900 History**. Neither scheme quite succeeds in solving the problem of ambiguous relationships between popular works of description and travel and other, perhaps more scholarly, books on national or regional social life and customs. The library user must search both the history and the geography shelves, and even the social sciences, to find all available materials on these topics.

There are some significant differences between LCC and DDC in organizing some materials. For example, LCC provides broad subclasses in class P for the literatures in various languages, subarranged by national literature, then chronology, and finally by individual author. Except for anthologies, it seldom groups literary works by form. DDC starts in its 800 class with a basic separation into national literatures, but it subdivides next by form (e.g., poetry, drama, fiction). Only subordinately does it provide for time divisions or individual authors.

The LC preference for grouping national literatures by time period and author extends to class **B-Philosophy**, but not to music or the graphic arts. In class **M-Music**, works are arranged first by form (e.g., opera, oratorio, symphony, chamber music), then by composer. There is no attempt to keep time periods, national schools, or genres of expression (e.g., classical, romantic, modern) distinct. Subclass **ML-Literature on Music** does use national, chronological, and similar groupings. In class **N-Fine Arts** materials are grouped first by form (e.g., sculpture, drawing, painting), then by nationality or chronology, and finally by artist.

LC formerly grouped literature in English by form in subclass **PZ-Fiction and Juvenile Belles Lettres**. Here a concession was made to a reader-interest orientation that proved to be controversial and a stumbling block to the full use of LCC by other research libraries with large holdings in literature. In 1980, LC discontinued use of PZ1, PZ3, and PZ4. American fiction is now classed in PS, English fiction in PR, and translations of fiction into English are classed with the original national literature. (Juvenile fiction in all languages remains classed in PZ.) Otherwise, LC's handling of literature has met with general approval. A recurring pattern of organization occurs within each literature:

1. General form divisions (e.g., periodicals, dictionaries)
2. History and criticism, subdivided
   a. Chronologically
   b. Then by form
3. Collections or anthologies, subdivided by period, region, and form
4. Individual authors, subdivided
   a. Chronologically
   b. Then alphabetically by author
      i.   Collective works
      ii. Individual works
      iii. Biography and criticism

LCC breaks the information and general works grouping in the 000 class of DDC into two classes at opposite ends of the alphabet. The **A-General Works** schedule employs for its subclasses rare instances of mnemonic notation. General encyclopedias are located in subclass AE, general indexes in AI, general museum publications in AM, and so forth. By contrast, the Z class, containing bibliographies and works on the book industries and on libraries, has had no two-letter subclasses at all until very recently. While its subject bibliographies are arranged alphabetically by topic in the Z5001-Z8000 span, there is nothing mnemonic about their notation. The only other notable instances of mnemonic class-letter associations in LCC are **G-Geography**, **M-Music**, **ML-Music Literature**, and **T-Technology**.

Similar to DDC, LCC relies on several types of notes to assist classifiers in their task, including: *scope notes*, *see notes* (both simple and complex), *confer notes*, and *including notes*. Scope notes, which may or may not be set off by the phrase *class here*, explain the nature of a topic or what a class covers. *See* notes direct classifiers to use another classification number for either the whole topic or a portion thereof. *See* notes are also provided for most obsolete numbers, indicated by the instruction *see*; others are explanatory in nature and often begin with the word *for*, but also contain the word *see*. *Confer* notes (indicated by the abbreviation *Cf.*) inform the classifier of other numbers that might be of interest in other parts of the schedules. *Including* notes list a subtopic(s) included within a class. *Including* notes are not indications of a concept being *in standing room*—a DDC concept that does not exist in LCC.

(GV673.S6-.S65)	South Africa
	See GV667-667.5
. . .	
	Sports for special classes of persons
	People with disabilities
	Including wheelchair sports in general
	For individual wheelchair sports, *see* the sport
	For wheelchair basketball *see* GV886.5
	Cf. GV722.5.P37 Paralympics
	Cf. GV722.5.S64 Special Olympics
GV709.3	General works
GV709.4	Coaching
. . .	
GV749.7	Extreme sports
	Class here general works and works on extreme activities not normally regarded as sports, e.g., Ironing

In the past, *divide-like notes* were used to direct classifiers to another part of the classification and to follow the pattern, table, or instructions found there; divide-like notes, mostly, have been removed from the system and replaced by explicit instructions. Occasionally, instructions direct classifiers to another part of the classification schedules to use the pattern, table, or instructions found there.

SCHEDULE FORMAT

Most of the LCC schedules exhibit certain common features of external and internal format. However, many of these format features are missing from certain schedules, a reminder that the scheme was intentionally decentralized in its development. Subject specialists were encouraged to adopt standard modes of organization, but were never forced to maintain a rigid formal pattern.

External Format

Both old and new editions of the print-formatted schedules, regardless of typography, actual format, or binding, tend to follow a familiar pattern of organization. They include the following features:

1. **A preface or prefatory note** nearly always follows the title page. These introductory remarks in recent editions have become briefer and less helpful for classification purposes than they formerly were.

```
                              SYNOPSIS


   H     Social Sciences (General)
   HA    Statistics
   HB    Economic Theory. Demography
   HC    Economic History and Conditions
   HD    Industries. Land Use. Labor
   HE    Transportation and Communications
   HF    Commerce
   HG    Finance
   HJ    Public Finance
   HM    Sociology (General)
   HN    Social History and Conditions. Social Problems. Social Reform
   HQ    The Family. Marriage. Women
   HS    Societies: Secret, Benevolent, etc.
   HT    Communities. Classes. Races
   HV    Social Pathology. Social and Public Welfare. Criminology
   HX    Socialism. Communism. Anarchism
```

FIGURE 18.1 An Example of an LCC Synopsis.

```
                              OUTLINE

   H     1-99              Social Sciences (General)

   HA    1-4737            Statistics
         29-32                Theory and method of social science statistics
         36-37                Statistical services. Statistical bureaus
         38-39                Registration of vital events. Vital records
         154-4737             Statistical data
         154-155                 Universal statistics
         175-4737                By region or country

   HB    1-3840            Economic theory. Demography
         71-74                Economics as a science. Relation to other subjects
         75-130               History of economics. History of economic theory
                                 Including special economic schools
         131-147              Methodology
         135-147                 Mathematical economics. Quantitative methods
                                    Including econometrics, input-output analysis,
                                    game theory
         201-206              Value. Utility
         221-236              Price.
         238-251              Competition. Production. Wealth
         501                  Capital. Capitalism
         522-715              Income. Factor shares
         535-551                 Interest
         601                     Profit
         615-715                 Entrepreneurship. Risk and uncertainty. Property
         801-843              Consumption. Demand
         846-846.8            Welfare theory
         848-3697             Demography. Population. Vital events
         3711-3840            Business cycles. Economic fluctuations
```

FIGURE 18.2 An Example of an LCC Outline.

2. **Brief synopses** next appear in many of the schedules, to show the primary subdivisions contained in those volumes. In most cases, these broad subclasses are readily identifiable by their brief double-letter notation, but class **K-Law** is issued in double-letter subclass volumes with synopses that frequently show mnemonic triple-letter divisions. One can learn at a glance that the law of Ontario is found in subclass KEO, whereas that of Quebec is in KEQ. A similar mnemonic arrangement applies to the American states in subclass KF, but their notation is more complicated since several states share initial letters. A typical synopsis is shown in Figure 18.1.

3. **An outline**, consisting not only of alphabetic subclasses, but also of significant alphanumeric sub-spans, is present in nearly every schedule. In schedules without synopses the outlines tend to be briefer and to show broader subdivisions; in schedules with synopses, they are longer and more detailed. Occasionally, as in the schedule for class **J-Political Science**, the synopsis is really an outline. These two kinds of preliminary overview offer the user supplementary techniques for arriving quickly at any given portion of the schedules. The outline for the first subclasses of class H appears in the schedule as shown in Figure 18.2.

4. **The schedule proper** enumerates specific class number assignments and sequences in their most explicit form. Page formatting devices, although slightly different in each of the schedule formats (i.e., printed or PDF schedules available from LC, schedules available on *ClassWeb*, and schedules available from Gale), demonstrate hierarchical subordinations and progressions. LCC printed schedules show left-margin indentions, with nested running titles on nearly every page or screen display to demonstrate hierarchy. In *ClassWeb* a complete hierarchy is displayed in the top frame of the divided screen for any notation on which a user clicks, although this display contains only the words of the hierarchy, not the notations; and it is not in the traditional indented form.

Many broad headings, which offer a useful survey of subtopics, are interpolated just ahead of the specific numbers that they embrace. They often carry no single class number of their own:

	Theory and practice of education
	Including philosophy
	Collected writings
	Including essays, monographs, papers
	Several authors
LB5	Serial collections
LB7	Minor collections
	Including selections, extracts, etc.
	Individual authors see LB51-885

There is no notation to be assigned for just *Theory and practice of education* or even for *Collected writings* on that subject. For this and related reasons, LCC does not work well for classifying small general collections or parts of collections. Nor are these spans very often accompanied by internal summary tables such as those DDC uses.

Most schedules do carry internal subdivision tables at key junctures, to provide schematic patterns for further localized development of class numbers or sequences. While LCC is basically enumerative, these generalized subdivision tables open up patterned arrangements that are usually not fully realized on the shelves. Scope notes occasionally refer to auxiliary tables or sometimes give useful instructions for number building. An excerpt from the **T-Technology** schedule shows most of these features (see Figure 18.3).

5. **Auxiliary tables**, designed for use with more than one specific notation or span, are located externally to the schedules proper. In most printed volumes they appear after the full schedule, immediately preceding the index. Tables for classes G, K, and P-PZ are published in completely separate volumes. In *ClassWeb* there is a separate button to click in order to view tables, which are numbered with the letter of the discipline followed by the table number (e.g., N1, N2, etc., for the fine arts tables). Some tables applicable to large portions of the entire classification scheme are presented in the CSM (e.g., tables for translations, societies, artists, biographies, regions, and countries in the form of Cutter numbers).

Tables can be used only when specifically instructed to do so by the schedules (except for the tables in the CSM; the instructions for their use are provided in the CSM with the table itself). Usually, a table number is given in the instructions in parentheses or directly in the text beside an entry in the schedule, to alert the user that the table should be applied. Such is the case in Figure 18.3 from the TD subclass. Sometimes the instructions for further division are right in the schedule, as seen at the end of this example:

T	**TECHNOLOGY (GENERAL)**
	Technical education. Technical schools
	Special schools
	Including technical departments of universities
	Cf. TT167.A+ Manual training schools
	American schools
171.A-Z	General. By name, A-Z
	Under each school:
	.xA1-.xA4 *Official serials*
	.xA5-.xA7 *Official monographs*
	.xA8-.xZ *Nonofficial publications. By author, A-Z*

TD	Environmental technology. Sanitary engineering
	Including the promotion and conservation of the public health, comfort, and convenience by the control of the environment
	Cf. GE170+ Environmental policy
	Cf. GF51 Human beings and the environment
	Cf. RA565+ Environmental health
	Cf. TH6014+ Environmental engineering in buildings
	Periodicals and societies. By language of publication
1	English
2	French
3	German
4	Other languages (not A-Z)
5	Congresses
	Exhibitions. Museums
6.A1	General works
6.A2-Z	By region or country, A-Z
	Subarrange each country by Table T4b
7	Collected works (nonserial)
9	Dictionaries and encyclopedias
12	Directories
	History
15	General works
16	Ancient
17	Medieval
18	Modern to 1800
19	Nineteenth century
20	Twentieth century
	Country and city subdivisions
	Including municipal reports of public sanitary works
	America
21	General works
	North America
22	General works
	United States
23	General works
23.1	Eastern states. Atlantic coast
23.15	New England
...	
24.A-.W	States, A-W
25.A-Z	Cities or other special, A-Z
	Canada
26.A1	General works
26.A6-Z	Provinces, A-Z
27.A-Z	Local (Cities, etc.), A-Z
27.5	Latin America
...	
127	Developing countries
	Biography
139	Collective
140.A-Z	Individual, A-Z
	General works
144	Early to 1850
145	1850-
146	Elementary textbooks
...	

FIGURE 18.3 Excerpt from LCC Schedule Showing Many Typical Features.

Figure 18.4 presents excerpts from Tables N1 and N2 in the **N-Fine Arts** schedules, showing how spans of 100 and 200 numbers can be distributed among the same list of terms. The notation span N5801-5896.3, which is for *Classical art—Special regions or countries—Other regions or countries*, is to be distributed according

```
                    N1: TABLE OF REGIONS OR COUNTRIES (100 NUMBERS)

              America
1                 General
                  Latin America
1.5                   General
                      By region or country see N1 14+
                  North America
2                     General
                      United States
3                         General
3.5                       Colonial period; 18th (and early 19th) century
3.7                       19th century
4                         20th century
4.2                       21st century
4.5                       Northeastern States
4.7                       Atlantic States
5                         New England
5.5                       Middle Atlantic States
6                         South
7                         Central
8                         West
8.5                       Northwestern States
8.6                       Southwestern States
9                         Pacific States
10.A-.W                   States, A-W
                              Each state may be subarranged:
                              .x              General works
                              .x2A-.x2Z       Local (other than cities), A-Z
...

                    N2: TABLE OF REGIONS OR COUNTRIES (200 NUMBERS)

              America
1                 General
                  Latin America
2                     General
                      By region or country see N1 14+
                  North America
3                     General
                      United States
5                         General
6                         Colonial period; 18th (and early 19th) century
7                         19th century
8                         20th century
8.2                       21st century
8.5                       Northeastern States
8.7                       Atlantic States
10                        New England
10.5                      Middle Atlantic States
11                        South
14                        Central
17                        West
18                        Northwestern States
18.6                      Southwestern States
19                        Pacific States
25.A-.W                   States, A-W
                              Each state may be subarranged:
                              .x              General works
                              .x2A-.x2Z       Local (other than cities), A-Z
...
```

FIGURE 18.4 Distribution of the Same Terms Between Different Spans of Numbers.

to Table N1, adding the appropriate number from the table to base number N5800. Table N1 distributes America and the United States within numbers 1 to 10 out of the 100-number span available. By contrast, NB1501-1685 for *sculptured monuments in special regions or countries* uses Table N2 as a guide for adding country numbers to base number NB1500. Table N2 distributes America and the United within numbers 1 to 25 out of the 200-number span. Number spans from the schedule and the table are matched according to the quantity of materials that the LC classifiers anticipate at any given location.

Table N1, used with the N schedule, is a *simple table* because it carries only one sequence of numbers that can be interpolated directly into the corresponding number spans in the schedule. In the past, many tables were *compound tables* (i.e., they supplied more than one number sequence for the same list of subtopics). Someone using older copies of schedules will still find these compound tables. All tables in new schedules and in the version available on *ClassWeb* are now simple tables.

Geographical and chronological subdivisions are often relegated to auxiliary tables. The two concepts may be combined as shown in Figure 18.4. Other principles of division may also be found in tabular form. Tables in class **J-Political Science** contain such categories as *Periodicals*, *Public administration*, *Political participation*, and the like. The heavily used P schedule has a separately published, extensive set of tables designed for use with literary author numbers. These tables run the gamut from long spans for prolific, often translated and discussed authors to brief expansions of cutter designations for recent or little-published authors.

6. **A detailed index** accompanies each printed schedule. These indexes vary in coverage and depth. References from synonyms or related terms, alphabetized and indented subordinate topical lists, and suggestions for placing related materials in other schedules are occasionally included.

Internal Format

While Herbert Putnam and Charles Martel left the local arrangement of topical and form divisions very much to the discretion of their subject specialists, they nevertheless identified certain basic features for use throughout the system. These organizational concepts—Martel's seven points—could be incorporated into the schedules at any level of hierarchical subdivision appropriate within the given context. They encompassed:

1. **General form divisions.** The approach here is similar to Dewey's Form Division Table, which evolved into T1: Standard Subdivisions. It assumes that library materials can often be effectively grouped according to their mode of presentation. Examples are periodicals;

society publications; collections; dictionaries or encyclopedias; conference, exhibition, or museum publications; annuals or yearbooks; directories; and specialized documents (e.g., official documents). Because of their general application, they belong near the beginning of any disciplinary or topical section, but LCC imposes no rigid order upon their location. Their importance in subclass **L-Education (General)** is observed in the following schedule outline:

L	EDUCATION (GENERAL)
7-97	Periodicals. Societies
(101)	Yearbooks, *see* L7-97
107	Congresses
111-791	Official documents, reports, etc.
797-899	Educational exhibitions and museums
899.A2-Z	School fairs
900-991	Directories of educational institutions

By contrast, Education subclasses **LD-LG-Individual Institutions** show no obvious use of the form division concept. Only in their auxiliary tables do a few of the forms emerge as useful ordering concepts.

2. **Theory. Philosophy.** In some schedules a single number is reserved for theory or philosophy of a topic; in others, a range of numbers is used. This concept is similar to the T1-01 Philosophy subdivision in DDC.

3. **History. Biography.** In the LC schedules, the history of a topic is sometimes subarranged by dates. This technique is used to break down the history of a topic by specific periods, with the dates referring to the time period covered in the work. In other cases, however, the same technique is used to separate more recent material from older material and the dates actually refer to the publication date of the work being classified.

HG Finance

    Money

        History

HG231	General works
	Primitive *see* GN450.5
HG237	Ancient
	Medieval
HG241	Contemporary works
HG243	Modern works
	16th-18th centuries

HG248	Contemporary works
HG249	Modern works
HG253	19th century
	20th century
HG255	General works
HG256	1971-

As you can see, there is a mix of the dates associated with the time periods covered in the content and the dates associated with publication of resources. For example, HG237 is for resources about money in ancient times, written at any point. HG241 and HG243 are both for resources about money in the Middle Ages, but HG241 is for those also written during that period and HG243 is for those written in modern times. This pattern is repeated in the next time period, ignored in the 19th century, and then changes in the 20th century to HG 255 for general works (see #4 below) on the 20th-century history of money, and HG256 for works specifically about the history of money during the period of 1971 to the present.

A biographical aspect also appears in most subjects. Often two numbers are reserved for biographical material. The first number is usually for *collective biographies* (i.e., a work that discusses the lives and/or contributions of two or more individuals). The second is for *individual biographies* (i.e., a continuous narrative that discusses the life of a single individual). The table that is used to subarrange most individual biographies classed in biography numbers is provided in the CSM.[19] In some schedules, such as **D-History**, **N-Fine Arts**, and **P-PZ-Literatures**, unique tables applicable to biographical material are provided. Biographies may also sometimes be classed in numbers that are not set aside only for biographies, and tables are not generally applied in those cases.

4. **General works.** The phrase *general works* appears throughout the LCC schedules under most topics and subtopics. A general work is a comprehensive work or a general treatise on a topic. It is a general monograph (or sometimes a serial) that does not fall within any of the other forms of work within the classification (e.g., biography, dictionary, textbooks). Related forms such as *popular works*, *juvenile works*, and *addresses, essays, and lectures* might appear near the general works class. Works falling under points 2-4 of Martel's Seven Points are often intermixed with those arranged according to physical form and with other locally useful groupings, as shown in the excerpt from **QE-Geology** in Figure 18.5.

5. **Law. Regulation. State relations.** Until the 1969 publication of the first **K-Law** subclass, this ordering principle was handy for grouping legal materials with their related topics, especially in the social sciences. The development of K classes inverts the relationship. Such

QE	GEOLOGY
1	Periodicals, societies, congresses, serial publications
3	Collected works (nonserial)
4	Voyages and expeditions
5	Dictionaries and encyclopedias
6	Philosophy
7	Nomenclature, terminology, notation, abbreviations
	History
11	General works
13	By region or country, A-Z
	Biography
21	Collective
22	Individual, A-Z
	e.g.
22.D25	Dana, James Dwight
22.S77	Steno, Nicolaus
23	Directories
25	Early works through 1800
	General works, treatises, and advanced textbooks
26	1801-1969
26.2	1970-2000
26.3	2001-
	Elementary textbooks
28	General
28.2	Physical geology
28.3	Historical geology
29	Juvenile works
31	Popular works
33	Special aspects of the subject as a whole
33.2.A-Z	Special topics, A-Z
33.2.A3	Aerial photography in geology
33.2.A7	Artificial satellites in geology
33.2.B6	Borings
...	

FIGURE 18.5 Excerpt Showing Different Kinds of Forms for the Geology Subclass.

works are now classified first as legal materials and only subordinately by discipline, and captions in the individual (non-law) classes have been removed. For example, resources dealing with government regulations for control of drugs as economic commodities were originally classified in HD9665.7-9. Those dealing with regulations for the manufacture, sale, and use of drugs were classified in RA402. Subclass **KF-Law of the United States** now places drug laws in KF3885-3895; works dealing with U.S. drug legislation and regulation are placed there.

6. **Study and teaching. Research. Textbooks.** Unlike DDC, LCC sometimes allows a unique place for textbooks, as well as for more theoretical works on how to study, teach, or research a topic. This is somewhat similar to DDC's T1-07 subdivision for education. An example was shown in Figure 18.5: QE 26-26.3 is for *General works, treatises, and advanced textbooks*, while QE28-28.3 is for *Elementary textbooks*. In other disciplines, LCC explicitly groups all textbooks

QH	BIOLOGY (GENERAL)
	Cytology
573	Periodicals, societies, congresses, serial publications
574	Collected works (nonserial)
575	Dictionaries and encyclopedias
	History
577	General works
578	By region or country, A-Z
	General works, treatises, and textbooks
581	Through 1969
581.2	1970-
581.5	Addresses, essays, lectures
582	Pictorial works and atlases
582.4	Popular works
582.5	Juvenile works
	Study and teaching. Research
583	General works
583.15	Outlines, syllabi
583.2	Laboratory manuals

FIGURE 18.6 Excerpt Showing Textbooks Grouped with General Works.

with general works and treatises, as shown under QH581-QH581.2 in Figure 18.6.

7. **Subjects and subdivisions of subjects**. Most modern classification systems are disciplinary rather than topical. That is, they normally proceed from broad general divisions of knowledge to narrower subdivisions, with more or less comprehensive coverage provided for each special topic in relation to the hierarchy. Any linear arrangement of books or other materials on shelves must resort to a series of cyclic progressions if it displays subject-related groupings based on logical considerations or practical associations. Just as Martel's fourth point reminds classifiers that *general works* should be shelved together, usually near the beginning of each new topical group, so this seventh point provides for further subject breakdown based on literary warrant or the amount of material requiring classification in such a group. These specific subjects and their subdivisions generally comprise the bulk of the classification schedules.

NOTATION

LCC notation is mixed and typically contains one to three letters, followed by one to four integers, and possibly a decimal extension. Decimal numbers were not used much until it became necessary to expand certain sections where no further integers were available. Decimals do not usually indicate subordination, but allow a new topic or aspect to be inserted into an established context. In the excerpt of QH schedules in Figure 18.6, the decimals belie the left-margin indentions of their associated topics. Clearly, the number for juvenile works on cytology, QH582.5, is hierarchically equivalent to and *not* subordinate to QH582, the notation used for pictorial works and atlases of cytology.

Another method of expanding LCC notations is by means of mnemonic letter-number combinations, which look like Cutter's author marks, but are derived from a different matrix (see chapter 19). These *cutter numbers* may represent topical concepts, geographic, personal, or corporate names, or titles. They are subordinated to schedule notations where an instruction to subdivide A-Z appears (e.g., *By region or country, A-Z*). Since they are part of the classification notation, some of the actual LC assignments, or at least some examples, are included within the schedules (see examples under QE22 in Figure 18.5). An alphabetical approach used with the caption, *Special topics, A-Z,* as seen at QE33.2 in Figure 18.5, often includes a number of examples of topics. If the special topics cutter is to represent persons, corporate bodies, geographic names, or titles of works, then the list is not considered to be all-inclusive and the cataloger may add to it locally on an as-needed basis. If the cutter is for a topical aspect, the cataloger may not add topics on an ad-hoc basis; new topics must be proposed to LC and approved before being used in the classification scheme. Geographic cutter numbers generally are not listed, however (see QE13 in Figure 18.5 and TD24 in Figure 18.3).

Alphabetical geographic sequences normally appear at subordinate places in the schedules, where they subarrange a single integer or decimal number. For broader disciplines or subjects, where the geographic arrangement covers an extensive number span, the organization follows a preferred pattern, as was noted earlier in the section on external format. Class N, Tables N1 and N2 (see Figure 18.4), show how such sequences begin with the classification's preferred geographic region (i.e., the Western Hemisphere and the United States), and then follow a pattern that covers the earth according to American perceptions of the nearness and importance of its neighbors.

In an LCC class mark, the primary group of letters and numbers (the classification notation) should be arranged first alphabetically, then by integers, until a decimal point is introduced into the notation. All schedules make the basic ordering by integer quite evident, as when PR509 follows PR51, but precedes PR5018. The secondary combinations of letters and numbers found in cutter numbers, by contrast, should be filed decimally. LC carefully inserts a decimal point in front of these cutter numbers, even if, as at QE33.2.A3 in Figure 18.5, a decimal is already part of the primary notation. Some libraries using LCC drop the cutter decimal from their notation, on the premise that users will remember to follow the convention. The practice may possibly cause confusion in cutter number runs where it is not clearly understood that a classification notation like PR4972.M33 should follow PR4972.M3 but precede PR4972.M5.

Occasionally a classification notation, or series of notations, appears in the schedules in angle brackets. These were formerly termed *shelflist numbers*, but today more often are called *alternative* or *reserved class numbers* (i.e., *optional* class numbers). They have not been assigned to works in the LC collections, but they are provided for the convenience of other libraries that may find the optional approach more attractive than the "official" approach enumerated in LCC. Some formerly reserved notations are now actively used in the classification. Alternative classification notations are nearly always accompanied by notes telling the user to see another notation. Libraries using LCC are welcome to adopt these alternative notations if their own classification needs are better realized by so doing. An example is <PS8001-8599> **Canadian litera-ture**, which to some libraries may be preferable to the shorter span PR9180-9199.4—the established location in LCC for Canadian literature in English.[20]

Some classification notations appear in the schedules in parentheses. These are *obsolete class numbers*, and as such, should generally not be used except for serial continuations, when the existing "run" of the serial is already classed there. These notations represent locations once actively used, but are now retired by LC for all monographs and new serial titles. Notes telling the classifier to see other notations nearly always accompany obsolete classification numbers. Subclass **SD-Forestry**, for example, has an entry (SD559) for Assessment and taxation, which instructs users to see HJ4167 instead.[21]

Following are a few examples of classification using LCC.

Example 1

DC203.4	Ashton, John, 1834-1911.
	English caricature and satire on Napoleon I
	. . .

D	History (General)
DC	History of France
139-249	Revolutionary and Napoleonic period, 1789-1815
203-212.5	Biography of Napoleon
203.4	Caricature and satire

Example 2

| QL696 | Turner, Angela K., 1954- |
| .P247 | Swallows & martins. . . |

Q	Science
QL	Zoology
605-739.3	Chordates. Vertebrates
671-699	Birds
696	Systematic divisions. By order and family, A-Z
.P2	Passeriformes
.P247	Hirundinidae (Swallows)

Example 3

RA407.3	American Hospital Association
	Comparative statistics on health facilities and population : metropolitan and nonmetropolitan areas . . .

R	Medicine (General)
RA	Public aspects of medicine
1-418.5	Medicine and the state
407-409.5	Health status indicators. Medical statistics & surveys
407.3-407.5	By region or country
407.3-407.4	United States.
407.3	General works

Example 4

HB1237	Marriage statistics for Sweden . . .

H	Social sciences
HB	Economic theory. Demography
848-3697	Demography. Population. Vital events
1111-1317	Marriages. Nuptiality
1121-1317	By region or country. Table H2 [Add country number in table to HB1120] [Table H2: 117-118 Sweden]
1201-1252.8	Europe
1229-1238	Scandinavia
1237	Sweden [General works]

CONCLUSION

Most libraries using LCC will continue to use officially assigned call numbers for any of their own materials that LC has already classified. However, it is a rare library that holds only resources also available in the LC collection. Classifiers should be able to create reasonably consistent notations with which to fit their unique holdings into the system. They may stumble over special practices at local points, but the general principles of arrangement are nearly always decipherable, especially now that one can search LC's and other libraries' online catalogs by LC call number and compare the results with the LCC schedules. Highly specific shelflisting (i.e., the rationale underlying many cutter numbers, as explained in chapter 19) is, on the other hand, not always so easy to explain. LCC is loosely coordinated and essentially pragmatic. It aims first to classify closely, then to identify uniquely, particular works, or issues of works, using the most economical notation available within its broad parameters of theory and practice.

NOTES

1. Lois Mai Chan, *A Guide to the Library of Congress Classification*, 5th ed. (Englewood, Colo.: Libraries Unlimited, 1999), 6-8.
2. Ibid., 8.
3. A table comparing the main classes of the Cutter and the LC schemes is given in chapter 20.
4. "Historical Notes: Library of Congress Classification," *Classification and Shelflisting Manual*, 1st ed. (Washington, D.C.: Cataloging Distribution Service, Library of Congress, 2013).
5. "Library of Congress Transitions to Free, Online-Only Cataloging Publications," *News from the Library of Congress*, accessed April 14, 2014, http://www.loc .gov/today/pr/2013/13-121.html.
6. "Update on Subject and Classification Documentation Plans," Library of Congress, accessed June 10, 2014, http://www.loc.gov/catdir/cpso/ catdocplans.html.
7. *Classification Web* (Washington, D.C.: Library of Congress, Cataloging Distribution Service), accessed June 12, 2015, https://classificationweb .net/ [requires ID and password]. Also known as *ClassWeb*. For subscription information: http://www.loc.gov/cds/classweb/.
8. *Classification and Shelflisting Manual*, 1st ed. (Washington, D.C.: Cataloging Distribution Service, Library of Congress, 2013). Also available in *Cataloger's Desktop*.
9. "Library of Congress Classification and Shelflisting Manual," Library of Congress, accessed June 24, 2014, http://www.loc.gov/aba/publications/ FreeCSM/freecsm.html.
10. "Classification," Library of Congress, Cataloging Distribution Service, accessed June 1, 2014, http://www.loc.gov/cds/products/lcClass.php.
11. "Library of Congress Classification Approved Lists," Library of Congress, accessed June 1, 2014, http://www.loc.gov/aba/cataloging/classification/.
12. For information regarding Gale and its publication of the cumulated editions of the Library of Congress Classification Schedules, see Gale Cengage Learning, http://shar.es/VFlE5.
13. Library of Congress, *Cataloging Service*, bulletin 1 (June 1945)-bulletin 125 (Spring 1978); *Cataloging Service Bulletin*, no. 1 (Summer 1978)-no. 128 (Fall 2010).
14. "Cataloging Service Bulletins," Library of Congress, accessed June 1, 2014, http://www.loc.gov/cds/PDFdownloads/csb/index.html.
15. Library of Congress Subject Headings, 13th-35th eds. (Washington, D.C.: Library of Congress, Office for Subject Cataloging Policy, 1990-2013). Also available in *Classification Web* and in PDF form. For a detailed discussion of LCSH, see chapter 13 of this text.
16. *Subject Headings Manual*, H365.
17. Library of Congress Shelflist (Ann Arbor, Mich.: UMI/Proquest, 1968-1979). Reprint information accessed June 1, 2014, http://www.proquest.com/ products-services/Library-of-Congress-Shelflist-330.html.
18. Mona L. Scott, *Conversion Tables: LC-Dewey, Dewey-LC, and LC Subject Headings-LC and Dewey*, 3rd ed. (Westport, Conn.: Libraries Unlimited, 2005).
19. *Classification and Shelflisting Manual*, F 275.
20. *Classification and Shelflisting Manual*, F 180.
21. *Classification and Shelflisting Manual*, F 185.

SUGGESTED READING

Chan, Lois M. *A Guide to the Library of Congress Classification.* 5th ed. Englewood, Colo.: Libraries Unlimited, 1999.

Dittmann, Helena, and Jane Hardy. *Learn Library of Congress Classification,* 2nd North American ed. Friendswood, Tex.: TotalRecall Publications, 2007.

Ferguson, Bobby. *Subject Analysis: Blitz Cataloging Workbook.* Englewood, Colo.: Libraries Unlimited, 1998. Chapter 4: Library of Congress Classification.

Foskett, A. C. *The Subject Approach to Information.* 5th ed. London: Library Association Publishing, 1996. Chapter 22: The Library of Congress Classification.

Olson, Hope A., and John J. Boll. *Subject Analysis in Online Catalogs.* 2nd ed. Englewood, Colo.: Libraries Unlimited, 2001, 240-264.

Chapter 19

Creation of Complete Call Numbers

INTRODUCTION

Library call numbers serve a double function. The classification notation portion groups related materials together. The second portion of the complete call number uniquely identifies different works in the same class. Traditionally, this second part of the call number is based on the primary access point (e.g., creator, title), which has been chosen for the work through descriptive cataloging. Various terms such as *author number*, *book number*, and *cutter number* have been applied over the years, but *author number* is not a good representation for those works with title as primary access point, while *book number* implies that it cannot be applied to non-book materials. Cutter number is also a bit misleading because the Library of Congress (LC) method of deriving it differs from the original tables devised by Charles A. Cutter. However, the designation *cutter number* has come into general use in practice regardless of the classification scheme used. Its general usage is a tribute to Cutter, who conceived the idea of using alphanumeric symbols to keep in alphabetical order all the items assigned the same classification notation. In this text, the term *cutter number* is used for any notation serving this function. The *term primary access point* is used in this chapter to refer to the entity that is chosen to be the basis for the cutter number in the call number. This entity is usually either the creator with the most responsibility for the work, or else the title.[1]

CUTTER NUMBERS DEVISED BY CHARLES A. CUTTER

Providing a classification notation with a supplementary cutter number enables the cataloger to design a fully unique call number for each item in a collection, sometimes with the inclusion of additional information (e.g., date, copy number) to distinguish between two or more items from the same expression or same manifestation that may be included in the collection. The cutter numbers most often used with *Dewey Decimal Classification* (DDC) classification notations are taken from a set of tables devised by Cutter. These tables equate surnames and other words with alphanumeric sequences. Cutter initially produced a table in a single alphabetical sequence of all consonants except *S*, followed by a sequence of vowels and the letter *S*.[2] This two-figure table (most of its combinations consist of a capital letter plus two digits) was later expanded by Kate E. Sanborn to provide more differentiation among names for use with larger collections.[3] Since she did not adhere to Cutter's schema, Cutter then developed his own expansion to permit growing libraries to assign more specific book numbers without disrupting the sequences they had already established from his two-figure table.[4] Of these three different *Cutter* tables, the Cutter-Sanborn version is the most widely used today, being preferred by many larger libraries because of its simpler design and notation. OCLC has developed Four-Figure Cutter Tables (one is an extension of Cutter and the other an extension of Cutter-Sanborn). A Dewey Cutter Program can be downloaded to automatically provide cutter numbers upon input of text.[5]

Although cutter numbers are most commonly used to arrange material by primary access points (usually authors' surnames, but occasionally forenames, corporate names, family names, or titles), they are also used in some instances to alphabetize material by subject, as in the case of biography. To illustrate the use of each table, let us suppose that we wish to assign a cutter number for the English poet John Donne. The three tables carry the following sequences:

Cutter Two-figure Table

Doll	69	Foh
Dom	71	Folg
Doo	72	Foll

Cutter Three-figure Table

Donk	718	Folk
Donnet	719	Folke
Doo	72	Foll

Cutter-Sanborn Table

Donk	684	Fonti
Donn	685	Fontr
Donner	686	Foo

According to the Cutter two-figure table, the number for Donne is D71 (choosing between *Dom* and *Doo* by using the number above where the name fits alphabetically). Using the Cutter three-figure table it is D718 (an expansion of the D71 assignment). But using the Cutter-Sanborn table it is D685. The above examples also demonstrate the three-column display used in the original form of the tables, in which the alphabetical letters on the left or the right are coordinated with the numbers in the middle. In 1969 Paul K. Swanson and

Esther M. Swift revised this arrangement into single continuous alphabets of two columns, with letters on the left corresponding to numbers on the right. The Swanson-Swift arrangement appears to be easier to use.

The *work letter* (or *workmark*) is the first letter of the title of the manifestation being cataloged, exclusive of articles. It follows the cutter number that comes after the classification number. For example, the complete Dewey Decimal call number for Henry James's novel *Wings of the Dove* is 813.4 J27w. Work letters do not inevitably ensure that a resource will be placed in alphabetical sequence within the author grouping; this depends upon the sequence of acquisition of the items. One additional letter from the title may be added if necessary. For example, a copy of James's *Washington Square* might be assigned the call number 813.4 J27wa. If the third acquisition is a volume entitled *The Works of Henry James*, it would most probably be given the call number 813.4 J27, with no *workmark*, as most libraries prefer to place collected works of an author ahead of the individual works.

With an author such as Lilian Jackson Braun, who began the title of each of her 29 mysteries with *The Cat Who . . .*, such a scheme is not feasible. Depending on the library's policy, the cataloger may choose one of several alternatives. For example, the cataloger can ignore completely the common phrase *the cat who* and proceed directly to the distinctive part of the title, or use two work letters: *c* for *cat*, plus an additional letter for the first distinctive word of the title (e.g., *The Cat Who Talked to Ghosts* might be assigned the work letters *ct*).

Biographies and criticism of a specific author pose a particular problem of library policy. The preferred way to classify biographies of literary authors in Dewey is with their work, in order to keep everything by and about a literary figure in one place. In such cases, a common method of distinguishing works by an author from works about an author is to insert an arbitrary letter— usually one toward the end of the alphabet (e.g., a capital *X*)—after the cutter number and to follow it with the initial of the author of the biography. This device puts all books about an author directly following all books by that author. For example, if the letter *X* is chosen as the biography letter, a biography of Henry James by Leon Edel could be cuttered J27Xe, and it would follow, in shelflist order, J27w. If James had written a novel beginning with the letter *z* only the work letter *z* would be used for the novel; and the convention is to file the lowercase workmarks before capitals. Some libraries using this system use *Y* for criticisms and *Z* for concordances. In the Dewey schedule, 928 is an optional biography number for literary figures (920 for Biography; 8 for Literature). Using this option, biographies of authors might be classified in 928, with subdivision for nationality. The cutter number in this case would be the number for the biographee with a workmark for the author of the biography. A capital letter would not be necessary.

Biographies of persons who are not authors or are not literary authors are classified in Dewey in a number corresponding to the subject area where the person is/was most prominent. The standard subdivision –092 is used with such a number. The cutter number for such a work usually stands for the person the work is about with a workmark for the author of the biography. For example, a biography of historian Marianne Awerbuch, an expert on Judaism and the Jewish people, by Clarissa Busse, would have the call number: 296.092 A966b.

The problem of the existence of a variety of editions occurs quite frequently in literature, but classic works in all other fields are also reprinted by the same or another publisher, especially since electronic and audio books have revived many worthwhile books that have long been out of print. One cataloging practice is to assign the date of publication as part of the call number to all editions of a single work issued by the same publisher and to assign a number following the work letter to all editions of the same work published by different publishers. For example, the first acquired copy of *Wings of the Dove* might be assigned the call number 813.4 J27w. If the library acquired a second copy of the novel, issued by a different publisher, the number might be 813.4 J27w2. If we assume that the second publisher was Modern Library and that the library received another edition of the novel, also published by Modern Library, in 1985, the call number might then be 813.4 J27w2 1985. A completely different edition published by a third publisher could be assigned 813.4 J27w3. Many variations of these practices exist. Keeping track of such numbering, however, is daunting, and many libraries have decided just to add the date of publication to a new edition's call number in all cases (e.g., 813.4 J27w 1983).

CUTTER NUMBERS DEVISED BY THE LIBRARY OF CONGRESS (LC)

LC call numbers also consist, in general, of two principal elements: classification notation and cutter number, to which are added, as required, symbols designating a particular manifestation of a work. While it is possible to use Cutter-Sanborn numbers with LC classification, most libraries prefer to use LC cutter numbers constructed from a table composed by LC for this purpose.

Policies and procedures used at LC in completing call numbers are available in the Library of Congress *Classification and Shelflisting Manual*.[6] This manual should be consulted for more detailed information than is discussed below. The shelflisting part of the LC manual provides instructions for the addition of letters, numbers, and/or symbols following a classification notation. Persons who perform this function may be called *shelflisters*, and at one time these were separate positions in library cataloging, because with card catalogs it was necessary to go physically to the shelflist to make sure that the additions made would cause the item to fall in alphabetical (or other) order as required, and that the completed call number would be unique to that item. Now, however, the process can be completed with an online look at the call numbers already in use and is usually done by the classifier.

LC cutter numbers are composed of the initial letter of the primary access point, followed by Arabic numerals representing succeeding letters on the basis shown in Figure 19.1.[7]

Some points need further comment. Note first of all that the numeral *1* appears nowhere in the table. LC avoids its use, so that it will not become necessary to use zeros to preserve alphabetic order. If, for instance, the name *Abbott* were given the cutter *.A1*, a subsequent cutter at the same location

---

LC Cutter Table

(1) After initial **vowels**

for the second letter:	b	d	l-m	n	p	r	s-t	u-y
use number:	2	3	4	5	6	7	8	9

(2) After initial letter **S**

for the second letter:	a	ch	e	h-i	m-p	t	u	w-z
use number:	2	3	4	5	6	7	8	9

(3) After initial letters **Qu**

for the third letter:	a	e	i	o	r	t	y
use number:	3	4	5	6	7	8	9

For initial letters **Qa-Qt**
use numbers: **2-29**

(4) After other initial **consonants**

for the second letter:	a	e	i	o	r	u	y
use number:	3	4	5	6	7	8	9

(5) For **expansion**

for the letter:	a-d	e-h	i-l	m-o	p-s	t-v	w-z
use number:	3	4	5	6	7	8	9

In the examples below, Cutters without asterisks conform to the table [above]. Cutters with single asterisks have been developed when a range of letters in the table has been provided e.g., **l-m**. Cutters with two asterisks have been developed when the second letter is not explicitly stated in the table, e.g., **h** after an initial consonant. In most cases, Cutters must be adjusted to file an entry correctly and to allow room for later entries.

Vowels		S		Q		Consonants	
IBM	.I26	Sadron	.S23	** Qadduri	.Q23	Campbell	.C36
Idaho	.I33	** Scanlon	.S29	** Qiao	.Q27	Ceccaldi	.C43
*Ilardo	.I4	Schreiber	.S37	Quade	.Q33	** Chertok	.C48
*Import	.I48	* Shillingburg	.S53	Queiroz	.Q45	** Clark	.C58
Inman	.I56	* Singer	.S57	Quinn	.Q56	Cobblestone	.C63
Ipswich	.I67	Stinson	.S75	Quorum	.Q67	Cryer	.C79
*Ito	.I87	Suranyi	.S87	Qutub	.Q88	Cuellar	.C84
*Ivy	.I94	* Symposium	.S96	** Qvortrup	.Q97	Cymbal	.C96

FIGURE 19.1 LC Cutter Table.

---

for *Aamondt* would have to be, say, *.A09*, while *Aagard* would go to *.A085* or something like it. Although most type-fonts distinguish between the digit zero and the capital letter *O*, it is still sometimes difficult for the human eye to distinguish them. In actual practice, LC catalogers would likely give *Abbott* a cutter such as *.A2* so that later assignments for names such as *Aagard* and *Aamodt* could have *.A12* and *.A15*, or similar decimals to ensure space for unlimited further alphabetical expansion if needed. In addition catalogers are instructed: "Do not end a Cutter with the numeral 1 or 0."[8]

All this brings out another characteristic of LC shelflisting. There is nothing sacrosanct about this table. It has been officially changed as shelflisting problems were encountered and new needs were perceived. Recently devised numbers may reflect accommodation to outmoded practices in order to avoid extensive re-shelflisting, rather than following current practice as outlined in the table. Cutter numbers assigned for the same person may also vary significantly from one classification notation to another. The examples below illustrate such a variation:

TL561	Splaver, Sarah, 1921-
.S65	Some day I'll be an aerospace engineer . . .

. . . .

Z682	Splaver, Sarah, 1921-
.S735	Some day I'll be a librarian . . .

Since cutter numbers are used by LC to extend some classification notations, as well as for shelflisting alphabetically by primary access point, many items have two cutter segments in their call numbers. An example is Niles M. Hansen's *French Regional Planning*, for which the LC call number, HT395.F7 H35, can be analyzed as follows:

H	Social sciences
HT	Communities. Classes. Races
101-395	Urban groups. The city. Urban sociology
390-395	Regional planning:
392-395	By region or country
392-394	United States
395.A-Z	Other regions or countries, A-Z
.F7	France
H35	The cutter number for Hansen

While double cutters are commonplace, triple cutters are rare. They have been used in class G for certain kinds of subject maps, but with a special disclaimer added. An example is the *New York City Community Health Atlas 1988* prepared by Melvin I. Krasner and the staff of the New York City Division of Research, Analysis, and Planning. Its call number, G1254.N4 E55 K7 1988, is analyzed as follows:

G	Geography. Anthropology. Recreation
1-9980	Geography (General). Atlases. Globes. Maps
1000-3122	World Atlases. Atlases of the Earth
1200-1534.24	United States
1205-1374	Eastern United States
1209.5-1277	Northeastern States
1250-1254	New York
1254	Cities, Towns, and Urban Townships, etc., A-Z **(Table G3803)**
	Apply Table G1a for subject
.N4	New York City

E55	Public Health [from Table G1a— Subject subdivisions. (These numbers have no alphabetical significance.)]
K7	Cutter number for Krasner
1988	Date of atlas publication

In other instances where double cutters are prescribed in the schedules to stand for two separate subdivisions of the subject, the second cutter is made to accommodate both the subject for which it stands and the alphabetical arrangement for which it stands. An example is:

HD3568	Cooperatives : pivot for economic development
.A6 L343	[a book about cooperatives in Lagos, Nigeria]
1996	

In the classification schedules under HD3441-3570.9, the notation run assigned to industrial cooperation by country, the notation for the country (in this case, HD3568 for Nigeria) is first cuttered by *.A6* for general cooperative societies and then is subdivided further "by state, province, etc." Therefore, *L343* stands both for Lagos State (L34) and for the alphabetical arrangement of the title primary access point among other works on the subject (i.e., the last digit "3" is an extension representing the primary access point).

Reserved Cutter Numbers

The LC schedules and tables frequently set aside the first few *.A* or the last several *.Z* possibilities in a cutter sequence for special purposes. Observe the example at TD26.A1-TD27.A-Z [Environmental technology. Sanitary engineering. Country and city subdivisions. Canada] (also shown in Figure 18.3):

	Canada
TD 26.A1	General works
TD 26.A6-Z	Provinces, A-Z
TD 27.A-Z	Local (Cities, etc.), A-Z

Assume that class T and the internal table in the schedule have been applied to derive the classification number TD26.A1 for a general work on sanitary engineering in Canada. Let us suppose that the first book classified here was written by a Robbyn Gomble. Using the LC cutter number table, we could complete the call number as TD26.A1 G6 or TD26.A1 G65. A second work on the same topic by a Rachael Goode might then receive the call number TD26. A1 G66, while still a third treatise by a Richard Goddard could be given something like TD26.A1 G58.

Assume now that we have a book on sanitary engineering in the Canadian province of Alberta. It cannot receive the usual cutter *.A4* or *.A43* because the internal table at TD26-TD27.A-Z has *reserved* TD26.A1 through TD26. A5 for general works. One knows this because the direction for cuttering for "Provinces, A-Z." is to use ".A6-Z," meaning that the first cutter that can be used for a province beginning with the letter *A* is "A6." Therefore we must accommodate the reservation by assigning the classification number TD26. A65, followed by an appropriate cutter number for the primary access point. Now suppose that still another book covers sanitary engineering in the city of Airdrie, Alberta, Canada. Our classification number will probably be TD27. A37, plus a second cutter for the primary access point.

Reservations for *.Z* cutters are most common in class P, where researchers like to have biography and criticism of an author shelved immediately following that author's works. In this class, separate integers frequently designate all authors of a given period whose surnames start with the same initial (e.g., PR6045 is for all English literary authors who wrote between 1900 and 1960 and whose surnames begin with "W"). The first cutter number is then based on the second letter of the surname. That is, the letter beginning the cutter is the second letter of the author's name, followed by a number representing the third letter (e.g., the cutter for Rebecca West is E8). A second cutter, based usually on an auxiliary table of reserved numbers, identifies collected works, selections, titles of separate works, adaptations, translations, or biography and criticism. The biography and criticism excerpt from Table 40 in the *P-PZ Language and Literature Tables*, for example, is as follows:

P-PZ40—Table for authors (1 Cutter no.)

. . .

	Biography and criticism
.xZ4581-.xZ4589	Periodicals. Societies. Serials
.xZ459	Dictionaries, indexes, etc. By date
.xZ46	Autobiography, journals, memoirs. By date
.xZ48	Letters (Collections). By date
	Including collections of letters to and from particular individuals
.xZ5-.xZ999	General works

The Selected Letters of Rebecca West, published in 2000, carries the LC call number PR6045.E8 Z48 2000, exemplifying application of the *.Z48* cutter for collections of letters arranged by date of publication.

Additions to LC Call Numbers

Workmarks, in the traditional sense of lowercase letters added to book numbers to alphabetize titles or writers of biographies, are not used by LC. Lowercase letters do serve a few special purposes in LC call numbers. They are sometimes used following dates, as discussed below. In addition, in subclass "PZ Fiction in English. Juvenile Literature" a unique combination of

upper- and lowercase letters (instead of second cutter numbers) alphabet-
izes the titles of a given author, while dates designate reissues or new editions. For example, the original 1938 Vanguard Press edition of Dr. Seuss's
The 500 Hats of Bartholomew Cubbins was given the call number PZ8.G326 Fi,
while the 1990 Random House edition has the call number PZ8.G326 Fi 1990.
(G326 represents Geisel, not Seuss—an artifact of the former practice of having primary access points assigned to birth names, not pseudonyms.) *Fi* was
used in the time when this title was to be filed as if spelled out: "Five Hundred
Hats. . . .") Formerly, numerals were used with juvenile literature call numbers
to designate new editions, so the 1966 Collins edition of this work was given
the call number PZ8.G326 Fi2.

The adding of dates to LC call numbers has increased with multiple publications in more than one country, in different imprints, in paperback as well
as hardcover, in later editions, and in reprints. LC began in 1982 to add dates
to all monographic call numbers.[9] One use of lowercase letters is to identify
bibliographically distinct issues of the same title published in the same year.
For example, Andrew M. Greeley's *Love Song* was published by G. K. Hall in
a large print version the same year it was published by Warner Books. The
second one to be cataloged was assigned the call number PS3557.R358 L68
1989b, the use of the letter "b" being the only difference between the two call
numbers. Another use of lowercase letters following dates is to distinguish
among works on the same subject and published in the same year that have
the same corporate body as primary access point.[10]

A few other exceptional notations show up in some schedules. For
example, dates are used not only as final elements, to distinguish issues
of the same title, but also they occasionally become secondary elements of
classification numbers, taking precedence over cutter numbers. Classification numbers "BX830-831—Christian denominations—Catholic Church—
Councils—Western (post-schismatic) councils" use this device to arrange
church councils by date of opening. An example is John W. O'Malley's *Tradition and Transition: Historical Perspectives on Vatican II*, which carries the
LC call number BX830 1962 .O45 1989. Also, in schedule "BL-BX—Religion"
some Bible texts are so specifically classified that LC shelflisters merely add
dates (no cutter numbers) to keep them in order. For example, the *NRSV-NIV
Parallel New Testament in Greek and English*, with interlinear translation by
Alfred Marshall, has been assigned the LC call number BS1965.5 1990.

CONCLUSION

Call numbers are of particular concern in libraries with open stacks where
browsing allows patrons to find physical resources on similar subjects in proximity, to find works of one author on a subject together, and to find editions
of a work together. Where there are closed stacks, an accession number can
serve as well as a call number for retrieval, although a greater burden is then
placed on the verbal subject headings to guide users to information resources
that may be found on particular subjects.

While use of cutter numbers is the most common method of creating complete call numbers, other means may sometimes be found more useful. In a

science and technology collection, for example, where recency of material may be of utmost importance, subarrangement under each classification notation may be by year of imprint. In very small general collections, on the other hand, one or more letters of the first word of the primary access point may be added after the classification notation, with no additional numbers given. This method, however, will usually not result in unique call numbers, which may be needed for shelving management.

NOTES

1. The *term primary access point* is no longer used in descriptive cataloging. At the time of this writing, however, a new phrase representing the same concept in call number creation and shelflisting has not yet emerged—thus, the use of an older term in this chapter.
2. Charles A. Cutter, *Two-Figure Author Table*, Swanson-Swift revision, 1969. Distributed by Libraries Unlimited, Inc., Littleton, Colo. (formerly distributed by H. R. Huntting Co.).
3. Charles A. Cutter, *Cutter-Sanborn Three-Figure Author Table*, Swanson-Swift revision, 1969. Distributed by Libraries Unlimited, Inc., Littleton, Colo. (formerly distributed by H. R. Huntting Co.).
4. Charles A. Cutter, *Three-Figure Author Table*, Swanson-Swift revision, 1969. Distributed by Libraries Unlimited, Inc., Littleton, Colo. (formerly distributed by H. R. Huntting Co.).
5. "Dewey Cutter Program: Speed Your Classification Efforts" OCLC, accessed October 24, 2014, http://www.oclc.org/support/services/dewey/program .en.html.
6. "Library of Congress Classification and Shelflisting Manual." Library of Congress, Acquisitions and Bibliographic Access Directorate, last updated February 5, 2015, http://www.loc.gov/aba/publications/FreeCSM/freecsm .html. Also available in *Cataloger's Desktop*.
7. "Library of Congress Classification and Shelflisting Manual: Cutter Numbers G 63," July 2013, http://www.loc.gov/aba/publications/FreeCSM/G063.pdf.
8. Ibid.
9. "Library of Congress Classification and Shelflisting Manual: Dates G 140," July 2013, http://www.loc.gov/aba/publications/FreeCSM/G140.pdf.
10. "Library of Congress Classification and Shelflisting Manual: Corporate Bodies G 220," July 2013, http://www.loc.gov/aba/publications/FreeCSM/G220.pdf.

SUGGESTED READING

Comaromi, John P. *Book Numbers: A Historical Study and Practical Guide to Their Use.* Littleton, Colo.: Libraries Unlimited, 1981.
Lehnus, Donald J. *Book Numbers: History, Principles, and Application.* Chicago: American Library Association, 1980.
Taylor, Arlene G. *The Organization of Information.* 2nd ed. Westport, Conn.: Libraries Unlimited, 2004. Chap. 12, "Arrangement and Display."
Taylor, Arlene G., and Daniel Joudrey. *The Organization of Information.* 3rd ed. Westport, Conn.: Libraries Unlimited, 2009. Appendix B, "Arrangement of Physical Information Resources in Libraries."

Chapter 20

Other Classification Systems

INTRODUCTION

This chapter provides a brief overview of some of the more significant modern classifications besides *Dewey Decimal Classification* (DDC) and *Library of Congress Classification* (LCC). Those discussed are Cutter's *Expansive Classification* (EC), Brown's *Subject Classification* (SC), Bliss's *Bibliographic Classification* (BC), and some special classifications, including some taxonomies. *Universal Decimal Classification* (UDC) is discussed at the end of chapter 17, and Ranganathan's *Colon Classification* (CC) is used as an example in the discussion of faceted classification in chapter 16. While the classifications discussed here by no means exhaust modern classification research and practice, they do illustrate many of the problems and solutions, or failures, of both the seminal and the well-entrenched systems discussed in the contemporary literature.[1]

CUTTER'S *EXPANSIVE CLASSIFICATION*

The *Expansive Classification*, like the DDC, was the brainchild of an eminent library pioneer. Charles A. Cutter (1837-1903) was 15 years older than Melvil Dewey (1851-1931), but took 15 years longer to publish his scheme. Both men devised their systems as practical efforts to organize collections that they knew and served. Just as DDC came out of Dewey's student employment in the Amherst College Library, so Cutter's cataloging efforts in the Harvard College Library, and for much longer at the Boston Athenaeum, gave rise to his *Expansive Classification*.

While the lives and achievements of the two men show many parallels, there are also significant differences. In classification, Dewey chose his pure decimal notation early on, making it such a key feature of his approach that it more or less governed all subsequent growth patterns. He saw that a simple basic design, easy-to-master mnemonic devices, and a certain sturdy inflexibility could provide a general system that would be applicable to the many libraries that were being established. With characteristic energy, he started a schedule of periodic revision to keep his system responsive to the rapidly changing cultural and publishing milieu. And he marketed his invention with zest and conviction. Cutter was of a more delicate physique and temperament, less exuberant, more institution-oriented. But he, too, was imbued with the gregarious optimism of his era and worked diligently to establish librarianship as a helping profession, with scientific organization as one of its basic assumptions.

Cutter's scheme stressed a sequence of classifications, or expansions, from a very simple set of categories for a small library to an intricate network of interrelated, highly specific subdivisions for the library of over a million volumes.[2] He did not live to finish his ultimate seventh expansion or to embark on a successive-edition program, but he did have the satisfaction of seeing the Library of Congress (LC) prefer many features of his scheme to those of his friendly rival. His willingness to take suggestions, and to compromise, worked to his credit and to the continuing influence of his system in spite of its limited adoption.

Cutter found the 10 broad classes of DDC too narrow a base for large collections. He therefore turned to the alphabet, with its easily ordered sequence of up to 26 primary groupings. For collections that "could be put into a single room" his first expansion used only seven letters, with an eighth double-letter subclass, as follows:

A   Works of reference and general works that include several of the following sections, and so could not go to any one

B   Philosophy and Religion

E   Biography

F   History and Geography and Travels

H   Social sciences

L   Natural sciences and Arts

Y   Language and Literature

YF   Fiction

Cutter's second expansion introduced a mixed alphanumeric notation that could be used if a small library should grow to require closer, more specific classes. It also subdivided the **F-History** and the new **G-Geography** classes by adding two Arabic numerals to the letter to signify identical geographic areas for each class. For example, F30 means History of Europe, while G30 means Geography of Europe. The second expansion holds 14 main classes, some redefinition of the original seven, and further differentiation of two classes along geographic lines.

The third expansion completes all but **P-Vertebrates** of the base 26 divisions and separates Religion from Philosophy, moving it to a second double-letter subclass. Part of the debt that LCC owes to Cutter can easily be traced through the outline comparison shown in Table 20.1.

TABLE 20.1 Comparison of the Main Outlines of EC and LCC.

	Cutter's *Expansive Classification* (3rd Expansion)		Library of Congress Classification (LCC)
A	General works	A	General works
B	Philosophy	B	Philosophy. Religion
BR	Non-Judaeo-Christian religions		
C	Judaism and Christianity	C	History. Auxiliary sciences
D	Ecclesiastical history	D	History (except America)
E	Biography	E-F	History of the Americas
F	History		
G	Geography	G	Geography. Anthropology
H	Social sciences	H	Social sciences
I	Sociology		
J	Political science	J	Political science
K	Law	K	Law
L	Natural sciences	L	Education
M	Natural history	M	Music
N	Botany	N	Fine arts
O	Zoology		
		P	Language and literature
Q	Medicine	Q	Science
R	Technology	R	Medicine
S	Engineering	S	Agriculture
T	Manufactures and Handicrafts	T	Technology
U	Defensive and preservative arts	U	Military science
V	Athletic and recreative arts	V	Naval science
W	Fine arts		
X	Languages		
Y	Literature		
YF	Fiction		
Z	Book arts	Z	Bibliography and Library science

The fourth expansion subdivides 12 main classes for the first time, increasing the double-letter subclasses to 50. It also carries an extensive supplementary table expanding the double-digit geographic numbers from the F and G classes into a *place* or *local* list.

The fifth expansion introduces the 26th single-letter class **P-Vertebrates** and subdivides all remaining undivided classes, using many triple- and a few quadruple-letter sections. The sixth expansion introduces no new techniques—only new additions to existing classes and subclasses.

The seventh expansion was published in 18 parts, edited and to some extent developed by William Parker Cutter after the originator's death.[3] All expansions were prepared on the theory that as a library outgrew its simpler modes of organization, partial dislocation and reclassification of the existing collection was preferable to complete reorganization. Although some books would have to be reclassed and relocated, not all would be, and certainly not all at once.

While it was never widely adopted, some 67 American, Canadian, and British libraries have been identified as past or present EC users.[4] Perhaps even more important is the influence it exerted on later, more popular classifications, such as that developed at LC.

BROWN'S *SUBJECT CLASSIFICATION*

Next in chronological development is a British scheme. James Duff Brown (1864-1914) was a Scottish counterpart of Dewey and Cutter, if somewhat younger. Coming to the profession from an early apprenticeship to publishers and booksellers, he became deeply involved in the public library movement in Great Britain. It is debatable whether his advocacy of open stacks was directly influenced by his travels in the United States in 1893. His breadth of knowledge was legendary, even though he did not have a university education, and his interest in music resulted in several music reference tools that he either compiled or sponsored.

Brown recognized the lack of good organization of materials in most British libraries. To make open stack access feasible, he and John Henry Quinn published in 1894 an article titled, "Classification of Books for Libraries in Which Readers Are Allowed Access to Shelves." Brown's own *Adjustable Classification* followed in 1898. As the name implies, it allowed for insertion of new divisions or topics as needed, but it was not worked out or indexed in much detail. Growing out of it, in 1906, was the first edition of the *Subject Classification* (SC). In 1914, shortly after Brown's death, came a second edition, and in 1939 James Douglas Stewart issued a revised and enlarged third edition.[5]

The basic scaffold of Brown's SC, as shown in Table 20.2, consists of 11 main classes, expressing four broad divisional concepts in orderly sequence. It is known for its *one-place* approach. In other words, each subject has a single logical place in the classification, rather than having many places scattered among different disciplines. The scheme does acknowledge:

> Every subject is capable of being treated from a large number of standpoints [i.e., facets or aspects] . . . . To illustrate this, I shall assume that there are some thousands of books existing, which have for their theme the Rose in every conceivable aspect. This subject may be considered from any of the following standpoints: —
> Biological, Botanical, Horticultural, Historical, Geographical, Ethical, Decorative, Legal, Emblematical, Bibliographical, Poetical, Musical, Sociological, and so on to any extent.

Works about the Rose may assume the form of Dictionaries, Periodicals, Societies, Catalogues, and so forth; while it may also be considered
in reference to Costume, Perfumery, Therapeutics, and similar subjects.
Now, it is quite evident that, . . . there would be enormous practical convenience to the Rose student [in an approach where all of these aspects
are brought together under a single general location].[6]

Primary notation in SC is alphabetical, with some classes assigned more than
one capital letter, to cover all subtopics without making the notation unduly
long. Each initial letter is followed by three Arabic numerals. Sequence, rather
than length of number, reveals hierarchy:

D600	METALLURGY	
601	Smelting	
602		Blast Furnaces
603		Open Hearth Furnaces
604	Ores	

These schedule numbers may be expanded like decimals (without the decimal
point) when new topics require insertion. The scheme allows several methods of building numbers: geographic numbers from the O-W classes may be
attached to topical numbers when needed. There is a Categorical Table and
an Index that contains "categories, forms, etc. for the subdivision of subjects."[7] Numbers from this table are attached after a period, which is not to be
regarded as a decimal point. A plus sign is used to connect two facets from the
same class. The underscore is used to stack parts of a number. Its purpose is
to keep an extended notation compact. For example, the *rose*, as a subject, is

TABLE 20.2 Broad Outline of Brown's Subject Classification.

Notation	Class	Division
A	Generalia	} Matter and force
B C D	Physical Science	
E F	Biological Science	
G H	Ethnological and Medical Science	} Life
I	Economic Biology and Domestic Arts	
J K	Philosophy and Religion	
L	Social and Political Science	} Mind
M	Language and Literature	
N	Literary forms	
O-W	History, Geography	} Record
X	Biography	

found in the E class at E600, but various standpoints, forms, and so on are represented through additional notation.

E600	**Rose, General**
E600.1	**Rose—Bibliography**
E600.2	**Rose—Encyclopædias**
E600.7	**Rose—Periodicals**
E600.10	**Rose—History**
E600.124	**Rose—Engravings**[8]

While Brown's *Subject Classification*, like Cutter's *Expansive Classification*, never gained the widespread adoption received by its American rivals, timing and the lack of a consistent, continuing update program may be the explanation, rather than the comparative merits of the four schemes. Brown's system stimulated research and development in British classification theory, much as Cutter's did in the United States. Both are now milestones of classification history, rather than popular modern schemes for arranging library materials.

BLISS'S *BIBLIOGRAPHIC CLASSIFICATION*

Henry Evelyn Bliss (1870-1955) was Librarian of the College of the City of New York, where he spent most of his career developing and testing his ideas on library classification. He was attempting to create a system based on logical principles of classification that he developed in his writing. After several periodical articles and books, he finished publication of his magnum opus only two years before his death.[9] Although Bliss's *Bibliographic Classification* (BC1 or Bliss) was created by an American librarian, it never really gained traction in the United States; it was used primarily in Great Britain.

Between 1940 and 1953, his four-volume BC1 was published. A *bibliographic classification* is, in Bliss's terminology, one designed to organize documentary materials (i.e., library collections, chiefly in print format). The sequence of main classes nonetheless preserves the discipline (rather than topical) orientation that Bliss interpreted as the basic structure of knowledge. Paul Dunkin called it "a sort of reader interest classification for scholars."[10] According to Bliss, it is important in classifying a book to decide in what main classes it falls. The literature on concrete topics like *bees* is not kept in one place (as Brown would try to do) but is distributed, as in DDC, according to the aspect from which it is viewed. For example, a book on bees from a scientific aspect goes to class **G-Zoology**, whereas a book on beekeeping is classed in **U-Useful Arts**.

The British Committee for the Bliss Classification, when it changed its name in 1967 to the Bliss Classification Association (BCA), began discussing the idea for a new and completely revised edition of the full classification. The *Bibliographic Classification*, Second Edition (BC2) is so radically revised that it is more accurately described as a new system, although it uses the broad outline developed by Bliss.[11] It derives techniques of facet analysis, as well as of explicit citation and filing orders, from Ranganathan's monumental contributions to classification theory.[12] The outline of BC2 is shown in Table 20.3.

TABLE 20.3 Outline of Main Classes in BC2.

Vol.	Title	Pub. Date	Online Version?
1	Introduction & Auxiliary schedules	1977	Yes
2/9	Generalia, phenomena, knowledge, information science & technology		Incomplete Draft
A/AL	Philosophy & Logic	1991	Yes
AM/AX	Mathematics, probability, statistics	1993	Yes
AY/B	General science, Physics	1999	
C	Chemistry	2012	Yes
D/DF	Astronomy		Draft
DG/DY	Earth sciences, including geography and geology		Draft
E/GQ	Biological sciences, including biology, genetics, virology, botany, and zoology		Incomplete Draft
GR/GZ	Applied biological sciences: agriculture and ecology		
H	Physical anthropology, human biology, health sciences	1980	
I	Psychology and psychiatry	1978	Yes
J	Education (Rev. ed.)	1990	Yes
K	Society (includes social sciences, sociology, and social anthropology)	1984	
L/O	History (including area studies, travel and topography, and biography)		Two Drafts
LA	Archaeology		Draft
P	Religion, occult, morals, and ethics	1977	Yes
Q	Social welfare & criminology (Rev. ed.)	1994	Yes
R	Politics and public administration	1996	Yes
S	Law	1996	Yes
T	Economics & management of economic enterprises	1987	
U/V	Technology and useful arts (including household management and services)		
W	The Arts	2007	Yes
WV/WX	Music		Draft
X/Y	Language and literature		Draft
ZA/ZW	Museology		Draft

The dates following the titles indicate the volumes that have appeared to date. Detailed draft schedules, usually in the form of PDFs, have been completed for many of the remaining classes, and are available from the BCA website.[13]

The BCA draws its membership largely from libraries using the scheme. It published, at least up until 2011, an annual *Bliss Classification Bulletin*, and has an annual meeting. The BCA arranges lectures and visits to libraries using the scheme. The BCA official website links to several BC sites, some of which are particular colleges within Cambridge University or Oxford University.[14]

Second edition notation consists of capital letters and numerals, omitting zero because of its similarity to the letter O. The classification numbers are as brief as possible, consistent with full expression of the various aspects of a topic. Each main class and each subclass is fully faceted. A comprehensive and consistent citation order is observed throughout; although it is suggested that if that order is not appropriate in a particular local situation, another order may be adopted. The notation is fully faceted and does not attempt the task of always reflecting hierarchy. The notation uses only letters and numbers divided into blocks of three. The first letter indicates the discipline of the information resource, as shown in the outline in Table 20.3. The next letter categorizes the subject into the broad areas of the discipline. It can be subdivided again for more specificity. An example of a notation for the nursing of children with cancer is HXO QEM Y:

HXO	Pediatrics
HQE	Cancer
HMY	Nursing

The initial letter for the class is dropped when combining subclasses.

The future of the *Bibliographic Classification* is dependent in large part on the timing and public acceptance of the new edition. That BC2's theory and practice has many advantages is recognized by anyone who knows it well enough to compare it with more widely accepted schemes. That it badly needed updating and further development is also clear. The gargantuan job of a complete overhaul by a few aficionados on a shoestring budget, if finished, should permit future sequential revision of different class schedules as needed (somewhat resembling the present revision program at LC). Establishment of the Bliss scheme as a major contender for library adoption will require not only efficient, dedicated work, but also a great deal of luck.

SPECIAL CLASSIFICATION SCHEMES

Classification schemes comprising the entire universe of knowledge must of necessity be general and cannot deal with specialties or fine detail. They are also largely inflexible, presenting the particular viewpoint of their designers (which in the case of DDC and LCC represents the late 19th century), and they often disperse subjects that, for the purposes of specialists, ought to be dealt with in close proximity (e.g., DDC has chemistry in 540 but chemical technology in 660, which is unhelpful for a chemistry library). Even UDC, although providing for very fine detail, suffers from many of the faults inherited from DDC (e.g., the chemistry dispersal) and often has long notations.

Librarians of collections devoted mainly or exclusively to one specific field of knowledge, a discipline, or one of its subfields have therefore often found it necessary to design special classification schemes, sometimes called *taxonomies*. The word *classification*, for most people, triggers the idea of a notation assigned to an information resource in order to put it in order among other resources. The word *taxonomy*, for most people, triggers the idea of a strict scientific arrangement of class/genus/species. The word comes from the Greek *taxis* (arrangement, order) and *nomos* (law). The term is still newly being used in place of *classification* and the current definition is still in flux. It can be used to mean classification schemes, thesauri, or simply lists of categories. The Montague Institute has defined it as "a system for naming and organizing things into groups that share similar characteristics."[15] Thomas Wason has defined it as "a knowledge map of a topic, typcially [i.e., typically] realized as a controlled vocabulary of terms and or phrases . . . an orderly classification of information according to presumed natural relationships. . . . The most typical form of a taxonomy is a hierarchy."[16]

The British Classification Research Group (CRG) was particularly active in designing special faceted classifications during the 1960s and 1970s, whereas in the United States special classifications were more often the work of individuals and organizations. Such special classifications have usually been bibliographic classifications, designed to provide ways of ordering physical resources in a specific subject area. Taxonomies have developed more recently, especially with the increased use of the web and other online systems for providing access to full text documents in specialized subject areas. Taxonomies are often categorized lists of terms and include classification schemes, subject heading lists, Internet directories, and subject gateways. They are often proprietary to the organizations that created them and, in such cases, they may not be freely used by others.

Special bibliographic classification schemes are mainly of two types: *general-special schemes*, which classify a special field or subject exhaustively while providing only very general class marks to peripheral or extraneous subjects, and *special schemes*, dealing only with a particular specialty in sometimes very fine detail but leaving the classing of other subjects to one of the general schemes. Hybrids of the two types are those schemes that expand an existing class of a general scheme or make use of an unused notation under which a special subject field is developed in detail.

Two examples of the latter type are widely used in U.S. libraries. The *National Library of Medicine* (NLM) *Classification* uses class W (which is vacant in LCC) and QS-QZ (classes which are also vacant) for the entire biomedical field.[17] There are 26 subclasses of W, subdivided by every letter of the Roman alphabet (even I and O, which are avoided by LCC because of possible confusion with the digits 1 and 0), followed by up to three digits used enumeratively and an occasional fourth digit used decimally, followed by more detailed subdivision using cuttering:

WD-Disorders of Systemic, Metabolic, or Environmental Origin, etc.

WD 200-226	Metabolic diseases
WD 205	Inborn errors of metabolism (General)
WD 205.5	Specific errors or groups of errors not elsewhere classified, A-Z
WD 205.5.A5	Amino acid metabolism

Since NLM's W class notations appear on many bibliographic records produced for distribution by NLM and also on some records produced by LC, most medical libraries use the W special classification.

Moys Classification and Thesaurus for Legal Materials,[18] which expands class K of LCC, found wide acceptance in law libraries after its publication in 1968, but completion of most of the K class by LC in recent years has reduced the need for the separate scheme. Another expansion of LCC is for a highly specialized subject; *An Alternative Classification for Catholic Books*[19] takes a section of the LC classification that was not in use by LC when the schedule was developed in 1937 and develops it as Christian literature with three major subclasses: BQT, theology; BQV, canon law; and BQX, church history, all further subdivided by enumerative digits and cuttering. The introduction gives detailed instructions on how to integrate these schedules into either LCC or DDC when these are used to classify other subjects in a library. (BQ is now used in LCC for Buddhism.)

The following examples are representatives of the special type of classification that combines a faceted structure and high flexibility with brief notations. The *London Education Classification*[20] fulfills a double role as a classification and a thesaurus and uses an alphabetical notation, with uppercase letters serving as facet indicators:

Mab	Curriculum
Mabb	Curriculum development
Mabf	Curriculum classification

The *London Classification of Business Studies*, first established in the late 1960s, is both a thesaurus and a classification.[21] It has three main categories: management responsibility within the enterprise (A-G), environment of the enterprise (J-R), and basic analytical techniques (S-X). In addition, there is a class set aside for information science (Y), which is based on the CRG's *Classification of Library & Information Science*.[22] There are also some auxiliary schedules (1-7) to address facets necessary for a business classification (such as occupational roles, products, and services), as well as standard subdivisions (e.g., geographical, chronological, and form divisions).[23] The notation consists of up to four uppercase letters.

K Industries	
KC	Confectionery and bakery industries
KCG	Sugar and sugar confectionery industries
KCGA	Chocolate and sweets industry

Notations can be combined by a forward slash.

> EE/KCGA   Financial management in the chocolate industry

Auxiliary table numbers are appended onto the end with a space between the classification letters and the table numbers. For example, if a cataloger were to classify case studies of the financial management in the Canadian chocolate industry, then 552 for Canada and 79 for case studies would be appended to the number above to get **EE/KCGA 522 79**. In the early 21st century, the scheme was used in about 40 British libraries and more than 20 libraries elsewhere. The London Business School Library is responsible for updating the scheme.

An example of a special scheme relying on another classification for supplementary topics is the *Classification of Library & Information Science*, designed by the CRG. This scheme, too, makes use of facets and lettered notation, but on occasion it may use notation from UDC for concepts outside the central topic of library and information science (e.g., geographic area, languages, other subjects). For example, the notation HQ-B481-AKQ is used for a directory of the National Library of Norway; 481, the notation for Norway, is taken directly from the UDC.

Special classifications are sometimes developed for extremely narrow subjects, such as the *Classification for London Literature*,[24] concerned with works only on that city, with decimal subdivisions for every place and event in its long history:

10	Religious life, history, influences, institutions	
12		St. Paul's Cathedral
12.4		Dome and roof

A 1982 bibliography of classification schemes and subject heading lists for hundreds of different subjects gives 2,250 items in several languages.[25] It may be assumed that hundreds more have been created in the intervening years.

As already mentioned, taxonomies are often not available for use by anyone other than the organizations that developed them. A few (mainly government-developed) are available on the web, however. One is the National Center for Biotechnology Information's taxonomy, which is "a curated classification and nomenclature for all of the organisms in the public [Entrez] sequence databases. This currently represents about 10% of the described species of life on the planet."[26] Another example is the GRIN (Germplasm Resources Information Network) Taxonomy.[27] As is true of virtually all taxonomies on the web, these two appear in hierarchical structures in which a term can be viewed in a tree structure. Records for individual terms may have a taxonomy ID (e.g., 36122 is the nomen number for *Syringa vulgaris L.*, commonly known as a *lilac*), but there is no classification notation to be used for the arrangement of information resources. The latter are indexed with the term and may be retrieved in response to a term search.

The ambiguity in use of the term *taxonomy* is illustrated by a website called "Taxonomy Warehouse," a "free online information resource . . . all about taxonomy: Content and links to everything you need to know about taxonomy in one convenient website. Explore our subject-oriented directory of taxonomies and their publishers."[28] When browsing the lists in the various categories provided, however, very few of them use the word *taxonomy* in their titles. Rather they are called *thesauri, terminology* or *subject lists,* or other such names.

A special classification scheme or taxonomy may initially have the advantage of being more detailed and more up to date than any of the general schemes, but it is unfortunately often the case that such schemes, once designed, are not further developed and therefore become obsolete and lacking in detail much quicker than general schemes. When adopting a special scheme, one must take care to choose a scheme that has a reasonably good chance of being further developed and updated—that is, one that is backed by an organization rather than being the one-time effort of a librarian in a special collection. Such homemade classification schemes are generally motivated by the fact that sooner or later almost any librarian will find that the scheme he or she uses, whether general or specific, is insufficiently detailed or does not contain a classification notation for a new subject. It is then easy to succumb to the temptation to create a new subdivision or an entirely new scheme for the missing topics or for sections of a scheme that seem to be misplaced. The proper design of a special classification is, however, a task best left to someone thoroughly familiar with the theory and principles of classification design (i.e., a classificationist), and the novice should refrain from attempting this enterprise until some considerable experience has been gained. Many hastily conceived and improperly designed special classification schemes have had to be abandoned sooner or later, to be replaced with an existing and proven scheme at great cost and inconvenience to a library or other organization and its users.

CONCLUSION

The classification systems briefly reviewed here differ from each other, and from the better known DDC and LCC systems, in many ways. In basic theory of the organization of knowledge, some emphasize the specific subject approach, clustering these unitary topics in related sequences, whereas most start from a broad disciplinary orientation, subdividing hierarchically, so that the various aspects or unitary topics become scattered to different parts of the system. In providing a schedule framework to arrange items on shelves, some systems (the more traditional) are primarily enumerative, whereas most newer ones are synthetic or faceted. Some maintain a comparatively pure notation, whereas others use combinations of letters and Arabic numerals; upper- and lowercase letters, Roman numerals, Greek letters, and a variety of arbitrary relational signs and symbols appear in still others. Systems designed for the web may be alphabetical but most are designed to display terminology in a hierarchical order.

Timeliness is a constant problem. Some systems maintain a program to announce additions and changes or issue new editions at intervals of 5 to 25 years. Many have outlived their originators, but some suffer more than others from age and lack of funds or organized promotion. Each has unique attractive features; each has practical and theoretical problems. Some are more useful for shelf arrangement of books and related formats. Others are better suited to in-depth indexing of periodical articles, technical reports, documents, and the like. Forces, such as networking, seem to favor general acceptance of one or two well-known, widely used schemes, overlooking functional disadvantages to achieve standardization and administrative coherence. Yet classification research, like that in all other areas of information organization, is very brisk and busy in the modern world of library and information science. Time may show that all the schemes catalogers study and use today, regardless of their present achievements or popularity, are chiefly important for the historic part they play as heralds of still better solutions to the problems of subject access.

NOTES

1. Four examples of specific applications using the systems discussed in this chapter, as well as DDC and LCC, are given in Bohdan S. Wynar, *Introduction to Cataloging and Classification*, 5th ed., prepared with the assistance of John Phillip Immroth (Littleton, Colo.: Libraries Unlimited, 1976), 314-328.
2. Charles A. Cutter, *Expansive Classification, Part I: The First Six Classifications* (Boston: Cutter, 1891-1893).
3. Charles A. Cutter, *Expansive Classification, Part II: Seventh Classification*, largely edited by William Parker Cutter (Boston and Northampton, Mass.: Cutter, 1896-1911), 2 vol., with supplementary pages.
4. Robert L. Mowery, "The Cutter Classification: Still at Work," *Library Resources & Technical Services* 20 (Spring 1976): 154.
5. James Duff Brown, *Subject Classification: With Tables, Indexes, etc., for the Subdivision of Subjects*, 3rd ed., rev. and enl. by James Douglas Stewart (London: Grafton, 1939).
6. Ibid., 8.
7. Ibid., 37.
8. Ibid., 9; 57-58.
9. Bliss's major works are the following: *The Organization of Knowledge and the System of the Sciences* (New York: Holt, 1929); *The Organization of Knowledge in Libraries*, 2nd ed., rev. and partly rewritten (New York: H. W. Wilson, 1939); *A Bibliographic Classification: Extended by Systematic Auxiliary Schedules for Composite Specification and Notation* (New York: H. W. Wilson, 1940-1953), 4 vol.
10. Paul S. Dunkin, *Cataloging U.S.A.* (Chicago: American Library Association, 1969), 126.
11. "The Bliss Bibliographic Classification: History & Description," Bliss Classification Association, accessed June 10, 2014, http://www.blissclassification.org.uk/bchist.shtml.
12. See, for instance, S. R. Ranganathan, *Prolegomena to Library Classification*, 3rd ed. (Bombay: Asia Pub. House, 1967).
13. "The Bliss Bibliographic Classification: Schedules," Bliss Classification Association, accessed June 10, 2014, http://www.blissclassification.org.uk/bcsched.shtml.
14. "Bliss Classification Association," accessed June 10, 2014, http://www.blissclassification.org.uk/index.shtml.

15. "Ten Taxonomy Myths," *Montague Institute Review*, accessed July 19, 2015, https://web.archive.org/web/20141216163734/http://www.montague.com/review/myths.html.

16. Thomas D. Wason, "Dr. Tom's Taxonomy Guide," Version 1.02, February 15, 2006, http://www.tomwason.com/drtomtaxonomiesguide.html.

17. "Outline of the NLM Classification," National Library of Medicine, 2015, http://www.nlm.nih.gov/class/OutlineofNLMClassificationSchedule.html.

18. Elizabeth M. Moys, *Moys Classification and Thesaurus for Legal Materials*, 5th ed., revised and expanded by Diana Morris, Helen Garner, Sara Wheeler (Berlin; Boston: De Gruyter Saur, 2013).

19. Jeannette Murphy Lynn, *An Alternative Classification for Catholic Books*, 2nd ed., revised by Gilbert C. Peterson (Washington, D.C.: Catholic University of America Press, 1954). Accompanied by *Supplement* (1954-1965) by Thomas G. Pater. (Washington, D.C.: Catholic University of America Press, 1965).

20. D. J. Foskett and Joy Foskett, *The London Education Classification: A Thesaurus-Classification of British Education Terms*, 2nd ed. (London: University of London Institute of Education Library, 1974).

21. K. D. C. Vernon and Valerie Lang, *The London Classification of Business Studies*, 2nd ed., rev. by K. G. B. Bakewell and David A. Cotton (London: Aslib, 1979).

22. Ruth Daniel and J. Mills, *A Classification of Library & Information Science* (London: Library Association, 1975).

23. London Business School Library, *Thesaurus: London Classification of Business Studies* (London: London Business School Library, 2009). The latest version, which comes in two volumes (one an alphabetical sequence; the other a classified sequence), is available electronically for a fee.

24. Guildhall Library, *Classification for London Literature Based upon the Collection in the Guildhall Library*, 3rd ed. (London: Guildhall Library, 1966).

25. *Classification Systems and Thesauri, 1950-1982*, International Classification and Indexing Bibliography 1 (Frankfurt, West Germany: Indeks Verlag, 1982).

26. "Taxonomy," National Center for Biotechnology Information, accessed July 19, 2015, http://www.ncbi.nlm.nih.gov/taxonomy.

27. "GRIN Taxonomy for Plants," USDA Agricultural Research Service (ARS), accessed July 19, 2015, http://www.ars-grin.gov/cgi-bin/npgs/html/index.pl.

28. "Taxonomy Warehouse," accessed July 19, 2015, http://taxonomywarehouse.com.

SUGGESTED READING

Chan, Lois Mai, with the assistance of Theodora L. Hodges. *Cataloging and Classification: An Introduction*. 3rd ed. Lanham, Md.: Scarecrow Press, 2007. Chapter 15: National Library of Medicine Classification and Other Modern Classification Systems.

Cutter, Charles A. *Expansive Classification. Part I: The First Six Classifications*. Boston: C. A. Cutter, 1891-1893.

Foskett, A. C. *The Subject Approach to Information*. 5th ed. London: Library Association Publishing, 1996. Chapter 10: General Classification Schemes. Chapter 19: The Bibliographic Classification. Chapter 20: The Broad System of Ordering.

Maltby, Arthur, and Lindy Gill. *The Case for Bliss: Modern Classification Practice and Principles in the Context of the Bibliographic Classification.* London: Clive Bingley, 1979.

Richardson, Ernest Cushing. *Classification, Theoretical and Practical: Together with an Appendix Containing an Essay Towards a Bibliographical History of Systems of Classification.* 3rd edition. New York, H. W. Wilson, 1930.

Rowley, Jennifer, and Richard Hartley. *Organizing Knowledge: An Introduction to Managing Access to Information.* 4th ed. Aldershot, Eng.; Burlington, VT: Ashgate, 2008. "Bibliographic Classification Schemes," 206-221; "Taxonomies and ontologies," 222-230.

Part V

Formatting and Presentation

Chapter 21

MARC Encoding

INTRODUCTION

In online systems, the content of catalog records must be electronically encoded in order to be machine-manipulable for searching and display. Encoding allows each element of a record to be distinguished from every other. This enables access to catalog record elements, either through searching (for author, title, subject, keyword, etc.) or for limiting via facets such as language, place of publication, date of publication, and so on. Encoding also underlies the markup that makes desired displays possible.

The MARC (MAchine-Readable Cataloging) encoding system has been used to create electronic catalog records since the mid-1960s. After an initial study begun in 1964, extensive experimentation proceeded with the MARC I and MARC II projects and subsequent initiatives, including the Retrospective Conversion (RECON), the Cooperative MAchine-Readable Cataloging (COMARC), and the British UK/MARC pilot projects. An excellent history of its development may be found in Deborah Byrne's *MARC Manual*.[1] The most current version for use in the United States is MARC 21, a harmonized version of USMARC and CAN/MARC, first published in 1999 and continually revised.[2]

Other encoding systems have been developed in response to the desire to make information (and accompanying metadata) available on the web. These approaches all started with the Standard Generalized Markup Language (SGML), which is an international standard for document markup. It is a *meta-language*—that is, a set of rules for designing a variety of markup languages that describe the structures of documents. The markup languages thus designed are SGML applications called *document type definitions* (DTDs). Around the turn of the century, a number of SGML DTDs were used for bibliographic data, including Text Encoding Initiative (TEI) and Encoded Archival Description (EAD). These SGML DTDs, however, have been revised to be compliant with the Extensible Markup Language (XML). XML is an application of SGML that added some features that solved earlier problems associated with SGML. As of 2015, XML has almost completely replaced SGML as the meta-language for web documents. XML has *schemas* as well as DTDs. Although they function similarly, schemas are more powerful for a variety of reasons. Unlike a DTD, a schema is written in XML itself, and it specifies the tags, attributes of tags, and rules for tags that will be used to encode records using the schema. Schemas have become the favored approach to providing structure to XML documents.

Because most open source software is XML compatible, and new generation integrated library systems (ILSs) support XML, the Library of Congress (LC) has developed a schema for translating MARC records into XML. Called MARCXML, it is very detailed in using all the MARC 21 tags and codes. The official website includes the specifications, example documents in MARCXML, tools for conversion of records into and out of MARCXML, and related information.[3] A simpler, but still highly compatible, schema has also been developed. This schema, called MODS (Metadata Object Description Schema), primarily comprises a subset of the MARC bibliographic format using language-based tags. More information about MODS can be found in the following chapter.

Currently, the MARC encoding system holds the position of being the one used for bibliographic records in the vast majority of the world's online catalogs, although this is poised for change. This chapter focuses on an introduction to MARC. A discussion of the Bibliographic Framework Initiative (BIBFRAME), designed to succeed MARC, follows in chapter 22.

INTRODUCTION TO MACHINE-READABLE CATALOGING (MARC)

Each MARC format is made up of three components: the record structure, the content designation, and the actual metadata content. The *record structure* "is an implementation of the international standard *Format for Information Exchange* (ISO 2709) and its American counterpart, *Bibliographic Information Interchange* (ANSI/NISO Z39.2)."[4] *Content designation* refers to the use of tags and sub-field codes to specifically identify and label the metadata held in parts of MARC records. Content designation allows automated library systems to process, index, and manipulate the data found in the record as needed. *Content* refers to the metadata contained in the record, formatted according to content standards, controlled vocabularies, classification schemes, and the like. In this chapter, the focus is on content designation; the record structure is highly technical and beyond the scope of this work. The content is addressed throughout the rest of this text. These three elements are present in each of the five MARC formats.

Formats

There are five MARC 21 formats for different types of data:

- **Bibliographic format**: for encoding bibliographic data in records that are surrogates for information resources
- **Authority format**: for encoding authority data collected in authority records created to help control the content of those surrogate record fields that are subject to authority control

- **Holdings format**: for encoding data elements in holdings records that show the holdings and location data for information resources described in surrogate records
- **Community information format**: for encoding data in records that contain information about events, programs, services, and the like
- **Classification data format**: for encoding data elements related to classification numbers, the captions associated with them, their hierarchies, and the subject headings with which they correlate[5]

This chapter provides an introduction to the MARC 21 bibliographic and authority formats, following brief descriptions of the others.

The *holdings format* provides metadata elements for the specific copies of resources to which individual libraries provide access. In the terms associated with FRBR, holdings format metadata is item-level metadata. Three broad categories of resources are included in the holdings format: items complete in a single physical part, multipart items intended to be complete with the issuance of a finite number of physical parts, and serial items issued in successive parts and intended to be continued indefinitely. Note that LC's introduction to the holdings format documentation specifies physical resources as the focus for the first two categories.[6]

Holdings metadata may include information about a specific copy of a resource and information about the library pertinent to the use or processing of the item, including its maintenance or preservation. For serials, holdings fields are used to designate the portion of a serial's run accessible through the library, including numbering (e.g., volume and part numbers or their equivalents) and dates. For single and multipart items, holdings fields may designate not only the library's ownership of the basic resource described in a bibliographic record, but supplemental material as well. Finally, MARC bibliographic and holdings records are not mutually exclusive; selected fields from either format may be present when appropriate and useful in records in the other format.

The *classification format* enables the recording of detailed information about classification numbers and their captions or descriptive text. Three types of records are included in this format: schedule records, in which the classification number recorded in field 153 is taken directly from the published classification scheme; table records, which include a single number or span of numbers from a published table, also recorded in field 153; and index term records, used to record explanatory terms pertinent to more than one classification number in a given scheme, entered in field 154. Schedule records may include classification numbers that have been built from instructions in the classification scheme, as well as those separately enumerated. The numbers recorded in table records, by contrast, are generally not to be used alone, but are to be added to base numbers.

There are multiple potential uses for classification records, including "online systems for library classifiers (e.g., for machine-assisted classification), systems for the maintenance and development of classification schedules, validation of classification numbers assigned to bibliographic records, and linking to MARC authority records."[7] Although the format is intended to be hospitable to any classification scheme, it was designed with particular attention to *Library of Congress Classification* and *Dewey Decimal Classification*, the two main systems in use in the United States.

The *community information format* was developed early in the 1990s and has not been widely implemented. The intention was to provide a means of recording information about community resources in a manner that could be tightly integrated with library resource metadata. For example, a user searching the library catalog for resources on the subject of family violence would also be able to find information about community agencies, government programs, individual speakers, and the like. However, this initiative was undermined by a development that few could have foreseen at that time: the explosion of the World Wide Web as a popular technology with the first releases of graphical browsers such as Mosaic.

There are five types of community information records. Records for individuals provide metadata about specific people who possess specific types of expertise and experience of value to a community. The second type is organization records, which are distinguished from the third type, records for programs or services offered by either individuals or organizations. Event records may be used for either individual or regularly offered events. The final category is designated as *other*, for resources that may not clearly belong to the other types.

Components of the MARC 21 Bibliographic Record

As already stated, the MARC 21 bibliographic format is used to encode metadata in records that act as surrogates for information resources in library catalogs. A bibliographic record contains both descriptive cataloging and subject cataloging data. It contains a large amount of detailed information about one or more particular resources. The metadata contained within the record reflects various levels of the FRBR Group 1 entities (works, expressions, manifestations, and items), as well as access points representing Group 2 entities (persons, families, and corporate bodies) and Group 3 entities (concepts, objects, places, and events). In other words, in a single record, a user finds information about a particular manifestation, but may also encounter details about (1) the specific item (e.g., a note about a signed copy), (2) the work contained within the resource, (3) the particular expression of that work (e.g., the language of a translation), (4) creator information, (5) the names and roles of various contributors, and (6) the subjects of the work. (See chapter 3 for a more in-depth discussion of FRBR.)

A MARC bibliographic record is a collection of fields. A field contains a unit of information within a record. A field may consist of one or more subfields. Tags (i.e., three-digit numerical codes) identify each field. Every field ends with a field terminator (in OCLC, for example, the field terminator may appear as a backward paragraph sign, appear as a left angle bracket, or be invisible). Each subfield is preceded by a delimiter sign or symbol (e.g., $ or | or ‡) followed by a single character code, which is usually alphabetical but can also be numerical (e.g., |2, $a, ‡v).

All MARC 21 records have the same four components:

1. A leader
2. A record directory

3. Control fields, including one referred to as the *fixed field*
4. Variable data fields

Leader

The leader identifies the beginning of a new record and provides coded information for record processing. The leader is fixed in length and contains 24 characters. The leader contains, among others, character positions for record length, type of record (e.g., language-based material, cartographic material, notated music), and bibliographic level/mode of issuance (e.g., monograph, serial, integrating resource). Many of the elements in the leader are system-generated data.

Record directory

The record directory contains a series of fixed length entries (12 characters long) that identify the tag, length, and starting position of each field in the record. Each entry in the directory is system-generated.

Control fields

Control field tags always begin with two zeros (00X). Control fields carry alphanumeric (often encoded) data elements. Most control fields are fixed in length, that is, each fixed-length field must consist of a set number of characters (see also *fixed field* below). The codes used in the control fields can be found at the Library of Congress's MARC standards website[8] or in OCLC's *Bibliographic Formats and Standards*.[9]

001   **Control number**: a control number assigned by an organization responsible for creating, using, or distributing the record.

001   45764

003   **Control number identifier**: a code that identifies the agency whose control number is recorded in field 001.

003   DLC

005   **Date and time of latest transaction**: 16 character positions representing the last date (i.e., yyyymmdd) and time (i.e., hhmmss.f) the record was edited. The timestamp is based on a 24-hour clock and includes fractions of a second at the end. This field is system-generated.

005   20150812103940.4

006   **Additional material characteristics**: positionally defined data elements about special aspects of the resource being cataloged that cannot be coded in field 008. This control field is used for characteristics of resources that are complex or feature aspects of multiple resource types, where these additional characteristics are considered important to code. For example, if a set of maps were published as a serial, 007 for maps would be used to record map characteristics, and 006 for serial characteristics. Input standards and values are the same as for field 008.

006   m   e   c

007 **Physical description fixed field**: positionally defined data elements about the physical characteristics of a resource, usually derived from explicit information in other fields of the record, but expressed here in coded form (i.e., separate character descriptions for map, electronic resource, globe, tactile material, projected graphic, microform, nonprojected graphic, motion picture, kit, notated music, remote-sensing image, sound recording, text, videorecording, and one for "unspecified").

007	vz czazuu	[LC formatting]
007	v $b z $d c $e z $f a $g z $h u $i u	[OCLC formatting]

008 **Fixed-length data elements**: 40 positionally defined data elements that provide coded information about the record as a whole or about special bibliographic aspects of the resource being cataloged. See the discussion immediately following for examples and more detail.

008   080822s2009   ctua   b   001 0 eng

Fixed field

There is one fixed length control field that is commonly referred to as "*the fixed field*." Field 008 carries general information about the content of the bibliographic record. This field is sometimes displayed in a single paragraph at the top of the screen and is often displayed with mnemonic tags. In other displays, it may appear as a single 40-character long text string with intermittent blanks. The data characters stored in this field are used to manipulate records for retrieval, indexing, limiting, and so on. A fixed field from a record for a book as it is displayed in OCLC is shown in Figure 21.1.

In the past, fill characters (displayed as ■ or _ or |) were sometimes used to indicate elements of the fixed field that were not in use when the record was created, or were not provided by the inputting library. This practice, although still noted in LC and OCLC documentation, does not provide meaningful metadata for current record creation. A blank space (sometimes written as a ƀ or a letter b with a forward slash through it), by contrast, is meaningful. That is, a blank is input to represent a coded value or to indicate that the element is not relevant to this resource. Some of the more common fixed field characteristics, particularly those for text, are listed in Table 21.1.

Type	a	**ELvl**		**Srce**		**Audn**		**Ctrl**		**Lang**	eng
BLvl	m	**Form**		**Conf**	0	**Biog**		**MRec**		**Ctry**	ctu
		Cont	b	**GPub**		**LitF**	0	**Indx**	1		
Desc	i	**Ills**	ab	**Fest**	0	**DtSt**	s	**Dates**	2009,		

FIGURE 21.1 OCLC Version of a Fixed Field. (Based on the OCLC format)

TABLE 21.1 Common Fixed Field Characteristics.

Characteristic	OCLC Label	Character Position	Explanation and Examples
Type of Record	Type	Leader/06	Not actually in the fixed field, but it appears with the fixed field in OCLC displays. Indicates the material type of the resource described in the record (e.g., a=language-based material).
Bibliographic Level	BLvl	Leader/07	Also, not in the fixed field. Indicates the mode of issuance of the resource (see ICC11 chapter 5; m=monograph, s=serial).
Descriptive Cataloging Form	Desc	Leader/18	Also, not in the fixed field. Indicates if the description conforms to the provisions of ISBD or other cataloging norms (e.g., a=AACR2, i=ISBD). The value i is used for RDA cataloging and the value RDA is recorded in 040 $e to specify which set of rules.
Encoding Level	ELvl	Leader/17	Also, not in the fixed field. Indicates the record's degree of completeness (e.g., a blank space indicates a full-level record prepared by LC or another national cataloging agency).
Form of Item	Form	008/29; 006/12	Indicates the form of material that is described in the record. The values generally represent variations on a standard print resource (e.g., a=microfilm, f=braille, o=online resource).
Nature of Contents	Cont	008/24-27; 006/07-10	Indicates a significant part of the item contains certain types of content or material (e.g., b=resource contains a bibliography or bibliographies).
Illustrations	Ills	008/18-21; 006/01-04	Indicates up to four kinds of illustrative content in the resource (e.g., a=general illustrations, b=maps).

(continued)

TABLE 21.1 (*continued*)

Characteristic	OCLC Label	Character Position	Explanation and Examples
Cataloging Source	Srce	008/39	Indicates the original cataloging source (e.g., a blank indicates that LC or another national cataloging agency initially created the record).
Conference Publication	Conf	008/29; 006/12	Indicates whether the resource is a conference proceedings, report, or summary (*0*=no, *1*=yes).
Government Publication	GPub	008/28; 006/11	Indicates whether the resource is a government publication and from which level of government it comes (e.g., a blank indicates it is not a government publication).
Festschrift	Fest	008/30; 006/13	Indicates if the resource is a *festschrift*, a resource published in honor of a person, an institution or a society on the occasion of an anniversary celebration (*0*=no, *1*=yes).
Audience	Audn	008/22; 006/05	Indicate the audience for the resource (e.g., a blank indicates that no audience type is specified. This is common for resources intended for general-adult audiences or readers).
Biography	Biog	008/34; 006/17	Indicates whether or not an item contains biographical material and at what level (e.g., a blank indicates it is not biographical).
Literary Form	LitF	008/33; 006/16	Indicates literary form of the work (e.g., *0*=non-fiction, *1*=fiction, letters indicate specific literary forms).
Type of Date/ Publication Status	DtSt	008/06	Indicates the type of date (e.g., *s*=single date, *k*=range of dates, *q*=questionable date, *t*=both a publication and a copyright date).

Type of Control	Ctrl	Leader/08	Also, not in the fixed field. Indicates a resource is described using archival descriptive principles and standards (e.g., *a* indicates it is, a blank says it is not).
Modified Record	MRec	008/38	Indicates if the metadata was modified for machine-readable encoding (e.g., a blank indicates it was not).
Index	Indx	008/31 006/14	Indicates if there is an index in the resource (*0*=no, *1*=yes).
Dates	Dates	008/07–14	Provides dates associated with the resource. Allows for two four-digit dates (e.g., 2009, along with s in DtSt, indicates this is a single publication date).
Language Code	Lang	008/35-37	Code that indicates the language of the content (e.g., eng indicates the resource is in English). The *MARC Code List for Languages* is used.
Country of Publication	Ctry	008/15-17	Code that indicates the country in which the resource was published. In the USA, UK, and Canada, the first two letters are the state, constituent country, or province (e.g., *ctu*=Connecticut—United States).

This table demonstrates that the values encoded in any fixed field position do not necessarily have mnemonic meanings. Even experienced catalogers cannot rely on their memories for all coded values; fortunately, online documentation is near at hand.

Variable data fields

Variable data fields carry alphanumeric data of variable length. The variable fields carry traditional cataloging data elements. Three-digit numeric tags identify variable fields (e.g., "490" identifies a series statement). In order to talk about these tags in groups, a convention is followed in which all fields beginning with *1* are identified as 1XX fields, those beginning with *2* as 2XX fields, and so on. Variable fields consist of (1) number and code fields, (2) fields for access points, and (3) descriptive fields. Variable fields may be repeatable, depending on the nature of the metadata designated. For example, although there may be only one 245 field (i.e., title statement) in a record, by contrast there may be, and frequently are, many 500 (general note) fields. With the implementation of RDA, fields were added to MARC 21 to enable RDA's more granular recording of information. Examples of the most common variable fields are given in the following lists (for the full lists see the MARC 21 documentation provided by LC or OCLC).

Numbers and Codes (01X-04X)

The number and code fields contain a variety of types of information. Some of the more common fields include the 010 field, which contains unique control numbers assigned to MARC records by LC, and the 016 field, which is similar but for control numbers assigned by other national libraries or agencies. ISBNs and ISSNs are recorded in the 020 and 022 fields respectively. It should be noted that the formatting of the numbers is different from the way in which they are presented in RDA (e.g., hyphens removed from ISBNs). The cataloging source (040) provides information about which cataloging agencies are responsible for the record. The 043, the geographic area code, provides a coded indication of the geographic subject matter.

> 010 — Library of Congress Control Number (LCCN)
>
> 015 — National Bibliography Number
>
> 016 — National Bibliographic Agency Control Number
>
> 020 — International Standard Book Number (ISBN)
>
> 022 — International Standard Serial Number (ISSN)
>
> 024 — Other standard identifier
>
> 030 — CODEN designation
>
> 033 — Date/Time and place of an event

040 — Cataloging source

041 — Language code

043 — Geographic area code

044 — Country of publishing/Producing entity code

045 — Time period of content

046 — Special coded dates

047 — Form of musical composition code

048 — Number of musical instruments or voices codes

Examples:

010   2013031454
016   20109071093

020   9781451665413 (hardcover : alk. paper)
022   0163-9374

040   DLC $b eng $e rda $c DLC $d IG# $d BTCTA

041 0_ cat $a fre $b eng $b fre
[Text in Catalan and French; summaries in English and French]

043   e-fr---   [Europe-France]
043   n-us-pa   [North American-United States-Pennsylvania]
043   mm-----   [Mediterranean Region; Mediterranean Sea]

Classification Notations and/or Call Numbers (05X-09X)

The classification fields include both full call numbers, including shelf marks, as well as partial call numbers including only classification notations proper. These fields are used by both national-level and local cataloging agencies. Though not delineated in LC's MARC documentation, fields 090 and 092 are frequently used. They are defined in OCLC's *Bibliographic Formats and Standards* as "Locally Assigned LC-type Call Number" and "Locally Assigned Dewey Call Number," respectively.[10]

050 — Library of Congress (LC) call number

070 — National Agricultural Library (NAL) call number

060 — National Library of Medicine (NLM) call number

080 — Universal Decimal Classification number

082 — Dewey Decimal Classification (DDC) number

084 — Other classification number

086 — Government Document Classification number

09X — Local call numbers

Examples:

050 00 TR679 $b .H45 2014

070 0_ 343 $b B236

060 10 W 84 AA1 $b F343 2007

082 00 778.9974692 $2 23

092 0_ 200.86642 $b T973b $2 22

090   BX8495 $b .R86 M4 2001

Main Entry Fields (1XX)

The concept of *main entry*, a central feature of cataloging codes through AACR2, is not present in RDA. This block of MARC fields could more appropriately be thought of as the area in which to record an authorized access point (AAP) for the single creator responsible for the resource being cataloged. Or it may be used to record the AAP for the first-named creator of a resource when there are multiple creators involved. Authorized access points for *other* creators and contributors are recorded in added entry fields (the 7XX fields, see below). It may seem somewhat strange to have a title listed in a block of tags referring to creators (i.e., the 130 field), but it is included here because title was sometimes chosen as main entry in AACR2. The formerly named *uniform title*, which is now referred to as the *preferred title for the work*, may be used for an anonymous work, a serial title, or a series title.

100 — Main entry—Personal name

110 — Main entry—Corporate name

111 — Main entry—Meeting name

130 — Main entry—Uniform title

Examples:

100 1_ De La Grange, Célestin.

100 1_ Charcot, J. M. $q (Jean Martin), $d 1825-1893.

100 1_ hooks, bell, $d 1952-

100 0_ Björk, $e composer, $e performer, $e producer.

100 3_ Clemente family.

110 2_ Sigur Rós (Musical group)

110 2_ 3M Leisure Time Products (Firm)

110 1_ United States. $b Army. $b Massachusetts
        Infantry Regiment, 15th (1861-1864)

110 2_ Association for Library Collections & Technical
        Services. $b Subject Analysis Committee.

111 2_ Aqua Art Miami.

111 2_ All India Numismatic Conference & Coin Fair
$d (2007 : $c Dinesh Mody Numismatic Museum)

111 2_ Philippine Historical Association Annual
Conference $d (2011 : $c Manila, Philippines)

111 2_ Expo (International Exhibitions Bureau) $d
(2010 : $c Shanghai, China)

130 0_ Beowulf.

130 0_ Beowulf. $l English $s (Swanton). $f 1997.

130 0_ Cataloging & classification quarterly.

130 0_ Eastern European economics.

Title and Title-Related Fields (20X-24X)

This block of fields is used primarily for recording title statements described in RDA 2.3. The concept of *uniform title*, designated by field 240, is derived from AACR2 and does not exist in RDA. In its place is *preferred title for the work*, described in RDA 6.2, with additional elements drawn from other sections of RDA chapter 6. The 240 and the 130 fields are used for different purposes. A 130 field contains a work title if a primary creator has not been identified for that work; a 240 field is used for the work title when a primary or first-named creator has been recorded in a 1XX field.

210 — Abbreviated title

222 — Key title

240 — Uniform title

242 — Translation of title by cataloging agency

243 — Collective uniform title

245 — Title statement

246 — Varying form of title

247 — Former title

Examples:

240 10 Hamlet

240 10 Hamlet. $l German

240 10 Story of British V.A.D. work in the Great War

240 10 Short stories. $k Selections

245 10 From starship captains to galactic rebels : $b leaders
in science fiction television / $c Kimberly Yost.

245 10 Novela/nivola / $c Miguel de Unamuno ;
translated, with an introduction, by Anthony
Kerrigan ; and with a foreword by Jean Cassou ;
annotated by Martin Nozick and Anthony Kerrigan.

245 10 Arrow. $n The complete first season.

245 13 Le seigneur des anneaux. $n Tome 2, $p Les deux tours / $c J.R.R. Tolkien ; [traduit de l'anglais par F. Ledoux].

245 10 East Africa : $b international road map = Ostafrika : internationale strassenkarte = Afrique orientale : carte routiere internationale / $c Ravenstein.

246 3_ Love and money

[*and* replaces ampersand in title proper]

246 1_ $i Corrected title: $a Linking conservation, tourism and sustainable development in the Caribbean

246 1_ $i At head of title: $a Little, Brown presents

246 30 Experiences of the United States Government Accountability Office

[subtitle made searchable]

Edition, Imprint, etc., Fields (25X-28X)

Included in this block of fields are the 260 and the 264 fields. The 260 was used with AACR2, but under RDA the 264 field has replaced it. The 260 field often contained information pertaining to publication, distribution, printing, and so on, all in the same field. The 264 resolves this cluttered situation by using the second indicator (see discussion of indicators below) to show whether the place, name, and dates are related to production (0), publication (1), distribution (2), manufacture (3), or copyright date (4).

250 — Edition statement

254 — Musical presentation statement

255 — Cartographic mathematical data

260 — Publication, distribution, etc. (Imprint: place, publisher, etc., date)

263 — Projected publication date

264 — Production, publication, distribution, manufacture, and copyright notice [added for RDA]

Examples:

250 First edition.

250 9an edizioa.

250 Third edition / $b edited by R.W. Burchfield.

250 Canadian ed. = $b Ed. canadienne.

250 Twenty-fifth anniversary edition, fully revised and updated.

254   Score and parts.

255   Scale approximately 1:450,000.

260   Cambridge, Mass. : $b CERA, $c c2002.

260   Cambridge [England] ; $a New York : $b Cambridge University Press, $c 2005.

260   [Lund] : $b Lund University ; $a Stockholm : $b distributed by Almqvist & Wiksell International, $c [2002]

264 _1 New York : $b Random House, $c 2014.

264 _1 New York : $b Random House, $c [2012]

264 _1 New York ; $a London : $b MacLehose Press, $c 2014.

264 _2 New York, NY : $b distributed in the United States and Canada by Random House Publisher Services

264 _4 $c ©2012

264 _1 Chicago : $b Chandler & Curtiss, $c [1874]

264 _3 Chicago : $b Lakeside Publishing & Printing Co. ; $b the electrotype music plates manufactured by R. R. Meredith & Sons

264 _4 $c ©1874.

264 _0 [Seattle, Wash.] : $b [Britta Johnson], $c 1998.

Physical Description, etc., Fields (3XX)

This area of the MARC format is used primarily for carrier elements, as specified in RDA chapter 3, although some, such as Planar coordinate data and Key, are found in RDA chapters 6 and 7.

300 — Physical description (extent of resource, other details, size, accompanying material)

306 — Playing time

310 — Current publication frequency

321 — Former publication frequency

336 — Content type [added for RDA]

337 — Media type [added for RDA]

338 — Carrier type [added for RDA]

342 — Geospatial reference data

343 — Planar coordinate data

344 — Sound characteristics

345 — Projection characteristics of moving image

346 — Video characteristics

347 — Digital file characteristics

362 — Dates of publication and/or sequential designation

380 — Form of work

381 — Other distinguishing characteristics of work or expression

382 — Medium of performance

383 — Numeric designation of musical work

384 — Key

Examples:

A book

300   xi, 116 pages : $b illustrations ; $c 22 cm

336   text $2 rdacontent

337   unmediated $2 rdamedia

338   volume $2 rdacarrier

A book with accompanying material

300   xi, 290 pages, 8 unnumbered pages of plates : $b illustrations (some color) ; $c 26 cm + $e 1 sound disc (24 min. : analog, 33 1/3 rpm, mono ; 12 in.)

336   text $2 rdacontent

337   unmediated $2 rdamedia

338   volume $2 rdacarrier

336   spoken word $2 rdacontent

337   audio $2 rdamedia

338   audio disc $2 rdacarrier

A DVD

300   1 video disc (6 min., 5 sec.) : $b sound, color ; $c 4 3/4 in.

336   two-dimensional moving image $b tdi $2 rdacontent

337   video $b v $2 rdamedia

337   computer $b c $2 rdamedia

338   videodisc $b vd $2 rdacarrier

347   video file $b DVD video $e region 1 $2 rda

A compact disc set

300   2 audio discs (1 hr., 45 min.) : $b digital, stereo ; $c 4 3/4 in.

306   014500

336	performed music $b prm $2 rdacontent
337	audio $b s $2 rdamedia
338	audio disc $b sd $2 rdacarrier
344	$3 Disc 1: $a digital $b optical $g stereo $2 rda
344	$3 Disc 2: $a digital $b optical $g stereo $g surround $h Dolby Digital 5.1 $2 rda
347	audio file $b CD audio $2 rda

Music score

300	1 score (4 unnumbered pages, 6 pages) ; $c 28 × 43 cm
306	000500
336	notated music $2 rdacontent
337	unmediated $2 rdamedia
338	volume $2 rdacarrier
382 01	piano $n 2 $v 4 hands $v performers also vocalize $s 2 $2 lcmpt

Series Statement Field (490)

The now obsolete 440 field was formerly used both to transcribe a series statement from the resource and to serve as an access point when the established form of the series title was identical with its appearance on the resource. At present, access points related to series are provided only in the 800-830 fields. Field 490 is used for transcription of series statements only, even when the form given on the resource is identical with the established form that is also given in an 800, 810, 811, or 830 field.

490 — Series statement

Examples:

490 0_ Essentia series

490 1_ Library and information science text series

490 1_ Lecture notes in mathematics. C.I.M.E. Foundation Subseries, $x 0075-8434 ; $v 2108

490 1_ Law, Governance and Technology series, $x 2352-1902 ; $v volume 15

490 1_ Perverse modernities / a series edited by Judith Halberstam and Lisa Lowe

Note Fields (5XX)

Note fields are used to record a variety of types of information about the resource not recorded elsewhere in the bibliographic record. Those most frequently appearing are given here. AACR2 prescribes an order in which notes relevant to a resource should appear in a typical record. This prescribed order is different from that given in a numerically ordered list of MARC tags. This sometimes causes confusion, but it must be remembered that MARC tags have no arithmetic value. A Summary note (520) is not in any sense greater than a Type of computer file note (516), just as a Personal name main entry (100) is not somehow lesser than a Geographic name subject heading (651). It is now typical for online systems to display notes in the order desired, regardless of the tag number. RDA does not give a prescribed order of notes. In any event, students, catalogers, and systems librarians should not expend any energy on what is essentially a non-issue.

500 — General note

502 — Dissertation note

504 — Bibliography, etc., note

505 — Formatted contents note

506 — Restrictions on access note

508 — Creation/production credits note

511 — Participant or performer note

516 — Type of computer file or data note

520 — Summary, etc., note

521 — Target audience note

530 — Additional physical form available note

533 — Reproduction note

534 — Original version note

538 — System details note

546 — Language note

547 — Former title complexity note

561 — Ownership and custodial history

580 — Linking entry complexity note

588 — Source of description

59X — Local notes

Examples:

500   Title supplied by cataloger.

504   Includes bibliographical references (pages 338-382) and index.

520   Presents the habits of fish, and includes information on keeping both freshwater and saltwater fish. Includes breeding and how to keep fish healthy.

505 0_ Tropical fish -- Fantastic fish -- What are they? -- Fishy habits -- Freshwater fish -- Whiskered fish -- Unusual fish -- Fighting fish -- Equipment -- A new home -- Feeding time -- Saltwater tank . . . .

588	Description based on print version record.
588	Title from home page (viewed Mar. 21, 2014).
502	$b Ph. D. $c University of Pittsburgh $d 2005.
546	$b Staff notation.
500	Reproduced from composer's manuscript.
500	Includes instructions for performance preceding score.
500	Microform reproduction of county maps of Ireland covering cities, towns and villages (not rural areas).

Subject Access Fields (6XX)

This block of fields is provided for the entry of both controlled-vocabulary and free-text (uncontrolled) subject terms. Terms such as genre/form or curriculum objective, or terms that express other facets of a work's content or nature, may be entered in the 6XX block as well. LC maintains an extensive list of subject heading and term source codes for use with the 600-651, 654, and 662 fields.[11]

600 — Subject added entry—Personal name

610 — Subject added entry—Corporate name

611 — Subject added entry—Meeting name

630 — Subject added entry—Uniform title

648 — Subject added entry—Chronological term

650 — Subject added entry—Topical term

651 — Subject added entry—Geographic name

653 — Index term—Uncontrolled

654 — Subject added entry—Faceted topical terms

655 — Index term—Genre/form

656 — Index term—Occupation

657 — Index term—Function

658 — Index term—Curriculum objective

662 — Subject added entry—Hierarchical place name

69X— Local subject access fields

Examples:

650 _0 Boating with dogs.

650 _0 Pear industry $z Oregon $z Hood River Valley $x Employees $v Case studies.

650 _0 Private presses $z England $x History $y 20th century.

650 _0 Space warfare $v Drama.

650 _1 Weights and measures $v Fiction.

650 _7 Metadata. $2 fast $0 (OCoLC)fst01017519

650 _7 Guerra $v Teatro. $2 bidex

651 _0 United States $x Civilization $x Hispanic
influences.

600 10 Sangiacomo, Angelo, $d 1930- $v Interviews.

610 20 Pear Tree Press.

611 20 San Diego Comic-Con $n (42nd : $c 2011)

630 00 Bible. $p Gospels $x Hermeneutics.

655 _7 Style manuals. $2 lcgft

655 _7 Thrillers (Fiction) $2 lcgft

655 _7 Satires (Literature) $2 lcgft

655 _7 Celestial charts. $2 lcgft

655 _7 Zombie television programs. $2 lcgft

Added Entry Fields (70x-75x)

The phrase *added entries* is not used in RDA. This block of fields includes
authorized access points for second or later-named creators, contributors,
and other entities associated with a resource, as well as any such authorized
access points in cases where the MARC record does not include a field from
the 1XX block. The 740 field is frequently used to record the title of a work
included in the resource being cataloged, for which a preferred title is not
provided by the cataloger.

700 — Added entry—Personal name

710 — Added entry—Corporate name

711 — Added entry—Meeting name

730 — Added entry—Uniform title

740 — Added entry—Uncontrolled related/analytical title

Examples:

700 1_ Lozano, Eduardo.

700 1_ Kimmel, Margaret Mary, $e joint author.

700 1_ Cloonan, Michèle Valerie, $d 1955- $e editor of
compilation.

700 1_ Sobule, Jill, $e singer.

700 1_ Mitchell, John Cameron, $e librettist.

710 2_ Simmons College (Boston, Mass.) $b Graduate School of
Library and Information Science.

710 1_ United States. $b Congress. $b House. $b Committee on
Ways and Means, $e compiler, $e issuing body.

710 2_ AAA (Organization : U.S.)

711 2_ North Carolina State Fair.

730 0_ Walking dead (Television program)

730 0_ $i Based on (work): $a Lord of the rings, the fellowship of the ring (Motion picture)

740 41 The sea gull.

740 01 Uncle Vanya.

740 41 The three sisters.

Linking Entry Fields (76X-78X)

These fields are used to identify different, sometimes complex, relationships between bibliographic resources. Fields 780 and 785 are frequently used in serials records to indicate serials that have changed their names or that have resulted from mergers or splits of previous titles.

760 — Main series entry

762 — Subseries entry

765 — Original language entry

767 — Translation entry

770 — Supplement/special issue entry

772 — Supplement parent entry

775 — Other edition entry

776 — Additional physical form entry

777 — Issued with entry

780 — Preceding entry

785 — Succeeding entry

787 — Other relationship entry

Examples:

780 00 $t Journal of documentary reproduction $x 0097-4250 $w (DLC) 39025582 $w (OCoLC)1696618

785 10 American Society for Information Science. $t Journal of the American Society for Information Science $x 0002-8231 $w (DLC) 75640174 $w (OCoLC)1798118

776 08 $i Online version: $t American documentation $w (OCoLC)564624778

776 08 $i Print version: $a United States. Congress. House. Committee on the Judiciary. $t Stop Online Piracy Act $w (OCoLC)841795713

772 08 $i Supplement to (work): $t Texas Wesleyan law review $x 1081-5449 $w (DLC) 2007219415 $w (OCoLC)31505688

Series Added Entry Fields (80X-840)

Although most series statements are established as uniform titles in field 830, some series are associated with individual authors (less often with corporate authors or meetings). For example, the series statement for a book in the *Diary of a Wimpy Kid* series is given in an 800 field as Kinney, Jeff. $t Diary of a wimpy kid (see the following discussion of subfield coding).

> 800 — Series added entry—Personal name
> 810 — Series added entry—Corporate name
> 811 — Series added entry—Meeting name
> 830 — Series added entry—Uniform title

Examples:

830 _0 Library and information science text series.

830 _0 Lecture notes in mathematics (Springer-Verlag). $p CIME Foundation Subseries, $x 0075-8434 ; $v 2108.

830 _0 Law, Governance and Technology Series, $x 2352-1902 ; $v v. 15.

830 _0 Perverse modernities.

800 1_ Austen, Jane, $d 1775-1817. $t Novels (1923)

810 2_ American Theological Library Association. $t ATLA religion indexes.

811 2_ International Congress of Nutrition $n (11th : $d 1978 : $c Rio de Janeiro, Brazil). $t Nutrition and food science ; $v v. 3.

Holdings, Location, Alternate Graphics, etc., Fields (841-88X)

The majority of the fields included in this block are shared with the MARC 21 holdings format. Of those originating as MARC 21 bibliographic fields, 856 and 880 are frequently used. The 856 field provides the address of an electronic resource, typically a URL. The 880 field provides a full representation of another field in the same record, but in a different script.

> 850 — Holding institution
> 852 — Location
> 856 — Electronic location and access
> 880 — Alternate graphic representation

Examples:

850   AAP $a CU $a DLC $a MiU

856 42 $u http://www.pbs.org/wgbh/pages/frontline/ shows/assault/ $z Companion website

856 41 $3 Table of contents only $u http://catdir.loc.gov/
catdir/toc/ecip0826/ 2008037446.html.

100 1_ $6 880-01 $a Suzuki, Akira, $d 1969-
880 1_ $6 100-01/$1 $a 鈴木彰, $d 1969-

Subfields

All subfields are distinct elements within fields. They generally contain one individual element of the description, although some subfields may contain two or more descriptive metadata elements (e.g., 300 $b). It is important to keep in mind that subfield definitions vary from field to field. Subfields are designated by the use of *delimiters* in combination with lowercase letters or numerals. Depending on the system used, delimiters are often input as dollar signs (**$**), as the pipe character (**|**), or the double dagger (**‡**). The dollar sign is used in this text. In the cataloging modules of local systems, it is common for there to be no space between the delimiter and the metadata encoded in the subfield. This may give rise to some confusion at first. For example, in AACR2, illustrations in 300 $b is abbreviated as *ill.* This may appear, disconcertingly, as *$bill.* A little experience in reading subfield codes separately from their contents will remove this difficulty. The meaning of seemingly identical designations, such as $a, is dependent entirely on the contexts of the fields themselves, as may be seen from these common examples:

050 LC call number

$a classification number

$b item number and date

082 Dewey Decimal Classification number

$a classification number

$b item number

$2 edition number [edition of DDC used]

X00 Personal name

[*X00 means that these subfields apply in fields 100, 600, 700, and 800.*]

$a personal name

$q fuller form of name (e.g., Lewis, C. S. $q (Clive Staples))

$b numeration

$c titles (e.g., Mrs., Sir, Bishop)

$d dates

$e relator (e.g., author or composer)

X10 Corporate name

$a corporate or jurisdiction name

$b subordinate unit

$e relator

$k form subheading

X11 Meeting name

$a meeting name

$c location of meeting

$d date of meeting

$n number of part/section/meeting

245 Title and statement of responsibility

$a title proper

$b remainder of title

$c statement of responsibility, etc.

264 Production, publication, distribution, manufacture, and copyright notice

$a place of production, publication, etc.

$b name of producer, publisher, etc.

$c date of production, publication, etc.

300 Physical description

$a extent of item

$b other physical details

$c dimensions

$e accompanying material

6XX Subject access fields

$a main subject (name, topic, etc.)

$x general (topical subject) subdivision

$y chronological subdivision

$z geographic subdivision

$v form subdivision

787 Other relationship entry

$a main entry heading

$d place, publisher, and date of publication

$i relationship information

$x ISSN

$z ISBN

8XX Series

$a personal, corporate, meeting or jurisdiction name as entry element; title

$t title of a work

$x ISSN

$v volume/sequential designation (numbering of series)

856 Electronic location and access

 $a host name

 $b access number

 $d path

 $h processor of request

 $u uniform resource identifier

The inclusion of Field 787 $i in the preceding examples is one indication of the expansion of MARC 21 to accommodate RDA. Specific instances of fields added in the bibliographic format were given earlier, and others will follow in the authorities format discussion below. Although the Linking Entry Fields (76X-78X), including their subfields, existed prior to RDA, the relationship metadata they are designed to include will likely be given greater emphasis from now on. It is widely understood that despite additions to the format, the MARC record is not optimal for fully integrating library-generated metadata in the linked data/Semantic Web environment. This is discussed more fully in chapter 22. Still, these additions are intended to help enable this transition by allowing for clearer coding of semantically more specific metadata elements.

Indicators

The two digits that follow the tags in a MARC field are called *indicators*. Each digit position has a certain meaning in the context of its particular field, allowing for correct processing of the metadata contained in the field. For example, in the OCLC-formatted 245 field shown here, the first indicator, *1*, tells the system that there should be an access point for the title, and the second indicator, *4*, tells the system that four non-filing characters (i.e., *T, h, e*, and a space) precede the first significant word of the title:

245 14 The dictionary of misinformation / $c Tom Burnam.

As with subfield designations, the meaning of a given numeral in an indicator position can only be understood in the context of the field itself. By contrast with the 245 field, in field 856 (Electronic Location and Access), the numeral *1* in the first position indicates that a remote resource is available via FTP. In subject access fields 600-651 and 655, the numeral *4* in the second position indicates that the subject term is drawn from an unspecified subject heading list or thesaurus.

Duplicate Information Entry in MARC 21

Students and working catalogers—experienced professionals as well as beginners—are often concerned by what appear to be requirements to enter the same information in two or three areas in a MARC 21 bibliographic record. Although this requirement is, to some extent, subject to local policy and practice, the basic concern is reasonable. This section provides a look at three examples of supposed duplication.

1. **Language of the resource.** There are three typical places in a bibliographic record where metadata for language of the resource may be recorded.

   - **008 character positions 35-37 (OCLC fixed field element *Lang*).** This is used to record a single three-character code, from the MARC code list for languages, for the language of the resource. Codes are also available for resources in sign language, undetermined languages, or with no linguistic content. Only a single language can be recorded here, which does not allow for full representation of multilingual resources. This requires a decision about what the predominant language is, which in some instances may be arbitrary. This element also cannot indicate the original language of a translation.

   - **041 Language Code.** This field may be used for highly granular metadata, including resources in multiple languages, the original and/or intermediate languages for translations, languages for subtitles or captions of moving-image materials, and even individual elements such as summaries and tables of contents. Originally, multiple MARC language codes were entered as a single string in one subfield, but beginning in 2001, the field was revised to allow for use of more specifically designated subfields. This changing pattern of use, unfortunately, has made it difficult for systems to parse and index the varied forms of this field as intended. Nevertheless, it allows for the potential of machine-intelligible sharing of language information at a great level of detail.

   - **546 Language Note.** This is a human-readable, free-text field, in comparison with fields 008/35-37 and 041.

2. **Illustrative matter.** Metadata about illustrations is generally recorded in two places.

   - **008 character positions 18-21 for Books (*Ills*).** Single-character codes are used here to record typical types of illustrative matter, including general illustrations as well as maps, portraits, charts, etc. Codes are also available for less common types, such as coats of arms and illuminations. This metadata may also be recorded in Control Field 006, positions 01-04.

   - **300 $b Other physical details.** This is a human-readable field. Its content is typically determined by the cataloging code in use. The metadata provided here may not exactly replicate that provided in 008/18-21.

3. **Place of Production, Publication, Distribution, and Manufacture.** The general concept of the place of a publishing or analogous entity is multifaceted in application.

   - **008 character positions 15-17 (*Ctry*).** Two- or three-character codes are used here. The potential complexity of place is indicated by LC: "For sound recordings, the code represents the place where the recording company is located. For still images that are original or historical graphics, if geographic information can be deduced (as with some photographs), a place code is recorded in this character position. For archival moving images, the code represents the country of producing entity from field 257. For mass-produced videorecordings, the code represents the place of publication in field 260 (Publication, Distribution, etc. (Imprint) [also 264]) . . . . For visual materials and music, if the work is a multi-country production, the code for the first country is recorded in 008/15-17. The code for the first country is repeated in field 044 (Country of Producer Code), followed by the codes for countries of other bodies involved in the production. For serials and integrating resources, the country code reflects the place of publication of the latest issue, part or iteration. If the record is updated at a later time and the place has changed, the place of publication code is updated. For mixed materials, the code represents the repository where the material is assembled."[12]

- **044 Country of Publishing/Producing Entity Code.** Similar to the relationship between the *Lang* fixed field position, and field 041, field 044 may be used for the publishing or similar entity when more than one place needs to be recorded.

- **260 $a Place of Publication, Distribution, etc.**

- **264 $a Place of Production, Publication, Distribution, Manufacture, and Copyright Notice.** As already noted, field 264 was added with the implementation of RDA. The use of either field is generally determined by the cataloging rules in use, as well as local policies. In both fields $a is repeatable to indicate multiple places of publication if desired. As with field 300 $b, the content of this subfield is determined by the cataloging rules.

From these three examples, it can be seen that what might be regarded as the same information, entered in theoretically duplicate or even triplicate form, serves different, non-overlapping functions. The most evident difference is between machine- and human-readable types of metadata. Although it is theoretically possible for computer software to parse and interpret free-text phrases, experiments toward this end have proved inconclusive. By contrast, it is too much to expect all but the most expert (and committed!) of human users to accurately interpret two- or three-digit codes, even if displayed to the public.

A more subtle, but pervasive, problem arises in the language and places examples. The 008 field positions are hospitable only to a single language or place, whereas fields 041 and 044 are designed to accommodate multiple values. Field 008 will suffice for those resources—plausibly still in the majority—where only one language or place is involved. However, the pervasiveness of multinational publishing and production, particularly with motion pictures, has rendered coding of a single place of publication inadequate or even misleading in many instances. The increasing sense of global interconnection, as well as the need for more accurate description of moving-image materials, necessitates a highly granular approach to recording languages.

The foregoing is not meant to imply that it is desirable to continue to record similar if not identical information in more than one place in a bibliographic record. Generations of catalog technology, simultaneously represented in a MARC 21 record, can be inferred from these different elements. Human-readable notes are obviously essential for printed cards and related text-based formats. A single language or location code is appropriate for rudimentary auto-mated systems, capable only of applying simple limits to search results. The detailed metadata recordable in the 04X fields is more suited to systems that exploit multiple values and that translate codes into human-readable display text. These latter fields suggest most clearly the transition into the detailed granularity required by linked data. They may come to remove the need to create separate human-readable text at all, and make obsolete the separate encoding of primary place or language.

At present, catalogers are for the most part not working directly in the linked data environment. It is still frequently important to record metadata for both direct human consumption and machine processing, even when this seems to mean duplicate effort. A full record showing the recording of some duplicate information is in Figure 21.2.

Components of MARC 21 Authority Records

MARC authority records have the same basic structure as bibliographic records: a leader and record directory, followed by control fields and vari-able data fields.[13] The leader and directory are similar in form and function to those in the bibliographic format. Only four control fields are defined. The 001 Control Number, 003 Control Number Identifier, and 005 Time and Date of Latest Transaction fields function in the same way as they do in bibliographic format. The 008 field is similar to the bibliographic 008 in its general function, but the definitions of many of the character positions are different, as it is used to record values pertinent to the authority record itself (e.g., Romanization scheme, cataloging source) and the authorized access point being established (e.g., cataloging rules used, subject head-ing list/thesaurus used, type of heading for which the entry is appropri-ate). An example of a 008 fixed field for a personal name authority record is shown in Figure 21.3. The fill character (■) is used to indicate that no value is given.

Not all catalogers create authority data. Those who create national-level authority records need to be much more conversant with the fixed-field posi-tions and their values for authority records than those catalogers who do not create authority data. It is useful, however, for all catalogers to understand what these positions mean. Common fixed field characteristics are listed in Table 21.2.

As with the bibliographic format, fields in the authority format were added with the implementation of RDA. Some of these are indicated in the lists of commonly used fields that follow.

```
OCLC  701031400    No holdings in SCL - 2 other holdings
Sound Recordings  Rec Stat c  Entered 20110131  Replaced 20140731192612.8
Type i      ELvl        Srce c    Audn        Ctrl        Lang eng
BLvl m      Form        Comp nn   AccM dghrs  MRec        Ctry dcu
            Part n      TrAr n
Desc i      FMus n      LTxt i    DtSt t      Dates 2011,2006
```

007		s $b d $d f $e u $f n $g g $h n $i n $j z $k m $l n $m e $n e
007		c $b o $d c $e g $g --- $h a $i u $j u $k m
040		BTCTA $b eng $e rda $c BTCTA $d CGU $d OCLCQ $d OCLCA $d OCLCF $d SCL
024	7_	00093070835429 $2 gtin-14
024	1_	093070835429
028	02	FI 8354 $b Smithsonian Folkways Recordings
041	0_	eng $d eng $e eng $g eng
042		pcc
055	_3	MT588 $b .S45 1955
082	04	787.8716213 $b S451f $2 23
049		SCL
100	1_	Seeger, Pete, $d 1919-2014, $e performer, $e teacher.
245	14	The folksinger's guitar guide : $b an instruction record / $c by Pete Seeger.
260		Washington, DC : $b Smithsonian Folkways Recordings, $c [2011?], Ⓟ2006.
300		1 audio disc : $b digital, CD audio ; $c 4 3/4 in.
336		spoken word $b spw $2 rdacontent
336		performed music $b prm $2 rdacontent
337		audio $b s $2 rdamedia
338		audio disc $b sd $2 rdacarrier
490	1_	Smithsonian Folkways archival
500		Instructional recording.
546		Taught and sung in English.
500		Container title.
511	0_	Pete Seeger, guitar, voice.
500		"This CD is a custom-made copy from our collection."--CD sleeve.
500		Previously issued in 1955 by Folkways Records.
500		Enhanced compact disc.
500		"The original liner notes are included as a PDF file on the disc."--CD sleeve.
538		System requirements: Adobe Acrobat Reader.
500		Liner notes include transcription of the instruction, song texts, and music (22 pages : illustrations, music).
505	0_	Tuning up (2:49) -- The first chord (1:59) -- Two more chords (2:02) -- Use of the capo (2:16) -- Methods of strumming (2:30) -- Bass runs (3:03) -- Bass countermelody (0:53) -- The "church lick" ; "Hammering on" (2:21) -- The blues (3:38) -- Two finger plucking (2:14) -- Other tunings (3:49) -- A hint of flamenco (1:54) -- A rhumba rhythm (1:47) -- The Mexican blues (2:18).
650	_0	Guitar $v Methods $v Self-instruction.
650	_0	Folk music $x Instruction and study.
650	_7	Folk music $x Instruction and study. $2 fast $0 (OCoLC)fst00929396
650	_7	Guitar. $2 fast $0 (OCoLC)fst00949140
655	_7	Methods $v Self-instruction. $2 fast $0 (OCoLC)fst01423708
830	_0	Smithsonian Folkways archival.

**FIGURE 21.2 MARC Record as Displayed in OCLC Connexion.
(Source: OCLC Connexion, WorldCat—record number 701031400)**

Type	z	Upd status	a	Enc lvl	n	Source	
Roman	■	Ref status	a	Mod rec		Name use	a
Govt agn	■	Auth status	a	Subj	a	Subj use	a
Series	n	Auth/ref	a	Geo subd	n	Ser use	b
Ser num	n	Name	a	Subdiv tp	n	Rules	z

**FIGURE 21.3 OCLC Version of a Fixed Field for an Authority Record.
(Based on the OCLC format)**

TABLE 21.2 Common Fixed Field Characteristics for Authority Records.

Characteristic	OCLC Label	Character Position	Explanation and Examples
Type of Record	Type	Leader/06	Not actually in the fixed field, but it appears with the fixed field in OCLC displays. Indicates the material type of the resource described in record. The value should be z to indicate authority data.
Romanization Scheme	Roman	008/07	Indicates the Romanization scheme used to transliterate the authorized access point (AAP) in the 1XX field. The fill character (■) indicates there was no attempt to code the information.
Type of Government Agency	Govt agn	008/28	Indicates the jurisdiction, *if* the AAP in the 1XX field is a government body. A blank indicates it is not a government body, f=federal, s=state or province, and so on.
Type of Series Code	Series	008/12	Indicates the type of series, *if* the AAP in the 1XX field is a series title (e.g., n=not applicable, a=monographic series, b=multipart item, etc.)
Numbered / Unnumbered Series Code	Ser Num	008/13	Indicates whether a series is numbered, unnumbered, or both. The values are as follows: a=numbered, b=unnumbered, c=numbering varies, n=not applicable, and the fill character indicates no attempt to code.
Record Update in Process	Upd Status	008/31	Indicates a change in any of the fields in the record. The values are a=record can be used, b=record is being updated, and the fill character indicates no attempt to code.
Reference Evaluation Code	Ref Status	008/29	Indicates whether the references (i.e., variant access points or VAPs) have been evaluated. In other words, the AAP/heading may have been updated to be compliant with the cataloging instructions, but the question is if the VAPs have been as well. The values are as follows: a=references are consistent with 1XX, b=references are not necessarily consistent with 1XX, n=not applicable, and the fill character indicates no attempt to code.

Level of Establishment	Auth Status	008/33	Indicates the status of the AAP/heading in the 1XX field. The values include *a*=fully established AAP/heading in 1XX, *c*=provisional 1XX, *n*=not applicable, among other values.
Kind of Record Code	Auth/ Ref	008/09	Indicates the type of entity found in the IXX field of the authority record. The values include *a*=record for established AAP/heading, *b*=untraced reference record, *c*=traced reference record, *d*=subdivision record, and *f*=established heading and subdivision.
Undifferentiated Personal Name Code	Name	008/32	Indicates whether the AAP is for a unique entity or if it is shared by more than one entity. The values are as follows: *a*=differentiated personal name, *b*=undifferentiated, *n*=not applicable, and the fill character indicates no attempt to code.
Encoding Level	Enc lvl	Leader/17	Not in the fixed field. Indicates the record's degree of completeness (*n*=complete, *o*=incomplete).
Modified Record Code	Mod Rec	008/38	Indicates if there are differences between the encoded and analog versions of an authority record. A blank space indicates it has not been modified; an *s* indicates a shortened record.
Subject Heading System	Subj	008/11	Indicates the subject heading system used (e.g., *a*=LCSH, *c*=MeSH, *s*=Sears).
Geographic Subdivision Code	Geo Subd	008/06	Indicates if the heading in the 1XX field can be subdivided geographically. The values are *i*=geographic subdivision allowed indirectly, blank=not allowed, *n*=not applicable, and the fill character indicates no attempt to code. The value *d* for directly subdivided geographically is not used in new authority records.

(continued)

TABLE 21.2 (*continued*)

Characteristic	OCLC Label	Character Position	Explanation and Examples
Type of Subdivision	Subd tp	008/17	Indicates the type of subdivision found in the 1XX field. The values are: *a*=topical, *b*=form, *c*=chronological, *d*=geographic, *e*=language, *n*=not applicable, and the fill character indicates no attempt to code.
Cataloging Source	Source	008/39	Indicates the original cataloging source of the authority data (e.g., blank space indicates that LC or another national cataloging agency initially created the record; *c* indicates it was a member of a cooperative cataloging program, such as the PCC).
AAP/Heading use—Main or Added Entry	Name Use	008/14	Indicates if the AAP/heading in the 1XX field may be used as a creator or a contributor in a bibliographic record. The values are *a*=appropriate, *b*=not appropriate, and the fill character indicates no attempt to code.
AAP/Heading use—Subject	Subj Use	008/15	Indicates if the AAP/heading in the 1XX field may be used as a subject in a bibliographic record. The values are *a*=appropriate, *b*=not appropriate, and the fill character indicates no attempt to code.
AAP/Heading use—Series	Ser Use	008/16	Indicates if the AAP/heading in the 1XX field may be used as a series in a bibliographic record. The values are *a*=appropriate, *b*=not appropriate, and the fill character indicates no attempt to code.
Descriptive Cataloging Rules Code	Rules	008/10	Indicates the cataloging code used to establish the name, title, name/title AAP in the 1XX field (e.g., *c*=AARCR2, *z*=other). The value z is used for RDA and the value *RDA* should be recorded in 040 $e to specify which set of rules.

Numbers and Codes (01X-09X)

This block of fields is closely similar, although not identical, to the parallel bibliographic format block. The metadata recorded, however, pertains not to bibliographic resources, but to the types of entities described in authority records. As examples, the 043 field is used for geographic areas associated with the entity, rather than the subject of a resource, and the 050 field is used for the classification of volumes in series instead of an individual resource.

010 — Library of Congress Control Number

016 — National Bibliographic Agency Control Number

040 — Cataloging source

043 — Geographic area code

046 — Special coded dates [added for RDA]

050 — Library of Congress Call Number

053 — Library of Congress (LC) Classification number

072 — Subject category code

073 — Subdivision usage

083 — Dewey Decimal Classification number

Examples:

010   no2006073134

010   n 79021164 $z sh 89001267 $z no 98029431

040   WaU $b eng $e rda $c WaU $d DLC

040   DLC $b eng $e rda $c DLC $d DLC $d MdU $d DLC

046    $s 1989 $t 2001

046    $f 18351130 $g 19100421

053 0_ PS1300 $b PS1348

072 _7 H 1145.5 $2 lcsh

073   H 1147 $a H 1164 $a H 1180 $z lcsh

Heading Fields (1XX)

As with the numbers and codes block, several of the fields here (particularly the 100-130 fields) appear similar to the analogous fields in the bibliographic format. The two should not be confused, however. These fields are used to record the established forms of AAPs for names, preferred titles, and subject/genre or other index terms, including subdivision terms. For the most part, the entities recorded in these fields will receive different MARC tags when used in bibliographic records. Topical terms recorded in the 150-155 fields will be tagged 650-655, for example, and subdivisions recorded in 180-185 will be given subfield coding. Entities recorded in 100-130 authority fields may also be so tagged in bibliographic records, but only if designated as main entries (to repeat the older terminology).

100 — Heading—Personal name

110 — Heading—Corporate name

111 — Heading—Meeting name

130 — Heading—Uniform title

148 — Heading—Chronological term

150 — Heading—Topical term

151 — Heading—Geographic name

155 — Heading—Genre/Form term

162 — Heading—Medium of performance term

180 — Heading—General subdivision

181 — Heading—Geographic subdivision

182 — Heading—Chronological subdivision

185 — Heading—Form subdivision

Examples:

100 1_ Kozelek, Mark

100 1_ King, Stephen, $d 1947-

100 3_ Agrant (Family : $d 1894-1976 : $c S.D.)

100 0_ Author of Rose Graham

100 1_ Shakespeare, William, $d 1564-1616. $t Coriolanus

110 2_ Red House Painters (Musical group)

110 2_ Royal Academy of Medicine in Ireland. $b Section of Bioengineering

111 2_ ACSA Annual Meeting & Technology Conference

130 _0 Committee on Lesbian and Gay History bibliographies

130 _0 Wire (Television program)

130 _0 Qur'an. $l English

150   Orchids

150   Generation X

151   Bluestone Lake (W. Va.)

155   Television public service announcements

180      $x Psychological testing

180      $x History $y 17th century

185      $v Indexes

Heading Information Fields (3XX)

This set of fields, introduced with RDA, allows for the recording of a wide variety of types of information associated with the entities named in the 100-130 fields, at a deeper level of granularity than was previously possible.

368 — Other attributes of person or corporate body

370 — Associated place

371 — Address

372 — Field of activity

373 — Associate group

374 — Occupation

375 — Gender

376 — Family information

377 — Associated language

378 — Fuller form of personal name

380 — Form of work

381 — Other distinguishing characteristics of work or expression

382 — Medium of performance

383 — Numeric designation of musical work

384 — Key

385 — Audience characteristics

386 — Creator/Contributor characteristics

Examples:

100 1_ King, Stephen, $d 1947-

370 Portland (Me.) $c United States $2 naf

372 Horror tales $2 lcsh

374 Novelists $2 lcsh

375 male

377 eng

378 $q Stephen Edwin

110 2_ Red House Painters (Musical group)

370 $e San Francisco (Calif.) $2 naf

372 Alternative rock music $a Folk-rock music $a Popular music $2 lcsh

100 1_ Griffin, Patty, $d 1964-

370 Old Town, Me.

374 Singers $2 lcsh

374 Songwriter

375 female

100 1_   Roberts, Janine, $d 1942-

370   England $c Australia $c Great Britain

371   $u http://www.sparks-of-light.org/Jan-CV-updated.html

372   Transgender people $2 lcsh $s 1975

372   Writing

371   Activism

373   Catholic Church

373   London School of Economics

374   Priest $s 1967 $t 1970

374   Writer

374   Activist

375   male $s 1942 $t 1975

375   female $s 1975

377   eng

110 2_   Leeds Initiative (Organization)

368   Organization

370   $e Leeds, England

371   Civic Hall $b Leeds $d United Kingdom $e LS1 1UR

372   Regional planning $2 lcsh

Complex Subject Reference Fields (260 and 360)

These two fields allow recording of information about forms of subject headings that differ from those established in the 150-155 fields, where the relationship cannot be easily recorded in the 4XX or 5XX fields.

150   Judaic . . .

260   $i subject headings beginning with or qualified by the word $a Jewish, $i e.g. $a Jewish art and symbolism; Short stories, Jewish

150   Social networks

360   $i subdivision $a Social networks $i under classes of people and ethnic groups

See From Tracing Fields (4XX)

In these fields, unauthorized heading forms and other variants of those in the 1XX fields are recorded. Online systems typically generate *see* references based on the variant access points entered in these fields. The term *tracing* is not current. As LC explains, "Tracing fields lead directly from one heading to a single other heading."[14] We can thus understand the use of this term in the sense of following a trail or trace.

400 — See from tracing—Personal name
410 — See from tracing—Corporate name
411 — See from tracing—Meeting name
430 — See from tracing—Uniform title
450 — See from tracing—Topical term
451 — See from tracing—Geographic name
455 — See from tracing—Genre/Form term
480 — See from tracing—General subdivision
485 — See from tracing—Form subdivision

Examples:
100 1_ King, J. B. S. $q (John Blair Smith), $d 1855-
400 1_ King, J. B. S. $q (John Blair Smith), $d b. 1855 $w nnea
400 1_ King, John Blair Smith, $d 1855-

100 1_ Twain, Mark, $d 1835-1910
400 1_ Tven, M. $q (Mark), $d 1835-1910
400 1_ 馬克吐温, $d 1835-1910

100 3_ Agrant (Family : $d 1894-1976 : $c S.D.)
400 3_ Agarant (Family : $d 1894-1976 : $c S.D.)

100 0_ Author of Rose Graham
400 0_ Rose Graham, Author of

110 2_ Archives of the Lithuanian KGB
410 2_ KGB Archive in Lithuania

111 2_ ACSA Annual Meeting & Technology Conference
410 2_ Association of Collegiate Schools of Architecture. $b Annual Meeting & Technology Conference

130 _0 Committee on Lesbian and Gay History bibliographies
410 2_ Committee on Lesbian and Gay History. $t Committee on Lesbian and Gay History bibliographies

130 _0 Qur'an. $l English
430 _0 Koran. $l English

150	Generation X
450	Gen X
450	X-ers
450	Baby bust generation
155	Horror fiction
455	Scary fiction
455	Terror fiction
180	$x Psychological testing
480	$x Psychology $x Testing
185	$v Indexes
485	$v Dictionaries, indexes, etc.
485	$v Bibliography $v Indexes

See Also From Tracing Fields (5XX)

Different authorized forms of headings, related to those in the 1XX fields, are recorded here. These are typically either Broader Terms or Related Terms for subject or genre/form headings or subdivisions (550-585) or related authorized access points for names and titles (500-530).

500 — See also from tracing—Personal name
510 — See also from tracing—Corporate name
511 — See also from tracing—Meeting name
530 — See also from tracing—Uniform title
550 — See also from tracing—Topical term
551 — See also from tracing—Geographic name
555 — See also from tracing—Genre/Form term
580 — See also from tracing—General subdivision
585 — See also from tracing—Form subdivision

Examples:

100 1_ Bachman, Richard

500 1_ $i Real identity: $a King, Stephen, $d 1947- $w r

100 1_ Twain, Mark, $d 1835-1910

500 1_ Clemens, Samuel Langhorne, $d 1835-1910
$w nnnc

500 1_ Snodgrass, Quintus Curtius, $d 1835-1910
$w nnnc

500 1_ Conte, Louis de, $d 1835-1910 $w nnnc

130 _0 Beowulf. $l English $s (Alexander). $f 2001

500 1_ $i Translator: $a Alexander, Michael, $d
        1941- $w r

110 2_ Exxon Mobil Corporation

510 2_ Exxon Corporation $w a

510 2_ Mobil Corporation $w a

111 2_ ACSA Annual Meeting & Technology Conference

510 2_ Association of Collegiate Schools of Architecture.
        $b Annual Meeting $w a

511 2_ ACSA Annual Meeting $w b

130 _0 Library and information science text series

530 _0 Library science text series $w a

150   Baby carriages

550   Carriages and carts $w g

550   Infants' supplies $w g

550   Baby strollers

Two subfields applicable to the 4XX and 5XX blocks should be pointed out. The first is **$i**, which contains relationship information. This subfield includes free-text phrases describing the specific relationship between the name or term in the 4XX or 5XX field with that in the 1XX field. Some examples of this subfield are:

110 2_ Royal Society of Medicine (Great Britain)

510 2_ $i Predecessor: $a Clinical Society of London $w r

110 2_ Civil Wars (Musical group)

500 1_ $i Group member: $a White, John Paul $w r

500 1_ $i Group member: $a Williams, Joy $c (Musician) $w r

100 3_ Berg (Family : $g Berg, Lars Mortensen,
        1829-1900)

500 1_ $i Progenitor: $a Berg, Lars Mortensen, $d
        1829-1900 $w r

The second subfield is **$w**, named the *control subfield*. This subfield includes four character positions (i.e., $w _ _ _ _, *but* with no spaces between the four positions) that make possible the coding of a variety of special instructions applicable to a specific name or term, as well as associated display texts. The first position codes a specific relationship that the 4XX or 5XX access point has with the authorized access point in the 1XX field. The values used in this position are:

a: Earlier heading
b: Later heading
d: Acronym
f: Musical composition
g: Broader term
h: Narrower term

i: Reference instruction phrase in subfield $i
n: Not applicable
r: Relationship designation in $i or $4
t: Immediate parent body

Examples:

110 2_ Exxon Mobil Corporation

510 2_ Exxon Corporation $w a

510 2_ Mobil Corporation $w a

150 1_ Siberian husky

550   Northern breed dogs $w g

550   Sled dogs $w g

The second position specifies the types of reference structures appropriate for cross-reference displays, if any, for the 1XX name or term involved. These may be name, subject, or series references, any two or all three of these, or none.

a: Name reference structure only
b: Subject reference structure only
c: Series reference structure only
d: Name and subject reference structures
e: Name and series reference structures

f: Subject and series reference structures
g: Name, subject, and series reference structures
h: No reference structures
n: Not applicable

The third position, applicable to 4XX variant access points that are earlier forms of the name or term, indicates the type of earlier form represented.

a: Pre-AACR 2 form of heading (national name authority file)
e: Earlier established form of heading (national authority file)
o: Earlier established form of heading (other authority file)
n: Not applicable

110 2_ University of Chicago

410 1_ Chicago. $b University $w nnaa

510 2_ $i Predecessor: $a University of Chicago (1857-1886) $w r

150 1_ Siberian husky

450   Siberian huskies $w nne

The fourth position includes codes for the suppression of cross-references in different cases.

a - Reference not displayed
b - Reference not displayed, field 664 used
c - Reference not displayed, field 663 used
d - Reference not displayed, field 665 used
n - Not applicable

Not every reference will have a subfield w. If it is there, however, not every position will be coded in every instance. In the University of Chicago example, the first two positions in the $w of the 410 field are coded *n* for not applicable, the third position is coded *a*, indicating that this field includes a form of the name that pre-dates AACR2, and the fourth position value of *a* indicates that this earlier form of name will not be displayed to the public.

Series Treatment Fields (64X)

These fields provide places to record different kinds of information about the treatment of series headings established in 1XX fields. As an example, field 641 is used for free-text descriptions of exceptions or anomalies in the numbering of individual resources issued as part of a series. By contrast, field 642 provides examples of the numbering patterns typically used. Field 644 is used to code analysis practice, that is, whether some, all, or none of the volumes in a series will be described in individual bibliographic records. Classification practice for volumes in a series is described in field 646, including the range(s) of volumes to which the practice applies. Subfield 5, found in the following examples, is used to indicate specific institutions to which these practices apply. These decisions are therefore not necessarily universal, although other institutions may also use them for local policy guidance. The codes entered in $5 come from the MARC Code List for Organizations: DPCC stands for the Program for Cooperative Cataloging, and AzTeS for Arizona State University.[15]

640 — Series dates of publication and/or Sequential designation

641 — Series numbering peculiarities

642 — Series numbering example

643 — Series place and publisher/Issuing body

644 — Series analysis practice—The values are: *f*=in full, *p*=in part, and *n*=analyzed.

645 — Series tracing practice—The values are: *t*=traced and *n*=not traced.

646 — Series classification practice—The values are: *s*=classify separately, *c*=classify together, and *m*=classify with main series.

Example:

130 _0 Bulletin of the Association for Childhood
Education International

410 2_ Association for Childhood Education International.
$t Bulletin of the Association for
Childhood Education International

430 _0 Bulletin (Association for Childhood Education
International)

530 _0 Bulletin of the Association for Childhood
Education $w a

642 no. 64 $5 DPCC $5 AzTeS

643 Washington, D.C. $b Association for Childhood
Education International

644 f $5 AzTeS

645 t $5 DPCC $5 AzTeS

646 s $5 AzTeS

Complex Name Reference Fields (633-666)

Similar to the 260 and 360 fields, these allow recording of information about
forms of name headings differing from those established in the 100-111 fields,
where the relationship cannot be easily recorded in the 4XX or 5XX fields.

663 — Complex see also reference—Name

664 — Complex see reference—Name

665 — History reference

666 — General explanatory reference

Examples:

100 1_ Snodgrass, Quintus Curtius, $d 1835-1910

663 Works by this author are entered under the name
used in the item. For a listing of other names used
by this author, search also under $b Twain, Mark,
1835-1910

110 2_ Exxon Corporation

665 The Standard Oil Company of New Jersey was
incorporated in 1882. In 1892 its name was
changed to Standard Oil Company. In 1972
the name Exxon Corporation was adopted. $a
Works by this body published before the change
of name in 1972 are found under $a Standard
Oil Company. $a Works published after that
change of name are found under $a Exxon
Corporation . . . .

Notes (667-68X)

This group addresses a mixture of needs, including general notes for the public (680) and notes for internal use only (667). Many of these notes are used to document sources that were consulted when conducting research to establish the heading. Field 681 Subject Example Tracing Note is frequently found in subject authority records. It is used to document the use of established subject terms, or authorized subdivisions, as examples in other authority records. Some of the note fields include the following:

667 — Nonpublic general note

670 — Source data found

672 — Title related to the entity

673 — Title not related to the entity

675 — Source data not found

678 — Biographical or historical data

680 — Public general note

681 — Subject example tracing note

Examples:

110 2_ Red House Painters (Musical group)

500 1_ $i Group member: $a Kozelek, Mark $w r

670   Songs for a blue guitar, p1996: $b label
(Red House Painters)

670   All music guide, c1994 $b (Red House Painters;
alternative pop/rock; leader, Mark Kozelek; first
recording released 1992)

670   Wikipedia, July 15, 2014 $b (Red House Painters;
alternative rock group formed 1989 in San
Francisco, Calif. by Mark Kozelek; genres: alt.
rock, folk-rock, dream pop, sadcore, slowcore,
indie rock; years active: 1989-2001)

110 2_ Warner Bros. Records

410 2_ Warner Brothers Records

410 2_ WBR

510 2_ $i Hierarchical superior: $a Warner Music
Group $w r

670   Bell, R. Careers with a record company,
c1983: $b CIP t.p. (Warner Bros.
Records, Inc.)

670   Exploding, c2002: $b CIP galley (Warner Bros.
Records; WBR; inc. 1958)

675   Stand. & Poor's, 1982.

100 1_ Snodgrass, Quintus Curtius, $d 1835-1910

667   SUBJECT USAGE: This heading is not valid for use as a subject. Works about this person are entered under Twain, Mark, 1835-1910

110 2_ Warner Bros.

667   Cannot determine relationship between Warner Bros. Pictures and Warner Bros.

180   x Testing

680    $ Use as a topical subdivision under topical headings, including languages, for tests and testing of native aptitude or acquired proficiency in a particular topic.

681    $i Reference under the heading $a Ability—Testing

155   Apocalyptic fiction

455   Doomsday fiction

455   End-of-the-world fiction

455   Post-apocalyptic fiction

455   Post-disaster fiction

555   Science fiction

680   This heading is used as a genre/form heading for works of fiction set in a world or civilization after a catastrophic event (e.g., nuclear war, an alien invasion), sometimes also including the period immediately preceding the event. Works set in an uncertain future, in a society ruled by an ineffectual, corrupt, or oppressive regime or by aliens, robots, etc., are entered under Dystopian fiction.

681   Note under Dystopian fiction

110 2_ XTO Energy Inc.

678 1_ Cross Timber Oil Company was formed in 1986. Its name was changed in 2001 to XTO Energy Inc. In 2010 it was acquired by Exxon Mobil Corporation and is now a subsidiary of that company. The corporate headquarters is located at 810 Houston St., Fort Worth, Texas, 76102-6298.

Heading Linking Entries (700-788)

These fields allow machine linking between controlled headings that demonstrate varying types of equivalence. They may refer to the same entity, as do authorized access points in different forms established in different authority files. They may be conceptually equivalent, as are topical or genre/form terms established in separate subject heading systems or thesauri. Equivalence may also be established between topical or genre/form terms and words or phrases used for subdivisions. This block of fields includes, among others, the following:

700 — Established heading linking entry—Personal name

710 — Established heading linking entry—Corporate name

750 — Established heading linking entry—Topical term

751 — Established heading linking entry—Geographic name

755 — Established heading linking entry—Genre/Form term

780 — Subdivision linking entry—General subdivision

781 — Subdivision linking entry—Geographic subdivision

788 — Complex linking entry data

Examples:[16]

100 1_ Augustinus, Aurelius $d 354-430
[German National Library AAP]

700 17 Augustine $d 354-430 $0 (DLC)n 80126290 $2 naf
$9 v:Saint, Bishop of Hippo [link to LCNAF]

110 2_ Deutsche Bibliothek (Francfort-sur-le Main, Alle-
magne) [Library and Archives Canada, French AAP]

710 25 Deutsche Bibliothek (Frankfurt am Main, Germany)
$0 (CaOONL)0067K1275E [LAC, English AAP]

150 Cancer $x Nursing [LCSH]

750 _0 Neoplasms $x Nursing [Medical Subject Headings]

111 _2 American Civil War (1861-1865) [FAST heading]

751 _0 United States $x History $y Civil War, 1861-1865
$0 (DLC)sh 85140205 [link to LCSH]

150 History

780 _0 $w a $x History [topical term used also as
general subdivision]

151 Milton (Mass.)

781 _0 $z Massachusetts $z Milton

Other Variable Fields (8XX)

The most commonly used field in this group is 856 (Electronic location and access), used as it is in bibliographic records to encode Uniform Resource Locators (URLs) for resources related to the entity documented in the authority record.

Example:

110 2_ National First Ladies' Library

856 4_ $u http://www.firstladies.org/

An example of a brief MARC authority record is presented in Figure 21.4.

Rec stat	c	Entered	19860807	Replaced	20131206073943.0		
Type	z	Upd status	a	Enc lvl	n	Source	
Roman	l	Ref status	n	Mod rec		Name use	a
Govt agn	l	Auth status	a	Subj	a	Subj use	a
Series	n	Auth/ref	a	Geo subd	n	Ser use	b
Ser num	n	Name	a	Subdiv tp	n	Rules	z

010	n 86107504
040	DLC $b eng $e rda $c DLC $d NNU
046	$f 19600910
100 1	Bechdel, Alison, $d 1960-
370	Lock Haven (Pa.) $e Bolton (Vt.)
372	Satire $a Autobiography $2 lcsh
374	Cartoonists--United States $2 lcsh
375	female
377	eng
670	Her Dykes to watch out for, 1986: $b CIP t.p. (Alison Bechdel) CIP data sheet (b. 9/10/60)
670	Fun home, 2006: $b title page (Alison Bechdel)
670	Dykes to watch out for website, 5 December 2013 $b (Alison Bechdel) $u http://dykestowatchoutfor.com/#

FIGURE 21.4 MARC Authority Record as Displayed in OCLC Connexion. (Source: OCLC Connexion, Authorities—record number 1684045)

MARC INPUT CONVENTIONS AND PUNCTUATION

The use of punctuation in creating bibliographic or authority metadata is not a concern for MARC in and of itself. Still, some guidelines for standard practice are, perhaps anomalously, only easily available via MARC 21-related documentation. To clarify this point it will help to outline three different sources for punctuation conventions made use of in library cataloging with MARC 21 and RDA.

The first source is RDA appendix E: Record Syntaxes for Access Point Control. Appendix E focuses on punctuation needed when formulating access points, as discussed in this text in chapter 7. An example is the authorized access point for Mary, Queen of Scots:

100 0_ Mary, $c Queen of Scots, $d 1542-1587

The comma-spaces before $c and $d are specified in appendix E, as the preceding punctuation for Title of the Person (RDA 9.4) and Date Associated with the Person (RDA 9.3), respectively. Note that there is no concluding punctuation specified for the access point itself, although there may be in the context of a specific bibliographic field.

As RDA does not prescribe syntax, either that of fields constructed from multiple metadata elements, or between fields, it also does not cover the punctuation used to indicate syntactical relationships. Most catalogers working in the MARC 21 format make use of ISBD punctuation, particularly for relating sub-elements within a descriptive field (see chapter 23). In the following example, the space-colon-space preceding $b, and the comma-space preceding $c, are specified by ISBD for Area 4 sub-elements 4.2 (Name of publisher, producer, and/or distributor) and 4.3 (Date of publication, production, and/or distribution) respectively.

260   Buffalo, N.Y. : $b Prometheus Books, $c 1992.

In the next example, the space-colon-space preceding $b and the space-semicolon-space preceding $c are specified by ISBD Area 5 sub-elements 5.2 (Other physical details) and 5.3 (Dimensions) respectively. The comma-space between color illustrations and color maps is justified by RDA 1.7.3, which states that catalogers should add punctuation for clarity if needed.

**300   iv, 57 leaves : $b color illustrations, color
maps ; $c 28 cm**

However, even this level of detail, where punctuation within a single field seems to interweave two quite different standards, does not cover all necessary elements of punctuation. What specifies the full stop following 1992 in the 260 field example, or the lack of final punctuation in the 300 field example? Surprisingly, these are not covered by either RDA or ISBD. Current practice is documented through the *input conventions* for individual MARC 21 bibliographic and authority fields, described at LC's MARC site.[17] The full, as opposed to the concise, version of the documentation for each field provides this guidance, sometimes at the subfield level. Applying this to the preceding examples, the documentation for field 260, subfield $c, says "Subfield $c ends with a period (.), hyphen (-) for open-ended dates, a closing bracket (]) or closing parenthesis ()). If subfield $c is followed by some other subfield, the period is omitted."[18] For field 300, the overall instruction is "Field 300 may end in no punctuation, may end in a right parenthesis when the last element of the field is a parenthetical qualifier, or may end in a period when the last element is an abbreviation ('cm' and 'mm' are not treated as abbreviations) or a 490 field is present in the record."[19] As the 300 example ends with cm, there is no period. Input conventions for a personal name, such as Mary, Queen of Scots, are given in a blanket instruction, "X00 - Personal Names-General Information," applying to personal names used as either authorized access points in bibliographic field 100 or subject headings in field 600. In addition to the notes given at the LC MARC site, an alternative source is the Library of Congress-Program for Cooperative Cataloging Policy Statement (LC-PCC PS) for RDA 1.7.1: General Guidelines on Transcription.

Fortunately, with experience, the practiced cataloger does not pause to ask, "Do I justify this comma by RDA, ISBD, or the MARC input standards?" The use of specified punctuation becomes second nature. Unfamiliar cases are often resolved with reference to examples in authoritative sources. Still, it is important to realize that practice is based in established standards, and to know what to consult in case of doubt.

DISPLAY OF MARC BIBLIOGRAPHIC RECORDS

MARC records are distributed in the MARC communications format. Each record consists of a single long character string. This begins with the leader, followed by the record directory, then all fields in sequence with no breaks, to the end of the record, concluding with a character to represent a record terminator. Such a record is practically unreadable if printed as transmitted, and so each system has a program that displays the record in a form that is more easily read. However, displays of the same record can look quite different from each other. Figure 21.5 shows the record as an unprocessed MARC character string. Figures 21.6, 21.7, and 21.8 show the same MARC record (containing AACR2 formatted cataloging data) as it is displayed in different systems.

03264cam 22005534a 45000010013000000030006000130050017000190080041000
36010001700077040014700094020001800241020001500259020003900274020003600
03130290020003490290019003690290018003880290022004060290023004280290
02100451029002100472035002100493042000800514043001200522050002700534082
00180056108200100057908400150058904900090060410002800613245005500641260
004000069630000037007365201005007735052000177860000550197865000580
20336550020020916550027021117760107021388560109022458560094023549380
039024489380040024879380071025279380029025989380071026279940012026980
ocm62127870 -OCoLC-20140731134205.0-051018s2006 maua 6 000 0aeng -
a 2005030304- aDLCbengcDLCdBAKERdC#PdVP@dlXAdCOOdIG#dBTCTA-
dYDXCPdBURdOCLCGdSTFdSMPdCQUdTEXdUBYdIAKdYUSdNLGGC-
dOCLCQdWAUdORKdOCLCOdP4I- a9780618477944- a0618477942- -
a9780618871711 (Mariner Books pbk.)- a0618871713 (Mariner Books pbk.)-1 alG#-
b0618477942-1 aYDXCPb2381798-1 aNZ1b10529863-1 aAU@b000028625609-1 -
alG#b9780618477944-1 aUNITYb117518611-1 aNLGGCb33182860X- -
a(OCoLC)62127870 - apcc- an-us----00aPN6727.B3757bZ46 2006-00a741.5/973-
222-04aB222- a18.062bcl- aDD0A-1 aBechdel, Alison,d1960--10aFun home :ba
family tragicomic /cAlison Bechdel.- aBoston :bHoughton Mifflin,cc2006.- a232 p.
:bchiefly ill. ;c24 cm.- aThis book takes its place alongside the unnerving,
memorable, darkly funny family memoirs of Augusten Burroughs and Mary Karr. It's
a father-daughter tale perfectly suited to the graphic memoir form. Meet Alison's
father, a historic preservation expert and obsessive restorer of the family's Victorian
house, a third-generation funeral home director, a high school English teacher, an icily
distant parent, and a closeted homosexual who, as it turns out, is involved with male
students and a family babysitter. Through narrative that is alternately heartbreaking
and fiercely funny, we are drawn into a daughter's complex yearning for her father . . .
--From publisher description.-0 aOld father, old artificer -- A happy death -- That old
catastrophe -- In the shadow of young girls in flower -- The canary-colored caravan of
death -- The ideal husband -- The antihero's journey.-10aBechdel, Alison,
d1960-vComic books, strips, etc.- 0aCartoonistszUnited StatesvComic books, strips,
etc.- 0aGraphic novels.- 7aGraphic novels.2lcgft-08iOnline version:aBechdel, Alison,
1960-tFun home.- dBoston : Houghton Mifflin, c2006w(OCoLC)654847254-423
Contributor biographical informationuhttp://catdir.loc.gov/catdir/enhancements/fy0736/
2005030304-b.html-423Publisher descriptionuhttp://catdir.loc.gov/catdir/
enhancements/fy0623/2005030304-d.html- aBaker and TaylorbBTCP-n2005030304-
aYBP Library ServicesbYANKn2381798- aBaker & TaylorbBKTYc13.95d10.46-
i0618871713n0007023825sactive- aIngrambINGRn0618477942- -aBaker & Taylor-
bBKTYc19.95d14.96i0618477942n0006620050sactive- aC0bDD0-^\

FIGURE 21.5 MARC Communications Format.

Books		Rec Stat	c	Entered	20051018	Replaced	20140222051220.0			
Type	a	ELvl	4	Srce		Audn		Ctrl	Lang	eng
BLvl	m	Form		Conf	0	Biog	a	MRec	Ctry	mau
		Cont	6	GPub		LitF	0	Indx	0	
Desc	a	Ills	a	Fest	0	DtSt	s	Dates	2006,	

010		2005030304
040		DLC $b eng $c DLC $d BAKER $d C#P $d VP@ $d IXA $d COO $d IG#
020		9780618477944
020		0618477942
042		pcc
043		n-us---
050	00	PN6727.B3757 $b Z46 2006
082	00	741.5/973 $2 22
082	04	B $2 22
084		18.06 $2 bcl
049		DD0A
100	1_	Bechdel, Alison, $d 1960-
245	10	Fun home : $b a family tragicomic / $c Alison Bechdel.
260		Boston : $b Houghton Mifflin, $c c2006.
300		232 p. : $b chiefly ill. ; $c 24 cm.
520		This book takes its place alongside the unnerving, memorable, darkly funny family memoirs of Augusten Burroughs and Mary Karr. It's a father-daughter tale perfectly suited to the graphic memoir form. Meet Alison's father, a historic reservation expert and obsessive restorer of the family's Victorian house, a third-generation funeral home director, a high school English teacher, an icily distant arent, and a closeted homosexual who, as it turns out, is involved with male students and a family babysitter. Through narrative that is alternately heartbreaking and fiercely funny, we are drawn into a daughter's complex yearning for her father.... --From publisher description.
505	0_	Old father, old artificer -- A happy death -- That old catastrophe -- In the shadow of young girls in flower -- The canary-colored caravan of death -- The ideal husband -- The antihero's journey.
600	10	Bechdel, Alison, $d 1960- $v Comic books, strips, etc.
650	_0	Cartoonists $z United States $v Comic books, strips, etc.
655	0	Graphic novels.
655	_7	Graphic novels. $2 lcgft
776	08	$i Online version: $a Bechdel, Alison, 1960- $t Fun home. $d Boston : Houghton Mifflin, c2006 $w (OCoLC)654847254
856	42	$3 Contributor biographical information $u http://catdir.loc.gov/catdir/enhancements/fy0736/2005030304-b.html
856	42	$3 Publisher description $u http://catdir.loc.gov/catdir/enhancements/fy0623/2005030304-d.html

FIGURE 21.6 MARC Record as Displayed in OCLC Connexion. (Source: OCLC Connexion, WorldCat—record number 62127870)

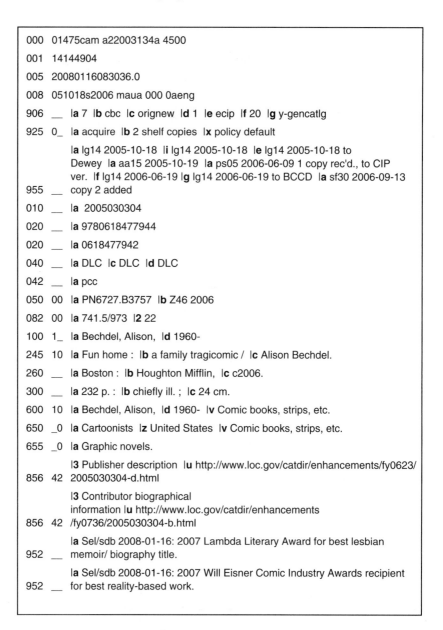

000   01475cam a22003134a 4500
001   14144904
005   20080116083036.0
008   051018s2006 maua 000 0aeng
906   __ |a 7 |b cbc |c orignew |d 1 |e ecip |f 20 |g y-gencatlg
925   0_ |a acquire |b 2 shelf copies |x policy default
955   __ |a lg14 2005-10-18 |i lg14 2005-10-18 |e lg14 2005-10-18 to Dewey |a aa15 2005-10-19 |a ps05 2006-06-09 1 copy rec'd., to CIP ver. |f lg14 2006-06-19 |g lg14 2006-06-19 to BCCD |a sf30 2006-09-13 copy 2 added
010   __ |a 2005030304
020   __ |a 9780618477944
020   __ |a 0618477942
040   __ |a DLC |c DLC |d DLC
042   __ |a pcc
050   00 |a PN6727.B3757 |b Z46 2006
082   00 |a 741.5/973 |2 22
100   1_ |a Bechdel, Alison, |d 1960-
245   10 |a Fun home : |b a family tragicomic / |c Alison Bechdel.
260   __ |a Boston : |b Houghton Mifflin, |c c2006.
300   __ |a 232 p. : |b chiefly ill. ; |c 24 cm.
600   10 |a Bechdel, Alison, |d 1960- |v Comic books, strips, etc.
650   _0 |a Cartoonists |z United States |v Comic books, strips, etc.
655   _0 |a Graphic novels.
856   42 |3 Publisher description |u http://www.loc.gov/catdir/enhancements/fy0623/2005030304-d.html
856   42 |3 Contributor biographical information |u http://www.loc.gov/catdir/enhancements/fy0736/2005030304-b.html
952   __ |a Sel/sdb 2008-01-16: 2007 Lambda Literary Award for best lesbian memoir/ biography title.
952   __ |a Sel/sdb 2008-01-16: 2007 Will Eisner Comic Industry Awards recipient for best reality-based work.

FIGURE 21.7 MARC Record as Displayed in the Library of Congress Online Catalog. (Based on the record display at: http://catalog.loc.gov/)

```
100:  1 : Bechdel, Alison,ld1960-

245: 10 : Fun home :lba family tragicomic /lcAlison Bechdel.

250:    : 1st Mariner Bks. ed.

260:    : Boston :lbHoughton Mifflin,lc2007, c2006.

300:    : 232 p. :lbchiefly ill. ;lc24 cm.

600: 10 : Bechdel, Alison,ld1960-lvComic books, strips, etc.

650:  0 : CartoonistslzUnited StateslvComic books, strips, etc.

650:  0 : Graphic novels.

520:    : This book takes its place alongside the unnerving, memorable,
          darkly funny family memoirs of Augusten Burroughs and Mary
          Karr. It's a father-daughter tale perfectly suited to the graphic
          memoir form. Meet Alison's father, a historic preservation expert
          and obsessive restorer of the family's Victorian house, a third-
          generation funeral home director, a high school English teacher,
          an icily distant parent, and a closeted homosexual who, as it turns
          out, is involved with male students and a family babysitter.
          Through narrative that is alternately heartbreaking and fiercely
          funny, we are drawn into a daughter's complex yearning for her
          father.... --From publisher description.

020:    : 0618871713 (pbk.)

020:    : 9780618871711 (pbk.)

001:    : 7312518
```

FIGURE 21.8 MARC Record as Displayed in the Catalog of the University of Toronto Libraries. (Based on the record display at: https://toroprod.library. utoronto.ca/)

NOTES

1. Deborah J. Byrne, "MARC Theory and Development," in Deborah J. Byrne, *MARC Manual: Understanding and Using MARC Records*, 2nd ed., (Englewood, Colo.: Libraries Unlimited, 1998), 1-15.
2. Library of Congress, Network Development and MARC Standards Office, *MARC 21 Format for Bibliographic Data*, accessed August 13, 2015, http://www .loc.gov/marc/bibliographic/ecbdhome.html.
3. MARC 21 XML Official Web Site, accessed May 11, 2014, http://www.loc.gov/ standards/marcxml/.
4. Library of Congress, Network Development and MARC Standards Office, "Introduction," *MARC 21 Format for Bibliographic Data*, accessed October 26, 2014, http://www.loc.gov/marc/bibliographic/bdintro.html.
5. Arlene G. Taylor and Daniel N. Joudrey, *The Organization of Information*, 3rd ed. (Westport, Conn.: Libraries Unlimited, 2009), 139.
6. Library of Congress, "Introduction: MARC 21 Holdings," accessed August 7, 2014, http://www.loc.gov/marc/holdings/hdintro.html.
7. Library of Congress, "Introduction: MARC 21 Classification," accessed August 7, 2014, http://www.loc.gov/marc/classification/cdintro.html.
8. LC, MARC 21.

9. OCLC, *Bibliographic Formats and Standards*, 4th ed. (Dublin, Ohio: OCLC, 2008), http://oclc.org/bibformats/en.html.

10. OCLC, *Bibliographic Formats and Standards*, accessed August 13, 2015, http://www.oclc.org/bibformats/en/0xx/090.html and http://www.oclc.org/bibformats/en/0xx/092.html.

11. Library of Congress, "Subject Heading and Term Source Codes," accessed August 6, 2014, http://www.loc.gov/standards/sourcelist/subject.html.

12. Library of Congress, "008—All Materials," accessed August 13, 2015, http://www.loc.gov/marc/bibliographic/bd008a.html.

13. Library of Congress, Network Development and MARC Standards Office, *MARC 21 Format for Authority Data*, accessed August 13, 2015, http://www.loc.gov/marc/authority/.

14. Library of Congress, "Tracings and References—General Information," accessed August 13, 2015, http://www.loc.gov/marc/authority/adtracing.html.

15. Library of Congress, Network Development and MARC Standards Office, *MARC Code List for Organizations*, accessed September 1, 2014, http://www.loc.gov/marc/organizations/orgshome.html.

16. Thanks to Paul Frank, Cooperative Programs Section, Library of Congress, for help with these examples.

17. Library of Congress, Network Development and MARC Standards Office, *MARC 21 Format for Bibliographic Data*, accessed August 13, 2015, http://www.loc.gov/marc/bibliographic/.

18. Library of Congress, "260 - Publication, Distribution, etc. (Imprint)," accessed August 7, 2014, http://www.loc.gov/marc/bibliographic/bd260.html.

19. Library of Congress, "300 - Physical Description," accessed August 7, 2014, http://www.loc.gov/marc/bibliographic/bd300.html.

SUGGESTED READING

Avram, Henriette D. *MARC, Its History and Implications.* Washington, D.C.: Library of Congress, 1975.

Beall, Julianne, and Joan S. Mitchell. "History of the Representation of the DDC in the MARC Classification Format," *Cataloging & Classification Quarterly* 48, no. 1 (2010): 48-63.

Ferguson, Bobby. *MARC/AACR2/Authority Control Tagging: Blitz Cataloging Workbook.* 2nd ed. Westport, Conn.: Libraries Unlimited, 2005.

Fritz, Deborah A., and Richard J. Fritz. *MARC21 for Everyone: A Practical Guide.* Chicago: American Library Association, 2003.

Furrie, Betty. *Understanding MARC Bibliographic: Machine-Readable Cataloging.* 8th ed. Washington, D.C.: Cataloging Distribution Service, Library of Congress, 2009. Also available online, accessed August 10, 2014, http://www.loc.gov/marc/umb.

"Implications of MARC Tag Usage on Library Metadata Practices." Dublin, Ohio: OCLC Research, 2010. Also available online, accessed August 10, 2014, http://www.oclc.org/content/dam/research/publications/library/2010/2010-06.pdf.

Mukhopadhyay, Asoknath. *Guide to MARC 21: For Cataloging of Books and Serials.* Oxford, England: Chandos Publishing, 2007.

Chapter 22

Alternative Containers for Metadata

INTRODUCTION

MAchine-Readable Cataloging (MARC) is still, at present, the predominant international family of formats that is used in libraries and other information institutions for encoding bibliographic and authority metadata. There are, nevertheless, alternative containers in use and under development. This chapter discusses three approaches that may be used to contain RDA metadata elements, authorized access points, subject headings, classification numbers, and other forms of cataloging data:

- **Dublin Core (DC)**: A descriptive metadata scheme that has been adopted by libraries and other institutions concerned with making their data widely available. Although DC is primarily a tool for describing resources, it may be communicated in a variety of formats; its development has been influenced by various non-MARC approaches to encoding.

- **Metadata Object Description Standard (MODS)**: A metadata scheme that provides a middle ground between MARC and DC; it is not as detailed as the MARC format, but it is not as simplistic as basic DC.

- **Bibliographic Framework Initiative (BIBFRAME)**: As of this writing, a new approach to recording metadata that is under development. It is intended to move library-generated metadata from the record-bound MARC structure to independent, yet authoritative, metadata statements that are part of the linked data that makes up the Semantic Web.

DUBLIN CORE

The complex of metadata projects and specifications comprising the Dublin Core Metadata Initiative (DCMI) originated in a series of workshops during the 1990s, beginning with the first one held in 1995 at OCLC headquarters in Dublin, Ohio. The objective of this first meeting was "to define a set of descriptive elements simple enough for non-catalogers, including authors themselves, to describe Web resources."[1] There was concern, given the explosion in the number of materials available on the still relatively new World Wide Web, that traditional approaches to information organization could not be successful. In addition, the effort was undertaken in the belief that non-librarian creators of web resources could effectively supply accurate metadata if a simple schema was made available. A set of 13 elements was developed in 1995, known as the *Dublin Core* (named after the host city of the first meeting). It was intended to be general enough that any type of resource, created in any sector or knowledge domain, could be described with enough metadata to allow for resource discovery. Within a few years, the element set expanded to 15 with the inclusion of the *Rights* and *Description* elements. This element set, now known as the *Dublin Core Metadata Element Set* (DCMES), may be all that many librarians associate with the phrase, though the DCMI's work has developed far beyond the core elements.

Dublin Core Basics

The 15 core elements of the DCMES are currently in version 1.1.[2] Each of the elements is optional, and each is repeatable. These elements are also given on the DCMI website as "Properties in the /elements/1.1/ namespace."[3] Each element has a minimum of five attributes: *Term Name, Label, Uniform Resource Identifiers* (URIs), *Definition*, and *Type of Term*. Although the attributes *Term Name* and *Label* serve different functions, in the case of the 15 core elements, they contain identical values; their only difference is in capitalization (e.g., *contributor* versus *Contributor*). A *URI* is a string of characters that identifies a resource on the web. The *Type of Term* for each of the core elements is *Property*. In the Dublin Core Abstract Model (DCAM), the process of describing a resource entails the creation of one or more *property-value* pairs.[4] A *property* is a descriptive element, such as a creator, a title, or a date; the *value* is the metadata supplied for that property to describe the resource. Both the property and its value must be clearly identified in order for the resource to be understood (by either person or machine). A partial example of a resource being described using property-value pairs is shown here:

> **identifier**: https://en.wikipedia.org/wiki/Main_Page
>
> **title**: Wikipedia: The Free Encyclopedia
>
> **language**: English

In the first pair, *identifier* is the property and "https://en.wikipedia.org/wiki/Main_Page" is the value; in the second pair *title* is the property and the value is "Wikipedia: The Free Encyclopedia"; and so on. For more information on the DCAM, see the Dublin Core website.[5]

The list of the 15 core elements, also known in the Dublin Core documentation as *terms* or *properties*, is found in the following bullets. Definitions and comments are taken or adapted from the DCMES Version 1.1 web page.[6]

- **Contributor**: *An entity responsible for making contributions to the resource. Contributor* types include persons, families, corporate bodies, and services. The name of a *Contributor* is typically used to indicate the entity, although a URI could be used in its stead. See also: *Creator.*

- **Coverage**: *The spatial or temporal topic of the resource, the spatial applicability of the resource, or the jurisdiction under which the resource is relevant. Coverage* refers to the content of the resource, not its publication or dissemination data. Spatial coverage may be represented by a named place or a location specified by its geographic coordinates. Temporal coverage may be represented by a named period, date, or date range. A jurisdiction may be represented by a named administrative entity or a geographic place to which the resource applies. Recommended best practice is to use a controlled vocabulary such as the *Thesaurus of Geographic Names.* Where appropriate, named places or time periods can be used in preference to numeric identifiers such as sets of coordinates or date ranges.

- **Creator**: *An entity primarily responsible for making the resource. Creator* types include persons, families, corporate bodies, and services. The name of a Creator is typically used to indicate the entity, although a URI could be used in its stead. See also: *Contributor.*

- **Date**: *A point or period of time associated with an event in the lifecycle of the resource. Date* may be used to express temporal information at any level of granularity. Recommended best practice is to use an encoding scheme, such as the W3C's profile for ISO 8601, the International Standards Organization representation of dates and times (e.g., YYYY-MM-DD).

- **Description**: *An account of the resource. Description* may include (but is not limited to) abstracts, tables of contents, graphical representations, or free-text accounts of the resource.

- **Format**: *The file format, physical medium, or dimensions of the resource. Format* differs from *Type*, in that *Type* refers to the nature or genre of a resource's content rather than its carrier(s). Examples of dimensions include size and duration. Recommended best practice is to use a controlled vocabulary such as the list of Internet Media Types (formerly known as *MIME types*). See also: *Type.*

- **Identifier**: *An unambiguous reference to the resource within a given context.* Recommended best practice is to identify the resource by means of a string conforming to a formal identification system. Familiar examples include URLs, URIs, ISBNs, ISSNs, and Universal Product Code (UPC) numbers.

- **Language**: *A language of the resource.* Recommended best practice is to use a controlled vocabulary or common standard, such as ISO 639-2, a set of three-letter codes for language names (e.g., *eng* for English, *tgl* for Tagalog).

- **Publisher**: *An entity responsible for making the resource available.* Similar to Contributor and Creator, the name of a *Publisher* is typically used to indicate the entity responsible for dissemination.

- **Relation**: *A related resource.* Distinguished from *Source* by the nature of the relationship between related resources. Examples include companion sites, commentaries, prequels, sequels, and reviews. Recommended best practice is to identify the related resource by means of a string conforming to a formal identification system. See also: *Source.*

- **Rights**: *Information about rights held in and over the resource.* Rights metadata typically includes a statement about various property rights associated with the resource, including intellectual property rights.

- **Source**: *A related resource from which the described resource is derived.* The described resource is derived from the source resource in whole or in part. Examples include reformatted versions, abridgements, and translations. Recommended best practice is to identify the original resource by means of a string conforming to a formal identification system. See also: *Relation.*

- **Subject**: *The topic of the resource.* Subject is typically represented using keywords, key phrases, subject headings, thesaurus terms, or classification codes.

- **Title**: *A name given to the resource.* Typically, title is a name by which the resource is formally known.

- **Type**: *The nature or genre of the resource.* Recommended best practice is to use a controlled vocabulary such as the *DCMI Type Vocabulary.* To describe the file format, physical medium, or dimensions of the resource, use the *Format* element. See also: *Format.*

The DCMES is a standard for resource description, not for encoding. It is discussed in this chapter because the set of 15 elements may be used in connection with the library content standard *RDA: Resource Description & Access.* The DC can act as an alternative container for simple RDA cataloging data. Just as catalogers are able to place RDA descriptive metadata into a MARC record with ISBD punctuation, they can also place RDA metadata into the 15 elements of the Dublin Core. The metadata may then be encoded in any of the formats that DC employs (HTML, XML, etc.). RDA data contained in the basic Dublin Core element set will not be particularly complex or granular because of the relative simplicity of the DCMES, but with the use of what were formerly called *qualifiers* (now referred to as *terms* or *properties*), which can provide additional refinements to the elements, the data may be more robust.

In place of the traditional concept of a bibliographic record, the DCMI promotes the concept of a *description set* in its abstract model. A *description set* consists "of one or more descriptions, each of which describes a single resource."[7] For example, a description set might comprise (1) a description of a painting and (2) a description of the artist responsible. Together the two individual descriptions make up the description set. An individual description is made up of "one or more *statements* (about one, and only one, *resource*) and zero or one *described resource URI* (a *URI* that identifies the *described resource*)."[8] The word *description* in this context has a different meaning than it does in more traditional cataloging rules. A description could theoretically consist of as little as one assertion about a resource (e.g., its title). Description sets may be presented, for end-user benefit, in the form of what appear to be traditional records, but the record concept is not primary. Recommended approaches for encoding description sets are provided as syntax guidelines.[9] They include text encoding for human consumption but focus on machine-processable formats, including the Resource Description Framework (RDF) for optimal Semantic Web presentation (see discussion of RDF later in this chapter).[10]

The DC Metadata Element Set has been approved by both the National Information Standards Organization (NISO) and the International Organization for Standardization (ISO) and published as ANSI/NISO Standard Z39.85-2012 (February 2013) and ISO Standard 15836:2009 (February 2009). But the Dublin Core encompasses a great deal more than just the 15 core elements. A variety of *properties, classes, types, syntax encoding schemes,* and *vocabulary encoding schemes,* collectively referred to as the *DCMI Metadata Terms,* provide robustness to what otherwise would be a simplistic scheme.

The DCMI currently identifies 55 properties that can be used to describe resources. This longer list of DC properties, shown in Figure 22.1, has

abstract	accessRights	accrualMethod	accrualPeriodicity
accrualPolicy	alternative	audience	available
bibliographicCitation	conformsTo	**contributor**	**coverage**
created	**creator**	**date**	dateAccepted
dateCopyrighted	dateSubmitted	**description**	educationLevel
extent	**format**	hasFormat	hasPart
hasVersion	**identifier**	instructionalMethod	isFormatOf
isPartOf	isReferencedBy	isReplacedBy	isRequiredBy
issued	isVersionOf	**language**	license
mediator	medium	modified	provenance
publisher	references	**relation**	replaces
requires	**rights**	rightsHolder	**source**
spatial	**subject**	tableOfContents	temporal
title	**type**	valid	

FIGURE 22.1 Current Set of 55 Properties in the Dublin Core.

TABLE 22.1 DC Properties Used to Refine Other Properties.

Independent Dublin Core Properties (terms)	Properties (terms) that Function as Refinements or Qualifiers
audience	educationLevel; mediator
coverage	spatial; temporal
date	available; created; dateAccepted; dateCopyrighted; dateSubmitted; issued; modified; valid
description	abstract; tableOfContents
format	extent; medium
identifier	bibliographicCitation
relation	conformsTo; hasFormat; hasPart; hasVersion; isFormatOf; isPartOf; isReferencedBy; isReplacedBy; isRequiredBy; isVersionOf; references; replaces; requires
rights	accessRights; license
title	alternative
accrualMethod accrualPeriodicity accrualPolicy **contributor** **creator** instructionalMethod **language** provenance **publisher** rightsHolder **source** **subject** **type**	n/a

incorporated the original set of 15 core elements known as the DCMES.[11] In Figure 22.1 and Table 22.1, the 15 core elements are shown in boldface type. Some properties are used independently; some properties are used to refine or qualify other properties. Table 22.1 shows which of the DC properties can be used to refine other properties. For example, the original DC element *date* may be qualified by using one of the properties listed in Table 22.1 in the row for *date* (e.g., date.valid). In some cases the refinement of a property is another property that is based on the original element (e.g., dateAccepted). In the following examples, all the variations based on the *date* element are shown.

- **Original DC element**: date
- **Refined DC element**: date.available
- **Refined DC element**: date.created
- **Refined DC element**: date.issued
- **Refined DC element**: date.modified
- **Refined DC element**: date.valid
- **Separate DC property**: dateAccepted
- **Separate DC property**: dateCopyrighted
- **Separate DC property**: dateSubmitted

The list of *DCMI Metadata Terms* also includes some special properties that have been added to describe education materials (such as *audience* and *instructionalMethod*), collections (such as *AccrualMethod* and *AccrualPolicy*), and provenance.

The grouping of terms called *Classes*, another category found in the *DCMI Metadata Terms*, is defined as "groups of resources having certain properties in common and therefore put together as members of one concept."[12] Some of the entries include explanatory comments. Examples of terms in the list, for which the *Type of Term* attribute is *class*, include the following:

- **Agent**: "A resource that acts or has the power to act. Examples of *Agent* include person, organization, and software agent."
- **LinguisticSystem**: "A system of signs, symbols, sounds, gestures, or rules used in communication. Examples include written, spoken, sign, and computer languages."
- **PhysicalMedium**: "A physical material or carrier. Examples include paper, canvas, or DVD."[13]

Other *classes* are perhaps less self-evident; for example, the class *Jurisdiction* is defined as "the extent or range of judicial, law enforcement, or other authority."[14] Each property may be related to a class by either a *has domain* or a *has range* relationship. In the *has domain* relationship, the domain indicates the class of resources for which the resource being described is an instance (e.g., a resource described by the property *accrualPolicy* is in the domain of the class *Collection*). In the *has range* relationship, the range indicates the class to which the values for that property belong (e.g., the property *conformsTo*, referring to an established standard, has the range of the class *Standard*).

The terms in the list of *DCMI Type Vocabulary*, which are also identified as *classes*, are established in order to populate the *type* element with resource types such as *Image*, *Dataset*, *Sound*, or *Text*. Each of these terms is also identified as *class* for its *Type of Term* attribute. The classes of the *DCMI Type Vocabulary* may have *broader than* or *narrower than* relationships. For example, *StillImage* is a type that is narrower than *Image*.

Syntax Encoding Schemes (SES), which provide guidelines for how a value is to be structured in an element, may be used for values for a variety of DC elements, such as *date* or *identifier*.[15] For example, country names may be represented by the two-letter codes of ISO 3166-1 (e.g., BG for Bulgaria, GH for

Ghana). *Vocabulary Encoding Schemes* (VES) include what are commonly known as *controlled vocabularies* (e.g., classification schemes, subject heading lists). A limited set of VES is provided, including familiar resources such as Library of Congress Subject Headings (LCSH) and the National Library of Medicine (NLM) Classification, as well as others, such as the list of DCMI Types itself.[16]

The Dublin Core Metadata Initiative carries out a number of additional activities. Prominent among these is the *Dublin Core Application Profile*.[17] An application profile is a structure for defining the parameters of metadata records developed for specific communities that require the use of terms from vocabularies beyond those defined in the DCMI. Semantic interoperability is key to the concept of the application profile. Application profiles are designed to be understood on the Semantic Web, as opposed to standalone record sets that require specifically constructed crosswalks in order to be shared.

Dublin Core and RDA

As stated previously, it is possible to encode RDA metadata using the Dublin Core. This is affirmed by RDA 0.2, which states, "The RDA element set is compatible with ISBD, MARC 21, and Dublin Core."[18] However, as of this writing, best practices have not yet emerged. The RDA Registry, a site maintained by the Joint Steering Committee for RDA, includes a page for application profiles, but no profiles are yet documented there.[19] The DCMI's page, "Guidelines for Dublin Core Application Profiles," likewise does not indicate the existence of any developed RDA profiles.[20] The RDA Toolkit does include a page titled "RDA to DC (Test)" located under the Tools tab and the Maps/Global maps sub-menu. The page is undated and no creator of the page is given credit. Nevertheless, suggestions for six of the DC elements are given. The Date element, for example, is mapped to RDA 2.7.6, 2.8.6, 2.9.6, and 2.10.6. This page should be regarded as tentative.[21]

Without clear guidance from the organizations most invested, efforts to encode RDA in Dublin Core are likely, for the time being, to be local and somewhat experimental. An article by Melanie Wacker, Myung-Ja Han, and Judith Dartt describe an early foray in encoding RDA in Dublin Core, as well as MODS (discussed later in this chapter) and Encoded Archival Description (EAD).[22] The experimenters discovered significant problems with semantic interoperability between RDA and Dublin Core, given that "the elements of RDA are as complex as those of MARC."[23] Among other outcomes, it was seen that 11 RDA elements mapped to *dc:title* and *dcterms:alternative*; four RDA elements corresponded to *dc:creator* and also to *dc:contributor*, and 19 to *dc:format*. The RDA elements *carrier type*, *media type*, and *content type* could not be encoded with sufficient specificity, as compared with the meaning defined in the MARC bibliographic fields 336, 337, and 338. One of the institutions involved in the test, the Columbia University Libraries, produced a Qualified Dublin Core schema for use with RDA, but this was a local effort. Such experiments are valuable and should be encouraged as preparations for an eventual, widely distributed application profile.

Table 22.2 presents a conceptual mapping from selected RDA core elements to DC metadata terms. This table can only suggest the direction in

TABLE 22.2 Mapping from RDA Core Elements to DC Metadata Terms.

RDA Element Grouping	Specific RDA Core Element	Corresponding DC Element (with Refining Term)
Attributes of Manifestation and Item		
Title	Title proper	Title
Statement of responsibility	Statement of responsibility relating to title proper	Creator and Contributor
Edition statement	Designation of edition	Relation (isVersionOf)
	Designation of a named revision of an edition	Relation (isVersionOf)
Numbering of serials	Numeric and/or alphabetic designation of first issue or part of sequence	[No equivalent element]
	Chronological designation of first issue or part of sequence	Date (Issued)
	Numeric and/or alphabetic designation of last issue or part of sequence	[No equivalent element]
	Chronological designation of last issue or part of sequence	Date (Issued)
Production statement	Date of production (for unpublished resource)	Date (Created)
Publication statement	Place of publication	[No equivalent element]
	Publisher's name	Publisher
	Date of publication	Date (Issued)
Distribution statement	Place of distribution	[No equivalent element]
	Distributor's name	[No equivalent element] (Possibly *Publisher*)
	Date of distribution	Date (Available)
Manufacture statement	Place of manufacture	[No equivalent element]
	Manufacturer's name	[No equivalent element] (Possibly *Publisher*)
	Date of manufacture	Date (Created)
Copyright date	Copyright date	Date (dateCopyrighted)

(*continued*)

TABLE 22.2 (*continued*)

RDA Element Grouping	Specific RDA Core Element	Corresponding DC Element (with Refining Term)
Series statement	Title proper of series	Relation (isPartof)
	Numbering within series	[No equivalent element]
	Title proper of subseries	Relation (isPartof)
	Numbering within subseries	[No equivalent element]
Identifier for the manifestation	Identifier for the manifestation	Identifier
Carrier type	Carrier type	Format (Medium)
Extent	Extent	Format (Extent)

Attributes of Work and Expression

Title	Preferred title for the work	Title

Differentiating elements for works and expressions

	Form of work	Type
	Date of work	Date (Created)
	Date of expression	Date (Created)
	Place of origin of the work	[No equivalent element]
	Other distinguishing characteristic	[No equivalent element]
	Medium of performance (for music)	[No equivalent element]
	Numeric designation of a musical work	[No equivalent element]
	Key (for music)	[No equivalent element]
Other elements	Identifier for the work	Identifier
	Identifier for the expression	Identifier
	Content type (expression)	Type
	Language of expression	Language
	Horizontal scale of cartographic content	[No equivalent element]
	Vertical scale of cartographic content	[No equivalent element]

Relationships between Group 1 and Group 2 Entities

	Creator	Creator
	Other person, family, or corporate body associated with a work	Contributor

TABLE 22.2 (*continued*)

RDA Element Grouping	Specific RDA Core Element	Corresponding DC Element (with Refining Term)
Subject Relationships		
	Subject of work	Subject Coverage (Temporal) Coverage (Spatial)

which an official mapping or application profile is likely to develop, but it does indicate areas of disjunction between RDA and DC. Notably, the table includes no mapped elements for RDA 0.6.4 (Attributes of Person, Family, and Corporate Body) or 0.6.5 (Primary Relationships between Work, Expression, Manifestation, and Item). With regard to 0.6.4, DCMI metadata terms have not been developed for PFC attributes. By contrast, although some DCMI terms, such as *hasVersion* or *replaces*, do indicate relationships among FRBR group 1 entities, they are not the primary relationships detailed in RDA 17.4.1:

- the relationship between a work and an expression through which that work is realized
- the relationship between an expression of a work and a manifestation that embodies that expression
- the relationship between a manifestation and an item that exemplifies that manifestation.[24]

Table 22.3 presents a conceptual mapping from the DCMES and its refining terms (i.e., *properties*) to relevant selected RDA instructions. In the first column, the 15 core elements are listed in boldface type; they are accompanied by qualified versions of the elements using the other DC terms that are used for refinements. A few DC terms are not used to qualify the original DC elements; these terms are listed separately at the end of the table. Some of the latter group have no evident equivalent concept in RDA. As is the case with the RDA to DC mapping previously discussed, this table also only suggests the direction in which an official mapping or application profile may develop.

Dublin Core Examples

Figures 22.2 and 22.3 show two different records for Alison Bechdel's *Fun Home* using DCMI metadata. These are the first of four transformations in this chapter of the MARC 21 record shown in Figure 21.6 (p. 843). The metadata shown in Figure 22.2 is derived from the DC template view of OCLC record

TABLE 22.3 Mapping from DC Metadata Terms to RDA Instructions.

DC Terms	RDA Instructions	
contributor	19.3:	Other Person, Family, or Corporate Body (PFC) Associated with a Work
	20.2:	Contributor
	21.2:	Producer of an Unpublished Resource
	21.6:	Other PFC Associated with a Manifestation
		See also: RDA appendix I.
coverage	7.3:	Coverage of the Content
coverage.spatial	7.4:	Coordinates of Cartographic Content
coverage.temporal	7.11.2:	Place of Capture
	7.11.3:	Date of Capture
	7.27:	Other Details of Cartographic Content
	23.4:	Subject Relationship
creator	19.2:	Creator
date	2.6.3:	Chronological Designation of First Issue or Part
date.available	2.6.5:	Chronological Designation of Last Issue or Part
date.created	2.7.6:	Date of Production
dateAccepted	2.8.6:	Date of Publication
dateCopyrighted	2.9.6:	Date of Distribution
dateSubmitted	2.10.6:	Date of Manufacture
date.issued	2.11:	Copyright Date
date.modified	2.17.10:	Note on Copyright Date
date.valid	2.17.7.3:	Details Relating to Publication Statement
	2.17.7.4:	Suspension of Publication
	2.17.12:	Note on Frequency
	2.19:	Immediate Source of Acquisition of Item
	6.4:	Date of Work
	6.10:	Date of Expression
	6.20:	Date of a Legal Work
	6.24:	Date of Expression of a Religious Work
	7.11.3:	Date of Capture
	7.9.4:	Year Degree Granted
	11.4.2:	Date of Conference, etc.
description	6.3:	Form of Work
description.abstract	7.2:	Nature of the Content
description.	7.10:	Summarization of the Content
tableOfContents	7.15:	Illustrative Content
	7.17:	Colour Content
		See also: chapters 25. Related works, 26. Related expressions, 27. Related manifestations, and appendix J.
format	3.2:	Media Type
format.extent	3.3:	Carrier Type
format.medium	3.4:	Extent
	3.5:	Dimensions

TABLE 22.3 (*continued*)

DC Terms	RDA Instructions	
	3.12:	Book Format
	3.20:	Equipment or System Requirement
	7.22:	Duration
		See: RDA chapter 3 for other carrier-related elements, especially 3.16-3.19 for special format characteristics.
identifier identifier. bibliographicCitation	2.15:	Identifier for the Manifestation
	2.16:	Preferred Citation
	2.20:	Identifier for the Item
	4.6:	Uniform Resource Locator
	6.8:	Identifier for the Work
	6:13:	Identifier for the Expression
language	6.11:	Language of Expression
	7.12:	Language of the Content
publisher	2.7.4:	Producer's Name
	2.7.5:	Parallel Producer's Name
	2.8.4:	Publisher's Name
	2.8.5:	Parallel Publisher's Name
	2.9.4:	Distributor's Name
	2.9.5:	Parallel Distributor's Name
	2.9.4:	Manufacturer's Name
	2.9.5:	Parallel Manufacturer's Name
relation relation.conformsTo relation.hasFormat relation.hasPart relation.hasVersion relation.isFormatOf relation.isPartOf relation.isReferencedBy relation.isReplacedBy relation.isRequiredBy relation.isVersionOf relation.References relation.Replaces relation.Requires	2.3.7:	Earlier Title Proper
	2.3.8:	Later Title Proper
	3.20:	Equipment or System Requirement
		See: RDA chapters 25-28 for discussion of related works, expressions, manifestation, and items. *See also*: Appendix J.
rights rights.accessRights rights.License	4.2:	Terms of Availability
	4.4:	Restrictions on Access
	4.5:	Restrictions on Use
source		*See*: RDA chapters 25-28 for discussion of related works, expressions, manifestation, and items. *See also*: Appendix J.
subject	23.4:	Subject Relationship

(*continued*)

TABLE 22.3 (*continued*)

DC Terms	RDA Instructions	
title	2.3:	Title
	6.2:	Title of the Work
	6.14:	Title of a Musical Work
	6.19:	Title of a Legal Work
	6.23:	Title of a Religious Work
	6.26:	Title of an Official Communication
title.alternative	2.3.3:	Parallel Title Proper
	2.3.4:	Other Title Information
	2.3.5:	Parallel Other Title Information
	2.3.6:	Variant Title
	2.3.9:	Key Title
	2.3.10:	Abbreviated Title
	6.2.3:	Variant Title for the Work
	6.14.3:	Variant Title for a Musical Work
	6.19.3:	Variant Title for a Legal Work
	6.23.3:	Variant Title for a Religious Work
	6.26.3:	Variant Title for an Official Communication
type	6.3:	Form of Work
	6.9:	Content Type

Additional DC Terms	RDA Instructions	
accrualMethod	N/A	
accrualPeriodicity	N/A	
accrualPolicy	N/A	
audience	7.7:	Intended Audience
educationLevel	7.7:	Intended Audience
instructionalMethod	N/A	
mediator	N/A	
provenance	2.18:	Custodial History of Item
rightsHolder	4.3:	Contact Information
	22.2:	Owner
	22.3:	Custodian

#62127870, using the Connexion browser software. Most of the elements and refinements in this figure are easily compared with the MARC 21 metadata in Figure 21.6. For Figure 22.3, the Dublin Core Generator site was used to demonstrate how the metadata in the DC template appears when encoded in XML.[25] By comparing the text entered in the *Element, Refinement,* and *Values* columns in Figure 22.2 with the XML tags in Figure 22.3, the latter figure becomes simpler to read and understand.

Element	Refinement	Value
Title		Fun home
	Alternative	a family tragicomic
Creator		Bechdel, Alison, 1960-
Subject	LCSH	Bechdel, Alison, 1960--Comic books, strips, etc.
	LCSH	Cartoonists--United States--Comicbooks, strips, etc.
	LCC	PN6727.B3757
	DDC	741.5973
Description		This book takes its place alongside the unnerving, memorable, darkly funny family memoirs of Augusten Burroughs and Mary Karr. It's a father-daughter tale perfectly suited to the graphic memoir form. Meet Alison's father, a historic preservation expert and obsessive restorer of the family's Victorian house, a third-generation funeral home director, a high school English teacher, an icily distant parent, and a closeted homosexual who, as it turns out, is involved with male students and a family babysitter. Through narrative that is alternately heartbreaking and fiercely funny, we are drawn into a daughter's complex yearning for her father. . . .--From publisher description.
Description	Table of Contents	Old father, old artificer -- A happy death -- That old catastrophe -- In the shadow of young girls in flower -- The canary-colored caravan of death -- The ideal husband -- The antihero's journey.
Publisher		Houghton Mifflin
Date	Copyrighted	©2006
Type	DCMI	Still image
	DCMI	Text
		Graphic novels
		Comic books, strips, etc.
Format	Extent	232 pages
	Medium	volume
Identifier		ISBN: 9780618871711
		LCCN: 2005030304
Language		eng
Coverage	Spatial	United States
	Spatial	n-us---

FIGURE 22.2 Dublin Core Metadata for Bechdel's *Fun Home* in a Dublin Core Template.

The DCMI maintains a number of communities "that bring together people interested in a specific topic related to Dublin Core metadata or metadata best practices in a particular domain."[26] Among the more active communities are those on the topics of Accessibility, Knowledge Management, Digital Preservation, Registries, Science & Metadata, Social Tagging, Vocabulary Management, and implementing metadata in the Education, Libraries, and Government Agencies domains. An Architecture Forum is dedicated to the development of "a model, strategy and roadmap for the practical deployment of Dublin Core metadata using mainstream web technologies (XML/RDF/XHTML)."[27] The DCMI sponsors periodic webinars, annual international conferences and workshops, as well as less-frequent regional conferences and meetings.

```
<?xml version="1.0" encoding="UTF-8"?>
<dc:title>Fun home</dc:title>
<dcterms:alternative>a family tragicomic</dcterms:alternative>
<dc:creator>Bechdel, Alison, 1960-</dc:creator>
<dc:subject xsi:type="dcterms:LCSH">Bechdel, Alison, 1960--Comic books, strips, etc.</dc:subject>
<dc:subject xsi:type="dcterms:LCSH">Cartoonists--United States--Comic books, strips,
etc.</dc:subject>
<dc:subject xsi:type="dcterms:LCC">PN6727.B3757</dc:subject>
<dc:subject xsi:type="dcterms:DDC">741.5973</dc:subject>
<dc:description>This book takes its place alongside the unnerving, memorable, darkly funny family
memoirs of Augusten Burroughs and Mary Karr. It's a father-daughter tale perfectly suited to the
graphic memoir form. Meet Alison's father, a historic preservation expert and obsessive restorer of the
family's Victorian house, a third-generation funeral home director, a high school English teacher, an
icily distant parent, and a closeted homosexual who, as it turns out, is involved with male students and
a family babysitter. Through narrative that is alternately heartbreaking and fiercely funny, we are
drawn into a daughter's complex yearning for her father. . . .--From publisher
description.</dc:description>
<dcterms:tableOfContents>Old father, old artificer -- A happy death -- That old catastrophe -- In the
shadow of young girls in flower -- The canary-colored caravan of death -- The ideal husband -- The
antihero's journey.</dcterms:tableOfContents>
<dc:publisher>Houghton Mifflin</dc:publisher>
<dcterms:dateCopyrighted>c2006</dcterms:dateCopyrighted>
<dc:type xsi:type="dcterms:DCMIType">Still image</dc:type>
<dc:type xsi:type="dcterms:DCMIType">Text</dc:type>
<dc:type>Graphic novel</dc:type>
<dc:type>Comic books, strips, etc.</dc:type>
<dcterms:extent>232 pages</dcterms:extent>
<dcterms:medium>volume</dcterms:medium>
<dc:identifier>ISBN:9780618871711</dc:identifier>
<dc:identifier>LCCN:2005030304</dc:identifier>
<dc:language>eng</dc:language>
<dcterms:spatial>United States</dcterms:spatial>
<dcterms:spatial>n-us---</dcterms:spatial>
```

FIGURE 22.3 Dublin Core Metadata for Bechdel's *Fun Home* in XML.

METADATA OBJECT DESCRIPTION SCHEMA (MODS)

In 2002, the Network Development and MARC Standards Office of the Library of Congress (LC), in collaboration with outside experts, developed MODS, a bibliographic element set expressed in XML. MODS is based on an extensive subset of fields from the MARC 21 bibliographic format, using language-based rather than numerical tags. MODS occupies a middle ground between the two other established standards: while it is richer than Dublin Core, it is less complex than MARC 21, although it inherits the latter's semantics to an extent. Usage of MODS is independent of any cataloging code or other content standard. This means that, like the Dublin Core, it may be used to convey RDA-based metadata typically communicated by MARC records.

MODS Basics

In comparison with the 15 DC elements, MODS specifies 20 top-level elements, as shown in Table 22.4. Each element is assigned attributes, and most have sub-elements. As an example, for the *subject* element, attributes include *authority, displayLabel,* and *usage,* and sub-elements include *geographic, temporal, name, genre,* and *occupation.* All elements and attributes are optional, but a MODS record must contain at least one element. This is similar to the minimal specification of a DCMI description, which must contain at least one assertion about a resource. Table 22.4 gives the MODS top-level elements, with their definitions, and the first level of sub-elements. Fuller information, including attributes and their definitions, notes on application, usage examples, and so on, is available at the MODS web site.[28]

TABLE 22.4 MODS Top-level Elements and Sub-elements.

MODS top-level element	Definition	Sub-elements
titleInfo	A word, phrase, character, or group of characters, normally appearing in a resource, that names it or the work contained in it.	title subTitle partNumber partName nonSort
name	The name of a person, organization, or event (conference, meeting, etc.) associated in some way with the resource.	namePart displayForm affiliation role description
typeOfResource	A term that specifies the characteristics and general type of content of the resource.	[None defined]
genre	A term(s) that designates a category characterizing a particular style, form, or content, such as artistic, musical, literary composition, etc.	[None defined]
originInfo	Information about the origin of the resource, including place of origin or publication, publisher/originator, and dates associated with the resource	place publisher dateIssued dateCreated dateCaptured dateValid dateModified copyrightDate dateOther edition issuance frequency

(continued)

TABLE 22.4 (*continued*)

MODS top-level element	Definition	Sub-elements
language	A designation of the language in which the content of a resource is expressed.	languageTerm
physical Description	[A "wrapper element" that containsall sub-elements relating to physical description information of the resource described. Data is input only within each sub-element.]	form reformattingQuality internetMediaType extent digitalOrigin note
abstract	A summary of the content of the resource.	[None defined]
tableOfContents	A description of the contents of a resource.	[None defined]
targetAudience	A description of the intellectual level of the audience for which the resource is intended.	[None defined]
note	General textual information relating to a resource.	[None defined]
subject	A term or phrase representing the primary topic(s) on which a work is focused.	topic geographic temporal titleInfo name genre hierarchicalGeographic cartographics geographicCode occupation
classification	A designation applied to a resource that indicates the subject by applying a formal system of coding and organizing resources according to subject areas.	[None defined]
relatedItem	Information that identifies other resources related to the one being described.	Any MODS element may be treated as a sub-element of relatedItem

TABLE 22.4 (*continued*)

MODS top-level element	Definition	Sub-elements
identifier	A unique standard number or code that distinctively identifies a resource.	[None defined]
location	The institution or repository holding the resource, or a remote location in the form of a URL where it is available.	physicalLocation shelfLocator url holdingSimple [with seven sub-subelements] holdingExternal
accessCondition	Information about restrictions imposed on access to a resource.	[None defined]
part	The designation of physical parts of a resource in a detailed form.	detail extent date text
extension	[Used to provide for additional information not covered by MODS.]	[None defined]
recordInfo	Information about the metadata record.	recordContentSource recordCreationDate recordChangeDate recordIdentifier recordOrigin languageOfCataloging descriptionStandard

Despite the restricted number of top-level elements, the mapping provided between MODS and MARC21 is extensive. In MODS Version 3.5, the element *titleInfo* maps more than 30 possible types of metadata found in 12 different MARC 21 fields and subfields dedicated to title information, showing the correlations of these different types to attributes and sub-elements of this single MODS element.[29] As one might infer, this mapping does not work in both directions: a record converted from MARC 21 to MODS cannot be converted back into MARC 21 without significant loss of specificity.

MODS and RDA

It is possible to create RDA metadata using MODS. The RDA Toolkit includes an RDA-to-MODS mapping, located under Tools/RDA Mappings.

RDA element names are correlated with MODS syntax, along with explanatory notes when relevant. For example, a statement of responsibility relating to title proper is mapped to the MODS element *note*, which then must be qualified with an attribute indicating that the note is of the type "statement of responsibility" (e.g., note type="statement of responsibility"). Sometimes more than one element in RDA is mapped to a single MODS element. For example, both the *extent* and the *dimensions* elements are mapped to the single sub-element *extent*, found under the top-level MODS element *physicalDescription*. In cases where RDA elements are inapplicable to MODS, the MODS syntax column is marked N/A.

The Network Development and MARC Standards Office has also developed the Metadata Authority Description Schema (MADS).[30] Similar to MODS, it allows the expression of MARC 21 data in XML, but in this case the schema is designed to contain authority data rather than bibliographic data. MADS is structured with three main elements:

- *authority*, which includes the sub-elements for names, titles, topics, genres, geographic locations, and other types of authority data

- *related*, which includes an identical set of sub-elements to contain names or terms that are related to the entity described in the *authority* element

- *variant*, which also includes an identical set of sub-elements to contain variant access points and unauthorized subject terms (e.g., *see* references)

MADS metadata may be recorded more specifically through a second sub-element level, if desired. Unlike MODS, MADS is not yet mapped to or from RDA, though mapping from MARC 21 is provided at LC's MADS website.[31]

Figure 22.4 shows a partial MODS record for Bechdel's *Fun Home*, derived from the LC catalog, using the same MARC 21 record as shown in Figure 21.6. Comparing Figure 22.4 to Figure 22.2 reveals many differences between the Dublin Core and MODS transformations. For example, the DC template record gives *Bechdel, Alison, 1960-* as a single character string in the Creator element, but the MODS record breaks it into two *namePart* elements, the latter qualified by the attribute *date*. By contrast, the MODS record presents *relatedItem* links to a publisher's description and to biographical information about the author, both of which were included in MARC 856 fields but were bypassed by the automated DC conversion process. These differences are highlighted in boldface type in Figure 22.4.

The MODS website includes a registry of current MODS implementation projects. These include, among others, LC's American Memory, Amherst College Digital Collections, Chopin Early Editions (University of Chicago), and National Library of Wales Digital Repository. For additional information on MODS, including tools, presentations, and versions of the schema from 3.0 forward, readers are encouraged to consult the MODS documentation at the LC website.[32]

```
<mods xmlns="http://www.loc.gov/mods/v3" xmlns:xsi="http://www.w3.org/2001/XML
Schema-instance" xsi:schemaLocation="http://www.loc.gov/mods/v3
http://www.loc.gov/standards/mods/v3/mods-3-5.xsd" version="3.5">

<titleInfo>
        <title>Fun home</title>
        <subTitle>a family tragicomic</subTitle>
</titleInfo>

<name type="personal" usage="primary">
        <namePart>Bechdel, Alison</namePart>
        <namePart type="date">1960-</namePart>
</name>

<typeOfResource>text</typeOfResource>

<genre authority="marcgt">biography</genre>
<genre authority="">Graphic novels.</genre>

<originInfo>
        <place>
                <placeTerm type="code" authority="marccountry">mau</placeTerm>
        </place>
        <place>
                <placeTerm type="text">Boston</placeTerm>
        </place>
        <publisher>Houghton Mifflin</publisher>
        <dateIssued>c2006</dateIssued>
        <dateIssued encoding="marc">2006</dateIssued>
        <issuance>monographic</issuance>
</originInfo>

<language>
        <languageTerm type="code" authority="iso639-2b">eng</languageTerm>
</language>

<physicalDescription>
        <form authority="marcform">print</form>
        <extent>232 p. : chiefly ill. ; 24 cm.</extent>
</physicalDescription>

<note type="statement of responsibility" altRepGroup="00">Alison Bechdel.</note>

<subject authority="lcsh">
        <name type="personal">
        <namePart>Bechdel, Alison</namePart>
        <namePart type="date">1960-</namePart>
        </name>
        <genre>Comic books, strips, etc</genre>
</subject>
<subject authority="lcsh">
        <topic>Cartoonists</topic>
        <geographic>United States</geographic>
        <genre>Comic books, strips, etc</genre>
</subject>

<classification authority="lcc">PN6727.B3757 Z46 2006</classification>
<classification authority="ddc" edition="22">741.5/973</classification>
```

FIGURE 22.4 MODS Record for Bechdel's *Fun Home*.   (*continued*)

```
<identifier type="isbn">9780618477944</identifier>
<identifier type="isbn">0618477942</identifier>
<identifier type="lccn">2005030304</identifier>

<relatedItem>
     <location>
          <url displayLabel="Publisher description">
          http://www.loc.gov/catdir/enhancements/fy0623/2005030304-d.html
          </url>
     </location>
</relatedItem>
<relatedItem>
     <location>
          <url displayLabel="Contributor biographical information">
          http://www.loc.gov/catdir/enhancements/fy0736/2005030304-b.html
          </url>
     </location>
</relatedItem>

<recordInfo>
     <descriptionStandard>aacr</descriptionStandard>
     <recordContentSource authority="marcorg">DLC</recordContentSource>
     <recordCreationDate encoding="marc">051018</recordCreationDate>
     <recordChangeDate encoding="iso8601">20080116083036.0</recordChangeDate>
     <recordIdentifier>14144904<  /recordIdentifier>
     <recordOrigin> Converted from MARCXML to MODS version 3.5 using
     MARC21slim2MODS3-5.xsl (Revision 1.96 2014/04/22)</recordOrigin>
</recordInfo>

</mods>
```

FIGURE 22.4   (*continued*)

BIBFRAME: SUCCESSOR TO MARC?

The first years of the current century saw increasingly urgent calls for the replacement of MARC as an encoding standard for library-generated metadata. Although the creation of MARC in the 1960s was consistently lauded as a groundbreaking achievement, and its ability to evolve over time was often noted, critics declared that MARC had reached the end of its useful life. Notable, or perhaps notorious, among these critiques was Roy Tennant's influential article, "MARC Must Die."[33] As the *Functional Requirements for Bibliographic Records* (FRBR) and the *Functional Requirements for Authority Data* (FRAD) entered the consciousness of librarians and were widely discussed, the multiple and diverse entity relationships emphasized by those models strained the limits of MARC's underlying design.

Angela Kroeger provides an overview of the developments occurring between 2002 and 2012 aimed toward a replacement of MARC as the primary encoding standard.[34] Her article discusses, among other things, key writings by Roy Tennant, Lorcan Dempsey, and Karen Coyle; *On the Record*, the report of the Library of Congress Working Group on the Future of Bibliographic Control; Martha Yee's inquiries toward an RDF-based cataloging code; and the statement-based rather than record-based emphasis of RDA.

In a prescient article from 2004, Roy Tennant outlined requirements for a new bibliographic metadata infrastructure. While respecting the achievements signaled by the creation of MARC and those occurring since that time, he asserted, "we must . . . assimilate MARC into a broader, richer, more diverse set of tools, standards, and protocols."[35] He named and discussed requirements for a new infrastructure:

- **Versatility**: the infrastructure will be "capable of ingesting, merging, indexing, enhancing, and presenting to the user, metadata from a variety of sources describing a variety of objects";

- **Extensibility**: the flexibility to incorporate additions to the base metadata, while allowing metadata users "to ignore extensions as they wish, without rending the base metadata unusable";

- **Openness and transparency**: qualities that allow "standards, protocols, and software" to be shared and tested efficiently "without restrictions that prevent their useful implementation";

- **Low threshold/high ceiling**: a condition which allows "as many people and organizations to participate as possible," while still supporting "the more complex requirements of those needing a more full-featured system";

- **Cooperative management**: an approach to creating and developing new standards "in as cooperative and inclusive [a] process as is practicable";

- **Modularity**: the ability "to replace a component that performs a specific function with a different component, without breaking the whole";

- **Hierarchy**: as the word implies, the ability to handle hierarchically structured information;

- **Granularity**: a requirement of the metadata itself, which must be coded at a level of sufficient detail "to support all intended uses";

- **Being graceful in failure**: the ability of a system to return some form of result to the user even if a given search, strictly interpreted, would result in "zero hits."[36]

At the same time, Karen Coyle asserted her own set of tasks that must be supported by future bibliographic records or equivalents. Beyond the four basic FRBR user tasks—*find, identify, select,* and *obtain*—Coyle includes *description, discovery, location, purchase, presentation,* and *promotion.*[37] Although these sets seem dissimilar, Kroeger links them by noting that where Tennant describes *qualities,* Coyle describes *functions.* However, despite discussions such as these, which challenge both MARC's record structure and that of the organizations that maintain it, there has not been a clear sense of what sort of encoding standard would replace it, particularly in view of the immense, and still increasing, quantity of essential bibliographic metadata encoded in MARC.

The way forward began to appear in the early years of the 2010s, as technologies associated with the Semantic Web matured and began to be widely implemented outside of librarianship. These developments provided a focus for MARC critiques as well as actionable plans for alternative encodings outside MARC. The following paragraphs discuss MARC's limitations in the Semantic Web environment.

With the rise of the Semantic Web, it has appeared that the rich and authoritative metadata statements created by catalogers are confined by the very concept of a record. Traditional bibliographic or authority records on the traditional World Wide Web are, in effect, documents in themselves, and are treated as such via established approaches to web linking. It is, for example, common practice to point to the record for a resource provided by a library, by embedding the URL for the specific record in the library's local catalog or discovery tool. Although this frequently addresses specific information needs, the context of an entire record is required to provide meaning for the majority of the metadata elements contained in it. For example, the relationship of a subject heading to a specific work can only be indicated by virtue of being associated with an access point for the work included in the same record.

The Semantic Web goes beyond the original web's linkage between *documents* to linking individual *data statements* about resources. The term *resource* is understood broadly here, to include not only information resources of the kinds traditionally provided by libraries, but also any type of entity (e.g., persons, families, corporate bodies) or any unit of conceptual analysis (e.g. classification number, subject heading, thesaurus term). Statements about the same resource, coming from different points of origin on the web, are encoded to allow computers to recognize them as semantically equivalent—thus the concept of the *Semantic* Web. Such encoded statements, and their aggregations into databases, are described as *linked data*, discussed more thoroughly below. By contrast, statements encoded in MARC records cannot participate in the Semantic Web because, as noted, they are encased in records-as-documents. The intellectual effort, sometimes considerable, required to create these authoritative statements is lost to the Semantic Web. Additionally, the fact that MARC-encoded statements cannot be directly linked on the Semantic Web means that they must be reproduced in multiple instantiations (e.g., copies of the same authority record existing in multiple local systems), sometimes thousands of times.

In addition, for all its detail, MARC is insufficiently granular to consistently encode meaningful metadata elements. For example, in MARC bibliographic field 300 $b, different types of illustrations (e.g., portraits or maps) cannot be coded distinctly, nor can the number of units (e.g., 5) be coded independently from the type of unit (e.g. volumes) in a statement of extent in field 300 $a, at least at the time of this writing. The Semantic Web regards these as independently meaningful, perhaps requiring separate and linkable statements.

In 2011, LC announced the "Bibliographic Framework Transition Initiative" aiming toward replacing MARC with protocols described as "an environment rather than a 'format.'"[38] In November 2012, the Library released the report *Bibliographic Framework as a Web of Data: Linked Data Model and Supporting Services*.[39] This report outlines what has become known as BIBFRAME, a "linked data entity-relationship model based on the Resource Description Framework (RDF)" and encoded in Extensible Markup Language (XML).[40] (See chapter 21 of this textbook for a brief discussion of XML.) BIBFRAME is intended to make it possible for library-originated bibliographic, authority, and holdings metadata to be provided via linked data statements capable of being shared on the Semantic Web. Additionally, BIBFRAME promises a means for repurposing existing MARC-encoded metadata for use as linked data. A discussion of linked data in the next section is followed by an introduction to BIBFRAME concepts.

Library Linked Data

As discussed above, traditional cataloging, using MARC, results in statements that are not shareable as linked data, and therefore cannot participate in the Semantic Web. This and the following sections describe in more detail the limitations of traditional library data in this context, provide an outline of linked data principles, explain why linked data should also be *open*, and give examples of use cases for linked data's relevance to library operations.

In 2011, the World Wide Web Consortium (W3C) Library Linked Data Incubator Group (LLDIG) outlined five factors that prevent traditional library data from fully participating in the Semantic Web:

1. *Library data is not integrated with web resources.* The databases in which traditional library metadata resides are not well integrated, if at all, with other web data sources.

2. *Library standards are designed only for the library community.* While the MARC format is the best-known example, the general focus on library-specific needs has meant limited relevance to the needs of and metadata created by other communities.

3. *Library data is expressed primarily in natural-language text.* The encoding of most traditional library metadata as end user-readable text (instead of as identifiers) means redundant effort and excess expense for metadata management. It also impedes linking and sharing of metadata.

4. *The library community and Semantic Web community have different terminology for similar metadata concepts.* This points, not to limitations of the data itself, but to the need to reconcile vocabularies and, to some extent, the assumptions that underlie them.

5. *Library technology changes depend on vendor systems development.* The utility of traditional library metadata is vulnerable to the tight dependency of libraries on a shrinking number of vendors in a small industry. Reliance on the technology development plans of these vendors, even when influenced to some extent by customer input, impedes full participation in the Semantic Web.[41]

In order to restructure library-created metadata, and move from reliance on *records* describing resources toward linked data *statements* about resources, it is necessary to use language that computers can interpret and use for international interchange of statements about entities, attributes, and relationships. Currently, the methodology being promoted focuses on Resource Description Framework *triples* and the use of Uniform Resource Identifiers (URIs).

The Resource Description Framework (RDF) was developed by the W3C as a standard model for data interchange on the web.[42] It enables the creation of metadata statements that "uniquely [identify] as Web resources all entities (resources), attributes, and relationships between entities."[43] Erik T. Mitchell writes that RDF "provides a method for making these simple statements and connecting statements together so that a series of statements can be viewed as a complete descriptive record of a resource."[44] The word *resource* in the two previous quotations has different meanings, which must be distinguished from each other. In the first statement, "web resources" denotes anything that may be designated on the web, "including physical things, documents, abstract concepts, numbers and [character] strings."[45] This reiterates a point stated in the previous Semantic Web discussion. Mitchell, by contrast, uses "resource" to designate what is traditionally thought of as *information resources* made available by libraries, such as books, maps, videos, and so on. RDF, therefore, makes possible the creation of statements about resources of the first type. Functioning as linked data, RDF statements may be aggregated to describe and provide access to resources of the second type: aggregations we might recognize as, for example, bibliographic or authority records. However, RDF itself is not concerned with such record-like presentations.

RDF statements are called *triples*. A triple consists of three elements: a subject, a predicate, and an object. For example, in the sentence, "Eleanor Roosevelt was born in New York City," the subject is "Eleanor Roosevelt," the phrase "was born in" is the predicate, and "New York City" is the object. Martha Yee contends that a triple's structure is reminiscent of relationships found in FRBR, correlating the FRBR concept *entity* with RDF's *subject*, attribute with object, and relationship with predicate.[46]

In an ideally constructed RDF triple, each element of a statement is represented not by human-readable language strings (i.e., *literals*), such as "Eleanor Roosevelt," but by HTTP URIs, which may be drawn from multiple sources. Expressed as HTTP URIs, it is possible for each component of a statement to be referenced by other RDF statements published anywhere else on the web. In this way, multiple statements about a given resource may be linked and assembled into more complete information displays, as needed. The relationships among resources expressed as subjects, predicates, and objects may be "used for navigating between, or integrating, information from multiple sources."[47]

The free-text statement about Eleanor Roosevelt may be expressed as this triple:

<http://viaf.org/viaf/76325766> <http://rdaregistry.info/Elements/a/P50119> <http://viaf.org/viaf/266415900>.

The first and third components, taken from the Virtual International Authority File (VIAF), represent the name authorities for Eleanor Roosevelt and for New York City. The second component, from the Open Metadata Registry, is the entry for the RDA Agent Property *has place of birth*. Although it may be possible to substitute other URIs for each of the elements of this triple (for example, "http://id.loc.gov/authorities/names/n79144645" is the URI for the LC Linked Data Service record representing Eleanor Roosevelt), each URI is nevertheless a globally unique identifier with an unambiguous reference. URIs, therefore, perform a function analogous to the traditional authority control provided by unique text strings (or literals) within a given database. Literals, however, cannot serve as direct links on the web, as HTTP URIs can and do.

Linked data separates the meaning of data (i.e., its semantics) from particular data structures (i.e., its syntax or format).[48] In the case of the statement about Eleanor Roosevelt, the concepts represented by subject, predicate, and object could be, as literals, represented in normal, human-readable language.

However, the elements of the example RDF triple shown can be machine-read and shared without computer parsing of human-readable language. Additionally, these statements provide meaningful elements for resource description without being dependent on their relationships with other statements in traditional bibliographic or authority records.

Linked Open Data

Most current discussions of linked data and libraries go further than the basic principles and mechanics of linked data proper, and concentrate on *Linked Open Data* (LOD). It is possible, after all, to create the structured statements that comprise linked data, and nevertheless leave it confined to restricted spaces available only to select authorized users and applications. The Semantic Web can only be truly realized when data is available with minimal or no restrictions on re-use. LOD, in fact, has been described as "a very Web-developer-friendly path to the Semantic Web."[49]

The four basic principles of LOD were formulated by Tim Berners-Lee in 2006. They are presented in boldface type in the subsequent bullet points, along with brief explanations.[50]

- **Use URIs as names for things**: This means that URIs should be used to identify any entity (information, resource, data, metadata record, etc.) that is made accessible through the web.

- **Use HTTP URIs so that people can look up those names**: This means that an HTTP identifier (URI) is the simplest mechanism for finding things. People understand HTTP addresses, and so do machines.

- **When someone looks up a URI, provide useful information, using the standards**: This means the data should be accessible using the most common web formats. Interoperability is key. If the data is not easily decipherable because of technological differences, it is not useful.

- **Include links to other URIs, so that they can discover more things**: This means to make data (information, resources, metadata, etc.) open and accessible, to share freely, and to link to other resources as much as possible.

These principles lay the groundwork for sharing information about the location and identity of a range of digital resources potentially much more vast than even the universe of web pages. The commonly understood HTTP protocol is mandated, instead of more specialized identifier schemes. LOD providers are encouraged to "share the wealth" by pointing to links created elsewhere.[51] The outcome is linked data that is "sharable, extensible, and easily re-usable."[52] It allows for the rich description of resources by institutions and/or individuals working in collaboration. This is a very different model from that of the solo cataloger, typically creating descriptions very much like those already created elsewhere, with much redundancy. The work of cataloging in an LOD environment has the potential, as well, to reduce or resolve the problematic, perennial pressures for minimal-level cataloging. Such mandates arose, after all, in a professional environment characterized by this redundancy. In an LOD environment, catalogers shift focus from creating authoritative *records* to authoritative and trusted *statements* about resources. With those statements linked, so as to create rich, structured information displays on the fly, the entire nature of catalogers' workloads and workflows may undergo a significant, positive change.

The types of linked data resources of probable greatest interest to libraries have been characterized as *datasets*, *value vocabularies*, and *metadata element sets*.[53] The concept of *datasets* generally refers to what we think of as record sets, such as the set of OCLC WorldCat bibliographic records, the British National Biography, or the records comprising a library's local catalog. *Value vocabularies* include controlled vocabulary terms and classification entries. Examples include LCSH and VIAF, which have been published as linked data.[54] *Metadata element sets* "define classes or attributes used to describe entities of interest."[55] Examples include, among others, MARC 21 fields, RDA's elements of description, and the ISBD elements.

Library LOD: Use Cases

It helps to visualize the value of linked open data through *use cases*—scenarios for possible real-world applications. As can be seen below, the BIBFRAME team has produced a set of use cases illustrating concrete scenarios. Additionally, the W3C Library Linked Data Incubator Group outlined its own set, at a broader level of generality.[56] The W3C use cases of greatest relevance to this discussion are described as pertaining to the bibliographic data cluster, authority data cluster, and vocabulary alignment cluster.

The W3C Incubator Group states that a bibliographic record "can be understood as a set of data elements describing the content and characteristics of an information object produced for human consumption."[57] The report outlines the following LOD bibliographic cluster use cases:

- Semantic standardization of bibliographic elements
- Deduplication and unification of records
- Tagging web resources with standardized bibliographic terms
- Integrated metadata search interfaces across several providers
- Bibliographic records annotation
- Information aggregation, which includes three scenarios:
  - Refine and expand search results
  - Identify recently-published bibliographic resources
  - Obtain access to online full-text versions of resources

One of the applications in the bibliographic data cluster with direct application to BIBFRAME is the potential for migrating library legacy data, including the conversion of MARC-encoded metadata, to RDF triples.[58]

The authority data cluster includes the following generalized use cases:

- Metadata enhancement by users uploading documents
- Extended search results based on authority data
- Authority data aggregation[59]

Here the use of LOD suggests many possibilities for authority data enrichment, including "the re-use of external data sets [relevant to an authority-controlled entity] by linking instead of copying and merging."[60] For example, library-created authority data may link out to data created by biographers or genealogists. VIAF already links its aggregated authority records to DBPedia, "a Linked Data extraction of Wikipedia."[61] In so doing, it provides direct access from one of the primary hubs of the Semantic Web to the authoritative metadata created by national libraries from around the world.

The vocabulary alignment cluster provides scenarios for the following:

- Vocabulary-based, multilingual, cross-domain enrichment and discovery
- Vocabulary enhancement and re-use
- Publication, discovery, and maintenance of tools or services of vocabulary alignment[62]

The W3C report gives a particularly vivid example of the value of LOD in this area: Civil War Data 150, which is a project "to share and connect American Civil War related data across local, state and federal institutions."[63] This project involves, in part, aligning multiple different source vocabularies so as to perform multiple-source searches for information about specific places, battles, officers, regiments, and so on.

Bibliographic Framework Initiative (BIBFRAME)

To date, the BIBFRAME initiative is the most ambitious attempt to replace MARC as the primary encoding standard for library-generated metadata. At the same time, it intends to retain the enormous investment made by librarians, since the card catalog era and even before, in the creation of metadata that is authoritative and reliable. As the November 2012 LC report, *Bibliographic Framework as a Web of Data*, puts it, "Libraries generate, maintain and curate an enormous amount of high-quality data . . . that is valuable well beyond traditional library boundaries . . . . In modeling the MARC 21 format as a Web of Data it is important to deconstruct and then reconstruct the informational assets that comprise MARC."[64] Beyond retaining the metadata itself, BIBFRAME is also designed to continue the basic MARC functions of "representation and communication of bibliographic and related information in machine-readable form."[65] Unlike previous calls for the replacement or "death" of MARC, BIBFRAME does not consign the billions of existing MARC records—in their many variant forms—to a sealed-off zone of legacy records, but moves their value forward into the Semantic Web. It is this difference that provides BIBFRAME's signal distinction, beyond its structural design.

The BIBFRAME initiative aims to achieve its objectives by (1) distinguishing conceptual content from physical manifestations, (2) unambiguously identifying information entities, and (3) creating well-defined and usable relationships between and among entities.[66] The model attempts to balance many factors, including the following:

- Flexibility to accommodate future cataloguing domains, and entirely new use scenarios and sources of information

- The web as an architectural model for expressing and connecting decentralized information

- Social and technical adoption outside the library community

- Social and technical deployment within the library community

- Previous efforts in expressing bibliographic material as Linked Data

- Application of machine technology for mechanical tasks while amply accommodating the subject matter expert (the librarian) as the explicit brain behind the mechanics

- Previous efforts for modeling bibliographic information in the library, publishing, archival, and museum communities

- The robust and beneficial history and aspects of a common method of bibliographic information transfer[67]

The model is built on four main classes: *Creative Work, Instance, Authority,* and *Annotation.* The first two classes may be correlated with FRBR's Group 1 entities (i.e., work, expression, manifestation, and item) but are not exactly analogous. *Creative Work* is defined as "a resource reflecting a conceptual essence of the cataloging resource."[68] The correlations between FRBR Group 1 entities and the first two BIBFRAME classes are generally asserted, but not necessarily absolute. This may not turn out to be a matter of real concern, however. Karen Coyle points out that the "criticism of BIBFRAME for presenting a two-entity bibliographic model instead of the four entities of FRBR" is based on "the mistaken idea that each Group 1 entity must be a record in whatever future bibliographic formats are developed. As entities in a conceptual model there is absolutely no direct transfer from conceptual entities to data records."[69] In this light, concern about categorical congruence between the two models is misplaced. What is important is an understanding of the models and their conceptual underpinnings, including their areas of overlap and divergence. It is clear, in any case, that BIBFRAME is closely informed by FRBR. A simple diagram is available demonstrating the connection between the first two BIBFRAME classes and describing the relationships between them and the *Authority* and *Annotation* classes.[70]

It is clear from the BIBFRAME documentation that *Creative Work* encompasses FRBR's work and expression entities. For example, the "BIBFRAME Relationships" document provides an example of a work-to-work relationship between the English text of Mark Twain's *The Adventures of Tom Sawyer* and a Hebrew translation.[71] A figure in the "BIBFRAME Profiles" document explicitly correlates the first two Group 1 entities with Creative Work, and the second two with Instance.[72] Other such assertions are found throughout the documentation, although there are some points of ambiguity. One of the BIBFRAME Annotation Model use cases, describing a researcher's discovery of a BIBFRAME Creative Work states, "The Work has valuable information about the book."[73] In FRBR, the term *book* would refer to a manifestation or item: the FRBR work and expression would likely not include any particularly valuable information about a book. The "Annotation Model" document also states, "The Work, Instance, and Authority are surrogates for the book, publication, and author."[74] BIBFRAME and FRBR demonstrate different concepts of work with the BIBFRAME class encompassing, but going beyond, the two most abstract FRBR entities. There is a multitude of properties associated with Creative Work, including those that might typically be associated with work in the FRBR sense (e.g., title) as well as expression (e.g., translationOf), and many that indicate relationships (e.g., accompanies, containedIn).

Instance is defined as "a resource reflecting an individual, material embodiment of the BIBFRAME Work that can be physical or digital in nature."[75] It is analogous to FRBR's manifestation and item, allowing for the fact that, except for manifestations existing as singletons with only one item, a manifestation is itself somewhat intangible. It is rare for anyone to be in the presence of the complete set of items produced in a physical manifestation, and essentially impossible to be in the presence of a complete set of digital items. Although Carol Jean Godby states that the "BIBFRAME Instance encompasses FRBR Manifestation and Item,"[76] she is also concerned that this BIBFRAME class is "too broad because of the many needs to distinguish between Manifestations and Items in a machine-processable description."[77] By contrast, Mitchell states that Instance "can roughly be described as a conflation between Expression and Manifestation,"[78] perhaps because, as he notes, the properties associated with Instance include some of those shared with Creative Work (for example, alternative title) and some that are closer to the FRBR manifestation (such as publication date). The "BIBFRAME Use Cases and Requirements" document includes examples of catalogers searching for an Instance either "with a specific ISBN" or to find a specific electronic publication—both examples of Instance related to FRBR's manifestation.

The BIBFRAME *Authority* concept must be distinguished from that of traditional authority records. As noted in the LC report, *Bibliographic Framework as a Web of Data*, BIBFRAME Authorities "provide a common abstraction layer over various different Web based authority records."[79] Mitchell comments, "Authority classes are roughly aligned with existing roles of authorities," but in keeping with basic principles of linked data, "authority entities should be unambiguously referenced using URIs rather than literal values."[80] Entities are defined in external vocabularies or ontologies only; the BIBFRAME Authority concept is not in itself an authority file such as the LC Name Authority File.

To understand the idea of an *abstraction layer*—a central concept in BIBFRAME Authorities—it is important to keep in mind that a BIBFRAME Authority is not intended as a replacement for library authority records.[81] It functions rather as a bridge between Work or Instance metadata and library authority records, or analogous metadata from other sources. To emphasize this distinction, the phrase *BIBFRAME Authority* is specifically distinguished from the single word, *authority*.[82] A BIBFRAME Authority may aggregate numerous links to authority-data statements, such as traditional authority records or records in VIAF. It "can easily enable implementers to augment entities for People, Organizations, Places, and Topics with information from other sources while still providing a means to offer implementers a way to leverage and make use of traditional, controlled library authority data."[83] A BIBFRAME Authority is therefore able to link in multiple directions: to a resource statement and to multiple library-type authority records.

The final BIBFRAME class is *Annotation*: an assertion or statement about a resource. The many types of information included in notes found in bibliographic records—from common statements referring to bibliographies and indexes to more specialized statements such as those about provenance—provide an immediate way to understand Annotations in the context of traditional cataloging. Annotations go beyond these familiar types of information, however. Additionally, they may register opinions about a resource, often in the form of reviews; record holdings or other information specific to an institution; or enhance the resource description through additions such as cover art.[84] The second category, institution-specific information, allows for recording of lifecycle metadata particular to a library's own specific copies or instances of resources, as well as discovery by users of copies available locally. The lifecycle of a BIBFRAME record itself may be noted via Annotations.[85] The summary descriptions included in the third category go beyond the cataloger's traditional summary notes to include content description available anywhere on the web. The potential of Annotations to aggregate widely distributed knowledge about Creative Works, and even Instances, gives rise to the statement that they are "key to creating a system driven by the knowledge capacity of libraries rather than the commercial interests that presently dominate the Web."[86]

Mitchell emphasizes that "outside of the rules governing the definition of these four main classes and the properties that connect them, the model does not have built-in content rules but rather defers to external standards and guidelines."[87] That is, BIBFRAME has nothing to do with the specific content of any of its statements or aggregated information displays. Instead, these are entirely determined by other metadata standards, from RDA and AACR2 to any of the hundreds of controlled vocabularies, and beyond to guidelines developed outside the library community.

As seen, the BIBFRAME model focuses on shareable statements about information resources and the entities responsible for them. This is a significant shift from the self-contained, conceptually complete record, the focus of cataloging since its earliest eras. It allows, however, for "cooperative cataloging at a far more granular level than before."[88] The cataloger's work does not disappear, but is focused on determining and recording authoritative statements. In concert with this, the installed base of existing MARC 21 records may be deconstructed into metadata elements, to be reassembled as needed; tools for making this translation are being developed. Although the work of description necessarily continues, the emphasis of a cataloger's work may move away from the aggregation of descriptive details required of an integral record, to specifying and linking relationships among statements about resources.[89] With the web itself serving as the architecture for BIBFRAME, updates to these statements may be automatically provided, or pushed, to systems that make use of the model.[90] This would be a welcome contrast to the long-time requirement to update statements, such as changes in the form of personal names or subject headings, either manually or in a semi-automated local process.

What might be some potential real-world applications of a transition from MARC 21 encoding to the BIBFRAME model? The document "BIBFRAME Use Cases and Requirements" gives several examples relevant for both external audiences (e.g., end users) and internal audiences (e.g., librarians and systems designers).[91] For end-users, these include the following:

- Finding a copy of a book in a nearby library (beyond searching in a consortium catalog), or "identify holdings of Instance" (section 3.1);
- Finding electronic books, with results pre-filtered to the type of electronic device used to search: "discover Instances by type" (3.2);
- Broadening a search to include adaptations: "discover Adaptations of a Work" (3.3);
- Searching for works by an author (again, beyond a local catalog or discovery tool): "BIBFRAME Authorities" (3.4).

For librarians, the many possibilities described include the following:

- Efficiently cataloging a new translation of an existing Work, by auto-populating the new Work statement with metadata from that of the existing Work statement (3.7). In this scenario, creation of the new Work information display also brings about a "Web trigger," an automated communication informing the creator of the original Work statement that the new statement has been created;
- Adding a local subject heading which, although not established in LCSH, has a relationship to an existing established term. In the process, the editors of LCSH are advised that the local heading is available for official consideration. This may happen via a *linkback*, a term designating one of several means by which web authors are informed when others link to one of their pages (3.0);
- Updating name authority records being pushed through the catalogs or discovery tools of multi-library systems (3.11);
- Establishing multilingual cataloging interfaces (3.15).

Figure 22.5 shows a set of BIBFRAME statements for the Creative Work, Bechdel's *Fun Home*. This set was generated from the "MARC to BIBFRAME Comparison Service" available on the BIBFRAME initiative's technical site, using the LC control number MARC bibliographic field 001 as the starting point.[92] The figure should be considered a snapshot of BIBFRAME thinking as of the time of this writing in 2015, rather than a definitive representation.

Comparison of Figure 22.5 with the previous figures in this chapter and the MARC 21 record shown in Figure 21.6 (p. 843) helps with understanding BIBFRAME's approach to creating and linking metadata statements. A couple of examples will be examined here. Metadata for Alison Bechdel, the creator of *Fun Home*, is presented in the block for the Creative Work property, *creator*. This block presents Bechdel's authorized access point (AAP) with both the MADS authority record and biographical information available on the LC site. In MARC 21, the latter is coded in the 856 field; in MODS, as previously shown, it is tagged as a relatedItem. In this way, the BIBFRAME *bf:creator* block aggregates types of metadata that have not been traditionally associated at this basic structural level. This block also gives the display form, or *label*, of the AAP for Bechdel. (Note also that the biographical information is presented as an Annotation of the *creator* property.)

The lengthy *hasInstance* block includes metadata statements easily recognizable as describing different elements of a FRBR manifestation including, for example, dimensions, extent, ISBNs, dissemination metadata, and statement of responsibility. Note that, while most of these values are presented as literals

```
@prefix bf: <http://bibframe.org/vocab/> .
@prefix madsrdf: <http://www.loc.gov/mads/rdf/v1#> .
@prefix rdf: <http://www.w3.org/1999/02/22-rdf-syntax-ns#> .
@prefix rdfs: <http://www.w3.org/2000/01/rdf-schema#> .
@prefix relators: <http://id.loc.gov/vocabulary/relators/> .
@prefix xml: <http://www.w3.org/XML/1998/namespace> .
@prefix xsd: <http://www.w3.org/2001/XMLSchema#> .

<http://id.loc.gov/resources/bibs/14144904> a bf:Text,
        bf:Work ;
    bf:authorizedAccessPoint "Bechdel, Alison, 1960- Fun home :a family tragicomic",
        "bechdelalison1960funhomeafamilytragicomicengworktext"@x-bf-hash ;
    bf:classification [ a bf:Classification ;
        bf:classificationEdition "22", "full" ;
        bf:classificationNumber "741.5/973" ;
        bf:classificationScheme "ddc" ;
        bf:label "741.5/973" ] ;
    bf:classificationLcc <http://id.loc.gov/authorities/classification/PN6727.B3757> ;
    bf:creator [ a bf:Person ;
        bf:authorizedAccessPoint "Bechdel, Alison, 1960-" ;
        bf:hasAnnotation [ a bf:Annotation ;
            bf:annotationBody <http://www.loc.gov/catdir/enhancements/fy0736/2005030304-b.html> ;
            bf:label "Contributor biographical information" ] ;
        bf:hasAuthority [ a madsrdf:Authority ;
            madsrdf:authoritativeLabel "Bechdel, Alison, 1960-" ] ;
        bf:label "Bechdel, Alison, 1960-" ] ;
    bf:derivedFrom <http://id.loc.gov/resources/bibs/14144904.marcxml.xml> ;
    bf:hasAnnotation [ a bf:Annotation ;
        bf:annotates <http://id.loc.gov/resources/bibs/14144904> ;
        bf:changeDate "2008-01-16T08:30" ;
        bf:derivedFrom <http://id.loc.gov/resources/bibs/14144904.marcxml.xml> ;
        bf:descriptionConventions <http://id.loc.gov/vocabulary/descriptionConventions/aacr2> ;
        bf:descriptionModifier <http://id.loc.gov/vocabulary/organizations/dlc> ;
        bf:descriptionSource <http://id.loc.gov/vocabulary/organizations/dlc> ;
        bf:generationProcess "DLC transform-tool:2014-10-31-T17:00:00" ],
        [ a bf:Summary ;
        bf:annotates <http://id.loc.gov/resources/bibs/14144904> ;
        bf:label "Publisher description" ;
        bf:review <http://www.loc.gov/catdir/enhancements/fy0623/2005030304-d.html> ] ;
    bf:hasInstance [ a bf:Instance,
            bf:Monograph ;
        bf:derivedFrom <http://id.loc.gov/resources/bibs/14144904.marcxml.xml> ;
        bf:dimensions "24 cm." ;
        bf:extent "232 p. :" ;
        bf:heldItem [ a bf:HeldItem ;
            bf:label "PN6727.B3757 Z46 2006" ;
```

```
        bf:shelfMarkLcc "PN6727.B3757 Z46 2006" ] ;
    bf:illustrationNote "chiefly ill. ;" ;
    bf:instanceOf <http://id.loc.gov/resources/bibs/14144904> ;
    bf:instanceTitle [ a bf:Title ;
        bf:subtitle "a family tragicomic " ;
        bf:titleValue "Fun home :" ] ;
    bf:isbn10 <http://isbn.example.org/0618477942> ;
    bf:isbn13 <http://isbn.example.org/9780618477944> ;
    bf:lccn [ a bf:Identifier ;
        bf:identifierScheme "lccn" ;
        bf:identifierValue "2005030304" ] ;
    bf:modeOfIssuance "single unit" ;
    bf:providerStatement "Boston : Houghton Mifflin, c2006." ;
    bf:publication [ a bf:Provider ;
        bf:copyrightDate "c2006." ;
        bf:providerName [ a bf:Organization ;
            bf:label "Houghton Mifflin" ] ;
        bf:providerPlace [ a bf:Place ;
            bf:label "Boston " ] ] ;
    bf:responsibilityStatement "Alison Bechdel." ;
    bf:titleStatement "Fun home : a family tragicomic" ] ;
bf:language <http://id.loc.gov/vocabulary/languages/eng> ;
bf:subject [ a bf:Person ;
    bf:authorizedAccessPoint "Bechdel, Alison, 1960---Comic books, strips, etc." ;
    bf:hasAuthority [ a madsrdf:Authority,
            madsrdf:ComplexSubject ;
        madsrdf:authoritativeLabel "Bechdel, Alison, 1960---Comic books, strips, etc." ;
        madsrdf:isMemberOfMADSScheme <http://id.loc.gov/authorities/subjects> ] ;
    bf:label "Bechdel, Alison, 1960---Comic books, strips, etc." ],
  [ a bf:Topic ;
    bf:authorizedAccessPoint "Graphic novels" ;
    bf:hasAuthority [ a madsrdf:Authority,
            madsrdf:GenreForm ;
        mads rdf:authoritativeLabel "Graphic novels" ;
        madsrdf:isMemberOfMADSScheme <http://id.loc.gov/authorities/subjects> ] ;
    bf:label "Graphic novels" ],
  [ a bf:Topic ;
    bf:authorizedAccessPoint "Cartoonists--United States--Comic books, strips, etc" ;
    bf:hasAuthority [ a madsrdf:Authority,
            madsrdf:ComplexSubject ;
        madsrdf:authoritativeLabel "Cartoonists--United States--Comic books, strips, etc" ;
        madsrdf:isMemberOfMADSScheme <http://id.loc.gov/authorities/subjects> ] ;
    bf:label "Cartoonists--United States--Comic books, strips, etc" ] ;
bf:workTitle [ a bf:Title ;
    bf:subtitle "a family tragicomic " ;
    bf:titleValue "Fun home :" ] .
```

FIGURE 22.5 BIBFRAME Statements for Bechdel's *Fun Home.*

(e.g., "c2006."), some are presented as HTTP URIs (although "example.org" is a fictitious domain name). The one sub-property in this block that might be taken as related to a FRBR item is *heldItem*, which essentially presents a call number. Although most institutions using Library of Congress Classification would be likely to share this call number, strictly speaking it refers to one that used for the copy in LC's own collection.

As of this writing, BIBFRAME is not operational, but is in active development. The reader should keep in mind that every BIBFRAME document cited in this chapter is subject to revision or cancellation, and the reader should consult the BIBFRAME website for the most current information. LC plans to initiate a pilot program to create cataloging data using BIBFRAME.[93] Regardless of whether BIBFRAME is widely implemented as currently envisioned, or perhaps in a significantly different form, it is safe to say that a viable replacement for MARC 21 is now possible, based on the principles of linked open data. As LC's *Bibliographic Framework as a Web of Data* report states, building on the pioneering LOD efforts of the past decade, "the BIBFRAME model is the library community's formal entry point for becoming part of a much larger web of data."[94] Therefore, the advantages for both the library community and the Semantic Web of library participation in LOD may be realized on a larger scale: "enhancing the Web through the addition of structured data" and contributing "trusted metadata for resources of long-term cultural importance."[95] The long-established strengths of library cataloging practice and the professional knowledge of catalogers are thus poised to become visible, and of value, in a much broader area.

CONCLUSION

"Linked data is here to stay," asserts an Indiana University group studying the future of non-MARC authority data. "The corporate world, search engines, social networking sites, international governments, *and libraries abroad* have already embraced and implemented linked data. Linked data isn't a pie in the sky; it's a viable means of conducting business."[96] Indeed, as of 2015, at least one library—the Oslo (Norway) Public Library—will use RDF as the primary cataloging format, abandoning not only the MARC record for new metadata creation, but the traditional ILS based on it.[97]

For librarians who have spent years, even decades, creating catalog records encoded in the MARC format, with the *Anglo-American Cataloguing Rules* as the content standard, it may very well seem as though library cataloging has irrevocably changed. Even more seriously, it may appear as though the fruits of their expertise and dedication are now obsolete. Fortunately, such conclusions are imprecise. To begin with, the likelihood is now great that, as MARC is gradually decommissioned, the greatest value of the work of traditional cataloging—the intellectual effort involved in formulating authoritative access points, expert descriptions, and multiple approaches to indexing and classification—will not only be preserved in the Semantic Web environment but given broader exposure than ever before. More fundamentally, the core professional competencies involved in the work of cataloging, as it has evolved over the centuries, will be carried forward and will find a new, but not completely alien, home.

As Asgeir Rekkavik puts it in his discussion of the plans for the Oslo Public Library, "It is a bit depressing that library cataloguing in 2014 still is pretty much about typing, and that much of the main focus in cataloguing is on strings, names and words. Cataloguing should be about linking resources, not typing; and the identity of the things we describe should be determined by unique identifiers, rather than by the strings that label them."[98] Regardless of whether BIBFRAME succeeds as intended, or another initiative takes its place, the cataloging profession is on the verge of simultaneously reducing the creation of redundant character strings and heightening participation in the broader world of information organization.

NOTES

1. Lois Mai Chan, *Cataloging and Classification: An Introduction*, 3rd ed. (Lanham, Md.: The Scarecrow Press, 2007), 117.
2. Dublin Core Metadata Initiative (DCMI), "Dublin Core Metadata Element Set, Version 1.1," accessed January 3, 2015, http://dublincore.org/documents/dces/.
3. DCMI, "DCMI Metadata Terms," accessed July 2, 2014, http://dublincore.org/documents/dcmi-terms/.
4. DCMI, "DCMI Abstract Model," section 2.1, accessed January 5, 2015, http://dublincore.org/documents/abstract-model/.
5. For more in-depth discussion, see "DCMI Abstract Model," accessed January 5, 2015, http://dublincore.org/documents/abstract-model/.
6. DCMI, "Dublin Core Metadata Element Set, Version 1.1."
7. DCMI, "DCMI Abstract Model," section 2.2.
8. Ibid.
9. DCMI, "DCMI Specifications," accessed July 2, 2014, http://dublincore.org/specifications/.
10. For a brief introduction to RDF, see chap. 4 in Arlene G. Taylor and Daniel N. Joudrey, *The Organization of Information*, 3rd ed. (Westport, Conn.: Libraries Unlimited, 2009).
11. DCMI, "DCMI Metadata Terms: Section 2: Properties in the /terms/ namespace," accessed July 2, 2014, http://dublincore.org/documents/2012/06/14/dcmi-terms/?v=terms#H2.
12. DCMI, "User Guide-DCMI_MediaWiki: Dublin Core Terms," accessed July 2, 2014, http://wiki.dublincore.org/index.php/User_Guide#Dublin_Core_Terms.
13. DCMI, "DCMI Metadata Terms: Section 6: Classes," accessed November 6, 2014, http://dublincore.org/documents/dcmi-terms/#H6.
14. Ibid.
15. DCMI, "DCMI Metadata Terms: Section 5: Syntax Encoding Schemes," accessed July 2, 2014, http://dublincore.org/documents/2012/06/14/dcmi-terms/?v=elements#H5.
16. DCMI, "DCMI Metadata Terms: Section 4: Vocabulary Encoding Schemes," accessed July 2, 2014, http://dublincore.org/documents/2012/06/14/dcmi-terms/?v=elements#H4.
17. DCMI, "Guidelines for Dublin Core Application Profiles," accessed November 30, 2014, http://dublincore.org/documents/profile-guidelines/.
18. RDA, 0.2: Relationship to Other Standards for Resource Description and Access.
19. "RDA Application Profiles," accessed November 30, 2014, http://www.rdaregistry.info/Profiles/.
20. DCMI, "Guidelines for Dublin Core Application Profiles."
21. "RDA to DC (Test)," accessed November 30, 2014, http://access.rdatoolkit.org/mpa25.html.
22. Melanie Wacker, Myung-Ja Han, and Judith Dartt, "Testing *Resource Description and Access* (RDA) with Non-MARC Metadata Standards," *Cataloging & Classification Quarterly* 49, nos. 7-8 (2011): 655-675.
23. Ibid., 670.

24. RDA, 17.4.1: Scope.
25. Nick Steffel, "The Advanced Dublin Core Generator," accessed December 2, 2014, http://www.dublincoregenerator.com/generator.html.
26. DCMI, "DCMI Work Structure," accessed July 2, 2014, http://dublincore.org/groups/.
27. DCMI, "DCMI Architecture Forum," accessed July 2, 2014, http://dublincore.org/groups/architecture/.
28. Library of Congress, "MODS User Guidelines Version 3," accessed December 19, 2014, http://www.loc.gov/standards/mods/v3/mods-userguide-elements.html.
29. Library of Congress, "MARC 21 to MODS 3.5 Mapping," accessed November 22, 2014, http://www.loc.gov/standards/mods/mods-mapping.html#title.
30. Library of Congress, "MADS: Metadata Authority Description Schema," accessed November 25, 2014, http://www.loc.gov/standards/mads/.
31. Ibid.
32. Library of Congress, "MODS: Metadata Object Description Schema," accessed July 2, 2014, http://www.loc.gov/standards/mods/.
33. Roy Tennant, "MARC Must Die," *Library Journal* 127, no. 17 (2002): 26-27.
34. Angela Kroeger, "The Road to BIBFRAME: The Evolution of the Idea of Bibliographic Transition into a Post-MARC Future," *Cataloging & Classification Quarterly* 51, no. 8 (2013): 873-890.
35. Roy Tennant, "A Bibliographic Metadata Infrastructure for the 21st Century," *Library Hi Tech* 22, no. 2 (2004): 176.
36. Ibid., 176-177.
37. Karen Coyle, "Future Considerations: The Functional Library Systems," *Library Hi Tech* 22, no. 2 (2004): 170-171 (cited in Kroeger, "The Road to BIBFRAME," 875).
38. Library of Congress, "A Bibliographic Framework for the Digital Age," accessed July 2, 2014, http://www.loc.gov/bibframe/news/framework-103111.html.
39. Library of Congress, "Bibliographic Framework as a Web of Data: Linked Data Model and Supporting Services," accessed July 2, 2014, http://www.loc.gov/bibframe/pdf/marcld-report-11-21-2012.pdf.
40. Kroeger, "The Road to BIBFRAME," 873.
41. W3C Incubator Group, "Library Linked Data Incubator Group Final Report," section 3.1, accessed July 2, 2014, http://www.w3.org/2005/Incubator/lld/XGR-lld-20111025/.
42. W3C, "Resource Description Framework (RDF)," accessed November 5, 2014, http://www.w3.org/RDF/.
43. Library of Congress, "Bibliographic Framework as a Web of Data," 9.
44. Erik T. Mitchell, *Library Linked Data: Research and Adoption* (Chicago: American Library Association, 2013), 13.
45. W3C, "RDF 1.1 Concepts and Abstract Syntax," section 1.2, accessed December 28, 2014, http://www.w3.org/TR/rdf11-concepts/.
46. Martha M. Yee, "Can Bibliographic Data be Put Directly onto the Semantic Web?" *Information Technology and Libraries* 28, no. 2 (2009): 64.
47. W3C, "Library Linked Data Incubator Group Final Report," section 1.
48. Ibid., section 2.3.
49. Library of Congress, "Bibliographic Framework as a Web of Data," 26.
50. Tim Berners-Lee, "Linked Data," accessed January 7, 2015, http://www.w3.org/DesignIssues/LinkedData.html.
51. Library of Congress, "Bibliographic Framework as a Web of Data," 25.
52. W3C, "Library Linked Data Incubator Group Final Report," section 2.
53. Ibid., appendix A.

54. Library of Congress, "LC Linked Data Service: Authorities and Vocabularies," accessed July 3, 2014, http://id.loc.gov/; "VIAF: Virtual International Authority File," accessed July 3, 2014, http://viaf.org/; "Dewey Decimal Classification / Linked Data," accessed July 3, 2014, http://dewey.info/.

55. W3C Incubator Group, "Library Linked Data Incubator Group: Datasets, Value Vocabularies, and Metadata Element Sets," section 1, accessed July 2, 2014, http://www.w3.org/2005/Incubator/lld/XGR-lld-vocabdataset-20111025/.

56. W3C Incubator Group, "Library Linked Data Incubator Group: Use Cases," accessed July 2, 2014, http://www.w3.org/2005/Incubator/lld/XGR-lld -usecase-20111025/.

57. Ibid., section 4.1.

58. Ibid., section 5.1.7.

59. Ibid., section 4.2.1.

60. Ibid., section 5.2.2.

61. W3C, "Library Linked Data Incubator Group Final Report," appendix C.

62. W3C, "Library Linked Data Incubator Group: Use Cases," section 4.3.1.

63. Ibid., section 5.3.3.

64. Library of Congress, "Bibliographic Framework as a Web of Data," 7.

65. Kevin M. Ford, "LC's Bibliographic Framework Initiative and the Attractiveness of Linked Data," *Information Standards Quarterly*, 24 no. 2/3 (2012): 47.

66. Library of Congress, "Bibliographic Framework as a Web of Data," 3.

67. Ibid., 8.

68. Library of Congress, "Overview of the BIBFRAME Model," accessed July 3, 2014, http://www.loc.gov/bibframe/docs/model.html.

69. Karen Coyle, "FRBR as a conceptual model," accessed July 3, 2014, http:// kcoyle.blogspot.com/2014/02/frbr-as-conceptual-model.html.

70. "The BIBFRAME Model," accessed June 7, 2015, http://bibframe.org/vocab -model/.

71. Library of Congress, "BIBFRAME Relationships: Draft Specification (25 April 2014)," accessed July 6, 2014, http://www.loc.gov/bibframe/docs/bibframe -relationships.html.

72. Library of Congress, "BIBFRAME Profiles: Introduction and Specification (Draft-5 May 2014)," section 6.2, accessed July 6, 2014, http://www.loc.gov/ bibframe/docs/bibframe-profiles.html.

73. Library of Congress, "BIBFRAME Annotation Model," section 1.2, accessed July 3, 2014, http://bibframe.org/documentation/annotations/.

74. Ibid., section 2.

75. "BIBFRAME Vocabulary: Terminology and Conventions," accessed July 6, 2014, http://www.loc.gov/bibframe/docs/vocab-conventions.html.

76. Carol Jean Godby, "The Relationship Between BIBFRAME and OCLC's Linked-Data Model of Bibliographic Description," 23, accessed November 18, 2014, http://oclc.org/content/dam/research/publications/library/2013/2013-05 .pdf.

77. Ibid., 25.

78. Mitchell, *Library Linked Data: Research and Adoption*, 27.

79. Library of Congress, "Bibliographic Framework as a Web of Data," 10.

80. Mitchell, *Library Linked Data: Research and Adoption*, 28.

81. Library of Congress, "On BIBFRAME Authority," accessed July 3, 2014, http://bibframe.org/documentation/bibframe-authority/.

82. Library of Congress, "BIBFRAME Authorities: Draft Specification (28 April 2014)," section 1, accessed July 6, 2014, http://www.loc.gov/bibframe/docs/ bibframe-authorities.html.

83. Library of Congress, "On BIBFRAME Authority," section 2.3.
84. Library of Congress, "BIBFRAME Annotation Model," section 2.
85. Library of Congress, "Bibliographic Framework as a Web of Data," 14.
86. Ibid., 15.
87. Mitchell, *Library Linked Data: Research and Adoption*, 27.
88. Library of Congress, "Overview of the BIBFRAME Model."
89. Library of Congress, "Bibliographic Framework as a Web of Data," 4.
90. Library of Congress, "Overview of the BIBFRAME Model."
91. Library of Congress, "BIBFRAME Use Cases and Requirements," accessed July 3, 2014, http://bibframe.org/documentation/bibframe-usecases/.
92. Library of Congress, "MARC to BIBFRAME Comparison Service," accessed December 4, 2014, http://bibframe.org/tools/compare/.
93. "Library of Congress, PCC and the BIBFRAME Model," accessed July 3, 2014, http://www.loc.gov/aba/pcc/documents/bibframe-pcc.html.
94. Library of Congress, "Bibliographic Framework as a Web of Data," 4.
95. W3C, "Library Linked Data Incubator Group Final Report," section 2.
96. Indiana University PCC Non-MARC Authorities Interest Group, "Brief on the Future of Non-MARC Authority," accessed December 31, 2014, https://scholarworks.iu.edu/dspace/handle/2022/18401 (emphasis in original).
97. Asgeir Rekkavik, "RDF linked data as new cataloguing format at Oslo Public Library," *SCATNews* 41 (2014): 13-16, http://www.ifla.org/files/assets/cataloguing/scatn/scat-news-41.pdf.
98. Ibid., 15.

SUGGESTED READING

Antoniou, Grogoris. *A Semantic Web Primer*. 3rd ed. Cambridge, Mass.: MIT Press, 2012.

"Bibliographic Framework as a Web of Data: Linked Data Model and Supporting Services." Accessed July 2, 2014. http://www.loc.gov/bibframe/pdf/marcld-report-11-21-2012.pdf.

Coyle, Karen. *Linked Data Tools: Connecting on the Web*. Chicago: ALA TechSource, 2012.

Coyle, Karen. *Understanding the Semantic Web: Bibliographic Data and Metadata*. Chicago: ALA TechSource, 2010.

The Dublin Core Metadata Element Set: An American National Standard. Bethesda, Md.: NISO Press, 2007.

Lubas, Rebecca L., Amy S. Jackson, and Ingrid Schneider. *The Metadata Manual: A Practical Workbook*. Oxford: Chandos Publishing, 2013. See especially chap. 3, "Using Dublin Core."

Miller, Steven J. *Metadata for Digital Collections: A How-to-Do-It Manual*. New York: Neal-Schuman Publishers, 2011. See especially chap. 2, "Introduction to Resource Description and Dublin Core"; chap. 3, "Resource Identification and Responsibility Elements"; chap. 4, "Resource Content and Relationship Elements"; and chap. 7, "MODS: The Metadata Object Description Schema."

Mitchell, Erik T. *Library Linked Data: Research and Adoption*. Chicago: American Library Association, 2013.

Van Hooland, Seth, and Ruben Verborgh. *Linked Data for Libraries, Archives and Museums: How to Clean, Link and Publish Your Metadata*. Chicago: Neal-Schuman, 2014.

Chapter 23

International Standard Bibliographic Description (ISBD)

INTRODUCTION

In this chapter, *International Standard Bibliographic Description* (ISBD) is discussed in some detail. Around the world, ISBD has long been known as an internationally agreed upon cataloging standard. It has been used as a format for the creation and sharing of bibliographic data. This chapter discusses ISBD as an intact global cataloging standard that may be used to describe resources of any type. In countries without a national content standard, ISBD provides order out of what could be chaos. In countries where RDA has been implemented, however, the role and importance of ISBD has been somewhat diminished because RDA has not adopted most of the substantial features of ISBD. Largely, ISBD has been relegated in RDA to a system of punctuation with which online catalogs display their data. In recent years, there has been a great deal of discussion over social media about how unnecessary ISBD has become, with participants in these discussions denigrating its role in bibliographic metadata. In 2014, Roy Tennant stated:

> If I ran into ISBD in a dark alley I would take it out with my pocket knife and do us all a big favor. Using punctuation to make a statement is so last century . . . . ISBD was made for catalog cards and it's long past time for us to realize that those days are long over. Display needs to be completely divorced from data. Semantics should not be embedded into text strings.[1]

What many of these catalogers and metadata librarians have failed to acknowledge is ISBD's rich background, noble intents (e.g., to provide a way for computer programs to be written so that descriptive elements could be recognized by the punctuation that preceded them), and its historical importance in the process of standardizing bibliographic data worldwide. While its role is likely to continue diminishing, and perhaps one day it will completely disappear from modern cataloging, its historical significance should not be forgotten—nor should its contemporary role as a cataloging standard for libraries still using catalog cards and for countries where little else is needed in terms of content standards.

THE ORIGINS OF ISBD

ISBD originated in 1969, in an International Meeting of Cataloguing Experts convened by the International Federation of Library Associations (IFLA) Committee on Cataloguing. One outcome of that meeting was a "resolution that proposed creation of standards to regularize the form and content of bibliographic descriptions," with the aim of sharing bibliographic descriptions, or records, internationally, regardless of language or script.[2] Michael Gorman became the chair of an ad hoc working group to develop the initial ISBD draft. With the working group, Gorman produced the first draft in 1969. In his memoir, Gorman recalls his approach to deriving the initial draft, provided as a report prepared for IFLA and UNESCO. He states that he "compared the descriptive sections . . . of many hundreds of catalogue records from the eight national bibliographies . . . selected and discovered a remarkable affinity in the choice and order of bibliographic data." Despite these similarities, there were obstacles in the way of sharing these national-level records: "the presentation of the data and the variations in punctuation and abbreviations varied widely, thus making it impossible, when dealing with unfamiliar languages, to decode the descriptions, and, crucially at that point, to create programs to translate the data automatically into the emerging machine-readable [MARC] format."[3]

The first ISBD text to appear was *International Standard Bibliographic Description for Monographic Publications* (ISBD(M)) published in 1971. Separate ISBD texts were produced for what were then considered separate and distinct resource types. The monographs text was followed in time by texts for serials, nonbook materials, cartographic materials, rare books, printed music, and computer files (with a later revision renamed *Electronic Resources*). A text for article-level publications was also developed, *Guidelines for the Application of the ISBDs to the Description of Component Parts*. The practice of maintaining separate texts for different material or publication types characterized ISBD publication history. However, a general text, ISBD(G), was developed after the first few format-specific ISBDs were issued. The experience of developing the separate ISBDs resulted in an understanding that an overarching text was needed, so that subsequent publications would be "harmonious in their treatment of data elements and prescribed punctuation."[4] ISBD(G), first published in 1977, served as a framework for further revisions of separate format texts, for as long as those were maintained.

The separate format-based ISBD texts have now been replaced by a consolidated edition, published by De Gruyter Saur in 2011. The consolidated text is intended to be used as the basis for "rules on description of library materials to describe all aspects of each resource, including its content, its carrier, and its mode of issuance."[5] As resource types and formats have become increasingly more complex and hybridized, the maintenance of separate texts became not only less efficient, but also less accurate as a representation of the bibliographic universe. The consolidated ISBD was prepared "in the effort to bring description of all materials to a common state of conformity"[6] with *Functional Requirements for Bibliographic Records* (FRBR).[7] Additional changes in the consolidated edition resulted from reviewing variations in editorial style, revising the introduction regarding application of the ISBD, "revision or addition of new definitions for removing ambiguity," and the provision of new examples.[8] The ISBD Consolidated Edition has been translated into Chinese, French, Spanish, Italian, Russian, Bulgarian, Lithuanian, and Catalan. An earlier version, the preliminary consolidated edition from 2007, has also been translated into French, Spanish, Italian, Latvian, Serbian, and Chinese. The translations are available at no charge from IFLA as is a PDF version of the English consolidated edition from 2011.[9] *Guidelines for the Application of the ISBDs to the Description of Component Parts* remains available in Romanian as well as English.[10] Additional translations of these documents may become available over time.

PURPOSE, OBJECTIVES, AND PRINCIPLES

ISBD "specifies the requirements for the description and identification of published resources that are likely to appear in library collections."[11] It was developed "to serve as a principal standard to promote universal bibliographic control, that is, to make universally and promptly available, in a form that is internationally acceptable, basic bibliographic data for all published resources in all countries."[12] National bibliographic agencies comprise its primary intended user base. Although not intended for use as a cataloging code in itself, it has provided the framework for many cataloging codes. At the same time, ISBD has in some cases been directly used in this fashion. For example, the Biblioteca Nacional de Portugal uses ISBD as its descriptive cataloging standard, supplementing it with rules for access points.

Use of ISBD has the following intended outcomes:

- Promoting interchangeability of records from different, generally international, sources, including producers and publishers as well as libraries;
- Assistance "in the interpretation of records across language barriers";
- Enabling conversion of bibliographic records from paper to electronic form;
- Enhancing "the portability of bibliographic data in the Semantic Web environment and the interoperability of the ISBD with other content standards."[13]

These outcomes all point, in different ways, toward sharing of bibliographic information. This is made possible by ISBD's provision of consistency in meta-data elements, order of presentation, and syntax. To guide catalogers, ISBD provides stipulation "to search for and to recognize data, to define the functions of each data element within the specific context and to ascertain the proper position for recording the data element within the areas of the description."[14] Two types of stipulations are given. The first provides consistency for all types of published resources, to the extent that there is uniformity among different resource types (e.g., that resources possess or are assigned titles, or that there are person(s) or organization(s) responsible for their creation). The second type comprises stipulations that are specific to given resource types possessing distinct characteristics (e.g., mathematical data present in cartographic resources). Overall, ISBD focuses on the elements of description and their order, rather than their use or display in specific information systems. If RDA is being used to catalog, then the elements are not determined by ISBD. The elements used are those enumerated in RDA and the order is generally determined by the encoding standard used (e.g., in MARC tag order) or by the retrieval tool (e.g., the layout determined for a partial, full, or some other view of a record).

In FRBR terms, ISBD descriptions take place at the manifestation level. Catalogers provide metadata elements in a predetermined sequence, serving as the description of the cataloged resource. Prescribed punctuation, within and between elements, is given "as a means of recognizing and displaying data elements and making them understandable independently of the language of the description."[15] ISBD is hospitable to varying levels of description—that is, descriptions with different granularity of detail—as required by different types of libraries. The data elements from ISBD form only part of a complete bibliographic description (i.e., a catalog or metadata record). ISBD "is not normally used by itself. The other elements that make up a complete bibliographic record, such as access points, and subject information, are not included."[16]

Figure 23.1 shows an ISBD description for a set of spoken word audio discs. It is adapted from an example in *Full ISBD Examples*, a publication of the ISBD

Spoken word : audio

South Africa's human spirit : an oral memoir of the Truth and Reconciliation Commission. — [Johannesburg] : SABC, cop. 2000.
6 sound discs (372 min) : digital ; 12 cm, in wire container 13 x 16 x 7 cm + 1 booklet (36 p. : 1 col. ill., col. port. ; 13 cm)
Title from booklet.
In various official South African languages with English voice-over.
Producers: Angie Kapelianis, Darren Taylor.
Sponsor: NORAD.
Booklet includes bibliographical references and glossary.
Contents: v.1. Bones of memory ; v. 2. Slices of life ; v. 3. Worlds of licence (2 discs) ; v. 4. Portraits of truth ; v. 5. Windows of history.
Production scripts also available on the Internet: http://www.sabctruth.co.za.
ISBN 0-86972-124-0 (set). — ISBN 978-0-86972-124-7 (set)

FIGURE 23.1 ISBD Description: Multiple Paragraphs Format.

Review Group.[17] The description in Figure 23.1 will be used to demonstrate the discussions of ISBD's structure and punctuation. Please note that the description includes some abbreviations that would not be used with RDA, and its formatting is similar to that found on catalog cards produced in the United States.

THE STRUCTURE OF THE ISBD

The first level of division in ISBD is the *area of description*. There are nine areas of description. Each ISBD *area* is "an aggregated statement with a structure given by the order, mandatory status, repeatability, and punctuation of a set [of] attributes."[18]

0. Content form and media type area
1. Title and statement of responsibility area
2. Edition area
3. Material or type of resource specific area
4. Publication, production, distribution, etc., area
5. Material description area
6. Series and multipart monographic resource area
7. Note area
8. Resource identifier and terms of availability area

An outline of ISBD areas, elements, and prescribed punctuation is provided in Table 23.1, which also contains examples to illustrate how the elements of description may be linked together in a bibliographic description.[19]

TABLE 23.1 ISBD Areas and Elements.

Areas	Prescribed Punctuation and Elements		Examples
0. Content Form and Media Type Area		0.1 Content form	Music
	.	• Subsequent content form (same media type)	Music. Sounds Text. Image
	+	• Subsequent content form (different media type)	Text + Dataset
	( )	0.1.1 Content qualification	Image (moving)
	;	• Subsequent content qualification	Image (moving ; 2-dimensional)
	:	0.2 Media type	Image (moving ; 2-dimensional) : projected

(continued)

TABLE 23.1 (*continued*)

Areas	Prescribed Punctuation and Elements	Examples
1. Title and Statement of Responsibility Area	1.1 Title proper	The organization of information
	= 1.2 Parallel title	Obras completas = Complete works
	: 1.3 Other title information	Retail hell : how I sold my soul to the store : confessions of a tortured sales associate
	1.4 Statement of responsibility / • First statement	The organization of information / Arlene G. Taylor and Daniel N. Joudrey
	; • Subsequent statements	The cultural life of Omsk in the 1920s and 1930s / by Mark Konecny ; edited with the assistance of Omsk State Technical University
	; 1.1.5.2 Subsequent title by same author	Sister Mary Ignatius explains it all for you ; and, The actor's nightmare : two plays / by Christopher Durang
	. 1.4.5.11.2 Subsequent title by different author	The suicide meet / Mary Humphrey Baldridge. Pickle / by Sheila Junor-Moore
2. Edition Area	2.1 Edition statement	. — Third ed. . — Improved edition
	2.3 Statement of responsibility for edition / • First statement ; • Subsequent statements	. — Fourth edition / revised and updated by Nicolas Pelham ; foreword by Michael Boire
	, 2.4 Additional edition statement	. — 2nd edition, corrected impression
	2.5 Statement of responsibility for additional ed. statement / • First statement ; • Subsequent statements	. — 2nd ed., revised / edited by Nicholas J. Heinemann ; assisted by Johanna Radding
3. Material or Type of Resource Specific Area	3.1 Mathematical data (Cartographic resources) • 3.1.1 Statement of scale ; • 3.1.2 Statement of projection ( ) • 3.1.3 Statement of coordinates and equinox ; • 3.1.3.3 Statement of equinox	. — Scale 1:9,000,000. ; azimuthal equidistant proj. (W 180°--E 180°/N 90°--N 50°) . — Scale not given (RA 0 hr. to 24 hr./Decl. +90˚ to -90˚ ; equinox 1980)

Areas	Prescribed Punctuation and Elements	Examples
	3.2 Music format statement (Notated music)	. — Full score
( )	3.3 Numbering (serials) • 3.3.2 Numeric designation • 3.3.3 Chronological designation [enclosed in parentheses only with a numeric designation]	. — Vol. 1, no. 1 (Jan. 1971)–vol. 5, no. 12 (Dec. 1975) . — Vol. 6, no. 2– = Vol. 13, no. 3 (Mar. 1969)–
= ;	• 3.3.6 Alternative numbering system • 3.3.7 New sequence of numbering	. — Vol. 1, no. 1 (Nov. 23, 1936)–vol. 73, no. 25 (Dec. 29, 1972) ; vol. 1, no. 1 (Oct. 1978)–
4. Publication, Production, Distribution, etc., Area	4.1 Place of publication, production, and/or distribution • First place • Subsequent place	. — Albany [New York] . — New York ; München
; :	4.2 Name of publisher, producer, and/or distributor	. — Albany [New York] : Peterson's . — München ; London ; New York : Prestel . — New York : Edition Julie Sylvester ; München : Schirmer/Mosel
,	4.3 Date of publication, production, and/or distribution	. — Berlin : Waxmann, 2010.
( )	Printing or manufacturing information	
: ,	• 4.4 Place of printing or manufacture • 4.5 Name of printer or manufacturer • 4.6 Date of printing or manufacture	. — New York : Dial Books for Young Readers, 1992 (Hong Kong : South China Printing Company, 1988)
5. Material Description Area	5.1 Extent	. — xii, 238 pages . — 1 sound disc
:	5.2 Other physical details	. — xii, 238 pages : illustrations . — 1 sound disc (ca 50 min) : digital, stereo

(continued)

TABLE 23.1 (*continued*)

Areas	Prescribed Punctuation and Elements	Examples
	; 5.3 Dimensions	. — xii, 238 pages : illustrations ; 22 cm . — 1 sound disc (ca 50 min) : digital, stereo ; 12 cm
	+ 5.4 Accompanying material statement	. — xii, 238 pages : illustrations ; 22 cm + 1 computer disc (sound, color ; 4 3/4 in.)
6. Series and Multipart Monographic ResourceArea	( ) 6.1 Title proper of a series	. — (Library and information science text series)
	= 6.2 Parallel title of a series	. — (White paper series = Liburu zurlen bilduma)
	: 6.3 Other title information of a series	. — (Orientaciones : revista de homosexualidades)
	6.4 Series statement of responsibility / • First statement ; • Subsequent statements	. — (Readings for liberal education / Louis Glenn Locke ; William Merriam Gibson)
	, 6.5 International standard number of a series or multipart monographic resource	. — (International business and management series, ISSN 1876-066X)
	; 6.6 Numbering within a series or multipart monographic resource	. — (Academia Dominicana de la Historia ; vol. 77)
7. Note Area	N/A 7. Notes	. — Originally published: New York : Harper, 2010 . —Includes bibliographical references (pages [439]-440) and index
8. Resource Identifier And Terms Of Availability Area	8.1 Resource identifier	. — ISBN 0521295319 (set of six paperback volumes). — ISBN 0521295262 (volume 2)
	= 8.2 Key title	. — 0360-0327 = Soviet astronomy letters
	: 8.3 Terms of availability	. — 9789051831429 (hbk.) : free

Many of the elements within ISBD areas are designated as *mandatory*, *mandatory if available*, or *mandatory if applicable*. The specification of some elements as *mandatory* is aligned with similar specifications in FRBR (see chapter 3 and later in this chapter). For example, although none of the ISBD area 2 elements are mandatory, element 2.3 is mandatory if available. That is, if an ISBD description includes an edition statement, and the resource includes a statement of responsibility relating to that edition, then that statement of responsibility must be provided in the description. The mandatory elements of ISBD do *not* correspond exactly with the core elements identified in RDA. There are differences between the two sets of elements despite each having a relationship to FRBR. Of the nine areas of description, only one of them is designated as mandatory: area 1. Although this may seem unusual, it makes sense. If nothing else, a resource needs a name of some sort (i.e., a title) even if the cataloger supplies it. All the other areas may be omitted if the information just is not there (however unlikely that would be).

In addition, ISBD also provides information about the repeatability of elements and areas. A resource being described may require more than one metadata value to adequately convey a resource's property or attribute. This means that some ISBD areas are allowed to appear more than once in the description. These are areas 3, 5, 6, 7, and 8. When an area is repeated, any punctuation preceding that area is repeated as well. Within those and the non-repeatable

TABLE 23.2 ISBD Elements: Mandatory Status and Repeatability.

Area	Mandatory Elements	Mandatory, if applicable or available	Repeatable
0	• Content form • Media type	• Content qualification	• Content form • Subsequent content forms • Subsequent content qualification
1		• Title proper • First statement of responsibility • Subsequent title by same author, etc. • Subsequent title by different author, etc.	• Parallel title • Other title information • Subsequent statement of responsibility • Subsequent title by same author, etc. • Subsequent title by different author, etc.
2		• Edition statement • First statement of responsibility for edition • Additional edition statement • First statement of responsibility for additional edition statement	• Subsequent statement of responsibility for edition • Additional edition statement • Subsequent statement of responsibility for additional edition statement

(*continued*)

TABLE 23.2 (*continued*)

Area	Mandatory Elements	Mandatory, if applicable or available	Repeatable

3		• Cartographic resources
		  o Mathematical data for
		  o Statement of scale
		  o Statement of coordinates and equinox
		• Music format statement
		• Serials
		  o Numeric designation
		  o Chronological designation
		  o Alternative numbering system
		  o New sequence of numbering
			• Mathematical data for
			• Statement of scale

4	• First place of publication, etc. • Name of publisher, etc. • Date of publication, etc.		• Subsequent place of publication, etc. • Name of publisher, etc. • Place of printing or manufacture • Name of printer or manufacturer
5			• Accompanying material statement
6		• Title proper of a series or multipart monographic resource • International standard number of a series • Numbering within a series	• Other title information of a series • Subsequent statement of responsibility
7		• Only some notes are mandatory if applicable and available; see ISBD instructions	• Some notes are repeatable
8		• Resource identifier • Key title	• Terms of availability

areas, individual ISBD elements also are repeatable. Any prescribed punctuation marks preceding these elements are also repeated. In some instances, the pattern of elements may be adjusted to accommodate any repeated information. In the publication area, catalogers are instructed to place the elements in patterns that are appropriate to the individual resource being cataloged. For example, compare the examples at ISBD 4.2 found in Table 23.1. It should be noted that when there are multiple place names in most of the examples they are recorded together. In one example, however, where there are multiple publishers as well, each place name is grouped with the corresponding publisher's name instead. In short, at times repeatability can change the order of ISBD elements. Elements that are mandatory and elements that are repeatable are listed in Table 23.2.

Figure 23.2 shows the description given in Figure 23.1, broken out by areas of description. In this example, the data elements have been formulated following RDA rules. The ISBD description includes no metadata for areas 2 or 6; presumably, this reflects an absence of information provided on the resource itself for editions or series. Area 3 simply does not pertain to this resource.

The addition of area 0 (Content Form and Media Type) to ISBD marked a major change instituted as part of the review leading to the consolidated edition and warrants its own discussion. Information analogous to that appearing in area 0 had previously been given in area 1, as a General Material Designation (GMD). The GMD, which provided information at an early point in the description but was never really part of any title element, was removed from area 1. It had long been noted that GMD terms were a mixture designating either the form of content of the resource, such as *technical drawing*, or its form of presentation, such as *electronic resource*. In addition, the lists of GMDs in practical use were not sufficiently granular to designate either form of content or form of presentation adequately for many types of inter- or cross-media resources.

As information provided by the GMD is nevertheless considered critical for end-users, the revised presentation of this part of the description, as area

---

Area 0: Spoken word : audio

Area 1: South Africa's human spirit : an oral memoir of the Truth and Reconciliation Commission.

Area 2:

Area 3:

Area 4: [Johannesburg] : SABC, ©2000.

Area 5: 6 sound discs (372 min.) : digital ; 12 cm, in wire container 13 x 16 x 7 cm + 1 booklet (36 pages : 1 color illustrations, color portraits ; 13 cm)

Area 6:

Area 7: Title from booklet. — In various official South African languages with English voice-over. — Producers: Angie Kapelianis, Darren Taylor. — Sponsor: NORAD. — Booklet includes bibliographical references and glossary. — Contents: volume 1. Bones of memory ; volume 2. Slices of life ; volume 3. Worlds of licence (2 discs) ; volume 4. Portraits of truth ; volume 5. Windows of history. — Production scripts also available on the Internet: http://www.sabctruth.co.za.

Area 8: ISBN 0-86972-124-0 (set). — ISBN 978-0-86972-124-7 (set)

FIGURE 23.2 ISBD Description: By Area.

0, is placed at the beginning of the record, before area 1. Whereas the GMD was optional, area 0 is required.[20] The area was numbered zero not simply to avoid renumbering the existing areas 1 through 8, though it does also have that beneficial side effect. The intent is to "indicate at the very beginning of the description both the fundamental form or forms in which the content of a resource is expressed and the type or types of carrier used to convey that content so as to assist catalogue users in identifying and selecting resources appropriate to their needs."[21] In the context of providing integral, structured bibliographic descriptions—similar to textual paragraphs—area 0 information would literally be read first.

The two area 0 elements are *content form* and *media type*. *Content form* has a sub-element, *content qualification*. *Content form* is defined as "the fundamental form or forms in which the content of a resource is expressed."[22] *Content qualification* is "the type of content, presence or absence of motion, dimensionality, or sensory nature of a resource."[23] The definition of *media type* is "the type or types of carrier used to convey the content of a resource; generally reflects the format of the storage medium and housing of a carrier in combination with the type of intermediation device required to render, view, run, etc., the content of a resource."[24] All three elements are provided with specified vocabularies in the ISBD text, which are similar though not identical to vocabularies specified in RDA. The terms used for content form and content qualification, in combination, are analogous to RDA's terms for its *content type* element. For example, where ISBD offers the term "music" as a form of content and provides qualifiers such as "notated" and "performed," RDA has the compound terms "notated music" and "performed music." ISBD's *media type* element is similar to RDA's *media type* although the term lists are not identical. By contrast, RDA's *carrier type* is closest to ISBD's *specific material designation*, but ISBD does not give a prescribed vocabulary for this element, as RDA does.

It can be seen in Table 23.3 that, in parallel with RDA, ISBD has moved deliberately toward providing information of much greater specificity regarding the nature of both a resource's content, and its physical/digital form, than did the previous editions of ISBD, with which AACR2 was in alignment. It is

TABLE 23.3 Comparison of ISBD Area 0 and RDA Elements.

ISBD		RDA	
Element	Example	Element	Example
0.1 Content form	image	6.9 Content type	two-dimensional moving image
0.2 Content qualification	moving		
0.3 Media type	video	3.2 Media type	video
5.1 Specific material designation and Extent	1 DVD	3.3 Carrier type 3.4 Extent	videodisc 1 videodisc or 1 DVD

desirable for a broad range of users to have content and form metadata presented either graphically, as material-type icons, or as facets presented via a checklist, or both. This is facilitated, in part, by the consistency of controlled vocabularies, such as those given by the ISBD.

Basis of Description and Sources of Information

The *basis of description* (i.e., "the bibliographic unit that is going to be described")[25] is given in ISBD A.4.1, with variations for single-part monographic resources, multipart monographic resources, serials, and integrating resources.[26] Though the basic principle is that "the whole resource constitutes the basis of the description,"[27] for serials and integrating resources there are specified bases for particular areas. For example, for serials the basis for the description of area 2 is the first or earliest issue or part, whereas with integrating resources, the basis for area 2 is the current iteration. This shows that there must be some necessary interpretation regarding what is taken to represent the whole resource.

Following the stipulations for basis of description are those for *preferred sources of information* within a given resource. It frequently happens that a given resource can present information suitable for a description in more than one place. A common instance of this is a DVD with its packaging: which should be preferred, the information on the packaging or that on the screen? Though stipulations for preferred sources vary with resource type, general criteria are given in A.4.2:

- the source that gives the fullest, clearest, and most authoritative information;
- the source that is nearest the content of the resource, such as an internal source;
- the source that is most enduring[28]

Details for specific cases, including cartographic resources, electronic resources, or resources without a common source of information, are given in sections A.4.2.1-A.4.2.6.

Preferred sources are distinguished from *prescribed sources of information*. The latter are particular to areas, and are defined as "the source or sources from which information is taken for each element or area of bibliographic description."[29] As an example, for printed textual and notated music resources the prescribed sources for area 4 are, in order of preference,

- the title page
- first page of music
- other preliminaries
- cover
- colophon
- the rest of the resource[30]

For the same materials, the prescribed source for area 5 is simply the entire resource.[31] Metadata elements taken from outside a prescribed source are given in square brackets.

Punctuation

Next to its specified nine (formerly eight) areas, ISBD's distinctive use of punctuation is possibly its best-known aspect. This has contributed, inadvertently, to the persistent but mistaken impression that it is primarily a standard for display (although in RDA cataloging that *is* its remaining function). Punctuation in ISBD serves two functions: identification of the elements within areas, and ordering their display.[32]

Each element of a description is "either preceded or enclosed by prescribed punctuation."[33] Enclosing punctuation consists of either parentheses ( ) or square brackets [ ]. These pairs are considered to be a single punctuation symbol. Examples of these include a place of publication taken from outside the prescribed source (4.1.12) and playing time for a cassette tape (5.1.5):

> **Place of publication**: [Hamburg?]
>
> **Playing time**: (90 min)

It is not intuitively obvious that, in general, ISBD punctuation *precedes* the element it designates. This becomes clearer when it is remembered that the function of such punctuation is to indicate the element that follows. Preceding punctuation is omitted when the element designated is the first element of an area, as areas do not begin with punctuation. Most prescribed punctuation marks are both preceded and followed by a single space, with the exception of the comma and the point (also known as a full stop or a period). Detailed prescriptions for punctuation are given in A.3.2.

The text for each ISBD area includes generic punctuation patterns for different combinations of the elements in that area. Table 23.4 gives an example of one punctuation pattern for each area, followed by the same pattern with bibliographic data.

One seemingly eccentric outcome of ISBD's putting a greater focus on delineating elements rather than on their presentation is the occasional occurrence of what appears to be double punctuation, particularly "where an area ends with a point and the following area is preceded by prescribed punctuation that begins with a point."[34] This can be seen in the following example:

> . — 2nd ed.. — Dublin

The example shows (1) the point, space, dash, space preceding the area; (2) the content associated with area 2, which, in this case, contains a designation of an edition using a point transcribed from the resource at the end of an abbreviation; (3) the point, space, dash, space preceding the next area; and (4) the beginnings of area 4 because ISBD area 3 is not applicable to the resource (area 3 is used infrequently, and only for certain types of materials).

TABLE 23.4 ISBD Punctuation Pattern Examples.

Area	Generic example pattern	Pattern with bibliographic data
Area 0	Content form (content qualification) : media type	Music (performed) : audio
Area 1	Title proper = Parallel title / statement of responsibility ; second statement of responsibility	Community & society = Gemeinschaft und Gesellschaft / Ferdinand Tönnies ; translated and edited by Charles P. Loomis
Area 2	. — Edition statement / statement of responsibility	. — Second revised English edition / prepared by Hilda Geiringer
Area 3	. — Number of the first issue or part (date of the first issue or part)–	. — Volume 1, number 1 (Jan./Feb. 1992)–
Area 4	. — Place of publication or production ; place of publication or production : name of publisher or producer, date	. — Cambridge ; New York : Cambridge University Press, 1976
Area 5	. — Specific material designation (extent) : other physical details statement ; dimensions + accompanying material statement (extent of accompanying material : other physical details of accompanying material ; dimensions of accompanying material)	. — 2 videodiscs (123 minutes) : sound, color ; 4 3/4 in. + 1 book (63 pages : color illustrations, portraits ; 19 cm)
Area 6	. — (Title proper of series ; numbering within series)	. — (Edward Cadbury lectures ; 1953-54)
Area 7	. — First note. — Subsequent note	. — Closed captioned for the hearing impaired. — Summary: Screen version of the life of Malcolm X, an influential civil rights leader.
Area 8	. — ISBN (qualification). — ISBN (qualification)	. — 0252017846 (cloth). — 0252062094 (paperback)

The appearance of two points may seem odd. However, for machine processing it is important that the same point not serve two different functions (e.g., as punctuation transcribed from the resource and also to indicate the break between areas). The sometimes-heard criticism that punctuation marks are used unnaturally in ISBD stems from a misunderstanding of its function— again, to designate elements in a bibliographic description rather than for use in parsing conventional prose. As Michael Gorman states, one of the fundamental ideas of ISBD has always been "that the main parts of the bibliographic description (*areas* in ISBD) and the parts of those areas (*elements*) would be given in an internationally agreed order and set off and delineated by distinctive punctuation."[35] Bianchini and Guerrini emphasize that ISBD "must not be confused with its punctuation." The punctuation "has a minor relationship with display issues. In fact, its most important function is to demarcate grammatical links between data elements and to clarify their respective (logical) position by giving them a specific, understandable, meaningful sequence."[36] Although their statement applies to bibliographic metadata presented on catalog cards or in other print catalogs, it is not completely relevant to most online catalogs and certainly not to those records created using RDA. As previously stated, in RDA the role of ISBD has been reduced to that of display punctuation.

ISBD: COMPARISONS TO OTHER STANDARDS

Functional Requirements for Bibliographic Records (FRBR) and ISBD

Following the publication of FRBR in 1998, the ISBD Review Group was charged by IFLA's Cataloguing Section to review each of the published ISBDs "to ensure conformity between the provisions of ISBDs and FRBR's data requirements for the 'basic level national bibliographic record.'"[37] This charge incidentally emphasized the nature of ISBD, not only as a basis for display defined by punctuation and delineation into paragraphs, but primarily as a descriptive standard for use by national bibliographic agencies. One outcome of this study was a reconsideration of those elements of ISBD considered mandatory. These were brought into conformity with the requirements for a basic level national bibliographic record as specified in FRBR.

The document *Mapping ISBD Elements to FRBR Entity Attributes and Relationships* provides a detailed correlation between the two.[38] It should be noted that this mapping was published in 2004, before the publication of the consolidated ISBD and the addition of area 0. Although this puts some limitations on its current validity, it nevertheless provides insights into ISBD's similarities with FRBR, as well as notable differences.

The most significant distinction is that, while FRBR is a conceptual model, ISBD is a data standard.[39] This has immediate significance for the question of whether FRBR's terminology, particularly for the Group 1 entities (*work, expression, manifestation,* and *item,* sometimes known as *WEMI*), should be incorporated into ISBD, and if so, how. The Review Group determined that to adopt the WEMI terminology and conceptualization of FRBR would be difficult "owing in large part to the fact that terms in FRBR were defined in the context of an entity-relationship model conceived at a higher level of abstraction than the specifications of the ISBDs."[40] The Review Group determined that it was not feasible to simply adopt FRBR terminology, but it was possible to make the relationship between ISBD and FRBR terms and concepts explicit. Some changes were nevertheless introduced into ISBD, notably "the

TABLE 23.5 Examples of Mapping Between ISBD and FRBR.

ISBD Area	ISBD Element	FRBR Entity	FRBR Attribute / Relationship
Area 3 Material	3.1 Statement of Scale	3.2.2 Expression	4.3.18 Scale
Area 6 Series	6.1 Title proper of series or sub-series	3.2.3 Manifestation	4.4.8 Series statement

use of the term *resource* rather than *item* or *publication*," partly to avoid confusion with FRBR terminology, especially its conceptually distinct use of the word *item*.[41]

The mapping document includes extensive endnotes, many of which explicate the conceptual points of comparison between ISBD and FRBR. The differences between their concepts of *title*—what it is that a title actually names—are given in this instance:

> The title proper *per se* (as defined in ISBD) corresponds to title of the *manifestation* in FRBR (an attribute of *manifestation*). However, the title proper may also correspond, *de facto*, to title of the *work* (an attribute of *work*), inasmuch as the title on the *manifestation* normally names the *work* contained in the *manifestation*. The title proper may also correspond to title of the *expression* (an attribute of *expression*), again inasmuch as the title on the *manifestation* may be associated with the particular *expression* of the work contained in the *manifestation* (e.g., the title associated with a translated text).[42]

Table 23.5 shows two instances of the mapping provided between ISBD and FRBR.

As Bianchini and Guerrini point out, "All the objects (entities, relationships, and attributes) delineated by FRBR are found within the ISBDs."[43] The ISBD Review Group continues to work with the Joint Steering Committee for Development of RDA, the ISSN Network, and other bodies toward harmonization of ISBD with FRBR, RDA "and other national and international cataloguing rules aligned with the FRBR model and the International Cataloguing Principles."[44] A critical aim of this work is "functional interoperability, so that records created according to at least one of these rules would be reusable by an agency employing one of the other standards."[45]

RDA: *Resource Description & Access* and ISBD

There was an explicit alignment between the structure and syntax of ISBD and that of Part I of the *Anglo-American Cataloguing Rules, Second Edition* (AACR2). ISBD areas 1-8 made up the core of an AACR2 description, and ISBD punctuation was required by AACR2. This situation has fundamentally changed with the publication and implementation of RDA. Although it is possible to prepare an RDA description according to ISBD standards—with points of exception noted below—RDA has been detached from ISBD. RDA's Appendix D provides textual instructions for ISBD punctuation and includes a link to an IFLA document featuring an extensive correlation between the order of elements in ISBD with RDA elements.[46] Beyond this, however, ISBD is not present as a structural underpinning, as it was in AACR2.

Bianchini and Guerrini express concern about "the role given to ISBD within RDA."[47] They emphasize ISBD as a descriptive standard, stating that "to facilitate human scanning of lists of descriptions [bibliographic records], certain aspects of descriptions need to be made uniform. These include the selection of data elements, the order in which they are displayed, and their punctuation, capitalization, and abbreviation."[48] RDA, by design, includes no section about the presentation of recorded metadata: it emphasizes the analysis and recording of metadata elements, to be assembled for display in different formats, and in different contexts, as needed. In contrast, Bianchini and Guerrini emphasize the importance of unity of description: "if we look at OPACs as they should be, that is, a means of description of, and access to, the bibliographic universe as a whole (to be used *also* to extract single pieces of information), we are obliged to recognize that, to make them comprehensible—to give them a meaningful sense—we still need both (a) access points—that provide for *how* the catalog can be arranged, structured, and browsed and (b) internationally agreed-on bibliographic descriptions that enable predictable, consistent displays of data."[49]

It is possible to structure and present a bibliographic description using RDA guidelines and ISBD paragraphing and punctuation. However, there are obstacles to creating a fully conforming ISBD description using RDA:

- **Square brackets**: ISBD specifies that information for areas 1, 2, 3, 4, and 6, if taken outside prescribed sources of information, is given in square brackets, unless given as a note in area 7. (A.4.3). RDA 2.2.4 specifies the use of square brackets as one possible option, when information to be transcribed is supplied from a source outside the resource itself. Brackets will be used in somewhat different sets of circumstances in this case.

- **Abbreviations**: ISBD mandates the use of Latin abbreviations, such as *et al.* (A.6.2.) or *s.l.* (4.1.14). Latin abbreviations have been abandoned by RDA, and the use of abbreviations in general is more restricted than in AACR2.

- **Misprints** (A.8): ISBD prescribes the transcription of misprints, but authorizes interpolations such as [sic] or [i.e.] followed by the corrected word. RDA does not allow this, following the representation principle. Instead, a phrase, such as a corrected title proper, would be additionally given as a separate element of the bibliographic description, if considered important for identification and selection.

The Semantic Web and ISBD

IFLA's ISBD Review Group is actively involved in the Semantic Web/linked open data environment. As Escolano Rodríguez notes, a current objective for ISBD is "to reposition the IFLA standard and its value as [an] important tool for the delivery and reuse of structured authorized bibliographic data in the Internet environment."[50] To this end, the ISBD/XML Study Group was established in 2008, during the IFLA World Library and Information Congress in Québec. Its primary purpose is "to position the ISBD as a relevant factor in assessing structured bibliographic information in the global information environment."[51] Actions of the group include

- positioning ISBD and other IFLA-developed standards as "authoritative documents for Semantic Web services and tools";
- analyzing "technical and modeling issues of ISBD in the RDF [Resource Description Framework]/XML environment";
- defining "uses and functions of ISBD in the RDF/XML syntax";
- analyzing and defining "the functionalities of ISBD elements in relation to FRBR, (UNI)MARC, and DC/XML schemas, new cataloguing rules such as RDA, [the Italian code] REICAT, and the Finnish cataloguing rules";
- analyzing and supporting "the concept of linked data, and [promoting] its relevance to vendors in support of the development of new generation library information systems."[52]

The consolidated ISBD also describes the intended place of ISBD with regard to the Semantic Web and linked data: to "enhance the portability of bibliographic data in the Semantic Web environment and the interoperability of the ISBD with other content standards."[53]

A fuller introduction to Semantic Web principles is found in chapter 22 of this text in relation to the BIBFRAME initiative. Here we note the value of enabling ISBD-based metadata to participate in the Semantic Web. Although bibliographic records have long been available via the web, they are generally only discoverable through narrow and specific channels: typically, as a result of an Internet user deliberately searching a library catalog. The metadata comprising a given record does not itself participate in the increasingly rich linked data environment. As Karen Coyle expresses it, metadata is "on the Web" but not "of the Web."[54] By contrast, Semantic Web statements, or RDF triples, based on metadata records created according to ISBD would be of great value in the larger network of linked data. They are "likely to be of higher quality than those generated by machines and by untrained humans."[55] In addition, given the specifications used by national cataloging agencies, such triples are "likely to be of greater granularity and specificity than metadata derived from core or simple records."[56]

Key to the inclusion of ISBD in the Semantic Web is its representation according to the Resource Description Framework (RDF) (see discussion of RDF in chapter 22). RDF, a model for interchange of Web metadata, enables the mixture of metadata from different sources, encoded originally according to different standards or schemas.

> RDF categorizes metadata elements as either classes or properties. A class is a type of thing that is described by a metadata statement; a property is a specific aspect of a thing or a relationship between one thing and another. The only type of thing described by ISBD is a bibliographic resource, labelled in the ISBD text simply as "resource". ISBD does not cover relationships between resources, so there are no RDF properties corresponding to relationships. All of the ISBD attributes, however, are specific aspects of a resource, so each attribute is represented as a property in RDF.[57]

Each ISBD class (resource) and property (attribute) has been assigned a Uniform Resource Identifier (URI) that uniquely represents it. The occurrence of such a URI in a Semantic Web triple will therefore indicate that, and only that, class or property named.

A concrete example of an RDF class is provided by the ISBD Study Group for the content form term *music* from area 0.1. The URI for this resource type is http://iflastandards.info/ns/isbd/terms/contentform/T1004. As is recommended practice, the URI is encoded in the form of a standard Uniform Resource Locator (URL). Entering this URI in a Web browser, in fact, brings you to the web page with multilingual entries for the properties assigned to *music*—in this case, scope note, preferred label, and definition. ISBD elements of description are also assigned unique URIs. The description for a particular piece of music (i.e., an instance of this specific class), would likely include elements such as

- has title proper: http://iflastandards.info/ns/isbd/elements/P1004
- has music format statement: http://iflastandards.info/ns/isbd/elements/P1014
- has name of publisher, producer, distributor: http://iflastandards.info/ns/isbd/elements/P1017

and many more.

The means exist, therefore, for the elements of ISBD descriptions to be represented in a form that allows bibliographic metadata to take its place in the Semantic Web. It is possible for other descriptive standards to also make use of the phrase, "has title proper." However, when an RDF triple designates the value "Capriccio for violin solo and 12 players, 1987" as corresponding to the ISBD URI "http://iflastandards.info/ns/isbd/elements/P1004," this is likely to mean that this metadata element may be regarded as originating from an authoritative source. Trust is critical to the effective functioning of the Semantic Web. Koivunen and Miller state that trustworthiness "is evaluated by each application that processes the information on the Web. The applications decide what they trust by using the context of the statements, e.g., who said what and when and what credentials they had to say it."[58] When metadata is identified as originating with a cataloging agency using the International

Standard Bibliographic Description, trust in the source credentials is likely to be enhanced.

NOTES

1. Roy Tennant to BIBFRAME mailing list, July 26, 2014, http://listserv.loc.gov/cgi-bin/wa?A2=ind1407&L=bibframe&T=0&O=D&P=25932.
2. John D. Byrum, "IFLA's ISBD Programme: Purpose, Process, and Prospects," in *IFLA Cataloguing Principles: Steps Toward an International Cataloguing Code*, edited by Barbara B. Tillett, Renate Gömpel and Susanne Oehlschläger. (München, Germany: K.G. Saur, 2004), 34.
3. Michael Gorman, *Broken Pieces: A Library Life, 1941-1978* (Chicago: American Library Association, 2011), 195.
4. Byrum, "IFLA's ISBD Programme," 34.
5. International Federation of Library Associations and Institutions, Cataloguing Section Standing Committee, *ISBD: International Standard Bibliographic Description*, Consolidated ed. (Berlin: De Gruyter Saur, 2011), section A.1.1. Also available online at the IFLA website: http://www.ifla.org/files/assets/cataloguing/isbd/isbd-cons_20110321.pdf. References given in these endnotes are to sections in the document, because paging differs somewhat in the different versions.
6. Ibid., introduction.
7. IFLA Study Group on the Functional Requirements for Bibliographic Records, *Functional Requirements for Bibliographic Records, Final Report* (München, Germany: K.G. Saur, 1998), http://www.ifla.org/publications/functional-requirements-for-bibliographic-records.
8. Elena Escolano Rodríguez, "ISBD Adaptation to SW of Bibliographic Data in Linked Data." *JLIS.it, Italian Journal of Library and Information Science* 4, no. 1 (2013): 132, http://leo.cilea.it/index.php/jlis/article/view/5484/7895.
9. Several translations are available, accessed July 26, 2014, http://www.ifla.org/publications/translations-of-isbd; a PDF version of the English Consolidated Edition from 2011 is available: http://www.ifla.org/files/assets/cataloguing/isbd/isbd-cons_20110321.pdf.
10. IFLA, *Guidelines for the Application of the ISBDs to the Description of Component Parts*, (Washington, D.C. : Cataloging Directorate, Library of Congress, 2003); also available online, http://www.ifla.org/files/assets/cataloguing/isbd/component-parts.pdf; Romanian translation: http://www.ifla.org/files/assets/cataloguing/isbd/component-parts_2003-ro.pdf.
11. IFLA, *ISBD*, section A.1.1.
12. Ibid., introduction.
13. Ibid., section A.1.2.
14. Carlo Bianchini and Mauro Guerrini, "From Bibliographic Models to Cataloging Rules: Remarks on FRBR, ICP, ISBD, and RDA and the Relationships between Them," *Cataloging & Classification Quarterly* 47, no. 2 (2009): 113.
15. IFLA, *ISBD*, section A.1.1.
16. Ibid., section A.1.3.
17. International Federation of Library Associations and Institutions, ISBD Review Group. "Full ISBD Examples: Supplement to the Consolidated Edition of the ISBD: International Standard Bibliographic Description," 58, accessed March 28, 2014, http://www.ifla.org/files/assets/cataloguing/isbd/isbd-examples_2011.pdf. The examples of cataloging are given in 16 languages.

18. Mirna Willer, Gordon Dunsire, and Boris Bosančić. "ISBD and the Semantic Web," *JLIS.it, Italian Journal of Library and Information Science* 1, no. 2 (2010): 226, http://leo.cilea.it/index.php/jlis/article/view/4536/4408.
19. IFLA, *ISBD*, section A.3.1.
20. Elena Escolano Rodríguez and Dorothy McGarry, "International Standard Bibliographic Description: Updating the Consolidated ISBD," *International Cataloguing and Bibliographic Control* 38, no. 1 (January/March 2009): 11.
21. IFLA, *ISBD*, section 0, Content Form and Media Type Area.
22. Ibid., Appendix E: Glossary.
23. Ibid.
24. Ibid.
25. Ibid., section A.4.1.
26. Ibid.
27. Ibid.
28. Ibid., section A.4.2.
29. Ibid., Appendix E, Glossary.
30. Ibid., section 3.2.
31. Ibid., section 5, Material Description Area.
32. Gordon Dunsire and Mirna Willer, "Initiatives to Make Standard Library Metadata Models and Structures Available to the Semantic Web," paper presented to the IFLA World Library and Information Congress, Gothenburg, Sweden, August 2010, 6, http://conference.ifla.org/past/2010/149-dunsire -en.pdf.
33. IFLA, *ISBD*, section A.3.2.1.
34. Ibid., History: Preliminary consolidated edition, 2007.
35. Gorman, *Broken Pieces*, 195.
36. Bianchini and Guerrini, "From Bibliographic Models to Cataloging Rules," 113.
37. Byrum, "IFLA's ISBD Programme," 35.
38. IFLA, "Mapping ISBD Elements to FRBR Entity Attributes and Relationships," published 2004-07-28, http://www.ifla.org/files/assets/cataloguing/isbd/ isbd-frbr-mapping.pdf.
39. Dunsire and Willer, "Initiatives to Make Standard Library Metadata Models and Structures Available to the Semantic Web," 5.
40. IFLA, *ISBD*, Introduction: ISBD and FRBR relationship.
41. Ibid.
42. IFLA, "Mapping ISBD Elements," 12 (endnote 1).
43. Bianchini and Guerrini, "From Bibliographic Models to Cataloging Rules," 109.
44. Escolano Rodríguez, "ISBD Adaptation to SW of Bibliographic Data in Linked Data," 133.
45. Ibid., 133-134.
46. Gordon Dunsire and IFLA Cataloguing Section's ISBD Review Group, "Alignment of the ISBD: International Standard Bibliographic Description element set with RDA: Resource Description & Access Element Set," accessed June 6, 2015, http://www.ifla.org/files/assets/cataloguing/isbd/OtherDocumentation/ isbd2rda_alignment_v3_1.pdf.
47. Bianchini and Guerrini, "From Bibliographic Models to Cataloging Rules," 107
48. Ibid., 111.
49. Ibid., 113.
50. Escolano Rodríguez, "ISBD Adaptation to SW of Bibliographic Data in Linked Data," 123.
51. Dunsire and Willer, "Initiatives to Make Standard Library Metadata Models and Structures Available to the Semantic Web," 3.
52. Ibid.

53. IFLA, *ISBD*, section A.1.2.
54. Karen Coyle, *Understanding the Semantic Web: Bibliographic Data and Metadata* (Chicago: American Library Association, 2010): 11.
55. Willer, Dunsire, and Bosančić. "ISBD and the Semantic Web," 233.
56. Ibid.
57. Ibid., 224.
58. Marja-Riitta Koivunen and Eric Miller, "W3C Semantic Web Activity," accessed August 20, 2014, http://www.w3.org/2001/12/semweb-fin/w3csw.

SUGGESTED READING

Bianchini, Carlo, and Mirna Willer. "ISBD Resource and Its Description in the Context of the Semantic Web." *Cataloging & Classification Quarterly* 52, no. 8 (2014): 869-887.

Bowman, J. H. "Development of Description in Cataloguing prior to ISBD." *Aslib Proceedings* 58, no. 1/2 (2006): 34-48.

Byrum, John D. "The Birth and Re-birth of the ISBDs: Process and Procedures for Creating and Revising the International Standard Bibliographic Descriptions." *IFLA Journal* 27, no. 1 (2001): 34-37. Also available online at the IFLA website: accessed August 31, 2014, http://archive.ifla.org/V/iflaj/art2701.pdf.

Dunsire, Gordon. "The Role of ISBD in the Linked Data Environment." *Cataloging & Classification Quarterly* 52, no. 8 (2014): 855-868.

Gorman, Michael. "The Origins and Making of the ISBD: A Personal History, 1966-1978." *Cataloging & Classification Quarterly* 52, no. 8 (2014): 821-834.

Howarth, Lynne C. "ISBD as Bibliographic Content Standard: Interweaving Threads, Contemplating a Future." *Cataloging & Classification Quarterly* 52, no. 8 (2014): 982-999.

Rodríguez, Elena Escolano. "ISBD Adaptation to SW [Semantic Web] of Bibliographic Data in Linked Data." *JLIS.it, Italian Journal of Library and Information Science* 4, no. 1 (2013): 119-137.

Rodríguez, Elena Escolano, and Dorothy McGarry. "Consolidated ISBD: a step forward." Prepared for the 73rd IFLA Council and General Conference, Durban, South Africa, 19th-23rd August 2007, accessed August 31, 2014, http://archive.ifla.org/IV/ifla73/papers/145-EscolanoRodriguez_McGarry-en.pdf.

Part VI

Administrative Issues

Chapter 24

Cataloging Management and Support

INTRODUCTION

Cataloging management, as considered in this book, involves decision-making and documentation regarding the multiple types of files incorporated in an *integrated library system* (ILS), with regard to the intended goals of bibliographic description and access. This chapter focuses on the relevant file types and their relationships, as well as the policy decisions that affect success in achieving these goals. The concept of *library services platforms* (LSPs), the likely successor to the ILS, is discussed. The management of a catalog department (which may go by many different names today) also takes place as part of an ecosystem of sources for records, training, and general operational support. This includes the many forms of external support for internal cataloging operations, including programs and services provided by the Library of Congress (LC), the Program for Cooperative Cataloging (PCC), vendors, bibliographic networks, and cooperative library efforts. Indeed, the line between what were previously considered internal and external operations has blurred considerably since the early 21st century.

Efficiency of bibliographic retrieval and the quality of bibliographic description are affected not only by the care and standards used to catalog each resource, but also by several other important factors:

- recording of local decisions and practices
- currency of system files and records
- organization and routines facilitating each phase of the process

- continuing maintenance and editing of metadata used in the catalog and related discovery tools

- oversight of any commercial processing for which the library has contracts

- involvement with external or cloud-based systems and/or vendor knowledgebases

Each of these factors should be carefully evaluated and efficiently administered. This chapter considers briefly the major responsibilities involved in cataloging management, summarizing those features for which patterns of implementation may vary from library to library. Organizational structure, including the specification of staff duties, is not within the scope of this text.[1]

THE CATALOG ENVIRONMENT

Integrated Library Systems and Discovery Environments

For the purposes of this textbook, the relevant catalog environment is the Online Public Access Catalog (OPAC), a basic component of the ILS, and associated discovery environments. The cataloging module, another basic ILS component, is the environment where local-system cataloging work is performed. Pre-ILS environments, including card and microform-based catalogs, are not considered here. The historical developments of various catalog formats are reviewed briefly in chapter 2. A discussion of catalog management in pre-ILS environments can be found in the 10th edition of this book. The supremacy of the ILS is, however, being challenged by the newer library services platforms (LSPs) discussed below.

The core elements of any ILS consist of a set of databases called files; software to support data ingestion, indexing, display, and transfer; and user interfaces, typically different for end-users and staff. The different files include bibliographic, authority, item, holdings (or copy), and patron records. In an ILS using a relational database management system, data elements in these files are linked using tables.[2] This allows, for example, the due date for an item checked out of the library to be displayed both in the library catalog and the patron record. The ILS supports functions for end-user discovery, database quality control, vendor information management, financial reporting, inventory, institutional accountability, and so on. Shared library standards, such as MARC 21 (including its expression in XML), Dublin Core, Metadata Object Description Schema (MODS), Metadata Encoding & Transmission Standard (METS), and NISO Circulation Interchange Protocol (NCIP), and analogous standards in the computing and networking industries—for example, the Open Archives Initiative Protocol for Metadata Harvesting (OAI-PMH), the Simple Object Access Protocol (SOAP), and the Resource Description Framework (RDF)—make integrated library automation possible.[3]

When library automation began in the 1970s, most systems were based on a hierarchical model, involving a host mainframe computer and one or more "dumb" terminals providing a text-only interface. Eventually, minicomputers replaced mainframes, but the basic model, featuring text-based, command or menu-driven OPACs with terminal emulation software, did not change. As microcomputer technology advanced into the 1990s, becoming the standard platform for desktop computing, tasks were distributed between the host, or server, and the requestor, or client, with standard communication methods such as Transmission Control Protocol/Internet Protocol (TCP/IP) and Z39.50 facilitating the sharing of information between client and server.

Until recently, most library networks have used a standard client/server configuration, in which servers are purchased, maintained, and upgraded by the library or its host institution. However, it is increasingly common for servers to be hosted remotely by a vendor, making local maintenance unnecessary. This in turn points to the ascendancy of cloud computing. The National Institute of Standards and Technology (NIST) defines cloud computing as "a model for enabling convenient, on-demand network access to a shared pool of configurable computing resources (e.g., networks, servers, storage, applications, and services) that can be rapidly provisioned and released with minimal management effort or service provider interaction."[4] For libraries, this means that, aside from not maintaining hardware or software locally, "network resources [may be] provided through remote data centers on a subscription basis; and network resources are delivered as services over the Web."[5] This has implications for the very nature of the ILS.

As the most visible part of an ILS, the OPAC displays location information, circulation/reserve status, and acquisitions information in the form of "on order/in processing" records. In addition to catalog records serving as surrogates for tangible resources, OPACs provide access to full-text resources, image files, and streaming audio and video, with associated metadata. OPACs are configured or customized according to a library's needs. They differ in the way in which data elements are displayed, the amount of data displayed, and the manner in which a user interacts with them. They typically allow users to limit searches by facets such as language, publication date, location, or format. It is common for these and other types of metadata to be presented to users via checkboxes or drop-down menus, as commercial web sites frequently do. The facets of location and format interact, in that the choice between physically and electronically available resources can be presented either in terms of format or location. ILS vendors provide varying degrees of authority control, from none at all to a complete authority record for every access point being linked to bibliographic records. OPACs also provide different kinds of access, ranging from those that essentially duplicate the access points of card catalogs to those that offer sophisticated levels of searching beyond the metadata in the ILS itself.

Within the cataloging module, catalogers create or edit bibliographic records and update holdings information. They may retrieve bibliographic records downloaded or transmitted via File Transfer Protocol (FTP) from a cataloging resource file for use in copy cataloging. They can copy a record into their own database and use it as the basis for a new bibliographic record. They can also access, with greater or lesser degrees of interaction, functions located in other modules within the integrated system, such as circulation, acquisitions, and reserves. Most online cataloging modules accommodate the creation of templates, often called *workforms*, which allow catalogers to call up blank MARC records that have been customized to describe a typical information resource of a given format. In the authority file, catalogers may create authority records, or edit records that have been generated from access points in bibliographic records.

The many other standard ILS functions include serials check-in and bindery information, circulation, commercial database access, flexible printing options, electronic reserves, vernacular display of languages, generation of statistics and reports, security and user authentication. Provisions for user ratings and reviews, shopping cart-like functionality enabling individual ad hoc collections of records, and tagging of individual resources are popular in some library environments. External vendors provide enhancements such as interfaces with vendors who specialize in order fulfillment from multiple publishers, table-of-contents services, and book cover images. Functions such as electronic interlibrary loan (ILL), reserves and resource management systems, reference linking software, and meta-search tools are common and expected features.

The older concept of meta-search tools relates to contemporary discovery environments, seen as either a complement of, or serious rival to, the traditional OPAC. Discovery environments combine Web 2.0 tools and popular features of sites like Google and Amazon with the traditional strengths of the library catalog. These end-user environments, now commonly provided by the major library system vendors, allow for integrated searching of types of resources that were traditionally segregated and separated by different interfaces. Products such as Innovative Interfaces' Encore Synergy and Serials Solutions' Summon incorporate features of major search engines, but go beyond them to mine traditional catalog/journal index data in ways that are more immediately useful to a broad range of users. Depending on what is available to the library, searches may also include results from e-books, streaming audio and video sets, and digital library resources.

C. C. Naun notes that discovery environments improve "the end user experience by creatively reinterpreting the data in the catalog."[6] These technologies deliver library content through an interface more consistent with what library users experience elsewhere on the web. They offer faceted search results, tag clouds, related search suggestions from library cataloging data, relevancy ranking, query-clarification functions (e.g., "Did you mean . . .?"), suggestions based on popularity and recent acquisitions, and other features. In addition, they first present users with a Google- or Amazon-like single search box; links to advanced searches or the "classic catalog" may also be presented, but are typically not prominent.

Marshall Breeding emphasizes that "the context of the current state of the web demands that libraries shift from sites of complex navigation and fragmented information delivery to streamlined destinations crafted to guide users to high-quality resources." He further states, "we are swimming in a very large pool of information providers. If libraries fail to offer more modern tools for discovery, our users will gravitate more towards the commercial destination."[7] Breeding describes next generation discovery interfaces as an attempt to provide access to all types of library resources, not only those managed in the traditional library catalog.

Although, for many users, there are undoubted benefits of removing multiple interfaces and search protocols, questions may remain as to the universal value of discovery environment displays. Not every searcher is looking for material on a topic, or by an author, with no regard for its form. Frequently, a searcher will know very clearly in advance that she would like a video specifically, a book specifically, or a journal article and nothing else; in these cases, combined result sets may be a distraction. The effectiveness of filtering by facets such as language and format, popular on consumer sites, is dependent on thoughtful and user-tested layout. It is also important to understand how the vendor derives filters from source files that may be very different in their construction and metadata values. One additional concern is the loss of quick access to simply ordered browse displays that standard catalog searches provide. These provide less visual information than the metadata-rich discovery environment screen, but by the same token, they may be scanned more quickly.

Taking these concerns into account, it is clear that discovery environments are now well established. The extent to which they are integrated with, or displace, the catalog, is a matter of ongoing experimentation. However, even in situations where a traditional catalog is no longer available to the typical end user (e.g., where the main catalog functions are folded into the discovery environment), cataloging metadata is still essential for quality indexing, display, faceting, and exploration among resource types. There is a solid role for catalogers to play in this environment.

Library Services Platforms

The second decade of the 21st century has seen the rise of the *library services platform* (LSP), viewed as either an improvement to or a replacement for the ILS. LSPs are designed to make better use of current technology and computing architecture and to address barriers to efficient resource use presented by the structure of traditional ILS modules. Chief among these is the divergent workflows that have arisen for managing traditional (physical) library resources, as compared with electronic resources of all kinds, whether e-books or other kinds of electronic monographs, databases, aggregations such as streaming video and electronic book collections, and local/institutional digital collections.

There is also strong interest in access to shared knowledgebases comprised of bibliographic and authority records as a core feature of otherwise local systems. Although the term *knowledgebase* is commonly used in the LSP literature, a simple definition is difficult to find. For the purposes of this text, a knowledgebase can be considered as a set of multiple different metadata types, traditionally housed in separate databases, but functionally integrated for the purposes of library resource management and discovery. To give an example, an LSP vendor's knowledgebase may include metadata for the offerings of e-book vendors (e.g. eBrary) and for the e-book packages to which a library subscribes. As a result, when users search in the LSP, their results will include dynamically updated results for individual e-books, without the need for librarians to manually add and delete bibliographic records from their vendors.

According to Marshall Breeding, there are four key LSP characteristics:

- unified "management of print and electronic library materials," eliminating the need for separate Electronic Resource Management (ERM) ILS modules;
- "reliance on global knowledgebases instead of localized databases," addressing the redundancy involved in thousands of local libraries maintaining their own individual copies of bibliographic and authority records;
- "deployment through multitenant SaaS [Software as a Service] based on a service-oriented architecture," where cloud computing allows for delivery of software applications to multiple users on an as-needed basis; and
- "the provision of a suite of application programming interfaces (APIs)," allowing LSP system software to interact with software outside the LSP.[8]

Kristen Wilson, using the phrase *next generation library management systems*, points out that the systems currently leading the field—OCLC's World-Share Management Services, Innovative Interfaces' Sierra, Ex Libris' Alma, and Serials Solutions' Intota—are "designed to replace two or more stand-alone library systems."[9] These may include the existing ILS (in its entirety), link resolver, knowledgebases, ERM systems, and so forth. In this respect, the LSP may come to replace the ILS through still greater integration with tools maintained in parallel.

Where this becomes most relevant for catalogers and catalog managers is that the integration of the ILS with a bibliographic knowledgebase may mean that a separate public catalog module (i.e., the OPAC) no longer exists. Instead, searching and discovery by users may happen exclusively within discovery environments as discussed above, with what would typically be catalog search results presented in the same displays as results from journal databases, digital repositories, and so on. As Wilson notes, "All of these systems will be discovery neutral, meaning that libraries will need to provide separate discovery platforms to make their holdings findable to users."[10] Managers will want to ask about interoperability among the different kinds of metadata representing these different materials: Are the same sets of facets presented to users for limiting or redirecting searches, regardless of the records' origins? How are controlled, authorized access points used and displayed? Does the discovery layer make use of the syndetic structure of authority records for the benefit of users? It is possible that the move away from a separate catalog to a unified discovery environment will accelerate the benefit to users if the system is able to skillfully exploit the intelligence built into bibliographic and catalog records. There is some evidence that this is taking place. For example, OCLC's WorldCat Local makes use of reference access points in authority records to improve search outcomes, when the user enters terms in advanced search fields for name, title, and subject.

Catalogers and managers will also want to learn if, and to what extent, end user searching in knowledgebases will incorporate the metadata added to local copies of bibliographic and authority records, commonly over a period of many decades. Cataloger stereotypes aside, this metadata often incorporates substantial changes that are relevant to home communities and institutions. The efficiencies involved in use of central knowledgebases should not come at the expense of discarding this expertise.

In 1997, Christine Borgman outlined four stages in library automation:

- efficiency of internal operations
- access to local library resources
- access to resources outside the library
- interoperability between information systems[11]

At the time of her article's publication, automation was just entering the fourth stage. Borgman's prediction that there would be a shift "from bibliographic data exchange between local integrated systems and between local systems and shared cataloging utilities to interoperability between digital libraries"[12] has proved accurate. With the rise of LSPs we may see not just the sharing of metadata, but also having centralized indexing, screen presentation of results, and software platforms broadly considered.

CATALOGING-RELATED METADATA

Authority Records and Files

Traditionally, the primary purpose of an authority file, or files, is to standardize and control a library's use of names, titles, and subject headings and their respective references. There is a difference between the existence of an authority file and the processes of creating and using an authority file. According to Arlene G. Taylor and Daniel N. Joudrey, *authority work* is

the process of determining and maintaining the form of a name, title, or subject concept to be used in creating access points. In the name and title areas, the process includes identifying all variant names or titles and relating the variants to the name or title forms chosen to be access points. In some cases it may also include relating names and/or titles to each other. In the verbal subject area, the process includes identifying and maintaining relationships among terms—relationships such as synonyms, broader terms, narrower terms, and related terms.[13]

The record that results from authority work is an *authority record*, which is entered into the *authority file*—a compilation of authority records. The file is then used for the process of *authority control*—that is, for maintaining the consistency of names, titles and subject headings in a bibliographic file and for showing relationships among them.

Until recently it was thought necessary to have one standardized form for every name, title, and subject known by variant forms. This was to be brought about by the establishment of unique, exact strings of characters representing the authorized forms for names, titles, or subjects that were to be used as access points in library catalogs internationally. Current practice still requires the use of uniquely established access points within a particular library cata-log or national authority file. However, in a globalized information system, it is recognized that multiple language and script forms can be authorized forms for access purposes, and that linked authority records may include all variant forms for an entity, without designating one as correct.

For names and titles, this is now in active development thanks to the Vir-tual International Authority File (VIAF), which links the authority files of more than 30 national libraries, plus selected regional and trans-national library agencies, from the Library of Congress and the British Library to the National Diet Library of Japan, the Deutsche Nationalbibliothek, and the Bibliotheca Alexandrina (Egypt), among many others.[14] As one example, searching VIAF for "Tchaikovsky, Peter Ilich, 1840-1893" brings a result set of nearly 600 authorized access points in different languages and scripts, for the composer's name alone and for his works. Figure 24.1 shows the first set of variant access points: the icons following each access point indicate the file or files including that form, as of August 2015.

According to the project home page, "Its creators envision the VIAF as a building block for the Semantic Web to enable switching of the displayed form of names for persons to the preferred language and script of the Web user." It accomplishes this by linking "national and regional-level authority records, creating a cluster record for each unique name" and in so doing, expands "the concept of universal bibliographic control by (1) allowing national and regional

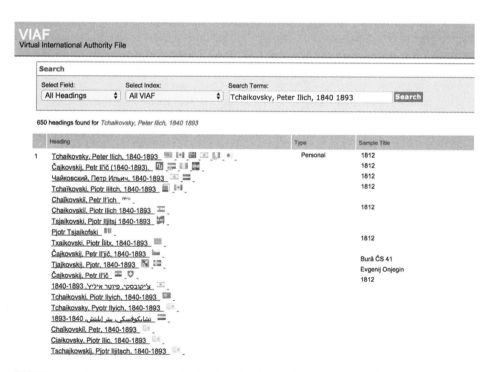

FIGURE 24.1 VIAF Entry for Tchaikovsky (partial). (Courtesy of OCLC/VIAF. Image ©2013 OCLC Online Computer Library Center, Inc., used with permission)

variations in authorized form to coexist; and (2) supporting needs for variations in preferred language, script and spelling."[15]

Nevertheless, the development of the VIAF has not made superfluous the need for national-level or local authority files. Librarians responsible for ILS systems, whether stand-alone or consortial, develop and implement policies for authority files, and the relationships between access points as established in those files and as present on bibliographic records. Some of these policies are, of course, influenced by the capabilities provided by vendors. Decision points include

- whether a file is hosted locally or remotely
- whether an authority record must be present for every access point in a bibliographic record
- whether purely local authority records are to be created
- whether the entire content of the relevant national authority file is loaded, regardless of bibliographic access points
- whether and how to implement local policies regarding access points, including variants
- whether and how to integrate changes in established access points into the local ILS

As library vendors and systems increasingly move to cloud-based architecture, the nature of many of these decisions will change. For example, if the access points in bibliographic records are linked to a remote-access authority file—*in the cloud*, to use the current expression—as those access points change, the bibliographic access points may be automatically updated.

Due to staffing and budget constraints some libraries neither maintain an authority file within the ILS nor link to an external file, and in many smaller libraries authority work has often been ignored or minimized in its application. Such libraries obviously depend on their prime cataloging sources (e.g., the Library of Congress) to suggest references and to keep the use of heading forms in standard order. The inconsistencies that inadvertently creep in, through rule changes, error, and the like, are remedied if and when found. In a limited operation there may be some economic justification for this ad hoc approach. In larger libraries, where inconsistent and erroneous names, titles, and subject headings cause misfiling and otherwise obscure valuable access points in extensive files, the commitment to authority work continues to escalate as more libraries join the Name Authorities Cooperative Program (NACO) of the Program for Cooperative Cataloging (PCC), discussed later in this chapter.

Outsourcing of the authority control process to commercial vendors has become an established aspect of catalog management. Among the principal vendors that provide authority control services to American libraries are Backstage Library Works, Library Technologies, Inc. (LTI), and MARCIVE. Services include retrospective cleanup, ongoing authority maintenance, and periodic updates and are accomplished using batch processing methods and FTP.[16] FTP technology facilitates transfer of records between libraries and vendors, allowing libraries to choose a monthly, weekly, or daily processing schedule. The vendors provide options for libraries to handle authority control in a mixed-standards environment, where authorized access points in bibliographic records may be formulated according to *RDA: Resource Description & Access* (RDA) or *Anglo-American Cataloguing Rules, Second Edition* (AACR2) prescriptions. RDA mandates a number of changes in the forms of authorized access points. For example, the abbreviation *fl.* (flourished) is replaced with *active* to indicate the period when a person with unknown birth or death dates was most productive.

OCLC and SkyRiver provide their members with LC's authority file online but do not maintain constant, global control over all authorized access points in their databases. Auto-Graphics' MARCit database does provide this, via "Online Interactive Authority Control." OCLC allows its users to control individual authorized access points in WorldCat records, by establishing links with authorized access points in authority records. These authorized access points are then automatically updated when the respective authorized forms of names, titles, or subjects change. This feature also provides a form of error checking in original or copy cataloging, if used. In systems that provide automated authority control, incoming authorized access points on bibliographic records are automatically checked against the authority file. For systems where bibliographic and authority records are linked, as with Ex Libris's Alma system (a library services platform), an authorized access point on a new bibliographic record that matches one in the authority file automatically links the bibliographic record to the authority record. In Alma, when the established form of the name, title, or subject in an authority record changes, the corresponding bibliographic record fields change as well. In systems with bibliographic/authority linking, when an authorized access point does not match, it may either be referred to the cataloger for checking, or the system may create a mini-authority record for it. In systems where the bibliographic and authority records are unlinked, a match of an incoming authorized access point with a reference will generate an invalid access point report, and a non-match will generate a new authorized access point report.[17]

It is rare today for libraries to maintain authority files in card form. Such files, if they exist, are closed and provide only retrospective information about authorized access point decisions not yet included in the ILS. Most have been discarded.

With the implementation of RDA, the functions of the authority record have begun a quiet but significant shift. This can be seen most clearly in RDA section 3, the guidelines for identifying persons, families, and corporate bodies. RDA calls for recording structured metadata, as compared with free-text notes, for a range of attributes beyond birth and death dates. These include, among others, gender, profession, field of activity, prominent family member, hereditary title, places, and addresses. One potential, indeed intended, outcome of these changes is that the authority record will move beyond its traditional purposes of standardizing and documenting authorized access points. As Jinfang Niu expresses it, "When they contain much more agent description information than what is needed for simply identifying agents, authority records are no longer merely supporting tools to facilitate the search and retrieval of works; they can be independent reference resources about agents and can, therefore, be called agent description records."[18]

In 2005, while RDA was still in development, Barbara Tillett noted that "authority records will be key building blocks for the infrastructure of the

Semantic Web" via links "to other resources, such as the home page for the entity described and links to digital resources such as biographical dictionaries, abstracting and indexing services, telephone directories, and other reference sources on the Web."[19] The VIAF model points to the further possibility, outlined by Tillett in 1988, that authority control itself may evolve into a process in which all names for an entity are recorded, or linked, as equal variants.[20] Niu has more recently suggested that authorized access points in authority records will be replaced by "globally unique IDs" used across "identity management systems," including library authority databases, to "disambiguate agents and collocate their works."[21] In whatever way these future possibilities develop—and the future is surely closer than many anticipate—the catalog manager will do well to maintain a grounded knowledge in the traditional purposes of authority control, while staying alert to its expanded horizons.

Lifecycle Metadata

Certain aspects of cataloging overlap with acquisitions. The process of maintaining information related to selection, ordering, receipt and payment, and eventual withdrawal of library materials, whether physical or electronic, has been transformed in nature as paper-based files are closed or discarded. Typically, in past practice, a singular file, whether maintained by the catalog manager or by the order librarian, showed "in process" information. Its records traced the status of each item from the time it was received in the library until it went to the shelf, with a full catalog record available to the public. In an intermediate phase of automation, some libraries used an online order record as the in-process record, later enhancing it as the catalog record.

Metadata that is used to record the lifecycle of an information resource is now dispersed across different files. It is common for libraries to load full-level bibliographic records from bibliographic networks or other vendors, and display these as linked to order or item records displaying an "In Processing" status. This allows library patrons interested in obtaining an "In Processing" item to request that it receive priority cataloging. A library's interlibrary loan (ILL) department may also request expedited cataloging of these items to fill ILL requests from other institutions.

Lifecycle metadata goes well beyond processing status, of course, and in this text we can only indicate some of the possibilities. Order records include elements such as the vendor from which the item was purchased, its cost, fund, intended location, and a code for the subject specialist who placed the order. Item records may include circulation status, due date if the item is in use, aggregated circulation data, and a code for the most recent borrower. Holdings records may be associated with any type of resource, but are most commonly used in association with continuing resources and monographic series. Often associated with check-in records, they show the volume or date ranges for such resources held by a library, as well as the most recently received items and anticipated dates for expected items. Even bibliographic records themselves may include lifecycle metadata, for example, if an information resource was received as a gift or included as part of a named collection. Any of the types of records mentioned in this paragraph may include other lifecycle metadata elements, allowing for sophisticated and detailed tracking and reporting.

Shelflists

As is the case with paper-based authority files, in regions where the ILS is the dominant form of access to the library catalog, shelflists in card form have been generally discarded or provide historical information only.[22] Historically, the shelflist was a complete record of all titles in a collection, arranged by call number as the library materials were found on the shelves. Its primary purpose was to provide an official inventory record of the collection. Its classified arrangement showed what titles were placed in specific class notations, which meant that it served a secondary purpose as an important classification aid, as catalogers consulted it to verify their library's use of each notation. The shelflist also displayed, within certain limitations, related materials more general and more specific on either side of the notation referred to. In addition, it furnished a matrix on which unique cutter numbers and workmarks were assigned, in order to differentiate titles collocated in the same classification. In current systems, the historical functions of the shelflist are incorporated via classification number indexes, combined with limiting search results by location within the library and/or material type. Catalogers are thus able to determine how intended call numbers will stand in relation to those already in use, and relate call number creation to practices which may differ for different parts of a collection. There has been no direct replacement of the shelflist's inventory function, although vendors typically offer system components or modules that compare shelf scans of barcodes or RFID tags with the physical items coded as being available.

CATALOGING ROUTINES

Copy Cataloging

Much of the cataloging performed in the United States today is derived from original cataloging created by LC (called *LC copy*).[23] A significant proportion of cataloging is derived from copy created by other members of a bibliographic network. Since LC uses International Standard Bibliographic Description (ISBD) and RDA (and prior to that, AACR2), most present-day descriptive cataloging embodies the precepts of these two internationally recognized standards. Local catalogers may use a description, as found on LC or other copy, as it stands or may alter it to reflect differences in an item received locally (e.g., a gift of a children's book autographed by its author), to correct occasional errors made on cataloging first created elsewhere, to adjust headings to fit the local authority file, or to add name or title access points that were not included originally.

In the area of subject analysis, LC provides in many of its records a suggested *Dewey Decimal Classification* (DDC) number,[24] as well as its own full LC call number, and sometimes provides possible alternative *Library of Congress Classification* (LCC) and DDC notations for such materials as bibliographies, biographies, and the separate parts of a monographic series. It also shows the subject headings it has chosen for the work. Local copy catalogers may use LC decisions as they stand, or may modify them: to reflect variations in edition, impression, or format; to complete the DDC classification numbers; to adjust official LC call numbers to their local classification sequences; to substitute *Sears List of Subject Headings* (*Sears*) or other subject list terms for the LC subject headings; and to omit, add, or change other access points, including those for genre or form. Searching for full-level bibliographic records that match the item in hand is a major part of the routine copy cataloging workflow: records are obtained in real time through pre-searching by a library's acquisitions department, through searching by copy catalogers, or by a service such as SkyRiver's SkySearch. If no record is available from LC, or if no usable record is available from the library's sources of catalog records, original cataloging is usually necessary.

To profit most from the availability of shared catalog records, it is a good idea to review all local variations from standard practice. This does not assume that all variations are unproductive. Many local prerogatives are necessary because of inconsistent precedents over the years on the part of LC itself. Others may be justified by local conditions. Cataloging managers in institutions that use OCLC may also choose to contribute locally created metadata to OCLC master records, by taking part in the Expert Community program.[25] While there are limits to the changes that can be made to master records under this program, it does allow considerable latitude for local expertise to be broadly shared. SkyRiver allows similar capabilities for making changes to master records, for customers who apply for and receive Direct Editing authority.[26] Even considering these potential benefits, librarians should review variations from standard acceptance of copy in the light of their costs and their effects on processing efficiency. Any decision made as a result of such a review will affect online cataloging in areas such as policies on the use of other libraries' records and the management of authority control processes.

Original Cataloging

Historically, cataloging has been based on the information resource, and on the iteration of a given work contained within that resource. This has resulted in the creation of multiple records with identical or related content.[27] However, with the implementation of RDA, based on the *Functional Requirements for Bibliographic Records* (FRBR)[28] (see discussion in chapter 3), catalogers will be better able to map relationships between bibliographic entities and to create more granular surrogates for information resources.

There are two phases in original cataloging: descriptive cataloging and subject cataloging. While most catalogers do both, there are different mental processes to be followed in conducting the two phases.

Descriptive Cataloging

Most libraries in the United States follow the practices of the Library of Congress, conforming to ISBD and RDA or AACR2 requirements, or some modification thereof. Bibliographic description requires transcription from the resource according to prescribed guidelines in the adopted cataloging code, as interpreted at a national level and/or modified in local practice. Whereas AACR2 was supplemented by the *Library of Congress Rule Interpretations* (LCRIs), critical guidance for RDA is provided by the *Library of Congress-Program for Cooperative Cataloging Policy Statements* (LC-PCC PSs). The LC-PCC PSs are available through the RDA Toolkit, although a subscription is not required for access. Whereas professionals may be needed to catalog some of the more complicated resources using RDA, AACR2, or another metadata standard (e.g., Dublin Core), much of descriptive cataloging is straightforward and is a task assigned to paraprofessional staff in many libraries.

AACR2 outlined three levels of description in cataloging, with increasing detail included at each of the two higher levels. It also offered options throughout, which frequently had to do with adding further details to the record. RDA 1.5: Type of Description also describes three types of description, but with a different focus than the degree of detail provided. These are *comprehensive description*, which is intended to apply to a resource considered as a unified whole; *analytical description*, which applies to a single part of a larger resource; and *hierarchical description*, which, in symmetrical contrast, is used with a resource considered as including more than one part. Any variations from LC-PCC PSs, or any RDA options exercised, should be described in a catalog department's manual. New headings may require new authority records, depending on the requirements of the system used. Catalogers in institutions that participate in NACO will contribute authority records for new headings to the Library of Congress Name Authority File (LCNAF) that are compliant with RDA, the LC-PCC PSs, and the guidelines on name and series authority records found in section Z1 of the LC *Descriptive Cataloging Manual*.[29] Authority control takes place as discussed earlier.

Subject Cataloging

In subject cataloging the cataloger examines the resource in order to determine what it is about. With its aboutness in mind, the subject heading lists and subject authority file used by the library are consulted for consistent selection and recording of accepted headings and references. Many information resources are complex enough in conceptual matter to require more than one, perhaps several, subject access points. Obsolete terminology may be caught and changed at once, although it may be better to postpone major overhauls until a designated time, in order to expedite new cataloging in progress.

For original cataloging, classifying an information resource requires judgment. The task requires the selection of an appropriate classification number that fits the existing collection in subject emphasis and then constructing the call number to fit uniquely into the existing collection. Although research on automatic classification of electronic resources has been conducted, for example by OCLC,[30] the results of these experiments have not yet suggested that fully automated classification can be used as a primary technique. Most resources still need to be classified by humans when no classification is provided on cataloging copy, and for original cataloging as well. For libraries that use LCC, the classification process has been facilitated by the introduction of *Classification Web* by LC's Cataloging Distribution Service, discussed later in this chapter.

After examining the resource to be cataloged in the light of the classification schedules used by the library, the cataloger usually consults the OPAC's classification number index (or formerly, the shelflist) to see if the classification notation chosen, or its possible alternative, has been previously used for similar or different materials. When the appropriate classification notation is selected, the distinguishing cutter number, with any necessary additions, such as workmark, edition date, or location symbol, is added. The full call number is typically recorded as part of the bibliographic record and on the resource itself (with volume and copy number if needed).

Catalog Department Manuals

The purpose of a department manual is to codify all pertinent decisions and procedures. The manual should be readily available to every member of the library staff, and it should contribute to the in-service training of every new cataloging employee. Public service staff should also be able and willing to consult it on problems of local catalog interpretation and use. Initially, most departmental manuals were in loose-leaf format so that the various tagged and indexed sections could be withdrawn and replaced by updated material as needed. It is now customary for department manuals to be available on the web, not only for internal use, but also to share with interested colleagues in other libraries.[31]

Donald Foster recommends that a departmental manual give complete coverage of responsibilities and practices and that it be easy to use, to read, and to revise. He gives the following points to remember during its preparation:

1. Arrange material in logical order so that related information is found together.
2. Use precise and concrete words, not abstract words. And illustrate whenever possible.
3. Be alert to details. Write the manual so that there is no question about procedures and so that the newcomer can easily understand and follow each routine.
4. But do not over-detail. Too much detail provides no room for individual variation and will not allow for minor changes without complete rewriting.
5. Anticipate future revisions and additions.
6. Before adding a new procedure into the manual, test it out to discover and correct unforeseen problems.
7. Take advantage of auxiliary sources, particularly publications from LC and, if the library is part of a network, publications distributed by network headquarters.[32]

On the first and last points, both related information and LC publications can be hyperlinked in online manuals. On the last point, the department manual may contain guidelines for input standards for automated systems or refer to those input standards of the bibliographic network to which the library belongs. In anticipation of the April 2013 implementation of RDA, a plethora of guidelines and best practice documents began to appear, and are invaluable for local training. Among the many good starting points are OCLC's RDA resource page,[33] the Catalogers Learning Workshop from the Library of Congress,[34] and RDA resources from the Program for Cooperative Cataloging.[35] Notably, the RDA Toolkit includes *workflows* (i.e., step-by-step guidelines for creating metadata for materials of different types and complexities) developed by national and local libraries, as well as experienced individuals, to help guide catalogers.[36] These workflows are available to Toolkit subscribers.

Some catalog department manuals also contain expectations for cataloging staff job performance with specific guidelines for performance standards. Such guidelines are very useful for a clear understanding of expectations when it is time for performance evaluations.

Workforms

Workforms or templates are useful to make procedures routine and to ensure full coverage of essential categories of metadata. In the past, it was typical for original catalogers to fill out workforms in print format (sheets, cards, or pre-printed slips), which were then given to library technicians to key into an online system. This workflow is now obsolete, as direct access to online systems is now the norm for cataloging personnel, and templates are completed directly at the keyboard. Workforms present metadata elements for typical information resources in different media, using preselected fields and tags that are then changed or expanded as needed. Figure 24.2 shows the OCLC workform for books. Figure 24.3 shows the analogous workform from SkyRiver.

Catalog Maintenance

Like any ongoing process, a developing catalog is subject to metadata obsolescence, inadvertent clerical and professional errors, inconsistency, and a variety of related ills. It therefore requires regular maintenance, although libraries, being continually shorthanded, often neglect or postpone the responsibility, to the detriment of effective service. As collections grow, the efforts needed to keep a catalog in satisfactory condition tend to increase exponentially. Call number changes, location changes, treatment changes, and blind references (i.e., references to or from authorized access points once used but incompletely or inaccurately withdrawn) are among the major maintenance problems. Data entry errors, invalid uniform resource locators (URLs), and incomplete or defective records due to faulty migration from a previous online system may cause major retrieval problems.

Maintenance of every catalog is also necessary to guard against obsolescence of terminology and to remedy the inconsistencies resulting from different rules for authority work, especially in online catalogs lacking a global update (i.e., global search and replace) capability. References must be maintained and old name and title access points must sometimes be changed when there are

Bibliographic Workform: Books
OCLC NEW

Rec Stat	n	Entered		Replaced			
Type		**ELvl**	**Srce**	**Audn**	**Ctrl**	**Lang**	
BLvl		**Form**	**Conf**	**Biog**	**MRec**	**Ctry**	
		Cont	**GPub**	**LitF**	**Indx**		
Desc		**Ills**	**Fest**	**DtSt**	**Dates,**		
040		SCL $e rda $c SCL					
020							
041		$h $b					
050		$b					
092		$b					
049		SCL					
1__		$e					
245		$b $c					
246							
250							
264		$b $c					
300		$b $c					
336		$b $2					
337		$b $2					
338		$b $2					
490		$x $v					
546		$b					
5__							
6__							
6__							
6__							
7__		$e $4					
7__		$e $4					
7__		$e $4					
856		$u					
8__		$v					

FIGURE 24.2 Workform for Monographs. (Based on OCLC Workform)

conflicts with new access points in the catalog. In addition there must be concern for maintenance of the equipment necessary for use. Equipment maintenance, however, usually is not performed by catalog department staff.

Re-cataloging and Re-classification

There is inevitably a certain amount of re-cataloging to be performed in any library. Re-cataloging may be either a mass production affair or an individualized, single item performance. During the 1960s and early 1970s, many medium-sized and larger libraries, especially academic ones, mounted full re-classification projects from DDC to LCC. Large-scale re-classification was sometimes undertaken on special collections or a selected part of a collection. In the course of most such efforts, brief, inaccurate, or obsolete cataloging could be caught and redone. Many collections were at the same time weeded and surveyed for needed new materials.

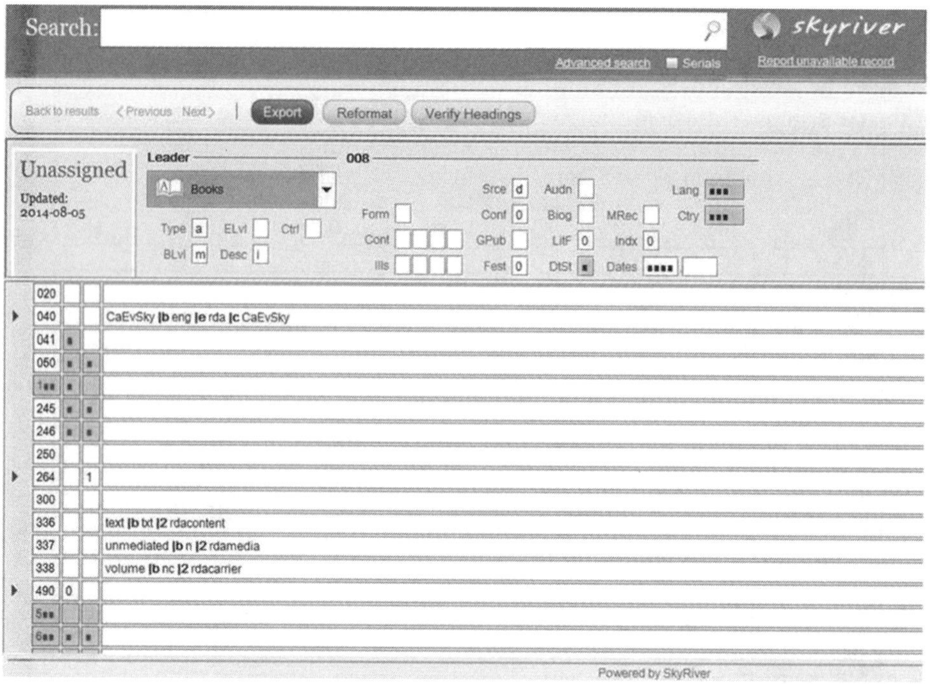

FIGURE 24.3 SkyRiver Workform for Monographs. (Software copyright Innovative Interfaces, Inc. Used with permission)

More commonly, however, re-cataloging is performed on individual items for which the former records prove unsatisfactory. Classification notations within a given classification scheme may need changing because the schedules have been revised or because of new interpretations and needs within the collection. Re-cataloging on a greater or lesser scale may also be the consequence of adopting a new or revised descriptive cataloging code. For instance, AACR2 called for many more corporate names to be entered directly under the body's own name. Previously, the rules called for entering most such names subordinately under a higher body (e.g., **Library of Congress** was entered previously as **United States. Library of Congress**). As noted above, RDA also mandates a number of changes in the forms of authorized access points.

Although it is not unusual for library catalogs to contain access points constructed using one or more sets of older rules, with linked authority control and/or global update capabilities, the problem can be fixed in OPACs. Old and new forms may also be identified and reconciled during preprocessing of record set loads or in subsequent cleanup of the database. Ongoing maintenance of changed forms of access points in online catalogs is also simplified through a global update capability.

CATALOGING SUPPORT

As mentioned in the introduction to this chapter, the management of a cataloging (or metadata, or access services) operation takes place within a context where there are many different types of support for internal operations. These prominently include sources of bibliographic and authority records, training materials, and even external management of internal operations. In the past, it was relatively simple to discuss cataloging management as consisting of distinct conceptual categories—typically, internal policies versus external sources for metadata records versus the functions provided by system vendors. Today, those categories are not so neatly separated. In this section, we discuss long-standing sources of metadata, services, and support, as well as vendor resources, centralized and cooperative systems, cataloging support tools, and commercial processing options.

Bibliographic Services of the Library of Congress

LC's bibliographic records offer extensive coverage for materials, both foreign and domestic, cataloged by the Library. LC is, of course, the copyright depository for domestic publications. Two federal legislative acts significantly increased LC's coverage of foreign materials starting in the early 1960s. One authorized certain foreign countries to pay some of their debts to the United States by sending printed materials. The other authorized LC to acquire, catalog, and distribute bibliographic records for all materials of research value published in foreign countries. The thrust of the legislation benefited not only LC, but also all American research libraries.

MARC Distribution Services

The importance of LC for setting catalog practice became even more evident with the introduction of the MARC Distribution Services, the source for purchase of LC's bibliographic and authority records.[37] A unit of LC's Cataloging Distribution Services, the MARC Distribution Services began operation in 1969.

At first, records were available only for English-language monographs, but formats were later developed for archival materials, audiovisual materials, digital resources, films, manuscripts, maps, music, and serials as well as for books. In addition, the Library of Congress does cataloging in more than 400 languages. MARC records for materials in several non–Roman-alphabet languages (i.e., Arabic, Hebrew, Chinese, Japanese, Korean, Persian, and Yiddish) are entered with those character sets. Other non–Roman-alphabet languages currently are transliterated as the MARC records are created, but work is proceeding toward UCS/Unicode implementation in library systems, after which all non–Roman-alphabet languages may be entered without transliteration.[38]

The Conversion of Serials (CONSER) automated database was sponsored by the Council on Library Resources (CLR), using the online facilities of OCLC, and initially distributed through the MARC Distribution Services—Serials. Beginning in mid-1976 with nearly 30,000 LC/MARC serial records, and accepting input from 14 North American libraries, it amassed over 200,000 records in its initial two years. Only one-third of them were authenticated by the designated centers of responsibility—LC and the National Library of Canada (now Library and Archives Canada)—but the number of verifications increased each year. Original plans were for LC to take over full support at the close of the two-year pilot program, but when it ran into difficulties in expanding its automation capacity, OCLC agreed to retain the master database, assuming managerial responsibility as well. LC continues to coordinate the project and to maintain the CONSER records, working with the Program for Cooperative Cataloging (PCC).

Another project to add machine-readable bibliographic records for materials previously cataloged on cards was the REMARC project, a retrospective conversion project. The REMARC database was created by Carrollton Press, beginning in 1980. The goal was to convert to the MARC format nearly five million titles cataloged by LC between 1897 and 1968 (the year that most English-language LC cataloging of monographs became available in the MARC format). Carrollton Press also converted some items cataloged by LC since 1968 that were not input into the MARC database by LC (e.g., foreign-language items that were phased into the MARC program throughout the 1970s). These records are available through Auto-Graphics, the current owner of REMARC. Users of LC's online catalog will see these records identified as "from old catalog," but they are not included in LC's MARC Distribution Services.

Other projects to add to the LC MARC database began as experiments in cooperative cataloging. In the early 1980s the University of Chicago and Harvard University joined with LC to create cataloging records in the MARC format. Library staff at both universities directly input bibliographic records into the LC database, which were then distributed along with LC records to MARC subscribers. This project expanded to become the National Cooperative Cataloging Project (NCCP), which in 1995 became the PCC.

The growth and nearly universal acceptance of the MARC formats, and even more, the publication of AACR2, highlighted the need for machine-readable authority records. A MARC format for name authority records was developed in the late 1970s, and LC began inputting name authority records in 1978. The MARC format for authorities was later expanded to accommodate subjects, series, and uniform titles. All new names, series, uniform titles, and subjects are currently entered into the LC database in the MARC authorities format, as well as those that have been retrospectively converted.

It is possible to obtain a subscription to one or more of the MARC Distribution Services, now a product of LC's Cataloging Distribution Service (CDS).[39] One can receive only books, visual materials, music, computer files, maps, or CONSER serials, or all of these. Also available are Name Authorities, Subject Authorities, and records for all Library of Congress Classification schedules. These services are described on LC's Cataloging Distribution Service website. All of the major bibliographic networks subscribe to the MARC Distribution Services. Manuals on the MARC 21 formats, and MARC code lists, are available for download at no charge.

In addition to the MARC 21 records created by LC and the National Library of Canada, other countries have accepted the MARC format with slight variations for creating machine-readable cataloging records. Some other countries use variations of the UNIMARC format established through the International Federation of Library Associations and Institutions (IFLA), or have their own national format, such as RUSMARC in Russia. Mapping across these formats enables sharing of records internationally.

Cataloging in Publication (CIP)

Most current American trade and academic books carry a partial biblio-graphic description, namely author, title, series statement, notes, subject and added entries, LC call number, DDC number, International Standard Book Number (ISBN), and LC control number (LCCN), on the verso of the title page. The program responsible for providing this bibliographic information is known as Cataloging in Publication (CIP). This program was initiated in 1971. Pub-lishers cooperate by sending paper or electronic data sheets and front mat-ter for books nearing publication to LC for preliminary cataloging prior to publication of their books. The E-CIP, or Electronic Cataloging in Publication, program allows for the submission of entire sets of typeset pages (i.e., galley proofs) to LC. This results in more consistently accurate subject analysis and classification, which may be difficult when only a few pages, or sketchy data elements, are provided. CIP records are available in the MARC format, being later supplanted when the full record becomes available. CIP records are use-ful as a ready source of LCCNs. They can also be used to assist in the estab-lishment of name headings. Some libraries use the CIP records for preliminary cataloging and later enhance the record when full LC records appear. Other libraries may use the brief CIP record instead of full cataloging, satisfied with the minimal-level record it provides. Figure 24.4 shows the current format and appearance of CIP data as printed. The content and appearance of CIP records will continue to evolve; in 2015, the CIP program announced that a labeled version of CIP data is to be implemented later in the year. Please see the CIP website for examples of the proposed new format.[40]

Program for Cooperative Cataloging

Initiated in February 1995, the Program for Cooperative Cataloging (PCC) grew out of cooperative activities of the previous 20 years. LC began NACO (then called the Name Authority Cooperative project) in the late 1970s and expanded the cooperative projects for contributing full bibliographic records in the then-National Coordinated Cataloging Program (NCCP). In November

---

Library of Congress Cataloging-in-Publication Data

Hand, Nick.
    Conversations on the Hudson / Nick Hand. — First Edition.
        pages cm
    Includes index.
    ISBN 978-1-61689-224-1
    1. Artisans—Hudson River Valley (N.Y. and N.J.)—Interviews. 2. Industries—Hudson River Valley (N.Y. and N.J.) 3. Hand, Nick—Travel—Hudson River Valley (N.Y. and N.J.) I. Title.

NK1411.5.H36 2014
745.09747´3—dc23   2013013839

FIGURE 24.4 Cataloging-in-Publication Record as Presented in Print.

1992 various participants from cooperative library programs met and formed the Cooperative Cataloging Council (CCC) that conducted studies to determine a strategic direction for future cooperative projects. The result was the PCC, which incorporated the CONSER program in October 1997. The PCC now has four components:

- NACO (name authority program)
- SACO (subject authority program)
- BIBCO (bibliographic record program)
- CONSER (cooperative online serials program)

According to its website, the PCC is "an international cooperative effort aimed at expanding access to library collections by providing useful, timely, and cost-effective cataloging which meets mutually accepted standards of libraries around the world."[41] Participants contribute records through OCLC or SkyRiver, and LC distributes those records through the MARC Distribution Services.

One of the early initiatives of the PCC was the promotion of a standard for what PCC calls the *core record*, a bibliographic record containing all essential bibliographic data elements, selected according to broad-based consensus. The purpose was to produce bibliographic records that could be created in a timely way and could be used by others with little or no editing, thus reducing the overall cost of cataloging. With the implementation of RDA, the PCC core record has been replaced by the BIBCO Standard Record (BSR).[42] The PCC's many other activities include the development of provider-neutral records for electronic resources available from multiple sources. The program has also developed guidelines and policy statements for easing the transition from AACR2 to RDA.[43]

Bibliographic Networks

Various definitions of *networking* spell out theoretical criteria or conditions. In practice, however, the term covers any systematic interchange of materials, metadata, services, or information, either between a central source and a number of recipients, or directly among peers. *Network* has been used to describe multi-library organizations designed to facilitate interlibrary loan, reference, duplicate exchange, processing, and the like. Our concern in this section is with the term in this sense.

The founding aims of bibliographic networks were to make catalog data widely and conveniently available, to foster processing speed and efficiency, to reduce the staff and cost of technical operations, and to facilitate resource sharing. Emphasis varies with the type(s) of library a network is designed to serve. The Research Libraries Information Network (RLIN), for example, catered to the needs of major research libraries, while OCLC evolved to appeal to a wider spectrum. As most bibliographic networks evolved, their goals broadened to include support for different library functions.

The Network Development Office of LC coined the term *bibliographic utility* for these online processing systems in 1978.[44] However, the providers of these services objected to the term, considering themselves to be networks of members. The term *utility* was an attempt to distinguish providers of computerized cataloging records from then-existing bibliographic service centers or regional networks, e.g., the Southeastern Library Network (SOLINET), which served as regional brokers, providing intermediate communication, training, and service for participating libraries. In recent years, the number of regional networks acting as brokers for OCLC products services has diminished dramatically, though a few, such as AMIGOS, MINITEX, and OHIONET, still exist. Others, including LYRASIS (formed from the merger of SOLINET, PALINET, and NELINET), continue as library membership organizations providing a range of products and training opportunities.

At present, the distinction has become blurred between bibliographic networks, as originally conceived, and library system vendors. OCLC has built its LSP, Worldshare Management Services, using the cooperatively developed WorldCat database—now considered a knowledgebase—as its basis.[45] Similarly, Ex Libris's Alma, and Serials Solutions's Intota, are developed with knowledgebases of multiple resource types at their centers.[46] In both instances, the long-standing assumption that one vendor provides the system software and architecture, while a different vendor provides the metadata, has been overturned. Given this development, which is likely to continue, the emphasis in the following discussion is on collectively built databases of bibliographic records, successors to the older concept of the union catalog. There are at present two major providers of such collective databases in the United States: SkyRiver[47] and OCLC,[48] which absorbed the Western Library Network (WLN) and RLIN. OCLC, the original bibliographic network, is still the largest; SkyRiver is offered by the ILS vendor Innovative Interfaces, Inc. A third source, Auto-Graphics, is based in Canada but also serves libraries in the United States.[49] Although SkyRiver is associated with a vendor, and Auto-Graphics is considered a vendor, their bibliographic databases are built, in part, through contributions by customers and can be considered as collective or cooperative ventures.

OCLC Online Computer Library Center (OCLC)

This oldest and largest of the bibliographic networks was incorporated in 1967 as the Ohio College Library Center, establishing an online, shared cataloging system with an online union catalog for the 54 academic libraries of Ohio. Online operations began in 1971 and expanded rapidly. In 1978 it changed its name to the acronym OCLC, Inc., downplaying the former regional connotation. At the same time, the governing structure was altered to allow libraries outside Ohio equal participation in its governance. In 1981 the official name was changed to OCLC Online Computer Library Center, Inc., in response to the fact that many people thought the initialism should stand for something.

OCLC serves individual libraries through a combination of the remaining United States regional networks, direct service, and offices for global regions. Governance is provided by three Regional Councils—Americas, Asia Pacific, and Europe, Middle East and Africa (EMEA)—who select a chairperson and administrative officers, plan live and virtual member meetings, and elect member delegates who represent the regions on the Global Council. The latter elects members to the OCLC Board of Trustees, makes recommendations to OCLC management and the board, and "serves as a key strategic discussion forum and the major communication link between member libraries, Regional Councils and OCLC."[50] Advisory committees include the Dewey Decimal Classification Editorial Policy Committee, the OCLC e-Resource Advisory Council, the Technology Advisory Board, and groups for metadata management, interlibrary loan, and FirstSearch.

The primary OCLC service has always been the online cataloging subsystem creating the WorldCat database (formerly known as the OCLC Online Union Catalog). Because of its widespread use, it is described briefly here, but this overview is not intended to be a full introduction to its operation.[51] A library using the subsystem has access to a database that numbers more than 339 million bibliographic records, for which there are more than 2.2 billion locations listed. The addition of LC bibliographic records and cataloging by member libraries enlarges the database at the rate of about one record every 10 seconds.[52] Most libraries download bibliographic and authority records directly into their local automated systems, while others receive their records via FTP or the web-based Product Services (PSWeb). OCLC still provides cards for those libraries with card catalogs, though this is a minor aspect of their record provision.

Connexion is the name for OCLC's primary cataloging service, providing access to WorldCat for original and copy cataloging. Connexion software is available for use with either a web browser or Windows-based client interface. Smaller libraries that do not need to create original catalog records may also use CatExpress, a simpler service based on the Connexion Web interface. WorldCat may be searched in a variety of ways. Keyword and/or phrase searching is available in more than 120 indexes, ranging from the traditional, such as Title, Author, and Subject, to the more specific, including LC Children's Subject Headings and National Agricultural Library Classification Number. Numeric searches (e.g., LCCN, ISBN, ISSN), title browse searches, and *derived searches* (i.e., searches based on the first few letters of name and/or title elements) are available. Multiple limits are available, including language, cataloging source, material format, language of cataloging, and others.

In addition to WorldCat, LC's name and subject authority files, commonly referred to as the NAF and SAF, are available for both searching and browsing. Authority records are displayed in separate windows, allowing the user to toggle between them and bibliographic records. Using this feature, one may copy and paste blocks of text into bibliographic records from either authority records or other bibliographic records. There is also a capability, available to NACO participants, to have a basic name authority record generated automatically from a heading in a bibliographic record.

OCLC's Connexion service software supports the cataloging of materials in multiple non-Roman scripts, including Chinese, Japanese, Korean, Arabic, Hebrew, Cyrillic, Greek, Thai, and Tamil scripts. System interfaces are available in Chinese (Simplified), Chinese (Traditional), English, German, Japanese, Korean, or Spanish. Search result sets may first be displayed in truncated or brief formats. New cataloging is usually entered into a MARC workform, although it is also possible to use a Dublin Core workform using the browser software. There are standard protocols for original cataloging entered into OCLC. Member libraries using AACR2 for cataloging are obliged to follow the latest version; local use of RDA is not required, as of early 2015. Libraries are also requested, when inputting original cataloging, to check all name, uniform title, and series headings in the LC MARC authority file. Headings found in the authority file that are coded as being AACR2 are to be input in that form into original cataloging. Records are coded to show compliance (or not) with these standards.[53] The system is highly flexible, allowing members to adapt local records to meet local practices and conventions.

Quality control exists in published standards to which participating libraries are expected to adhere. Participants are encouraged to report any errors they find in the database. OCLC staff members check and correct the master records from these reports. Although certain libraries have been authorized to correct errors directly since 1984, all member libraries with full-level cataloging authorizations have been able to enrich records since 2009. This Expert Community program undertakes decentralized, if informal, quality control by correcting errors in many MARC fields, verifying headings, and upgrading record levels, as well as adding or updating metadata elements ranging from notes to classification numbers, subject headings, URLs, and a variety of standard numbers.[54]

OCLC's cataloging services are constantly developing and changing. A great quantity of documentation and training materials is available from the support site for OCLC's Connexion.[55] Also valuable are OCLC's Technical Bulletins, which provide updates for using the system.[56] OCLC also offers many other cataloging services including custom cataloging, automated copy cataloging, and retrospective conversion. OCLC Research works in a number of areas relevant to cataloging, including web-based services for controlled vocabularies, study of MARC fields and tags in WorldCat, and the application of IFLA's *Functional Requirements for Bibliographic Records* (FRBR), among other projects.[57]

SkyRiver

SkyRiver was created in 2009 by Jerry Kline, founder and then CEO of Innovative Interfaces, Inc. (III), sometimes referred to informally as *Triple-I*. In 2006, OCLC merged with the Research Libraries Group (RLG). With the absorption of RLG's RLIN, this left WorldCat as the only major bibliographic database in the United States. Many librarians were concerned about the loss of choice that this implied. In addition, OCLC's redeveloped record use policy[58] was seen by many as unnecessarily restrictive, a perception heightened by the debates leading to the promulgation of the new policy.[59] In this environment, SkyRiver was founded to provide libraries with an alternative bibliographic record service. It remained as a sister company to III until 2013, when it was fully integrated with Innovative. However, it is not necessary to be an Innovative Interfaces customer to use SkyRiver. Customers pay a flat annual fee.

The SkyRiver bibliographic database includes over 44 million records, including the full LC MARC and CONSER files. It grows, as does WorldCat, by records contributed from member libraries. Libraries may use the web-based client to contribute original bibliographic and authority records, or may contribute via batch loads. Similar to Expert Community users in OCLC, SkyRiver customers with "Direct Editing" authority may make changes to master database records.

If a search on the database does not return an appropriate record, customers may use SkySearch to request that a record be returned within 48 hours. After receiving SkySearch requests, a team of searchers uses an internal SkyRiver program that queries a collection of source databases not typically used for the main bibliographic database. If an appropriate record is retrieved, it is added to the main database and the requestor is notified. SkyWatch, an optional product, provides notice of CIP record upgrades. RDA-cataloging support is provided to the extent desired by a library, including creation of hybrid RDA/AACR2 records. eMARC Express provides MARC records for electronic resources available from Overdrive and 3M Cloud Library, vendors who specialize in supplying to libraries remote access electronic resources (e.g., e-book and streaming videos). Although SkyRiver does not provide contract-cataloging services, it can provide shelf-ready materials with MARC records, through SkyMatch.

SkyRiver has asserted an open data policy with regard to the records in its database: "SkyRiver holds as a guiding principle that bibliographic metadata exist within the public domain. Thus, SkyRiver makes no claims to ownership of any bibliographic metadata and imposes no restrictions on subsequent use of bibliographic metadata that its customers obtain from the SkyRiver database."[60]

Auto-Graphics

Canadian efforts toward computer-based network cataloging were sparked largely by the University of Toronto Library Automation Systems (UTLAS), which became a separate corporation in 1983 and changed its name in 1988 to Utlas International. In 1963 the Ontario New Universities Library Project had started work on computer-produced book catalogs representing the initial library collections for five new campuses in the province. The project was to facilitate selection, acquisition, and cataloging, while remaining flexible in its record format, access, and products. Implementation in 1965 led to the University's participation in the LC MARC project. By 1970 it was producing cards from MARC tapes for sale to clients, including in 1971 the College Bibliocentre, a processing center for 19 colleges of applied technology. It started supplying computer-based systems and services to libraries in 1973.

The UTLAS system was purchased in the early 1990s and became ISM Information Systems Management Manitoba Corporation. In June 1997 A-G Canada, a wholly owned subsidiary of the library automation company Auto-Graphics, was formed and purchased ISM. It offers cataloging products and services primarily to Canadian libraries, but with a number of customers in the United States.

Auto-Graphics offers MARCit, a cooperatively developed database consisting of over 30 million bibliographic and authority records, including the Library of Congress bibliographic database and user-contributed records. MARCit is included as a custom module in VERSO, the company's ILS product. Auto-Graphics provides a range of other bibliographic services, including authority control, record de-duplication, and record upgrades.

CENTRALIZED PROCESSING AND COOPERATIVE SYSTEMS

In library systems serving an entire region, county, municipality, university, public school district, commercial enterprise, or government agency, a central processing office normally handles the acquisition and preparation of materials for all public service branches. Subunits may do a final checking of records, but if any significant revision of the work is needed, it usually goes back to the central office. This type of organization received strong emphasis with the rapid growth of library systems after World War II.

The term *centralized processing* may be broadly defined as any consolidated effort to bring under one control the technical operations necessary to prepare library materials for access and use at different service points. In the ensuing discussion several comments are made that apply equally well—perhaps with some slight modification—to cooperative efforts and even to commercial sources of cataloging. The reader can carry over such observations into those discussions where they have a bearing.

Processing centers can provide a variety of services depending on the needs of their constituencies:[61]

- cataloging and classification
- complete technical processing, including physical marking and/or jacketing
- electronic resource management
- serials management
- material selection (as distinct from acquisitions, which may simply concern the obtaining of selected materials and budgetary tracking)
- material repair and preservation
- digitization

There are, of course, advantages to setting up a processing center for a group of libraries or branches:

- increased efficiency in handling more material at less cost
- higher quality cataloging
- centralization and simplification of business routines
- better deployment of staff through specialization
- growth and maintenance of shared databases
- centralization of ILS support

Problems or challenges may also be encountered in the operation of processing centers, including:

- careful determination of the economic justification for the operation
- determination of the optimal volume and size of the operation
- balancing the requirements of different library types and sizes

- identification, coordination, and possible elimination of local variations in practice
- time and cost involved in transferring materials
- objectivity in self-appraisal and reports

Cooperative Systems

The chief trait differentiating cooperative systems from centralized processing is that the cooperative approach involves several independent libraries or systems. Each member usually continues to perform some of its own technical service work, with the responsibility for maintaining the overall integrity of the database and maintenance of the ILS resting with a centralized body. Again, better use of resources, personnel, and equipment, as well as higher discounts on bulk purchases, are anticipated. The need for more standardization in ordering and cataloging may become either an advantage or a disruptive factor. Processing decisions often rest with the independent organizations within the cooperative.

Cataloging Support Tools

A range of electronic and web-based products, services, and resources has evolved to support the cataloging process. One of the most commonly used is *Cataloger's Desktop*, a product of LC's Cataloging Distribution Service, which features over three hundred resources, including:

- access to the RDA Toolkit (separate subscription required)
- LC-PCC policy statements for RDA
- AACR2 (through the RDA Toolkit) and its LCRIs
- manuals for classification, shelflisting, and subject headings
- MARC 21 formats for bibliographic, authority, holdings, and classification data, and community information
- the latest editions of code lists for MARC 21
- ISBD: International Standard Bibliographic Description
- numerous other useful cataloging tools

Classification Web, also available from CDS, is an online compilation of the LCC schedules, LC subject and genre/form headings, and other LC supplementary vocabularies. It features correlations between *Library of Congress Subject Headings* (LCSH) and LC classification numbers, and between DDC and LCC numbers.[62]

OCLC, like LC, offers cataloging support services via its Connexion service. In addition to WorldCat, Connexion provides access to a wide variety of integrated cataloging tools, including NACO support for authorities functionality, local files, macros, and batch and real time processing. OCLC's *Bibliographic Formats and Standards*, a guide to "tagging conventions, input standards and guidelines for entering information into WorldCat," is freely available on the web.[63]

For performing original cataloging and complex copy cataloging via RDA, access to the RDA Toolkit is essential.[64] During the process of RDA development, it became clear that the complexities of the new code required a database presentation. Although a printed version of RDA is available, it is a cumbersome tool and a poor compromise, as compared with the Toolkit, which integrates a host of other cataloging resources with the RDA instructions.

Toolkit resources are organized under three tabs presented in a left-hand column. The *RDA* tab presents RDA's sections and chapters in an expandable table of contents, allowing the user to drill down to specific rules. The text of each rule includes links to other rules when they are referenced, and to LC-PCC PSs where they apply. The rules may be viewed in English, or in translations including French, German, and Spanish. It is possible to filter the results to only those for core elements or to the basic instructions, and to either display or hide examples. A *quick search* window enables a keyword search on the rules, with the results list linked back into the body of the rules, enabling a jump into relevant chapters. The glossary is also searchable.

The *Tools* tab features resources that relate RDA rules to other standards and models, including FRBR and FRAD entities and MARC tags. PDF files containing examples of full RDA bibliographic and authority records provided by the Joint Steering Committee are given under this tab. Each example is shown first in RDA rule order, and then in MARC tag order, with ISBD punctuation as applicable. *Workflows*, which provide navigation through RDA and are of great value to the cataloger, are also provided under this tab. Global workflows are those that have been created by individuals and institutions and shared via the Toolkit. They include topics ranging from basic book or sound recording cataloging, to highly specialized activities, including the relevant RDA rules for cataloging braille music records. The set of global workflows is constantly expanding. Individual catalogers and departments may choose which of these is best for them to use, keeping in mind that global workflows are created according to other local needs and standards and are not necessarily updated. A space for local workflows for an institution's own documentation is also provided. Local workflows are available only to that institution via the appropriate login.

The third tab, *Resources*, features most notably the text of AACR2. This is provided not only for historical reference, but also for navigation purposes. Individual rules in AACR2 are internally linked where relevant, but they are also linked to (1) corresponding RDA rules, (2) the Library of Congress and Library and Archives Canada rule interpretations for AACR2, and (3) MARC tags. It should be noted that access to some of these external resources requires a subscription to Cataloger's Desktop. The *Resources* tab also includes sets of policy statements from various national libraries (e.g., LC-PCC PSs), and a growing set of external sites such as the Dublin Core Metadata Initiative, the RDA Registry, the XC Extensible Catalog site, and many others.

Many organizations, including groups with a focus on specific topics in librarianship, provide tutorials and best-practice guides. For example, the Online Audiovisual Catalogers (OLAC) group has developed tools and training documents, ranging from authority sources for audiovisual materials to a guide to summary notes for catalog records and a compiled list of LC Genre-Form Terms for Moving Image materials.[65] The Music OCLC Users Group links to a number of tools and guides, useful for music catalogers.[66] The American

Association of Law Libraries Technical Services Special Interest Section provides links to useful resources, as well as forums for asking questions about classification and proposing new subject headings.[67] An investigation of cataloger's interest groups, and local/regional library organizations, will typically reveal more useful compilations and tools of this sort.

First unveiled in 1999 and continually developed since then, MarcEdit is a very popular cataloging and metadata editing utility, available at no charge from the developer, Terry Reese of Oregon State University.[68] Among its many features are a highly flexible set of record editing functions, an *RDA Helper* that adds RDA-specific metadata to existing MARC records, a *Delimited Text Translator* allowing the conversion of metadata in Excel and other delimited formats to MARC, a character set converter, tools to validate MARC data and correct incorrectly structured data, as well as the ability to work with metadata formats beyond MARC, including MARCXML and MODS, among others.

Commercial Processing

In the mid-1800s, Charles C. Jewett, librarian of the Smithsonian Institution, proposed "A Plan for Stereotyping Catalogues by Separate Titles. . . ."[69] The Smithsonian was, at that time, a copyright depository. As it produced bibliographic records, they could, he suggested, be preserved on stereotype plates for a variety of applications, including the printing of cards for sale to other libraries on demand. While Jewett's proposal did not itself endure, it presaged the marketing of printed cards undertaken by LC in 1901. Neither venture was commercial in the strict sense, although they were later imitated by a host of business concerns. Barbara Westby defined *commercial cataloging* as "centralized cataloging performed and sold by a non-library agency operating for profit."[70] In some cases it has been a by-product of other commercial interests, e.g., the Standard Catalog compilations of H. W. Wilson, the vending emphasis of a book jobber such as Yankee Book Peddler, or the promotional activities of a corporation like the Society for Visual Education.

The Wilson Printed Catalog Card Service supplied many school and public libraries with simple but adequate card copy at nominal cost for widely read books from 1938 to 1975. During that period more than 100 other distributors and publishers followed the Wilson example of supplying a packet of cards with each book sold. In 1976 the first edition of *Cataloging with Copy* listed 15 commercial processing services and 5 additional commercial sources of card sets.[71] Technological advances have caused considerable changes in the scene since then. Some of the services are no longer in business. All of the others have radically changed their character. In recent years commercial processors have added catalogers to their staffs and provide *contract cataloging services*, a type of *outsourcing*.

Outsourcing

Outsourcing can be defined as the purchase from an outside vendor of specific services or functions that would otherwise be provided by in-house staff. Services that have been outsourced in libraries include collection development, cataloging, and processing. Libraries have contracted out services for years, commonly obtaining catalog cards and catalog records from LC, OCLC, and many vendors. Catalog departments often seek outside help for projects such as the cataloging of backlogs, special collections, and foreign language materials. However, a controversial trend arose, beginning in the 1990s, of outsourcing entire library departments, or even entire libraries. Libraries reduced cataloging staff and hired for-profit vendors for regular cataloging services, beyond obtaining records. Some publications from that decade discussed these services and analyzed their potential impacts on libraries.[72]

Why do libraries work with outside vendors to fulfill their cataloging needs? When a vendor can provide better quality catalog records at a faster pace and at a cheaper rate than in-house staff can provide, the library benefits. Cost savings may be realized because of reduced overhead costs. Physical space can be saved, and in some situations staff may be moved into other areas of need. In perhaps extreme cases, some libraries outsourced cataloging in response to problems with personnel and productivity.

In the second decade of the 21st century, outsourcing is accepted as a standard component of a catalog manager's toolkit. The practice has not given rise to the mass elimination of cataloging/metadata departments, as was feared, in part due to a renewed emphasis on providing metadata for local, unique, and/or digital materials.[73] There is flexibility in determining what portions of a library's cataloging load will be contracted out, and it is possible to write careful specifications for different degrees of customization. Still, it is worthwhile to recapitulate the concerns debated in previous decades, as these issues remain relevant.

Some proponents of the outsourcing of cataloging services claimed that cataloging was not a core function of libraries, and that those personnel resources formerly spent in cataloging should be geared towards functions such as reference service. That organizing information is a core library service, and that the catalog is the key to the library, is not something that all library administrators agreed or agree upon.

Many librarians, though, regarded outsourcing as anathema to the obligations of professional librarianship. Outsourcing cataloging can mean that lower-skilled, lower-paid personnel replace highly trained (and presumably higher-paid) catalogers. Catalog records that are inaccurate and incomplete can be produced as a result. This results in long-term problems with the catalog database; despite the presumed quick availability of cataloged materials, patron access to collections can be hindered rather than helped.

More arguments against outsourcing are connected with the library's dependency on the vendor. If a library commits to a vendor to perform a function such as cataloging, problems can arise if the vendor changes its core service, no longer supports certain technology, or goes out of business. When cataloging staff members are replaced by outside vendors, local knowledge of collections and user needs is lost. Human costs are high: jobs can be lost. If cataloging staff remain employed by the institution, they can lose promotional opportunities and benefits. If displaced staff members are moved to other departments, those other departments may be negatively affected. Morale throughout the library can be damaged.

The success of outsourced cataloging depends on how the vendor contract is negotiated and on how library administration manages the change, including careful writing of specifications and monitoring outcomes. Poorly planned and/or managed outsourcing projects can be very detrimental to staff, to the catalog, and to the bottom line. When outsourcing cataloging, there must be a way to measure in-house performance and costs in order to compare them to outsourced performance and costs. Experienced catalogers must become contract managers, oversee quality control of the vendor's product, and constantly monitor costs and the value of the contract.

Beyond the questions raised here, it is important to note that a move from an ILS to a LSP may change the entire discussion with regard to locally provided versus vendor-provided metadata. The need for processing of physical items will no doubt persist. But if knowledgebases stand at the core of these systems, the concern may shift from local customization of *records,* and toward association of discrete local metadata *elements* with master records.

CONCLUSION

The management of a cataloging and metadata services department (again, an operation that may go by many names) involves not only a grasp of current and evolving standards, but also fluency with a continually evolving landscape of resource and training provision. The older boundaries between decisions and policies that are strictly internal to a given library, and the options made possible by the larger ecosystem, have largely disappeared. These borders were perhaps never absolute. But more than ever, the relationships are thickening among, for example: authority control and manual, automated, or even global processing; the choice of vendor as a source of system architecture and/or key knowledgebases; or the impacts of traditional cataloging practices in contexts where the catalog as traditionally understood, as a distinct tool for access to information, may no longer seem to exist. Although a sequential approach to decision-making still supports clear analysis of complex situations, it seems that now the cataloging manager must be also capable of making multiple key choices almost simultaneously.

NOTES

1. A good text for this purpose is Sheila S. Intner and Peggy Johnson, *Fundamentals of Technical Services Management* (Chicago: American Library Association, 2008).
2. Thomas R. Kochtanek and Joseph R. Matthews, *Library Information Systems: From Library Automation to Distributed Access Information Systems* (Westport, Conn.: Libraries Unlimited, 2002), 29-30.
3. Roy Tennant, "A Bibliographic Metadata Infrastructure for the Twenty-first Century," *Library Hi-Tech* 22, no. 2 (2004): 179.
4. United States Department of Commerce. National Institute of Standards and Technology, "NIST Cloud Computing Program," accessed August 11, 2014, http://www.nist.gov/itl/cloud/.
5. Yan Han, "On the Clouds: A New Way of Computing," *Information Technology and Libraries* 29, no. 2 (June 2010): 87.

6. C. C. Naun, "Next Generation OPACs: A Cataloging Viewpoint," *Cataloging & Classification Quarterly* 48, no. 4 (2010): 330-342.

7. Marshall Breeding, "The State of the Art in Library Discovery 2010," *Computers in Libraries* 30, no. 1 (2010): 31-34.

8. Marshall Breeding, "Agents of Change," *Library Journal* 137, no. 6 (2012): 33.

9. Kristen Wilson, "Introducing the Next Generation of Library Management Systems," *Serials Review* 38, no. 2 (2012): 110.

10. Ibid.

11. Christine L. Borgman, "From Acting Locally to Thinking Globally: A Brief History of Library Automation," *Library Quarterly* 67, no. 3 (July 1997): 218. Kochtanek and Matthews also provide a good overview of the development of library automation in *Library Information Systems*, Chapter 1: "The Evolution of LIS and Enabling Technologies," 3-13.

12. Borgman, "From Acting Locally to Thinking Globally," 230.

13. Arlene G. Taylor and Daniel N. Joudrey, *The Organization of Information*, 3rd ed. (Westport, Conn.: Libraries Unlimited, 2009), 445.

14. VIAF: The Virtual International Authority File, accessed August 11, 2014, http://viaf.org/.

15. OCLC, VIAF: Virtual International Authority File, accessed August 11, 2014, http://www.oclc.org/viaf.en.html.

16. Sherry L. Vellucci, "Commercial Services for Providing Authority Control: Outsourcing the Process," *Cataloging & Classification Quarterly* 39, no. 1-2 (2004): 443-456; also published in *Authority Control in Organizing and Accessing Information: Definition and International Experience*, edited by Arlene G. Taylor and Barbara B. Tillett (New York: Haworth Information Press, 2004), 443-456.

17. For more background information on automated authority control, see Arlene G. Taylor, "Authority Control: Where It's Been and Where It's Going," and other papers from the conference "Authority Control: Why It Matters," sponsored by NELINET, November 1, 1999, Worcester, Mass, http://www.pitt.edu/~agtaylor/presentations/NELINET-1999.htm.

18. Jinfang Niu, "Evolving Landscape in Name Authority Control," *Cataloging & Classification Quarterly* 51, no. 4 (2013): 406.

19. Barbara B. Tillett, "Library Authority Files as Building Blocks for the Semantic Web," in *Knowledge Without Boundaries: Organizing Information for the Future*, edited by Michael A. Chopey (Chicago: Association for Library Collections & Technical Services, American Library Association, 2005), 47, 39.

20. Barbara B. Tillett, "Access Control: a Model for Descriptive, Holding, and Control Records," in *Convergence: Proceedings of the Second National Conference of the Library and Information Technology Association, October 2-6, 1988, Boston, Massachusetts*, edited by Michael Gorman (Chicago: American Library Association, 1990), 48-56.

21. Niu, "Evolving Landscape in Name Authority Control," 418.

22. Thanks to Qiang Jin (University of Illinois, Urbana/Champaign) and Rebecca L. Mugridge (University at Albany) for their assistance with this discussion.

23. For discussion of what was formerly required to adapt copy in the cataloging process, see Arlene G. Taylor, with the assistance of Rosanna M. O'Neil, *Cataloging with Copy: A Decision-Maker's Handbook*, 2nd ed. (Englewood, Colo.: Libraries Unlimited, 1988).

24. Melvil Dewey, *Dewey Decimal Classification and Relative Index*, Edition 23, edited by Joan S. Mitchell et al. (Dublin, OH: OCLC, 2011); *Abridged Dewey Decimal Classification and Relative Index*, Edition 15, edited by Joan S. Mitchell et al. (Dublin, Ohio: OCLC, 2012). DDC, Dewey, Dewey Decimal Classification, and WebDewey are registered trademarks of OCLC.

25. OCLC, "Expert Community," accessed August 11, 2014, http://www.oclc.org/en-US/services/metadata/quality/expert.html.
26. Jennifer Dupuis, Personal communication, August 7, 2013.
27. Tennant, "A Bibliographic Metadata Infrastructure for the Twenty-first Century," 175.
28. IFLA Study Group on the Functional Requirements for Bibliographic Records, *Functional Requirements for Bibliographic Records* (München, Germany: K.G. Saur, 1998), http://www.ifla.org/publications/functional-requirements-for-bibliographic-records.
29. Library of Congress, "Z1: Name And Series Authority Records," *Descriptive Cataloging Manual*, prepared by the Policy and Standards Division, Library of Congress (Washington, D.C.: Library of Congress, 2014), http://www.loc.gov/catdir/cpso/dcmz1.pdf.
30. OCLC Office of Research, "Automatic Classification Research at OCLC," accessed August 11, 2014, http://www.oclc.org/research/activities/auto_class.html?urlm=159709.
31. Examples of web-based manuals include Ohio State University Libraries http://library.osu.edu/staff/cataloging/catman.php; University of Colorado Boulder http://ucblibraries.colorado.edu/cataloging/cpm/; Maine Balsam Libraries consortium http://www.mainebalsamlibraries.org/documents/Cataloging%20with%20Evergreen.pdf, all accessed August 11, 2014.
32. Donald L. Foster, *Managing the Catalog Department*, 3rd ed. (Metuchen, N.J.: Scarecrow, 1987), 225-226.
33. OCLC, "About RDA," accessed August 11, 2014, http://www.oclc.org/en-US/rda/about.html.
34. Library of Congress, Program for Cooperative Cataloging, "Catalogers Learning Workshop (CLW)," accessed August 11, 2014, http://www.loc.gov/catworkshop/.
35. Library of Congress, Program for Cooperative Cataloging, "RDA and PCC," accessed August 11, 2014, http://www.loc.gov/aba/pcc/rda/RDA%20Resources.html.
36. RDA Toolkit, accessed August 11, 2014, http://access.rdatoolkit.org/.
37. Henriette D. Avram, *MARC, Its History and Implications* (Washington, D.C.: Library of Congress, 1975).
38. Library of Congress, Cataloging Policy and Support Office, Unicode Implementation at the Library of Congress: Cataloging Policy Position. March 16, 2006, http://www.loc.gov/catdir/cpso/unicode.pdf.
39. Library of Congress, Cataloging Distribution Service, accessed August 11, 2014, http://www.loc.gov/cds/.
40. Library of Congress, "Cataloging in Publication Program," accessed August 13, 2015, http://www.loc.gov/publish/cip/.
41. Program for Cooperative Cataloging, "Program for Cooperative Cataloging," accessed August 11, 2014, http://www.loc.gov/aba/pcc/.
42. PCC, *BIBCO Participants' Manual*, accessed July 30, 2014, http://www.loc.gov/aba/pcc/bibco/documents/BPM.doc.
43. Library of Congress, Program for Cooperative Cataloging, RDA and PCC, accessed August 3, 2014, http://www.loc.gov/aba/pcc/rda/RDA Resources.html.
44. Library of Congress, Network Development Office, "A Glossary for Library Networking," *Network Planning Paper, no. 2* (Washington, D.C.: Library of Congress, 1978), 7.
45. OCLC, "WorldCat Knowledge Base," accessed August 11, 2014, http://www.oclc.org/knowledge-base.en.html.

46. Burke, Jane. "Knowledgebase: The Foundation for Serials Solutions Intota," accessed August 11, 2014, http://www.proquest.com/blog/2012/knowledge -base-the-foundation-for-serials-solutions-intota1.html.

47. SkyRiver, accessed August 11, 2014, http://www.iii.com/products/skyriver.

48. OCLC, "OCLC Online Computer Library Center," accessed August 11, 2014, http://www.oclc.org/.

49. "Auto-Graphics," accessed August 11, 2014, http://www4.auto-graphics .com/.

50. OCLC, "OCLC Global and Regional Councils," accessed August 11, 2014, http://oclc.org/en-US/councils.html.

51. OCLC, "OCLC WorldCat®," accessed August 11, 2014, http://www.oclc.org/ en-US/worldcat.html. Detailed information is available via this site and its related pages.

52. OCLC, "WorldCat Facts and Statistics," accessed July 30, 2014, http://www .oclc.org/worldcat/catalog.en.html.

53. OCLC, "Online Cataloging," accessed August 11, 2014, http://www.oclc.org/ bibformats/en/onlinecataloging.html.

54. OCLC, "Quality Assurance," accessed August 11, 2014, http://www.oclc.org/ bibformats/en/quality.html.

55. OCLC, "Connexion Support," accessed August 11, 2014, http://www.oclc .org/support/services/connexion.en.html.

56. OCLC, "Technical Bulletins," accessed August 11, 2014, http://www.oclc .org/support/documentation/technicalbulletins.en.html.

57. OCLC, "OCLC Research," accessed August 11, 2014, http://www.oclc.org/ research.html.

58. OCLC, "WorldCat record use and data licensing," accessed August 11, 2014, http://www.oclc.org/worldcat/community/record-use.en.html.

59. International Coalition of Library Consortia, "Statement on the Proposed OCLC Policy for Use and Transfer of WorldCat Records," accessed August 11, 2014, http://icolc.net/statement/statement-proposed-oclc-policy-use-and -transfer-worldcat-records.

60. SkyRiver, "Frequently Asked Questions," accessed August 8, 2014, https:// web.archive.org/web/20131207100849/http://theskyriver.com/faqs.

61. Thanks to Jeremy Goldstein (Minuteman Library Network), for valuable input on this section. Personal communication, September 5, 2013.

62. *Classification Web* (Washington, D.C.: Library of Congress, Cataloging Distribution Service), accessed August 11, 2014, http://classificationweb.net [requires ID and password]. For subscription information: http://www.loc .gov/cds/classweb/classweborder.html.

63. OCLC, "About This Guide," *Bibliographic Formats and Standards*, accessed July 31, 2014, http://oclc.org/bibformats/en/about.html.

64. RDA Toolkit, accessed August 2, 2014, http://access.rdatoolkit.org/.

65. Online Audiovisual Catalogers, "Cataloging Tools and Training Documents," accessed August 11, 2014, http://olacinc.org/drupal/?q=node/358.

66. Music OCLC Users Group, "Cataloging Tools," accessed August 11, 2014, http://www.musicoclcusers.org/catools.htm.

67. American Association of Law Libraries, Technical Services Special Interest Section, "Resources," accessed August 11, 2014, http://www.aallnet.org/ sections/ts/Resources.

68. MarcEdit, accessed August 11, 2014, http://marcedit.reeset.net/.

69. Charles Coffin Jewett, *On the Construction of Catalogues of Libraries, and Their Publication by Means of Separate, Stereotyped Titles*, 2nd ed. (Washington, D.C.: Smithsonian Institution, 1853).

70. Barbara M. Westby, "Commercial Services," *Library Trends* 16, no. 1 (July 1967): 46.

71. Arlene Taylor Dowell, *Cataloging with Copy: A Decision-Maker's Handbook* (Littleton, Colo.: Libraries Unlimited, 1976), 248-257.

72. Clare B. Dunkle, "Outsourcing the Catalog Department: A Meditation Inspired by the Business and Library Literature," *Journal of Academic Librarianship* 22, no. 1 (January 1996): 33-43; "Intellectual Freedom Toolkits: Outsourcing and Privatization" [includes links to several documents], accessed August 11, 2014, http://www.ala.org/tools/outsourcing; Marie A. Kascus and Dawn Hale, eds., *Outsourcing Cataloging, Authority Work, and Physical Processing: A Checklist of Considerations* (Chicago: American Library Association, 1995); Robert S. Martin et al., "The Impact of Outsourcing and Privatization on Library Services and Management: A Study for the American Library Association," School of Library and Information Studies, Texas Woman's University, June 2000, http://www.ala.org/tools/sites/ala.org .tools/files/content/outsourcing/outsourcing_doc.pdf; Karen A. Wilson and Marylou Colver, eds, *Outsourcing Library Technical Services Operations: Practices in Public, Academic, and Special Libraries* (Chicago: American Library Association, 1997).

73. See for example, Working Group on the Future of Bibliographic Control, *On the Record: Report of The Library of Congress Working Group on the Future of Bibliographic Control*, 21-24, accessed August 11, 2014, http://www.loc.gov/ bibliographic-future/news/lcwg-ontherecord-jan08-final.pdf.

SUGGESTED READING

Bénaud, Claire-Lise, and Sever Bordeianu. *Outsourcing Library Operations in Academic Libraries: An Overview of Issues and Outcomes*. Englewood, Colo.: Libraries Unlimited, 1998.

Blackman, Cathy, Erica Rae Moore, Michele Seikel, and Mandi Smith. "WorldCat and SkyRiver: A Comparison of Record Quantity and Fullness." *Library Resources and Technical Services* 58, no. 3 (July 2014): 178-186.

Eden, Bradford Lee, ed. *Twenty-first Century Metadata Operations: Challenges, Opportunities, Directions*. London: Routledge, 2012.

Evans, G. Edward, Sheila S. Intner, and Jean Weihs. *Introduction to Technical Services*. 8th ed. Santa Barbara, Calif.: Libraries Unlimited, 2011.

Grant, Carl. "The Future of Library Systems: Library Services Platforms." *Information Standards Quarterly* 24, no. 4 (Fall 2012): 4-15.

Hider, Philip, with Ross Harvey. *Organising Knowledge in a Global Society: Principles and Practice in Libraries and Information Centres*. Wagga Wagga, NSW, Australia: Centre for Information Studies, 2008. Chapter 11: Arrangements for Bibliographic Data Exchange. Chapter 12: Bibliographic Utilities. Chapter 14: Local systems and OPACs.

Intner Sheila S., and Peggy Johnson. *Fundamentals of Technical Services Management*. Chicago: American Library Association, 2008.

Intner, Sheila S., and Jean Weihs. *Standard Cataloging for School and Public Libraries*. 5th ed. Santa Barbara, Calif.: Libraries Unlimited, 2014.

Oddy, Pat. "Bibliographic Standards and the Globalization of Bibliographic Control." In *Technical Services Today and Tomorrow*. 2nd ed., edited by Michael Gorman, 67-78. Englewood, Colo.: Libraries Unlimited, 1998.

Potter, William Gray. "The Online Catalogue in Academic Libraries." In *Technical Services Today and Tomorrow*. 2nd ed., edited by Michael Gorman, 141-155. Englewood, Colo.: Libraries Unlimited, 1998.

Rohrbach, Peter T. *Find: Automation at the Library of Congress: The First Twenty-five Years and Beyond*. Washington, D.C.: Library of Congress, 1985.

Sellberg, Roxanne. "Cataloguing Management: Managing the Bibliographic Control Process." In *Technical Services Today and Tomorrow*. 2nd ed., edited by Michael Gorman, 111-127. Englewood, Colo.: Libraries Unlimited, 1998.

Taylor, Arlene G., with the assistance of Rosanna M. O'Neil. *Cataloging with Copy: A Decision-Maker's Handbook*. 2nd ed. Englewood, Colo.: Libraries Unlimited, 1988. Chapters 1 and 9.

Yee, Martha. "Guidelines for OPAC Displays." Prepared for the 65th IFLA Council and General Conference, Bangkok, Thailand, 20th-28th August 1999, http://archive.ifla.org/IV/ifla65/papers/098-131e.htm.

Appendix A: RDA Outline

Section 4: Recording Attributes of Concept, Object, Event & Place

12: General Guidelines on Recording Attributes of Concepts, Objects, Events, and Places   *[Currently empty]*

13: Identifying Concepts   *[Currently empty]*

14: Identifying Objects   *[Currently empty]*

15: Identifying Events   *[Currently empty]*

16: Identifying Places
16.0 Purpose and Scope
16.1 General Guidelines on Identifying Places
16.2 Name of the Place
16.3 Identifier for the Place
16.4 Constructing Access Points to Represent Places

Section 5: Recording Primary Relationships between Work, Expression, Manifestation, & Item

17: General Guidelines on Recording Primary Relationships
17.0 Purpose and Scope
17.1 Terminology
17.2 Functional Objectives and Principles
17.3 Core Elements
17.4 Recording Primary Relationships
17.5 Expression of Work
17.6 Work Expressed
17.7 Manifestation of Work
17.8 Work Manifested
17.9 Manifestation of Expression
17.10 Expression Manifested
17.11 Exemplar of Manifestation
17.12 Manifestation Exemplified

Section 6: Recording Relationships to Persons, Families, & Corporate Bodies

18: General Guidelines on Recording Relationships to Persons, Families, and Corporate Bodies Associated with a Resource
18.0 Scope
18.1 Terminology
18.2 Functional Objectives and Principles
18.3 Core Elements
18.4 Recording Relationships to Persons, Families, and Corporate Bodies Associated with a Resource
18.5 Relationship Designator
18.6 Note on Persons, Families, and Corporate Bodies Associated with a Resource

19: Persons, Families, and Corporate Bodies Associated with a Work
19.0 Purpose and Scope
19.1 General Guidelines on Recording Persons, Families, and Corporate Bodies Associated with a Work

24.7   Source Consulted
24.8   Cataloguer's Note

25: Related Works
25.0   Purpose and Scope
25.1   Related Work
25.2   Explanation of Relationship

26: Related Expressions
26.0   Purpose and Scope
26.1   Related Expression
26.2   Explanation of Relationship

27: Related Manifestations
27.0   Purpose and Scope
27.1   Related Manifestation

28: Related Items
28.0   Purpose and Scope
28.1   Related Item

Section 9: Recording Relationships between Persons, Families, & Corporate Bodies

29: General Guidelines on Recording Relationships between Persons, Families, and Corporate Bodies
29.0   Scope
29.1   Terminology
29.2   Functional Objectives and Principles
29.3   Core Elements
29.4   Recording Relationships between Persons, Families, and Corporate Bodies
29.5   Relationship Designator
29.6   Source Consulted
29.7   Cataloguer's Note

30: Related Persons
30.0   Purpose and Scope
30.1   Related Person
30.2   Explanation of Relationship

31: Related Families
31.0   Purpose and Scope
31.1   Related Family
31.2   Explanation of Relationship

32: Related Corporate Bodies
32.0   Purpose and Scope
32.1   Related Corporate Body
32.2   Explanation of Relationship

Section 10: Recording Relationships between Concepts, Objects, Events, & Places

33: General Guidelines on Recording Relationships between Concepts, Objects, Events, and Places   *[Currently empty]*

34: Related Concepts   *[Currently empty]*

35: Related Objects   *[Currently empty]*

36: Related Events   *[Currently empty]*

37: Related Places   *[Currently empty]*

Appendices

A: Capitalization
B: Abbreviations and Symbols
C: Initial Articles
D: Record Syntaxes for Descriptive Data
E: Record Syntaxes for Access Point Control
F: Additional Instructions on Names of Persons
G: Titles of Nobility, Terms of Rank, Etc.
H: Dates in the Christian Calendar
I: Relationship Designators: Relationships between a Resource and Persons, Families, and Corporate Bodies Associated with the Resource
J: Relationship Designators: Relationships between Works, Expressions, Manifestations, and Items
K: Relationship Designators: Relationships between Persons, Families, and Corporate Bodies
L: Relationship Designators: Relationships between Concepts, Objects, Events, and Places
M: Relationship Designators: Subject Relationships

Glossary

Appendix B:
ICC11 RDA Book Template

The ICC11 RDA Book Template is presented here for quick reference. Due to publishing constraints, it is presented in a format that is unusable for actual cataloging purposes because the *Metadata Content* column has been greatly reduced so that the other columns can be more easily read. A more functional version of the template is available online in PDF, RTF, and DOC formats at **http://web.simmons.edu/~joudrey/ICC11/**.

ICC11 RDA Book Template				
(for single-part monographs)				
Key: **RDA**: RDA instruction number				
Element: RDA element name; includes *Core, Core-if, LC Core,* and *ICC11 Core* for books				
(T): Transcribed data				
Metadata content: Place to record the data				
MARC: Typical MARC fields and subfields				
ISBD: Preceding ISBD punctuation when used in MARC				
RDA	**Element**	**Metadata Content**	**MARC**	**ISBD**
Manifestations and Items				
2.3.2	Title proper (T)		245 $a	n/a
2.3.2.6	Collective titles & titles of individual contents (T)		245 $a 505 $t 7XX $t	n/a
2.3.3	Parallel title proper (T)		245 $b	=

2.3.4	Other title information (T)		245 $b	:
2.3.6	Variant titles		246 $a	
	Other titles not listed above			
2.4.2	Statement of responsibility for title proper (T)		245 $c	/
	Subsequent statements of responsibility (T)		245 $c	;
2.5	Designation of edition (T)		250 $a	n/a
2.5.4	Statement of responsibility for edition (T)		250 $b	/
2.5.6	Designation of a named revision of an edition (T)		250 $a	,
	Other edition information			
2.8.2	Place of publication (T)		264 #1 $a	n/a
2.8.4	Publisher's name (T)		264 #1 $b	:
2.8.6	Date of publication		264 #1 $c	,
2.9.2	Place of distribution (T)		264 #2 $a	n/a
2.9.4	Distributor's name (T)		264 #2 $b	:
2.9.6	Date of distribution		264 #2 $c	,
2.10.2	Place of manufacture (T)		264 #3 $a	n/a
2.10.4	Manufacturer's name (T)		264 #3 $b	:
2.10.6	Date of manufacture		264 #3 $c	,
2.11	Copyright date		264 #4 $c	n/a
	Other dissemination information			
2.12.2	Title proper of series and subseries (T)		490 $a	n/a
2.12.8	ISSN of series		490 $x	,
2.12.9	Numbering within series (T)		490 $v	;
2.12.10	Title proper of subseries (T)		490 $a	.
2.12.16	ISSN of subseries		490 $x	,
2.12.17	Numbering within subseries (T)		490 $v	;
	Other series information			
2.13	Mode of issuance		Ldr/07 Value=m	
2.15	Identifier for manifestation		020 $a	n/a
2.17.2	Note on title		5XX	n/a
	Other manifestation data		5XX	n/a
Carriers				
3.2	Media type		337	n/a
3.3	Carrier type		338	n/a
3.4	Extent		330 $a	n/a
3.5	Dimensions		300 $c	;
4.6	Uniform resource locator (URL)		856 $u	

	Other carrier elements			
	Carrier description of accompanying material		300 $e	+
Works and Expressions				
6.2.2	Preferred title for the work or expression		130 $a 240 $a 7XX $t 730	n/a n/a . n/a
6.9	Content type		336	n/a
	Other work or expression level information needed in the bibliographic description			
Content				
7.7	Intended audience		008/22 521 $a	n/a
7.9	Dissertation or thesis information		500 $a 502 $a-$c	n/a
7.10	Summarization of the content		520 $a	n/a
7.12	Language of the content		008/35-37 546	n/a
7.15	Illustrative content		300 $b	:
7.16	Supplementary content		500 $a 504 $a	n/a
	Other content elements			
Persons, Families, and Corporate Bodies (PFCs) Associated with Resource				
19.2	Principal or First-named Creator		1XX $a	n/a
19.2	Additional creators		7XX $a	n/a
19.3	Other PFCs associated with a work		7XX $a 1XX $a	n/a
20.2	Contributors		7XX $a	n/a
	Additional information regarding PFCs			
Related Resources				
25.1	Related work		500/505/ 7XX/490/ 8XX	
26.1	Related expression		500/7XX	
27.1	Related manifestation		500/7XX	
	Other relationship information			
Other Needed Metadata				

Glossary of Selected Terms and Abbreviations

Defined in this glossary are selected basic terms for students of cataloging, including a number of terms and identifiers used in information organization, descriptive cataloging, classification, subject heading work, filing, document indexing, networking, and other topics treated in this text. Readers may wish to consult other sources for other terms used in the library and information professions. Some concepts are marked *obsolete* to indicate that the term is no longer used; these terms remain in the glossary, however, because they may be encountered in older LIS literature.

20% rule. *See* **Twenty-percent rule**.

AACR (*Anglo-American Cataloguing Rules*). A set of cataloging rules, first published in 1967, for producing the descriptive metadata and name-and-title access points in a surrogate record for a resource; later editions were published in 1978, 1988, 1998, and 2002; replaced in 2010 by *RDA: Resource Description & Access*; the creation of these rules was the result of collaboration among representatives from Australia, Canada, Great Britain, and the United States.

AAP. *See* **Authorized access point**.

Aboutness. The subject of a work contained in a resource, which is translated into controlled subject languages (e.g., classification schemes, subject headings lists); includes topical aspects and also genre and form. *See also* **Conceptual analysis**; **Is-ness**; **Subject analysis**; **Translation (Subject cataloging)**.

Abstract. A condensed narrative description of a resource that may serve as a surrogate for the resource in a retrieval system.

Abstracting. The process of creating abstracts. *See also* **Indexing**.

Access. That portion of cataloging in which access points are selected and formulated by a cataloger. *See also* **Description**; **Descriptive cataloging**.

Access point. Any word or phrase used to obtain information from a retrieval tool or other organized system; in cataloging and indexing, *access points* are specific names, titles, and subjects chosen by the cataloger or indexer, when creating a surrogate/metadata record, to allow for the retrieval of the record. *See also* **Authorized access point**; **Controlled access point**; **Uncontrolled access point**; **Variant access point**.

Accession number. A number assigned to each item as it is received in the library. Accession numbers may be assigned through continuous numbering (e.g., 30291, 30292) or a coded system (2015-00201, 2015-00202, etc.).

Accompanying materials. Dependent materials, such as answer books, teacher's manuals, atlases, portfolios of plates, slides, sound recordings, or computer disks, that accompany and are cataloged with the main component of the resource.

Acquiring function. The function of information organization that allows a user to obtain access to a resource or to determine where it is located physically in a library, archives, museum, or the like.

Add instructions. Notes in classification schedules that specify what digits to add to a base number. *See also* **Base number**.

Added entry. *Obsolete.* In AACR2, a secondary access point; any access point other than the main entry or primary access point; replaced in RDA by *access point*, and access points are not considered to be primary or secondary unless a work identifier is being selected.

Alphabetical catalog. A catalog with entries arranged or displayed in alphabetical order rather than according to the symbolic notation of a classification. *See also* **Classified catalog**; **Dictionary catalog**; **Divided catalog**.

Alphabetico-classed catalog. A catalog in which subject categories are used for arrangement of surrogate records; broad categories are subdivided by narrower categories that are placed alphabetically within each broad category.

Alternative title. The second title of a work, which is joined to the first title with the word *or* (e.g., *Maria, or, The Wrongs of Woman*) or its equivalent (*Candide, ou, l'Optimisme*). Both titles together are considered to constitute the title proper of the work. *See also* **Title**; **Title proper**.

Analytical description. A description of a part or parts of a resource (as opposed to a description of the whole resource). *See also* **Comprehensive description**; **Hierarchical description**.

Analytico-synthetic classification. *See* **Faceted classification**.

Anonymous work. A work in which the creator's name does not appear anywhere in the resource; a work of unknown authorship.

Approximate the whole. In DDC, a phrase used to describe the relationships between a topic and the class that contains it; a topic that "approximates the whole" is coextensive (i.e., a nearly perfect fit) with the full meaning of the class number; status often indicated by a class-here note. *See also* **Class-here note**.

Area. A major section of an ISBD bibliographic description; the nine areas of description are: area 0—Content form and media type area; 1—Title and statement of responsibility area; 2—Edition area; 3—Material or type of resource specific area; 4—Publication, production, distribution, etc., area; 5—Material description area; 6—Series and multipart monographic resource area; 7—Note area; and 8—Resource identifier and terms of availability area. *See also* **ISBD**.

Asynchronous responsibility. The situation in which the persons, families, or corporate bodies involved in the creation or expression of a work have made different kinds of contributions (e.g., author and illustrator; performer, conductor, choreographer, and producer); also called *mixed responsibility*. *See also* **Mixed responsibility**; **Shared responsibility**; **Synchronous responsibility**.

Attribute. A characteristic or property of an entity; useful in description.

Author. A specific type of creator primarily associated with writing books or other forms of text; a person who is responsible for all or some of the intellectual or artistic content of a work. *See also* **Creator**.

Author number. *See* **Cutter number**.

Authority control. The result of the process of maintaining consistency in the verbal form used to represent an access point and the further process of showing the relationships among names, works, and subjects; also, the result of the process of doing authority work with or without the necessity of choosing one form of name or title or one subject term to be the authorized selection. If every variant name, title, or term is given equal status, then one form is chosen for default display. Whether or not an authorized form is chosen to represent the name, title, or term, a searcher may use any of the forms in the authority record to gain access to resources related to the name, title, or subject. *See also* **Authority work**.

Authority file. A grouping of authority records.

Authority record. Documentation of the decisions made during the course of authority work. An authority record contains a variety of data about the entity being described, including all the forms used for a particular name, title, or subject; typically the record designates one of the forms as the authorized or default one to use in catalog records.

Authority work. The process of determining and maintaining the form of a name or title and/or determining and maintaining an authorized term or phrase to stand for a subject concept. In the name and title areas, the process includes identifying all variant names or titles and relating the variants to the name or title forms chosen to be access points. In some cases it may also include relating different names and/or titles to each other. In the verbal subject area, the process includes identifying and maintaining relationships among terms—relationships such as synonyms, broader terms, narrower terms, and related terms. *See also* **Authority control**.

Authorized access point. The standardized character string established in an authority record that is used to represent an entity (e.g., person, family, corporate body, a work, a subject) consistently in bibliographic descriptions. *See also* **Controlled access point**; **Reference**; **Uncontrolled access point**; **Variant access point**.

Auto-Graphics (A-G). A bibliographic network offering its database and services to a variety of Canadian libraries and also to a few libraries in the northeastern United States; formerly Utlas International, ISM/LIS, and A-G Canada.

Auxiliary table. A generalized subdivision table appended to a classification schedule for use in building specific classification numbers where indicated in the schedule proper.

Base number. A classification number to which other digits are appended or added. *See also* **Add instructions**.

BIBCO (Monographic Bibliographic Record Cooperative Program). A part of the Program for Cooperative Cataloging (PCC); the program has led to the widespread availability of high quality cataloging records for monographs in international bibliographic databases; provides a description of what is expected in a standard record created by participants. *See also* **CONSER**; **NACO**; **PCC**; **SACO**.

BIBCO Standard Record (BSR). The PCC model for a typical, shareable bibliographic record.

BIBFRAME. Bibliographic Framework Initiative, a project started by the Library of Congress to provide a replacement for MARC as the primary encoding standard for library-generated metadata. Based on linked data principles, BIBFRAME replaces self-contained bibliographic and authority records with authoritative statements about resources coded for participation in the Semantic Web.

Bibliographic   control.   *See*   **Information   organization**;   **Universal Bibliographic Control**.

Bibliographic   data.   Information   gathered   in   the   process   of   creating bibliographic records; also refers to any discrete element(s) in a bibliographic record. *See also* **Metadata**.

Bibliographic database. A collection of bibliographic records held in the format of a database. *See also* **Catalog**.

Bibliographic family. A set of related works that are derived from a common progenitor.

Bibliographic file. A grouping of bibliographic records. In a catalog or bibliographic database, a bibliographic file is distinct from, but might be linked to, one or more authority files and/or holdings files.

Bibliographic Framework Initiative. *See* **BIBFRAME**.

Bibliographic identity. The concept that creators of works may use separate personae when creating different types of works. For example, Charles L. Dodgson and Lewis Carroll are two bibliographic identities used by a single person; one wrote about mathematics and the other wrote stories for children. *See also* **Pseudonym**.

Bibliographic network. A corporate entity that has as its main resource a bibliographic database; access to the database is available for a price, and members of the network can contribute new records and download existing ones; sometimes called a *bibliographic utility*.

Bibliographic record. Catalog data in card, microform, machine-readable, or other form carrying full cataloging information for a resource; a set of metadata statements referring to the same resource. *See also* **Metadata**; **Surrogate record**.

Bibliographic tool. *See* **Bibliographic database**; **Bibliography**; **Catalog**; **Index**; **Retrieval tool**.

Bibliographic universe. The concept that encompasses all instances of recorded knowledge.

Bibliographic utility. *See* **Bibliographic network**.

Bibliography. A list of resources on a given subject, by a given author, from a particular time period or place, or the like.

BL. British Library, London, England.

Blind Reference. A reference that directs the user of a catalog or other such database to a place where nothing is found. *See also* **Reference**.

Book catalog. A catalog in which surrogate records are printed on pages that are bound into book form.

Book number. *See* **Cutter number**.

Boolean operators. The terms *and*, *or*, and *not* as used to construct search topics in a retrieval tool that uses post-coordinate indexing and/or keyword searching.

Broad classification. A method of applying a classification scheme that omits detailed subdivision of its main classes or that facilitates the use in smaller libraries of only its main classes and subdivisions. *See also* **Close classification**.

Broader term (BT). A term one level up from the term being examined in a listing where terms for subject concepts have been organized into relationships that are hierarchical. *See also* **Narrower term**; **Related term**.

BSR. *See* **BIBCO Standard Record**.

Call number. A notation on an item that matches the same notation in the surrogate/metadata record and is used to identify and locate the particular item; it often consists of a classification notation and a cutter number, and it may also include a workmark and/or a date. It is the number used to "call" for an item in a closed stack library—thus the source of the name *call number*. *See also* **Cutter number**; **Workmark**.

Card catalog. A catalog in which every record is printed or typed on a card (usually 3" × 5") and placed in a file drawer in a particular order (usually alphabetical or classified order).

Carrier. The physical format in which the content of a resource is stored.

Carrier type. A category reflecting the physical format of a resource (e.g., volume, audio disc, filmstrip cartridge).

Catalog. An organized compilation of bibliographic metadata or an organized set of surrogate records that represent the holdings of a particular collection and/or resources to which access may be gained. It may be arranged alphabetically, by classification notation, by subject, or, in the case of an online catalog, the display may be arranged by date or any one of several other elements. *See also* **Bibliographic database**; **Index**.

Catalog record. *See* **Bibliographic record**; **Metadata**; **Surrogate record**.

Cataloger. Person in a library or another information or cultural heritage organization who creates surrogate records for the resources collected by the organization and who works to maintain the system through which those surrogate records are made available to users; the person may also be an independent contractor. *See also* **Indexer**.

Cataloging. The process of creating metadata for resources by describing a resource, choosing name and title access points, conducting subject analysis, assigning subject headings and classification numbers, and maintaining the system through which the cataloging data is made available. *See also* **Copy cataloging**; **Descriptive cataloging**; **Indexing**; **Original cataloging**; **Subject cataloging**.

Cataloging in Publication. *See* **CIP**.

Centered entry. In DDC, a span of numbers used to represent a concept; it is referred to as *centered* because the span is printed in the center of a page in the print volumes of DDC; it is denoted by a greater than sign (>).

Centralized processing. Any cooperative effort that results in the centralization of one or more of the technical processes involved in getting material ready for use in a library.

Characteristic of division. In classification, the attribute or property chosen to sort members of a class into subclasses; for example, in a literature class, the characteristics of division may include language, form, and time period; the order of the characteristics of division determines citation order. *See also* **Citation order**.

Chief source of information. *Obsolete.* The source in an information resource that is prescribed by AACR2 as the major source of data for use in preparing a bibliographic description; replaced in RDA by *preferred sources of information*. *See also* **Preferred sources of information**; **Title page**.

CIP (Cataloging-In-Publication). A program in which cataloging is provided by an authorized agency to the publisher or producer of a resource so that the cataloging can be issued with the resource; often the phrase or acronym is applied in the case of cataloging provided by the Library of Congress to the publishers of books.

Citation order. In classification, the sequence of the characteristics of division used for dividing a class; citation order determines which concepts are collocated and which are scattered. *See also* **Characteristics of division**.

Class. The first order of structure in a hierarchical classification, at which level major disciplines are represented. A class may incorporate one or more divisions, which in turn may incorporate one or more sections or subdivisions. *See also* **Division**; **Hierarchical classification**; **Section**; **Subdivision**.

Class-here note. In DDC, a note used to identify major topics that are coextensive or nearly coextensive with the topic listed in the caption; such topics are said to "approximate the whole" of the number under which the note appears. *See also* **Approximate the whole**.

Classification. The placing of subjects into categories; in information organization, classification is the process of determining where a work fits in a given hierarchy and then assigning the notation that is associated with the most appropriate concept to the resource and to its metadata (e.g., a catalog record). *See also* **Broad classification**; **Close classification**; **Faceted classification**; **Hierarchical classification**.

Classification notation. The set of numbers, letters, symbols, or a combination of these that is assigned to a certain concept in a classification scheme.

Classification schedule. The list of concepts found in a classification system in classified order.

Classification scheme. An organized framework for the systematic organization of knowledge, usually organized by subject.

Classification table. Supplementary part of a classification scheme in which a hierarchy is developed and notations are assigned for concepts that can be applied in conjunction with many different topical subjects. Tables commonly exist for geographic locations, time periods, standard subdivisions (e.g., dictionaries, theory, serial publications, historical treatment), ethnic and national groups, languages, and so on.

Classified catalog. A catalog arranged or displayed in the order of symbols, numbers, or other notations that represent the various subjects or aspects of subjects covered by the resources housed in the institution. *See also* **Alphabetical catalog**; **Shelflist**.

Close classification. The use of minute subdivisions to arrange materials by highly specific topics. *See also* **Broad classification**.

Closed stacks. The name given to the situation where collections are not open to public access or are limited to only a small group of users. *See also* **Open stacks**; **Stacks**.

Code (as a noun). (1) A set of rules. (2) A specific designation in an encoding standard that defines and limits the kinds of data that can be stored at that point.

Code (as a verb). The process of assigning the appropriate specified designations of an encoding standard. *See also* **Content designation**.

Coextensive subject entry. A principle of subject analysis, by which a term, phrase, or set of terms defines precisely the complete intellectual contents, but no more than the contents, of a resource.

Collaborative work. A single work created by two or more persons, families, or corporate bodies, in which (1) responsibility is shared and (2) the individual contributions of the creators cannot be distinguished. *See also* **Joint author**; **Shared responsibility**.

Collation. *Obsolete.* In AACR2 and earlier, referred to the physical description of a resource, which contained the extent, other physical details (e.g., illustrative content), dimensions, and accompanying material. These elements are identified in RDA by such terms as Media type, Carrier type, Extent, Dimensions, Production method, Video characteristic, Reduction ratio, and so on.

Collective title. An inclusive title that represents a compilation that contains two or more individually titled parts. *See also* **Title**.

Collocating function. The function of information organization that relates bibliographic entities to each other through the process of collocation; also called *gathering function*.

Collocation. The process of bringing together records and/or resources that are related in some way (e.g., same author, same work, same subject).

Colon Classification. Classification scheme first devised by S. R. Ranganathan in the early 1930s; it was the first fully faceted classification scheme.

Colophon. A statement of publication data found at the end of a resource.

COM. Computer Output Microform.

COM catalog. A catalog produced on COM and requiring a microform reader for its use.

Compilation. A collection of works (or parts of works) by one author published together, or two or more works or parts of works by more than one author published together. Each work in a compilation was originally written independently or as part of an independent publication.

Compiler. A creator who brings together selections (e.g., articles, chapters) from the works of various authors or the works of a single author to create an aggregate new work, or, who brings together separate pieces of information (e.g., citations, data) to create a new work such as a bibliography, a directory, or the like. *See also* **Creator**; **Editor**.

Comprehensive description. A description of a resource as a whole (as opposed to descriptions of individual parts). *See also* **Analytical description**; **Hierarchical description**.

Comprehensive number. In DDC, a classification number that encompasses all the facets of a topic treated within the single discipline in which that topic appears; often identified by a note instructing, "Class here comprehensive works" on the topic. *See also* **Interdisciplinary number**.

Conceptual analysis. The first stage of the subject analysis process in which a resource is analyzed to determine its aboutness. *See also* **Aboutness**; **Subject analysis**; **Translation (Subject cataloging)**.

CONSER (Cooperative Online Serials Program). A part of the Program for Cooperative Cataloging (PCC); the program has led to the widespread availability of high quality serials records in bibliographic databases. *See also* **BIBCO**; **NACO**; **PCC**; **SACO**.

Content. The intellectual or artistic substance of a work.

Content designation. The act of making a bibliographic or authority record machine-readable by encoding its various elements using the MARC formats. *See also* **Code (as a verb)**; **MARC**.

Content standard. A set of rules or instructions to guide catalogers, indexers, and the like in the creation and formatting of data for a bibliographic or index record, an authority record, a metadata statement, or some other form of resource description.

Content type. In RDA, a category representing how the content of a work is communicated or perceived (e.g., text, performed music, still image, cartographic three-dimensional form).

Contextualize. A FRAD user task; to put an entity (person, family, subject, etc.) in context; in RDA, the comparable user task is identified as *clarify*.

Continuation. (1) A work issued as a supplement to an earlier one. (2) A part issued in continuance of a book, a serial, or a series.

Continuing resource. *See* **Integrating resource**; **Serial**.

Contract cataloging. A type of outsourcing in which an institution contracts with a person or agency to provide bibliographic records, and sometimes authority records, that represent the institution's collection. *See also* **Outsourcing**.

Contributor. A person, family, or corporate body that helps to realize an expression of a work—sometimes in the original creation of the work and sometimes in later expressions of the work—with supplementary content (such as illustrated editions or versions with commentary) that was not present in the original expression.

Control field. A field in the MARC format (00X) that includes numeric or other encoded data for retrieval. *See also* **Field**; **Fixed field**; **Variable field**.

Controlled access point. A name, term, or code found in an authority record; may be an authorized access point or a reference. *See also* **Authorized access point**; **Reference**; **Uncontrolled access point**; **Variant access point**.

Controlled vocabulary. A list or database of terms (usually subject or genre/form terms) in which all terms or phrases representing a concept are brought together. Often a preferred term or phrase is designated for use in surrogate records in a retrieval tool; the non-preferred terms have references from them to the chosen term or phrase, and relationships among used terms are identified (e.g., broader terms, narrower terms, related terms). There may also be scope notes. *See also* **Subject heading list**; **Thesaurus**.

Conventional collective title. In RDA, a collective title referring to the form of the work used for a compilation containing two or more works by a person, family, or corporate body (e.g., *Plays, Works, Speeches*), or it may be used for two or more parts of a work (e.g., *Selections*); formerly called a *uniform title* in AACR2. *See also* **Title**.

Cooperative cataloging. The working together of independent institutions to share network memberships or to create cataloging that can be used by others.

Coordinate indexing. The enabling of information retrieval through the use of single concept terms in a catalog or database. *See also* **Post-coordinate indexing**; **Pre-coordinate indexing**.

Copy cataloging. Adapting the original cataloging created by one library for use in another institution's catalog. *See also* **Original cataloging**.

Core elements. In RDA, the minimal set of elements required for an adequate bibliographic description.

Core-if elements. Required metadata elements, in addition to the minimum set of elements, that are recorded if applicable and if available.

Core record. *Obsolete. See* **BIBCO Standard Record**.

Corporate body. An organization or a group of persons that is identified by a collective name and that acts as an entity.

Creator. A person, family, or corporate body that is responsible for the intellectual or artistic content of a work; includes authors, writers, compilers, composers, artists, photographers, and the like.

Cross-reference. *See* **Reference**.

Crosswalk. A table, chart, or other device that indicates equivalence relationships among concepts, elements, or values in two or more controlled vocabularies, metadata schemes, encoding standards, and so on. *See also* **Switching language**.

Cutter number. The symbols, usually a combination of letters and numbers, used to distinguish items with the same classification number; used to maintain alphabetical order (by author, title, etc.) of items on the shelves; sometimes called *author number* or *book number*. The word *cutter* is derived from the widespread use of the tables first devised by Charles A. Cutter to provide alphabetical sub-arrangement. *See also* **Call number**; **Workmark**.

Database. A set of records that are all constructed in the same way and are often connected by relationship links; the structure underlying retrieval tools.

DC. *See* **Dublin Core**.

DDC. *See Dewey Decimal Classification*.

Depth indexing. Assignment of subject terms to represent all of the main concepts in a document, including many subtopics and subthemes. *See also* **Exhaustivity**; **Summarization**.

Description. That portion of the descriptive cataloging process in which elements that identify a resource are transcribed into a bibliographic record; also, the portion of the bibliographic record (i.e., descriptive data) that results from this process. *See also* **Access**; **Descriptive cataloging**; **Descriptive data**; **Metadata**.

Descriptive cataloging. That phase of the cataloging process that is concerned with the identification and description of a resource, the recording of this information in a bibliographic record, and the selection and formation of access points—with the exception of subject access points. *See also* **Access**; **Description**.

Descriptive data. Data that describes a resource, such as its title, its associated names, its edition, its date of publication, its extent, and notes identifying pertinent features.

Descriptor. A subject term, representing a single concept, usually found in thesauri and used in indexes. *See also* **Subject heading**; **Term**.

Designation of edition. A word or number identifying the edition to which a resource belongs.

Dewey Decimal Classification (DDC). Classification devised by Melvil Dewey in 1876; it divides the world of knowledge hierarchically into 10 classes, which are in turn divided into 10 divisions, then into 10 sections, and so on with additional subdivisions, using the 10 digits of the Arabic numeral system (i.e., 0-9). DDC is enumerative but has many faceting capabilities, especially in its later editions.

Diacritic. Modifying mark over, under, or through a character to indicate that pronunciation is different from that of the character without the diacritic; also called *diacritical mark*.

Dictionary catalog. A catalog arranged or displayed in alphabetical order with records for names, titles, and subjects all intermixed. *See also* **Divided catalog**.

Direct entry. A principle of formulation of controlled vocabularies that stipulates the entry of a concept directly under the term that names it, rather than as a subdivision of a broader concept (e.g., Child rearing, *not* Children—Development and guidance).

Distributor. Corporate body, person, or family responsible for delivering resources.

Divided catalog. A catalog in which different types of records are arranged or displayed in separate files or displays. In print catalogs, usually the subject entries are separated from other entries, and sometimes titles are also separated. Order is usually alphabetical in each section, but the subject section may be in classified order. Online catalogs are de facto divided catalogs when authors, titles, and subjects are searched and displayed separately. *See also* **Dictionary catalog**.

Division. In hierarchical classification, the second structural level at which major components of a discipline are represented. A division is a subset of a class and may incorporate one or more sections or subdivisions. *See also* **Class**; **Hierarchical classification**; **Section**; **Subdivision**.

Document. A resource; often associated in people's minds with text and illustrations having been produced on paper, but increasingly associated with other forms of information resources.

DTD (Document type definition). An SGML or XML application; defines the structure of a particular type of document.

Dublin Core. A set of metadata elements, with associated attributes and properties, developed and maintained by the Dublin Core Metadata Initiative as a simple standard for resource description.

Edition. A particular version of a resource; a specific expression of the intellectual content of the work found in a resource.

Edition, Designation of. *See Designation of edition.*

Editor. A contributor to a resource who supervises the preparation and/or the publication of a new expression of a work or of a collection of works or articles authored by others; editing responsibility may extend to revising, providing introductory matter, and similar functions that are not considered to be activities that result in new works. See also **Compiler**; **Contributor**.

Electronic resource. Resource that requires the use of a computer to access its intellectual or artistic contents.

Element. An individual category or field that holds a single piece of the description of a resource (e.g., extent is an element used to describe a resource's carrier).

Encoding. Using a record syntax or a coding scheme to make metadata electronically accessible. Encoding ensures that metadata is structured logically and that it may be communicated, shared, and displayed easily. Encoding entails the setting off of each part of a record (or each metadata statement) so that (1) each of the parts can be identified clearly; (2) the parts or statements may be displayed in certain positions according to the wishes of those creating a display mechanism; and (3) certain parts of a record can be searchable.

Entity. A thing (a person, subject, work, resource, etc.); in cataloging, entities are described by listing their various attributes.

Entry. *Obsolete. See* **Access point**; **Bibliographic record**; **Heading**.

Entry term. A reference in a controlled vocabulary; it points users to authorized subject terms.

Enumerative classification. A classification arrangement that attempts to assign a designation for every subject concept (simple or complex) required in the system. *See also* **Faceted classification**; **Hierarchical classification**.

Evaluating function. *See* **Selecting function**.

Exhaustivity. The number of concepts that will be considered in the process of providing subject analysis. *See also* **Depth indexing**; **Summarization**.

Expansive Classification. A classification scheme created by Charles A. Cutter in which a set of coordinated schedules gives successive development possibilities from very simple (broad) to very detailed (close) subdivision.

Explanatory reference. A reference that gives detailed guidance necessary for understanding the relationships among the entities involved, explaining such things as history or complex relationships. *See also* **Scope note**.

Expression. The second level in describing a Group 1 entity in the FRBR conceptual model; an expression is the way that a work is communicated through alphanumeric characters, signs, images, movement, sounds, or the like. *See also* **Item**; **Manifestation**; **Work**.

Extent. The number and type of units and/or subunits that make up the carrier of a resource.

Facet. A component (piece, side, or aspect) of a subject.

Facet indicator. A symbol, punctuation mark, or reserved digit signifying that the digits or letters following that symbol represent another aspect of the topic.

Faceted Application of Subject Terminology. *See* **FAST**.

Faceted classification. A subject concept arrangement that has small notations standing for sub-parts of the whole topic, which, when strung together, usually in prescribed sequence, create a complete classification notation for a multipart concept. *See also* **Enumerative classification**; **Hierarchical classification**.

Faceting. An approach to categorizing terms in a controlled vocabulary or organizing discrete concepts in a classification scheme so that terms/concepts with a similar function or a shared characteristic are clustered together.

Facsimile. A reproduction in which the producer tries to recreate the appearance of an original manifestation in addition to reproducing its content exactly.

FAST. A faceted controlled vocabulary based on LCSH.

FID. Fédération Internationale de Documentation (International Federation for Documentation).

Field. A separately designated segment of an encoded record. A field may contain one or more subfields. *See also* **Control field**; **Fixed field**; **Subfield**; **Variable field**.

Filing. The process of placing paper records (e.g., catalog cards, acquisition forms) in order, usually in drawers.

Finding function. The function of information organization that allows a user to search for a resource or a set of resources based on specific criteria.

First-order political division. In LCSH, the level of political jurisdiction below the country level (e.g., state, province).

Fixed field. A field in an encoded record that is of a set length. There are three major fixed fields in a standard MARC 21 record: 008 (fixed length data elements), 007 (physical description fixed field), and 006 (additional material characteristics), of which the 008 field is often referred to as *the* fixed field. *See also* **Control field**; **Field**; **Subfield**; **Variable field**.

Fixed location. A set place where a physical resource will always be found or to which it will be returned after having been removed for use. *See also* **Relative location**.

Form division. *See* **Standard subdivision**.

Form/genre heading. *See* **Genre/form heading**.

FRAD. *See Functional Requirements for Authority Data*.

FRBR. *See Functional Requirements for Bibliographic Records*.

Free-floating subdivision. A term that can be added to a subject heading, as needed, whether or not it is written in the published list following that heading. In the LCSH system, however, *free-floating subdivisions* have scope notes that express limitations on the use of some such terms.

Front matter. *See* **Preliminaries (in a book)**.

FRSAD. *See Functional Requirements for Subject Authority Data*.

Full entry. *See* **Main entry (record)**.

Functional Requirements for Authority Data **(FRAD).** A conceptual model developed by IFLA, designed as a companion to FRBR; it focuses on authority data, particularly on controlled access points used to represent persons, families, corporate bodies, and works.

Functional Requirements for Bibliographic Records **(FRBR).** A conceptual model of the bibliographic universe developed by IFLA that provides a way of describing entities and relationships between them. FRBR describes three groups of entities. Group 1 identifies entities that are the products of intellectual endeavors: *work, expression, manifestation, item.* Group 2 identifies entities responsible for such products: *person, corporate body,* and *family* (later added by FRAD*)*. Group 3 identifies entities that may serve as the subjects of intellectual or artistic endeavor: *concept, object, event,* and *place,* in addition to any group 1 or group 2 entity.

Functional Requirements for Subject Authority Data **(FRSAD).** A conceptual model developed by IFLA, designed as a companion to FRBR and

FRAD, which focuses on subject authority data, particularly on *thema* (subject) and *nomen* (labels or names for those subjects).

Gateway. A computer system or Web location that provides access to many different databases or other resources, using the same interface.

Gathering function. *See* **Collocating function**.

General works. In LCC, comprehensive works covering a topic.

Genre/form heading. A controlled vocabulary term that refers to the literary genre or artistic form or the publication format of a work rather than to its topical content; sometimes said to reflect an item's *is-ness* when discussed in opposition to *aboutness*. *See also* **Is-ness**.

Geographic name. The place name usually used in reference to a geographic area. It is not necessarily the political name. *See also* **Jurisdiction**.

Global update. A function in the back-end of a retrieval tool that allows for searching and replacing data strings in a record, a document, or throughout an entire database.

GMD (General Material Designation). *Obsolete.* A term that is given in an AACR2 record to indicate the class of material to which a resource belongs (e.g., art original, electronic resource, motion picture); replaced in RDA with three metadata elements: *content type*, *media type*, and *carrier type*. *See also* **Content type**; **Media type**; **Carrier type**.

Heading. *Obsolete* (in descriptive cataloging). (1) An access point printed at the top of a copy of a surrogate record or at the top of a listing of related works in an online retrieval tool. (2) The exact string of characters of the authorized form of an access point as it appears in the authority record. Replaced in RDA with *authorized access point*. Still used in subject cataloging in the term *subject heading*. *See also* **Access point**; **Subject heading**; **Term**.

Hierarchical classification. A classification that attempts to arrange subjects in a series of ordered groups, some of which are subordinate to others—proceeding from broad classes to more specific subdivisions. *See also* **Enumerative classification**; **Faceted classification**.

Hierarchical description. A description of two levels of a resource: a *comprehensive description* of the whole resource with *analytical descriptions* of one or more of its parts; also called *multi-level description*; generally not used in U.S. cataloging. *See also* **Analytical description**; **Comprehensive description**.

Hierarchical force. In DDC, the concept that what applies to a broader class applies to the more specific numbers in the subdivisions that fall under it hierarchically (i.e., topics inherit the attributes of the classes above them).

Hierarchical notation. In classification, the use of symbol groups of varying combinations and lengths to reflect a hierarchy of topics and subdivisions. Also called *expressive notation*.

Hierarchy. An arrangement by which categories are grouped in such a way that a concept (e.g., class or discipline) is subdivided into sub-concepts of an equal level of specificity, each of those sub-concepts are further subdivided into subcategories, and so on. In science, for example, living organisms are in the hierarchy: phylum, class, order, family, genus, species.

Holdings. A designation of physical items contained in a collection; sometimes also used to include electronic resources to which a library provides access.

Holdings file. A group of holdings records. In an OPAC or a bibliographic database, a holdings file is usually distinct from, but might be linked to, a bibliographic file.

Holdings note. One note in the bibliographic record for a serial that tells which parts of the serial are held by the library.

Holdings record. A record in a holdings file that gives complete holdings for a resource (volumes, parts, issues, etc.).

ICC11 PS. *See* ***Introduction to Cataloging and Classification, 11th ed. Policy Statements***.

ICP. *See* ***Statement of International Cataloguing Principles***.

Identifier. A unique character string (e.g., an ISBN, URI, a record number) associated with an entity (e.g., a person, a resource, a concept) that differentiates it from other entities.

Identifying function. The function of information organization that allows a user to recognize a specific resource.

IFLA. International Federation of Library Associations and Institutions, formerly International Federation of Library Associations; an international organization for the promotion of library standards and the sharing of ideas and research.

ILL. Interlibrary loan; the process of acquiring a physical resource or a copy of it from a library that owns it by a library that does not own it, usually for the purpose of re-lending it to a patron.

ILS. *See* **Integrated Library System**.

Imprint. The information in a textual publication that tells where it was published, who published it, and when it was published.

Including note. In DDC, a note beginning with the word *Including*, indicating that a topic is considered to be in *standing room*. *See also* **Standing room**.

Index. A bibliographic tool that provides access to the analyzed contents of resources (e.g., articles in journals, short stories in collections, papers in conference proceedings). A back-of-the-book index provides access to the analyzed contents of one work.

Indexer. A person who determines access points (usually subject terms, but may also be authors or titles) that are needed in order to make surrogate records available to searchers; an indexer also may create surrogate records. *See also* **Cataloger**.

Indexing. The process of creating surrogate records, especially the access points, for resources; such work done in commercial enterprises is often called *indexing*, while similar work done in nonprofit agencies is usually called *cataloging. See also* **Cataloging**.

Indexing vocabulary. *See* **Controlled vocabulary**.

Indicators. In the MARC encoding standards, indicators for a field contain coded information that is needed for interpreting or supplementing data in the field.

Infoglut. A state of information overload.

Information organization. The process of describing resources in the bibliographic universe and then providing name, title, and subject access to the descriptions, resulting in records that serve as surrogates for the actual items of recorded information, and also resulting in resources that are logically arranged. Information organization further requires that surrogate records be placed into retrieval systems where they act as pointers to the actual resources.

Information resource. *See* **Resource**.

Information retrieval. The process of gaining access to stored data for the purpose of becoming informed.

Integrated Library System (ILS). Computer system that includes various modules to perform different functions while sharing access to the same database. *See also* **Library services platform**.

Integrating resource. A bibliographic resource that is added to or changed by means of updates that are integrated into the whole resource (includes updating loose-leafs and updating websites). *See also* **Mode of issuance**.

Interdisciplinary number. In DDC, (1) a classification number established for works that approach a topic from multiple points of view (i.e., from different disciplinary approaches); often identified by a note instructing, "Class here interdisciplinary works" on the topic; and (2) in DDC's relative index, the classification number displayed on the same line as the main caption for the concept. *See also* **Comprehensive number**.

Interlibrary loan. *See* **ILL**.

Introduction to Cataloging and Classification, 11th ed. Policy Statements* (ICC11 PS)**. Interpretations or decisions—that have been made by the authors of this text—as to how catalogers should interpret and apply specific RDA instructions. Meant to supplement other institutions' policy statements. *See also **Library of Congress–Program for Cooperative Cataloging Policy Statements* (LC-PCC PSs)**; ***RDA: Resource Description & Access.

ISBD (*International Standard Bibliographic Description*). An internationally accepted format for the representation of descriptive information in bibliographic records that standardizes the elements to be used, assigns an order to these elements, and specifies a system of symbols to be used in punctuating the elements. Although ISBD may serve as a stand-alone descriptive standard, with the implementation of RDA the role of ISBD in relation to RDA has been reduced to that of a display standard. ISBD punctuation is placed between data elements in MARC records for display in OPACs and for printing on catalog cards. *See also* **Area**.

ISBD areas of description. *See* **Area**.

ISBN (International Standard Book Number). An internationally distinctive and unique number assigned to a monographic item.

ISDS (International Serials Data System). A network of national and international centers, sponsored by UNESCO, that develops and maintains registers of serial publications; this includes the assignment of ISSNs and key titles.

Is-ness. The form or genre of a work; what the work is, rather than what it is about. *See also* **Aboutness**; **Genre/form headings**.

ISSN (International Standard Serial Number). A distinctive and unique number assigned to a serial by ISDS.

Item. One copy of a manifestation of a work, such as a book, a map, an electronic file, or a sound recording, as distinct from its intellectual content (i.e., the work or expression of the work that it contains); the fourth level in describing a resource in the FRBR conceptual model. *See also* **Expression**; **Manifestation**; **Work**.

Joint author. A person who collaborates with one or more associates to produce a work in which the individual contributions of the authors cannot be distinguished. *See also* **Collaborative work**; **Shared responsibility**; **Synchronous responsibility**.

Jurisdiction. The proper name of a geographical area according to the law. This name may change with a change in government. *See also* **Geographic name**.

Justify. A FRAD user task; to document the choice of name of, or inclusion of other attributes about, an entity (person, family, subject, etc.); in RDA, the user task is identified as *understand*.

Key heading. *See* **Pattern heading**.

Keyword. A term that is chosen, either from actual text or from a searcher's mind, that is considered to be a *key* to finding certain information.

Keyword indexing. Use of significant words from a title or a text as index entries. *See also* **Coordinate indexing**.

Keyword searching. The use of one or more keywords as the intellectual content of a search command.

Knowledgebase. A set of multiple different products, traditionally housed in separate databases, but functionally integrated for the purposes of library resource management and discovery. Knowledgebases underlying library services platforms (LSPs) go beyond the functions typically included in integrated library systems (e.g., cataloging, authority control, circulation information) to include the offerings of library materials vendors (e.g., descriptions of accessibility of e-journals and e-books, URL link resolvers, discovery tools), dynamically updated within the LSP.

KWAC indexing. Key Word And Context, a format for showing index entries within the context in which they occur, but which also isolates or highlights the significant words ensuring that the keywords are easily identified; a combination of KWIC and KWOC indexing.

KWIC indexing. Key Word In Context, a format for showing index entries within the context in which they occur.

KWOC indexing. Key Word Out of Context, the use of significant words from titles for subject index entries, each followed by the whole title from which the word was taken.

LC. Library of Congress.

LC-PCC PS. *See **Library of Congress–Program for Cooperative Cataloging Policy Statements**.*

LCC. *See **Library of Congress Classification**.*

LCNAF (Library of Congress Name Authority File). A file housed at the Library of Congress containing not only the authority records created by LC and PCC contributors, but also records contributed from Australia, Canada, Great Britain, and others. More recently called *LC/NACO Authority File*.

LCRIs. *See **Library of Congress Rule Interpretations**.*

LCSH. *See **Library of Congress Subject Headings**.*

Leaf. A single sheet of paper that contains two sides (i.e., pages); when numbering is on both sides of a leaf, the extent of text is counted in terms of the number of pages, but when numbering is printed only on one side it is provided in terms of the number of leaves.

Letter-by-letter filing. An arrangement of terms in a retrieval tool in which spaces and some punctuation marks are ignored so that a term files as if it is all run together into one word (e.g., *New York* is treated as *Newyork* and follows *Newark*). *See also **Word-by-word filing**.*

Lexical ontology. In natural language processing, a formal representation of language that identifies specific terms, usually from a defined subject area, and lays out the relationships that exist between the terms. *See also **Ontology**.*

***Library of Congress Classification* (LCC).** Classification scheme created by the Library of Congress beginning in the late 1890s; it divides the world of knowledge hierarchically into categories using letters of the English alphabet and then using Arabic numerals for further subdivisions. LCC is basically an enumerative scheme, allowing only a limited amount of faceting.

Library of Congress Name Authority File. *See* **LCNAF**.

***Library of Congress–Program for Cooperative Cataloging Policy Statements* (LC-PCC PSs).** Interpretations or decisions—that have been made by LC's Policy and Standards Division, the PCC, or both—as to how catalogers will interpret and apply specific RDA instructions; the replacement for the *Library of Congress Rule Interpretations* (LCRIs).

***Library of Congress Rule Interpretations* (LCRIs).** *Obsolete.* A collection of the decisions that were made by the Library of Congress's Cataloging Policy and Support Office as to how catalogers at the Library of Congress would interpret and apply AACR2; replaced by the *Library of Congress–Program for Cooperative Cataloging Policy Statements* (LC-PCC PSs).

***Library of Congress Subject Headings* (LCSH).** List of terms to be used as controlled vocabulary for subject concepts by the Library of Congress and by any other agency that wishes to provide such controlled subject access to surrogate records.

Library services platform (LSP). An extension of traditional integrated library systems, using current technology to address barriers to efficient use of divergent material types, particularly electronic resources. Typical characteristics include unified management of physical and electronic materials; use of global knowledgebases in addition to, or rather than, local databases; cloud computing as the basis for system architecture; and development of application programming interfaces to facilitate interaction of LSP system software with that of external vendors. *See also* **Integrated library system**.

Linkage. A relationship between or among access points or records that is manifested implicitly or explicitly in a bibliographic retrieval system.

Linked data. An approach to encoding data from a wide range of different sources, and publishing it on the Web, such that it may be understood by computers as related to the same resource or concept. Linked data makes possible the discovery of knowledge about entities that would otherwise have been separated by disassociated means of encoding or by different data silos. Linked data is referred to as *open* if it is made freely available with minimal or no restrictions on access or re-use. *See also* **Semantic Web**.

Literary warrant. The concept that new notations are created for a classification scheme and new terms are added to a controlled vocabulary only when resources actually exist about a concept.

Locating function. *See* **Acquiring function**; **Finding function**.

Location device. A number or other designation on an item to tell where it is physically located.

LOD. Linked Open Data. *See* **Linked data**.

LSP. *See* **Library services platform**.

MAchine-Readable Cataloging. *See* **MARC**.

Main class. *See* **Class**.

Main entry (access point). *Obsolete. See* **Primary access point**.

Main entry (record). *Obsolete.* A full catalog record, headed by the primary access point, that gives all the elements necessary for the complete identification of a manifestation of a work. This record also bears the tracings of all the other headings under which the work is entered.

Manifestation. The physical form in which an expression of a work can be found; the third level in describing a resource in the FRBR conceptual model. *See also* **Expression**; **Item**; **Work**.

Manufacturer. The agency that has made (e.g., printed, pressed, fabricated, mass-produced) the manifestation being cataloged.

Manuscripts. Papers created by an individual (not papers of a corporate body); original word-processed, handwritten, or typed documents that usually exist in single copies (unless they have been carbon-copied, photocopied, or printed multiple times).

Map series. A group of map sheets having the same scale and cartographic specifications, identified collectively by the producing agency. When the series is completed, it covers a given geographic area.

MARC (MAchine-Readable Cataloging). A standard that prescribes codes that precede and identify specific elements of a bibliographic, authority, or holdings record, allowing the record to be read by a machine, which then displays the data in a fashion designed to make the record intelligible to users. *See also* **MARC 21**; **UNIMARC**.

MARC 21. A MARC standard agreed upon by Canadian and U.S. representatives ("21" stands for the 21st century). MARC 21, which represents a consolidation of USMARC and CAN/MARC, two previous national MARC schemes, also has been adopted by Great Britain and other countries, as well.

MARC record. An electronic bibliographic record that has its content designated according to MARC conventions.

MARC tag. A number that designates the kind of field in a MARC record.

Media type. A category indicating the type of intermediation device (e.g., a computer, a projector) needed in order to interact with a resource; there are eight possible categories (*audio, computer, microform, microscopic, projected, stereographic, unmediated,* and *video*) as well as *other* and *unspecified*.

Medical Subject Headings (MeSH). List of terms created by the National Library of Medicine to be used as controlled vocabulary for subject concepts in the field of medicine.

Metadata. Structured information that describes the attributes of resources for the purposes of identification, discovery, selection, use, access, and management; an encoded description of a resource (e.g., an RDA record encoded with MARC, a Dublin Core record); the purpose of metadata is to provide a level of data at which choices can be made as to which resources one wishes to view without having to search through massive amounts of irrelevant full text.

Metadata statement. An assertion about a single attribute or property of a resource; metadata statements are the foundation of bibliographic or metadata records.

Meta-language. A set of rules for designing markup languages.

Microfiche. A flat sheet of photographic film designed for storage of complete texts in multiple micro-images and having an index entry visible to the naked eye displayed at the top.

Microfilm. A length of photographic film containing sequences of micro-images of texts, title pages, bibliographic records, etc.

Microform. Usually a reproduction photographically reduced to a size difficult or impossible to read with the naked eye; some microforms are not reproductions, but rather original editions. Microforms include microfilm, microfiche, micro-opaques, and aperture cards.

Mixed notation. A notation that combines two or more kinds of symbols, such as a combination of letters and numbers.

Mixed responsibility. A situation that occurs when two or more entities make different types of contributions during the creation of a work (e.g., one creator illustrates the story that is written by a different creator). *See also* **Asynchronous responsibility**; **Shared responsibility**.

Mode of issuance. A category reflecting how a resource is produced in terms of the number of parts, distribution, updating, and termination. *See also* **Integrating resource**; **Monograph**; **Multipart monograph**; **Serial**.

MODS (Metadata Object Description Schema). An encoding standard developed by the Library of Congress based on an extensive subset of fields from the MARC 21 bibliographic format, but using language-based rather than numerical tags.

Monograph. A complete bibliographic unit or resource. It may be a single resource or a collection that is not a serial. *See also* **Mode of issuance**; **Multipart monograph**.

Monographic series. A sequence of monographs with a collective title.

Monographs in collected sets. Collections or compilations by one or more authors issued in two or more volumes.

Multipart monograph. A monograph issued in a finite number of parts; it may be issued in successive parts at regular or irregular intervals, but it is not intended to continue indefinitely. *See also* **Mode of issuance**.

Musical presentation statement. A statement in a chief source of information for music that indicates its physical form.

NACO (Name Authority Cooperative Program). A part of the Program for Cooperative Cataloging (PCC); the program has led to the widespread availability of high quality authority records for persons, families, corporate bodies, geographic jurisdictions, standardized work titles, and series titles. *See also* **BIBCO**; **CONSER**; **PCC**; **SACO**.

NAL. National Agricultural Library, Washington, D.C.

Name authority file. A file containing the authority records for names used in a given catalog.

Name-title access point. An authorized access point that includes the authorized name of a person, family, or corporate body and the preferred title for a work. It serves to identify a work that is included in a larger work that is being cataloged, to identify a work that is the subject of a work being cataloged, to identify a larger work of which a work being cataloged is part, or to identify another work to which a work being cataloged is closely related (e.g., an index).

Narrower term (NT). A term one level down from the term being considered in a listing where terms for subject concepts have been conceived in relationships that are hierarchical. *See also* **Broader term**; **Related term**.

***National Union Catalog* (NUC).** A publication in the Library of Congress Catalogs series that cumulated cataloging records from many libraries and indicated by NUC symbol those libraries that owned a particular resource; ceased publication in 2002.

Network. An interconnected system (wired or wireless) of telecommunications that allows the exchange of data between nodes. *See also* **Bibliographic network**.

NLA. The National Library of Australia, Canberra.

NLM. The National Library of Medicine, Washington, D.C.

Nomen. In FRSAD, the particular label or term applied to a concept. See also ***Functional Requirements for Subject Authority Data***; **Thema**.

Non-book materials. Term used to designate collectively maps, globes, motion pictures, filmstrips, electronic resources, video recordings, sound recordings, and other resources that do not consist of text in book form.

Notation. A representation in a system, such as a classification system, with a set of marks, usually consisting of letters, numbers, and/or symbols.

Number building. In DDC, the process of developing a complex classification number for a resource by appending digits from tables or other parts of the schedules to a base number.

Obtaining function. *See* **Acquiring function**.

OCLC Connexion. The cataloging interface to OCLC's database.

OCLC Online Computer Library Center. A bibliographic network, based in Dublin, Ohio, that is the largest and most comprehensive bibliographic network in the world.

Online catalog. A catalog in which surrogate records are encoded for computer display.

Online Computer Library Center. *See* **OCLC Online Computer Library Center**.

Online public access catalog (OPAC). A catalog that is available for use by the general public; part of an integrated library system (ILS).

Ontology. In the field of artificial intelligence, a formal representation of what, to a human, is common sense or reality; an attempt to define the essence of a situation, domain, or conceptual framework. *See also* **Lexical ontology**.

OPAC. *See* **Online public access catalog**.

Open stacks. The name given to the situation where all users of a facility are admitted directly to the areas where resources are stored. *See also* **Closed stacks**; **Stacks**.

Organization of information. *See* **Information organization**.

Original cataloging. The process of creating a bibliographic record "from scratch," especially without reference to other records for the same resource; also, the cataloging data created by this process. *See also* **Copy cataloging**.

Other title information. Words or phrases (e.g., a subtitle) that appear in conjunction with and are subordinate to the title proper of a resource. *See also* **Subtitle**; **Title**; **Title proper**.

Outsourcing. A management technique used by an institution whereby some activities, formerly conducted in house (e.g., acquisitions, cataloging, serials control, reference work), are contracted out for completion by a contracting agency. *See also* **Contract cataloging**.

Parallel title. The title proper written in another language or in another script. *See also* **Title**; **Title proper**.

Paris Principles. The conventional name of the Statement of Principles agreed upon by attendees at the International Conference on Cataloging Principles in Paris, October 9-18, 1961; more recently replaced by IFLA's *Statement of International Cataloguing Principles*. *See also* **Statement of International Cataloguing Principles**.

Pattern heading. A representative heading, with its subdivisions, from a category of terms that would normally be excluded from a subject heading list (e.g., names of individuals), included as an example of normal subdivision practice within that category.

PCC (Program for Cooperative Cataloging). An international cooperative program coordinated jointly by the Library of Congress and participants around the world; effort is aimed at expanding access to collections through useful, timely, and cost-effective cataloging that meets internationally accepted standards. *See also* **BIBCO**; **CONSER**; **NACO**; **SACO**.

Periodical. A publication with a distinctive title, which appears in successive numbers or parts at stated or regular intervals and which is intended to continue indefinitely. Usually each issue contains articles by several contributors. *See also* **Serial**.

Person. In RDA, *person* refers not only to an individual human being, but also to personas or bibliographic identities used by one or more individuals, to fictitious or literary characters, to legendary figures, to deities and mythological figures, and to individually named animals.

Plate. An illustrative leaf that is not included in the pagination of the text; it is not an integral part of a text gathering; it is often printed on paper different from that used for the text (e.g., glossy paper).

Plate number. A number used by a music publisher to identify a set of printing plates used to print a musical work.

Post-coordinate indexing. Indexing that enters subject concepts as single concepts so that searchers are required to coordinate them using such techniques as Boolean searching in order to locate resources on the compound and/or complex subjects in which the searchers are interested.

Pre-coordinate indexing. The assigning of subject terms to surrogate records in such a way that some concepts, sub-concepts, place names, time periods, and form concepts are put together in subject strings, and searchers of the system do not have to coordinate these particular terms themselves.

Preferred sources of information. In RDA, the source or sources in an information resource considered to be the major supply of bibliographic data for use in preparing a description; unlike the concept it replaced (i.e., *chief source of information* in AACR2), more than one location within the resource may be considered primary; varies according to the type of resource.

Preferred title for the work. A standardized title chosen to identify a work that has been known by various titles over time or across multiple languages; formerly known as *Uniform title*. *See also* **Title**; **Work**.

Preliminaries (in a book). The title page or title pages, the verso of each title page, the cover, and any pages preceding the title page; may also include prefatory matter such as a preface or foreword; also called *front matter*.

Prescribed source of information. *Obsolete.* One of the sources in an information resource that is prescribed by AACR2 as a source from which certain parts of the description should be taken; replaced in RDA by individual instructions about the appropriate, but not prescribed, source of information for each descriptive element.

Primary access point. *Obsolete.* In pre-RDA cataloging, the access point that was chosen as the main or primary one; was usually referred to as *main entry* in libraries and archives, where the other access points were called *added entries*.

Printed catalogs. A catalog in which the surrogate records appear in static printed form (e.g., cards in a card catalog, columns in a book or on microform).

Processing center. A central office where the materials of more than one library are processed and distributed. Such a center may also handle the purchasing of materials for its constituents.

Producer (Film, television, media, etc.). A person or agency responsible for financial and administrative production of a non-book item, such as a motion picture, television or radio programming, streaming audio or video, and so on; a producer may be responsible for various financial and managerial aspects of production.

Producer (Unpublished resources). In RDA, a person, family, or corporate body responsible for fabricating or building an unpublished resource.

Pseudonym. An assumed name used by a creator of a work to conceal identity or to establish a separate bibliographic identity. *See also* **Bibliographic identity**.

Publisher. The person, family, or corporate body responsible for issuing resources to make them available for public use.

Pure notation. In classification, a notation that consistently uses only one kind of symbol (e.g., either letters or numbers, but not both).

RDA: Resource Description & Access. A set of cataloging instructions based on FRBR and FRAD, published in 2010 and implemented in 2013, for producing the description and name and title access points representing a resource; the descriptive cataloging standard that replaced AACR2. The creation of RDA was the result of collaboration among representatives from Australia, Canada, Germany, Great Britain, and the United States.

Realia. *Obsolete.* Term referring to objects or three-dimensional forms (artifacts, specimens, etc.).

Recon or RECON. *See* **Retrospective conversion**.

Record. *See* **Bibliographic record**; **Metadata**; **Surrogate record**.

Recto. In a book, the page on the right (or the page on the left in cultures that read from right to left); the front side of a leaf. *See also* **Verso**.

Reference. An instruction in a catalog or other retrieval tool that directs a user to another place in the catalog or other tool; also called *cross-reference*. *See also* **Authorized access point**; **Blind reference**; **Controlled access point**; **Explanatory reference**; **Variant access point**.

Related term (RT). A term at the same level of specificity or bearing a non-hierarchical relationship to another term in a listing where terms for subject concepts have been conceived in relationships that are hierarchical. *See also* **Broader term**; **Narrower term**.

Relational database. A form of database architecture in which records are structured in such a way that information is not all stored in the same file; files for different kinds of information are created (e.g., a bibliographic file, a personal name file, a corporate name file, a subject file, a classification file). Pointers establish relationships among records. A relational database structure conserves storage space, allows for faster searching, and allows for easier modification of records.

Relationship. A reciprocal association or connection between two entities.

Relationship designator. A device (i.e., a label, phrase, or term) that indicates the kind or type of relationship that exists between one entity and another (e.g., between two works, between a person and a work).

Relative index. An index to a classification scheme that not only provides alphabetical references to the subjects and terms in the classification but also shows some of the relations between subjects and aspects of subjects.

Relative location. A classificatory arrangement of library materials, allowing the insertion of new material in its proper relation to that already on the shelves; as a result, an item might be shelved in a somewhat different physical location each time it is re-shelved. *See also* **Fixed location**.

Reprint. A new printing of an item either by photographic methods or by resetting substantially unchanged text.

Resource. A term used in the field of information organization to indicate an instance of recorded information (e.g., book, article, video, Internet document, sound recording, electronic journal); *resource* is used in order to avoid using *book*, *DVD*, or other such specific designations; also called *document*, *information resource*, *information package*, *library materials*, or *object*.

Retrieval tool. Device such as a catalog, an index, a search engine, and the like, created for use as an information retrieval system; also called *bibliographic tool*.

Retrospective conversion. The process of changing information in printed surrogate records into machine-readable form; sometimes referred to as *recon* or *RECON*.

Romanization. The representation of the characters or script of a nonroman alphabet by roman characters. *See also* **Transliteration**.

Rule of 3 (Classification). In DDC, an instruction that states that if a work is about three or more subjects that are all part of a broader classification number, one assigns the broader number to the work.

Rule of 3 (Descriptive cataloging). *Obsolete.* In AACR2, a restriction placed on the number of access points for creators of and contributors to the resource—if more than three were involved, only the first of each kind was recorded; also, a restriction on the numbers of persons or corporate bodies listed in statements of responsibility—if more than three were found on the chief source of information, only the first was recorded and the others were replaced by the Latin abbreviation *et al.* (meaning *and others*). In RDA, no such restrictions apply.

Rule of 3 (Subject cataloging). In LCSH, an instruction that if a work is about two or three subtopics of a broader concept, catalogers are to assign the two to three individual topics; if the work is about more than three subtopics, the cataloger may assign the broader heading, unless the *Rule of 4* applies.

Rule of 4. In LCSH, an instruction that in some cases where a work discusses four subtopics of a broader concept, the cataloger may find it more suitable to assign four individual topics, rather than a broader heading, if the broader topic is much more extensive than the aboutness of the work.

SACO (Subject Authority Cooperative Program). A part of the Program for Cooperative Cataloging (PCC); the program allows members to propose new headings for the *Library of Congress Subject Headings* list and new classifications numbers for the *Library of Congress Classification*. *See also* **BIBCO**; **CONSER**; **NACO**; **PCC**.

Schedule. *See* **Classification schedule**.

Schema neutral. The idea that a content standard, controlled vocabulary, or some other standard may be used with more than one metadata scheme or encoding format.

Scope note. A statement defining and/or delimiting the meaning and associative relations of a subject heading, index term, or a classification notation. *See also* **Explanatory reference**.

Score. An arrangement of all of the parts of a piece of music one under another on different staves. A series of staves on which is written music composed originally for one instrument is not considered a score; for example, *piano score* is used to designate, not music written originally for the piano, but music written originally for instrumental or vocal parts that has been arranged for the piano.

Search engine. A computerized retrieval tool that, in general, matches keywords input by a user to words found in documents of the site being searched; the more sophisticated search engines may allow other than keyword searching.

***Sears List of Subject Headings* (Sears).** A controlled vocabulary of terms and phrases that is used mostly in small libraries to provide subject access to resources available in those libraries.

Section. In DDC, the third-level of structure in the classification; the level below a division. *See also* **Class**; **Division**; **Hierarchical classification**; **Subdivision**.

***See also* reference.** A reference indicating related entities; the relationships may be lateral or hierarchical. *See also* **Broader term**; **Narrower term**; **Related term**.

***See from* reference.** A designation in an authority record showing a variant name or term from which a reference is to be made in the catalog to the authorized access point. *See also* **Used for**.

***See* reference.** A reference from a name or term not used to the authorized access point that is used. *See also* **USE**.

Selecting function. The function of information organization that allows a patron to make an informed choice of materials from a bibliographic tool.

Semantic Web. An extension of the World Wide Web. The traditional Web provides linkages between online resources, generally at the level of the whole resource or a discrete part of it. The Semantic Web provides linkages among data, or statements about resources, in a format semantically meaningful to, and actionable by, computers. Linked data is generally considered to be the basis for the Semantic Web. *See also* **Linked data**.

Serial. A publication (physical or electronic) issued in successive parts at regular or irregular intervals, intended to continue indefinitely, and usually bearing numbering. Included are periodicals, newspapers, proceedings, reports, memoirs, annuals, numbered monographic series, and online journals. *See also* **Periodical**; **Mode of issuance**.

Series. A number of separate works, usually related in subject or form, that are issued successively. They are usually issued by the same publisher, distributor, etc., and are in uniform style, with a collective title.

Series access point. An authority-controlled series title established for the purpose of collocation in retrieval tools; contained in a series *authority record*, which is found in a *series authority file*.

Series authority file. A file of series authority records containing authorized access points for series titles, with references made to them from other forms, and a record of their treatment as to analysis, tracing, and classification.

Series statement. A transcribed statement identifying the series to which the resource belongs; it is recorded in a description as found on the resource itself.

Series title. The collective title given to volumes or parts issued in a series. *See also* **Title**.

Shared authorship. *See* **Shared responsibility**.

Shared responsibility. The situation in which more than one person is responsible for the creation of the intellectual content of a work. *See also* **Asynchronous responsibility**; **Collaborative work**; **Joint author**; **Mixed responsibility**; **Synchronous responsibility**.

Shelflist. Originally, a record of the resources owned by a library with descriptions arranged in the order of the resources on the shelves. In time the meaning has developed to indicate classification order of surrogate records for resources, which now allows for intangible as well as physical resources.

S.l. (sine loco). *Obsolete.* Place of publication, distribution, etc., unknown; replaced in RDA by the phrase *Place of publication not identified*.

S.n. (sine nomine). *Obsolete.* Name of publisher, distributor, etc., unknown; replaced in RDA by the phrase *Publisher not identified*.

Sound recording. Aural recording, including discs, cartridges, cassettes, cylinders, and the like.

Specific entry. A principle observed in application of controlled vocabularies, by which a resource is listed under the most precise term(s) available in the controlled vocabulary (or allowed to be created by the rules of the vocabulary), rather than under a broader heading. *See also* **Specificity**.

Specificity. The level of semantic depth that is addressed by a particular controlled vocabulary (e.g., LCSH has greater specificity in its established headings than does *Sears*). *See also* **Specific entry**.

Square brackets. Symbols (i.e., [ ]) used in RDA to indicate that metadata came from outside the resource itself.

Stacks. The areas in libraries where materials are stored or shelved; these areas may or may not be accessible to the public. *See also* **Open stacks**; **Closed stacks**.

Standard subdivisions. Divisions used in DDC that apply to the form of a work. Form may be physical (e.g., a periodical or a dictionary) or it may be the approach used (e.g., a philosophy or history of a subject). Formerly called *form divisions*.

Standing room. In DDC, the idea that some subjects may not yet have settled into their permanent places in the classification; it is a metaphor taken from the phrase, *standing room only,* where a person may stand in a theatre if there are no seats available at that time; topics in standing room may not undergo number building. *See also* **Including note**.

Statement of International Cataloguing Principles. An IFLA document that outlines principles and values associated with cataloging; designed as a replacement for the 1961 *Paris Principles*. *See also* **Paris Principles**.

Statement of responsibility. A statement in the resource that names persons, families, and corporate bodies responsible for the intellectual or artistic content of the work, contributions to the expression, performances of the content, revisions of a work, subsequent editions, and so on.

Subdivision. (1) A level of structure in a hierarchical classification at which subordinate concepts are represented (the level below a class, division, section, etc.). (2) A restrictive word or group of words added to a main subject heading to limit it to a more specific meaning or treatment. *See also* **Class**; **Division**; **Hierarchical classification**; **Section**; **Subject subdivision**.

Subfield. A separately designated segment of a field in an encoded record. *See also* **Field**.

Subject access. The provision to users of the means of locating information using subject terminology and/or classification notations.

Subject analysis. The part of indexing or cataloging that deals with the conceptual analysis of a resource, translating that conceptual analysis into a particular classification, subject heading, or indexing system, and then assigning specific notations or terminology to the resource and its surrogate record. *See also* **Aboutness**; **Conceptual analysis**; **Translation (Subject cataloging)**.

Subject authority file. A file containing records of choices made in the development of a controlled vocabulary. The authority file contains such things as justification for the choice of one synonym over another; references from unused synonyms or near-synonyms; references for broader terms, narrower terms, and related terms; scope notes; citations for references used; and so on. *See also* **Subject heading list**; **Thesaurus**.

Subject cataloging. The process of providing subject analysis, including subject headings and classification notations, when creating catalog records.

Subject heading. Subject concept term or phrase found in a subject heading list and used in catalog records; sometimes used in indexes. *See also* **Descriptor**; **Term**.

Subject heading list. A list of authorized controlled vocabulary terms or phrases together with any references, scope notes, and subdivisions associated with each term or phrase. *See also* **Controlled vocabulary**; **Subject authority file**; **Thesaurus**.

Subject subdivision. A method of pre-coordinating subject headings by using terms or phrases following main concepts to show special treatment of a subject.

Subseries. A series within a series.

Subtitle. A secondary title, often used to expand or limit the title proper; considered to be one kind of "other title information." *See also* **Other title information**; **Title**; **Title proper**.

Summarization. A level of subject analysis in which only the dominant or main theme of a document is recognized. *See also* **Depth indexing**; **Exhaustivity**.

Superimposition. A Library of Congress policy decision that only entries being established for the first time would follow AACR rules for form of entry and that only works new to LC would follow AACR rules for choice of entry. When LC adopted AACR2, the policy of superimposition was dropped.

Surrogate record. A presentation of the attributes or characteristics of a resource (title, and usually one or more of the following: creator, physical description if appropriate, subject(s), date of creation, etc.). *See also* **Bibliographic record**; **Metadata**.

Switching language. A mediating or communication indexing language used to establish equivalencies between or among various subject indexing languages, classification schemes, or encoding schemes (e.g., Unified Medical Language System [UMLS]); often found as a computer program in which equivalencies between two encoding or indexing languages are made so that, for example, entry of an encoded surrogate record into the system will switch it to the other encoding scheme involved (e.g., UNIMARC, Z39.50). *See also* **Crosswalk**; **UNIMARC**; **Z39.50**.

Synchronous responsibility. The situation in which all persons or corporate bodies involved in the creation of a resource have made the same kind of contribution to the creation of the work (e.g., joint authors). *See also* **Asynchronous responsibility**; **Joint author**; **Mixed responsibility**; **Shared responsibility**.

Syndetic structure. An organizational framework in which related names, topics, and other controlled terms are linked to each other via connective terms such as *See* and *See also*, or the thesaural indicators BT, NT, RT, USE, and UF. *See also* **Broader term**; **Narrower term**; **Related term**; **USE**; **Used for**.

Tag. A number, set of letters, certain set of punctuation marks, or other identification, that designates the kind of field in an encoding standard.

Tagging (Encoding). *See* **Content designation**.

Tagging (Web 2.0). An activity in social media in which users assign terms (keywords, subjects, etc.) related to the resource being described. These terms (i.e., tags) are used for identifying properties of the resource and for retrieving the resource at a later time. In recent years, tagging has been widely criticized for: its lack of terminological control (e.g., using tags like *Science Fiction, Sciencefiction, Science_Fiction, Science-Fiction, SciFi, ScienceFiction, SyFy,* and *SF* to represent the same concept in a single system); its highly subjective and personal nature (e.g., using tags like *NeedToBuy, mine*); and for its unpredictable objectives, for example, to describe a subject (e.g., *soap*), to describe the status or relationship to the tagger (e.g. *ToRead*), to provide a review (e.g., *Terrible, great!*), and the like.

Taxonomist. The creator of a controlled vocabulary or classification scheme.

Taxonomy. *See* **Classification**; **Controlled vocabulary**.

Technical reading. The process of getting acquainted with a resource prior to cataloging, in which various internal sources of information are identified and examined.

Technical services. The group of activities in an institution that involves acquiring, organizing, housing, maintaining, and conserving collections and automating these activities. In some places circulation services are also considered to be part of technical services.

Term. A separately represented concept in a thesaurus. *See also* **Descriptor**; **Subject heading**.

Terms of availability. Stipulations or conditions by which a resource is available for purchase or use.

Thema. In FRSAD, a concept or subject. *See also Functional Requirements for Subject Authority Data (FRSAD)*; **Nomen**.

Thesaurus. A specialized authority list of controlled vocabulary terms (usually restricted to a particular subject area) used with information retrieval systems; terms represent single concepts, together with any references, scope notes, and subdivisions associated with each term, and are organized so that the relationships between concepts are made explicit; similar to a list of subject headings, except for the emphasis on single terms rather than phrases. *See also* **Controlled vocabulary**; **Subject heading list**.

Title. The name of a resource (or the work contained within), usually identified from the preferred sources of information of a resource. *See also* **Alternative title**; **Collective title**; **Conventional collective title**; **Other title information**; **Parallel title**; **Preferred title for the work**; **Series title**; **Subtitle**; **Title proper**; **Uniform title**.

Title frame. An opening frame or screen on a moving image resource that contains the most complete bibliographic information about the resource. Also referred to as *title screen*. *See also* **Title page**.

Title page. A page that occurs very near the beginning of a book or other printed document and that contains the most complete bibliographic information about the resource, such as the creator's name, the fullest form of the title, the name and/or number of the edition, the name of the publisher, and the place and date of publication. In RDA it is considered to be a preferred source of information for resources consisting of pages or leaves; for resources made up of cards or sheets, a *title card* or *title sheet* plays an equivalent role. *See also* **Title frame**.

Title proper. The title that is the chief name of a resource; excludes any parallel title or other title information; includes alternative title and part title. *See also* **Title**.

Tracing. *Obsolete.* The listing on a printed surrogate record (e.g., a catalog card) of the set of name, title, and subject access points, other than the primary access point (i.e., main entry) under which the work is listed in the catalog; used to find (i.e., trace) all copies of a record in a printed catalog.

Transcription. The recording of data or information as it is found on a resource; it generally means that the cataloger takes the data as found in terms of wording, spelling, and order, with perhaps slight changes in capitalization and punctuation.

Translation. The conveyance of the content of a work in another language. In RDA, a translation is considered a different expression of a work, not a new work.

Translation (Subject cataloging). The second stage of the subject analysis process, in which the aboutness is converted into controlled terminology (e.g., subject headings and classification notations). *See also* **Aboutness**; **Conceptual analysis**; **Subject analysis**.

Transliteration. A representation of the characters of one alphabet by those of another. *See also* **Romanization**.

Twenty-percent rule. In LCSH, an instruction that states that only topics that encompass 20% or more of a resource are represented in subject headings.

UBC. *See* **Universal Bibliographic Control**.

UDC. *See* **Universal Decimal Classification**.

Uncontrolled access point. A name, title, and term that does not appear in an authority record; for example, a title proper is an access point but one that is transcribed and not standardized. *See also* **Authorized access point**; **Controlled access point**.

Uniform title. *Obsolete.* The title chosen for cataloging purposes when a work has appeared under varying titles or in more than one form; allows display of all manifestations of a work together. Uniform titles also are used to distinguish between and among different works that have the same title; concept replaced in RDA by *preferred title for the work*. *See also* **Conventional collective title**; **Preferred title for the work**; **Title**; **Work**.

UNIMARC (Universal MARC). A MARC format, first developed in 1977 by the Library of Congress, to be used as an international communications format for the exchange of machine-readable cataloging records between national bibliographic agencies; now overseen by IFLA. A number of countries have adopted it as their national MARC format. *See also* **MARC (MAchine-Readable Cataloging)**.

Union catalog. A catalog that lists, completely or in part, the holdings of more than one library or collection.

Universal Bibliographic Control (UBC). The concept that it will someday be possible to have access to metadata for all the world's important information resources.

***Universal Decimal Classification* (UDC).** A classification devised by Otlet and La Fontaine in the late 1890s; originally based on the 5th edition of DDC, but has evolved into a much more faceted scheme than DDC.

USE. In controlled vocabulary lists, a relationship indicator or instruction that indicates that the entry term is not authorized for use and that one should see the authorized term instead. *See also* **Reference**; **Used for**.

Used for (UF). In controlled vocabulary lists, a relationship indicator that signifies terms that are considered equivalent to or nearly synonymous to the authorized subject heading or descriptor; has a reciprocal relationship with **USE**. *See also* **Reference**; **USE**.

User tasks. The reasons users approach an information retrieval tool; they reflect functions of the catalog. They are expressed differently in various cataloging standards. The user tasks are identified in FRBR as: *find, identify, select,* and *obtain*. In FRAD, they are: *find, identify, contextualize,* and *justify*. In FRSAD, they are: *find, identify, select,* and *explore*. The *Statement of International Cataloguing Principles* lists: *find, identify, select, obtain,* and *navigate*.

USMARC. A machine-readable bibliographic record format developed by the Library of Congress and originally called LC-MARC. USMARC was replaced by MARC 21. *See also* **MARC (MAchine-Readable Cataloging)**; **MARC 21**.

USNAF. *See* **LCNAF**.

Variable field. A field in an encoded record that can be as long or as short as the data to be placed into that field. *See also* **Control field**; **Field**; **Fixed field**.

Variant access point. A string of alphanumeric characters, which represents an entity, but is not authorized for use in bibliographic records; a variant access point refers users to an authorized access point. *See also* **Authorized access point**; **Reference**.

Variant title. A title associated with a resource, but one that is not the title proper, other title information, a parallel title, or any of the other specific title sub-elements identified in RDA.

Verification. Determining the existence of a creator and the form of name as well as the correct title of a particular work; in short, using bibliographic sources to verify (i.e., prove) the existence of a creator and/or work. Alternatively, verification can refer to the process of determining whether an authorized access point input in a record matches one in an authority file. Automatic verification is a desirable feature for a cataloging subsystem of an ILS or LSP.

Vernacular name. A name in the form used in reference sources in the country of origin of the name.

Verso. In a book, the page on the left (or the page on the right in cultures that read from right to left); the back side of a leaf. *See also* **Recto**.

Vocabulary control. The process of creating and using a controlled vocabulary.

Volume. (1) One or more sheets bound together to form a single unit. (2) In the bibliographical sense, a major division of a multipart resource distinguished from the other major divisions by having its own chief source of information.

Word-by-word filing. An arrangement of terms in a retrieval tool in such a way that spaces between words take precedence over any letter that may follow (e.g., *New York* appears before *Newark*). *See also* **Letter-by-letter filing**.

Work. A distinct intellectual or artistic creation; an abstract instance of content or ideas, regardless of the packaging in which the content or ideas may be expressed; the first level of conceptualization in the FRBR model. *See also* **Expression**; **Item**; **Manifestation**.

Workflow. Step-by-step guidelines for creating metadata for materials of different types and complexities.

Workform. A structured form into which information can be placed to create a catalog record; it can also include other information pertinent to the maintenance of a collection.

Workmark. A designation (usually a letter or letters) placed after a cutter number in a call number; also called *work letter*. A workmark is often the first letter of the title of a work (exclusive of articles), but may stand for other entities, such as the name of a biographee, depending upon the circumstances. *See also* **Call number**; **Cutter number**.

Z39.50. A national standard that provides for exchange of information, such as surrogate records or full text, between otherwise non-compatible computer systems. *See also* **Switching language**.

Selected Bibliography

This selected bibliography contains resources consulted in the preparation of this text, resources deemed useful for further exploration of the topics addressed in this text, and resources useful for keeping current in the field. The bibliography contains not only contemporary resources, but also some significant historical works. Some works appear in more than one section. The bibliographic entries are divided into the following sections:

- General works on cataloging and classification, including works on metadata, information organization, and technical services
- History of cataloging and classification
- Descriptive cataloging, including works on bibliographic description, access, and bibliographic relationships
- Authority control
- Subject cataloging, including works on determining aboutness, controlled vocabularies, and classification
- Arrangement
- Formatting and presentation, including works on MARC, ISBD, Dublin Core, BIBFRAME, the Semantic Web, and linked data
- Administrative issues, including works on Integrated Library Systems and Library Services Platforms
- Resources for current information and updating

GENERAL WORKS

Anderson, James D., and José Pérez-Carballo. *Information Retrieval Design: Principles and Options for Information Description, Organization, Display, and Access in Information Retrieval Databases, Digital Libraries, Catalogs, and Indexes.* St. Petersburg, Fla.: Ometeca Institute, 2005.

Berman, Sanford. *Joy of Cataloging.* Phoenix, Ariz.: Oryx Press, 1981.

Borgman, Christine L. *From Gutenberg to the Global Information Infrastructure: Access to Information in the Networked World.* Cambridge, Mass.: MIT Press, 2000.

Caplan, Priscilla. *Metadata Fundamentals for All Librarians.* Chicago: American Library Association, 2003.

Carpenter, Michael, and Elaine Svenonius, eds. *Foundations of Cataloging: A Sourcebook.* Littleton, Colo.: Libraries Unlimited, 1985.

Chan, Lois Mai, with the assistance of Theodora L. Hodges. *Cataloging and Classification: An Introduction.* 3rd ed. Lanham, Md.: Scarecrow Press, 2007.

Coyle, Karen. *Understanding the Semantic Web: Bibliographic Data and Metadata.* Chicago: American Library Association, 2010.

Evans, G. Edward, Sheila S. Intner, and Jean Weihs. *Introduction to Technical Services.* 8th ed. Santa Barbara, Calif.: Libraries Unlimited, 2011.

Foster, Allen, and Pauline Rafferty, eds. *Managing Digital Cultural Objects: Analysis, Discovery and Retrieval.* London: Facet Publishing, 2014.

Hagler, Ronald. *The Bibliographic Record and Information Technology.* 3rd ed. Chicago: American Library Association, 1997.

Haynes, Elizabeth, Joanna F. Fountain, and Michele Zwierski. *Unlocking the Mysteries of Cataloging: A Workbook of Examples.* 2nd ed. Santa Barbara, Calif.: Libraries Unlimited, 2015.

Hider, Philip. *Information Resource Description: Creating and Managing Metadata.* Chicago: ALA Editions, 2013.

Hider, Philip, with Ross Harvey. *Organising Knowledge in a Global Society: Principles and Practice in Libraries and Information Centres.* Revised ed. Wagga Wagga, NSW, Australia: Centre for Information Studies, 2008.

International Conference on Cataloguing Principles. Paris, 9th-18th October, 1961. *Report.* London: International Federation of Library Associations, 1963.

International Federation of Library Associations and Institutions. Cataloguing Section and IFLA Meetings of Experts on an International Cataloguing Code. *The Statement of International Cataloguing Principles.* The Hague: IFLA, 2009.

International Federation of Library Associations and Institutions. Study Group on the Functional Requirements for Bibliographic Records. *Functional Requirements for Bibliographic Records, Final Report.* München, Germany: K.G. Saur, 1998.

International Federation of Library Associations and Institutions. Working Group on Functional Requirements and Numbering of Authority Records. *Functional Requirements for Authority Data: A Conceptual Model (FRAD).* Edited by Glenn E. Patton. München, Germany: K.G. Saur, 2009.

International Federation of Library Associations and Institutions. Working Group on the Functional Requirements for Subject Authority Records. *Functional Requirements for Subject Authority Data (FRSAD): A Conceptual Model.* München, Germany: De Gruyter Saur, 2011.

Intner, Sheila S., and Jean Weihs. *Standard Cataloging for School and Public Libraries.* 5th ed. Santa Barbara, Calif.: Libraries Unlimited, 2014.

Intner, Sheila S., Joanna F. Fountain, and Jean Weihs, eds. *Cataloging Correctly for Kids: An Introduction to the Tools.* 5th ed. Chicago: American Library Association, 2011.

Intner, Sheila S., Susan S. Lazinger, and Jean Weihs. *Metadata and Its Impact on Libraries*. Westport, Conn.: Libraries Unlimited, 2006.

Jewett, Charles Coffin. *On the Construction of Catalogues of Libraries, and Their Publication by Means of Separate, Stereotyped Titles*. 2nd ed. Washington, D.C.: Smithsonian Institution, 1853.

Lai, Lingling, and Arlene G. Taylor. "Knowledge Organization in Knowledge Management Systems of Global Consulting Firms." *Cataloging & Classification Quarterly* 49, no. 5 (2011): 387-407.

Levy, David M. "Cataloging in the Digital Order." Accessed December 31, 2014. http://www.csdl.tamu.edu/DL95/papers/levy/levy.html.

Mann, Thomas. *The Oxford Guide to Library Research*. 4th ed. New York: Oxford University Press, 2015.

Panizzi, Antonio. "Rules for the Compilation of the Catalogue." In *The Catalogue of Printed Books in the British Museum*. London: British Museum, 1841.

Ranganathan, S. R. *The Five Laws of Library Science*. 2nd ed. Bombay: Asia Pub. House, 1963.

Rowley, Jennifer, and Richard Hartley. *Organizing Knowledge: An Introduction to Managing Access to Information*. 4th ed. Aldershot, Eng.; Burlington, Vt.: Ashgate, 2008.

Sanchez, Elaine R., ed. *Conversations with Catalogers in the 21st Century*. Foreword by Michael Gorman. Santa Barbara, Calif.: Libraries Unlimited, 2011.

Sleeman, Bill, and Pamela Bluh, eds. *From Catalog to Gateway: Charting a Course for Future Access: Briefings from the ALCTS Catalog Form and Function Committee*. Chicago: Association for Library Collections & Technical Services, American Library Association, 2005.

Smiraglia, Richard. *The Nature of "A Work": Implications for Knowledge Organization*. Lanham, Md.: Scarecrow Press, 2001.

Soergel, Dagobert. *Organizing Information: Principles of Data Base and Retrieval Systems*. Orlando, Fla.: Academic Press, 1985.

Svenonius, Elaine. *The Intellectual Foundation of Information Organization*. Cambridge, Mass.: The MIT Press, 2000.

Taylor, Arlene G. "The Information Universe: Will We Have Chaos or Control?" *American Libraries* 25, no. 7 (July/August 1994): 629-632.

Taylor, Arlene G. "Organization and Representation of Information/Knowledge." In *The Portable MLIS: Insights from the Experts*, edited by Ken Haycock and Brooke Sheldon, 98-111. Westport. Conn.: Libraries Unlimited, 2008.

Taylor, Arlene G., and Daniel N. Joudrey. "Cataloging." In *Encyclopedia of Library and Information Science*, 3rd ed., edited by Marcia J. Bates and Mary Niles Maack, 798-807. New York: Taylor and Francis, 2009.

Taylor, Arlene G., and Daniel N. Joudrey. *The Organization of Information*. 3rd ed. Westport, Conn.: Libraries Unlimited, 2009.

Taylor, Arlene G., with the assistance of Rosanna M. O'Neil. *Cataloging with Copy: A Decision-Maker's Handbook*. 2nd ed. Englewood, Colo.: Libraries Unlimited, 1988.

Wilson, Patrick. "The Catalog as Access Mechanism: Background and Concepts." In *Foundations of Cataloging: A Sourcebook*, edited by Michael Carpenter and Elaine Svenonius, 253-268. Littleton, Colo.: Libraries Unlimited, 1985.

Wilson, Patrick. *Two Kinds of Power: An Essay on Bibliographic Control*. Berkeley: University of California Press, 1968.

Working Group on the Future of Bibliographic Control. *On the Record: Report of The Library of Congress Working Group on the Future of Bibliographic Control.* Washington, DC: Library of Congress, 2008. http://www.loc.gov/biblio graphic-future/news/lcwg-ontherecord-jan08-final.pdf.

Zeng, Marcia Lei, and Jian Qin. *Metadata.* 2nd rev. ed. Chicago: American Library Association, 2014.

HISTORY

Baker, Nicholson. "Discards." *The New Yorker* 70, no. 7 (April 4, 1994): 64-86.

Bowman, J. H. "Development of Description in Cataloguing Prior to ISBD." *Aslib Proceedings* 58, no. 1/2 (2006): 34-48.

Denton, William. "FRBR and the History of Cataloging." In *Understanding FRBR: What It Is and How It Will Affect Our Retrieval Tools,* edited by Arlene G. Taylor, 35-57. Westport, Conn.: Libraries Unlimited, 2007.

Dunkin, Paul S. *Cataloging U.S.A.* Chicago: American Library Association, 1969. See esp. chap. 1, "Mr. Cutter's Catalog" and chap. 2, "The Prophet and the Law: Codes after Cutter."

Gorman, Michael. *Broken Pieces: A Library Life, 1941-1978.* Chicago: American Library Association, 2011.

Gorman, Michael. "The Origins and Making of the ISBD: A Personal History, 1966-1978." *Cataloging & Classification Quarterly* 52, no. 8 (2014): 821-834.

Hanson, J. C. M. *The Anglo-American Agreement on Cataloging Rules and Its Bearing on International Cooperation in Cataloging of Books.* Bruxelles: Academies Royales de Belgique, 1908.

Hanson, J. C. M. "The Subject Catalogs of the Library of Congress." *Bulletin of the American Library Association* 3 (September 1909): 385-397.

Hensen, Steven L. *Archives, Personal Papers, and Manuscripts: A Cataloging Manual for Archival Repositories, Historical Societies, and Manuscript Libraries.* 2nd ed. Chicago: Society of American Archivists, 1989.

Hopkins, Judith. "The 1791 French Cataloging Code and the Origins of the Card Catalog." *Libraries & Culture* 27, no. 4 (Fall 1992): 378-404.

Joachim, Martin D., ed. *Historical Aspects of Cataloging and Classification.* Binghamton, NY: Haworth Information Press, 2003.

LaMontagne, Leo E. "Historical Background of Classification." In *The Subject Analysis of Library Materials.* New York: Columbia University School of Library Service, 1953.

Lubetzky, Seymour. "The Fundamentals of Bibliographic Cataloging and *AACR 2.*" In International Conference on AACR 2, Florida State University, 1979, *The Making of a Code,* 18-23. Chicago: American Library Association, 1980.

Martel, Charles, "Cataloging: 1876-1926." Reprinted in *The Catalog and Cataloging,* edited by A. R. Rowland, 40-50. Hamden, Conn.: Shoe String Press, 1969.

Miksa, Francis L. *The Development of Classification at the Library of Congress.* Champaign: University of Illinois, Graduate School of Library and Information Science, 1984.

Miksa, Francis L. *The Subject in the Dictionary Catalog from Cutter to the Present.* Chicago: American Library Association, 1983.

Norris, Dorothy May. *A History of Cataloguing and Cataloguing Methods 1100-1850: With an Introductory Survey of Ancient Times.* Ann Arbor, Mich.: University Microfilms, 1982. (Facsimile of: London: Grafton & Co., 1939).

Osborn, Andrew. "The Crisis in Cataloging." *Library Quarterly* 11 (October 1941): 393-411; also reprinted in: Carpenter, Michael, and Elaine Svenonius, eds. *Foundations of Cataloging: A Sourcebook*, 90-103. Littleton, Colo.: Libraries Unlimited, 1985.

Pettee, Julia. *Subject Headings: The History and Theory of the Alphabetical Approach to Books*. New York: H. W. Wilson, 1946.

Rayward, W. Boyd. "The UDC and FID: A Historical Perspective." *Library Quarterly* 37 (July 1967): 259-278.

Rayward, W. Boyd. *The Universe of Information: The Work of Paul Otlet for Documentation and International Organisation*. Moscow: FID, 1975.

Rohrbach, Peter T. *Find: Automation at the Library of Congress: The First Twenty-five Years and Beyond*. Washington, D.C.: Library of Congress, 1985.

Russell, Beth M. "Hidden Wisdom and Unseen Treasure: Revisiting Cataloging in Medieval Libraries." *Cataloging & Classification Quarterly* 26, no. 3 (1998): 21-30.

Smalley, Joseph. "The French Cataloging Code of 1791: A Translation." *Library Quarterly* 61, no. 1 (January 1991): 1-14.

Strout, Ruth French. "The Development of the Catalog and Cataloging Codes." *Library Quarterly* 26, no. 4 (October 1956): 254-275.

Tate, Elizabeth L. "Examining the 'Main' in Main Entry Headings." In International Conference on AACR 2, Florida State University, 1979, *The Making of a Code*, 109-140. Chicago: American Library Association, 1980.

Taylor, Arlene G. "Cataloguing." In *World Encyclopedia of Library and Information Services*. 3rd ed., 117-181. Chicago: American Library Association, 1993.

Taylor, Arlene G. "Implementing AACR and AACR2: A Personal Perspective and Lessons Learned." *Library Resources & Technical Services* 56, no. 3 (July 2012): 122-126.

Taylor, Arlene G., and Barbara Paff. "Looking Back: Implementation of AACR 2." *Library Quarterly* 56, no. 3 (July 1986): 272-285.

Taylor, Arlene G., and Daniel N. Joudrey. "Development of the Organization of Recorded Information in Western Civilization." Chap. 3 in *The Organization of Information*, 3rd ed. Westport, Conn.: Libraries Unlimited, 2009.

Weinberg, Bella Hass. "Indexing: History and Theory." In *Encyclopedia of Library and Information Sciences*, 3rd ed., edited by Marcia J. Bates and Mary Niles Maack, 2277-2290. New York: Taylor and Francis, 2009.

Wiegand, Wayne A. *Irrepressible Reformer: A Biography of Melvil Dewey*. Chicago: American Library Association, 1996.

DESCRIPTIVE CATALOGING

Description and Access

ALA/ALCTS/CCS Committee on Cataloging: Description and Access. *The Future of AACR* (April 2003). http://www.libraries.psu.edu/tas/jca/ccda/future1 .html.

Anglo-American Cataloguing Rules, Second Edition, 2002 Revision, prepared under the direction of the Joint Steering Committee for Revision of AACR. Chicago: American Library Association, 2002. (Also available in RDA Toolkit. http:// rdatoolkit.org/).

Carpenter, Michael. "Does Cataloging Theory Rest on a Mistake?" In *Origins, Content, and Future of AACR2 Revisited*, edited by Richard P. Smiraglia, 95-102. Chicago: American Library Association, 1992.

Carpenter, Michael, and Elaine Svenonius, eds. *Foundations of Cataloging: A Sourcebook.* Littleton, Colo.: Libraries Unlimited, 1985.

CONSER Editing Guide. Prepared by staff of the Serial Record Division under the direction of the CONSER operations coordinator. 2002 Cumulation. Washington, D.C.: Cataloging Distribution Service, Library of Congress, 2002-date. Looseleaf, with updates. (Also available in *Cataloger's Desktop.*)

Cutter, Charles A. *Rules for a Dictionary Catalog.* 4th ed., rewritten. Washington, D.C.: Government Printing Office, 1904; republished, London: Library Association, 1972. The original version of this work was: Charles A. Cutter. "Rules for a Printed Dictionary Catalogue." In *Public Libraries in the United States of America: Their History, Condition, and Management,* U.S. Bureau of Education. Part II. Washington, D.C.: Government Printing Office, 1876.

Describing Archives: A Content Standard. 2nd ed. Chicago: The Society of American Archivists, 2013. http://files.archivists.org/pubs/DACS2E-2013.pdf.

Differences Between, Changes Within: Guidelines on When to Create a New Record. Prepared by the Task Force on an Appendix of Major and Minor Changes of the Committee on Cataloging: Description and Access, Association for Library Collections & Technical Services (A division of the American Library Association) Cataloging and Classification Section. 2003. http://www.libraries.psu.edu/tas/jca/ccda/docs/tf-appx10.doc.

Dowell, Arlene Taylor. *AACR 2 Headings: A Five-Year Projection of Their Impact on Catalogs.* Littleton, Colo.: Libraries Unlimited, 1982.

El-Sherbini, Magda. *RDA: Strategies for Implementation.* Chicago: American Library Association, 2013.

Gorman, Michael. "*AACR 2*: Main Themes." In International Conference on AACR 2, Florida State University, 1979, *The Making of a Code,* 45-46. Chicago: American Library Association, 1980.

Hagler, Ronald. "Access Points for Works." In *The Principles and Future of AACR2,* edited by Jean Weihs, 214-228. Chicago: American Library Association, 1998.

Hart, Amy. *RDA Made Simple: A Practical Guide to the New Cataloging Rules.* Santa Barbara, Calif.: Libraries Unlimited, 2014.

International Conference on AACR 2, Florida State University, 1979. *The Making of a Code: The Issues Underlying AACR 2.* Chicago: American Library Association, 1980.

International Conference on Cataloguing Principles. Paris, 9th-18th October, 1961. *Report.* London: International Federation of Library Associations, 1963.

International Federation of Library Associations and Institutions. Cataloguing Section and IFLA Meetings of Experts on an International Cataloguing Code. *Statement of International Cataloguing Principles.* The Hague, Netherlands: IFLA, 2009. http://www.ifla.org/files/assets/cataloguing/icp/icp_2009-en.pdf.

International Federation of Library Associations and Institutions. Study Group on the Functional Requirements for Bibliographic Records. *Functional Requirements for Bibliographic Records, Final Report.* München, Germany: K.G. Saur, 1998. http://www.ifla.org/publications/functional-requirements-for-bibliographic-records.

Jones, Ed. *RDA and Serials Cataloging.* Chicago: American Library Association, 2013.

Kincy, Chamya Pompey, with Sara Shatford Layne. *Making the Move to RDA: A Self-Study Primer for Catalogers.* Lanham, Md.: Rowman & Littlefield, 2014.

Library of Congress, Program for Cooperative Cataloging. *Integrating Resources: A Cataloging Manual.* 2011 revision. http://www.loc.gov/aba/pcc/bibco/documents/irman.pdf.

Lubetzky, Seymour. *Cataloging Rules and Principles: A Critique of the A.L.A. Rules for Entry and a Proposed Design for Their Revision.* Washington, D.C.: Processing Dept., Library of Congress, 1953.

Lubetzky, Seymour. *Code of Cataloging Rules, Author and Title: An Unfinished Draft . . . with an Explanatory Commentary by Paul Dunkin.* Chicago: American Library Association, 1960.

Lubetzky, Seymour. *Code of Cataloging Rules, Author and Title Entry: Additions, Revisions, and Changes Prepared in Light of Discussions of the March 1960 Draft for Consideration of the Catalog Code Revision Committee.* Chicago: American Library Association, 1961.

Maxwell, Robert L. *FRBR: A Guide for the Perplexed.* Chicago: American Library Association, 2008.

Maxwell, Robert L. *Maxwell's Handbook for RDA, Resource Description & Access: Explaining and Illustrating RDA: Resource Description and Access Using MARC 21.* Chicago: ALA Editions, 2013.

Mering, Margaret, ed. *The RDA Workbook: Learning the Basics of Resource Description and Access.* Santa Barbara, Calif.: Libraries Unlimited, 2014.

Oliver, Chris. *Introducing RDA: A Guide to the Basics.* Chicago: American Library Association, 2010.

Online Audiovisual Catalogers, Inc., Cataloging Policy Committee. *Guide to Cataloging DVD and Blu-ray Discs Using AACR2r and MARC 21.* 2008 Update. http://www.olacinc.org/drupal/capc_files/DVD_guide_final.pdf.

Paige G. Andrew, Susan M. Moore, and Mary Larsgaard. *RDA and Cartographic Resources.* Chicago: American Library Association, 2015.

RDA: Resource Description & Access. Joint Steering Committee for Development of RDA. Chicago: American Library Association, 2010. http://www.rdatoolkit .org/.

Tate, Elizabeth L. "Access Points and Citations: A Comparison of Four Cataloging Codes." *Library Research* 1 (Winter 1979): 347-359.

Taylor, Arlene G., ed. *Understanding FRBR: What It is and How It Will Affect Our Retrieval Tools.* Westport, Conn.: Libraries Unlimited, 2007.

Tillett, Barbara. "Keeping Libraries Relevant in the Semantic Web with Resource Description and Access (RDA)." *Serials* 24, no. 3 (2011): 270-271.

Tillett, Barbara. *What Is FRBR? A Conceptual Model for the Bibliographic Universe.* Washington, D.C.: Library of Congress Cataloging Distribution Service, 2004. http://www.loc.gov/cds/downloads/FRBR.PDF.

Weihs, Jean, ed. *The Principles and Future of AACR: Proceedings of the International Conference on the Principles and Future Development of AACR.* Ottawa: Canadian Library Association; Chicago: American Library Association, 1998.

Welsh, Anne. *Cataloguing and Decision-making in a Hybrid Environment: The Transition from AACR2 to RDA.* London: Facet Publishing, 2014.

Zhang, Yin, and Athena Salaba. *Implementing FRBR in Libraries: Key Issues and Future Directions.* New York: Neal-Schuman Publishers, 2009.

Bibliographic Relationships

Smiraglia, Richard P. "Derivative Bibliographic Relationships: Linkages in the Bibliographic Universe." In *Navigating the Networks: Proceedings of the ASIS Mid-Year Meeting, Portland, Oregon, May 21-25, 1994,* 167-183. Medford, N.J.: Learned Information, 1994.

Smiraglia, Richard P. "Bibliographic Families and Superworks." In *Understanding FRBR: What It Is and How It Will Affect Our Retrieval Tools*, edited by Arlene G. Taylor, 35-57. Westport, Conn.: Libraries Unlimited, 2007.

Taylor, Arlene G., and Daniel N. Joudrey. "Metadata: Access and Authority Control." Chap. 8 in *The Organization of Information*. 3rd ed. Westport, Conn.: Libraries Unlimited, 2009.

Tillett, Barbara B. "Bibliographic Relationships: An Empirical Study of the LC Machine-Readable Records." *Library Resources & Technical Services* 36 (April 1992): 162-188.

Tillett, Barbara B. "The History of Linking Devices." *Library Resources & Technical Services* 36 (January 1992): 23-36.

Tillett, Barbara B. "A Summary of the Treatment of Bibliographic Relationships in Cataloging Rules." *Library Resources & Technical Services* 35 (October 1991): 393-405.

Tillett, Barbara B. "A Taxonomy of Bibliographic Relationships." *Library Resources & Technical Services* 35 (April 1991): 150-158.

Vellucci, Sherry L. "Bibliographic Relationships." In *The Principles and Future of AACR2*, edited by Jean Weihs, 105-146. Chicago: American Library Association, 1998.

Vellucci, Sherry L. "Bibliographic Relationships among Musical Bibliographic Entities: A Conceptual Analysis of Music Represented in the Library Catalog with a Taxonomy of the Relationships Discovered." DLS diss., Columbia University, 1995.

AUTHORITY CONTROL

Authority Control in the 21st Century: An Invitational Conference, March 31-April 1, 1996. Dublin, Ohio: OCLC Online Computer Library Center. http://world cat.org/arcviewer/1/OCC/2003/06/20/0000003520/viewer/file1.html.

Authority Control: Why It Matters. Conference sponsored by NELINET, 1 November 1999, Worcester, Mass. http://web.archive.org/web/20090106070603/ http://www.nelinet.net/edserv/conf/cataloging/cts/1999/cts99.htm.

Barnhart, Linda. "Access Control Records: Prospects and Challenges." In *Authority Control in the 21st Century, Invitational Conference, March 31-April 1, 1996*. http://worldcat.org/arcviewer/1/OCC/2003/06/20/0000003520/viewer/ file1.html.

Bratton, Robert, ed. "Authority Tools for Audiovisual and Music Catalogers: An Annotated List of Useful Resources." Online Audiovisual Catalogers, Inc., 2003- . http://www.olacinc.org/drupal/?q=node/13.

Hickey, Thomas B. "WorldCat Identities: Another View of the Catalog." *NextSpace*, Issue 6 (April 2007): 18-20.

International Federation of Library Associations and Institutions. Working Group on Functional Requirements and Numbering of Authority Records. *Functional Requirements for Authority Data (FRAD): A Conceptual Model*. Edited by Glenn E. Patton. München, Germany: K.G. Saur, 2009. http://www.ifla.org/ publications/functional-requirements-for-authority-data.

Jin, Qiang. *Demystifying FRAD: Functional Requirements for Authority Data*. Santa Barbara, Calif.: Libraries Unlimited, 2012.

Library of Congress. "Z1: Name and Series Authority Records." In *Descriptive Cataloging Manual*, prepared by the Policy and Standards Division, Library of Congress. Washington, D.C.: Library of Congress, 2014, http://www.loc .gov/catdir/cpso/dcmz1.pdf.

"NACO: Name Authority Cooperative Program." Program for Cooperative Cataloging. Accessed November 23, 2014. http://www.loc.gov/aba/pcc/naco/.

Patton, Glenn E. "FRANAR: A Conceptual Model for Authority Data." *Cataloging & Classification Quarterly* 38, no 3/4 (2004): 91-104; also published in *Authority Control in Organizing and Accessing Information: Definition and International Experience*, edited by Arlene G. Taylor and Barbara B. Tillett, 91-104. New York: Haworth Information Press, 2004.

"SACO Subject Authority Cooperative Program." Program Description: Program for Cooperative Cataloging. Accessed November 23, 2014. http://www.loc.gov/aba/pcc/saco/index.html.

Smiraglia, Richard. "Authority Control of Works: Cataloging's Chimera?" *Cataloging & Classification Quarterly* 38, no 3/4 (2004): 291-308; also published in *Authority Control in Organizing and Accessing Information: Definition and International Experience*, edited by Arlene G. Taylor and Barbara B. Tillett, 291-308. New York: Haworth Information Press, 2004.

Taylor, Arlene G. "Authority Control and System Design." In *Policy and Practice in the Bibliographic Control of Nonbook Media*, edited by Sheila S. Intner and Richard P. Smiraglia, 64-81. Chicago: American Library Association, 1987.

Taylor, Arlene G. "Authority Control: Where It's Been and Where It's Going." In "Authority Control: Why It Matters," conference sponsored by NELINET, 1 November 1999, Worcester, Mass. http://www.pitt.edu/~agtaylor/presentations/NELINET-1999.htm.

Taylor, Arlene G. "Research and Theoretical Considerations in Authority Control." *Cataloging & Classification Quarterly* 9, no. 3 (1989): 29-56.

Taylor, Arlene G., and Barbara B. Tillett, eds. *Authority Control in Organizing and Accessing Information: Definition and International Experience*. New York: Haworth Information Press, 2004.

Tillett, Barbara B. "Authority Control: State of the Art and New Perspectives." *Cataloging & Classification Quarterly* 38, no. 3/4 (2004): 23-41; also published in *Authority Control in Organizing and Accessing Information: Definition and International Experience*, edited by Arlene G. Taylor and Barbara B. Tillett, 23-41. New York: Haworth Information Press, 2004.

Tillett, Barbara B. "International Shared Resource Records for Controlled Access." In *From Catalog to Gateway: Briefings from the CFFC*, paper no. 12. *ALCTS Newsletter Online* 10, no. 1 (December 1998); also published in *From Catalog to Gateway: Charting a Course for Future Access: Briefings from the ALCTS Catalog Form and Function Committee*, edited by Bill Sleeman and Pamela Bluh, 69-74. Chicago: Association for Library Collections & Technical Services, American Library Association, 2005.

Vellucci, Sherry L. "Metadata and Authority Control." *Library Resources & Technical Services* 44, no. 1 (January 2000): 33-43.

SUBJECT ANALYSIS

General

Abbas, June. *Structures for Organizing Knowledge: Exploring Taxonomies, Ontologies, and Other Schema*. New York: Neal-Schuman, 2010.

Bates, Marcia J. "Rethinking Subject Cataloging in the Online Environment." *Library Resources & Technical Services* 33, no. 4 (October 1989): 400-419.

Bates, Marcia J. "Subject Access in Online Catalogs: A Design Model." *Journal of the American Society for Information Science* 37, no. 6 (November 1986): 357-376.

Chan, Lois Mai, Phyllis A. Richmond, and Elaine Svenonius, eds. *Theory of Subject Analysis: A Sourcebook.* Littleton, Colo.: Libraries Unlimited, 1985.

Coates, E. J. *Subject Catalogues: Heading and Structure.* London: Library Association, 1960.

Foskett, A. C. *The Subject Approach to Information.* 5th ed. London: Library Association Publishing, 1996.

Fugmann, Robert. *Subject Analysis and Indexing: Theoretical Foundation and Practical Advice.* Frankfurt am Main: Indeks Verlag, 1993.

International Organization for Standardization. *Documentation: Methods for Examining Documents, Determining Their Subjects and Selecting Indexing Terms.* Geneva, Switzerland: ISO, 1985.

Haykin, David Judson. *Subject Headings: A Practical Guide.* Washington, D.C.: Government Printing Office, 1951.

International Federation of Library Associations and Institutions. Working Group on the Functional Requirements for Subject Authority Records, *Functional Requirements for Subject Authority Data (FRSAD): A Conceptual Model.* München, Germany: De Gruyter Saur, 2011.

Joudrey, Daniel N. "Building Puzzles and Growing Pearls: A Qualitative Exploration of Determining Aboutness." PhD diss., University of Pittsburgh, 2005. http://d-scholarship.pitt.edu/10357/.

Joudrey, Daniel N. "Building Puzzles and Growing Pearls: A Qualitative Exploration of the Subject Determination Process." In *Proceedings from 7th ISKO-Spain Conference: The Human Dimension of Knowledge Organization, Barcelona 6-8 July 2005.* Barcelona: Universitat de Barcelona, 2005.

Lakoff, George. *Women, Fire, and Dangerous Things: What Categories Reveal about the Mind.* Chicago: University of Chicago Press, 1987.

Langridge, D. W. *Subject Analysis: Principles and Procedures.* London: Bowker-Saur, 1989.

Mann, Thomas. *Doing Research at the Library of Congress: A Guide to Subject Searching in a Closed Stacks Library.* 2nd ed. Washington, D.C.: Library of Congress, Humanities and Social Sciences Division, 2005.

Mann, Thomas. *Library Research Models: A Guide to Classification, Cataloging, and Computers.* New York: Oxford University Press, 1993.

Markey, Karen. "The Online Library Catalog: Paradise Lost and Paradise Regained?" *D-Lib Magazine* 13, no. 1/2 (Jan./Feb. 2007). http://www.dlib.org/dlib/january07/markey/01markey.html.

Markey, Karen. *Subject Searching in Library Catalogs: Before and After the Introduction of Online Catalogs.* Dublin, Ohio: OCLC, 1984.

Miller, David, Tony Olson, and Sara Shatford Layne. "Promoting Research and Best Practices in Subject Reference Structures: A Decade of Work by the Subject Analysis Committee." *Library Resources & Technical Services* 49, no. 3 (July 2005): 154-166.

Olson, Hope A., and John J. Boll. *Subject Analysis in Online Catalogs.* 2nd ed. Englewood, Colo.: Libraries Unlimited, 2001.

Petersen, Toni, and Pat Molholt, eds. *Beyond the Book: Extending MARC for Subject Access.* Boston: G. K. Hall, 1990.

"SACO Subject Authority Cooperative Program." Program Description: Program for Cooperative Cataloging. Accessed November 23, 2014. http://www.loc.gov/aba/pcc/saco/index.html.

Šauperl, Alenka. *Subject Determination during the Cataloging Process.* Lanham, Md.: Scarecrow Press, 2002.

Subject Data in the Metadata Record: Recommendations and Rationale: A Report from the ALCTS/CCS/SAC Subcommittee on Metadata and Subject

Analysis, July 1999. http://www.ala.org/alcts/resources/org/cat/subjectdata
_record.

*Subject Indexing: Principles and Practices in the 90's: Proceedings of the IFLA Sat-
ellite Meeting Held in Lisbon, Portugal, 17-18 August 1993.* München, Germany: K.G. Saur, 1995.

Taylor, Arlene G. "On the Subject of Subjects." *Journal of Academic Librarianship*
21, no. 6 (November 1995): 484-491.

Wellish, Hans H. "Aboutness and Selection of Topics." *Key Words* 4, no. 2 (March/
April 1996): 7-9.

Wilson, Patrick. "Subjects and the Sense of Position." In *Theory of Subject Analysis: A Sourcebook,* edited by Lois Mai Chan, Phyllis A. Richmond, and Elaine
Svenonius, 253-268. Littleton, Colo.: Libraries Unlimited, 1985.

Žumer, Maja, Marcia Lei Zeng, and Athena Salaba. *FRSAD: Conceptual Modeling of
Aboutness.* Santa Barbara, Calif.: Libraries Unlimited, 2012.

Verbal Subject Access

Allemang, Dean, and James Hendler. *Semantic Web for the Working Ontologist:
Effective Modeling in RDFS and OWL.* Amsterdam: Morgan Kaufmann,
2008.

American Library Association. *List of Subject Headings for Use in Dictionary Catalogs.* Boston: Library Bureau, 1895.

American Library Association. Subject Analysis Committee. "Definition of Form
Data." 1993. http://www.pitt.edu/~agtaylor/ala/form-def.htm.

American Library Association. Subject Analysis Committee. Subcommittee on
Subject Access to Individual Works of Fiction, Drama, etc. *Guidelines on
Subject Access to Individual Works of Fiction, Drama, etc.* 2nd ed. Chicago:
American Library Association, 2000.

Angell, Richard S. "Library of Congress Subject Headings—Review and Forecast."
In *Subject Retrieval in the Seventies: New Directions,* edited by Hans Wellisch
and Thomas D. Wilson. Westport, Conn.: Greenwood Publishing, 1972.

Berman, Sanford. *Prejudices and Antipathies: A Tract on the LC Subject Heads
Concerning People.* Jefferson, N.C.: McFarland, 1993.

Broughton, Vanda. *Essential Library of Congress Subject Headings.* New York:
Neal-Schuman Publishers, 2012.

Brown, A. G., in collaboration with D. W. Langridge, and J. Mills. *An Introduction to
Subject Indexing.* 2nd ed. London: Bingley, 1982. [Programmed text.]

Canadian Subject Headings: Supplement. 3rd ed. Ottawa: National Library of Canada, 1996.

Chan, Lois Mai. *Library of Congress Subject Headings: Principles and Application.*
4th ed. Westport, Conn.: Libraries Unlimited, 2005.

Chan, Lois Mai, and Edward T. O'Neill. *FAST: Faceted Application of Subject Terminology: Principles and Application.* Santa Barbara, Calif.: Libraries Unlimited,
2010.

Clack, Doris H. *Black Literature Resources: Analysis and Organization.* New York:
Marcel Dekker, 1975.

Dykstra, Mary. "LC Subject Headings Disguised as a Thesaurus." *Library Journal*
113 (March 1, 1988): 42-46.

Fountain, Joanna F. *Subject Headings for School and Public Libraries.* Bilingual 4th
ed. Santa Barbara, Calif.: Libraries Unlimited, 2012.

Ganendran, Jacki, and Lynn Farkas. *Learn Library of Congress Subject Access.*
2nd North American ed. Friendswood, Tex.: TotalRecall Publications, 2007.

Getty. *Art & Architecture Thesaurus Online.* Accessed November 23, 2014. http://www.getty.edu/research/tools/vocabularies/aat/.

Gross, Tina, and Arlene G. Taylor, "What Have We Got to Lose? The Effect of Controlled Vocabulary on Keyword Searching Results." *College & Research Libraries* 66, no. 3 (May 2005): 212-230.

Gross, Tina, Arlene G. Taylor, and Daniel N. Joudrey, "Still a Lot to Lose: The Role of Controlled Vocabulary in Keyword Searching." *Cataloging & Classification Quarterly* 53, no. 1 (2015): 1-39.

Hemmasi, Harriette, David Miller, and Mary Charles Lasater; edited by Arlene G. Taylor. "Access to Form Data in Online Catalogs." In "From Catalog to Gateway: Briefings from the CFFC," paper no. 13. *ALCTS Newsletter Online* 10, no. 4 (July 1999); also published in *From Catalog to Gateway: Charting a Course for Future Access: Briefings from the ALCTS Catalog Form and Function Committee*, edited by Bill Sleeman and Pamela Bluh, 75-81. Chicago: Association for Library Collections & Technical Services, American Library Association, 2005.

International Organization for Standardization. *Information and Documentation. Thesauri and Interoperability with Other Vocabularies*, ISO 25964-1:2011, Part 1: Thesauri for Information Retrieval. Geneva: ISO, 2011.

International Organization for Standardization. *Information and Documentation. Thesauri and Interoperability with Other Vocabularies*, ISO 25964-2:2013, Part 2: Interoperability with Other Vocabularies. Geneva: ISO, 2013.

Lancaster, F. W. *Indexing and Abstracting in Theory and Practice.* 3rd ed. Champaign: University of Illinois, Graduate School of Library and Information Science, 2003. [Also published: London: Facet Publishing, 2003.]

Lancaster, F. W. "Trends in Subject Indexing from 1957 to 2000." In *New Trends in Documentation and Information: Proceedings of the 39th FID Congress, 1978*, 223-233. London: Aslib, 1980.

Lancaster, F. W. *Vocabulary Control For Information Retrieval.* 2nd ed. Arlington, Va.: Information Resources Press, 1986.

Lee-Smeltzer, Kuang-Hwei (Janet). "Finding the Needle: Controlled Vocabularies, Resource Discovery, and Dublin Core." *Library Collections, Acquisitions, & Technical Services* 24 (2000): 205-215.

Library of Congress Subject Headings. "Introduction." Accessed November 23, 2014. http://www.loc.gov/aba/publications/FreeLCSH/freelcsh.html.

Library of Congress Subject Headings. 13th-35th eds. Washington, D.C.: Office for Subject Cataloging Policy, Library of Congress, 1990-2013 [ceased print publication in 2013]. (Available in *Classification Web* and at the Library of Congress website.) http://www.loc.gov/aba/publications/FreeLCSH/freelcsh.html.

Library of Congress Subject Headings Monthly Lists. Washington, D.C.: Cataloging Policy and Support Office, Library of Congress, January 1997- [date]. http://www.loc.gov/aba/cataloging/subject/.

Lighthall, Lynne Isberg, ed. *Sears List of Subject Headings: Canadian Companion.* 6th ed. New York: H. W. Wilson, 2001.

Luhn, Hans Peter. "Keyword in Context Index for Technical Literature (KWIC Index)." *American Documentation* 11 (1960): 288-295.

Mann, Thomas. "Research at Risk." *Library Journal* (July 15, 2005). http://lj.libraryjournal.com/2005/07/ljarchives/research-at-risk/.

Mann, Thomas. "Will Google's Keyword Searching Eliminate the Need for LC Cataloging and Classification?" AFSCME 2910. Last updated August 15, 2005. http://www.guild2910.org/searching.htm.

Markey, Karen. *Subject Searching in Library Catalogs: Before and After the Introduction of Online Catalogs.* Dublin, Ohio: OCLC Online Computer Library Center, 1984.

Marshall, Joan K. *On Equal Terms: A Thesaurus for Nonsexist Indexing and Cataloging.* Santa Barbara, Calif.: American Bibliographical Center-CLIO Press, 1977.

National Information Standards Organization. *Guidelines for the Construction, Format, and Management of Monolingual Controlled Vocabularies.* ANSI/NISO Z39.19-2005 (R2010). Bethesda, Md.: NISO Press, 2010. http://www.niso.org/apps/group_public/download.php/12591/z39-19-2005r2010.pdf.

National Library of Medicine. "PubMed." Accessed November 23, 2014. http://www.ncbi.nlm.nih.gov/pubmed.

National Library of Medicine. "UMLS Metathesaurus: Fact Sheet." Accessed November 23, 2014. http://www.nlm.nih.gov/pubs/factsheets/umlsmeta.html.

National Library of Medicine. "Unified Medical Language System (UMLS)." Accessed November 23, 2014. http://www.nlm.nih.gov/research/umls/.

Noy, Natalya F., and Deborah L. McGuinness. *Ontology Development 101: A Guide to Creating Your First Ontology.* Knowledge Systems Laboratory, Stanford University, 2000. http://www.ksl.stanford.edu/people/dlm/papers/ontology-tutorial-noy-mcguinness.pdf.

Olson, Hope A. *The Power to Name: Locating the Limits of Subject Representation in Libraries.* Dordrecht, The Netherlands; Boston: Kluwer Academic Publishers, 2002.

O'Neill, Edward T., Lois Mai Chan, Eric Childress, Rebecca Dean, Lynn M. El-Hoshy, and Diane Visine-Goetz. "Form Subdivisions: Their Identification and Use in LCSH." *Library Resources & Technical Services* 45, no. 4 (October 2001): 187-197.

"Principles of the Sears List of Subject Headings." In *Sears List of Subject Headings.* 21st ed., Barbara A. Bristow, editor; Christi Showman Farrar, associate editor. Ipswich, Mass.: H. W. Wilson, a division of EBSCO Information Services; Armenia, N.Y.: Grey House Publishing, 2014.

Satija, M. P., and Elizabeth Haynes. *User's Guide to Sears List of Subject Headings.* Lanham, Md.: Scarecrow Press, 2008.

Sears List of Subject Headings. 21st ed., Barbara A. Bristow, editor; Christi Showman Farrar, associate editor. Ipswich, Mass.: H. W. Wilson, a division of EBSCO Information Services; Armenia, N.Y.: Grey House Publishing, 2014.

Sears: Lista de Encabezamientos de Materia: Nueva Traducción y Adaptación de la Lista Sears, Iván E. Calimano, editor; Ageo García, editor asociado; Judy Medina, Carmen Torres, traductores; incorporando el trabajo de 1984 de Carmen Rovira. New York: H. W. Wilson, 2008.

Sinkankis, George M. "A Study in the Syndetic Structure of the Library of Congress List of Subject Headings." PhD diss., University of Pittsburgh, 1972.

Subject Headings Manual. 1st ed. Washington, D.C.: Cataloging Distribution Service, Library of Congress, 2008. Updates, 2008- . (Also available in *Cataloger's Desktop.*) http://www.loc.gov/aba/publications/FreeSHM/freeshm.html.

Subject Headings Used in the Dictionary Catalogues of the Library of Congress, [1st]-3rd eds. Washington, D.C.: Catalog Division, Library of Congress, 1910-1928; *Subject Headings Used in the Dictionary Catalogs of the Library of Congress,* 4th-7th eds. Washington, D.C.: Subject Cataloging Division, Library of Congress, 1943-1966; *Library of Congress Subject Headings,* 8th-12th eds. Washington, D.C.: Subject Cataloging Division, Library of Congress, 1975-1989; *Library of Congress Subject Headings,* 13th-35th eds. Washington, D.C.: Office for Subject Cataloging Policy, 1990-2013.

Svenonius, Elaine. "LCSH: Semantics, Syntax and Specificity." *Cataloging & Classification Quarterly* 29, no. 1/2 (2000): 17-30.

Taube, Mortimer, and Associates. *Studies in Coordinate Indexing.* Washington, D.C.: Documentation, Inc., 1953.

Classification

Bliss, Henry Evelyn. *The Organization of Knowledge in Libraries and the Subject-approach to Books.* New York: H. W. Wilson, 1933.

Bliss Classification Association. "Bliss Classification Association: homepage." http://www.blissclassification.org.uk/.

Bowker, Geoffrey C., and Susan Leigh Star. *Sorting Things Out: Classification and Its Consequences.* Cambridge, Mass.: MIT Press, 1999.

Broughton, Vanda. *Essential Classification.* U.S. ed. New York: Neal-Schuman, 2004.

Chan, Lois M. *A Guide to the Library of Congress Classification.* 5th ed. Englewood, Colo.: Libraries Unlimited, 1999.

Chan, Lois Mai, and Joan S. Mitchell. *Dewey Decimal Classification: Principles and Application.* 3rd ed. Dublin, Ohio: OCLC, 2003.

Classification and Shelflisting Manual. 2013 ed. Washington, D.C.: Library of Congress, 2013. (Also available in *Cataloger's Desktop* and at the Library of Congress website.) http://www.loc.gov/aba/publications/FreeCSM/freecsm .html.

Classification Research Group. "The Need for a Faceted Classification as the Basis of all Methods of Information Retrieval." In *Theory of Subject Analysis: A Sourcebook,* edited by Lois Mai Chan, Phyllis A. Richmond, and Elaine Svenonius, 154-167. Littleton, Colo.: Libraries Unlimited, 1985.

Dewey, Melvil. *Abridged Dewey Decimal Classification and Relative Index.* 15th ed. Edited by Joan S. Mitchell et al. Dublin, OH: OCLC, 2012. DDC, Dewey, Dewey Decimal Classification, and WebDewey are registered trademarks of OCLC.

Dewey, Melvil. *Dewey Decimal Classification and Relative Index.* 23rd ed. Edited by Joan S. Mitchell et al. Dublin, OH: OCLC, 2011. DDC, Dewey, Dewey Decimal Classification, and WebDewey are registered trademarks of OCLC.

Dittmann, Helena, and Jane Hardy. *Learn Library of Congress Classification.* 2nd North American ed. Friendswood, Tex: TotalRecall Publications, 2007.

Gorman, Michael. "The Longer the Number, the Smaller the Spine; or, Up and Down with Melvil and Elsie." *American Libraries* 12 (September 1981): 498-499.

Hunter, Eric J. *Classification Made Simple.* 3rd ed. Aldershot, Eng.; Burlington, Vt.: Ashgate, 2009.

Koch, Traugott, and Michael Day. *The Role of Classification Schemes in Internet Resource Description and Discovery.* Accessed November 23, 2014. http:// www.ukoln.ac.uk/metadata/desire/classification/.

Langridge, D. W. *Classification: Its Kinds, Elements, Systems and Applications.* London: Bowker-Saur, 1992.

Library of Congress Classification: Classes A-Z. Var. eds. Washington, D.C.: Cataloging Distribution Service, Library of Congress, 1976-2013. [Print publication ceased in 2013.] (Also available online at *Classification Web* and at the Library of Congress website.) http://www.loc.gov/aba/publications/ FreeLCC/freelcc.html.

Maltby, Arthur, and Lindy Gill. *The Case for Bliss: Modern Classification Practice and Principles in the Context of the Bibliographic Classification.* London : Clive Bingley, 1979.

Marcella, Rita, and Arthur Maltby, eds. *The Future of Classification.* Aldershot, Eng.; Brookfield, Vt.: Gower, 2000.

Marcella, Rita, and Robert Newton. *A New Manual of Classification.* Aldershot, Eng.; Brookfield, Vt.: Gower, 1994.

McIlwaine, I. C. *The Universal Decimal Classification: A Guide to Its Use.* Rev. ed. The Hague: UDC Consortium, 2007.

Miksa, Francis L. *The DDC, the Universe of Knowledge, and the Post-Modern Library.* Paper presented at the Fourth International ISKO Conference, July 15-18, 1996, Washington, D.C.; Albany, N.Y.: OCLC Forest Press, 1998.

National Library of Medicine. *NLM Classification 2014.* http://www.nlm.nih.gov/class/.

OCLC. "Dewey Services." Accessed November 23, 2014. http://www.oclc.org/dewey/updates/default.htm.

Ranganathan, S. R. *Colon Classification: Basic Classification.* 6th ed., completely revised. Bombay; New York: Asia Publishing House, 1960.

Ranganathan, S. R. *Colon Classification.* 7th ed., revised and edited by M. A. Gopinath. Bangalore: Ranganathan Endowment for Library Science, 1989.

Ranganathan, S. R. *Prolegomena to Library Classification.* 3rd ed., assisted by M. A. Gopinath. London, Asia Pub. House, 1967.

Richardson, Ernest Cushing. *Classification, Theoretical and Practical: Together with an Appendix Containing an Essay towards a Bibliographical History of Systems of Classification.* 3rd ed. New York, H. W. Wilson, 1930.

Satija, M. P. *The Theory and Practice of the Dewey Decimal Classification System.* Oxford: Chandos, 2007.

Sayers, W. C. Berwick. *Sayers' Manual of Classification for Librarians.* 5th ed., revised by Arthur Maltby. London: Deutsch, 1975.

Sweeney, Russell. "The Atlantic Divide: Classification Outside the United States." In *Classification of Library Materials,* edited by Betty G. Bengtson and Janet Swan Hill, 40-51. New York: Neal-Schuman, 1990.

UDC Consortium. "About Universal Decimal Classification (UDC)." Accessed November 23, 2014. http://www.udcc.org/index.php/site/page?view=about.

"UDC Online." Accessed November 23, 2014. http://www.udc-hub.com/index.php.

Universal Decimal Classification. 3rd ed., standard ed. London: British Standards Institution, 2006.

Vickery, B. C. *Faceted Classification: A Guide to the Construction and Use of Special Schemes.* London: Aslib, 1960.

Wason, Thomas D. "Dr. Tom's Taxonomy Guide: Description, Use and Selections," Version 1.01, 15 February 2006. http://www.tomwason.com/drtomtaxonomiesguide.html.

Williamson, Nancy. "Classification in the Millennium." *Online & CDROM Review* 21, no. 5 (October 1997): 298-301.

ARRANGEMENT

ALA Filing Rules. Chicago: American Library Association, 1980.

A.L.A. Rules for Filing Catalog Cards. Chicago: American Library Association, 1942.

ALA Rules for Filing Catalog Cards. 2nd ed. Chicago: American Library Association, 1968.

Buckland, Michael K., Barbara A. Norgard, and Christian Plaunt. "Filing, Filtering and the First Few Found." *Information Technology and Libraries* 12, no. 3 (September 1993): 311-319.

Classification and Shelflisting Manual. 2013 ed. Washington, D.C.: Library of Congress, 2013. (Also available in *Cataloger's Desktop* and at the Library of Congress website. http://www.loc.gov/aba/publications/FreeCSM/freecsm .html.)

Comaromi, John P. *Book Numbers: A Historical Study and Practical Guide to Their Use.* Littleton, Colo.: Libraries Unlimited, 1981.

Cutter, Charles A. *Cutter-Sanborn Three-Figure Author Table,* Swanson-Swift revision, 1969. Distributed by Libraries Unlimited, Inc., Englewood, Colo.

Cutter, Charles A. *Three-Figure Author Table,* Swanson-Swift revision, 1969. Distributed by Libraries Unlimited, Inc., Englewood, Colo.

Cutter, Charles A. *Two-Figure Author Table,* Swanson-Swift revision, 1969. Distributed by Libraries Unlimited, Inc., Englewood, Colo.

Lehnus, Donald J. *Book Numbers: History, Principles, and Application.* Chicago: American Library Association, 1980.

Library of Congress Filing Rules. Washington, D.C.: Library of Congress, 1980.

Taylor, Arlene G. "Appendix: Arrangement Dilemmas and Filing Rules." In Taylor, Arlene G., with the assistance of David P. Miller. *Introduction to Cataloging and Classification,* 10th ed., 509-524. Westport, Conn.: Libraries Unlimited, 2006.

Taylor, Arlene G. "Arrangement and Display." Chap. 12 in *The Organization of Information.* 2nd ed. Westport, Conn.: Libraries Unlimited, 2004.

Taylor, Arlene G., and Daniel Joudrey. "Arrangement of Physical Information Resources in Libraries." Appendix B in *The Organization of Information.* 3rd ed. Westport, Conn.: Libraries Unlimited, 2009.

FORMATTING AND PRESENTATION

Andresen, Leif. "After MARC—What Then?" *Library Hi Tech* 22, no. 1 (January 2004): 41-51.

Antoniou, Grogoris. *A Semantic Web Primer.* 3rd ed. Cambridge, Mass.: MIT Press, 2012.

Avram, Henriette D. *MARC, Its History and Implications.* Washington, D.C.: Library of Congress, 1975.

Bianchini, Carlo, and Mirna Willer. "ISBD Resource and Its Description in the Context of the Semantic Web." *Cataloging & Classification Quarterly* 52, no. 8 (2014): 869-887.

"Bibliographic Framework as a Web of Data: Linked Data Model and Supporting Services." Accessed July 2, 2014. http://www.loc.gov/bibframe/pdf/marcld -report-11-21-2012.pdf.

Bowman, J. H. "Development of Description in Cataloguing prior to ISBD." *Aslib Proceedings* 58, no. 1/2 (2006): 34-48.

Byrne, Deborah J. "MARC Theory and Development." In *MARC Manual: Understanding and Using MARC Records.* 2nd ed., 1–15. Englewood, Colo.: Libraries Unlimited, 1998.

Byrum, John D. "The Birth and Re-birth of the ISBDs: Process and Procedures for Creating and Revising the International Standard Bibliographic Descriptions." *IFLA Journal* 27, no. 1 (2001): 34-37. http://archive.ifla.org/V/iflaj/ art2701.pdf.

Coyle, Karen. *Linked Data Tools: Connecting on the Web.* Chicago, Ill.: ALA Tech-
Source, 2012.

Coyle, Karen. *Understanding the Semantic Web: Bibliographic Data and Metadata.*
Chicago, Ill.: ALA TechSource, 2010.

The Dublin Core Metadata Element Set: An American National Standard. Bethesda,
Md.: NISO Press, 2007.

Dunsire, Gordon. "The Role of ISBD in the Linked Data Environment." *Cataloging
& Classification Quarterly* 52, no. 8 (2014): 855-868.

Ferguson, Bobby. *MARC/AACR2/Authority Control Tagging: Blitz Cataloging Workbook.* 2nd ed. Westport, Conn.: Libraries Unlimited, 2005.

Ford, Kevin M. "LC's Bibliographic Framework Initiative and the Attractiveness of
Linked Data." *Information Standards Quarterly,* 24 no. 2/3 (2012): 46-50.

Fritz, Deborah A. *Cataloging with AACR2 and MARC21, for Books, Electronic
Resources, Sound Recordings, Videorecordings, and Serials.* 2nd ed., 2006
cumulation. Chicago: American Library Association, 2007.

Fritz, Deborah A., and Richard J. Fritz. *MARC21 for Everyone: A Practical Guide.*
Chicago: American Library Association, 2003.

Furrie, Betty. *Understanding MARC Bibliographic: Machine-Readable Cataloging.*
8th ed. Washington, D.C.: Library of Congress Cataloging Distribution Service, 2009. http://www.loc.gov/marc/umb/.

Godby, Carol Jean. "The Relationship between BIBFRAME and OCLC's Linked-Data
Model of Bibliographic Description." Accessed November 18, 2014. http://
oclc.org/content/dam/research/publications/library/2013/2013-05.pdf.

Howarth, Lynne C. "ISBD as Bibliographic Content Standard: Interweaving
Threads, Contemplating a Future." *Cataloging & Classification Quarterly* 52,
no. 8 (2014): 982-999.

"Implications of MARC Tag Usage on Library Metadata Practices." Dublin, Ohio: OCLC
Research, 2010. http://www.oclc.org/content/dam/research/publications/
library/2010/2010-06.pdf.

International Federation of Library Associations and Institutions. Cataloguing Section and ISBD Review Group. *International Standard Bibliographic Description.* Consolidated ed. Berlin: De Gruyter Saur, 2011. http://www.ifla.org/
files/assets/cataloguing/isbd/isbd-cons_20110321.pdf.

Kroeger, Angela. "The Road to BIBFRAME: The Evolution of the Idea of Bibliographic Transition into a Post-MARC Future." *Cataloging & Classification
Quarterly* 51, no. 8 (2013): 873-890.

Library of Congress. "MARC in XML." Network Development and MARC Standards
Office, Library of Congress. Washington, DC: Library of Congress. Accessed
November 23, 2014. http://www.loc.gov/marc/marcxml.html.

Lubas, Rebecca L., Amy S. Jackson, and Ingrid Schneider. *The Metadata Manual:
A Practical Workbook.* Oxford: Chandos Publishing, 2013. See esp. chap. 3,
"Using Dublin Core."

MARC 21 Format for Authority Data. 1999 ed. Washington, D.C.: Cataloging Distribution Service, Library of Congress, 2014. http://www.loc.gov/marc/
authority/ecadhome.html.

MARC 21 Format for Bibliographic Data. 1999 ed. Washington, D.C.: Cataloging
Distribution Service, Library of Congress, 2014. http://www.loc.gov/marc/
bibliographic/.

MARC 21 Format for Classification Data. 2000 ed. Washington, D.C.: Cataloging
Distribution Service, Library of Congress, 2014. http://www.loc.gov/marc/
classification/eccdhome.html.

MARC 21 Format for Community Information. 2000 ed. Washington, D.C.: Cataloging Distribution Service, Library of Congress, 2014. http://www.loc.gov/
marc/community/eccihome.html.

MARC 21 Format for Holdings Data. 2000 ed. Washington, D.C.: Cataloging Distribution Service, Library of Congress, 2014. http://www.loc.gov/marc/holdings/echdhome.html.

"The MARC 21 Formats: Background and Principles." Prepared by MARBI in conjunction with Network Development and MARC Standards Office, Library of Congress. Washington, D.C.: Library of Congress, 1996. http://www.loc.gov/marc/96principl.html.

McCallum, Sally H. "An Introduction to the Metadata Object Description Schema." *Library Hi Tech* 22, no. 1 (January 2004): 82-88.

Miller, Steven J. *Metadata for Digital Collections: A How-To-Do-It Manual.* New York: Neal-Schuman Publishers, 2011. See esp. chap. 2, "Introduction to Resource Description and Dublin Core"; chap. 3, "Resource Identification and Responsibility Elements"; chap. 4, "Resource Content and Relationship Elements"; and chap. 7, "MODS: The Metadata Object Description Schema."

Mitchell, Erik T. *Library Linked Data: Research and Adoption.* Chicago: American Library Association, 2013.

Mukhopadhyay, Asoknath. *Guide to MARC 21: For Cataloging of Books and Serials.* Oxford, England: Chandos Publishing, 2007.

OCLC. *Bibliographic Formats and Standards.* 4th ed. Dublin, Ohio: OCLC, 2008. http://www.oclc.org/bibformats.

Rodríguez, Elena Escolano. "ISBD Adaptation to SW [Semantic Web] of Bibliographic Data in Linked Data." *JLIS.it, Italian Journal of Library and Information Science* 4, no. 1 (2013): 199-137.

Rodríguez, Elena Escolano, and Dorothy McGarry. "Consolidated ISBD: A Step Forward." Prepared for the 73rd IFLA Council and General Conference, Durban, South Africa, 19th-23rd August 2007. http://archive.ifla.org/IV/ifla73/papers/145-EscolanoRodriguez_McGarry-en.pdf.

Smith-Yoshimura, Karen, et al. *Implications of MARC Tag Usage on Library Metadata Practices.* Dublin, Ohio: OCLC, 2010. Published online at www.oclc.org/research/publications/library/2010/2010-06.pdf.

Tennant, Roy. "A Bibliographic Metadata Infrastructure for the 21st Century." *Library Hi Tech* 22, no. 2 (2004): 176.

Tennant, Roy. "MARC Must Die." *Library Journal* 127, no. 17 (2002): 26-27.

UNIMARC Manual: Bibliographic Format. 3rd ed. München, Germany: K.G. Saur, 2008. http://www.ifla.org/publications/ifla-series-on-bibliographic-control-36.

Van Hooland, Seth, and Ruben Verborgh. *Linked Data for Libraries, Archives and Museums: How to Clean, Link and Publish Your Metadata.* Chicago: Neal-Schuman, 2014.

Wacker, Melanie, Myung-Ja Han, and Judith Dartt. "Testing Resource Description and Access (RDA) with Non-MARC Metadata Standards." *Cataloging & Classification Quarterly* 49, nos. 7-8 (2011): 655-675.

Willer, Mirna, ed. *UNIMARC Manual: Authorities Format.* 3rd ed. München, Germany: K.G. Saur, 2009.

ADMINISTRATIVE ISSUES

Auto-Graphics. "Auto-Graphics Library Automation." Accessed November 23, 2014. http://www4.auto-graphics.com/.

Bénaud, Claire Lise, and Sever Bordeianu. *Outsourcing Library Operations in Academic Libraries: An Overview of Issues and Outcomes.* Englewood, Colo.: Libraries Unlimited, 1998.

Bilal, Dania. *Automating Media Centers and Small Libraries: A Microcomputer-Based Approach.* 2nd ed. Greenwood Village, Colo.: Libraries Unlimited, 2002.

Blackman, Cathy, Erica Rae Moore, Michele Seikel, and Mandi Smith. "World-Cat and SkyRiver: A Comparison of Record Quantity and Fullness." *Library Resources & Technical Services* 58, no. 3 (July 2014): 178-186.

Borgman, Christine L. "From Acting Locally to Thinking Globally: A Brief History of Library Automation." *Library Quarterly* 67, no. 3 (July 1997): 215-249.

Borgman, Christine L. "Why Are Online Catalogs *Still* Hard to Use?" *Journal of the American Society for Information Science* 47, no. 7 (July 1996): 493-503.

Brisson, Roger, and Janet McCue. "Retooling Technical Services." In *Encyclopedia of Library and Information Science*, vol. 58, suppl. 21, 281-301. New York: Marcel Dekker, 1996.

Buttlar, Lois, and Rajinder Garcha. "Catalogers in Academic Libraries: Their Evolving and Expanding Roles." *College & Research Libraries* 59, no. 4 (July 1998): 311-321.

Calhoun, Karen, and Bill Kara. "Aggregation or Aggravation? Optimizing Access to Full-Text Journals." In *From Catalog to Gateway: Briefings from the CFFC*, paper no. 15. *ALCTS Newsletter Online* 11, no. 1 (Spring 2000); also published in *From Catalog to Gateway: Charting a Course for Future Access: Briefings from the ALCTS Catalog Form and Function Committee*, edited by Bill Sleeman and Pamela Bluh, 91-97. Chicago: Association for Library Collections & Technical Services, American Library Association, 2005.

Carlyle, Allyson. "Fulfilling the Second Objective in the Online Catalog: Schemes for Organizing Author and Work Records into Usable Displays." *Library Resources & Technical Services* 41, no. 2 (April 1997): 79-100.

Carlyle, Allyson, and Sara Ranger. "Facilitating Retrieval of Fiction Works in Online Catalogs." *Proceedings of the 12th ASIS&T/CR Classification Research Workshop, November 4, 2001*, Silver Spring, Md.: ASIST&T, c1997 [i.e., 2001]: 1-11.

Carlyle, Allyson, and Traci Timmons. "Default Record Displays in Web-Based Catalogs." *Library Quarterly* 72, no. 2 (April 2002): 179-204.

Colver, Marylou, and Karen Wilson, eds. *Outsourcing Library Technical Services Operations.* Chicago: American Library Association, 1997.

Crawford, Walt. "The Card Catalog and Other Digital Controversies: What's Obsolete and What's Not in the Age of Information." *American Libraries* 30, no. 1 (January 1999): 52-58.

Dunkle, Clare B. "Outsourcing the Catalog Department: A Meditation Inspired by the Business and Library Literature." *Journal of Academic Librarianship* 22, no. 1 (January 1996).

Eden, Bradford Lee, ed. *Twenty-first Century Metadata Operations: Challenges, Opportunities, Directions.* London: Routledge, 2012.

Evans, G. Edward, Sheila S. Intner, and Jean Weihs. *Introduction to Technical Services.* 8th ed. Santa Barbara, Calif.: Libraries Unlimited, 2011.

Farb, Sharon. "Universal Design and the Americans with Disabilities Act: Not All Systems Are Created Equal—How Systems Design Can Expand Information Access." In *From Catalog to Gateway: Briefings from the CFFC*, paper no. 16. *ALCTS Newsletter Online* 11, no. 1 (Spring 2000); also published in *From Catalog to Gateway: Charting a Course for Future Access: Briefings from the ALCTS Catalog Form and Function Committee*, edited by Bill Sleeman and Pamela Bluh, 99-106. Chicago: Association for Library Collections & Technical Services, American Library Association, 2005.

Foster, Donald L. *Managing the Catalog Department*. 3rd ed. Metuchen, N.J.: Scarecrow Press, 1987.

Gassie, L. W. "What Do We Expect from the Next Generation of Library Systems?" *LLA Bulletin* 60, no. 2 (Fall 1997): 97.

Grant, Carl. "The Future of Library Systems: Library Services Platforms." *Information Standards Quarterly* 24, no. 4 (Fall 2012): 4-15.

Helfer, Doris, and Helen Heinrich. "Library Technical Services." In *Encyclopedia of Library and Information Science*, 3rd ed., edited by Marcia J. Bates and Mary Niles Maack, 3460-3467. New York: Taylor and Francis, 2009.

Hirshon, Arnold, and Barbara Winters. *Outsourcing Library Technical Services: A How-to-do-it Manual for Librarians*. New York: Neal-Schumer Publishers, 1996.

"Intellectual Freedom Toolkits: Outsourcing and Privatization in Libraries" (includes links to several documents). Accessed November 23, 2014. http://www.ala.org/tools/outsourcing.

Intner, Sheila S., and Peggy Johnson. *Fundamentals of Technical Services Management*. Chicago: American Library Association, 2008.

Kaplan, Michael, ed. *Planning and Implementing Technical Services Workstations*. Chicago: American Library Association, 1997.

Kascus, Marie A., and Dawn Hale, eds. *Outsourcing Cataloging, Authority Work, and Physical Processing: A Checklist of Considerations*. Chicago: American Library Association, 1995.

Kochtanek, Thomas R., and Joseph R. Matthews. *Library Information Systems: From Library Automation to Distributed Access Information Systems*. Westport, Conn.: Libraries Unlimited, 2002.

Long, Chris Evin. "The Internet's Value to Catalogers: Results of a Survey." *Cataloging & Classification Quarterly* 23, no. 3-4 (1997): 65-74.

Machovec, George. "ILS System Selection: Second Time Around." *Colorado Libraries* 23, no. 4 (Winter 1997): 6.

Martin, Robert S., et al. "The Impact of Outsourcing and Privatization on Library Services and Management: A Study for the American Library Association." School of Library and Information Studies, Texas Woman's University, June 2000. http://www.ala.org/tools/outsourcing/outsourcingprivatization.

Matthews, Joseph R., Gary S. Lawrence, and Douglas K. Ferguson, eds. *Using Online Catalogs: A Nationwide Survey*. Sponsored by the Council on Library Resources. New York: Neal-Schuman, 1983.

Morris, Dilys E., and Gregory Wool. "Cataloging: Librarianship's Best Bargain." *Library Journal* 124, no. 11 (June 15, 1999): 44-46.

Naun, C. C. "Next Generation OPACs: A Cataloging Viewpoint." *Cataloging & Classification Quarterly* 48, no. 4 (2010): 330-342.

OCLC. "OCLC Connexion." Accessed November 23, 2014. http://connexion.oclc.org/.

OCLC. "OCLC Online Computer Library Center, Inc." Accessed November 23, 2014. http://www.oclc.org/.

Oddy, Pat. "Bibliographic Standards and the Globalization of Bibliographic Control." In *Technical Services Today and Tomorrow*. 2nd ed., edited by Michael Gorman, 67-78. Englewood, Colo.: Libraries Unlimited, 1998.

Potter, William Gray. "The Online Catalogue in Academic Libraries." In *Technical Services Today and Tomorrow*. 2nd ed., edited by Michael Gorman, 141-155. Englewood, Colo., Libraries Unlimited, 1998.

Program for Cooperative Cataloging. "BIBCO: Monographic Bibliographic Record Cooperative Program." Accessed November 23, 2014. http://www.loc.gov/aba/pcc/bibco/index.html.

Program for Cooperative Cataloging. "Program for Cooperative Cataloging." Accessed November 23, 2014. http://www.loc.gov/aba/pcc/.

Reynolds, Dennis. *Library Automation: Issues and Applications*. New York: R. R. Bowker, 1985.

Rushoff, Carlen. "Cataloging's Prospects: Responding to Austerity with Innovation." *Journal of Academic Librarianship* 21, no. 1 (January 1995): 51-57.

Saffady, William. "Commercial Sources of Cataloging Data: Bibliographic Utilities and Other Vendors." *Library Technology Reports* 34, no. 3 (May/June 1998): 281-432.

Sellberg, Roxanne. "Cataloguing Management: Managing the Bibliographic Control Process." In *Technical Services Today and Tomorrow*, 2nd ed., edited by Michael Gorman, 111-127. Englewood, Colo.: Libraries Unlimited, 1998.

Taylor, Arlene G., with the assistance of Rosanna M. O'Neil. *Cataloging with Copy: A Decision- Maker's Handbook*. 2nd ed. Englewood, Colo.: Libraries Unlimited, 1988. See esp. chap 1, "Catalogs, Procedures, and Personnel," and chap. 9, "Merits and Problems of Copy Cataloging."

Vellucci, Sherry L. "Future Catalogers: Essential Colleagues or Anachronisms?" *College & Research Library News* 7 (1996): 442-443.

Watson, Mark. "Top Five Reasons Why Library Administrators Should Support Participation in the Program for Cooperative Cataloging." Accessed November 23, 2014. https://scholarsbank.uoregon.edu/xmlui/bitstream/handle/1794/2427/pcc_topfive.pdf?sequence=1.

Wilson, Karen A., and Marylou Colver, eds. *Outsourcing Library Technical Services Operations: Practices in Public, Academic, and Special Libraries*. Chicago: American Library Association, 1997.

Yee, Martha. "Guidelines for OPAC Displays." In "From Catalog to Gateway: Briefings from the CFFC," paper no. 14. *ALCTS Newsletter Online* 10, no. 6 (December 1999); also published in *From Catalog to Gateway: Charting a Course for Future Access: Briefings from the ALCTS Catalog Form and Function Committee*, edited by Bill Sleeman and Pamela Bluh, 83-90. Chicago: Association for Library Collections & Technical Services, American Library Association, 2005.

Yee, Martha. "Guidelines for OPAC Displays." Prepared for the 65th IFLA Council and General Conference, Bangkok, Thailand, August 20-28, 1999. http://archive.ifla.org/IV/ifla65/papers/098-131e.htm.

Yee, Martha M., and Sara Shatford Layne. *Improving Online Public Access Catalogs*. Chicago: American Library Association, 1998.

Zyroff, Ellen. "Cataloging Is a Prime Number." *American Libraries* 27, no. 5 (May 1996): 47-48, 50.

RESOURCES FOR CURRENT INFORMATION AND UPDATING

Banerjee, Kyle. "The Cataloging Calculator." Accessed November 23, 2014. http://calculate.alptown.com/.

Cataloger's Desktop. Washington, D.C.: Library of Congress, Cataloging Distribution Service. Accessed November 23, 2014. http://desktop.loc.gov/ [requires ID and password]. For subscription information: http://www.loc.gov/cds/desktop/.

Cataloging & Classification Quarterly. Philadelphia, Pa.: Taylor & Francis, 1979- . Quarterly. http://catalogingandclassificationquarterly.com/index.html.

Cataloging Service Bulletin, no. 1-128. Washington, D.C.: Library of Congress, 1978-2010.

Classification Web. Washington, D.C.: Library of Congress, Cataloging Distribution Service. Accessed November 23, 2014. http://classificationweb.net/ [requires ID and password]. For subscription information: http://www.loc .gov/cds/classweb/.

Library of Congress Authorities. Accessed November 23, 2014. http://authorities .loc.gov/.

Library of Congress. "Cataloging and Acquisitions Home: Home page of the Acquisitions and Bibliographic Access Directorate." Accessed November 23, 2014. http://www.loc.gov/aba/.

Library of Congress. "Cataloging Distribution Service." Accessed November 23, 2014. http://www.loc.gov/cds/.

Library of Congress Online Catalog. Accessed November 23, 2014. http://catalog .loc.gov/.

Library Resources & Technical Services. Chicago: American Library Association, 1957- . Quarterly. http://www.ala.org/alcts/resources/lrts.

OCLC. "Support and Training." Accessed November 23, 2014. http://www.oclc .org/support/home.en.html.

OCLC. "Technical Bulletins." Accessed November 23, 2014. http://www.oclc.org/ support/documentation/technicalbulletins.en.html/.

INDEX

Note: Page numbers followed by 'f' or 't' refer to figures and tables.

About the Authors

DANIEL N. JOUDREY, MLIS, PhD, is Associate Professor, School of Library and Information Science, Simmons College, Boston, Massachusetts, where he teaches information organization, subject cataloging and classification, and descriptive cataloging. His published works include the third edition of *The Organization of Information*, with Dr. Arlene G. Taylor; "Cataloging," in *The Encyclopedia of Library and Information Science*; and several articles, including some on cataloging education, published in *Cataloging & Classification Quarterly*. His research interests include aboutness determination, subject access to information, and cataloging education. He holds an MLIS and a PhD from the School of Information Sciences at the University of Pittsburgh, where his studies, guided by Dr. Taylor, focused on subject cataloging, particularly that of determining aboutness.

ARLENE G. TAYLOR, MSLS, PhD, is Professor Emerita, School of Information Sciences, University of Pittsburgh, and Distinguished Adjunct Professor, School of Information and Library Science, University of North Carolina, Chapel Hill. She is author of numerous articles and books, including *The Organization of Information*, 3rd ed. (with Dr. Daniel N. Joudrey, Libraries Unlimited, 2009) and *Understanding FRBR: What It Is and How It Will Affect Our Retrieval Tools* (Libraries Unlimited, 2007). Dr. Taylor received the 1996 Margaret Mann Citation and the 2000 ALA/Highsmith Library Literature Award, and was the 2011 recipient of the Distinguished Alumnus Award from the Graduate School of Library and Information Science of the University of Illinois.

DAVID P. MILLER, MA, MSLIS, is Professor and Head of Technical Services, Levin Library, Curry College, Milton, Massachusetts. His published works include anthology contributions and journal articles for *Cataloging & Classification Quarterly*, *Library Resources & Technical Services*, and other publications. With Filiberto Felipe Martínez Arellano, he co-edited *Salsa de tópicos = Subjects in SALSA : Spanish and Latin American subject access* (ALCTS, 2007).